INTERNATIONAL FINANCE

RAJIV SRIVASTAVA
Professor, Finance
Indian Institute of Foreign Trade, New Delhi

OXFORD
UNIVERSITY PRESS

OXFORD
UNIVERSITY PRESS

Oxford University Press is a department of the University of Oxford.
It furthers the University's objective of excellence in research, scholarship,
and education by publishing worldwide. Oxford is a registered trademark of
Oxford University Press in the UK and in certain other countries.

Published in India by
Oxford University Press
22 Workspace, 2nd Floor, 1/22 Asaf Ali Road, New Delhi 110 002

© Oxford University Press 2015

The moral rights of the author/s have been asserted.

First published in 2015
Eighth impression 2023

All rights reserved. No part of this publication may be reproduced, stored in
a retrieval system, or transmitted, in any form or by any means, without the
prior permission in writing of Oxford University Press, or as expressly permitted
by law, by licence, or under terms agreed with the appropriate reprographics
rights organization. Enquiries concerning reproduction outside the scope of the
above should be sent to the Rights Department, Oxford University Press, at the
address above.

You must not circulate this book in any other form
and you must impose this same condition on any acquirer.

ISBN-13: 978-0-19-945359-7
ISBN-10: 0-19-945359-4

Typeset in Garamond
by Ideal Publishing Solutions, Delhi
Printed in India by Rakmo Press, New Delhi 110 020

For product information and current price, please visit www.india.oup.com

Third-party website addresses mentioned in this book are provided
by Oxford University Press in good faith and for information only.
Oxford University Press disclaims any responsibility for the material contained therein.

In memory of my loving daughter

Juhi

Features of

Chapter on Taxation and Transfer Pricing discusses tax havens and how MNCs use them to their advantage along with regulations of transfer pricing in India with latest data.

Chapter on Accounting for International Operations describes principles used in translating accounts from one currency to another and resulting differences due to exchange rate variations.

Figures and Tables illustrate and analyse data given in the chapter in an easy-to-retain format.

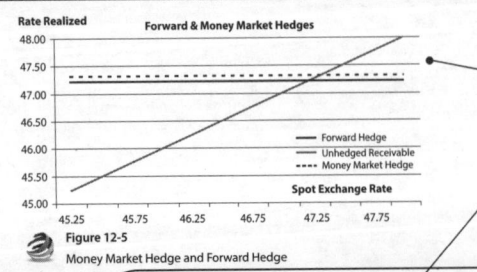

the Book

Concepts in Practice included in the text support, reinforce, and enhance learning of the concepts discussed.

CONCEPTS IN PRACTICE
Taxing Foreign Capital Flows

THE CHILLY CHILEAN *ENCAJE*

For long period of more than a decade, Chile practised capital controls to avoid real appreciation problem and unwarranted build-up of short-term debt on Chilean economy by unique way of reducing the attractiveness of increased returns while simultaneously ensuring a long-term flows. During the late 1980s and early 1990s, international capital began to return to Chile because of its sound economic policies and low levels of debt as also due to slow growth and low interest rates in the developed world.

The Chilean authorities feared that these capital inflows would complicate monetary policy decisions—perhaps causing real appreciation of the exchange rate—and they also were wary of the danger of building up short-term debt. Chile had long restricted capital flows and these limits were updated in the early 1990s to deal with the surge in capital inflows. Direct investment was made subject to a 10-year holding requirement in 1982; this period was reduced to three years in 1991 and to one year in 1993. Portfolio flows were made subject to the *encaje*—a one-year, mandatory, non-interest paying deposit with the central bank—created in 1991 to regulate capital inflows. The *encaje* was initially 20% but was increased to 30% in 1992. The penalty for early withdrawal was 3%. This effectively ensured long-term capital flows to Chile while reducing the gap in returns between developed and developing world. The effect of the *encaje* was to tax foreign capital inflows, with short-term flows being taxed much more heavily than long-term flows.

Exercise 11-3
Borrower's Hedge with Eurodollar

Three months from now London Motors Limited (LML) needs to raise short-term loan of US$20 million for three months. Current LIBOR is 6.50% and the Eurodollar futures contract with three months to expire is quoted at 93.00 (implying an interest rate of 7%). The LML expects the interest rate to rise to 8%.
(a) How can LML hedge against the rising interest rates?
(b) What would be the effective cost if the interest rate actually rises to 8%?
(c) Analyse the interest cost if LIBOR actually falls to 6%.

Solution
(a) LML faces the risk of rising interest rate for its contemplated borrowing three months from now. It needs to go short on Eurodollar futures worth an amount equal to US$20 million. Therefore, it needs to short 20 Eurodollar futures contracts to freeze the borrowing cost to around 7%, the current yield reflected in Eurodollar futures. After three months, it buys back the Eurodollar futures and resorts to borrowing at market rates prevailing then.
(b) If LIBOR rises to 8%, the Eurodollar price would fall to 92.00. The profit of each futures contract would be

Profit/loss on Eurodollar futures (for short position)

$$= \$1,000,000 \times \frac{F_0 - F_1}{100} \times \frac{90}{360}$$

$$= \$1,000,000 \times \frac{93.00 - 92.00}{100} \times \frac{90}{360} = \$2,500$$

The borrowing cost for $20 million = 20,000,000 × 0.08 × 90/360 = $400,000
Less: Profit from 20 Eurodollar futures contracts = 2,500 × 20 = $ 50,000

Solved Exercises aid students' understanding of the concepts and provide adequate practice.

QUESTIONS

13-1 What do you understand by translation exposure?
13-2 Why do you think that management of translation exposure is more important than management of economic exposure?
13-3 Critically evaluate the statement 'Managing translation exposure is a waste of precious time of management'.
13-4 Briefly explain the following translation methods:
 (a) Current/non-current method
 (b) Monetary/non-monetary method
 (c) All current method
13-5 'Translation exposure would be same irrespective of the method used for translation.' Discuss.
13-6 How is economic exposure different from transaction exposure?
13-7 China has pegged its currency to US dollar and, therefore, Chinese companies do not face any economic exposure. Do you agree with the statement? Give reasons.

Chapter-end Exercises contain concept review questions and problems, which could be used by faculty to test students' knowledge of the concepts.

PROBLEMS

13-1 Assume an American firm has a subsidiary in Germany having the following assets and liabilities denominated in euros:

Balance Sheet — Euros in Thousands

Fixed Assets	12.00	Net Worth	12.00
Stocks	5.00	Term Liabilities	5.00
Debtors	4.00	Trade Creditors	6.00
Cash	2.00		
	23.00		23.00

PREFACE

International Finance has gained more importance recently because of the expansion of businesses from local to global or national to international domains. With increased globalization and due to policies of liberalization of international trade followed by developed nations, the perspective of decisions of finance too has undergone a sea change. Developing economies like India have commenced their journey towards increased integration with the world in all domains of businesses. It has now become almost inevitable for firms to take decisions of finance in a global perspective. This requires increased understanding of world's economy, familiarity with international trade, valuation principles of foreign currencies, differentiating features of various monetary systems prevailing, and intricacies of foreign exchange markets.

It is important to understand that international finance is not a mere extension of financial concepts stated in foreign currency. It further includes an understanding of international economic environment, trade policies and barriers, cross-border flows of capital, risk profile of international investors, ways of managing risk emanating from newer and unchartered sources of risk, changing trade-off between desired return and risk, etc.

Therefore, it has become imperative for the students of finance to understand global economic environment as also expand the study of international trade and economics. Foreign exchange markets provide a link for the domestic economy with rest of the world, and hence an understanding of foreign exchange markets is also mandatory. In fact, the study of international finance has become an amalgamation of economics and finance, and mere substitution of one currency with another does not suffice. The ambit of international finance therefore expands from domestic finance to include its inter-linkages with international trade policies and global economics. This book attempts to present concepts of finance in a manner that integrates three domains of economics, trade, and finance. Besides, it presents the nuts and bolts of foreign exchange markets and an introduction to specific financial instruments designed for hedging against the foreign exchange risks.

About the Book

International Finance is specially designed to meet the requirements of postgraduate management students specializing in finance by presenting a comprehensive overview of the international economic environment, foreign exchange markets, foreign exchange risk management, and controls. The book also provides a discussion of exchange rate systems, economic policies, cost of capital, its structure, and international capital budgeting. International activities on accounting and taxation in India are also detailed for readers to gain a wider perspective. Latest environment and regulatory changes in the Indian economy and financial markets for international operations are included for readers to identify with and recognize the market conditions.

The distinguishing feature of the book is the emphasis on Indian multinationals which are becoming increasingly relevant in the world by looking beyond national domain. The book has extensive discussions on India's balance of payments, its foreign exchange reserves, etc. It also contains details on International Monetary Fund, euro currencies and markets, trends and guidelines for foreign direct investment (FDI) in India, RBI guidelines on external commercial borrowings, etc. through Online Resource Centre. This would give the students the knowledge about the actual happenings in financial markets of the world.

Online Resources

The online resource centre provides the following resources for the faculty using the text.

- Instructor's Manual
- PowerPoint Slides

Additional readings relating to India's balance of payments, its foreign exchange reserves and more are provided for both faculty and students.

Coverage and Structure

For better understanding of this vast subject, the book has been divided into six parts as follows:

- Part I deals with international economic environment covering historical events that have led to development of various monetary systems in vogue.
- Part II emphasizes foreign exchange markets and exchange rate theories.
- Part III delves into various derivative instruments involving foreign currency used for hedging foreign exchange risk.
- Part IV concentrates on different kinds of risks faced in international finance and strategies of managing these risks.
- Part V covers distinguishing features of international equity and debt markets. It also covers the ways of regulating and motivation foreign investments, and how foreign investments effect domestic economy.
- Part VI deals with differentiating financial concepts and issues that concern a multinational corporation.

The contents of the chapters are discussed in detail here.

Chapter 1, *Introduction to International Finance*, discusses the role of a finance manager and the objectives of an MNC, and describes risks including political and exchange rate faced by them. The factors responsible for firms becoming MNCs are also covered. Chapter 2, *Balance of Payment*, explains the meaning of balance of payment (BOP) and its structure along with various approaches for correcting the adverse BOP. It also provides an understanding of India's BOP and foreign exchange reserve position. Chapter 3, *International Monetary Systems*, discusses the history and development of monetary systems. It provides discussion on various aspects of the Bretton Woods system and its intervention mechanism; and how European Monetary System evolved and culminated in new currency euro. Chapter 4, *Exchange Rate Systems*, discusses various exchange rate systems prevailing in the world, and how various currency crises have developed and the lessons that can be driven from the management of these crises.

Chapter 5, *Foreign Exchange Rates and Markets*, focuses on the features of foreign exchange markets, and their growth and development. It also discusses nominal, real, and effective exchange rates, and spot and forward contracts. Chapter 6, *International Parity Conditions*, discusses absolute purchasing power parity (PPP) and factors that cause distortion in PPP. The Fisher effect and its

implications for international capital flows are also covered. Chapter 7, *Exchange Rate, Economic and Monetary Policies*, discusses how fiscal and monetary policies impact national economy and exchange rate and explains the varying effectiveness of fiscal and monetary policies under fixed and floating rate regimes.

Chapter 8, *Currency Forwards and Futures*, covers the features of forward and futures contracts on currencies and also discusses non-deliverable forwards, their evolution, and applications. Chapter 9, *Currency Options*, discusses options and how they are different from forwards and futures. It also explains barrier options and Asian options and their cost effectiveness in hedging foreign currency exposures. Chapter 10, *Currency and Interest Rate Swaps*, discusses historical development that caused swaps to come into being and distinguishes between different types of interest rate and currency swaps. Hedging interest rate risk and exchange rate risk through swaps are also included in detail. Chapter 11, *Interest Rate Risk and Hedging*, explains the importance of interest rate risk management and also describes forward rate agreement, their features, and hedging with them. Eurodollar futures and hedging with them are also covered.

Chapter 12, *Measurement and Management of Transaction Exposure*, explains various risks related to foreign exchange rates and provides a differentiation between transaction, translation, and economic exposures. The mechanisms of hedging with financial instruments are included in detail too. Chapter 13, *Measurement and Management of Translation and Economic Exposure*, explains translation, consolidation, and resultant exposures, and different methods of translation of financial statements. It also covers the methods and desirability of management of economic exposure. Chapter 14, *Political and Country Risk*, defines and describes political and country risks. The methods of assigning country rating and the strategic ways of managing political risk are also covered.

Chapter 15, *International Debt Markets*, focuses discussion on international bond and debt markets. It also provides differentiation between foreign bonds and Eurobonds and their markets. It also offers discussion on comprehending risks in international bonds. Chapter 16, *International Equity Investment*, discusses the features of international capital markets and the composition of secondary markets worldwide. It also covers Sharpe ratio, trade-off of risk and return, and trends of FII investment in India. Chapter 17, *Foreign Direct Investment*, discusses the theory of absolute and comparative advantage as the basis for international trade, and various modes of making an entry into a foreign nation to invest. It also discusses the trends of FDI capital flows worldwide and in India. Chapter 18, *Managing Capital Flows*, explains the need for capital control measures especially for emerging economies and gives a brief history of capital controls with a view to understand the objective achieved in different times.

Chapter 19, *Capital Asset Pricing Model—Local and Global*, differentiates between systematic risk and unsystematic risk in local and global context and describes dual listing and depository receipts as modes of integrating the financial markets. Chapter 20, *Cost of Capital and Capital Structure for Multinational Firms*, discusses the features of cost of capital and capital structure of a multinational corporation and lists the practical considerations in determining the capital structure of a subsidiary. Chapter 21, *International Capital Budgeting*, provides discussion on the basic framework used in capital budgeting exercises and discusses the advantages and disadvantages of WACC model and FTE model. It also gives an understanding of the relevance of using the correct discount rates in different currencies and different situations. Chapter 22, *Financing Foreign Trade*, explains various modes of payments in international trade, letter of credit, bill financing, and the advantages of counter trade for nations. Chapter 23, *Taxation and Transfer Pricing in India*, provides the rules and features of the Indian income tax, with types of taxes, rates of corporate tax, and tax incentives. General Anti Avoidance Rules and Double Taxation Avoidance Agreements are also covered. Chapter 24, *Accounting for International Operations*, explains how accounting for transactions denominated in foreign currency is carried out and describes the principles used in translating accounts from one currency to another, and resulting differences due to exchange rate variations.

Acknowledgements

The motivation to undertake this project has been provided by my students who always ask thought-provoking questions. I have tried to answer some of them in the form of this book.

I am also thankful to the management and my faculty colleagues of Indian Institute of Foreign Trade, New Delhi, who have provided me with an extremely conducive atmosphere and the encouragement to undertake the endeavour.

I am particularly thankful to Dr Anil Misra, Associate Professor at Management Development Institute, Gurgaon, for having graciously agreed to allow me to use some part of the contents of my earlier book titled *Financial Management* in which he is the co-author.

I sincerely appreciate reviewers for their constructive criticism and useful inputs. I would like to thank the editorial team at Oxford University Press, India, for enabling several improvements in the contents and presentation of this book.

I am extremely thankful to my wife, Anita Srivastava, for her endurance, support, and encouragement during the preparation of this work.

Any suggestion or improvement could be sent to me directly on my email address rajiv1234@hotmail.com or through Oxford University Press and would be highly appreciated.

Rajiv Srivastava

Brief Contents

Features of the Book   iv
Preface   vi
Detailed Contents   xi

PART I INTERNATIONAL ECONOMIC ENVIRONMENT	1
1. Introduction to International Finance	2
2. Balance of Payment	14
3. International Monetary Systems	44
4. Exchange Rate Systems	74

PART II FOREIGN EXCHANGE MARKETS AND EQUILIBRIUM	109
5. Foreign Exchange Rates and Markets	110
6. International Parity Conditions	156
7. Exchange Rate, Economic and Monetary Policies	193

PART III FOREIGN EXCHANGE DERIVATIVES	229
8. Currency Forwards and Futures	230
9. Currency Options	273
10. Currency and Interest Rate Swaps	311
11. Interest Rate Risk and Hedging	338

PART IV FOREIGN EXCHANGE RISK MANAGEMENT	361
12. Measurement and Management of Transaction Exposure	362
13. Measurement and Management of Translation and Economic Exposure	398
14. Political and Country Risk	419

PART V INTERNATIONAL FINANCIAL MARKETS AND CONTROLS	437
15. International Debt Markets	438
16. International Equity Investment	469
17. Foreign Direct Investment	494
18. Managing Capital Flows	521

PART VI MULTINATIONAL FINANCIAL MANAGEMENT	543
19. Capital Asset Pricing Model—Local and Global	544
20. Cost of Capital and Capital Structure for Multinational Firms	576
21. International Capital Budgeting	610
22. Financing Foreign Trade	643
23. Taxation and Transfer Pricing in India	669
24. Accounting for International Operations	699

Selected ISO Currency Codes   729
Index   731
About the Author   737

Detailed Contents

Features of the Book iv
Preface vi
Brief Contents x

PART I INTERNATIONAL ECONOMIC ENVIRONMENT 1

1. Introduction to International Finance 2
Introduction 3
Finance Decisions for Multinational Corporations 4
  Investment Decision 4
  Capital Structure Decision 5
  Dividend Decision 5
Additional Risks 5
  Political Risk 6
  Exchange Rate Risk 6
Risk Composition in International Finance 6
Objective of Multinational Corporation 7
Role of a Finance Manager 9
Why and How Firms Become Multinational 10
  Imperfect Markets 10
  New Markets, Products, and Technologies 11
  Asynchronous Business Cycles 11
  Tax Advantages 11

2. Balance of Payment 14
Balance of Payment—Definition 16
Structure of Balance of Payment 17
  Current Account 18
  Capital Account 19
  Reserve Account 19
  Errors and Omissions 20
Accounting for Balance of Payment 21
Imbalances in Balance of Payment 24
  Current Account Balance 24
  Trade Account Balance 25
  Capital Account Balance 25
Balance of Payment and Domestic Economy 26
Multipliers 27
  Current Account Multipliers 30
Correcting Balance of Payment 31
  Currency Devaluation/Depreciation 31
  Protectionism 37
  Controlling Capital Flows 38
  Domestic Savings Rate 41

3. International Monetary Systems 44
Introduction 45
  The Barter System 45
  Gold Specie Standard 45
Classical Gold Standard 46
  Variants of Gold Standard 48
  How Gold Standard Works 48
Bretton Woods System 53
  Features of Bretton Woods System 53
  Intervention Mechanism under Bretton Woods System 54
  Progress of Bretton Woods System 57
  Reasons of Failure of Bretton Woods System 58
European Monetary System 60
  Intervention Mechanism under European Monetary System 62
  Benefits of European Monetary System 64
Beyond European Monetary System: Monetary and Economic Union 65
  The Maastricht Treaty 66
Optimum Currency Area 70

4. Exchange Rate Systems 74
Introduction 75
Fixed and Floating Exchange Rate Systems 76
Advantages of Fixed Exchange Rates 77

    Promoting International Trade 77
    Uniformity in Economic Policies of the World 77
    Containing Inflation 78
    Reduced Volatility 78
Advantages of Floating Exchange Rate System 78
    Monetary Independence 79
    Less Painful Adjustment 80
    No Need for Foreign Exchange Reserves 80
    No Sharp Changes 81
    Avoiding Peso Problem 83
Dollarization 84

Currency Board 86
Pegged Exchange Rate System 88
Trilemma of Economics 94
Crawling Pegs 97
Managed/Dirty Float 98
    Benefits of Managed Float 99
    Sterilization 101
Free Float 102
Cooperative Interventions and Target Zone Arrangements 103
Choice of Exchange Rate Regime 104

PART II   FOREIGN EXCHANGE MARKETS AND EQUILIBRIUM   109

5. Foreign Exchange Rates and Markets   110

Introduction 111
Foreign Exchange Markets—Structures and Features 111
Foreign Exchange Rates 116
    Bid and Ask Rates 117
    Direct and Indirect Rates 118
    Merchant and Interbank Rates 119
    Cross Rates and Vehicle Currency 119
Spot Rates and Arbitrage 121
Spot and Forward Contracts 125
    Forward Premium/Discount 126
    Swap Transaction 128
    Outright Forward vs Swap 130
    Forward–Forward Swap 133
    Option Forwards 133
Merchant Rates 135
Nominal and Real Effective Exchange Rates (NEER and REER) 137
    Need for Basket of Currencies for Nominal and Real Effective Exchange Rates 139
Foreign Exchange Markets in India 142
Historical Background 153
Growth of Euro Dollar 153
Instruments of Euro Dollars 154

6. International Parity Conditions   156

Introduction 157
Law of One Price 157

Absolute Purchasing Power Parity 158
Relative Purchasing Power Parity 163
    Nominal and Real Exchange Rates 165
    Exchange Rate Pass-through 168
Fisher Effect 170
International Fisher Effect 171
Interest Rate Parity 176
    Covered Interest Arbitrage 176
    Forward Premium and Discount 183
    Interest Rate Parity with Transaction Costs 184
Reconciling Parities 189

7. Exchange Rate, Economic and Monetary Policies   193

Introduction 194
National Income 194
Internal Balance and External Balance 195
    External Balance 195
Swan Diagram 196
Mundell–Fleming Model: IS-LM-BP Approach 199
    IS Schedule 199
    LM Schedule 201
Equilibrium in a Closed Economy 203
    BP Schedule 205
Exchange Rate Expectations 207
    Effect of Exchange Rate Changes on IS, LM, and BP Schedules 208
    Achieving Equilibrium 209

Detailed Contents **xiii**

Fixed Exchange Rate and Monetary Expansion 211
Fixed Exchange Rate and Fiscal Expansion 212
Flexible Exchange Rate and Monetary Expansion 214
Flexible Exchange Rate and Fiscal Expansion 216
Limitations of IS-LM-BP Approach *217*
Monetary Models of Exchange Rate Determination *217*
Dornbusch's Sticky Price Model *220*
Portfolio Balance Model *222*
Forecasting Exchange Rate *224*
Chartist/Technical Approach *225*

PART III FOREIGN EXCHANGE DERIVATIVES   229

8. Currency Forwards and Futures   230

Introduction *231*
Forward and Futures Contracts *231*
 Forward Contract—Payoffs of Receivable and Payable 233
Hedging with Forwards *235*
 Hedging Receivable with Forward Contract 236
 Hedging Payable with Forward Contract 238
 When to Hedge 240
 Obligations under Forward Contracts 240
 Cancellation of Forward Contracts 241
 Cost of Forward Hedge 242
Speculation with Forward Contract *243*
Non-Deliverable Forward Contract *244*
 Hedging with Non-Deliverable Forward 245
 Evolution and Growth of Non-Deliverable Forward 248
 Non-Deliverable Forward and Interest Rate Parity 248
Currency Futures *251*
Limitations of Forward Contract *252*
Futures Contract vs Forward Contract *254*
Terminology of Futures *255*
Hedging with Currency Futures *259*
 Basis 262
 Basis Risk 263
 Sources of Basis Risk 264
Pricing Currency Futures *265*
 Convergence of Futures Price to Spot 267
Arbitrage with Currency Futures *267*
Speculation with Currency Futures *269*

9. Currency Options   273

Introduction *274*
Option Contracts—Call and Put *274*
Terminology of Options *275*
Payoffs of Options *276*
 Call Option 276
 Put Option 278
 Commitments under Options 282
Moneyness of Options: In-the-Money, At-the-Money, and Out-of-the-Money Options *283*
Exchange-traded and Over-the-Counter options *284*
Understanding Options Quotations *286*
 Assignment 288
 Margins in Options 289
Options and Forwards/Futures *289*
Black Scholes Option Pricing Model *291*
Hedging with Currency Options *295*
 Hedging Foreign Currency Receivable with Put Option 295
 Hedging Foreign Currency Payable with Call Option 298
Modifying Option Terms *301*
 Range Forward—Zero Cost Collar 301
 Participating Forward 304
 Barrier Options 305
 Asian Options 306
 Innovations in Options 308

10. Currency and Interest Rate Swaps   311

Introduction *312*
 Interest Rate and Exchange Rate Risks 312
 Swap—Definition and Development 313
Types of Swaps *316*
■ Currency Swaps *317*
Hedging against Exchange Rate Risk with Currency Swap *318*

Reducing Cost of Funds with Currency Swap *321*

■ **Interest Rate Swaps 324**

Features of Interest Rate Swap *324*

Applications of Interest Rate Swaps *326*
  Transforming Fixed Rate/Floating Rate Liabilities *327*
  Transforming Nature of Assets *328*
  Hedging with Interest Rate Swaps *329*
  Reducing Cost of Funds *330*

Rationale for Swap *331*

Need for Swap Intermediary *332*

Types of Interest Rate Swaps *335*

11. Interest Rate Risk and Hedging 338

Introduction *339*

Benchmark Interest Rates *339*

Forward Rate Agreement *340*
  Features of Forward Rate Agreement *340*
  Borrower's Forward Rate Agreement *342*
  Investor's Forward Rate Agreement *343*
  Pricing Forward Rate Agreement *344*

Interest Rate Futures *346*
  Eurodollar Futures *346*
  Value of Eurodollar Futures *346*
  Hedging with Eurodollar Futures *347*

Interest Rate Options *349*
  Call Option on Interest Rate *349*
  Put Option on Interest Rate *351*

Caps *352*
Floor *355*
Collar *356*

PART IV FOREIGN EXCHANGE RISK MANAGEMENT 361

12. Measurement and Management of Transaction Exposure 362

Introduction *363*

Transaction Exposure *363*
  When does Transaction Exposure Arise? *364*
  Which Transactions to Include *364*
  Factors Affecting Transaction Exposure *364*
  Measuring Transaction Exposure *365*

Translation Exposure and Economic Exposure—Defined *367*

Management of Transaction Exposure *368*

Importance of Managing Transaction Exposure *369*
  Hedge or Not to Hedge: Selective Hedging *370*

Hedging Strategies *371*

Internal Hedging Strategies *371*
  Invoicing *371*
  Exposure Netting *372*
  Leading and Lagging *374*
  Risk Sharing *375*

Hedging with Financial Instruments *377*
  Forward Hedge *377*
  Hedging with Option Forward *380*

Money Market Hedge *381*

Futures Hedge *386*
Options Hedge *391*

13. Measurement and Management of Translation and Economic Exposure 398

Introduction *399*

■ **Translation Exposure 399**

Translation Exposure—Explained *400*

Does Translation Exposure Matter? *401*

Determinants of Translation Exposure *401*

Methods of Translation *402*
  Current/Non-current Method *402*
  Monetary/Non-monetary Method *403*
  Temporal Method *404*
  All Current Method *404*
  Recognition of Translation Gain/Loss *404*

Measuring Translation Exposure *406*

Management of Translation Exposure *407*
  Balance Sheet Hedge *408*
  Derivatives Hedge *408*

■ **Economic Exposure 409**

Measuring Economic Exposure *410*
  Scenario Analysis *411*

    Market Value of the Firm—A Proxy for Cash Flow 412
    Real vs Nominal Exchange Rates 413
    Pegging and Economic Exposure 415
  Managing Economic Exposure 415
    Manage or Not to Manage 415
    Strategic Management of Economic Exposure 416

14. Political and Country Risk   419

  Introduction 420
  Sources of Political Risk 420
  Measuring Country/Political Risk 421
    Economic Risk 422
    Financial Risk 423
  Sovereign Rating and Political Risk 424
  Forms of Political Risk 426
    Expropriation 429
    Politics and Business 430
  Political Risk and Capital Budgeting 432
  Managing Political Risk 433
    Hire Locals 433
    Seek Local Listing 433
    Borrow Locally 434
    Repatriate Quickly 434

PART V INTERNATIONAL FINANCIAL MARKETS AND CONTROLS   437

15. International Debt Markets   438

  Introduction 439
  International Debt markets 440
  International Bonds market 440
  Types of Bonds 444
  Features of Foreign Bond 445
    Nature of Coupon and Coupon Rate 445
    Currency of Denomination 447
  Eurobonds Market 449
  Features of Eurobonds 451
  Investing in International Bonds 453
  Yield on the Bonds 453
  Comparing Costs of Foreign Bonds 453
    All-in Cost for Bonds 455
  Risks in International Bonds 457
    Exchange Rate Risk 457
    Interest Rate Risk 457
    Inflation Risk 458
    Political Risk 458
  International Banking 460
    Syndicated Loans and Project Finance 461
    Offshore Banking 462
    Development Banks 463
  Foreign Currency Loans in India 464

16. International Equity Investment   469

  Introduction 470
  Equity Markets 470
  International Investment 474
    Returns and Exchange Rates 474
    Risk in International Investing 479
  Rationale for International Diversification 483
  International Portfolio—The Risk Return Trade-off 485
  Foreign Portfolio Investment in India 491

17. Foreign Direct Investment   494

  Introduction 495
  Theory of International Trade 495
  Theory of Comparative Advantage 496
    Sharing Benefits of International Trade 498
    Exchange Rate and Terms-of-trade 499
    Limitations of Theory of Comparative Advantage 500
  Motives for Foreign Investment 501
    Imperfect Market 501
    Horizontal Expansion 502
    Vertical Expansion 502
    Risk Diversification 503
  Benefits of Foreign Direct Investment 507
  Barriers to International Trade and Foreign Direct Investment 509
    Tariff Barriers 509
    Non-tariff Barriers 510
    Protection and Need 513
  Modes of Foreign Direct Investment 514
    Licensing 514

xvi Detailed Contents

Joint Venture 515
Wholly Owned Subsidiary 515
Foreign Direct Investment in India 516

18. Managing Capital Flows — 521
Introduction 522
Nature of Capital Flows 522
Foreign Direct Investment 523
Commercial Borrowings and Other Inflows 523
Portfolio Investments 523
History of Capital Controls 524
Implications of Capital Flows for Domestic Economy 525
Capital Controls and Impossible Trinity 527
Features of Capital Control Measures 530
Ways of Capital Control 532
Effectiveness of Capital Control Measures 538
Capital Controls in India 538

PART VI MULTINATIONAL FINANCIAL MANAGEMENT — 543

19. Capital Asset Pricing Model—Local and Global — 544
Introduction 545
■ Domestic Capital Asset Pricing Model Revisited 545
Return and Risk of a Portfolio 545
The Efficient Frontier 546
Capital Market Line 547
Pricing the Asset. The Expected Return 548
Benchmark Values 549
Portfolio Diversification—Domestic Markets 550
Relevant Risk Measure, the Beta 551
■ Global/International Capital Asset Pricing Model 552
The Efficient Frontier, Global 552
Portfolio Diversification—Global Markets 553
Systematic and Unsystematic Risk for Global Portfolio 555
Global vs Local Betas of Firms 555
Exchange Rate Risk 557
Incorporating Exchange Rate Risk 560
■ Segmented and Integrated Markets 562
Country-specific Capital Asset Pricing Model for Segmented Markets 562
Integrating Capital Markets 564
Dual Listing 564
American Depository Receipts and Global Depository Receipts 565
Indian Depository Receipts 569
Diversifying Globally 571

20. Cost of Capital and Capital Structure for Multinational Firms — 576
Introduction 577
Weighted Average Cost of Capital 577
Review of Weighted Average Cost of Capital and Capital Structure 578
Cost of Debt 580
Cost of Equity 580
Direct Investment in Multinational Corporations 580
Cost of Equity for a Foreign Project 581
Capital Asset Pricing Model and Foreign Project 582
Beta of a Foreign Project 585
Market Risk Premium for a Foreign Project 588
Pure-play Approach 590
Cost of Capital for Foreign Project 592
Exchange Rate Risk and Sovereign Risk 595
Cost of Foreign Currency Debt 596
■ Capital Structure of Foreign Subsidiary 599
Capital Structure of Multinational Corporation on Global Basis 600
Irrelevance of Capital Structure of Subsidiary 601
Practical Considerations in Deciding Subsidiary's Capital Structure 604
Managing Political Risk 604
Desire for Control and Management Decision-making 604

Detailed Contents xvii

   Currency Convertibility 605
   Eliminating Currency Risk 605
   Tax Considerations 605
Low Cost Financing 606
   Valuation of Tax Holiday 607

21. International Capital Budgeting   610

Introduction 611
Capital Budgeting: A General Framework 611
Differences in Domestic and International Capital Budgeting 612
   Differences in Cash Flows 613
   Cash Flow—Subsidiary or Parent 613
   Currency of the Cash Flow 614
   Discount Rate 615
Illustration: Euronet—Equivalence of Net Present Value in Foreign and Home Currency 616
   Properties of Discount Rate 620
Review of Net Present Value Framework 621
Illustration: Equivalence of Weighted Average Cost of Capital and Flow to Equity Methods 622
   Flow to Equity Approach 624
   Weighted Average Cost of Capital Approach 625
   Limitations of Weighted Average Cost of Capital and Flow to Equity Approaches 625
Adjusted Present Value Method 628
   Debt and Discount Rate 629
Illustrative Case: DVS Limited—Adjusted Present Value Method 630
   Project Details and Features 630
   Exchange Rate Projection 631
   Cash Flow Projection 632
   Tax Considerations 632
   Post-tax Incremental Cash Flow 633
   Discount Rate for Operating Cash Flows 634
   All Equity Net Present Value 634
   Depreciation Tax Shield 634
   Concessionary Loan 636
   Use of Blocked Funds 638
   Value of Debt Capacity 638
   Value of Royalty to Parent 639
   Value of Inputs Supplied 640

22. Financing Foreign Trade   643

Introduction 644
Supply and Terms of Payments 644
Letter of Credit Explained 645
Documents under Letter of Credit 647
   Invoice 649
   Packing List 649
   Inspection Certificate 649
   Bill of Lading 649
Bills of Exchange (Drafts) 651
   Insurance 652
   Certificate of Origin 652
Types of Letter of Credit 653
   Banks in Letter of Credit 654
Advantages of Letter of Credit 655
Financing under Letter of Credit 655
Financing International Trade 657
Packing Credit—Pre-shipment and Post-shipment 657
Bill Discounting 658
   Banker's Acceptance 659
Factoring 659
   Invoice Financing 661
Forfaiting 662
Countertrade 663
   Countertrade without Money 663
   Countertrade with Money/Credit 664
   Objectives of Countertrade 665

23. Taxation and Transfer Pricing in India   669

Introduction 670
■ Income Tax 671
Types of Taxes 671
Taxable Income 671
Residential Status 672
Tax Rates 672
   Minimum Alternate Tax 673
   Capital Gains 673
   Transactions in Securities 674
   Dividend Distribution Tax 675
   Withholding Tax 675

xviii Detailed Contents

Tax Incentives 675
■ Transfer Pricing 676
  Introduction 676
  Transfer Pricing Regulation in India 679
    Associated Enterprises 679
    Nature of Transactions Covered 680
  Arm's Length Price 680
  Methods of Determining Arm's Length Price 681
    Comparable Uncontrolled Price (CUP) Method 682
    Resale Price Method 683
    Cost Plus Method 684
    Profit Split Method 685
    Transactional Net Margin (TNM) Method 685
    Any Other Method 686
  Relaxations in Transfer Pricing and Arm's Length Price 687
■ Tax Havens 688
■ General Anti Avoidance Rules 690
■ Double Taxation Avoidance Agreements 692
■ Advance Rulings 695

24. Accounting for International Operations 699

Introduction 700
Accounting for Transactions in Foreign Currency 701
  Accounting with Forward Contract 703
  Transactions in Non-monetary Items 706
Accounting for Foreign Currency Loan 706
Translation of Foreign Operations 710
Accounting for Net Investment in Foreign Operations 712
Hedge Accounting for Foreign Currency Exposure 714
  Cash Flow Hedge 715
  Fair Value Hedge 716
Accounting for Investment in Associates 716
  Equity Method 717
Accounting for Interests in Joint Ventures 720
  Proportionate Consolidation 721
Consolidation of Accounts of Subsidiaries 723

Selected ISO Currency Codes 729
Index 731
About the Author 737

PART I
International Economic Environment

1. Introduction to International Finance
2. Balance of Payment
3. International Monetary Systems
4. Exchange Rate Systems

Introduction to International Finance

LEARNING OBJECTIVES

This chapter aims at

- explaining how international finance is different from the conventional study of finance
- discussing how the three decisions of corporate finance—investment, capital structure, and dividend—change when the domain becomes international
- describing the additional risks faced by multinational corporations
- dissecting the composition of risk and how it changes in international domain in terms of systematic risk and its implication on Capital Asset Pricing Model, the cornerstone of financial management
- explaining how corporate objectives remain unchanged despite several new dimensions added
- describing the difference in the role of a finance manager for a multinational corporation (MNC)
- explaining why and how firms become multinational

CONTENTS

Introduction
Finance Decisions for Multinational Corporations
   Investment Decision
   Capital Structure Decision
   Dividend Decision
Additional Risks
   Political Risk
   Exchange Rate Risk
Risk Composition in International Finance

Objective of Multinational Corporation
Role of a Finance Manager
Why and How Firms Become Multinational
   Imperfect Markets
   New Markets, Products, and Technologies
   Asynchronous Business Cycles
   Tax Advantages

INTRODUCTION

Globalization of business is the theme of almost all firms in the world. As the economies are growing and becoming increasingly open by relaxation of regulations concerning international trade, the firms are expanding businesses from local markets in domestic currencies to global markets in multiple currencies. International markets present a number of challenges including an additional one regarding selection of currency of trade and finance, that requires complete understanding of financial markets on global basis. As the world economy becomes more and more integrated, a finance manager is required to make additional decisions with respect to strategic issues such as currency of borrowing, impact of globalization on capital structure, cost of capital in various currencies, and tactical issues such as currency of invoicing and hedging against changing exchange rates. These new dimensions have added complexities in the trade and business management. The dynamics of derivative markets in terms of newer products too have witnessed a major change.

Many people believe that international finance is a mere substitution of local currency with foreign currency using an exchange rate and the rest all must remain same. Just as the distance from one place to another does not change whether specified in kilometres or in miles, the concepts of finance too remain same irrespective of the unit of measurement, be it rupee, dollar, or euro. However, such a belief is too naïve. International finance is not a mere substitution of local currency with foreign currency, but it is a substitution of local perspective with global perspective. When we replace metres with centimetres, the conclusions do not change because the conversion factor does not change. Such is not the case for currencies even when the exchange rate is fixed. The decisions of finance such as capital budgeting, capital structure, or dividend may require careful considerations when we change the denomination of currency. The attitude that a mere substitution of one currency with another, assuming conclusions won't change, does not help.

The exchange rate is not just a conversion factor but is also linked to several macroeconomic parameters. It is a bridge between two economies and reflective of consistencies or otherwise of the economic, monetary, and trade polices of two nations, though it happens to be a number. Since exchange rate is part of global decision-making, it cannot be treated just as a multiplication factor. Instead, it is a dynamic phenomenon that requires constant managerial intervention over the financial decision-making of the firm with far-reaching implications on the survival and growth of the firm.

Besides the selection of currency for finance and trade, another important dimension that figures prominently on the agenda of the finance manager is the exposure of additional risk emanating from dealing in the currency other than the domestic currency. Apart from broadening of the conceptual scope for understanding of interest rate structures in various countries and financial assets denominated in a foreign currency, a finance manager has the onerous task of gathering, assimilating, and analysing the vast information that is generated all over the world. In this way, an international firm, referred to as a multinational corporation (MNC), becomes different from a pure domestic firm, which essentially deals in a single currency.

FINANCE DECISIONS FOR MULTINATIONAL CORPORATIONS

One may argue that the concepts of corporate finance must essentially remain the same irrespective of the currency being evaluated. All the three major decisions in finance—investment, financing, and dividend—should be independent of the currency being considered. The argument is valid but the presence of multiple currencies makes each of these decisions more complicated as the number of choices available increases significantly. Numerically it is a simple multiplication of exchange rate to convert one currency into another, but the decision-making framework changes drastically with regard to international business as managerial inputs are significantly larger, more complex, and different.

The finance function distinguishes among three important decisions—the investment decision including working capital, the capital structure decision, and the dividend decision. Each of the three decisions undergoes a substantial change when a firm takes them in global perspective. One would wonder as to why the nature of decision must change when a firm transgresses from a domestic environment to the global environment. We examine all the three decisions to highlight the change that would take place when the firm becomes global from local.

Investment Decision

First consider the capital budgeting decision, that is, the decision to invest in a project or not. The universal principle of capital budgeting is to accept all the projects with positive net present values (NPVs). The decision requires two vital inputs— the expected cash flows for the life of the project and return expectation of the capital suppliers called the hurdle rate or discount rate. Whether multinational or domestic, the decision-making rule continues to remain same. However, the perspective for the two inputs of projected cash flows and the discount rate changes considerably in case of multinationals.

An MNC as a firm is regarded as collection of several projects in vastly different economic, political, and social environments. More often than not, for an MNC the starting point of the exercise is the cash flows of the project which are considered equal to cash flows to the firm too. We face the first difficulty here. The cash flows that need to be evaluated are the cash flows that accrue to the capital suppliers of the project. In case of the multinational firm, the cash flows of the project, that is, the subsidiary, could be different from those accruing to the parent. For example, royalty payments by subsidiary are cash outflows, whereas they are cash inflows to the parent. Similarly, for the captive supplies to the subsidiary by the parent, there is an element of profit included in them.

One additional dimension besides the cash flows is the question of denomination of currency. The cash flows of the subsidiary and the parent would be in different currencies, and hence an exercise to forecast the exchange rate for the life of the project is an inevitable, challenging, and integral part of the international capital budgeting decision.

Discount Rate The second input for capital budgeting decision is the determination of appropriate discount rate. Recall that discount rate used for discounting the cash flows must satisfy certain properties for capital budgeting decision to be correct. It must be consistent with (a) riskiness of the cash flows, and (b) expectations of capital suppliers. The source of cash flows is the subsidiary in a different location that carries the risk of the host nation, whereas the capital suppliers belong to the parent in a different nation, both of which are subject to different risk profiles being in different economic environments and possibly in opposing political philosophies. Reconciling the cash flows and discount rate perhaps requires a change in the conceptual framework for investment decisions for an MNC as distinct for a domestic firm.

Capital Structure Decision

The second finance decision relates to capital structure, that is, the optimum level of debt a firm that maximizes for the shareholders' wealth. This decision too places several limitations. Most developing nations offer many kinds of incentives to attract foreign investment, which includes grants of capital subsidy and concessional loans, besides imposing restrictions on foreign equity holding. These constraints and incentives can cause deviations in the target capital structure of the MNCs that otherwise would be optimal. The choice is further compounded by another decision whether or not to replicate the parent's capital structure on to the subsidiary because the debt levels are also a function of the varying norms in different economic environments, availability of domestic capital, and nature of capital controls. Here we must be reminded that norms of capital structure in a nation are most often decided on the basis of experience rather than any mathematical model.

Dividend Decision

The third decision of dividend too is constrained by the several conditions imposed in the host nation. Whether or not one believes in the relevance of dividend decision to the value of the firm, the constraints imposed on dividend pay-out play a vital role in the dividend decision at apex level. These conditions relate to restrictions on repatriation of profits, differential rates of taxation for retained and repatriated profits, varying withholding taxes or tax credits or double taxation avoidance agreements, exchange control regulations, etc. The free flow of capital from parent to subsidiary and vice versa when constrained creates gaps in availability of cash at different subsidiaries. Matching needs and resources of various subsidiaries poses difficulties in pursuing contemplated dividend policies for the multinational.

All the concerns raised here are addressed in subsequent chapters.

ADDITIONAL RISKS

Dealing in foreign currency and different economic and political environments adds new dimensions to all decisions of finance. The risk profile undergoes substantial change not only in terms of new additional risk factors as compared to a domestic firm, but also in terms of the characteristics of risk. Risk is perceived and classified in many ways. For an MNC, two new sources of risk that otherwise would be absent in the risk profile of a domestic firm are political risk and exchange rate risk.

Political Risk

Political risk, as the name implies, emanates from political factors—the fact that MNCs operate in a different environment with which they are not completely familiar. They are treated like strangers who are at risk of losing their possessions through what is referred to as expropriation by the government or nationalization of assets in the larger public interest. This risk is the maximum in the initial stages of expansion in the new territory and reduces gradually with time as the MNC becomes more familiar with the environment and learns to cope with uncertainties. As the MNC becomes older in its operations in a foreign country, it becomes more like a resident and achieves greater acceptance. The risk of expropriation or nationalization recedes with time. An exposition to political risk is provided in a separate chapter later.

Exchange Rate Risk

The second element of risk is called the exchange rate risk. There is a constant movement of capital from MNCs to their subsidiaries and vice versa. Initial investment must flow from the parent to the subsidiary till the time the latter becomes self-sufficient. Yet there would be regular cash interchange on revenue account for sale, purchase, fees, royalty, etc. and on capital account for repatriation of profit and meeting dividend obligations. The cash interchange would require the conversion of one currency into another and the value of same cash in one currency would differ when converted to another currency depending upon the time. Therefore, the value of the MNC becomes extremely dependent upon the exchange rate and its expected and actual behaviour.

RISK COMPOSITION IN INTERNATIONAL FINANCE

Besides two new dimensions added to the risk, the concept of risk too gets altered in the context of an MNC. In terms of composition of risk, we distinguish between systematic and unsystematic under the Capital Asset Pricing Model (CAPM). The systematic risk emanates from the factors that have market-wide impact, and the measurement is done against a benchmark usually a stock market index. Under the domestic version of CAPM, the systematic/market risk is contained in a single factor called beta measured against domestic market portfolio. Is the use of the same benchmark appropriate for an MNC? In the international context, the benchmark for market risk undergoes a change from the domestic market portfolio to the global market portfolio because investors in MNCs are supposed to have global portfolio. In contrast, the investors in domestic firms are assumed to have diversified domestic portfolio.

Besides benchmarking issue, the definition of systematic risk is also questionable. Systematic risk is supposed to emanate from the factors that affect market as a whole and majority of financial assets albeit to different degrees. As such, fiscal, monetary, trade policies, etc. of a nation are among the factors included in systematic risk in a national context for a domestic portfolio. However, in the perspective of a global portfolio, the fiscal/monetary/trade policies of individual nations would have rather little significance in affecting returns of a global portfolio. As such, the variability of returns due to such factors is diversifiable when one is presumed to hold stocks from different nations and, hence, such factors must be classified as unsystematic. The CAPM has been considered as the most robust model to arrive at the cost of equity to be included in discount rate. With the composition of risk factors changed, the returns expected by investors for investment in a subsidiary in a different nation, one perhaps cannot use domestic CAPM to compute cost of equity or cost of capital. There would be a substantial change in the application of CAPM in the context of an MNC.

In addition, the basic message of the CAPM is that the risk that is diversifiable would not be rewarded and, hence, the cost of capital must be estimated by providing risk premium for assuming only the systematic risk. In the context of international financial management, because of the haziness of classification of systematic and unsystematic nature of risk, the preferred and more appropriate approach to determine the cost of capital must be to consider the total risk rather than systematic risk alone. In theory, the currency risk and project risk should be diversifiable because the MNC has diversified projects in most countries of the world. However, in practice very few MNCs would qualify to have sufficient diversification that they can afford to ignore unsystematic risk for rewarding shareholders. Consideration of total risk of the project would in any way not distort the return expectations.

OBJECTIVE OF MULTINATIONAL CORPORATION

As the very first lesson in finance, we learnt that for a firm, the three decisions of investing, financing, and dividend are taken with a single objective of maximization of shareholders' wealth. The argument rests on the principle that the shareholder being the owner of the residual would maximize only after meeting all obligations towards the rest of the stakeholders such as employees, customers, suppliers, lenders, and government. Only after meeting commitments towards one and all, who contribute to the value of the firm, the remainder belongs to the shareholders. Hence, the objective of maximization of shareholders' wealth is consistent with those of rest all stakeholders, and not contradictory.

In the context of an MNC, does the objective of maximization of shareholders' wealth hold? In contrast to a pure domestic firm, the number of stakeholders in case of an MNC is more. An MNC operates in at least two nations and, therefore, would have customers, suppliers, employees, etc. from different nations. In case of a joint venture, the shareholders too would have at least two different nationalities. There would also be two different governments involved—one for the parent nation and the other for the host nation. Therefore, in terms of stakeholders, one additional dimension that gets added in case of an MNC is the different nationalities of all kinds of stakeholders. How does that change the objective of the firm?

Loyalty to Nation vs Loyalty to Firm In the context of an MNC typically shareholders belong to one nation where the multinational is resident. For example, most shareholders of IBM, which is a US firm, would be US citizens. Likewise, most shareholders of Nokia would be Finnish. It is common to see for MNCs that while shareholders are predominantly from one nation, the rest of the stakeholders are likely to be from different nationalities. One may construe that maximization of shareholders' wealth would often get replaced and confused with the welfare of the nation to which the shareholders belong. By extension of the same logic, it is often presumed that the welfare of one nation is at the cost of the other. At best this is a misplaced notion.

The New Agency Problem   Differing nationalities of employees and classes of shareholders aggravate the agency problem. We are familiar with two agency problems: (a) employees not always acting in the interest of shareholders, and (b) agency problem of debt. In case of an MNC, there would be a third kind of agency problem. The local employees may place national interest before corporate interest. For example, in a subsidiary, procurement of raw material from the parent at higher cost than what could be available locally would be constraining the cash flows of the subsidiary and yet may increase the cash flows of the parent. Not only such a decision would be against the national interest of the nation hosting the subsidiary, but enrichment of the majority shareholders would also be at cost of minority shareholders in case the subsidiary is a joint venture with local shareholders. Similarly, the decision to remit cash flows to the parent for dividend distribution or to retain them at subsidiary for furthering growth may be considered as conflicting with interests of subsidiary (and hence the host nation) and the parent.

No doubt such instances would often give rise to more complex situations where the corporate and national interests could be at loggerheads. Therefore, nature and cost of agency in case of an MNC would be different and significantly more. For containing such problem, the MNC would possibly have to make extra efforts to contain agency problem.

Capitalist vs Socialist Philosophies   Another aspect that comes in the way is the political philosophy of the nations. While in capitalist countries emphasis on creation of private wealth implies most efficient allocation and utilization of capital leading to increased national welfare, such is not the political thought in a socialist country. Many socialist countries believe in equitable distribution of wealth rather than creation and concentration of private wealth. Hence, the allocation and utilization of resources is governed by public welfare philosophy at large in contrast to private welfare. The ownership of resources and therefore the ways of utilization is denied to private individuals. In case an MNC attempts to expand to a socialist state, it may have to compromise on the objective of maximization of shareholders' wealth.

It, however, need not be the case. An MNC operating in a socialist country does not have to consider that the objective is being diluted or needs to be replaced. It continues with the same objective considering the conditions imposed by the socialist government as additional constraints among the several others, which perhaps exist in the homeland. For example, changing rates of taxation in the homeland is one constraint in operations of MNC that possibly is opposed to the maximization of shareholders' wealth. Similarly, conditions imposed by the host government must be treated as additional constraints, but the objective of maximization of shareholders' wealth remains intact.

Should such situations alter the objective of the firm from maximization of shareholders' wealth? Certainly not! Just as we state that enrichment of shareholders cannot take place without satisfying the commitments made to other stakeholders, the differing nationalities should not come in the way of this objective. In case of a joint venture where there could be different nationalities of the shareholders, the majority prevails. Just as in a domestic corporation, the welfare of minority shareholders is supposed to be coincidental with that of majority shareholders, the same may be extended to MNCs no matter if minority shareholders have a different nationality than the majority shareholders. Therefore, the objective of maximization of shareholders' wealth remains undisputed and unchanged for an MNC.

Centralized vs Decentralized Control One way of containing the agency problem is to have centralized decision-making. The method of control—decentralized or centralized—is neither good nor bad per se with both having advantages and disadvantages of their own. While in some cases, such as procurement of raw material, decentralized control may be more effective, in some other situations, such as promotions and training, the centralized control may be more apt.

ROLE OF A FINANCE MANAGER

The study of international finance is in effect a study of finance in an integrated market where markets expand to the globe. The role of the finance managers of a multinational would expand to (a) identifying global investment opportunities, (b) accessing international capital and debt markets for augmenting financial resources of the firm, (c) establishing ethical and healthy corporate practices and governance standards because adherence to laws of the single nation does not suffice, (d) forecasting exchange rate behaviour, (e) estimating political/country risk, and (f) devising suitable hedging strategies to cover exchange rate risk, political risk, inflation risk, etc.

An important difference in the role of a finance manager for a domestic firm and that of an MNC is the consideration of inflation. In most situations for a domestic firm, inflation is given and common to all propositions under consideration. Therefore, absence or presence of inflation does not enter the process of financial decision-making based on differential cash flows. Since the finance manager in an MNC is considering alternatives in terms of different nations that are subject to different inflation rates, the decision must necessarily consider effects of inflation. The consideration of inflation is of tremendous importance while raising capital in international markets, because the cost of funds has strong linkages to inflation as manifested in the exchange rate forecasting.

The hedging decision in case of MNCs has vastly different scope as compared to a domestic firm. A domestic firm is mostly concerned only with price risk and, therefore, concentrates on it by managing through domestic markets. However, in case of an MNC, there exist exchange rate risk and political risk too. Currency risk can be managed with derivatives, and many available financial markets across the world where hedging can be undertaken. For example, a US-based MNC operating in Europe has a choice of covering euro exchange rate risk in Chicago, USA, or any of the major financial centres in Europe. Political risk must be managed through insurance-like products. The ambit of hedging in case of MNCs is much wider.

For a finance manager in an MNC, the canvas of study expands from local to global events. The concern for business is how international events affect survival and growth opportunities as well as threats emanating from there. With increasing integration taking place, the business is no more isolated and protected. Instead the good and bad effects of global events get transmitted to business. Example of global crisis of 2008, though originated from sub-prime lending in USA, impacted the businesses all over the world. Similarly, Asian currency crisis as well as Greek crisis expanded to the neighbouring nations due to contagion and strong linkages of the economies in the region. Since capital controls are getting gradually dismantled, the transgression of crisis happens at a very fast pace for financial markets. The impact of broader economic phenomenon is not as severe and rapid in the goods market because of its inertia as it happens in case of financial markets. Study of such events and learning from them become an integral part of the role of the finance manager in an MNC.

WHY AND HOW FIRMS BECOME MULTINATIONAL

There are many ways one can look at the growth of MNCs and motives of businesses becoming larger and larger. It would be hard to come out with a universally true hypothesis that could explain the phenomenal growth of MNCs, some of which have become so huge to control a resource base possibly as large as if not greater than some of the smaller economies.

Motives for expanding business and becoming an MNC are many including increasing market share, reducing cost, controlling supply chain, creating brand image, exploiting natural resources, meeting competition, etc. One may get an impression that all these objectives are not consistent with the objective of maximization of shareholders' wealth. However, such mission and vision statements are only manifestations of the objective that is stated in finance function.

Imperfect Markets

One theory explaining the growth of firms is 'imperfect markets'. Due to differences in endowment of production resources such as material, manpower, capital, and technology, the factors of production are not uniformly priced in different nations. This results in different costs of production at different locations. For example, manpower in developing nations is much cheaper than the manpower in developed nations, which causes movement of production facilities from developed economies to developing economies such as China, India, and Bangladesh.

For example, hardware production base of Nokia phones moved to India. Many Japanese entertainment brands chose Thailand as production base. The differential of cost of production has been and is a motivation strong enough to expand operations in another country. Not only are the markets for factors of production imperfect, but the markets for finished goods too are imperfect because of varying income levels and purchasing powers in different nations. Firms constantly strive for new markets to increase volume and drive the economies of scale.

New Markets, Products, and Technologies

Every business starts small. They first cater to local markets and then evolve into a regional player and gradually become national. When the markets at home become saturated, the only way to grow and increase business is to either explore newer markets or innovate new products. This causes a national firm to become multinational. Growing competition and depleting profit margins force firms to look beyond their national frontiers and become multinationals.

Typically, a firm first explores foreign markets by exporting goods. This is either motivated by increasing profits by increasing volumes or extra price that foreign market may fetch.

As the markets and products become familiar in the foreign country, the local competition by way of close imitations develops, which invariably is cheaper and causes pressure on multinational exporting firms to cut margins. To have protection against imitations and conserve margins, an MNC sets up production facilities abroad. Thus, the growth never stops since markets for factors of production and that of finished goods would always remain imperfect, though the degree of imperfection would reduce with time and increased openness and integration of world economy and markets. Would it ever become perfect remains utopian?

Asynchronous Business Cycles

Another reason for firms to explore new markets and territories is diversification of risk. Every economic environment in which a firm operates is subject to business cycles that cause variability to revenue, cash flows, and profits for different time periods. Diversification to different economies should even out the variability because business cycles of different regions are asynchronous. Asynchronous business cycles provide natural cash flow hedge. The MNCs that generate revenues in different nations are likely to face more stable cash flows year after year because recession/boom conditions world over would never be identical.

Loss of revenue or cash flow in one economy may be made good by extra gains of revenue and cash flow from another economy making profit more stable. Imparting stability to cash flows brings down the cost of capital because return expectations of investors are directly proportional to the risk. The cost of capital for MNCs, therefore, should be less as compared to a domestic firm due to more stable cash flows.

For example, UK-based Vodafone's entry into India or India-based Airtel's acquisition of Zain in Africa should make consolidated cash flows of these firms more stable because of asynchronous business cycles of growth or recession prevailing in Europe, Asia, and Africa.

Tax Advantages

Domestic firms while expanding business choose locations based on pure techno-economic reasons. Being in the same tax jurisdiction, seldom do they find tax advantage of one location over another. Though tax incentives for a region are a common practice in developing nations to have balance regional development, they perhaps do not differentiate between domestic

firms and MNCs. The MNCs face location choice in different nations that have different tax rates. Therefore, the choice of location can be influenced by tax considerations because each national boundary has different sets of tax laws, rates, and administration, which would make certain locations more preferable as compared to others.

Taking advantage of liberal tax regimes, a number of MNCs have started operating in Middle-East and Gulf regions due to absence of taxes.

Thus, though international finance can be considered an extension of financial management, it becomes substantially different because of several new dimensions that are presumed to be given and constant in the conventional study of finance. Perceptions of inflation, exchange rates, asset pricing, risks, etc. undergo substantial changes when the domain expands from domestic markets to world markets and local finance to global finance. The key to study international finance lies in the understanding of monetary systems, their evolving nature, determination, and forecasting of foreign exchange rates, and the domestic macroeconomic policies and variables that affect exchange rates and choosing monetary system. In this book, all these issues are addressed first, to be followed by foreign exchange rate markets, derivatives on them, and exchange rate risk management, and finally shift to the concepts of corporate finance for MNCs, its financing, and few commercial aspects.

SUMMARY

In view of increased globalization of the world, converging financial markets in terms of returns with freer flow of capital, the domain of finance too is becoming increasingly complicated and different from conventional finance. Some people wrongly have the notion that a simple replacement of domestic currency with foreign currency would translate study of finance from local to international. The challenge of a finance manager lies in the understanding of global financial markets, exchange rate determination, and forecasting.

There are three major decisions of finance—investment, capital structure, and dividend. All the three decisions get altered when the perspective changes from domestic to international. Investment decision poses issues in forecasting of cash flows and choice of discount rate. Capital structure decision gets influenced by cheaper debt financing, incentives on offer, and tax breaks available besides financing norms prevailing in the host nation where subsidiary is incorporated. Dividend decision is constrained by regulation on repatriation of profit, extra withholding tax, and tax treaties.

In the international domain, at least two new risks—political and exchange rate—require additional exposure to the understanding of international financial markets. Besides additional risk, the composition of risk as understood in conventional corporate finance also undergoes change because it is not easy to segregate systematic and unsystematic risk. Due to hazy segregation, the applicability of CAPM for the determination of cost of equity and cost of capital becomes subjective and consideration of total risk gains credence.

The objective of an MNC remains identical to that of a domestic firm, that is, maximization of shareholders' wealth, though there are several more impediments, such as agency costs and contradicting national policies of achieving economic welfare. For additional constraints in risk and impediments in achieving objective, the role of finance manager is significantly expanded as compared to that of his counterpart in a domestic firm.

The firms become multinational because of several reasons. Imperfect markets for factors of production give rise to cost differential. Internal competition compels the firms to explore new markets. Asynchronous business cycles in the different economies of the world lend stability to revenues and cash flows when firms diversify globally. Also tax arbitrage sometimes becomes crucial to decision-making in an MNC.

QUESTIONS

1-1 'When domestic currency gets replaced by foreign currency, finance becomes international finance.' Comment.
1-2 How do the three decisions of finance—capital budgeting, capital structure, and dividend—get changed for a multinational firm as compared to a domestic firm?
1-3 What new risks are faced by MNCs as compared to their domestic counterparts?
1-4 'Due to different nationalities of shareholders in a multinational corporation, the maximization of shareholders' wealth implies the sacrifice of minority interest and unjust welfare of one nation at the cost of another nation.' Comment.
1-5 What are imperfect markets?

Balance of Payment

LEARNING OBJECTIVES

This chapter aims at

- explaining the meaning of balance of payment (BOP) and its structure
- describing imbalances in BOP
- finding linkages of BOP to the domestic economy
- discussing various approaches for correcting adverse BOP
- reviewing India's BOP and foreign exchange reserve position

CONTENTS

Introduction
Balance of Payment—Definition
Structure of Balance of Payment
    Current Account
    Capital Account
    Reserve Account
    Errors and Omissions
Accounting for Balance of Payment
Imbalances in Balance of Payment
    Current Account Balance
    Trade Account Balance
    Capital Account Balance
Balance of Payment and Domestic Economy
Multipliers
    Current Account Multipliers
Correcting Balance of Payment
    Currency Devaluation/Depreciation
    Protectionism
    Controlling Capital Flows
    Domestic Savings Rate

INTRODUCTION

In modern times it is hard to believe that a nation can be self-sufficient and remain economically independent of other nations. The economic performance of a nation is dependent and is closely related to the way the economy interacts itself with the rest of the world. Due to the political systems and sovereignty of nations that entitle the control of a geographical area, the economic, monetary, and other policies can be controlled in a way the national leaders deem them right. Through transactions of trade with other nations, a country links itself with rest of the world. Within the economy the policies can be implemented to provide directional growth, but no controls and tools—except in the form of preventing or liberalizing foreign trade—exist that can make radical changes in international trade.

From the perspective of a single nation, the international environment can largely be said to be independent and governed by free and competitive forces. Although the course of global changes cannot be guided by a single nation, the national policies are substantially affected by global trade and environment. The external environment deeply affects the internal controls and policy measures that a nation can adopt. Ignoring development across the world would leave the nation isolated—politically, economically, and socially. The internal policies have to be consistent with the world, and should be least conflicting. Since international trade can provide important signals and directions to the domestic economy, it is important to have some framework that provides a planned assimilation of global changes and forms a basis for making national macroeconomic policy.

No country can produce everything that it needs more efficiently than others. While a nation can produce some goods better than others, then by the same logic other nations too can produce certain other goods better in terms of cost and quality. The objective of increasing the welfare of people by providing better quality products at cheaper price can only be achieved by promoting international trade. Exporting goods that are efficiently produced in a country and importing goods that are produced more efficiently in other countries either in absolute or relative terms form the basis of international trade in most situations.

The transactions of an economy with the outside world are captured, contained, and consolidated in a statement called *balance of payment* (BOP). It contains all the information needed by those concerned much in the same way as a balance sheet of a firm does for all its stakeholders. A profit and loss (P&L) account and a balance sheet record all the transactions with others and depict the position of a firm for a period or as on a date respectively for assimilations of all the stakeholders. Similarly, the balance of payment of a nation is a statement of all transactions undertaken by its residents with those of other nations, that is, the rest of the world. The BOP provides a bird's eye view of a nation's interaction with the rest of the world. Please refer to the **Online Resource Centre** for a detailed discussion on India's BOP.

A balance of payment also provides important guidelines to economists and policy makers to influence exchange rates and domestic economic, monetary, and trade policies. It may help estimate the impact of trade policies and fixing tariffs on import and exports, which has revenue implications and may augment or deplete resources of the government. These are vital for directional growth and development of an economy, as may be considered appropriate by the policy makers.

The figures of balance of payment may be regarded as good or bad. These figures create an impression about a nation's own domestic economy and policies as well as its global competitiveness. Balance of payment is an important set of numbers both for foreigners and residents. For foreigners, it is important to understand whether or not it is a safe place to invest. To the local residents, it is important because it quantifies a nation's interlinkages with rest of the world, in terms of its dependence on others and the need for changes in the domestic economic, trade, and monetary policies to enhance its global competitiveness. It helps form notions of how strong a nation is compared to the rest of the world. Before discussing the economic interpretations of BOP, it is necessary to understand its composition, content, and meaning.

BALANCE OF PAYMENT—DEFINITION

By definition, balance of payment is a record of all transactions of the residents of a country with the rest of the world in a given period. Transactions of the residents amongst themselves are not part of balance of payment. An Indian undertaking a transaction with an American would form part of the balance of payment but a transaction with a fellow Indian would not. For example, a transaction of an Indian farmer selling wheat to an American would be reflected in the balance of payment, while wheat sold to another Indian would be excluded from the balance of payment.

Normally, a statement of BOPs is condensed on annual basis for smoothing out seasonal variations. However, for the purpose of analysis and to initiate timely corrections, the provisional data is made available and monitored on monthly or quarterly basis. International transactions primarily comprise exports and imports of goods and services. However, the trade alone does not reflect the complete picture of BOPs. There are transactions that do not relate to exports or imports of goods and services, such as borrowing in foreign currency or mobilizing equity capital from foreign residents, and yet are part of BOPs.

The transactions have one crucial element, that is, establishing the residential status of entity. Residents comprise government, firms, and individuals. A subsidiary of a multinational corporation (MNC) incorporated locally is a resident even though the shareholders of the parent company—the owners—are foreigners. From the perspective of corporate finance, it would be considered a foreign entity but for BOP purposes, the subsidiary is a resident in the host nation being incorporated there. Therefore, the subsidiary's exports and imports, including to and from its parent, would be treated as transactions with non-residents and are included in the balance of payment. Similarly, international bodies such as International Monetary Fund (IMF) and United Nations Organization (UNO) are treated as non-residents irrespective of their locations.

The difficulties in the compilation of balance of payments are many. It is a record of all transactions of residents with non-residents, and no single entity can ever monitor all kinds of transactions, especially in an open economy where there are no approvals or regulations required. The statistics are generally compiled by the central bank of a country based on the inputs provided by various agencies involved in regulating and monitoring the foreign exchange transactions. In the absence of regulations, there is no way of assuring whether the flow of goods and money is from residents or non-residents. For example, for import and export of physical goods, the clearance at border could provide the value of transaction.

However, in case of services, the transaction does not enter the records of the same agency. Another source of information is commercial banks that exchange one currency into another. However, these transactions can be misleading if the remittances made are on a net basis. For example, for import of goods worth US$100 and export of goods worth US$90, a net payment of US$10 is made and recording the same would lead to misleading conclusions.

Naturally there would be aberrations in data when they are compiled from various sources and agencies with no mutual obligations to cross-check with one another. In an unregulated economy, such dissemination of information is voluntary. Therefore, some of the transactions can go unrecorded. For example, the transactions that do not involve cash flows would not be entered in records of any of the regulating agency or banks, and hence may remain unreported. Therefore, balance of payment is always an estimate, whether official or unofficial. It is explicitly recognized as a separate head *error and omissions* in BOP that reconciles the difference between debits and credits.

STRUCTURE OF BALANCE OF PAYMENT

There exists no standard format for reporting balance of payment statistics. Although IMF publishes the balance of payment statistics in a standardized format, it has to make adjustment to the reported statistics of the nation that may follow a different pattern to compile the balance of payment. India presents its balance of payments in the format given in Table 2-1.

Table 2-1
Structure of Balance of Payment—India

	A. Current Account
1. Merchandise	Includes export and import of goods.
2. Invisibles	Comprises services such as (a) software, travel, and transport insurance; (b) private and official transfers; and (c) income from investment and compensation to employees.
Total Current Account (1 + 2)	
	B. Capital Account
1. Foreign Investment	Includes (a) foreign direct investment and (b) portfolio investment. Items disclosed include portfolio investment by foreign institutional investment (FIIs), American Depository Receipts (ADRs), and Global Depository Receipts (GDRs).
2. Loan	Includes (a) external assistance; (b) commercial borrowing; and (c) short term funds to India that comprises (i) suppliers' credit >180 days and buyers' credit and (ii) suppliers' credit up to 180 days.
3. Banking Capital	It comprises three components: (a) foreign assets of commercial banks called authorized dealers (ADs), (b) foreign liabilities of ADs, and (c) others. 'Foreign assets' of commercial banks consist of (i) foreign currency holdings, and (ii) rupee overdrafts to non-resident banks. 'Foreign liabilities' of commercial banks consist of (i) Non-resident deposits, which comprise receipt and redemption of various non-resident deposit schemes, and (ii) liabilities other than non-resident deposits which comprise rupee and foreign currency liabilities to non-resident banks and official and semi-official institutions. 'Others' under banking capital include movement in balances of foreign central banks and international institutions such as IBRD, IDA, ADB, IFC, and IFAD, maintained with RBI as well as movement in balances held abroad by the embassies of India. Separately disclosed are non-resident deposits.

(Contd)

18 International Finance

Table 2-1 (Contd)

	B. Capital Account
4. Rupee Debt Service	Comprises interest and repayment of principal on debts from Rupee Payment Area.
5. Other Capital	Other capital comprises mainly the leads and lags in export receipts. Besides this, other items included are funds held abroad, India's subscription to international institutions, quota payments to IMF, remittances towards recouping the losses of branches/subsidiaries, and residual item of other capital transaction not included elsewhere.
	C. Reserve Account
	Movement in reserves comprises changes in the foreign currency assets held by the RBI and SDR balances held by the Government of India. These are recorded after excluding changes on account of valuation.
	D. Errors and Omissions
	To provide equality of debit and credit because of different data sources used for compilation of BOP statistics that are non-reconcilable.
	E. Overall Balance
	Total Current Account, Capital Account, and Errors & Omissions
	F. Monetary Movements
1. IMF	**Comprises changes in special drawing rights (SDRs) and Rupee Tranche Position with IMF. SDRs** are international *reserve assets* that are periodically allocated to IMF and not considered as liabilities of the IMF and its members. SDRs can be used to acquire other members' currencies (foreign exchange), to settle financial obligations, and to extend loans. **Reserve Tranche Position of IMF member** is the position in the IMF's General Resource Account as the sum of the reserve tranche purchases that India may draw upon and any indebtedness of the Fund.
2. Changes in Foreign Exchange Reserves	Negative denotes increase and positive signifies decrease in reserves.

Irrespective of the conventions followed by respective nations, BOP is divided into two parts—*the current account* and *capital account*—that distinguish the nature of transactions. Foreign currency reserve, which is forming the part of capital account, is grouped separately.

Current Account

Current account is akin to the P&L account of a firm. It comprises transactions of export (sales to non-residents) and import (purchases from non-residents) of goods and services. The current account further constitutes two accounts—*merchandise* and *invisibles*.

Merchandise relates to export and import of goods. It is normally a major account and a key to balance of trade. All goods exported and imported irrespective of their nature, that is, consumption goods or capital goods are part of the merchandise account. Steel plants, food grains, clothes, chemicals, and oil are all part of merchandise account. In case of India, oil constitutes major portion of imports.

Invisibles constitute services such as tourism, insurance, transport, and software. In case of India, software export forms a significant part of invisibles and is separately disclosed. The second component of invisibles is unilateral or unrequited transfers (those where the transferor does not require anything in return). These transfers can be done by private individuals (such as residents working abroad sending money) or by the government (such as financial aid by the government to the country ravaged by disasters). In case of India, considerable amount of remittances is sent by non-resident Indians working abroad. These transfers are classified as unilateral or unrequited. The donations may be inwards or outwards. They too are unilateral as the flow of funds is only in one direction and the counter flow is absent. Subscription to international bodies such as UNO, IMF, and Asian Development Bank (ADB) is classified as government transfers on the debit side.

The last item in the current account is investment income, which includes income from investments in the form of dividend and interest. Outflow is a debit and inflow is a credit. Some reserves of India are invested in treasuries of the USA that provide small yield. The income accruing on such investment is classified under investment income.

Current account is like the P&L account of a firm. The exports are sales of goods and services from the nation and the imports are analogous to purchases of materials. Services are similar to wages and investment income includes other sources of income such as dividend and interest. With the exception of depreciation, current account is like a P&L statement for a nation, where exports exceeding imports would denote a profit and imports exceeding exports signify a loss.

Capital Account

Transactions that are purely claims on financial assets are classified as capital account transactions. They have many parts as shown in Table 2-1. Foreign direct investment (FDI) and portfolio investments comprise a significant portion of capital account. Borrowings by Indian firms in foreign currency, mobilizing equity capital from residents abroad, portfolio investments by foreign institutional investors (FIIs), and FDI—both inwards and outwards—are some of the common transactions that appear in capital account. The profits of the foreign equity participation by way of FDI, if retained, are classified as 'reinvested earning'.

The profit distributed as dividend would go to current account in investment income on the debit side. Significant amount of foreign investment in India comes as portfolio investment. These investments are done by those in financial securities by hedge funds, mutual funds, banks, and investment institutions. An inflow is recorded as credit in the capital account by debit to reserves account. Withdrawal of investment would deplete reserves.

Reserve Account

Reserve account is a part of capital account, but the changes in the position of reserves are separately indicated. A debit entry in reserves indicates accretion, whereas a credit entry denotes depletion of reserve. This often leads to confusion, but it must be seen in the context of accounting. Reserves are assets from national perspective. Increasing debit implies increasing assets, and decreasing debit means decreasing liabilities. Generally, foreign exchange reserves are created when exports are more than imports. Exports increase the supply of foreign currency, whereas imports consume foreign currency. Since exports are credits, the increases in asset would be debits.

Reserve account comprises assets that are acceptable across the world for settlement of international transactions. Historically, gold was the most acceptable medium of settlement of international trade transactions. Thereafter, it was IMF. The global bank had its currency denoted as special drawing rights (SDRs), which could also be used as means of international settlement. Today, international payments are made in several currencies, depending upon the confidence of the world in them. Therefore, the reserve position of a nation is gauged by the amount of (a) gold, (b) SDRs—the currency of IMF, and (c) other freely convertible currencies, such as US dollar, euro, pound sterling, and Japanese yen, that a nation possesses. Please refer to the *Online Resource Centre* for India's foreign exchange reserves.

Just as the P&L account of a firm is a summary of its activities during a period, the current account of the nation is a reflection of the sale and purchase of goods and services to and from other nations. The capital account is more like a balance sheet or a cash flow statement reflecting receipts and payments from the outside world. It provides details of a nation's claim on assets and liabilities created during a period towards the rest of the world. A borrowing in foreign exchange would create a liability with increase in reserves, just in the same way as a loan does for a firm increasing liability and cash/bank balance. Therefore, reserves are equivalent to cash and bank balance of a firm in its balance sheet.

Errors and Omissions

Errors and omissions refer to the recognition of the statistical errors in the compilation of BOPs. Compilation of data for BOP is a Herculean task and errors are inevitable part of the process. It is next to impossible to keep track of all the transactions of residents with non-residents. Errors and omissions arise because of the following reasons:

1. The data for exports and imports is neither available at single source nor are the entries passed on double entry basis. There are different bodies responsible for various constituents of balance of payment. A firm involved in exports would only submit details of exports to one controlling organization, whereas the payments would be advised to another. There exists no check of debit and credit equivalence. The submission of data to various organizations responsible for BOP is at best a single entry system.
2. Besides mismatch of two legs of entries, there is another problem of lead and lag. Sometimes payments may lead exports; while at some other time, payments may lag. With no countercheck possible on outstanding transactions, there would be mismatch due to time lags. These mismatches cause statistical discrepancy. The only alternative is to give credence to one leg of the transaction, assuming that the counter-leg follows. The net difference is accounted for as errors and omissions.
3. Some of the data compiled may be based on samples that may not represent a true figure. This may lead to error.

ACCOUNTING FOR BALANCE OF PAYMENT

The rules for recording the transactions of balance of payment are fairly simple. At an aggregate level the accounting system for BOP transactions follows the standard accounting practice of double entry. In simple terms, it means that there is an equivalent debit for every credit and vice versa. Therefore, the sum total of balance of payments would always be zero.

All transactions are recorded in domestic currency. As a country would trade in different currencies, the common denominator is the local currency. Thus, for India, all transactions would be recorded in rupees, whereas the trade may actually be denominated in several currencies such as dollar, euro, yen, and pound.

All exports are credits and all imports are debits. This would imply that credits in BOP would indicate the supply of foreign currency and debit would mean the demand for it. For example, consider the export of goods on credit from India worth ₹1,000. It would be reflected as

Debit	Short term claims (in capital account)	1,000
Credit	Mechandise export (in current account)	1,000

All payments received would lead to an increase in reserves. This may happen by increase in foreign assets or decrease in foreign liabilities. When this payment is received after the credit period is over, there would be a monetary movement. The entries passed are as follows:

Debit	Foreign exchange reserve (in capital account)	1,000
Credit	Short-term claims (in capital account)	1,000

There are basically five types of transactions that can take place. We consider each of the transaction for India with an example, each demonstrating double entry system as follows:

1. *Exchange of goods/services for a financial asset*

   Consider the import of computers worth ₹50,000 by an Indian. The entries in the BOPs would be

	Credit	Debit
Merchandise import (computers)		50,000
Short-term claims	50,000	

   Credit to the short-term claim indicates increase in liability. When paid, the liability would be extinguished by depletion of reserves.

2. *Exchange of goods/services for a return of other goods/services, commonly called barter or countertrade*

   Consider that India imports oil from one of the Gulf countries in exchange of supply of wheat. The value is placed at ₹60,000. The entries would be

	Credit	Debit
Merchandise import (oil)		60,000
Merchandise export (wheat)	60,000	

Both the transactions are recorded in the current account portion of BOP. There would be no cash flow and, hence, the position of foreign exchange reserves remains unaffected.

3. *Exchange of financial asset in return of another financial asset*

   An example of exchange of a financial asset for another would be an Indian firm borrowing from a foreign bank. Consider, for example, Tata Steel borrows US$1,000 from a bank abroad because of a lower interest rate in the US dollar as compared to borrowing in Indian rupee. At an exchange rate of ₹45/$ the transaction recorded would be

	Credit	Debit
Foreign exchange reserves		45,000
Commercial borrowing	45,000	

   Commercial borrowing forms the part of capital account and so do the reserves. Both the entries are in capital account with one entry indicating an increase in liability for India, whereas the counter entry denotes equivalent increase in foreign currency reserve.

4. *Transfer of goods and services with no corresponding quid pro quo*

   Transfer of goods and services without any obligation to return would include unilateral or unrequited transfers. Several governments provide financial assistance to countries in the form of medical supplies or food grains. For example, consider India providing clothes worth ₹35,000 to another nation devastated by floods. The BOP entries would be

	Credit	Debit
Unilateral transfers—Govt		35,000
Merchandise export (clothes)	35,000	

   Both the transactions shown here are contained in the current account portion of BOP. Since no flow of funds is involved, the reserve position remains unchanged.

5. *Transfer of financial assets with no corresponding quid pro quo*

   Transfer of financial assets without any return would include unilateral or unrequited transfers. Consider the aid in the form of cash rather than in goods as in the earlier example. If the aid were a donation in cash, the first entry would remain same, whereas the second entry of merchandise export would be replaced by credit to foreign exchange reserve position, indicating a depletion of reserves by ₹35,000.

   Another frequent transaction of this nature is the remittance sent by non-resident Indians. For example, consider that a software engineer from India sends US$1,000. At an exchange rate of ₹46, the transaction in the BOP would be recorded as

	Credit	Debit
Foreign exchange reserves		46,000
Unilateral transfers—Private	46,000	

In the remittances, the cash flow takes place in foreign currency in India. The debit entry in the foreign exchange reserves account indicates increasing reserves.

The BOP for India after the five entries just discussed would be as given in Table 2-2.

Table 2-2
Final BOP of Examples

Description	Credit	Debit	Net (Credit − Debit)
I. Current Account			
Merchandise	95,000[1]	1,10,000[2]	−15,000
Trade Balance			
Transfers—Govt		35,000	−35,000
Transfers—Private	46,000		46,000
Total Current Account	1,41,000	1,45,000	−4,000
II. Capital Account			
Commercial borrowings	45,000		45,000
Short-term claims	50,000		50,000
Total Capital Account	95,000	–	95,000
Overall Balance	2,36,000	1,45,000	91,000
III. Monetary Movements			
Changes in foreign exchange reserves[3]		91,000	−91,000

[1] Total of merchandise export of wheat and clothes.
[2] Total of imports of oil and computers.
[3] Comprises external commercial borrowing and private remittance.

Exercise 2-1
BOP—Accounting

What entries in the BOP of India would be passed for the following transactions?
1. An American tourist arrives India and encashes US$2,000 at the exchange rate of ₹44.00 at the airport.
2. An Indian remits a fee of £1,000 at ₹75/£ for his son studying in Britain.
3. An Indian firm provides software in exchange of receiving hardware from Germany for €1,000 when the exchange rate is ₹55/€.
4. An American investor redeems ADRs worth $200 when the exchange rate is ₹48/$.
5. A firm exports rice worth $3,000 and adjusts $2,000 towards the payment of the representative of the importer and receives the remaining US$1,000 in the bank account. The exchange rate is ₹45/$.

Solution
The entries passed in the BOPs would be as follows:

Transaction	Description	Credit	Debit
1.	Invisibles—Travel	88,000	
	Reserves account		88,000
2.	Invisibles—Miscellaneous		75,000
	Reserves account	75,000	

Transaction	Description	Credit	Debit
3	Invisibles—Services	55,000	
	Merchandise		55,000
4.	Portfolio Investment		9,600
	Reserves account	9,600	
5.	Merchandise	1,35,000	
	Invisibles—Compensation to employees		90,000
	Reserves account		45,000

A debit in reserves account indicates an increase in Reserves and vice versa.

IMBALANCES IN BALANCE OF PAYMENT

All transactions done on the double entry system have equal debit and credit. Therefore, BOP would always balance just as the balance sheet of a firm does. Sources and uses of funds have to be always equal. Yet colloquially we speak of imbalances in BOP either as deficit or as surplus. Let us examine what really it means?

Current Account Balance

In totality, BOP cannot be imbalanced. The key to the study of BOP lies in the data contained in the current account portion; or more closely those contained in the trade account (merchandise). The strength of a nation is often judged from the competitiveness of its export. Foreign exchange reserves that are created through exports are considered more permanent in nature, with no corresponding future liability to fulfil. If exports exceed imports, there would be an accumulation of foreign currency reserves. Analysts, economists, and academicians focus only on current account balance since the state of current account indicates the inherent strength or weakness of an economy. The balance in the current account may imply need for structural changes in the economy.

When one speaks of deficit or surplus in the balance of payment, it means the balance in the current account, that is, the merchandise and invisibles. A deficit BOP means that the value of export of goods and services is less than the value of import of goods and services. Similarly, a surplus BOP implies that the value of export of goods and services exceeds the value of import of goods and services.

$$\text{Total exports} - \text{Total imports} \quad \begin{array}{l} > 0 \quad \text{Surplus BOP} \\ < 0 \quad \text{Deficit BOP} \end{array}$$

Countertrade has no impact on the current account balance because the imports and exports cancel out each other. However, unilateral transfers do have implications on the current account balance.

Trade Account Balance

When one refers to the merchandise account ignoring transactions in the invisibles, it is referred as trade balance. When export of goods is less than import of goods, the trade balance is in deficit and vice versa, that is,

$$\text{Merchandise exports} - \text{Merchandise imports} \quad \begin{array}{l} > 0 \quad \text{Surplus balance of trade} \\ < 0 \quad \text{Deficit balance of trade} \end{array}$$

Trade account balance depicts the competitiveness in the manufacturing sector because trade balance excludes invisibles (services). In the olden days, it was a correct measure as services were not forming significant proportion of international trade. As the world economy is growing, the proportion of services in the gross domestic product (GDP) as well as in the international trade is continuously growing. Earlier, the current accounts of nations were dominated by trade in the manufactured products. With growing services sector, the trade account deficit may be offset by invisibles. In that case, the services sector is more competitive internationally than the manufacturing sector.

Capital Account Balance

Since BOP is always balanced, the surplus or deficit in current account balance should be equal to the same deficit or surplus in capital account, including the changes in reserves. The following identity must always remain true (with the exception of errors and omissions):

$$\text{Current account deficit/surplus} = \text{Capital account surplus/deficit} \tag{2-1}$$

As a natural extension of Eq. 2-1, one may expect that excess of exports over imports must result in increase in reserves (a debit in the capital/reserve account). If reserves do not increase, the capital must leave the country and the surplus must result in investment abroad, that is, holding of foreign assets, which is again a debit in the capital account. In case imports exceed exports, the extra payment must be financed by borrowings or depletion of reserves. The capital required to finance the deficit would result in an increase in holding of domestic financial assets by the foreigners. It is analogous to funding of losses of a firm through borrowings, which is clearly an undesirable option in the long run. Therefore, there is a need to bifurcate the capital account into two—short-term and long-term capital accounts.

Economists also tend to distinguish the transactions of balance of payments as *autonomous* or *accommodating*. Autonomous transactions take place independent of BOP. Accommodating transactions result due to financing of autonomous transactions. Excess of receipts of autonomous transactions over payments for them is a surplus. Further, this surplus is accommodated by acquiring foreign assets. Conversely, if payments exceed receipts for autonomous transactions, it would cause borrowings. These borrowings, which are consequential to the autonomous transaction, then become accommodating transactions. The difficulty of classifying the transactions as autonomous or accommodating arises due to the lack of knowledge of motive of undertaking a transaction. It is indeed difficult to determine if the transaction was independent or otherwise.

BALANCE OF PAYMENT AND DOMESTIC ECONOMY

The balance of payment of a nation summarizes its performance with the external world. It is a linkage of domestic economy with the rest of the world. The study of BOP may throw light on the competitiveness of the nation as compared to other nations. The performance in the external sector, as can be interpreted by BOP, is not aloof from domestic economic developments.

The imports and exports affect consumption and production in an economy. National income, Y, must be either consumed, C, or saved, S. Similarly, national expenditure must equal consumption, C, and investment, I. Therefore, a closed economy under equilibrium must have savings equal to the investment.

$$\text{Savings} = \text{Investment} \tag{2-2}$$

In an open economy, the nation would not only consume or produce domestically but also have imports and exports. Consumption would comprise domestic products and imported products. National product would include production for domestic use and exports. Therefore,

$$\text{Savings} - \text{Investment} = \text{Exports} - \text{Imports} \tag{2-3}$$

No role of government is assumed in Eqs 2-2 and 2-3. National income with government expenditure G, indicated separately is given by

$$Y = C + I + G \tag{2-4}$$

For an open economy with exports and imports, the national income with government expenditure indicated separately for private consumption and including export, X, and import, M, we have

$$Y = C + I + G + X - M \tag{2-5}$$

National income consists of disposable income, D, and taxes, T. Similarly, consumption equals disposable income and savings. Therefore, Eq. 2-5 becomes

$$D + T = D - S + I + G + X - M \tag{2-6}$$

Rearranging according to the groups, that is, government expenditure and taxes, savings and investment, and exports and imports, we get a relationship given by Eq. 2-7 that links the external sector performance with the domestic scenario of saving, investment, and fiscal policies as

$$\begin{array}{ccccc} (X-M) & = & (T-G) & + & (S-I) \\ \text{Current Account Surplus} & = & \text{Budget Surplus} & + & \text{Saving Surplus} \end{array} \tag{2-7}$$

$(S - I)$ represents private savings and $(T - G)$ represents government savings, that is, budget surplus. $(X - M)$ is the savings provided by foreigners or conversely $(M - X)$ is the savings of an economy used for funding foreigners. According to Eq. 2-7 the current account surplus must equal the budget surplus and the private savings surplus. If there is saving surplus and budget is balanced, then the private savings must be channelized abroad. This would cause the capital account of BOP to have deficit, which equals the current account surplus. If not channelized abroad, the surplus would remain idle in the form of reserves.

Moreover, assuming balanced budget for current account deficit would equal shortfall of savings over investment needs. These investments would need to be funded by capital from abroad.

Generally, worsening of BOP is considered a sign of worsening economy. It also signifies dependence on other nations for meeting consumption needs. In the context of Eq. 2-7, the deficit in the current account must be accompanied by a combination of budget deficit and savings deficit. If budget deficit results from planned expenditure on capacity generation, and the savings deficit is compensated by foreign inflows to create capacities, it would lead to increased income and production in future. Hopefully with passage of time the current account deficit would improve. This is an important result that communicates that adverse BOP need not be detrimental to the national objective of development and growth of the economy.

Equation 2-7 remains an accounting equality and does not imply causation. It is an identity that provides relationship among current account imbalance, fiscal deficit, and savings inadequacy. The accounting equality must hold true. It provides how the variables are related, and given any two constants, what needs to be done with the third. One cannot say that budget deficit would cause current account deficit and vice versa. One may attribute that current account deficit is due to fiscal deficit and lack of private savings over needs of capital formation. The relationship provides directions to policy makers.

MULTIPLIERS

Equation 2-7 provides a relationship of domestic economic environment as captured by savings and consumption habits, external sector as measured by supply of products to the world and consumption of imported products, and fiscal policies as reflected in the budget deficit/surplus. The fact that budget deficit can cure adverse BOP enhances the role and importance of government intervention. In fact, the impact of seemingly small policy changes is fairly large due to the multiplier effect.

The effect of government intervention by fiscal policy on the national income was suggested by Lord John Keynes in 1936 in his work titled *The General Theory of Employment, Interest and Money*. He demonstrated that a small impetus by the government can cause manifold increase in national income. Though applicable for a closed economy, the concept of multiplier can be extended for an open economy too.

For a closed economy if the government decides to increase expenditure on infrastructure by ₹100, the increase in national income would be manifold, depending upon the marginal propensity to consume (MPC). An additional impetus of ₹100 would increase the national income instantly by ₹100. This additional income would be either consumed or saved. Assume that MPC is 0.80 and marginal propensity to save (MPS) is 0.20. There would be additional consumption of ₹80, which raises output by 80. This in turn enhances the income by ₹80, which again may be partly consumed (80%) and partly saved. The next round makes the income rise by ₹64 (80 × 0.8). This goes on forever and the effect on income would be

$$= 100 + 100 \times 0.8 + 100 \times 0.8 \times 0.8 + 100 \times 0.8 \times 0.8 \times 0.8 + \ldots\ldots\ldots$$
$$= 100/(1 - 0.8) = ₹500$$

This multiplier is known as Keynesian multiplier. Its value is 5 (1/MPS) in the example discussed. The higher the consumption, the greater is the impact of fiscal stimulus. For an underemployed economy, the consumption-led growth is the key to improve national welfare. When the economy is fully employed, additional capacity must be created or efficiency of existing resource base must be increased to meet the increase in consumption. Increasing consumption becomes a constraint in a fully employed economy. The need to create capacity is paramount. In such a situation, savings-based development, which ultimately translates into investment, becomes more important.

In developing nations, the economies remain underemployed and are unable to exploit the full potential of resources available at hand. Higher savings in these countries would translate in investment that creates a platform for increased capacity for production of goods and services and, hence, the increased consumption. In developed economies, resources are fully deployed, and additional capacity creation would only be motivated by increased demand for goods and services. The recipe for success changes from one situation to another. Increased consumption is not a panacea of all problems.

In the description of multiplier, we assumed that (a) increase in government expenditure by way of deficit financing is nominal and would not lead to price rise, but instead the economy would gear up the output, (b) the economy is less than fully employed to enable increase in production, and (c) the interest rates remain constant.

The concept of multiplier can be extended to open economy where the assumption of economy less than fully employed can be relaxed as the increased consumption can be met by imports. However, an additional assumption needs to be made regarding constant prices. For an open economy, the value of foreign currency must also remain constant, that is, exchange rate does not change.

In an open economy, the national income as given by Eq. 2-5 is restated here:

$$Y = C + I + G + X - M$$

As income rises, the (a) consumption and (b) import also rise. Increase in income causes increase in consumption and import, but not by the same amount as the increase in income. Increase in income would be consumed and saved and increase in consumption would be met by domestic and imported goods.

The changes in consumption and imports of a nation are dependent upon the inclination of its residents to consume and import. Assuming both consumption and import as increasing linear function of income, they can be represented as follows:

$$C = C_a + cY \qquad (2\text{-}8)$$
$$M = M_a + mY \qquad (2\text{-}9)$$

Where C_a and M_a are autonomous values of consumption and imports, and c and m are marginal propensity of consume and marginal propensity to import, respectively.

The coefficients c and m represent what part of increased income would be consumed and what part is spent on import, respectively. The assumption of consumption and import as an increasing linear function of income seems reasonable. It simply implies that more the income, more the consumption and imports. Substituting Eqs 2-8 and 2-9 in Eq. 2-5, we get

$$Y = C_a + cY + I + G + X - M_a - mY$$

Therefore,

$$(1 - c + m)Y = C_a + I + G + X - M_a$$

If c is MPC, then $1 - c$ is MPS, s. Hence,

$$(s + m)Y = C_a + I + G + X - M_a \qquad (2\text{-}10)$$

If Δ denotes the change, then on marginal basis we have

$$(s + m)\Delta Y = \Delta C_a + \Delta I + \Delta G + \Delta X - \Delta M_a$$

$$\text{or } \Delta Y = \frac{1}{(s+m)}(\Delta C_a + \Delta I + \Delta G + \Delta X - \Delta M_a) \qquad (2\text{-}11)$$

Therefore, the multiplier changes from $1/s$ in closed economy to $1/(s + m)$ in an open economy. The multipliers for government expenditure and export would be

$$\frac{\Delta Y}{\Delta G} = \frac{1}{(s+m)} \quad \text{or} \quad \Delta Y = \frac{1}{(s+m)}\Delta G \qquad (2\text{-}12)$$

$$\frac{\Delta Y}{\Delta X} = \frac{1}{(s+m)} \quad \text{or} \quad \Delta Y = \frac{1}{(s+m)}\Delta X \qquad (2\text{-}13)$$

Since marginal propensity to import m is positive, the multiplier effect would be less in an open economy as compared to the closed economy for a given impetus in government expenditure. The reason is not far to seek. To the extent the increased consumption is met by imports, it does not benefit the nation. The increased consumption is met by increase in production of the other nation rather than its own. From the increased consumption, the foreign country benefits to the extent the consumption is met by imports. If the increased consumption is met entirely by local resources, the economy is benefited more. A part of increased consumption is passed on to the other nation and to that extent the local economy is deprived of the benefit of increased consumption.

Exercise 2-2
Impact of Government Expenditure on National Income

In India, marginal propensities to save and import are 25% and 10%, respectively. What changes in national income are expected if the Government of India decides to increase its expenditure by ₹100 crore to boost the local economy?

If the Government of India decides to ban import of goods, what growth in national income do you see?

Solution

The change in the national income, ΔY, as a result of the increase in government expenditure, ΔG, using Eq. 2-12 is given as

$$\Delta Y = \frac{1}{(s+m)} \Delta G = \frac{1}{0.25+0.10} \times 100 = ₹285.71 \text{ crore}$$

If no imports are allowed, then ($m = 0$); due to ban on imports the change in national income would be

$$\Delta Y = \frac{1}{(s+m)} \Delta G = \frac{1}{0.25+0.00} \times 100 = ₹400 \text{ crore}$$

The impact on national income for exports would be same as the effect of increased government expenditure, as can be seen from Eq. 2-13. Exercise 2-3 will elaborate on the effectiveness of export-led growth—a model followed by many developing countries with Japan and China being the prominent amongst them.

Exercise 2-3
Impact of Government Expenditure on National Income

In Exercise 2-2, if the increase in government expenditure is in the form of export subsidy and if exports register an equivalent growth, what changes in income are expected?

If Government of India's expenditure on subsidy of exports makes Indian goods cheaper and exports increase by ₹300 crore, what changes in the national income do you expect?

Solution

The change in the national income, ΔY, as result of increase in the government expenditure, ΔG, translated into increase in exports using Eq. 2-13 is

$$\Delta Y = \frac{1}{(s+m)} \Delta X = \frac{1}{0.25+0.10} \times 100 = ₹285.71 \text{ crore}$$

If no imports are allowed, the change in national income would be

$$\Delta Y = \frac{1}{(s+m)} \Delta X = \frac{1}{0.25+0.00} \times 300 = ₹857.14 \text{ crore}$$

Current Account Multipliers

The relationship of current account deficit with other economic variables too may be determined. Rearranging Equation 2-10 current account balance is given by

Current account balance, $CA = X - M = X - M_a - mY$

Using Eq. 2-10, we have

$$mY = \frac{m}{(s+m)}(C_a + I + G + X - M_a)$$

and $\quad CA = X - M_a - \dfrac{m}{(s+m)}(C_a + I + G + X - M_a)$

In the incremental form, we have

$$\Delta CA = \Delta X - \Delta M_a - \dfrac{m}{(s+m)}(\Delta C_a + \Delta I + \Delta G + \Delta X - \Delta M_a) \qquad (2\text{-}14)$$

The multipliers for current account balance for government expenditure and exports can be worked out by Eq.2-14 leaving all other parameters constant and are $-m/(s+m)$ and $s/(s+m)$, respectively, as shown below

$$\Delta CA = -\dfrac{m}{(s+m)} \Delta G \qquad (2\text{-}15)$$

$$\Delta CA = \Delta X - \dfrac{m}{(s+m)} \Delta X \quad \text{or} \quad \Delta CA = \dfrac{s}{(s+m)} \Delta X \qquad (2\text{-}16)$$

Negative sign in Eq. 2-15 indicates deteriorating balance of payment situation, that is, increased current account deficit with increased government expenditure, that is, budget deficit.

CORRECTING BALANCE OF PAYMENT

As stated earlier, the persistent and continuous deficit in current account implies continuous dependence of the nation on foreign capital to fund the excess of imports. If the deficit is persistent and large, it is regarded as a bad sign for the economy and is a constant source of worry for all economists the world over. In an ideal situation, the balance of payment in the current account must be balanced, that is, exports must finance the imports exactly. However, most of the countries, predominantly developing ones, have persistent deficits in their BOPs.

The current account deficit may be financed by external debt or other capital account transactions. Sadly, developing countries are also not favourite destinations of multinational corporations for investments abroad. Financing the current account deficit by debt has its own dangers because it merely defers the adversity by creating larger future liabilities. To avoid the dangers of debt, nations must adopt internal measures to contain the deficit to a reasonable level. The preceding section highlights the relationship of domestic economic conditions with the external sector. Here we discuss some policy measures that greatly affect external sector.

Currency Devaluation/Depreciation

The propensity to import and encouragement to exports are the functions of the value of the domestic currency. Devaluation or depreciation of local currency makes exports competitive as compared to competing products from other nations. Besides, it also makes imports expensive. Undervalued currency is a boost for exports and discourages imports.

For correcting the deficit in the current account, that is, reducing the excess of imports over exports currency devaluation is considered a very convenient option by academicians, economists, political leaders, and business people alike. Most of them believe that adjusting the exchange rate to favour exports and to discourage imports is an effective remedy to control the adverse BOP

CONCEPTS IN PRACTICE
Revaluation Concern

YUAN HIGHS AND LOWS

In January 2010, amidst the brouhaha generated by the start of the five-day annual jamboree of the World Economic Forum in Davos, Switzerland, and the continued bloodbath in stock markets the world over, the significance of a positive export performance by Japan was overlooked and instead focus was on Chinese policy on the valuation of its currency, yuan.

The concerns arose from the uncertainty in the Chinese stance on the dollar–yuan exchange rate and not to revalue yuan. The Chinese policy of keeping yuan artificially low keeps Chinese export prices low and stable, which allows its suppliers to maintain trade relations with the Chinese import-intensive industrial and export sectors.

Even developed countries like the USA have benefited from the Chinese currency policy during the period of recession just before 2010. The undervalued currency has enabled such countries to finance the vast sums they needed to stimulate their economies. But with world economy improving, there is an increasing pressure on China to revalue yuan and, then, float their currency freely just as dollar, euro, and yen do. That would make Chinese exports more expensive, allowing other nations to compete better.

According to Paul Krugman's 'back-of-the-envelope' calculations, China's weak-yuan policy has cost 1.4 million American jobs (out of the more than 27 million jobs lost in the USA in the recession), many in manufacturing, as American producers find it hard to compete with cheap Chinese goods. Notwithstanding the fact that the Chinese weak-yuan policy accounted for a mere 5% of all American job losses in this recession, the call for revaluation of yuan is gaining momentum to reduce 'global imbalances'. Stronger yuan is considered necessary to turn the Chinese economy inward and relieve the nation's excessive dependence on external demand.

But will the Chinese play ball? Unlike the Japan of yore, it has not been easy for the international community to pressurize China into adopting policies that they deem not suited or ill-timed for their national interests.

Source: Extracted from Karmakar, Suparna, *Business Line*, 29 January 2010.

situation. One of the most powerful economies in the world, China, has achieved continuous growth for long periods by maintaining an undervalued domestic currency, that is, yuan. The value of yuan has evoked sharp reactions worldwide as the impact of this strategy is not only confined to China and its neighbours, but also affects far-off and powerful economies like USA. USA often blames undervalued yuan for its high and persistent adverse balance of payment.

The proponents of currency depreciation as a solution to adverse BOP hold a view that correct exchange rate is one at which demand and supply of foreign currency are equal. Adverse balance of payment implies greater imports than the exports can fund. Hence, the supply of foreign currency is less than what is demanded by importers. Making foreign currency expensive would enhance supply and contain its demand.

Elasticity Approach It is uncertain that the currency devaluation would lead to improvement in the position of current account. It is so because the devaluation has two opposing effects—*price effect* and *volume effect*. While price effect of devaluation worsens balance of payment, the volume effect improves it. Till the time price effect dominates the volume effect, currency devaluation would fail to achieve its objective.

For ease of understanding, consider a simple example. Assume that India exports a product with a quantity of 120 at the rate of ₹20 each, with value of exports at ₹2,400. It also imports another product with a quantity of 12 at the rate of $4 each, with the total import bill at $48. At current exchange rate of ₹50/$, the balance of payment is balanced. For simplicity of exposition, assume that these are the only transactions in the current account.

To improve the balance of payment, the Government of India decides to devalue rupee by 20% from ₹50/$ to ₹60/$. With no change in the volume of export, the balance of payment worsens to $8 or ₹420, as the price of the products exported and imported remain same. However, the worth of exports reduces from $48 to $40, whereas the value of import remains at $48, worsening the BOP. This is due to price effect as shown in Panel I of Table 2-3.

Table 2-3
Elasticity Approach to Devaluation and Balance of Payment

			Balance of Payment		Remarks
	Quantity	Price	Value (₹)	Value ($)	
Panel I: Price Effect					
Exports	120	₹20	2,400	40	Price effect alone worsens the BOP
Imports	12	$4	2,880	48	
BOP			−420	−8	
Panel II: Volume Effect < Price Effect					
Exports	126	₹20	2,520	42	Volume effect does not offset the price effect; BOP worsens but not as much as with price effect alone
Imports	11	$4	2,640	44	
BOP			−120	−2	
Panel III: Volume Effect > Price Effect					
Exports	132	₹20	2,640	44	Volume effect more than offsets the price effect to improve BOP
Imports	10	$4	2,400	40	
BOP			+240	+4	

Now assume that as a result of devaluation, the export quantity increases by 5% and import quantity decreases by 8.33%. For the new quantity of imports and exports, the BOP worsens by $2 as compared to the position prior to devaluation. Refer to Panel II of Table 2-3. The change in volume (increase in exports and decrease in imports) does not compensate or offset the adverse price effect due to devaluation.

Now, consider that exports increase by 20% and imports fall by 16.67% in terms of volume. The changes in the volume are large enough to offset the adverse price effect. The BOP turns positive to $4 or ₹240 from earlier balanced position pre-devaluation. Refer to Panel III of Table 2-3.

From this exposition, it is clear that the improvement in the balance of payment position is dependent upon the elasticity of exports and imports, that is, how sensitive is the volume to the price change. If international trade is more responsive to the changes in the exchange rate, the chances of improving balance of payment are more. The responsiveness of the quantities of import and exports to the changes in the exchange rates are defined as

$$\text{Elasticity of Export, } \eta_e = \frac{\text{\% change in export quantity}}{\text{\% change in exchange rate}} \qquad (2\text{-}17)$$

$$\text{Elasticity of Import, } \eta_m = -\frac{\text{\% change in import quantity}}{\text{\% change in exchange rate}} \qquad (2\text{-}18)$$

Elasticity of export/import is the percentage change in quantities for 1% change in exchange rate. The elasticity of export in the first case is 5/20 = 0.25 and in the second case is 10/20 = 0.5. Similarly, the import elasticity in the first and second cases are 8.33/20 = 0.416 and 16.67/20 = 0.833, respectively. Note that import elasticity is negative as increase in the exchange rate results in decrease in the quantity.

For devaluation to result in improvement in the BOP, the sum of foreign elasticity of demand for exports and home country's elasticity of imports must exceed one.[1] Here, the absolute value of import is considered without its negative sign

Absorption Approach Under the elasticity approach, it is assumed that currency devaluation does not impact national income or consumption when exchange rate changes balance the supply and demand for foreign currency. The effects of currency devaluation on income, besides those on imports and exports, need to be examined for a more comprehensive view.

We know that $Y = C + I + G + X - M$, or

Current Account Balance, $CA = X - M = Y - (C + I + G) = Y - A$
or $\Delta CA = \Delta Y - \Delta A$

Absorption, A, relates to the changes in the consumption including investment and government expenditure ($C + I + G$). The devaluation, therefore, depends upon income level

---

[1] This is known as Marshall–Lerner condition that is valid only approximately.

and absorption. From the perspective of changes in the exchange rate, the absorption has two components: (a) the indirect changes in absorption, a, as a function of change in income, Y, from sources other than devaluation and (b) the second component related to devaluation, that is, direct changes due to devaluation, A_d.

$$\Delta A = a\, \Delta Y - \Delta A_d$$
$$\text{or} \quad \Delta CA = (1-a)\, \Delta Y - \Delta A_d \tag{2-19}$$

With a less than one, the current account must improve, provided national income increases. If a is greater than one, the increased income would cause deterioration in the current account. More than proportionate absorption is likely to happen when the increased income induces borrowing for investment for a further rise in future income. Hence, marginal propensity to absorb in the short run decides the fate of current account balance.

The change in the income level is also dependent upon whether the economy is fully employed or underemployed. If the economy is fully employed, there is no possibility of increasing income and, hence $\Delta Y = 0$. The current account position remains unaffected if direct change in direct absorption ΔA_d too is zero.

If the economy is less than fully employed, devaluation may increase production. The exports would increase and so would the income. But increased income leads to increased imports too. If increased imports are more than the increased exports, then the net result could be a fall in income.

Considered from the viewpoint of prices, the devaluation must lead to marginal increase in price of exports, P. The domestic price of imports is $S \times P^*$, where S is the spot exchange rate post devaluation and P^* is the price of import in foreign currency. In terms of foreign trade with devaluation of currency, the imports become costlier. If the increase in price of export is less than the increase in domestic price, the terms of trade becomes negative. A negative terms of trade implies that the country needs to export more to import the same quantity of imports; hence, it would lead to decrease in national income.

The elasticity approach and the absorption approaches to examine the impact of devaluation on the current account are not contradictory but complementary. Raising exports more than imports as per elasticity approach implies that income would rise with marginal propensity to absorb, a less than one. If marginal propensity to absorb, a is more than one, then the income would not rise.

The J-Curve Another consideration in currency depreciation to resolve balance of payment situation is the reaction time of the economy to respond to the initiative for exchange rate change. Due to the inertia of the economy and reluctance of people to refrain from imports even when they become expensive, the impact of currency devaluation on balance of payment would not be immediate. Though exports become cheaper, increasing exports is also dependent upon capacity creation and the readiness of the foreign market to accept the cheaper exports. The response to currency devaluation would in most cases be delayed as it takes a while for (a) resident consumers to curb imports, (b) resident producers to create capacities, and (c) foreigners to consume more of cheaper exports. It is not surprising to see that the immediate impact of currency devaluation on balance of payment could be opposite of what is intended, that is, further deterioration rather than improvement in balance of payment because of two possible lagging effects:

Producers' lag Though the exports become cheaper and more competitive in the international markets with currency depreciation, the volumes do not increase immediately partly due to producers' inability to produce more and partly due to importers' considerations other than price. This makes the value of exports decline as price effects precede the compensating volume adjustment.

Consumers' lag Similar to producers' lag, consumers of imported goods need time to reduce volume to the higher price level. Though the imports become expensive, volumes do not reduce immediately. Here, price effect again precedes volume changes. With the same volume and raised prices of foreign goods, the value of import may actually increase in the short run.

The correction of adverse BOP is dependent upon the change in prices of goods and change in volumes of imports and exports. Currency devaluation causes the price change immediately, but changes in the volumes take longer to adjust. The initial worsening of BOP before it moves in the contemplated direction is called J-Curve effect (due to its resemblance with the letter J), as depicted in Figure 2-1.

The impact of devaluation on domestic economy is fuelling inflation. As inflows of foreign currency increase and reserves mount, the domestic money supply increases. To an extent, increased local money supply is absorbed in increased production and national income. It is only a matter of time that money supply exceeds the value of goods and services in the economy.

However, for developing countries, the transactions on capital account are expected to be nominal and devaluation of currency remains an effective way of correcting the imbalance in the

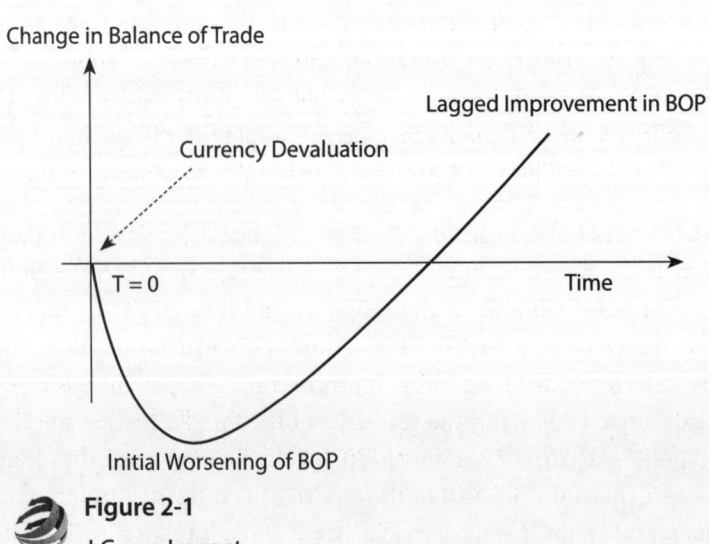

Figure 2-1
J Curve Impact

CONCEPTS IN PRACTICE
Keeping Currency Undervalued

COST OF UNDERVALUATION

A rapid rise in current account surplus and associated build-up of reserves pose mounting challenge for the Chinese central bank to keep its currency undervalued.

The basic premise of an undervalued currency is that the central bank has to intervene in the foreign exchange market to postpone current consumption and delay inflation. The increased money supply on account of foreign exchange receipts has to be sterilized by mopping up the surplus local money. If it does not, then the excess liquidity causes inflation and appreciation of local currency.

In 2010 following the collapse of interest rates in the USA, the interest rates in China exceeded those of the USA. Therefore, the cost of issuing sterilization bills increased. The central bank had to rely more on upward adjustment of statutory reserve requirement of local banks, thereby passing part of the cost to commercial banks. However, from long-term perspective, interest rates in China had to be kept low to avert the capital inflows, necessitating further sterilization.

Exchange rates are not decided by pure economic forces. Faced with extreme competition with Japan and hefty current account deficit in 1985, the USA deliberately devalued dollar under Plaza Accord. Many analysts also believed that expensive Japanese yen had been largely responsible for halting its unprecedented economic progress since the 1950s. The case of Japan provides impetus to the policy of continuing to keep currency devalued. Though devalued currency of China may be partly responsible for unemployment in the USA it refrained from imposing penalties of any form because under Sino-US mutual economic dependence, China remains the largest holder of US treasuries at US$800 billion. The dollar that goes from the USA to China on current account transaction returns back to the USA in the form of capital account inflow.

Source: Extracted from ShahidulIslam, M., 'The Renminbi Challenge', *Business Line*, 5 January 2010.

balance of payment. China has been running consistent and large current account surplus for long. Keeping its currency undervalued is attributed as the primary reason for the export-led growth.

Protectionism

Besides playing with the exchange rate, another tool available with polity to correct adverse balance of payment is to consider the regulatory means of (a) encouraging exports and (b) discouraging imports. In currency depreciation, the intervention was by fixing the lower value for domestic currency and waiting for the open market forces to respond to the new price level of the currency.

Boosting exports by way of incentives and discouraging imports by imposing tariff provides protection to domestic producers against foreign competition.

Increasing exports by providing export subsidy and tax holidays, setting export processing zones, and stipulating export commitments are some of the common measures adopted by governments. These measures are more in the nature of incentives to export so as to bring down the prices and make them more competitive in the international markets. These measures compensate exporters for the cost of production, enabling them to supply goods at lower prices and compete with other nations.

Simultaneously with or independently of export promotion measures, one can check the foreign currency outflows by imposing tariffs and/or quota for import of goods. Tariff relates to imposition of customs duty on imported goods, making them expensive with tariff amount collected by the government. Quota is a quantitative restriction on the quantity of goods that can be imported in a given period. As compared to quota restrictions, resorting to tariff on import is a more lucrative option for governments in developing nations. These nations not only remedy the adverse balance of payment but also generate revenue because besides solving BOP problem, developing nations also suffer from acute shortage of financial resources to implement the developmental programmes and face fiscal deficit.

Imposition of tariff serves dual purpose of containing imports and augmenting the revenue collection of the government. The additional revenue collected by tariff can be used for subsidizing exports or funding the developmental programmes. Hence, import tariff may be deemed as a mere re-allocation of financial resources from supposedly affluent importers to the not-so-affluent general population, and exporters perceived to be serving the national cause. Politically, raising tariffs as revenue generation tool is considered better as compared to raising income tax. Tariff is a consumption tax that is not felt as much as income tax which leaves tax payers with lesser disposable income and more aggrieved.

Nature of goods is an important consideration in imposing tariff. Tariffs can be effective tools for containing the deficit in the balance of payment as long as they are imposed only on finished goods and not on intermediate goods or inputs. If imposed on intermediate goods or raw materials, the cost of production increases for the finished goods. This harms the domestic users. Moreover, if these goods are exportable, then they become expensive too, thereby neutralizing the impact of tariff. The reduction in imports will be offset by reduction in exports, keeping the deficit at original level.

Controlling Capital Flows

Besides currency depreciation and protectionism, another way of monitoring and checking the adverse BOP is controlling the capital flows on account of transactions of financial assets. We know that current account deficit must be supported by equal capital account surplus. Without implying causation whether capital account surplus causes current account deficit or vice versa, the accounting entity essentially remains true. Of late, the fact that developing countries invest their reserves in US treasuries, the current account deficit in the USA is being funded by capital inflows, providing surplus in capital account of its balance of payment.

CONCEPTS IN PRACTICE
Resorting to Protectionism

SLOW JOBLESS RECOVERY BREEDS PROTECTIONISM

Comparing the recent (2008–10) Great Recession with the Great Depression of the 1930s can be comforting for politicians and policy makers in the sense that there is no return to tit-for-tat protectionism. It is based on the belief that the recovery would be swift and sustained as compared to the 1930s. If the global economy is stuck with low-growth, high-unemployment rut, there could be no escape from increased protectionism. The year 2008–2009 saw this. Trade statistics of top 10 trading nations, in this year, showed a decline of 22% in total trade, as shown in the following table.

Despite the magnanimous stimulus provided in 2010, the recovery has been feeble and short-lived. The traditional tools—cutting interest

Trade Statistics - Top 10 Nations								$ billions
Country	Calendar Year 2009				Calendar Year 2008			
	Export	Import	Total	Surplus/Deficit	Export	Import	Total	Surplus/Deficit
USA	1,056	1,605	2,661	–549	1,287	2,169	3,456	–882
China	1,201	1,005	2,206	196	1,430	1,133	2,563	297
Germany	1,126	938	2,064	188	1,446	1,185	2,631	261
Japan	581	552	1,133	29	782	763	1,545	19
France	485	560	1,045	–75	616	715	1,331	–99
Holland	498	445	943	53	638	581	1,219	57
UK	352	481	833	–129	460	633	1,093	–173
Italy	406	413	819	–7	543	562	1,105	–19
Belgium	370	352	722	18	472	466	938	6
Korea	364	323	687	41	422	435	857	–13
Total	**6,439**	**6,674**	**13,113**		**8,096**	**8,642**	**16,738**	
India	*163*	*250*	*413*	*–87*	*195*	*321*	*516*	*–126*

> rates and spending more public money—were not enough. After having cut the interest rate to abysmally low levels, politicians and central banks have already exhausted one tool. Yet there is pressure for continuing and increasing the stimulus.
>
> As a tool of last resort, the only feasible option seems manipulating the currency exchange rates or increase trade barriers. In October 2010 Guido Mantega, Brazil's finance minister, warned that 'international currency war' had broken out. It is not difficult to understand why nations are engaged in such wars. The history of the 1930s provides an evidence of those who devalue earlier steal a march over competition. But devaluation is different from protectionism. The question is whether commitment to free international trade is as deep as it seems. The trade liberalization process that commenced in 2001 in Doha remains tardy or at best moves at snail's pace. There is always a common problem with all trade ministers. All of them talk of free trade but act like mercantilists—seeking maximum concessions while giving away as little as possible in return in terms of access to their own domestic markets.
>
> *Source*: Based on Elliot, Larry, 'The Guardian', *Hindustan Times*, 25 October 2010.

The deficit in the balance of trade must be financed by borrowings such as external commercial borrowings and loans. Portfolio investments too are inflows that go to support the deficit in current account. The underlying thought in regulating the capital flows on financial assets is that when no foreign exchange is available, the imports cannot be supported. Similarly, when no avenues other than exports are available for creating supplies of foreign exchange, the nation would import only as much as the export can support. Foreigners too would import only as much as they can export.

Emerging markets such as China, India, and Brazil have become very attractive and favourite destinations for portfolio investment due to the high returns they offer. Often the capital moves in on account of *carry trade*. Capital always chases higher returns. Carry trade refers to the transaction of borrowing in currencies with low interest rates such as yen and Swiss francs and investing in currencies offering higher yields. Such carry trades are naturally extremely volatile and reverse the direction of capital flows with big volumes. In the system where exchange rate is determined by market forces and not controlled by government, the initial flow of foreign currency would see the value of local currency rise, whereas when the capital outflows are sudden and large, the local currency can depreciate extremely fast.

The capital flows on portfolio investments are certainly volatile, and an issue of great concern is whether to tax or stop the capital flows on account of FDI. From the perspective of development of economy, FDIs are essential so as to sustain the competitive edge in the market by constant upgrading of technology and enhancing productivity.

As foreign currency investment continued to flow in Brazil making its currency *real* appreciate as much as 36% in less than first 10 months of 2009, it imposed a 2% tax on foreign inflows for investment in equity and debt markets of Brazil in November 2009. With the imposition of tax on inflows, the carry trade became less attractive and desired inflow on account of more stable foreign direct investment (FDI) remains unaffected. Various means and their effectiveness in managing the balance of payment as well as the economy are discussed in greater detail in a chapter exclusively devoted to the subject.

Domestic Savings Rate

Another accounting identity provides a clue to tackle the deficit on current account. We know that current account deficit is a combination of budget deficit and savings deficit as shown in Eq. 2-7. Making an economy savings surplus would lead to an improvement in the current account. If private savings improve, they help in two ways:

1. Savings get channelized in (a) investment to build productive capacities if economy is underemployed, thereby increasing production or (b) flow out for financial asset acquisition abroad if fully employed, creating capital account deficit. In both cases, one must see an improvement in the current account of the balance of payment.
2. Increased savings imply reduced consumption and, hence lesser import of goods, which again helps improve the balance of payment. However, it opposes the view of having consumption-led development as the value of multiplier ($1/s$) falls down.

Heavy trade surplus in Japan can be attributed partly to the high savings rate they have. Savings habit is more a function of social values and social security. Western economies have fairly advanced social security system that reduces the need to save for future or for rainy days. Hence, the growth is mainly driven by consumption function. In developing nations absence of social security system forces higher savings (it does not mean to suggest that social security systems are bad). Incentivizing savings can be one of the lasting solutions to reduce worsening foreign trade. Providing tax breaks for savings and reduced taxation are some of the effective measures that can go a long way in correcting the adverse balance of payment situation.

It is indeed difficult to find out which of the measures is suitable to remove imbalances. The economic variables within the economy as well as with that of the world are so intricately linked that selecting one strategy while rejecting others would be hazardous. Tinkering with one variable in the economy automatically implies changes in the other variables. What could be effective in one situation may be ineffective in another. While China can focus on currency devaluation, Japan can rely on savings rate, and Brazil can regulate capital flows. Different ways of managing the balance of payment suggests that there is merit in each method of improving interaction with rest of the world and yet achieve the desired results in the domestic economy.

SUMMARY

Economies in the world are becoming dependent on each other. This emphasizes the recognition of benefits of international trade. Due to inherent advantages in importing some goods and exporting some, the nations derive the advantages of specialization and economies of scale, resulting in better quality products and lower pricing. International trade is inevitable for the development of a country and welfare of the world.

A balance of payment contains the records of the residents of one country with those of the rest of the world. It is an important document in terms of its implication on the domestic economy. It is like the financial statement of a firm that indicates its health. It provides a link of the nation with rest of the world just as a financial statement does for the firm. The balance of payment is recorded on double entry system. Exports are credits, whereas imports are debits.

The balance of payment comprises two parts—current account and capital account. Current account is the record of exports and imports of goods and services, whereas capital account records the inflows and outflows of foreign capital. The broad components of current accounts are merchandise dealing with physical goods and invisibles, comprising services. Capital account mainly consists of foreign direct investment, portfolio investment, and borrowing and lending of foreign capital. It also includes a reserve account, representing the foreign currency assets the country possesses. Since there are many agencies involved in the compilation of BOP statistics, errors creep, which are represented separately.

Accounting of balance of payment is done on double entry system, and as such, it must always be balanced. The surplus or deficit in BOP relates to the excess/deficit of exports over imports. When imports and exports of merchandise are considered, it is referred to as trade balance. Excessive deficit in balance of payment is regarded as detrimental to the long-term prospects of an economy. Since it must always be balanced, the deficit in the current account is always equal to surplus in capital account.

The balance of payment is intricately linked to domestic economic statistics. Under ideal conditions, the surplus current account must be equal to savings surplus. Small impetus by the government can result in more than proportionate increase in the national income. Similarly, current account deficit too can be impacted by small changes in seemingly domestic economic parameters, such as government expenditure and export promotion.

Amongst the more popular measures of controlling the adverse position in BOPs are currency devaluation and policies of protectionism. Currency devaluation makes exports cheaper and imports expensive. Protectionism relates to regulating the flow of foreign goods and promoting exports. Both the strategies are expected to remove the deficit in the current account. However, currency devaluation would improve the current account balance only when the volume effect dominates the price effect. Further, the favourable impact of currency devaluation is not likely to result in immediate improvement in the current account position. Due to consumers' lag and producers' lag, the impact would be deferred. This is called J-Curve effect. Since current account deficit is accompanied by equal amount of capital account surplus, many believe that controlling the surplus on capital account would lead to improvement in current account position. More radical and fundamental measures to control the adverse BOP would be enhancing the domestic savings rate because savings surplus would lead to current account surplus.

QUESTIONS

2-1 Write a note on the following:
    (a) Meaning of balance of payment
    (b) Uses of balance of payment
    (c) Structure of balance of payment
    (d) Deficit and surplus in balance of payment

2-2 Comment upon the following statements:
   (a) An adverse balance of payment is always a sign of weakness in the economy.
   (b) No foreign exchange reserves can be generated unless the country's exports exceed its imports.
   (c) Foreign exchange reserves are unnecessary drain on an economy since they represent idle resource.
2-3 What remedies can be suggested to overcome the deficit in balance of payment? Discuss the various options available and their suitability.
2-4 Differentiate between the following terms:
   (a) Adverse balance of trade and adverse balance of payment
   (b) Current account and capital account
   (c) Capital account and reserve account
2-5 What impact would the following events have on India's balance of payment if
   (a) India encourages capital inflows for investment in government securities and portfolio investment?
   (b) China devalues its currency?
   (c) Indian government provides cash compensatory support for export of leather?
   (d) Reserve Bank of India increases rates of deposits for non-resident Indians?
   (e) USA imposes a quota on import of garments from India?
   (f) Thai Baht appreciates with respect to all major currencies?

PROBLEMS

2-1 **Accounting for Balance of Payment**
   What would be the accounting entries for the following transactions in India's balance of payments?
   (a) Government of India provides US$50 million aid to African countries as medical aid.
   (b) Indian parent remits US$50,000 for his son studying at Harvard.
   (c) Indian government buys 1,00,000 barrels of oil for supplying potatoes to UAE both worth US$7 million.
   (d) An Indian firm issues pound denominated bonds to British nationals with face value at par of £100 million worth US$150 million.
   (e) A foreign mutual fund registered with SEBI divests stocks in India worth US$75 million and remits it to home country.
   (f) Infosys mobilizes US$25 million by issue of American Depository Receipts for investors in USA.

2-2 **Foreign Exchange Reserves**
   How would the foreign exchange reserve position of India get affected by the following transactions?
   (a) Wipro invoices software to a Japanese client for US$100,000 payable after 4 months.
   (b) Bharti Telecom acquires a firm in South Africa for an aggregate value of US$1 billion of which 10% is payable in cash and 90% by issue of shares of Bharti listed in India.
   (c) Holders of ADRs of $50 million outstanding of Wipro convert their depository receipts into local shares.

2-3 **Fiscal Stimulus**
   France has marginal propensity to save and import at 20% and 25%, respectively. An infusion of €100 million is planned by French Government by way of export subsidy, expecting a three-fold rise in exports. What change in income and current account is expected?

2-4 **Understanding Changes in Balance of Payment**
   Assume that Tata Steel imported equipment worth US$200 million by raising equivalent amount of borrowing abroad in the year 2010. The borrowing was payable in bullet repayment after 5 years and no interest was payable in the year 2010. What is the impact of the transaction on (a) current account, (b) capital account, (c) foreign exchange reserves, and (d) overall balance of payment?

3

International Monetary Systems

LEARNING OBJECTIVES

This chapter aims at

+ knowing the history and development of monetary systems
+ realizing how gold standard worked
+ understanding the causes of failure of gold standard
+ knowing various aspects of the Bretton Woods system and its intervention mechanism
+ learning how European Monetary System evolved and culminated in the new currency euro
+ appreciating the necessary conditions for a common currency
+ realizing how certain economic crises erupt within a monetary system

CONTENTS

Introduction
    The Barter System
    Gold Specie Standard
Classical Gold Standard
    Variants of Gold Standard
    How Gold Standard Works
Bretton Woods System
    Features
    Intervention Mechanism

Progress
    Reasons for Failure
European Monetary System
    Intervention Mechanism
    Benefits
Beyond European Monetary System:
Monetary and Economic Union
    The Maastricht Treaty
Optimum Currency Area

INTRODUCTION

Determination of exchange rate for currencies of various nations has always been intriguing. Over several centuries, the issue of how much is the worth of one currency in terms of another has been the central thought for traders and speculators. International trade has been going on from the primitive time, even when there existed no currency or money. When there was no currency, the most primitive mode of settlement of trade had been the barter system, in which a certain quantity of goods was exchanged for other goods as a trade settlement. Even in the modern-day society, trade on barter takes place where nations adopt exchange of oil for food grains, arms for medicines, etc.

For several centuries, politicians, traders, and economists have struggled to find a mechanism for settlement of trade within and outside a nation. In this chapter, we shall take a look at the history of development in the monetary systems that evolved over a period of time, with a view to explain some economic factors that govern the international payment mechanism and its impact on the domestic economy. For close to about 200 years preceding 1982, the international monetary system has been stable with almost no changes taking place.

However, since the 1970s and thereafter, the developments in the monetary systems have been too hectic and revolutionary. The implications of these developments have been far reaching, affecting global as well as local economic, monetary, and political systems. The increasing role of governments in regulating the foreign currency inflows and outflows, controlling interest rates and money supply, modulating fiscal policies, changing trade policies, etc. has started affecting the exchange rate values to a great extent. The wide array of fiscal, monetary, and regulatory instruments have led to several exchange rate systems prevail simultaneously in the world in the various economies.

The Barter System

Perhaps the most primitive method of settlement of payment was the exchange of one commodity for another in domestic as well as international trade. Exchange of one commodity for another as a mode of settlement of trade has been extremely inconvenient not only in terms of logistics but also in addressing the broader and more basic question of what quantity of a commodity must be exchanged for another. Barter indirectly determines the prices of goods. The price of one commodity is determined in terms of another commodity. For example, 1 barrel of oil is equal to 10 tonnes of wheat and 1 tonne of wheat is equal to 2 tonnes of rice.

In the barter system, there is no common denominator in which the worth of a commodity is determined. The barter system was the only choice of settlement as there were no currencies such as dollar, euro, yen, and rupee in which the value of goods and services could be denominated.

Gold Specie Standard

Inconveniences of barter mechanism for settlement of trade forced the traders to find a solution, that is, a common denominator in which the value of goods could be established. Much before the metal coins and the paper currency that we see now, gold coins evolved as the medium of exchange for settlement of domestic as well as international trade. All old civilizations such as Roman, Greek, Indian, and Chinese have used gold coins as a medium of exchange and store of value. For several centuries, the tradition continued. The wealth of the person was measured in terms of gold one possessed.

The primary reason why gold and no other metal or commodity became a lasting and satisfactory means of payment is that gold has the following five important and distinguishing characteristics:

1. Durability 2. Storability 3. Portability 4. Divisibility 5. Standardizability

These five features are unique to gold and all of them cannot be found in any other commodity/metal. Durability implies no deterioration in value with the passage of time. Coins of other metals such as iron are subject to rust as time progresses. Gold is weather proof. Ease of storability implies little storage space required to hold money. Portability refers to the ease of transportation from one place to another, making the settlement of payment easier. Divisibility is another convenience that gold can offer. It can be broken down in minute values without much effort. This makes it suitable for settling large as well as small payments. Elimination of ambiguity of value is another key determinant in settlement of trade transaction. The purity of gold can be established by simple means. This feature of gold is referred to as standardizability. These features have made gold the most acceptable medium of exchange all over the world, and it has served as a common denominator of value of all goods.

With the passage of time, gold coins were mixed with other metals, predominantly silver, which is usually the closest substitute of gold in terms of the features. Several countries came out with what is referred to as debased coins or bimetallic standard. Civilized world tended to use the silver standard. Silver pennies became the staple coin of Britain around 796 AD. Silver was typically the main circulating medium, with gold serving as the metal of monetary reserve.

CLASSICAL GOLD STANDARD

Starting with Great Britain, the gold standard came in vogue and became accepted in almost all the countries. Great Britain minted pound out of gold. Later, paper or coin currency, which was convertible into gold at a specified fixed rate, was issued. In modern times, the British West Indies was one of the first regions to adopt a gold specie standard. In the year 1717, Sir Isaac Newton, who was the master of the Royal Mint, established a new mint ratio between silver and gold that had the effect of driving silver out of circulation and putting Britain on a gold standard. However, it was not until the year 1821, following the introduction of the gold sovereign coins by the new Royal Mint at Tower Hill in the year 1816, that the United Kingdom was formally put on a gold specie standard. The United Kingdom was the first of the great industrial powers to switch from the silver standard to a gold specie standard. See Table 3-1 which gives the years when countries adopted gold standard.

Table 3-1
Adoption of Gold Standard

Year	Description
1704	The British West Indies 'de facto' following Queen Anne's proclamation.
1717	Kingdom of Great Britain 'de facto' following Isaac Newton's revision of the mint ratio, at 1 guinea to 129.438 grains (8.38 g) of 22 carat crown gold.
1821	United Kingdom 'de jure' at one sovereign to 123.27447 grains of 22 carat crown gold.
1818	Netherlands at 1 guilder to 0.60561 g gold.
1853	Canada in conjunction with the American Gold Eagle coin equal to ten US dollars and also the British gold sovereign equal to four dollars eighty-six and two-thirds cents. The Canadian unit was made equal to the American unit in the year 1858.
1854	Portugal at 1000 réis to 1.62585 g gold.
1873	German Empire at 2790 Goldmarks to 1 kg gold.
1873	United States 'de facto' at US$20.67 to 1 troy oz (31.1 g) gold. Belgium, Italy, Switzerland, and France at 31 francs to 9.0 g gold.
1875	Denmark, Norway, and Sweden at 2480 kroner to 1 kg gold.
1876	France who founded Latin Monetary Union in 1865 fixed the value of franc at 0.2903 gm of gold.
1876	Spain at 31 pesetas to 9.0 g gold.
1878	Grand Duchy of Finland at 31 marks to 9.0 g gold.
1879	Austrian Empire.
1881	Argentina at 1 peso to 1.4516 g gold.
1885	Egypt fixed the value of its currency Egyptian pound to 7.4375 gm of gold.
1897	Russia at 31 roubles to 24.0 g gold.
1897	Japan at 1 yen devalued to 0.75 g gold.
1898	India when its silver rupee was pegged to pound sterling at 1s 4d.
1903	The Philippines gold exchange/US dollar.

Source: www.wikipedia.com

Commencing 1873, all countries soon after one another started following the gold standard. The currencies issued by these nations were convertible into gold at fixed rates. The determination of the exchange rate was fairly simple and straight forward as the ratio of gold content decided the exchange rate of two currencies. If the USA fixed its currency convertible into gold at the fixed rate of US$20.67 per ounce, whereas Britain converted at the rate of £4.2474 per ounce of gold, then $20.67 equals £4.2474, giving an implicit exchange rate of $4.8665/£. As long as the two currencies were freely convertible into gold at the given rates, the exchange rate between the two currencies would remain fixed. It did so till the World War I, when trade disruptions took place and free flow of gold was checked.

By the nineteenth century the remaining silver standard countries began to peg their silver coin units to the gold standard of the United Kingdom or the USA. In 1898, British India pegged the silver rupee to the pound sterling at a fixed rate of 1s 4d, whereas in 1906, the Straits Settlements adopted a gold exchange standard against the pound sterling with the silver Straits dollar being fixed at 2s 4d. The Philippines pegged the silver Peso to US dollar at 50 cents. By 1908, only China and Hong Kong were on the silver standard.

Variants of Gold Standard

Under the gold standard, the monetary unit, in any shape, is equal to a fixed amount of gold. Three distinct kinds of gold standard can be identified.

Gold Specie Standard The gold specie standard is a system in which the monetary unit is associated with circulating gold coins, or with the unit of value defined in terms of one particular circulating gold coin in conjunction with subsidiary coinage made from a lesser valuable metal.

Gold Bullion Standard In gold bullion standard, the circulating currency is not gold but the monetary unit is convertible into gold at a fixed price. The value of the currency in question is determined by its content of gold. The authorities issuing the currency have agreed to sell gold bullion on demand at a fixed price in exchange for the circulating currency.

Gold Exchange Standard In the gold exchange standard, the country issuing the currency undertakes to convert it into another currency that is on gold bullion. The conversion into the currency would be at a predetermined rate and, therefore, the issued currency is de facto on gold standard.

Issuance of the currency was backed by 100% gold reserves which meant that all the amount of currency issued could be converted into gold at any time.

How Gold Standard Works

The major advantage of gold standard was its feature of self-correction and adjustment of international trade, which led to the settlement and balance of payment (BOP) that provided stability of prices and balanced trade. This is referred to as *price specie flow*. Any change in the environment would prompt changes in the international trade and settlement. The trade needs to correct itself as balance of payment gets affected adversely for some nations, whereas it becomes favourable for the rest. The gold standard would operate automatically and restore the balance through price adjustment and flow of gold from one country to another.

Consider a small example for understanding how the gold standard works. Beyond the scope of fiscal and monetary policies that dominate and guide the economic growth and development in modern days, no such elaborate policy changes were required in the era of gold standard. Let us assume that due to some technological innovation the productivity increases which results in increased volume and reduced prices of a product. Increased volume and decreased prices would make the product cheaper, thereby boosting exports. The importing country would have to pay for it in terms of gold, thus depleting its gold reserves.

On the other hand, the exporting country would have larger reserves of gold. The BOP would become favourable for the exporting nation. These larger reserves of gold would lead to issuance of more local currency. With the increase in domestic money supply the prices of goods would increase, making exports expensive and imports more attractive. Thus, the favourable change in BOP would be offset by increased prices due to increased money supply. The sequential changes in the events are shown in Figure 3-1.

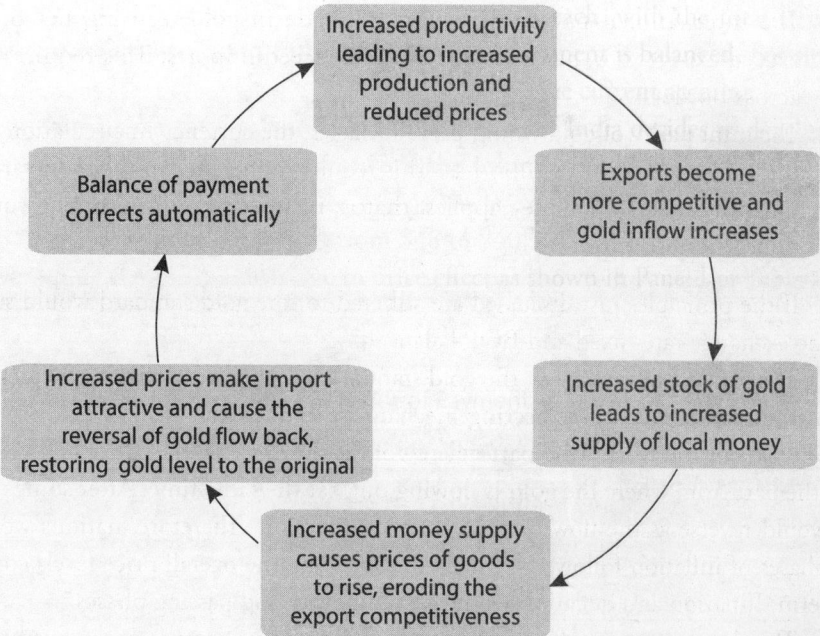

Increased productivity ⇒ Reduced prices of goods/services ⇒ Exports become more competitive ⇒ Imports become less attractive ⇒ Increased export and reduced import ⇒ Flow of gold inside ⇒ Issue more currency ⇒ Increase in prices ⇒ Exports become expensive ⇒ Imports become more economic and attractive

(OFFSETS THE EARLIER EFFECT of increased productivity, reduced prices and exports and imports)

Figure 3-1
Self-correcting Mechanism under Gold Standard

For importing nations, the reverse process of the one exhibited in Figure 3-1 would apply. The adverse impact on balance of payments causing outflow of gold would lead to shrinking money supply. This would decrease local price levels, reducing pressure on imports. Increased prices in the exporting country would cause the gold to return, thereby correcting the imbalance (the deficit) in balance of payments.

In modern-day economics, the demand for import or a deficit in balance of payments implies greater demand for foreign currency or increased supply of domestic currency. In terms of gold standard, since the currencies have their values attached to fixed amount of gold the increased foreign currency (gold) would be offset by decreased domestic currency (gold). The aggregate of foreign and domestic currency would remain same at all times. Hence, the form in which the gold is held changes, but the aggregate amount of currencies across the world remains constant. The aggregate amount could only change upon further mining of gold.

The self-correcting mechanism of the gold standard rests on the following principles:

1. The international payments would be made in gold, causing net outflow if imports exceed exports and net inflow if exports exceed imports. This requires free flow of gold across borders.
2. The mint parity of gold would prevail, that is, the currency in circulation is proportional to the gold reserves the country has. This requires adherence to the monetary discipline.
3. Quantity theory of money applies, that is, increase in money supply would cause proportional increase in prices.

If the principles just discussed are adhered to, the gold standard would succeed in keeping the exchange rates fixed and BOP balanced.

The greatest advantage of the gold standard is its ability to keep inflation at near zero levels in the world. The self-correcting mechanism implies that while there would be inflation in one part of the world (the part where gold is flowing in), the other half would face deflation (the part from where the gold is flowing out), at the same time. After some time, the situation would reverse as the flow of gold changes direction. Therefore, nations would see successive phases of inflation followed by deflation, keeping the overall price levels constant in the long term. Inflation and deflation would be temporary and passing phases.

The alternate cycles of inflation and deflation occur because of the fixed and limited supply of gold in the world. If one could create gold, then the supply of money being proportional to gold too would increase causing upward pressure on prices.

The effectiveness of the gold standard can be visualized from the fact that for close to about 200 years from the 1700s to 1914, the start of World War I, the prices remained constant. During this period, most nations were on gold standard. In the modern times, the credibility of gold standard gains even more importance due to the fact that ever since gold standard has been abandoned, inflation has been a global phenomenon, occupying the greatest attention and concern of economists and governments all over the world alike and remains unabated.

One important fact responsible for the success of gold standard in containing inflation was that the total amount of gold available across the globe was more or less constant. Therefore, the aggregate money supply would be constant if it is equal or proportional to the available amount of gold. The paper currency would change only in form from one currency to another, say from dollar to pound and vice versa. The increased supply of one implies automatic decreased supply of another through specie-flow mechanism. Since aggregate money supply over the world is constant, the inflation rate in the world would aggregate to zero as there is no money expansion. Money expansion could take place only with new discovery of gold. Upon new discovery, the additional gold would again find its way to spread across the globe through price-specie-flow mechanism.

One of the major objections to the gold standard is that the economic growth is limited to fresh mining of gold. Since money supply has to grow as economic development takes place, development would be constrained if one adheres to the tenets of gold standard, limiting money supply. It may also be construed that because of alternate bouts of inflation and deflation to maintain the price stability, the economic situations may warrant actions contrary to those propagated in the gold standard. There is considerable debate over the extent and length of the Great Depression of the 1930s; many believe that it could have been lesser in intensity and time duration had gold standard not been in vogue.

There is a common belief among economists that given a choice between moderate rates of inflation and deflation, the former is preferable because combating moderate inflation is easier than overcoming deflation. A deflation may lead to continued and persistent reduced consumption which is considered detrimental to economic growth. Overcoming consumption patterns is not a problem that economists alone can solve; perhaps it needs support from behavioural economists and marketing professionals too.

In the present day, economists who are the proponents of gold standard are in clear minority. Perhaps this is because of the absence of freedom that gold standard does not allow.

The gold standard functioned smoothly till the onset of World War I in 1914. The period prior to 1914 is characterized by consistent economic development with stable prices and fixed exchange rates. Proponents of gold standard can cite these facts for its re-introduction.

However, to many, the gold standard was too rigid and was seen as a constraining factor for development as it did not allow for expansionary policies. In the aftermath of World War I, the constraining factor heightened, when nations after the war were preoccupied with rehabilitation of people devastated in the war. Perhaps that necessitated expansionary fiscal policies and increased money supply to propel growth and development. Financing of war by increased money supply also led to the abandonment of financial discipline of keeping money supply strictly in accordance with gold reserves—an all-important tenet for the success of gold standard.

The Fiat Money The issue of excess money without having the requisite gold for its redemption is called fiat money. Fiat money is issued by governments on the faith alone (and not tangible gold) that the money would be converted into gold at the prescribed rate. Fiat money is for free as no gold needs to be acquired to issue it. In the intervening period of two World Wars fiat money became a widespread phenomenon for the war-torn countries trying to rebuild the nations.

After World War II, countries tried to re-establish the gold standard with the same gold parity that existed in the pre-war period with the exception of Germany and Austria. In the 1920s, the pre-war parities created problems as pound became overvalued. Post World War I in 1925,

Concepts in Practice
Back to Gold Standard

GOLD: THE ONCE AND FUTURE MONEY

It may take many more years, even decades, but the era of soft money is coming to a close, predicts Nathan Lewis, a noted economist, in his book titled *Gold: The Once and Future Money*. The world really has no choice but to move back towards a framework of hard money, because the never-ending and completely unnecessary difficulties of floating currencies cannot be solved in any other way.

The best system that can maintain stability of values of currencies over long periods of time, and the one easiest to implement without disruptions is the gold standard. He says, 'As for accomplishing this task there are no serious challengers to a gold standard, not even in the form of proposal and certainly none that has weathered the test of history.'

The hard money system of the future would be based on gold, just as the hard money system of the past. According to Lewis, 'Gold has not been flawless foundation for monetary systems. Perfection does not exist in human affairs. It has, however, been the most flawless.'

It was the most powerful monetary system that was ever created. Nathan Lewis advocates the principle of *stable money and low taxes* to be remembered by all policy makers and politicians during financial crises. What is happening today is exactly the opposite in Europe. Pressure for austerity (high taxes) and calls for disintegration of weaker economies from Eurozone (instability) are gathering momentum. Adherence to gold standard would not have let things reach that stage. Japan achieved phenomenal growth during 1950 to 1975 when it reduced taxes and yen was tied to gold providing stable currency. Is that the reason for similar rise of China in today's world when its currency yuan is pegged to dollar?

All solutions and bail-outs are apparently failing to resolve the economic and financial crises in the past 25 years. According to Nathan Lewis, the solution lies in returning to gold standard that has demonstrated to work far better than any other system because yellow metal has a fixed intrinsic value.

the gold standard was reintroduced in the form of gold exchange standard as recommended by Genoa Conference in 1922. It lasted for a brief period. Under the gold exchange standard, the USA and England could hold gold as reserves, whereas other nations could have gold, US dollar, and sterling pound as reserves.

The accumulation of gold, pound, and dollar was a managed gold standard that allowed settlement of international trade obligations to be settled not only in gold but also in dollars and pounds. The USA that had been exporting to Europe during the World War I and in later years accumulated large reserves of gold as it ran huge trade surplus. This also meant that gold reserves across Europe depleted, but money supply kept increasing. To get the gold back, France insisted the payment to be made only in gold. The central bank of France also refused to accept pound-denominated assets held by its commercial banks. This compelled redemption of pound-denominated assets into gold.

Coupled with the redemption pressure and expansionary policy of the British government, England had no option but to devalue the pound in 1930. Gold was back in demand as it became the only mode of international settlement despite managed gold standard. The devaluation of pound and depression in 1930s commenced war of competitive devaluations across Europe. One country after another devalued its currency to gain competitive edge over others to increase exports and propel economies.

This was a virtual collapse of gold standard as the underlying tenets were abandoned. This resulted in the development of trading blocs that did business in currencies of their convenience. France, Belgium, Italy, the Netherlands, Sweden, and Switzerland formed a Gold Bloc. England, Scandinavian countries, and Commonwealth countries (excluding Canada) formed Sterling Bloc. Countries in North and South America became Dollar Bloc. Germany and Austria had their own value of the currency and did not join any bloc. The intra-bloc trade continued on fixed exchange rate, whereas inter-bloc trade used varying exchange rates.

On the whole, the exchange rate system remained in a flux with no direction. The onset of World War II led to further confusion and aborting of little efforts that were being made to stabilize the inter-bloc exchange rate scenario.

BRETTON WOODS SYSTEM

With a view to provide stability to exchange rate system that evaded during 1930s, a conference at Bretton Woods, New Hampshire, USA took place and devised a new order for determination of exchange rates. The conference had two groups—one led by Harry White from the USA and the other by John Keynes from England. Attended by 44 countries, the critics dubbed it as a conference of one and a half nations, given the fact that the USA dominated the outcome of the conference. It also symbolized the increasing dominance of the US dollar and to that extent the diminishing influence of British pound in the determination of exchange rates.

With clear three blocs of gold, dollar, and pound, the exchange rates needed to be stabilized. An attempt was made to eliminate the problems that faced the world in the 1930s. Hyperinflation in Germany, depression in the USA, wide spread policies of protectionism, and competitive devaluations were some of the events dominated by politics that led to anarchy in the determination of trade and exchange rates and prevented stability to exchange rate.

Features of Bretton Woods System

The new system came to be known as the Bretton Woods system. Implemented in 1946, the salient features of the system were as follows:

1. Each government was to fix the exchange rate of its currency in terms of US dollar or gold, referred to as *par value*.
2. The US dollar was convertible into gold. The value of gold was fixed at US$35 per ounce. This provided the value of currency in terms of gold and, therefore, with respect to all other currencies.

54 International Finance

3. Monetary authorities in each country were obligated to defend the exchange rate fixed in a band of ±1%. Thus, though fixed in terms of gold, the value of a currency was not absolutely fixed as in gold standard but was adjustable in a limited band of ±1%. Therefore, the system is also referred to as 'adjustable peg'.
4. The exchange rate within the band would be maintained by the central bank with intervention of buying and selling of US dollars, as the case may be. If the value of the currency appreciated beyond +1% the central bank would buy enough US dollars required to bring back the exchange rate within the prescribed band. On the contrary, if the currency depreciated by more than 1%, the central bank would sell the US dollar to lift the value up and come back in the prescribed band.
5. The US dollar required by the country would be provided by the International Monetary Fund (IMF) that was set up with the exclusive objective of maintaining the stability of exchange rates. The IMF would provide requisite US dollars for intervention in the foreign exchange market against the gold pledged by each nation and quota assigned on the basis thereof. The quota was decided using the exchange rate of US$35 per ounce.
6. If the exchange rate variations happen temporarily, the instability would be overcome by intervention. However, in case the country is unable to defend the exchange rate within the initially fixed band due to *fundamental disequilibrium* (never defined), it could adjust the par value by ±5% subject to approval from the IMF.

Thus, under the Bretton Woods system, the de facto intervention could be done by US dollars alone, making dollar a world currency in single stroke. It was a gold exchange system that provided some flexibility to governments to adjust the money supply as per the needs of the economic and monetary conditions. The governments could pursue the desired economic and monetary policies by compromising somewhat on exchange rates. Some leeway was provided for domestic policies. The flexibility had the objective of eliminating the use of trade restrictive measures and exchange control.

Intervention Mechanism under Bretton Woods System

The key to the Bretton Woods system was the intervention mechanism. This is explained with the help of an example. Assume that India pegs its exchange rate at ₹10/$, supposedly the intersection of the demand curve (DD) and supply curve (SS) of US dollar as shown in Figure 3-2. The equilibrium quantity of dollars is Q_0.

Intervention by central banks in the currency markets hopes to make exchange rate stable. Then, the prescribed band under the Bretton Woods system would let the value of rupee change from a maximum of ₹9.90 to a minimum of ₹10.10 (within ±1% of the par value) only. In case the free market forces make the exchange rate go beyond this range, then the Reserve Bank of India (RBI), the central bank of India, is obligated to intervene in the foreign exchange markets by buying or selling the US dollar, as the case may be, to bring back the exchange rate within the prescribed band of ₹9.90 to ₹10.10.

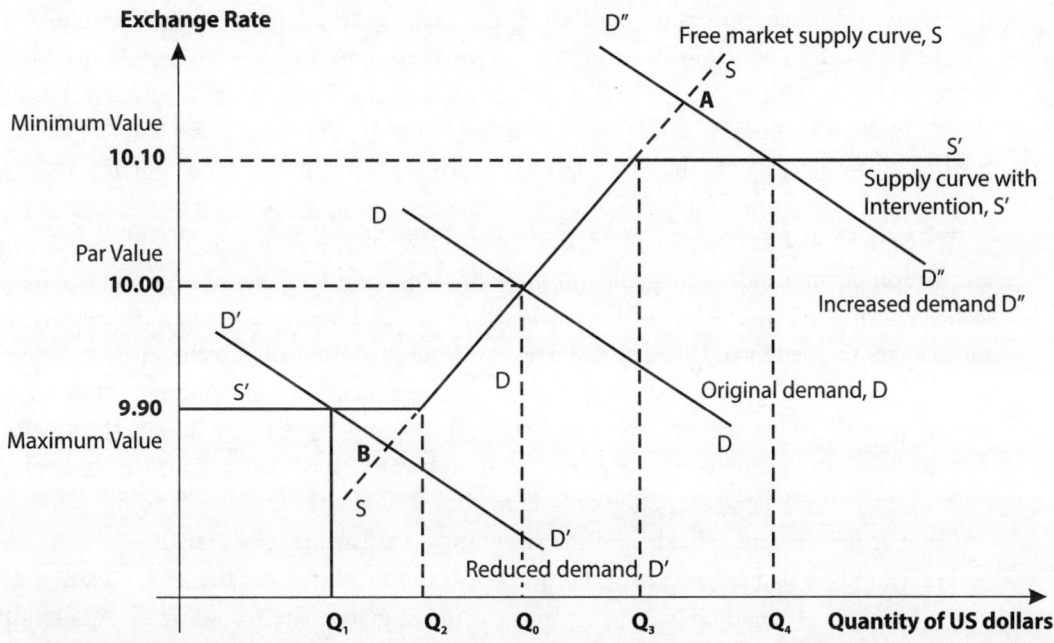

Figure 3-2
Intervention Mechanism under Bretton Woods System

Suppose India follows expansionary policy which leads to inflation. The Indian goods become expensive and the condition worsens (reduced surplus or increased deficit) the balance of payment. With imports becoming more attractive, the demand for US dollars would increase leading to depreciation of rupee and appreciation of US dollar. Till such time, the depreciation of rupee is within 1%, that is, the exchange rate of rupee falls to ₹10.10/$ from ₹10.00/$, there is no need for intervention by RBI.

However, if the new demand curve DD" now intersects the supply curve SS at A, that is, beyond ₹10.10, the exchange rate would move there, if left unchecked. The increased demand for US dollar would have to be met by Reserve Bank of India (RBI) by selling US dollar such that the value of dollar decreases and rupee appreciates to a level of ₹10.10. The quantity of US dollars to be supplied by RBI would be equal to Q_4–Q_3, as may be seen from Figure 3-2.

Depletion of reserves of dollar would constrain imports. Besides, selling dollars would mean buying local currency, rupee. Hence, foreign currency market operations would offset the expansionary monetary policy. Continuation of expansionary policy means continuing depletion of reserves. Sooner or later, when the reserves deplete to dangerously low levels through intervention, the country would be forced to reverse its expansionary policy.

Instead now suppose India follows the policy of contraction of money. The value of local currency would now increase, reducing the demand for imported goods, making dollar depreciate and rupee appreciate. Till the rise in value is less than the exchange rate to be ₹9.90, RBI keeps quiet. However, if rupee appreciates further beyond ₹9.90, RBI would need to buy dollars to lift its value. Buying of dollars would increase the supply of local currency, offsetting the contraction that initiated the rise in value of rupee. If the new reduced demand intersects the free market SS at more than ₹9.90, the quantity of dollars needs to be bought is Q_2–Q_1 as may be again seen from Figure 3-2.

The Bretton Woods system of maintaining exchange rate focuses on supply-side management and not on demand side management of foreign exchange rates. The intervention mechanism influences the supply schedule of the foreign currency and not its demand schedule. To affect the changes in the demand schedule, the nation would have to bring in the structural changes in the economy, the outcome of which is uncertain and time-consuming. At maximum and minimum exchange rates, the supply schedule is supposed to become perfectly elastic. Theoretically, irrespective of exchange rate beyond the prescribed band, any quantity of foreign exchange, that is, dollar, is supplied or bought.

Comparing the demand-side and the supply-side management of exchange rate, it can be said that supply-side management is far quicker. It is difficult to alter the demand curve. Even if one could do so, the time required to affect demand preferences would be large. Sometimes the demand schedule may also be rather inelastic. In contrast, the supply-side management can be influenced by monetary authorities while attempting to change more fundamental forces of demand and supply of foreign exchange requires fiscal intervention. Though influencing structural changes to alter the demand and supply schedule is long-lasting, its impact takes time. Altering supply schedule is instantaneous that offers a quick-fix solution to the exchange rate fluctuations.

Role of International Monetary Fund It is only when the intervention efforts fail to maintain the exchange rate around par value that the need to change the par value would arise. In most cases, it would be downward revision in value when the initial par value suggested overvaluation of the currency. In such cases, the reserves of dollar would deplete faster than one could imagine. Additional foreign currency, that is, US dollars would have to be obtained for further intervention. This would be supplied by IMF.

The IMF would provide dollars for intervention on the basis of quota. The quota was fixed on the basis of size of its subscription to the IMF. Countries could draw 25% of its prescribed quota of dollars should it need to correct the BOP problems or for stabilizing the exchange rate. Further, withdrawals could be made in tranches of 25% with aggregate not exceeding 125% of the subscription. With each tranche of 25%, the IMF would place increasing austere conditions for monetary and fiscal policies to be followed.

Under the Articles of Agreement, the member countries were required to make the currency convertible for current account transactions on the balance of payment. Full convertibility, that is, conversion of currency for capital account transactions was not insisted upon, communicating the view that capital flows on financial assets could prove dangerous and destabilizing for the economies. Please see the ***Online Resource Centre*** for discussion on IMF.

Progress of Bretton Woods System

When the Bretton Woods system was introduced, the economy of the USA was very sound with massive surplus in balance of payment and huge gold reserves. These were created by exports to European nations during war days. Simultaneously, European countries were running huge deficits as they had no reserves of gold left with heavy imports from USA. Possibly that was the reason why all the conditions favourable to the USA were acceded to, while devising the new system of exchange rate determination with US dollar being the fulcrum.

With abundant funds and gold, the USA provided huge aid to European countries to reconstruct their economies. The availability of gold/dollar was a major constraint. Under Marshall Plan, an aid of US$11.6 billion as grants and US$1.8 billion as loan were provided. Realizing the shortage of US dollar, the aid to European countries was conditional on settling their own trades in currencies other than US dollars.

In 1949, several devaluations took place when countries realized having pegged their currencies at levels higher than their economies could sustain. England, France, and Scandinavian countries sought devaluation of par value, recognizing that initial par values set by them made their currencies overvalued and, hence, they needed devaluation. These devaluations were made to make exports extremely competitive.

Things changed rapidly thereafter and the 1950s saw the reversal of BOP situations. The trade balance of the USA started turning negative, but those of Europe and Japan started turning to surplus from deficit. West Germany and Japan dominated with their export-led growth and started accumulating dollars. Trade and capital controls across Europe started vanishing, and by 1958, the European currencies started becoming convertible.

The deterioration of balance of payment of the USA prompted conversion of dollars into gold by central banks of several nations. European currencies started gaining strength and Deutsche marks (DMs) and Dutch guilders were revalued by 5% each in 1961. Starting in the 1959 till 1970, President Charles de Gaulle of France reduced the country's dollar reserves, exchanging them for gold at the official exchange rate, reducing the US economic influence. Meanwhile, the prices of gold were mounting in London markets making it evidently clear that gold was undervalued and dollar was overvalued.

With the mounting price of gold in the open market, there was a loss of confidence in the ability of dollar to convert the liabilities into gold if such need arises. In 1962, the system of *Gold Pool* was devised by the UK, France, Germany, Italy, Belgium, the Netherlands, and Switzerland to repose faith in gold and dollar. They tried to sell gold to maintain US$35 per ounce, but the USA was supposed to restrict the deficit trade balance. This could not hold as the USA could not contain the deficit in balance of payment.

Vietnam War added to the loss of confidence when the USA decided to fund the war with deficit financing rather than by raising taxes. By 1967, the devaluation of dollar was clear. There were imminent signs of breakdown of the system. In 1967, British pound was devalued by 14.6% and French franc (FF) by 11%. No serious attempt was made by the USA to contain its deficit in the balance of payment. In May 1971, West Germany had to buy US$2 billion in two days to lift up the value of dollar. The DM was revalued by 7% besides its preceding revaluation by 9.3% in 1969.

In August 1971, the USA announced several measures which made the system collapse. It announced that dollar was no more convertible into gold, imposed a 10% duty of imports, and announced price and wage controls to check inflation. It was a signal that the USA was not prepared to devalue but instead wanted all other currencies to revalue against dollar. Rather than revaluation—which meant loss of export competitiveness—the major currencies preferred floating their currencies, that is, the value to be determined by market forces.

According to an estimate, by 1971 the USA owed $88 billion in short-term liquid liabilities to foreigners due to heavy and consistent deficit in balance of payment, whereas the USA had gold only worth $12 billion. By December 1971, the fall of the Bretton Woods system was imminent. In a last minute effort to save the system, top 10 nations met at Smithsonian Institute in Washington where (a) dollar was devalued to US$38.02 per ounce of gold, a devaluation of dollar by 8.87%, (b) other currencies with surplus BOP were revalued upwards in the range of 7.4% for Canadian dollar and 16.9% for Japanese yen, (c) fluctuation margin of ±2.25% was allowed instead of ±1% to reduce pressure on dollar, and (d) the USA agreed to remove 10% tariff imposed on its imports. Devaluation of dollar was done to reduce the demand for dollar. The intervention band was increased to ±2.25% with the view that increased band would require lesser intervention and, hence, the demand for dollar would fall, easing liquidity. Larger size of the band would also provide greater autonomy to the nations to manage their monetary and fiscal policies.

By 1972, the BOP deficit of the USA reached a record proportion of $6.99 billion on trade account and $9.81 billion on current account. The USA devalued dollar further to $42.22 per ounce of gold. Massive flow of capital in favour of countries with surplus BOP took place. The flow was so great that foreign exchange markets had to be closed in March 1973.

In 1976, Jamaica Agreement was signed legalizing the floating exchange rate system and ***demonetization*** of gold as the currency of reserves (IMF quota could be paid in foreign currencies). Henceforth, gold would be like any other commodity and was abandoned as a Reserve Asset. The IMF returned 50% of gold reserves to respective nations and also sold one-third of its gold reserves to aid poor nations. This sale was completed by 1980.

Please see the ***Online Resource Centre*** for a detailed discussion on SDRs, the currency of IMF.

Reasons of Failure of Bretton Woods System

As may be seen from the history of the Bretton Woods system that it started off well but cracks in the system started developing slowly. Rather than improving with time, the situation kept on worsening, and it deteriorated rapidly in the last four years, from 1969 to 1972. Some of the reasons for the failure of the system are discussed here.

Crisis of Confidence: Triffin's Dilemma The Bretton Woods system ran well till 1962 till the time the world at large was confident of the ability of the USA to maintain the promise of converting dollars into gold at the agreed rate of $35 per ounce. As the balance of payments deteriorated from surplus to deficit, there was a gradual loss of confidence. Around 1960, when the crack in the system started developing, Robert Triffin almost predicted the breakdown of the system. According to him, the Bretton Woods system had an inherent contradiction. Referred to as Triffin dilemma, the success of the system depended on dollar performing its role as a key currency. Increased levels of income and international trade demanded increased supply of gold or gold equivalent, that is, US dollar. Other countries could accumulate dollars only if the USA ran a persistent deficit in balance of payment. The surplus countries would cash in the dollars for gold, depleting the reserves of the USA. Continued depletion of gold reserves would create a confidence crisis. Hence, the dilemma was that if the USA took corrective steps to contain the BOP deficit, the growth and development of the world would suffer due to shortage of resources. On the other hand, if it did not check the adverse balance of payment the confidence crisis would emerge. Therefore, with a catch 22 situation the Bretton Woods system is inherently unstable.

True to the analysis, the actual reserves, as a ratio of the liability of the USA, fell from a healthy 2.73 in 1950 to a paltry 0.14 in 1974. Table 3-2 provides the trend of decline of the ratio of gold reserves to liabilities of the USA. This is akin to the debt coverage ratio which is used for assessing the repaying capacity of the debt. The root cause of the failure lies in continued large deficit BOP situation. These ratios are indicative of the delicate reserve position of gold which could not have remained hidden. The loss of confidence in the USA's ability to defend the conversion price was too great for the system of Bretton Woods to continue. Under such a situation, nations would be reluctant to peg the exchange rate to US dollar. Instead they would prefer the value of the currency to be determined on the basis of the fundamentals and performances of their own economies rather than on the economy of the USA over which they exercised no control.

Table 3-2
Ratio of Gold Reserves to Liabilities of USA[1]

Year	Ratio
1950	2.73
1954	1.84
1958	1.34
1962	0.71
1966	0.50
1970	0.31
1974	0.14

[1]*Source*: Pilbeam, Keith (2006), *International Finance*, Third Edition, Palgrave Mcmillan, p. 269.

The Seigniorage Gains Another reason attributed to the failure of the system was the lopsided way the system was devised. The system placed the USA in an extremely advantageous position. When all other nations had to earn their dollars, USA could simply reap the benefits

by additional supply of dollars. To export more, the nations were supposed to sacrifice their own consumption. The USA, on the other hand did not have to make any such sacrifice. To enable shore up the gold/dollar reserves, the goods produced by other nations could be exported to the USA. If the USA follows an expansionary policy in the name of maintaining international liquidity or otherwise, the benefits of the best products at very competitive prices in the world can be enjoyed by Americans.

Further, the dollars earned by the nations were invested back in the treasuries of the USA that yielded little return in real terms due to inflation in the USA that was caused by its expansionary policies. The payment crisis is averted as dollars that went as payment on current account transactions flowed back to the USA on capital account. Besides highlighting the virtues of gold, President De Gaulle of France called it 'exorbitant privilege' conferred by the system to the USA, the value of which cannot be reckoned. There was none that could enforce financial discipline on the USA. Of its own, the USA was not willing to devalue dollar with respect to gold, for fear of loss of credibility.

EUROPEAN MONETARY SYSTEM

Concurrent with the failure of the Bretton Woods system several nations in Europe decided to remove the peg to dollar and preferred to float their currencies. In order to resolve its adverse balance of payment, Britain decided to float the pound in 1972. Switzerland and Japan followed soon in early 1973.

While floating of currencies against the US dollar was announced, the concern for stability of the exchange rate remained. If the exchange rates were to be determined solely by market forces, the volatility may become too large to cope with. In the absence of any formidable substitute to the Bretton Woods system European community decided to maintain

(a) fluctuations of their own currencies in the band of ±1.125% with one another, and
(b) a band of ± 2.25% with respect to dollar as agreed under Smithsonian Agreement.

This system was referred to as 'snake in the tunnel' with band of ±1.125% with respect to European currencies against one another as snake and broader band of ±2.25% with respect to US dollar as tunnel. The system was conceived by European Economic Community (EEC) to promote trade within Europe to which the fluctuating exchange rates were considered as a deterrent.

The system of reduced band within the currencies was started by six original members of EEC (BENELUX, that is, Belgium, Netherlands, and Luxembourg, France, Italy, and Germany) in April 1972. The system had volatile membership apparently due to uncertainties with the system. Soon England and Denmark joined but left almost immediately. Denmark rejoined later. Italy too left in 1973. France also left in 1974 and rejoined later in 1975 again to leave in 1976. The system had clearly failed in the objectives of rendering stability and promoting economic cooperation among European nations. The system was no more alive.

In 1978, the system of 'snake in the tunnel' was revived and rechristened European Monetary System (EMS), bringing back France and Italy. The primary motive that caused the reintroduction was the realization of the need for stable trade within the region despite existence of economic divergences in BOP situation, growth rates, and inflation rates of the participating nations. It was felt that greater cooperation, not just in maintaining exchange rates but otherwise too, was necessary to remove economic divergences.

Led by West Germany and France, EMS was introduced in 1979 with the following three salient features:

1. *A Parity Grid for Bilateral Exchange Rates:* Each participating nation had a central value (akin to par value in Bretton Woods) and a band for its exchange rate against each of the currencies. The grid of bilateral rates and band was fixed for the purpose of deciding when the corrective measures, currency intervention, or other ways would be initiated and become obligatory on the nations in the joint interests of all members. This was called the Exchange Rate Mechanism (ERM). Broadly this grid used a band of ±2.25% around central rate as was the case under Smithsonian Agreement.

2. *Concept of European Currency Unit (ECU):* Besides bilateral rates, each currency was also assigned a central value against a hypothetical currency called European Currency Unit (ECU), which became real later as well as a band in which the exchange rate was to be maintained. This hypothetical currency was a basket of currencies made of weighted average of 12 European currencies of the members and others in proportion of their respective trade contributions. The purpose of ECU was to assign the responsibility of intervention and corrective measures to be taken to restore the currency value within the original band, explained later. Table 3-3 gives the composition of ECU as in September 1989. It is noteworthy that despite Britain not being a member, pound sterling was included in ECU.

3. *Creating European Monetary Cooperation Fund (EMCF):* In order to provide resources for intervention by nations, a fund was created for providing credit facilities. The ECMF would be funded by 20% of reserves of gold and dollar of each nation as contribution

Table 3-3
Composition of ECU as on 21 September 1989

Currency	% Weight	Currency	% Weight
Deutsche mark	30.10	Spanish peseta	5.30
French franc	19.00	Danish krone	2.45
Pound sterling	13.00	Irish punt	1.10
Italian lira	10.15	Greek drachma	0.80
Netherlands guilder	9.40	Portuguese escudo	0.80
Belgian franc	7.60	Luxembourg franc	0.30

Source: Clark, Ephraim (2004), *International Finance*, Second Edition, Thomson Asia Pte Ltd, Singapore, p. 108.

and get equivalent ECUs. It was expected that interventions to defend the value of the currency would be made in ECU and settlement of trade too would be made in ECU. The fund could also be accessed for solving the problems of deficit in balance of payments. The funding would be done on the basis of credit facilities. This may be deemed equivalent of the IMF under the Bretton Woods system, which provided necessary resources to enable member countries intervene in the foreign exchange markets.

At the outset, the EMS may look no different than the Bretton Woods system. The parity grid of bilateral rates was no different than the band of ±1% fixed for US dollar. The concept was akin to US dollar as intervention currency. Establishing of EMCF was much the same as creation of the IMF as supplier of the intervention currency.

There were, however, conceptual differences in EMS that eliminated some of the shortcomings of the Bretton Woods system. The EMS differed fundamentally in (a) the intervention mechanism by not fixing responsibility on single nation, (b) not conferring an absolute advantage on single nation/currency, and (c) varying bands of exchange rates for each currency, instead of flat ±1% for all currencies in Bretton Woods, that recognized the individual characteristics and needs of each nation.

Intervention Mechanism under European Monetary System

The fundamental difference between Bretton Woods and EMS can be appreciated in the way the correction mechanism to restore the exchange rate within the prescribed band was devised. For the participating countries in the EMS and with bilateral bands fixed, the responsibility to come back within the band was not determined on the basis of the bilateral exchange rates alone. The onus of correcting the exchange rate to come back to the parity grid was not the sole responsibility of one nation.

In addition, the correction was not confined to intervention in the foreign exchange markets alone. Instead the defaulting nation could alter its monetary policies too, to correct the adverse BOP, which was the primary reason for exchange rate moving beyond the prescribed band.

Purpose of Parity Grid Consider an example illustrating the fundamental difference in the intervention mechanisms under the Bretton Woods system and the EMS. Assume that the parity between Deutsche Mark (DM) and French Franc (FF) is at 1 DM = FF 3.40 with a band of ±5%. The band would then be FF 3.57 (1.05 × 3.40) and FF 3.23 (0.95 × 3.40) per DM. For trade, economic, or monetary reason, assume that FF depreciates more than 5% and goes below FF 3.57/DM. The depreciation of FF can be attributed to higher prices of French exports to Germany so as to cause depreciation of its currency or lower prices of German exports to France so as to cause its appreciation, or both. The intervention mechanism of EMS would not distinguish between the two and would put the onus of correcting the exchange rate on both the nations. The situation can be corrected with buying of FF, lifting its value and selling of DM decreasing its value in terms of FF.

Under EMS intervention mechanism, both Germany and France would participate in restoring the exchange rate within the prescribed band. Germany would buy FF and France would sell DM to restore the exchange rate. This was unlike Bretton Woods where the onus of correcting the exchange rate with respect to US dollar rested with one nation only and the USA was under no obligation to correct the exchange rate. With onus on single nation, the correction was difficult as the cost of correction and the inconvenience would have to be borne by one nation only. In an integrated world where international business is to be encouraged, the responsibility of rectifying the situation cannot lie with one nation. Consistent with the issue of equal responsibilities, the correction mechanism of the EMS was fair in as much as the sharing of the burden between the two. Besides, such an intervention mechanism would achieve results with more certainty and much faster than if it were the sole responsibility of one nation.

Implication of European Currency Unit: The Divergence Indicator The nature of intervention in the EMS was not determined by the parity grid of bilateral exchange rates alone. Each currency also had a band with respect to the hypothetical currency ECU, a basket of all currencies in the EMS. Each currency was required to maintain exchange rate equilibrium with ECU too. By the bilateral bands the currencies could be assessed regarding their performance with each nation, but how did a currency do in the entire region could be monitored against a benchmark that incorporated all the exchange rates. The performance of the currency with ECU was an indicator of the relative strength or weakness of the nation with respect to the entire region.

The implications of ECU on the intervention in maintaining the exchange rates was that if only bilateral bands are violated, then the onus of correcting the exchange rate would be on the two nations, and if a currency violated its band with ECU, then the single nation would have to take corrective measures. The violation of band with ECU would mean that bilateral rates with several nations are violated, and hence the onus of correction lies with that nation only. For example, if FF is unable to maintain the exchange rate with ECU, it is likely that grid parity with several currencies would be violated too. In such a case, France would be required to take corrective steps in its economic and monetary policies including intervention to maintain the exchange rate within the bands of bilateral rates as well as ECU. Violation of band with ECU would call for more basic and structural changes in the economy.

The concept of the basket helps in gauging whether the economic and monetary policies of a nation are coherent with those of the rest of the nations whose currencies constitute the basket.

The Currency Basket The value of ECU 'a basket of currency' was determined by 12 currencies with heavy weights to Duetsche mark, French franc, and British pound (despite Britain not being a member). The features of the basket are as follows:

- Changes in the value of a currency with respect to a basket better indicates the strength than changes with respect to one currency.
- When bilateral rates change, the weights in the basket also change.
- Appreciation of one currency with respect to all will increase its weight in the basket.
- Basket tends to follow the stronger currencies because of greater weight assigned to them in the composition of the basket.
- Change in the value of the basket is equal to the proportionate change in the bilateral rates.

Since ECU assigned weights in proportion of the trade in each currency, the change in the values of currencies with larger weights would be small as compared to the change in values of currencies of smaller weights. Therefore, the threshold for currencies with small weights was higher.

The ECU was used as a divergence indicator, which does not have a parallel in the Bretton Woods system. Breaching of ECU band signalled that the economy was at divergence with the policies of the rest of the nations. The intervention mechanism differed substantially from the one prescribed under Bretton Woods.

The performance of EMS has not been considered very effective by many critics. There were several realignments of exchange rates. France and Italy had constant devaluation to combat inflation, which was low in West Germany. To match the inflation rate and yet maintain the exchange rate mechanism, it was necessary that the interest rates in the region too must converge. Speculators took advantage of the system as the direction and magnitude of realignment of exchange rate was almost predictable. Only the timing of realignment was unknown. Since the changes were infrequent but large, the cost of speculation was borne by treasuries of the nations. In order to defend the ERM, an exorbitant sum of around US$4–6 billion is estimated to have been spent.

Despite the extraordinary cost of defending ERM, Britain and Italy dropped out of it. Spain, Portugal, and Ireland devalued their currencies. Scandinavian countries too, though not formally a part of ERM, broke their informal links with it.

Currency attacks in Europe caused heavy losses during July–August 1993. As there were no capital controls, the speculators could take almost certain profit-making positions of buying DMs and selling all other currencies. Inability to defend the original ERM the bands were expanded to ±15% for seven currencies. Portugal and Spain were to operate in a band of ±6%, whereas Germany and the Netherlands remained in the original band of ±2.25%. With such wide bands, the ERM practically had conceded its objective of providing stable exchange rates, and currencies could be deemed as floating.

Despite the severe adversity and exorbitant cost of maintaining ERM, EMS cannot be regarded as a failure. During that period, it was able to achieve lower inflation rates across nations. Over a decade, from 1980 to 1990 the inflation rates in the region converged to that of Germany; the lowest inflation rate in the region. The gap of 16% in 1980 between the highest inflation rate, that is, 21.2% for Italy and the lowest inflation rate, that is, 5.2% for Germany in 1980 reduced to 4% in 1990. The hard stance of Germany of not compromising its monetary policy proved a blessing in disguise for other member nations as they had to adjust their economic and monetary policies in line with that of Germany of balanced budgets and contained money supply.

Benefits of European Monetary System

The EMS was launched with the purpose of providing stable and fixed exchange rates for different currencies in the region. The underlying motive possibly arose from the performance of US dollar in the Bretton Woods system, especially when convertibility to gold was suspended.

Devaluation of US dollar also caused losses to the reserve positions held by all nations in the form of gold and dollar. However, these nations did see the virtues of fixed exchange rate system and hence formed a monetary union.

The benefits of EMS were several. Fixed exchange rate sets up the stage for monetary union where only single currency is in circulation. It is a fixed exchange rate system in the hardest form.

Increased Trade Volumes Stable and fixed exchange rates help in expanding the market with greater confidence among exporters and importers. Though there was already a high volume of trade within the European countries, stable exchange rate would enhance the volumes. At the level of consumers, the enhanced trade provides them with wider selection and more economical choices of products. From the producers' view point, greater markets become available and larger volumes can be produced providing economies of scale and helping in reducing cost. Further, fixed exchange rates enable better planning of resources for all firms all over Europe.

Saving Hedging Cost Fixed exchange rates eliminate hedging needs too. Firms hedge to make cash flows certain, as had been the case with the currencies that were not part of EMS. Under EMS if the trade confined to the region the suppliers were assured of almost certain cash flows. This would naturally change the preferences of the suppliers to the trading in area with fixed exchange rate system in place rather than carry currency exchange rate risk by trading with non-member nations.

BEYOND EUROPEAN MONETARY SYSTEM: MONETARY AND ECONOMIC UNION

It is remarkable that despite heavy cost of defending the ERM, that practically was reduced to zero with widening of band to as high as ±15%, the members of EMS thought that there is a need to move towards monetary and economic union from mere maintaining of the exchange rates. Possibly the motivating factor behind it was the lowering of the inflation rates towards that of Germany. Monetary union, as distinct from fixed exchange rate system, called for no margin for change in the exchange rate. If the bands of exchange rate become zero, then for all purposes and intent it is a single currency that works in the entire region.

Monetary union would also mean removal of all controls in the movement of capital across nations. All capital markets become integrated. Fixed exchange rates and independent monetary policies cannot coexist. Different monetary policies of different nations would increase/decrease the relative supply of one currency against another and hence the exchange rate cannot remain constant. It is easy to see that one central bank and single monetary policy are the basic pre-requisites for a monetary union to succeed. The question of realignment of exchange rates becomes redundant if the currency of use is one. Having different currencies with absolutely fixed exchange rates is not only impractical but also impossible theoretically. If different currencies prevail with fixed exchange rates, then would the value of one currency remain same socially, politically, and economically, is a big question mark.

The Maastricht Treaty

The idea of having a common currency perhaps emanated from the desire to have uniform fiscal and monetary policies, possibly as well as that of Germany all across Europe. The experiment of EMS had mixed results. However, in 1988 the member countries of EEC decided to set up a committee headed by Jacques Delors to propose a strategy to achieve monetary union. It seemed recognition of the fact that ERM would be difficult to sustain unless the harmony in economic and monetary policies across nations is achieved. Greater convergence of economic and monetary policies among member countries would remove the disparities in the economic performance of the nations.

Delors Plan was approved in February 1992 at Maastricht and came in force in November 1993.

The first stage, which had already started in 1990, focused on removal of capital controls and allowed free flow of capital across region. In January 1994, the ERM bands were tightened again.

It provided for three important timelines for transition to common currency that later became euro:

1. Selection of countries that met the Maastricht criteria of inclusion in the European Monetary Union (EMU) by May 1998.
2. Fixing of permanent rates of conversion to euro by 1 January 1999 for each eligible member and forming of European Central Bank (ECB). The exchange rates were to be pegged irrevocably for next three years.
3. Starting January 2002 introduce euro notes and coins alongside the existing local currency for a period of six months. After July 2002, the individual currencies would cease to exist and only euro would be the legal tender.

Economic Convergence Delor's plan called for achieving absolute economic and monetary convergence. The Maastricht criteria for being eligible to join the EMU were fairly strict. The five criteria that each nation must satisfy to become part of EMU were as follows:

1. Nominal inflation rate in the country must not exceed more than 1.5% of the average of best three performing nations.
2. Budget deficit must not exceed 3% of the GDP.
3. Public debt must not exceed 60% of the GDP.
4. Long-term interest rates must not exceed by more than 2% of the average of the best three performing nations.
5. Should have maintained the exchange rate band for its currency for at least two years.

The strict convergence criterion of Maastricht Treaty came under a lot of criticism. One criticism was that the criteria were fixed rather arbitrarily. The heaviest criticism was the condition of 'no bail-out' set. The debt issued by respective governments would remain the sole responsibility of the government that issued it. Others would not come to its rescue. Further, no other conditions were imposed after the country joined the monetary union, whereas economic and monetary convergence was achieved prior to joining. Initially there

International Monetary Systems 67

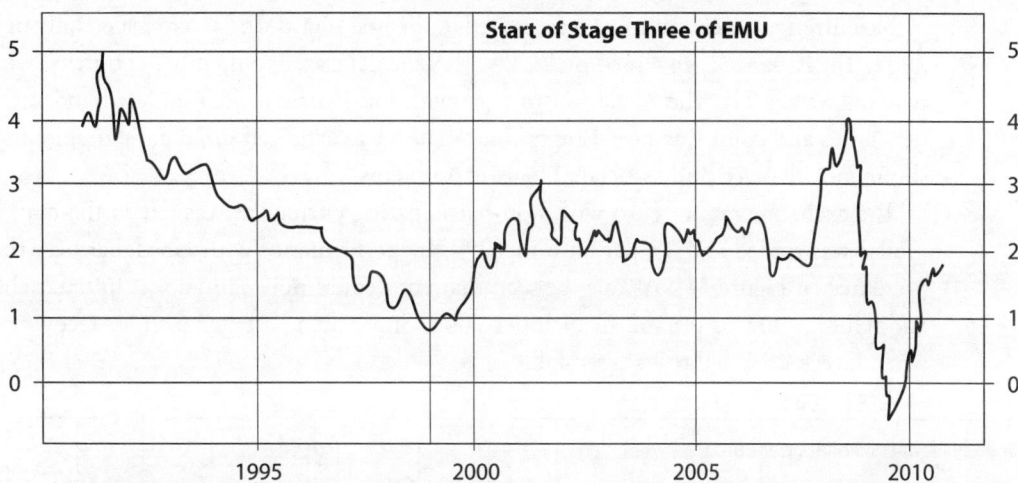

Inflation refers to a general increase in consumer prices and is measured by an index that has been harmonized across all EU member states: Harmonized Index of Consumer Prices (HICP). The HICP is the measure of inflation which the Governing Council uses to define and assess price stability in the euro area as a whole, in quantitative terms.

Source: European Central Bank, 5 October 2010.

Figure 3-3

Average Inflation Rate in Euro Area (Annual % Changes, Non-seasonally Adjusted)

were 11 members and in January 2001 Greece met the economic convergence criteria and was admitted as the twelfth member.

The new currency euro was introduced in January 1999 replacing ECU. The exchange was 1:1. The currencies of the countries also existed alongside. As on 31 December 1998, based on the then prevailing exchange rates, the conversion rates for various currencies are given in Table 3-4. These irrevocable rates were to remain till such time the euro was introduced in January 2002.

Table 3-4

Conversion Rates for Euro*

Currency	For 1 euro	Currency	For 1 euro
Austrian schilling	13.7613	German mark	1.95583
Belgian franc	40.3399	Irish punt	0.787564
Netherlands guilder	2.20371	Italian lira	1936.27
Finnish markka	5.94573	Luxembourg franc	40.3399
French franc	5.94573	Portuguese escudo	200.482
Greek drachma	340.75	Spanish peseta	166.386

*Source: Shapiro, Alan C. (2003), Multinational Financial Management, Seventh Edition, John Wiley & Sons, p. 103.

No currency notes and coins were issued in the first phase. They were issued only in February 2002. The issuance is governed by ECB with 92% delegated to member countries, whereas 8% remains with ECB. The transition to euro with local currency surrendered and exchange for new notes and coins was surprisingly smooth and was achieved in 20 days, despite the massive shipments involved and associated logistic problems.

The exchange rate of euro with non-participating currencies was left to the market forces. Dollar was traded at 1.17 per euro in 1999. Its performance with US dollar over the years is presented in Figure 3-4. As may be seen that euro could not maintain its initial exchange rate and fell to as low as 0.8252 in October 2000. Since then it staged a smart recovery till 2009 when Greek crisis led to its steep fall.

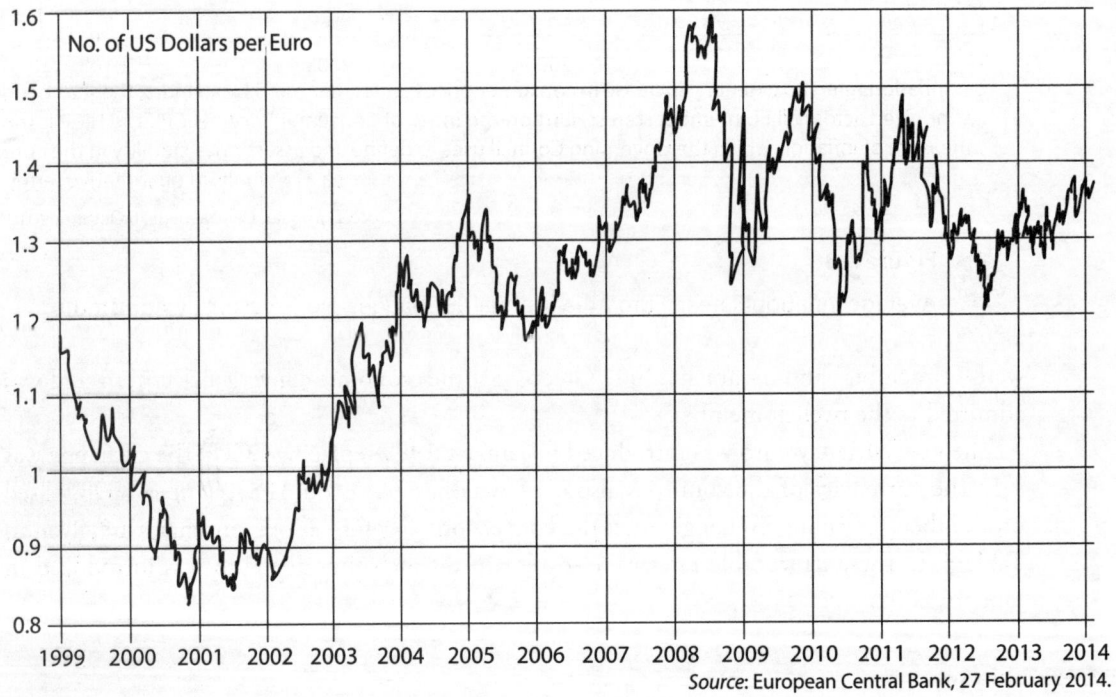

Source: European Central Bank, 27 February 2014.

Figure 3-4

Performance of Euro since 4 January 1999

Britain chose not to join the EMU for several reasons. Possibly they did not want to cede control over their monetary policies and interest rates. They also believed that ECB cannot find the right interest rates for the whole region. Four large economies of euro, namely Germany, France, Spain, and Italy, are growing at substantially different rates. Britain also had higher deficit than the Eurozone nations and in order to comply they had to cut public expenditure and raise taxes, which were lower than the levels in Eurozone. Lower tax rates in Britain were considered enough for attracting foreign capital. Further inflation and unemployment in Britain were lower, whereas their growth rate was higher.

CONCEPTS IN PRACTICE
Currency Union

EUROZONE CRISIS: THE OPTIONS

In 2012 at the height of crises of Greece and Ireland apprehensions are high on survival of euro as a currency of several nations in Europe. Greece running huge budget and current account deficits was completely out of line with rest of the nations sharing the currency. The zero growth rate in the economy and high interest rate have prompted several options. One option could be printing more money to reduce redemption pressure or buy back the bonds issued. The other alternative could be to have a political and economic union of Europe that forces the common fiscal policy across euro zone besides already existing common monetary policy.

Some have opined that in the first place Greece should not have been admitted and once taken into the fold they should have been told to follow norms.

Quantitative Easing: One solution is for European Central Bank (ECB) to buy back the bonds issued by troubled economies like Greece, Ireland, and Portugal. This would mean printing more money to bring down the borrowing cost for these nations. Though ECB has been buying the bonds otherwise but at the same time negating the purchase in money market operations. This is considered a delicate and short-term solution as it is likely to fuel inflation across all euro zone.

Default: Another solution to the problem is to let the weaker nations default on the bonds. According to many including Angela Markel, the Chancellor of Germany it is opined that the bond holders must bear the cost of the wrong doing of their governments rather than entire region and IMF bear the cost by bailing them out. Bond holders must take the losses on the debt the government's own. If so the doubts are abound that how the euro zone would stay together in times to come when Germany goes ahead with its opinion.

Make Germany Pay: A contrasting solution to letting default occur is that the strongest nation in the region should contribute towards the bail-out to reap future benefits that would accrue by remaining together. The question that remains is if desire for Germans to have economic and monetary union is strong enough to pay for the bail-out.

Let Greece, Ireland, etc. Leave: Another idea to preserve the union is to let the troubled nations leave till they become strong enough to follow the fiscal norms. This implies that the troubled nations would have to make a default on borrowings. The question is whether to defend euro at all cost or would it be better to let weaker nations leave, sort out their economies, and let them rejoin later.

Two-stage Euro: An opposite view is proposed is that the weak nations let Germany leave the euro and let other countries like the Netherlands, Austria, Germany and Finland from another common currency area. This allows for devaluation of euro and come out of crises.

United States of Europe: To some experts the only way to keep the euro zone together is to create more convergence. To mimic the United States of America the Europe too should become united with common politics and fiscal policies. How feasible and acceptable would it be for 16 current members of euro zone is a moot point.

Today Britain is paying high price for isolation; foreign investment critical to development is in jeopardy, as it gets diverted to Eurozone, being a larger market. In addition, British MNCs have to bear higher transaction cost for trade and managing exchange rate risks, and trade with nations in Eurozone (50% of total) is stagnating, whereas those in the common zone have seen increasing trade among themselves.

For some contrasting reasons, Sweden too opted out of Eurozone. In September 2003 in a referendum Swedish voted against joining euro. Sweden is budget surplus with high tax rates and an elaborate social security spending. They may have to cut expenditure on public spending and lower tax rates as most nations in Eurozone had budget deficits. Additionally, interest rate and unemployment in Sweden was lower than most nations in Eurozone.

OPTIMUM CURRENCY AREA

The Maastricht Treaty highlighted the economic convergence of nations as a prerequisite for adoption of euro as common currency for the participating nations. The question that arises is whether there is an optimal region to have a common currency. Recent crises in Eurozone would surely raise the question with greater vigour. Determining a set of criteria is indeed difficult.

Degree of Factor Mobility   Higher the degree of mobility of factors of production, more beneficial would be the monetary union. Free flow of labour and capital would ensure that deficit is made good by factors of production moving across the borders obviating the need for exchange rate changes. High mobility of labour implies that deficit nation can more easily deflate their economies without associated problem of creating unemployment as workers can migrate to other regions. If labour cannot move freely then depreciation of the currency would be the alternative to keep employment levels intact.

Degree of Financial Integration   Degree of financial integration related to factor mobility is concerned with the ability of the nation to mobilize external financial resources to finance the trade deficit, and to that extent, provide lesser need to change exchange rate to correct the BOP situation. Financial integration also would cause similar lending and borrowing norms including interest rates in the region.

Inflation Rates   Inflation rates in the region are indicative of similarity of economic and monetary policies. It also reflects more even distribution of resources financial or otherwise across the region. According to purchasing power parity the exchange rates need to adjust by the differential of the inflation rates. Closer inflation rates in the region would mean that the exchange rates would remain constant over a period of time with respect to one another in the region.

Emphasizing the single factor as sufficient condition for common currency would be misplaced. Some other observers have suggested other criteria too like ratio of tradable goods to non-tradable goods in the balance of payment of international trade. In addition, a more diversified range of goods and services in export and import makes balance of payment less vulnerable to changes and renders stability of international trade.

Besides economic convergence (as was the case under Maastricht Treaty) social and cultural integration of the people of the region would also be a requirement for common currency. Religion could also be a factor crucial for common currency. Most of the non-economic factors are difficult to measure and as also to determine the threshold for currency integration, though we have some idea about economic convergence factors as preceded in the case of euro.

CONCEPTS IN PRACTICE
Optimum Currency Area

WOULD EURO SURVIVE?

Since the eruption of Greek crisis in 2012, the debate for survival of euro has intensified. The euro area is perceived as fragile in coping with the sovereign debt crisis. Though the debt to GDP ratio is smaller and growing at slower pace than that of the USA, the reason that the sovereign debt crisis erupted in Eurozone is the vastly different economic conditions for different nations in the area. The public debt in Japan is 200% of GDP; around 2.5 times higher than the Eurozone average. The debt is heavy in certain nations like Greece and Italy, whereas it is low in other nations and hence the average remains within manageable bounds. Since Greece constitutes only 2% of the Eurozone GDP, the excessive debt should have been manageable. In the absence of political union the budget deficit cannot be transferred to other states. Greek government announced in October 2012 that its budget deficit would be 9% of GDP as against 8.1% as agreed with European Union and the IMF. The contagion would take its course.

In contrast to Greece, which never met the requirement of joining euro, Ireland was a performing economy. They took sufficient austerity measures and cut jobs to contain the budget deficit. After accepting a US$120 billion bail-out the Irish government initiated the toughest measures by announcing cutting about 25,000 jobs (10% of government workforce) and curtailing social security cost amounting to about 8% of average wages.

Portugal too ran high-budget deficit of 9.3% only behind Ireland, Greece, and Spain. Bond yield was constantly rising. Spain was not far behind with expected budget deficit for 2010 of the order of 9.3%. Italy though having manageable budget deficit had inordinately high public debt for the over spending done in the past.

The divergence in the area was great. For Greece it was fiscal indiscipline, and for Ireland it was asset bubble of property prices with banking system collapsing. So was the case with Spain together with mountainous fiscal deficit. Each country would have a different trigger for the crisis to erupt that would erode financial confidence. The economies are too divergent to allow a single central bank to manage all of them. Fixing one would mean loosening another. Would euro survive with diversities in economies or is it just an 11-year-old boy learning to cope with pressures and come out stronger in times to come?

SUMMARY

The value of a currency is a critical input and most intriguing. The most primitive settlement of trade was barter system where one commodity was exchanged for another. Later as barter system became inconvenient as trade grew both in volume and geographical spread, a need for a common denominator for valuing various commodities arose. Gold served as the most acceptable medium because of its unique properties of durability, storability, portability, divisibility, and standardizability that no other medium satisfied.

Usage of gold as medium of exchange for value of the products initiated an era called gold standard. Under gold specie, standard coins were made of gold. When paper currency came into being the currency of any country was convertible into gold. The content of gold in currencies automatically determined the exchange rate. This was called gold bullion standard. Where the value of a currency was linked to another currency that was on gold bullion it was referred as gold exchange standard.

Gold standard worked very well for international trade settlements based on flow of gold into exporting country, issuance of local currency in proportion of gold the country possesses, and prices being directly proportional to money. Since the quantity of gold world over was fixed, gold standard succeeded in maintaining the global prices at constant level. Post World War I the priorities of nations changed leading to creation of fiat money and non-adherence of principles of gold standard due to more pressing needs of economic development, creating employment, resettlement, infrastructure, etc. The situation remained fluid till 1944 when for restoring the order a conference was organized in Bretton Woods, New Hampshire, USA.

The system that evolved at the conference became known as the Bretton Woods system. Under the system each nation was to fix the value of its currency in terms of US dollar with gold assured at US$35 per ounce by the USA. Each nation was required to maintain the exchange rate with ±1% of the initial rate fixed. For doing so central banks were required to intervene in the foreign exchange markets. The need for supplying US dollars was to be fulfilled by a global organization called IMF.

The Bretton Woods system cracked in a short span of about 25 years because continued supply of US dollar to all nations could be maintained only if USA ran a persistent huge current account deficit. Another problem was of seigniorage implying that the USA could get all goods by simply printing more money not supported by accumulation of gold. The deficiency of the Bretton Woods system caused its failure and complete delinking of value of currency with gold. With the collapse of the Bretton Woods system, with the final nail in its coffin in 1976 Jamaica Agreement, which was not much different from the gold standard except for concentration of power to single nation and disciplined behaviour on part of the USA, most strong nations adopted flexible exchange rate system delinking the values from dollar and hence gold.

Almost at the same time when the Bretton woods system was collapsing another fixed exchange rate regime in Europe was working. It came to be known as 'snake in tunnel' when major European nations decided to maintain a narrower band for their own exchange rate but a broader range with US dollar. The system also called EMS operated on similar principles as that of Bretton Woods but differed in terms of less concentrated responsibilities of nations for correcting the exchange rates and BOP situations. The system did not fix onus of maintaining exchange rate of single nation, unlike Bretton Woods since it created a hypothetical currency called ECU. The system with initial hiccups worked well and ultimately culminated in the adoption of single currency called euro, the new name for ECU.

Of late, several crises have happened that are attributed to the creation of a unified currency of 16 nations called euro. These crises have raised the question of optimum common currency area and whether the adoption of euro for different set of economies and disparities was judicious.

QUESTIONS

3-1 Why did gold become the universally acceptable common medium of exchange for values of different commodities?
3-2 Differentiate gold specie standard from (a) gold bullion standard and (b) gold exchange standard.
3-3 What are the distinctive features of the Bretton Woods system that evolved in 1944?
3-4 Differentiate between the following terms:
  (a) Intervention mechanisms of Bretton Woods and European Monetary System
  (b) Gold standard and Bretton Woods system
  (c) Bretton Woods system and European Monetary system
3-5 What is Triffen's dilemma?
3-6 What do you understand by optimum currency area?

PROBLEMS

3-1 **Direct Intervention**
In a study of exchange rate fluctuations, it was estimated that an inflow of foreign currency of 100 billion leads to 5% rise in the exchange rate of local currency. What intervention amount of the foreign currency would keep the exchange rate within ±1% of the existing exchange?

3-2 **Managed Float**
In Problem 3-1 if the country wanted to depreciate the value of its currency by 5% from the existing levels, what does its central bank need to do?

Exchange Rate Systems

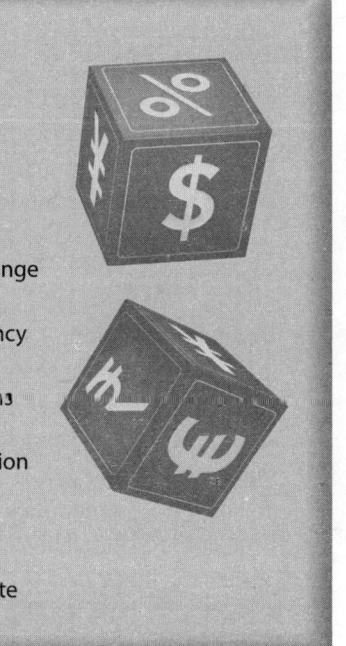

LEARNING OBJECTIVES

This chapter aims at

+ knowing various exchange rate systems prevailing in the world
+ understanding the differences between fixed and floating exchange rate systems
+ describing the advantages and disadvantages of fixed and floating exchange rate systems
+ understanding various currency rate regimes such as dollarization, currency board, pegging, managed float, and clean float
+ realizing how various currency crises have developed and learning lessons from the management of these crises
+ understanding the system of managed, float, interventions, and sterilization
+ understanding the free/clean float system
+ understanding the concept of trinity of impossible
+ knowing cooperative interventions and target zone arrangements
+ discussing the factors that determine the choice of currency exchange rate systems

CONTENTS

Introduction
Fixed and Floating Exchange Rate Systems
Advantages of Fixed Exchange Rates
    Promoting International Trade
    Uniformity in Economic Policies of the World
    Containing Inflation
    Reduced Volatility
Advantages of Floating Exchange Rate System
    Monetary Independence
    Less Painful Adjustment
    No Need for Foreign Exchange Reserves
    No Sharp Changes
    Avoiding Peso Problem

Dollarization
Currency Board
Pegged Exchange Rate System
Trilemma of Economics
Crawling Pegs
Managed/Dirty Float
    Benefits of Managed Float
    Sterilization
Free Float
Cooperative Interventions and Target Zone
    Arrangements
Choice of Exchange Rate Regime

INTRODUCTION

Till the time the Bretton Woods system of exchange rate determination was in vogue, the values of the currencies were determined by the content of gold the currency had. A gradual demise of the Bretton Woods system led to a situation where the determination of the value of the currency, and, therefore, exchange rate became an issue. If not the content of gold, what else must determine the value of currency? Beginning 1971, more and more countries started believing that the value must be determined by the free market forces rather than pegging to dollar or gold, as was prevailing then.

All exchange rate systems prior to 1971 were fixed exchange rate systems where the value of the currency would not change except by devaluation or revaluation by the respective issuing authorities. The change would take place by way of devaluation or revaluation depending upon the perspective of politicians, economists, etc. Whenever the revaluation or devaluation would take place, it would be relatively large but infrequent. For considerable periods of time, the values would remain unchanged and if at all they change, it would be in a limited band already prescribed, as was the case under the Bretton Woods system. Nations would generally be reluctant to revalue or devalue frequently as such moves send signals of not only the instability of exchange rate but also the unsteady and directionless monetary and fiscal policies.

Viewed differently, fixation of a band was recognition of the fact that free market forces have a role to play in the determination of exchange rates, albeit this role is limited, and the exchange rates essentially remain fixed by law. The failure of the Bretton Woods system and the desire of politicians and economists to have more fiscal and monetary freedom to guide the developmental programmes of nations led to evolution of the thought that foreign currency is just like any other commodity whose price should be determined by free forces of demand and supply.

Since 1973, the exchange rates of currencies were allowed to be determined by the sovereign concerned. Though choice of determining exchange rate by free market forces was available to all nations, only a few countries have actually chosen to do so. There is a huge number of variants of exchange rate systems existing today. On one end of spectrum is fixed exchange rate system, characterized by no legal tender of its own, while on the other end is floating exchange rate system. Figure 4-1 depicts the major exchange rate regimes that are in practice today by different nations in the world.

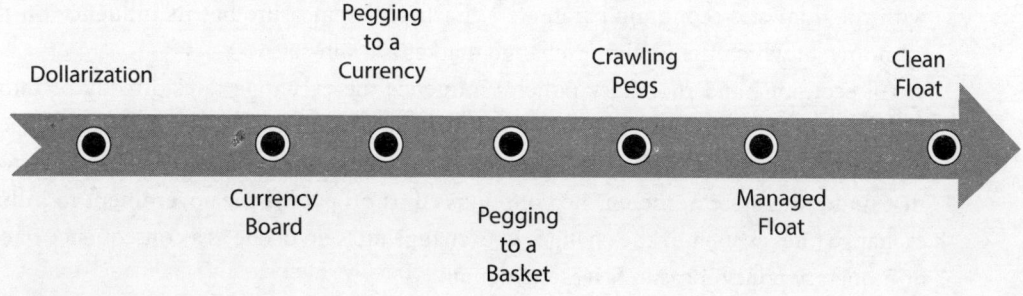

Figure 4-1
Spectrum of Exchange Rate Regimes

Both fixed exchange rate system and floating exchange rate system (also called free float or clean float) are in vogue in different parts of the world because each has its own merits and demerits. Broad economic conditions and political considerations may warrant the use of a particular exchange rate system. The experience with both fixed and floating rate systems has been mixed. In this chapter, we will discuss the advantages and disadvantages of both the systems, as also the features of these intermediate systems which are some combination of fixed and floating rates.

FIXED AND FLOATING EXCHANGE RATE SYSTEMS

Fixed exchange rate systems are those where the value of local currency is not allowed to change. The effects of economic, monetary, and financial policies of the nation are not transmitted to the foreign exchange markets by enforcing the official exchange rate. Minor variations may be allowed within a permissible band. In fact, under fixed exchange rate system, there is a conscious effort on the part of government and economists to adopt economic and monetary policies consistent with maintaining the exchange rate.

However, the economy of the nation is dynamic and what is right today may not be good tomorrow. As long as the economy supports the predetermined and regulated exchange rates, they would remain stable. However, needs of the economy would change over time warranting changes in some economic and monetary policies. Hence, pre-fixed exchange rate would no longer remain consistent with national economic policies. In case large changes are required in the exchange rate, the government would have to revalue or devalue the currency with the passage of time.

Revaluation and devaluation provide signals to the world at large, rightly or wrongly regarding the state of economy and its progress. It must be emphasized here that neither revaluation nor devaluation per se is regarded as bad or good. It must be seen in the perspective of history and background of the way the exchange rates are determined and have moved.

In contrast to fixed, floating exchange rate system, also called free float, allows for free determination of exchange rate by market forces of supply and demand with no participation by the government. It is difficult indeed to believe that governments would turn a blind eye to the happenings in the foreign exchange markets and do nothing. As such it is not possible for governments to remain indifferent because of the linkages the foreign exchange markets have with the domestic economic parameters. Each policy measure has its influence on the entire economy, of which the foreign exchange market is a sub-set.

All economic and monetary policies influence the exchange rates directly or indirectly in some way or the other, but they would not amount to interference in foreign exchange markets if they are not initiated only to influence the exchange rates. What is meant by free float is that under this system, there is no conscious effort on part of the government to influence the exchange rates as such. If the changes in exchange rates do occur as a consequence of economic or monetary policy measures, it is incidental.

ADVANTAGES OF FIXED EXCHANGE RATES

Fixed exchange rates have their own merits. Highlighting the advantages of fixed exchange rate system does not imply that it becomes superior to flexible exchange rate system. The history and experience of floating exchange rate system has been too short (they became a reality only in the 1970s), whereas the experience with fixed exchange rate systems has lasted for several centuries. Therefore, we refrain from making any conclusive judgement of superiority or inferiority of one system over the other.

Promoting International Trade

Fixed exchange rate system implies stability of cash flows for business enterprises dealing in exports and imports. If the exchange rates are fluctuating, the cash flows in local currency become uncertain, whereas cash flows in foreign currency remain same as invoicing takes place in foreign currency. Reduction in uncertainty of the local currency cash flows is conducive for increased international trade and better cash flow planning for importers and exporters.

Fixed exchange rate system is not only good for the producers but also serves the community well. Since producers seek reward in proportion to the risk they assume, the business community would be willing to work with lower profit margins in the wake of reduced risk. This offers scope for reduction in price. Hence, the consumers should get the same product at a lower price under fixed exchange rate system than under floating exchange rate system. The welfare of the economy lies in reducing uncertainty in the environment. In the domain of exchange rates that govern the international environment, fixed exchange rate system, therefore, must render stability for producers and consumers alike.

Uniformity in Economic Policies of the World

Commitment to fixed exchange rate system, in a way, amounts to consent to follow the world's economic order. Fixed exchange rate system forces a discipline on the domestic economic policies. Example of Germany to keep the inflation and interest rates down under European Monetary System (EMS) forced the other participating nations to do away with their own agendas, political or economic, and follow the practices so as to make the differential of inflation rates come down in the region. Further, if the other nations were not convinced about the policies of Germany, a dominant force, there were no compelling reasons for them to have agreed to merge their own identities in favour of single currency, euro, representing an example of the ultimate form of fixed exchange rate system.

On the contrary, under the Bretton Woods system the dominant force was the USA. If the expansionary policies of the USA were to be followed by the rest of the world, it could have been detrimental. They were not acceptable and, hence, European nations and a few stronger economies abandoned the system. The bottom line is that world follows the leaders and when the leader is pragmatic the world too is pragmatic; if not, it is no more worthy of being followed. Fixed exchange rate system, therefore, would promote adoption of uniform and converging economic, fiscal, and monetary policies in the world.

Containing Inflation

The success of gold standard is evaluated in terms of its ability to keep world prices constant for long periods of time. This is amply demonstrated in the past data of the gold standard era that suggested no inflation over the long 150–200 years prior to the Bretton Woods system. In contrast, the inflation data after 1973 reveals varying and high-inflation rates in different periods of time. In addition, the convergence of inflation rates across Europe, as reflected in the inflation rate differentials falling under EMS prior to introduction of euro, is also a testimony to the capability of fixed exchange rate system to contain worldwide inflation.

The reason for no or little inflation is not far to seek. With total availability of gold almost constant all over the world and currency supply maintained in proportion to the gold, the aggregate money supply around the world would remain constant. With gold flowing from one nation to another the supply of one currency would increase, causing inflation while that of the other decrease causing deflation. Increased prices make goods more expensive, result in outflow of gold and reduction in supply of currency, reversing the inflationary impact caused earlier.

Reduced Volatility

An argument, not as much in favour of fixed exchange rate system as against floating exchange rate system, is that currency markets in the latter can be extremely volatile. It can be a destabilizing factor for the world as speculation is encouraged. Speculation in currency has the potential to distort the true value of a currency as supported by fundamentals. Speculators always overreact to a situation and blow incidents out of proportion. For example, news of deteriorating balance of payment (BOP) may warrant a depreciation of the currency in question. The speculators would make the currency depreciate more than what is dictated by the actual data. To this extent, the value in floating rate system may become detached from the fundamentals.

Herd mentality also contributes to this distortion. Speculators take positions not on the basis of what has happened, but on what is likely to happen in future. They anticipate the changes and act in advance discounting forthcoming events. These anticipations at time are unfounded and, hence, can lead to mispricing of the currency.

Another argument in favour of fixed exchange rate is that floating rate does not suit small economies.

ADVANTAGES OF FLOATING EXCHANGE RATE SYSTEM

As stated earlier, under floating rate system the exchange rate is determined by market forces without being influenced by law or government actions. There are many advantages of the system that either are inherent with the system or are disadvantages of fixed rate system.

Monetary Independence

Floating exchange rate system allows politicians and economists to pursue independent monetary policies as they deem fit for the nation's development and growth. This freedom is not available under fixed exchange rate system where a nation is forced to follow the monetary policies of a dominant trading partner.

Consider an example for better understanding. Assume that the USA is the major trading partner of Canada. Under fixed exchange rate system, the monetary policies of the USA are forced upon Canada. To maintain the exchange rate under fixed regime, the actions in the foreign exchange markets impact the domestic monetary situation. If the USA follows expansionary policy, the prices there would go up and make its exports more expensive and imports more attractive. This deteriorates the BOP for the USA. Its counter effect takes place in Canada whose BOP improves.

Under fixed exchange rate system, Canada would be obligated to defend the exchange rate. To stave off the appreciation of Canadian dollar originating from external environment, the Bank of Canada would have to intervene in the foreign exchange markets to buy US dollar. This action would mean selling Canadian dollar and, as such, inadvertently the local money supply increases. This leads to inflationary conditions in Canada that is not of its own making but results due to the expansionary policy followed by its major trading partner. This is also referred to as *importing inflation*.

Importing inflation should not draw a negative connotation. It has its positive side too, as follows:

1. Inflation would be imported in Canada if their economy was fully employed. The increased money supply would cause inflation. However, if the economy is underemployed, the increased money supply may raise production, GDP, and employment.
2. In case the major trading partner follows deflationary policy, it would be transferred to the other nation. Fixed exchange rate system necessarily forces a uniform rate of inflation. If the dominant force believes in containing inflation, the smaller nations would, and should, accept fixed exchange rate system.

Under flexible exchange rate system, the Bank of Canada is under no obligation to defend the fixed parity with US dollar and, therefore, there would be no intervention. Hence, in the currency markets, US dollar would depreciate and equivalently Canadian dollar would appreciate. Changes in the exchange rate would restore BOP to the original level. How the variables change under fixed and floating rate systems is contrasted in Figure 4-2. In fixed exchange rate system, the intervention would impact the local economy, whereas in floating exchange rate system the exchange rate changes would act to correct the BOP situation.

Thus, floating exchange rate system provides increased independence for devising monetary policy. Under fixed rate system, the monetary policy is constrained by the policies adopted by the dominant trading partner.

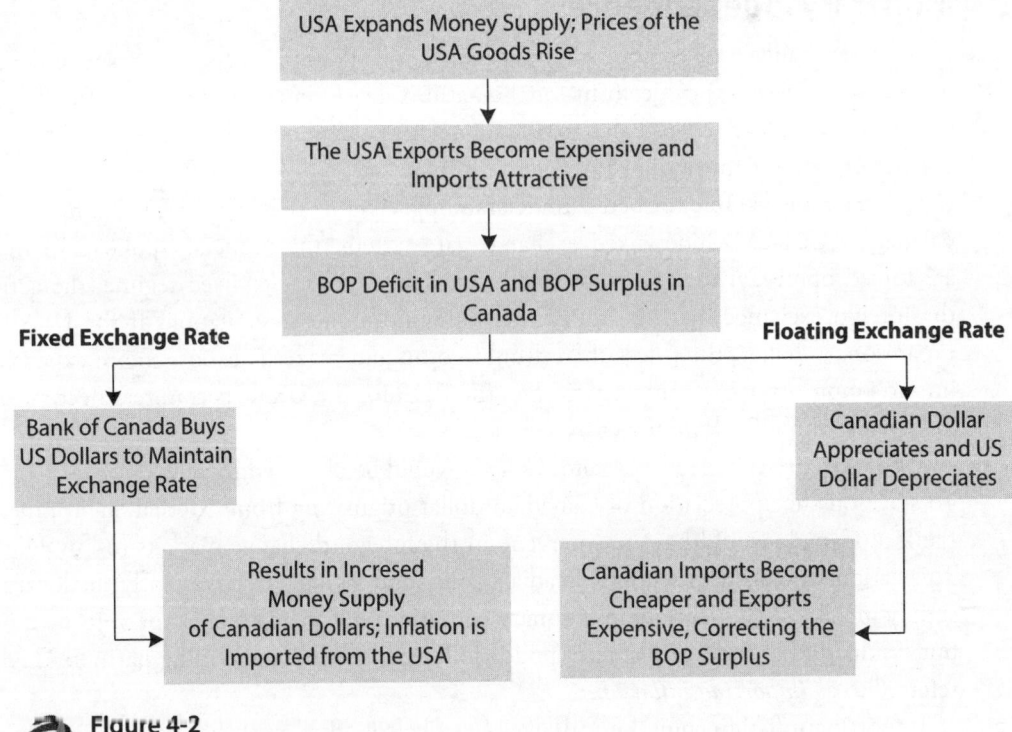

Figure 4-2
Importing Inflation—Fixed Exchange Rate System

Less Painful Adjustment

The adjustment process in floating exchange rate system is through continuous changes in the exchange rates. Under fixed exchange rate system, the adjustment for any external changes is through income route affecting wages. A persistent deficit in an economy would be corrected by depreciation in the value of the local currency. The appreciation of foreign currency would make imports expensive. Under fixed exchange rate system, the value of currency would not change but instead consumption would have to adjust by reducing real income and wages. For many, this is a rather high cost to pay, especially when the situation could be corrected by modifying exchange rates. Reduction in real wages would be suicidal from the political viewpoint too.

No Need for Foreign Exchange Reserves

One perceptible major advantage of flexible exchange rate system is that a country does not need to maintain any foreign currency reserves for the purpose of intervention in the foreign exchange markets to stabilize the value of the currency. The reserves can be used for more productive purposes. Foreign currency earned by way of exports can be utilized for financing import of goods required in the economy. There are better and more productive uses of foreign currency than throwing it in the market to change the value. The precious foreign exchange used for intervention is a direct loss to the nation. The profit is ultimately made by speculators alone when central banks throw money in the currency markets.

No Sharp Changes

Another advantage of flexible exchange rate system is that the exchange rate changes are frequent and small just as the economic changes. The economy keeps absorbing these frequent small changes. Under fixed exchange rate system, the changes in the exchange rates keep getting postponed. In addition, when a change takes place, the change is usually large. Small frequent changes provide time for adjustment by producers and consumers alike. Under fixed rate system even though the direction of change is well-anticipated, its quantum and timing are unknown. As and when revaluation or devaluation occurs, it is sharp. A 10% depreciation spread over a period of 365 days or a devaluation of 10% on a single day after a year though are equivalent monetarily but have different impact. Abrupt changes are always painful and appear unjust for some as such changes make one section of society (exporters, in case of devaluation) gain suddenly at the expense of another (importers, in case of devaluation). A slow and steady change is less predictable for speculators as exchange rate moves both ways. In fixed exchange rate regimes, the direction of change is predictable benefitting the speculators.

Likely paths of exchange rate changes under fixed and floating rate systems are depicted in Figure 4-3 where the final exchange rate is the same but the path taken is different. Under fixed rate system, the currency is devalued thrice to be at the same level of exchange rate as under floating rate system.

Recognizing that change is inevitable, the two systems differ only in the way the change is managed. Ultimately, the exchange rates have to follow what the economy can sustain and support. Consider the following arguments for and against fixed and floating exchange rate systems:

1. The proponents of fixed exchange rate system may argue that changes in the exchange rates under floating rate are destabilizing and are not conducive for international

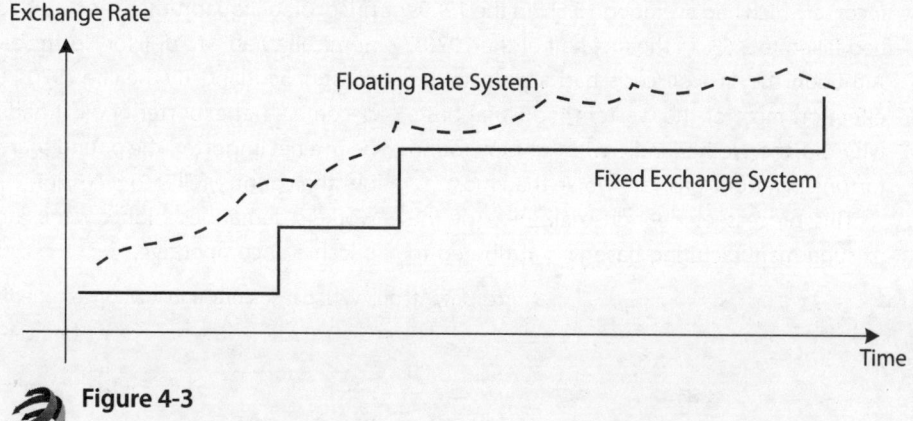

Figure 4-3
Changes in Exchange Rates under Fixed Rate and Floating Rate System

cooperation and increasing trade. Those favouring floating rate system may counter argue that it is the abrupt and large changes that have more destabilizing effect rather than the gradual and small changes.

2. Those who favour floating rate system may argue that since the hedging tools of forward, futures, options, and swaps are available, small changes in exchange rates can always be hedged. These derivative tools, however, are not apt to manage large changes. The counter argument could be to consider who bears the cost of hedging. Since the changes in the exchange rate under fixed rate system are abrupt with the direction of change almost predictable, the speculators can benefit at the expense of public exchequer.

CONCEPTS IN PRACTICE
Flexible Rates and Dutch Disease

DUTCH DISEASE DISTURBING THE UNIVERSE

In 1959, a large reservoir of natural gas was discovered in the Netherlands, which by 1976 earned them revenues of some $2 billion in addition to an estimated $3.5 billion of savings in imports. By the mid-1970s, gross corporate investment had fallen by 15% since the start of the decade, while employment in manufacturing had declined by 16%. The total level of unemployment had risen from a modest 1.1% to 5.1%, whereas the share of profits in national income which had averaged 16.8% in the 1960s had fallen to 3.5% in the first half of the 1970s. Although the first oil crisis had a devastating effect on most of the western industrial base, why did the Netherlands, with its new-found fortune in natural gas, fare worse than most?

This process of de-industrialization of the existing manufacturing base was attributed to the upward pressure that the energy discovery placed on the Guilder and the wage rate and was dubbed as *the Dutch Disease*. Since then, the term's use has widened considerably to encompass any situation whereby a country's apparent good economic fortune ultimately proves to have a net detrimental effect. This is also called the law of unintended consequences.

Similarly, in the 1970s, the same economic condition occurred in Great Britain, when the price of oil quadrupled and it became economically viable to drill for North Sea oil off the coast of Scotland. By the late 1970s, Britain had become a net exporter of oil; it had previously been a net importer. The pound soared in value, but the country fell into recession when British workers demanded higher wages and exports became uncompetitive.

Source: Dey, Atanu, www.deesha.org, and www.investopedia.com, both accessed on 7 October 2010.

Exchange Rate Systems

Avoiding Peso Problem

The peso problem gets its name from the events that took place in the 1980s in Mexico. Mexico was maintaining the fixed rate with US dollar at unrealistically high levels, and it was widely anticipated that peso would be devalued. To prevent the withdrawal of foreign investment, Mexico maintained high interest rates. High interest rate stifled investment, reducing job opportunities. This economic downturn was attributed to the prevalence of fixed exchange rate. Ultimately, Mexico devalued peso. High interest rates only delayed the inevitable devaluation. This is referred to as *peso problem*. One believes that with flexible exchange rate, the peso problem could have been avoided.

From the foregoing discussion one can clearly see that both systems have their merits and demerits, and one cannot assume superiority of one over the other. Therefore, there exist many variants of exchange rate systems that countries adopt to meet their individual needs.

The International Monetary Fund (IMF) has classified various exchange control systems that are prevailing, as presented in Table 4-1. These systems range from dollarization to clean or free float and the IMF has classified the exchange rate systems of various countries. We discuss some of them here.

Table 4-1
De Facto Classification of Exchange Rate Arrangements as of 30 April 2012

1. Exchange Arrangements with No Separate Legal Tender (14)	Ecuador, El Salvador, Marshall Islands, Micronesia, Palau, Panama, Timor-Leste, Zimbabwe, Kosovo, Montenegro, San Marino, Kiribati, Tuvalu
2. Currency Board Arrangement (12)	Antigua and Barbuda, Dominicia, Djibouti, Grenada, Hong Kong SAR, St Kitts and Nevis, St Lucia, St Vincent & the Grenadines, Bosnia and Herzegovina, Bulgaria, Lithuania, Brunei Darussalam
3. Conventional Peg Arrangements (43)	Aruba, Bahamas, Bahrain, Barbados, Belize, Curacao and Saint Maarten, Eritrea, Jordan, Oman, Qatar, Saudi Arabia, Turkmenistan, United Arab Emirates, Venezuela, Cape Verde, Comoros, Denmark, Latvia, Sao Tome Principe **WAEMU**: Benin, Burkina Faso, Cote d'Ivoire, Guinea-Bissau, Mali, Niger, Senegal, Togo **CAEMC**: Cameroon, Central African Republic, Chad, Congo, Equatorial Guinea, Gabon, Fiji, Kuwait, Libya, Morocco, Samoa, Bhutan, Lesotho, Namibia, Nepal, Swaziland
4. Stabilized Arrangements (16)	Cambodia, Guyana, Iraq, Lebanon, Maldives, Surinam, Trinidad & Tobago, FYR Macedonia, Vietnam, Tajikistan, Ukraine, Gautemala, Angola, Azerbaijan, Egypt, Lao PDR
5. Pegged Exchange Rates within Horizontal Bands (1)	Tonga
6. Crawling Pegs (3)	Nicaragua (US Dollar), Botswana (Composite), Bolivia (de facto US dollar)

(Contd)

Table 4-1 Contd

7. Exchange Rates within Crawling Bands (12)	Ethiopia, Honduras, Jamaica, Kazakhstan, Croatia, Argentina, China, Rwanda, Uzbekistan, Dominican Republic, Haiti, Tunisia	
8. Other Managed Arrangements (24)	Liberia, Algeria, Iran, Singapore, Syria, Vanuatu, Bangladesh, Burundi, Congo Democratic Republic, Guinea, Kyrgyz Republic, Malawi, Nigeria, Paraguay, Yemen, Belarus, Costa Rica, Malaysia, Mauritania, Myanmar, Russia, Solomon Islands, Sudan, Switzerland	
9. Floating Arrangement (35)	Afghanistan, Gambia, Kenya, Madagascar, Mongolia, Mozambique, Pakistan, Papua New Guinea, Seychelles, Sierra Leone, Sri Lanka, Tanzania, Uganda, Zambia, Albania, Armenia, Brazil, Columbia, Georgia, Ghana, Hungary, Iceland, Indonesia, Korea, Moldova, Peru, Philippines, Romania, Serbia, South Africa, Thailand, Turkey, Uruguay, India, Mauritius	
10. Free Floating (31)	Australia, Canada, Chile, Czech Republic, Israel, Mexico, New Zealand, Norway, Poland, Sweden, United Kingdom, Japan, Somalia, United States, **EUROZONE**: Austria, Belgium, Cyprus, Estonia, Finland, France, Germany, Greece, Ireland, Italy, Luxembourg, Malta, Netherlands, Portugal, Slovak Republic, Slovenia, Spain	

Note: Figure in brackets represent number of nations in the category.
Source: IMF Annual Report on Exchange Rate Arrangements and Exchange Restrictions, October 2012.

DOLLARIZATION

As per the IMF, dollarization refers to the circulation of currency of another country as legal tender. Since most countries use US dollar as their currency, the term dollarization has come to denote such a practice, even though the currency is other than US dollar. The country does not have its own currency, and hence the question of monetary policy adjustments does not arise. Adopting such regimes implies the complete surrender of the monetary authorities' independent control over domestic monetary policy. The major advantage of dollarization is promoting fiscal discipline and, thus, greater financial stability and lower inflation.

One can have its own currency backed by reserves of foreign currency as is the case with currency board arrangement (discussed next), but dollarization has more credibility than currency board because reversing dollarization is harder than the currency board arrangement (Argentina abandoned currency board in 2002).

Official dollarization has gained prominence as several countries have considered and implemented it as an official policy. Dollarization can occur unofficially when private agents prefer the foreign currency over the domestic currency. For example, private agents may hold deposits in the foreign currency because of a bad track record of the local currency; semiofficially (or officially bi-monetary systems), where foreign currency is a legal tender but plays a secondary role to domestic currency; or officially, when a country ceases to issue the domestic currency and uses only foreign currency. It adopts the foreign currency as its legal tender.

CONCEPTS IN PRACTICE
Unofficial Dollarization

THE GHOST OF DOLLARIZATION IN ZIMBABWE

Dollarization, the holding by residents of a significant share of their assets in the form of foreign-currency-denominated assets is a common feature of developing countries and some transitional economies. However, as Zimbabwe's experience has shown, dollarization can, and does occur, when the 'flight from domestic currency' gets under way.

Chronic inflation does not necessarily degenerate into hyperinflation, which is triggered by an uncontrolled expansion in the money supply that is fuelled by endemic fiscal imbalances. Though in official terms Zimbabwe's dollarization (or Randization) is of unknown quantity, the country already has a high, but unknown, degree of unofficial dollarization. The phenomenon started with the practice of prices of cars and houses, fees for services, and salaries of scarce personnel, either paid or calculated in US dollars. This was followed by licensed foreign currency shops, where virtually most goods, including local manufactured ones, are priced in US dollars. With the virtual collapse of the domestic currency as a means of transacting business, most business is now transacted in foreign currency. Nearly all goods and services in Zimbabwe are paid for with hard currency, and the Zimbabwe dollar has fallen out of use except for paying certain official fees and fines.

Zimbabwe has skirted the adoption of official or full dollarization where a foreign currency—possibly rand or US dollar—has the exclusive, predominant status as full legal tender so that the domestic currency is phased out and replaced by the US dollar or South African rand. There were two policy moves in 2009 that were very promising: (a) Zimbabwe was abandoning the production of its own currency and (b) it was allowing foreign currencies to be used as a legal tender.

Zimbabwe's dollarization is near complete. Joint circulation of an anchor currency, in this case the US dollar and the Zimbabwe dollar, for a period would help restoring the Zimbabwe dollar as the sole legal tender.

Countries that adopt this model can no longer have an independent monetary policy and set their own interest rates but must 'import' the monetary policy of the country whose currency is chosen.

Alternatively, Zimbabwe can continue with its current unofficial dollarization but regularize its exchange rate through some pre-determined fixed rate, and at the same time look for an appropriate monetary anchor.

Source: Ndlela, Daniel B., Short Briefing Note, www.epolotics.org.za, 8 October 2010.

For small countries with large neighbours, dollarization makes sense. Ecuador, El Salvador, and Panama are among the countries that use US dollar as their currency. Montenegro and San Marino use euro and Kiribati uses Australian dollar.

Besides large number of nations using hard peg with US dollar or euro, South African rand serves an anchor currency of its three neighbours—Lesotho, Namibia, and Swaziland. Liechtenstein used Swiss francs, Nepal and Bhutan use Indian rupee as anchor, and Andorra and Monaco use euro as their currency.

CURRENCY BOARD

A currency board is a monetary authority that issues notes and coins freely convertible into a foreign currency at a fixed rate and on demand. The foreign currency is referred to as anchor or reserve currency. A currency board's foreign currency reserves must be sufficient to ensure that all money issued can be converted into the reserve currency with no restrictions on the nature of transactions, on current account or capital account. There is a free flow of cross border capital. Currency board arrangements are a very strong form of fixed exchange rate regime. Like the gold standard, they rely on market forces, rather than on foreign exchange controls or interventions, to fix the exchange rate. A gold standard is a special case of a currency board where the value of the national currency is linked to the value of gold instead of a foreign currency or a set of foreign currencies.

The net effect of a currency board is that it has no discretionary powers to affect any monetary policy. The board would issue only as much local currency as can be converted into reserve/anchor currency. As such the money supply is determined by market forces. Exporters need to earn foreign currency first before importers can have it. Besides loss of authority to issue local currency, the currency board also does not influence interest rates, which is another monetary tool. By doing so the board tends to keep interest rates and inflation very closely aligned to the anchor currency.

Thus, governments have only fiscal tools, such as taxes and control of budgetary expenditure to execute their growth and developmental plans.

Thus, currency boards are characterized by (a) anchor currency, (b) full convertibility at fixed pre-determined exchange rate, (c) absence of capital control measures, (d) 100% back up of reserves in anchor currency, and (e) absence of monetary policy. Since there is no interest rate determination, arbitrage ensures alignment of inflation rate and interest rates of the anchor currency.

Among the economies that have adopted currency board arrangement, only Argentina (in the past) and Hong Kong are large, whereas the remaining countries are too small. Typically, currency boards have advantages for small, open economies which would find an independent monetary policy difficult to sustain. By adopting currency board arrangement they can have a credible commitment to low inflation, as demonstrated by Argentina in the past, when they adopted currency board arrangement to come out of hyper inflationary situation, as described here.

Case: Argentina's Currency Board The Argentine Currency Board pegged the Argentine peso to the US dollar between 1991 and 2002 in an attempt to eliminate hyperinflation and stimulate economic growth. For most of the period between 1975 and 1990, Argentina had experienced hyperinflation (averaging 325% a year), poor or negative GDP growth, a severe lack of confidence in the national government and the Central Bank, and low levels of capital investment. Inflation peaked in 1989, reaching 5,000% that year. GDP was 10% lower than that in 1980 and per capita GDP had fallen by over 20%. Fixed investment fell by over half. Social indicators deteriorated seriously, real wages collapsed to about half of their 1974 peak, and poverty rates increased from 27% in 1980 to 47% in 1989.

To a large extent, the main reason behind this long period of hyperinflation was unsustainable growth of the money supply to finance the large fiscal deficits maintained by successive governments. Since Argentina could not participate meaningfully in world capital markets, given the great investment risk it posed, the only course available was the financing of these fiscal deficits by monetizing them.

Argentina implemented its currency board in April 1991 by adopting the following: (a) changing currency from austral to peso and (b) choosing US dollar as anchor currency. New peso could be issued only when US dollar was available as backup. Its main achievement was in controlling inflation, which was brought down from more than 3000% in 1989 to 3.4% in 1994, getting aligned with the inflation rate of the USA. Another major accomplishment of the system was renewed economic growth. Although the currency board in Argentina initially met with considerable success, when the recession and the bank's massive withdrawals started in 2000, Argentina abandoned currency board arrangements in 2002.

A currency board only earns profit from interests on foreign reserves. A currency board does not act as a lender of last resort to commercial banks and does not regulate reserve requirements. It only issues local currency in exchange of anchor currency.

Williamson[1] lists the following seven disadvantages with currency board:

1. The *seigniorage* problem: Due to the necessity of keeping assets in foreign currency as reserves, a currency board may earn less if domestic investments provide a better yield.
2. The *start-up* problem: A currency board may not have enough foreign assets; for the initial launching a minimum threshold level of foreign currency would be required.
3. The *transition* problem: A currency board may start from a highly inflationary situation and the transition to a fixed exchange rate may rapidly result in an overvaluation of the domestic currency.
4. The *adjustment* problem: A currency board cannot resort to exchange rate changes to secure BOP adjustments even in the case of external shocks; the problems will be acute if flexibility in the real sector is not high.
5. The *management* problem: A currency board cannot run an independent monetary policy.
6. The *crisis* problem: A currency board may not be able to act as a lender of last resort to financial institutions because it violates the 'basic precept of issuing domestic currency only in exchange for foreign currency rather than against domestic assets'.
7. The *political* problem: A currency board may not be able to impose fiscal discipline because politics may weigh in favour of the finance ministry.

In Hong Kong, currency board arrangement was instituted on 17 October 1983 as a rescue measure in a currency crisis caused by Sino-British political conflict over the future of the territory. It fixed the exchange rate of HK$7.80 to the US dollar that continues till today. The British overseas territories of Gibraltar, the Falkland Islands, and St Helena continue to operate currency boards, backing their locally printed currency notes with pound sterling reserves. Estonia and Lithuania too have used euro as anchor, whereas Brunei continues to use Singapore dollar in their currency board arrangement. In January 2011, Estonia adopted Euro as its currency.

---

[1] Williamson, John (1995), *What Role for Currency Boards?* Institute for International Economics, USA.

CONCEPTS IN PRACTICE
Currency Board

BRUNEI'S CURRENCY BOARD

The Brunei Currency Board (BCB) was established by the 1967 Currency Act in Chapter 32 of the Laws of Brunei. It has the sole right to manage and issue currency notes and coins in Brunei Darussalam. The currency issued by the Board is designated to serve as legal tender within the state.

Brunei Darussalam commenced issuance of its own currency on 12 June 1967. Prior to this date, the Board of Commissioners of Currency, which was reconstituted under the Malaya British Borneo Currency Agreement, 1960, was the sole currency issuing authority in Malaysia, the Republic of Singapore, and Brunei Darussalam. Under an arrangement, the Government of Malaysia replaced the Board by Bank Negara Malaysia as the sole currency issuing authority in Malaysia. Similarly, the Board of Commissioners of Currency, Singapore, became the currency issuing authority in Singapore.

A currency interchangeability agreement was established between Singapore and Brunei Darussalam, which remains in effect till today and continues to play a central role in relations between the two countries. This agreement allows both the countries to interchange their currencies at par without either country running the risk of currency exchange rate fluctuations and, thus, further facilitates trade and commerce between the two countries. The individual currencies are acceptable as customary tender when circulating in the country in which they are not legal tender.

Its main mission is to ensure the integrity of the currency issue and safeguard public interest. At the same time, BCB also seeks to provide the highest standard of service to both the banks and the public.

BCB maintains strict control over the amount of currency in circulation whereby the external and liquid assets must exceed the statutory limits of 70% and 30%, respectively.

Source: www.finance.gov.bn, accessed on 8 October 2010.

PEGGED EXCHANGE RATE SYSTEM

Pegged exchange rate system, which is used by a large number of developing countries, implies a fixed exchange rate with respect to one currency or a basket of currencies called composite. According to the IMF, classification pegging is defined as follows:

1. The country (formally or de facto) pegs its currency at a fixed rate to another currency or a basket of currencies, where the basket is formed from the currencies of major trading or financial partners, and the weights assigned reflect the geographical distribution of trade, services, or capital flows. The currency composites can also be standardized, as in the case of the special drawing rights (SDRs).

2. There is no commitment to keep the parity irrevocably. The exchange rate may fluctuate within narrow margins of less than ±1% around a central rate—or the maximum and minimum values of the exchange rate may remain within a narrow margin of 2%—for at least three months.
3. The monetary authority stands ready to maintain the fixed parity through direct intervention (i.e. via sale/purchase of foreign exchange in the market) or indirect intervention (e.g. via aggressive use of interest rate policy, imposition of foreign exchange regulations, exercise of moral suasion that constrains foreign exchange activity, or through intervention by other public institutions).
4. Flexibility of monetary policy, though limited, is greater than in the case of exchange arrangements with no separate legal tender and currency boards because traditional central banking functions are still possible and the monetary authority can adjust the level of the exchange rate, although relatively infrequently.

Under the pegged exchange rate system, a country fixes the value of its currency with respect to another currency or with a basket of currencies. This currency/basket to which the value is pegged is chosen on the basis of two major considerations—the international acceptability of the currency and, if major trade is denominated, in the chosen currency. Most likely, the currency to which pegging is done would normally be the one whose value is flexible. The US dollar is the most popular currency followed by euro to which nations peg their currencies because of its worldwide acceptability, flexible values, and the fact that most international trade even though not with USA or Eurozone, is denominated in them.

Currency board arrangement discussed earlier is also pegging that implies foregoing the monetary independence of tinkering with money supply and domestic interest rates. Under pegging, the value of currency is fixed but the tools of monetary policy are also retained by the government. Exchange rate mechanism in Europe prior to single currency of euro was also one form of pegging as various currencies were pegged to each other by very limited movement permitted around the central rate. Each of the participating nations retained monetary freedom.

The notion that the value of currency remains fixed under pegging is misplaced. It does remain fixed with one currency for a limited period of time but varies with other currencies as does the anchor currency. The value moves as the value of the currency to which it is pegged moves. For example, if Thai Baht is pegged to US dollar which depreciates 10% against British pound, then the value of Thai Baht automatically depreciates with respect to British pound by the same amount of 10% as US dollar did. Hence, under fixed exchange rate system, the appreciation and depreciation of the currency would be same as that of the currency to which it is pegged. With respect to all other currencies, the value of Thai baht would appreciate or depreciate just as the US dollar does. The value remains fixed with dollar and not with the remaining currencies.

The pegging rate is fixed in a manner that supposedly keeps the BOP neutral. Since the value of the currency changes except to which it is pegged, the BOP with other nations changes to the extent the trade is denominated in other currencies. In addition, other changes in the economic environment disturb the peg and may soon create an imbalance. For example, Thailand having pegged its currency to dollar competes with Japan for trading with the USA. If Japanese yen depreciates with US dollar, then exports from Japan become more competitive. For the USA, importing from Japan rather than from Thailand becomes cheaper and it replaces import from

Thailand with Japanese goods, causing trade deficit in Thailand. Hence, pegged rate is no guarantee that the trade balance would be maintained.

Dynamic nature of the economy, trading with other nations, and changes in the competitive position all warrant monetary interventions to maintain the pegged exchange rate. These interventions can be in the form of fiscal incentives for exports, changing tariff structure, etc. or monetary tools of changing interest rates and/or money supply, or of regulatory nature of directing the foreign capital flows. The kind of response would depend upon whether the changes are deemed temporary or permanent, warranting structural changes by the government. Usually governments assume that the changes are temporary. If changes are structural, the remedy lies in re-pegging (substantial devaluation in most cases) of the exchange rate that many governments tend to use only as measure of last resort.

The pegged or fixed exchange rate system has mixed results. Fixed exchange system as that of EMS has culminated in the unification of 12 currencies into euro. The currency board arrangements of Hong Kong and Argentina, besides some smaller economies, have also delivered desired results. China's pegging has also demonstrated achieving consistent growth for several years. On the contrary, there have been failures too. Mexican peso crisis and Asian currency crisis are the two examples of failure of pegging of exchange rates. By understanding the reasons for failure of pegging in Mexico and Asia, we can draw some basic pre-requisites of pegged exchange rates.

Case: Mexican Peso Crisis In 1991, Mexico used pegged exchange rate with a tight band. The pegging kept the inflation rate in Mexico at around the same level as that of the USA. Later, it widened the band for the exchange rate fluctuations, riding high on expectations with overcoming of the debt crisis, opening up of the economy and capital account transactions, and joining the North America Free Trade Treaty. Mexico attracted massive foreign investment. The Mexican peso appreciated to the maximum in the prescribed band due to heavy inflow of dollars. With good inflow of foreign currency, Mexico had issued short-term securities denominated in US dollars to attract foreign capital inflows.

Large inflows of foreign capital caused appreciation of peso to the maximum in the widened band. This appreciation led to huge deficit in BOPs running as high as 8% of GDP. However, there were significant political developments with armed rebellion in early 1994 causing much of the uncertainty in business. The external environment too changed substantially with the USA increasing interest rates. With political uncertainty looming large, increased returns in the USA coupled with free capital account transactions—the reverse capital flight started. Withdrawal of dollars created tremendous demand for dollars raising its value. In order to retain the foreign capital, Mexico too had to raise interest rates so that capital keeps flowing in, else the trade deficit could not be funded. Mexican peso depreciated to the lower end of the band.

Throughout 1994, the position of reserves fell drastically to meet the heavy demand of dollars and also to lift the value of peso. The short-term securities denominated in dollars too matured for redemption causing further demand for dollars. There was excessive money supply of peso. Speculation too mounted expecting a massive devaluation of peso. Foreign capital started flowing out at a much greater speed than it flowed in when circumstances were favourable. Local residents too had more confidence in dollar than in peso and wanted to hold dollar. To the extent of the demand for dollars increased the local currency would be absorbed from the market, and there would not have been so adverse outcome.

Instead of keeping the peso with it, the central bank, Banco de Mexico, cycled these pesos back into the economy by redeeming securities. It did so because of the fear that constrained supply of peso would cause interest rate to rise. The unintended consequence was further loss of confidence in peso and almost certain devaluation. This led to unabated rush for conversion to dollars.

Mexico could not sustain the pressure on peso and on 20 December 1994, it devalued from peso 3.50/$ to peso 4.025/$, that is, about 15% lower than the lower limit of the band. Panic set in the capital markets as foreign investors sold securities to get back dollars as quickly as possible anticipating further devaluation. Capital markets crashed by 11%.

Within two days of devaluation, that is, on 22 December 1994, the Mexican government, unable to sustain the value of peso, had to change from pegging to de-pegging of peso. The peso was now on free float with the value determined by market forces. The free float caused peso to fall to peso 7.00/$ by March 1995 and to peso 7.70/$ by end 1995, implying more than 100% devaluation in one year. To discourage withdrawal of capital, Mexico had to raise the domestic interest rates.

The crisis of peso put the country on the brink of default on external debt. A bail-out package was quickly worked out. The bail-out package amounting to $53 billion consisted $20 billion from US Treasury Guarantee Fund, $10 billion from the IMF and balance from other nations. The oil reserves of Mexico were to serve as collateral for these loans and strict austerity conditions were placed on them. These conditions included (a) tightening of monetary policy to shore up the value of peso, (b) tax cuts to induce employment, and (c) tough targets for money supply, domestic credit, fiscal budgets, and foreign borrowings.

Whether or not the disaster could be averted if Mexico had not pegged its currency remains an unanswered question.

Case: Asian Currency Crisis Another currency crisis with large ramifications, both in terms of its geographical coverage and the financial impact, occurred in 1997 with the sudden devaluation of Thai Baht on 2 July 1997—an event widely regarded having triggered the crisis. The massive damage caused can be estimated from the fact that major currencies in the entire region, that is, Thai baht, Indonesian rupiah, South Korean won, Malaysian ringgit, and Philippines peso declined in the range of 40%–80% in value. All these currencies were pegged to dollar with the exception of South Korean won, which was on crawling peg.

Entire South East Asia had been doing exceedingly well, and there were no signs of any forthcoming danger till 2 July 1997 when Thailand suddenly announced devaluation of baht, its currency. No financial analyst, research house as well as monitoring agencies like the IMF could ever see any signs of weaknesses in the growing economy before it actually occurred. The crisis took all of them by surprise.

The South East Asian currency crisis originated from Thailand, known as Asian Tiger due to its great export competiveness, ability to attract foreign investment, booming economy and markets, controlled inflation, and all round prosperity and growth witnessed in the immediately preceding decade. Economic fundamentals of the economy were sound with good growth rate,

low unemployment levels, booming stock markets, and inflow of FDI. There were no signs of the impending crisis of the proportions that the world witnessed in 1997.

The growth rate always exceeded 6% and had touched even 11% in 1990s. Inflation rates too were well within the manageable limits of around 5% or below. With fixed nominal exchange rates, the higher domestic inflation rate would cause appreciation of domestic currency in real terms. Appreciation of currency in real terms causes loss of export competitiveness. With controlled inflation, the currency (though fixed in nominal terms) in fact showed real appreciation.

Despite booming exports, the current account was in deficit primarily due to high consumption including that of imported goods. However, the deficit in the current account is expected for developing economies and analysts regard that there is no cause for alarm if it remains within 4% – 5% of the GDP. Thailand had an alarmingly high level of deficit of around 8% of GDP prior to the crisis. Though there is no causal relationship in current account deficit and capital account surplus but it seems that excessive capital flows were causing current account imbalance. With fixed exchange rates and no capital controls, foreign capital was flowing in. Thailand was the prominent recipient of foreign investment in the region. These foreign flows also included foreign direct investment (FDI) predominantly from Japan, an export-driven economy, looking for locations with low wages and skilled and educated workforce to gain advantage in the exports of the manufactured products. This was perhaps due to the reason that Japanese yen had appreciated against dollar making exports from Japan expensive.

The capital flows in the region (five countries—Indonesia, Korea, Malaysia, Philippines, and Thailand) during 1996 and first half of 1997 were $56 billion and $49 billion, respectively, as per the estimates of Bank of International Settlements. The fiscal position was in surplus in case of Thailand and other nations except in case of Taiwan. Hence, at a more fundamental level, the deficit in the current account could be caused only by savings deficit and not budget deficit.

Looking at the sound fundamentals of the entire region, rating agencies such as Standard and Poor and Moody's made no changes in the assigned ratings of these countries. Ironically, the downgrades came only three to four months after the crises occurred.

The research post Asian currency crisis to examine its causes has focused on the external factors to the region rather than the signs of shortcomings in the economic fundamentals of the affected nations. It is largely believed that external factors precipitated the crisis and not the internal conditions. Foreign investors seem to have ignored the hard realities of how financial markets operate in the Asian societies. Some of these external factors are mentioned and described as follows:

1. *Loss of Export Competitiveness*: The economic growth of the region was largely dependent upon its export. The USA was the most prominent destination for their products. The following developments were crucial:

    (a) *Appreciation of US dollar*: From mid-1995 US dollar appreciated with respect to Japanese yen and European currencies making US imports cheaper from Japan and Europe rather the emerging economies of Asia.

    (b) *Devaluation of Chinese yuan*: In 1994, China in its attempt to gain competitive edge over its competitors devalued yuan by about 50% making Chinese product cheaper to that extent. Countries in South East Asia were competing with China.

The appreciation of US dollar and devaluation of yuan implied reduction in export competiveness of the region of South East Asian, especially when the currencies were pegged to US dollar.

2. *Short-term Nature of Capital Inflows*: With prospering capital markets and booming real estate, the entire region was an attractive destination for portfolio investments. Pegged exchange rates with absence of capital controls guaranteed high returns from the investments in the region. For example, if Thailand offered 15% return with pegged exchange rates as against 5% in the USA, the dollar investment in Thailand can capture all the baht returns in dollar terms without having the risk of exchange rate loss. The region was also too glad to receive these funds perceived as sign of strength of the economy rather than structural imbalance.

With government guaranteed exchange rates, attractive portfolio investments, and willingness of the recipient nations to absorb the capital inflows, the foreign investors had no hesitation in remitting money. However, short-term foreign capital flows are extremely volatile, and they disappear more quickly than they appear, when circumstances reverse.

With no fiscal deficit in the countries, the current account deficit implied savings deficit. The foreign inflows were used in the non-productive assets such as investment in real estate and stocks. As a result, booming conditions prevailed in the financial and real estate markets.

3. *Crony Capitalism*: Flush with funds and with not as much need for the investment in productive assets created laxity in the lending norms. The balance sheets of firms showed excessive borrowing. Governments too played its part when commercial lending was directed to support the perceived strategic businesses. The lending was based on immediate past performance and collateral-based lending became routine with the rising prices of assets such as real estate and stocks. Sooner or later, these loans were to turn into non-performing assets making banking industry fragile.

With mounting current account deficit and massive inflows of short-term foreign funds, there were concerns about fragility of the economy. During 1996, stocks markets in Thailand fell by 30% and by another 30% in first half of 1997. Similar patterns were seen in Korean and Malaysian markets too. Simultaneously, the property prices too started falling. The collateral securities backing loans declined in value and, hence, credit was not renewed or rolled over. Withdrawal of short-term funds started. The high short-term capital inflows make a nation highly susceptible to equally large capital outflows with slightest of adversity. Political developments caused a fall of 11% in Thai stocks on a single day of 19 June 1997. The Bank of Thailand, the central bank intervened with sale of dollars to prop up the value of Thai baht. The intervention proved ineffective in the face of massive demand for dollars ready for withdrawal. Eventually, Thai baht had to be devalued.

Due to strong trading links and similar economic conditions, the crisis spread to other nations. Speculative pressures on all currencies started mounting. Announcement of capital controls prohibiting financing in real estate caused a fall in the stock markets in neighbouring and trading nations of Thailand. By July 1997, Philippines peso and Malaysian ringgit were floating. Indonesian rupiah and South Korean won got affected later due to similar reasons of political uncertainty and economic similarity.

The bail-out by the IMF amounted to $118 billion that stipulated several conditions. Some of the conditions were (a) adherence to fiscal discipline, the IMF favoured a budget surplus of 1% of GDP to restore investors' confidence and help improve BOP situation, (b) observing monetary discipline, the IMF stipulated rise in the interest rates to prevent pressure on local currency and retain foreign funds despite knowing that increased interest rates may come in the way of economic development, and (c) reform and strengthen the financial and banking sector, the IMF stipulated progressively higher capital adequacy ratios and closure of some weak banks.

TRILEMMA OF ECONOMICS

The cases of Mexico and Asian currency crises and many others have led to a thought whether the pegged exchange rate system is a viable option for countries wanting complete freedom that the countries practicing free float enjoy. Free float is characterized by market-based determination of foreign exchange and governments merely guide and control the economic and monetary policies as felt necessary for economic development, checking inflation, etc. treating foreign exchange rates as only one of the incidental outcome.

Trilemma of economics, also known as 'trinity of impossible', attributed to Robert Mundell, a Nobel laureate, states that simultaneous sustainability of the following three alternative policy tools is impossible:

1. Fixed or pegged exchange rate system
2. Independent monetary policy
3. Free flow of capital

This is usually represented as a triangular-shaped diagram with three policy tools at three corners of a triangle as shown in Figure 4-4. The trilemma of economics states that any two

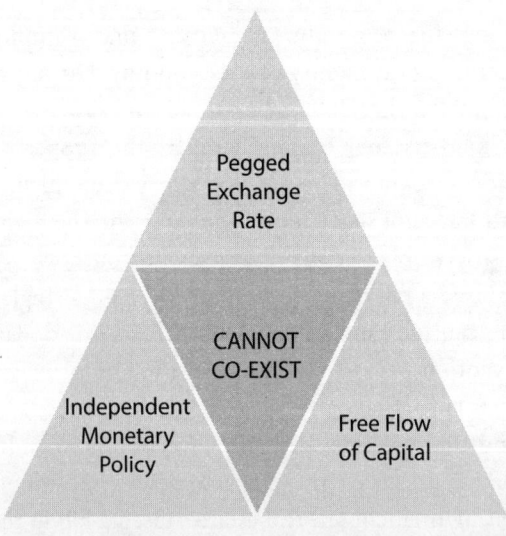

Figure 4-4
The Impossible Trinity

combinations of policy tools along one side of the triangle can be chosen for stability of economy. Pursuing all the three tools necessarily means tracing two sides of the triangle. This is an unsustainable position in an economy. Ultimately, the country would have to abandon at least one of the three policy tools.

A country can follow freedom of monetary policy (regulating the money supply and/or interest rates) and free flow of capital, but cannot have pegged exchange rates. Pegged exchange rate with free flow of capital implies that that a country would necessarily have to align its interest rates with those of the currency to which it is pegged. If not, there would be unidirectional flow of capital from low interest region to the high interest region. This would be so till the interest rate becomes same in the two countries. Indirectly, the money growth would also become the same, making monetary policy of the country pegging its currency redundant.

Examples of the pegging and free flow of capital are the countries that follow currency board arrangement, such as Hong Kong. The countries opting for currency board arrangement forego their monetary policies. The monetary policy is governed by the currency to which they are pegged. Unification of currency is nothing but a currency board arrangement with pegging rate at 1.00. Euro is the classic example where the participating nations have the same currency and free flow of capital but common monetary policy for all nations.

Pegged exchange rate with independent monetary policy is another combination that is feasible. For these two tools the country would have to exercise capital controls. It cannot have free flow of capital. Classic example of such strategy is China which has pegged its currency to US dollar and keeps its independent monetary policy but restrains flow of capital. The flow of capital on account of underlying trade transactions is a necessity. Restricted flow of capital is for the capital on transactions other than current account transactions. The flow of capital arising out of underlying trade transaction is a necessity and is not governed by profit motive and arbitrage on interest rates/yields.

All countries that follow free float have free flow of capital and independent monetary policies, and as such is a sustainable strategy. The exchange rate is determined by market forces including those from external environment.

The refusal of Britain to join euro is a case in point supporting the trinity of impossibility. Britain realized that impossible trinity could not be violated. If Britain wanted to retain the interest rate autonomy there was no way it could have acceded to join euro.

The trilemma can offer vital insights to the peso and Asian currency crises. All the nations involved in the Asian currency crisis followed pegged exchange rates, independent monetary policies with free flow of capital. The countries such as China and India, which remained relatively unaffected, did not have all the three dimensions. China pursued pegged exchange rate with independent monetary policies but exercised substantial capital controls. India had independent monetary policies with managed floating rather than pegged exchange rates and managing capital controls by limiting the end-use of foreign capital such as investment in real estate and stock markets. Investment of foreign capital in real estate and stocks does not add to the productive capacity but instead leads to asset price bubble that does not justify fundamentals in the economy and is prone to burst anytime.

CONCEPTS IN PRACTICE
The Contagion Effect

WHY INDIA SURVIVED ASIAN CURRENCY CRISIS

The impact of the Asian currency crisis was minimal in India presumably due to different conditions related to fiscal position, monetary policies, and capital controls. According to Reserve Bank of India (RBI),

'In retrospect, India was successful in containing the contagion effect of the Asian crisis due to swift policy responses to manage the crisis and favourable macro-economic condition. During the period of crisis, India had
   (a) a low current account deficit,
   (b) comfortable foreign exchange reserves amounting to import cover of over seven months,
   (c) a market determined exchange rate,
   (d) low level of short-term debt, and
   (e) absence of asset price inflation or credit boom.

These positive features were the result of prudent policies pursued over the years, notably,
   (a) cap on external commercial borrowings with restrictions on end-use,
   (b) low exposure of banks to real estate and the stock market,
   (c) insulation from large intermediation of overseas capital by the banking sector,
   (d) close monitoring of off-balance sheet items and tight legislative, regulatory, and prudential control over non-banking entities.'

Some capital controls also helped in insulating the economy from the contagion effect of the East Asian crisis. The ultimate result could be seen in terms of low volatility in the exchange rate of the Indian rupee, during the second half of the 1990s, when most of the Asian currencies witnessed high level of volatility.

A comparison of volatility of various currencies in Asia is presented here:

Daily Exchange Rate Volatility in Select Emerging Economies (Annualized; in %)

Currency	1993–1995	1996–2000	2004	2005	2006
Indian Rupee	7.5	4.3	4.7	3.5	4.0
South Korean Won	2.6	22.2	6.5	6.8	6.9
Indonesian Rupiah	2.1	43.4	7.7	9.1	8.9
Thai Baht	1.7	18.3	4.3	4.7	6.2
New Taiwan Dollar	3.7	5.3	4.9	4.9	4.9
Singapore Dollar	3.7	7.4	4.6	4.4	3.9
Philippine Peso	6.8	12.9	3.1	4.1	4.6

Note: Volatility has been calculated by taking the standard deviation of percentage change in daily exchange rates.

Source: *RBI Report on Currency and Finance*, January 2010.

There is a view that if impossible trinity was well-recognized, then why did Asian nations affected in the Asian crisis choose pegging, control over interest rates, and free flow of capital. More importantly, international organizations and economists did not point out the non-sustainability of the policy. Apparently, there could be a grey area. Pegged exchange rate is neither fixed nor floating. Hence, the impossible trinity could be defied. If so, the logic could be that (a) with control of monetary policy and free flow of capital the exchange rate is independent and (b) with free flow of capital and fixed exchange rate the monetary policy is independent. Hence, interest rates could be modulated. As long as interest rates were low, the local currency would not be depreciating in real terms and, hence, the nominal anchor would truly reflect the real worth. However, when interest rates increased, the situation reversed and became unsustainable.

CRAWLING PEGS

Crawling peg is the modified form of pegged exchange rates that allows for adjustment of exchange rate periodically depending upon the economic fundamentals. According to the IMF, the crawling pegs are where

1. the exchange rate is adjusted periodically in small amounts at a fixed rate or in response to changes in selective quantitative indicators, such as past inflation differentials vis-à-vis major trading partners, differentials between the inflation target and expected inflation in major trading partners, and so forth.
2. the rate of crawl can be set to generate inflation-adjusted changes in the exchange rate (backward looking), or set at a preannounced fixed rate and/or below the projected inflation differentials (forward looking).
3. maintaining a crawling peg imposes constraints on monetary policy in a manner similar to a fixed peg system.
4. exchange rate within crawling bands is maintained within certain fluctuation margins of at least ±1% around a central rate, or the margin between the maximum and minimum value of the exchange rate exceeds 2% and the central rate or margins are adjusted periodically at a fixed rate or in response to changes in selective quantitative indicators.
5. the degree of exchange rate flexibility is a function of the bandwidth. Bands are either symmetric around a crawling central parity or are widened gradually with an asymmetric choice of the crawl of upper and lower bands.

A typical crawling peg is depicted in Figure 4-5 with four adjustments of the peg and the band shown. Adjustment of peg would be triggered by some quantitative factor and not with time. In case of inflation rate, targeting the peg may be adjusted depending upon the differential of inflation rates. The advantage of crawling peg is that it limits the fluctuations in the short term while providing useful guidance to the future exchange rates' behaviour in the long term encouraging better planning for business.

Most trade transactions of receivables and payables mature in a short period of time for the corporate sector. There is a fair degree of certainty under crawling peg and hence provides a

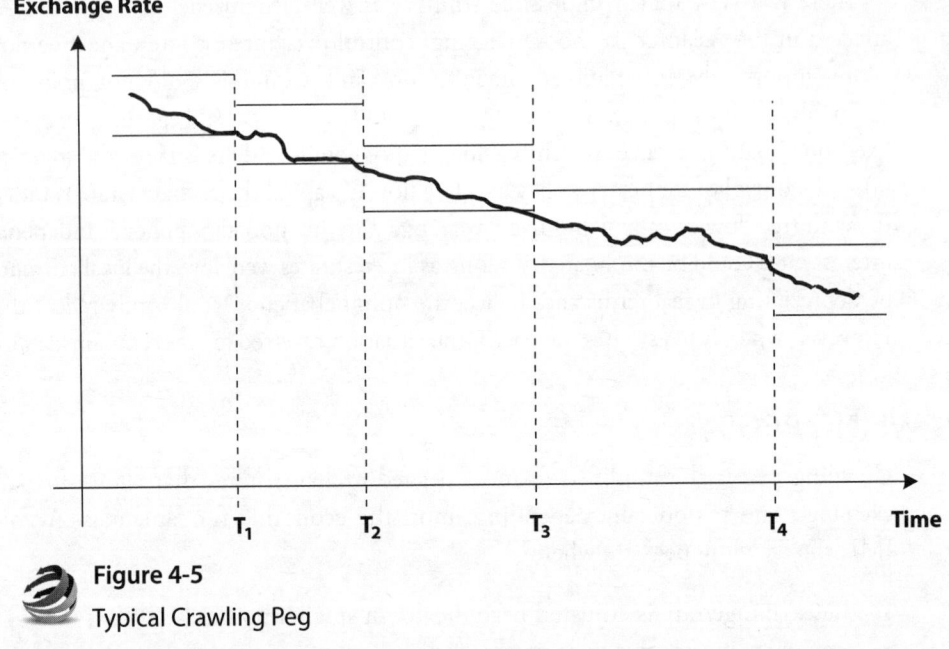

Figure 4-5
Typical Crawling Peg

fair degree of planning ease. Central bank intervenes in the currency market at the support points, yet it pays exorbitantly to maintain the band and it revises the peg downwards based on average rates during a period with the same or slightly different bands. Therefore, exchange rate moves according to fundamental economic factors like inflation rate yet provides the stability to exchange rates and promotes environment conducive for international trade. The crawling peg can move according to some other variable, such as BOP or external borrowing levels.

MANAGED/DIRTY FLOAT

Briefly described by the IMF, a managed float is an attempt to influence the exchange rate without having a specific exchange rate path or target. Indicators for managing the rate are broadly judgemental (e.g., BOP position, international reserves, parallel market developments, etc.), and adjustments may not be automatic. Intervention may be direct or indirect.

As explained under the intervention mechanism of Bretton Woods, we know that by adjusting the supply curve of the foreign currency the exchange rate can be influenced almost instantaneously. This supply curve can be changed by buying and selling of the foreign currency in the currency markets. When government believes that exports are becoming uncompetitive and there is need to reduce the value of local currency, it may buy foreign currency. When it is desired that local currency must appreciate in value possibly to induce imports it would decide to sell the foreign currency. Buying and selling of foreign currency is called direct intervention.

Indirect intervention involves amending the usual monetary tools, such as interest rates. Increasing interest rate would attract foreign capital with local currency appreciating and foreign currency depreciating. Decreasing interest rate would result in the opposite. Such direct or indirect interventions also take place under pegging and crawling peg arrangements but managed float is different in the following two aspects:

1. There is neither a declared or a pre-announced exchange rate of pegging nor a policy for the crawl or a band, and
2. The band under managed float is also usually much larger than what is associated with pegging or crawling peg. The usual bands in pegging or crawling peg is ±1% around the central rate.

We may say that while pegging or crawling peg is formal, managed float is informal. Managed float is advantageous in the sense that it provides an informal understanding to the corporate sector to have an exchange rate which would not be too high or low, without any commitment to maintain the rate. The system of managed float is also referred to as *dirty float*.

Benefits of Managed Float

There are many advantages of managed float system. It is a balanced system taking into account the realities of an economy and desirability of fixed exchange rates to promote international trade. Some of the advantages of the managed float are as follows.

Prevent Speculative Attacks Since there is no commitment to maintain a specific rate or a band, the speculative attacks on the currency are less likely knowing that the central bank would not defend the exchange rate and exhaust precious foreign exchange. In case rates change much, the central bank would prefer to let the exchange rate move rather than wastefully spend the precious foreign exchange in defending the exchange rate. In most currency crises emanating from pegged exchange rate system, speculators have gained at the expense of central banks by taking positions knowing well that the pegged exchange rate is indefensible and ultimate devaluation/revaluation is inevitable.

Speculative attacks are extremely pronounced when a nation follows unrealistic exchange rate policy not supported by economic fundamentals. Speculators know that the exchange rate is unsustainable. Though governed by their private motive of profiting from the situation at the expense of exchequer, they in fact hasten the inevitable by taking actions that suggest a corrective course. We know that earlier the remedial action is taken faster is the cure and lesser is the loss to the central bank. Some examples of failure of pegged exchange rate that resulted in heavy losses and corrections in the value of the currency are condensed here:

Country	Currency	Time	Events
Russia	Rouble	October 1994	Depreciation by 27% on a single day. Adopting free float from pegging.
Venezuela	Bolivar	April 1996	Depreciation by 42% on a single day. Removal of exchange controls.
Brazil	Real	December 1998	8% devaluation followed by 40% depreciation upon adoption of floating rate.

Smoothen the Exchange Rate Changes Intervention in the foreign exchange markets helps reduce the volatility. Abrupt movements due to seasonality are smoothed out due to intervention. It may guide the flow of exchange rate smoothly even though it is unidirectional.

The fixing of informal bands under the managed float is based on many considerations. It is a compromise between need and ability to maintain the band. Sustainability of the deficit in the BOP, criticality of developmental expenditure for the growth objective, saving and investment pattern in the economy, containing inflation levels, etc. are some of the parameters that determine the need for intervention and maintaining of the specific bands. On the other hand, ability to intervene is largely governed by the adequacy of foreign exchange reserves and the import cover desired.

India has been classified by the IMF under managed float, where RBI makes conscious efforts to keep the exchange rate under control to assure exporters and importers an approximate exchange rate for their respective revenue and cost. Even the developed nations that are on free float have used intervention in the foreign exchange markets some time or the other with the intention of keeping exchange rate at the desired level.

The effect of intervention is depicted in Figure 4-6. DD and SS are the demand and supply schedules, respectively, without any role for the central bank leading to the exchange rate of P_0. If central bank assumes that P_0 is too high and the domestic currency needs to be depreciated, then it would have to buy the foreign currency in the currency market restricting its supply in the economy. This is shown in Figure 4-6 (a) with supply curve shifting left upwards at SS' and new value of domestic currency at P'. Similarly, if appreciation of domestic currency is required, the central bank sells the foreign currency in the foreign exchange markets. This is shown in Figure 4-6 (b) where supply curve of the economy shifts downwards at SS, providing new exchange rate at P'. These interventions are tactical and short-term in nature, as they do not cause much structural changes if done on a moderate scale. For sustaining the new exchange rate post-intervention the structural economic changes must follow.

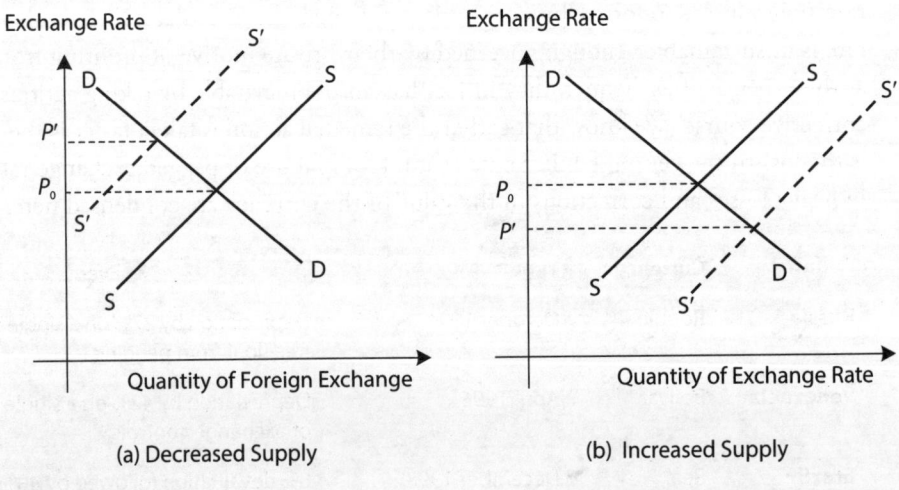

Figure 4-6
Direct Intervention and Exchange Rates

Sterilization

Direct intervention in the foreign currency markets of buying/selling of intervention currency, usually US dollars, has its impact on the domestic economy. Increasing supply of foreign currency implies decreasing supply of local currency (mopping up of local currency) and vice versa. By intervening in the foreign exchange markets with the objective of achieving the desired value for the local currency, the central bank inadvertently affects the monetary policy by affecting the money supply in the domestic economy.

For example, consider India wants to decrease the value of rupee to promote exports and correct the adverse BOP. To achieve the lower value of rupee, RBI needs to buy US dollars, the intervention currency. Buying of dollars would imply selling rupee, thereby increasing its supply. Increased supply of rupee causes inflation. This is clearly an undesirable and unintended outcome for the economy as a whole. Further, the price rise due to inflation negates the purpose of intervention as exports become more expensive.

In order to insulate the domestic economy for its act in the foreign currency markets, RBI consciously has to mop up the increased supply of Indian rupee. It can be achieved by redeeming the treasury bills of equivalent amount. For example, if RBI bought $10 million with an average rate of exchange of ₹45, it caused an increase in rupee supply by ₹450 million. To offset the inflationary effect RBI would now have to issue T-bills worth ₹450 million.

Buying and selling of government securities is referred as *open market operation* usually deployed to regulate the money supply in the economy. It is one of the most prominent components of monetary policy. If the intervention in the currency markets is not followed by appropriate open market operations it is referred to as non-sterilized intervention. Insulating economy from effects of intervention in currency markets by appropriate open market operations is called sterilized intervention. The difference in non-sterilized and sterilized intervention is highlighted as depicted in Figure 4-7.

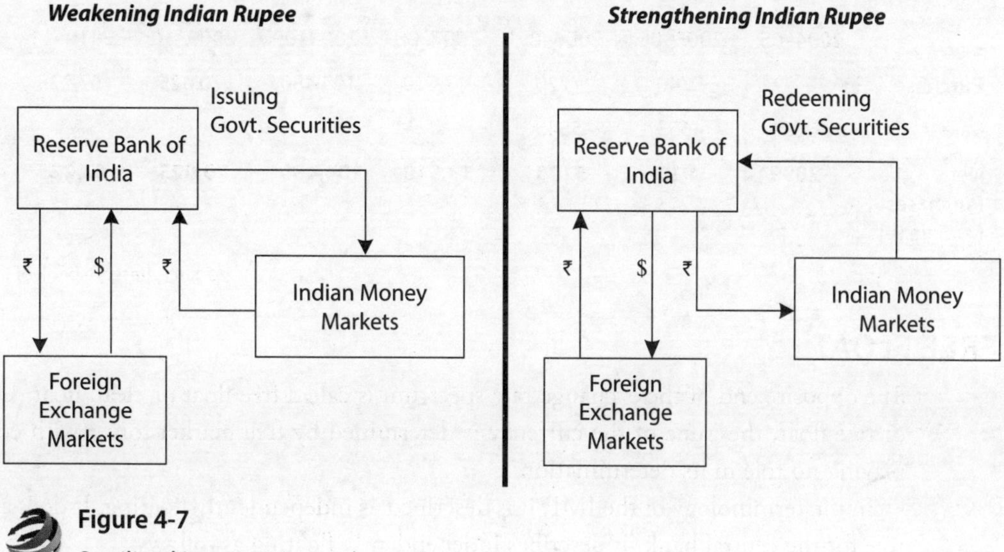

Figure 4-7
Sterilized Intervention

Under non-sterilized intervention the appreciation of domestic currency would cause inflationary conditions as follows

Appreciation of domestic currency → Central bank needs to buy foreign currency to restore original rate → Implies increased supply of domestic currency → *Inflationary conditions*

To sterilize the domestic economy corrective measures would be taken as follows

Inflationary conditions → Need to mop up the increased supply of domestic currency → Issue the government securities (called open market operations) → Get back the additional domestic currency equal to the amount released by intervention

A similar argument can be offered in case India wants to increase the value of rupee if it finds it is depreciating more and faster than desired. The difference in non-sterilized and sterilized interventions would be as follows.

Non-sterilized intervention

Depreciation of domestic currency → Needs selling of foreign currency to restore original rate → Implies decreased supply of domestic currency → *Deflationary conditions*

Sterilized intervention

Deflationary conditions → Need to increase supply of domestic currency → Redeem the government securities → Infuse back the domestic currency equal to the amount mopped up by intervention

Figure 4-7 depicts the actions of sterilized intervention for the two cases of Indian rupee with Reserve Bank servicing as balancing the money supply from currency markets and money markets on an aggregate basis. Table 4-2 provides the details of open market operations undertaken by RBI from 2004–05 onwards.

Table 4-2
Open Market Operations of Dated Securities (₹ crores)

	2004–05	2005–06	2006–07	2007–08	2008–09	2009–10	2010–11	2011–12
Purchase	–	740	720	13,510	104,480	70,025	67,225	134,086
Sale	2899	4653	5845	–	–	–	–	–
Net Purchases (+)/Sale (–)	–2899	–3913	–5125	13,510	104,480	70,025	67,225	134,086

Source: Reserve bank of India bulletins.

FREE FLOAT

The opposite end of the exchange rate spectrum is called free float or clean float. Under clean or free float, the value of the currency is determined by free market forces with central bank playing no role in its determination.

In the terminology of the IMF, it is described as independently floating. It does assign some role for the central bank. It describes independently floating as follows:

'Exchange rate is market-determined, with any official foreign exchange market intervention aimed at moderating the rate of change and preventing undue fluctuations in the exchange rate, rather than at establishing a level for it.'

It is noteworthy that the role of central bank is not eliminated even in the economies categorized as independently floating regimes. It is possible in the recognition of the opinion that undue fluctuations and volatility in the exchange rate is damaging for the world economy. The possible difference lies in that the par values in the independently floating regimes are not fixed, but the intervention is providing the moderating effect to the volatility. In the managed float category, the par value of the currencies may be fixed (may not be disclosed) and central banks strive to achieve it.

Free float or independently floating currencies belong to the developed economies where the matured and large markets have the capacity to absorb abrupt events arising in the economic environment. The country itself should be strong enough to absorb the political changes, economic phases and speculative attacks. Needless to mention that such a system of free float may not be suitable for developing economies as they do not have enough depth in the financial markets to absorb shocks. Further the developmental needs may warrant undervaluation of currency that free market forces may not support.

COOPERATIVE INTERVENTIONS AND TARGET ZONE ARRANGEMENTS

The need for managing the exchange rates can be best illustrated by what happened immediately after failure of the Bretton Woods system, when the exchange rate regimes were still evolving. Countries were in the midst of choosing between fixed and floating exchange rate systems. The migration for the developed nations from fixed exchange rates to floating rate system was not abrupt. They too had to resort to managed or dirty float before adopting flexible rates.

From 1980 to 1985, the dollar appreciated phenomenally by about 50%. It touched a level of Japanese yen of 250 per dollar in 1985. There were conflicting opinions for soaring value of dollar. One opinion attributed the rise of dollar to the large budget deficit and tight fiscal policy followed in the USA. According to some the mounting budget deficit was so huge ($204 billion in 1985) that it could not be financed by capital within the USA. The issues of treasuries to fund the fiscal deficit had to be subscribed by foreigners. These subscriptions came predominantly from Japan and Germany. With capital flowing from abroad, the capital account of the BOP was in surplus with corresponding deficit in the current account. Hence, funding the deficits in current account and fiscal budget were no cause for concern. The contrary opinion was that appreciation of dollar was not a problem and instead reflected greater confidence in US dollar and was considered good for global economy.

Though increased exports to the USA from Japan and Europe were desirable, the dollars so earned were recycled back as capital flows to the USA to fund the budget deficit. This caused international concern about the fiscal policy of the USA. Europeans and Japanese believed that fiscal deficit will ultimately cause the monetary expansion that would be inflationary. Concerned about the evil effects of inflation it was thought that containing fiscal deficit was essential.

On the assurances by the USA to contain its fiscal deficit, it was agreed upon in September 1985 at Plaza Hotel in New York (hence termed as Plaza Accord) among the group of five countries (USA, UK, Japan, Germany, and France) to collectively manipulate exchange rate to stem the soaring dollar and correct the trade imbalance. The decline of dollar in fact had begun before Plaza Accord. The participants agreed to spend $18 billion over a period of six weeks. The US dollar was considered overvalued and Japanese yen undervalued. Substantial buying effort was made for Deutsche mark and yen.

The fall of dollar was steeper than its rise. By 1987, the value of US dollar had fallen enough to cause opposite concern of arresting the decline in its value. By then, G-5 stood expanded by Canada and Italy to become G-7. In February 1987, G-7 met at Louvre Museum in Paris, known as Louvre Accord, wherein it was agreed to keep dollar within 5% of the current levels with deutsche mark and yen. It was thought that extreme volatility in the exchange rate is not conducive for international trade and needs to be contained. This target band was to be achieved with cooperative effort because no nation was considered resourceful enough to achieve the objective by itself. Louvre Accord was successful in arresting the decline in the value of dollar. The cooperative arrangement was acceptance of joint managed float system where target zones for the values of currencies were decided with joint interventions.

CHOICE OF EXCHANGE RATE REGIME

Which of the exchange rate system is best for the nation remains a moot point. Japan suffered a great deal in adopting the policies imposed on it by others. Monetary expansion to allay the fears of recession in the second half of the 1980s caused Japanese economy to go into a tailspin. With rising yen, the export led growth of Japan received a severe dent. Japan experienced the worst phase by acceding to interventions in the manner imposed by other nations and letting its currency appreciate. Interventions aimed at exchange rate target that is inconsistent with the economic fundamentals serve no purpose except that this provides an opportunity to the private speculators to gain at the expense of central bank.

At present, China seems to be avoiding all pressures to let yuan appreciate. Since there exist no theory or formulae that can provide optimum exchange rate, it is the political considerations that dictate the exchange rate policy.

RBI's *Report on Currency and Finance*, January 2009, provides an excellent review of exchange rate regimes and the conditions that dictate the choice of exchange rate system. Some of these observations are as follows:

- The distribution of exchange rate regimes over time has remained almost constant, and as such state of economy—developed or developing—has no bearing.
- Floating is not a necessarily a preferred or durable state of exchange rate regime as it demands very robust institutional monetary framework. Some countries have been switching the exchange rate regimes depending upon the circumstances. Most Latin American countries, such as Argentina, Chile, and Brazil have seen multiple exchange rate regimes over time.
- Small economies normally find floating exchange rate system difficult to maintain.

CONCEPTS IN PRACTICE
Swiss Franc Pegging

FREE FLOAT TO INTERVENTION

Amidst fledgling and sagging fortunes of euro, the central bank of Switzerland on 6 September 2011 announced an extremely surprising decision to put a cap on the value of their currency; the Swiss franc (CHF). The decision was unilateral and effective immediate. The decision shocked the financial markets because the cap placed on the value of CHF—considered as a very strong currency—in terms of euro was an act of extreme confidence expressed in survival and strength of euro and Eurozone at a time when the whole world debated its very existence. The value of euro was capped at CHF 1.20.

The motive of doing so was to safeguard the Swiss economy falling into deflationary development due to massive overvaluation of Swiss franc. The Swiss National Bank while capping the value signaled that it was ready to intervene in the foreign exchange market and buy euro, if needed, by printing CHF. At the risk of inflating the CHF money supply Swiss bank was risking exports of its chocolates and watches.

Euros so bought could be used to buy government bonds in the Eurozone increasing bond prices and decreasing yields on them. If it decides to buy Spanish or Italian bonds the gap in the bond yields of Eurozone members would shrink. This in turn would help solve Eurozone crisis by convergence of bond yields in financial markets. On the other hand, if euro accumulated by Switzerland are used for buying government bonds of stronger nations, say France or Germany, the gap in the bond yields across Eurozone would widen, aggravating the crisis further.

The move of capping or pegging the value of CHF to euro produced the desired result rather immediately as euro strengthened by about 9% against CHF within weeks of the announcement. However, by linking its fate to euro Swiss economy became closely connected with the events in the Eurozone for good or bad.

The key determinants in the selection of exchange rate regimes are as follows:

1. It is essential for countries to pursue sound and credible macroeconomic policies so as to avoid the build-up of major macro imbalances in the economy.
2. It is essential for such economies to improve the flexibility of their product and factor markets to cope with and adjust to shocks arising from the volatility of currency markets and swings in the terms of trade in world product markets.
3. It is crucial to develop and strengthen the financial systems to enhance resilience to shocks. This warrants a sound and efficient banking system together with deep and liquid capital markets. This contributes to the efficient intermediation of financial flows and minimization of unsound lending practices that lead to the build-up of excessive leveraging in the corporate sector and exposure to foreign currency borrowings.

4. Countries would need to build regulatory and supervisory capabilities to keep pace with financial innovations and the emergence of new financial institutions' activities, and new products and services, which have complicated the conduct of exchange rate policy.
5. Policy makers need to promote greater disclosures and transparency.

SUMMARY

The collapse of the Bretton Woods system in the early 1970s brought an end to fixed exchange rate regime that left the choice of adopting an appropriate exchange rate policy rest with the nations. Over a period of time since the 1970s, there have been several systems ranging from fixed/pegged exchange rates to completely market determined floating rate system.

The two extremes of the exchange rate systems, that is, fixed and floating, have their own merits and demerits and none could be assumed to be superior to another. Fixed exchange rate system, where the value of the currency does not change, eliminates the volatility. Volatility is supposed to hinder the growth of international trade. If nations follow fixed exchange rates, the inflation rates tend to converge across the nations. It stabilizes the world trade and economic growth. Flexible exchange rate system has the advantages such as providing flexibility in the monetary policies as per the needs of the country, slow and gradual adjustment as against abrupt changes, elimination of need for maintaining foreign exchange reserves, and so on.

The extreme form of fixed rate is the adoption of some other nation's currency as legal tender. As most such countries have adopted US dollar as the currency the phenomena is called dollarization. In such economies the monetary policy is not an economic variable. The next exchange rate system closer to fixed rates is called currency board. Under the currency board, the local currency issued is equal to the reserves of the foreign currency the country. The exchange rate is fixed and the currency is fully convertible but there is no independent monetary policy. Inflation and interest rates, therefore, become same as that of reserve currency.

Pegged exchange rate is perhaps the most common amongst developing nations. The local currency has a fixed exchange rate with a foreign currency, referred to as anchor or a basket of currencies with which the nation trades. The currency is fully convertible but the country retains control over local interest rates. In such a system though the interest rates of local and anchor currencies can be somewhat different but large differentials could be destabilizing with massive and instantaneous inflows and outflows of foreign capital for interest arbitrage. Many crises in the past have been attributed to pegged exchange rate system. Crawling peg is another form where the value of the currency though fixed but moves with the pre-determined disclosed path based on some broad economic parameter, such as inflation rate.

The most common and important system is a managed float which is a mix of pure fixed rate and floating rate system. Under managed float the central government makes conscious effort to maintain the desired exchange rate that may be disclosed or undisclosed. The effort of central government mostly is by way of intervention in the foreign exchange market. Such intervention inadvertently affects the monetary policy as it alters the supply of domestic currency. The increased/decreased supply of local currency has to be nullified by undertaking open market operations of issuing/redeeming of the treasury bills. Intervention followed by nullifying open market operations is called sterilized intervention.

Completely flexible rates determined by free market forces with no government intervention are adopted by developed economies that have well-developed and deep financial markets capable of absorbing the external shocks.

A considerable work has been done to examine what kinds of policies related to the exchange rate are sustainable. The trinity of impossibility asserts that three policy measures—free capital mobility, fixed exchange rates, and independent monetary policy—cannot be sustained. Any two of them are sustainable. A currency board has fixed rates and free mobility and no independent monetary policy and is, therefore, stable. Floating exchange rates have independent monetary policy and free flow of foreign capital. Pegged exchange rate system defies trinity of impossibility unless monetary policy is tuned to the anchor currency.

Cooperative intervention is a joint effort to maintain an exchange rate deemed to be in the interest of all, by contributing their respective resources.

Among the wide variety of exchange rate systems, a nation faces a difficult menu to choose the appropriate system that meets the requirement of the country in terms of its developmental needs, increasing international competitiveness, the position of foreign exchange reserves position, etc.

QUESTIONS

4-1 What do you understand by fixed and flexible exchange rate systems?
4-2 Compare the advantages and disadvantages of fixed and floating exchange rate systems.
4-3 'Fixed exchange rate system imposes the monetary policy of the strong nation to the weaker nations.' Comment.
4-4 Write short notes on the following terms:
   (a) Importing inflation
   (b) Dutch disease
   (c) Peso problem
4-5 'Currency board is a stable and lasting exchange rate system for smaller economies.' Do you agree with the statement? Give reasons.
4-6 Differentiate between the following terms:
   (a) Pegged and crawling peg exchange rate system
   (b) Dollarization and currency board arrangement
   (c) Sterilized intervention and unsterilized intervention
4-7 How is managed float system different from pegged exchange rate system?
4-8: 'Managed float is superior to pegged exchange rate system because it conserves foreign exchange reserves in case of speculative attacks on the currency.' Comment with reason.

PROBLEM

4-1 **Intervention under Managed Float**
   In a study of exchange rate fluctuations, it was revealed that Indian rupee appreciates by 1% with a net inflow of $1,000 million. India has managed float system. The current exchange rate is at the upper bound of the desired band of ₹44.50 to ₹45.50. Reserve Bank of India expects massive inflows in the next couple of days and hence wants the exchange rate to reach the lower bound of the band. Find out
   (a) How much of the intervention currency should be traded to achieve the objective?
   (b) If treasury bills maturing after 45 days are trading at a discount yield of 5%, what amount of treasury bill should be bought or sold by Reserve Bank of India?
   (c) If Reserve Bank of India chooses to make an indirect intervention by modulating the interest rates, should it result in decline or enhancing the yield on the short-term securities?

PART II
Foreign Exchange Markets and Equilibrium

5. Foreign Exchange Rates and Markets
6. International Parity Conditions
7. Exchange Rate, Economic and Monetary Policies

5

Foreign Exchange Rates and Markets

LEARNING OBJECTIVES

This chapter aims at

- knowing features of foreign exchange market and its growth and development
- understanding various kinds of exchange rate quotations
- describing cross rates and vehicle currency
- realizing how arbitrage establishes equilibrium in the exchange rate quotations
- understanding the meaning of effective exchange rates on nominal and real basis and how they are calculated
- describing spot and forward transactions
- discussing the utility of option forward contracts
- understanding how to arrive at merchant rates from interbank rates

Contents

Introduction
Foreign Exchange Markets—Structures and Features
Foreign Exchange Rates
    Bid and Ask Rates
    Direct and Indirect Rates
    Merchant and Interbank Rates
    Cross Rates and Vehicle Currency
Spot Rates and Arbitrage
Spot and Forward Contracts
    Forward Premium/Discount
    Swap Transaction

Outright Forward vs Swap
Forward–Forward Swap
Option Forward
Merchant Rates
    Bill Buying Rate
Nominal and Real Effective Exchange Rates
Need for Basket of Currencies for NEER and REER
Foreign Exchange Markets in India

Annexure A5-1: Euro Currencies and Markets

INTRODUCTION

Since the breakdown of the Bretton Woods era of fixed exchange rate after Jamaica Agreement in 1976 officially demonetizing gold, the system of determination of values of currency has become extremely complex. Each nation has its own way of determining or fixing the value of its currency. We have discussed the issue of determination of currency values in previous chapters, but in this chapter we focus on the various foreign currency rates and markets which too are complex.

Today, foreign exchange market is perhaps the largest financial market in the world. The reasons for expansion in foreign exchange markets are many, ranging from increased globalization to floating exchange rate regimes to risk management and speculation. However, primarily they include bona fide trade transactions as globalization of business has become almost a necessity for survival and increased competiveness, shrinking profit margins, and inevitable needs of hedging the foreign currency risks.

There have been conscious political efforts through initiatives such as World Trade Organization (WTO) to remove the barriers to trade that are being pursued by different nations with varying vigour and justifications. With decreasing trade restrictions, larger markets are thrown open for multinational corporations. Firms have started competing globally rather than confining their operations nationally. Ironically, the businesses, though becoming large in terms of volume, have also become more sensitive to levels of profit that are under pressure due to global competition.

With increased globalization and growth of multinational corporations, the businesses are moving across nations and are now denominating transactions in several currencies. This poses serious issues for the managers working in the multinational corporations (MNCs). First, they need to understand the nuances of foreign exchange markets and conventions. Second, they need to understand the causes of exchange rates to change. Third, the fluctuating exchange rates pose a serious challenge to the already slim bottom lines of the firms they work for. Lastly, the issue of foreign exchange rates assumes significance because the factors that change them are beyond the control of these managers. In this chapter, we discuss the features of foreign exchange markets and their conventions, and the various kinds of rates that prevail, whereas strategies to counter the challenges the vagaries of rates and markets are dealt with in later chapters.

FOREIGN EXCHANGE MARKETS—STRUCTURES AND FEATURES

Foreign exchange markets have several distinguishing features that separate them from markets for other financial assets. They also have implications for operators and managers in MNCs. Some of these features are discussed as follows.

Exchange Traded and Over-the-counter Markets Unlike most financial securities and markets, the foreign exchange markets are mainly over-the-counter (OTC) markets. An OTC market means that the buyers and sellers negotiate the price and other terms of the contract between themselves. The price and other terms need not be disclosed to public at large. It implies that the exchange rate can vary from person to person, time to time, and place to place. The exchange rate can be different for two different people at the same time and place. Other factors affecting the exchange rate are size and place of the contract, nature of participants, etc.

In contrast to OTC markets, we have exchange-traded markets where the buying and selling takes place at specific places (now on all-pervasive computer terminals attached to a common server hosting all the data) with all the past information readily available, such as the last traded price, volumes traded, open interest, and demand for and supply of assets at different prices. In OTC contracts, disclosure of price and other information is discretionary and not obligatory upon the participants of the contract.

While spot markets in the foreign currencies are mainly OTC, the derivatives on foreign currency are traded on exchanges as well as OTC. Currency futures are exchange-traded. Forward contracts, swaps, etc. on foreign currency are OTC. Options are mostly OTC but are also exchange-traded.

The OTC nature of foreign exchange markets places additional onus on corporate managers. For their requirements of foreign exchange, several counterparties need to be contacted before a decision could be taken. This is followed by analysis and negotiations. The negotiation for the best rates becomes time-consuming job besides requiring domain knowledge.

Participants Every market is characterized by the nature of its participants. The OTC market in foreign exchange mainly consists of the following:

1. *Exporter, importers, and MNCs*, who are mostly the actual users of foreign currency who need to convert foreign currency into local currency or vice versa for their business needs.
2. *Commercial banks*, who mostly offer the services of arranging the sale/purchase of foreign currency for remuneration and act as counterparties to actual users, and may also undertake transactions on their own account.
3. *Central banks*, who intervene in the foreign exchange markets on their own mostly to influence the exchange rate for a value they deem fit.
4. *International organizations*, who participate to facilitate the international settlements as also for lending in different currencies, such as the International Monetary Fund (IMF), the World Bank, and the Asian Development Bank (ADB).

The participants in the foreign exchange markets can also be classified on the basis of their objectives, as in other markets. There are (a) *hedgers* who need to avoid exchange rate risk emanating from underlying trade transactions, (b) *speculators* who assume risk in the hope of gains from favourable movement of exchange rates, and (c) *arbitrageurs* who assume risk-free positions exploiting the mispricing in the exchange rates in different markets thereby make exchange rate consistent in various markets.

Like any other markets, the foreign exchange markets are also dominated by speculators who take positions on their own in a currency with the motive of making profit on the future exchange rate by cancelling the original position.

A very distinctive feature of the foreign exchange markets is the role the central bank plays. This role can be divided into two—direct participation in the market by trading in foreign currency referred to as *intervention* and indirect role of influencing the exchange rate by exercising regulatory powers conferred. Normally, in other financial markets, such as, those for stocks, bonds, and commodities, regulators are not the participants in the market and other participants are not the regulators. Due to the conflicting interest, markets are demutualized by avoiding the overlap of participants and regulators. In the foreign exchange markets, central banks not only participate but also exercise significant influence by direct intervention as well as by directing the policies and designing the rules for the participants for orderly functioning. The unique position of the central bank is intended to provide protection to genuine users of foreign exchange and prevent speculative attacks by placing suitable capital controls and monitoring mechanisms. Thus, they have considerable influence on the process of determination of values of the currencies.

Timings Unlike exchange-traded markets that remain open only for fixed duration, the foreign exchange markets work round-the-clock. The major centres of foreign exchange trades are New York, London, Paris, Zurich, Tokyo, Sydney, Singapore, etc. Some markets open before the others close, thus providing continuous trading and exchange rates. Banking hours govern the trading duration in the foreign exchange markets in a country because banks dominate the trading volumes and serve as market makers in the OTC markets to fulfil the needs of hedgers and speculators alike.

Geographical/Currency Concentrations Trading in foreign currencies is dominated by few currencies as well as in terms of trading centres. Table 5-1 gives shares of 12 top currencies that constitute about 92% of the total turnover in foreign currency markets. The dominance of US dollar as most active currency is evident from Table 5-1 as it constitutes 43.5% (87/2) of global trade. Euro is a distant second with about 17% of global trade. The dominance of US dollar in global trading may be attributed to the legacy of Bretton Woods making the availability of US dollar in abundance and the practice of international settlement in US dollars. In modern times, another reason for dominance of US dollar is because oil trade is denominated in it.

Developing countries such as India, Brazil, and South Africa constituted about ½% each of the foreign exchange turnover in April 2013.

Table 5-1
Share of Top 12 Currencies in Foreign Exchange Trading (as in April 2013)

Currency	% share	Currency	% share	Currency	% share
US Dollar	87.0	Australian Dollar	8.6	Chinese Yuan	2.2
Euro	33.4	Swiss Franc	5.2	New Zealand Dollar	2.0
Japanese Yen	23.0	Canadian Dollar	4.6	Swedish Kroner	1.8
British Pound	11.8	Mexican Peso	2.5	Russian Rouble	1.6

Source: *Triennial Central Bank Survey* (2013), Bank of International Settlements.
Since foreign currency trading involves two currencies the figures are for a base of 200 and not 100.
To arrive at approximate percentage share the figures in the table may be divided by 2.

As is the case with turnover, the foreign currency trading is concentrated in few centres. The United Kingdom (London) is the top trading centre for spot as well as derivatives trading in foreign exchange followed by USA. Table 5-2 provides the percentage share of trading of top 12 centres in the world for foreign exchange trading.

Table 5-2
Share of Top 12 Centres in Foreign Exchange Trading (as in April 2013)

Country	Spot	All Instruments	Country	Spot	All Instruments
United Kingdom	41.96	40.86	Hong Kong	2.08	4.12
USA	25.18	18.92	Australia	1.94	2.72
Japan	6.37	5.61	France	1.51	2.85
Singapore	4.20	5.74	Denmark	1.41	1.54
Switzerland	2.55	3.24	Germany	0.98	1.66
Netherlands	2.22	1.68	Canada	0.01	0.97

Source: Triennial Central Bank Survey (2013), Bank of International Settlements.
Compiled on the basis of data available in Tables 11 and 12 of above survey.

Volumes Despite over-the-counter market the turnover in the foreign exchange markets has been growing. From a daily turnover of about US$1527 billion in April 1998, it has increased more than three and a half times to US$5345 billion per day in April 2013. In addition, the exchange-traded derivatives segment occupies a very little proportion. This is in contrast to turnover in the other financial securities. The growth of foreign exchange markets in spot and various derivatives like forwards, swaps, and options is shown in Table 5-3. Exchange traded products like futures contracts on foreign exchange and some standardized options traded on the exchange constitute a miniscule proportion of total markets (160/5,345 = 3%), as may be observed from the data in Table 5-3.

A comparative of share foreign exchange trading in developing markets can be seen from Table 5-4 providing the data of trading in spot and 'all instruments'. Even though in terms of percentage share or volumes compared with developed nations the contribution of developing nations is rather negligible. However, the data would be revealing if analysed in the perspective of lack of financial illiteracy, inefficiencies of capital markets, and existing currency controls that prevail in developing nations in varying degrees.

Most markets such as stocks and commodities are mostly influenced by local economic, fiscal, monetary, and trade policies with global factors playing marginal role. In contrast, the foreign exchange markets are mainly affected by global factors. In an exchange rate, at least two currencies, if not more, are involved and hence the impact is driven by what happens in two nations apart from other parts of the world. For example, rupee dollar exchange rate is

Table 5-3
Global Foreign Exchange Market Turnover by Instrument[1]

	Average daily turnover in April 2013, in billions of US$					
Instrument	**1998**	**2001**	**2004**	**2007**	**2010**	**2013**
Foreign Exchange Instruments	**1,527**	**1,239**	**1,934**	**3,324**	**3,971**	**5,345**
Spot Transactions[2]	568	386	631	1,005	1,488	2,046
Outright Forwards[2]	128	130	209	362	475	680
Foreign Exchange Swaps[2]	734	656	954	1,714	1,759	2,228
Currency Swaps	10	7	21	31	43	54
Options and Other Products[3]	87	60	119	212	207	337
Turnover at April 2013 Exchange Rates[4]	*1,705*	*1,505*	*2,040*	*3,370*	*3,969*	*5,345*
Exchange-traded Derivatives	*11*	*12*	*26*	*80*	*155*	*160*

[1]Adjusted for local and cross-border inter-dealer double-counting (i.e. 'net–net' basis).
[2]Previously classified as part of the so-called 'Traditional FX market'.
[3]The category 'other FX products' covers highly leveraged transactions and/or trades whose notional amount is variable and where decomposition into individual plain vanilla components was impractical or impossible.
[4]Non-US dollar legs of foreign currency transactions were converted into original currency amounts at average exchange rates for April of each survey year and then reconverted into US dollar amounts at average April 2013 exchange rates.
Source: Triennial Central Bank Survey (2013), Bank of International Settlements.

Table 5-4
Trading Volumes in Developing Economies (as in April 2013)

				Average daily turnover in millions of US$	
Country	**Spot**	**All Instruments**	**Country**	**Spot**	**All Instruments**
China	23,128	44,251	South Africa	4,820	20,946
India	15,475	31,276	Russia	25,883	60,725
Brazil	7,613	17,203	Mexico	7,060	32,112

Source: Triennial Central Bank Survey (2013), Bank of International Settlements.

determined by not only what happens in India but also what happens in the USA. Though the foreign exchange rates change in the same way as do the stocks, but the prices of Indian stocks are primarily influenced by economic factors in India. In contrast, rupee dollar exchange rate would be influenced by economic and political environments in India and the USA, apart from what happens in the rest of the world.

Another peculiarity of foreign exchange markets is the problem of *numéraire*—the unit of account in which the measurement is done. Since the exchange rate involves a pair of currencies and the exchange rates change continuously, we have statistical issue of measurement. For example, trading in euro and dollars could be measured in either of the two currencies. Similarly, trading in euro and yen could also be measured in either of the two. Such measurements are difficult to comprehend as they lack common denominator. However, US dollar remains the major currency in which the global data is presented, as is done in Table 5-1 to Table 5-3 that gives trading in major currencies from 1998 to 2013.

Among the major currency pairs, the most popular combinations are US dollar with euro (24%), with yen (18%), and with British pounds (9%). These pairs constitute about 51% of the aggregate turnover in the foreign exchange markets. Indian rupee is gaining importance and from 2010 its pairing with US dollar has been included in the main currency pair constituting about 1%.

Communication Communication among the participants in the foreign exchange markets takes place on a medium called Society for Worldwide Interbank Financial Telecommunication (SWIFT). Since every nation specifies its currency in its own way (e.g. ₹ in India), it is hard to assume that other nations would be following the same conventions for business communication. In order to eliminate any miscommunication and misunderstanding, all currencies in the world have been assigned a three-letter code that is used while communicating internationally. While USA, Britain, and India may continue to use $, £, and ₹, respectively, as the symbols of their currencies, it cannot be done so internationally. They have been assigned three-letter codes of USD, GBP, and INR, respectively, which need to be used in banks and all official cross-border communications. Likewise, all currencies have been assigned these codes mentioned in the Appendix to the book.

FOREIGN EXCHANGE RATES

In an exchange-traded transaction, the last traded price is available in public domain. Buyers and sellers of the asset pay a brokerage to the broker who facilitates the transactions and is a member of the exchange. For example, if a share is trading at ₹100 and the brokerage is 1%, then the buyer would pay ₹101 (price plus brokerage) for the asset and seller would receive ₹99 (price minus brokerage). The OTC markets such as foreign exchange operate on a different basis as there is no public display of the exchange rates. The exchange rates that are available in the print or electronic media are only indicative. The banks function more as a *market maker* rather than a broker. A market maker offers a two-way quote, provides liquidity, and may trade on his own behalf. With two-way quote, the market maker is obligated to buy and sell at quoted rates and the counterparty decides whether to buy or sell the foreign currency. In contrast, a broker merely executes the orders of the client at a given price for a commission.

There are many rates available in the foreign exchange markets and are quoted in several different fashions. These are described as follows.

Bid and Ask Rates

As stated, foreign exchange dealers offer two-way quotes. Foreign exchange markets are OTC with various banks quoting rates in pairs of bid and ask—one for buying and another for selling the foreign currency. In the example just cited, the bid rate would be ₹99 and the ask rate would be ₹101 with ₹2 accruing as profit. For foreign currency markets, bid rate and ask rate are defined as follows:

Bid rate Bid is the rate at which bank/dealer buys foreign currency.
Ask rate Ask is the rate at which bank/dealer sells foreign currency.

Bid rate is the appropriate rate for exporters who sell foreign currency, and ask rate is relevant for importers who need to buy foreign currency. Bid rate would also be applied by dealer when selling local currency and ask rate when buying local currency.

Exercise 5-1
Foreign Exchange Rates and Spread

A bank in India has quoted the following rate for US dollar and euro:

US dollar	₹/US$	45.00	–	45.50
Euro	₹/€	60.00	–	60.60

Find out the following:
(a) At what rate would the bank sell US dollar?
(b) At what rate would the bank buy euro?
(c) An importer needs €1,000. How much Indian currency would he pay?
(d) An exporter has US$2,000 to render to the bank. How much would the exporter get on Indian currency?
(e) If the bank has to buy and sell one dollar, how much profit can it make? What is the percentage of profit?
(f) If the bank has to buy and sell one euro, how much profit can it make? What is the percentage of profit?

Solution
(a) The bank would sell at ask rate. It would charge ₹45.50 for each dollar sold.
(b) The bank would buy at bid rate. It would pay ₹60.00 for each euro bought.
(c) An importer buys euro. Therefore, bank sells euro. It would charge the ask rate of ₹60.60/€. For buying €1,000, the importer would pay ₹60,600 (1,000 × 60.60)
(d) An exporter sells dollar. Therefore, bank buys dollar. It would charge the bid rate of ₹45.00/$. For selling $2,000, the exporter would get ₹90,000 (2,000 × 45.00)
(e) and f.

The profit margin for the bank is given by Eq. 5-1.
For US dollar the spread is ₹0.50 per dollar and for euro the spread is ₹0.60 per euro. The % spreads are as follows:

$$\text{For US dollar: } \% \text{ Spread} = \frac{\text{Ask Rate} - \text{Bid Rate}}{\text{Mid Rate}} \times 100 = \frac{45.50 - 45.00}{45.25} \times 100 = 1.10\%$$

$$\text{For euro: } \% \text{ Spread} = \frac{\text{Ask Rate} - \text{Bid Rate}}{\text{Mid Rate}} \times 100 = \frac{60.60 - 60.00}{60.30} \times 100 = 0.99\%$$

The exchange rate for US dollar, for example, may be quoted as ₹45.15 – ₹45.75. It implies that a bank would buy US dollar at ₹45.15, but it would sell at ₹45.75. In the process of buying and selling one dollar, the bank would make ₹0.60 (₹45.75 – 45.15) as profit. The difference between ask and bid rates is called bid–ask spread representing profit for the bank in a round-trip transaction. For a dealer, the spread is more important than the absolute values of the exchange rates.

% spread is defined as follows:

$$\% \text{ Spread} = \frac{\text{Ask Rate} - \text{Bid Rate}}{\text{Mid Rate}} \times 100 \tag{5-1}$$

Bid rate is always less than ask rate in case of direct quotation (discussed later) to enable the dealer earn profit.

For few currencies, such as Japanese yen, the exchange rates are quoted for 100 units. An exchange rate of ₹55.00 in India for Japanese yen would mean that J¥100 = ₹55.00. Rates quoted are usually up to four decimal places, but for currencies whose base is 100 units the rates are quoted up to two decimal places.

In India, Reserve Bank publishes exchange rates for US dollar, euro, British pound, and Japanese yen called RBI reference rates. These rates are only indicative rates and do not imply actual transactions at these rates. However, they serve an important function in currency derivative trading in India. These RBI reference rates are used for final cash settlement of the derivatives trades in foreign currencies.

Direct and Indirect Rates

Exchange rate is the price of one currency in terms of another. For currency A and B it can be expressed in two ways—price of A in terms of B or price of B in terms of A. For example, an exchange rate of ₹50.00/US$ can also be expressed as $0.02/₹. Both are same but expressions are different. The two ways of quoting the exchange rates are called direct and indirect rates. These are defined as follows.

Direct rate Direct rate is the number of units of home currency per unit of foreign currency. For example ₹50/$ or ₹60/€ would be a direct quote in India. Similarly, US$1.60/£ would be a direct quote in the USA.

Indirect rate Indirect rate is the number of units of foreign currency per unit of home currency. An exchange rate of $0.02/₹ would be an indirect quote in India.

Most countries in the world follow the direct rate convention. However, in London indirect rate is prevalent where rates are quoted as the number of units of a currency per British pound. Similarly, in Eurozone euro is being quoted under indirect convention, that is, number of units of a currency per unit of euro.

Direct rates can be converted into indirect rates and vice versa. They simply have to be inverted for changing one form to another. However, the inverting bid rate would give the ask rate and inverting ask rate would give the bid rate. An exercise follows.

> **Exercise 5-2**
> **Direct and Indirect Rates**
>
> The exchange rates in Exercise 5-1 are direct rates in India. What would be the equivalent rate for Indian rupee in the USA and in Germany if they were to follow the direct rate convention?
>
> *Solution*
>
> In India the direct rate for US dollar is ₹/US$: 45.00 – 45.50
>
> The equivalent rate for Indian rupee in the USA would be
> Bid rate = 1/Ask rate = 1/45.50 = $0.0220/₹; and
> Ask rate = 1/Bid rate = 1/45.00 = $0.0222/₹
>
> In the USA the direct rate for Indian rupee is   US$/₹:   0.0220 – 0.0222
>
> In India the direct rate for euro is   ₹/€:   60.00 – 60.60
>
> The equivalent rate for Indian rupee in Germany would be
> Bid rate = 1/Ask rate = 1/60.60 = € 0.0165/₹; and
> Ask rate = 1/Bid rate = 1/60.00 = € 0.0167/₹
>
> In Germany the direct rate for Indian rupee is   €/₹:   0.0165 – 0.0167

Merchant and Interbank Rates

There are two distinct tiers in the foreign exchange markets—one comprising transactions between the banks and its customers, who are the actual users of foreign exchange, and the other consisting of transactions among the banks themselves called the interbank market. The transactions with the customers are called merchant transactions and the rates used for these transactions are merchant rates.

The transactions among banks are done at interbank rates and the market is referred to as interbank market. Merchant rates are derived from interbank rates. Interbank rates are quoted up to four decimal places except for some currencies with small (not to be construed as weak) currencies such as Japanese yen and Indonesian rupiah. However, merchant rates in India are quoted up to two decimal places. Calculation of merchant rates from interbank rates is discussed later.

Basis Points and Points-in-Points Merchant rates are normally quoted up to two decimal places, for example, ₹46.25/$ or $1.20/€. Like interbank rates they are also quoted in pairs of bid and ask. To shorten the quotation the practice is to communicate only the two decimal places. For example, a quote of 45.25 – 45.75 for rupee dollar rate may be shortened to 25/75. The first two decimal places are called *basis points (bps)*. One *bp* is equal to 1/100. In the interbank market the convention is to specify rates up to four decimal places, for example, $1.2320 – 1.2380 per euro. The last two decimal places are called *points-in-points (pips)*. In terms of *pips* the quotation could be 20/80. Hundred bps make one point and 100 pips make one basis point.

Cross Rates and Vehicle Currency

The foreign exchange markets are not equally efficient in all currencies, that is, not all currencies are traded and equally popular at all places. The efficiency in the foreign exchange markets is dependent upon the volumes traded for each currency. For example, there would be a little demand and supply of Mexican peso in India. It is due to the fact that exports in India may not be denominated in Mexican peso nor a Mexican exporter would invoice in Indian rupee. In such cases, it would be difficult to obtain a direct market-based quote for Mexican peso in India. So would be the case in Mexico where direct quote for Indian rupee may not be available as the markets in the two currencies are not deep and liquid enough.

Under such circumstances, the exchange rates are synthesized from other rates. The synthetic rate uses a common currency denominator for working out the rates. The common denominator is the currency against which the two currencies whose exchange rates is to be worked out are actively traded. We know that both Indian rupee and Mexican peso are traded actively against US dollar. Therefore, US dollar exchange rates for Indian rupee and Mexican peso can be combined to arrive at the desired exchange rate. In such a case, US dollar serves as a vehicle to get the desired exchange rate and is called *vehicle currency*. The rates arrived at using a vehicle currency is also called synthetic rate or *cross rate*.

As an example, consider that an Indian national has Mexican peso and needs to convert them to Indian rupees. The banks do not offer exchange rate for rupee to peso. Instead it would synthesize the exchange rate as follows:

1. Sell Mexican peso for US dollar, say at Mex peso 12/$
2. Then sell US dollar to convert in Indian rupee, say at ₹45/$

Exercise 5-3
Cross Rates

The exchange rates for Mexican peso and Indian rupee with respect to US dollar are as follows:

	₹/$	45.00	–	45.50
	Mex peso/$	12.00	–	12.25

Find out at what rate would the bank (a) buy Mexican peso and (b) sell Mexican peso?

Solution

In India the direct rate for US dollar is   ₹/US$:   ₹45.00   –   45.50

Since the US dollar has been quoted in terms of Mexican peso, the exchange rate needs to be inverted. This may be converted into an expression that gives the number of US dollar per Mexican peso as follows:

No. of pesos per dollar	12.00	12.25
No. of dollars per peso	1/12.25	1/12.00
	0.0816	0.0833

The bank buys peso at bid rate; Bid rate (₹/peso)   = 45.00 × 0.0816 = 3.6735
The bank sells peso at ask rate; Ask rate (₹/peso)   = 45.50 × 0.0833 = 3.7916

This would result in an exchange rate of ₹3.75 per peso.

$$\text{Number of Indian rupee/Mexican peso} = \frac{\text{₹}}{\text{US\$}} \times \frac{\text{US\$}}{\text{Mex Peso}} = \frac{\text{₹}}{\text{US\$}} \bigg/ \frac{\text{Mex Peso}}{\text{US\$}}$$

$$= \frac{45.00}{12.00} = ₹3.75/\text{peso}$$

The bid ask spread is referred to as the transaction cost also as this is the amount of money that the bank makes and a customer loses in a round-trip transaction of foreign currency. The spread in case of synthetic rates would be larger. The reason is simple. In case of synthetic rates, the transaction cost is incurred twice as much as that of direct rates, as one needs to convert a currency into an intermediate currency before obtaining the desired currency.

The use of cross rates reduces the number of quotations drastically. If all currencies are to be expressed with respect to all others, the number of quotations for n convertible currencies are $n(n-1)/2$, while with cross rates, only $(n-1)$ quotations would be required as all currency rates can be expressed in terms of single identified common currency, termed as vehicle currency. Using the vehicle currency, all exchange rates may be computed.

SPOT RATES AND ARBITRAGE

As stated earlier, foreign exchange markets are over-the-counter where the exchange rates at which the transactions take place are not in the public domain. Individual dealers and banks quote prices of their own without knowledge of one another and it is possible that different dealers quote different exchange rates. Naively, one would imagine that there exists a possibility of arbitrage because one can buy foreign currency from one dealer offering lower price and, then, sell to the dealer quoting higher price. How are different dealers able to converge on a price range that does not offer arbitrage? We address this question now.

Remember that we are not attempting to find out how spot exchange rates are determined, which is separate matter. At a macro-level, there are a large number of economic factors that impact the prices of various currencies almost continuously. Attempting to understand the factors that determine the foreign exchange rates is a subject matter of economics. At micro-level or day-to-day operations, we are more concerned about how the rates from different sources are arrived. We shall explore this process in this section.

The question of determination of rates is analogous to stock market quotations, without the concern about the fair value of a financial asset, such as stocks or bonds. The arbitrage principle states that in an efficiently functioning market, an asset cannot command two prices. Having two prices provides an opportunity to investors to have immediate profit without making any investment or assuming any risk. When doing arbitrage, the focus is on price differential in two markets rather than the fair value of the asset in either of the markets.

Arbitrage opportunities in foreign exchange markets are not as visible as in case of exchange traded assets where the price is in public domain and remains same for buying and selling. The primary reasons are—the foreign exchange markets are OTC markets where the rates remain confidential, and the foreign exchange quotations are two-way quotes with bid and ask rates.

Let us consider a simple example where two dealers A and B in India offer the following rates for buying and selling euro (normally interbank markets specify rates up to four decimal places):

Nos of ₹ per Euro	Bid	Ask
Dealer A	60.3125	60.3250
Dealer B	60.3275	60.3350

The rates of Dealer A mean that he would buy euro at ₹60.3125 and sell at ₹60.3250. Therefore one can buy euro at ₹60.3250 from Dealer A. Similarly, the quotation of Dealer B means that he would buy euro at ₹60.3275 and sell at ₹60.3350. Therefore, one can sell euro to Dealer B and get ₹60.3275. By doing so, a profit of ₹0.0025 can be made (₹60.3275 – ₹60.3250) for every euro transacted.

A customer sells the foreign currency at bid rate and buys foreign currency at ask rate. To derive profit one needs to 'sell high and buy low'. In the foreign exchange markets, if the bid rate of one is higher than the ask rate of another, it would offer an arbitrage opportunity and the difference of ask of one and bid of another can be earned as profit. The condition for arbitrage is exhibited in Figure 5-1.

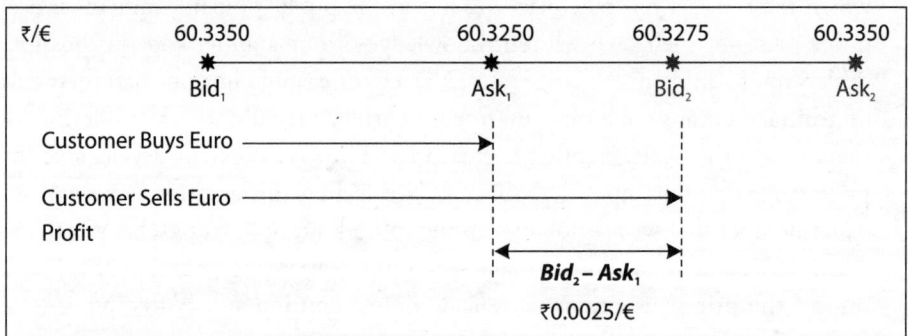

Figure 5-1
Condition for Arbitrage

The outcome of such rates would automatically become evident to the dealers because dealers tend to operate on the basis of no inventory of foreign exchange. At the end of the day, buying and selling of foreign currency must be equal with no change of inventory at hand. Hence, Dealer A would soon discover that customers are buying euro from him depleting his stock of euro, whereas no one sells euro to him. Hence, he automatically revises upwards the ask rate. Similarly, Dealer B would be accumulating euro and to discourage selling by customers would decrease the bid rate. This process of revising rates happens far quicker than one would imagine. An accumulation of foreign currency with dealer indicates that the bid rate is too low and, hence, must be revised downwards. Similarly, depletion of stock of foreign currency suggests that dealer sells at too low a price and, hence, revises the ask rate upwards.

The arbitrage opportunities vanish very quickly—almost as soon as they appear. Even though the dealers are unaware of rates offered by others, the market forces as monitored with the level of inventory of foreign exchange will communicate a lot to them about the quantum and the direction of revision in exchange rates.

Condition for No Arbitrage Traders would not be able to generate profit by buying from one and selling to another if the banks revise the rates as follows:

No. of ₹ per Euro	Bid	Ask
Dealer A	60.3125	60.3275
Dealer B	60.3225	60.3350

Here, the rates are overlapping and, hence, offer no scope of arbitrage. The condition for no arbitrage to exist is depicted in Figure 5-2. Here, the loss would be ₹0.0050 per euro if the trader deploys the same strategy of buying from Dealer A and selling to Dealer B. The no arbitrage condition can also be stated as

$$\text{For no arbitrage:} \quad \text{Bid}_2 < \text{Ask}_1$$

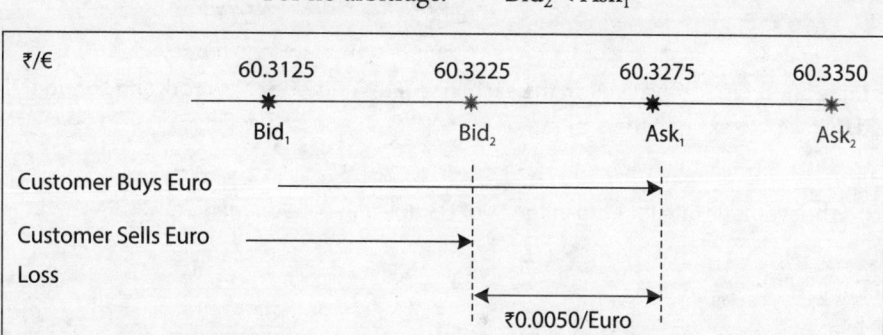

Figure 5-2
Condition for No Arbitrage

Arbitrage in Two Markets Although it was easy to identify the arbitrage opportunities in the same location/country, the opportunities are not that easily visible in the international scenario by simply comparing the bid of one dealer with the ask rate of another. If nations follow the same convention of quoting direct/indirect rates, the additional task would be to convert the rates in the identical format. However, the principle of arbitrage essentially remains same.

For example, consider the Indian bank and the German bank, following direct rate convention with rates as follows:

	Bid	Ask
Indian Dealer (₹/€)	60.3125	60.3250
German Dealer (€/₹)	0.0160	0.0165

Here, the identification of arbitrage is not apparent till we convert one of the rates in the same format as that of other. We convert the direct quote of the German bank into indirect by inverting the rates. Ask rate is inverted to get the bid rate and vice versa. This is shown here.

German Bank (€/₹) (Direct Quote)   0.0160   0.0165
(₹/€) (Indirect Quote)   60.6060   62.5000
                           (1/0.0165) (1/0.0160)

Here the bid rate of German bank is higher than the ask rate of Indian bank. One can buy euro at ₹60.3250 from Indian bank and sell the same to German bank at ₹60.6060 generating a profit of ₹0.2810 for every euro purchased. Note that arbitrage profit is not available if the transaction is reversed, that is, buying euro from German bank and, then, selling it to Indian bank.

Exercise 5-4
Three-point Arbitrage

In New York, the following price of euro is quoted as follows:

$\$/€$ 1.2500   –   1.2600

In London, the values of US dollar and euro against British pound are as follows:

$\$/£$ 1.5650   –   1.5750
$€/£$ 1.2200   –   1.2300

Is there any arbitrage available in the exchange rates quoted at New York and London? If so, what action would be taken to execute the arbitrage?

Solution
We find the synthetic rate for euro in terms of US dollar in London market.

$$(\$/€)_{Bid} = \left(\frac{\$}{£}\right)_{Bid} \times \left(\frac{£}{€}\right)_{Bid}$$

$= 1.5650 \times 1/1.2300 = 1.2724$

$$(\$/€)_{Ask} = \left(\frac{\$}{£}\right)_{Ask} \times \left(\frac{£}{€}\right)_{Ask}$$

$= 1.5750 \times 1/1.2200 = 1.2910$

The exchange rates in New York and London are therefore as follows:

In New York (Direct)	$\$/€$	1.2500	–	1.2600
In London (Synthetic)	$\$/€$	1.2724	–	1.2910

Clearly, there is arbitrage in the ask rate of direct quote and bid rate of synthetic quote. One can buy euro at $1.2600 in New York and sell euro in London at $1.2724 to gain $0.0124 per euro.

The steps in arbitrage would be as follows:
1. Buy €10,000 by paying US$12,600 in New York
2. Sell €10,000 to get £10,000/1.2300 = £ 8,130.08
3. Sell £8,130.08 to get $1.5650 × 8,130.08 = $12,724; $124 more than what was paid to acquire €10,000.

Arbitrage using only two currencies is referred to as two-point arbitrage. When three currencies are involved, it is referred to as three-point arbitrage. Three-point arbitrage is further complex as it involves not only inverting the rate but also finding synthetic rates from two currencies to compare with the direct quotes. Refer to Exercise 5-4.

SPOT AND FORWARD CONTRACTS

Transactions in the foreign exchange markets are settled by exchanging the currencies involved. If one buys US dollar at ₹45, the transactions would complete only when the buyer delivers ₹45 to the seller and the seller delivers US$1 to the buyer. Ideally, the exchange of the currencies must be simultaneous. Since the currencies belong to the different nations that are geographically apart and are in different time zones, the simultaneous mutual exchange of currencies may not be operationally feasible. The settlement, that is, the conclusion of mutual obligations, takes place by way of debiting and crediting the accounts of one bank with another. The debit and credit must take place on the same day to avoid credit/default risk[1]. Further, the bank may not have direct arrangements or its account in all the currencies and may have to depend on the correspondents for routing the remittances. Recognizing the difficulties of settlement, the spot transactions in foreign exchange are settled within two business days for the exchange rate negotiated.

If a spot transaction has taken place on Thursday, then the actual debit and credit would be executed on the following Monday, that is, after two business days (Saturdays and Sundays being holidays in the foreign exchange markets). The settlement date is also known as *value date* as a date which shall be used in determining the exchange rate. Since the determination of two business days in international transactions has its problems, the practice of specifying the value date removes uncertainty of the exchange rate. Because of intervening banking holidays and settlement locations falling in different countries and time zones, the rule of two business days poses a problem. There are several conventions and practices that are followed in the international markets depending upon the currencies involved. For example, countries in Middle East observe Fridays as holidays but are open on Saturdays, whereas most nations have Saturdays and Sundays as holidays. Normally in transactions of foreign exchange, the value date is specified rather than being computed.

Sometimes the settlement is feasible on the following day. In such cases the exchange rate is called *tom rate* (tomorrow's rate). If the transaction has to be settled on 'here and now' basis, then the exchange rate for such transaction is called *cash rate*. The exchange rates offered for immediate conversion of currency at banks, airports, etc. are cash rates and not spot rates.

Keeping the issue of counting two business days aside, we concentrate on forward contracts on foreign exchange. Besides dealing in the spot transactions, the contracts for buying and selling of foreign exchange can also be made for settlement at future dates. Such transactions are called forward contracts, and the exchange rate agreed therein is called *forward rate*.

---

[1]This is also referred to as *Hershatt Risk*, named after a German bank that denied transactions undertaken and denied its cash flow obligations, having lost on its speculative positions.

Forward contracts in foreign exchange, like any other forward contract of other commodities or underlying assets, fix the exchange rate today for settlement at some future date. By settlement means the actual exchange of currencies involved. For example, a 1-m forward contract of buying US dollar negotiated at an exchange rate of ₹45/$ means that although the exchange rate is fixed now, actual exchange of the currencies involved would take place after one month by buyer paying ₹45 and receiving $1.

Forward contract is very useful as it provides a hedge against the uncertain future conditions. Consider, for example, an importer with a liability to pay US$10,000 one month later for the raw materials purchased. The importer has two options in the spot market—(a) buy the US dollar spot and retain it till liability matures after a month or (b) buy the dollar spot one month later. Under the first option, the importer blocks the capital for one month and the very purpose of availing credit is lost. Instead the importer can pay now and avail cash discount. Under the second alternative, the importer can buy the US dollar when the liability actually matures after one month. In this case, the importer carries the risk because what the spot rate will be after one month is unknown. If dollar appreciated in the meanwhile, the importer ends up paying more. However, the importer also stands to gain if dollar depreciated.

With forward market, there is yet another feasible option. It is to book a 1-m forward contract for buying dollars. Although forward contract enables fixing the exchange rate now for delivery and settlement later, after one month in this case eliminating the exchange rate risk and at the same time avail the credit. Under forward contract, the exchange rate is fixed now but settled by actual delivery of the currencies involved at the expiry of forward period. Thus, the cash flow that is ascertained now is deferred for one month. Hence, with forward contract of buying dollars, the importer neither needs funds now nor carries the risk of fluctuating exchange rates.

Forward Premium/Discount

If forward rate has the advantage of removing uncertainty of spot rate, then would it be same/more/less than the spot rate? From the nature of forward contract one may believe that since the settlement of the contract is deferred but the exchange rate is fixed now, the forward rate necessarily must be higher than the current spot rate. However, such belief is not true. We would discuss how the forward exchange rate is worked out later. Suffice would be to say here that the forward price can be lower than, higher than, or equal to the spot. First, we focus on the difference of forward and spot prices, referred to as forward premium or discount.

Under the system of direct rates, the value of foreign currency is stated in terms of number of units of domestic currency per unit of foreign currency, for example, ₹45/US$ in India or US$1.20/€ in the USA. System of direct rate is prevailing across the world except for few countries. Under direct rate convention, if forward rate is higher than the spot, it means that foreign currency is more expensive in future than it is now. Here, the foreign currency is said to be at premium. Similarly, if forward rate is lower than the spot rate, it implies that foreign currency is cheaper in future than it is now and is said to be at discount. Under indirect system of quoting rates, the interpretation would reverse.

Conventionally, the forward premium of discount is stated in annualized terms. Forward rates are generally available for varying forward periods ranging from one to six months and sometimes up to 12 months. Being OTC market one can get the foreign exchange rates for any forward period on demand, but it is more common to find forward rates available at monthly intervals. The annual premium or discount on the foreign currency can be computed by using the forward rate as follows:

$$\text{Annualized Forward Premium/Discount (\%)} = \frac{\text{Forward Rate}_{mid} - \text{Spot Rate}_{mid}}{\text{Spot Rate}_{mid}} \times \frac{12}{\text{Forward Period (in months)}} \times 100$$

Exercise 5-5
Forward Premium or Discount

Consider following rates of foreign exchange for British pound

Spot (₹ per £)	77.90	78.10
1-m Forward (₹ per £)	77.50	77.80

(a) Find out whether the British pound is at premium or discount.
(b) What is the annualized premium or discount for British pound?
(c) Based on the answer to (b) what average (mid)-rate for 3-m, 6-m, and 12-m forward contracts are likely?

Solution

(a) Since 1-m forward rates are lower than the spot rate the foreign currency, that is, pound is at discount to rupee.

(b) The amount of discount is computed from mid rates. The spot mid-rate is ₹78.00/£ and the forward mid-rate is ₹77.65/£. Therefore,

$$\text{Annualized Forward Premium/Discount (\%)}$$
$$= \frac{\text{Forward Rate}_{mid} - \text{Spot Rate}_{mid}}{\text{Spot Rate}_{mid}} \times \frac{12}{\text{Forward Period (in months)}} \times 100$$
$$= \frac{77.65 - 78.00}{78.00} \times 12 \times 100 = -5.38\%$$

The annualized discount of 5.38% means that pound is likely to depreciate by the same amount in a year.

(c) Assuming that the premium/discount calculated using the 1-m forward rate is fair representative of forward rates for the whole year, the likely forward rates for three months, six months, and 12 months are

3-m forward rate (mid) = 78.00 × (1 − 0.0538/4) = ₹76.95/£
6-m forward rate (mid) = 78.00 × (1 − 0.0538/2) = ₹75.90/£
12-m forward rate (mid) = 78.00 × (1 − 0.0538)   = ₹73.80/£

Forward rates for different periods are available. The calculations of annualized premium/discount based on 1-m, 3-m, or 6-m are likely to differ from each other. In such situations one faces a dilemma as to which of the forward periods is most appropriate for calculating the annualized premium/discount. Generally speaking, greater the liquidity, more fair the price. In addition, longer the horizon, lesser is the liquidity. It suggests that 6-m forward contract would be less liquid than 3-m forward and still less liquid than 1-m forward. Therefore, the premium reflected in 1-m forward contract should be more accurate.

However, there is a disadvantage too if we use 1-m forward price for projecting the annualized premium/discount. Computing annualized premium using 1-m forward price requires multiplication by 12, and hence if there is distortion in the price it would be magnified 12 times. The magnification of error would be less if we use 3-m forward price and still less if 6-m forward price is used. Therefore, for appropriate annualized premium/discount, the choice is difficult for truer and more accurate projection. However, most analysts prefer to use the most liquid contract for finding annualized premium/discount because of the greater liquidity in the near month contracts.

Another practical rule about the forward rate is regarding the bid-ask spread in the forward rates. Since forward rates are only an estimate, the banks/dealers are exposed to greater risk at the time of dealing with the forward contracts. For the increased amount of risk, banks would expect a greater reward, which is derived from spread (the difference between ask and bid rates). Therefore, spread in the forward quotations is larger than the spread in the spot rates. As uncertainty compounds with time the bid–ask spread increases with increasing forward period, that is, the spread in 6-m forward contract should be higher than the spread in 1-m forward rates.

In the forward markets, banks usually quote forward rates for periods in whole number of months. It is common to find quotations for forward periods of 1, 2, 3, 6, and 9 months. One year forward contracts are also quoted. Forward period beyond one year is uncommon in the market. Therefore, forward contracts are appropriate for hedging for a short period of time. However, banks can also quote rates for forward periods that are not exact multiples of month. Such contracts are called **broken date contracts** or **odd date contracts**.

Swap Transaction

The forward transaction defined earlier is a stand-alone contract where a bank may buy/sell foreign currency forward from/to its customers. It is called an outright forward contract. In contrast, we have a *swap transaction*, a composite contract which consists of two opposite and equal transactions at two different points of time. A swap transaction is a combination of spot and forward transactions[2]. The spot and forward legs of the swap are opposite and equal in value. They are depicted in Figure 5-3.

Buying foreign currency 1-m forward and selling the same amount 3-m forward is an example of forward–forward swap. For example, a bank may buy $5000 spot from another

---

[2]A swap where both the legs are forward with differing maturities is called a forward–forward swap. Buying foreign currency 1-m forward and selling the same amount 3-m forward is an example of forward–forward swap.

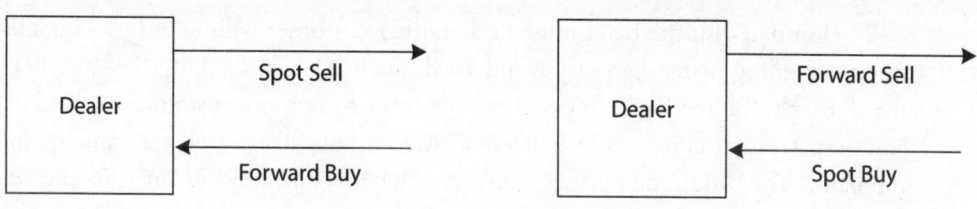

Figure 5-3
Schematic View of Swap Transaction

bank and, simultaneously, enter into a 1-m forward contract to sell $5000 to the same bank. The rates for buying spot and selling forward would be different. This is a swap transaction. Alternatively, the bank may sell spot and buy forward. The swap transaction seems like a lending/borrowing transaction for both the counterparties but in different currencies. The bank selling US dollar spot and buying it 1-m forward is akin to lending US dollar for one month. Similarly, for the counterparty buying dollar spot (selling rupee) and selling dollar 1-m forward (buying rupee) is a lending transaction in rupee. Swap is a temporary short-term arrangement to borrow one currency for another with a promise to reverse the same later. It is akin to repo or reverse repo transaction.

With both buying and selling rates known the bank is not exposed to any risk of changing exchange rates. The position of swap is also obtainable with two independent but opposite and equal contracts—one spot and another forward. An independent forward contract is called an *outright forward contract*. Two independent contracts—one spot and another outright forward—are more expensive than an equivalent and composite swap contract.

Rationale for Swap Transactions Most transactions in the interbank markets are swaps and most merchant transactions are outright forward contracts. Composite swap contracts are of great utility to banks as they avoid assuming exchange rate risk for the bank. It also eliminates the problem of finding exactly matching counterparty for a customer. Swap, having offsetting positions in a single contract, enables achieve both the issues of elimination of risk and matching counterparty.

Banks usually do trading on behalf of their customers—exporters and importers, who sell and buy on outright basis. Assume that a bank buys 1-m forward $10,000 at ₹45/$ on outright basis from an exporter. The contract means that after one month, the exporter would deliver $10,000 to the bank and receive ₹4,50,000 from it. One month later, after paying ₹4,50,000 to the exporter, the bank would end up with $10,000. Although the rupee amount payable by the bank is certain, after one month it does not know at what exact rate it would be able to sell $10,000. This implies the risk of foreign exchange rates. If the exchange rate after one month is more than ₹45, the bank makes profit else it ends up with a loss. The risk that was supposed to be borne by exporter is being assumed by the bank, indeed a function not in the scope of banking activities.

To eliminate risk the bank must find another customer willing to buy US dollar after one month. Finding matching party is indeed difficult. Hence, bank decides to sell 1-m forward the dollars to be received after one month from the export customer to another party. The counterparty that agrees to buy dollar forward would like to sell the same quantity spot to the bank. This would be a swap transaction where bank buys dollar spot and sells forward. Such a situation is a lending transaction in dollars for the counterparty. The rate at which the swap would be transacted is known. By doing so, the cash flows of dollar after one month are matched. Once the swap transaction is negotiated, the bank would do as follows:

1. The dollars received by the bank now under the swap are sold in the spot market at the rate known, and
2. The foreign currency to be received by the bank from the exporter already stands sold to the counterparty to the swap.

Thus, the cash flows of the bank are frozen as depicted in Figure 5-4. For the bank, this eliminates the risk of exchange rate as well as the problem of finding matching customer to square off its position in foreign exchange.

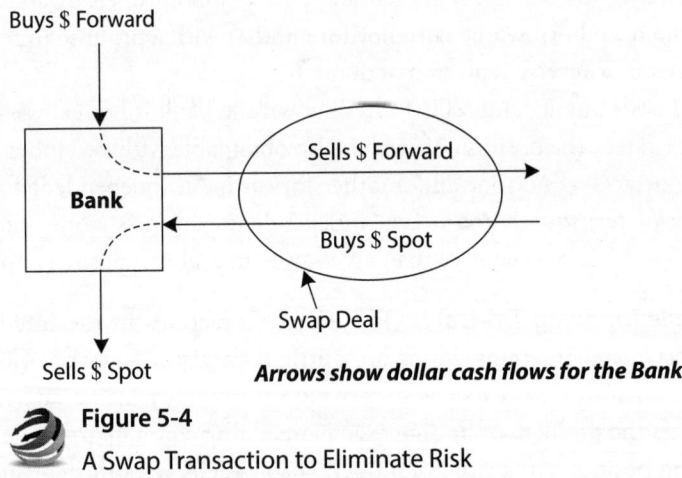

Figure 5-4
A Swap Transaction to Eliminate Risk

Outright Forward vs Swap

We described a swap transaction as either of the following:

> Buy foreign currency spot and sell forward, or
> Sell foreign currency spot and buy forward.

A swap is a composite deal that has two equal legs; one spot and another forward that is equal and opposite to spot. The exposure to foreign currency is nullified at the end of the swap period. Both legs being equal and opposite, the net flow of foreign exchange is zero. A swap contract merely changes the timings of the cash inflow and the cash outflow of foreign currency.

Swap Quotes Swap deals are quoted in a different way. Although spot rates are readily available, the rates for the forward leg are quoted through the swap points instead of an explicit quotation. Spot rates with swap points are used to arrive at the rate applicable for the forward leg. The rate for forward leg would depend upon whether it is a swap or an outright forward.

The working can be explained with an example. Assume that Trader A wants to buy euro now and sell one month later. This is a swap transaction where the spot leg is a buy and forward leg is a sell for the trader. Now, assume that in the interbank market, the exchange rate is quoted as follows:

Spot (₹/€)   62.5800 – 62.6000
Swap points[3] 1 m   500/700

If Trader A has to buy euro spot in the interbank market, it can do so at ask rate of ₹62.6000. If the forward leg is independent of spot transaction, it would be an outright forward. For given swap points, the rate for the outright forward is computed as follows:

When swap points are low/high The foreign currency is at premium and the rate for the forward deal is arrived by adding the swap points to the spot rates.

When swap points are high/low The foreign currency is at discount and rate for the forward deal is arrived by subtracting the swap points from the spot rates.

As a cross check whether the forward rate by adding or subtracting is realistic we must observe the following:

1. *Positive spread*: The ask rate must always be higher than the bid rate, and
2. *Increasing spread with time*: The spread between the ask and the bid rates must widen as we extend the forward period, that is, 3-m forward must have larger spread than 1-m forward and 1-m forward to have larger spread than spot.

The first rule ensures a profit margin for the bank for 'buying low and selling high' and the second rule implies greater margin for more uncertain positions since risk increases as forward period extends. In case we inadvertently add rather than subtract or vice versa either of the above common sense rules would be violated.

Using the above rule, the rate for the forward contract is arrived as follows:

Spot (₹/€)   62.5800 – 62.6000
1-m Swap points   500/700
1-m outright forward rate   62.6300 – 62.6700
(*Swap points being low/high are added to the spot rates*)

Here, the spread in the spot is 200 pips, and in forward, it is 400 pips. If we had subtracted the swap points instead of adding, the 1-m forward quote would be 62.5300 – 62.5300, the spread is zero, which violates both the conditions of positive spread and increasing spread in forward mentioned above.

---

[3]In the Interbank market the rates are quoted in pips.

As independent contracts, Trader A buys euro spot at 62.6000 (the ask rate for spot deal) and sells euro 1-m forward on outright basis at 62.6300 (the bid rate for the forward deal). In this process, Trader A would gain 300 pips (₹0.03) per euro.

Instead of booking two independent contracts, Trader A can book a composite swap contract. In such a contract, the profit for Trader A would be larger than two independent contracts. Under the swap, the first leg of spot transaction would be done at the same rate (the ask rate) of ₹62.6000/€. However, the rate for the forward leg would differ and is arrived in the following fashion:

1. The rate for the spot leg becomes the *reference rate* to which relevant swap points are either added or subtracted.
2. If swap points are low/high, they would be added to the spot rate and if high/low, they would be subtracted from the spot rate.
3. If the forward leg is 'buy' in the interbank market for the dealer, the bid points are relevant and if it is 'sell', then ask points are relevant.

Here, the reference rate is 62.6000; being the spot rate for buying. The second leg is a forward 'buy' for the dealer in the foreign exchange interbank market. Therefore, bid points become relevant. Bid points are added because swap points are low/high. The rate applicable for the forward leg under the swap would be *reference rate* + bid points, that is, 62.6000 + 500 pips = 62.6500. The swap deal would result in a profit of ₹0.0500 per euro for Bank A.

The position of Trader A under swap transactions and with outright forward would be as follows:

	Under swap	Under outright forward
Trader A buys euro at	62.6000	62.6000
Trader A sells euro at	62.6500	62.6300
Profit for Trader A	0.0500	0.0300

A composite contract of swap is always cheaper than the combination of two independent contracts of a spot followed by an outright forward contract.

The swap points directly give profit and loss under swap transaction. Lower points are the profit and higher points are the losses. The following rules are convenient:

1. For swap points in order of low/high, the foreign currency is at premium and buying now and selling later would yield profit. If one sells now and buys later the swap would be loss making.
2. For swap points in order of high/low, the foreign currency is at discount and buying now and selling later would yield loss. If one sells now and buys later the swap would be profit making.

Essentially the swap points are of essence in the swap transactions and it is rather immaterial what the spot rate is. The swap rates are the profit/loss in a given swap transaction because rates for the initial leg of the swap serves only as reference rate for the second leg that is in opposite direction. This mechanism makes gains/losses in the swap independent of the rate used for initial leg, that is, the spot rate. Hence, the focus is on what derives the swap points, which shall be discussed in another chapter later.

Forward–Forward Swap

In a swap arrangement if both the legs are forward, it would be a forward–forward swap. For example, one may agree to sell Japanese yen against US dollar three months from now and buy back the same six months from now. It is a swap arrangement with first leg after three months and second leg after six months. It can be taken as a combination of two swaps—the first one being spot buy and 3-m forward sell of Japanese yen and the second one is spot sell and 6-m buy of Japanese yen. The spot legs of the two contracts cancel out with forward legs remaining. This is depicted in Figure 5-5. Swap points for three months and six months are required for pricing of forward–forward swap. The gain/loss would be determined by the differential of swap points for the two forward legs.

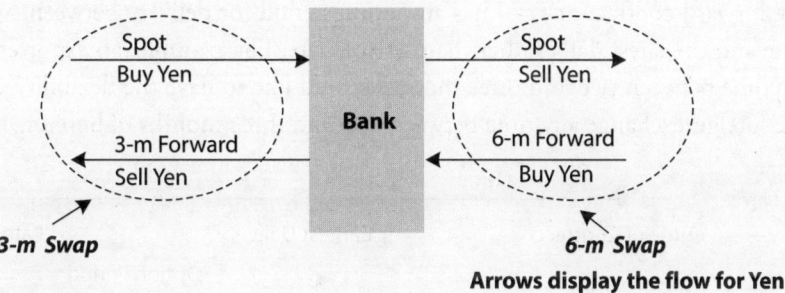

Figure 5-5
Forward–Forward Swap

One application of forward–forward swap may be for a bank to meet the requirements of its exporter and importer customers with same quantity of foreign currency but at different points of time. For example, an export customer of the bank may sell foreign currency three months forward and an import customer of the same bank may buy foreign currency six months forward. To cover such positions the bank may enter a forward–forward swap.

Option Forward

Forward contracts are exact date contracts. In addition, the contractual obligations under forward contract are independent of obligations in the spot market. In fact whether one has a position in the spot or not is irrelevant to booking of a forward contract. While booking forward contracts, the parties are committed to settle their mutual obligations on the due date.

While banks are in a better position to meet these commitments exactly on the specific date as they deal regularly in currencies and have foreign currencies, the merchants dealing in exports and imports do not have such a flexible position. The commitments made under the forward contract are dependent upon whether the underlying spot transaction for the merchant would fructify. For example, an exporter expecting a payment in one month's time from his customer may decide to sell the foreign currency 1-m forward. Although the commitment has been made to sell the foreign currency to the bank, the exporter may not realize his payment on due date as expected. In such a case, the exporter would default as he is not ready with the foreign currency to be delivered to the bank on the scheduled date. A similar case may happen with the importer who may not be in position to buy the foreign currency on the date fixed against the forward contract booked by him. It certainly does not imply that merchants do not want to honour the contractual commitments at all.

Some flexibility in timing of the maturity of the forward contract is desired by merchants as they can predict their cash flows only on an approximate basis due to their nature of business. Therefore, delivery date commitments have to be somewhat flexible. A forward contract with some flexible window of time meets this requirement. This window for delivery is called option period and the forward contract with delivery commitments within a time range rather than on specific exact date is called *option forward*. Such a contract is called an option forward contract and is depicted in Figure 5-6. Under option forward contract, the merchant having booked the forward contract at $t = 0$ has an option period for delivery between two dates, the earliest date and the latest date, rather than a fixed date. For example, an exporter expecting payment anytime between two and three months would like to have the flexibility where he can deliver the foreign exchange any time between two and three months of booking a forward contract.

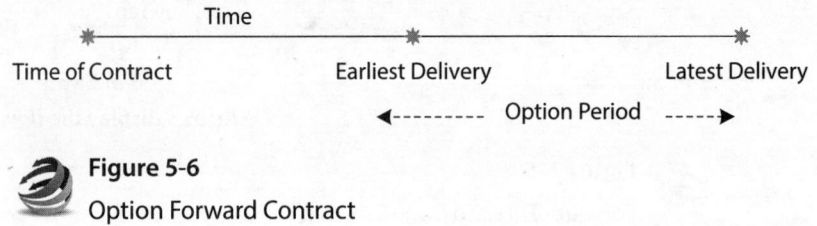

Figure 5-6
Option Forward Contract

Rates offered by the bank in option forward contract are based on the principle of least risk and maximum gain. Again swap points are used to determine the quote to merchants for the option period. It would depend upon

(i) whether the bank is buying or selling, and
(ii) whether the foreign currency is at premium or discount.

If the foreign currency is at premium, the bank would like to buy it as early as possible since foreign currency becomes more expensive as time elapses. Hence, the bank prefers earliest buying. For discount on foreign currency buying as late as possible is preferred as it becomes cheaper with time. The rules would reverse if the bank were to sell the foreign currency. The decision rules for quoting the option forward rates are as follows:

	Buy	Sell
Premium	Earliest	Latest
Discount	Latest	Earliest

For example, if the bank is dealing with an exporter who wants to tender foreign currency anytime between two and three months forward and the currency is at premium, the bank would use 2-m forward rate rather than 3-m forward for quoting to the customer. Since the foreign currency is at premium, it is advantageous for the bank to buy sooner rather than later as foreign currency is more expensive then.

MERCHANT RATES

We already stated that foreign exchange market has two tiers—the interbank where banks participate among themselves and the merchant where banks deal with the customers. The rates quoted to customers known as merchant rates are derived from the rates prevailing in the interbank markets.

Consistent with the practice of interbank markets there are two merchant rates—one for buying foreign currency and the other for selling it. For the customers, bank also performs several other functions apart from converting one currency to another, related to the import and export. Therefore, in each of buying and selling category, there are two rates—one for acting merely as money changer, converting one currency into another, and the other for performing other functions for its customers. The fees for performing functions other than those related to the exchanging money are built into the exchange rates.

Banks act only as agents and the deals done by them with their customers are covered in the interbank market. For example, if an exporter client sells foreign currency to the bank, it in turn further sells in the interbank market. Hence, the rate at which the bank would buy foreign currency from the customer depends upon at what rate it can dispose-off the currency in the interbank markets. The rates quoted to customers for only converting one currency into another are called *Telegraphic Transfer (TT) rates*.

Prevailing interbank bid rate becomes the basis of quote to the export customers for buying the foreign currency. This is known as TT buying rate. Similarly, if an import customer needs foreign currency the bank would buy it from the interbank market, at interbank ask rate. The rate at which the bank sells foreign currency to its customers is called TT selling rate. In providing services of exchanging money, the bank would like to earn exchange commission over above its cost in the interbank markets. Therefore,

> TT Buying Rate = Base Rate (Interbank bid rate) − Exchange Margin, and
> TT Selling Rate = Base Rate (Interbank ask rate) + Exchange Margin

In case the bank performs other functions too, then it is entitled to a fee for the services rendered. Buying and selling of currency by customers also require associated functions, such as handling of documents and providing credit before bank actually gets credited. For such transactions the *bill rate* is applicable. Hence, there would be bill selling rate applicable for importers and bill buying rate applicable for exporters.

Importers remit money against documents like bills drawn on them by their suppliers. The bank charges a separate margin for handling such documents. Therefore, bill selling rate would be as follows:

> Bill Selling Rate = TT Selling Rate + Exchange Margin for handling

If the importer needs to book a forward buy contract, then the base would be interbank ask rate for the forward period.

The bill buying rate presents some problems in computation. Exporters tender documents and need to sell the foreign currency of the amount stated in the invoice. The bank provides local currency immediately while it gets credited later. The time that would elapse between providing credit to the exporter and getting itself reimbursed depends upon (a) the time it takes to deliver the documents to the payee called the *transit period* and (b) the credit period provided by the exporter to his customer called the *usance period*. Thus, the bill buying rate is essentially a forward transaction with forward period equal to transit period + usance period. Therefore, for bill buying, the base rate would be the forward bid for period equal to transit and usance periods. In case exporter needs to sell the currency even before the submission of document that period too would be added.

The forward market operates on the basis of whole number of months. Therefore, the forward period applicable in the bill buying rate would have to be rounded off to the multiple of whole month. If the foreign currency is at premium, the rounding off would be to lower the number of months and if at discount then to higher number of months. The reason for doing so is apparent in as much as that bank likes to buy foreign currency as cheap as possible. For example, if the transit and usance period add to three months 10 days, then if the foreign currency is at premium, then the 3-m forward bid rate forms the basis and if at discount then 4-m forward becomes the basis for deriving bill buying rate. The calculation for finding the bill buying rate can be stated as follows:

Bill Buying Rate = Base Rate (spot buy) − Forward discount for transit plus usance plus forward period (rounded to higher month) less exchange margin; or

= Base Rate (spot buy) + Forward premium for transit plus usance plus forward period (rounded to lower month) less exchange margin

Refer to Exercise 5-6 for elaboration.

Exercise 5-6
Merchant Rates

The following information is given: (₹/US$)

Spot		45.6000/6500		
SWAP	1-m	3500/3000	2-m	5500/5000
	3-m	8500/8000	4-m	1.1500/1.1000
	5-m	1.3500/1.3000	6-m	1.5500/1.5000

With a transit period of 20 days, the exchange margin of 0.15%, and bill selling exchange margin of 0.20%, calculate the following:

(a) Ready Bill Buying Rate
(b) 2-m Forward Rate for buying Demand Bill
(c) 2-m Forward Rate for 60 day Usance Bill
(d) 3-m Forward TT Selling Rate
(e) 3-m Forward Bill Selling Rate

Solution

(a) Ready Bill Buying Rate

Forward + Usance + Transit = 0 + 0 + 20 days = 20 days (round off higher to 1-m)

	Spot Buying Rate	45.6000	
Less:	Forward Discount 1-m	−0.3500	
		45.2500	
Less:	Exchange Margin 0.15%	−0.0679	
	Merchant Rate	**45.1821**	(r/o 45.18)

(b) 2-m Forward Ready Buying Rate

	Spot Buying Rate	45.6000	
Less:	Forward Discount 3-m	−0.8500	
		44.7500	
Less:	Exchange Margin 0.15%	−0.0671	
	Merchant Rate	**44.6829**	(r/o 44.68)

(c) 2-m Forward 60-d Usance Bill Buying Rate

Forward + Usance + Transit = 2 + 2 + 20-d = 4-m 20-d (round off to 5 months)

	Spot Buying Rate	45.6000	
Less:	Forward Discount 5-m	−1.3500	
		44.2500	
Less:	Exchange Margin 0.15%	−0.0664	
	Merchant Bill Buying Rate	**44.1836**	(r/o 44.18)

(d) 3-m Forward TT Selling Rates

	Spot Selling Rate	45.6500	
Less:	Forward Discount 3-m	−0.8000	
		44.8500	
Add:	Exchange Margin 0.15%	+0.0673	
	Merchant TT Selling Rate	**44.9173**	(r/o 44.92)

(e) 3-m Forward Bill Selling Rate

	Merchant TT Selling Rate	44.9173	
Add:	Bill Exchange 0.20%	+0.0898	
	Merchant Bill Selling Rate	**45.0071**	(r/o 45.01)

NOMINAL AND REAL EFFECTIVE EXCHANGE RATES (NEER AND REER)

Nominal exchange rate is the value of one currency in terms of another at any given point of time. The exchange rates that we get to see on daily basis and are available in public domain are called nominal exchange rates. If in 1995, the exchange rate for US dollar was ₹35 and in 2010 it moved to ₹45, then we say that rupee has depreciated by 28.57% (10/35) in 15 years. Is it the true change in value, that is, the buying power of rupee? Most of us would tend to disagree because we think that in purchasing power terms, this may be untrue because not only the buying power of rupee has changed but the same has also happened to the buying power of US dollar.

Nominal exchange rates do not account for the purchasing powers of the currencies. The change over 15-year period from 1995 to 2010 is (45 − 35)/35 = 28.57% called a nominal change in value. Therefore, rupee has depreciated by 28.57% against US dollar over a period of 15 years in nominal terms.

In case of countries whose currency is pegged, the nominal exchange rate remains fixed and is not allowed to change by law. Chinese yuan and Hong Kong dollar are prominent examples as on today, whose values are not allowed to change much by the act of law. Since exchange rate is fixed, nominal exchange rate is practically of no use. However, fixing nominal exchange rate does not mean that no change in value of the currency has occurred in terms of purchasing power. In fact the purchasing power of the currencies has changed even though it appears to be constant in terms of fixed nominal exchange rate. In true sense, a fairer view can be taken only if one analyses the purchasing power of the two currencies involved with the changes in the nominal exchange rates.

Real exchange rate is the nominal exchange rate adjusted for purchasing power of the two currencies. With nominal spot exchange rate S_1 (direct quotation, that is, units of home currency per unit of foreign currency), the real exchange rate would be as per Eq. 5-2.

$$\text{Real Exchange Rate} = \frac{S_0}{S_1} \times \frac{\text{Relative price level in home country}}{\text{Relative price level in foreign country}} \times 100 \qquad (5\text{-}2)$$

Where S_0 and S_1 are the spot exchange rates at time $t = 0$ and $t = 1$ expressed in direct terms. Normally, real exchange rate is measured in terms of some base year where the index value is set at 100. As an example, consider the following data:

Year	Nominal Exchange Rate	Price level in India	Price level in the USA
2000	₹42.00/$	1,000	700
2005	₹45.00/$	1,100	735

Both nominal and real exchange rates are expressed on an index basis that is, the base year value is normalized to 100. Hence the exchange rate of ₹42 in any year, say beginning of year 2000, is indexed to 100. The nominal exchange rate on index basis would be (42/45) × 100 = 93.33 indicating depreciation of Indian currency with respect to US dollar by 6.67%. On index basis nominal exchange rate greater than 100 indicates appreciation of domestic currency.

Does the rupee depreciation by 6.67% in nominal terms implies that one would be buying 6.67% less than what a US dollar can in the year 2005 as compared to year 2000. Not really so. The buying power would be dependent upon the inflation rates in the two countries during the period. Assume that price levels as measured by the indices are 1000 in India and 700 in USA in the year 2000. However, the purchasing power of rupee stands reduced by 10% with rise in prices in India, whereas in case of dollar the purchasing power declines by

5% during the same period. The real exchange rate on index basis using Eq. 5-2 would be 97.78, as follows:

$$\text{Real Exchange Rate} = \frac{S_0}{S_1} \times \frac{\text{Relative price level in home country}}{\text{Relative price level in foreign country}} \times 100$$

$$= \frac{42}{45} \times \frac{1100/1000}{735/700} \times 100 = 97.78$$

The real exchange rate shows depreciation of 2.22%. This implies that the purchasing power of rupee has decreased by 2.22% from the year 2000 to the year 2005 as compared to US dollar; not same as 6.67% as indicated by nominal depreciation. Real exchange rate less than 100, that is, from the base year indicates real depreciation, whereas more than 100 implies real appreciation of domestic currency.

Need for Basket of Currencies for Nominal and Real Effective Exchange Rates

Normally people adjudge the economic performance of a nation by several economic and monetary factors. The exchange rate of domestic currency is one of the factors that provide some impression about the state of the economy with respect to external sector. Policy makers are also concerned about how the changes in the exchange rates impact domestic economy. The understanding of changes in the exchange rates provides useful clues about the cause of adverse balance of payment and helps decide the corrective measures.

Like an economy has to be viewed along several parameters and not one to make an objective assessment of its performance and causes, the appreciation or depreciation of the domestic currency with respect to several currencies rather than single foreign currency would be a truer measure of the strength of any economy or its external trade. The reason is simple. A nation trades with many nations and not with one. Therefore, the performance of the domestic currency and its impact must be measured (a) with respect to several currencies rather than one and (b) in the proportions of the trade with those countries. For example, if Britain trades only with European countries that use euro as their currency, the exchange rate of British pound with US dollar seems irrelevant. If Britain trades with Eurozone, Japan and the USA then the changes in the exchange rates of British pound with respect to euro, yen, and US dollar are important to the extent of the magnitude of trade with each nation/region.

Effective exchange rate is one such measure that helps find how the domestic currency fares with respect to all the nations with whom it trades. Effective exchange rate is the weighted average of the changes in the exchange rates from a base year set at 100. It is computed by Eq. 5-3 as follows:

$$\text{Effective Exchange Rate} = \sum_{1}^{n} w_i \times \frac{S_{0i}}{S_{1i}} \tag{5-3}$$

where

w_i is the proportion of trade in currency i, and

S_{0i} and S_{1i} are the exchange rates in the base year and now for currency i, respectively

When effective exchange rates used are nominal, then we get Nominal Effective Exchange Rate (NEER). A simple example would illustrate the computation of NEER. Assume that India has exports and imports from USA of ₹1,500 crore and ₹2,500 crore respectively. India also trades with Eurozone by exporting worth ₹3,500 crore and importing worth ₹2,500 crore. The aggregate trade is, therefore, ₹10,000 crore. The USA accounts for 40%, whereas Eurozone accounts for 60%. The exchange rate in the base year of 2000 assumed are ₹39/$ and ₹51/€, respectively. The price rise in India after 2000 was 15%, whereas that in the USA and Eurozone was 10% and 5%, respectively, as condensed in Table 5-5.

Table 5-5
Computation of NEER and REER

Country	Exports (₹ crore)	Imports (₹ crore)	% Share of Trade	Exchange Rate Now	Exchange Rate in the Base Year	Price Appreciation
USA	1,500	2,500	40%	₹44/$	₹39/$	10%
Eurozone	2,500	3,500	60%	₹56/€	₹51/€	5%

The NEER is the weighted average of the new exchange rate relative to the exchange rate of the base year. Rupee has depreciated by 11.36% and 8.92% against US dollar and euro, respectively. The combined effect is depreciation of rupee by 9.91% as computed here with NEER of 90.09.

$$\text{Nominal Effective Exchange Rate} = \left[\frac{39}{44} \times 0.4 + \frac{51}{56} \times 0.6\right] \times 100$$
$$= (0.3545 + 0.5464) \times 100 = 90.09$$

The Real Effective Exchange Rate (REER) would indicate the change in the exchange rate after accounting for the purchasing powers of the currencies involved. The indexed real exchange rate for US dollar is (39/44)(1.15/1.10) = 0.9266 or 92.66, and for euro is (51/56)(1.15/1.05) = 0.9974 or 99.74. This means that in real terms, rupee depreciated by 7.34% and 0.26% against US dollar and euro, respectively. Using real exchange rates for dollar and euro, REER is worked out below suggesting a real depreciation of 3.08% as against nominal depreciation of 9.91%:

$$\text{Real Effective Exchange Rate} = \left[\frac{39}{44} \times \frac{1.15}{1.10} \times 0.4 + \frac{51}{56} \times \frac{1.15}{1.05} \times 0.6\right] \times 100$$
$$= (0.3707 + 0.5985) \times 100 = 96.92$$

Nominal and Real Effective Exchange Rates in India The Reserve Bank of India (RBI) computes the indices of NEER and REER as indicators of external competitiveness of India. The NEER is the weighted average of bilateral nominal exchange rates of the home currency in terms of foreign currencies. Currency-wise imports and exports in % terms are given in Table 5-6, which establishes that most foreign trade in India is denominated in US dollars.

Table 5-6
Currency-wise Invoicing of India's Exports and Imports (%)

Name of Currency	Exports					Imports				
	2008–09	2009–10	2010–11	2011–12	2012–13	2008–09	2009–10	2010–11	2011–12	2012–13
Pounds Sterling	2.77	2.81	2.47	2.31	2.31	0.89	0.66	0.71	0.5	0.42
US Dollar	84.06	84.75	86.41	87.01	88.41	86.06	83.91	85.38	88.67	86.06
Japanese Yen	0.48	0.35	0.22	0.26	0.15	2.3	1.98	1.73	1.41	1.47
Euro	10.85	10.13	8.88	8.14	6.97	9.82	12.61	11.13	8.29	9.44
All Other Currencies	1.84	1.96	2.02	2.28	2.16	0.93	0.84	1.05	1.13	2.61

Source: Reserve Bank of India Press Release 2013-14/1329, 1 January 2014.

The RBI computes NEER and REER for two different baskets of currencies—against 6-currency basket and 36-currency basket. The six currencies are US dollar, euro, British pounds, Japanese yen, Chinese yuan, and Hong Kong dollar. The weights are assigned according to the volume of trade from the country and not as per the currency denominating the trade. For a base of 1993–94, the values of REER and NEER are shown in Table 5-7.

Table 5-7
Trends in External Value of Indian Rupee

	36-Currency Basket				6-Currency Basket			
	REER	% Variation	NEER	% Variation	REER	% Variation	NEER	% Variation
1993–94	100.00	0.0	100.00	0.0	100.00	0.0	100.00	0.0
1994–95	104.32	4.3	98.91	–1.1	105.71	5.7	96.86	–3.1
1995–96	98.19	–5.9	91.54	–7.5	101.14	–4.3	88.45	–8.7
1996–97	96.83	–1.4	89.27	–2.5	100.97	–0.2	86.73	–1.9
1997–98	100.77	4.1	92.04	3.1	104.24	3.2	87.80	1.2
1998–99	93.04	–7.7	89.05	–3.2	95.99	–7.9	77.37	–11.9
1999–00	95.99	3.2	91.02	2.2	97.52	1.6	77.04	–0.4
2000–01	100.09	4.3	92.12	1.2	102.64	5.3	77.30	0.3
2001–02	100.86	0.8	91.58	–0.6	102.49	–0.1	75.89	–1.8
2002–03	98.18	–2.7	89.12	–2.7	97.43	–4.9	71.09	–6.3
2003–04	99.56	1.4	87.14	–2.2	98.85	1.5	69.75	–1.9
2004–05	100.09	0.5	87.31	0.2	101.36	2.5	69.26	–0.7
2005–06	102.34	2.2	89.84	2.9	106.67	5.2	71.41	3.1
2006–07	98.07	–4.2	85.80	–4.5	104.91	–1.6	68.13	–4.6

(+) indicates appreciation and (–) indicates depreciation.
Note: Both REER and NEER are bilateral trade weight-based indices with 1993–94 as the base year.
Source: Reserve Bank of India.

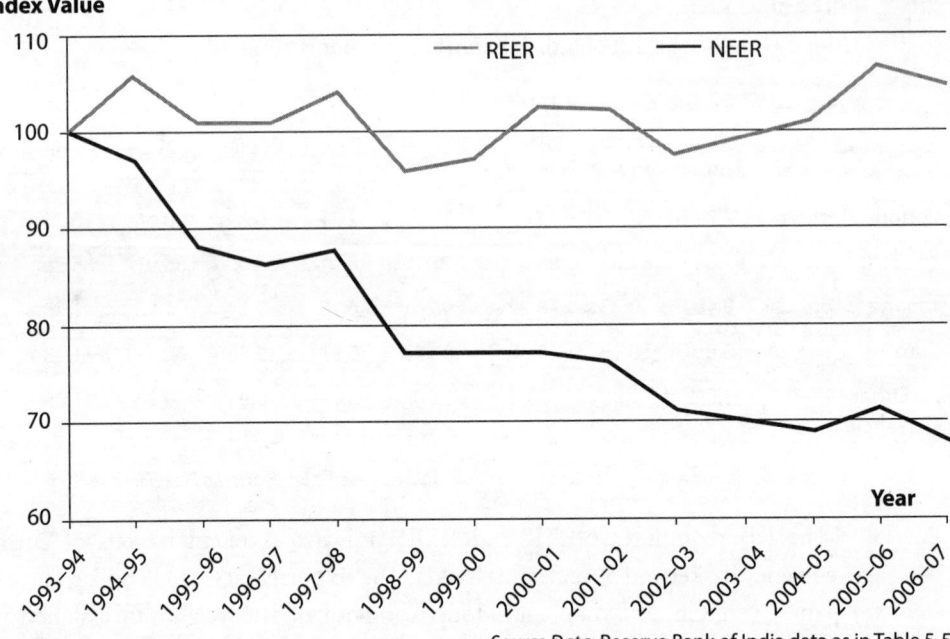

Figure 5-7
External Value of Indian Rupee (Base 1994–95)

Figure 5-7 depicts the value of Indian rupee compared to six currencies from 1993–94 to 2006–07. While in nominal terms the value of rupee has fallen to 68% of its value from the base year of 1993–94, it has appreciated marginally in real terms. This is due to higher inflation in India as compared to the region covered by six currencies. However, in real terms, the rupee is almost kept pace and in fact has appreciated by about 4.91%.

The base of calculation was revised in 2004–05 and reset at 100 to facilitate more recent comparison. The values of REER and NEER since 2004–05 are shown in Figure 5-8. Since 2004–05, Indian rupee has depreciated by about 35% in nominal terms, but in real terms the depreciation is only about 4%.

The relative performance of the various currencies in the Asian region for a 10-year period from 1995 to 2005 is condensed in Table 5-8. Note that in real terms, while Indian rupee has appreciated, currencies of other countries have depreciated during the 10-year period.

FOREIGN EXCHANGE MARKETS IN INDIA

Since independence in 1947 till about 1971, that is, in the era of the Bretton Wood system India followed par value system with rupee value pegged to 4.15 grains of gold with variations band of ±1% band and intervention currency as British pound. The intervention currency did not matter as British pound and US dollar had fixed exchange rate. Rupee was devalued to 2.88 grains of gold in September 1949 and to 1.83 grains in June 1966. Due to fixed exchange rate system, the foreign currency markets were practically non-existent.

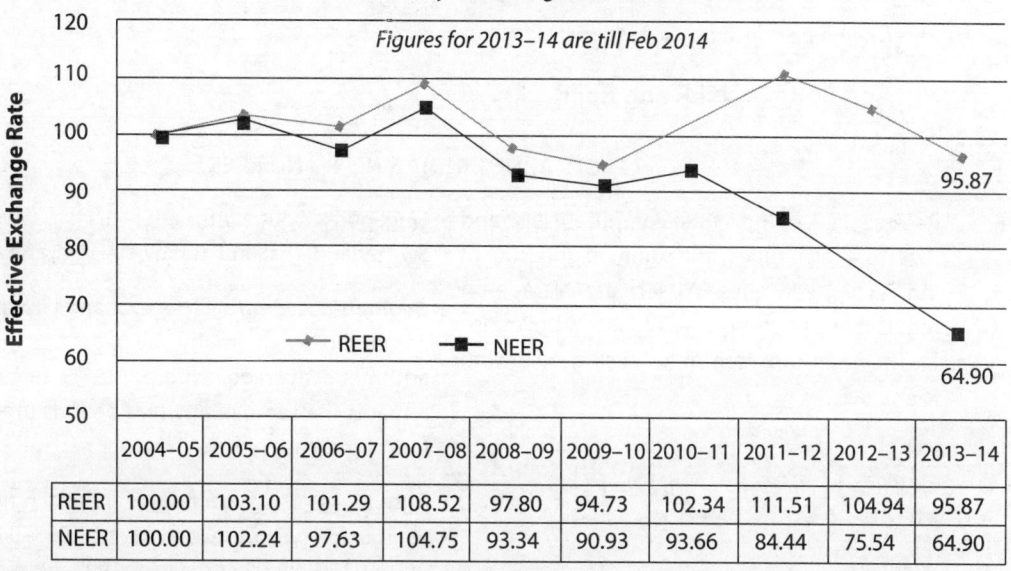

Figure 5-8

External Value of Indian Rupee (Base 1994–95)

Table 5-8
REER and NEER of Select Asian Countries (Base: 2000 = 100)

Country	1995	1997	2000	2001	2002	2003	2004	2005
REER								
China	84.7	100.4	100.0	104.3	101.9	95.2	92.7	92.5
India	101.7	103.0	100.0	100.9	96.9	96.6	98.4	103.7
Japan	108.2	85.3	100.0	89.0	83.0	83.6	84.5	79.4
Malaysia	122.7	122.6	100.0	104.9	105.0	99.2	94.9	95.2
Philippines	120.4	128.7	100.0	95.6	96.2	89.1	86.2	92.3
Singapore	106.2	110.2	100.0	100.5	97.9	94.3	93.3	92.1
NEER								
China	82.2	92.5	100.0	105.5	105.1	98.6	94.2	94.3
India	117.0	114.3	100.0	97.9	93.3	90.1	88.6	91.3
Japan	99.4	81.3	100.0	90.5	85.7	85.4	87.1	85.3
Malaysia	127.6	126.8	100.0	105.4	104.8	99.6	95.9	95.5
Philippines	145.8	142.5	100.0	90.9	89.7	81.3	75.7	76.9
Singapore	97.1	105.6	100.0	101.6	100.8	98.4	97.9	98.7

Note: Rise in index implies appreciation.
For India data pertain to 6 currency trade-based index.
Source: International Financial Statistics, IMF (2006) and Reserve Bank of India.

CONCEPTS IN PRACTICE
Nut and Bolts of NEER and REER

FEW FACTS ABOUT INDIA'S NEER AND REER

Reserve Bank of India (RBI) computes NEER and REER for Indian rupee, as a summary measure of India's competitiveness in international trade, on regular basis published in its monthly bulletins.

The rates are computed using following formulae:

$$NEER = \prod_{i}^{N} \left(\frac{S}{S_i}\right)^{w_i} \qquad REER = \prod_{1}^{N} \left[\frac{S}{S_i} \times \frac{P}{P_i}\right]^{w_i}$$

where

S = Exchange rate of Indian rupee in terms of numeraire, that is, SDR in index form expressed as number of rupees per SDR in index form

S_i = Exchange rate of foreign currency, i in terms of numeraire, that is, SDR in index form expressed as number of rupees per SDR in index form

W_i = Weight of Indian trade in currency i

P = Price index in India

P_i = Price index in currency i

Two Sets of Rates RBI calculates two sets of rates—for 6 currencies and for 36 currencies called 6-currency NEER and REER, and 36-currency NEER and REER.

Six currencies are US dollar, euro, British pound, Japanese yen, Chinese yuan, and Hong Kong dollar.

Thirty-six currencies belong to the regions of Argentina, Australia, Bangladesh, Brazil, Canada, China, Hong Kong, Denmark, Egypt, Euro, Indonesia, Iran, Israel, Japan, Kenya, Korea, Kuwait, Malaysia, Mexico, Myanmar, Nigeria, Pakistan, Philippines, Qatar, Russia, Saudi Arabia, Singapore, South Africa, Sri Lanka, Sweden, Switzerland, Thailand, Turkey, UAE, UK, and USA.

Geometric Average The exchange rates are computed as geometric average and not as arithmetic average, where the % difference remains the same in any two periods irrespective of the base period chosen.

Base Years Base year figures are benchmarked as 100 for two base periods of 1993–94 and 2003–04. While base year of 1993–94 remains fixed, the second base currently as 2003–04 is moving to reflect the latest trends in exchange rate movements by making comparison with relatively more recent data. The fixed base of 1993–94 is chosen due to radical and fundamental changes that took place in Indian economy and market structures in 1990–91 when Indian rupee exchange rate became market determined.

Numeraire The exchange rates use the numeraire of SDR in index form rather than a single currency. SDR is basket of currencies that smoothen the effects of the changes in exchange rate when compared with the changes in exchange rate with a single currency say US dollar. The changes with respect to a basket of currencies better reflects the competitive position of a currency.

Exchange rates are measured as indirect quotes, that is, number of units of SDR in index form per unit of currency, i. Hence an increase in exchange rate, S_i or ratio S/S_i reflects its appreciation and a decrease signifies depreciation.

Weights Weights of the currencies are decided on the basis of proportion of bilateral trade denominated in different currencies. The bilateral trade is the sum of exports and imports. The weights are not fixed but are 3-year moving averages to reflect the changes in the trade patterns with time in different nations. Weights are normalized as

$$\sum_{1}^{N} W_i = 1$$

Price Indices Price indices for computation of REER are on the basis of WPI for India and CPI for other currencies. Since WPI reflects producer's cost it is considered a more appropriate base for exports but CPI is considered a better indicator of imports.

After the collapse of the Bretton Wood system, Indian rupee was pegged to British pound till September 1975 when it decided to peg to a basket of currencies to have better understanding of the value of the domestic currency which could be misleading in case of pegging to single currency. The composition of basket remained undisclosed to prevent arbitrage and speculation.

In 1978, the foreign exchange markets made a small beginning when trading by banks in the currency markets were allowed by RBI with intra-day trading on 'near square' basis and daily limits on intra-day exposure and carrying overnight open positions, at banks' discretion. The RBI continued to advise buying and selling rates to bank while rupee remained pegged. The bid–ask spread was fixed at 0.5%. Till 1990, the markets remained regulated with thin trading and regulations gave rise to 'havala' markets.

The balance of payment position became precarious and it was soon realized that macroeconomic and structural changes were required to correct the same and regulating exchange rates was not a remedy. In 1992 as part of policy changes and in a move to transform the market from regulated regime to market-determined exchange rates India introduced dual-rate system in March 1992 when exporters were permitted to sell 60% in the open market while 40% needed to be surrendered at official rate. True to its purpose the exchange rate regime moved to unified rate when in a year's time in 1993 the compulsion of surrendering the 40% at official rate too was removed. This was an important step towards integrating the Indian foreign exchange markets to global factors.

RBI continued to take baby steps towards opening of foreign exchange markets by (a) allowing firms to hedge, (b) providing discretion to banks for intra-day exposures, (c) permitting cross currency positions, (d) only selective intervention, and (e) permitting positions in derivatives on fully covered basis.

The exchange rates during the period from 1994–95 till 2002–03 as depicted in Figure 5-9 indicate that since the unified market determined currency markets the value of Indian rupee consistently depreciated almost at a uniform rate reaching a value of about ₹49 in 2003–04 from ₹31.37 in 1994–95. This was perhaps due to the fact that RBI continuously pursued

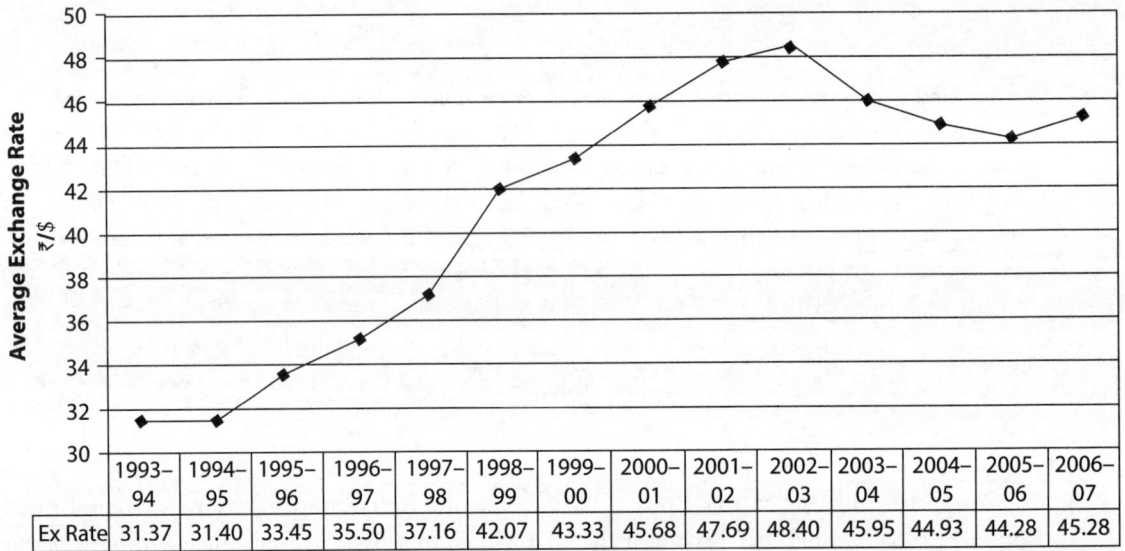

Source: Report on Currency and Finance (2009), Vol. III, Reserve Bank of India.

Figure 5-9
Trends in Exchange Rate of Indian Rupee

buying of US dollar letting local currency depreciate continuously for promoting exports concerned with the abysmal levels of reserve that it faced in 1992–93. Also during this period the volatility in the exchange rates was witnessed due to Asian currency crisis during 1997–98 demanding frequent interventions. Indian rupee came out relatively unaffected by the crisis due to several policy measures with timely interventions and capital flow controls imposed. The trend of Indian rupee for the period is exhibited in Figure 5-9 with steady depreciation till 2003–04. Unidirectional movement witnessed in the past indicates futility of the intervention by central bank in the foreign exchange markets providing a virtual insurance to the hedgers and speculators alike. Of course the intervention by central banks by buying or selling of currency is not free of cost.

After 2003–04, the exchange rate reversed its trend and it started seeing two-way sharp and large movements. Increased volatility is indicative of increased openness of the Indian economy and better alignment with the world events, lesser interventions, volatility of capital inflows, etc. The value of rupee against US dollar since 1993–94 is depicted in Figure 5-10 with its appreciation and depreciation.

Foreign exchange market in India has been growing at a phenomenal rate. Average daily turnover during 1997–98 stood at about US$5 billion. It rose to US$18 billion by 2005–06 with interbank markets forming about three-fourth of the turnover. The spot and derivatives have about the equal share of the trading. Some indicators of activity and structure of the market are presented in Table 5-9.

The foreign exchange markets currently stand at a turnover of more than US$55 billion per day estimated based on the turnover in the month of September 2012. The figures and

Foreign Exchange Rates and Markets **147**

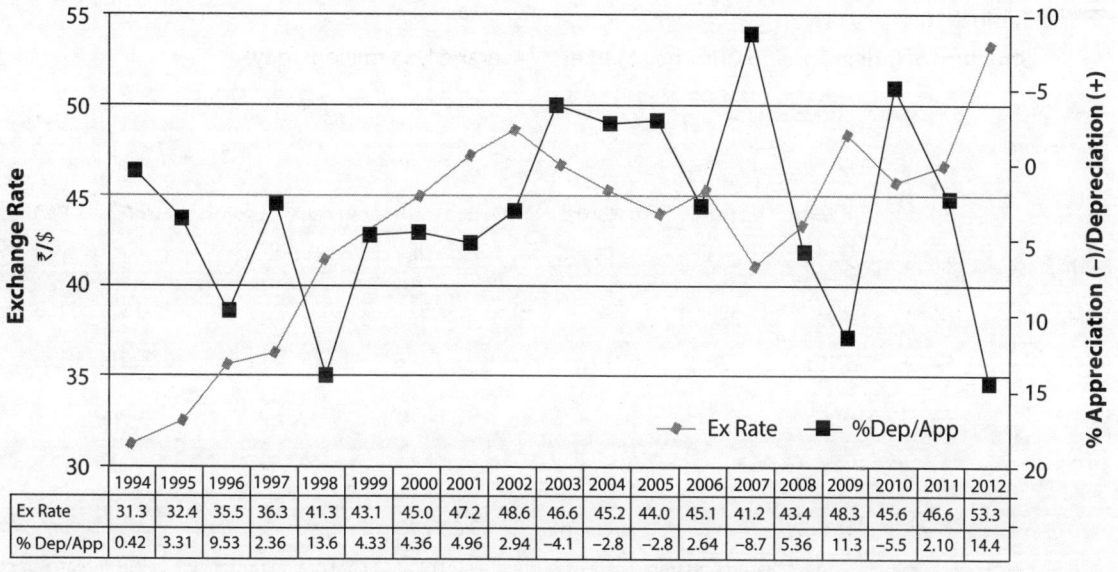

	1994	1995	1996	1997	1998	1999	2000	2001	2002	2003	2004	2005	2006	2007	2008	2009	2010	2011	2012
Ex Rate	31.3	32.4	35.5	36.3	41.3	43.1	45.0	47.2	48.6	46.6	45.2	44.0	45.1	41.2	43.4	48.3	45.6	46.6	53.3
% Dep/App	0.42	3.31	9.53	2.36	13.6	4.33	4.36	4.96	2.94	−4.1	−2.8	−2.8	2.64	−8.7	5.36	11.3	−5.5	2.10	14.4

Source: Report on Currency and Finance (2009), Vol. III, Reserve Bank of India.

Figure 5-10

External Value of Indian Rupee

its break-up in terms of (a) merchant and interbank markets, (b) spot and derivatives, and (c) with rupee (INR–FCY) and not involving rupee (FCY–FCY) are presented in Table 5-10 and depicted in Figure 5-11. Average daily turnover during 2012–13 was US$51.021 billion (RBI Bulletin Table 29, 10 February 2014). The growth in the trading has been about three times in the last five years. Though the volumes have increased considerably, the structure in terms of proportions of merchant and derivative turnover remain almost the same.

Table 5-9

Indicators of Indian Foreign Exchange Market Activity (US$ billion)

Item	1997–98	2005–06	2006–07
Total Annual Turnover	1,306	4,413	5,734
Average Daily Turnover	5	18	23
Average Daily Merchant Turnover	1	5	7
Average Daily Interbank Turnover	4	13	18
Interbank to Merchant Ratio	5.2	2.6	2.6
Spot/Total Turnover (%)	51.6	50.5	52.4
Forward/Total Turnover (%)	12.0	19.0	18.0
Swap/Total Turnover (%)	36.4	30.5	29.6

Source: Report on Currency and Finance (2005–06), Vol. III, Reserve Bank of India.

Table 5-10
Structure of Indian Foreign Currency Markets* (Average US$ millions/day)

	Merchant				Interbank					
	FCY–INR		FCY–FCY		FCY–INR			FCY–FCY		
	Spot	Forward	Spot	Forward	Spot	Swap	Forward	Spot	Swap	Forward
Purchase	2,836	2,578	437	917	7,291	7,601	787	4,007	1,484	160
Sale	2,583	2,617	299	802	7,170	7,525	788	4,030	1,512	168
	5,419	5,195	736	1,719	14,461	15,126	1,575	8,037	2,996	328
	10,614		2,455		31,163			11,362		
TOTAL	13,069				42,525					
	55,594									

*Based on sample data of September 2012   FCY: Foreign Currency   INR: Indian Rupee
Forward in the merchant segments includes cancellations
Source: Reserve Bank of India, December 2012.

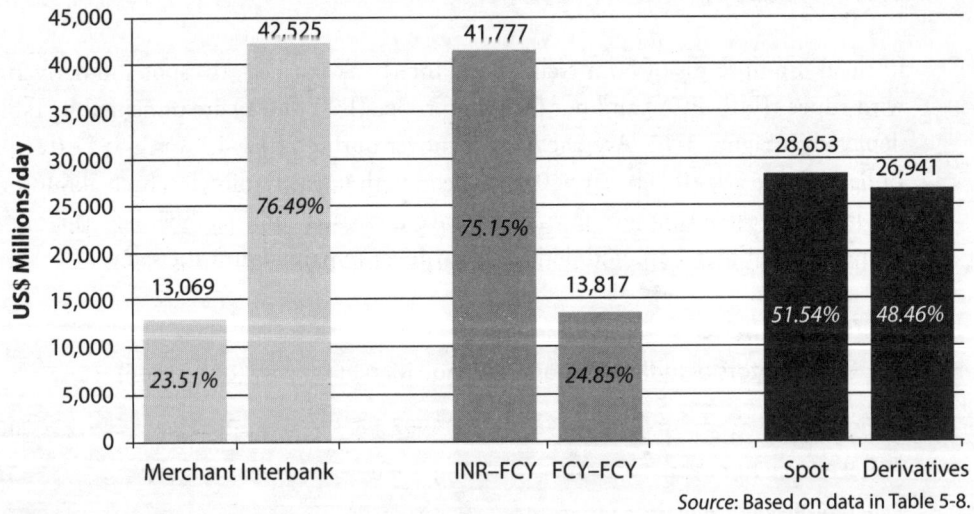

Figure 5-11
Structure of Indian Foreign Exchange Markets

Volumes in Derivatives The volumes in derivatives are comparable to those in the spot. Forwards contract, the basic derivative product, constitutes about 50% of the derivatives. In the past, we have seen that the exchange rate movement in India had been unidirectional for considerable period. The utility of forward contract is limited when the direction of change of exchange rate is more or less predictable. When spot rates are unpredictable, forward contract as hedging tool becomes extremely attractive. The volumes in the forward are constrained because for booking of forward contracts, the firms in India need to have an underlying trade transaction—perhaps unique to Indian foreign exchange markets. If there were to be no compulsions of having underlying exposures for booking, cancellations, and rebooking of forward contract the turnover in the derivatives segments would be much higher, as is the case in most developed and open market economies.

The other popular derivative product is swap primarily used in the interbank markets for managing currency risk. Options are virtually non-existent since firms in India are not permitted to write options and, therefore, limiting the depth and number of participants in the foreign exchange markets.

Despite rapid increase in trading activity in the foreign exchange markets in India, it constitutes a fraction (roughly ½%) of global trade. In future, we only expect to see increased activity and increased proportions in the world trade as India progresses towards greater integration with world markets, larger imports and exports, and fuller capital account convertibility.

SUMMARY

Beginning early 1970s, when the flexible exchange rate system came in vogue the foreign exchange markets have multiplied manifolds. Increased globalization, cut-throat competition, and volatility in the exchange rate since the dismantling of fixed exchange rate system have added to the need of understanding foreign exchange markets and the way exchange rates are quoted.

Foreign exchange markets are over-the-counter and operate round-the-clock. One of the major participants in the foreign exchange markets is the central bank that also exercises considerable influence, control, and regulatory powers on the policy matters related to the functioning of the foreign exchange markets. This is peculiar because normally policy makers are not the participants in the market. Major centres of foreign exchange are New York, London, Zurich, Tokyo, Hong Kong, Singapore, etc. Volumes both in the spot and derivative markets are rising.

There are several rates prevailing in the foreign exchange markets. The foreign exchange rates are a two-way quote—the bid rate for buying and the ask rate for selling the foreign currency. The difference between the two known as bid–ask spread is the profit for the bank. The convention in most parts of the world is to quote direct rates, that is, the number of units of home currency per unit of foreign currency. However, few nations notably Britain, follow indirect rates, that is, the number of units of foreign currency per unit of home currency. Foreign exchange market has two distinct tiers—a segment comprising banks only and another segment comprising banks and their customers. The rates quoted by the banks among themselves are called interbank rates, whereas those quoted by banks to their customers are merchant rates, which are derived from interbank rates. The market for every pair of currency is not deep enough. In such cases, the exchange rates are synthesized using a common currency called vehicle currency. These rates are also called cross rates.

Foreign exchange markets despite being OTC where the transactions are not in public domain are fairly efficient. Different dealers in different locations offer competitive arbitrage-free rates based on the stock of currencies available with them. The rates of different dealers are normally overlapping so as to eliminate the arbitrage opportunities.

The changes in exchange rates are normally associated with the performance of the economy. The performance measurement with respect to single currency is fallacious. Further the exchange rates must be adjusted for purchasing power of the currency. Nominal rates adjusted for purchasing power are called real rates. Therefore, exchange rate changes with respect to a basket of currencies in which a nation trades are measured. Such rates, called effective exchange rates, are computed on index basis. When nominal exchange rates are used, we get NEER and when real rates are used, we get REER.

Spot transaction in the foreign currency markets are settled in two business days. Foreign exchange transactions can also be settled in future. Such contracts are called forward contracts. Banks regularly offer whole months forward contracts. The forward rates are normally expressed as annualized % premium over spot rates.

In the interbank market, outright forward transactions are rare. Instead they enter swap transaction which consists of two legs. These two legs are opposite and equal. The swap transactions cost less than an equivalent combination of spot transaction followed by an opposite forward deal.

Forward contracts that are not exact date contract but instead provide a window of time for settlement are called option forwards. The option forward contracts are very expensive because they provide flexibility in the timing of settlement. They are offered by banks to the clients to overcome their inability to forecast exact timings of requirements of foreign exchange.

Merchant rates are of two types—one for undertaking pure exchange function called TT rates and the other for carrying out other banking functions called bill rates. Buying and selling bill rates are derived from interbank rates.

QUESTIONS

5-1 How do you compare foreign exchange markets with those of other financial assets?
5-2 Differentiate among hedgers, speculators, and arbitrageurs.
5-3 What do you understand by cross rates and vehicle currency? What is the necessity of having synthetic rates?
5-4 Differentiate between the following terms:
   (a) Bid rate and ask rate
   (b) Spot rate and forward rate
   (c) Direct rate and indirect rate
   (d) Interbank rate and merchant rate
5-5 Synthetic rate would always be more inefficient than market rate. Explain.
5-6 Differentiate between the following terms:
   (a) Nominal rate and real rate
   (b) Exchange rate and effective exchange rate
   (c) NEER and REER
5-7 Why should banks undertake swap transactions rather than spot followed by an opposite and equal outright forward contract?
5-8 What are option forwards and their uses?

PROBLEMS

5-1 Bid & Ask Rates

In Japan a bank has quoted the following rate for US dollar and euro:

US dollar	JY/US$	115.00 –	120.00
Euro	JY/€	160.00 –	170.00

Find out the following:
(a) At what rate would the bank sell US dollar?
(b) At what rate would the bank buy euro?
(c) An importer needs €1000. How much Japanese yen would he pay?
(d) An exporter has US$2000 to render to the bank. How much would the exporter get on Japanese yen?
(e) If the bank has to buy and sell one dollar, how much % profit can it make?
(f) If the bank has to buy and sell one euro, how much % profit can it make?

5-2 Direct & Indirect Rates

The following rates are direct rates:

		Bid	Ask
In Switzerland	CHF/US$	1.01	1.03
In Germany	Euro/US$	0.89	0.92
In Bangladesh	Taka/Euro	95.00	99.00
In South Africa	Rand/Pound	10.00	11.00
In Australia	Aus$/NZ$	0.90	1.00
In China	Chinese yuan/Euro	9.80	10.20
In Japan	Yen/Singapore $	75.00	81.00

Convert the rates into indirect rates.

5-3 Cross Rates

In Problem 5-2, what rate would you quote for (a) Taka/US$ (b) Yuan/CHF?

5-4 Arbitrage in Foreign Exchange Markets

The following rates are quoted by two dealers in New York and Sydney:

In New York	US$/Aus $	0.9050	0.9250
In Sydney	Aus$/US$	1.0100	1.0250

(a) Is there an arbitrage opportunity?
(b) If so, how do you execute the arbitrage?
(a) What is the amount of profit if a transaction of Australian $1 million is made?

5-5 Forward Premium/Discount

Consider the following rates of foreign exchange for euro:

Spot (₹ per €)	55.90	56.10
1-m forward (₹ per €)	57.50	57.80

(a) Find out whether the euro is at premium or discount.
(b) What is the annualized premium or discount for euro?
(c) Based on the answer to (b) what average (mid)-rate for 3-month, 6-month, and 12-month forward contracts are likely?

5-6 **Forward & Swap**

Consider the following rates of foreign exchange for British pound

Spot (₹ per £)	76.5000	77.2200
3-m Swap points	300/200	

(a) Find out whether the British pound is at premium or discount.
(b) What is 3-m forward quote?
(c) If a trader buys pound spot and sells 3-m forward as two independent contracts, what would be the applicable rates? In case of swap, what rates would be applicable for spot and forward legs?
(d) If a trader sells pound spot and buys 3-m forward as two independent contracts, what would be the applicable rates? In case of swap, what rates would be applicable for spot and forward legs?
(e) Compute profit/loss of the trader for outright and swap deals for (c) and (d).

Annexure A5-1

EURO CURRENCIES AND MARKETS

Euro currency is the currency held outside its home country. Thus, a US dollar deposit held outside the USA, say London or Paris, would be called Eurodollar. The currency can be in the form of an asset, that is, a deposit or a liability, that is, a debt. The first currency that came to be called a euro currency was US dollar and applied to a loan or deposit denominated in US dollar in a bank outside the USA. Originally applied to US dollar in Europe, the term has expanded its scope. Later it became applicable to all currencies being transacted outside their homeland. EuroCHF, eurosterling, and euroyen, therefore, would be a loan or deposit denominated in Swiss franc (CHF), pound sterling, and yen outside Switzerland, Britain, and Japan, respectively. With the advent of euro as a currency, a euro deposit or loan made in Hong Kong, Singapore, or Dubai would be confusingly termed as euroeuro. While terming a currency as euro currency, the location of the deposit or loan and not the ownership is of significance.

HISTORICAL BACKGROUND

It is important to understand why a currency should be deposited or loaned outside the homeland. The reasons are historic. Erstwhile Russia is credited with the evolution of Eurodollar. Soviet Union in the 1950s sold gold and other products to get US dollar to obtain grains from international markets. Moscow Narodny Bank, the central bank, needed to park these dollars for short term. Banks in the USA would willingly accept such deposits and provide some returns. However, Soviet Union was reluctant to park these dollars with US banks for fear of cold war between USA and Russia turning hot. During the Cold War period, especially after the invasion of Hungary in 1956, Soviet Union feared that its deposits in North American banks would be frozen as retaliation. Therefore, these dollars were kept in banks in Britain and France. On 28 February 1957, a sum of $800,000 was transferred to a French bank whose telex address was EUROBANK, creating the first eurodollars.[1] In order to provide some returns on these deposits, the banks in London and Paris would grant loans denominated in US dollars. Thus, both deposits and loans in US dollars originated outside the USA and a small market evolved.

GROWTH OF EURO DOLLAR

Though the birth of Eurodollar was due to political circumstances, the growth of the euro markets is largely attributed to the absence of regulation for such deposits and loans. Regulatory changes in the 1960s and 1970s coupled with large availability of US dollars outside the

---

[1] en.wikipedia.org accessed on 3 January 2011

USA since World War II as consequence of large BOP deficit of USA have contributed to the explosive growth of Eurodollars. These regulatory changes regarding interest rates, reserve requirements, and insurance were applicable to deposits and advances in the USA, whereas the dollars held outside even if with branches of the US banks outside the USA, these regulations were not applicable. The dollar outside USA escaped the jurisdiction of Federal Reserve. Since dollar held outside the USA was free from regulatory framework, the deposit and lending rates were purely governed by free market forces. These regulations were

Regulation Q In the 1960s and 1970s, the interest rates on deposits by US banks were subject to ceilings. Branches of US banks in London and other places outside of USA did not have to comply with these ceilings. Interest higher than ceiling could be paid on dollar deposits outside the USA. These dollars found its way back to the USA as loans.

Regulation M Like Cash Reserve Ratio in India, the Regulation M requires keeping of some reserve against dollar deposits with Federal Reserve. Until 1969, this regulation did not apply to deposits abroad. Complying with reserve requirement means deploying part of funds in non-earning assets. The regulation increased the cost of deposits which meant that loans in the USA would be more expensive than the ones lent outside it.

Premium on insuring dollars The deposits were subject to insurance for the depositors. The insurance premium on these deposits also added to the cost of funds. This again was not applicable to deposits held outside the USA, which could be without insurance.

Interest Equalization Tax in 1963 US government imposed a tax on foreign debt, which forced the US companies to pay more to foreign investors to attract investment, raising cost of borrowing.

Major implication of these regulations was the increasing cost of funds for the banks and hence the lending rates. Conversely, escaping the regulation meant the ability of banks to offer (a) higher rates to depositors and (b) lower interest rates to borrowers. Hence, the market for Eurodollars became extremely attractive for both sides of the balance sheet.

The supply of dollars outside the USA too was not a constraint as huge quantities were in circulation outside the USA due to (a) dollar being an international currency and (b) unwillingness of the USA to contain huge and persistent deficit in balance of payment. Growing international trade and presence of tax havens were other factors that provided impetus to growth of Eurodollars.

INSTRUMENTS OF EURO DOLLARS

The common instrument of Eurodollar deposits is a non-negotiable term deposit, or Certificate of Deposits (CDs): Negotiable deposits that are traded in secondary markets are more liquid and avoid penalty for premature withdrawal. The markets and instruments have become so popular that interest rate derivatives are also designed with Eurodollar deposits as an underlying asset.

Most regulations of Federal Reserve mentioned earlier were removed in the 1970s, but Eurodollar continued to grow. Persistent BOP deficit of the USA continued to increase the supply of dollars worldwide. This deficit was partly overcome by recycling of petro-dollars. These dollars were finally parked in banks outside the USA.

Regulations such as credit deposit ratio, deposit insurance, and reserve requirement have got cash impact on bank deposit rates and lendable resources and its pricing. Eurodollar market being free from major regulations having cash flow implications become more competitive as compared to the market dealing in dollars. Eurodollar deposits would attract higher deposit rates for a similar deposit in the USA in a US bank. Similarly, Eurodollar loans would be available at cheaper rate than the loans in dollars in the USA.

International Parity Conditions

LEARNING OBJECTIVES

This chapter aims at

- explaining the law of one price
- explaining absolute purchasing power parity (PPP) and the likely factors that cause distortion in it
- explaining relative PPP as a tool for forecasting exchange rate changes as differential of inflation rates
- explaining the difference between nominal and real exchange rates
- explaining Fisher effect and its implications for international capital flows
- explaining International Fisher Effect for understanding the relationship between interest rates and exchange rates
- explaining interest rate parity and the determination of forward rates
- forecasting exchange rates using various parity conditions

CONTENTS

Introduction
Law of One Price
Absolute Purchasing Power Parity
Relative Purchasing Power Parity
    Nominal and Real Exchange Rates
    Exchange Rate Pass-through
Fisher Effect
International Fisher Effect

Interest Rate Parity
    Covered Interest Arbitrage
    Forward Premium and Discount
    Interest Rate Parity with Transaction Costs
Reconciling Parities

INTRODUCTION

We have already discussed gold standard and its many variants including the Bretton Woods system describing how the exchange rates were determined in olden days. With fixed exchange rate systems almost vanished except for pegging and currency board arrangements, the determinants of exchange rates have become too diverse. Prior to 1976 when the Bretton Woods system ended, the exchange rates were changed periodically (not continuously) by authorities with a view to bring about the desired changes in the economy and balance of payments (BOPs). The focus was to examine the impact of exchange rate changes in the flow of capital across the world.

The situation stands changed today, from fixed rate to floating rate system where exchange rates for major currencies around the world are now determined by free forces of demand and supply of foreign currency. With the advent of floating exchange rate system, attention has turned to the understanding of the factors that influence the exchange rates. Several theories and studies have been advanced to understand the complex behaviour of exchange rates. Though exchange rates seem to have a direct bearing on BOP, they are intricately linked to other economic fundamentals, such as employment, growth, money supply, and interest rates.

Parameters describing an economy are interrelated with each other. Exchange rate links the domestic economy and the external economies. The interlinkages of these variables make the understanding of exchange rate behaviour complex. For managers in the multinational corporations, forecasting exchange rates is a primary and critical activity because it is a major input for decision-making. This necessitates the understanding of factors that determine and influence the exchange rate changes.

The preceding chapters have highlighted the dependence of exchange rates on many factors such as interest rates and price levels. The basic relationship of exchange rates with interest rates and price levels is discussed in this chapter. These relationships are commonly called international parity conditions. Interestingly, the application of these parity conditions leads to the same forecast of future exchange rates in a perfect world. It is important to realize how each economic parameter affects the exchange rates given that other determinants remain constant.

In real-life situations, using different parity conditions there may be variations in the forecast exchange rates because parity conditions become distorted in real world. In such situations, managerial discretion becomes important in determining what emphasis is to be placed on the specific parity condition. Therefore, it is imperative for the managers in multinational corporations to have a comprehensive view of these parity conditions with regard to their outcomes and underlying assumptions.

LAW OF ONE PRICE

An underlying principle that requires no elaboration is the law of one price. Any commodity or product cannot command two prices in two different markets. If so, one would buy in one market at lower price and sell in the other at higher price to derive profit. Buying pressure in the market with lower price would cause the value of the product to go up. Similarly, selling pressure in the market with higher price would drive its value down. The process continues till prices in both the markets become equal. The foreign exchange is also a commodity that has no back up tangible asset under flexible exchange rate system. Under gold standard of exchange rates we stated the law of one price as 'mint parity of gold' that governed the exchange rates of currencies because each currency was supported by equivalent amount of gold.

The important assumptions for the law of one price to hold are same as that of perfect markets. We must satisfy the conditions of free markets. In respect of foreign currency these would be (a) free trade across international markets, (b) absence of transportation costs from one market to the other implying that difference in prices can prevail in two markets to the extent of transportation cost, (c) absence of transaction costs, (d) absence of trade barriers such as tariffs, incentives for promotion of trade like subsidy of exports, and (e) no single nation to be strong enough to influence the exchange rates. Such practices are termed as frictions in the trade and are distortions in free markets. Subject to the absence of such frictions the law of one price holds.

ABSOLUTE PURCHASING POWER PARITY

From the 1700s to the 1970s, gold formed the basis of values of the currencies and, hence, exchange rates on the premise that gold must command one price across nations and their currencies. Today, gold is just like any other commodity since its demonetization in 1976 under Jamaica Agreement. However, arguably the principle of law of one price must still hold. The difference is that exchange rate determination is not governed by a single commodity like gold. It now comprises a basket of commodities, with gold being only one of them.

If one can form a basket of goods that represents common utility across nations and cultures, then the price of the basket of goods must be same around the world. In the international scenario, the value of the common basket of goods in two cross-border markets is linked by exchange rate. For example, if the price of the basket of goods is P_f in the USA, denominated in US dollar, and P_d in India, denominated in Indian rupees; then, for the value of the basket of goods to be equal in India and the USA, we must have $P_f \times S = P_d$ where S is the spot exchange rate in India as direct quote, that is, ₹/$.

The equality of value of the common basket of goods is known as purchasing power parity (PPP) in absolute form. According to PPP, the exchange rate of two currencies must be equal to the ratio of prices of the common basket of goods denominated in their respective currencies. The law of one price provides the basis for the determination of exchange rate, which may be stated as follows:

$$\text{Exchange Rate} = \frac{\text{Price of common basket of goods in domestic market, } P_d}{\text{Price of common basket of goods in foreign country, } P_f} \quad (6\text{-}1)$$

Here, exchange rate is stated in direct terms, that is, the number of units of home currency per unit of foreign currency. For example, if a basket of goods in India costs ₹4,500 and the same basket is priced at US$100 in the USA, then as per PPP the exchange rate that must prevail is ₹4,500/US$100 = ₹45.00. If the exchange rate is any different than ₹45/$, then the balance between the goods market and currency market would be disturbed. The balance would be restored by the process of arbitrage in goods. If the exchange rate were ₹46, then (a) one would buy the basket of goods in India at ₹4,500, (b) sell the same basket in the USA for US$100, and (c) convert dollars back to Indian rupees to get ₹4,600, making a profit of ₹100. Similarly, if the exchange rate were ₹44.00, then (a) one would buy the basket in the USA at US$100, (b) sell in India to realize ₹4,500, and (c) convert back to US dollar to obtain 4,500/44 = US$102.27 and profit by $2.27.

Exercise 6-1
Exchange Rates and PPP

Assume that economic conditions of France and Britain are almost the same and so are their social and cultural values. A basket of goods representing the same utility in both the countries is costing £1,200 in Britain and €1,800 in France.
(a) Find the exchange rate of two currencies according to PPP.
(b) If the actual exchange rate happens to be €1.40/£, which of the currency is overvalued and by how much?

Solution
(a) According to PPP, the exchange rate must be the ratio of the prices of the same basket of goods and, hence, £1,200 in Britain and €1,800 in France must be equal. Therefore,

$$\text{Exchange rate} = 1,800/1,200 = €1.50/£$$

(b) The actual rate is €1.40/£ as compared to PPP rate of 1.50. Hence, euro is overvalued and pound is undervalued. The overvaluation of euro is by 7.14% as given by

$$\text{Overvaluation (+)/Undervaluation (−)} = \frac{\text{PPP rate} - \text{Actual rate}}{\text{Actual rate}} \times 100 = \frac{1.50 - 1.40}{1.40} \times 100 = 7.14\%$$

One would immediately realize that the effectiveness or validity of PPP rests on the feasibility of arbitrage in goods. Without much debate, one can possibly reason out that arbitrage in goods across nations is impractical due to several apparent and real-life factors in the world. Some of the factors that apparently distort the PPP are described as follows.

Composition of Common Basket of Goods In order to measure the price level changes, all nations develop a basket of goods that represents the choice of products and their respective proportions. The changes in the prices of these goods are monitored to measure inflation over different periods of time. The baskets of goods representing consumers' preferences in different nations cannot be identical. For example, the proportion of vegetables in the composition of basket in a predominantly vegetarian nation like India would be larger as compared to that in

American and European societies. If so, different compositions of the basket cannot form the basis of exchange rate determination by PPP.

Identical Utility   The utility of goods is different in different countries. For example, clothing has different utilities in different nations. In hot and humid conditions, like the regions close to equator, the utility of woollen garments is almost nil, whereas for nations in temperate regions, woollens are almost a necessity. For PPP verification, not only the composition of basket must be identical but also the utility value must be the same.

Quality of Goods   Quality of goods is also one of the major issues because in each class of goods, there are huge varieties that are priced differently. Even if the utility of wheat as major staple diet is presumed to be identical across different regions, in the composition of the basket, the quality of wheat would be a major issue. In advanced countries, the quality requirement may be much more stringent than that in the developing nations. Advanced nations would be ready to pay a much higher price for the same product on account of quality differentials as can be seen from vastly different prices cars command for performing the same basic function of transportation from one place to another.

Styling   Marketing of products plays a very important role in segmenting the market, differentiating the basic functions, and devising newer products, and therefore the pricing of products but seems to serve the same basic need. For example, the food having same calorific value would be priced several times higher if consumed in a five-star hotel environment rather than a college canteen, apparently due to difference in styling rather than content.

Trade Barriers   Trade barriers cause hindrances in executing the arbitrage; the process that removes distortion in prices in different markets. In PPP, it is implied that free trade exists. Most countries in the world for their own different reasons impose a variety of trade restrictions. Tariff- and non-tariff-based trade barriers create price differentials. These trade barriers either result in raised prices or curtailed consumption. If arbitrage is constrained legally, politically, or economically, the law of one price cannot hold and the distortions in the prices across nations would prevail. The exchange rate would no more be governed by PPP.

Transportation, Inconvenience, and Cost   For executing the arbitrage and eliminating the price differential, goods need to be transported from one place to another. This may pose two kinds of problems—one concerning the logistics and the other concerning the cost. Besides, there could be substantial time loss in transportation, making perishable goods not subject to arbitrage. Bulky goods may be inconvenient to move from one place to another.

Non-tradable Goods   Another major problem with PPP is that it only considers goods that are tradable. The underlying concept is goods arbitrage. An economy is governed by prices of goods and services. Of the three sectors of the economy—that is, agriculture, manufacturing, and services—the proportion of services in the GDP is rising with time and the increasing emphasis on skills of human resources. Services being skill-based are not subject to arbitrage. Similarly, land, although a tangible asset, is also not subject to arbitrage. Determination of exchange rates would not only consider manufactured and agricultural products, but also include services. With increasing proportions of GDP coming from services such as consultancy, telecommunication, and software, it would be wrong to base the exchange rate determination only on the prices of manufactured and tradable goods.

Normally, price indices in different countries are used as proxy to the basket of goods. These price indices also include non-tradable goods. Since non-tradable goods are not subject to arbitrage, the empirical testing of PPP would pose problems. The PPP as a determinant of exchange rate would yield better results if price indices of only traded goods are used.

Time Lag in Changes Another reason that can cause distortion in PPP is that changes in the exchange rates and prices of goods do not happen in the same period and at the same speed. The changes in the exchange rates are rather instantaneous, large, and frequent. They possibly discount the likely future changes in the price levels. Foreign exchange markets being supple and proactive rather than reactive, there is a great likelihood of overreaction for anticipated changes. As compared to the foreign exchange markets, the changes in the price levels of physical goods are steady, mostly unidirectional and tardy. Physical goods market has its own inertia that reacts for changes rather slowly. As such, movements of prices in the goods market are likely to lag the changes in the exchange rates. Prices of goods are sticky in the short run, as most producers fear price rise for commercial considerations. At best, changes in the exchange rates can be leading indicators of the changes in the price levels and not vice versa, as postulated in PPP. Changes in prices are likely to lag the changes in the exchange rates. Hence, ascertaining the validity of PPP with change in prices of goods causing changes in the exchange rate is difficult to establish.

Other Factors Affecting Exchange Rates Besides prices of goods, the flow of foreign money has motives other than exploiting goods arbitrage. The changes in the exchange rates are also caused by changes in the interest rates, portfolio returns, etc. The process of arbitrage is easier to execute for financial assets rather than physical assets in the absence of logistic difficulties and with immediate realization of financial gains. Therefore, effect on exchange rates of factors other than prices of goods may be more pronounced.

One of the most popular and talked about studies to establish the validity of PPP is the Big Mac study done by *The Economist* since 1986 where the prices of McDonald's burger are observed at different locations around the world. The PPP would hold if it were valued same across all locations. The choice of McDonald's burger as a universal product with same taste, style, presentation, and environment with which it is served across the globe seems unmatched by any other product. Big Mac seems to represent a universal product with factors that cause distortions in PPP more likely to be absent.

CONCEPTS IN PRACTICE
Eating Purchasing Power Parity

BIG MAC: A COMMON BASKET OF GOODS

The Big Mac index was introduced in *The Economist* in September 1986 by Pam Woodall and is being published by the magazine annually since then. The index gave rise to the word *burgernomics*. As per *The Economist*, 'Burgernomics' is based on the theory of PPP; the notion that a dollar should buy the same amount in all countries. Thus, in the long run, the exchange rate between two countries should move towards the rate that equalizes the prices of an identical basket of goods and services in each country. Our 'basket' is a McDonald's Big Mac, which is produced in about 120 countries. The Big Mac PPP is the exchange rate that would mean hamburgers cost the same in America as abroad. Comparing actual exchange rates with PPPs indicates whether a currency is undervalued or overvalued.

The UBS Wealth Management Research has expanded the idea of the Big Mac index to include the amount of time that an average worker in a given country must work to earn enough to buy a Big Mac. The working-time-based Big Mac index might give a more realistic view of the purchasing power of the average worker, as it takes into account more factors, such as local wages. In the Big Mac index, the basket in question is a single Big Mac burger as sold by the McDonald's fast food restaurant chain.

The Big Mac was chosen because it is available to a common specification in many countries around the world as local McDonald's franchisees at least in theory have significant responsibility for negotiating input prices. For these reasons, the index enables a comparison between many countries' currencies.

The Big Mac PPP exchange rate between two countries is obtained by dividing the price of a Big Mac in one country (in its currency) by the price of a Big Mac in another country (in its currency). This value is then compared with the actual exchange rate; if it is lower, then the first currency is undervalued (according to PPP theory) compared with the second, and conversely, if it is higher, then the first currency is overvalued. For example, using figures in July 2008

1. The price of a Big Mac was $3.57 in the United States (Varies by store)
2. The price of a Big Mac was £2.29 in the United Kingdom (Britain) (Varies by region)
3. The implied PPP was $1.56 to £1, that is $3.57/£2.29 = 1.56
4. This compares with an actual exchange rate of $2.00 to £1 at the time
5. The per cent differential in the price is [(1.56 − 2.00)/2.00]*100 = −22%
6. British pound was thus overvalued against the dollar by 22%

The burger methodology has limitations in its estimates of the PPP. In many countries, eating at international fast-food chain restaurants such as McDonald's is relatively expensive in comparison to eating at a local restaurant and the demand for Big Macs is not as large in countries like India as it is in the United States. Social status of eating at fast food restaurants like McDonald's in a local market, what proportion of sales might be to expatriates, local taxes, levels of competition, and import duties on selected items may not be representative of the country's economy as a whole.

Source: Based on *The Economist* and www.wikipedia.com, accessed on 25 October 2010.

RELATIVE PURCHASING POWER PARITY

According to the absolute version of PPP, the exchange rate of the two currencies must be equal to the ratio of prices of the common basket of goods. For several reasons, as discussed in the preceding section, this is more likely to be untrue than true. Does this imply that PPP is of no value in forecasting the exchange rates? No, it still can be used fruitfully in forecasting exchange rate changes. For illustrative purposes, let us assume that the common basket of goods in India and the USA cost ₹5,000 and US$100, respectively. As per absolute PPP the exchange rate should be ₹50/$. Further assume that the actual exchange rate is ₹45 defying absolute PPP.

The distortion in the PPP could be on account of any of the factors that are already discussed in the previous section. However, as managers in the multinational corporation, the focus is not as much on the true or fair values of currencies as much is on the direction and magnitude of changes in the exchange rates. Given that the exchange rate is ₹45.00 today, the issue of critical importance for finance function is to know where the rupee–dollar exchange rate is headed to, from its current value. Knowing the direction and quantum of change would help the manager plan for the cash flows better and make strategic decisions such as costing, pricing, and hedging in the international trade.

Now we focus on the likely changes in the exchange rates rather than on its absolute value. Continuing with the same basket of goods, assume that inflation rates in India and the USA are 10% and 5%, respectively. This implies the basket of goods after a year in India would cost ₹5,500, whereas in the USA it would be $105. Now as per PPP the exchange rate should be 5,500/105 = ₹52.38/$. Given the distortion in the pricing of currency in the beginning of the year would it be right to assume that changes according to the PPP would get transferred to the actual exchange rate? What appears reasonable is that if the PPP was distorted initially for whatever reasons, the same reasons continue from one period to another as these factors seem to be of permanent nature. Even if the causes of distortions in true value were to vanish, it would happen too slowly.

To generalize what is just stated, let us assume at time period $t = 0$ the price levels in domestic economy, India, and foreign economy, USA, are P_0^d and P_0^f. Hence, the exchange rate as per PPP, S_0 at $t = 0$ is

$$\text{Spot Exchange Rate (₹/\$) } S_0 = \frac{\text{Price of basket of goods in India}}{\text{Price of same basket of goods in USA}} = \frac{P_0^d}{P_0^f}$$

These price levels change by the amount of inflation in period $t = 1$ to P_1^d and P_1^f, respectively. If domestic and foreign inflation rates are I_d and I_f, respectively, then the exchange rate again according to PPP in period 1, S_1 would be as follows:

$$\text{Spot Exchange Rate (₹/\$) } S_1 = \frac{\text{Price of basket of goods in India in Period 1}}{\text{Price of same basket of goods in USA in Period 1}} = \frac{P_1^d}{P_1^f} = \frac{P_0^d(1+I_d)}{P_0^f(1+I_f)} \quad (6\text{-}2)$$

We know that both S_0 and S_1 as per PPP are not likely to be correct. Therefore, we do not use PPP as a predictor of exchange rate but rather focus on the change of spot rate in period 1,

S_1 from the exchange rate in period 0, S_0. This may be done as follows:

$$\text{Spot Exchange Rate (₹/\$) } S_1 = \frac{P_1^d}{P_1^f} = \frac{P_0^d(1+I_d)}{P_0^f(1+I_f)} = S_0 \frac{(1+I_d)}{(1+I_f)}$$

$$\frac{S_1}{S_0} = \frac{(1+I_d)}{(1+I_f)}$$

$$\text{Or} \quad \frac{S_1 - S_0}{S_0} = \frac{\Delta S}{S_0} = \frac{(I_d - I_f)}{(1+I_f)} \tag{6-3}$$

Even though the PPP as given in Eq. 6-1 may not hold, Eq. 6-3 may still hold because if factors distorting PPP remain same during the period they would annul each other in a ratio, even though the absolute values are distorted. It implies that even though spot exchange rate cannot be forecast on the basis of PPP, but it can still form the basis for forecasting the changes in the spot exchange rates. Equation 6-3 is referred to as *relative purchasing power parity (Relative PPP)*.

Exercise 6-2
Forecasting Changes in Exchange Rates with Relative PPP

The actual exchange rate of €1.40/£ in Exercise 6-1 does not conform to PPP. Assume that the distortion leading to disparity in the actual and PPP exchange rate would continue and the expected inflation rates in Eurozone and Britain are 3% and 5%, respectively. Based on the actual exchange rate as of now
(a) Which of the currency is likely to depreciate?
(b) What would be the magnitude of depreciation?
(c) What is the likely exchange rate after (a) 6 months, (b) 1 year, and (c) 2 years if the inflation rates remain same?

Solution
(a) Since inflation rate in Britain is higher, pound would depreciate and euro would appreciate.
(b) The extent of depreciation for British pound would be approximately 2% annually being the differential of inflation rates in Britain and Eurozone.
(c) The likely spot exchange rates after 6 months, 1 year, and 2 years can be found using Eq. 6-5 as follows

After 6 months $\quad S_{1/2} = S_0 \left(\frac{1+I_d}{1+I_f}\right)^{1/2} = 1.40 \times \left(\frac{1.03}{1.05}\right)^{1/2} = €1.3867/£$

After 1 year $\quad S_1 = S_0 \left(\frac{1+I_d}{1+I_f}\right) = 1.40 \times \left(\frac{1.03}{1.05}\right) = €1.3733/£$

After 2 years $\quad S_2 = S_0 \left(\frac{1+I_d}{1+I_f}\right)^2 = 1.40 \times \left(\frac{1.03}{1.05}\right)^2 = €1.3478/£$

If the foreign inflation rate is assumed low so that $1 + I_f \approx 1$, then relative PPP means that the percent change in the spot exchange rate, $\Delta S/S_0$ is approximately equal to the differential in the inflation rates of two countries, that is,

$$\frac{\Delta S}{S_0} \approx (I_d - I_f) \qquad (6\text{-}4)$$

It is worth noting that in forecasting the changes in the exchange rates, we only need the inflation differential of the countries. The currency that has higher inflation would depreciate. The amount of depreciation would be equal to the excess of inflation over the currency with smaller inflation rate. Hence, if inflation rate in India and the USA were 10% and 5%, Indian rupee must depreciate by about 5% (5/1.05 to be exact) annually.

If inflation rates are expressed in annual terms and time period is also specified in terms of years, then Eq. 6-3 can be modified as

$$\frac{S_1}{S_0} = \left[\frac{(1+I_d)}{(1+I_f)}\right]^t \qquad (6\text{-}5)$$

Nominal and Real Exchange Rates

Attached with the theory of PPP is the concept of real and nominal exchange rates, as discussed in the previous chapter.

We know from relative PPP that currency with higher inflation rate must depreciate, whereas that with lower inflation rate must appreciate. If currency depreciates exactly to the extent of inflation differential, it implies that the purchasing power of the foreign currency in the local market has remained intact over the period with respect to another. For example, assume that spot exchange rate of US dollar at the beginning of the year is ₹42. The inflation rates are 15% and 5% in India and the USA, respectively. Then as per relative PPP the Indian rupee must depreciate by 9.52% (10/1.05) to ₹46.00/$ by the end of the year. If indeed this is the actual rate at the year end, then a dollar converted to Indian rupee would buy the same amount of goods in India as it would buy in the USA.

In India if the price of a product is ₹42.00 in the beginning it would become ₹48.30 (42 × 1.15) by year end. Similarly, goods costing US$1 in the USA in the beginning of the year would be available at $1.05 by the year end. If $1.05 is exchanged to Indian rupee and used for buying products in India at the year end, then it would buy goods worth ₹48.30 (1.05 × 46.00). Hence, if the exchange rate moved as per PPP, there would be no erosion of purchasing power of any of the currency.

In nominal terms rupee has depreciated from ₹42/$ to ₹46/$. However, there is no erosion in the value of either of the currencies, that is, rupee or dollar despite depreciation of rupee. Therefore, real rate has not changed. If rupee depreciated beyond ₹46/$, the purchasing power of rupee would be eroded as compared to dollar but if the exchange rate is less than ₹46, then the value of dollar would be eroded as compared to rupee.

Nominal rates adjusted for the purchasing power would signify the real change in exchange rate. Inflation adjusted exchange rates are real exchange rates. To measure changes in the real exchange rate, we need to have a base year in which we assume that nominal rate and real rates are equal. From the base year changes in nominal exchange rates are measured by adjusting for inflation rates/purchasing power. Real exchange rate S' is given by Eq. 6-6 where S is the nominal exchange rate and I_f and I_d are the inflation rates of foreign country and home country, respectively.

$$S' = S \frac{(1+I_f)}{(1+I_d)} \quad (6\text{-}6)$$

For finding the changes in the real rates, we assume that in the base year, real and nominal rates are identical at S_0. Then the change in real exchange rate is given by Eq. 6-7.

$$\text{Change in real exchange rate} = \frac{S' - S_0}{S_0} \quad (6\text{-}7)$$

For example, the exchange rate of US dollar was ₹35 in the year 2000 and it changed to ₹45 in the year 2010. The increase in prices in India and the USA during the period of 10 years was 50% and 20%, respectively, then the real exchange rate in the year 2010 is

$$S' = S \frac{(1+I_f)}{(1+I_d)} = 45 \times \frac{1.2}{1.5} = ₹36.00/\$$$

Therefore, change in the real value of Indian rupee is

$$\text{Change in real exchange rate} = \frac{36-35}{35} = 0.0286 \equiv 2.86\%$$

This can also be calculated by deviation of the actual rate from PPP rate of ₹43.75/$ (35 × 1.5/1.2) as follows:

Overvaluation (−) / Undervaluation (+)

$$= \frac{\text{Actual rate} - \text{PPP rate}}{\text{PPP rate}} \times 100 = \frac{45.00 - 43.75}{43.75} \times 100 = 2.86\%$$

According to PPP, the rupee should have depreciated to ₹43.75/$. Had the nominal rate been ₹43.75/$, there would have been no erosion in the value of rupee. The nominal exchange rate of ₹45/$ indicates that rupee depreciated by 2.86% in real terms, as against 28.57% [(45 − 35)/35] in nominal terms.

Changes in real exchange rates are more meaningful in determining the competitive position of a nation in the world. Nominal change in accordance with the differential of inflation rates is not regarded as dangerous to the economy in terms of its international competitive position, though higher inflation is undesirable for domestic economy. A real depreciation of domestic currency increases export competitiveness of the host nation, whereas real appreciation is damaging to exports, and BOP. Real depreciation would lead to the creation of an employment in an economy that is not at full employment. In determining the relative competitive position, the changes in real exchange rates depict a truer view than the changes in nominal exchange rates.

To illustrate, how export competitiveness improves with real depreciation, let us consider an example of an Indian exporter who makes a supply to German customer worth €100. With a cost of ₹4,000 and revenue of ₹6,000 at the current exchange rate of ₹60/€ (Period 0), the current profit is ₹2,000. With assumed inflation rates of 20% and 10%, respectively, in India and Germany, Indian rupee must depreciate to ₹65.45 in nominal terms.

Depreciation beyond ₹65.45 after one year would improve the competitive position of the Indian exporter because with inflation rate of 10% in Germany, the buyer must be indifferent to pay €110 for the exports from India as prices of all local goods have gone up by 10%. At the same time, the costs of Indian exporter have gone up by 20% to ₹4,800 from ₹4,000. The profit of exporter is now dependent upon what the exchange rate of euro is after one year. Assume three scenarios:

(a) Rupee deteriorates more than what the relative PPP predicts, say to ₹68/€.
(b) Rupee deteriorates exactly as per relative PPP, say to ₹65.45/€.
(c) Rupee does not deteriorate as much as the relative PPP warrants, say to ₹62/€.

These three scenarios are tabulated in Table 6-1. If rupee deteriorates to ₹68, that is, beyond PPP rate the profit of exporter would be ₹2,680, and in real terms of the previous year it is in ₹2,233 (2,680/1.2). To be equivalent in real terms, the exporter needs a profit of ₹2,400. Therefore, the price can be made €105.88 rather than €110 to remain unaffected. Thus, the Indian exporter can compete more effectively with the price of €105.88.

If the nominal rate changes to ₹65.45 the exporter needs to price the goods at €110 to derive same profits. The competitive position remains unaffected.

In case the nominal exchange rate moves to ₹62, that is, rupee appreciates in real terms, the competitive position would deteriorate because the exporter needs to charge a price of €116. 13, that is, in excess of €110 to have the same level of profit as that before the exchange rate changed.

Table 6-1
Competitive Position and Real Exchange Rate (₹)

	Rupee Depreciates Excessively beyond PPP	Rupee Depreciates Normally as per PPP	Rupee does not Depreciate as much as PPP Rate
Nominal Exchange Rate (₹/€)	68.00	65.45	62.00
Sales Realization of €110	7,480	7,200	6,820
Cost	4,800	4,800	4,800
Profit	2,680	2,400	2,020
Profit in Terms of Period 0 Prices	2,233	2,000	1,683
Competitive Position	Improves	Remains same	Deteriorates
Real Exchange Rate (₹/€)	64.17	60.00	56.83
New Price in Euro to Maintain the Same Profit	105.88	110.00	116.13

Exchange Rate Pass-through

Exchange rate pass-through is the trade response in terms of prices as a result of change in the exchange rates. If all the changes in the exchange rates are passed on from the seller to the buyer by suitably adjusting the price, then the exchange rate pass-through is complete. For example, an Indian exporter supplies goods worth ₹6,000 at €100. If rupee appreciates by 10% against euro from ₹60 to ₹54, then the equivalent price must also rise by 10%. However, if the Indian exporter decides to raise the price from €100 to €105, then only 5% of the rise has been passed on to the customer whereas the remaining has been absorbed by the Indian exporter. The exchange rate pass-through is partial. On the contrary, if the price is raised to €115 in response to the same change in the exchange rate, the supplier has benefitted at the expense of the customer.

The exchange rate pass-through is dependent upon the relative positions of the exporter and importer, and elasticity of demand. Exchange rate pass-through is seldom complete and it results in distortions in the PPP theory. Due to partial exchange rate pass-through, the empirical testing of PPP is constrained.

CONCEPTS IN PRACTICE
Exchange Rate Pass-through

RESERVE BANK'S VIEW ON PASS-THROUGH

The general argument is that lower average inflation and its volatility was an outcome of credible monetary policy. In such an environment, firms believe that monetary policy will be successful in stabilizing prices and are less keen to alter prices of their products resulting in lower pass-through.

The impact of exchange rate volatility on pass-through is less unambiguous. One view is that currencies of countries with lower exchange rate variability imply a stable monetary policy, and consequently, would be chosen as the invoice currency. Hence, the pass-through would be lower. The counter view is that greater exchange rate volatility implies common and transitory fluctuation, and makes firms wary of changing prices as they fear losing market share. Firms are therefore more willing to adjust profit margins. Increasing share of trade in GDP by increasing the share of imports in consumption and the participation of foreign firms in domestic economy would lead to higher pass-through. Pass-through to imports such as energy, raw materials, and food with inelastic and less competitive supply is found to be higher than that to manufactured products, the supply of which is elastic and more competitive. Thus, change in import composition would affect the aggregate pass-through even when the pass-through in individual components remains the same.

Trade barriers such as tariffs and quantitative restrictions act as a barrier to arbitrage of goods between countries and have a negative impact on pass-through. Reducing these barriers would, thus, lead to higher pass-through. These factors underwent significant transformations in the early 1990s with economic reforms. Thus, exchange rate pass-through to domestic prices in India would have undergone a change during the post-economic reforms as found in other countries.

A recent study for the period August 1991 to March 2005 that estimated the pass-through coefficients found that a 10% change in exchange rate leads to change in final prices by about 0.6% in short run and 0.9% in the long run. The statistical tests on temporal behaviour of pass-through obtained from rolling regressions show that, unlike in case of many countries, there was no evidence of decline in pass-through. This was much more evident in the long run than in the short run and was observed to be the result of rise in inflation persistence.

Further, pass-through from appreciation was also found to be higher than that from depreciation. In an increasingly open economy where foreign firms' objective would expectedly be to capture a larger market share, they would be more willing to pass on the benefit of lower prices from appreciation and avoid passing on the higher prices from depreciation that cause loss of market share. The pass-through was higher for small exchange rate changes than large exchange rate changes. This could be explained by the invoicing of imports in India in US dollars (80%–90%) and the presence of menu cost in changing invoice price. For small exchange rate change, it is not worthwhile to change the invoice price of imports in its own currency due to the menu cost (a fixed cost involved in altering invoice price).

Thus, the import price in local currency (domestic prices) would change by the extent of the exchange rate change, that is, a higher pass-through. The opposite will be the case for large exchange rate change, as it would be worthwhile for foreign firms to change the invoice price in their currency in order to absorb a part of the exchange rate change on import price in local currency. Invoicing pattern of trade, exchange rate movements and exchange rate pass-through to domestic prices, thus, have implications for exchange rate management and trade competitiveness.

Source: Khundrakpam, J.K. (2007), 'Economic Reforms and Exchange Rate Pass-through to Domestic Prices in India', *BIS Working Paper No. 225*, as published in *RBI Report on Currency and Finance*, 31 May.

Exercise 6-3
Nominal and Real Exchange Rates

Assume that exchange rate of British pound in India in 1990 was ₹45.00/£ and in 2005 the same was quoted as ₹65.00/£. The price levels during the 15-year period increased by 75% and 50% in India and Britain, respectively. Assuming 1990 as the base year, what is the real appreciation/depreciation of Indian rupee in 2005?

Solution
In the nominal terms the depreciation of Indian rupee is $\frac{S_1}{S_0} - 1 = \frac{65}{45} - 1 = 1.44 \equiv 144\%$

As per the PPP the exchange rate for pound in 2005 must be $S_1 = 45 \dfrac{1.75}{1.50} = ₹52.50$

The real depreciation of rupee is

Real depreciation (+)/Appreciation (−)

$= \dfrac{\text{Actual rate} - \text{PPP rate}}{\text{PPP rate}} \times 100 = \dfrac{65.00 - 52.50}{52.50} \times 100 = 23.81\%$

FISHER EFFECT

Named after economist Irving Fisher, the concept of real rates is extended to investment. According to Fisher, the investment behaviour is guided by real returns rather than nominal returns. One of the motives for making an investment is the hope for better reward for deferring consumption. By making investment one foregoes current consumption to have enhanced consumption in future. One would prefer to invest now only when matured investment results in better consumption value later.

For example, consider that a bank deposit offers a return of 8%. Does it mean that the investor would be better off by 8%? If the inflation rate in the economy is 5%, then of the 8% gain 5% is eroded due to inflation and increased future consumption would be close to 3%. Fisher effect implies that investors look for returns that cover the inflation as well as provide some desired real return. If inflation rate were 10% and nominal returns were 8%, there is no incentive to invest because the investor would be poorer by investing. The investor would consume the wealth now rather than save and invest. The real return is the true increase in wealth by investing. The relationship of real returns, nominal return, and inflation rate is given as Eq. 6-8 as

$$1 + r = (1 + I) \times (1 + a) \qquad (6\text{-}8)$$

where r and a are nominal and real rates of return, and I is the inflation rate.

In case the inflation rates are low, the product term of $a \times I$ can be ignored Eq. 6-8 can be approximated as Eq. 6-9:

$$r \approx I + a \qquad \text{or} \qquad a \approx r - I \qquad (6\text{-}9)$$

The concept of real returns is extended to international investing. The implication of Fisher effect is that international investing is guided by real returns and not nominal returns. For example, consider nominal rates of return in India and Mexico as 10% and 15% respectively. For an American or European investor Mexico appears a more favourable destination for investment rather than India as it offers 5% extra returns in nominal terms. Wrongly so, such a decision based on nominal returns ignores the inflation rates in the two nations. If the inflation rates in India and Mexico are 4% and 12%, respectively, the real gains would approximately be 6% in India and 3% in Mexico. That must reverse the decision and capital flows must be directed towards India rather than to Mexico for investment.

The other implication of Fisher effect is that how international investing would restore the balance. Assume that foreign investment is made in bonds in the two countries, and inflation rates are not affected by foreign capital flows. Increased inflows in India would raise the prices of bonds, bringing down the nominal returns, whereas in Mexico the relative dearth of investing capital would reduce prices of bonds increasing nominal returns. Assuming inflation remains unaffected by foreign capital flows, the real return in India would fall and that of Mexico would increase. The process on international capital flow would continue till the time real rates of return in the two nations become equal. Therefore, under steady conditions, real rates of return across the world would equalize. So, international flow of capital would tend to equalize real rates of return across nations.

Another important conclusion of Fisher effect is that varying nominal returns in different nations is not a sign of instability but can be persisting, assuming that interest rates are guided by much larger macroeconomic factors, of which foreign flow of capital is one.

Fisher effect also throws light on the effectiveness of monetary policy for attracting foreign capital. Several developing countries tend to raise the nominal rates of interest to attract foreign capital. The need for doing so automatically arises because most developing nations face current account deficit in the BOP. This deficit needs to be funded by capital account surplus and, hence, the need to raise the interest rates. Fisher effect reveals that the foreign capital could also be attracted by attempting to control inflation rates. It would have the same but more lasting impact on the economy. Such an approach would be beneficial in the longer term. Since most politicians and economists realize difficulties in controlling inflation rates, the easier route of changing the nominal interest rates is preferred. In addition, managing inflation rates is a longer term uncertain phenomena, whereas interest rate changes are easily manipulated, perceived, and have immediate impact.

The applicability of the Fisher effect is constrained by the psychological preference of investors to favour domestic investment. Foreign investors despite higher returns in another country may not invest for reasons of political risk or non-sustainability of high nominal returns attached with high inflation rates. Nations with high rates of inflation and high nominal interest rates are viewed risky destinations. Besides the domestic investors, politicians and economists alike are skeptical of foreign investment as they are regarded as volatile. Hence, most developing countries exercise some form of capital controls. Further, capital flows for investment in financial assets are usually regarded as detrimental to exports, considered as engine of growth, as these capital flows based on returns cause local currency to appreciate.

INTERNATIONAL FISHER EFFECT

From the Fisher effect the relationship between the inflation rate and interest rate is evident. It is normally seen that countries that have high inflation rates also have high nominal interest rates in order to provide positive real returns. According to Fisher effect the nominal interest rates in any country must compensate for the anticipated inflation and desired returns. If real rates of returns are equalized across world then interest rates must keep pace with inflation rates. If for two countries, A and B, the inflation rates are I_A and I_B, respectively, with nominal returns of r_A and r_B then as per Fisher effect real returns must equalize. This implies that differential of nominal returns and inflation rates must equalize across nations, mathematically represented as

$$r_A - I_A = r_B - I_B$$

We can now attempt to establish the relationship of spot exchange rates with interest rates because the relationship of exchange rate with the inflation rate is already known through relative PPP. If interest rates are related to inflation rates for equality of real returns, then spot exchange rates must change according to changes in the interest rates as well and in similar fashion as with inflation rates.

As per Fisher condition, the interest rates and inflation rates are related by Eq. 6-8, that is, $1 + r = (1 + I) \times (1 + a)$. Assuming domestic and foreign inflation, real returns and nominal interest rates with subscript d and f, respectively, we may restate the Fisher condition as follows:

$$1 + I_d = \left[\frac{(1+r_d)}{(1+a_d)}\right] \quad \text{and} \quad 1 + I_f = \left[\frac{(1+r_f)}{(1+a_f)}\right]$$

Since international capital flows should make $a_d = a_f$ as Fisher condition, we may combine relative PPP and Fisher effect to get the relationship between spot exchange rates and interest rates as follows:

$$\frac{S_t}{S_0} = \left[\frac{(1+I_d)}{(1+I_f)}\right]^t = \left[\frac{(1+r_d)/(1+a_d)}{(1+r_f)/(1+a_f)}\right]^t = \left[\frac{(1+r_d)}{(1+r_f)}\right]^t \quad (6\text{-}10)$$

Equation 6-10 is known as International Fisher Effect (IFE).

The implications of IFE are similar to that of relative PPP. According to IFE the spot rate must change according to interest rates. The country with higher nominal interest rates would see its currency depreciate. The extent of annual depreciation of domestic currency/appreciation of foreign currency for $t = 1$ as specified by per cent change is given Eq. 6-11.

$$\frac{S_1 - S_0}{S_0} = \frac{\Delta S}{S_0} = \frac{(r_d - r_f)}{(1+r_f)} \quad (6\text{-}11)$$

Equation 6-11 for low foreign interest rate can be approximated as

$$\frac{\Delta S}{S_0} \approx (r_d - r_f) \quad (6\text{-}12)$$

The implication of IFE for international investing is straightforward. The investment made in view of higher nominal interest rates prevailing abroad would yield higher nominal returns than investing domestically. However, the excess returns so achieved would be offset exactly by the loss in the exchange rate as the currency invested in would depreciate. For example, let us say, interest rates in the USA and Japan are 8% and 1%, respectively. This would prompt

Japanese investors to invest in the USA to book the extra 7% gain. Assume that current exchange rate is ¥100/$ and Japanese investor invests ¥100 exchanging it for $1 in the USA, which after a year becomes $1.08. The exchange rate after one year would be:

$$S_1 = S_0 \left[\frac{(1+r_d)}{(1+r_f)}\right]^t = 100\frac{1.01}{1.08} = ¥93.5185/\$$$

When converted back to yen the matured amount of $1.08 becomes ¥101 (93.5185 × 1.08) providing exactly the same return as the Japanese would get by investing home. Hence, the extra return of 7% in dollar by investing abroad is eroded by its depreciation to the same extent.

IFE assumes free flow of capital among countries. It also assumes dependence of spot exchange rates on interest rates and not vice versa. Interest rate being a much wider economic phenomenon does not get affected by spot rates, instead spot rates respond to interest rate changes.

Exercise 6-4
International Fisher Effect

Investment in 90-day, 180-day, and 360-day treasury bills denominated in euro provide annualized yields of 6.00%, 6.50%, and 7.00%, respectively, whereas those of identical maturities in the USA in US dollars offer 4%, 4.25%, and 4.50%, respectively.

(a) If the current exchange rate is €1.20/$, what should be the value of euro in terms of US dollar after 90 days, 180 days, and 360 days?
(b) If there were capital controls by the USA to Europe, do you believe that exchange rates forecast in a) would hold?
(c) If there were no exchange controls and if euro were pegged to dollar what change must occur in Europe?

Solution

(a) The likely spot exchange rates after 90 days, 180 days, and 360 days assuming 360 days per year (for simplicity of calculation only) can be found using Eq. 6-10, as follows:

(i) After 90 days $\quad S_{1/4} = S_0\left[\frac{(1+r_{euro})}{(1+r_\$)}\right]^t = 1.20 \times \left(\frac{1.06}{1.04}\right)^{1/4} = €1.2057/\$$

(ii) After 180 days $\quad S_{1/2} = S_0\left[\frac{(1+r_{euro})}{(1+r_\$)}\right]^t = 1.20 \times \left(\frac{1.065}{1.0425}\right)^{1/2} = €1.2129/\$$

(iii) After 360 days $\quad S_1 = S_0\left[\frac{(1+r_{euro})}{(1+r_\$)}\right]^t = 1.20 \times \left(\frac{1.07}{1.045}\right) = €1.2287/\$$

(b) If there are controls on the capital flows across the USA and Europe, the rates obtained in (a) may not hold good. In case there is complete control, the exchange rate may stay same as $1.20/€.
(c) If euro were pegged to dollar with free flow of capital the interest rates for treasuries in euro must fall to those in the USA.

IFE is depicted in Figure 6-1 by way of 45° line with two axes as differential of interest rates and % change in exchange rates. The region above the IFE line denotes extra returns and the region below it represents lesser returns by investing abroad. Assume domestic interest rate in India, I_d, is 10%, whereas that of the USA, I_f, is 4%. There is 6% extra return for a US investor by investing in India. Point A is on IFE where excess returns in India get eroded exactly by depreciation of Indian rupee by about 6%. At Point B, the US investor gets extra return, but the depreciation of Indian rupee is less than the differential of interest rates, providing US investor some extra gains. Point C below the IFE line represents excessive depreciation more than offsetting interest rate differential. At Point D, Indian interest rate is lower than USA, yet can give excessive return to US investor when the appreciation of Indian rupee is larger.

In actual practice, the changes in spot rates as per differential of interest rates may only hold approximately as depicted by the dotted line in Figure 6-1. With IFE being followed only approximately the distortions may present some short-term opportunities for investment abroad to make extra gains.

There are few limitations in applicability of IFE. Some of them are discussed here.

Risk Premium Interest rates are returns on investment and must be commensurate with the risk associated with the investment. In an economy, there are several kinds of interest rates. Yield on investment in treasuries are quite different than the returns on investment in real estate or financial markets like stocks. Exchange rate changes respond to all returns in the economy and not one kind of investment. For example, vibrant stock markets would attract foreign investment in an open economy causing appreciation of local currency. For empirical

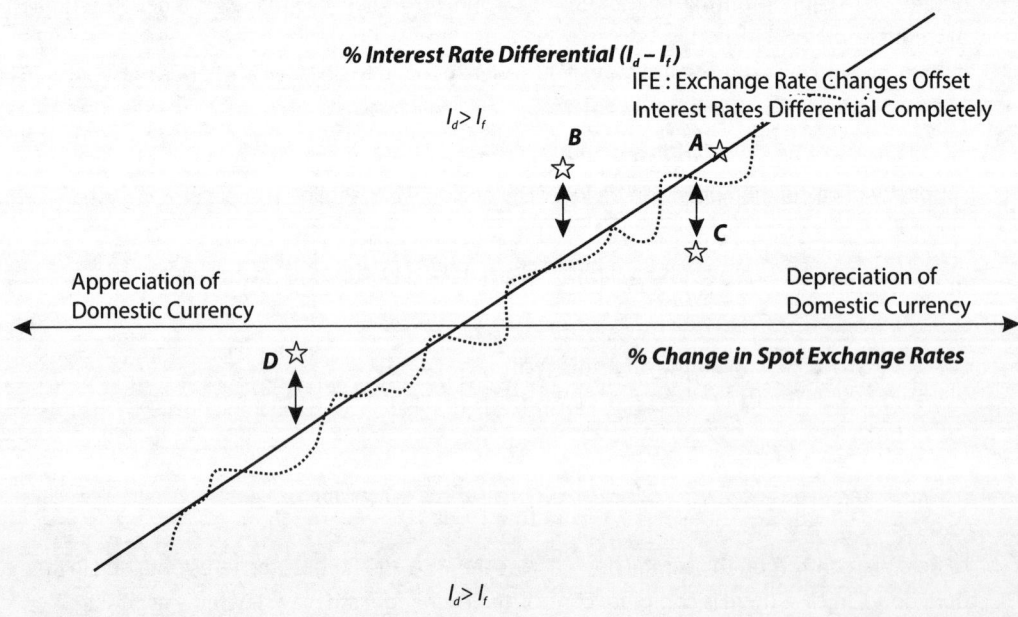

Figure 6-1

International Fisher Effect—Graphical View

testing of IFE, we have choice of (a) risk-free returns in two countries or (b) a weighted average of the interest rates prevailing in the economies. With the first option of using risk-free rate, there is little concern (except for the country risk attached with the treasuries of different nations), but with the second option a factor of risk premium would have to be added as risk of returns in two countries would be different.

Home Bias   Another factor that must be considered in applicability of IFE is the uncertainty of returns by investing abroad. If there is no differential in interest rates of two countries, the investors in each country would prefer to invest in their own countries, being more certain of return. Home environment has greater familiarity and confidence than the foreign environment. Investing abroad makes returns dependent upon the exchange rate at the maturity of investment, thereby making it riskier. With IFE, there should be no change in exchange rate, but it is fraught with risk. Hence, the foreign investment must offer some extra return to compensate for the extra uncertainty associated with foreign investment as compared to domestic investment.

Herd Mentality   Normally, foreign inflows for portfolio investment act in two ways—increase the stock prices and cause local currency to appreciate. While appreciation of local currency and stock prices happen simultaneously, it presents an excellent opportunity to book extraordinary gains. For example, US dollar inflows into India cause Indian rupee and stock markets to appreciate simultaneously. For example, assume one invests $1 when the exchange rate is ₹50. As foreign capital flows in (a) the stock market returns become 20%, far exceeding the normal rates and (b) rupee appreciates 25% to ₹40/$. If the investor makes timely exit, he can have $1.50 for every dollar invested and book handsome gain of 50% (1.20 × 1.25) compounding stock markets gains with currency appreciation. However, in the long run, IFE must hold. As appreciation of currency and stock market returns happen simultaneously, it would be logical to assume reversal of the process too must happen simultaneously. As foreign capital flows out, portfolio returns fall and currency too depreciates. Any delay in exiting the investment would cause speedier depreciation of currency as well as steeper fall in portfolio returns. This has been witnessed in several currency crises where capital outflows have been much quicker than the capital inflows.

IFE and Pegged Exchange Rate   IFE has implications on the pegged exchange rate system. With pegged exchange rate the returns in foreign country become independent of future exchange rate. That necessarily implies alignment of interest rates in two countries. If interest rates of the pegged currency and the anchor currency are not aligned, the foreign capital would continue to flow in the nation with higher interest rates. When country A pegs its currency to that of another country B and maintains a higher interest rate, it would attract capital from country B. However, pegging and higher interest rate cannot prevail for a long time. Continued flow of capital from country B must cause pressure for appreciation of currency of country A which is pegged. Such pressure acts against pegging. To prevent appreciation/depreciation of local/foreign currency to maintain the peg, intervention to buy the foreign currency is required causing increased supply of domestic currency fuelling inflation.

If defied, the pressure for appreciating domestic currency causes inflation, making investment risky. As and when the trigger for withdrawals takes place the capital flows out more quickly. This would lead to pressure for appreciation of foreign currency. To defend pegged exchange rate the foreign currency reserve would be used up. Therefore, for how long the pegged exchange rate without alignment of interest rates would last is a matter of conjecture, but the cost of depleting reserve would have to be borne by the nation.

INTEREST RATE PARITY

Arbitrage is normally associated with discrepancies in prices of an asset in two different markets at the same point of time. Arbitrage causes the price of the asset to converge in two markets. The prospects of arbitrage are better when the two markets are unaware of each other's prices, as it happens in foreign exchange markets being over-the-counter (OTC). In exchange-traded contracts the prices of assets are known to all, and as such arbitrage opportunities vanish almost instantly. In OTC markets, the arbitrage may last for slightly longer but sooner or later the process makes the two markets know that they are in imbalance.

In the previous chapter, we discussed two- and three-point arbitrages. Under two-point arbitrage, also known as locational arbitrage, the values of the two currencies in the markets converge. With three-point arbitrage, also called *triangular arbitrage*, the cross rates of currencies also remain in balance. Now we discuss another kind of arbitrage called *covered interest arbitrage* that may be available in spot and forward markets.

Covered Interest Arbitrage

We know that in the foreign exchange markets the spot transactions are settled in two business days. The markets also offer rates for settlement at a later point of time with the exchange rates quoted today. This is true for most financial and other assets where the prices can be fixed much prior to delivery and settlement. Contracts for deferred settlement are called forward contracts. These are derivatives where the price of the contract is dependent upon the spot exchange rate. In a way the spot and forward market are different because the maturities of the two occur at different points of time. As maturities differ, the two markets can be seen differently and independently in terms of fulfillment of obligations undertaken. In case of mispricing, arbitrage opportunities may arise if the spot and forward markets do not work in tandem with each other.

Spot and forward foreign exchange markets differ in terms of their maturities, and hence the prices in the two must differ with the time value of money. Therefore, intuitively we may guess that spot and forward rates must be linked with the interest rates prevailing in the markets for two currencies. Assuming no forward markets the arbitrage may be executed by (a) borrowing in one currency with lower interest rate and (b) investing in another with higher interest rate. In the absence of forward markets, the maturity amount of borrowing is not covered. This is often referred to as *carry trade*. The risk of future exchange rate would arise. Hence, it would be uncovered interest arbitrage since borrowing in currency with lower interest rate and investing in currency with higher interest rate must yield excess returns assuming that exchange rates at beginning and end of investment horizon remain same. Such would be the case if exchange rate is pegged.

Now assume the exchange rates are not fixed. The interest arbitrage, that is, the carry trade is fraught with risk since at maturity of the investment the exchange rate would be different and gain/loss would not be equal to the interest rate differential but would be modulated by exchange rate changes. The uncertainty of future exchange rate can be removed with a forward contract whose maturity coincides with that of investment and borrowing. If a forward contract is booked when borrowing and investment are made, there would be no uncertainty. One may gain a definite sum. Such a strategy is called *covered interest arbitrage*. Can this difference in investing value and borrowed sum be exploited by using the spot exchange rate and the forward exchange rate? Let us illustrate how covered interest arbitrage works with the help of an example.

Assume that the spot rate of US dollar in India is ₹45.00. A 12-m forward contract is quoted at ₹46.70. Further assume that interest rates in India and the USA are 10% and 5%, respectively. One may set up an arbitrage as follows:

Today: At $t = 0$, take the following four actions simultaneously:

1. Borrow $1 at 5% the interest rate prevailing in US dollar for 12 months, creating a liability with the maturity amount of $1.05 (1 + 0.05).
2. Convert the $1.00 borrowed in Indian rupees using the spot markets at prevailing rate of ₹45.00. Now we have ₹45.00 instead of $1.00.
3. Invest Indian rupee at the interest rates prevailing in Indian rupees at 10% for one year.
4. Finally, sell the matured amount of Indian rupees forward for US dollars at forward rate of ₹46.70 so as to repay the liability in US dollars.

By taking the actions just discussed, one has invested no money of one's own and also has assumed no risk since all the cash flows are frozen now. The maturity of borrowing one currency, that is, US dollar coincides with the maturity of the investment in the other currency, that is, Indian rupees. Both these maturities also coincide with the maturity of the forward contract. Amounts of liability and investment asset are also known. In addition, the amount to be paid against borrowed amount is covered by the forward contract leaving no uncertainty of changing exchange rates.

After 12 months: The following actions would happen automatically as a result of steps initiated at $t = 0$:

1. Collect the matured amount of investment in Indian rupees, that is, ₹49.50 (45 × 1.10) known for sure.
2. Tender Indian rupees to get US dollar under the forward contract. The amount realized would be US$1.06.
3. Pay borrowing with interest thereon in US dollar at US$1.05, providing a profit of US$0.01. The profit of US$0.01 when converted at forward rate of ₹46.70 is equal to ₹0.4670.

178   International Finance

As the amount payable US$1.05 is less than the amount receivable US$1.06, it gives US$0.01 as a profit for every dollar borrowed. The actions at $t = 0$ and subsequently after a year are tabulated in Table 6-2 and depicted in Figure 6-2.

Table 6-2
Covered Interest Arbitrage (Borrow Abroad and Invest Local)

	Actions at $t = 0\,m$			Actions at $t = 12\,m$		
Cash Flow	$	₹	Cash Flow	$	₹
Borrow in US Dollar	+1.00	–	Realize Investment in Indian Rupees	–	+49.50
Convert to Indian Rupee	–1.00	+45.00	Convert to US$ under Forward Contract	+1.06	–49.50
Investment in Indian Rupee	–	–45.00	Pay Borrowing with Interest	–1.05	
Sell Indian Rupee Forward	–	–			
Net Cash Flow	–	–		+0.01	–

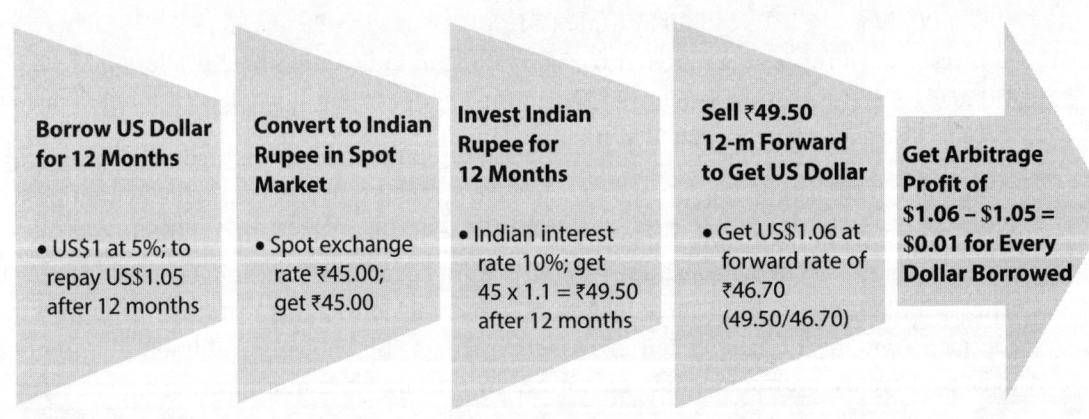

Figure 6-2
Covered Interest Arbitrage (Borrow Abroad and Invest Local)

For the execution of the arbitrage resulting in a profit of US$0.01 we used four parameters—(1) the spot exchange rate, (2) the interest rate for investment in India, (3) the interest rate for borrowing in US dollars, and (4) the forward exchange rate.

The process of arbitrage would cause downward pressure on US dollar as they are sold to get Indian rupee. Similarly, borrowing US dollar would raise dollar interest rates and increased investment in rupee would cause downward pressure on rupee interest rates. It is easy to see that of the four parameters, spot exchange rates and interest rates in the USA and India are rather inflexible as they are long-term broader economic phenomenon. Clearly, the fourth parameter of forward exchange rate of ₹47.60/$ is unsustainable and must undergo a change so as to eliminate the arbitrage profit.

Revised Forward Exchange Rates Assume that the spot rate of US dollar in India and the interest rates of 10% and 5% in India and the USA remain same as before. Borrowing US dollar at 5% and investing at a higher rate of 10% in India seemed motivated with the gain of 5%. Although there was a gain but not as much as anticipated 5% due to depreciation of rupee in the forward market.

It was apparent from the exposition just discussed that any downward revision of forward rate from ₹46.70 would only increase the arbitrage profit. Such gains come at the expense of forward market participants. Not having any idea about the upward revision, we revise in an ad hoc manner that the 12-m forward contract rate is now ₹47.60. If so, the arbitrage can be executed in the following manner that is opposite to the one executed by borrowing US dollar and investing in Indian rupee.

Today: At $t = 0$, take the following four actions simultaneously:

1. Borrow ₹45 at 10% for 12 months at the interest rates prevailing in Indian rupee, creating a liability with the maturity amount of ₹49.50 (45 × 1.1).
2. Convert ₹45 borrowed in US dollar using the spot markets at the prevailing rate of ₹45.00. Now, we have US$1.00 instead of ₹45.00.
3. Invest US dollar for one year at the interest rates prevailing in US dollar at 5% to get US$1.05 at maturity.
4. Finally, sell the matured amount of US dollar forward at forward rate of ₹47.60 so as to pay the amount of liability.

As before, by the actions just discussed, you have neither invested any money of your own nor assumed any risk. All the cash flows are known and certain. The maturity of liability of borrowing one currency, that is, Indian rupee coincides with the maturity of the investment in the other currency, that is, US dollar. In addition, the amount to be paid against borrowing amount is also covered by the forward contract.

After 12 months: The following actions would happen automatically as a result of steps initiated at $t = 0$:

1. Collect the matured amount of investment in US dollar, that is, $1.05 (1 × 1.10).
2. Deliver US dollar to get Indian rupees under the forward contract. The amount realized would be ₹49.98.
3. Pay borrowing with interest thereon in Indian rupees at ₹49.50, providing profit of ₹0.48.

As the amount payable ₹49.50 is less than the amount receivable ₹49.98, it gives ₹0.48 as profit for every ₹45 borrowed. The actions at $t = 0$ and subsequently a year are tabulated in Table 6-3 and depicted in Figure 6-3.

Table 6-3
Covered Interest Arbitrage (Borrow Local and Invest Abroad)

	Actions at $t = 0\ m$			Actions at $t = 12\ m$		
Cash Flow	$	₹	Cash Flow	$	₹
Borrow in Indian Rupee	–	+45.00	Realize Investment in US Dollar	+1.05	–
Convert to US Dollar	+1.00	–45.00	Convert to Indian Rupee under Forward Contract	–1.05	+49.98
Investment in US Dollar	–1.00	–	Pay borrowing with Interest	–	–49.50
Sell Indian Rupee Forward	–	–			
Net Cash Flow	–	–		–	+0.48

Borrow Indian Rupee for 12 Months
- Indian rupee 45 at 10%; To repay ₹49.50 after 12 months

Convert to US Dollar in Spot Market
- Spot exchange rate ₹45.00; get US$1.00

Invest US Dollar for 12 Months
- US interest rate 5%; Get 1.00 × 1.05 = US$1.05 after 12 months

Sell US$1.05 12-m Forward to Get Indian Rupee
- Sell US$1.05 at forward rate of ₹47.60 and get ₹49.98

Get Arbitrage Profit of ₹49.98 – ₹49.50 = ₹0.48 for Every Dollar Invested

Figure 6-3
Covered Interest Arbitrage (Borrow Local and Invest Abroad)

Finding Equilibrium Forward Rate Thus, we see that if the forward rate were either too low or too high, the arbitrageurs would make profit by taking positions in the money market by borrowing one currency, converting spot, and investing in another with an appropriate forward contract. The only way to eliminate the arbitrage profit is to adjust the forward rate. Neither the spot rate, nor the money market rates in the two currencies can be influenced. In the first case of borrowing dollar, the foreign currency, the forward rate must be adjusted upwards just enough to eliminate the profit of ₹0.47. Similarly, in the second case of borrowing in rupee, that is, the domestic currency, the forward rate must be revised downwards just enough to eliminate the profit of ₹0.48. Any revision in excess would make arbitrage possible in one way or the other. We need to find a state of equilibrium.

To obtain a solution to find an arbitrage free forward rate, let us work with symbols. Let the spot exchange rate be S_0 and the forward rate be F_0 for one period case. The interest rates in the domestic and foreign money markets are r_d and r_f, respectively.

By borrowing one unit of the foreign currency and converting it at the spot rate, we get S_0 of the domestic currency. Investing in the domestic currency, we create an asset that matures to a value of $S_0 \times (1 + r_d)$. At the same time, we create a liability of $(1 + r_f)$ by borrowing one unit of foreign currency, which matures into an equivalent liability of $(1 + r_f) \times F_0$ in domestic currency using forward market. If the value of the asset exceeds the value of the liability of borrowing, the arbitrage profit would result. For no arbitrage to take place, the asset value must be less than the liability. Hence

$$S_0(1+r_d) \leq F_0(1+r_f)$$

$$F_0 \geq S_0 \frac{(1+r_d)}{(1+r_f)} \qquad \text{Condition 6-1}$$

Similarly, in the other process of borrowing one unit of the domestic currency and converting it at the spot rate, we get $1/S_0$ of the foreign currency. Investment in the foreign currency would create an asset that matures to a value of $(1/S_0) \times (1 + r_f)$. At the same time, we have created a liability of $(1 + r_d)$ in domestic currency, which is equivalent to $(1 + r_d)/F_0$ in foreign currency. Again for no arbitrage, the matured asset must be less than the matured liability. Hence

$$\frac{(1+r_f)}{S_0} \leq \frac{(1+r_d)}{F_0}$$

$$F_0 \leq S_0 \frac{(1+r_d)}{(1+r_f)} \qquad \text{Condition 6-2}$$

Both the inequalities specified as Conditions 6-1 and 6-2 can be satisfied simultaneously to eliminate arbitrage if and only if

$$F_0 = S_0 \frac{(1+r_d)}{(1+r_f)} \tag{6-13}$$

Equation 6-13 is referred to as interest rate parity (IRP) that establishes the relationship between the forward rate and the spot rates. With the example just described, the arbitrage free 12-m forward rate would be

$$F_0 = S_0 \frac{(1+r_d)}{(1+r_f)} = 45 \frac{1.10}{1.05} = ₹47.14/\$$$

With the 12-m forward rate of ₹47.14

1. In the first case of borrowing dollars, the matured liability was $1.05 and the value of investment in Indian rupees was ₹49.50. Sold at 12-m forward rate of ₹47.14, the asset would convert to $1.05, exactly equal to the amount of liability.
2. In the second case of borrowing Indian currency matured at ₹49.50, the investment asset matured into US$1.05, which is equal to ₹ 49.50, which is exactly equal to the amount of liability at the given 12-m forward rate.

For other than annual period, the IRP is stated forward rate at time $t = 0$ for forward period of, t, shown as follows:

$$F_0^t = S_0 \left[\frac{(1+r_d)}{(1+r_f)}\right]^t \qquad (6\text{-}14)$$

Exercise 6-5
Interest Rate Parity

The exchange rate in New York for British pound is $1.8500/£. The interest rates prevailing in the USA and Britain are 8% and 12%, respectively, with flat-term structure. 90-day and 180-day forward contracts are quoted at $1.8400/£ and $1.7900/£, respectively.

(a) What should be the arbitrage free forward exchange rates for periods of 90 days and 180 days?
(b) In what way you can execute covered interest arbitrage with 90-day forward contract rate?
(c) Could you execute the same covered interest arbitrage with 180-day forward? Explain how this arbitrage would be different.

Solution

(a) The forward rate exchange rates as per IRP for 90 days and 180 days can be found using Eq. 6-14 as follows:
   i. After 90 days

$$F_0^{90} = S_0\left[\frac{(1+r_d)}{(1+r_f)}\right]^t = 1.85\left[\frac{1.02}{1.03}\right] = 1.85 \times 0.9903 = \$1.8320/£$$

   ii. After 180 days

$$F_0^{180} = S_0\left[\frac{(1+r_d)}{(1+r_f)}\right]^t = 1.85\left[\frac{1.04}{1.06}\right] = 1.85 \times 0.9811 = \$1.8151/£$$

(b) For 90 days, we find that the actual forward rate is $1.8400/£ as against $1.8320/£ valuing US dollar more than what IRP suggests. In the forward market, US dollar is underpriced. Hence, it must be bought in forward. To execute arbitrage, one must (i) borrow US dollar at 8% for 90 days, (ii) convert spot to British pound, (iii) invest pounds, so obtained at 12% for 90 days, and (iv) sell maturity value of pounds at 90-day forward rate to get the US dollars. For every US dollar borrowed, the maturity value of pound investment is $\frac{1}{1.85} \times 1.03 = £0.5568$. Sold at the forward rate of $1.8400/£, it would fetch $1.0245 exceeding the liability of $1.0200.

(c) For the 180 days, we find that the actual forward rate is $1.7900/£ as against $1.8151/£, valuing US dollar less than what IRP suggests. In the forward market, US dollar is overpriced. Hence, it must be sold in forward. To execute arbitrage, one must (i) borrow pounds at 12% for 180 days, (ii) convert spot to US dollar, (iii) invest US dollars so-obtained at 8% for 180 days, and (iv) sell maturity value of US dollar at forward rate to get the pounds. For every pound borrowed, the maturity value of dollar investment is $1.8500 \times 1.06 = \$1.9610$. When sold at 180-day forward rate, we get $\frac{1}{1.7900} \times 1.9610 = £1.0955$ that is in excess of liability of £1.0400, providing arbitrage gains.

Forward Premium and Discount

The IRP as given in Eq. 6-14 is normally stated in an alternate form in terms of premium or discount with respect to spot rates. If domestic interest rates are higher than the foreign interest rates, the foreign currency must be more expensive in future than it is in spot. In such a case, the foreign currency is said to be at premium and equivalently domestic currency is at discount. Equation 6-13 can be stated in terms of forward premium/discount as

$$\text{Forward Premium}(+)/\text{Discount}(-) = \frac{F_0 - S_0}{S_0} = \frac{(r_d - r_f)}{(1+r_f)} \qquad (6\text{-}15)$$
$$\approx (r_d - r_f), \text{ if } r_f \text{ is low}$$

The IRP version of Eq. 6-15 has implications for the covered interest arbitrage. The differential of the interest rates in two currencies represents additional gain by borrowing in cheaper currency and investing in currency with higher interest rates. Borrowing and investing are the operations in the money markets of the two currencies.

However, in order to capitalize on the interest rate differential, investors need to buy back the borrowed currency on maturity of the investment. The currency borrowed (the one with lower interest rates) would be at premium in the forward market. The extra gains made by borrowing and investing would be eroded by the premium in the forward market. This means tendering greater number of units of invested currency than what one obtained in the spot market.

The other implication of IRP is that by investing abroad, the investors can earn only as much as they can by investing domestically. For example, consider that interest rates in India and the USA are 10% and 4%, respectively. Investors in the USA may be tempted to invest in India for a seeming advantage of 6%. The IRP says that extra returns of the US investors by investing in Indian rupee would be eroded by the premium of 6% on US dollar in the forward market. When the capital has to be repatriated upon maturity of investment in India the US investors would find dollar 6% more expensive, that is, extra rupee returns of 6% would be foregone by buying dollars 6% more expensive, making their dollar return equal to 4%; the returns obtainable by investing in the USA.

The reverse also happens to be true. If Indian investors want to invest in the USA at 4%, they would still get 10%; same if they were to invest domestically. Indian investors can get only 4% by investing in the USA, thereby losing 6% in the money markets. However, this loss is compensated by 6% extra rupees obtained at the maturity of the investment as dollar being expensive now fetches 6% more rupees.

The IRP implies that transactional gains/losses in the money markets are completely offset by losses/gains in the forward markets. This is depicted in Figure 6-4 where a 45° line with interest rate differential on vertical axis and forward premium/discount on horizontal axis represents IRP. Point A signifies that extra returns in the domestic money markets are offset by equal premium on foreign currency. Similarly, Point B represents that lower domestic interest rate would be compensated by discount on foreign currency.

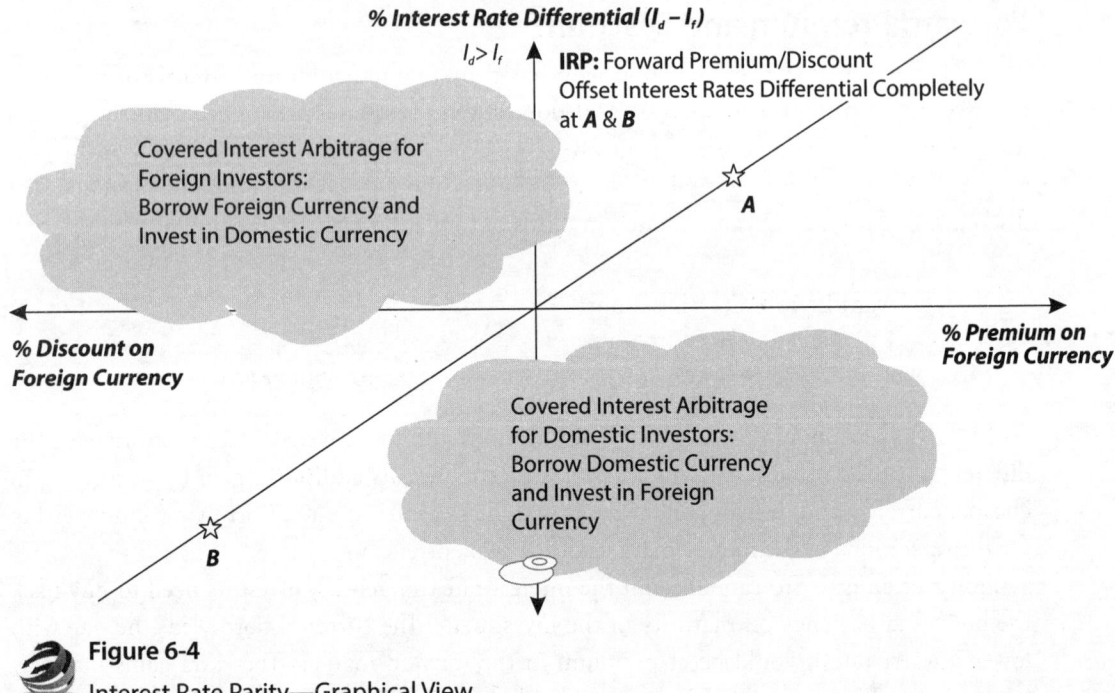

Figure 6-4
Interest Rate Parity—Graphical View

The region below the IRP line represents covered interest arbitrage for domestic investors. Borrowing domestic currency and investing abroad would fetch more returns than by investing domestically because the premium/discount on foreign currency would be greater/smaller. The region above the IRP line represents covered interest arbitrage opportunities for foreign investors. They may borrow foreign currency (their home currency) to invest in domestic currency (their foreign currency). The premium/discount would be smaller/greater than the extra returns in the money markets.

Interest Rate Parity with Transaction Costs

For IRP to hold, we must have free flow of capital across nations, implying freedom to invest and borrow in any currency irrespective of residential status of the borrowers and investors. In addition, it was assumed that investors do not have apprehensions about borrowing or investing abroad. Both of these assumptions seem to be invalid as most nations exercise some control on the flow of capital in some form or the other, and investors do have home bias for investments. Besides, we also assumed that (i) borrowing and lending could be done at the same rate and (ii) buying and selling of foreign currency can also be done at the same rate. In practice, we have borrowing rates higher than lending rates and ask rates greater than bid rates.

The differentials in lending and borrowing, and buying and selling of foreign currency are referred to as transaction costs. The presence of transaction costs does not invalidate the IRP but only places limitations on the process of arbitrage. The gains under arbitrage must exceed the transaction costs for it to be fruitful. Therefore, IRP would hold only approximately, that is, interest rate differential may only be approximately offset by premium/discount in the forward markets.

Let us examine the IRP and the underlying arbitrage process when transaction costs are present with an example. The borrowing rates are higher than the lending rates and so is the ask rate with respect to the bid rate. With direct rate convention for the USA, we assume that the following rates are quoted in the currency and money markets in the USA and Europe:

Spot Rates (US$/€)		1.3000	1.3100
Interest Rates	US$	5.50%	5.75%
	Euro	4.00%	4.25%

Without losing the substance and for the sake of simplicity, let us consider forward markets for a 12-month period. We need to find the arbitrage free forward rates. To arrive at valid 12-m forward rates that do not permit arbitrage, we follow the same process of borrowing and investing in different currencies and using spot and forward markets for converting currencies. The presence of transaction cost would place lower and upper bounds on ask and bid forward rates. Assume that the 12-m forward bid and ask rates are F_b and F_a, respectively.

(a) Borrow Euro and Invest in US dollar

First, we consider borrowing in euro and investing in US dollar and proceed as follows:

1. We borrow €1 at 4.25% for a year. The amount payable after one year would be €1.0425.
2. In order to invest in US dollar we need to convert euro at spot bid rate of 1.3000. For each euro, we get $1.30.
3. The dollars are invested at 5.50% maturing into US$1.30 × 1.055 after one year.
4. Finally, in order to cover for the uncertainty of future spot rate, we sell the maturity amount of US dollar forward at ask rate F_a to get euro back to enable liquidate the liability created by borrowing.

The maturity amount of US dollar invested when sold at forward rate would convert to specific and certain amount of euro. The euro receivable after one year would be $\frac{1.055 \times 1.30}{F_a}$.

The maturity amount payable for euro borrowed is €1.0425. For no arbitrage forward ask rate, euro receivable under forward contract must be less than the liability created by borrowing, that is,

$$\frac{1.055 \times 1.30}{F_a} \leq 1.0425$$

$$F_a \geq \frac{1.055 \times 1.30}{1.0425} \geq \frac{1.3715}{1.0425} \geq \text{US\$}1.3156/€$$

The inequality thus obtained places a lower bound on the forward ask rate. As long as exchange rate is above US$1.3156/€, there would not be any covered interest arbitrage available by borrowing euro and investing in dollars. In terms of domestic and foreign investment the inequality for lower bound on the forward ask rate may be stated as follows:

$$F_a \geq \frac{(1+r_d^l)}{(1+r_f^b)} S_b \qquad (6\text{-}16)$$

Subscripts f and d on interest rate, r, denote the foreign and domestic rates, respectively, whereas superscripts b and l denote borrowing and lending rates, respectively. S_b denotes the spot bid rate.

(b) Borrow US dollar and Invest in Euro

We now reverse the process just discussed to find the limits on the forward bid rate. We now borrow US dollars and invest in euro as follows:

1. We borrow $1 at 5.75% for a year. The amount payable after one year would be $/€1.0575.
2. In order to invest in euro we need to convert dollars at spot ask rate of 1.3100. For each dollar we get €1/1.3100 = €0.7634.
3. Euro is invested at 4.00% maturing into €0.7634 × 1.04 after one year.
4. Finally, In order to cover for the uncertainty of future spot rate, we sell the maturity amount of euro forward at bid rate, F_b, to get US dollar back to enable liquidate the liability created by borrowing.

The maturity amount of euro invested when sold at forward rate would convert to specific and certain amount of euro. The dollar receivable after one year would be $\frac{1.04 \times F_b}{1.3100}$.

The maturity amount payable for dollar borrowed is $1.0575. For no arbitrage forward bid rate, dollar receivable under forward contract must be less than the liability created by borrowing it, that is

$$\frac{1.04 \times F_b}{1.3100} \leq 1.0575$$

$$F_b \leq \frac{1.0575 \times 1.3100}{1.0400} \leq \frac{1.3853}{1.0400} \leq US\$1.3320/€$$

The inequality thus obtained places an upper bound on the forward bid rate. As long as the exchange rate is less than US$1.3320/€, there would not be any covered interest arbitrage available by borrowing dollar and investing in euro. In terms of domestic and foreign investment, the inequality for lower bound on the forward ask rate may be stated as

$$F_b \leq \frac{(1+r_d^b)}{(1+r_f^l)} S_a \qquad (6\text{-}17)$$

As stated earlier, subscripts, f and d, on interest rate, r, denote the foreign and domestic rates, respectively, whereas superscripts b and l denote the borrowing and lending rates, respectively. S_a denotes the spot ask rate.

Inequalities 6-16 and 6-17 by placing a lower and upper bounds on the forward bid and ask rate, respectively, make large sets of forward exchange rates feasible that do not offer arbitrage. Several rates may persist in the forward markets as long as they satisfy the inequalities. In the example just discussed, we must have (a) forward ask rate more than US$1.3156/€ and (b) forward bid rate less than rate US$1.3320/€.

Besides satisfying no arbitrage conditions, the forward markets must have other consistencies. For realistic forward rates at least these additional principles must be followed:

1. Ask rates must be higher than the bid rates.
2. Recognition of increased risk in forward rates as compared to spot rates by increased bid–ask spread in forward rates.
3. Consistency with IRP.

For example, consider the forward quotation of US$/€1.3300 – 1.3200. Both, the bid and ask rates satisfy the no arbitrage conditions, but they are impractical. These rates would depict a loss for the dealer as he buys euro at $1.33, whereas he sells it for $1.32. Clearly, the ask rate must be higher than the bid rate.

Another practical consideration is the spread in the bid–ask spread in the forward contracts. We know that forward transaction has greater uncertainty than the spot. Since the dealer assumes greater risk in forward deals and uncertainties increase with the increase in the forward period, the remuneration for forward contract must be more. Therefore, bid–ask spread must increase as forward period extends. The increased spread must be dependent upon the interest rate differential so as to make foreign exchange transactions more attractive than the borrowing and lending transactions. For example, 12-m forward rates of US$/€1.3200 – 1.3250 again satisfy the no arbitrage conditions but offer lesser spread in the forward transaction than in the spot. The spread in spot is 100 bps and, hence, forward transaction must yield more than 100 bps for the foreign exchange dealer.

Finally, and possibly most importantly, the forward exchange rate must obey IRP. The forward premium/discount must reflect the differential of the interest rates in the two currencies. In the example just discussed, the mid-points of interest rates in dollars and euro are 5.625% and 4.125%, respectively. This represents differential of 1.5%, indicating that US dollar must depreciate approximately by 1.5% annually with respect to euro. Therefore, forward mid rate must be higher by 1.5% than the spot mid rate, that is, $1.015 \times 1.3050 = \$1.3245/€$.

Now we are in a position to arrive at practical forward rates. With forward mid rate known at $1.3245/€, we may have a spread of about 200 bps (decided arbitrarily) in forward as against 100 bps in the spot. That would give forward rates as $/€1.3145 – 1.3345. These rates also satisfy no arbitrage conditions.

The IRP links money markets of the two currencies with the exchange rate markets. Violation of the IRP would make borrowing in one currency and investing in another profitable.

Exercise 6-6
Interest Rate Parity with Transaction Costs

The spot foreign exchange rate in India for US dollar is:

	Spot (₹/$)	44.00	44.25

Interest rates in India are between 10.00% and 10.50%, whereas those of the USA are between 8.00% and 8.50%. What valid forward rates for 6 months must prevail in the market?

Solution
Using Inequality (6-15) for the forward ask rate, we get lower bound by (i) borrowing US dollar for 6 months at 8.50%, (ii) converting to Indian rupee at spot bid rate of ₹44.00/$, (iii) investing in Indian rupee for 6 months at 10%, and (iv) selling the matured investment forward at ask rate for getting US dollar back.

$$F_a \geq \frac{(1+r_d^l)}{(1+r_f^b)} S_b = \frac{1.05}{1.0425} 44.00 = ₹44.32/\$$$

Using Inequality (6-16) for the forward bid rate, we get the upper bound by (i) borrowing Indian rupee for 6 months at 10.50%, (ii) converting to US dollar at spot ask rate of ₹44.25/$, (iii) investing in US dollar for 6 months at 8%, and (iv) selling the matured investment forward at bid rate for getting Indian rupee back.

$$F_b \leq \frac{(1+r_d^b)}{(1+r_f^l)} S_a = \frac{1.0525}{1.04} 44.25 = ₹44.78/\$$$

As per IRP, US dollar should be at 2% annualized premium. Therefore, approximate mid forward rate for 6 months period must be 1% higher that the spot mid rate. Hence forward mid rate is $1.01 \times 44.125 \approx$ ₹44.58/$.

Assuming a spread of ₹0.50 in the forward as against ₹0.25 in the spot, we subtract and add ₹0.25 in the forward mid rate to obtain bid and ask rates as follows:

6-m forward rates (₹/$) : 44.33 – 44.83

Therefore, money markets and foreign exchange market have to operate in tandem to eliminate any arbitrage profits. Forward rates, being facilitator of currency risk management, have to align to the broader economic fundamentals governing the money market conditions in the two economies. Any increase in the domestic interest rate compared to foreign interest rates would see increasing forward rate and vice versa.

With the exception of transaction costs, all other factors causing mismatch in the forward and the spot rates must be minimized. All nations including developed ones do place some kinds of restrictions on the flow of capital in and out of the country. Are competitive and politically independent exchange rates and financial instruments available? The nearest instruments that satisfy the conditions for IRP to hold are present in the euromarkets.[1] Therefore, in order to

---

[1] Refer Annexure A5-1. Euro markets are markets for deposit and lending of money outside the home country. For example, US$ deposited or lent in London would be called Eurodollar. Likewise, Japanese yen transacted outside Japan would be referred as Euroyen.

test the validity of the IRP, the rates prevailing in the euro-markets are often considered most appropriate because these markets offer very competitive rates and are free from exchange control mechanisms as also from the political interference.

RECONCILING PARITIES

We discussed several parity conditions that attempted to forecast the future exchange rate based on economic fundamentals of the economies of the two currencies. The parity conditions presented a simplistic view of complex exchange rate behaviour. The fundamentals that govern the exchange rate determination based on domestic and external macroeconomic factors help the comprehension of likely changes that exchange rates may exhibit. From the perspective of a manager in a multinational firm, the understanding of macroeconomic factors is vital for the bottom line of the firms.

Should all parity conditions lead to a similar outcome? Under ideal conditions of perfect markets where macroeconomic variables are perfectly correlated and there exists free capital mobility across borders, the parity relationships should lead to identical forecast. However, in the real world, these variables never behave in the exact manner that they are expected by academicians, economists, and policy makers. If so, forecasting would have been one of the easiest assignments. For example, interest rates and inflation rates would move in the same direction albeit not maintaining the same differentials.

The relationship of future exchange rate with various parities is presented in Figure 6-5. Exchange rates can be forecast on the basis of absolute and relative purchasing power parities in the long run of say five years, since the exchange rate behaviour must conform to some broad economic parameters like inflation rates being a long-term phenomenon. With free mobility of capital across borders, Fisher effect must prevail. Do the differentials of inflation

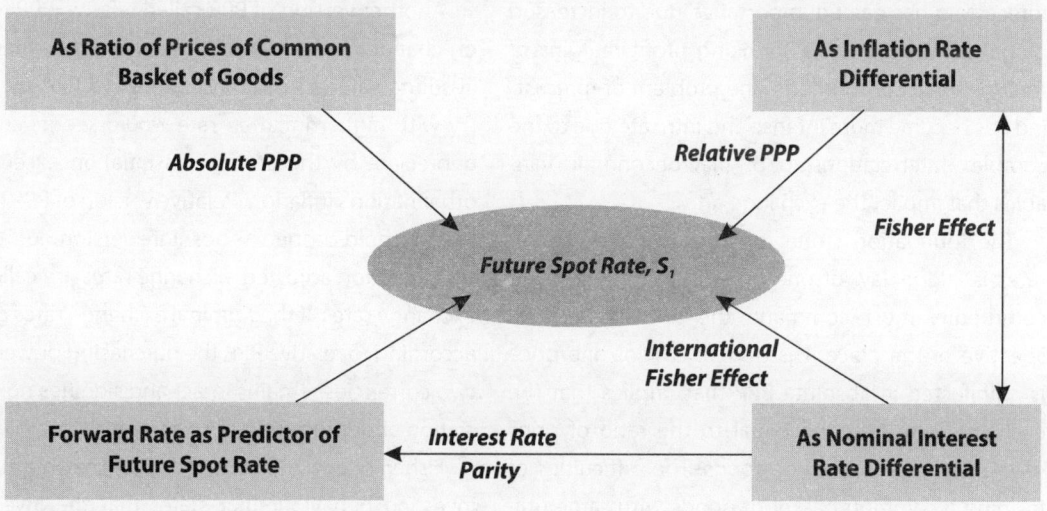

Figure 6-5
Reconciling Parity Conditions for Exchange Rate Forecasting

and interest rates equalize is again a long-term phenomena and more critically dependent upon the unchecked flow of capital free from home-bias and purely guided by returns. In the shorter term of say—one to two years, the interest rate must play a dominant role in the determination of exchange rates since interest rates can be influenced rather easily as compared to controlling the inflation rates. Therefore, the prediction on the basis of forward rate as unbiased predictor of future spot rate could be a more reliable indicator.

Hence, as manager's choice of technique of forecasting exchange rate depends upon *interalia*, the time horizon, regulatory environment for flow of capital, returns in the debt and capital markets, political risks, interdependence of interest and inflation rates, willingness of investors abroad to invest/disinvest, etc. These factors are economic, political, social, and regulatory in nature, the assessment of which becomes extremely subjective and discretionary. Therefore, applicability of the parity conditions is dependent upon how close the real environment is to theoretical positions.

Recognizing the subjectivity and discretionary nature, one can say that any or none of the parity conditions may or may not hold. It is the divergence of opinions that creates varying forecasts. Yet these parity conditions remain formidable tools of forecasting exchange rates fairly accurately and are worth taking cognizance for well-informed and conscious decisions in the foreign exchange markets by managers in the multinational firms. Simply because they may or may not hold is not a good reason enough to ignore them.

SUMMARY

When the exchange rates were fixed, the question of forecasting future exchange rates was rather trivial. With the advent of flexible exchange rate system, the forecasting has gained importance due to increased global competition and shrinking profit margins of multinational corporations. The problem of forecasting has become more intense and intricate due to the complex interrelationship of macroeconomic variables that impact the exchange rates.

The foundation stone for forecasting exchange rates is laid in 'law of one price' that implies that a commodity must command the same price irrespective of the place it is traded. Law of one price is manifested in absolute PPP that implies that the exchange rate must be equal to the ratio of price of the common basket of goods. The difficulties of forming a common basket of goods with same utility and styling, trade barriers, product differentiation, transportation costs, and increasing proportions of non-tradable goods are some of the factors that limit the applicability of the PPP.

Another version of PPP called relative PPP focuses on changes in spot exchange rates rather than their absolute values. According to relative PPP, the country with higher inflation rate would see its currency depreciate by the amount its inflation exceeds the other nation's inflation. Relative version of PPP is more likely to hold despite its absolute version not holding true. Inflation adjusted exchange rates are called real exchange rates. If the nominal exchange rates change according to relative PPP, the purchasing power of the two currencies remains intact and signifies no appreciation or depreciation of currencies.

Fisher effect is concerned with the international investing behaviour that states that the investment abroad is guided by the real returns rather than the nominal returns. Real returns are defined as excess of nominal returns over inflation rates. The flow of capital across nations would equalize real returns in the world. Linking Fisher effect with relative PPP, we obtain IFE. As per IFE, the spot exchange rate would change according to the nominal interest rates. The currency with a higher interest rate would depreciate by the differential of interest rates. The implication of IFE for international investing is that excess returns obtained by investing in currency with higher interest rate would be eroded by its depreciation by an equal amount. Hence, investing at home or abroad would yield identical returns.

The IRP based on covered interest arbitrage illustrates how the forward contracts in currencies would be priced. According to IRP, the premium or discount of the forward over spot rate is approximately equal to the difference of the interest rates in two currencies. IRP, therefore, links the money markets of two countries with the foreign exchange markets. Defying IRP would produce arbitrage profits by borrowing in one currency and investing in another and covering the liability of the borrowed amount with the forward contract. The presence of transaction costs in the form of bid–ask spread and different lending and borrowing rates places the upper and lower bounds to forward rates and, hence, vastly different forward rates may exist yet providing no arbitrage gains.

Different parity conditions linking inflation rates, interest rates, international flow of capital, forward markets, etc. can be used to forecast the spot exchange rates. Which of the parity conditions would more accurately forecast the future spot rate is subject to how distortions in the real world are perceived by the person concerned. Under ideal circumstances where broad variables of the economy behave in the anticipated way, any of the parity conditions may be used because all of them would lead to the same forecast.

QUESTIONS

6-1 Write a short note on the following:
   (a) Law of one price
   (b) Exchange rate pass-through
   (c) Real returns and nominal returns
   (d) Applicability of International Fisher effect under pegged exchange rate

6-2 Comment on the following statements:
   (a) Relative purchasing power parity cannot be true because the absolute version of purchasing power parity has serious limitations that distort the outcome.
   (b) No one should invest abroad because by doing so, no excess returns than by investing home can be made.
   (c) There would always be some scope of deriving arbitrage profits in forward markets because the forward rates quoted by different dealers are vastly different.

6-3 What do you understand by absolute purchasing power parity? Describe some of the factors that are likely to invalidate the outcome of purchasing power parity.

6-4 Differentiate between the following terms:
   (a) Absolute and relative purchasing power parity
   (b) Fisher Effect and International Fisher Effect
   (c) Nominal and real exchange rates

6-5 Explain the covered interest arbitrage when forward rates are (a) too high and (b) too low.

PROBLEMS

6-1 Purchasing Power Parity & Exchange Rates

Assume that price indices in India and Britain for a common basket of goods are as follows:

Year	India	Britain
1996	2,000	45
1999	2,750	54
2002	3,450	65
2005	3,725	73

(a) What would be your estimate of the exchange rate of Indian rupee with British pound in various years?

(b) If the actual exchange rate in 2002 happens to be ₹54.50/£, which of the currencies is overpriced and by how much, if purchasing power parity is assumed to hold?

6-2 Relative Purchasing Power Parity

Inflation rates in the USA and Japan are 5% and 1%, respectively. The exchange rate is J¥100/US$. What exchange rates are likely to prevail after (a) 6 months, (b) 1 year, and (c) 2 years?

6-3 Overvaluation & Undervaluation of Currency

In Problem 6-2, if the actual rate after one year is J¥110/US$, find the overvaluation/undervaluation of the currency.

6-4 International Investing

The YTM of government bonds in India and Indonesia are 10% and 20%, respectively. As a US investor, in which country would you like to invest if inflation rates of India and Indonesia are 5% and 16%, respectively? Would your decision change if the exchange rate in Indonesia were pegged to US dollar?

6-5 Forward Exchange Rates

Exchange rate in New Delhi for British pound is ₹85.00/£. The interest rates prevailing in India and Britain are 12% and 8%, respectively with flat-term structure. What should be the arbitrage free forward exchange rates for periods of 90 days and 180 days?

6-6 Forward Exchange Rates—Upper & Lower Bounds

In Problem 6-5, the exchange rate has a spread of 100 bps between bid and ask, whereas that of the interest rates is 50 bps. Assume the rates mentioned in Problem 6-5 are mid rates. Find the lower and upper bound to the 12-month forward rate.

Exchange Rate, Economic and Monetary Policies

LEARNING OBJECTIVES

This chapter aims at

- understanding how fiscal and monetary policies impact national economy and exchange rate
- knowing the meaning of internal and external balance
- comprehending how to achieve simultaneous internal and external balance
- understanding the IS-LM-BP approach
- knowing the process of exchange rate adjustment to the fiscal and monetary changes
- understanding the difference in effectiveness of fiscal and monetary policies under fixed and floating rate regimes
- understanding why exchange rates overreact to monetary changes
- knowing monetarists' views on exchange rate forecasting
- getting familiar with portfolio balance model

CONTENTS

Introduction
National Income
Internal Balance and External Balance
    External Balance
Swan Diagram
Mundell–Fleming Model: IS-LM-BP Approach
    IS Schedule
    LM Schedule
Equilibrium in Closed Economy
    BP Schedule
Exchange Rate Expectations
    Effect of Exchange Rate Changes on IS, LM, and BP Schedules

Achieving Equilibrium
Fixed Exchange Rate and Monetary Expansion
Fixed Exchange Rate and Fiscal Expansion
Undervaluation and Overvaluation of Exchange Rate
Flexible Exchange Rate and Monetary Policies
Flexible Exchange Rate and Fiscal Policies
Limitations of IS-LM-BP Approach
Monetary Models of Exchange Rate Determination
Dornbusch's Sticky Price Model
Portfolio Balance Model
Forecasting Exchange Rate
Chartist/Technical Approach

INTRODUCTION

International parity conditions discussed earlier, especially purchasing power parity (PPP), are concerned with the determination of exchange rates based on goods arbitrage, inflation, and interest rates. Besides the fundamental factors influencing exchange rate in today's world, there are numerous other determinants of the exchange rates ranging from balance of payment (BOP) situation to political uncertainties, and fiscal and monetary policies to exchange rate regimes. Increased globalization and integration of economies with the rest of the world have multiplied the variables that determine exchange rates. Free flow of capital across borders too has increased providing broader investment avenues causing prices and returns on the financial assets to converge across the world. Increased integration of capital markets has created additional dimensions to the economic policies of a nation as they are no more closed to or isolated from the happenings in the rest of the world.

In this chapter, we examine the complex relationship between fiscal and monetary policies, on one side, and the exchange rate changes and flow of foreign capital, on the other. It must be recognized that exchange rate changes represent the nation's interaction with the rest of the world and economic policies and exchange rate regimes are interdependent.

NATIONAL INCOME

Recall from Chapter 2 that national income in an open economy is given by sum of consumption (C), Investment (I), Government Expenditure (G), and Net Exports ($X - M$), where X is Exports and M is Imports.

$$Y = C + I + G + X - M \qquad (7\text{-}1)$$

Further, consumption, C, and import, M, are positive functions of income comprising an autonomous component and a dependent component as increasing function of income. A higher level of income means higher consumption of both domestic and imported goods. Therefore, imports become an increasing function of income. Exports, X, and government expenditure, G, are considered autonomous. Exports are determined by the income level of foreigners and the relative value of goods and not as much by domestic income and, therefore, are considered autonomous of domestic output. Imports would imply expenditure on foreign goods instead of domestic goods, and therefore, domestic output need not be higher by the amount of imports.

Exports represent how much foreigners have spent on a nation's goods and services and imports represent how much a nation has spent on foreign goods and services. Therefore, export would imply increase in domestic output and import would reduce the domestic output. Exports are determined by the income level of foreigners and the relative value of goods expressed by the exchange rate. If domestic currency depreciates and foreign income level remains constant, foreigners demand more goods because they become relatively cheaper, thereby increasing exports. Similarly, with depreciating domestic currency, the imports become more expensive, and exports increase. Hence, it is easy to assume that depreciation of domestic currency would cause current account surplus. Conversely, appreciation of domestic currency would lead to current account deficit.

INTERNAL BALANCE AND EXTERNAL BALANCE

The objective of economic policies of a nation is to achieve full employment with stable prices. This is rather never achieved though authorities continuously strive for it. Therefore, the objective can be restated as (a) achieving high economic growth, (b) with low unemployment, and (c) almost zero inflation. If a nation can do so, it is referred to as internal balance. For a closed economy, which permits no international trade or capital flows, the internal balance can be achieved without consideration to the exchange rate and international environment.

The tools available to achieve the internal balance are fiscal and monetary policies. Fiscal policies are concerned with modifying consumption pattern and savings behaviour, channelizing savings to investment, and providing impetus to the economy by government's development expenditure to increase output/GDP and create employment. The fiscal policy predominantly revolves around government budget, that is, ways of generating revenue for the government by altering taxes and undertaking developmental programmes with regard to providing infrastructure, resources, social security, etc. The taxes modify the disposable income in the hands of public and modulate consumption and savings. In a given period, the budget is called (a) a balanced budget when government's revenue equals government's expenditure, (b) a deficit budget when expenditure exceeds revenue, and (c) a surplus budget when revenue exceeds expenditure. The internal balance should not be construed as having a balanced budget but instead a budget that aims at fuller employment with stable prices.

In most developing countries, a deficit budget is common. Even the developed economies have fiscal deficits. The deficit can be financed in three ways—by raising money nationally from residents, called public debt, or by simply printing the money called deficit financing, or by raising money from non-residents called external debt.

Monetary policies are focused on the mode of financing of development programme and controlling the money supply, thereby attempting to achieve price stability. Monetary policy is mainly affected by three tools—(a) through open market operations, that is, issuing and redeeming of government securities to directly impact the money supply in the economy, (b) by regulating reserve requirements which primarily affects the capacity of the banking system to create money, and (c) by changing interest/discount rates (the repo and reverse repo rates), that is, encouraging or discouraging the borrowings by the financial system. Besides these three tools, monetary policy can also control directional flow of credit to the desired sectors by imposing selective conditions on sanction of credits for various sectors such as food, agriculture, housing, and industries or providing incentives and refinancing for credit in certain sectors.

Since monetary policies are quick to implement, they are viewed as a more effective tool than fiscal policies for managing the economy in the short run.

External Balance

When an economy engages in international trade and allows international flows of capital, it is called an open economy. However, the degree of openness may vary from country to country. The trade policy of the nation and the controls placed on the movement of international capital across borders would determine the degree of dependence or independence of the economy on the rest of the world. The tools of trade policies are increasing/decreasing import tariffs, defining quota for import and export, and other administrative trade barriers. The interaction of goods and services and resultant capital flows across borders adds another dimension to money, that is, the exchange rate, which is the value of local currency in terms of foreign currency.

The flow of goods, services, and money across borders is dependent upon several factors including the relative values of goods and services in the two nations. A summary measure of international trade could be the changes in the exchange rate, that is, the appreciating or depreciating value of local currency in terms of foreign currency. If non-residents find it is cheaper to import a product than to buy domestically, they would engage in imports. Similarly, if residents find it cheaper to import than to buy it domestically, they would import. These imports could be altered by influencing the consumption pattern and the trade policy of the nation.

The external linkages of the economy with the rest of the world are captured in the balance of payments. As we know that it has two components—the current account (CA), that is, the exports and imports of goods and services, and the capital account (KA), that is, the flow of capital on financial assets. The combined position of CA and KA determines the foreign exchange reserves. The positions of CA and KA are dependent upon the economic policies of the nation, the competitiveness of its products, efficiency of capital markets, etc.

We may define the external balance of the economy as a position that warrants no change in the foreign exchange reserve position of an economy. A condition requiring no change in the reserve position implies that inflows/outflows on current account exactly match the outflows/inflows on capital account. A persistent surplus or deficit on balance of payment is considered unsustainable in the long term because no nation can accumulate either foreign assets or liabilities on a continuous basis for ever. At some point of time, these accumulations must vanish through exchange of goods and services or financial assets.

SWAN DIAGRAM

In an open economy, a nation has to achieve simultaneous equilibrium internally and externally. This was best illustrated in 1955 by Trevor Swan, an Australian economist, who used relative cost (exchange rate) and fiscal deficit (national income/output) as the two key determinants of the simultaneous external and internal equilibrium. The diagram is used to evaluate the changes to the economy that result from policies that affect either the domestic expenditure or the relative demand for foreign and domestic goods. Exchange rate coupled with a set of economic policies would determine both internal and external balance.

Figure 7-1 depicts the various combinations of real exchange rate and the real income levels where the economy is in internal balance, that is, no unemployment with stable prices. Exchange rate is expressed in direct terms so that increasing exchange rate represents the depreciation of local currency. The locus is downward sloping to the right because an appreciation of domestic currency would reduce exports and increase imports. Therefore, to maintain full employment, income levels have to rise. If the economy is below the internal balance line it represents

Exchange Rate, Economic and Monetary Policies   197

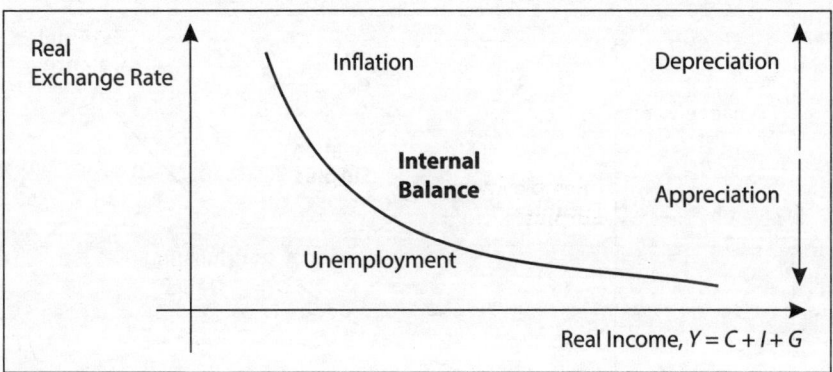

Figure 7-1
Internal Balance

unemployment and if above it implies inflation. For a given exchange rate, if the economy is above the internal balance schedule, it is inflationary because the income levels are greater than what is required for full employment.

The external balance schedule depicts combinations of different exchange rates with income for which the nation is in external balance, that is, requiring no change in foreign exchange reserves. For a given level of income, the area above the external balance schedule indicates BOP surplus because a depreciated local currency would encourage exports and reduced imports, creating a current account surplus. The external balance schedule is upward sloping because depreciation of local currency creates current account surplus, and to offset it one needs to increase the income levels to increase imports. Figure 7-2 depicts the external balance.

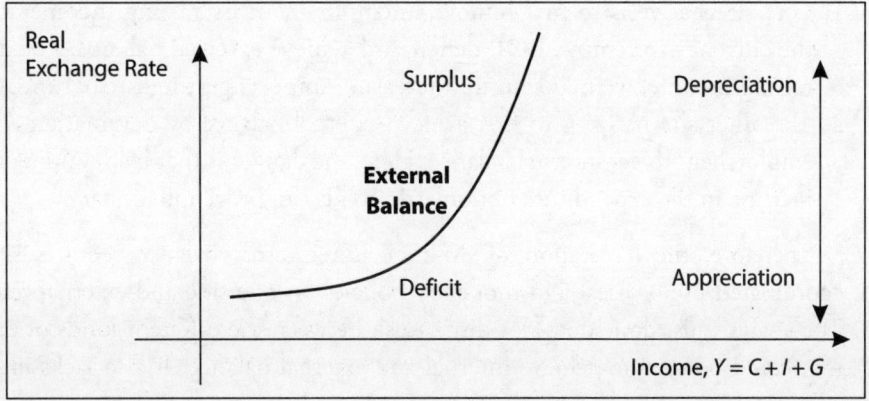

Figure 7-2
External Balance

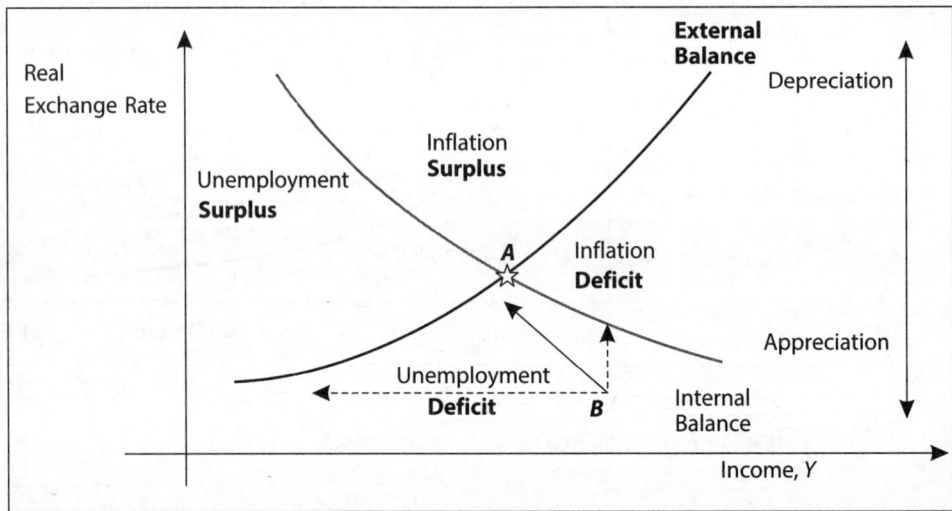

Figure 7-3
Internal and External Balance

Figure 7-3 is the simultaneous depiction of internal and external balances which takes place at only one point, A, surrounded by four regions—inflation with surplus BOP, inflation with deficit BOP, unemployment with surplus BOP, and unemployment with deficit BOP. These regions are clearly marked in Figure 7-3. Only at Point A, the economy is at internal as well as external balance, that is, full employment with no inflation and balanced BOP with current account offsetting capital account and no change in reserves.

If we are in the region of unemployment and deficit, at Point B we have two ways to restore external and internal balance to go back to A—via internal balance curve or via external balance curve.

1. One alternative is to first remove unemployment by raising income and then devalue the currency to remove BOP deficit and achieve external balance. The danger is that by raising income, we may end up increasing imports getting further into BOP deficit.
2. The other alternative is to first achieve external balance by devaluation and then enhance employment to get internal balance. Here, the danger is that by devaluing the currency, the increase in the expenditure of domestic goods can prove inflationary.

Therefore, the restoration of external and internal balance requires simultaneous and coordinated use of fiscal and monetary policies on one side and external trade on the other. The analysis just done does not distinguish between the different kinds of economic policies that could be used to achieve internal and external balance. It also lacks in determining the efficacy of monetary and fiscal policies used in addressing the problem. To better understand the adjustment process, with the internal and external linkages getting more and more complex in today's world, we need a more comprehensive framework that distinguishes between various fiscal and monetary policies with their implications on free capital flows across borders.

MUNDELL–FLEMING MODEL: IS-LM-BP APPROACH

The IS-LM-BP model is one framework that is the most comprehensive, suggesting the suitable tools and remedies that could be used in solving domestic economic issues along with the external environment. It uses three variables—the income/output in the economy, the interest rate, and exchange rate along which the targets can be specified, measured, and affected by fiscal, monetary, and trade policies. It addresses the issue of how to achieve internal and external balance in an economy.

The IS-LM-BP framework, attributed to Robert Mundell and James Fleming and also called Mundell–Fleming model, is an extension of Keynesian macroeconomic model incorporating the international capital movement. *IS* meaning Investment and Savings focuses on fiscal policies; *LM* that stands for Liquid Money deals with monetary policies; and *BP* signifying the Balance of Payment concentrates on exchange rate policies. The impact of fiscal, monetary, and exchange rate policies is examined on income/output, interest rates, and exchange rates.

IS Schedule

IS schedule is the locus of various combinations of income levels and interest rates that equates the savings and investment. The economy is in internal balance at all the points on the IS schedule. In a closed economy with no exports, E, and imports, M, the national income, Y, is the sum of consumption, C, investment, I, and government expenditure, G. In an open economy, exports and imports influence the national income leading to the expression already stated as Eq. 7-1:

$$Y = C + I + G + X - M$$

Savings, S, is given by $(Y - C)$ and hence $S = I + G + X - M$

The nature of investment, exports and imports, and government expenditure is as follows:

- Consumption, savings, and imports are an increasing function of income, depending upon the marginal propensity to consume, save, and import, represented by c, s, and m, respectively, that is, the fraction of additional income that would be spent on consumption, savings, and investment. Larger the values of c, s, and m, larger would be the change with increased income. Parts of consumption, savings, and import are autonomous, denoted by C_a, S_a, and M_a, respectively, that does not depend on income level. The consumption function, savings function, and import function are, therefore, represented as follows:

$$C = C_a + cY \tag{7-2}$$

$$S = S_a + sY \tag{7-3}$$

$$M = M_a + mY \tag{7-4}$$

- Investment is a decreasing function of interest rates, that is, lower the interest rates, higher is the investment, and can be represented by Eq. 7-5.

$$I = I_a - br \tag{7-5}$$

- Government expenditure and exports are assumed exogenous, that is, independent of interest rates and income levels in the economy. Exports would be a function of income level of foreigners and not that of residents.

For tax rate of t, private savings would be equal to disposable income less consumption, that is, $(1-t)Y - C$ and government savings would be $tY - G$. In an open economy, the foreigners too would impact the savings. If a nation exports more than it imports, then the extra consumption by foreigners is funded by the nation and differential would flow out as investment abroad by the residents. If imports are more than exports, then foreigners are funding the consumption of the residents. Therefore, in an open economy, the savings would be as follows:

$$S = \text{Savings by residents} + \text{Savings by government} + \text{savings by foreigners}$$
$$= \{(1-t)Y - C\} + \{(tY - G)\} + \{M - X\}$$

For a closed economy, $X = M = 0$ and $Y = C + I + G$ and $S = \{(1-t)Y - C\} + \{(tY - G)\}$.

The IS curve implies that at all points on it, the goods market is in equilibrium and investment equals savings. The IS curve is plotted with income on horizontal axis and interest rate on vertical axis. The horizontal axis can also be seen as output or employment. The IS curve is the locus of all points for different levels of income and interest rates at which savings equal investment.

With increasing levels of income, savings would rise and so would the investment. To achieve equality of higher levels of savings, the investment too must increase. Therefore, the interest rate would have to fall to restore the equality because investment is an inverse function of the interest rate. Therefore, the IS curve would be negatively sloped. This is shown in Figure 7-4. Normally, a curved function, the IS curve is depicted here as a linear function for simplicity but without losing the efficacy of the outcome of analysis of changes. The area above the IS curve to the right implies that savings are more than the investment and the region to the left and below the IS curve states that investment is greater than savings.

Fiscal Expansion and Contraction   Increase in consumption or increase in investment shifts the IS curve to the right, increasing the income/output for each level of interest rate. Fiscal policy relates to the government's spending and collection. Expansionary fiscal policy, implying either widening fiscal deficit or shrinking fiscal surplus, would move the IS schedule to the right, increasing the income. Increased government spending would raise income levels manifold depending upon the propensity to consume/save if interest rate is held constant. If income does not increase with increased fiscal deficit, the savings would come down (since government savings decline). To restore the equality, the investment must come down and, therefore, interest rate must increase. Hence, fiscal expansion would cause increase in income/output or increase in interest rate or some combination of both. The effect on investment is ambiguous because rising income warrants rising investment, whereas increasing interest causes decline in investment. The net impact would be aggregate of the two effects depending on which of the two opposing effects is larger.

Reduction in fiscal deficit or increasing the fiscal surplus would have the opposite effect on income. Figure 7-4 also depicts the effects of fiscal expansion and contraction on the IS curve.

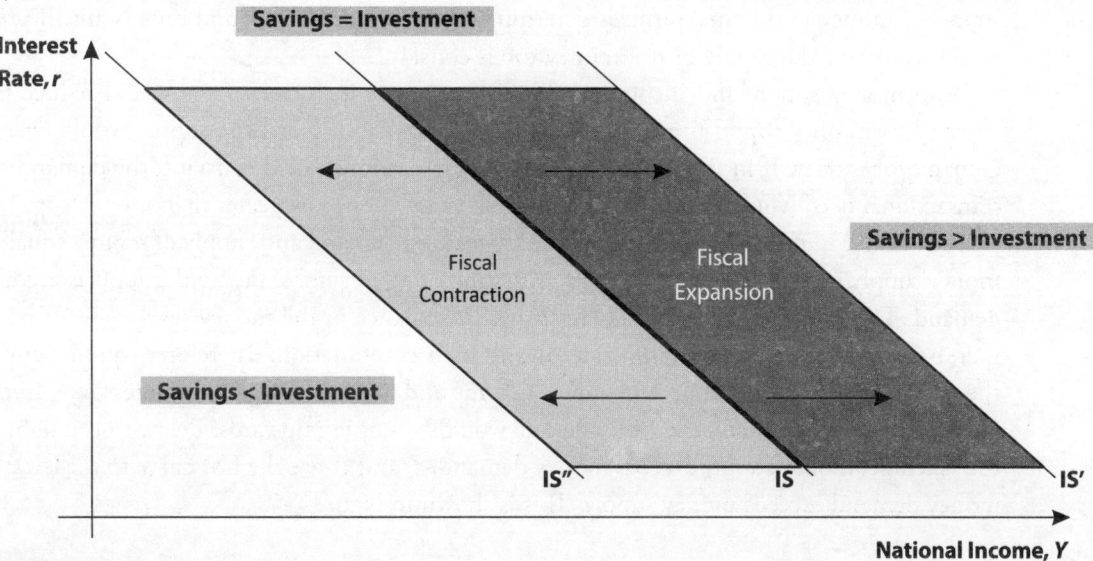

Figure 7-4
Investment Saving (IS) Schedule, Fiscal Expansion, and Contraction

LM Schedule

Just as the IS curve describes the equilibrium of goods market, LM curve is the equilibrium in the money markets. It equates the demand for money with supply of money. LM schedule is the locus of various combinations of income/output and interest rates that keep money market in balance, that is, quantity of money demanded is equal to the quantity of money supplied. This is also termed as liquidity preference.

Demand for money constitutes two components—for transactional needs and for speculative purposes. Just as two purposes money can be said to have two forms—cash and bonds. Transaction needs, fulfilled by having cash, are related to consumption and, hence, depend upon the income level. Higher the income level, higher is the demand for cash money. The money saved goes in the form of speculation. Cash is required for transaction needs, whereas speculative needs are kept in the form of bonds. All money available is in the form of cash or bonds, and consumers do portfolio balancing in allocating the money in the two forms of cash and bonds.

As said before, any money held in excess of transactional needs is for speculative purposes. If interest rates rise, people shift to bonds. The demand for money for speculative purposes would be higher if the interest rate is higher. It is because higher the interest rate, higher is the opportunity cost of holding money for transactional purposes. Hence, with rising interest rate, the demand for speculative money would rise, whereas demand for transactional needs would fall.

The LM curve with respect to income would be positively sloped because if for any reason the income level rises, the need for cash would rise. This implies that less is available for bonds. Therefore, interest rate must rise for consumers to have bonds. Here, it is assumed that the supply of money in nominal terms is determined by the central bank and is constant. If price level is constant, the supply of real money too is constant.

With money supply and income held constant, a rise in interest rates would reduce the demand for money (opportunity cost of holding cash rises). Here, the supply would exceed demand for money. If income increases with supply of money held constant, the demand for transactional need would go up. Here, the demand for money is greater than money supply.

The balance in money market is achieved by making demand and supply of money equal. If money supply is increased, then we have a situation of money imbalance with supply exceeding demand. To increase the demand for restoring the balance in the money market, we need to increase income or reduce interest rate or any such combination. Therefore, equilibrium in the money market is a positive function of income and inverse function of interest rate. In the income–interest rate space, the LM schedule would be sloping upwards. Below to the right of the schedule, money supply exceeds money demanded, and above the LM curve to the left, the money demand exceeds money supply. This is shown in Figure 7-5.

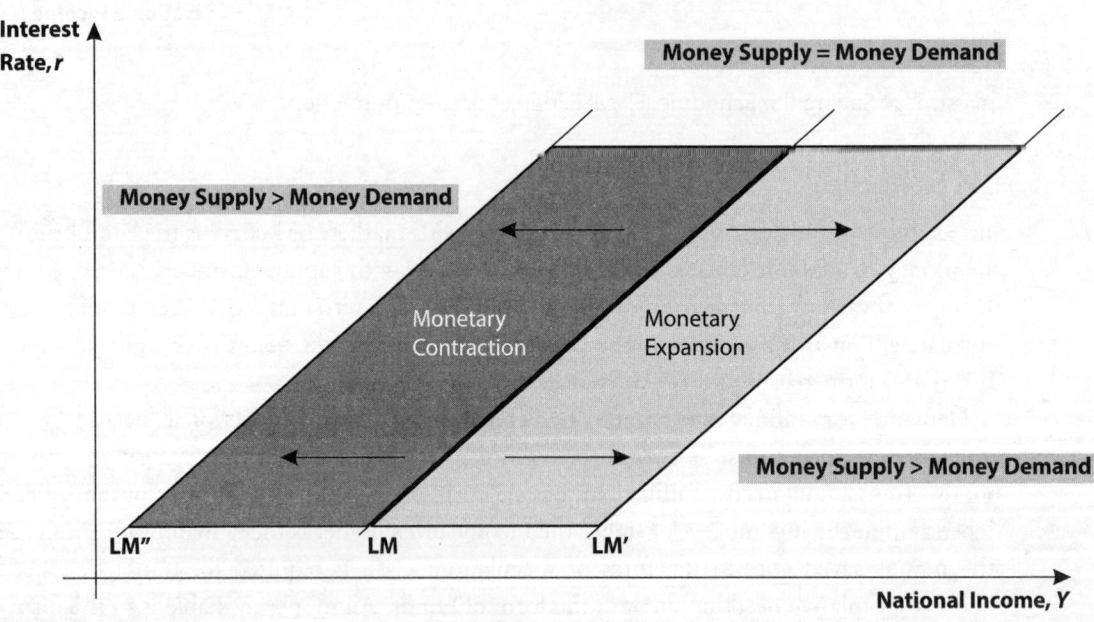

Figure 7-5
LM Schedule, Monetary Expansion, and Contraction

Monetary Expansion and Contraction Money supply is exogenously determined by central bank. The central bank may take a number of steps, directly or indirectly, to alter the supply of money or influence the demand for money. Changing interest rates is an attempt to influence the demand, whereas open market operations of buying and selling of government securities has direct implication on the supply of money. The measures that create situations where supply of money becomes greater than its demand are termed as monetary expansion. Monetary expansion would shift the LM curve down to the right. The situations that make demand for money greater than the supply are termed as monetary contractions, which shift the LM curve up to the left. These too are shown in Figure 7-5.

EQUILIBRIUM IN A CLOSED ECONOMY

With the understanding of IS and LM curves, we are now ready to understand the equilibrium position in the closed economy. For a closed economy, the equilibrium is provided by the intersection of the IS and LM schedules, where both the goods market and money market are in equilibrium. This is a combination of income and interest rate at which economy is in equilibrium in the goods and money markets. This would be true for a closed economy having no international linkages.

Every nation attempts (though has never reached) to reach an equilibrium, both in the goods market and in the money market. These attempts are made by constantly changing fiscal and monetary policies striving for the balance and achieving economic objectives of raising income and employment, containing inflation, etc.

Fiscal policies are concerned with the expenditure and revenue of the government. Revenues are generated by taxes which change the disposable income of the nation affecting the consumption. Expenditure by government increases total spending in the economy. It has multiplier effect and increases the national income manifold depending upon marginal propensity to consume/save. If the marginal propensity of save is s, the income multiplier is $1/s$.

If fiscal expansion is financed by printing money, the money supply would increase and the LM curve too would shift. If deficit is financed by public debt the money supply remains constant, because finance raised by issuing bonds gets ploughed back in the economy by way of increased government expenditure. If fiscal expansion is by way of reduced taxes, the increased disposable income would increase consumption, propelling growth in output and reducing unemployment.

Fiscal expansion would shift the IS curve to the right so as to intersect the LM curve at a higher level. The new equilibrium would be at a higher output level with higher interest rate. This is shown in Figure 7-6 where the equilibrium moves from Point A to Point B on the new IS schedule, IS_2.

Fiscal policy is a very effective tool for managing an economy and combating business cycles. Increase in government expenditure has multiplier effect and boosts the income level creating increased demand for goods and services. It can lead to increased output or increased prices. If the economy is at less than full employment, the supply catches up with the demand and there is little increase in prices. But if the economy is at full employment, the effect of fiscal expansion is inflationary with output not changing. When the focus is on reducing unemployment, expansionary fiscal policy can be followed but when the concern is on controlling inflation, a strategy of running a budget surplus (contractionary fiscal policy) is more appropriate.

Monetary expansion would increase money supply lowering the interest rate. The increase in money supply would be through buying of the bonds raising their prices and, therefore, reducing yield. The LM curve shifts down and to the right. Fall in interest rate leads to higher income. Higher income forces increased output and employment. The income would increase till the quantity demanded for money matches the increased supply of money. Increased money supply should also reduce budget deficit because for a given tax rate and expenditure level, the government revenue increases due to rise in income. The effect of monetary expansion is shown in Figure 7-7.

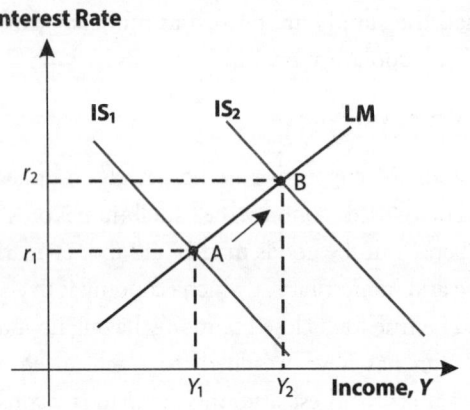

Fiscal expansion by raising government expenditure would shift the original IS curve, IS_1 to the right at IS_2 intersecting LM curve at a higher income level Y_2 and a higher interest rate r_2.

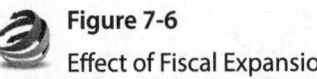

Figure 7-6
Effect of Fiscal Expansion

The effects of fiscal and monetary policies on the income and interest rates are summarized as follows:

1. An expansionary fiscal policy results in a rightward shift in IS, an increase in the interest rate, and an increase in output.
2. A contractionary fiscal policy results in leftward shift in IS, a decrease in the interest rate, and a decrease in output.
3. An expansionary monetary policy results in a rightward shift in LM, a decrease in the interest rate, and an increase in output.
4. A contractionary monetary policy results in a leftward shift in LM, an increase in the interest rate, and a decrease in output.

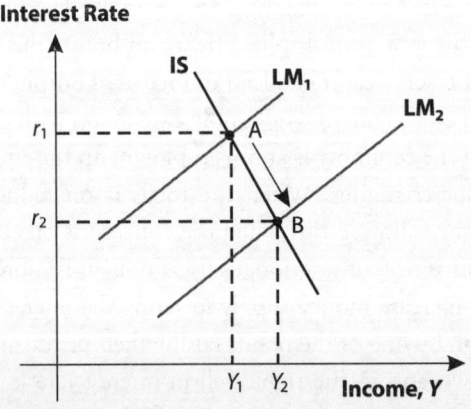

Monetary expansion by raising money supply shifts LM_1 curve down and right to LM_2 intersecting the IS curve at a lower interest rate, r_2 but at a higher Income level, Y_2.

Figure 7-7
Effect of Monetary Expansion

BP Schedule

In an open economy, the demand and supply of domestic money can be affected by preferences of foreigners—both in terms of flow of goods and flow of capital. The exports and imports would affect the output and therefore the income levels. Interest rate changes would govern the capital flows. Therefore, non-residents too become participants in the economy and bear the consequences of economic policies that a nation follows.

The transactions of the non-residents are captured in the balance of payment. The equilibrium in the balance of payment is defined as the position where foreign currency reserves remain unchanged. We know that BOP can be divided into two parts—current account and capital account. The CA records the trade in goods and services, and the KA records capital flows on financial assets. The net change in the two is reflected in changes the foreign currency reserves the nation has. If the reserves remain unchanged, it implies that deficit (liabilities)/surplus (assets) in CA are exactly matched by the surplus (assets)/deficit (liabilities) in the KA. If the nation can have unchanged foreign currency reserves, we deem the economy to be in external balance.

Like IS and LM curves, which are the loci of the different levels of income and interest rates with respect to equality of savings and investment and money demand and supply, respectively, the BP schedule is the locus of points in the space of income–interest rate at which the BOP is in equilibrium, that is, no change in the foreign exchange reserves position. For simultaneous internal as well as external balance, all three schedules—IS, LM, and BP—must intersect at one point.

Shape of BP Curve Assume that in the income–interest rate space, we are at equilibrium with respect to external world. For some reason (say fiscal expansion) the income rises. The economy would no more be in balance with the external world and has to find a new equilibrium. As income rises, the consumption including those of imported goods increases. With export considered independent, the rise in income would result in current account deficit. To keep reserves unchanged, the current account deficit has to be offset by foreign capital inflows. If the real interest rate increases, foreigners would buy financial assets and capital would flow in. Therefore, the interest rate must increase just enough to offset the current account deficit caused by increased income. Therefore, the BP curve should be sloping upwards.

Therefore, the BP schedule would be an increasing function of income. The slope of the BP schedule would depend upon the marginal propensity to import (the fraction of income spent on foreign goods) and the degree of capital mobility across nations. If the degree of capital mobility is high, then a smaller rise in the interest rate would cause relatively larger capital inflows in the country. For offsetting the current account deficit, a smaller rise in interest rate is required to attract equivalent capital inflows to restore the BOP. The area up to the left of the BP curve implies BOP surplus and below to the right implies BOP deficit, as shown in Figure 7-8.

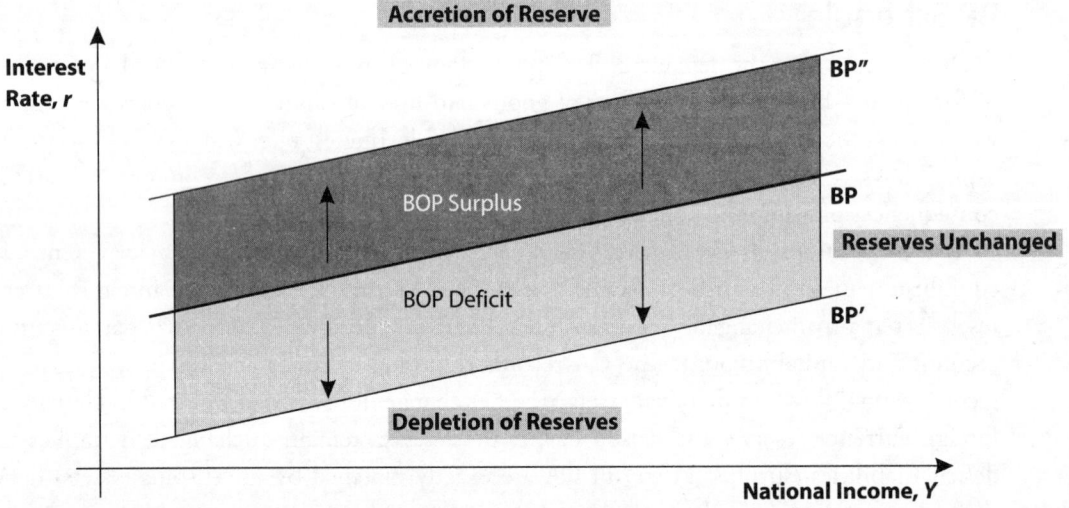

Figure 7-8
BP Curve: BOP Surplus and Deficit

Slope of BP Curve The slope of BP schedule can be defined as the change in interest rate required for a given change in the income, that is, $\Delta r/\Delta Y$ to restore the foreign currency reserves to the original level. The income level of a nation may change due to several reasons. For a given increase in income if a smaller increase in interest rate is required, the BP curve would be flatter. The slope of BP curve indicates the degree of capital mobility, that is, how much the international flow of funds responds to changes in interest rate. A flatter BP schedule represents high capital mobility. A vertical BP schedule means no capital flows at all and a horizontal BP schedule represents perfect mobility of capital. A miniscule rise in domestic interest rate with world interest rate constant would result in massive inflow of foreign capital and a slightly lower domestic interest rate implies massive outflow of foreign capital.

These small changes in the flow of foreign capital place tremendous pressure on the exchange rate to change in floating exchange rate system. Under fixed exchange rate system, the capital flows from outside the economy would have to be met by domestic money. A vertical BP schedule means domestic interest rate is independent of world's interest rate, whereas a horizontal BP schedule represents domestic interest rates are aligned with foreign interest rate.

In a closed economy, both imports and exports are zero and the slope of the IS curve is determined by marginal propensity to save, s, whose value is $1/s$. In an open economy, the multiplier would be lesser at $1/(s + m)$. Therefore, for the IS curve in case of open economy, the impact of fiscal stimulus on the changes in national income would be smaller than in case of closed economy.

Similarly, the slope of LM curve is the elasticity of money with respect to interest and income. With participation of non-residents in the domestic economy, the question of exchange rate viz-à-viz interest rate gains importance. The relative slopes of LM curve and

BP curve indicate the substitutability of foreign money and domestic money. If the BP curve is flatter than the LM curve, the foreign flow of capital is more mobile and responsive to the changes in the interest rate as compared to the domestic money. If the LM curve is flatter than the BP curve, it implies that foreign money is not as mobile as domestic money.

EXCHANGE RATE EXPECTATIONS

The effect of opening the economy to trade in goods and services and capital flows is that exchange rate policies also enter the prescription domain for curing the economy. Therefore, all three schedules need to be understood with respect to the exchange rate changes. We need to recapture international parity conditions.

International parity conditions involved interest rate parity that linked the forward rate to the differential of the interest rates in two currencies. It was derived with the conditions of no arbitrage by setting up a risk-free position by borrowing in one currency and investing in another, and covering the borrowed amount through a forward contract.

International Fisher effect related the interest rates to the changes in the future spot exchange rates. We view a similar position in a slightly different context here in the sense that expected interest rate differential would drive the changes in the current spot exchange rates. For example, consider the position of an international investor facing an option to invest in India and the USA in the bonds issued by the respective governments. The investor deems the investment in India and the USA equally risky and is indifferent to the currency of investment. Further, we assume that the capital flow across India and the USA is unrestricted. If conditions of perfect mobility of capital and risk neutrality of the investor are assumed to be true, then the currency exchange markets would ensure that returns in the two investment avenues are equalized.

Assume that yields in the bonds of India and the USA are 8% and 3%, respectively. The investor in the USA can invest in US bond to have yield of 3%, whereas in India he can get a return of 8%. To invest in India, he needs to convert US dollars in Indian rupee at spot rate, invest in rupee, and finally on maturity of investment reconvert the rupee back to US dollars. If the spot exchange rate remains unchanged during the period, the investor locks-in a return of 8% in US dollar terms. However, this arbitrage condition cannot exist in perfect capital markets. The 5% extra returns must be compensated by changes in the exchange rates with Indian rupee depreciating by 5%. This is referred to as Uncovered Interest Rate Parity (UIP) according to which, to equalize returns the expected spot rate after one year would indicate depreciation of rupee by 5%. If the current spot exchange rate is ₹50.00/$, then the expected spot rate after one year should be ₹52.50/$.

Would the current spot rate remain unaffected? The UIP condition states that the spot rate is influenced by differential of expected interest rates. Assume that yields on the Indian bonds now rise from 8% to 9% due to contractionary monetary policy initiated by Indian government. The situation can be assimilated in UIP if rupee is depreciated immediately by 1% in the spot market to equalize real returns. If the exchange rate is not allowed to change, as would be the case under the fixed exchange rate regime, the extra nominal gains must be eroded by increased inflation.

Effect of Exchange Rate Changes on IS, LM, and BP Schedules

In an open economy, the exchange rate changes and regime add another dimension to economic policies because these changes influence all the three schedules—IS, LM, and BP. Holding all other things constant, let us examine the impact of exchange rate changes on each of the three schedules. The change in exchange rate is a policy matter with the nations and they may choose any exchange rate regime. The frequency, timing, and quantum of exchange rate changes are essentially determined by the authorities. Irrespective of the exchange rate regime, exchange rate does change. In case of flexible exchange rate system, the adjustment is continuous and small, whereas in case of fixed exchange rate system the changes are abrupt and large.

Impact on IS Schedule Any depreciation in the local currency would increase exports and decrease imports improving the current account. For the same interest rate and to restore the earlier position of current account, the imports must increase (exports are more a function income of foreigners) to offset the increased exports. Therefore, the income must rise to increase consumption of imported goods. Hence, the IS schedule must shift to the right. If income is held constant, the improved current account position indicates that the contribution of foreigners to the savings, that is, $(X - M)$ has decreased. Equivalently, the investment must fall which can happen only by increasing the interest rate. The effects of appreciation of local currency would shift the IS curve to the left, decreasing income and decreasing interest rate.

Under fixed exchange rate system, the IS schedule remains unaffected till authorities devalue or revalue the currency.

Impact on LM Schedule Depreciation of local currency makes imported goods expensive. With increase in the prices of imported goods, the real supply of money decreases. If the demand for money for transaction purposes remains same, we have a position where demand for money exceeds supply of money. To reduce the demand for money, the income level must fall. Therefore, LM schedule must shift left, indicating lower income. Another way of reducing the transaction demand for money is to increase the opportunity cost of holding money. This can be done by increased interest rate. It is easy to see why appreciation of local currency would shift the LM schedule to the right.

Impact on BP Schedule It is already stated that depreciation of local currency discourages imports and encourages exports, improving the current account balance. To remedy the situation, the nation either must increase imports or offset the improved current account balance with equal deterioration in capital account. Imports can be increased by increasing income, holding interest rate constant. Capital inflows would deteriorate with decrease in the interest rate. Therefore, depreciation of local currency would shift the BP schedule to the right with increased income and reduced interest rate. The effect of appreciation of the local currency would be the opposite.

The impact of local currency depreciation on IS, LM, and BP curves is shown in Figure 7-9 (a), (b), and (c).

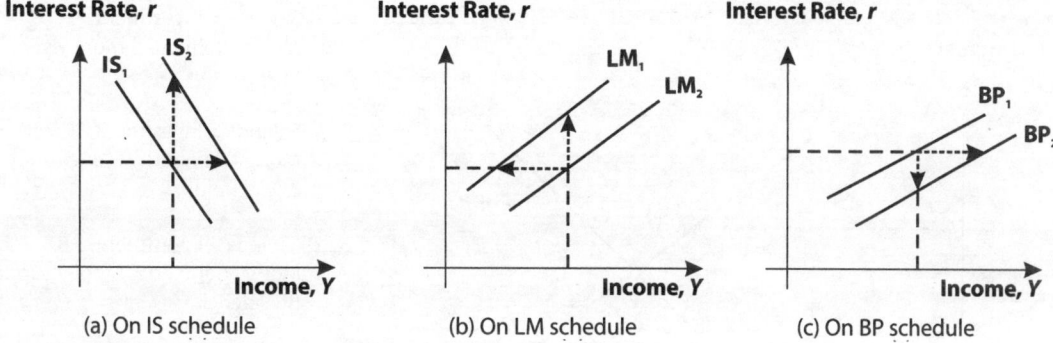

Figure 7-9
Impact of Depreciation of Local Currency

Achieving Equilibrium

Given that an economy is in internal balance, the equilibrium may lie either in the BOP deficit region (below to the right of BP curve) or in BOP surplus region (above to the left of BP curve). Under the fixed exchange rate system, neither the IS curve nor the BP curve undergoes a change. Only LM curve moves. The adjustment is done by monetary policy controlling the supply of domestic money.

Under flexible exchange rate system, exchange rate is allowed to change and, hence, imports and exports are affected. Therefore, IS curve gets altered besides the BP curve. If the internal equilibrium (the intersection of IS and LM curves) is above the BP curve, the internal balance is in the BOP surplus region indicating exports exceeding imports. To wipe out the surplus, imports must rise. Therefore, income must rise to induce consumption of imported goods and IS schedule must shift to the right.

Internal and external equilibrium under the IS-LM-BP model is depicted at the common intersection of the IS, LM, and BP schedules as shown at point E in Figure 7-10. At E, the economy would have equality of savings and investment, money demand and money supply, and unchanged foreign currency reserves. At any other point, the economy would not be in equilibrium. In all, there are six regions denoted as I to VI that are economically different and would require different shock treatments from fiscal, monetary, and exchange rate policies to restore the equilibrium. The appropriateness and efficacy of shock treatments in each case would be different.

Let us examine a point in Region I. Any point in Region I is characterized by savings exceeding investment being above the IS curve, money demand in exceeding money supply being on the left of LM curve, and BOP in surplus again being to the left of BP curve. To reach equilibrium, we have fiscal, monetary, and exchange rate policies available to guide the economy, with the following objectives to be achieved simultaneously:

(a) Equalize savings and investment by reducing savings/increasing investment.
(b) Match supply and demand of money by reducing demand for money/increasing supply of money.
(c) Balance BOP by removing surplus by controlling CA/KA transactions.

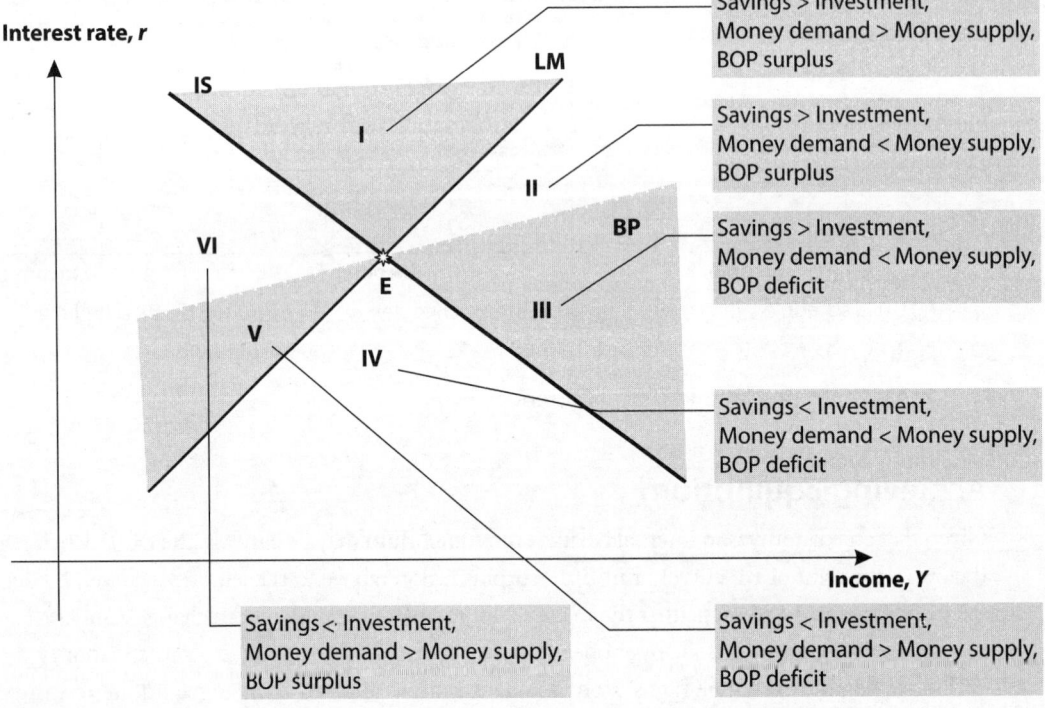

Figure 7-10
Equilibrium and Disequilibrium under IS-LM-BP Model

Let us consider the effect of fiscal policy alone. Fiscal expansion, by way of increased government expenditure, financed by public debt would increase income and hence, increase imports. This would tend to reduce the BOP surplus. The shift of IS schedule to the right also implies increase in interest rate which has impact on domestic investment and capital flows. Assuming that decreased investment due to rise in interest rate would more than offset the decrease in income due to multiplier effect of fiscal stimulus, the outcome on BOP surplus, thus, becomes uncertain. For the LM schedule too, the likely outcome is opposite to what is desired. Increased income also increases demand for transaction money and the result would be exacerbating the gap between money demand and supply rather than shrinking the gap. Hence, fiscal measure alone may not work for restoring the equilibrium.

Now consider monetary expansion to meet the excess demand of money by increased supply. Increased money supply reduces interest rate. With the IS curve remaining unchanged, the exports and imports are assumed constant and, hence, there is no impact on current account due to income changes. However, a fall in interest rate would make (a) local currency appreciate making exports uncompetitive and imports attractive, reducing current account surplus, and/or (b) foreign capital flow dry up also deteriorating capital account. Therefore, BOP surplus position moves towards equilibrium consistent with the objective. The impact on IS curve too would be favourable because decreased interest rate induces investment reducing the gap between savings and investment. Hence, under the circumstances, monetary policy should prove extremely appropriate and effective.

The authorities have other measures that have direct impact on BOP position. Under fixed exchange rate regime, revaluation of local currency would make imports attractive and exports uncompetitive. This brings down the BOP surplus. Under flexible exchange rate system, the exchange rate would respond to economic conditions automatically. Other measures that are independent of exchange rate regime to reduce BOP surplus could be to regulate the capital inflows without changing the interest rate, including taxing the inflows, or posing other barriers to inflows of foreign capital such as through FDI policy.

It may be now noted that solutions to the problems of the economy are situation specific. Because of the intricate linkages of economic parameters, the effects of various policy measures are multi-dimensional with non-uniform impact. Some measures may be more desirable and effective than others. We analyse eight different combinations of the IS-LM-BP configurations with respect to effectiveness of fiscal and monetary policies under fixed and flexible exchange rate systems.

Under flexible exchange rate system, the broad framework is that the focus is to determine interest rate through the BP curve, then find corresponding money supply from the LM curve, and move to IS curve. Under fixed exchange rates system, the exchange rate is exogenously determined by the law and money supply is adjusted through interventions in the currency markets to maintain the desired exchange rate. Therefore, we move from the BP curve to the IS curve, and then determine desired money supply from the LM curve.

We now analyse four different situations of IS-LM-BP configurations, that is, fixed exchange rate system with monetary and fiscal expansion and flexible exchange rate system with monetary and fiscal expansion.

Fixed Exchange Rate and Monetary Expansion

Under fixed exchange rate, monetary expansion would be undertaken by redeeming of government securities causing the prices of government bonds to increase and yield to fall. The LM schedule shifts down and right from LM_1 to LM_2 as shown in Figure 7-11. With downward pressure on interest rates, the internal equilibrium tends to move from A to B with income tending to rise. The seemingly favourable scenario of decreasing interest rate and rising income is extremely transitory and illusory in nature. The external factors start acting to counter the monetary expansion.

At Point A, the economy had external as well as internal balance. With internal balance moving to B below the BP schedule (in the deficit region), the external balance is yet to be achieved. With open economy, the fall in yield would dry up capital inflows and they prove insufficient to offset the current account deficit. The deficit puts pressure for local currency devaluation. Since the economy pursues fixed exchange rate, the central bank intervenes to sell foreign currency/buy local currency to ward off the pressure to devalue the local currency. The intervention in the currency markets, buying local currency, nullifies the earlier policy of monetary expansion, restoring the money supply back to the original level. The outcome is that the economy retraces back to A from B.

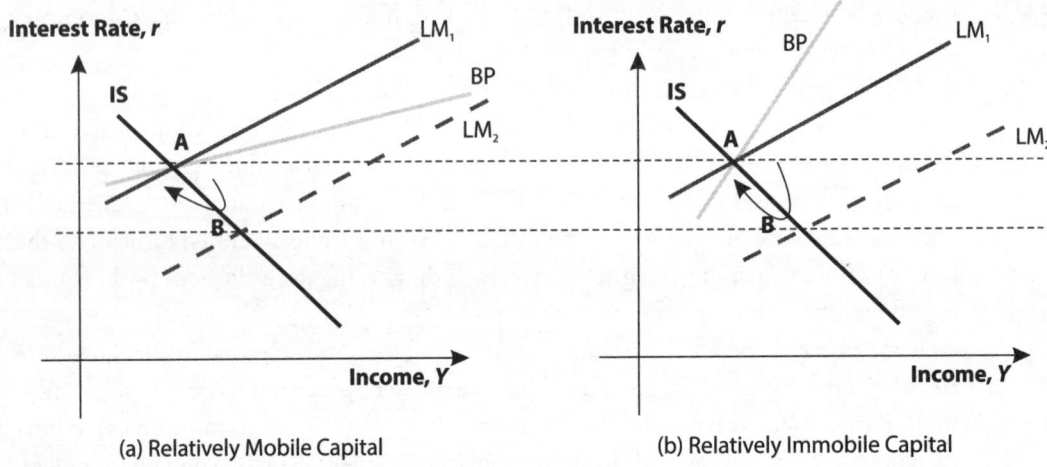

Figure 7-11
Fixed Exchange Rate System—Monetary Expansion

Therefore, monetary expansion would not result in increase of income or decrease of interest rate since intervention in the foreign currency markets nullifies the supposedly honest and sincere objectives of monetary expansion policy and would prove to be ineffective.

The degree of openness of the economy to external trade and capital flows is immaterial, as may be seen from Figure 7-11 (a) and (b). Figure 7-11 (a) and (b) show positions with relatively mobile capital (flatter BP schedule than LM schedule) and relatively immobile capital (steeper BP schedule than LM schedule). At best, relative mobility of foreign capital impacts only on the time required for adjustment in the economy. In case of mobile capital, adjustment back would be quicker than the time taken in case of immobile capital.

Under the fixed exchange rate system, the monetary policy changes prove ineffective. It essentially implies that economies having fixed exchange rate system need to align the monetary policies with those of major trading partners or the home nation of the currency in which the international trade is denominated.

Under fixed rate system, following independent monetary policy also poses a threat of inflation. In case the economy is not having the unemployment as one of the major problems, the increased money supply has potential to result in inflation as supply side is not matched with increased money supply. Monetary policy as a tool to achieve full employment could indeed misfire.

Fixed Exchange Rate and Fiscal Expansion

While the monetary policies affect the LM schedule leaving IS schedule unchanged, the fiscal policies impact the IS schedule. The IS schedule, being more fundamental in nature, remains unaffected by monetary policies. By the same token, we may say that attempts to change the IS schedule can force the LM schedule to alter. The money supply has to respond to fundamentals in the economy, whereas money supply may or may not cause or force a change in the fundamentals.

Fiscal expansion can be achieved by either reducing taxes or spending more, widening the fiscal deficit. In either case, the IS schedule, IS_1, would shift to the right as IS_2 intersecting the existing LM schedule, LM_1, at higher levels of income and interest rates. The internal balance would shift from A to B as shown in Figure 7-12.

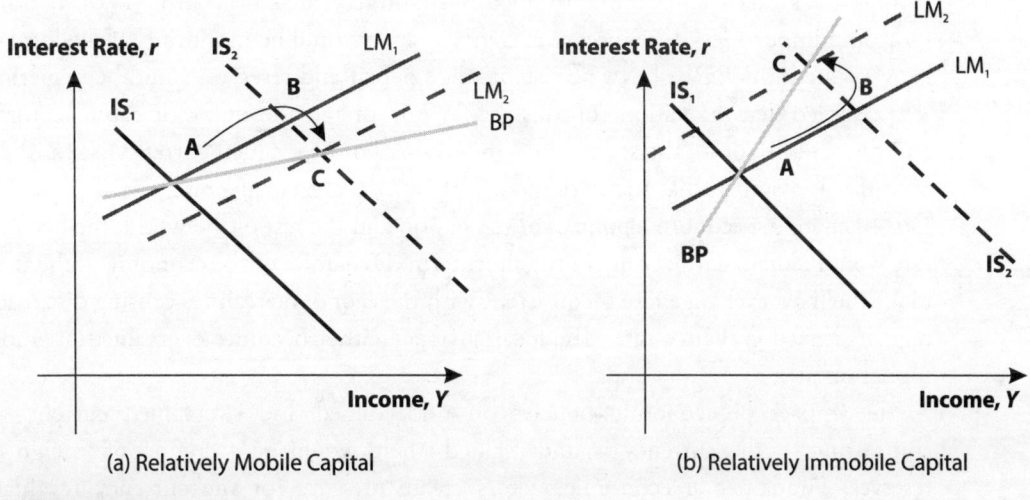

(a) Relatively Mobile Capital   (b) Relatively Immobile Capital

Figure 7-12
Fixed Exchange Rate System—Fiscal Expansion

The behaviour of LM schedule would depend upon the relative mobility of foreign capital, as contrasted in Figure 7-12(a) and (b).

When foreign capital is more mobile (BP curve flatter than LM curve) the fiscal expansion causes IS curve to move right from IS_1 to IS_2 indicating higher income level and higher interest rate as shown by Point B in Figure 7-12(a). Foreign capital, being extremely mobile, moves in to take advantage of raised interest rate. Foreign capital flows are more than what is required to offset the current account deficit. To keep exchange rate unchanged the central banks needs to buy foreign currency and in the process increase supply of local currency. This inadvertent monetary expansion shifts the LM curve down to the right from LM_1 to LM_2. Thus, economy moves from B to C at higher income level but lower interest rates. Hence fiscal expansion would be extremely effective in case of mobile foreign capital.

However, if foreign capital is not as mobile (BP curve steeper than LM curve) the rise in income level due to fiscal expansion would cause deficit in BOP. This must be matched by capital surplus to keep reserve position same. Here, the local currency would depreciate. To keep the exchange rate fixed the central bank needs to buy local currency. This would be inadvertent monetary contraction shifting LM curve upwards to the left from LM_1 to LM_2 as shown by Point C in Figure 7-12(b). Thus, the impact of fiscal stimulus would be partly offset and would not be as effective as was the case with greater mobility of foreign capital.

Undervaluation and Overvaluation of Exchange Rate Another issue that is of concern under the fixed exchange rate system is how appropriate is the fixed exchange rate with respect to what the economy can take. Seldom do we find that exchange rate is correctly fixed by authorities. The undervaluation or overvaluation of the exchange rate can be gauged by monitoring the trends of BOP. If the balance of payment shows persistent and large trade surplus, the local currency is undervalued. With undervalued local currency, the nation exports more and imports less. The foreign currency reserve would be mounting. If the local currency is overvalued, the BOP shows persistent trade deficit and reserves would be depleting. Here, it is assumed that the nation controls the flow of foreign and domestic capital across borders and does sterilization. The scenario of undervalued or overvalued currency is realistic because even if it is assumed that the nation correctly fixes the exchange rate, at best it is temporary. Due to changing economic policies of the nation and the rest of the world, the fixed exchange rate would remain correct only in the short term. Dynamics of the economy of the world soon make the fixed exchange rate inconsistent with the economic realities causing distortion in the regulated fixed exchange rate. The local currency either becomes overvalued or undervalued sooner or later.

The impact of economic policies on undervalued and overvalued currency is quite contrasting. If the currency is undervalued, there would be accretion of foreign currency reserves. Fundamental economic factors create pressure for the currency revaluation. To maintain undervalued currency, the monetary authorities increase the supply of local currency since they have to absorb the foreign currency inflows on trade account. Hence, the central bank must sterilize through open market operations by issuing government securities. With no sterilization, the real interest rate falls. If capital flows are allowed, there would be outflow of capital both foreign and local. If capital flows are controlled and no sterilization is done the increased local currency would cause inflation.

In case the currency is overvalued, there would be deficit in the current account creating pressure to devalue the currency. To maintain overvalued currency, the central bank needs to mop up the local currency. This causes rise in the real interest rate leading to foreign capital inflows. Again, the central bank must either sterilize or impose capital controls or execute a combination of both. In the absence of sterilization and capital flow controls, the rise in interest rate would stifle investment, reduce income, and increase unemployment.

Flexible Exchange Rate and Monetary Expansion

Expansionary monetary policy can be administered either by redeeming bonds, raising their prices and lowering the yield, or decreasing interest rates directly. Either way, the money supply increases.

Increased money supply shifts the LM schedule to the right from LM_1 to LM_2 finding an intermediate equilibrium at B in Figure 7-13 (a) and (b) at a higher output with lower interest rate. Lower interest rate stimulates demand causing income to rise. The intersection of IS and LM curve at B is temporary because external balance is yet to be achieved. Under flexible exchange rate, the BP curve too would adjust to monetary changes. Increased income level and fall in interest rate causes two changes in balance of payment position:

1. Increase the income level, increasing imports being a positive function of income, causing current account deficit or worsening of the balance of trade.
2. Fall in interest rate impacts the capital inflows adversely by (a) reducing the foreign capital inflows, and/or (b) increasing the outflow of domestic capital, worsening the capital account of the balance of payment.

Worsening of BOP both on current account and capital account causes local currency to depreciate.

As an outcome of depreciation of local currency, the exports improve. This again has two effects:

1. The IS schedule shifts to right to IS_2 due to rise in income level further than the intermediate equilibrium, and increasing the interest rate too from the intermediate equilibrium.
2. The BP schedule too shifts right with improving deficit from the intermediate equilibrium position.

The final equilibrium is at C in Figure 7-13 at a higher income level and higher interest rate than intermediate equilibrium at B, amplifying the impact of monetary expansion. The amplification of income is due to (a) fall in interest rate due to monetary expansion and (b) depreciation of local currency increasing net exports.

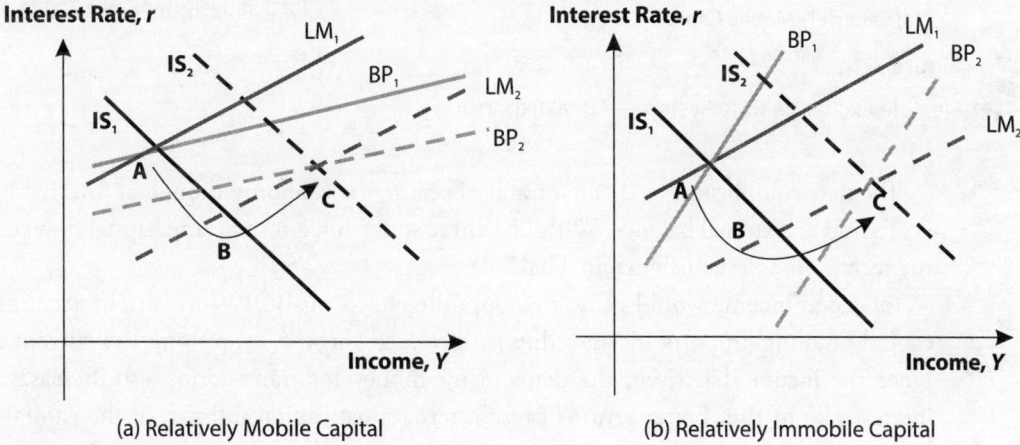

Figure 7-13
Flexible Exchange Rate System—Monetary Expansion

Relative mobility of foreign capital, that is, BP curve being flatter or steeper than LM schedule, does not change the outcome of rising income and depreciation of local currency. However, the slope of BP curve has an impact on magnitude of income and depreciation as just described.

Flexible Exchange Rate and Fiscal Expansion

Assume the economy is in internal and external equilibrium at A (refer to Figure 7-14) at the intersection of IS, LM, and BP curves. Expansionary fiscal policy, because of increase in government expenditure, shifts the IS schedule to the right raising the income level. Government expenditure is financed by public debt by issuing securities. The prices of government securities fall and the yield rises. The money supply does not change because money mobilized by way of public debt gets infused in the economy by way of government expenditure. Hence, the LM curve does not move. The equilibrium, therefore, moves temporarily from A to B as shown in Figure 7-14.

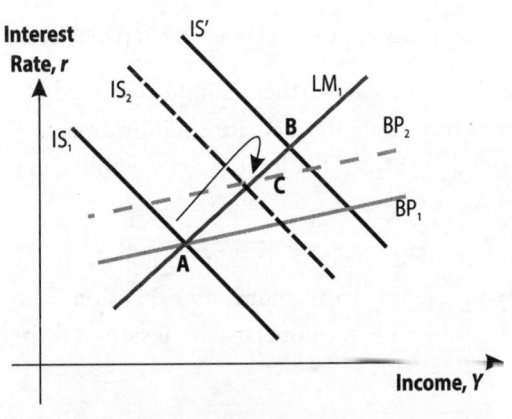
(a) Relatively Mobile Capital

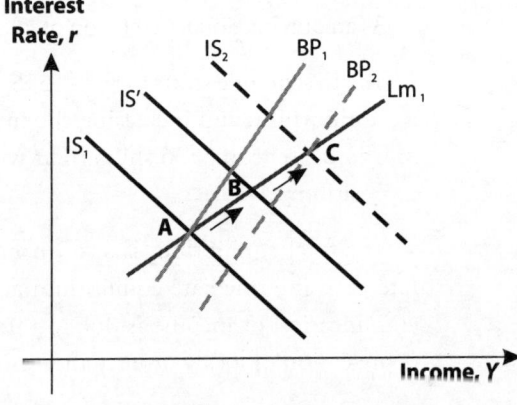
(b) Relatively Immobile Capital

Figure 7-14
Flexible Exchange Rate System—Fiscal Expansion

The new equilibrium at B is temporary because the economy though at internal balance is yet to find an external balance. With LM curve static, foreign trade and capital flows come into the reckoning to establish external balance.

Increased income would cause two opposite effects on BOP—on current account and on capital account. Imports increase due to increased income, worsening the current account. Since the income has risen, the demand for money for transactions also increases, causing interest rate to rise. Better returns cause international capital inflows, in the capital account improving the balance of payment.

The net impact on the balance of payment would depend on the relative mobility of the foreign capital flows. If foreign capital is more mobile, the capital inflows would outpace the increased liabilities of the imports. In such a case, the BOP would show a surplus (Refer Figure 7-14 (a). The local currency appreciates. It again has two impacts:

1. *On the BP curve*: As the local currency appreciates, exports become more expensive and imports cheaper shifting the BP curve to the left (worsening the current account position) of the intermediate equilibrium Point B.

2. *On the IS curve*: As net exports fall, the income too has to fall shifting the IS curve to the left of the intermediate equilibrium Point B.

Therefore, income retraces back somewhat and the final equilibrium would be at an income level lesser than the intermediate equilibrium.

However, if foreign capital is not mobile enough for capital inflows to overcome current account deficit (refer Figure 7-14 (b)), the BOP remains in deficit and, hence, local currency depreciates. This would have the following effects:

1. *On the BP curve*: As the local currency depreciates, exports become more attractive and imports expensive, shifting the BP curve to the right of the intermediate equilibrium Point B.
2. *On the IS curve*: As net exports increase, the income too has to rise, shifting the IS curve to the right of the intermediate equilibrium Point B.

Therefore, income enhances further and the final equilibrium would be at an income level higher than the intermediate equilibrium.

Therefore, under flexible exchange rate system, monetary policies are more effective than fiscal policies, as may be observed by comparing Figures 7-13 and 7-14.

LIMITATIONS OF IS-LM-BP APPROACH

Though the IS-LM-BP framework is perhaps the most comprehensive framework explaining the linkages of fiscal, monetary, and exchange rate policies, it is said to suffer from many limitations. One of the limitations is the assumption that continued current account deficit can be financed by continued capital inflows. Though this is possible in the short run, it seems unsustainable in the long term. The deficit in the current account cannot be financed by creating financial liabilities indefinitely because capital inflows would be guided by interest rate. Persistent capital flows imply that the nation keeps raising the interest rate indefinitely; clearly an impossible situation. Ultimately, the economy must develop competencies to finance imports with exports.

Another limitation is concerning the expectations of exchange rate changes by investors. Under flexible exchange rate regime, the changes in the exchange rate are consequent upon fiscal and monetary stimulus, and they are not anticipated by the investors.

MONETARY MODELS OF EXCHANGE RATE DETERMINATION

Monetary models of exchange rate determination focus on the money markets. It is surmised that capital flows based on prices of assets take place at an astonishing speed. The flow of capital on the financial assets responds to changes in interest rates and inflation expectations. The monetarists treat markets for financial assets as extremely efficient and, therefore, cross-border flow of capital is guided by the returns offered on the financial assets and the exchange rate expectations.

The returns expected by investing internationally in different currencies comprise (a) the nominal returns offered in currency of investment and (b) the expected appreciation/

depreciation of currency of investment with respect to currency of the investor. For example, consider an American investor wanting to invest in India for investment horizon of one year, and the current exchange rate is ₹50/$. If he buys an asset priced at ₹100, he would invest US$2.00. If the financial markets of India offer a rupee return of 10% the investment would grow to ₹110 in one-year time. If the exchange rate stays the same, the dollar return too would be 10%. If rupee depreciates by 10%, the exchange rate would be ₹55/$ and the investment of the American investor remains at US$2.00 providing him no returns. The gains made in the financial markets of India are nullified by the erosion in the exchange rate depreciation. Instead, if rupee appreciated by 10% to ₹45, the investor would get 110/45 = US$2.44 magnifying his dollar returns to 22.22%, which can be said to be consisting of 10% rupee gain and remaining generated through foreign exchange markets.

Monetarists believe that international financial assets are perfect substitutes and international investor is indifferent to investing at home or abroad. They chase higher returns and keep shuffling the portfolio of financial assets based on nominal returns offered in financial markets and the expectations of exchange rate changes in the foreign exchange markets. Exchange rate changes happen with immediate effect to reflect interest rate changes. In this world where currency transfers are agile and currency controls absent, capital flows across border become the key determinant of exchange rates. Monetarists, therefore, make the following assumptions for the determination of exchange rate:

(a) If demand for nominal money is M with price level of P, the real demand for money is M/P.
(b) The demand for money should be proportional to income level, Y, because people need more money for transaction purposes, consuming more with increased income level.
(c) The demand for money should be inversely proportional to nominal interest rate, r, as the opportunity cost of holding money rises with the rising interest rate.
(d) In an economy, we may write money demand function as

$$\frac{M}{P} = b\frac{Y}{r} \tag{7-6}$$

where b is a constant representing sensitivity of demand of real money with income and interest rate.

(e) Using subscripts d and f for domestic money demand and foreign money demand, we may write the demand function for the domestic and foreign economy as

$$\frac{M_d}{P_d} = b_d \frac{Y_d}{r_d} \quad \text{or} \quad P_d = \frac{1}{b_d} \times \frac{M_d \times r_d}{Y_d} \tag{7-7}$$

$$\frac{M_f}{P_f} = b_f \frac{Y_f}{r_f} \quad \text{or} \quad P_f = \frac{1}{b_f} \times \frac{M_f \times r_f}{Y_f} \tag{7-8}$$

(f) Assuming PPP holds we have exchange rate as ratio of prices. Therefore, spot exchange rate, s, is given by

$$s = \frac{P_d}{P_f}$$

$$s = k_m \frac{M_d}{M_f} \times k_y \frac{Y_f}{Y_d} \times k_r \frac{r_d}{r_f} \quad (7\text{-}9)$$

Therefore, spot exchange rate is a function of (a) relative nominal money supply in domestic and foreign markets, (b) relative income levels of domestic and foreign markets, and (c) relative nominal interest rates in domestic and foreign markets. Since we are concerned with the direction and quantum of changes, we may concentrate on relative values and ignore the constants k_m, k_f, and k_r.

Equation 7-9 can be expressed in terms of expected inflation rate too. The nominal interest rate comprises real interest rate and expected inflation rate. A rise in interest rate implies rise in expected inflation, given constant real interest rate. Further, if real interest rates are assumed equal in domestic and foreign markets (i.e. equal all over the world), the relative nominal interest rate can be replaced by relative expected inflation rates. If expected inflation rates are $e(I_d)$ and $e(I_f)$, respectively, for domestic and foreign economies, then Eq. 7-9 can be rewritten as

$$s = k_m \frac{M_d}{M_f} \times k_y \frac{Y_f}{Y_d} \times k_r \frac{e(I_d)}{e(I_f)} \quad (7\text{-}10)$$

The behaviour of spot exchange rate with respect to changes in one variable, holding all other things constant, would be as follows:

(a) If domestic money supply increases by 10% the exchange rate, the relative supply of domestic money would increase by 10% causing 10% increase in exchange rate. This implies depreciation of domestic currency by 10%. A similar impact can be assumed if foreign money supply decreases. The immediate change in the spot exchange rate is based on the assumptions (a) that changes in money supply are immediately reflected in the prices of goods, that is, the quantity theory of money holds and is effective immediately, and (b) PPP continues to hold.

(b) According to Equation 7-10 if domestic income rises the local currency must appreciate. If foreign income rises relative to domestic income, the local currency must depreciate. Converse would be true for rising domestic income and falling foreign income. If domestic income rises, the demand for transaction money too rises. Since supply of nominal money and nominal interest rates are unchanged, the increased demand for money for transaction purposes can only be met by fall in domestic prices. For PPP to hold the fall in domestic prices warrants appreciation of local currency. By same logic if the foreign income rises, the foreign prices have to adjust downwards. This requires appreciation of foreign currency, that is, depreciation of local currency for PPP to hold.

(c) Changes in nominal interest rate would have similar impact as that of money supply. An increase in the domestic nominal interest rates causes a depreciation of local currency. As stated earlier, an increase in the interest rate increases the opportunity cost of holding money and, therefore, the demand of money comes down. Rise in nominal interest rate is associated with expectations of inflation rate, leading to rise in price level in the domestic market. Since PPP is maintained, the local currency depreciates. Similarly, a rise in foreign nominal interest rate would cause depreciation of foreign currency and appreciation of local currency.

The monetary model just described made the following assumptions:

(a) Financial assets at home or abroad are perfect substitutes and investors are indifferent to investment in domestic and foreign markets.
(b) Prices adjust to money supply immediately in response to money supply changes, that is, quantity theory of money holds in the short term.
(c) The PPP holds and exchange rate changes respond to price changes.
(d) Exchange rate markets react immediately to interest rate changes, that is, UIP holds all the time.

Though more likely to be untrue than true, these assumptions provide an insight to exchange rate behaviour incorporating the impact of money supplies, income levels, nominal interest rates, and inflation rates.

DORNBUSCH'S STICKY PRICE MODEL

In the above analysis, it was assumed that prices in the goods market and money markets adjust with equal speed and instantaneously. It implies that conditions of PPP and UIP hold continuously.

However, it is believed that money markets respond much faster than goods markets. For determination of exchange rate, the unequal speed at which the money markets and goods markets respond throws light on behaviour of exchange rates in the short run and the long run. It is assumed that while financial markets react immediately, goods markets are resistant to change (especially downwards) and react slowly. How does the adjustment take place was explained by Rudger Dornbusch in his model, also referred to as 'sticky price' model or 'overshooting' model.

In this model, the financial markets tend to react to the given stimulus rather fast, whereas prices in the goods and labour market being sticky react later. Since financial markets, including the currency markets being efficient must remain in balance all the time, and the exchange rate has the tendency to overreact to a given fiscal or monetary impetus. How do we achieve short- and long-term equilibria is shown in Figure 7-15 and discussed here.

Assume that an economy is infused with 10% increase in money supply. The reasons for doing so are immaterial for the exposition. According to the monetarists' view, this 10% increase in money supply must result in 10% increase in prices in the goods market accompanied by

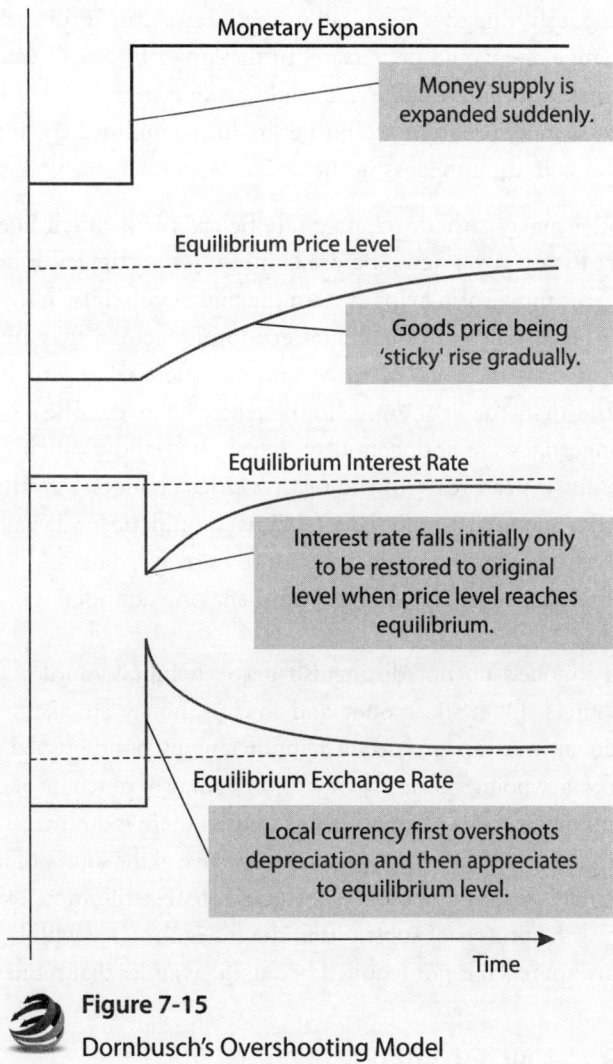

Figure 7-15
Dornbusch's Overshooting Model

10% depreciation of local currency. While this outcome remains unchallenged in the long run, the process of adjustment would be somewhat different as follows:

1. An increase in money supply by 10% would not immediately show on the goods market as prices of goods and labour are sticky. They would rise in proportion of increase in money supply slower than the adjustment in the financial markets.
2. The excess supply of money should find its way into the financial assets market because goods continue to be available at cheaper rates compared to money balances available. The surplus money in financial markets would raise prices of bonds and decrease yields. The drop in the interest rate would exceed the equilibrium level. After dropping more than warranted, the interest rate would rise slowly towards equilibrium level as prices in the goods market rise.

3. Simultaneously, due to sudden fall in the interest rate, capital flows out of the country and the exchange rate would depreciate. In the long run, the depreciation must equal 10% but in the short run, the exchange rate market would overshoot the long-term equilibrium level. The excessive depreciation would be gradually nullified by appreciation of domestic currency, compensating the loss in the interest income by capital gains in the exchange rate.

The model suggests that exchange rate behaviour is much like stock markets which tend to overreact to any given news, before coming to the true level; normally termed as technical correction. The model also helps explain the higher volatility in the exchange rates. If exchange rates are to be driven by fundamental economic factors, they must change only slowly and marginally as does the pace of the economy. The changes in the exchange rates are much more volatile than the economic fundamental changes. The IS-LM-BP approach assumed that exchange rates are endogenously determined and as such do not cause relative prices to change, but instead react to the relative price changes. Another implication of monetary model is that monetary policy corrections should be undertaken only gradually because goods price equilibrium can only be achieved slowly. Massive dosages of monetary treatment result in instability of money markets only, shaking confidence of domestic and international investors alike.

Monetary models do not distinguish between inflows/outflows of money from foreign or domestic sources. Domestic money and foreign money are assumed to be perfect substitutes, as international investors are deemed indifferent to bonds issued by various countries. From central bank's viewpoint, monetary expansion by way of purchase of domestic bonds is considered equivalent to buying foreign currency. As long as there is an increase in money supply, it would have the same effect on the exchange rate irrespective of the source of money—domestic or foreign. Therefore, under monetary approach, the question of sterilization loses all significance. Recall that sterilization is the process of substituting the foreign money with domestic money, which under the monetary approach is not required because it assumes that money has only one colour.

PORTFOLIO BALANCE MODEL

Another monetary model based on asset prices is portfolio balance model. Monetary model as discussed assumed that foreign bonds and domestic assets are perfect substitutes except that they are denominated in different currencies. The returns on foreign bonds are equalized because the differential in yields on bonds is compensated by changes in the exchange rate, that is, uncovered interest parity holds. For example, if domestic bonds offered 8% return and foreign bonds offer 11% return, then domestic currency appreciation and/or foreign currency depreciation aggregating to 3% would take place to equate the two returns.

The implication of perfect substitute is that there is no difference in the perceived risk of domestic and foreign bonds. However, when domestic and foreign bonds are not perfect substitutes, the return expectations do not remain identical. The investors demand extra return, that is, the risk premium, on the more risky bond. The demand for risk premium has its roots in political uncertainty, exchange controls, inflation, etc.

There are three key vital differences in the assumptions of monetary models and portfolio balance model. Under monetary models (a) exchange rate is a function of relative money supplies of two currencies, (b) because foreign bonds and domestic bonds are perfect substitutes with no extra risk premium desired, and (c) therefore, UIP holds. Under portfolio balance model (a) exchange rate becomes a function of relative supplies of domestic and foreign bonds, (b) because they are not perfect substitutes; hence, risk premium is desired on more risky bond, and (c) hence UIP does not hold.

Under portfolio balance model, there are only two forms of money—base money and bonds. Investors and authorities can have a portfolio of money, domestic bonds, and foreign bonds. The demand for money is the function of (a) domestic interest rate, (b) income level, and (c) expected return on foreign bonds which is a product of foreign interest rate and expected change in the exchange rate. They are related as follows:

(a) Demand for money is directly proportional to income and inversely proportional to (i) domestic interest rate and (ii) foreign interest rate, that is, expected yield on them.
(b) Demand for domestic bonds is directly proportional to domestic interest rate and inversely proportional to (i) expected return on foreign bonds and (ii) income.
(c) Demand for foreign bonds is directly proportional to expected return on foreign bonds and inversely proportional to (i) domestic interest rate and (ii) income.

The equilibrium exchange rate would be one at which the supply of and demand for money and assets are denominated in two currencies. Hence, the preferences of investors for holding domestic bonds and foreign bonds would affect the exchange rate. Investors keep rebalancing the portfolio depending upon the expected returns, and, therefore, the demand function of domestic and foreign bonds change.

Increased risk perception of foreign bonds would cause rebalancing of the portfolio with more proportion allocated to domestic bonds. Buying of domestic bonds and selling of foreign bonds would lead domestic interest rate to fall and foreign interest rates to rise. Thus, foreign currency would depreciate and domestic currency would appreciate. Similarly, perception of increased risk on domestic assets may lead to depreciation of domestic currency and rise in domestic interest rate.

The position of BOP too can be analysed on similar lines. A current account surplus implies accumulation of foreign currency reserves or acquisition of foreign bonds. The wealth of the investors, therefore, increases. Keeping the portfolio composition of domestic bonds, foreign bonds, and money same as before, the increased proportion of foreign bonds would require proportionate increase in the domestic bond holding. Buying of domestic bonds due to increased wealth raises prices of bonds and interest rate falls. This would cause domestic currency appreciation, which would restore the current account balance removing surplus. The reverse holds good for current account deficit.

The outcome of changes in the fiscal policy on exchange rate is rather uncertain. A fiscal expansion financed by purchase of bonds keeps aggregate money supply same as money gathered by central bank is circulated back in the economy by way of government expenditure. Increased income of the investors due to fiscal expansion raises domestic interest rate leading to fall in demand of foreign bonds. On the other hand, increased proportion of domestic bonds requires acquisition of foreign bonds in the same proportion, increasing demand for them. If increase in demand for foreign bonds is greater than the fall in demand for them (due to rising interest rate), then the domestic currency depreciates. If the fall in demand is greater than the rise in demand due to bond financed fiscal expansion, the domestic currency would appreciate.

FORECASTING EXCHANGE RATE

The models for exchange rate determination discussed so far were based on economic fundamentals and analysed the impact of fiscal, monetary, and trade policies on the exchange rate. They concentrated on the equilibrium exchange rate and its behaviour, given certain fiscal or monetary shocks. These fiscal and monetary shocks are decided by authorities to achieve broader objectives of economic welfare in terms of generating income, employment, and controlling inflation. With the exception of policies of intervention in currency markets and its sterilization, seldom are economic policies directed towards correcting exchange rate. As such exchange rate remains a by-product of all such economic treatments.

Forecasting exchange rate is of primary concern to multinational corporations and firms engaged in exports and imports because their competitive position is extremely dependent on the exchange rate behaviour. The likely changes in the exchange rate determine day-to-day corporate decisions such as pricing, hedging, and credit periods. While implications of economic policies of the nation are vital for forecasting long-term equilibrium values and may determine competitiveness of a nation as a whole, firms are usually more concerned with the behaviour of exchange rate over a period that possibly does not stretch beyond one year.

Foreign exchange markets behave much like any other financial markets such as stocks and bonds. We all know that the value of share is fundamentally determined by the cash flows of the firm. At the same time, we also know that multitude of factors also govern the value of a share. Identification of such factors is an uphill task. Even though factors could be identified, there seems no logical way of incorporating the expectations about changes in these factors in a model which has reasonable accuracy of prediction.

As exchange rates tend to discount all the information available, it is believed that changes in exchange rates are on account of unanticipated factors. All the anticipated factors like policy measures with regard to economic, monetary, and trade matters are widely known and are announced to follow a predetermined path which is well anticipated. Therefore, all these measures guiding the economy are already discounted in the present exchange rates, much in the same manner as stock price discounts future earnings of the firm. It is only when the policy measures and economic fundamentals do not follow a predestined path the exchange rates become volatile, else they too must move in a predestined manner.

Fortunately, we have fairly well-developed forward markets in foreign exchange and for major currencies in the world forward rates are available. Under efficient market assumption, the forward rates can be assumed to be an unbiased predictor of future spot rate, that is, if 1-m forward rate is ₹64/$, it is expected that one month later the spot exchange rate would be ₹64.

If the future spot rate turns out to be equal to forward rate, then there is no element of surprise in the behaviour of exchange rates. However, if future spot rate does not turn out to be same as what forward rate predicted, the deviation needs to be attributed to the changes that occurred in the interim forward period.

Some firms and analysts use regression approach to forecast the exchange rate based on the values of the parameters that they believe influence the exchange rate movement. A general regression equation for forecast for time, t, as differential of forward rate, made at time $t-1$ may be given as

$$S_t - F_t = a + bX_t + cY_t \ldots\ldots + e \tag{7-11}$$

where

S_t and F_t are forecast spot exchange rate for time t and forward rate at time $t-1$ for time, t, respectively,

$X_t, Y_t, \ldots$ are expected values of fundamental determinants for time t at time $t-1$, as considered appropriate by the forecaster,

$b, c, \ldots$ are sensitivity coefficients of the exchange rate with the respective determinants denoting the direction (the signs of coefficients) and extent of dependence (the values of the coefficients) of exchange rate on the determinants, and e is the error term in the regression.

The determinants of exchange rate are at the discretion of the forecaster. For example, these determinants could be economic fundamental variables, such as growth/changes in GDP, inflation rates, money supply, current account surplus/deficit, foreign currency reserves, stock market returns, bond yields, or interest rates, or could be seemingly unrelated variables such as growth in tourism, growth in infrastructure, and sovereign credit rating changes. The following points may be noted about the choice of exchange rate determinants in the model:

1. The determinants could be the relative values of two countries or changes from one period to another for the same economy. The choice of the determinants is also a function of forecast horizon. If the long-term forecast is required then using more fundamental determinants such as inflation and growth rates may be more appropriate, whereas for short-term forecast, transient issues may be of concern.
2. Another choice available with the forecaster is to find values of determinants based either on other measurable parameters prevailing at the time of the forecast or on using time series of the determinants itself. For example, for finding the value of X_t, we may use past values of the same variable, $X_{t-1}, X_{t-2}, X_{t-3} \ldots\ldots$

CHARTIST/TECHNICAL APPROACH

Another way of forecasting exchange rate is based on the technical analysis, where the past trends are presumed to form the future. Based on the premise that past patterns of prices have the tendency to repeat themselves, one can expect same trends to continue if one can discern these patterns. Commonly called chartists, they are at divergence with the efficient market hypothesis and with fundamentalists approach.

Chartists study the past behaviour of exchange rate and discern patterns in them in the hope that same patterns would be repeated in future and, hence, can be used for predicting the future spot rate. These patterns are given fancy names such as double top, double bottom, wedge and hammer, and head and shoulder. They also study moving averages and attempt to find the minimum level called support and the maximum level called resistance. Some of them also use Fibonacci numbers to predict the retracements and up moves. The application of chartist is same as that applied to forecast stock prices.

SUMMARY

At the time of discussing the parity conditions for forecasting the exchange rates, we considered broad parameters of inflation, interest rates, etc. ignoring the policies pursued by individual nations to control or regulate the inflation rate and interest rate. The fiscal policies and monetary policies of the nation are intricately linked to the exchange rate regime in an open economy.

Through fiscal and monetary policies, an economy attempts to strike an internal balance, that is, achieving economic growth with low unemployment and preferably with no inflation. Fiscal policies attempt to modify the consumption and saving pattern and providing impetus to the economic development. Monetary policies are focused on achieving price stability by controlling the money supply. In an open economy not only is the internal balance important but also the external balance. External balance is defined as achieving a balance of payment position that leaves the reserve position unchanged by controlling the imports, exports, and capital flows. While fiscal policies are difficult to implement having uncertain and delayed outcome, monetary policies are easy and fast to execute.

Swan diagram is a tool to understand linkages between real income and exchange rate that shows a negatively sloped line of internal balance which is a locus of income–exchange rate combinations at which economy is in internal balance. Similarly, an upward sloping line representing a locus of income–exchange rate combinations depicts external balance. The intersection of the two lines would represent income–exchange rate level where internal as well as external balance is attained, with four quadrants segregating different economic conditions with inflation, unemployment, deficit, or surplus BOP.

The Mundell–Fleming model (called IS-LM-BP approach) is the most comprehensive model suggesting the suitable tools and remedies that could be used in solving domestic economic issues along with the external environment. It uses three variables—the income/output in the economy, the interest rate, and exchange rate—along which the targets can be specified, measured, and affected by fiscal, monetary, and trade policies. It addresses the issue of how to achieve internal and external balance in an economy. It assumes consumption, savings, and import as increasing function of income, while investment as decreasing function of interest rate, with government spending and export as exogenous. With national income on the horizontal axis and interest rate on the vertical axis, the IS curve on which savings equals investment is downward sloping. Fiscal expansion would shift the IS curve to the right and fiscal contraction would take the IS curve to the left.

The LM schedule depicts money market equilibrium on the national income and interest rate space as upward sloping. Monetary expansion shifts LM schedule to the right, whereas monetary contraction shifts LM schedule to the left. Intersection of IS and LM curves represents equilibrium in a closed economy where goods market and money market are in simultaneous equilibrium. An expansionary fiscal policy results in an increase in the interest rate and an increase in output, whereas a contractionary fiscal policy works in the opposite direction. An expansionary monetary policy results in a decrease in the interest rate and an increase in output and a contractionary monetary policy results in opposite.

The BP schedule represents equilibrium in BOPs, that is, reserves unchanged for different combinations of income and interest rate. BP curve slopes upwards because rise in income would increase imports to push deficit in CA. To offset current account deficit capital must flow in, which happens when interest rate rises. Intersection of IS, LM, and BP curves would imply internal as well as external balance. Depreciation of local currency would shift (a) IS schedule to the right, (b) LM schedule up to the left, and (c) BP schedule down to the right.

The effectiveness of the fiscal and monetary policies is dependent upon whether the exchange rate regime is fixed or flexible. Under fixed exchange rate system, monetary policies are rather ineffective in raising the income level, whereas fiscal policies are more effective. Under flexible exchange rate system, monetary policies are better and faster to address economic issues.

Monetary models of exchange rate determination focus on the money markets. Monetarists believe that international financial assets are perfect substitutes and international investor is indifferent to investing at home or abroad. Spot exchange rate is a function of (a) relative nominal money supply in domestic and foreign markets, (b) relative income levels of domestic and foreign markets, and (c) relative nominal interest rates or expected inflation rates in domestic and foreign markets.

It is believed that money markets respond much faster than the goods market. For determination of exchange rate the unequal speeds at which the money markets and goods markets respond throws light on the behaviour of exchange rates in the short run and the long run. In the short run due to greater speed of money market adjustment there is a tendency for exchange rate to overreact first before coming to true level.

QUESTIONS

7-1 What do you understand by internal balance and external balance?
7-2 Depict Swan diagram indicating simultaneous internal and external balance with the description of four regions surrounding the equilibrium point.
7-3 Briefly describe IS, LM, and BP schedules and how they react to changing fiscal and monetary policies.
7-4 How would IS, LM, and BP schedules change with the appreciation of local currency? Depict graphically.
7-5 Under the fixed exchange rate system, describe the equilibrium adjustment process with (a) monetary expansion, and (b) fiscal expansion.
7-6 Under flexible exchange rate system, describe the equilibrium adjustment process with (a) monetary expansion, and (b) fiscal expansion.
7-7 What are the monetary models of exchange rate determination?
7-8 What do you understand by overshooting?

Part III
Foreign Exchange Derivatives

8. Currency Forwards and Futures
9. Currency Options
10. Currency and Interest Rate Swaps
11. Interest Rate Risk and Hedging

Currency Forwards and Futures

LEARNING OBJECTIVES

This chapter aims at

- explaining the features of forward and futures contracts on currencies
- discussing how to hedge with forwards and futures
- discussing non-deliverable forwards, their evolution, and applications
- explaining the salient features of futures contract
- discussing basis, basis risk, perfect and imperfect hedge, and convergence
- explaining how to price forwards and futures
- explaining how to speculate and arbitrage with futures

CONTENTS

Introduction
Forward and Futures Contracts
    Forward Contract—Payoffs of Receivable and Payable
Hedging with Forwards
    Hedging Receivable with Forward Contract
    Hedging Payable with Forward Contract
    When to Hedge
    Obligations under Forward Contracts
    Cancellation of Forward Contracts
    Cost of Forward Hedge
Speculation with Forward Contract
Non-Deliverable Forward Contract
    Hedging with Non-Deliverable Forward
    Evolution and Growth of Non-Deliverable Forward
    Non-Deliverable Forward and Interest Rate Parity
Currency Futures
Limitations of Forward Contract
Futures Contract vs Forward Contract
Terminology of Futures
Hedging with Currency Futures
    Basis
    Basis Risk
    Sources of Basis Risk
Pricing Currency Futures
    Convergence of Futures Price to Spot
Arbitrage with Currency Futures
Speculation with Currency Futures

INTRODUCTION

Foreign exchange markets are perhaps as volatile as the stock markets, if not more. This may be because of the fact that the volatility in the foreign exchange rates is determined by global factors which are too many and far complex to understand, whereas stock markets predominantly respond to local changes. The volatility in exchange rates is naturally distinct than in the stock markets that are mainly governed by domestic economic, political, and business environments, though global factors do have implications on the returns from stocks and bonds. Possibly, the proportion of global factors affecting volatility of foreign exchange rates is more than that on stock returns. For example, the value of US dollar with respect to Indian rupee would be governed not only by what happens in India, but also by the economic, political, and business events in the USA. As compared to this, the returns on stocks listed in the Indian stock exchanges would be primarily determined by local microeconomic and macroeconomic factors. Changes in the foreign exchange rates are mainly caused by macroeconomic factors worldwide.

In the preceding chapters, we have examined the influence of economic policies, monetary policies, and government intervention in the currency markets on exchange rates. Inflation rates, interest rates, economic growth, employment levels, savings and consumption patterns, trade policies, etc. are the major determinants of the exchange rates and likely changes in them. Besides government's policies of interventions also have significant influence on exchange rates. In most countries except where free float is in vogue, the government through central bank is also a major participant in the foreign exchange markets, unlike stock markets where governments do not participate but their policies influence the returns. From the perspective of a firm, all these factors are beyond their control. Some of these factors are more fundamental in nature affecting exchange rates rather slowly, whereas some such as interventions and trade policies impact exchange rates rather instantaneously.

FORWARD AND FUTURES CONTRACTS

We have already discussed various foreign exchange rates and markets including forward rates as well as the factors affecting them in an earlier chapter. In view of the complexities of the movement of foreign exchange prices and the volatility, it is imperative for the firms to find ways and means to reduce or eliminate the exposures faced by them. No business likes uncertainties. They continuously and consciously strive to eliminate uncertainties to the extent they can.

For multinational firms, fluctuating exchange rates is a major threat since they operate in several countries conducting transactions in different currencies. Changes in foreign exchange rates have direct bearing on the top line as well as the bottom line. Unfortunately, very little can be done by these firms to influence economic, social, or political fundamentals; the major determinants of exchange rates change. Instead they have to learn to cope with these incessant changes to insulate themselves. The risk emanating from the fluctuations in exchange rates would have to be managed independently through specific financial instruments that came into existence for a precise reason of managing such risks.

Among the most frequently used tools of managing the exposure of foreign exchange is a derivative instrument. *A **derivative instrument** is one that drives its value from the underlying asset/markets.* Derivatives can have any asset as underlying such as commodities, currencies, interest rates, stocks, and indices. Here, we are concerned with the derivatives that have only currencies as underlying asset. Derivatives on currencies are used for hedging exposures in foreign currency.

Forward contract on foreign currency is the most basic derivative product, the underlying asset being the spot exchange rates. Forward contract can be called the mother of all derivatives. Another derivative product is a futures contract (discussed later in this chapter) that is similar to the forward contract fundamentally but is different operationally. Derivative products can be traded in two ways—*over-the-counter* (OTC) or on an *exchange*. The OTC products involve one-to-one negotiations of the terms and conditions of the contract, whereas in an exchange-traded product, the specifications of the product are standardized with pricing information available in the public domain.

The OTC products (forward contracts) dominate the foreign exchange trading despite the availability of exchange-traded modern derivative products like futures. Few reasons that can be attributed to the dominance of forward contracts over other derivatives, especially the exchange-traded futures, are as follows:

- The users of foreign currency, that is, importers and exporters necessarily have to deal with banks for their other business and commercial requirements. The relationship of clients and banks serves many needs like credit, rating, discounting, payments, collections, etc. Therefore, banks in their own business development offer forward contracts on currencies to complement their own portfolio of services. For users of foreign currency, the bank becomes a convenient medium for meeting hedging requirements.
- The transactions in foreign currency emanate from selling of goods and services by exporters to importers, necessitating the transfer of title from seller to the buyer. These documents of transfer of title are normally routed through the banks for reasons of credibility, timing, possession, and payments. Hence, banks are aware of the underlying trade transaction as well as need for hedging. They can provide important and crucial consultancy inputs to their clients that help mitigate other risks such as solvency, credit that are inherent in commercial transactions.
- Since payments are realized/made in foreign currency, the task of converting it back to domestic/foreign currency is performed by the banks, and there does not exist an exchange where currencies are traded for spot deliveries. Hence, spot foreign exchange markets essentially remain OTC.
- Since the spot market in currencies is over-the-counter, the derivatives' market is also in the nature of over-the-counter, explaining the dominance of forwards contracts over the exchange-traded products like futures.

In OTC markets, the exchange rates vary from source to source for commercial reasons. Foreign exchange contracts are usually made through banks where they buy/sell foreign currencies for client firms which are exporters and importers. The necessity of the firms to deal with banks for their regular requirements, wide network and correspondent arrangements of banks across the world, enabling prompt and credible information gathering, the reliability of the delivery of title documents from exporter to importers, etc. are some of the factors that have made OTC markets in foreign exchange more dominant than the exchange-traded markets.

Forward Contract—Payoffs of Receivable and Payable

Most exporters invoice their products to customers in internationally acceptable currencies, such as US dollar, euro, and yen. In addition, most invoices provide for a credit period. Firms receive the payment only after the end of the credit period. Importers make payment in the invoiced currency (may not be the domestic currency). Though the amount of foreign currency is fixed, the equivalent domestic currency amount is subject to change depending upon the exchange rate prevailing at the time of settlement of transaction. It essentially makes the spot rate prevailing at the time of initiation of trade transaction irrelevant.

The outlook of exporters and importers with the fluctuations of exchange rate is opposite to one another. Although exporters are happy with the appreciation of foreign currency (invoiced) during the credit period because it enables them to realize more of domestic currency, they fear depreciation of foreign currency. On the contrary, importers dread the appreciation of foreign currency (invoiced) as it increases the liability amount in domestic currency.

Consider, for example, an Indian exporter invoiced for US$1,000 today and expects to receive payment three months later with an expected exchange rate of ₹55/$. If the exchange rate after three months happens to be ₹56/$ his rupee cash flow would be ₹56,000 instead of targeted ₹55,000. However, if the exchange rate were to be ₹54/$, then the cash flow would suffer to ₹54,000.

Similarly, importers receive invoice first and pay later at the expiry of the credit period, and the amount payable in domestic currency would be governed by the exchange rate prevailing at the time of payment for the same amount of foreign currency as invoiced. They fear appreciation of foreign currency during the period from when the liability was fixed and to when it was actually liquidated.

The exchange rates at the time of invoice and at the time of realization/payment are likely to differ (except in situations where domestic currency is pegged) and, hence, the amount in domestic currency is not constant, causing uncertainty of cash flows for firms. The risks of exchange rate changes faced by importers and exporters are consolidated in the Table 8-1.

The pain or pleasure of a credit transaction is often measured in terms of payoff, that is, the difference between spot exchange rates on the dates of initiation and maturity of the trade transaction. Assuming invoicing in foreign currency that is appreciating (domestic currency depreciating)

(a) the value of receivable would rise resulting in the greater realization than expected; hence, a positive payoff for the exporter, and
(b) the cost of payable too would be higher than expected; hence, a negative payoff for the importer.

Table 8-1
Impact of Exchange Rate Changes

Nature of Exposure		Exchange Rate Scenario	
		Appreciation of Foreign Currency	Depreciation of Foreign Currency
Exporters	Assets denominated in foreign currency to be realized later	Increased cash inflow in domestic currency than contemplated. **(Desirable)**	Decreased cash inflow in domestic currency than contemplated. **(Not desirable)**
Importers	Liabilities denominated in foreign currency to be liquidated later	Increased cash outflow in domestic currency than contemplated. **(Not desirable)**	Decreased cash outflow in domestic currency than contemplated. **(Desirable)**

The situation would reverse if foreign currency were to depreciate.

When the exchange rate at maturity of payable/receivable, S_T (referred to as target exchange rate) happens to be the same as the current spot rate, S_0, the importer/exporter neither gains nor loses. If spot rates, S_T and S_0 are different, there would be either a gain or a loss. The positions of exporter for receivable and importer for payable are shown in Figure 8-1. It is evident that the position of exporters and importers are opposite to each other.

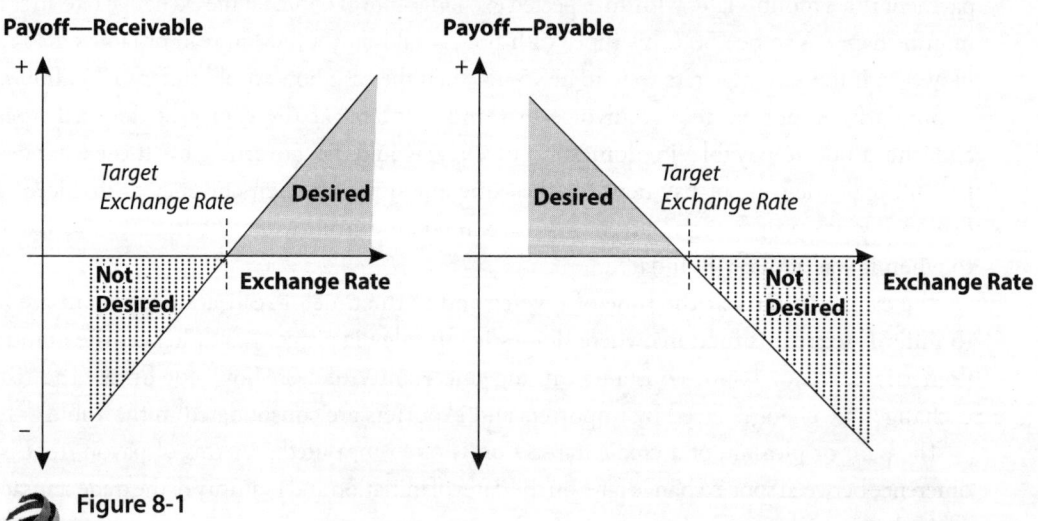

Figure 8-1
Payoff of Receivable and Payable

Payoffs of Forward Positions The risk of receivable from depreciation foreign currency and of payable from appreciating foreign currency can be eliminated by selling/buying the foreign currency forward. A forward contract in foreign currency is normally offered by banks. As described earlier, a forward contract to buy or sell the foreign currency requires exchange of cash flows upon maturity of the forward period at an exchange rate fixed now. Hence, the spot exchange rate at the maturity of forward period becomes irrelevant for determination of the cash flow in domestic currency.

Exporters sell the foreign currency receivable forward. It is referred to as short position in forward. A forward contract to sell foreign currency means that irrespective of the spot change rate at maturity, the forward rate, F, applies. For the perfect hedge, the dates of maturity of the receivable and the forward contract must coincide. The payoff of short position in forward contract is given by $F - S_T$. If the spot exchange rate at maturity, S_T, is less than the forward rate, F, then the exporter gains in forward contract by an amount equal to $F - S_T$.

Similarly, importers needing foreign currency in future buy the foreign currency payable forward. It is called a long position in forward. It means that irrespective of the exchange rate at maturity, the importer would buy at the contracted rate. The payoff of long position in forward contract is given by $S_T - F$. If the spot exchange rate at maturity, S_T, is more than the forward rate, F, then long position gains by an amount $S_T - F$.

Payoffs of long position and short position applicable to importers and exporters, respectively, are depicted in Figure 8-2. Note that the payoff of forward is opposite of the payoff of position in the asset, that is, receivable/payable depicted in Figure 8-1.

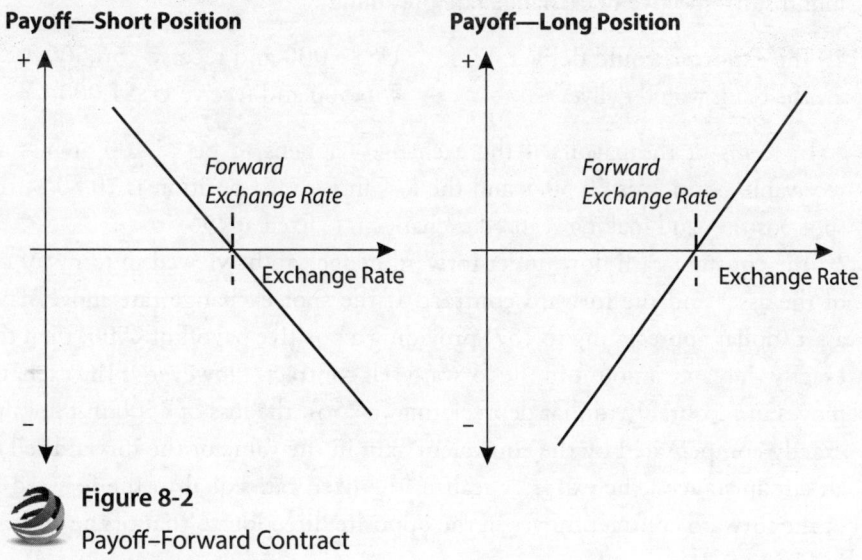

Figure 8-2
Payoff–Forward Contract

HEDGING WITH FORWARDS

An exporter would hedge with a short position in forward contract. The combined payoffs of receivable (as in Figure 8-1) and a short position in forward (as in Figure 8-2) would be the aggregate position of the exporter. With rise in the exchange rate, the receivable position gains but the forward short position loses equally, thereby freezing the exchange rate that would be realized for the receivable amount. The loss/gain in the receivable position is completely offset by gain/loss in the forward short position.

For an importer, the hedging would be achieved by long position in forward; the agreement to buy foreign currency forward at a rate fixed today. The unhedged position would lose with rise in the exchange rate. If hedged with a forward contract, the gain in forward position would offset the loss in payable completely, thereby ensuring the constancy of the domestic currency amount payable required to liquidate the liability in foreign currency.

Hedging strategies for exporters and importers with forward contract are as follows:

	Position	*Hedging Strategy*
Exporters	Receivable in foreign currency	Sell foreign currency forward
Importers	Payable in foreign currency	Buy foreign currency forward

Hedging Receivable with Forward Contract

For illustrative purposes, consider an exporter with US$1,000 receivable after three months. The exporter books a 3-m forward contract to sell US$1,000 to a bank, say at an exchange rate of ₹56.50 (forward rate assumed as target rate). Then, at end of forward period of three months, irrespective of exchange rate prevailing

1. The exporter would deliver   US$1,000 and receive ₹56,500
2. The bank would deliver   ₹56,500 and receive US$1,000

In terms of the payoffs if the exchange happens to be ₹57.00 at maturity, the gain in receivable position is ₹0.50/$ and the loss in forward position is ₹0.50/$, thereby offsetting spot position and making realized exchange rate fixed at ₹56.50.

The constant cash flow under forward hedge can be viewed in terms of combined payoff of the asset and the forward contract. If the spot exchange rate moves favourably for the asset (dollar appreciating to ₹57) providing a positive payoff of ₹500, then the exporter loses exactly the same amount in the forward sell contract. However, if the exchange rate scenario moves unfavourably (dollar depreciating to ₹56), the loss of ₹500 in the value of the asset is exactly compensated by the equivalent gain in the value of the forward sell contract. Under all circumstances, the exporter realizes the fixed rate equal to the forward rate. The payoff of the forward contract moves in the opposite direction to that of the asset. This is depicted in Figure 8-3.

As stated earlier, exporters have assets of receivables denominated in foreign currency. Appreciating foreign currency increases the value of asset and, hence, is a favourable situation for outstanding receivables. However, they would like to avoid situations that diminish the value of asset, that is, depreciating foreign currency. To avoid the erosion in the value of the asset, exporters can sell the foreign currency forward to the counterparty, usually a bank.

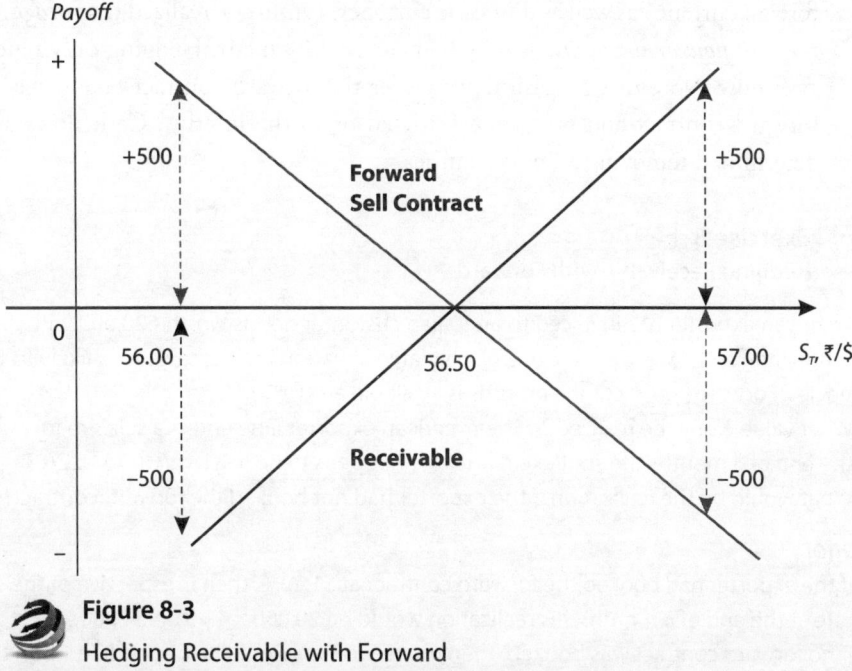

Figure 8-3
Hedging Receivable with Forward

If the exporter were unhedged, the amount realized in domestic currency remains uncertain. By booking a forward sell contract with the bank, the exporter commits to deliver US$1,000 and receive ₹56,500 to/from the bank. By doing so, the uncertainty of the rupee amount is removed. The cash flows for three different spot rates with unhedged and hedged receivable are presented in Table 8-2.

Table 8-2
Forward Hedge for Receivables

Exchange Rate at Maturity of Receivable	Unhedged	Forward Hedge		
	Value of Receivable	Value of Receivable	Payoff of Forward Sell Contract	Total–Net Realization
56.00	56,000	56,000	+500	56,500
56.50	56,500	56,500	0	56,500
57.00	57,000	57,000	−500	56,500

With the booking of a forward sell contract, the exporter is able to realize the fixed certain sum for the receivable in domestic currency irrespective of the spot exchange rate prevailing at the maturity of the receivable. Therefore, forward contract implies a fixed and certain sum in foreign currency as well as domestic currency. It must be realized that *hedging does not maximize the cash flow or the profit*, as may be perceived by many. Hedging only renders stability to the cash flow. Note that all cash flows under the forward contract take place only at maturity of forward contract and not when initiated or in the interim. Cash flows at maturity are pre-determined removing all uncertainties.

> ### Exercise 8-1
> **Hedging Receivable with Forward**
>
> An American exporter has invoiced to an Italian customer goods worth €20,000 with 3-m credit. The spot exchange rate is $1.25/€. Due to extremely volatile situation in Greece, euro is likely to weaken against all currencies. Forward contract for 3 months is available at $1.20/€.
> (a) What value would be realized by the American exporter if he enters a sell 3-m forward contract and at the end of 3 months the spot exchange rate happens to be (i) $1.12/€ (ii) $1.22/€?
> (b) What would be the realization if the exporter had not booked the forward contract?
>
> **Solution**
> (a) If the exporter had booked the forward contract at $1.20/€, then irrespective of the spot exchange rate at the end of 3 months, his realization would be 20,000 × 1.20 = $24,000.
> (b) If no forward contract was booked, then the realization would be dependent upon the spot rate prevailing at the time of realization. Therefore,
>
> | Exchange Rate | Amount Realized |
> |---|---|
> | $1.12/€ | 20,000 × 1.12 = $22,400 |
> | $1.22/€ | 20,000 × 1.22 = $24,400 |

Hedging Payable with Forward Contract

Similar to the receivable, we may hedge a liability of payable. Assume that an importer has to pay US$1,000 after three months. Hedging for a liability (payable denominated in foreign currency) would involve buying foreign currency forward for the required amount and the period equal to the maturity of liability. Forward buy contract would entail the payment of a fixed amount of local currency for the specified foreign currency at the end of forward period.

A 3-m forward contract to buy US$1,000 from a bank at an exchange rate of ₹56.50 is entered wherein at the end of forward period of three months, irrespective of exchange rate prevailing

1. The importer would deliver ₹56,500 and receive US$1,000
2. The bank would deliver US$1,000 and receive ₹56,500

If the exchange happens to be ₹57.00 at maturity of payable and forward contract, then in terms of the payoffs the gain in forward position is ₹0.50/$ and the loss in payable position is ₹0.50/$ again offsetting each other and fixing the exchange rate of payable at ₹56.50 irrespective of exchange rate prevailing at the time of maturity of payable.

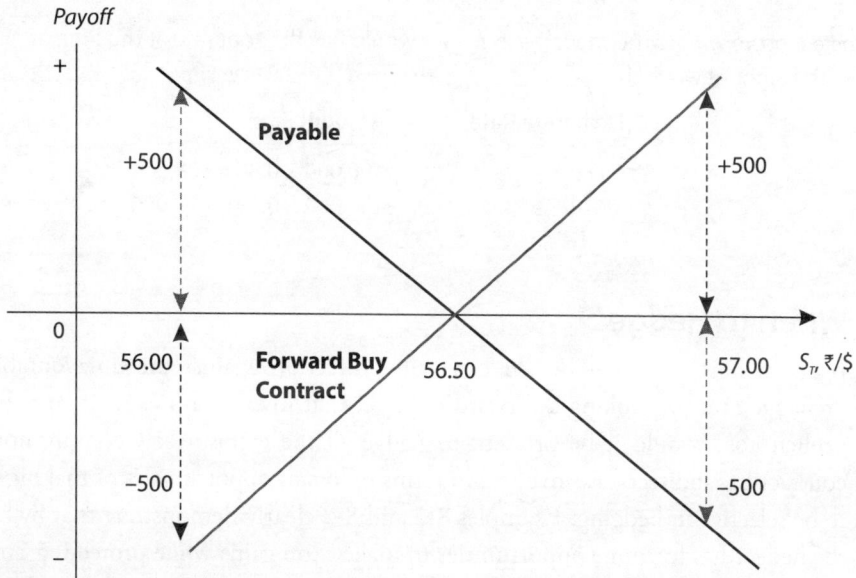

Figure 8-4
Hedging Payable with Forward

The payoff diagram of payable would be negatively sloped with increasing exchange rate, whereas that of forward buy contract is positively sloped. The payoffs of the two would be exactly compensating and would render the amount of payment in local currency fixed. It is shown in Figure 8-4 which is identical with Figure 8-3 with the positions in underlying foreign currency and the forward contract interchanged.

Exercise 8-2
Hedging Payable with Forward

A French wine producer has imported fragrances from California, USA, for US$100,000 for which the payment is due after six months. Due to uncertainties in Europe, euro has been weakening against US dollar in the past. The importer is worried about appreciation of US dollar as 6-m forward contract is available at a premium of about 5% at €0.84/$ against current spot of €0.80/$. The importer expects US dollar to move up further.
(a) Should the importer hedge with the forward contract?
(b) What would be the amount paid by the French for his import under forward hedge at the end of six months when spot exchange rate happens to be (i) €0.88/$ (ii) €0.78/$?
(c) What would be the payment amount if the importer did not hedge?

Solution
(a) As US dollar is expected to appreciate beyond the forward rate of €0.84/$, the importer must hedge the exposure of US$100,000 with the 6-m forward buy contract of equal amount.
(b) If the importer books the forward contract at €0.84/$, then irrespective of the spot exchange rate at the end of six months, he would end up paying 100,000 × 0.84 = €84,000.

(c) If the exposure was not hedged, the importer would pay the spot rate at the time of maturity of payable. The amount would be

Exchange Rate	Amount Paid
€0.88/$	100,000 × 0.88 = €88,000
€0.78/$	100,000 × 0.78 = €78,000

When to Hedge

By now, it is clear that hedger can gain protection against the unfavourable movement of exchange rate by booking a forward contract that involves no explicit cost. In the absence of explicit cost, would it be prudent to hedge all the exposures? Certainly not. Since forward contract has indirect cost involved in terms of loss of opportunities of making gains, one needs to be selective in hedging. Examples 8-1 and 8-2 clearly demonstrate that by booking forward, the hedger has foregone opportunities to make extra gains while protecting downside risk. The decision to hedge rests on the expected spot exchange rate at the maturity of receivable/payable, S_T, and the forward rate for the coinciding period, F. The prevailing spot exchange rate, S_0, is trivial to the decision-making for hedging. The decision rules for hedging the transactions are summarized as follows:

	ACTION	DECISION
For Receivable	Compare S_T and F	If $F > S_T$ Sell Forward Else Remain Unhedged
For Payable	Compare S_T and F	If $F < S_T$ Buy Forward Else Remain Unhedged

Obligations under Forward Contracts

While discussing hedging of receivable and payable, it was mentioned that at the end of the forward period that coincides with the maturity of receivable or payable, the exchange of cash flows would take place. Under forward sell, the exporter would deliver the foreign currency and receive local currency; and under forward buy, the importer would pay local currency to receive foreign currency. This makes obligations of the exporter and the importer under forward contract dependent upon the conclusion of underlying trade transaction. The exporter must realize the receivable from its customer to deliver foreign currency and importer must be ready to pay the foreign bill and pay domestic currency.

What happens when the underlying trade transaction is not completed? Can the obligations under the forward be deferred or cancelled if the underlying trade transaction is not completed? It must be mentioned that neither the existence of underlying transaction nor its completion is a prerequisite to the booking of a forward transaction, subject to laws of the land. Obligations of cash flow under the forward contract at its maturity have to be honoured and are independent of the underlying transaction.

From the foregoing, we may summarize the features of a hedge through a forward contract as follows:

1. It is an OTC product that involves no front-end payment.
2. Obligations of counterparties are mutual and arise only at the end of forward period.
3. Forward contract is independent of the underlying trade transactions and the commitments undertaken have to be honoured irrespective of whether underlying trade transaction matures or not.
4. If forward contract is backed by underlying trade transaction, it is hedging else the position of forward contract is speculative.

Cancellation of Forward Contracts

Reverting back to the transaction of forward sell of US$1,000 by the exporter, at its maturity the exporter was required to deliver US$1,000 and receive ₹56,500. The commitment of the exporter to deliver US$1,000 is dependent upon receivable fructifying no later than the maturity of forward contract. What if the receivable does not mature? Nevertheless, the exporter must honour the commitment towards the bank under the forward contract. Since it does not have the required dollars, it can comply with the requirement of forward contract in one of the following two ways:

(a) Obtain US$1,000 at spot and deliver to the bank and receive ₹56,500. If the spot rate is ₹57.50, the net payoff for the exporter would be

Purchase of US$1,000 from spot market	−₹57,500
Receipt from bank under forward contract	+₹56,500
Net cash flow	**−₹1,000**

(b) In case the exporter learns that receivable would not mature as scheduled, then he could enter into an opposite forward contract with the bank with maturity and amount coinciding with those of the initial forward contract and exchange the differential of the value of the two forward contracts. For example, if the exporter learns about the failure to receive US$1,000 from his customer one month prior, then he can have a 1-m forward buy contract. Say, this is done at the forward price of ₹56.00. By doing so, the obligations of foreign exchange under the two forward contracts would nullify and differential of local currency obligation would remain as can be seen from the following:

	US$	₹
Under the first contract, 3-m forward sell	−1,000	+56,500
Under the later contract, 1-m forward buy	+1,000	−56,000
Net cash flow	**0**	**+500**

Thus, by receiving ₹500, the exporter can absolve himself of obligations of forward contract without actually delivering the foreign currency.

Cost of Forward Hedge

In the preceding paragraphs, we demonstrated that by forward contract the exporter/importer was able to realize the fixed predetermined exchange rate, thereby eliminating the uncertainty but no upfront payment was made while booking a forward contract. Only upon the maturity of the forward period, the contracted obligations are settled and sums of money at predetermined rate are exchanged.

Common sense demands that hedger must pay a cost to eliminate the risk, as no risk-free position can be obtained without some cost being incurred. There cannot be any free lunch. Under forward hedge, the hedger does not pay directly but indirectly. The future spot exchange rate can move either way, favourably or unfavourably. Through a forward contract, the hedger gains protection against an unfavourable movement of exchange rates. The cost that the hedger pays is in the form of sacrificing the potential gain with favourable movement in which case the counterparty gains. Depreciation (appreciation) of foreign currency is detrimental to the interest of exporter (importer) and it is protected by booking a forward sell (buy) contract by foregoing the opportunity of making gains by its appreciation (depreciation).

Another related question is that of why the bank, the counterparty, should offer a forward contract for assuming risk. Again the answer lies in balancing the opportunity for making a gain and loss. The counterparty sees exactly the opposite way. The payoff of the counterparty is exactly equal and opposite to that of hedger. What is foregone by hedger is gained by the counterparty. The combined payoff of the two counterparties would always add up to zero.

Cost of forward hedge is measured in notional terms by premium or discount over the spot exchange rate. When foreign currency is more expensive in future than in spot, that is, $F > S_0$, it is said to be at premium and when cheaper than spot, that is, $F < S_0$, it is at discount. The cost of forward hedge is measured as % premium or discount over the current spot price as follows:

$$\text{Cost of Hedging} = \text{Premium or discount } (+/-) = (F - S_0)/S_0 \qquad (8\text{-}1)$$

However, whether the forward hedge has been beneficial or otherwise can only be determined at the end of hedge, that is, at the end of forward contract period. The real cost or benefit of the forward hedge must be measured not when it was set up but when it ended. The cost of forward at the time of set-up only tells that what premium or discount the foreign exchange is available. The real measure of effectiveness of forward hedge comes from the spot price S_1 at the end of period of hedge, which tells whether or not we actually benefited from the forward hedge. Therefore, real cost of hedging is

$$\text{Real Cost of Forward Hedge} = (F - S_1)/S_0 \qquad (8\text{-}2)$$

Real cost of hedging for receivable would be measured in terms of benefits. In case the spot exchange rate at the end of hedge, S_1 happens to be lower than the forward rate, the export hedge has proved better. In case of importer, the hedge would be beneficial if the spot rate at the end is higher than the forward rate.

Since the future spot rate is unknown, the cost of hedge is measured in terms of the current spot exchange rate and forward rate as given by Eq. 8-1.

SPECULATION WITH FORWARD CONTRACT

Since commitments of the forward contracts are independent of the underlying trade transactions, one can book the forward buy/sell contract separately, that is, without the underlying transaction. If there is no actual need of converting foreign currency into local or vice versa, the booking of a forward contract would imply a view on future spot exchange rate that is different than what is communicated by the forward rate.

For example, assume that the 6-m forward rate for US dollar is ₹57.50. It implies that the likely spot rate after six months would be ₹57.50. One may or may not agree with this rate. If one believes that the likely rate after 6 months would be greater than the forward rate, say ₹58.00, then to make profit, he can buy US dollar forward at ₹57.50 now. If the anticipated rate turns out to be true, then at the end of six months, he can sell US dollar spot at ₹58.00. The cash flows at the end of six months would be

	US$	₹
Under forward buy contract	+1.00	−57.50
Spot sell	−1.00	+58.00
Net cash flow	0.00	+0.50

Naturally, if the spot rate at the end of six months were to be less than the forward rate of ₹57.00, there would be a loss in the transaction.

Similarly, if one believes that at forward contract at ₹57.50/$ is overpriced (i.e. the likely price after six months would be less than ₹57.50 say ₹57.00), one can sell now and buy spot at the expiry of the forward period. If the forecast is true, then the cash flow would be

	US$	₹
Under forward sell contract	−1.00	+57.50
Spot buy	+1.00	−57.00
Net cash flow	0.00	+0.50

Whether the position in forward is speculative depends upon if (a) one has underlying trade transaction to honour the cash flow commitment under forward and (b) the forecast spot rate is viewed different than the forward rate. Under hedging, the position in the forward market must be equal to that of the exposure of foreign currency in the trade transaction. For an exposure of US$10,000 as receivable, if forward sell is for US$7,000, then the exporter would be under hedged as he leaves the exposure of US$3,000 uncovered. Similarly, if the forward cover is taken for US$15,000, then the exporter is covered for US$10,000 and is assuming speculative position for the remaining US$5,000.

The payoffs of the speculative positions for forward price of F for forward period of T and spot price at the end of forward period S_T are as follows:

Forward Rate	Speculative Position	Payoff at Maturity
Foreign Currency Underpriced	Buy foreign currency forward and sell spot at maturity	$S_T - F$
Foreign Currency Overpriced	Sell foreign currency forward and buy spot at maturity	$F - S_T$

An example follows.

Exercise 8-3
Speculation with Forward

A foreign exchange trader in Singapore finds that US dollar is trading at S$1.4050 in the spot market, whereas 6-m forward is quoted at about 8% annualized premium at S$1.4625. He believes forward market is overestimating the depreciation of Singapore dollar against his own estimate that depreciation of Singapore dollar would not be more than 5%.

(a) How can the trader benefit from his forecast?
(b) What profit/loss would result if at the end of six months the spot exchange rate happens to be (i) S$1.4650 and (ii) S$1.4325?

Solution

(a) The foreign exchange trader believes that 8% premium for US dollar is rather high, hence foreign currency is overpriced and local currency is underpriced. Therefore, he can now sell US dollar 6-m forward and buy spot six months later when the forward contract matures. If US dollar rises only by 5% as the trader expected, he would stand to gain about 3% (annualized).

(b) At the end of six months, the trader would have the following cash flows in Singapore dollar per US dollar:

Spot (S$/US$)	1.4650	1.4325
Under forward contract	+1.4625	+1.4625
Bought US$ in the spot market	−1.4650	−1.4325
Profit/Loss (S$ per US$)	−0.0025	+0.0300

NON-DELIVERABLE FORWARD CONTRACT

We have already mentioned the obligations under the forward contract, which upon maturity, required delivery of foreign currency from one party to another for exchange of local currency. In case the underlying trade transaction exists, the commitments of the exchange of foreign currency can be met easily. The exporter would realize receivables in foreign currency, deliver it against the forward contract, and receive the local currency. Importers wanting to make the payment in foreign currency under the forward contract would deliver local currency to receive foreign currency and remit the same to the suppliers of goods.

However, if the forward contract is booked not for hedging but with speculative motive, then delivery/receipt of foreign currency would require buying/selling the foreign currency in the spot market to meet the obligations under forward contract. There is no explicit need of foreign currency to satisfy trade transaction. Capital controls of the nation may prohibit speculation in foreign currencies. In addition, some controls in the foreign exchange markets may be placed on non-residents to deal with local currency.

Currency controls exist in many nations, including India, where transactions in the currency derivatives are permissible for hedging but not for speculative motives. Currencies in which such restrictions exist typically are not freely convertible. These capital controls or restrictions are placed by governments of many countries (mostly developing) with different and multiple objectives, such as the need for accumulating foreign currency reserves, promoting exports, reducing volatility in the foreign exchange markets by preventing speculation, regulating exports and imports, and promoting local industries and entrepreneurship.

Obligations under the forward contract are settled in one of the following ways:

Settlement by delivery Where on maturity of forward contract, the required foreign currency delivered for the local currency is called *settlement by delivery*. Further, the required foreign currency may be delivered either (a) from underlying trade transaction, for example, receivable realized from customer or (b) by procuring the same in the spot market.

Cash settled Where the obligations of foreign exchange under the forward contract are nullified by entering into an equal and opposite contract with matching maturity, and the difference of the two is settled in cash is called *cash settlement* (refer to the section on *cancellation of forward contracts* in preceding pages).

For currencies/nations where capital controls exist, the settlement by delivery is feasible only for hedging purposes, otherwise not. The only way the forward contracts with speculative motive can be satisfied is cash settlement.

Financial markets have responded to these controls by devising a product called *Non-Deliverable Forward (NDF)*, obviating the need for the delivery of the underlying asset, and instead make cash settlement as the only mode of fulfilling the obligations under forward contracts. These contracts could be traded either onshore or offshore. When NDF is onshore (where NDF is traded within the same geography), as was the case in Australia, the differential of forward prices were cash settled in local currency, that is, in Australian dollar.

In offshore NDF markets, the contracts are opened and closed outside the jurisdiction of the host nation/currency. For example, Indian rupee or Korean won may be quoted in the offshore markets in Singapore, Hong Kong or Dubai. Since capital controls exist in the currency of the host nation, the cash settlement of offshore NDF is done necessarily in foreign currency that is freely convertible, usually US dollar.

Hedging with Non-Deliverable Forward

Since NDFs are cash settled, one may get a notion that the product is devised for speculative purposes. It may be emphasized here that irrespective of whether the settlement is by delivery or by cash, the hedging remains equally effective. Only the operative mechanism under NDF changes and its hedging effectiveness remains same as that of deliverable forward contract.

Consider an example of an Australian exporter expecting to receive US$10,000 in three months' time. The spot price of US$ is A$1.28, whereas 3-m forward suggesting depreciation of US dollar is quoted at A$1.22/US$. If the exporter decides to hedge through deliverable forward, he would sell US$10,000. After three months, he would realize A$12,200, irrespective of the spot rate prevailing then.

In case of hedging with NDF, the delivery of foreign currency is ruled out and instead the position in NDF is cash settled on the notional amount as follows:

Settlement Amount (in foreign currency)
$$= (1 - \text{Forward rate/Settlement rate}) \times \text{Notional Principal} \tag{8-3}$$

The settlement rate is determined on the basis of spot rate prevailing at the end of the forward period. If the spot rate after 3 months is A$1.25, that is, the settlement rate is equal to spot. The amount receivable by the exporter would be as follows:

Under offshore NDF: $(1 - 1.22/1.25) \times 10{,}000 = $ US$240
Under onshore NDF: US$240 × 1.25 = A$300

We now analyse hedging with onshore and offshore NDFs.

- Under onshore NDF contract, the Australian exporter would sell US$10,000 now and buy back at maturity of three months at the settlement price of NDF. He would pay/receive the difference of the opening price and settlement price in Australian dollars, the local currency. He would sell his receivable at the spot rate prevailing then. The total value in Australian dollar would be same and is independent of the spot rate prevailing at maturity.
- If the NDF is done offshore, the difference of the opening and settlement price would be paid or received in a freely convertible currency, say US dollar and not in Australian dollar. The receivable would again be sold in the spot market.

Table 8-3 demonstrates that hedging with NDF both onshore and offshore would be as effective as the hedging with the deliverable forward.

Table 8-3
Hedging with NDF

Spot Rate, Settlement Rate (A$/US$)	1.25	1.22	1.20
Onshore NDF			
Value of Receivable (A$)	12,500	12,200	12,000
Cash Settlement of NDF			
Sold US$ Forward at A$1.22/US$	12,000	12,200	12,200
Bought US$ Spot on Settlement Day	−12,500	−12,200	−12,000
Net Cash Flow under NDF (A$)	−300	0	+200
Net Value of Receivables Realized (A$)	12,200	12,200	12,200
Offshore NDF			
US$ Sold under NDF	10,000	10,000	10,000
Cash Settlement of NDF (US$)	−240	–	166.67
Net US$ realized	9,760	10,000	10,167
Value Realized in Local Currency(A$)	12,200	12,200	12,200

Exercise 8-4
Settlement of Non-Deliverable Forward

Assume on 19 July 20XX, a firm in Manila, Philippines, has 3-m payable of US$1 million. The value of US dollar is expected to appreciate in three months. It can hedge only in the offshore NDF market as no forward contract is available to the firm in Manila. A bank in Dubai offers three months NDF for value 20 September 20XX at the rate of Philippine Peso (PHP)/USD at 54.00. The firm sells PHP54 million. The NDF settlement date is 19 September 20XX with 11:00 a.m. Manila time exchange rate.

Examine the cash flow for the firm in case the settlement rate at 11:00 a.m. in Manila is (a) PHP54.00, (b) PHP60.00, and (c) PHP48.00.

Solution
By transacting the above, the firm locks in the three-month forward PHP selling rate at PHP54.00/USD, which is equivalent to buying US$1 million (PHP54 million). The settlement would be done in cash in US dollar and not in Philippine Peso. For settlement, the exchange rate at 11.00 a.m., 19 September would be compared with the NDF rate of 54.00.

(a) **The settlement rate is equal to the NDF rate:**
If the settlement rate is exactly PHP54.00 on 19 September, 20XX, there is no difference between the NDF and the settlement rate; hence, no payment is made by either parties at the expiry of NDF. The firm buys US$1 million at the spot rate of PHP54.00/$. The cash outflow would be PHP54 million.

(b) **The settlement rate is higher than the NDF rate, that is, 60.00 on 19 September 20XX:**
Here, the PHP has weakened. Hence, the bank in Dubai will pay the difference, that is, US$100,000 to the firm on the settlement date of 20 September 20XX.

Dollar receivable by the firm at NDF rate
= PHP 54 million/PHP54/$ = US$1,000,000

Dollar payable by the firm on NDF settlement date
= PHP 54 million/PHP60/$ = US$900,000

The NDF is settled in US$. The firm gets US$100,000 under NDF contract and procures balance US$900,000 at PHP60/$, costing PHP54 million.

(c) **The settlement rate is higher than the NDF rate, that is, 48.00 on 19 September 20XX:**
In this instance, PHP has strengthened and, hence, the firm would pay to the bank in Dubai the difference, that is, US$125,000, on the settlement date of 20 September 20XX.

Dollar receivable by the firm at NDF rate
= PHP54 million/PHP54/$ = US$1,000,000

Dollar payable by the firm on NDF settlement date
= PHP54 million/PHP48/$ = US$1,125,000

The firm would now buy US$1,125,000 to pay US$125,000 under NDF and US$1 million for the payable. The cash out flow would be 1,125,000 × 48.00 = PHP54 million.

Evolution and Growth of Non-Deliverable Forward

The NDFs evolved in the 1970s with Australian dollar when the currency was subjected to capital controls. It was done with the objective of providing effective hedge and yet causing no flows of foreign capital. They came into being because of increased volatility in the interest rates which made hedging difficult with the onshore banking system through deliverable forward market. Transactions for hedging were conducted in the NDF market, and hence they are also referred to as *hedge market*. In case of Australia, the development of the NDF market was onshore with settlement in local currency of Australian dollar.

Today, the NDF market primarily consists of six Asian currencies, namely Chinese renminbi, Indian rupee, Korean won, Indonesian rupiah, Philippine peso, and Taiwanese dollar, all of which have capital controls in varying degree. Foreign currency movements are controlled depending upon the end-use. Since obligations in the derivatives markets are independent of the underlying trade transactions, one of the popular measures to exercise control is to ban forward trading in currency markets.

Further, if allowed they would be cash settled in local currency only so as to eliminate the demand/supply of foreign currency. Due to regulations and constraints, legal and practical; in the movement of a currency, NDF contracts are normally traded offshore, that is, outside the jurisdiction of the country. For example, if Indian rupee is subject to non-delivery outside India, the NDF contract could be traded outside India, say at Dubai or Singapore without involving rupee and settled in freely convertible currency like US dollar.

Banking system in a nation may prohibit booking of forward contract in the absence of exposure in the underlying currency. Such controls make hedging feasible but other activities of speculation and arbitrage are denied restricting the depth of the forward markets.

The NDFs provide alternative hedging avenues for the non-resident who cannot participate in the onshore deliverable market. Further, onshore deliverable market may be illiquid too. Capital controls are aimed at restricting the short-term capital flows that are not trade-related. Growth in NDFs in the 1990s is believed to be related to Asian currency crisis that led to tightening the currency controls further. The participation by foreign nationals in the onshore forward markets was regarded as speculative enough to destabilize the currency value by making the exchange rate extremely volatile.[1]

Non-Deliverable Forward and Interest Rate Parity

Under the circumstances where both the forward contract and NDF exist simultaneously, like for Asian currencies, would the pricing of the two be identical? All we can say is that neither one of them is likely to reflect the true value of the forward contract though for different reasons. None of the markets seems complete. Onshore forward contracts available for hedging purposes only would lack volumes as speculators and arbitrageurs are kept at bay. Since capital

---

[1] Higgins, Patrick and Owen M. Humpage (2005), *Non-Deliverable Forwards: Can We Tell Where Renminbi Is Headed*, Federal Reserve Bank of Cleveland, 1 September.

controls exist, the pricing is not determined by free market forces. The NDF market, though indifferent to capital controls (the reason they exist), lacks depth due to limited participation.

The pricing of the forward contract is governed by interest rate parity as discussed in the earlier chapter. It was based on the premise of free flow of capital across borders and, thus, the premium/discount is governed by interest rate differentials of two currencies. When capital markets are freely accessible offering choice of borrowing in one currency and investing in another, the forward markets and spot markets are linked by Eq. 8-4 as follows:

$$F_n = S_0 \frac{(1+r_d)^n}{(1+r_f)^n} \qquad (8\text{-}4)$$

where F_n is the forward rate for n periods, S_0 is the spot rate, and r_d and r_f are the interest rates in home and foreign countries, respectively.

However, when capital account controls exist the lending and borrowing onshore is restricted distorting the IRP. This gives rise to offshore market. The rate of NDF, therefore, would imply an interest rate differential that is not same as the differential reflected in the deliverable forward markets onshore. Since NDF is not subject to capital controls the validity of IRP tends to be greater.

Assuming a 12-month NDF contract in Indian rupee is quoted at ₹44.60 per dollar as against the spot rate of ₹44.00 with 5% interest rate in US dollar implied interest rate for Indian rupee in the NDF would be 6.43%:

$$(1 + r_{\text{NDF}}) = 1.05 \times \frac{44.60}{44.00} = 1.0643 \text{ or } r_{\text{NDF}} = 6.43\%$$

Similarly, the forward rate in the deliverable onshore markets would indicate another implied rate. Assume that forward rate in deliverable market is ₹45.00, then the implied interest rate in India will be 7.38%:

$$(1 + r) = 1.05 \times \frac{45.00}{44.00} = 1.0738 \text{ or } r = 7.38\%$$

The differential of two implied interest rates indicates the effectiveness of the capital control measures. Greater the difference, greater is the effectiveness of measures of capital control. We can make the following observations of the two implied interest rates:

1. Changing policies of capital control are likely to impact onshore deliverable markets and not the NDF as much.
2. Changes in the premium/discount of the NDF are more governed by free market forces and, hence, volatility in NDF would better indicate relative strength or weakness of the currencies.
3. Shrinking gap between the two implied interest rates would suggest that currency can move towards full convertibility, or decreasing need or desirability of the capital controls.
4. Interest rate implied in the NDF premium/discount rather than the onshore deliverable forward market would be a truer measure of likely future spot rates.

An active NDF market and lesser differential of the offshore and onshore interest rates would be an indicator or precursor of the likely scenario of the exchange rate markets if the capital flow controls were to vanish.

In the context of interest rate parity, more reliance must be placed on the forward rate prevailing in the NDF market rather than onshore deliverable forward market. Where local residents operating in the onshore markets also have access to offshore markets, the differential in the offshore and onshore forward rates (or the differential of yields) would give rise to arbitrage opportunities. This would make offshore and onshore yields and forward rates to be in close proximity with one another with nominal differential that probably does not exceed the transaction costs in two markets.

The NDF markets are often viewed with suspicion as they circumvent the local exchange control rules and provide easy alternatives to those who cannot access the onshore deliverable forward market. However, they must be viewed in a different perspective. Onshore deliverable markets in regulated environment provide hedging applications, but they inhibit speculative and arbitrage activities. In contrast, those who need to hedge through NDF would be few but offshore NDF would present opportunities for speculators. Both stand-alone markets would lack depth, and only when combined can present a truer and competitive picture regarding the status of a currency.

The differential is likely to be greater where interventions by governments in the foreign exchange markets are frequent and large. In the situation of fixed exchange rates and restrictions on local residents to access offshore market, the NDF rates may suggest the likely revaluation/devaluation of the currency.

CONCEPTS IN PRACTICE
Non-Deliverable Forward as Predictor of Future Spot Exchange Rate

RENMINBI LEAVES THE PEG, NON-DELIVERABLE FORWARD PROVIDED CLUE?

After a long standing pressure and lobbying from the USA and other nations concerned about extremely undervalued yuan (renminbi), the Chinese currency, China finally relented on 21 June 2010 but gave very little by announcing de-pegging of yuan with US dollar. It merely stated that it would allow more flexible policy of fixing the value of its currency. Although most nations would crave for a double-digit revaluation, China gave little by opting for a crawling peg, that too a very slow one.

From 1997 till July 2005, yuan was pegged to US dollar at about yuan 8.30/$. The central bank of China abolished the peg and permitted a slow rise in the value of yuan. After initial appreciation of 2%, yuan appreciated by 21% in three years by mid-2008 when in the wake of global financial crisis, it opted to re-peg the exchange rate at yuan 6.83/$ to protect its export-led economic growth.

In July 2005, when China permitted a more flexible exchange rate regime by abandoning the explicit peg to US dollar, all that China's central bank did was to set a reference rate against US dollar every day and then allow a change not exceeding 0.5% around the mid-point. Actual fluctuations were much smaller as is reflected in facts that over a period of three years till mid-2008 yuan rose only by 21%. For over two years, the exchange rate remained pegged at 6.83.

The implied PPP rate by estimates of IMF in June 2010 is about yuan 3.60 as against the pegged rate of 6.83, indicating and undervaluing by about 47%. On 21 June 2010, while there was no change in the official exchange rate, the NDFs shot higher. The NDFs that allow bets on the future exchange rate rose by about 1% to RMB6.6425 for 12-m NDF—the most liquid contract. It implied an expected annual appreciation of 2.3% against US dollar. The NDF market is generally used for taking speculative positions in the value of a currency. The scenario in the NDF market seems to belie general expectations as at that rate, it would take more than a decade to eliminate the undervaluation believed to be in the range of 25%–40%.

The faith of the world that NDFs would correctly reflect the believed value seems misplaced. The NDF markets place due cognizance to the past when in the previous period when relaxation in rate was granted yuan rose only by 21% over two years despite a permissible band of 0.5% per day. The NDF markets seem more practical, giving due cognizance to the intervention ability and other economic factors while determining the NDF quotes, than the guesstimates about the valuation by other nations and experts, IMF inclusive. Possibly, the annual appreciation of 2.3% is valid for one year and seemingly the degree of freedom over an observation period that China has really relented, the NDF rate would correct as expected by world's leading nations and economists. Inhibitions in the NDF market appear to be closer to reality than the overoptimism and expectations that China would take radical steps to correct the exchange rate overnight.

Further, it is believed that the NDF market[2] (1) facilitates smoother transition of an economy from controlled regime to full convertibility, as it serves as an intermediate bridge for the interim period and (2) provides skills and expertise developed in the NDF markets to be adapted in the deliverable forward market as and when capital controls are lifted or full convertibility of the currency achieved.

CURRENCY FUTURES

In the previous section, we discussed the applications of currency forwards and NDFs for hedging foreign currency risk, both for exporters and importers. In this section, we discuss a rather similar instrument called futures that has similar applications and fundamentals as that of a forward contract. Futures contract too is a derivative product that derives its price from some underlying asset. Currency futures would have exchange rates as underlying asset.

In respect of pricing, fundamentals and applications futures are identical to forward contracts. However, they differ substantially from forward contracts in terms of their markets,

---

[2] Based on Debelle, Guy, Jacob Gyntelberg, and Michael Plumb (2006), 'Forward Currency Markets in Asia; Lesson from Australian Experience', *BIS Quarterly Review*, September.

operations, and settlement. Although forwards are in existence for long, futures contract is relatively a recent development.

Currency futures came into being in the 1970s. Till about 1973, the exchange rates for various currencies were fixed. In the era of gold standard that remained in vogue till 1926, the fixed amount of gold that the currency could buy determined the exchange rates. Gold specie flow self-correcting mechanism ensured stability of exchange rates for decades. When gold standard broke down during the two world wars and in between, the Bretton Woods system was devised in 1944 which provided limited flexibility to exchange rates by making intervention in the currency markets obligatory on the central banks to maintain the desired exchange rates and contain volatility. The values of the currencies continued to be determined by content of gold or US dollar as dollar meant a fixed quantity of gold.

In the late 1970s, when the Bretton Woods system collapsed, the exchange rates of various currencies started becoming more and more market-determined and the world started moving from fixed exchange rate system to floating exchange rate system. The number of countries opting for floating rate system is increasing with the passage of time. In the floating rate system, the factors impacting the exchange rates become too many and form part of broader economic policies, causing exchange rates to move continuously.

As the major currencies of the world moved towards floating rate system increasing volatility in the exchange rates, so did the need for hedging foreign currency exposures. The need for hedging also caused innovations in the financial markets, devising newer and newer instruments with time to cover exposures. Futures contract is one such product that covers the needs of hedging. Currency futures contract is suitable for exporters and importers who are exposed to exchange rate risk for their receivables and payables just in the same manner as did the forward contracts.

Before we take a look at the specifics of futures contract, let us discuss some of the shortcomings/issues with forward contract.

LIMITATIONS OF FORWARD CONTRACT

Forward contract is an OTC product that required the counterparties to negotiate and finalize the terms of the contract, that is, amount, price, and maturity date. The terms of the contract remain confidential with the two contracting parties and are not in public domain. Most contracts are initiated by corporate clients with their bankers. Contract terms being confidential, it is not hard to find the same bank offering different forward prices to two different customers at the same point of time. Whether differing prices of two similar contracts is a sign of competiveness of the market or otherwise is a moot point.

Forward contracts have certain limitations as enumerated here.

Fairness of Forward Price Negotiation of price in OTC contracts is always subject to the relative bargaining power of the counterparties involved. The identity of parties is known to each other and not to others. The strengths of the two parties are likely to be unequal rather than equal. If the counterparties are equal in stature, need, size, etc. one could presume the price would be competitive, fair, and market-determined. However, the forward exchange rate becomes the function of relative strengths of the two parties and is likely to favour the stronger of the two counterparties. Due to disclosed identities and uneven bargaining strength of counterparties, the pricing of forward contract is likely to be unfair to one and favourable to the other. It cannot be said to be a fair and market-determined price.

Free Flow of Information   In the markets for currency forwards, the potential participants are not aware of the price the forward contracts are being negotiated. They are also in dark about the volumes, trends, etc. Though the information is exchanged through informal interaction of participants, the market competitiveness depends upon the willingness of the participants to exchange views in open. The confidentiality clause in a forward contract may impede free flow of information. Though informal channels for exchange of price and other data are open, there exists no organized way for disclosures. With the advent of information technology and computers, there are platforms such as Bloomberg and Reuters that collate and display information about currency forwards. However, bid ask spreads displayed there, a measurement of market efficiency, are likely to be high.

Delivery-based Settlement   Forward contracts are normally settled by delivery of the underlying asset, that is, foreign currency, though there are provisions of cancellation of forward by entering an equal and opposite contract with same maturity. In practice, the subsequent contract is normally entered with the same party with whom the initial contract was negotiated so as to nullify the delivery of foreign exchange. This requires mutual consent of two parties, which again limits the competitiveness of the market. Entering two opposite contracts with different parties though cancels the foreign exchange obligations on net basis, and it involves the flow of local currency from one party to another. The feasibility of such operations is subject to operational constraints and legal barriers. Practical compulsions of delivery-based settlement, mutual consent for cancellation of the forward contract, and legal environment governing foreign exchange transactions are few factors that would constrain the market efficiency.

Default Risk (Counterparty Risk)   While entering the forward contract, the two counterparties agree to fulfil their mutual obligations at the end of forward period. One party delivers the foreign currency and the other delivers the local currency. Either of the parties can fail to meet its obligation undertaken while initiating the forward contract. Further, the price scenario at the end of the forward period would favour one party and disfavour the other. For example, consider an exporter enters a 3-m forward sell contract at ₹56/$. If after three months, the spot rate is ₹55 (less than the forward rate), the exporter is too happy to deliver US dollars, whereas the counterparty facing a loss would be reluctant. If the price scenario is the other way round, that is, ₹57, the reverse would happen. The exporter would be a reluctant party to meet his obligation. Since the payoffs of the counterparties to the forward contracts are opposite and equal, the price scenario would favour one party and equally disfavour another, giving rise to great likelihood of default.

Thus, forward contracts may suffer from somewhat distorted pricing, constrained flow of price information, operational difficulties in cancellation of contracts, compulsion of delivery-based settlement, and existence of default risk. Futures contracts attempt to overcome these constraints by

(a) providing a trading platform through an exchange without disclosing the identities of counterparties and thereby removing the distortion of price due to the size of counterparties,

(b) displaying information with respect to the last trade price, best offers, bids, etc. continuously and, therefore, aiding the participants with well-informed decision-making,

(c) providing for cash settlement as well along with delivery-based settlement, obviating the need for obtaining mutual consent for cancellation from the counterparty, and

(d) acting as counterparty to all buyers and sellers virtually eliminating the counterparty risk.

FUTURES CONTRACT VS FORWARD CONTRACT

How these deficiencies of forward markets are covered by futures is explained by describing the futures contract. The shortest possible way a futures contract can be described or defined is that it is an exchange-traded forward contract. Recall that forward contract is one that is negotiated for price now and to be settled at a future date. So is the futures contract. Forward and future contracts differ only operationally as are depicted in Figure 8-5.

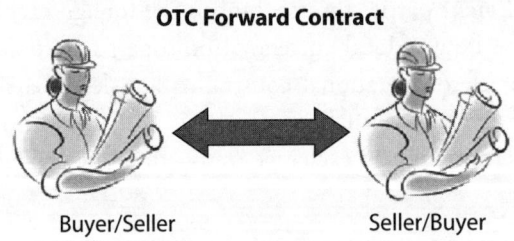

Figure 8-5
Forward and Futures Contracts

Price Information in Public Domain In a futures contract, the exchange is the interface and it conceals the identities of the counterparties from each other. The exchange serves as a buyer to each seller and a seller to each buyer. This facilitates the price discovery in more efficient manner. The exchange continuously provides the price information by displaying the last traded price (LTP). It also displays the best bids and best offers along with the pending demand at different price levels. When the LTP, demand and supply information at various levels, etc. is visible different all, it induces various participants to place their bids and offers. This makes the markets more efficient and competitive. Therefore, with increased participation, the pricing of the futures contract should be more true and fair as compared to OTC forward contract, where such information is not readily available and visible.

Cash Settlement and Ease of Entry/Exit At the maturity of the futures contract, the settlement procedures are extremely well-defined. Cash settlement in contrast to delivery-based settlement is more in practice that provides easy entry and exit routes to the participants. It must be mentioned here that delivery-based settlements are not ruled out because delinking of delivery would tend to distort the link between the spot markets and the derivatives markets. Cash settlement increases participation in the market and helps increase volumes. Increased participation and increased volumes are the desirable characteristics of any competitive market.

Eliminating Counterparty Risk Since exchange serves as counterparty to each buyer and seller, the risk of default becomes negligible. The exchange ensures that the commitments made under the contract on an exchange are honoured on the due date by delivery and price differential. In case one party defaults, the obligations to the counterparty are met by the exchange, preventing the chain of defaults and systemic risk. To ensure that all commitments are honoured, the exchange takes suitable measures to contain the risk of default. For this purpose, the exchange has elaborate auctioning system and margining system that each participant has to comply with.

TERMINOLOGY OF FUTURES

Intervention by the exchange to facilitate trading of contracts to be settled at a later date demands operational changes to the forward contract. For active trading to take place, the contracts have to be standardized in terms of their size, delivery dates, methods of quoting, settlements, etc. We describe the same with respect to currency contracts traded in India through National Stock Exchange (NSE) and Multi-Commodity Exchange (MCX). Specifications of the contracts available in India at NSE and MCX are given in Table 8-4.

Contract Size Each participant can buy or sell the specified currency for specified quantities. With the exception of Japanese yen, the standard contract size is fixed at 1,000 units of foreign currency. For Japanese yen, the contract size is 100,000. To facilitate participation by small enterprises, the lot size in India is kept substantially below the international markets, for example, the lot size for British pound at CME is 62,500. The exposures in multiples of the contract size

Table 8-4
Currency Futures Contract Specifications in India

	US Dollar	Euro	British Pound	Japanese Yen
Contract Size	$1,000	€1,000	£1,000	¥100,000
Expiry Date	2 days prior to the last trading day of the month for spot transaction			
Nos of Contracts	12 monthly contracts for next 12 months			
Price Quotation	₹ per unit of foreign currency up to four decimal places			₹ per ¥100 up to four decimal places
Tick Size	₹0.0025 or ₹2.50 per contract			
Settlement Mode	Cash Settled			
Daily Settlement Price (DSP)	Weighted average of last 30 minutes of trading			
Settlement Price	Daily: DSP with T + 1 Final settlement: RBI reference rate with T + 2			
Base Price	Theoretical price for the first day of the contract and DSP for remaining days			
Margin	NSE: SPAN based MCX: Initial margin of 1.75% on the first day and 1% thereafter and extreme loss margin of 1% of MTM value of gross open position			
Daily Price Variation	±3% for contracts up to 6 months ±5% for contracts greater than 6 months			

Source: Based on websites of NSE and MCX-SX, 25 June 2013.

can be hedged. Exposures not in multiple of contract size would have to be rounded off. For example, exporter needing to hedge receivables of US$15,500 would have to trade either 15 or 16 contracts of US dollar.

Contract Expiry Forward contracts need to be settled at a future date depending upon the mutual convenience of counterparties. Such cannot be the case for futures. Futures contracts are standardized for the delivery dates. Each contract matures on a specific date, known in advance to all participants. In India, we have monthly contracts in contrast to quarterly contracts at CME. All futures contracts have to be settled at the end of the respective month. The expiry date is fixed so that the settlement finishes within the contract month. Since spot markets provide for two business days for settlement, the expiry date of futures contracts are fixed two days prior to the last date of spot transaction for the month. For example, June 2013 contract expired on 26 June 2013.

Number of Contracts Available At any point of time, there are 12 futures contracts available expiring every month. On 20 June 2013, there would be contracts available for next 12 month covering the period till May 2014. This implies that maximum hedging period is limited to 12 months. At CME and most other exchanges, there are four quarterly contracts available, again restricting the hedging period to one year.

The contracts are specified by the currency pairs and followed by expiry date. For example, futures contract of *USDINR260613* means that the futures contract is for US dollar against Indian rupee (INR) and expires on 26 June 2013.

Price/Quotation The price of the currency futures follows direct convention, that is, number of units of home currency per unit of foreign currency. For convenience of quotation Japanese yen is quoted for 100 yens. Futures markets follow the same convention as that of spot. In India and most other nations, the currencies are quoted up to four decimal places. Price quotation of ₹57.3725 per dollar for US dollar contract is the value of one unit of US dollar in terms of Indian rupee. For standard size of US$1,000, the contract value would be $57.3725 \times 1,000 = ₹57,372.50$.

Tick Size Tick size is the minimum movement of the price quotation in either direction. The tick size for futures in India has been fixed at ₹0.0025. Hence, from the existing price of ₹57.3725/$, the next move could either be ₹57.3750 or 57.3700. In terms of the value of the futures contract, the minimum change would be ₹2.50 ($0.0025 \times 1,000$).

Settlement The normal way of settling the futures contract is not by delivery but by entering into an offsetting contract and, then, exchanging the price differential. For example, one investor buys a contract of USDINR260613 at a price of ₹57.3725 on 4 June 2013. This implies that the investor would receive US$1,000 and pay ₹57,372.50 on 26 June 2013. However, the investor need not wait till then. Any time prior to the last trading day of the same contract, the investor can sell one USDINR260613 contract under which he would deliver US$1,000 on 26 June 2013 and receive equivalent rupee.

Assume that the price of the contract USDINR260613 on 15 June is ₹58.3725 and the investor sells the contract. On the settlement day, his US$ obligation of foreign exchange would nullify, but he is to pay ₹57,372.50 under the first contract and receive ₹58,372.50 under the second contract. The net receivable is ₹1,000. By entering the offsetting contract, obligations under both the contracts are met. This is known as cash settlement. In India because of exchange control restrictions, all futures contracts are compulsorily cash settled. Outstanding positions, if not squared off by the investor till the last day, are assumed to be closed by exchange and settled at RBI reference rate.

Margin System To enable exchange, assume the responsibility of meeting the future obligations on the due date, some deposit is required by both the counterparties. This deposit should suffice for the losses that could be incurred in the futures contract. In the event of loss, the exchange would refund the deposit only after adjusting for the losses.

There are various ways by which the amount of margin is computed. Initial margin is the money to be deposited for opening a position and normally covers a maximum possible loss

Currency Derivatives Watch

MARKET OPEN
As on Jun 28, 2013 16:52:12 IST

RBI Reference Rate As on Jun 28, 12:00:00

1 $ ₹ 59.6995   1 £ ₹ 91.1432   1 € ₹ 77.9760   100 ¥ ₹ 60.4900

Option Chain | Daily Reports

Price Watch | Live Chart | Spread Contracts | Most Active | Trade History | Information

Contracts	Best Bid Qty	Best Bid Price	Best Ask Price	Best Ask Qty	Spread	Chng	% Chng	LTP	OI	Volume (Contracts)	Turnover (crs)	No. Of Trades
USDINR												
USDINR 290713	110	59.7375	59.7425	192	0.0050	-0.83	-1.37	59.7450	1,650,295	3221850	19,295.33	109889
USDINR 280813	94	60.0050	60.0175	127	0.0125	-0.84	-1.39	60.0150	332,969	143035	860.48	8512
USDINR 260913	50	60.2525	60.2675	213	0.0150	-0.85	-1.39	60.2625	123,963	26247	158.40	1548
More Contracts ▼												
EURINR												
EURINR 290713	10	78.0525	78.0625	1	0.0100	-0.78	-1.00	78.0450	73,314	41376	323.41	6471
EURINR 280813	8	78.3350	78.3650	2	0.0300	-0.82	-1.03	78.3400	8,923	2513	19.72	435
EURINR 260913	7	78.5450	78.6875	2	0.1425	-0.76	-0.96	78.6050	2,450	477	3.75	75
More Contracts ▼												
GBPINR												
GBPINR 290713	19	91.0225	91.0350	20	0.0125	-1.49	-1.61	91.0225	27,862	37927	346.16	7030
GBPINR 280813	24	91.3250	91.3625	25	0.0375	-1.50	-1.61	91.3275	5,324	2910	26.62	734
GBPINR 260913	6	91.5650	91.6600	1	0.0950	-1.49	-1.60	91.6575	1,205	781	7.17	99
More Contracts ▼												
JPYINR												
JPYINR 290713	14	60.3075	60.3150	18	0.0075	-1.37	-2.22	60.2775	13,099	27183	164.57	4835
JPYINR 280813	1	60.5625	60.5925	10	0.0300	-1.35	-2.19	60.5400	1,200	1345	8.17	445
JPYINR 260913	10	60.3525	61.4750	5	1.1225	-0.74	-1.18	61.4750	87	37	.23	9

Source: www.nseindia.com as on 30 June 2014.

Figure 8-6

Currency Futures Prices at National Stock Exchange

over a period of one day. At the end of each day, all the outstanding contracts are brought to a price called Daily Settlement Price (DSP) at which profit and loss is computed. This process is called marking-to-market. The loss is recovered from the loss-making position and passed on to the profit-making position. Profit and loss are adjusted the next day, referred to as $(T+1)$. On the last day of the contract, the settlement of the contract is not on DSP but on the RBI reference rate. The final profit or loss based on RBI reference rate is adjusted on $(T+2)$ days basis.

The futures contract for four currencies, that is, US dollar, euro, British pound, and Japanese yen are available in India both at NSE and MCX. Figures 8-6 and 8-7 display the LTP, best bid, and best ask rates with respective quantities, volume traded, etc. of the active contracts traded at NSE and MCX, respectively.

Open interest represents the number of contracts yet to be squared up. As is known, futures trades are mostly settled by entering into offsetting contracts before the expiry. Hence, at expiry when all contracts are settled, the open interest must reduce to zero. Open interest over the life of a contract starts building up after its introduction and diminishes as maturity nears. It is a vital statistic used by analysts to forecast and interpret the market behaviour.

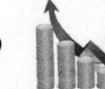

MCX-SX > Market > Currency Derivatives > Live Report > Price Watch

RBI Reference Rate 28-Jun-2013 — 1$:₹59.6995 — 1€:₹77.9760 — 1£:₹91.1432 — 100¥:₹60.4900

Price Watch | Expand All | As on 28 Jun, 2013 16:59:59 IST — All prices in ₹

Option Calculator

Contract	Buy		Sell		Spread	Change		LTP	Volume (In Lots)	OI (In Lots)	Value* (₹ in Crores)	No. of Trades
	QTY	Price	Price	QTY		Price	%					
USDINR												
USDINR 290713	66	59.7450	59.7500	19	0.0050	-0.8325	-1.37	59.7450	23,23,362	7,50,758	13,914.97	1,06,679
USDINR 280813	4	60.0100	60.0200	50	0.0100	-0.8300	-1.36	60.0125	99,236	1,96,021	596.61	7,269
USDINR 260913	9	60.2500	60.2675	61	0.0175	-0.8350	-1.37	60.2550	12,911	72,044	77.93	917
More Contracts												
EURINR												
EURINR 290713	55	78.0350	78.0500	1	0.0150	-0.8100	-1.03	78.0325	46,016	57,803	359.83	9,716
EURINR 280813	5	78.3150	78.3475	1	0.0325	-0.7875	-1.00	78.3300	1,173	2,703	9.21	324
EURINR 260913	15	78.2050	78.7950	15	0.5900	-1.3625	-1.71	78.3800	6	21	0.05	6
More Contracts												
GBPINR												
GBPINR 290713	86	91.0125	91.0175	1	0.0050	-1.5075	-1.63	91.0125	36,876	25,128	336.62	10,389
GBPINR 280813	1	91.3200	91.3375	8	0.0175	-1.4725	-1.59	91.3475	1,600	1,714	14.66	560
GBPINR 260913	1	91.5525	92.1075	5	0.5550	-1.5700	-1.69	91.4300	47	236	0.43	19
More Contracts												
JPYINR												
JPYINR 290713	12	60.2700	60.2800	1	0.0100	-1.3825	-2.24	60.2700	27,145	13,177	164.29	6,979
JPYINR 280813	10	60.5175	60.5500	1	0.0325	-1.3325	-2.15	60.5625	475	433	2.89	187
JPYINR 260913	10	60.0000	62.7500	20	2.7500	-	-	-	-	0	-	-
More Contracts												

Source: www.mcx-sx.com as on 28 June 2013.

Figure 8-7
Currency Futures Prices at Multi-Commodity Exchange

HEDGING WITH CURRENCY FUTURES

Currency futures are used for hedging much in the same way as the forward contract. With the forward contract, an exporter/importer enters a forward sell/buy contract with coinciding maturity of the receivable/payable. Irrespective of spot rate prevailing at the maturity of the receivable/payable, the required foreign currency is sold/bought at the forward price negotiated.

Hedging with futures is done in similar fashion with a slightly different outcome. The price received/paid under the forward contract is exactly equal to the forward price. Hedging with futures would result in the ultimate price that is not exactly but approximately equal to the futures price at the time of the initiation of futures position.

Hedging with futures would involve the following steps:

1. Determine the amount of exposure, that is, receivable or payable in foreign currency, called underlying and its maturity. Receivable is referred as a long position, whereas payable is called a short position, the payoffs of which remain same as depicted in Figure 8-1.

2. Determine the suitable futures contract that is nearest to the maturity of the underlying.
3. Determine the number of futures contracts that approximately equals the amount of exposure that must be traded for hedging. The position in futures contract must be opposite to that of underlying. Following is the hedging strategy:

    (a) For long position of underlying (receivable), short (sell) the futures
    (b) For short position of underlying (payable), long (buy) the futures

4. The position in futures in terms of amount and maturity must match the position in the underlying to the extent possible, for an effective hedge.
5. Nullify the futures position by entering the offsetting contract, that is, buy futures if initially short or sell futures if initially long, around the maturity of the underlying.
6. Trade the underlying position at the spot rate prevailing then.

By following the aforementioned steps, the result of the hedging with futures would closely resemble the hedging outcome with forward contract. We illustrate this with an example. Assume today is 7 June 2013 and an exporter has outstanding receivable of US$15,000 due 75 days. Implementing the hedging steps outlined above the exporter would do the following:

1. The exporter is long for US$15,000 in the underlying and, therefore, he needs to go short on the futures.
2. The due date of receivable is 21 August 2013 (7 June 2010 + 75 days).
3. The exposure of the exporter is for US$15,000 till 21 August 2013, and the suitable futures contract to hedge that is closest to his exposure is USDINR280813 as it expires on 28 August 2013.
4. With the contract size of US$1,000, the exporter would short 15 futures contracts USDINR280813, which can be done at *best bid* rate. Referring to Figure 8-6, we find that the best bid rate of this contract is ₹60.0050. For convenience, assume that in OTC, forward market is identical at ₹60.0050.
5. On 21 August 2013, when his receivables mature, the exporter lifts the hedge by buying the futures contract USDINR280813 at the rate that would prevail at the futures exchange, and
6. Sells US$15,000 at the spot rate that would prevail then.

For various assumed spot rates and the futures price at the time of lifting the hedge, the net realization by the exporter is shown in Table 8-5.

Table 8-5
Realization under Futures Hedge (₹/US$)

(a) Spot rate*	58.0075	59.0000	59.0500	60.0050	60.0550	61.2500	61.0800	62.0500
(b) Futures Price*	58.0100	59.0050	59.0575	60.0025	60.0575	61.2450	61.0775	62.0450
(c) Profit/loss on Futures (60.0050 − (b))	1.9950	1.0000	0.9475	0.0025	−0.0525	−1.2400	−1.0725	−2.0400
Total Realized (a) + (c)	60.0025	60.0000	59.9975	60.0075	60.0025	60.0100	60.0075	60.0100

*Assumed prices

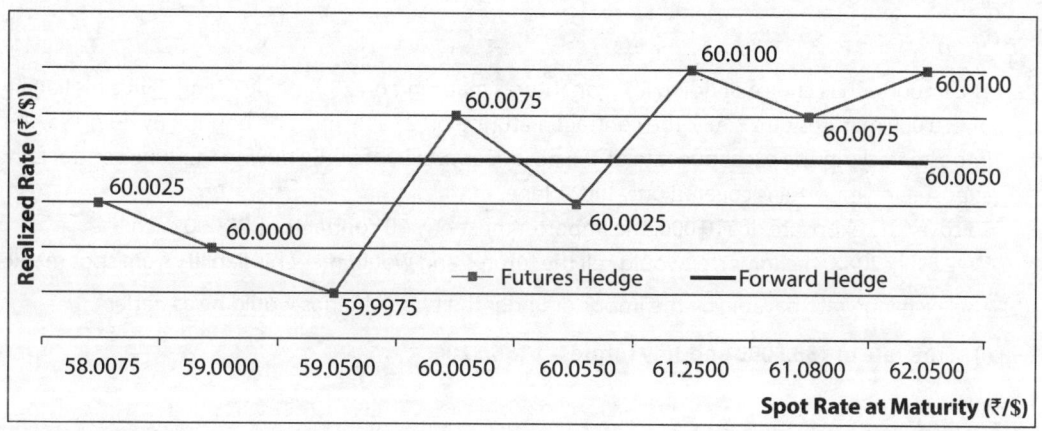

Figure 8-8
Comparing Forward and Futures Hedge for Receivable

The effective rate under futures hedge is dependent upon (a) the futures price of the initial contract and (b) the spread between spot price and futures price when the hedge is lifted. Only upon maturity of the futures contract, its price would be exactly equal to the spot price to eliminate arbitrage. When maturities of the exposure and the futures contract do not coincide, there would be minor difference in the futures price and spot price causing the deviation to the effective exchange rate than the forward. Although the forward hedge provides exact exchange rate, the futures hedge attempts to provide exchange rate close to the futures price while initiating the hedge. This may be seen from Figure 8-8.

The hedging by exporters for the receivables is referred to as *short hedge*. The hedge for the receivable is set up by shorting the futures and is lifted by buying the same futures contract before or on maturity.

Importers are in need of foreign currency. This is a short position in foreign currency. To cover the risk of appreciating foreign currency, the payable position is covered by going long on futures contract and, hence, called a *long hedge*. At the maturity, the futures contract is offset by selling. An example of long hedge follows.

Exercise 8-5
Long Hedge with Currency Futures–Payable

On 7 June 20XX, an importing firm in India has payable of €10,000 after 45 days falling due on 22 July 20XX. The futures contracts of the size of €1,000 maturing on 28 June 20XX and 27 July 20XX are selling for ₹56.5500/€ and ₹56.6850/€, respectively. The importer expects that by July end the euro would appreciate to minimum to about ₹57.00.

(a) Describe the hedging strategy of the importer in terms of maturity and value of contracts to be traded.
(b) What would be the effective exchange rate payable by the importer if on 22 July the following scenarios of spot and futures market exist: (i) spot rate of ₹56.5000 and July futures trades at ₹56.5200 and (ii) spot rate of ₹58.0000 and July futures selling at ₹58.0300.

Solution

(a) The importer has choice of going long on futures maturing on 28 June or 27 July. Since his liability of €10,000 matures on 22 July, the contract maturing on 27 July must be bought. By doing so, the importer locks in the exchange rate of ₹56.6850/€ approximately. By buying the June contract, the exposure of importer is covered only till 28 June.

To cover the exposure of €10,000, the importer must buy 10 contracts of €1,000 each.

On 22 July 20XX, the importer would sell the futures and would meet his liability from spot market.

(b) The exchange rate payable by the importer under the two scenarios would be as under

  (i) **Spot rate of ₹56.5000 and July futures at ₹56.5200**

	₹
The importer buys €10,000 at spot rate with cost = 10,000 × 56.5000 =	5,65,000
Gain/loss in futures:	
Futures bought at 56.6850 Indian rupee payable = 10,000 × 56.6850 =	5,66,850
Futures sold at ₹56.5200 Indian rupee receivable = 10,000 × 56.5200 =	5,65,200
Add: Loss on futures	1,650
Total cost of payable	5,66,650

Effective exchange rate = 5,66,650/10,000 = ₹56.6550/€

  (ii) **Spot rate of ₹58.0000 and July futures at ₹58.0300**

	₹
The importer buys €10,000 at spot rate with cost = 10,000 × 58.0000 =	5,80,000
Gain/loss in futures:	
Futures bought at 56.6850 Indian rupee payable = 10,000 × 56.6850 =	5,66,850
Futures sold at ₹58.0200 Indian rupee receivable = 10,000 × 58.0300 =	5,80,300
Less: Profit on futures	13,450
Total cost of payable	5,66,550

Effective exchange rate = 5,66,550/10,000 = ₹56.6550/€

Basis

In the aforementioned example, we observed that the effective exchange rate was not exact but close to the futures price of the initial contract. The difference arises due to mismatch of futures price and the spot price at the time of lifting of the hedge. Ideally, maturity of positions in futures and underlying trade transaction must coincide when futures price converges to spot. Any of the two positions maturing earlier amounts to lifting of hedge. The difference of futures price and the spot price is called basis. Basis[3] at the end of hedging period ($t = 1$)

---

[3] Usual definition of basis is $S_1 - F_1$. For financial assets the definition is $F_1 - S_1$.

would be

$$\text{Basis} = \text{Futures Price, } F_1 - \text{Spot Price, } S_1 = F_1 - S_1$$

Under futures hedge, if F_0 is the futures price at inception of the hedge, the effective exchange rate at the time of lifting it at $t = 1$ would be:

$$\text{Effective Exchange Rate} = F_0 - (F_1 - S_1) \quad (8\text{-}5)$$

Exercise 8-6
Basis and Exchange Rate

In Example 8-5, what is the basis under two scenarios of 22 July of spot and futures markets at (a) spot rate of ₹56.5000 and July futures trades at ₹56.5200 and (b) spot rate of ₹58.0000 and July futures selling at ₹58.0300? Work out the exchange rates payable from the basis as given by Eq. 8-5.

Solution
(a) **Spot rate of ₹56.5000 and July futures at ₹56.5200**
Basis = 56.5200 − 56.5000 = 0.0200
Initial futures price = 56.6850
Exchange rate payable = −{$F_0 - (F_1 - S_1)$} = −(56.6850 − 0.0200) = −56.6650

(b) **Spot rate of ₹56.5000 and July futures at ₹56.5200**
Basis = 58.0300 − 58.0000 = 0.0300
Initial futures price = 56.6850
Exchange rate payable = −{$F_0 - (F_1 - S_1)$} = −(56.6850 − 0.0300) = −56.6550
Negative sign implies cash outflow in local currency

Basis Risk

The effective exchange rate without hedging would be S_1, which is extremely volatile and unpredictable. The effective exchange rate with forward contract would be F_0, which is fixed now and known with complete certainty. The effective exchange rate with futures hedge would be around F_0 and deviate by the differential of futures price and the spot price; the basis at the end of hedging horizon. The uncertainty with the futures hedge would be nominal as the basis at the end of the hedge is much less volatile than the spot price at the end of hedging period, S_1. Hence, hedging with the futures replaces price risk with the basis risk, that is, the variability of the differential of futures and spot price. Basis risk would be much smaller than the price risk because of the shrinking of the time remaining for maturity of futures contract.

Perfect and Imperfect Hedge Hedging through the forward contract is normally referred to as perfect hedge as it exactly provides a guaranteed exchange rate for the receivables and payables, which is equal to the forward price. This may be viewed in terms of the payoffs as depicted in Figures 8-3 and 8-4. The payoff of the underlying asset and the forward position are exactly equal and opposite, thereby effective exchange rate is exact. Under futures hedge, the same principle of offsetting the gain/loss in the position of underlying with the loss/gain in futures is implemented. However, the offsetting would not be exact but only be approximate because of the basis.

Forward and futures hedge are compared in Figure 8-8 where it can be observed that while forward hedge is perfect, futures hedge results in effective exchange rate to the level around initial futures price. The imperfection in the futures hedge may be acceptable to most hedgers if (a) cost of such hedging is less as compared to forward, (b) it is more convenient in terms of ease of entry and exit, and (c) continuous flow of transparent information of latest price, supply, and demand conditions is available, facilitating continuous monitoring of effectiveness of the hedge at all times.

Sources of Basis Risk

Why should there be uncertainty of the effective exchange rate under futures hedge? If at the time of maturity or lifting of the hedge, the spot price and futures price are identical, the effective exchange rate would be equal to F_0; same as obtainable under forward hedge. Recall that under futures hedge, the effective exchange rate is determined by transacting the underlying at the prevailing spot rate and the squaring up of position in the futures. However, there could be several reasons why the effective exchange rate may differ from the expected fixed rate of F_0. Three possible reasons for the difference caused by the mismatch of the spot and futures prices are discussed as follows.

Mismatch of Exposures in Underlying and Futures For the perfect hedge, the positions in the underlying and the futures on them must be of identical size. For example, just described, the exposure of receivable was US$15,000 and the contract size of the futures was US$1,000. Therefore, by shorting 15 futures contract, the exposure was fully covered. Such situations may not be common in the real life. Due to standardization of the futures contract in terms of the size, it may not be feasible to have identical exposures in futures and underlying. If the amount of receivables were US$14,200, the exporter would have to short either 14 contracts worth US$14,000 leaving US$200 exposed or 15 contracts worth US$15,000 assuming speculative position for the excess US$800. Due to unequal positions, the offsetting effect would not be complete even if the futures price were to be same as spot price.

Mismatch of Maturities of Underlying and Futures Contract Again, for the perfect hedge to take place, the maturity of the underlying must coincide with that of the futures contract. In the example just discussed, the receivables matured on 21 August, whereas the futures matured seven days later on 28 August. The hedge was lifted on 21 August by selling receivables at the spot price and squaring up of short position of futures. These two prices were different and, therefore, the compensating effect was not full. If only these two prices were same, the realized exchange rate would have been exactly equal to the futures price when hedge was established.

Mismatch of Asset in Underlying and Futures Another source of imperfection in the hedge would be when the futures contract is not available in the currency of the underlying exposure. In such a situation, futures hedge could still be implemented by taking futures position in the currency that is closely related to the currency of exposure. For example, if receivables were in British pound and no futures contracts were available in it, the futures hedge could be implemented by shorting equivalent contracts in US dollars, under the presumption that changes in the spot rates of British pound and US dollar are identical. Hedge that involves exposures in underlying and futures on different but related assets, is called *cross hedge*.

The two currencies are assumed to move in tandem, and it is hoped that the changes in the position of underlying asset denominated in British pounds would be offset by the changes in the futures position in US dollars. The extent to which these changes would be offset would of course depend upon the strength of the relationship of the two currencies, that is, US dollar and British pound. The amount of exposure in the underlying and the futures market would be governed by the coefficient of correlation on the exchange rate of US dollar and British pound. In practice, the expected changes would rarely come out to be true, and hence the hedge would not be perfect.

PRICING CURRENCY FUTURES

Entering a forward or a futures contract is an agreement for the settlement of delivery at a future date. When one enters a spot contract, the delivery and payments are instantaneous and simultaneous. A forward or futures contract is a deferred delivery contract at a price negotiated now. This price is dependent upon the spot exchange rate. With the given spot value, at what price would be the forward contract negotiated? The question can be answered with the help of the argument of economic equivalency of present and future using the concept of time value of money.

Consider that a foreign exchange dealer needs €1 after 12 months. Assume that the spot rate, S_0 is ₹60.00/€. He has two alternatives:

(a) **Buy euro now**: By doing so he would have to part away ₹60 now, but he could invest euro for 12 months. If interest rates in euro, r_f, were 5% per annum, he would need to buy only $1/(1 + r_f) = 1/1.05$ so that after six months, it becomes €1. The rupee required now are $S_0/(1 + r_f) = 60/1.05$, or

(b) **Buy euro forward at a price F_1**: The other alternative is to enter into a forward contract at an exchange rate of F_1. By doing so, the foreign exchange dealer is obligated to pay F_1 in domestic currency, that is, Indian rupee, after 12 months. If he could invest Indian rupees at an interest rate of r_d say at 10%, the cash flow commitments would be met by having funds of $F_1/(1 + r_d)$ now.

The two positions have to be are equivalent else they give rise to arbitrage. Therefore

$$\frac{S_0}{(1+r_f)} = \frac{F_1}{(1+r_d)}$$

$$\text{or } F_1 = S_0 \frac{(1+r_d)}{(1+r_f)}$$

(8-6)

Equation 8-6 provides the value of the 12-m futures/forward contract. If we assume continuous compounding, the price of the futures contract maturing after time t is given by

$$F_t = S_0 e^{(r_d - r_f)t} \qquad (8\text{-}7)$$

$(r_d - r_f) \cdot t$ is the net cost of carry for the remaining time to expiry. Equations 8-6 and 8-7 are referred to as the cost of carry model for pricing futures contract for discrete and continuous compounding, respectively. The futures price can also be written as

Futures price = Spot price + Cost of carry for time left for expiration

It may be seen that if domestic interest rate, r_d, is higher than the foreign interest rate, r_f, the forward/futures contract price would be higher than the spot price. The foreign currency then would be at premium to spot. If foreign interest rate is higher than the domestic interest rate, the forward price would be lower than the spot price, and foreign currency is said to be at discount. Forward premium or discount is normally expressed in annualized per cent terms and is supposed to represent the differential of domestic and foreign interest rates.

Exercise 8-7
Pricing Currency Futures

Refer to Figure 8-6. The following are the last traded futures price on 28 June 2013 for contracts in US dollar:

USDINR290713	₹59.7450
USDINR280813	₹60.0150
USDINR290913	₹60.2625

Assuming the spot rate of 28 June at ₹59.6995 and the price of the futures expiring 29 July as correctly reflecting the cost of carry, what should be the futures price for contracts expiring on 28 August and 29 September? What do you infer about the interest rates in India and the USA from the futures price?

Solution

The cost of carry for the futures contract expiring 29 July with 31 remaining is

$$\text{Cost of carry} = \frac{F_1 - S_0}{S_0} \times 100 = \frac{59.7450 - 59.6995}{59.6995} \times 100 = 0.0762\%$$

Using the same cost of carry, the futures price for contract expiring on 28 August with 61 days remaining for maturity is calculated by adding the cost of carry for 61 days to the current spot value. That is

$$\text{August futures price} = 59.6995 \left[1 + 0.0762\% \times \frac{61}{31} \right] = ₹59.7890$$

Similarly, with the same cost of carry, the futures price for contract expiring on 29 September with 61 + 31 = 92 days remaining for maturity is calculated by adding the cost of carry for 92 days to the current spot:

$$\text{September futures price} = 59.6995 \left[1 + 0.0762\% \times \frac{92}{31} \right] = ₹59.8345$$

The annual cost of carry implied by July futures is $0.0762\% \times 365/31 = 0.8972\%$ indicating that the interest rate in India should be higher by about 0.90% as compared to that of the USA.

Convergence of Futures Price to Spot

The difference of futures and spot price is proportional to the time left for the expiry of the futures contract. As maturity of the futures approaches, the net cost of carry $(r_d - r_f) \times t$ also decreases. As time progresses, the futures price becomes closer and closer to the spot price. At maturity, the time left for expiration is zero and, hence, the cost of carry must be zero. This would make the futures price equal to the spot price at the time of maturity. This is called *convergence* of the futures price to the spot price.

Irrespective of whether initially the futures contract is at premium or at discount to spot price, it would converge to the spot as time progresses, as shown in Figure 8-9. Alternatively, we may say that as time progresses, the basis reduces and approaches zero. If basis reduces to zero, the basis risk too would be zero.

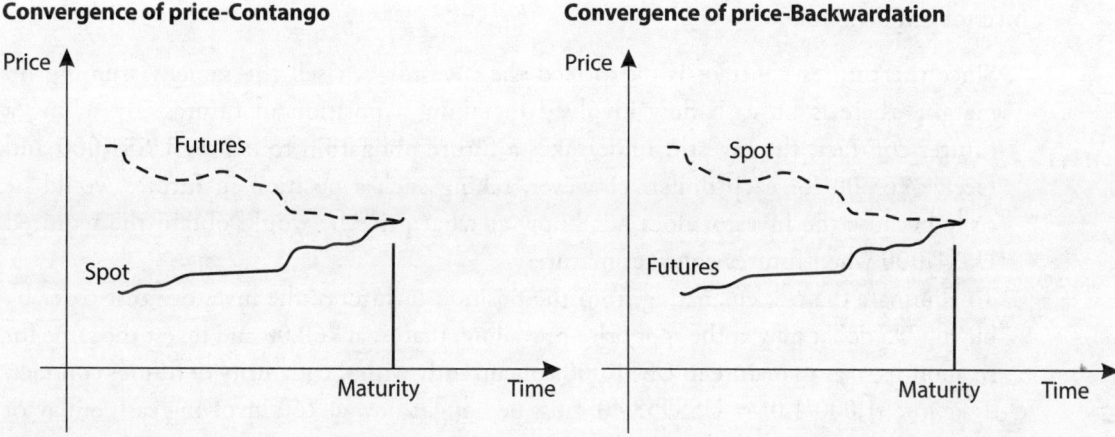

Figure 8-9
Convergence of Futures and Spot Exchange Rates

The implication of convergence to hedging is important. When hedge is established with futures position close to maturity of the underlying, the cost of carry would be large. However, when hedge is lifted, the underlying asset is traded at spot price and the futures position is offset at futures price. The futures contract is closer to its maturity and, therefore, its price would be close to the spot price. Therefore, closer the maturities of underlying and the futures, more effective is the hedging outcome.

ARBITRAGE WITH CURRENCY FUTURES

The cost of carry model provides a basis to arrive at the theoretical price of the futures contract. In practice, futures price may or may not conform to the theoretical price due to several aberrations that may exist. If so, arbitrage opportunities exist and they can be exploited by simultaneous positions in the spot and futures market.

Assume that spot exchange rate for US dollar is ₹60. The interest rate in the USA and India are 10% and 20% (taken artificially high for magnified illustrative purposes), respectively. The theoretical price of the futures contract expiring six months later would be given by Eq. 8-6 as follows:

$$F_1 = S_0 \frac{(1+r_d)}{(1+r_f)} = 60 \frac{1.10}{1.05} = ₹62.8571 \approx ₹62.86$$

If the futures price is different than the theoretical price as computed in the equation just solved, the opportunity to profit can be exploited by taking risk-less positions in the futures and the spot market simultaneously.

If the futures price is overpriced, that is, futures price is > its theoretical price Assume that the 6-m futures contract is trading at ₹63.00 as against its theoretical price of ₹62.86. If so, an investor can do as follows:

1. Since the futures contract is overpriced the investor can sell the same. Assuming no margin, there is no cash flow involved in taking a position in futures. By selling a futures contract, the investor undertakes a future obligation to deliver US$1,000 and receive ₹63.00 for each dollar. However, taking such a position in futures would be risky because the investor does not know at what price he would obtain the required US$1,000 when futures contract matures.
2. To eliminate the risk emanating from the position in futures, the investor must cover by buying US dollar now at the spot price prevailing, that is, at ₹60.00 and invest the same for six months so as to mature to US$1,000 concurrently with the maturity of futures contract. Therefore, 1,000/1.05 = US$952.40 must be bought now at ₹60 involving cash outlay of 952.40 × 60.00 = ₹57,144.
3. The cash required to procure US dollar now would be borrowed at domestic interest rate of 20%. After six months the amount payable would be ₹57,144 × 1.10 = ₹62,858.40.
4. At maturity of the futures contract the investor would (a) deliver the US dollar already owned, (b) receive ₹63,000 under futures contract, and (c) pay the borrowed sum with interest, that is, ₹62,858.40.

These actions would result in a profit of ₹141.60 or 0.14 per US$ without undertaking any risk or investment. Such a profit is called arbitrage profit.

If futures contract is underpriced, that is, futures price is < its theoretical price When futures contract is underpriced, that is, it is quoted at less than its theoretical price, the arbitrage profit can still be made simply by reversing the aforementioned actions. If futures contract is underpriced, say at ₹62.00, the investor would

1. Buy US dollar futures.
2. Borrow US$952.40 (1,000/1.05) at 10%, sell them spot to get ₹57,144, and invest for six months at 20%.

3. Pay the required rupees under the futures, that is, ₹62,000 from the investment matured ₹62,858 (952.40 × 60 × 1.10).
4. Repay US$1,000 to the lender which is received under futures contract. The rupee amount payable under futures would be less than the maturity value of the investment providing an arbitrage profit of ₹858.

These actions of driving the arbitrage profit whenever the futures are mispriced help in correcting the aberrations in the spot and futures markets. When futures are overpriced, investors would sell futures and buy spot. If many investors do so, the value of futures would fall, thereby overpricing of futures would be corrected. Similarly, if futures are underpriced, the investor would buy futures creating upward pressure on the futures prices, whereas simultaneously sell in the spot market would cause a downward pressure on prices in the spot market, automatically correcting the under pricing of futures. Thus, the process of arbitrage restores the balance between spot and futures prices in case they become out-of-line with each other.

Exercise 8-8
Arbitrage with Currency Futures

Refer to Figure 8-6 and Example 8-7. How can you execute arbitrage assuming that the July futures contract is correctly priced?

Solution
The actual price for August futures contract is ₹60.0150 as against the fair price of ₹59.7890. The futures contract is overpriced. Hence, one can sell futures contract for August and buy US dollar spot at ₹59.6995, driving the profit of ₹0.2260 (the differential of actual and theoretical futures prices) for every dollar bought.

SPECULATION WITH CURRENCY FUTURES

Arbitrage actions just explained were riskless and did not require any investment of own. The investment was funded by borrowing/lending. Further, these actions were dependent upon the estimates of fair or theoretical price of futures. While the actual price is known and observable, the theoretical price is unknown and not observable. It is only an estimate. This estimate is based on interest rates in two currencies. One must guard against the pitfall of estimating the theoretical futures price. Theoretical price is more a function of expectations of interest rates in two currencies rather than the prevailing interest rates, which are known. Hence, there is always an element of risk in the estimate of fair value of futures when one assumes the present interest rates as sacrosanct.

Further, arbitrage also warrants borrowing or lending at the same rates. In actual practice, the lending and borrowing rates may differ from those used in determining the fair value of futures, constraining the execution of arbitrage mechanism. In view of these constraints, one may not like to resort to borrowing or lending to have risk-free position, and instead may assume a risky position. Taking a position in futures requires no investment and is speculative.

Speculative positions are taken with the motive of driving profit when one does not agree with the futures price. Futures price can be thought of as collective wisdom of investors in the market of what they think that the future spot price be. For example, we find that August futures is trading at ₹60.0150 as on 28 June. It implies from there that the market expects the spot price of US dollar on 28 August to be ₹60.0150. This the best estimate and the collective wisdom of the investors in the foreign exchange markets.

However, each individual is entitled to hold his opinion about the future spot price and one may or may not agree with the price projected by futures trading. If one has sufficient conviction in the views that do not conform to futures price, it presents an opportunity to speculate. For example, if one forecasts that spot price of US dollar would be in excess of ₹60.0150 as on 28 August as suggested by futures, one could buy futures now. At maturity, if the forecast comes true and spot price of US dollar is ₹61.000, the investor can take delivery of US dollars against the futures contract and, then, sell them in the spot market making a gain of ₹0.9850/US$. Of course, if the actual spot price turns out to be less than ₹60.0150, the position would result in a loss.

In case the investor feels that the futures contract is overpriced, that is, its price is less than the forecast, then one would sell now. On maturity, the obligation of delivery of foreign exchange would be met by buying in the spot market.

Taking position in futures is risky because future spot price is unknown. Actions under speculation may be summarized as follows.

When futures price, F_1 < Expected spot price, S_1 Buy futures now and on maturity take the delivery of foreign exchange under futures contract and sell in the spot market.

When futures price, F_1 > Expected spot price, S_1 Sell futures now and on maturity, meet the delivery obligations under futures contract by buying foreign exchange in the spot market.

SUMMARY

Since the advent of flexible exchange rate systems, the uncertainties of exchange rates have increased manifold. One of the most effective and efficient ways of handling the risk of foreign exchange exposure is through forward contracts. Forward is a derivative product. Forward contract is settled later with the exchange rate fixed now. Receivable/payable can be hedged by selling/buying foreign currency forward, assuring exporter/importer of an exchange rate. This is possible due to the complimentary payoffs of spot and forward positions. One must hedge for receivable/payable only when expected spot rate is lesser/greater that the forward rate. The cost of forward hedge is implicit as hedger foregoes the potential gain to prevent potential losses. Explicitly, the cost of forward hedge is measured by premium/discount of forward rate over spot.

Obligations under forward contract are independent of those of spot market. The obligations in forward have to be settled irrespective of spot transaction. However, obligations may be nullified by cancellation of the original forward contract by entering an equal and opposite contract with the same time left for maturity of original contract. Since forward contract does not involve any initial cash outflows, one can make speculative gains if forward rate is not in line with the expected spot rate at the end of forward period.

The NDFs are forward contracts where delivery requirements can be obviated as they are cash settled. The NDFs can be onshore or offshore. These contracts are generally available offshore for currencies that have some controls over capital flows and are prominently available in six Asian currencies, including Indian rupee. NDFs are effective as deliverable forwards are for hedging as well as speculative purposes.

Currency futures are exchange-traded forward contracts that overcome the deficiencies of forward markets. Forward markets are OTC with constrained flow of information, delivery-based settlement, and counterparty risk. The limitations of forward contract are overcome by trading on exchanges which offer standardized contracts in convenient sizes and deliveries. They also eliminate counterparty risk by an elaborate margin system. Currency futures also help price discovery by instantaneous dissemination of information of prices, demand, and supply conditions. Futures contracts also offer an easy entry and exit as compared to the forwards.

Hedging with futures is done by assuming opposite position in futures as that of spot. The position in underlying is traded in the spot market while offsetting the futures position. However, the hedge with futures would not be perfect due to the presence of basis. Basis is the difference of futures and spot price. Under futures hedge, the price risk is replaced by much smaller basis risk. Since the basis must approach zero with maturity of the futures contract, the risk would be lesser.

Futures are fairly priced by the differential of interest rates in two currencies called cost of carry model. If the fair price and the actual price are different, then opportunities for arbitrage arise. Arbitrage can be exploited by taking simultaneous positions in spot and futures markets. Further, if one believes that futures price does not represent the future spot price or the forecast exchange rate, he can take speculative position to benefit from the forecast.

QUESTIONS

8-1 Write short notes on the following:
  (a) Convergence of futures price to spot
  (b) Long and short positions
  (c) Cost of carry
  (d) Sources of basis risk
8-2 Comment on the following statements:
  (a) The markets for NDF are good for the currencies that are subject to control by their governments.
  (b) Forward markets are extremely inefficient when compared with futures market.
  (c) Futures contract are no good as they cannot offer perfect hedge.
8-3 What are the limitations of forward contract and how does a futures contract overcome them?
8-4 Differentiate between the following terms:
  (a) Forward and non-deliverable forward contracts
  (b) Forward and futures contract
  (c) Price risk and basis risk
8-5 Explain hedging of payable and receivable with a forward contract.
8-6 Explain hedging with futures contract for receivable and payable.
8-7 What are the salient features of specifications of a currency futures contract?
8-8 Pricing of forward and futures contracts by cost of carry model is no different than interest rate parity. Comment.
8-9 With the help of an example, describe the process of arbitrage with currency futures.
8-10 How does futures contract facilitate speculation?

PROBLEMS

8-1 Forward Hedge

Multi-Motors Limited has exported induction motors worth US$2 million for which the payment is due after 3 months. The projected profits assume the current spot rate of ₹46.00/$. US dollar is expected to decline in its value in coming days. The following rates are quoted by the bank:

$$\text{Spot (₹/US\$)} \quad 45.90 \quad 46.10$$
$$\text{3-m forward} \quad 45.50 \quad 45.80$$

(a) Should the firm hedge its receivable?
(b) What realization could be made in Indian rupees if it decides to hedge?

8-2 Futures Hedge

Three months from now, you are expecting to receive US$200,000. The spot price of US$ is ₹46.00, whereas 3-m futures at MCX is trading at ₹45.30, indicating depreciation of US dollar. Under what circumstances would you like to hedge? What would be the hedging strategy?

8-3 Settlement of NDF

In Hong Kong foreign exchange market, non-deliverable forwards are quoted for Chinese renminbi (RMB). Being offshore contracts, they are settled in US dollar. An importer based in Hong Kong has RMB1 million payable after three months. RMB is likely to appreciate. The NDF is being offered at RMB7.90/$ and booked by the importer. If on the settlement date, the fixing rate is RMB7.80/$, what amount would the importer pay/receive?

8-4 Pricing Cost & Futures of Carry

The following are the futures prices on 7 June 20XX for contracts in US dollar:

$$\text{USDINR 2806XX} \quad ₹47.3725$$
$$\text{USDINR 2807XX} \quad ₹47.4100$$
$$\text{USDINR 2708XX} \quad ₹47.4600$$

Assuming the spot rate of 7 June 20XX at ₹47.3000 and the price of the futures expiring 28 June 20XX as correctly reflecting the cost of carry, what should be the futures price for contracts expiring on 28 July 20XX and 27 August 20XX? What do you infer about the interest rates in India and the USA from the futures price?

8-5 Effective Exchange Rate with Futures Hedge

An Indian firm has payable of €20,000 after 60 days. The futures contracts of the size of €1,000 maturing after 65 days are selling for ₹56.6500/€. The importer expects that euro would appreciate to minimum to about ₹58.2500. Describe the hedging strategy of the importer. What would be the effective exchange rate payable by the importer if the maturity spot and futures market are ₹56.5000 and 56.5200, respectively?

Currency Options

LEARNING OBJECTIVES

This chapter aims at

- learning what options are and how they are different from forwards and futures
- understanding the terminology of options, their payoffs, and commitments
- knowing the differences between call and put options, and exchange-traded and OTC options
- becoming familiar with option valuation, factors governing option premium, and relationship of call and put prices
- learning how to hedge with options
- appreciating the cost involved in options hedge
- understanding cost-reducing structures
- understanding what barrier options and Asian options are and their cost-effectiveness in hedging foreign currency exposures

CONTENTS

Introduction
Option Contracts—Call and Put
Terminology of Options
Payoffs of Options
    Call Option
    Put Option
    Commitments under Options
Moneyness of Options: In-the-Money, At-the-Money, and Out-of-the-Money Options
Exchange-traded and Over-the-Counter Options
Understanding Options Quotations
    Assignment
    Margins in Options

Options and Forwards/Futures
Black Scholes Option Pricing Model
Hedging with Currency Options
    Hedging Foreign Currency Receivable with Put Option
    Hedging Foreign Currency Payable with Call Option
Modifying Option Terms
    Range Forward—Zero Cost Collar
    Participating Forward
Barrier Options
Asian Options
Innovations in Options

INTRODUCTION

Forwards and futures discussed in the previous chapter were contracts where the mutual obligations of the two contracting parties towards each other were even, that is, both the parties were equally likely to gain or lose. The magnitudes of loss or profit, that is, the payoffs were linear and equal for a given change in the price of the underlying asset. For a forward selling price of ₹45/$, the exporter gained ₹1 if the spot exchange rate turned out to be ₹44/$ and lost ₹1 if the exchange were to be ₹46/$. The gain/loss was equal for a same change in either direction. At the same time, the obligations under forwards were binding and one could not back out of the contract in case the exchange rate scenario turned out to be unfavourable.

The question that arises is whether there exists a financial contract that allows retention of gains while protecting the loss. Fortunately, the answer is yes. Such an instrument that fulfils the requirement is called an option. An option is a unique instrument that confers a *right without an obligation* to buy or sell the underlying asset. The underlying asset in our case would be a foreign currency such as dollar, euro, pound, and yen. Like forwards and futures, option too is a derivative instrument because the value of the right so-conferred would depend on the price at which the underlying asset is traded in the spot market. As such options derive their values inter alia from the spot exchange rate.

OPTION CONTRACTS—CALL AND PUT

Consider an example for understanding of how an option contract works. An importer needs to buy foreign currency when the payable, say US$20,000 is due after three months. The current exchange rate is ₹55/$. The importer carries the risk of appreciating dollar. If dollar appreciates to ₹58 in three months, his liability would increase. However, he would be happy to see a favourable situation of dollar depreciating. In case the importer buys dollar forward, the exchange rate is frozen. Assume the 3-m forward rate to be ₹56.00/$. If the exchange rate is ₹58.00 at the end of three months, the importer benefits by buying dollar forward by ₹2/$. However, if the exchange rate happens to be ₹55.00/$ at the end of three months, the importer regrets the decision to buy dollar forward because he is obligated to honour the commitment made under the forward contract.

Ideally, the importer would like to protect against the appreciating dollar while retaining the advantage of depreciating dollar. Such a situation warrants that the importer should be able to buy dollar at ₹56, if he desires so. However, buying the dollar at ₹56.00 should not be imposed as is obligatory under forward contract. Instead, under the situation of dollar depreciating below ₹56, the importer wants flexibility to meet the dollar obligations from the market. Such a contract that gives *the right without an obligation to buy* is known as **call option**.

Similarly, consider the position of an exporter. An exporter needs to sell foreign currency receivable in future. An appreciation foreign currency is a favourable situation, whereas its depreciation is damaging. The exporter would want protection against depreciating foreign currency. A forward contract provides such protection, but at the same time takes away the advantage of gaining from appreciation of dollar. Ideally, exporters need to protect against depreciation of foreign currency while retaining the advantage of gaining from appreciation of foreign currency. Such a position is provided by a *right to sell the foreign currency without an obligation* to do so. This is called a *put option*.

The unique feature of the option is that although it confers the right to buy or sell the underlying asset (foreign currency in our case), the holder is not obligated to perform. The holder, at his option, can force the counterparty to honour the commitment made. Obligations of the holder would arise only when he decides to exercise the right. Therefore, a currency option may be defined as a contract that gives the owner the right but no obligation to buy or sell foreign currency at predetermined exchange rate within a given time frame. It is the absence of obligation to perform for one of the parties that makes the option contract a substantially different derivative product from others like forwards and futures, where there is an equal and binding obligation on both the parties. This unique feature of an option of a right without obligation makes several applications possible that are not feasible with other derivative products.

Option contract would be an excellent hedging tool enabling protection against unfavourable movement of exchange rate as well as providing opportunities for gain with favourable movement. Such a contract that limits losses but retains potential for gain must be priced explicitly. In futures and forwards, the probability of gains and losses is equal for both the counterparties who are likely to gain or lose equally, and as such they do not have any explicit cost. Since option contracts are favourable to one party and not favourable to another, such contracts have an explicit price payable upfront.

TERMINOLOGY OF OPTIONS

For full comprehension of options, it is essential to understand the terms associated with them that are used in the description. Though options can have any underlying asset such as stocks, interest rates, indices, currencies, and commodities, here we describe the features of the options in the context of foreign currency only even though the terms used are common to all underlying assets.

The basic terms of options are described here:

Call Option A right but no obligation to BUY the foreign currency at predetermined exchange rate within a specified interval of time is called a CALL option.

Put Option A right but no obligation to SELL the foreign currency at predetermined exchange rate within specified interval of time is called PUT option.

Buyer or Holder The person who obtains the right to buy or sell but has no obligation to perform is called the buyer or holder of the option. One who buys the option has to pay a premium to obtain the right.

Writer or Seller One who confers the right and undertakes the obligation to the holder is called the seller or the writer of an option. For a call, the writer has an obligation to sell, whereas for put, the writer has an obligation to buy the foreign currency at the specified exchange rate from the holder of the option.

Premium While conferring a right to buy or sell to the holder, the writer who is under obligation to perform is entitled to charge a fee upfront. This upfront fee is called the premium. This is paid by the holder to the writer and is also called the price of the option. The premium induces the writer to confer the right, hoping that the holder would not exercise the right and he can pocket the premium. In the absence of premium, the writer has no incentive to make any profit.

Strike Price The predetermined exchange rate at the time of initiation of option contract at which the right of buying/selling the foreign currency would be exercised is called the strike price. It is the price at which the holder of an option buys/sells the foreign currency to the seller/writer of the option.

Strike Date/Maturity Date The right to exercise the option cannot be given for indefinite period. It is valid for limited time. The latest time by when the option can be exercised is called the time to maturity. It is also referred to as expiry/maturity date.

American and European Option When the option to buy or sell can be exercised at any time before the maturity of the option, it is called an American option. However, when an option can be exercised only on its maturity, it is referred to as a European option. Most literature on option relates to European options.

PAYOFFS OF OPTIONS

With the terms used in describing options being defined, we now have a look at gains and losses, referred to as payoffs that the holder can have on call and put options. Depending upon the value of the underlying asset at maturity of options contract, the two parties, that is, the holder and the writer would gain or lose an equal amount. The gain/loss at maturity of the options contract is described as payoffs of options.

Call Option

We described a call option in respect of an importer. Assume that an importer needs to buy US dollar three months later. It may be mentioned that for trading of option, one need not be an actual user, that is, importer or exporter. It is assumed only for the ease of explanation. The US dollar is currently trading at ₹46. The importer believes that dollar would rise at least to ₹48 in immediate future of three months.

The following 3-m call options with different strikes are available through a bank:

	Strike Exchange Rate, X	Premium, c
Call 1	₹46.00/$	₹0.75
Call 2	₹46.50/$	₹0.50
Call 3	₹47.00/$	₹0.40

Each of these call options confers a right on the buyer to buy US dollar at strike exchange rates, X by paying the upfront premium, c to the writer. Assuming European option, the right can be exercised only at the end of three months. Assume the importer buys call option with $X = 46.50$ by paying a premium of ₹0.50 to the writer.

What happens after three months when the call option expires? The importer compares the strike price with the spot exchange rate prevailing. If the spot exchange rate is more than the strike, X, of ₹46.50, the importer exercises the option of buying the required dollars from the writer. If the market rate is less than ₹46.50, the importer would prefer to buy dollars from the open market and let the option lapse. In case the spot exchange rate is ₹47.25, his gain from exercising the option would be ₹0.75 per dollar (47.25 − 46.50). Adjusting for the premium paid, his gain would reduce to ₹0.25 per dollar (47.25 − 46.50 − 0.50). His cost of buying dollar would be ₹47.00 as against spot value of ₹47.25. In case the spot rate after three months happens to be ₹45, the cost of buying dollar would be ₹45.50 including the option premium. Hence, the maximum price of the dollar that would be paid by the importer is ₹47.00.

We may generalize the outcome of a call option in the following manner:

As long as the price of the underlying asset, S, remains below the strike price, X, the buyer of the call option will not exercise it; and the loss of the buyer would be limited to the premium paid on the call option, c. If the spot price is more than the exercise price, the holder exercises the option and generates profit equal to the difference of the two prices. Alternatively,

Exchange Rate Scenario	Action by Holder	Payoff of Holder
When $S < X$	Buyer lets the call expire	$-c$
When $S = X$	Buyer is indifferent	$-c$
When $S > X$	Buyer exercises the call	$S - X - c$

Mathematically, the value of the call option at expiry is given by Eq. (9-1).

$$\text{Value of the Call Option} = \text{Max}(0, S - X) - c \tag{9-1}$$

We can analyse other calls in similar fashion. A graphical depiction of the payoffs of the holder for the three calls with different strike prices is presented in Figure 9-1. The payoff for writer of the option is opposite and equal to that of the holder. The holder gains at the expense of writer and vice versa. The payoff of holder and writer is shown in Figure 9-2.

With payoffs of holder and writer being opposite and equal, the combined payoff would always add up to zero. For example, if the exchange rate at the end of option period, that is, after three months, is ₹47.50 the call holder benefits by ₹0.50. The writer loses the equal amount of ₹0.50. The payoff of the writer under different exchange rate scenarios at expiry of option is shown as follows:

Exchange Rate Scenario	Action by Holder	Payoff of Writer
When $S < X$	Buyer lets the call expire	$+c$
When $S = X$	Buyer is indifferent	$+c$
When $S > X$	Buyer exercises the call option	$-(S - X - c)$

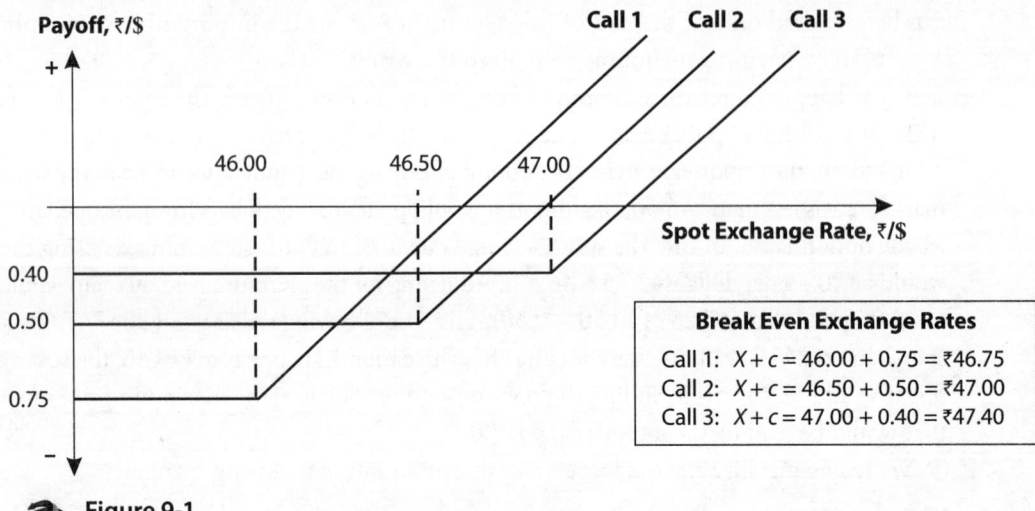

Figure 9-1
Graphical View: Payoff of Call Option for Holder

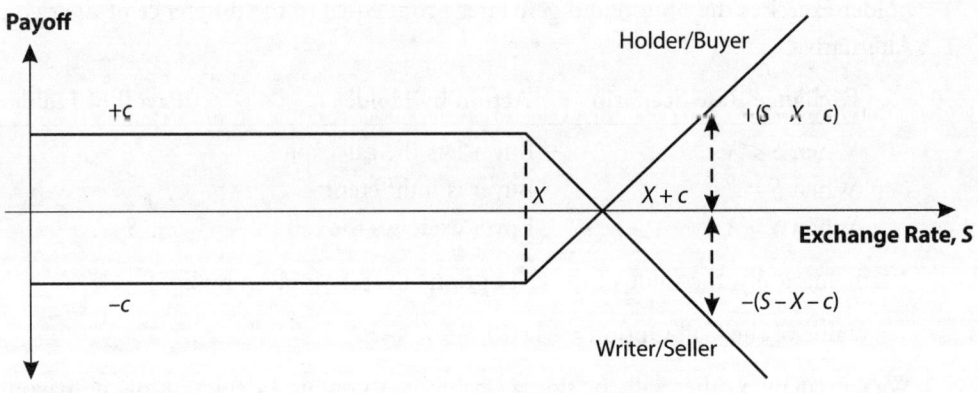

Figure 9-2
Graphical View: Payoff of Call Option for Buyer and Seller

A look at Figure 9-2 would reveal that (a) the call holder has loss limited to call premium with unlimited potential to gain with the increasing exchange rate (appreciating foreign currency or depreciating local currency) and (b) the call writer has a maximum income of premium earned while writing the option with potentially unlimited losses. Payoffs of holder and writer being equal and opposite options are also referred to as zero sum game.

Put Option

Put option on foreign currency is a right without obligation to sell it at a predetermined exchange rate. Like calls if the option is exercisable only on its expiry, it is European option, and if at any time before maturity, it is called American option.

Put option is useful for exporters as they need to sell the foreign currency receivable when realized. Assume that an exporter needs to sell US dollar three months later. Assume that US dollar is currently trading at ₹45 and the exporter believes that dollar would fall at least to ₹42 in immediate future of three months. The following put options are available through a bank:

	Strike Exchange Rate, X	Premium, p
Put 1	₹44.00/$	₹0.60
Put 2	₹43.50/$	₹0.40
Put 3	₹43.00/$	₹0.30

Each of these put options confers a right on the buyer to sell US dollar at strike exchange rates, X, by paying the premium, p, to the writer. Assuming European option the right can be exercised only at the end of three months. Assume the exporter buys put option with $X = 43.50$ by paying a premium of ₹0.40 to the writer.

After three months, the exporter compares the strike price with the spot exchange rate. If the spot exchange rate is less than the strike, X, of ₹43.50, the exporter exercises the option of selling the received dollars to the writer. If the exchange rate is more than ₹43.50, the exporter would prefer to sell dollars in the open market and let the put option lapse. In case the spot exchange rate is ₹42.25, his gain from exercising the option would be ₹1.25 per dollar (43.50 – 42.25). Adjusting for the premium paid, his gain would be ₹0.85 per dollar (43.50 – 42.25 – 0.40). His realization by selling dollar would be at a minimum of ₹43.10 (43.50 – 0.40). In case the spot rate happens to be ₹45, the exporter can realize the same in open market. The effective exchange rate realized would then be ₹44.60 after adjusting the premium paid.

We may generalize the outcome of a put option in the following manner:

If the price of the underlying asset, S, remains above the strike price, X, the buyer of the put option will not exercise it; the loss of the buyer would be limited to the premium paid on the put option, p. If the price is less than exercise price, the holder exercises the option and generates profit equal to the difference of the two prices.

Alternatively,

Exchange Rate Scenario	Action by Holder	Payoff of Holder
When $S < X$	Buyer exercises the put	$(X - S - p)$
When $S = X$	Buyer is indifferent	$-p$
When $S > X$	Buyer lets the put expire	$-p$

Mathematically, the value of the put is given by Eq. 9-2.

$$\text{Value of the Put Option} = \text{Max}(0, X - S) - p \tag{9-2}$$

A graphical depiction of the payoffs of the holder for the three put with different strike prices is presented in Figure 9-3. The payoff for writer of the option is opposite and equal to

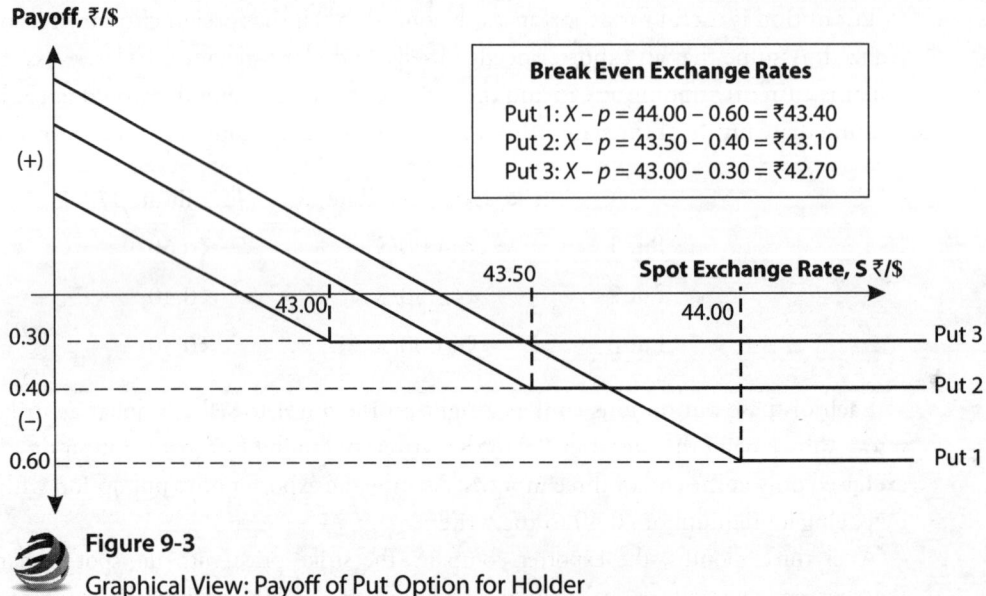

Figure 9-3
Graphical View: Payoff of Put Option for Holder

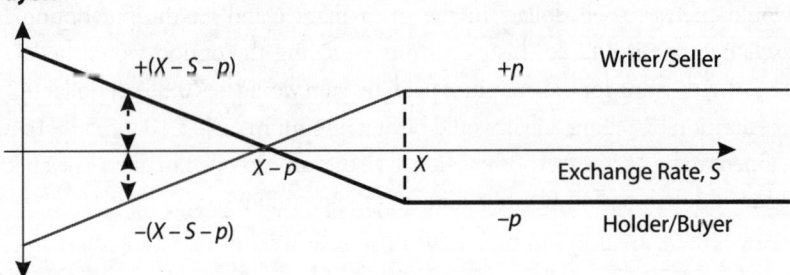

Figure 9-4
Graphical View: Payoff of Put Option for Buyer and Seller

that of the holder. The holder gains at the expense of writer. The payoffs of holder and writer are shown in Figure 9-4.

Just as with calls, the payoff of holder and writer for puts is also opposite and equal with combined payoff always adding to zero. For example, if the exchange rate at the end of option period, that is, after three months is ₹42.50, the put holder benefits by ₹0.60. The writer loses the equal amount of ₹0.60. The payoff of the writer under different exchange rate scenarios at expiry of option is shown here:

Exchange Rate Scenario	Action by Holder	Payoff of Writer
When $S < X$	Buyer exercises the put option	$-(X - S - p)$
When $S = X$	Buyer is indifferent	$+p$
When $S > X$	Buyer lets the put expire	$+p$

Currency Options 281

A look at Figure 9-4 would reveal that (a) the put holder has loss limited to the put premium with rather unlimited potential (with $S = 0$) to gain with the decreasing exchange rate (depreciating foreign currency or appreciating local currency) and (b) the put writer has a maximum income of premium earned while writing the option with potentially unlimited losses with $S = 0$.

 Exercise 9-1
Payoff of Call and Put Options

A 6-m call option on euro has exercise price of ₹63.00 and is selling at ₹1.20. At the same time, put option with the same strike is priced at ₹0.90. Depict payoff of call and put holder.

(a) At what exchange rate would the call and put option holders break even?
(b) What is the payoff of the holders of call and put options on euro if on expiry the exchange rate is
   (i) ₹61.00, (ii) ₹63.50, and (iii) ₹65.00?

Solution
The payoff of the long position of call on euro is depicted as follows:

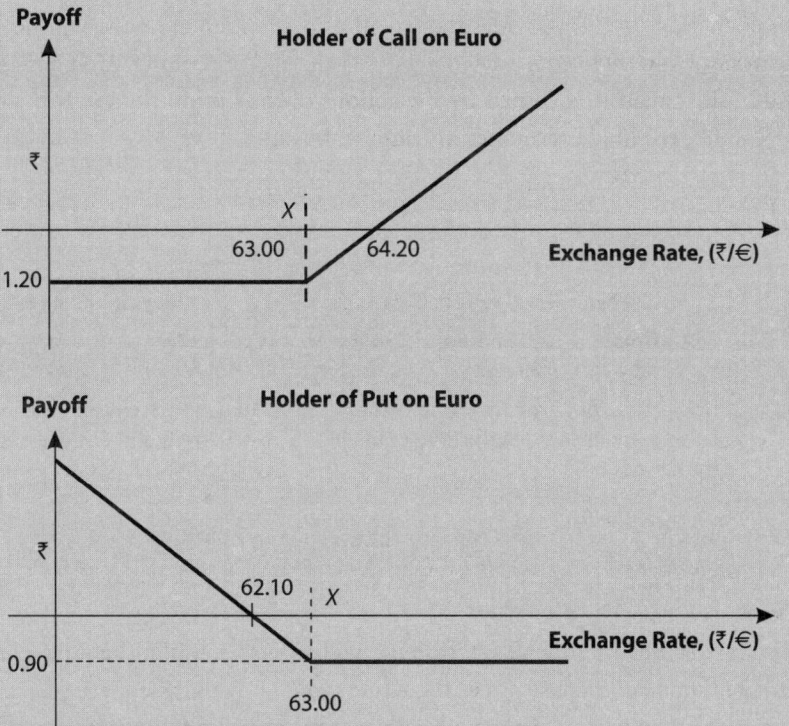

(a) The call position would break even when the exchange rate reaches level of ₹64.20/€, that is, $X + c = 63.00 + 1.20 = ₹64.20/€$.
Similarly, put position would break even when the exchange rate reaches level of ₹62.10/€, that is, $X − p = 63.00 − 0.90 = ₹63.10/€$.

(b) Payoff of call at expiration is given by Max $(S - X - c, -c)$.
   (i) For the price of ₹61.00, the call expires worthless. The payoff is the loss of premium of ₹1.20 paid by the holder of call.
   (ii) For price of ₹63.50 the call would be exercised gaining ₹0.50. The payoff would be – ₹0.70 recovering part of the premium paid.
   (iii) For price of ₹65.00 the gain from exercise is ₹4.00. Net of premium paid the payoff is ₹2.80.

Payoff of put at expiration is given by Max $(X - S - p, -p)$.
   (iv) For the price of ₹65.00, the put expires worthless. The payoff is loss of premium of ₹0.90 paid by the holder of put.
   (v) For price of ₹63.50, the put expires worthless. The payoff would be loss of premium of ₹0.90.
   (vi) For price of ₹61.00, the put from exercise is ₹2.00. Net of premium paid, the payoff is ₹1.10.

Commitments under Options

All derivatives including options are a zero-sum game; what is gained by the holder of an option exactly the same amount is lost by the writer. Similarly, the gain of the writer is the loss of the holder. Table 9-1(a) provides the payoff of the holder and writer of the call option with exercise price of ₹46.00 for the exchange rates at the end of option period ranging from ₹45.00 to ₹47.00. The payoff is governed by the actions of the option holder. If the exchange rate is beyond ₹46.00, the holder exercises his right to buy.

Table 9-1(a)
Payoff of Call Option $X = 46.00$

Exchange Rate ₹/$	Payoff—Call Holder (₹/$)			Payoff—Call Writer (₹/$)		
	Buy from Writer	Sell in the Market	Profit (+)/ Loss (–)	Sell to Holder	Buy from Market	Profit (+)/ Loss (–)
45.00	Holder does not exercise the call option; Loses premium paid at the time of buying the call option			Obligation of writer does not arise; Gains premium received at the time of writing the call option		
45.50						
46.00						
46.50	46.00	46.50	0.50	46.00	46.50	–0.50
47.00	46.00	47.00	1.00	46.00	47.00	–1.00

Assuming that he instantly sells the foreign exchange at prevailing spot rate, his gain would be differential of spot and exercise price. The writer would buy the asset at the exercise price and sell the same asset in the market. To meet his obligation the call option writer would have to obtain the foreign exchange at the prevailing spot rate and realize only the exercise price. Market price being higher, he would incur a loss. If the price remains below the exercise price, the holder does not exercise the option and the writer pockets the premium as profit.

Table 9-1(b) shows the payoff of the put option for the holder and the writer. Here, the option becomes profitable if the price remains below exercise price and, therefore, the holder

Table 9-1(b)
Payoff of Put Option X = 42.50

Exchange Rate ₹/$	Payoff—Put Holder (₹/$)			Payoff—Put Writer (₹/$)		
	Sell to Writer	Buy from the Market	Profit (+)/ Loss (−)	Pay to Holder	Sell in the Market	Profit (+)/ Loss (−)
41.50	42.50	41.50	1.00	42.50	41.50	−1.00
42.00	42.50	42.00	0.50	42.50	42.00	−0.50
42.50	Holder does not exercise the put option; Loses premium paid at the time of buying the put option			Obligation of writer does not arise; Gains premium received at the time of writing the put option		
43.00						
43.50						

exercises his option. Here, he would sell at the exercise price and buy back the asset from the market. The writer would have to buy from the holder and sell in the market.

The rights and obligations of the holder and writer of options on foreign currency at an exchange rate of X are as follows:

	Holder	*Writer*
Call Option	Right to buy at X	Obligated to sell at X
Put Option	Right to sell at X	Obligated to buy at X

MONEYNESS OF OPTIONS: IN-THE-MONEY, AT-THE-MONEY, AND OUT-OF-THE-MONEY OPTIONS

Options are normally stated in terms of the money they can provide to the holder. The payoff of the option keeps changing with time as the spot exchange rate changes. Recall that the payoff of option is the differential of the price of the underlying asset and the exercise price.

Depending upon the payoff of the options, they are referred to as either In-the-Money (ITM), At-the-Money (ATM), or Out-of-the-Money (OTM). At any time, ITM options are those which if exercised would result in positive cash flow to the holder. Similarly, ATM options would have no cash flows if exercised. The OTM options would result in cash out flow, if exercised. Since exercise is optional, OTM option would not be exercised and, hence, there would be no cash flow.

A call option provides a positive payoff when the price of the underlying asset exceeds the exercise price. Similarly, a put option is worth exercising when the price of the asset is less than the exercise price. Therefore, call option is in-the-money when asset price (spot exchange rate in our case) exceeds exercise price. A put option would be in-the-money when asset price is lower than the exercise price.

When asset price, that is, the spot exchange rate, is equal to the exercise price, it is called ATM option. The ATM option, whether call or put, results in no net cash flow, if exercised.

Similarly, when asset price is lower than exercise price, the call option is out-of-the-money; whereas the put option is out-of-the-money when asset price exceeds the exercise price. The following table captures the state of call and put options.

Underlying Value, S	S < X	S = X	S > X
Call option	Out of the Money	At the Money	In the Money
Put option	In the Money	At the Money	Out of the Money

EXCHANGE-TRADED AND OVER-THE-COUNTER OPTIONS

Options have several features that forwards and futures do not have. While forward is an Over-the-Counter (OTC) product, futures are exchange-traded. Options can be both; either exchange-traded or over-the-counter. Currency options are mostly over-the-counter because of the flexibility of making strike prices and maturity dates available as per the needs of the users primarily the corporate houses. On the contrary, exchange-traded options are standardized in terms of contract sizes, strike prices, and maturity dates.

The standardization of option contract is at the discretion of the exchange and may vary from exchange to exchange, though various exchanges attempt to make such contracts as similar as possible. The standardization is done in terms of the following:

Quantity (Size) Only specific quantity of the underlying asset, that is, foreign currency could be traded on the exchange and needs to be predetermined.

Strike Prices Only specific strike prices can be handled in a standardized product traded on the exchanges. An OTC product can have any strike price as agreed by the two contracting parties.

Expiration Dates Like strike price, the expiration dates too must be known before trading can take place in options at the exchanges.

Price Quotation Price quotation is the way prices are specified. It would be the number of rupees up to four decimal places per unit of foreign currency.

Tick Size Tick size is the minimum change in the price quotation that would be recognized by the exchange concerned.

Nature of Exercise Whether the options are American or European in nature too must be known to traders in options.

Settlement Whether the option contract is to be settled by delivery of foreign exchange or is cash settled at the expiry by exchange of difference between the exercise price and the price of the underlying asset must be known. They can also be settled by cancellation of the original contract by entering into an equal and opposite contract.

Due to tremendous flexibility in OTC products, the proportion of exchange-traded options is small. Exchange-traded options may not meet the exact requirements of users. Internationally, Philadelphia Stock Exchange in the USA offers both European and American currency options in several currencies. CME Group also offers currency options on various currencies offering choice of American and European options. Quotations are based on premium or implied volatility, globally on terminals, or voice trading.

In India, United Stock Exchange (USE) and National Stock Exchange (NSE) launched currency options for US dollar on 29 October 2010. Multi-Commodity Exchange (MCX) launched USDINR options contracts on 10 August 2012. The contract size is US$1,000 with strike intervals of ₹0.25/$. The price quotation is in rupees per dollar with the tick size of ₹0.0025, therefore a minimum change in the contract value would be $0.0025 \times 1,000 =$ ₹2.50. There are three monthly contracts covering a quarter, and then three quarterly contracts expiring in March, June, September, and December. The specification of the product at USE is given in Table 9-2. Other exchanges too have same specifications of the option contracts.

Table 9-2
Option Contract Specification at United Stock Exchange

Size of Contract	1 contract is for US$1,000 (Lot size)
Underlying	US Dollar–Indian Rupee spot rate
Quotation	Premium in Rupee terms. Outstanding position in USD terms
Type of Option	Premium-styled European call and put options
Tick Size	0.25 paise or ₹0.0025
Available Contracts	Three serial monthly contracts followed by three quarterly contracts of the cycle March/June/September/December
Last Trading Day	Two working days prior to the last business day of the expiry month at 12 noon
Strike Price	Minimum of 12 ITM, 12 Out-of-the-Money and 1 Near-the-Money strikes would be provided for all available contracts
Strike Interval	25 paise or ₹0.25
Final Settlement Day	Last working day (excluding Saturdays) of the expiry month. The last working day would be taken to be the same as that for Interbank Settlements in Mumbai.
Exercise at Expiry	On expiry date, all open long ITM contracts, on a particular strike of a series, at the close of trading hours would be automatically exercised at the final settlement price and assigned on a random basis to the open short positions of the same strike and series
Initial Margin	The Initial Margin requirement would be based on a worst scenario loss of a portfolio of an individual client comprising his positions in options and futures contracts on the same underlying across different maturities and across various scenarios of price and volatility changes. In order to achieve this, the price range for generating the scenarios would be 3.5 time standard deviation and volatility range for generating the scenarios would be 3%.
Extreme Loss Margin	Extreme loss margin equal to 1.5% of the Notional Value of the open short option position.
Settlement of Premium	Premium would be paid in by the buyer in cash and paid out to the seller in cash on T + 1 day. Until the buyer pays in the premium, the premium due shall be deducted from the available Liquid Net Worth on a real time basis.
Mode of Settlement	Cash settled in Indian Rupees

Premium Style and Future Style Options While all terms in the exchange-traded option specifications are well-understood or -explained before, a word about *type of options* needs to be mentioned. Options can be of two types—*premium style* or *futures style*. In an options contract, the holder pays the premium front-end. The holder has no liability that can exceed the premium payable. In the worst case, scenario option holder does not exercise the option and his maximum loss is limited to the premium that has already been paid. However, these premiums change continuously as the spot exchange rate changes. If the holder squares up before maturity of option, he becomes liable to pay/receive the difference of the premiums by way of settlement.

If it is assumed that the option holder waits till maturity, he does not need to provide for additional loss on his position in options. Though for writer, the losses can keep mounting and is required to make good the loss to the exchange. Where the exchange does not require option holder to pay/receive additional amounts of differential in premiums, such options are called *premium style options*.

On the contrary, if it is assumed that the option holder has taken a speculative position and squares up before maturity, the difference of premiums in original and offsetting contracts becomes payable or receivable. Under this scenario, the option holder would have to pay or receive the difference in premiums of options. If so, the contract would be called a *future style* contract. If the exchange stipulates that difference of premiums is paid/received till the position remains open (initial contract not squared up), such an option contract would be classified as *future style option*.

In India exchange-traded options at all exchanges are *premium style*.

UNDERSTANDING OPTIONS QUOTATIONS

Option prices for currencies are read in the same manner as that for any other underlying asset.

Table 9-3 depicts the select actual option chain data for call and put options traded at NSE on 1 July 2013 for the contracts on US dollar expiring on 29 July 2013. The value of the underlying asset as represented by RBI reference rate at 12 noon is ₹59.1490/$. Contracts with strike prices in steps of ₹0.25 from strike prices of ₹57.00 to ₹61.00 are presented.

The column in the middle represents different strike prices. The strike prices move in the steps of ₹0.25, and exchanges intend to cover at least 12 strike prices above and below the spot rate prevailing. Hence, there are a minimum of 25 strike prices available for investors to trade. Call and put prices respectively are given in the left and right of the middle column. They include ask and bid prices and quantities representing the demand and supply positions at the next immediate level. The next column contains last-traded price (LTP), the price at which the last transaction took place.

The column next to LTP denotes *implied volatility, IV* (explained later). A major constituent of the option price is the volatility in the spot exchange rate. Greater the volatility, higher is the price. Absolute prices of the options do not communicate much about the state of the market. Option prices are supposed to reflect the volatility of the spot markets. Note that call and put

Currency Options 287

Table 9-3
Option Chain Data for Select Active Contracts on US Dollar Option

Contract Expiry: 29 July 2013
RBI Reference Rate 1 July 2013 12:00 Hr = ₹59.1490

	CALLS							Strike Price	PUTS							
OI	Volume	IV	LTP	Bid Qty	Bid Price	Ask Price	Ask Qty		Bid Qty	Bid Price	Ask Price	Ask Qty	LTP	IV	Volume	OI
20,111	695	7.84	2.8500	10	2.8300	2.8525	1	57.00	1,914	0.0600	0.0650	400	0.0600	11.91	37,910	87,417
5	–	8.11	1.2800	–	–	3.0500	500	57.25	1,200	0.0150	0.1175	1,200	0.0950	12.31	1	1,091
19,185	2,332	7.85	2.1600	250	2.3675	2.6450	100	57.50	1,200	0.0975	0.1050	50	0.1050	11.81	9,754	23,224
546	10	4.93	1.8500	500	1.5725	2.6000	500	57.75	1,200	0.1275	0.1975	1,200	0.1275	11.45	506	2,157
111,482	1,697	11.02	1.9250	50	1.9125	1.9575	10	58.00	25	0.1600	0.1625	500	0.1575	11.36	45,204	117,547
213	–	26.70	2.6000	–	–	2.1500	500	58.25	1,200	0.1800	0.2125	1,200	0.1850	10.82	10,694	22,300
74,801	10,636	11.64	1.5425	200	1.4525	1.5600	100	58.50	100	0.2575	0.2600	42	0.2600	11.15	37,262	57,428
2,589	396	10.33	1.3075	1,000	1.1525	1.7275	1,000	58.75	47	0.3200	0.3300	1,191	0.3250	11.13	3,240	7,492
74,661	31,010	11.73	1.2175	1,000	1.1950	1.2075	10	59.00	23	0.3975	0.4000	387	0.3950	11.16	117,327	117,463
17,374	7,053	11.79	1.0500	1,000	1.0425	1.0575	1,000	59.25	39	0.4900	0.4975	144	0.4800	11.16	22,886	11,496
69,714	73,805	11.69	0.9100	1,030	0.9000	0.9050	4	59.50	1,026	0.5925	0.6000	66	0.5925	11.15	75,748	57,171
38,040	18,995	11.51	0.7800	20	0.7700	0.7800	21	59.75	1,185	0.7100	0.7200	1	0.7200	11.31	13,972	18,132
203,937	198,790	11.59	0.6675	127	0.6525	0.6575	495	60.00	243	0.8425	0.8550	1,027	0.8400	11.16	76,970	124,184
15,282	11,235	11.75	0.5500	20	0.5525	0.5625	1,075	60.25	200	0.9800	1.4200	50	1.0000	11.42	1,941	6,975
101,671	55,586	11.77	0.4750	6	0.4675	0.4725	110	60.50	200	1.1450	1.1675	1,006	1.1750	11.85	5,015	64,436
17,425	9,605	11.79	0.3975	1,119	0.3875	0.4000	1,168	60.75	–	–	–	–	1.3450	11.88	144	4,031
216,919	160,597	12.03	0.3300	1	0.3275	0.3325	30	61.00	175	1.5025	1.5250	500	1.5200	11.61	15,319	106,355
6,573	6,678	11.77	0.2725	200	0.2700	0.2800	1,200	61.25	25	1.5300	2.2475	25	1.2225	2.81	–	220
24,860	27,479	12.17	0.2300	254	0.2250	0.2300	1,200	61.50	–	–	1.9950	175	1.9000	11.64	20	25,344
26,747	7,970	12.04	0.1775	1,200	0.1700	0.2025	1,200	61.75	30	1.7150	2.3500	30	–	0.00	–	–
59,945	28,846	12.42	0.1650	163	0.1500	0.1550	237	62.00	200	2.0025	2.4025	500	2.0025	6.71	–	252

Source: www.nseindia.com on 1 July 2013.
Note: Dark portions represent In-the-Money options.

option prices for different strike rates vary substantially in absolute terms but represent almost similar implied volatility.

Volume represents the number of contracts traded during the day. It is indicative of activity and investor's interest in a particular contract. *Open interest* represents the number of contracts yet to be squared up. As explained in the previous chapter, open interest is a vital statistic used by analysts for study of market sentiments.

Most traded options are ATM options apparently because they have maximum chance to become In-the-Money. The OTM option requires a larger price movement to become In-the-Money. The ITM options already have some intrinsic value and, therefore, become expensive.

In India, all contracts in options are cash settled, that is, the difference in the prices is exchanged in Indian rupees rather than by delivery of foreign currency.

Since currency options in India are European in nature, they can only be exercised on maturity. The following procedures are usual with exchange-traded options:

- Prior to the expiry, all outstanding contracts need to be closed else the exchange clears all contracts at the clearing price on the last day of the trading. Prior to the expiry of the options, traders must square up the positions to have cash settlement and avoid deliveries. Long contracts are nullified by going short and vice versa. As a measure of abundant precaution, it must be stated that a call written would be nullified by buying a call only and not by trading in put options. Consider, for example, a call written (obligation to sell) US dollar for strike price of ₹58.00. It would stand nullified by buying a call (right to buy) on US dollar with the same strike price and same expiry and not by buying a put which is a right to sell. An obligation to sell/buy stands nullified by a right to buy/sell and not by creating another obligation to buy/sell.

If not cancelled prior to expiry, then for exchange-traded options, at the closing of business hours on the last day of trading

1. All long positions (holders of options) in options that are Out-of-the-Money lapse automatically with expiry. Exercising options is prerogative of holder and it is well within his right to exercise even if the option is Out-of-the-Money. However, exercise of the Out-of-the-Money options is ruled out by exchanges.
2. Long positions in the options that are In-the-Money are deemed exercised at the end of closing hours at the final settlement price, which is RBI reference rate on the expiry date of the contract. The short positions (writers of options) outstanding for the same contract with the same exercise would be assigned to meet the obligations towards holder of options.

Assignment

In case of OTC options, the buyer and the seller of options enter the contract directly and, therefore, the holder knows whom to approach if and when he decides to exercise his right. The writer of the option has to fulfil the obligation.

In an exchange-traded option, the buyer and seller enter the contract through an exchange, with buyer and seller not known to each other. To each of them the counterparty is exchange. If buyer needs to exercise the option, he has to advise the decision to the exchange only. In such a case, the exchange has the task of making good the claim made by the holder of the option. A suitable writer needs to be identified among several option sellers. This process is called assignment.

Margins in Options

Options are one-sided contracts in which the buyer has no obligations to perform except upon exercise. In case of call, the holder has to deliver cash equal to exercise price and in case of put, the underlying asset. On initiating position the buyer of the option satisfies his obligations by paying the premium. On the contrary, the writer of the options assumes unlimited risk in case price of the asset moves unfavourably. Since exchange has the responsibility for settlement, it faces risk from seller of the options. Options are cash settled. It is assumed that the writer of the option would nullify the liability by buying the option back. Thus, his obligations would limit to the premium payable on buying less premium received from selling the option.

Since exchanges in India have only premium-style options on currencies, the exchange keeps all marked-to-market (MTM) losses collected from writers with itself and not pass on to the gainers. Only writers of the options have to make good the MTM losses.

OPTIONS AND FORWARDS/FUTURES

It is interesting to compare long position in futures/forwards with that of long call, and short position in futures/forwards with long put. The payoffs of forwards/futures and options are distinctly different. Forwards/futures have an equal amount of loss or profit for the same change in the exchange rate in either direction, whereas options have uneven loss or profit. Consider, for example, futures and options position on US dollar at ₹45.00 and a call option with $X = 45.00$ at a premium of ₹0.50. What would be the risk return profile under two situations?

With two opposite scenarios of increased and decreased price, the payoffs of forward and option strategies would be different. With long forward/futures contract, the holder gained if dollar appreciated and lost if dollar depreciated. With call option contract one gains with appreciation, but the depreciation of dollar limits the loss to the premium paid. The payoffs for equal change in exchange rate in either direction (exchange rate moving from ₹40 to ₹50) with long futures and long call are as follows:

Exchange Rate	Long Futures Position	Long Call Option
₹40.00	−₹5.00	−₹0.50
₹50.00	₹5.00	₹4.50

As can be seen, the payoffs under long position in forward/futures contract are equal under situations of favourable and unfavourable movements in exchange rate. It is uneven in case of option which permits the gain but limits the loss. The payoffs are depicted in Figure 9-5.

Similarly, one can compare payoffs of short position in futures and long put. A put option permits gains with decline in price (depreciation of foreign currency), whereas contains losses

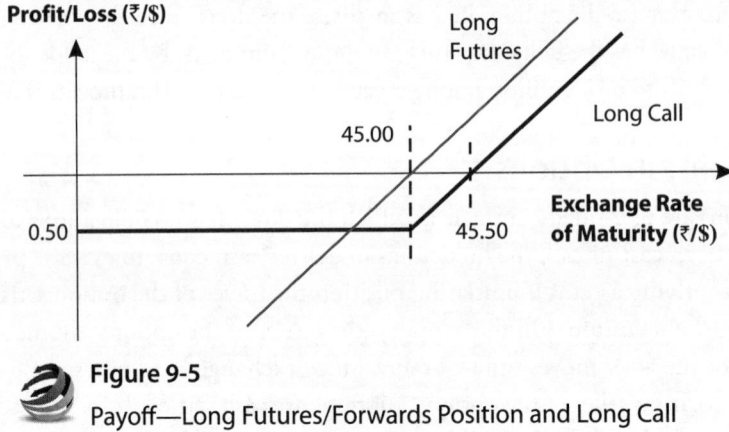

Figure 9-5
Payoff—Long Futures/Forwards Position and Long Call

due to rise in price (appreciation of foreign currency). Assume that an exporter takes (i) a short position in US dollars at exchange rate of ₹45/$ and (ii) buys put with the same strike of ₹45, paying a premium of ₹0.30. The following would be the payoffs of short futures and long put when the price at maturity is lesser at ₹40 or higher at ₹50:

Asset Price	Short Futures Position	Long Put Option
₹40.00	₹5.00	₹4.70
₹50.00	−₹5.00	−₹0.30

The payoffs of short position in forwards/futures and long put are shown in Figure 9-6. A look at Figures 9-5 and 9-6 would reveal that loss-making areas in case of long options are curtailed, whereas profit-making area is retained with payoff lesser by the extent of premiums paid. Short positions in options, that is, short call or short put, are non-descript in terms of forward/futures positions. A short call in terms of futures appears like a short position in

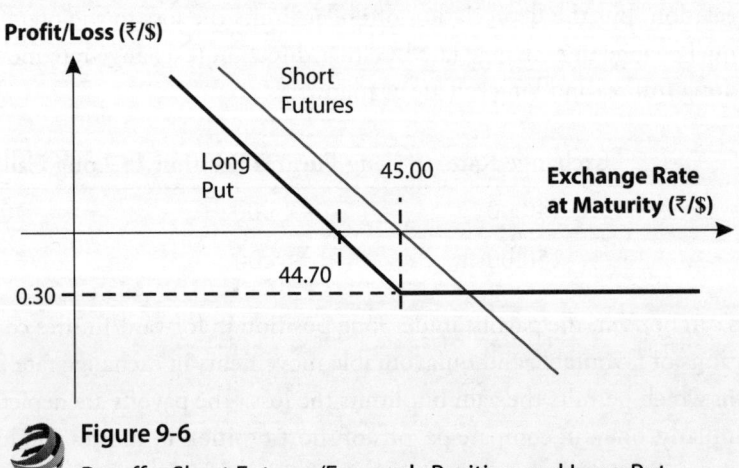

Figure 9-6
Payoff—Short Futures/Forwards Position and Long Put

Table 9-4
Differences of Forward/Futures and Options

	Forward	Futures	Options
Payoff	Linear	Linear	Non-linear
Obligation to Perform	Both on buyer and seller	Both on buyer and seller	Only on seller of option with right to the buyer
Trading	OTC	Exchange-traded	Both OTC and Exchange-traded
Margin	None	As required by exchange	None if OTC and as per exchange requirement if exchange-traded
Initial Payment	None	None	Buyer pays premium to seller
Settlement	On maturity	Daily for futures	Daily if exchange-traded and once on maturity if OTC

futures with gain making area curtailed substantially and retaining all the loss making positions. Similarly, a short put is like a long position in futures with almost entire profit-making region removed and whole of loss-making range retained. Why short positions in options do not have a parallel in futures is due to uneven payoff of options and even payoff of futures.

Differences in payoff of options have a remarkable effect on the hedging strategies that are discussed later. For easier comprehension, the differences between forward/futures and options are condensed in Table 9-4.

BLACK SCHOLES OPTION PRICING MODEL

We looked at the intrinsic and time value of the option. While it is easy to understand the changes in the value of the option qualitatively and apply arbitrage arguments to the pricing of options, the quantification of the changes in the value of option is extremely difficult. The determination of exact value of the option requires comprehensive understanding of many complex concepts in mathematics, which is beyond the scope of this book.

The backbone of option pricing is formulated by a model developed by Black and Scholes applicable to non-dividend paying European options commonly referred to as Black Scholes Model (BSM). The BSM modified for value of currency options is given as Eqs 9-3 and 9-4.

The option pricing model as given by Eqs 9-3 and 9-4 can be expressed in terms of the forward price F for the option period T. We know the relationship of spot and forward price from interest rate parity as follows:

$$F = S \frac{e^{rT}}{e^{r_f T}} = S e^{(r-r_f)T}$$

Price of Foreign Currency Options

$$c = S \cdot e^{-r_f T} \cdot N(d_1) - X \cdot e^{-rT} \cdot N(d_2) \quad (9\text{-}3)$$

$$p = X \cdot e^{-rT} \cdot N(-d_2) - S \cdot e^{-r_f T} \cdot N(-d_1) \quad (9\text{-}4)$$

where

$$d_1 = \frac{\ln(S/X) + (r - r_f + \sigma^2/2)T}{\sigma\sqrt{T}}; \text{ and}$$

$$d_2 = \frac{\ln(S/X) + (r - r_f - \sigma^2/2)T}{\sigma\sqrt{T}} \text{ or } d_2 = d_1 - \sigma\sqrt{T}$$

r_f = Risk-free interest rate in foreign currency,
r = Risk-free interest rate in domestic currency,
σ = Volatility of spot exchange rate,

S = Spot exchange rate
X = Exercise price
T = Time to expiry

$N(d)$ = Standard normal distribution $= \dfrac{1}{\sqrt{2\pi}} \displaystyle\int_{-\infty}^{d} e^{-z^2/2} \, dz$

where z is standard normal distribution

Substituting spot exchange rate with the forward rate from interest rate parity, we get the call and put prices as per Eqs 9-5 and 9-6 in terms of forward rate.

Price of Foreign Currency Options

$$c = e^{-rT}\{F \cdot N(d_1) - X \cdot N(d_2)\} \quad (9\text{-}5)$$

$$p = e^{-rT}\{X \cdot N(-d_2) - F \cdot N(-d_1)\} \quad (9\text{-}6)$$

where

$$d_1 = \frac{\ln(F/X) + (\sigma^2/2)T}{\sigma\sqrt{T}}; \text{ and}$$

$$d_2 = \frac{\ln(F/X) - (\sigma^2/2)T}{\sigma\sqrt{T}} \text{ or } d_2 = d_1 - \sigma\sqrt{T}$$

F = Forward exchange rate
r = Risk-free interest rate in domestic currency,
σ = Volatility of spot exchange rate,

X = Exercise price
T = Time to expiry

$N(d)$ = Standard normal distribution $= \dfrac{1}{\sqrt{2\pi}} \displaystyle\int_{-\infty}^{d} e^{-z^2/2} \, dz$

Let us consider 3-m ATM European call and put options on euro with spot exchange rate at ₹65/€. The risk-free interest rates in rupee and euro are 8% and 4%, respectively. The volatility of exchange rate for euro is 15%.

Here, $S = 65$, $X = 65$, $r = 8\%$, $r_f = 4\%$, $T = 3$ months (0.25 years), and $\sigma = 0.15$. Putting these values in Eqs 9-3 and 9-4 for valuing call and put options, respectively, we get

$$d_1 = \frac{\ln(65/65) + (0.08 - 0.04 + 0.15 \times 0.15/2) \times 0.25}{0.15 \times \sqrt{0.25}} = 0.1708$$

$$d_2 = d_1 - 0.15 \times \sqrt{0.25} = 0.0958$$

$N(d_1) = 0.5678 \quad N(d_2) = 0.5382 \quad N(-d_1) = 0.4322 \quad N(-d_2) = 0.4618$

Call Price, $c = S\,e^{-r_f T} N(d_1) - Xe^{-rT} N(d_2)$

$\qquad = 65.00 \times e^{-0.04 \times 0.25} \times 0.5678 - 65^{-0.08 \times 0.25} \times 0.5382$

$\qquad = 61.7129 \times 0.5678 - 64.3532 \times 0.5382 = 36.1776 - 34.6332$

$\qquad = ₹1.5444$

Put Price, $p = Xe^{-rT} N(-d_2) - S\,e^{-r_f T} N(-d_1)$

$\qquad = 65.00 \times e^{0.08 \times 0.25} \times 0.4618 - 65.00 \times e^{-0.04 \times 0.25} \times 0.4322$

$\qquad = 64.3532 \times 0.4618 - 63.7129 \times 0.4322$

$\qquad = 29.7183 - 27.5253 = ₹2.1930$

For ATM options, the intrinsic value is zero. The entire premiums worked out for call and put options, therefore, represent the time values.

Exercise 9-2
Application of Black Scholes Model: Call and Put Prices

In the foreign exchange markets, US dollar 3-m forward is quoting ₹46.00/$. The volatility of dollar rupee exchange rate is estimated at 20%. With domestic interest rate at 5%, find out the value of 3-m call and put options on US dollar with exercise prices of (a) ₹45 (b) ₹46, and (c) ₹47.

Solution
As per Eqs 9-5 and 9-6, the values of the call and put are given by

$$c = e^{-rT}\{F.N(d_1) - X.N(d_2)\}$$
$$p = e^{-rT}\{X.N(-d_2) - F.N(-d_1)\}$$

where $\quad d_1 = \dfrac{\ln(F/X) + (\sigma^2/2)T}{\sigma\sqrt{T}};\ $ and

$\qquad\qquad d_2 = \dfrac{\ln(F/X) - (\sigma^2/2)T}{\sigma\sqrt{T}}\ $ or $\ d_2 = d_1 - \sigma\sqrt{T}$

(a) For exercise price of ₹40

First, we find the values of d_1 and d_2. All values used are annual and in decimal form. We have $F = 46.00$, $X = 45.00$, $r = 0.10$, $T = 0.25$, and $\sigma = 0.20$. These are plugged in the formula.

$$d_1 = \frac{\ln(46/45) + (0.20 \times 0.20/2) \times 0.25}{0.20 \times \sqrt{0.25}} = 0.2698$$

$$d_2 = d_1 - 0.20 \times \sqrt{0.25} = 0.2698 - 0.01 = 0.1698$$

From Normal distribution tables or using Excel function NORMSDIST(d), we find out the area under the Normal distribution for values less than d_1 and d_2. We get

$N(d_1) = 0.6063$ and $N(d_2) = 0.5674$
$N(-d_1) = 0.3937$ and $N(-d_2) = 0.4326$

Inserting the values in the equations for the call premium, c and put premium, p

$$c = e^{-rT}\{FN(d_1) - XN(d_2)\} = 0.9876(46 \times 0.6063 - 45 \times 0.5674) = ₹2.3275$$

$$p = e^{-rT}\{XN(-d_2) - FN(-d_1)\} = 0.9876(45 \times 0.4326 - 46 \times 0.3937) = ₹1.3399$$

(b) **For exercise price of ₹46**

$$d_1 = \frac{\ln(46/46) + (0.20 \times 0.20/2) \times 0.25}{0.20 \times \sqrt{0.25}} = 0.0500$$

$$d_2 = d_1 - 0.20 \times \sqrt{0.25} = 0.0500 - 0.01 = 0.0500$$

From Normal distribution tables or using Excel function NORMSDIST(d), we find out the area under the Normal distribution for values less than d_1 and d_2. We get

$N(d_1) = 0.5199$ and $N(d_2) = 0.4801$
$N(-d_1) = 0.4801$ and $N(-d_2) = 0.5199$

Inserting the values in the equations for the call premium, c and put premium, p

$$c = e^{-rT}\{FN(d_1) - XN(d_2)\} = 0.9876(46 \times 0.5199 - 46 \times 0.4801) = ₹1.8081$$

$$p = e^{-rT}\{XN(-d_2) - FN(-d_1)\} = 0.9876(46 \times 0.5199 - 46 \times 0.4801) = ₹1.8081$$

(c) **For exercise price of ₹47, we get**

$$d_1 = \frac{\ln(46/47) + (0.20 \times 0.20/2) \times 0.25}{0.20 \times \sqrt{0.25}} = -0.1651$$

$$d_2 = d_1 - 0.20 \times \sqrt{0.25} = -0.1651 - 0.01 = -0.2651$$

$N(d_1) = 0.4344$ and $N(d_2) = 0.3955$
$N(-d_1) = 0.5656$ and $N(-d_2) = 0.6045$

Inserting the values in the equations for the call premium, c and put premium, p

$$c = e^{-rT}\{FN(d_1) - XN(d_2)\} = 0.9876(46 \times 0.4344 - 47 \times 0.3955) = ₹1.3766$$

$$p = e^{-rT}\{XN(-d_2) - FN(-d_1)\} = 0.9876(47 \times 0.6045 - 46 \times 0.5656) = ₹2.3642$$

HEDGING WITH CURRENCY OPTIONS

Like any other derivative, options too have applications of hedging, speculation, and arbitrage. We discuss the hedging applications of currency options here. The spot exchange rate is subject to change due to national as well as international factors. The two situations that are most likely and warrant hedging are

1. risk of depreciating foreign currency for exporters for credit invoices denominated in foreign currency, and
2. risk of appreciating foreign currency for importers for deferred payment of liabilities in foreign exchange.

We discuss these two basic situations for hedging with conventional call and put options as basic hedging strategies with the help of an example on each.

Hedging Foreign Currency Receivable with Put Option

Exporters provide goods and services on credit by raising invoice in foreign currency such as US dollar and euro. The invoicing is done on the basis of a target exchange rate of realization. An appreciation of foreign currency beyond the target rate is beneficial as it leads to enhanced profit. For example, with cost at ₹40 and a target profit of ₹5, the exporter may invoice $1.00 if the exchange rate is ₹45/$. However, if the money is realized later when dollar appreciates to ₹46, the profit would stand increased to ₹6. But, depreciation of US dollar below ₹45 would reduce the targeted profit.

In order to protect against the depreciation of foreign currency, one of the instruments available is a put option on US dollar. Assume that an exporter has invoiced US$1 million receivable after three months. The value of dollar after three months is uncertain. It is equally likely to go up or down. The exporter has planned his profit by assuming that dollar receivable would give him ₹45. Realizing more than ₹45 (dollar appreciating) would be a pleasing situation but anything less than ₹45 would be seriously damaging.

The exporter can protect the position by buying a put with the strike price of ₹45 with three months to expire by paying a small premium of say ₹0.25 per $.

If exporter hedges the position with a put, the net realization would always be greater than ₹44.75 (strike exchange rate − premium). If the rate happens to be less than ₹45, say ₹43.00, the exporter can exercise his put resulting in the profit of 2.00 (45 − S). The exporter sells his dollars at ₹43.00 in the spot market losing ₹2.00 from the target profit. The shortfall is made good by exercising the put which gives ₹2 as payoff. The realized exchange rate with a put under two different scenarios of exchange rate at the time of actual receipt of foreign currency is shown as follows:

Spot price	Position of Put	Put Pay-off	Asset Value	₹ Realized Price
S < 45.00	Exercise put	45.00 − S − 0.25	S	44.75
S < 45.00	Let put lapse	−0.25	S	S − 0.25 (always ≥ ₹44.75)

The payoffs and value of receivable with and without put are presented in Table 9-5 and Figures 9-7(a) and 9.7(b).

Table 9-5
Hedging Receivable with Put Option

Strike Price, ₹/$		45.00		
Cost of Put, ₹		0.25		*Figures in ₹/$*
Exchange Rate	Value of Receivable	Receivable Payoff	Put Payoff	Net Realized
40.00	40.00	−5.00	4.75	44.75
41.00	41.00	−4.00	3.75	44.75
42.00	42.00	−3.00	2.75	44.75
43.00	43.00	−2.00	1.75	44.75
44.00	44.00	−1.00	0.75	44.75
45.00	45.00	0.00	−0.25	44.75
46.00	46.00	1.00	−0.25	45.75
47.00	47.00	2.00	−0.25	46.75
48.00	48.00	3.00	−0.25	47.75
49.00	49.00	4.00	−0.25	48.75
50.00	50.00	5.00	−0.25	49.75

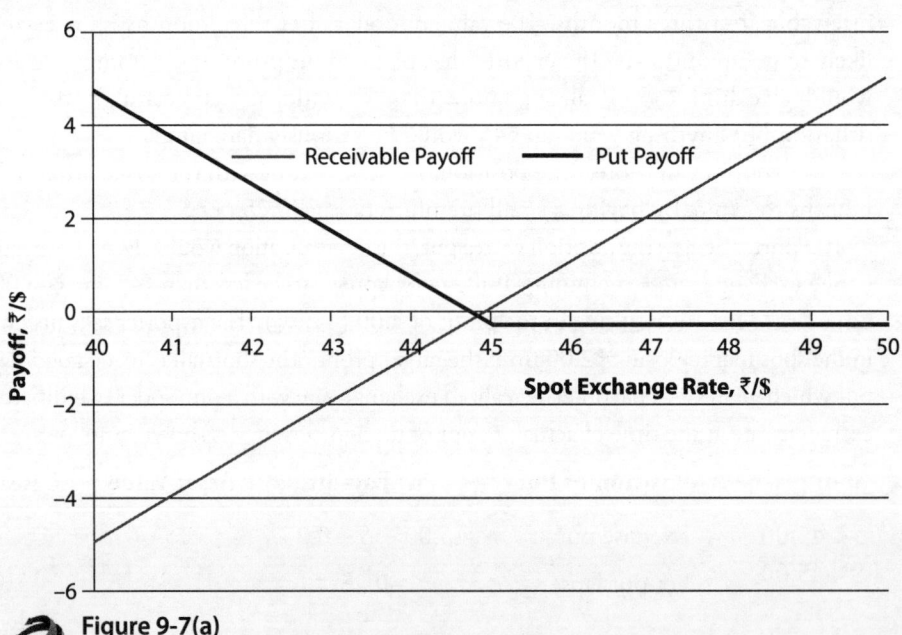

Figure 9-7(a)
Payoff—Receivable and Put

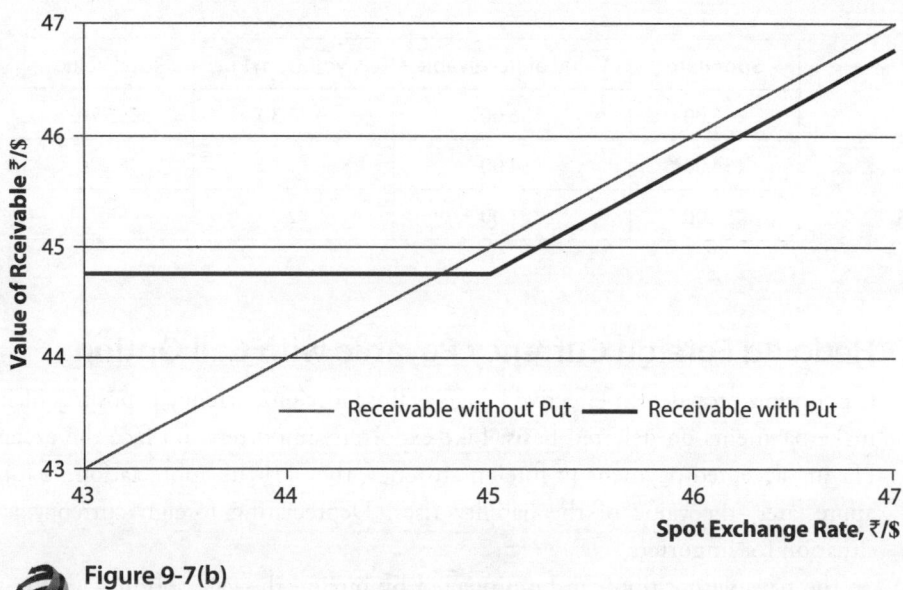

Figure 9-7(b)
Value of Receivable with and without Put

As can be seen from the Figure 9-7(b) that hedging receivable through put not only protects the value to some floor level but also helps in retaining the potential gain if the currency appreciates. If at the time of realization the spot price were ₹48, the exporter would end up getting ₹47.75 for each dollar.

Exercise 9-3
Hedging Foreign Currency Receivable with Put Option

Today is 10 January and spot exchange rate is ₹55.00/$. An exporter is expecting to receive US$10,000 on 31 March. He is expecting US dollar to depreciate and expects it to fall by about 5% in this period, whereas realization of less than ₹53.00/dollar would cause a significant erosion in his profit. A European put option maturing on 31 March with a strike price of ₹54.00 is available at a premium of ₹0.30.

(a) How should the exporter hedge his receivable?
(b) If the exporter hedges, what would be his realized exchange rate if on 31 March the exchange rate happens to be (i) ₹56.00 (ii) ₹54.00, and (iii) ₹51.00?

Solution
(a) The exporter must buy the put option with strike price of ₹54.00 by paying a premium of ₹0.30, thereby ensuring the minimum realization of ₹53.70 ($X - p$) for his receivables. If at maturity, the spot rate falls below ₹54.00, the exporter can exercise the put option. In case the spot happens to be more than ₹54, the exporter would let his put option lapse.
(b) The following would be the position of his receivables under different exchange rate scenarios:

Spot Rate	Value of Receivable	Payoff from Put	Total Value
₹56.00	₹56.00	– ₹0.30	₹55.70
₹54.00	₹54.00	– ₹0.30	₹53.70
₹51.00	₹51.00	– ₹2.70	₹53.70

Hedging Foreign Currency Payable with Call Option

Call option provides an effective hedge against foreign currency exposures of importers who make payments on deferred basis. Like exporters, importers too face the exchange rate risk. Having accepted payment in foreign currency, they fear its appreciation. If foreign currency appreciates, the value of the liability rises. Depreciating foreign currency is a favourable situation for importers.

The payable position can be protected by buying the call option with the strike price at which the protection is desired. Assume that an importer has to pay US$10,000 in three-month time. The current exchange rate is ₹45. The value of dollar after three months is uncertain. The importer has planned his profit by assuming that dollar payable would not exceed ₹45. Paying more than ₹45 (dollar appreciating) would be disastrous for the bottom line. The importer can protect the position by buying a call option with the strike price of ₹45 valid for three months by paying a small premium of say ₹0.50/$.

If importer hedges the position with a call, the maximum payment is capped at ₹45.50 (strike exchange rate + premium). If the exchange rate happens to be less than ₹45, say ₹43.00, the importer can buy the foreign currency at ₹43.00 from the market and let the call option lapse limiting the overall cost to ₹43.50. However, if the rate happens to be in excess of ₹45, the importer exercises the call option to get the foreign currency at ₹45 limiting the overall cost to ₹45.50. This is shown in the following table:

Figures in ₹

Spot Price	Position of Call	Call Pay-off	Payable Value	Net Lost
$S < 45.00$	Let call lapse	–0.50	S	$S – 0.50$
$S > 45.00$	Exercise call	$S – 45.00 – 0.50$	S	45.50

(always ≤45.50)

Like put works for receivable, hedging payable through call not only protects the cost but also helps in retaining the potential for gain if the currency depreciates. If at the time of payment, the spot price is ₹48, then importer would end up paying ₹45.50 for each dollar. However, if the spot exchange rate is say ₹43.00, the cost of payable would be ₹43.50.

The payoffs and cost of payable with and without call are presented in Table 9-6 and depicted in Figures 9-8(a) and 9-8(b). The payable is capped at ₹45.50 with call of strike at ₹45.00.

Table 9-6

Hedging Payable with Call Option

Strike Price,	₹/$	45.00		
Cost of Call,	₹	0.50		₹/$
Exchange Rate	Value of Payable	Payoff of Payable	Call Payoff	Net Paid
40.00	40.00	5.00	−0.50	40.50
41.00	41.00	4.00	−0.50	41.50
42.00	42.00	3.00	−0.50	42.50
43.00	43.00	2.00	−0.50	43.50
44.00	44.00	1.00	−0.50	44.50
45.00	45.00	0.00	−0.50	45.50
46.00	46.00	−1.00	0.50	45.50
47.00	47.00	−2.00	1.50	45.50
48.00	48.00	−3.00	2.50	45.50
49.00	49.00	−4.00	3.50	45.50
50.00	50.00	−5.00	4.50	45.50

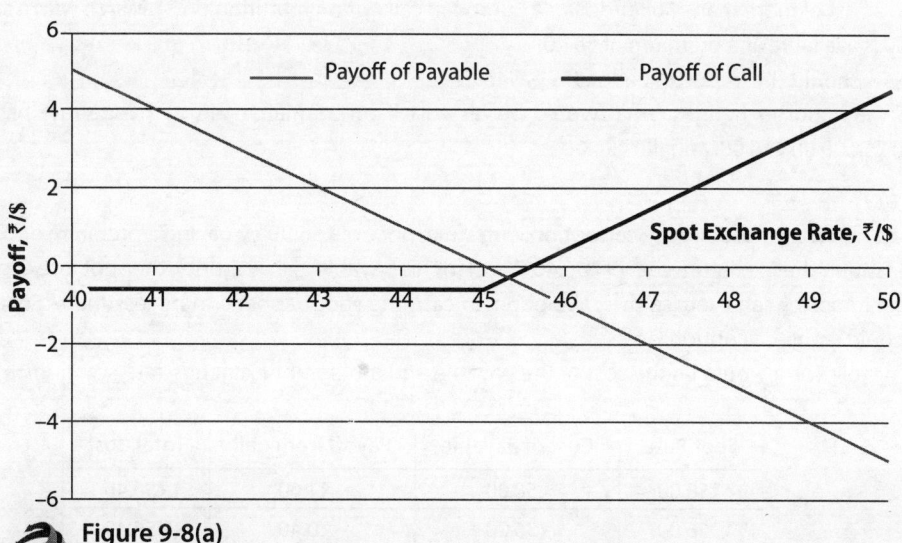

Figure 9-8(a)

Payoff—Payable and Call

300 International Finance

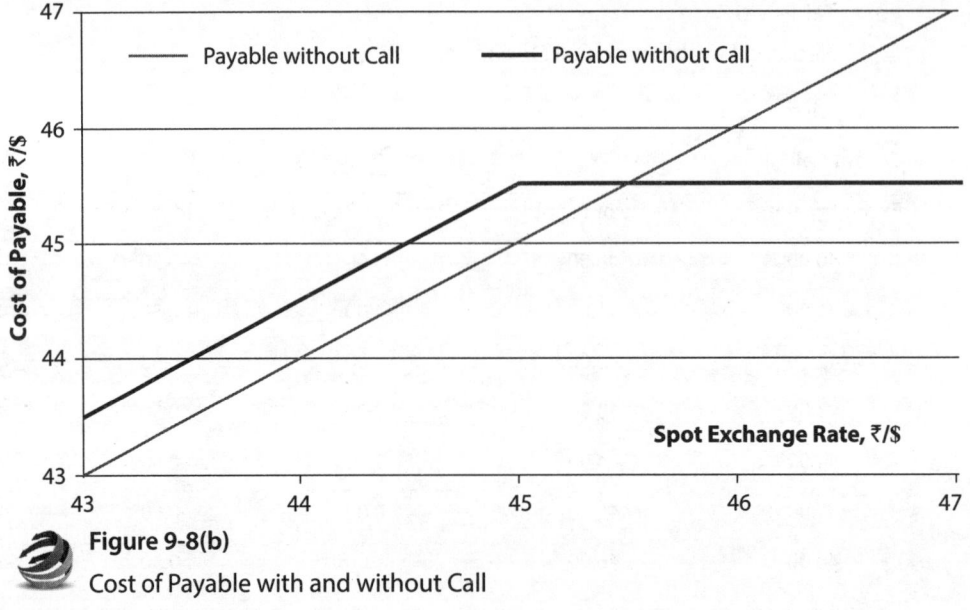

Figure 9-8(b)
Cost of Payable with and without Call

Exercise 9-4
Hedging Foreign Currency Payable with Call Option

Today is 10 January and spot exchange rate is ₹55.00/$. An importer has to pay US$10,000 on 31 March. He is expecting US dollar to appreciate and expects it to rise by about 5% in this period. The importer cannot afford a cost of more than ₹56.50/dollar. A European call option maturing on 31 March with a strike price of ₹56.00 is available at a premium of ₹0.40.

(a) How should the importer hedge his payable?
(b) If the importer hedges, what would be his cost if on 31 March the exchange rate happens to be (i) ₹58.00 (ii) ₹56.00, and (iii) ₹54.00

Solution
(a) The importer must buy the call option with strike price of ₹56.00 by paying a premium of ₹0.40, thereby ensuring the maximum cost of ₹56.40 ($X + c$) for his payable. If at maturity, the spot rate exceeds ₹56.00, the importer can exercise the call option. In case the spot happens to be less than ₹56, the importer would let his call option lapse.
(b) The following would be the cost of the payable under different exchange rate scenarios:

Spot Rate	Cost of Payable	Payoff from Call	Total Cost
₹58.00	₹58.00	₹1.60	₹56.40
₹56.00	₹56.00	– ₹0.40	₹56.40
₹54.00	₹54.00	– ₹0.40	₹54.40

MODIFYING OPTION TERMS

Hedging with routine call and put options was discussed in the previous section. One of the disadvantages of hedging with options is the explicit cost associated while setting up the hedge. The premium is payable upfront and is not adjustable against the exercise price. The initial outlay in options hedge is a source of constant concern for all firms as they strive to curtail the cost and yet like to achieve desired hedging outcome.

We discuss some of the complex options normally referred to as exotics that enable us to reduce the cost by compromising with lesser or no payoff for some unlikely situations. The compromises on payoffs would lead to the reduction of option premiums since in option valuation all situations howsoever unlikely are accounted for. By excluding such unlikely scenarios, the cost of hedging with options can be reduced. Another way of reducing cost is to share the payoff with option writer. Yet another strategy is to write options to earn some premium back from the premium paid for the option bought.

Range Forward—Zero Cost Collar

We considered the hedging of long position with buying a put and short position with buying a call. Both the strategies required initial cost equal to the price of the option that needs to be paid front-end. While put assured a minimum value of the underlying asset, the call ensured the maximum value for a liability.

Hedging through options involve cost as buying an option requires payment. The one who sells the option earns the premium. One can reduce the cost by buying one option while writing another. For example, an exporter to hedge against the falling foreign currency buys a put retaining the potential to gain from appreciation of foreign currency. With decreasing strike price, the value of the put falls, whereas that of call increases. In order to contain cost, the exporter may consider buying a put with lower strike, say at ₹44, that would cost lesser than the put with strike of ₹45. However, this would reduce the floor level to less than ₹44.00.

Alternatively, the exporter while buying a put can also write a call with the same underlying and maturity but with higher and suitable exercise price to earn some premium offsetting, partially or fully, the cost of put bought. Buying a put is a right to sell foreign currency, whereas writing a call is an obligation to sell foreign currency. The strategy of buying a put and selling a call is consistent with the position of exporter owning the underlying foreign currency asset that needs to be sold. Similarly, an importer can buy a call and write a put since importer needs to buy currency. A long position in call with a short position in put is consistent with his position in the underlying asset. The position of buying one call/put and simultaneously writing a put/call with different strike prices is called a *range forward*.

When following the second strategy simultaneously with buying an option while writing another, part of the premium is recovered. Such a strategy/product is called a range forward. The range forward for exporter comprises long put with lower strike and short call with higher strike. For an importer, the range forward is consisting of buying a call and writing a put. If the premium payable on option bought equals the premium receivable on option sold, the cost can become zero. For this strike, prices of options need to be carefully selected. Such a combination is called a zero-cost collar.

What is the implication of strategy of range forward? Clearly if the cost of the strategy has become zero or reduced considerably, the hedging objective would have to be compromised. Let us examine the payoff of range forward with an example. Assume the case of an exporter who believes that current spot exchange rate of ₹45.00/$ is reasonable and fairly stable but needs protection below ₹44.00/$ in the next three months. Therefore, rather than buying a put with strike of ₹45.00/$, he buys a put with strike of ₹44.00/$ that would cost him less but would not provide protection if spot exchange rate ends between ₹44.00 and ₹45.00. The exporter foregoes protection below ₹45.00 till ₹44.00 to save the cost of hedging.

The exporter also believes that in the span of three months, the period of his exposure, the rupee is not going to depreciate below ₹47.00; hence, he creates an obligation to pay by writing a call with strike of ₹47.00/$. It implies that if exchange rate ends higher than ₹47.00, the call holder would exercise the option and the exporter would have to pay the differential. Since the exporter holds US dollar, he foregoes the opportunity to convert the dollar receivable at higher exchange rate.

Assuming the put of strike of ₹44.00 and call of strike of ₹47.00, both sell for ₹0.25 each, the cost of range forward for exporter would be zero. Therefore, it is referred to as *zero cost collar* too. The value of receivable under different scenarios of exchange rate at the maturity of receivable and the options for a range of ₹40/$ to ₹50/$ is presented in Table 9-7.

Table 9-7
Hedging Receivable with Range Forward

Put with X = 45 Bought and Call with X = 47 sold					
Put Option Bought			**Call Option Sold**		
Premium Paid, ₹	0.25		Premium Earned, ₹		0.25
Strike Price, ₹/$	44.00		Strike Price, ₹/$		47.00
					₹/$
Spot Exchange Rate	**Receivable**	**Receivable Payoff**	**Put Payoff**	**Call Payoff**	**Net Realized**
40.00	40.00	−5.00	3.75	0.25	44.00
41.00	41.00	−4.00	2.75	0.25	44.00
42.00	42.00	−3.00	1.75	0.25	44.00
43.00	43.00	−2.00	0.75	0.25	44.00
44.00	44.00	−1.00	−0.25	0.25	44.00
45.00	45.00	0.00	−0.25	0.25	45.00
46.00	46.00	1.00	−0.25	0.25	46.00
47.00	47.00	2.00	−0.25	0.25	47.00
48.00	48.00	3.00	−0.25	−0.75	47.00
49.00	49.00	4.00	−0.25	−1.75	47.00
50.00	50.00	5.00	−0.25	−2.75	47.00

The net impact of buying a put at ₹44.00 and selling a call at ₹47.00 means that

1. The exporter protects the receivable at ₹44.00 when the exchange rate falls below 44.00/$, by exercising the put.
2. When the exchange rate is between ₹44.00/$ and ₹47.00/$, the put is worthless. The call too is worthless and the liability of call written does not arise. The exporter sells the foreign exchange at the prevailing market rates.
3. When the exchange rate at the end of option period and maturity of receivable is more than 47.00/$ the exporter sells US dollar at prevailing market rate. However, any amount in excess of ₹47.00/$ is foregone as the same would have to be paid to the call holder. Therefore, the maximum exchange rate that can be realized is ₹47.00/$.

The position of exporter with range forward is depicted in Figure 9-9.

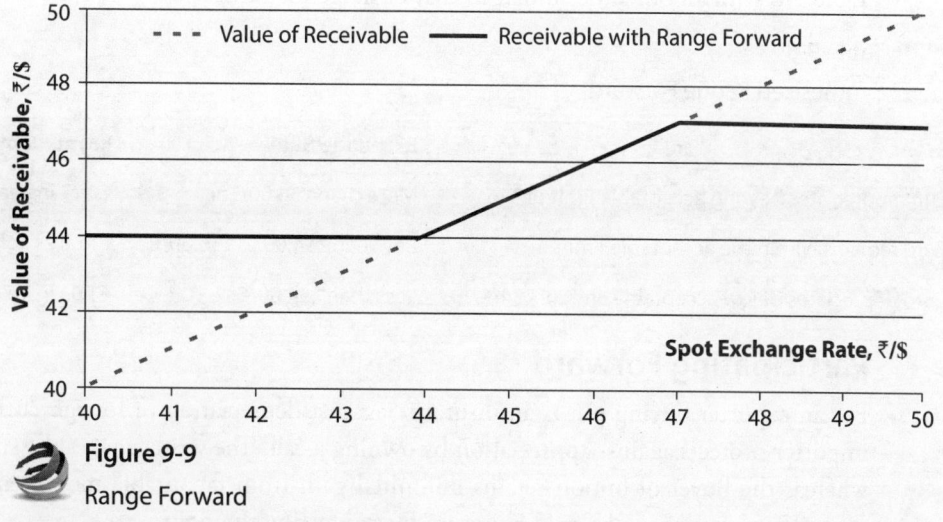

Figure 9-9
Range Forward

Range forward for importer is created by buying a call with higher strike, X_2, and writing a put with lower strike, X_1. Buying a call is a right to buy and selling a put is an obligation to buy. For spot price above X_2, the call would provide protection; between X_1 and X_2 market price prevails; and below X_1 the benefits of lesser cost are foregone as put become activated.

The difference between the two strike prices is the exposed range of exchange rate where the hedger realizes the market rates. Of the two strike rates, one is normally chosen by the hedger (put strike by exporter/call strike by importer), while the strike for the other option is chosen by market maker to make the cost of set-up zero. Normally, both the strikes are OTM and the forward rate is approximately the mid-point of two strikes. Sometimes, zero-cost is achieved by writing more options than bought or vice versa. The ratio of calls and puts is other than unity. The structures with put and call ratios other than unity are called *ratio range forward*.

Range forward as a combination of a put and a call can be comprehended without understanding of options. Without resorting to pure financial instruments, the same objective and payoff can be achieved directly between a supplier and customer. In order to share the risk of exchange rate, it is common in long-term contracts involving cash flows stretched over long periods, to incorporate a clause making payment depending upon the exchange rate prevailing. For example, a customer may be asked to (i) pay a lower amount if the foreign currency appreciated from a benchmark range, (ii) pay the contracted amount if exchange rate remains within a range, and (c) pay a higher amount if foreign currency depreciated beyond the benchmark range.

As an example, consider an Indian contractor building a bridge in Greece that takes two years to complete with several payment tranches. The contractor prices the contract on the basis of spot euro exchange rate of ₹55 and is willing to assume risk of exchange in the range of ₹54 to ₹56. The counterparty may agree to pay more number of euros if it depreciated below ₹54 and less number of euros if it appreciated beyond ₹56 so as to protect the contractor for a floor but not allowing the potential gain from appreciation of euro. It is analogous to owning a put option at ₹54 and writing a call at ₹56. The payoff of such position is presented in Table 9-8 with an outcome similar to that of range forward.

Table 9-8
Synthesized Range Forward

Event	Exchange Rate	Payment by Customer
Euro appreciates beyond acceptable limit of ₹56	More than ₹56.00/Euro	€0.97 instead of €1.00
Euro remains within the acceptable limits	Between ₹54.00 to ₹56.00/€	€1.00 as agreed
Euro depreciates below acceptable limit of ₹54/€	Less than ₹54.00/€	€1.03 instead of €1.00

Participating Forward

For an exporter buying put is an insurance against depreciation of foreign currency, whereas importer protects against appreciation by owning a call. The writer makes the small premium, whereas the buyer of option retains unlimited gain from favourable movement of exchange rates. The writer has to be paid premium for conferring the right.

Alternatively, the writer may forego the premium if he is allowed to participate in the likely profit. Such a situation where the writer participates in the profit of the holder of the option is called a *participating forward contract*. Let us examine participating forward with an example for an exporter.

An exporter wants to hedge the 3-m euro receivable with a forward contract at ₹55/€. A put option with same strike is available for ₹1.00. If exporter goes for forward hedge, he is assured of ₹55/€ irrespective of exchange rate at maturity. If exporter hedges with put, he is assured of ₹54/€ (put strike less premium) with potential of making gain with appreciation of euro. A participating forward may be set at say ₹53.00/€ where the payoff would be as follows:

Exchange Rate at Expiry		Value for the Exporter (₹/€)
If the spot at expiry	$S < ₹53/€$	53.00
	$S > ₹53/€$	$53 + \lambda(S - 53)$

where λ is between 0 and 1 and is called participation ratio

The payoff of participation forward can also be represented as 53 + Max (0, S − 53), which is same as ₹53 (F_1) plus the call with the strike of ₹53 $c(X = F_1)$. Since λ is chosen in such a way that the participation forward costs zero as does an outright forward of ₹54 (F), the cost of the two must be equal. Hence,

$$Fe^{-rT} = F_1 e^{-rT} + \lambda c(X = F_1) \tag{9-7}$$

Equation 9-7 may be used to find the desired participation ratio for zero cost.

Barrier Options

From the considerations of cost, barrier option offers are another set of alternatives to hedge against foreign currency exposures. Barrier options are among the most popular and most traded exotic options. Conventional options have exercise price predetermined and based on the spot price at maturity the payoff is computed. The strike price serves as a reference point for determination of payoff. In barrier options, there is another price reference for the spot exchange rate called the barrier price. The function of the barrier price is not to determine the payoff but to know if the option is alive or dead. If alive, payoff is made based on spot exchange rate at maturity and the exercise price, just as it would be in case of conventional option. No payoff is made if option is dead.

The fact that the barrier options can become worthless before expiry upon touching of the barrier it should cost less. Barrier options are also known as path-dependent options as the value of these options not only depends upon the value of the underlying asset at maturity but also on what path the underlying value, that is, the spot exchange rate followed till maturity.

Barrier options are of two types with respect to the life they can have. Barrier options can be either **knock in** or **knock out**. *Knock-in* options come to life only when the barrier is touched, otherwise they remain worthless. *Knock-out* options are those which may be alive at inception but become worthless if the spot touches the barrier. Once alive the barrier options become just like standard options.

The direction, that is, up or down from which the barrier is touched gives rise to two more possibilities for knock-in or knock-out options. They can be *Up* and *In* meaning that if spot goes above barrier they become alive. Similarly, *Down* and *In* options would be alive if spot goes below the barrier. Knock-out options remain a standard option till they expire upon spot touching barrier. They too can be *Up* and *Out* or *Down* and *Out*. Spot price going above the barrier makes option worthless for *Up* and *Out*. Similarly, for *Down* and *Out*, the option expires when spot goes below the barrier. Remember that once out is always out and once alive is always alive.

Barrier options would cost less than the standard options simply because they are not expected to remain alive for the entire time till maturity. If during the life of the option, barrier is never touched then knock-out option would always remain alive and knock-in option would never come to life. While pricing options, the premium includes the entire duration of the option. For barrier options, the life cannot exceed that of standard option, but there are chances that it may (a) become alive for the part of the option period if dead at inception and

(b) become dead during the option period if alive at inception. Hence, lesser premium would be payable for barrier options.

For example, consider a call option on euro with ₹55/€ as strike and ₹60/€ as barrier when spot exchange rate is ₹54/€. An *Up* and *In* option would be one which remains dead till the spot touches a barrier of ₹60/€. Once the exchange rate goes above, the barrier the option comes to life. It remains alive irrespective of the subsequent exchange rates. The payoff would be decided as in case of vanilla call option. Similarly, if the barrier were ₹45/€, a *Down* and *In* option would remain dead till spot is above ₹45/€ and becomes alive when spot goes below ₹45/€. Four types of barrier call options are described in Table 9-9.

Table 9-9
Barrier Options—Call   Assumed Spot Exchange Rate = ₹55/€

KNOCK-IN OPTIONS				
TYPE	Exercise Price, X	Barrier Price, B	Description	Features
Up and In	55	60	Option comes to life only when S goes above the barrier of ₹60/€; else option remains is worthless	Call option suddenly gains intrinsic worth of ₹5/€ the moment it comes to life.
Down and In	55	45	Option comes to life only when S goes below ₹45/€; else option is worthless	A call option gets activated only when spot falls to the barrier of ₹45/€. Thereafter, it behaves like a regular option. The payoff would be zero if ending spot rate is less than exercise, i.e. ₹55/€.
KNOCK-OUT OPTIONS				
Up and Out	55	60	Option is valuable till the S does not touch ₹60/€. It expires when S goes above ₹60/€.	The call option gaining in value with rise in price suddenly loses the entire intrinsic worth of ₹5/€ upon touching the barrier.
Down and Out	55	45	If S goes below ₹45/€ the option becomes worthless.	Call option becomes out-of-money prior to spot touching the barrier. The value consists only of time value. Time value becomes zero upon touching of barrier.

There would be four similar combinations of barrier options involving put.

Asian Options

Asian options also called average options are also popular among importing and exporting firms and for multinationals. Regular options have a payoff based on spot values at the end of option period. Asian options have payoff that is not linked to the price of the underlying asset at maturity, but is determined by the average price during the period of the option. Therefore, they are also called average options. Like barrier options, they too are path-dependent because average during a period is governed by the values of exchange rates at different points of time during the option period. The payoff of average option is given by Eq. 9-8:

$$\text{For Call} \quad \text{Max}(0, S_a - X)$$
$$\text{For Put} \quad \text{Max}(0, X - S_a) \tag{9-8}$$

where S_a is the average of the spot price during the option period

Another kind of Asian option is average strike option in which the strike price is based on the average of the exchange rate that prevailed during the option period. The payoff of the average strike option is based on the final price, S_T, and the average price during the period as given by Eq. 9-9:

$$\text{For Call} \quad \text{Max}(0, S_T - S_a)$$
$$\text{For Put} \quad \text{Max}(0, S_a - S_T) \tag{9-9}$$

where S_a is the average of the spot price during the option period and S_T is the price at maturity of the option

Average strike options ensure that the final price realized or paid during the period is close to average spot rate during the period.

Average options are cheaper than the regular options because the payoff is based on average during the period. Options drive their values from the volatility of the prices. More the volatility, more expensive is the option irrespective of it being a call or a put. End of the period price would be more volatile than the average. Because average itself is a smoothing phenomenon the volatility of average would be less than that of spot rates. Therefore, options based on average would cost less.

Asian options are preferred by many firms for several reasons. One reason is of course the reduced cost of hedging because options based on average cost less than the options based on end-values of spot exchange rate. Besides, average options achieve other objectives better. Most firms are judged by average performance during the period. For example, consider a constantly upward trend of dollar rupee exchange rate during a quarter. The performance of an exporting firm would be considered good if it realized dollar receivables at exchange rate of ₹46, whereas the average during the period was say ₹45 with end-of-quarter value standing at ₹47. When compared with end-of-the-period value, the performance does not appear good.

In Asian option, the payoff is determined on the average. An exporter would buy put option and an importer a call option that has payoff based on for average over the quarter rather than ending values. For example, consider as an alternative to average option, buying of 13 weekly options covering the quarter. The payoff in case of 13 weekly options would be better than the one quarterly average option. The logic is simple. Of the 13 weekly options, some of the options would expire worthless as options may become out-of-the-money. In

case of put options for exporters, the spot rate could be higher than the strike in some of the weeks. These spot values are not counted. In case of average option, none of the values would be ignored as they are used in calculating the average. All the values would be included in the average, and hence the payoff would be smaller than the series of independent equivalent options. This makes average options cheaper than vanilla options. If they hedge for the average rate the performance quarter after quarter would be steadier than if they chose to have conventional options. Hedging strategy based on average rather than end-values would have better credibility.

Asian options are popular because (a) of the convention of judging the performance for a given period over average price for the period rather than end-of-the-period values, (b) averages are more difficult to manipulate than the prices at any single point of time, (c) averages represent fairer view of trends and prices than the end-of-the-period prices, and (d) they are cheaper than the plain vanilla options.

Innovations in Options

Options being primarily OTC product have huge possibilities for innovations by (a) changing the manner of exercising, (b) altering the frequency of exercising (c) specifying different payoff or sharing payoffs (d) switching positions from call to put and put to call (d) combining calls and puts, (e) changing exercising price, etc. Since they are negotiated between the buyer and the seller of options, any of the features of the option can be modified to suit the needs of the hedger. The list continues to grow. We have described here only few of the modifications that are more popular. There exist a vast number of OTC options contracts that are not in public domain. There is a huge variety of options like products that firms have entered to suit their specific needs in terms of hedging and its cost.

SUMMARY

Options are somewhat unique instruments that confer a right to one of the parties to buy/sell an asset (foreign exchange), whereas the other party is obligated to perform at the instance of former. An option to buy foreign currency is known as call and an option to sell is a put. Holder of the option pays a premium to the counterparty called writer or seller to induce him to confer the right on him. The price at which the foreign currency is sold or bought is called the strike price, and the time till which the right can be exercised is called time to expiry. If the option is exercisable only on maturity it is European option else it is American.

Call option provides a positive payoff when spot exchange rate at maturity is more than the exercise price. They are bought when spot exchange rates are expected to rise beyond the strike price of the call. A put option is used when one expects exchange rate to fall and it is exercised when spot price falls below the exercise price. Option is a zero sum game where the gain of the holder is equal to the loss of the writer and vice versa.

Options can either be traded at the exchange or customized between two parties called OTC. Though options contracts are available on exchange, but most users find OTC options more attractive due to their ability to meet specific needs of hedging and negotiation of the option premium.

There is substantial difference between the position taken in options as compared to other derivatives like forwards and futures. Since options do not have equal obligations on counterparties, the payoff is uneven. Options protect the downside while retaining the potential for capturing upside, and therefore they become unique instruments. The exact pricing of options is based on the formulation given by Black and Scholes.

Foreign currency options provide an effective hedge against exposures of foreign currency assumed by exporting and importing firms. Hedging with option is unique. It permits retention of potential of profit in case of favourable movement of exchange rate simultaneously with protection from losses due to unfavourable movement. The protection from unfavorable movement while permitting gains from favourable movement comes at a price that is paid up front. For importer the appropriate hedging instrument is a call option, whereas for exporter seeking protection against depreciating foreign currency, the appropriate strategy is buying a put option.

One of the major issues with hedging through options is the front-end premium. To save on the explicit hedging cost, several innovations have been made in the options market. The cost reduction strategies centre around the writing option to offset fully or partially the cost of options bought for hedging, such as range forwards, sharing part of the risk, sharing part of the payoff, changing exercise prices, and limiting the life of the option. With the same objectives of cost reduction and matching hedging needs, the landscape of options is ever-changing with a lot of innovations taking place in the field.

QUESTIONS

9-1 Describe the following terms briefly with respect to options:
   (a) Payoffs for buyer and seller of call option and put option
   (b) Long and short positions of call and put options
   (c) Determinants of option price
   (d) In-the-Money, At-the-Money, and Out-of-the-Money options
9-2 Comment on the following statements:
   (a) A long position in a call option can be nullified by a short position in put option and vice versa.
   (b) Options are better product to hedge as compared to forwards and futures because they protect downside while retaining potential for upside.
   (c) Option contracts are no good as they cannot offer perfect hedge.
9-3 What are the salient features of the specifications of a currency options contract?
9-4 Differentiate between the following terms:
   (a) Call option and put option
   (b) American option and European option
9-5 Explain hedging with options for receivable and payable.
9-6 Describe the features and advantages of range forward and participating forward contracts?
9-7 Options are lopsided contacts that favour one party at the expense of the other party. Comment.
9-8 What are the barrier options and why do you think they would be cheaper than the conventional options?
9-9 How do Asian options work and why do you think that they are better hedging tools as compared to the conventional options?

PROBLEMS

9-1 Payoff of Currency Options

Find out the payoffs of the following positions on European options on US dollar whose end-of-the-period value is ₹60:
(a) Long call with exercise price of ₹55
(b) Short call with exercise price of ₹80
(c) Long put with exercise price of ₹65
(d) Short put with exercise price of ₹55

9-2 Payoff—Short Call

You have written a call on the exchange rate of US dollar with Rupee with the strike price of ₹55/$, charging a premium of ₹1.00. Find the payoff at various exchange rates, ranging from ₹50 to ₹60. At what levels of exchange rate, would you turn from profit to loss?

9-3 Payoff—Long Put

As an exporter, you are expecting to receive euro 10,000. You have bought a put option with strike exchange rate of ₹70 per euro and have paid a premium of ₹1.75. Depict the payoff of put option, receivable, and receivable combined with the put, from exchange rate of ₹65 to ₹75 per euro.

9-4 Black Scholes Valuation for Options on Currency

The spot rate for euro is ₹68.00. A call option with strike of ₹69.00 expiring in three months is available. What would be the premium on the call option if risk-free interest rate for Indian rupee and euro are 12% and 8%, respectively, and the volatility of rupee-euro exchange rates is 20%. Find the value of the put for same parameters.

9-5 Hedging with Call

Good Health Ltd (GHL) has imported a capsule-making machine from Britain worth £100,000 for which the payment is due in six months' time. The exchange rate prevailing is ₹85/£. In six months' time, British pound is likely to appreciate to an estimated level of ₹90/£. A call option and a put option with strike exchange rate of ₹87/£ are available at ₹1.50 and ₹3.00 respectively. Why and with what option should GHL hedge its exposure of British pound? If it does, what maximum exchange rate would it pay to liquidate the liability?

9-6 Hedging with Range Forward

Auto Comp Ltd is an exporting firm and is very conscious of exchange rates they realize on their receivables as well as cost of hedging. The current spot rate is ₹50.50/$ and they believe that rupee would be depreciating further. However, they decide to hedge by buying put option with strike of ₹50.50 at a cost of ₹0.70. In order to offset the cost, they also write a call option with a strike of 51.50 because they can afford to forego any gains beyond this level. Since they believe that rupee would not be appreciating, and in order to recover the cost of hedging they also write a put option with strike of ₹49.50 also selling at ₹0.35.

For a range of possible exchange rates at the end from ₹48.00 to ₹55.00, (a) find out the payoff of all the three positions, (b) find out the value of receivable, and (c) depict the position graphically.

9-7 Hedging with Options

Assume that the spot exchange rate for US dollar is ₹45, 3-m forward contract is offered at ₹45.50 per dollar. Also call and put options at various strikes are available. A put for strike of ₹45.50/$ sells at a premium of ₹0.70 and a call with strike of ₹46.50 is selling at ₹0.35. For a likely range of exchange rates from ₹40.00 to ₹50.00 at the end of three months, tabulate the value of receivable for the exporter if (a) he is unhedged, (b) buys a forward contract at ₹45.50 (c) buys a put with strike of ₹45.50, and (d) buys a range forward with market between ₹45.50 and ₹46.50. Depict the payoffs and values under different scenarios.

Currency and Interest Rate Swaps

LEARNING OBJECTIVES

This chapter aims at

+ knowing about the historical development that caused swaps to come into being
+ describing the basic concept of swaps
+ distinguishing between different types of interest rates and currency swaps
+ hedging interest rate risk and exchange rate risk through swaps
+ using swap as an instrument of reducing financing cost
+ describing the role of swap intermediary
+ valuing swaps as pair of bonds and/or as series of forward contracts

CONTENTS

Introduction
    Interest Rate and Exchange Rate Risks
    Swap—Definition and Development
Types of Swaps
Currency Swaps
Hedging against Exchange Rate Risk with Currency Swap
Reducing Cost of Funds with Currency Swap
    Distinguishing Features of Currency Swap
Interest Rate Swaps
Features of Interest Rate Swap

Applications of Interest Rate Swaps
    Transforming Fixed/Floating Rate Liabilities
    Transforming Nature of Assets
    Hedging with Interest Rate Swaps
    Reducing Cost of Funds
Rationale for Swaps—The Comparative Advantage
Need for Swap Intermediary
Types of Interest Rate Swaps
    Fixed to Floating, Floating to Fixed, Basis Swap

INTRODUCTION

In this world of increasing globalization and fast reduction in barriers to flow of capital, the scope of corporate treasurers as well as financial intermediaries has widened considerably. Corporate managers and financial intermediaries are today required to evaluate borrowing and investing alternatives on global basis. It is no more necessary for borrowers and investors to remain confined to the local currency.

The good part of increasing globalization is the expanding menu of investment alternatives, and the flip side being that as the choices increase, the risk associated with these alternatives too becomes complicated. Borrowing and investing in different currencies expose the firms to other risks that are absent with domestic investing/borrowing. These risks are emanating from the fluctuations in exchange rates in the tenure of investment/borrowing. While the exchange rates are known in the beginning, the ending exchange rates at the time of maturity are unknown. In this chapter, we shall attempt to comprehend such risks and ways of managing them specifically with a typical instrument called swap.

Interest Rate and Exchange Rate Risks

All global firms conduct business in multiple currencies and generate cash flows in local currencies. This necessitates a raise in financial resources in currencies other than the home currency of the multinational corporation (MNC). Though an MNC may have a choice of funding the subsidiary's operations by remittances from home, but at times it may become rather inconvenient to manage. There would be too many transactions converting currencies back and forth. Further, the MNCs also have a choice of raising loans in various currencies due to their presence in global markets and access to multilateral financial agencies. They also have requisite credibility to raise resources in multiple currencies. For example, they may face a choice of loans as follows:

- A US dollar loan with 4% fixed coupon
- A Japanese yen denominated loan with LIBOR + 1% floating rate interest
- A British pound floating rate note at LIBOR + 100 bps
- Indian rupee denominated bond with 10% coupon

These choices give rise to many questions such as the following: 'Would 4% dollar loan be cheaper than LIBOR + 100 bps of yen loan or would 4% dollar loan be cheaper than 10% rupee loan? Such questions clearly reflect the interlinkages of currencies, their exchange rates, and interest rates applicable. The relationship of exchange rates and interest rates is a complex matter in the real life, though under ideal conditions international Fisher effect discussed earlier presents a simple relationship. Under ideal conditions, interest rates and exchange rates must move in tandem and simultaneously.

In this and the following chapter, we examine various instruments that are available to manage exchange rate risk and interest rate risk.

Swap—Definition and Development

In very simple terms, swap is an exchange of series of cash flows where one party pays a stream of cash in exchange of receiving another stream of cash over a period of time. The value of cash flows is decided on the basis of two different sets of parametes. For example, one may receive periodic cash flows in terms of rupees and pay periodic cash flows in US dollars. Similarly, the exchange of series of cash flows at periodic intervals can take place with one series determined on fixed interest rate basis, whereas the other series may be governed by latest interest rates prevailing at the time of cash flows, the floating rate of interest.

The concept of swap is said to have emerged from the regulatory environment for capital flows that prevailed in the 1970s. Forced with the problem of funding the subsidiaries in foreign countries, MNCs helped each other by funding foreign operations through parallel or back-to-back loans. When MNCs operating in various countries could not remit funds back and forth among their subsidiaries due to exchange controls exercised by various governments on the capital flows, they came out with innovations of back-to-back or parallel loans among themselves.

Parallel loans involve four parties—two MNCs and two subsidiaries in two different countries. Imagine Firm A in Country A and Firm B in Country B. Both the firms have subsidiaries in the other country. These subsidiaries require funding in the currency of the country where they are located but funded by the parent. Since the currencies of the parent and the subsidiary are different, it requires flow of money from one country to another and currency conversion. If there were no controls over cross-border flow of capital, no problem is encountered in funding the subsidiaries by the parent MNCs. However, when the capital controls are enforced the flow of funds back and forth between the parent and the subsidiary becomes impossible. To overcome the regulation, Firm A in Country A can fund the subsidiary of B in exchange of Firm B, agreeing to fund the subsidiary of Firm A in Country B. This would obviate the need of flow of capital as well as conversion of one currency into another. Such an arrangement is called back-to-back or parallel loans and is depicted in Figure 10-1.

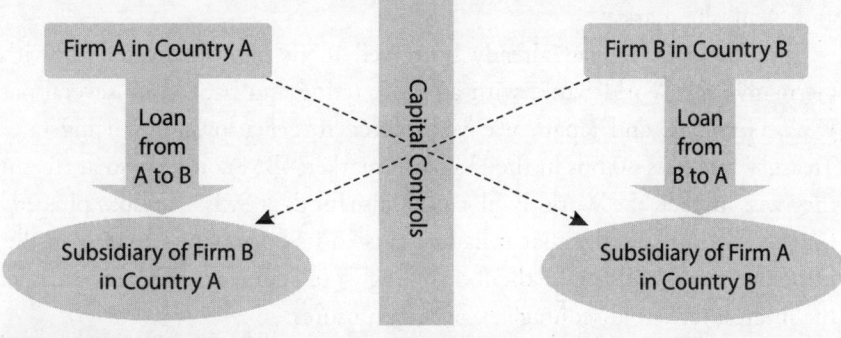

Figure 10-1
Schematic Representation of Parallel Loans

Besides overcoming the regulatory controls, there are other economic advantages that caused the development of swaps as a full-blown financial product and became popular even

after the removal of regulatory controls. By this simple arrangement, each firm has access to capital markets in foreign country and make use of their comparative advantage of borrowing in different capital markets. The growth of the swaps has been so phenomenal that in 1984, a need for standardization, uniform practices for documentation, trading, and settlement was felt that led to the formation of International Swaps and Derivatives Association (ISDA).

The evolution of swap as a financial instrument took place out of the constraints and the regulatory controls with respect to cross-border capital flows faced by the large corporations in the 1970s. Upon removal of restrictions on the capital flows, these loans later developed into a full financial product called swaps because it was realized that in overcoming the regulatory environment, these loans saved the transaction costs associated with currency conversion. Due to cost-effectiveness of the arrangement, the market has grown many times despite removal of capital flow controls.

The World Bank IBM Currency Swap The idea of swap was provided by a historical deal in August 1981 when the World Bank entered a swap deal with IBM through Saloman Brothers. IBM and the World Bank entered a deal where the two exchanged the liabilities of US dollar on one hand and Swiss franc and Deutsche marks on the other side. It was the first-ever currency swap that recognized the potential of the instrument in saving the cost of borrowing for both the parties involved.

The World Bank involved in lending to developing countries for various projects was looking for funding at least cost. The cost consideration was paramount for them because of their inability to charge higher rates of interest from developing countries. As in August 1981, the prevailing interest rates in US dollar were as high as 17%. In contrast, the interest rates in Switzerland and Germany were 8% and 11%, respectively. The interest rate scenario suggested depreciation of dollar by about 9% against Swiss franc and 6% against Deutsche mark. The World Bank believed that depreciation of dollar would not be as much as suggested by interest rate differentials and, hence, it is cheaper to borrow in Swiss franc and Deutsche mark.

The World Bank had already borrowed to its allowed limits in Switzerland and West Germany. The World Bank, with an AAA rating and backed by several nations, such as the USA, Germany, and Japan, was well-placed to get a lower financing rate in US dollars at Treasury rate plus 40 bps in the US bond market. IBM could do so at treasury plus 55 bps. In the Swiss market, the World Bank could raise funds at Swiss Treasury plus 20 bps. The problem for the World Bank was that it had exhausted its borrowing capacity in the Swiss francs and Deutsche marks and any further borrowing would come at a higher cost as lenders start raising the interest rates to discourage excessive exposures.

In contrast to this, IBM could raise funds in Swiss market at the best rate. It could borrow at Swiss treasury rate and held advantage of 20 bps over the World Bank, but had a poorer rate than the World Bank if it were to borrow in US dollars. At the same time, IBM believed that US dollar would depreciate much beyond the interest rate differentials of US dollar vis-á-vis Swiss franc and Deutsche mark and, therefore, funding in US dollar is more beneficial. IBM already had the loans outstanding in Swiss francs and Deutsche marks as given in Table 10-1, which if serviced in US dollar would save cost.

The desire of the World Bank to raise money in Swiss franc and Deutsche mark and the existing obligations of IBM in these currencies along with its willingness to raise funds in US dollar created a common meeting ground for the two. Contrasting views of IBM and the World Bank regarding expected depreciation of US dollar (World Bank anticipated lesser depreciation and IBM expected more depreciation of dollar than reflected by interest rate differentials) were contributing to fruitful engagement of a swap deal.

The liabilities of IBM for loans in Swiss franc and Deutsche mark added to US$205.48 million in present value terms as shown in Table 10-1. IBM was willing to pay 16% on US dollar loan. After adjusting for the issue expenses, the World Bank issued debt aggregating US$210 million with maturity of 31 March 1986 coinciding with IBM's loans. Subsequent to the debt raised by the World Bank, cash flows were exchanged where IBM paid US dollar obligations at 16% for a principal of US$210 million and the World Bank paid Swiss franc and Deutsche mark obligations of IBM. A schematic diagram of the swap is presented in Figure 10-2. The flow of principal from the World Bank to IBM and vice versa and its repayment at the end of swap were not required. These flows are shown only for the completeness of understanding of the swap mechanism.

Table 10-1
Details of Loans of IBM for Swap with World Bank

	Swiss Franc Loan	Deutsche Mark Loan
Principal, *Millions*	200.00	300.00
Due date for bullet repayment of principal	30 March 1986	30 March 1986
Annual interest out flow due 30 March each year, *Millions*	12.375	30.000
Effective interest rate	6.187%	10.000%
Interest rate prevailing in August 1981	8.00%	11.00%
Present value of loans in August 1981, *Millions*	191.37	301.32
Exchange Rate prevailing in August 1981, *Units/$*	2.18	2.56
Equivalent dollar of present value of loans, *Millions*	87.78	117.70

The advantage of the swap arrangement was that IBM got US dollar at a cheaper rate, whereas the World Bank got Swiss franc and Deutsche mark loan at a cheaper rate, capitalizing on the strength of each other in the respective currencies. Both IBM and the World Bank got what they wanted at cheaper rate. If the World Bank borrowed US dollars and lent them to IBM at US Treasury + 40 bps, it would lose no money and IBM would get a better rate. If IBM borrowed Swiss francs and lent them to the World Bank at Swiss Treasury + 10 bps, IBM would make 10 bps, and so would the World Bank. If both of these loans were done, it would result in a profit of 15 bps to IBM and a profit of 10 bps to the World Bank.

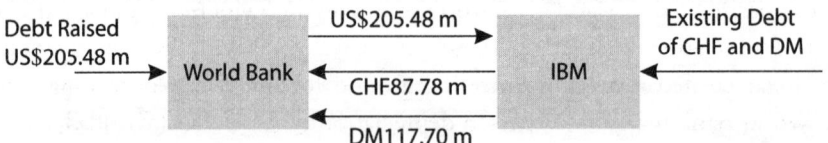

August 1981: Raising Loans and Exchanging Principal

March 1982–March 1986: Exchanging Interest Obligations and Re-exchange of Principal

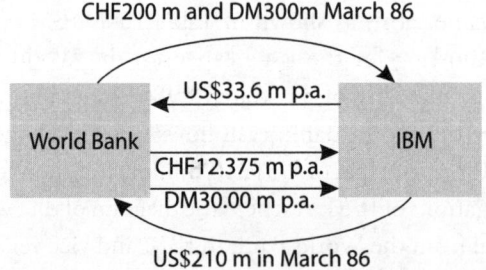

Figure 10-2
Swap Transaction of IBM and World Bank

Banks and financial intermediaries were quick to grab the idea and soon started broking the deals of swaps for a fee. The swap had greater appeal in saving the borrowing cost rather than managing the risk. Since the IBM–World Bank swap, the swap market has grown leaps and bounds and has possibly become the largest derivative product in terms of notional values involved.

Back-to-back/Parallel loans posed several difficulties of finding matching parties with identical needs in terms of amount of principal, timing, and duration of loans; periodicity and nature (fixed or variable) of interest payments, all of which must match to conclude as a successful deal. Solutions to these problems were found by intermediary banks, and they later became dealers in swaps from mere arrangers of swaps between two parties. They assumed the counterparty risk, did warehousing and became market makers by offering swap rates. Swap then became an extremely popular full blown financial product.

The underlying principle that forms the basis of swap is the exploitation of the comparative advantage of the two counterparties, as was done in the World Bank–IBM swap. Although the first swap was a currency swap between the World Bank and IBM, the swap market has been mainly driven by the fixed for floating interest rate swaps market.

TYPES OF SWAPS

We defined swap as an exchange of a series of cash flows between two parties as agreed upon according to the terms of the contract. There are a minimum of two legs and a minimum of two parties to a swap. What one party pays, the counterparty receives. The two legs of the cash flows are determined on different bases. Swaps are mainly of two types:

1. Currency swaps
2. Interest rate swaps

In a *currency swap*, the basis of exchange of future cash flows is exchange rate. For example, one party agrees to pay in US dollars and in exchange receives euros based on the spot exchange rate prevailing at the inception of the swap.

In an *interest rate swap*, the basis of exchange of cash flows between two parties is interest rate. One leg of the swap may be on fixed interest rate, whereas the other would be on floating rate. This is referred to as plain vanilla swap.

Apart from interest rates and currency rates, the formula for determination of the periodic cash flows can be equity returns, commodity prices, etc. In essence, one of the cash flow would be fixed, called fixed leg, whereas the other cash flow called floating leg would be variable, depending upon the value of the variable identified for the swap.

Swap for the exchange of floating rate in one currency with a floating rate in another currency is referred to as a *basis swap*. More complex swap structures involve two currencies with varying interest rates, that is, fixed interest for one and floating rate for another currency. Such swaps are called *cocktail swaps*.

Swap may also be categorized as asset swap or liability swap. Where the exchange of cash flows is for one liability, for another it is called liability swap. Similarly, we may have the same structure for one kind of asset for another called an *asset swap*.

Financial engineers have also created various forms of exotic swaps as mentioned here:

- *Forward swap*: A swap that is entered now but starts in future.
- *Amortizing swap*: A swap where the notional principal amount reduces in a predetermined way.
- *Quanto swap*: A swap where the payment is done in another currency than the one in which the swap is denominated.
- *Equity swap*: A swap that is between the dividend and capital gain realized on an equity index and a floating (or fixed) leg.
- *Credit default swap*: A swap where one pays a fixed spread to be protected against certain credit event or default of a specified bond.

We shall be discussing now currency swaps and interest rate swaps in details with their features and applications.

CURRENCY SWAPS

Where the exchange of cash flows is in two different currencies determined on the basis of exchange rates, it is known as currency swap. The first swap between the World Bank and IBM was a currency swap where the cash flows in different currencies were made on the basis of fixed interest rates on all the three currencies involved. Currency swaps can be used in several ways as described here:

HEDGING AGAINST EXCHANGE RATE RISK WITH CURRENCY SWAP

Currency swaps cover the exchange rate risk. It is a way of converting liabilities or assets from one currency to another. By doing so, asset and liabilities can be hedged against exchange rate risks. For example, an Indian firm having a foreign currency loan assumes foreign exchange risk in servicing the loan. The firm can convert it into a rupee loan with a swap and eliminate exchange rate risk on foreign currency loan.

Let us consider an example to see how MNCs face currency risks and how these risks can be overcome through a swap deal. Assume that an Indian firm needs funds for its European operations. For example, Tata Steel may need to fund its operation in Europe through Corus being a subsidiary. The firm raises funds in Indian rupees at a fixed interest rate and services this loan in Indian rupees. The funds raised in rupees are converted in euro to fund operations in Europe. The operations in Europe generate income in euro. The cash flows in euro are converted back to rupee to service the loan. The Indian firm is facing a risk if rupee strengthens against euro as it receives lesser rupee amount for the fixed income earned in euro.

Similarly, imagine a Swiss firm Holcim (a cement major) looking for global business in cement needs to fund acquisition of ACC and Ambuja Cement in India. It does so by raising funds in euro. The Swiss firm faces the same risk. Its earnings are in Indian rupees and the liabilities need to be serviced in euro. Like an Indian firm, Holcim also faces the risk of shortfall in euro if it appreciates (or rupee depreciates/weakens).

The vulnerability of both Tata Steel and Holcim is due to the uncertainty of exchange rate fluctuations that may be in either direction because assets and liabilities are in different currencies. While depreciation of euro harms the Indian firm, it benefits the Swiss firm. In case euro appreciates, the Swiss firm is at a loss, whereas the Indian firm gains. The risks for both the firms arise because it is not known what direction exchange rates would take. Even though it is possible to make an estimate of the likely direction of exchange rates based on many theories, such as Purchasing Power Parity and Interest Rate Parity, there could be contrary views as was the case with the World Bank and IBM. However, we are concerned here with the unexpected and adverse movement of exchange rates as everybody factors-in the likely movement by making estimates. We also recognize that these estimates are likely to fall apart.

The element of risk can be removed if the Indian firm and the Swiss firm enter into a swap as depicted in Figure 10-3. A look at this would reveal that the Indian firm has financed its European assets by creating rupee liability. This liability to be serviced by income generations in euro faces currency exchange rate risk as euro may depreciate in future. Likewise, the Swiss firm having funded Indian operations through borrowing in euro would be serviced by rupee income that needs to be converted to euro. Rupee depreciation would be damaging for the Swiss firm because it would make lesser euro available for service of the euro loan.

Under the swap transaction, the Indian firm may agree to pay the euro liability of the Swiss firm from its operations in Europe, obviating the need of conversion of euro into Indian rupees to service the Indian rupee liability. Similarly, the Swiss firm can use its Indian rupee cash to repay the liabilities of the Indian firm, again eliminating the need of exchanging the currency. Since no currency crosses its borders, the risk of fluctuating the exchange rate is automatically extinguished.

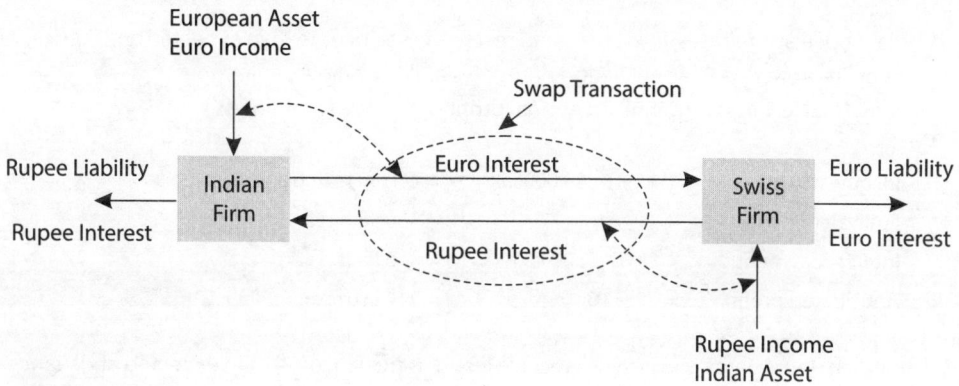

Figure 10-3
Currency Swap: Converting Liability from One Currency to Another

The mismatch of cash flows for both the firms can be eliminated by the Swiss firm agreeing to pay rupee generated out of its Indian operations to Indian firm in exchange of Indian firm agreeing to pay euro generated out of its European operations. Thus, the rupee asset income that flows to the Indian firm facilitates the service of rupee liability of the Swiss firm and vice versa (indicated by dotted interconnecting lines in Figure 10-3). Through the swap, both the firms will have assets (income) and liabilities (loan) translated in the same currency, eliminating the currency risk.

Exercise 10-1
Swap to Hedge against Exchange Rate Risk

Assume that an Indian software firm Inso Ltd wants to acquire a US firm with a cost of $2.00 crore. For this purpose, it raises the required capital of ₹90 crore (current exchange rate of ₹45/$) at 12%. The US acquisition is expected to yield 15% return. At the same time, a US engineering firm USENG Inc. is negotiating a joint venture to contribute US$2.00 crore which promises to yield 15% return in India. USENG Inc. raises the required dollars at a cost of 8%. Assume that all liabilities need annual payments.
1. Examine the risk faced by Inso Ltd and USENG Inc. if
   - Rupee appreciates to 44, 42, 40, 38, and 36 per dollar for next five years
   - Rupee depreciates to 46, 48, 50, 52, and 54 per dollar for next five years
2. Show how a swap arrangement between the two can help eliminate the risk of exchange rate fluctuations.

Solution
Inso Ltd is targeting an annual profit of ₹270 lakh as follows:

Income in US dollar	= 15% of $200 lakh	= $30 lakh p.a.
Equivalent rupee		= ₹1,350 lakh p.a.
Interest payment	= 12% of ₹9,000 lakh	= ₹1,080 lakh p.a.
Anticipated profit	= 1,350 − 1,080	= ₹270 lakh p.a.

If Indian rupee appreciates, Inso Ltd would receive lesser income than expected and, hence, carries a risk of reduction in profit due to appreciation of rupee, liability being fixed in rupee.

Similarly, USENG Inc. is targeting an annual profit of $14 lakh as follows:

Income in rupees	= 15% of $9,000 lakh	= ₹1,350 lakh p.a.
Equivalent dollar		= $30 lakh p.a.
Interest payment	= 8% of $200 lakh	= $16 lakh p.a.
Anticipated profit	= 30 – 16	= $14 lakh p.a.

If Indian rupee depreciates, the firm will receive lesser annual income than expected and, hence, face a risk of reduction in profit to the extent of depreciation in rupee, liability being fixed in US dollar.

While appreciation of rupee is good for the US firm and detrimental to the Indian firm, the position reverses if rupee depreciates. The impact on the spreads of both the firms for the exchange rate scenario is presented as follows:

All figures in lakhs

Year	Exchange Rate (₹/$)	Indian Firm			US Firm			
		Income US$	Equivalent ₹	₹ Spread	Income ₹	Equivalent $	$ Spread	
5	54.00	30.00	1,620.00	540.00	1,350.00	25.00	9.00	Favourable for Indian Firm and Unfavourable for US Firm
4	52.00	30.00	1,560.00	480.00	1,350.00	25.96	9.96	
3	50.00	30.00	1,500.00	420.00	1,350.00	27.00	11.00	
2	48.00	30.00	1,440.00	360.00	1,350.00	28.13	12.13	
1	46.00	30.00	1,380.00	300.00	1,350.00	29.35	13.35	
Now	45.00	30.00	1,350.00	270.00	1,350.00	30.00	14.00	
1	44.00	30.00	1,320.00	240.00	1,350.00	30.68	14.68	Favourable for US Firm and Unfavourable for Indian Firm
2	42.00	30.00	1,260.00	180.00	1,350.00	32.14	16.14	
3	40.00	30.00	1,200.00	120.00	1,350.00	33.75	17.75	
4	38.00	30.00	1,140.00	60.00	1,350.00	35.53	19.53	
5	36.00	30.00	1,080.00	–	1,350.00	37.50	21.50	

2. By entering into a swap arrangement, both the firms eliminate the volatility of spread. Under the swap arrangement at a current rate of ₹45/$

US firm will pay Indian ₹1,350 lakh annually earned out of its joint venture in India.

Indian firm will pay $30 lakh annually earned out of acquisition in the USA.

A schematic diagram of the swap arrangement is shown below. The spread after the swap arrangement becomes fixed for both the firms irrespective of exchange rate. The US firm will lock in a return of $14 lakh and the Indian firm will assure a profit of ₹270 lakh after the swap arrangement. Without the swap, the income for both the firms in the USA and India were subject to fluctuations due to currency exchange rate.

Currency Swap: Converting Liability from one Currency to Another

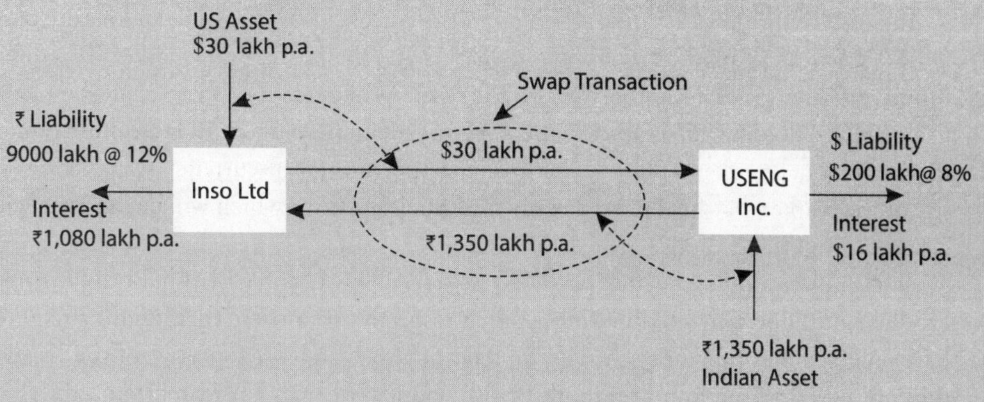

Cash Flows after Swap	Figures in Lakh p.a.	
	Inso Ltd	USENG Inc.
Income earned abroad	+ $30	+₹1,350
Paid to counterparty	− $30	−₹1,350
Received from counterparty	+₹1,350	+ $30
Interest obligation	−₹1,080	− $16
Spread	+₹270	+ $14

REDUCING COST OF FUNDS WITH CURRENCY SWAP

Besides hedging, currency swap can also be effectively used for reducing the cost of funds. The ability of MNCs to leverage their size, name, and reputation makes swap an attractive tool for reducing cost. The guiding principle is the theory of comparative advantage. Comparative advantage results from two distinct and separate markets governed by an altogether different set of rules and operating in vastly different economic conditions.

Credit Quality Spread The credit quality spread refers to charging a different cost or price (interest rate) because of the quality of the buyer. In terms of borrowing, a firm may hold an advantage over another firm because of its larger size, better name, and reputation. Due to the difference in the credibility of the firms, the financial markets offer different lending rates called the quality spread. The quality spread in domestic and international markets is based on the credit rating of the parties.

In the International markets, the credit rating for the same firm may vary substantially across nations as firms are generally better known in their own country and lesser known in a foreign country. Further, exchange control regulations of the land may discourage borrowing by non-residents by stipulating a higher rate than what is applicable for residents. Therefore, the quality spread could be greater in international financial markets.

The quality spread varies depending upon the currency of borrowing and nature of interest rates. The spread changes in the fixed rate market and the floating rate market. This differential in interest rates generates opportunities for swap. While quality spread could be identical in fixed rate and floating rate market in the domestic financial markets, they are more pronounced in international markets. This creates greater opportunities in currency swaps. However, the size of the market may be limited to only multinational firms which will be the beneficiaries of currency swap transactions.

As a simple example, consider two MNCs—an American and a British. Both the firms enjoy excellent and equivalent credit ratings in their respective countries. Their funding requirements have enlarged and they need to raise capital at cheapest rate, irrespective of the location and the currency. An American firm needs British pounds, whereas a British firm needs US dollars. The following is the cost of capital for two firms in the USA and Britain in their respective currencies:

	US Market Dollar Funds	British Market Pound Funds
US Firm	8%	6%
British Firm	12%	4%
Advantage—British Firm	−4%	2%

Clearly and naturally, the US firm enjoys an advantage over the British firm in the USA, and British firm commands more credibility than the US firm in Britain. The comparative advantage here is 6%. If the two firms borrow in the required currency, the total cost of funds will be 18%, that is, the US firm borrows pound at 6% and the British firm borrows US dollar at 12%. However, if they borrow as per the comparative advantage theory and exchange each other's commitment, the total cost of funds can be reduced to 12% with the British firm borrowing in British pound at 4% and the US firm borrowing dollar at 8%. Both the firms can benefit by 6% in aggregate if they enter into a swap arrangement wherein

(a) US firm mobilizes capital in the USA in dollars at 8%,
(b) British firm raises funds in the British market in pound at 4%,
(c) The two firms complement the requirements of each other by entering a swap where the US firm lends dollars to the British firm and in exchange the British firm lends British pounds to the US firm,
(d) They service the debt of each other till maturity, and
(e) Finally, exchange back the principal amounts upon redemption.

The schematic diagram of the swap arrangement and the cost of funds for both the firms is shown in Figure 10-4.

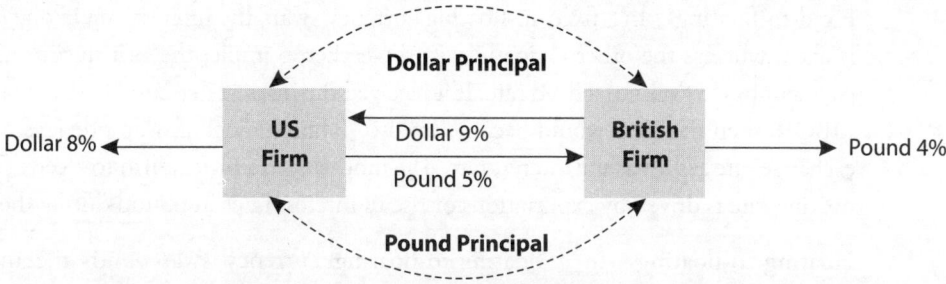

	US Firm	British Firm
1. Payment to investors	US Dollar 8%	Pound 4%
2. Payment to counter party	Pound 5%	US Dollar 9%
3. Receipt from counter party	US Dollar 9%	Pound 5%
Cost of borrowing (1 + 2 − 3)	Pound 4%	US Dollar 8%

Figure 10-4
Currency Swap to Reduce Cost of Funds

It is assumed in the example that the US firm and the British firm exchanged the principal amount of borrowing as well as repaid the principal at maturity. Since the flow of principal would be at the prevailing exchange rates, the spot market could be used to convert one currency into another, both at the time of raising funds and at its redemption.

Through the swap, the US firm obtains the required pounds at 4% as against 6% if it accessed the British market on its own; a benefit of 2%. Similarly, if the British firm accessed the US market for dollar funds, it would cost 12% but with US firm accessing the US market and then entering into a swap would provide a saving of 4%. The aggregate benefit of the two firms is equal to the comparative advantage of 6%. This advantage may be shared between the two firms in the desired ratio. Here, it is 2% for the US firm and 4% for the British firm. Sharing of benefit of swap is a matter of negotiations between the two parties that decides the quantum of cash flows to be exchanged between the two.

Currency swap just described is a classic structure. However, innovations in the field are ample and each swap entered by the firms has its own features. It is not a standardized product but remains an over-the-counter (OTC) product, which leaves much scope to the negotiating parties to settle terms and conditions of the swap. Currency swaps may be broadly classified as follows:

Fixed-to-fixed In a fixed-to-fixed currency swap, the interest rates in the two currencies involved are fixed. In the example just discussed, both the firms were paying fixed interest rates and, hence, the swap was fixed-to-fixed.

Fixed-to-floating In a fixed-to-floating currency swap, the interest rate in one of the currencies is fixed, whereas the other is floating. In the earlier example, the British firm made the interest payment in US dollar at a fixed rate. If it received the interest in pound based on a benchmark, say LIBOR, then the swap would become fixed-to-floating. Such a swap provides hedge against the exchange rate as well as the interest rate. The motive of the British firm to receive pound interest at floating rate is driven by expectations of rise in interest rates in pound during the tenure of swap.

Floating-to-floating In a floating-to-floating currency swap, both the interest rates are floating but in different currencies. In the earlier example, if the British firm made interest payment in dollar based at a prime rate in the USA while receiving pound interest based on LIBOR from the US firm, then such a swap would be floating-to-floating.

INTEREST RATE SWAPS

Though the first swap deal was essentially a currency swap, the more dominant of the swaps in today's market is interest rate swap. Of the two legs of cash flows in an interest rate swap, one is based on fixed rate and another is based on floating rate. Such a swap is also called a plain vanilla swap. A swap between two firms A and B is depicted in Figure 10-5 with A paying fixed interest rate at 6.50%, whereas receiving floating at LIBOR + 10 bps. The currency involved in the swap is same.

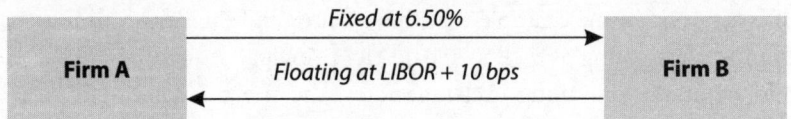

Firm A pays fixed and receives floating, and Firm B pays floating and receives fixed. At inception of swap, both payments are equal. Firm A and Firm B hold opposite views regarding future interest rates.

Figure 10-5
Plain Vanilla Interest Rate Swap

When two parties enter a swap agreement, they essentially believe that the fixed and floating rates are equal. In Figure 10-5, it would be fair to assume that at the inception of the swap, Firm A believes that fixed payment of 6.50% is equal to the receipt of LIBOR + 10 bps. Firm B too believes in similar fashion when it agrees to pay LIBOR + 10 bps for receiving fixed 6.50%. However, their views with regard to future scenarios of interest rate are opposite. Firm A believes that the interest rate would go up in future and intends to receive in the floating leg more than what it pays in the fixed leg. Firm B holds contrary views of falling interest rates and, hence, anticipates lesser payment in future for receiving a higher amount of fixed interest.

FEATURES OF INTEREST RATE SWAP

With the rationale of swap explained, let us have a look at some of the terminologies used in swap. Assuming that the swap between Firm A and Firm B as depicted in Figure 10-5 is (i) for a period of five years, (ii) with semi-annual payment of interest, (iii) on a notional principal of US$500 million, the cash flows for Firm A for 10 semi-annual periods for an assumed LIBOR would be as per Table 10-2. The cash flows of Firm B would be opposite to that of Firm A.

Table 10-2
Cash Flow under Swap for Firm A

Notional Principal: US$500 Million

Time Months	Assumed LIBOR	Cash flow, $ million		
		Fixed Leg	Floating Leg	Net
0	6.30%			
6	6.45%	−16.250	16.000	−0.250
12	6.55%	−16.250	16.375	0.175
18	6.60%	−16.250	16.625	0.375
24	6.45%	−16.250	16.750	0.500
30	6.50%	−16.250	16.375	0.125
36	6.20%	−16.250	16.500	0.250
42	6.00%	−16.250	15.750	−0.500
48	6.15%	−16.250	15.250	−1.000
54	6.35%	−16.250	15.625	−0.625
60		−16.250	16.125	−0.125

With the context of the example just described, the following salient features of the swap may be noted:

1. **Effective date:** As per the definition of ISDA, the trade date is the date on which the parties agree to the terms of a contract. The *effective date* is the date on which the parties begin calculating accrued obligations, such as fixed and floating interest payment obligations on an interest rate swap. All the cash flows pertaining to fixed leg (as in column 3 of Table 10-2) are known at the time of entering the swap at $T = 0$. The cash flow for the first floating rate is also known on the effective date.
2. **Resetting of floating leg cash flow:** With known cash flows of the fixed leg, the cash flow for floating leg of the swap is determined one period in advance when the floating rate becomes known. Therefore, at the time of entering the swap, both the amount cash flows are known. However, the first exchange of cash flow would occur only at $T = 6$ m with the floating rate determined at $T = 0$. With LIBOR at 6.30%, the cash flow for $T = 6$ m for the floating leg would be 6.40% (LIBOR + 10 bps). The cash flow of the next floating leg at $T = 12$ m would be similarly set at $T = 6$ m. The date on which the next floating rate payment is decided is called *Reset Date*. One may observe that LIBOR at $T = 60$ m is immaterial to the swap as the final cash flow of floating leg at $T = 60$ m would be set at LIBOR prevailing at $T = 54$ m.
3. **Notional principal:** In an interest rate swap, the exchange of principal is not required. It is an instrument to hedge against the interest rate changes. No purpose is served by exchanging the

principal. However, for determination of cash flows of interest, a principal is assumed. This is notional in nature. As per ISDA, notional principal of a derivative contract is a hypothetical underlying quantity upon which interest rate or other payment obligations are computed.

4. **Differential (net) cash flow**: Like the principal is not required to be exchanged, the cash flows of the two legs of swap need not be exchanged separately. Exchanging the net cash flow would serve the purpose of hedging. For example, for Firm A, the first cash flow of the swap requires a payment of $16.25 million under fixed leg for a receipt of US$16.00 million under floating leg, which is equivalent to the net payment of US$0.250 million by Firm A to Firm B. For an assumed rate of LIBOR, the net cash flows for Firm A are shown in the last column of Table 10-2. Negative sign implies cash outflows for Firm A. The cash flows of the Firm B would be opposite to that of Firm A.

5. **Convention for fixed and floating legs**: The figures of cash flows shown in Table 10-2 are simplified assuming the two semi-annual payments as equal and half of annual interest rate. However, the practice may be somewhat different. The method of calculation of interest on the two legs can be defined in the swap agreement being an OTC product. However, the convention to calculate the two legs of interest may be different. For example, it may be as follows:

For Fixed Leg : Actual/365
For Floating Leg : Actual/360,
(As is the practice in the money markets)

Actual implies that cash flows would be computed on the basis of the actual number of days elapsed in the semi-annual period. Fixed leg and floating leg would assume 365 days and 360 days in a year, respectively. To illustrate, if the actual number of days in the a six-month period is 182, the amount of interest for both the legs for the first cash flow would be somewhat different and would be as follows:

$$\text{For fixed leg: Principal} \times \text{Interest rate} \times \frac{\text{No. of days}}{365}$$

$$= 500,00,000 \times 0.065 \times \frac{182}{365} = \$16,205,479$$

$$\text{For floating leg: Principal} \times \text{Interest rate} \times \frac{\text{No. of days}}{360}$$

$$= 500,000,000 \times 0.064 \times \frac{182}{360} = \$16,177,778$$

APPLICATIONS OF INTEREST RATE SWAPS

Interest rate swaps have several applications like any other derivative. Swaps can be used for transforming the floating rate asset/liability to fixed rate asset/liability or vice versa that are required for purposes of hedging against interest rate risk. However, the major application that has led to tremendous growth of this financial instrument is the potential of saving the borrowing cost. These are discussed as follows.

Transforming Fixed Rate/Floating Rate Liabilities

Interest rate swap is a very efficient and effective instrument that transforms the nature of liability either from fixed to floating rate or from floating to fixed interest rate. Consider that Firm A has issued semi-annual floating rate bonds at MIBOR plus 25 bps. The bonds have five years remaining for maturity. The yields in the bond have been rising. The bond indenture does not allow calling back of the bonds and firm faces rising cost of capital.

Swap offers an easy solution wherein the firm agrees to pay fixed rate in exchange of receiving floating for next five years on semi-annual basis. Such a swap would appear like the one shown in Figure 10-6(a). By doing so, the liability of the firm would become fixed and insulate against the rising interest rate in future.

Similar swap can be used in an opposite manner to transform fixed rate liability into a floating one. It is useful for a firm which after having issued fixed coupon instruments faces falling yields. The firm may enter a swap paying floating and receiving fixed interest rate. The fixed obligation of coupon cancels with the fixed payment received under swap. The floating rate payment becomes the cost of the debt. This is shown in Figure 10-6(b).

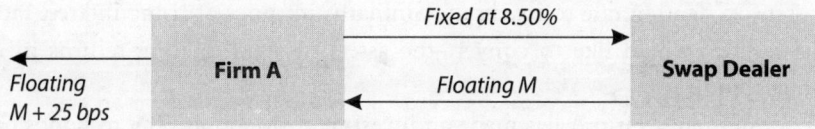

Firm A pays fixed and receives floating from swap dealer. The revised cost after swap would be fixed at 8.75%.

Figure 10-6(a)
Transforming Floating Rate Liability to Fixed Rate Liability

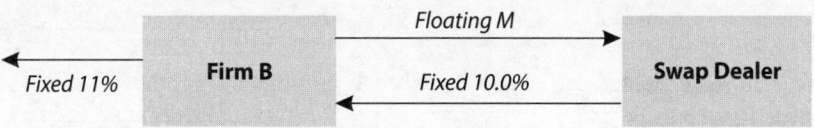

Firm B pays floating and receives fixed from swap dealer. The revised cost of funds after swap would be floating at M + 100 bps.

Figure 10-6(b)
Transforming Fixed Rate Liability to Floating Rate Liability

Besides converting the liability from one form to another, swap has additional advantage of maintaining the confidentiality of the actions of the firms. Under the situation in which indenture does not permit changes in terms of the original offer without the consent of counterparty (the debt holders), swap becomes handy. By entering the swap, the firms can achieve the desired change without letting the subscribers know. The commitments under swap are independent of the underlying debt obligations.

Another advantage would be the flexibility to revert back to the original position because the swap can be cancelled at any time by exchanging the value of the swap. This allows the desired changes in the position of liability as the interest rate scenario changes and may be done as frequently as desired without disturbing the original loan contract. For example, a firm expecting a rise in the interest rate may swap to convert a floating rate debt into a fixed rate. If the scenario changes after some time and the interest rate is expected to fall, the firm can revert back to the original liability at floating rate by cancelling the swap or entering into another swap with a different swap dealer.

Transforming Nature of Assets

Just as the way swaps can be used to transform the nature of liability, the complexion of assets too can be changed. Changing nature of liability is the need of borrowing firm. Swaps can be used by investing firms as they have income-yielding assets that may be providing a fixed or variable income. Assets provide income to investing firms based on the interest rates. The income rises and falls with interest.

In the circumstance of falling interest rates, the firms would like to change the complexion of assets on floating rate to fixed rate. Similarly, in times of rising interest rates, firms earning fixed interest would like to convert the assets to yield floating returns to remain with the market trend.

For example, a Firm A has made an investment by subscribing to bonds carrying 9% fixed coupon. The yields in the market are rising and the trend is expected to continue. The firm faces a potential loss of income and to lock-in the increased yield may like to convert investment from fixed rate to floating rate. The objective may be achieved by entering a swap receiving floating rate, MIBOR, and paying a fixed rate of 8%. By doing so the nature of income transforms from fixed 9.00% to MIBOR + 100 bps as shown in Figure 10-7.

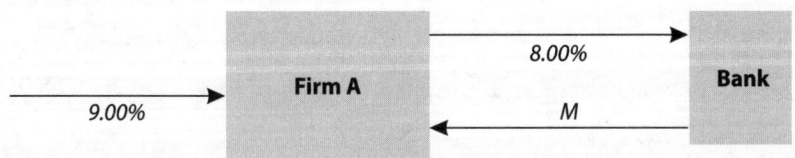

Firm has fixed income of 9%. Under the swap, it pays fixed interest of 8% and receives benchmark MIBOR. The income now is MIBOR + 100 bps.

Figure 10-7
Swap to Transform Fixed Rate Asset to Floating Rate

Assuming that the current rate of MIBOR is 8%, the income remains the same. In future if MIBOR rises as expected, the income too would rise. Instead if MIBOR falls subsequent to the swap, the firm turns out to be a loser.

Similarly, an asset providing income on variable rate can be converted to fixed rate by entering a suitable swap.

Exercise 10-2
Changing Floating Rate Asset to Fixed Rate

Assume that Indian Technology Limited (ITL) has subscribed to 8-year bonds that pay MIBOR + 120 bps as coupon. Coupons are payable semi-annually. Since the time of subscribing for two years, the interest rates have been falling. It is worse that the downtrend is likely to continue. There are 10 more coupons to be received. ITL wants to convert the floating rate asset into a fixed rate asset. The current swap rate offered by the bank is 7.5% for MIBOR. Structure a swap for ITL. What would be the investment income if ITL agrees for the swap offered by the bank?

Solution
ITL can enter the swap as follows:

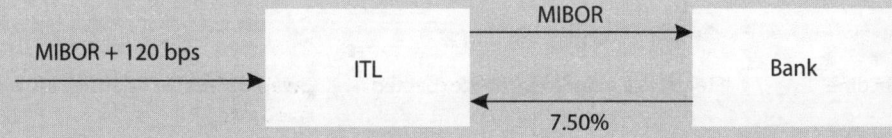

After the swap, the investment income would be 8.20% as follows:

Income from investment	=	MIBOR + 120 bps
Less: Payment under swap	=	MIBOR
Receipt under swap	=	7.50%
Investment income after swap	=	8.70%

Hedging with Interest Rate Swaps

Transformation of assets or liabilities from floating to fixed rate or vice versa is used as a hedge against fluctuations of interest rates. The need to change the complexion of assets and liabilities arises when firms expect unfavourable movement of interest rates. Though there are other instruments available for covering interest rate risk (to be discussed in next chapter), swaps as a composite contract may offer a cost-effective and efficient solution for long-term hedging. Like any forwards and futures, swap too works well only if the actual movement of interest rate is as anticipated, and when the actual is contrary to expectation, the swap results in a loss. Swaps also offer an opportunity to exit just like forwards and futures by entering another swap reversing the initial contract, amounting to its cancellation.

Normally, changes in interest rates are steady and unidirectional and not as wild as compared to changes in other financial assets like stocks, indices, and spot exchange rates. The values of other financial assets are heavily dependent upon changes in the interest rates which themselves respond to macroeconomic changes. The hedgers prefer to cover the short-term risk with instruments, such as forwards and futures, which have shorter maturity. The changes in interest rates in developed and stable economies are rather slow. In an extremely volatile economy where interest rates change frequently and sometimes wildly, swap as a hedging instrument is not appropriate. Unfortunately, volatile economies do not have well-developed capital markets and products like swaps. For covering a short-term interest rate risk (say for a period of less than a year), there are better derivatives like forward rate agreements and interest rate futures. Only when the interest rate risk is intended to be covered over a longer time horizon, say 3–5 years, swap becomes an attractive instrument.

Various actions under different situations of the firm and the prospective scenario are presented in Table 10-3.

Table 10-3
Hedging Strategies with Swaps

Nature	Risk Situation	Hedging Action
ASSETS		
Fixed Rate Income	Steady rise in interest rates expected	Swap to receive floating rate and pay fixed rate.
Floating Rate Income	Steady fall in interest rates expected	Swap to pay floating rate to receive fixed interest rate.
LIABILITIES		
Fixed Rate Borrowing	Falling interest rates	Swap to pay floating interest rate and receive fixed interest rate
Floating Rate Borrowing	Rising interest rates	Swap to receive floating interest rate for paying fixed rate.

There are other ways to hedge against adverse situations but at times swap could prove more convenient. For example, a firm may have borrowed on fixed rate basis for 10 years. After a few years, if the interest rates start downward movement, the possible recourse with the firm is to approach the lender to change the nature of loan from fixed to variable. This would be resisted by the lender. A better course of action is to enter into a swap arrangement with another. The firm achieves its objective without the resorting to the original lender.

Reducing Cost of Funds

Swaps are not used as much for hedging requirements as they are for reducing the cost of funds, making use of differential of credit quality spread that prevails in the financial markets. Reducing the cost of borrowing through swaps is more attractive. Ability of the swaps to take advantage of market imperfection of differential credit spread is primarily responsible for its popularity and growth. As per ISDA of the total of US$24,115 billion of notional principal outstanding, about 92% was accounted for by interest rate swaps as at the end of the first half of 1997. The driving force behind usage of swap would be its potential for cost saving rather than hedging; else the notional principal in currency and interest rate swaps would have been of equal magnitude.

To demonstrate the utility of swap for reducing the cost of borrowing, let us consider an example. Assume that a AAA rated firm needs to raise funds on floating rate basis. The firm can mobilize in the fixed rate market at 9% and in the floating rate market at MIBOR + 100 bps. In contrast, another firm not rated as high but at AA can mobilize capital at 11.5% in the fixed rate market and at MIBOR + 200 bps in the floating rate market. The AA rated firm is interested in availing funds at fixed rate because it believes the interest rates would move up. If each of them mobilizes capital independently, AAA rated firm can borrow floating at MIBOR + 100 bps and AA rated firm at fixed rate of 11.5%.

We shall examine if the two firms collaborate with each other, can they benefit from the market distortion to their advantage. Clearly, firm AAA has advantage over firm AA in both kinds of the markets—fixed and floating, as can be seen here:

	Firm AAA	Firm AA	Advantage AAA
Fixed Rate	9%	11.5%	250 bps
Floating Rate	MIBOR + 100 bps	MIBOR + 200 bps	100 bps

RATIONALE FOR SWAP

Despite an absolute advantage of AAA rated firm in both the fixed rate and floating rate markets, what must be focused that the absolute advantage is not identical in the two markets. There seems no distortion in the market to a naïve person since the firm rated higher gets funds cheaper. However, the distortion comes in the relative pricing that different markets offer. The matter of significance is the comparative advantage and not the absolute advantage.

Firm AAA holds absolute advantage of 250 bps in the fixed rate market and 100 bps in the floating rate market. Alternatively, we can say that Firm AAA has comparative advantage of 150 bps (difference of two absolute advantages) in the fixed rate market. This comparative advantage of 150 bps can be exploited by both the firms.

The comparative advantage forms the basis of the swap wherein depending upon the relative strengths of the firms involved the cost savings can be negotiated. Assume that the advantage of 150 bps is to be shared in the ratio of 2 : 1 in favour of AAA rated firm. If so, the cost of funds for AAA rated firm and AA rated firm must come down by 100 bps and 50 bps, respectively. This can be achieved as follows:

1. Firm AAA mobilizes funds from fixed rate market instead of its preferred option of floating rate market. The cost payable by AAA would be 9%.
2. Similarly, AA rated firm accesses the floating rate market by issuing debt at MIBOR + 200 bps rather than fixed rate instrument.
3. Having accessed different markets against their preferred habitats, the two firms enter a swap as follows:
   (a) AAA pays AA floating at MIBOR
   (b) AA pays AAA a fixed rate of 9%.

Post swap (i) the nature of liabilities of the two firms would change, that is, for AAA from fixed to floating, and for AA from floating to fixed rates, and (ii) the cost of funds would come down by 100 bps and 50 bps, respectively, for AAA and AA if the two had accessed the markets independently and had not entered the swap arrangement. The schematic diagram of swap and the resultant cost of the two firms are shown in Figure 10-8.

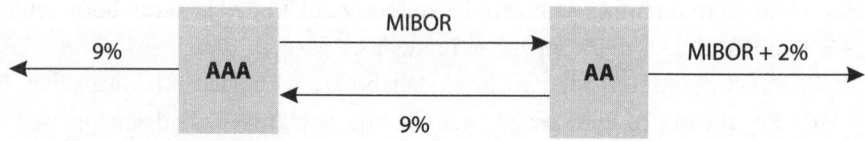

Cost of funds for two firms after swap

	AAA	AA
1. Payment to investors	9%	MIBOR + 2%
2. Payment to counterparty	MIBOR	9.0%
3. Receipt from counterparty	9.0%	MIBOR
Cost of borrowing (1 + 2 − 3)	MIBOR	11.0%
IMPACT	Firm can raise funds at MIBOR as against MIBOR + 1% without the swap; gaining 1.00%	Firm can raise funds at 11.0% as against 11.5% without the swap; gaining 0.50%

Figure 10-8
Interest Rate Swap—Reducing Cost of Borrowing

The exploitation of the comparative advantage by the firms is a clear case of arbitrage on the credit rating. The fixed rate market demanded a greater premium, that is, 250 bps from the lower rated firm than it did for the floating rate borrowing, that is, 100 bps. The quality spread based on ratings appears justified in financial markets. However, there is apparently no reason to have different spreads in fixed and floating rate markets if the market is competitive. Unequal credit quality spreads may be attributed to several factors such as information gap, subjectivity in assigning credit quality spread, and past experiences. One possible reason for lower credit quality spread in the floating rate market is the assured and definite level of profit to lender, irrespective of the prevailing interest rate. The inability of financial market to assign equal credit quality spreads paves the way for the swap. Swap, therefore, is an example of exploitation of credit quality arbitrage. The arbitrage should have vanished over a period of time. However, the rising volume of swaps indicates otherwise. Arbitrage on credit rating continues to grow.

NEED FOR SWAP INTERMEDIARY

One of the factors that seem to be contributing to the explosive growth in swaps is the active role the bankers play in facilitating the deals. As illustrated in examples discussed, swap would be very beneficial to the two firms if one can find a perfect match in (a) the principal amount of borrowing (b) its timings of commencement and maturity, (c) periodicity of coupon payments, etc. These conditions are difficult to fulfil.

Matching Requirement Further, for unexplained reasons, most firms refrain from making funding requirements public. The borrowing and its acceptable terms are generally known to the bankers of the firm. Banks have supposedly confidential information about credit requirements of various firms. For a fee, they can perform the role of match-making with the identities of the counterparties kept confidential, a preferred route by the all firms alike.

Counterparty Risk Swap is a promise to exchange of cash flows in future. The cash flows become unequal as time progresses and, therefore, one of the counterparties would be at disadvantage. This makes swaps prone to default risk. The paying firm is likely to default on the payment in future. In the absence of a bank, the two counterparties assume default risk on each other. The swap intermediary, being a bank, can assume default risk in a swap becoming the counterparty to each of the two firms in the swap. Both the counterparties are likely to have greater comfort level if the counterparty is a bank rather than a firm.

Warehousing Further, the banks can fulfil the gaps in the requirements of funding by warehousing the swaps. Till the time a matching party is found, the banks can swap on their own behalf. With banks serving as counterparty, the large swap deal can be broken into smaller and several parts increasing the participation in the market. For example, a 10-year borrowing of ₹100 million may be split in two parts of ₹40 million and ₹60 million and can be placed with two different firms. This would be possible only when banks become intermediaries.

The swap intermediaries earn their commission for facilitating swaps, assuming counterparty risk and warehousing. Firms do not mind paying such fee because such fee comes from sharing of the comparative advantage available. In fact with banks as intermediary, the swaps may lead to better cost reduction due to expanded market participants. With the bank as intermediary, each party deals with the bank rather than each other. In that case, the comparative advantage needs to be shared among three parties rather than two. Exercise 10-3 illustrates the sharing arrangement of the aggregate benefit with intermediary involved.

Exercise 10-3
Interest Rate Swap with Swap Intermediary to Reduce Cost

Assume two British firms A and B need £100 million for a period of three years. Firm A believes that the interest rates would be falling in future and, hence, prefers issue of floating rate bonds. It can do so at LIBOR + 50 bps. Alternatively, debt can be issued at a fixed coupon of 7%.

Firm B believes that interest rates would rise in future and, hence, issuing floating rate instrument would be disadvantageous. It prefers a bond with 8.50% fixed coupon. If Firm B were to issue a floating rate bond, it needs to offer coupon at LIBOR + 100 bps to the subscribers.

Bank of North England (BNE) is a common banker to both A and B and is aware of borrowing needs and their preferences. It is ready to negotiate a swap between the two serving as intermediary for a fee of 5 bps from each party.

(a) Find out what benefit Firm A and Firm B can have if BNE needs 10 bps as charges for intermediation.
(b) If the benefit has to be shared between Firm A and Firm B in the ratio of 5 : 4, what savings in the cost of funds each one of them can derive?
(c) Show the schematic diagram of the swap indicating the cash flows from Firm A and Firm B.
(d) Assuming annual payment of the debt instruments and LIBOR rates today, after one year, and two years as 6.50%, 6.75%, and 6.25%, respectively, draw the cash flows of Firm A, Firm B, and BNE on gross and net basis.

Solution

(a) The advantage of Firm A over Firm B in the two markets is as follows:

	Firm A	Firm B	Advantage A over B
Fixed Rate Market	7.00%	8.50%	150 bps
Floating Rate Market	LIBOR + 50 bps	LIBOR + 100 bps	50 bps

The comparative advantage of Firm A over Firm B is 100 bps (150 – 50). Of this, total comparative advantage 10 bps is required by BNE, whereas the remaining 90 bps may be shared between Firm A and Firm B.

(b) If the sharing is 5 : 4 of the net benefit, an advantage of 50 bps goes to Firm A and 40 bps to Firm B. After the swap, the cost of funds for Firm A should be 50 bps less at LIBOR and for Firm B, it would be 8.10%, that is, 40 bps less. The remaining 10 bps would accrue to BNE.

(c) BNE advises Firm A to issue fixed coupon bond at 7% and Firm B to issue floating rate bonds at LIBOR + 100 bps, and then enter into swap with BNE as mentioned in the given table.

Interest Rate Swap: A Schematic View with Intermediary

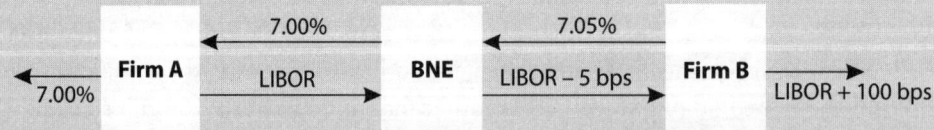

The cost of funds after the swap would be as follows:

	Firm A	Firm B
1. Payment to investors	7.00%	LIBOR + 100 bps
2. Payment to Bank	LIBOR	7.05%
3. Receipt from Bank	7.00%	LIBOR – 5 bps
Cost of borrowing (1 + 2 – 3)	LIBOR	8.10%

(d) The cash flows on notional principal of £100 million and given floating leg LIBOR rates, the three annual cash flows would be as mentioned in the given table.

Cash Flows for Firm A, Firm B, and BNE			£ millions
	Firm A	Firm B	BNE
First Year Cash Flows	LIBOR at $T = 0$ year: 6.50%		
Payment to Debt Holders	−7.00	−7.50	−
Receipt from Bank	+7.00	+6.45	−13.45
Payment to Bank	−6.50	−7.05	+13.55
Net Cash Flow under Swap	+1.50	−1.60	+0.10
Net Cash Flow	−6.50	−8.10	+0.10
Second Year Cash Flows	LIBOR at $T = 1$ year: 6.75%		
Payment to Debt Holders	−7.00	−7.75	−
Receipt from Bank	+7.00	+6.70	−13.70
Payment to Bank	−6.75	−7.05	+13.80
Net Cash Flow under Swap	+0.25	−0.35	+0.10
Net Cash Flow	−6.75	−8.10	+0.10
Third Year Cash Flows	LIBOR at $T = 2$ years: 6.25%		
Payment to Debt Holders	−7.00	−7.25	−
Receipt from Bank	+7.00	+6.20	−13.20
Payment to Bank	−6.25	−7.05	+13.30
Net Cash Flow under Swap	+0.75	−0.85	+0.10
Net Cash Flow	−6.25	−8.10	+0.10

TYPES OF INTEREST RATE SWAPS

Interest rate swaps can be categorized as follows:

Fixed-to-floating In the fixed-to-floating rate swaps, the party pays fixed rate of interest and receives floating rate from the bank.

Floating-to-fixed In this kind of swap, the party pays floating rate of interest to the bank and receives a fixed rate interest.

Basis swap Fixed-to-floating or floating-to-fixed swaps have one leg fixed, whereas the other leg is based on floating rate. The floating rate is decided by a benchmark, such as LIBOR and MIBOR. A swap where both the legs are floating but tied to different benchmarks is referred to as basis swap. Basis swaps are used where parties in the contract are tied to one asset or liability based on one reference rate and want to convert the same to another reference rate.

SUMMARY

Swaps were born out of compulsions of MNCs to overcome the capital flow controls imposed by governments. MNCs devised mutual parallel loans to fund their operations overseas. Later, when capital controls were removed, these parallel loans developed into full blown financial product now known as swap.

Swap is the exchange of series of cash flows at periodic intervals for specified time where one party receives and pays to another. The value of cash flows to be exchanged between two parties would be decided on a parameter. If the basis is interest rates, it is called interest rate swap; and if it is the exchange rate, it is called financial/currency swap.

Currency swaps have two legs of cash flows which are denominated in two different currencies. This enables firms to transform the assets/liabilities from one currency to another. Thus, currency swap can be used for hedging against exchange rate risk because assets and liabilities denominated in one currency can be transformed in another supposedly stable currency.

In an interest rate swap, one leg of cash flow is based on the fixed interest rate on a notional principal, whereas the other leg called floating is based on the market-based floating rate. No principal is exchanged either at initiation or conclusion of swap. Only the differential of the cash flow is exchanged. Interest rate swap can alter the complexion of nature of liability or asset from fixed rate to floating rate or vice versa, without necessity of disturbing the original contract. This enables hedging against the interest rate risk. When interest rates are rising, a borrowing firm likes to convert a floating rate liability to fixed rate. When interest rates are falling, firms like to have floating rate liability and not fixed rate. An investing firm would like to have opposite for their assets. Besides working as a tool to hedge against the interest rate risk swap has potential to save funding cost which perhaps is the important factor in its popularity. Cost saving results due to market imperfection that has unequal credit spreads in fixed and floating markets for borrowing. The differential in the spread, referred to as comparative advantage can be utilized for the benefit of two firms to reduce borrowing cost.

The swap normally requires exact matching of needs of the two counterparties in terms of amount, maturity, timing, and periodicity of interest payments which are difficult to fulfil and constrain the development of market. Another drawback is that swap gives rise to a counterparty risk. Bank by acting as a facilitator provides the much-needed depth to the swap markets. It also fills the gaps in matching needs and acts as a counterparty to a swap transaction. The ready market of swaps provided by banks also makes entry and exit from swap easier. For valuation, the swap may be either treated as a pair of fixed rate and floating rate bonds or as a series of forward agreements.

QUESTIONS

10-1 What do you understand by parallel loans? Explain with an example.
10-2 How does a currency swap transforms assets/liabilities from one currency to another? Explain.
10-3 If a firm has an asset and a liability denominated in two different currencies, how can it eliminate the exchange rate risk? Draw a schematic diagram to explain your answer.
10-4 Explain the hedging of fixed rate and floating rate loans using swap.
10-5 How are currency swaps and interest rate swaps used for reducing cost? What are the problems in arranging a swap and how are they overcome by a swap intermediary/bank?
10-6 If an enterprise has invested funds in securities providing floating rate of income, what risk does it face? How would you hedge such a risk using an interest rate swap?

PROBLEMS

10-1 Currency Swap Structure

Two firms, A and B, can raise money in British pounds and euro at the following rates:

	British Pounds	Euro
Firm A	6.00%	9.80%
Firm B	8.00%	10.00%

(a) What would be the cost of funds when Firm A raises money in Euro and Firm B raises money in British pound?

(b) If Firm A and Firm B decide to arrange a swap, what would be the cost of funds for each of them if the benefit of swap is to be shared equally between the two? Draw a diagram of swap indicating the cash flows.

(c) If a swap intermediary expecting 10 bps from each party is involved to facilitate the deal, what would be the swap structure and the cost of funds for each firm? Draw a swap diagram indicating the cash flows.

10-2 Interest Rate Swap Structure

Two firms, A and B, need ₹100 crore for five years. Firm A prefers floating rate liability, whereas Firm B wants a fixed rate liability. They can issue fixed or floating rate bonds with coupons as follows:

	Fixed Rate	Floating Rate
Firm A	6.00%	MIBOR + 50 bps
Firm B	8.00%	MIBOR + 100 bps

(a) What would be cost of funds when Firm A issues floating rate bonds and Firm B issues fixed coupon bonds?

(b) If Firm A and Firm B decide to arrange a swap, what would be the cost of funds for each of them if the benefit of swap is to be shared in favour of A in the ratio 2 : 1? Draw a diagram of swap indicating the cash flows.

(c) If a swap intermediary expecting 10 bps from each party is involved to facilitate the deal, what would be the swap structure and the cost of funds for each firm if the benefit of swap is to be shared equally? Draw a swap diagram indicating the cash flows.

10-3 Hedge against Falling Yield

A firm had issued 10-year bonds worth ₹10 crore at fixed coupon of 12% payable semi-annually. The coupon was consistent with the yield prevailing at the time of the issue. Since then, the yield has fallen and the bond has five years remaining for maturity.

Swap rate offered by the bank is 9.00%–9.20% against floating rate based on MIBOR. Depict the swap arrangement of the firm with the bank and find out the cost of the bond after the swap is entered.

11

Interest Rate Risk and Hedging

LEARNING OBJECTIVES

This chapter aims at

- understanding the importance of interest rate risk management
- understanding the features of benchmark interest rate
- describing the forward rate agreement, their features, and hedging with them
- explaining Eurodollar futures and hedging with them
- understanding the operation, payoffs, and hedging with interest rate options
- describing caps, floors, and collars

CONTENTS

Introduction
Benchmark Interest Rates
Forward Rate Agreement
    Features of Forward Rate Agreement
    Borrower's Forward Rate Agreement
    Investor's Forward Rate Agreement
    Pricing Forward Rate Agreement
Interest Rate Futures
    Eurodollar Futures

Value of Eurodollar Futures
    Hedging with Eurodollar Futures
Interest Rate Options
    Call Option on Interest Rate
    Put Option on Interest Rate
Caps
    Floor
    Collar

INTRODUCTION

In the previous chapter, we have seen how to hedge against changes in exchange rates. We also learnt about the strong linkages of interest rates and exchange rates in an economy and, therefore, dependence of the performance of MNCs upon the behaviour of interest rates and exchange rates. With increased globalization, understanding of behaviour of interest rates is becoming increasingly complex. In segmented markets, the changes in interest rates are predominantly governed by local monetary and fiscal policies. However, in integrated or semi-integrated financial markets, an economy needs to respond to not only local factors but also global factors. The scope of policy making by local politicians and economists gets expanded. For managers in multinational corporations (MNCs), the situation becomes more complex because they are mere puppets to the policy changes and practically have no role in guiding the interest rates. They simply have to react to this exogenous variable.

The need for management of interest rate risk depends upon how crucially the performance of MNC is dependent on changes in interest rate. Firms in the automobiles, housing, and real estate face greater threats. Banks and financial services are perhaps the most affected by changes in interest rates since their asset (loans) and liabilities (deposits) are valued on the basis of interest rate, and profitability is a pure function of spreads in lending and deposit rates.

This chapter deals with describing the instruments for management of interest rate risk. We know about the four derivatives products—forwards, futures, options, and swaps. Of these, swaps have been discussed in the previous chapter. In this chapter, we discuss the remaining three with interest rate as underlying.

BENCHMARK INTEREST RATES

Interest rate derivatives have the interest rate as the underlying asset. The underlying asset must be such that its value must be determined purely on the basis of the market interest rates. Though we can say that values of all assets, such as stocks, currencies, and commodities, depend in some way or the other on the interest rates, it is indeed difficult for one to identify the asset whose value is almost entirely dependent on interest rates.

For the quotation of interest rates and the measurement of interest rate risk, we need a reference rate. In an economy there are several interest rates that prevail. These include bank rate, repo rate, reverse repo rates, prime lending rate, yields on T-bills and government securities, etc. Which of them is the right interest rate that should be considered appropriate as a benchmark rate for the purposes of reference and measurement of changes? A benchmark reference rate must be

(a) *market determined* and must represent true yields;
(b) *devoid of default risk;* interest rates usually incorporate the premium for the default risk of the borrowers;
(c) *available in public domain on continuing basis*; interest rate for the transaction are settled by two parties and remain confidential leaving scope for variations in interest rates for similar transaction with different parties; and
(d) *devoid of investment preferences in terms of incentives and time to maturity*; interest rates are also a function of environmental compulsions like Statutory Liquidity Ratio (SLR),

motivated by tax incentives, etc. which may differ from the returns desired by investment out of free will guided purely by commercial considerations. Besides, expected return is also a function of time to maturity of the investment, that is, the returns desired for investments of one year are different from that of three or five years.

Yields on T-bills and government securities can be regarded risk free as default can be presumed to be non-existent. However, these cannot serve as a benchmark for market-determined rate because investment in these securities is driven by tax benefits attached and compulsions imposed by central banks. Therefore, yields on government securities do not represent true market rates. The rates quoted by banks on daily basis of acceptance of deposits and lending among themselves are driven by pure commercial considerations reflecting the true supply and demand of funds. Transactions among the reputed banks can also be deemed as risk free. For these reasons, market-determined rates like LIBOR in international markets are considered as appropriate benchmark. For domestic instruments, the equivalent reference rate is Mumbai Inter Bank Offer Rate (MIBOR).

The design of interest rate derivative products, monitoring of changes in interest rates, and determination of the payoff are based on LIBOR or any other such rate that is market-based, transparent, free from default risk, and free from investment preferences and influence.

FORWARD RATE AGREEMENT

A forward contract calls for the price of the underlying asset for settlement at future date. In case of forward rate agreement (FRA), the interest rate is the underlying asset. Interest rate is the price of capital, invested or borrowed. If the price of capital is fixed in advance for future investing and borrowing, it becomes a forward product with interest rate as underlying.

An instrument that fixes an interest rate today for investing or borrowing in future is called a Forward Rate Agreement (FRA). This is an agreement to lend or accept deposits in future at an interest rate determined today. For example, a firm needing funds six months later can freeze the interest rate of borrowing through an FRA of six months.

Features of Forward Rate Agreement

An FRA is defined as a forward contract for agreeing to advance a loan or accept a deposit at an interest rate at a future date for a notional amount of principal. A typical FRA is quoted as depicted in Figure 11-1.

The quotation of FRA means that the quoting bank is prepared to accept deposit or extend lending in US dollar starting 6 months from now and ending 12 months. For placing a deposit,

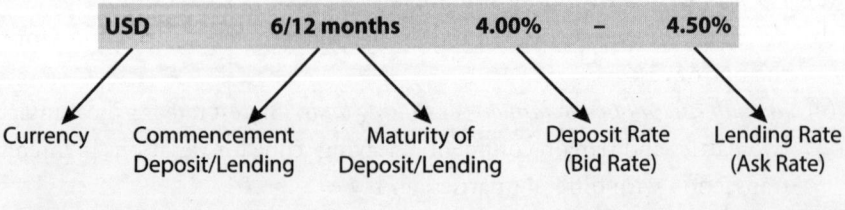

Figure 11-1
Quotation of FRA

the interest rate would be 4% (the bid rate), whereas the bank would lend at 4.50% (the ask rate). The difference between the bid and ask rates represents the spread for the bank. By offering such rate, the investing firm or company can lock in a return of 4% for 6-m investment beginning six months from now. Similarly, the borrowing firm can lock in the future borrowing cost at 4.5%.

Hedging Product It must be noted that FRA is a short-term hedging product and is not an agreement to either accept deposits or lend funds. It merely is an assurance of interest rate. For long-term hedging of interest rate risk, swaps are used. This assures a future interest rate payable or receivable. The investment or borrowing as the case may be can be done with any other party. The FRA is a promise to compensate the loss or claim the profit that counterparty incurs in its investment/borrowing programme. The FRA is an instrument independent of underlying investment or borrowing of a certain amount of principal.

Notional Principal The amount of principal mentioned in an FRA essentially remains notional and is used for computing only the payoffs.

Benchmarking Since FRA is detached from actual borrowing and investing the interest rate quotations are based on some benchmark rate that is market-determined in a transparent manner and available in public domain on a continuous basis. Most often used benchmark is LIBOR. The FRA can be said to be the best future estimate of LIBOR. For example, a USD 6/9 FRA quoted at 3.45–3.55% suggests that for US dollar the three-month LIBOR rate after six months is expected to be 3.50%.

Cash Settlement FRAs are settled in cash with the differential of actual and contracted forward rate for the corresponding period upon its maturity as given by Eq.11-1.

$$\text{Interest Payment} = \text{Notional Principal} \times \frac{[\text{Reference Rate} - \text{Forward Rate}]\frac{\text{Days}}{360}}{1 + \text{Reference Rate}\frac{\text{Days}}{360}} \quad (11\text{-}1)$$

For example, a borrowing firm books USD 6/12 FRA at 4.50% for a notional amount of US$10 million. It implies that for a borrowing of US$10 million for a period of six months, commencing six months from now should not exceed 4.50%. If the 6-m LIBOR after six months is found to be 5.5%, then the firm should receive the discounted value of 1% for six months (approximately US$50,000) towards compensation for the additional interest that the firm would have to bear in borrowing. The exact amount of US$49,188 is found based on *Actual*/360 convention discounted at observed reference rate for the relevant period using Eq. 11-1.

$$\text{Interest payment} = \text{Notional principal} \times \frac{[\text{Reference rate} - \text{Forward rate}]\frac{\text{Days}}{360}}{1 + \text{Reference rate}\frac{\text{Days}}{360}}$$

$$= 10,000,000 \times \frac{(0.055 - 0.045)\frac{182}{360}}{1 + 0.055\frac{182}{360}} = \text{US\$49,188}$$

Tailor-made Over-the-counter Product The FRA is an over-the-counter (OTC) product and quotations are available on demand as per the requirement of the investing or borrowing firms. For example, a firm desirous of investing/borrowing ₹1 million for 12 months commencing 3 months from now can ask for quotation of INR 3/15FRA for notional principal of ₹1 million. Just as exporters and importers ask for forward rate for foreign currency receivable and payable maturing at different points of time, the investing and borrowing firms can ask for forward interest rates.

The FRAs can be used for freezing the borrowing cost or investment returns over short term provided the firm knows the requirements in advance. Since FRAs and other interest rate derivatives (discussed later) are benchmarked against a reference rate, only the changes in reference rate can be hedged. The firms would continue to pay/receive the spread over reference rate. Assuming constant spread, the hedging against interest rate can be done through interest rate derivatives. For changes in the spread during the period under consideration no hedging is possible.

Borrower's Forward Rate Agreement

The buyer of an FRA would be a borrowing firm which needs funds in future and apprehends that interest rate would rise by then. The firm is aware of its borrowing requirements now but would need them in future. A typical circumstance would be the expectation of a huge order to be processed in a short period of time and the firm requiring working capital funds. It is a situation in which firms need increased borrowings on temporary basis. In order to hedge against the rising borrowing cost, the firms can book FRA at the ask rate.

Assume that an MNC needs additional funds of €10 million after three months for execution of an order. The expected completion time for this order is six months after which additional funds would not be required and extra borrowing would be liquidated from the proceeds of the order. The current 6-m LIBOR is 6% and the firm expects it to rise to 7% in three-month time. Assume that ask rate of Euro 3/9 FRA is 6.50%. The firm books the FRA.

At the end of three months, the cash settlement of FRA would take place based on the actual 6-m LIBOR. If it happens to be more than the contracted rate of 6.50%, the differential would be received by the firm and if it is less than 6.50%, the differential would be payable by the firm. Assuming 182 days in the six-month period, the exact amounts would be as follows:

If actual 6-m LIBOR is 7.00%, the firm would receive €21,414

$$\text{Interest payment} = 10{,}000{,}000 \times \frac{(0.07 - 0.065)\frac{182}{360}}{1 + 0.07\frac{182}{360}} = €21{,}414$$

If actual LIBOR is 6.00%, the firm would pay €24,534

$$\text{Interest payment} = 10{,}000{,}000 \times \frac{(0.06 - 0.065)\frac{182}{360}}{1 + 0.06\frac{182}{360}} = €24{,}534$$

The MNC can have borrowing from any other source and cash settlement of FRA would freeze the borrowing cost to 6.50% (ignoring the credit quality risk premium).

Investor's Forward Rate Agreement

Like in borrower's FRA, that locks in the rate of borrowing in times of rising interest rates an investor's FRA enables locking in of the investment returns over a short horizon, when one expects future interest rates to fall.

The investing firm would book an FRA at the bid rate. The cash settlement would be done in the same manner as Eq. 11-1 with signs reversed. Refer to Exercise 11-1.

Exercise 11-1
Investor's Forward Rate Agreement

Capital Constructions is expecting to receive mobilization advance after six months for a project of US$15 million which is not required for business operations for the next six months. The current rate of return earned by the firm is 6.00%. The liquidity situation in the banking circle indicates that yields are going to fall. A bank has offered 6/12 FRA at bid rate of 6.00% based on 6-m LIBOR.
(1) How can Capital Constructions hedge against the falling yields?
(2) Find out the settlement amount of FRA if after six months the LIBOR is (a) 7.00% and (b) 5%. Assume 182 days in the six month period.

Solution

(1) For a notional principal of US$15 million, Capital Construction buys an FRA at 6.00%. It would lock in the rate of return at 6%. The differential of actual LIBOR and 6% discounted at LIBOR would be paid or received by Capital Construction after six months.
(2) The settlement amount in FRA would be such that yield on the investment is frozen at around 6%. The minor difference arises due to computation of cash settlement based on different conventions.

   (a) If 6-m LIBOR rises to 7%
   After six months, Capital Construction would pay 1% (actual rate − FRA rate) for six months discounted at LIBOR.

   $$\text{Interest payment} = 15{,}000{,}000 \times \frac{(0.07-0.06)\frac{182}{360}}{1+0.07\frac{182}{360}} = -\text{US\$73{,}241}$$

   After making payment under FRA and investing the surplus funds at higher rate of 7%, the return for the firm would be around 6%.

   (b) If 6-m LIBOR falls to 5%
   After three months, Capital Construction would receive 1% (actual rate − FRA rate) for six months discounted at LIBOR.

   $$\text{Interest payment} = 15{,}000{,}000 \times \frac{(0.05-0.06)\frac{182}{360}}{1+0.05\frac{182}{360}} = \text{US\$73{,}964}$$

   Here, the firm would invest at yields of 5%, but the shortfall would be made good by FRA seller so as to enable return at around 6% as contemplated.

Pricing Forward Rate Agreement

We now discuss how an FRA seller arrives at the quotation of bid and ask rate that are likely to prevail in future. In fact that information is contained in the current term structure of interest rate. The term structure of interest rates provides the rate of return based on maturity of investment. It reflects the investors' expectations of returns with the maturity of investment. For example, consider the following term structure of interest rates from 3 to 12 months in the steps of three months:

Investment Horizon (Months)	3	6	9	12
Yields (% Annualized)	5.00	5.30	5.60	6.00

The yield for three-month investment is 5%, whereas for six-month investment, the desired return is 5.30%. It is derived from the prices of different financial securities at any given point of time. Here, the term structure, also known as yield curve, is a rising one, indicating rising yields (annualized) with increased maturities.

From the given yield curve (zeros) we can find the expectations of interest rate 3 months from now for investment horizons till 12 months. First we find the expected interest rate after 3 months for 3-m investment, that is, $_3r_6$. By equivalency of (a) direct investment for six months at the rate of 5.30%, $_0r_6$ with (b) initial investment for three months at $_0r_3$, and then rolling it over for another three months at $_3r_6$, we can find the 3-m interest rate expected to prevail after three months. This depicted in Figure 11-2. In competitive markets direct investment strategy and roll-over strategy must result in same return. Such a principle could be used as a guide to quote 3/6 FRA. Mathematically,

$$(1 + {}_0r_3)(1 + {}_3r_6) = (1 + {}_0r_6)$$

or (11-2)

$$(1 + {}_3r_6) = (1 + {}_0r_6)/(1 + {}_0r_3)$$

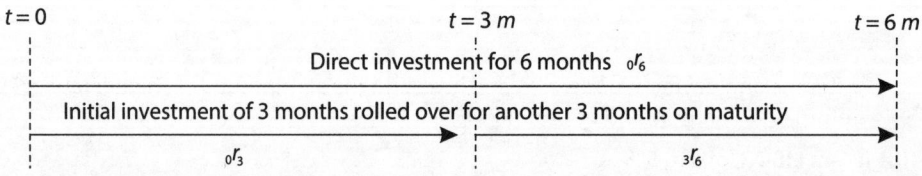

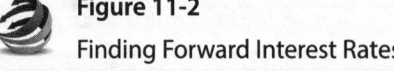

Figure 11-2
Finding Forward Interest Rates

We have assumed 180 days and 90 days in a six-month period and three-month period, respectively, for simplicity of calculation. We can find $_3r_6$, that is, the forward interest rate for three-month investment after three months. In terms of the given yield curve, substituting the values in Eq. 11-2, we have

$$(1 + {}_3r_6) = \frac{1 + 0.053 \times \frac{180}{360}}{1 + 0.050 \times \frac{90}{360}} = \frac{1.0265}{1.0125} = 1.01383;$$

gives ${}_3r_6 = 0.01383$, or equivalent to annualised ${}_3r_6 = 5.53\%$

The rate of 5.53% can serve as guide for the mid-rate of 3/6 FRA. Assuming a spread of 20 bps, we can quote 3/6 FRA at 5.43–5.63%.

Continuing with the same process of equivalency of direct investment with the roll-over strategies, we can find the 3-m forward rates for investments maturing 9 months and 12 months later. From the given yield, we may also find 6-m and 9-m forward interest rate for investment horizon up to 12 months. These are shown in Table 11-1.

Table 11-1
Forward Rates as Implied in Term Structure

Maturity from Today (Months)	6	9	12
Forward Rate (% Annualized)			
Three months from now	5.531	5.827	6.255
Six months from now	–	6.040	6.527
Nine months from now	–	–	6.910

Exercise 11-2
Determining Forward Interest Rates

Three zero-coupon bonds A, B, and C each having face value of ₹100 maturing after 1, 2, and 3 years, respectively, are trading at ₹95.43, ₹90.68, and ₹85.04, respectively.
(1) Find out the yield offered by each of the bond.
(2) What forward rates of interest do you expect for (a) one-year and two-year investment after one year and (b) one-year investment after two years?

Solution
(1) The yields offered by Bond A, B, and C for one-year, two-year, and three-year investment can be found as follows:

$95.43 \times (1 + {}_0r_1) = 100$ gives ${}_0r_1 = 4.79\%$
$90.68 \times (1 + {}_0r_2)^2 = 100$ gives ${}_0r_2 = 5.01\%$
$85.04 \times (1 + {}_0r_3)^3 = 100$ gives ${}_0r_3 = 5.55\%$

(2) Implied forward rates are
  (a) One year later $\quad (1 + {}_0r_1)(1 + {}_1r_2) = (1 + {}_0r_2)^2$
   Gives $\quad (1 + {}_1r_2) = 1.1028/1.0429$ or ${}_1r_2 = 5.24\%$

Gives $(1 + {}_0r_1)(1 + {}_1r_3)^2 = (1 + {}_0r_3)^3$
$(1 + {}_1r_3)^2 = 1.1759/1.0429$ or ${}_1r_3 = 5.93\%$

(b) $(1 + {}_0r_2)^2(1 + {}_2r_3) = (1 + {}_0r_3)^3$ Gives $(1 + {}_2r_3) = 1.1759/1.1028$ or ${}_2r_3 = 6.63\%$

INTEREST RATE FUTURES

The exchange-traded equivalent instrument of a forward contract is a futures contract. As FRAs are available in the OTC markets, we have interest rate futures based on financial instruments whose value directly and almost solely depends upon the interest rate; such assets are T-bills, dated securities, bonds, etc. In the international financial markets, the most popular asset is Eurodollar deposit.

Eurodollar deposit is an offshore deposit denominated in US dollars. Since these deposits are placed with a non-US bank, they are not subject to US regulations, and hence the yields on them are deemed to be freely market-determined. They are also considered free from default risk because they are placed in a reputed bank. There is sufficient liquidity available in these instruments because of abundance of US dollar offshore. Thus, Eurodollar deposits serve as an ideal underlying asset for an interest rate futures contract.

Eurodollar Futures

Ideally futures contract like forward requires delivery of underlying asset on its expiry. For example, a futures contract on T-Bill requires delivery of T-bills worth face value of US$1 million that matures 91 days thereafter. In theory, a future contract on Eurodollar requires delivery of deposit of US$1 million that matures three months thereafter. Delivery of Eurodollar deposits being non-transferable is not possible. They cannot serve as collateral for loans. Therefore, futures contract on Eurodollar deposit is cash-settled, that is, the difference of price on initial contract and offsetting contract is exchanged.

Futures on Eurodollar deposits are quoted on index basis—that is, 100 – annualized forward rate, I, as given by Eq. 11-3.

$$\text{Eurodollar futures price, } F = 100 - \text{3-m LIBOR rate} = 100 - I \qquad (11\text{-}3)$$

A futures price of 91.50 would imply annualized yield of 8.50%, that is, 100 – 91.50. Index-based quotation of futures contract is a convention to be consistent with other futures market where a long position gains with the increase of the underlying asset. Since there is an inverse relationship of the value of fixed income security with interest rate, the index-based quotations are used.

Value of Eurodollar Futures

The value of the futures contract on Eurodollar initiated at 91.50 would be reckoned as given by Eq. 11-4. Eurodollar being a three-month deposit, the annualized rate is converted to quarterly rate by using a factor of 90/360.

$$\text{Value of Eurodollar futures contract} = \$1{,}000{,}000 \times \left[1 - I\,\frac{90}{360}\right] \qquad (11\text{-}4)$$

As the interest rate increases, the value of futures contract would also increase. At 91.50, the value of Eurodollar futures contract is US$978,750

$$\text{Value of Eurodollar futures contract} = \$1{,}000{,}000 \times \left[1 - 0.085\,\frac{90}{360}\right] = \text{US}\$978{,}750$$

At maturity of the futures contract, the buyer is supposed to pay US$978,750 and get delivery of Eurodollar deposit that matures 91 days thereafter. However, a Eurodollar deposit is a non-transferable instrument and, hence, the futures contract cannot be satisfied with delivery. One would have to cash settle it by entering an offsetting contract before or on maturity. The value of the offsetting contract would also be found using Eq. 11-4. Assume that yields have fallen to 8% when an offsetting contract is entered. The value of futures contract would rise to US$980,000.

$$\text{Value of Eurodollar futures contract} = \$1{,}000{,}000 \times \left[1 - 0.080\,\frac{90}{360}\right] = \text{US}\$980{,}000$$

For the initial buy contract one would sell for offsetting. Seller of the Eurodollar futures would receive US$980,000. For initial buy and offsetting sell contract one ends up making a profit of US$1,250.

The yield on the Eurodollar deposit is quoted on add-on basis, whereas most fixed income instruments are quoted on the basis of discount yield, that is, debt instruments mature at the face value and are sold at discount to the face value. Eurodollar deposits have a face value to which yield is added. Add-on yield[1] is higher than discount yield. Irrespective of yield being on discount or add-on basis traders in Eurodollar futures are only concerned about changes in the yield because position has to be cash-settled. One basis point change in yield would change the Eurodollar futures value to change by US$25 (1,000,000 × 0.0001/4). Change in the yield from 8.00% to 8.50% implies a cash flow of US$1,250 (50 bps × 25).

Hedging with Eurodollar Futures

The illustration just discussed on Eurodollar futures lays down the rule for hedging with them. We may conclude as follows:

(1) One who goes long on futures would make profit if yield falls and lose if yields rise.
(2) Conversely, who goes short on futures ends up with profit if interest rate rises and with loss if interest rate falls.

---

[1] $\text{Add-on yield} = \dfrac{\text{Discount}}{\text{Face value} - \text{Discount}} \times \dfrac{360}{\text{Days to maturity}}$

Exercise 11-3
Borrower's Hedge with Eurodollar

Three months from now London Motors Limited (LML) needs to raise short-term loan of US$20 million for three months. Current LIBOR is 6.50% and the Eurodollar futures contract with three months to expire is quoted at 93.00 (implying an interest rate of 7%). The LML expects the interest rate to rise to 8%.
(a) How can LML hedge against the rising interest rates?
(b) What would be the effective cost if the interest rate actually rises to 8%?
(c) Analyse the interest cost if LIBOR actually falls to 6%.

Solution
(a) LML faces the risk of rising interest rate for its contemplated borrowing three months from now. It needs to go short on Eurodollar futures worth an amount equal to US$20 million. Therefore, it needs to short 20 Eurodollar futures contracts to freeze the borrowing cost to around 7%, the current yield reflected in Eurodollar futures. After three months, it buys back the Eurodollar futures and resorts to borrowing at market rates prevailing then.

(b) If LIBOR rises to 8%, the Eurodollar price would fall to 92.00. The profit of each futures contract would be

Profit/loss on Eurodollar futures (for short position)

$$= \$1,000,000 \times \frac{F_0 - F_1}{100} \times \frac{90}{360}$$

$$= \$1,000,000 \times \frac{93.00 - 92.00}{100} \times \frac{90}{360} = \$2,500$$

The borrowing cost for $20 million = 20,000,000 × 0.08 × 90/360 = $400,000
Less: Profit from 20 Eurodollar futures contracts = 2,500 × 20 = $50,000
Effective interest paid = $350,000

$$\text{Effective interest rate} = \frac{350,000}{20,000,000} \times \frac{360}{90} = 7.00\%$$

This is the rate implicit in the futures contract now that can be locked in.

(c) If LIBOR falls to 6%, the Eurodollar price would rise to 94.00. The loss of each futures contract would be

Profit/loss on Eurodollar futures (for short position)

$$= \$1,000,000 \times \frac{F_0 - F_1}{100} \times \frac{90}{360}$$

$$= \$1,000,000 \times \frac{93.00 - 94.00}{100} \times \frac{90}{360} = -\$2,500$$

The borrowing cost for $20 million = 20,000,000 × 0.06 × 90/360 = $300,000
Add: Loss from 20 Eurodollar futures contracts = 2,500 × 20 = $50,000
Effective interest paid = $350,000

$$\text{Effective interest rate} = \frac{350,000}{20,000,000} \times \frac{360}{90} = 7.00\%$$

With fall in the interest rates, the firm would not benefit. It still has to pay the same cost of 7%, the rate implicit in the futures contract now.

A borrowing firm is apprehensive of rising interest rates and faces a loss. By taking a short position on Eurodollar futures, the expected loss from the rising interest rate can be made good through futures. An investing firm is apprehensive of falling yields and faces a loss if they do. By taking a long position on Eurodollar futures, the expected loss from falling interest rate can be made good through futures. Simply stated, the hedging rule would be

(1) A *borrowing firm* wishing to lock in borrowing cost with rising yield must *go short on Eurodollar futures*, and

(2) An *investing firm* wanting to lock in a return on investment with falling yield must *go long on Eurodollar futures*.

INTEREST RATE OPTIONS

Interest rate forwards and futures are the products that provide protection from adverse movement of interest at the expense of sacrificing the potential gain that may accrue due to favourable movement of interest rates. Like options on any other asset protect the downside while retaining the upside, interest rate options do the same for interest rates. One cannot have protection from downside simultaneously with the retention of upside gain without incurring a cost. Hence, interest rate options like options on any other asset would require payment of premium upfront by the buyer of the option. The premium is specified in terms of percentage of the face value of the contract representing the notional principal.

As usual we need to highlight that forward contracts on interest rate, that is, FRAs and futures, discussed earlier are obligatory in nature. The commitments under FRA are binding irrespective of the outcome at the maturity. Booking an FRA by the borrower would freeze the borrowing rate. In case the interest rate fell, the borrowers would not be able to take advantage of the situation. Therefore, hedging with forwards and futures has implicit cost in terms of sacrificing the potential gain from favourable changes in interest rate.

Options on interest rate would provide a right without creating obligations, just as any other option on any asset, and thereby let the advantage be availed. The options that have interest rate as underlying asset are referred to as interest rate options. They are called CAPs, FLOORs, and COLLARs. Unlike FRAs, futures, and swaps, options on interest rate are not firm commitments but are rights for which a price has to be paid upfront. Such options on interest rates are OTC products. In addition, many bonds have these options embedded in the product itself.

Call Option on Interest Rate

Consider, for example, a borrowing firm having issued bonds with semi-annual coupon determined on the basis of MIBOR. Assume that the firm pays interest to the subscribers of the bond at each six-month interval on the basis of MIBOR that prevailed at the beginning of the period (coupons on floating rate are decided one period in advance). If MIBOR goes up, the liability of the firm too goes up. Can anything be done to contain the rising cost of debt? Let us examine how an interest rate option can limit the borrowing cost with an example.

Assume that a firm is planning to issue three months from now a five-year bond with the face value of ₹100 million, coupon payable semi-annually. The coupon would be decided 100 bps over 6-m MIBOR prevailing at the time of the issue. The firm can afford a maximum coupon of 9.00% but cannot defer the issue for urgent need of funds. The way out for the firm is to buy a European call option on interest rate with a strike of 8.00% based on 6-m MIBOR. The call option on interest rate gives right to the holder to exercise without obligation. It provides for flexibility as well as opportunities to avail profitable opportunities. A call option on interest rate would have contract specifications as follows:

Notional Principal	₹100 million
Strike Interest Rate	8.00%
Underlying Interest Rate	6-m MIBOR
Time to Expiry	91 days
Premium	20 bps (₹200,000)

The firm buys the option by paying a premium of ₹200,000 with cap on interest rate. When interest rate exceeds the strike interest rate, the holder exercises the call else lets it expire. If at the end of 91 days, 6-m MIBOR is above strike of 8.00%, the holder gets the differential interest rate for 182 days on notional principal discounted at MIBOR. The cash flow under the call option is based on a notional principal just as was the case under FRAs and swaps. The payoff of the interest rate option is calculated in Figure 11-3 where an amount of ₹962,454 becomes payable to the holder if after 91 days 6-m MIBOR turns out to be 10%.

It is evident from the presentation that call option on interest rate is suitable for borrowing firms who want to limit the cost of borrowing without surrendering the advantage of availing funds at lower cost.

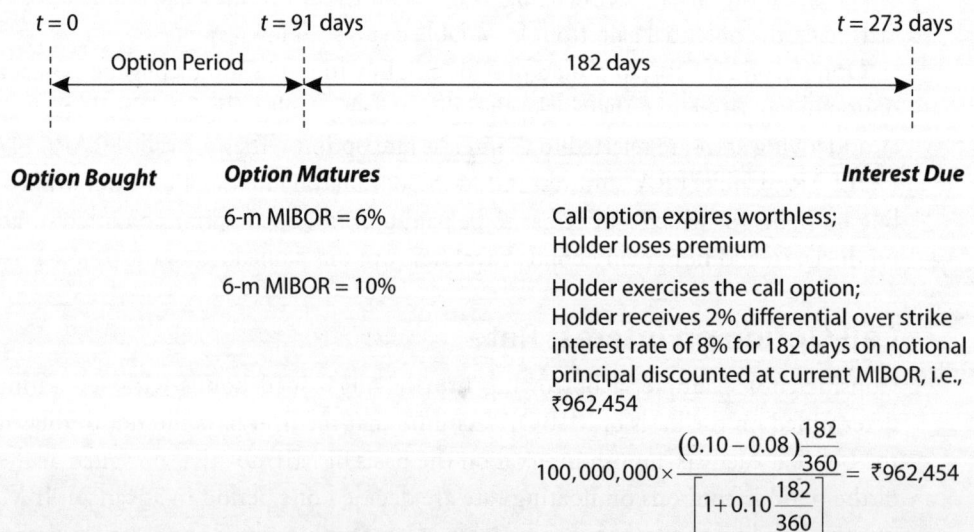

Figure 11-3
Interest Rate Option—Call

$$100,000,000 \times \frac{(0.10 - 0.08)\frac{182}{360}}{\left[1 + 0.10 \frac{182}{360}\right]} = ₹962,454$$

Put Option on Interest Rate

Just as call options provide a cap on the cost of fund, a put option on interest rate assures a minimum return on investment. It is suitable for investing firms which want to assure a floor on the investment while retaining the advantage of availing opportunities of getting higher return.

We explain put option on interest with an example. We now assume that a firm is interested in investing surplus funds of ₹100 million available to them after 91 days from now. The returns are MIBOR-based and they expect to get 6-m MIBOR + 50 bps. The first lot of interest would be paid 273 days later based on the 6-m MIBOR determined 91 days from now. MIBOR has been falling and the firm wants to assure itself of a minimum return of 8.00%. It can buy a put option as follows:

Notional Principal	₹100 million
Strike Interest Rate	8.00%
Underlying Interest Rate	6-m MIBOR
Time to Expiry	91 days
Premium	30 bps (₹300,000)

The firm buys the put option by paying a premium of ₹300,000 with floor on interest rate. When interest rate exceeds the strike interest rate, the holder lets the put option expire and invest the surplus at the higher rate prevailing. If at the end of 91 days, 6-m MIBOR is lower than the strike of 8%, the holder gets the differential interest rate for 182 days on notional principal discounted at MIBOR. The cash flow under the put option is based on a notional principal just as was the case under FRAs and swaps. The payoff of the interest rate option is calculated in Figure 11-4 where an amount of ₹981,344 becomes payable to the holder if after 91 days 6-m MIBOR turns out to be 6.00%.

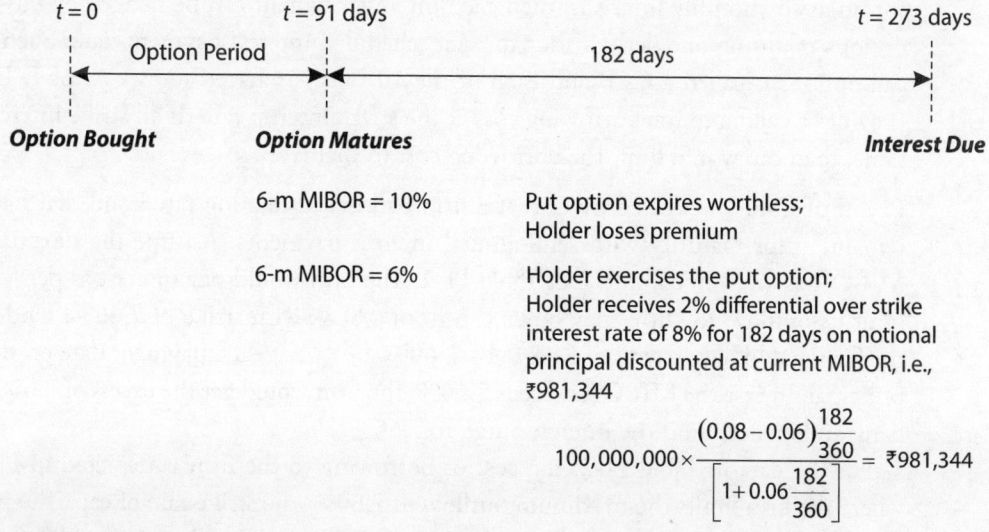

$$100,000,000 \times \frac{(0.08 - 0.06)\frac{182}{360}}{\left[1 + 0.06 \frac{182}{360}\right]} = ₹981,344$$

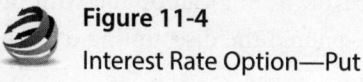

Figure 11-4
Interest Rate Option—Put

The payoff of call and put options on interest rate is shown in Figure 11-5. Note that the payoff of call and put on interest rate is curved and not linear at the strike rate. The reason is that the payoff in case of interest rate options is discounted at the interest rate which is the underlying itself, while for options on other asset the payoff is not discounted.

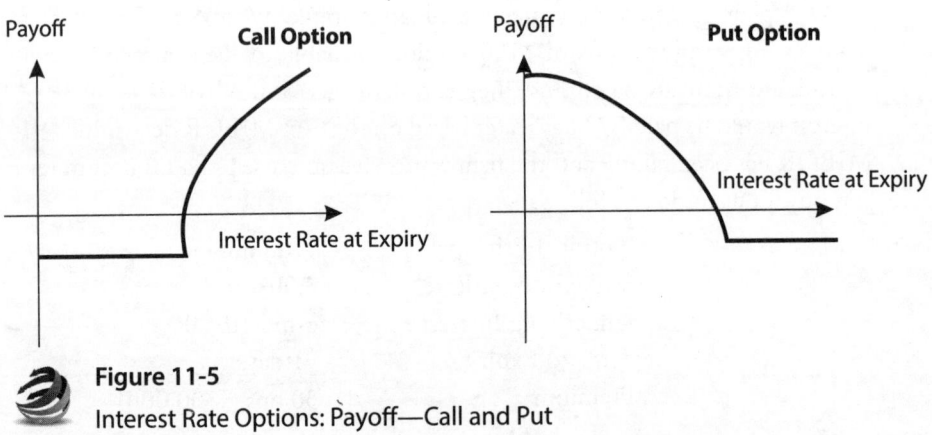

Figure 11-5
Interest Rate Options: Payoff—Call and Put

CAPS

We saw how a single cash flow of interest payable or receivable in future based on floating rate can be hedged with call or put option on interest rate. Investment or borrowing is normally made for an extended period of time with interest flows at periodic intervals. Each subsequent cash flow of interest spreads over life of borrowing/investment with call and put options with maturity of option matching time when interest rate is fixed.

For example, if a borrowing firm issues a five-year bond with semi-annual interest payment spread at six monthly intervals, then each interest payment can be hedged by buying 10 call options maturing one period prior to each scheduled interest payment date. Such a series of call options is called a CAP and each of the 10 calls is referred to as CAPLET. Each caplet provides a ceiling to the borrowing cost at the strike interest rate. If all strike interest rates are same, then cap would limit the borrowing cost to that level.

Payoff of Cap: Let us consider that a firm had issued floating rate bond that has five years remaining for maturity with semi-annual interest payments. Assume the next 10 values of MIBOR as given in column 2 of Table 11-2. The firm would pay interest as per MIBOR. To limit its outflow, the firm may buy a cap from a bank with strike of 7.60%. Under this cap, the firm would have payoff of Max (M − 7.60%, 0) × ½ at each payment date on the notional principal. In case the MIBOR exceeds 7.60%, the firm would get the excess of 7.60% from the bank and, hence, limit the interest outgo to 7.60%.

For the data in Table 11-2, the cost of borrowing to the firm is depicted in Figure 11-6, where the firm limits the maximum outflow to 7.60%, the strike rate of cap. The payoff from cap at each exercise date, called a *caplet* is like payoff from a call option with interest rate as underlying as depicted in Figure 11-6. We have ignored the discounting of each payment to keep the exposition simple.

Table 11-2
Interest with and without CAP

Time Months	MIBOR %	Floating Rate Interest %	Interest with Cap %
0	7.00	–	–
6	7.25	7.00	7.00
12	8.00	7.25	7.25
18	7.50	8.00	7.60
24	8.50	7.50	7.50
30	7.60	8.50	7.60
36	7.80	7.60	7.60
42	8.20	7.80	7.60
48	8.50	8.20	7.60
54	7.80	8.50	7.60
60	–	7.80	7.60

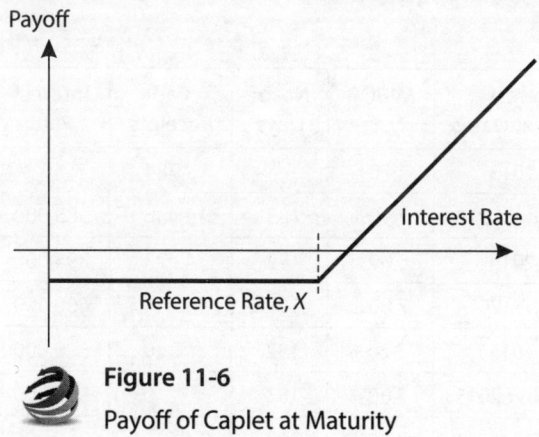

Figure 11-6
Payoff of Caplet at Maturity

Payoff of cap on each exercise date would depend upon (a) the reference rate, M, (b) the cap rate, X, (c) notional loan amount, L, and (d) how many times per year the interest is paid, m. The payoff on each exercise date is given by Eq. 11-5.

$$\frac{L}{m} \times \text{Max}\,(M-X,0) \qquad (11\text{-}5)$$

Like FRA and swap, cap is an independent product and it is immaterial whether the actual liability of floating rate interest rate payment exists or not.

Exercise 11-4
Capping Borrowing Cost

Today is October 2012. A firm needs to raise ₹1 crore in April 2013 for five years with interest payable every six months based on 6-m MIBOR. MIBOR currently at 7.40% is showing a rising trend. A cap is available to the firm with strike of 7.50% at 1% of notional amount consisting of 10 caplets.

(a) What would be the maximum cost of borrowing if the firm buys the cap?
(b) Assume that 6-m MIBOR on 1 of April and October for next five years are as follows:

1 April 2013	1 October 2013	1 April 2014	1 October 2014	1 April 2015
7.70%	7.90%	8.00%	7.80%	7.20%
1 October 2015	1 April 2016	1 October 2016	1 April 2017	1 October 2017
7.00%	7.80%	8.50%	8.30%	7.90%

Find out the cost of borrowing with and without the cap.

Solution

(a) If the firm buys a cap with strike of 7.5%, the cost of funds would not exceed 7.50%. In case the MIBOR turns out to be more than 7.50%, then the excess interest would be paid by the cap seller to the firm. The reimbursement of the extra interest payable would contain the cost to 7.50%. However, for buying the cap, the firm has to incur upfront cost of 1% which would increase the cost. Assuming an approximate amortization of the cost over five years the approximate cost of funds would increase to 7.70%.

(b) The cash flows of the borrowing with assumed MIBOR with and without cap are given in the following table:

S. No.	Interest Payment Dates	MIBOR	No. of Days	Cap Receipts	Interest Paid	Cash Flow under Cap	Cash Flow without Cap
0	1 April 2013	7.70%		9,784		−99,09,784	−10,000,000
1	1 October 2013	7.90%	183	19,446	385,000	365,554	385,000
2	1 April 2014	8.00%	182	24,423	395,000	370,577	395,000
3	1 October 2014	7.80%	183	14,591	400,000	385,409	400,000
4	1 April 2015	7.20%	182	0	390,000	390,000	390,000
5	1 October 2015	7.00%	183	0	360,000	360,000	360,000
6	1 April 2016	7.80%	183	14,668	350,000	335,332	350,000
7	1 October 2016	8.50%	183	48,473	390,000	341,527	390,000
8	1 April 2017	8.30%	182	39,020	425,000	385,980	425,000
9	1 October 2017	7.90%	183	19,446	415,000	395,554	415,000
10	1 April 2018		182	0	395,000	10,395,000	10,395,000
Effective Cost of Borrowing		Semi-annual				3.83%	3.90%
		Annual				7.66%	7.80%

The IRR of the cash flows of the borrowing would be its cost. With cap, the cost comes to 7.66% and without cap the cost is 7.80%.

The amounts are calculated based on Actual/360 days with one period in advance and discounted at 6-m MIBOR. For payment of 1 October 2014, the calculations are as follows:

(1) The amount payable to the lender on 1 October 2014 is determined on the basis of 6-m MIBOR on 1 April 2014 observed at 8%.
(2) Interest payable to lender, therefore, would be 8%/2 × 10,000,000 = ₹400,000
(3) Since 6-m MIBOR is determined on 1 April 2014, the cap writer would pay the differential interest rate of 0.5% towards loan servicing payment due on 1 October 2014 as follows:

$$\frac{1,00,00,000 \times (0.080 - 0.075)\frac{183}{360}}{\left[1 + 0.08\frac{183}{360}\right]} = ₹24,423$$

Floor

Similar to the cap, a series of put options maturing at equally spaced intervals matching with the date of receipt of each interest is called a FLOOR. A single put option in a FLOOR is called a *floorlet*. The strike interest rate of each floorlet is the minimum return assured for single interest received, whereas that of the floor is the minimum return assured for entire duration of investment.

Payoff of Floor: As stated a floor is a series of put options on interest rate. The payoff of the floorlet would be Max $(X - M, 0)$, where X is the floor rate and M is the floating rate on the maturity of the floorlet. When interest falls below X, the investing firm receives M from investment and $X - M$ from the floorlet, ensuring minimum aggregate return of X. On each exercise date, the payoff would be determined and a guaranteed return as fixed by floor value can be achieved for the desired tenure. The payoff of floorlet is depicted in Figure 11-7,

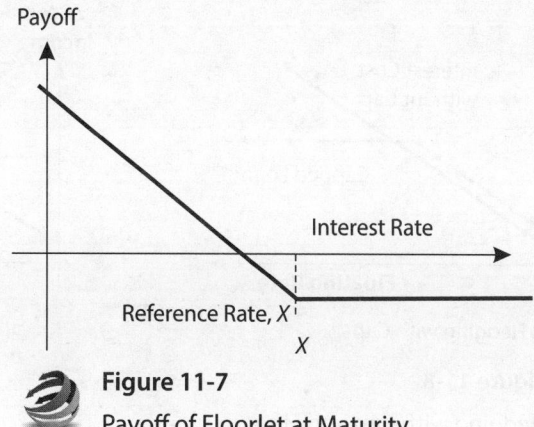

Figure 11-7
Payoff of Floorlet at Maturity

which is similar to the put holder with interest rate as underlying. Again, we have ignored the discounting of cash flow under floor. Like cap, floor is also independent of the investment contract. Since the investment and the position in floor can be with different parties, it is not necessary that the underlying investment asset must exist to have position on floor option.

Relationship between Cap and Floor   There exists a relationship between the values of caps and floors. Each caplet is like a call option and each floorlet is like a put option. Buying a cap and selling a floor with the same strike is like entering into a swap with fixed rate equal to the strike rate. For example, consider buying a cap and selling floor both at strike of 10%. It always results in the inflow of M, floating rate, and cash outflow of 10%, the strike. This is identical with the cash flows of a swap to receive floating and pay fixed as shown here:

	Cash flow		Interest in %
	Sold Floor	Bought Cap	Total
When $M < 10$	$-(10 - M)$	–	$M - 10$
When $M > 10$	–	$(M - 10)$	$M - 10$

Therefore, we may say

$$\text{Value of Cap} - \text{Value of Floor} = \text{Value of Swap}$$

Collar

For a borrowing firm, the cost of funds can be contained to a maximum level of strike rate of the cap. The buyer of such option has to pay a premium for obtaining the protection. Similarly, an investing firm can assure a minimum return by buying a floor. In addition, to get assured minimum return, the investor must pay a premium. The writers of cap and floor receive this premium to provide protection from rising cost or assuring minimum return.

Like any option, the payoffs of caps and floors for the seller (writer) would be opposite to those of the holder. The writer of cap or floor earns the premium paid by the holder.

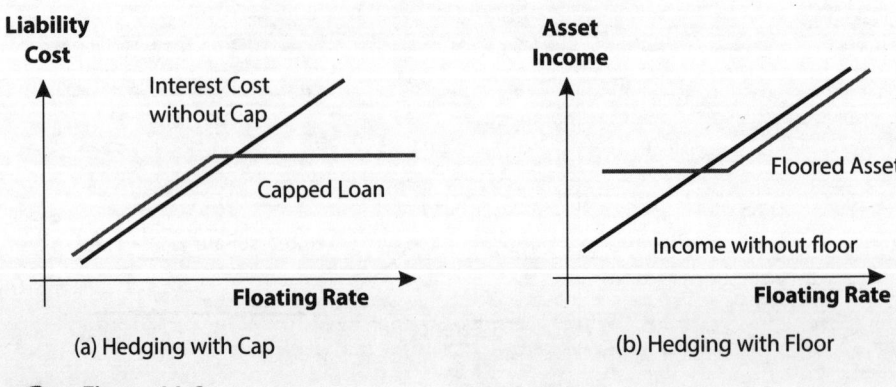

Figure 11-8
Hedging with Cap and Floor

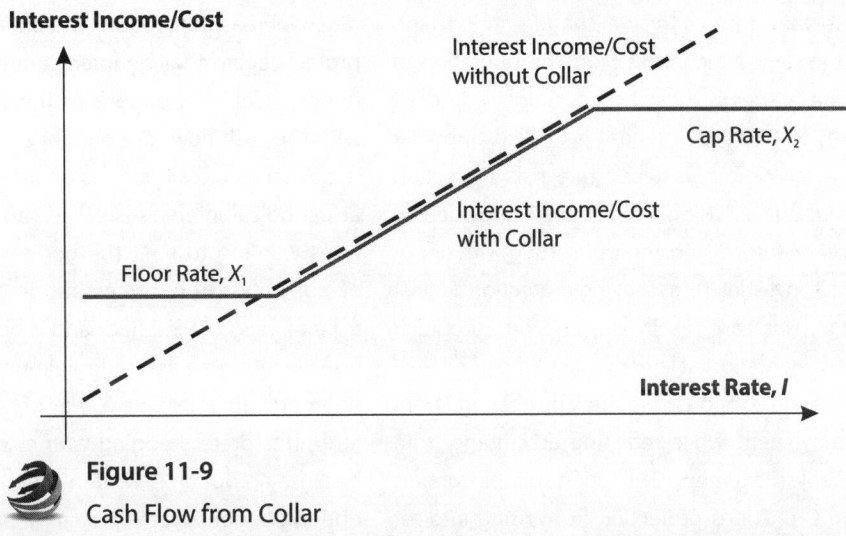

Figure 11-9
Cash Flow from Collar

As a strategy of cost cutting, just as we used range forward for foreign exchange risk, a borrowing firm may buy a cap and simultaneously sell a floor to earn some premium. This offsets the cost of cap either completely or partially. The cap rate and floor rate may be adjusted such that the premium on cap equals the premium on floor for achieving zero cost. Buying cap and writing floor or buying a floor and writing a cap is called a collar. Premiums of cap and floor depend upon the strike rate chosen. Choosing appropriate strikes of cap and floor may result in a collar with zero cost. Such a collar is referred to as zero-cost collar.

To attain zero cost, a borrowing firm buys cap and sells floor. In such a collar, the borrowing firm would give up some of the gains that could accrue on down side movement of interest rate. Hedging with cap, floor, and collar are depicted in Figures 11-8 and 11-9.

SUMMARY

All firms are affected by fluctuating interest rates. Firms in sectors such as auto and real estate have relatively larger impact on profitability. Firms in banking and financial services are most affected as their profitability almost entirely dependent upon spreads.

The risk from changing interest rate can be managed by derivatives on interest rate. To design a derivative product, we need underlying assets whose value is almost entirely dependent upon interest rates. The value of assets must reflect the return expectation that does not include the risk premium. Yields on government securities are considered risk free, but they are not regarded as a suitable benchmark because investment in these securities is motivated by tax considerations and environmental compulsions. It is assumed that rates offered by bans in a competitive manner truly reflect the market and can also be presumed to be risk-free. Therefore, polled rates like LIBOR are considered a suitable benchmark interest rate for design and determination of payoff of interest rate derivatives.

Basic derivative products of forwards, futures, options, and swaps are available on interest rates. The FRA quotes two-way rates for deposit and lending at a future date for a notional principal amount. This cash-settled OTC product enables fixing of interest rate in advance for investment and borrowing over short term.

Interest rate futures are exchange-traded and perform the same function as FRA. The quotation of interest rate futures is index-based. Globally, interest rate futures on Eurodollar deposit is the most popular instrument for hedging interest rate risk. Protection to borrowers against rising interest rate is provided by going short on futures and, then, offsetting with opposite contract. Investing firms seeking protection against the falling yields can initially go long on Eurodollar futures and, then, short at later point of time.

Interest rate options provide protection from adverse movement while retaining advantage from the favourable movement. Call option suitable for borrowing firms provides protection from rising interest rate, whereas put option suitable for investing firms protects against falling interest rates. For a long-term hedge, a series of options with maturities coinciding with the cash flows are bought as a composite product. A series of call options on interest rate maturing at periodical intervals is called cap and is bought by firms wanting to limit the borrowing costs. A series of put options on interest rate maturing at periodical intervals is called floor and is bought by investing firms wanting an assured minimum return. Caps and floors are rather expensive way of hedging, and therefore firms prefer hedging with collar which cost less because an option is written simultaneously with the option bought offsetting a part of premium.

QUESTIONS

11-1 What are the desirable features of a benchmark interest rate that can serve as a reference rate for designing interest rate derivatives?
11-2 What do you understand by a forward rate agreement quoted as INR6/9 10.00–10.25? How would this forward rate agreement be settled?
11-3 How would a borrowing firm hedge with an forward rate agreement? Explain with an example.
11-4 What is a Eurodollar deposit? Describe the working of futures on them.
11-6 Explain hedging for investing and borrowing firm with Eurodollar futures.
11-7 How is options hedge for interest rate different from forwards and futures hedge?
11-8 Explain the following terms:
    (a) Caplet   (b) Floorlet   (c) Cap   (d) Floor
11-9 What is a collar and why are collars a more popular way of hedging interest rate risk?

PROBLEMS

11-1 **Hedging with FRA-Borrower**
A firm needs to borrow US$50 million in next three months for a period of six months. In view of the extremely volatile situation in the money markets, they wish to lock in their borrowing rate. A 3/9 forward rate agreement on US dollars is quoted at 6.00–6.50%.
 (a) How should the firm hedge?
 (b) How would forward rate agreement be settled at the end of three months from now if reference rate is (i) 5.50% and (ii) 7.50%? Assume 182 days in the 6-m period.
 (c) What would be the borrowing cost of the firm under each circumstance described above?

11-2 **Hedging with FRA-Investor**
Refer to Problem 11-1. Describe how an investing firm would lock in the return. What returns would the firm get if the interest rate at the end of three months is (a) 5.50% and (b) 7.50%?

11-3 Hedging with Eurodollar Futures

A firm while projecting a cash flow statement realizes that it would have a shortfall of US$10 million after three months for the next three months. To overcome liquidity problems, it would have to borrow at LIBOR + 100 bps. LIBOR is on the rise. A 3-m Eurodollar futures is currently trading at 95.18. Explain how the firm can lock in the borrowing rate. If 3-m LIBOR after three months is 5%, what would be the cash flow under Eurodollar futures contract?

11-4 Hedging with Eurodollar Futures

Refer to Problem 11-3 and discuss the same question if the firm was having a surplus of US$10 million for three months and LIBOR were showing a falling trend.

11-5 Hedging with Cap

A firm has an outstanding loan of ₹50 million with six semi-annual payments due on each 15 March and 15 September based on MIBOR + 100 bps. It buys a cap for three years with the following terms:

Notional Principal	₹50 million
Strike Interest Rate	8%
Underlying Rate	6-m MIBOR
Reset Dates	15 March and 15 September
Premium	1% of notional value

Draw a cash flow for the firm assuming the following rates of 6-m MIBOR in the next three years:

15 March 20X1	9.0%	15 March 20X2	8.3%	15 March 20X3	9.2%
15 September 20X1	8.5%	15 September 20X2	9.5%	15 September 20X3	8.3%

What is the effective cost of loan with and without cap?

Part IV
Foreign Exchange Risk Management

12. Measurement and Management of Transaction Exposure
13. Measurement and Management of Translation and Economic Exposure
14. Political and Country Risk

12

Measurement and Management of Transaction Exposure

LEARNING OBJECTIVES

This chapter aims at

- explaining the various risks related to foreign exchange rates
- defining and differentiating among transaction, translation, and economic exposures
- explaining the importance of managing transaction exposure
- describing the internal hedging strategies
- explaining the mechanisms of hedging with financial instruments
- explaining and differentiating among forward hedge, money market hedge, futures hedge, and options hedge

CONTENTS

Introduction
Transaction Exposure
    When does Transaction Exposure Arise
    Which Transactions to Include
    Factors Affecting Transaction Exposure
    Measuring Transaction Exposure
Translation Exposure and Economic
    Exposure—Defined
Management of Transaction Exposure
Importance of Managing Transaction Exposure
    Hedge or Not to Hedge: Selective Hedging
Hedging Strategies

Internal Hedging Strategies
    Invoicing
    Exposure Netting
    Leading and Lagging
    Risk Sharing
Hedging with Financial Instruments
    Forward Hedge
    Effectiveness of Forward Hedge
    Underbooking/Overbooking of Forward Contract
    Money Market Hedge
    Futures Hedge
    Options Hedge

INTRODUCTION

Conducting business denominated in foreign currency gives rise to the risk of uncertain cash flows in domestic currency due to uncertainty of exchange rates. Since most costs, such as raw material (if not imported), wages, utility payments, interest, and taxes, are denominated in local currency, the need for conversion of foreign currency transactions into local currency is inevitable. With almost continuous fluctuations in exchange rates and sometimes very large, the firm is generally exposed to the uncertainty of the cash flows in local currency. These uncertainties in cash flows arising due to changes in exchange rates are referred to as exposures in the context of international finance and multinational firms.

The containment of risk arising due to exchange rate fluctuations is dependent upon many factors, such as proportion of business in foreign currency, volatility of exchange rates, and forecasting abilities and its accuracy. While proportion of business denominated in foreign currencies and volatility of exchange rate fall in the uncontrollable domain, the crucial element in the risk remains that of forecasting abilities. Forecasting of exchange rate is possibly more hazardous than forecasting stock prices merely due to the fact that the number of variables affecting exchange rates is much larger being global in nature than those affecting stock prices predominantly dependent on domestic factors. Therefore, apart from coping with normal business uncertainties, multinational corporations (MNCs), exporters, and importers have to contend with additional dimension of foreign exchange risk.

Besides business transactions, MNCs also deal in assets and liabilities denominated in the foreign currencies. The values of these assets and liabilities are also subject to variations when converted in local currency at different points of time. These values would depend upon the exchange rate prevailing at the time when valuation is done.

As stated earlier, uncertainties in the valuation of assets and liabilities emanating from the business transaction fall in the category of foreign exchange risk often referred to as exposure in the parlance of international finance. These exposures can be classified into three categories as follows:

1. Transaction exposure
2. Translation exposure
3. Economic exposure

This chapter would deal with the measurement and management of transaction exposure. The remaining two exposures will be discussed in the subsequent chapter.

TRANSACTION EXPOSURE

Transaction exposure arises from the transactions that are ***denominated in foreign currency but are not yet settled.*** These would include the exports invoiced in foreign currency for which the payment is not received, and the imports made in foreign currency that are not yet paid. Cash transactions invoiced in foreign currency are immediately settled at the spot rates that are known at the time of entering the transaction. As such they do not face any uncertainties with regard to how much money in local currency is received or paid. However, credit transactions of buying or selling of goods/services denominated in foreign currency are settled only after the credit period ends. The amounts in local currencies can only be ascertained only when actual payment fructifies on the basis of spot rates prevailing then. Since the spot rates at the end of credit period are unknown, the risk of uncertain cash flows in domestic currency arises.

When does Transaction Exposure Arise?

Transaction exposures do not include deals for which foreign currency amounts have not been crystallized. Typically, this would include orders in progress that have not been invoiced yet. Some people regard that transaction exposure arises even before the dispatch of goods and services are made and invoiced. In case the firm has agreed to supply the goods/services based on the quoted prices and confirmed the order received, the transaction exposure is deemed to arise then. Here, invoicing is a mere part of the routine and the supplier has no flexibility of adjusting the invoice as per the exchange rate changes. Transaction exposure must be reckoned from the time when the firm loses the right to adjust the price due to changes in the exchange rates. It may happen any time from the time of quoting for a tender to the acceptance of tender or completion of supply. Transaction exposure, therefore, arises not on the day of invoicing but on the day when the price is frozen.

Which Transactions to Include

The nature of transaction exposure is not confined to trade transactions alone. It includes transactions on capital account too where firms may have raised foreign currency loans or foreign equity by way of ADR/GDR issue. Loans are serviced by interest and finally redeemed while equity too needs to be rewarded with periodic dividends.

The transaction exposure may be defined as impact on the immediate cash flows of the firm in local currency due to transactions entered in foreign currency that are not yet settled. Interest on loans and dividend on foreign equity are examples of that. Since the cash flows of the firm in the immediate future are affected, the transaction exposure becomes important from the perspective of liquidity of the firm. Persistent liquidity problems could lead to structural problems later when it translates into a situation that could be threatening the survival of the enterprise. Persistent lack of liquidity is a precursor to ominously deteriorating profitability.

Factors Affecting Transaction Exposure

The exposure to exchange rate fluctuation would depend upon (i) the amount or proportion of trade denominated in foreign currencies, (ii) the length of the credit period granted, and (iii) the unanticipated change in exchange rate from the date of invoicing to the date of realization/payment, that is, the volatility in the spot exchange rate.

Proportion of Trade in Foreign Currencies Larger the amount or proportion of trade in foreign currency, larger would be the exposure/risk of foreign exchange rate fluctuations at any given point of time. Naturally, businesses that depend heavily on imported materials and exporting finished goods are more prone to changes in the exchange rate environment than those substantially or wholly dependent upon domestic markets. The firms having larger proportion of international business face larger transaction exposure.

Time Lag between Actual Cash Flow and Invoicing Similarly, firms which avail or extend larger credit periods are exposed to greater exchange rate fluctuations than those extending/accepting smaller credit periods. This is based on the premise that uncertainties compound with time. One would be less confident of the forecast of exchange rate for six months than for the forecast of one month. For example, consider an American exporting goods to China and accepting payment in Chinese yuan. In view of the fact that yuan is pegged to US dollar, the exporter does not face any foreign currency exposure because the payable amount is fixed in Chinese yuan as well as in US dollars. This may be true in near future. However, if the credit period is extended to say one year, when the Chinese currency is likely to move more and more towards flexible exchange rate system, the American exporter may have apprehensions in receiving payment in yuan.

Volatility of Exchange Rates Finally, the exposure would depend upon how strong or weak the foreign currency is. The volatility of the currency in the international markets is a function of several factors complexly interlinked with each other. The ability of the currency to maintain the exchange rate and absorb shocks of economic, monetary, and political changes taking place across the world governs the strength of the currency. Firms are more willing to invoice in the currencies that have demonstrated stability in the exchange rate for protracted period of time in the past given no exchange controls. If the change in the exchange rate does not deviate much from the forecast exchange rate, the exposure to foreign exchange rate is nominal.

The variability in the exchange rate can be gauged by many parameters. Standard deviation of the exchange rate movements is one common and well-accepted measure of risk or strength of a currency. Larger the standard deviation of exchange rate of a currency, riskier is the transaction in that currency. Such statement is valid for currencies whose value is decided by market forces alone. The standard deviation of currencies that are subject to pegging or managed float the standard deviations would be too small and is not a factor in choosing the currency of trade. Pegged currencies are not considered as strong currencies. When exchange rates are pegged, for example, Chinese yuan, the standard deviation would be too low but it should not be construed as a sign of strong currency.

Especially for currencies that are pegged or are under managed float, quite often the changes in the exchange rates are drastic. Several such incidents have happened in the past that have made exchange rate movements extremely volatile. The crisis of Mexican peso, Asian currency crisis of 1997–98, both attributed to pegging of currencies, and more recent Greek crisis for euro attributed to fiscal indiscipline and structural differences among nations in the Eurozone are some examples of sudden and relatively large changes in small periods of time. Re-occurrence of such crises in future is not ruled out. By and large these changes were unexpected and wild.

Measuring Transaction Exposure

The impact of transaction exposure is measured by the extent to which cash flows in local currency are affected by the conversion of receipts and payments of transactions denominated in foreign

currency. Therefore, measurement of transaction exposure involves (a) aggregation of exposures in different foreign currencies, (b) netting the inflows and out flows, (c) forecasting the changes in exchange rates and their volatilities, and (d) studying correlations between different currencies.

Netting is required because cash inflows and out flows of the same foreign currency have opposite effect. If appreciation of foreign currency is good for exporters (inflow), it becomes bad for importers (outflows). For example, if a firm expects to receive US$100 from one customer and pay US$100 to a supplier, both at the same point of time, the firm faces no risk of fluctuating exchange rate as positive/negative impact of changes are passed on from the customer to the supplier with the firm remaining unaffected. Receivables and payables are said to provide a *natural hedge* against foreign exchange rate risk.

If two currencies are positively correlated, the transaction exposure of both the currencies is additive. However, if there is a negative correlation among the currencies, the transaction exposure may be nullifying. For example, imagine a situation that when Japanese yen rises with respect to Indian rupee when the value of dollar falls. In such a case, for an Indian exporter invoicing in Japanese yen to Japanese customer and in US dollars to American customer the transaction exposures would tend to cancel out to the extent of the lesser of the amounts. However, if yen and US dollar move in the same direction, the exposures in Japanese yen and US dollars would be additive.

Therefore, the factors that would govern the quantum of transaction exposure would be dependent upon (a) the volatility as measured by standard deviation of the currency of exposure and (b) the nature and degree of the coefficient of correlation in the various currencies of exposure.

Exercise 12-1
Computing Transaction Exposure

Flex Industries Limited imports petroleum intermediates and converts them into polyfilms for sale including exports. For the next year, it has the following foreign exchange transactions expected in US dollar and euro:

In millions	US dollars	Euros
Payment for Import of a Machine from Europe	–	7.0
Payment for Import of Raw Material from Europe		3.5
Payment for Import of Raw Material from USA	5.5	–
Receipt of Export of Finished Goods from Europe	–	6.5
Receipt of Export of Finished Goods from USA	8.5	–

(a) Find out the amount of transaction exposure the firm has in different currencies.
(b) What would be the impact on cash flows of the firm if US dollar and euro appreciate by 10% during the period? Current spot rates are ₹50/$ and ₹65/€.
(c) If the exchange rates of US dollar and euro with respect to Indian rupee are perfectly positively correlated, what exposure does Flex Industries face?
(d) Is it favourable for the firm if US dollar and euro appreciate?

> **Solution**
> (a) Exposure in each currency is computed separately in terms of net cash flow.
> In US dollar = Receipts − Payments = 8.5 − 5.5 = US$3.0 million (receivable)
> In Euros = Receipts − Payments = 6.5 − 10.5 = −€US 4.0 million (payable)
> At current spot rate of ₹50/$ and ₹65/€, the exposure in terms of local currency is 3 × 50 − 4 × 65 = −₹110 million (payable).
> (b) If US dollar appreciates by 10% between now and time of receipts, the firm would gain extra cash inflow of approx. US$300,000.
>
> If euro appreciates by 10% between now and time of payment, the firm would lose by extra cash outflow of approx €400,000.
> (c) At current spot rates €1 = $1.30 and if exchange rates with respect to rupee have perfectly positive correlation, then the exposures of US dollar and euro can be added. In such a case, the exposure would be
> In euros = −4 + 3/1.3 = −€1.6923 million
> In US dollars = −4 × 1.3 + 3 = −$2.2 million
> (d) If euro and US dollar appreciate by the same rate, the firm would be a loser, but depreciating foreign currencies would improve the cash flows.

Another way of measurement of transaction exposure is based on VaR (Value at Risk). VaR is a comprehensive measure that quantifies n-day maximum loss with X level of confidence on a portfolio. It is based on statistical method using portfolio approach to assess risk in terms of standard deviation and coefficient of correlations of historical data of prices of the assets comprising the portfolio. Large multinational corporations and banks are increasingly adopting this measure for the assessment of transaction exposure. They provide adequate cushion of capital adequacy based on VaR.

TRANSLATION EXPOSURE AND ECONOMIC EXPOSURE—DEFINED

For the purpose of better clarity on kinds of risks of foreign exchange, we deviate from discussions on transaction exposure to briefly define the other two exposures, that is, translation and economic exposures.

Features of transaction exposure are foreign-currency denominated transactions that have not been settled as yet having potential to impact the immediate cash flows due to unexpected changes in exchange rates.

To understand translation exposure, let us consider an example. A pharmaceutical multinational corporation of India wants to establish a Greenfield project through a subsidiary in Japan and acquires a piece of land for ¥100 million paying in cash. At an exchange rate of ₹1 = ¥2, the equivalent rupee value of the land in Japan is ₹50 million, at which the asset is valued in the financial statements of Indian MNC. Assume that a year passes without any further development but yen has appreciated by 10% to 1.80; therefore, the value of land in equivalent rupee increases to ₹55.55 million. Is this a transaction exposure? The answer is no because there is no cash flow implication of appreciation of yen. It is an asset denominated in foreign currency, the value of which remains same when stated in foreign currency but stands increased when stated in local currency. Same asset is translated at two different times using two different exchange rates. The change in value affects the accounting statement but not the cash flow. Therefore, translation exposure is also referred to as accounting exposure. The change is notional and not real in nature. If the payment for the land were to be made after a year, then it would have also become transaction exposure.

Translation exposure is defined as an effect on the values of assets and liabilities denominated in foreign currency, in terms of local currency. It remains notional in nature as values of assets and liabilities keep changing as the exchange rate changes from period to period. Gains or losses are, therefore, notional having no cash flow implications. Cash flow implications would arise only when assets/liabilities are liquidated.

Economic exposure is defined as changes in competitive position of the firm due to changes in the exchange rates. To understand this let us assume an Indian firm producing and selling cars in India only. For simplicity, assume that there is no foreign currency transaction for this firm as it neither imports nor exports anything. Therefore, it faces no transaction exposure. However, this firm competes with imported cars from Germany and the USA. Would exchange rate changes affect the cash flows of the Indian firm? Obviously, yes! Depreciation of rupee would make imported cars more expensive, thereby improving the competitive position of the Indian firm. Appreciation of rupee would have opposite impact. Being an entirely domestic firm, the Indian automaker faces neither transaction exposure nor translation exposure but faces economic exposure. Competitive positions of all firms change whether domestic or MNC due to changes in exchange rates, though the effect on MNCs may be greater because of their exposures to different currencies.

Distinguishing features of three exposures are presented in Table 12-1.

Table 12-1
Foreign Currency Exposures—Differences

Translation	Transaction	Economic
Changes in the income statement, and *values of assets and liabilities*; denominated in foreign currency	Changes in the amount of future cash flows, for contracts *entered in foreign currency but not settled*	Changes in the amount of future cash flows determined by future *competitive position*
Notional	Real	Real
Retrospective in nature; deals with activities happened in the past	Retrospective and prospective as well; Contracts entered: past but not settled: prospective	Prospective;
Concerns only foreign currency	Concerns only foreign currency	Concerns both local and foreign currency

MANAGEMENT OF TRANSACTION EXPOSURE

The changes in the cash flows of the firm due to exchange rate fluctuations for foreign-currency denominated transactions need to be controlled by making the cash flows in local currency as steady as possible. Such an attempt is called hedging against the fluctuations in foreign exchange rates. It provides protection against the unexpected gains or losses from the expected cash flows that a transaction can result into.

The fluctuations in the exchange rate though appear to be small when viewed in relation to the aggregate revenue but are dangerously large when viewed from in relation with the net cash flow or profit. For example, consider an exporter having invoiced goods for US$1,000 with three months credit has a target realization rate of ₹46/$. His planned revenue is ₹46,000 and net profit at 5% of sales is ₹920. After three months, the exporter realizes US$1,000 when the spot rate happens to be ₹45/$. He faces a revenue loss of ₹1,000 from the target in mind which is around 2% less. However, the net cash flow or profit from the sales becomes negative at ₹80 rather than contemplated ₹920, that is, a reduction of about 108%. Thus, the impact of foreign exchange fluctuation on bottom line is much larger and is more damaging than one expects in terms of top line.

The example highlights another issue. A relevant issue here is what exchange rate must be considered in profit planning. While planning profit, should the exporter consider the spot rate at the time of invoicing or should he consider the expected spot rate at the time of realization. Clearly the appropriate exchange rate is the rate that is likely to prevail at the time of realization rather that at the time of invoicing exports. The profit planning must be done of the basis of the expected future spot rate rather than current spot rate. Therefore, the forward rate rather that current spot is an indicator of the exchange rate that is likely to prevail and provides a better estimate of the expected future exchange rate. Forward rate incorporates the expected changes in the markets. Since transaction exposure is concerned with unexpected changes, forward rate provides a better base for estimating transaction exposure.

IMPORTANCE OF MANAGING TRANSACTION EXPOSURE

Exposure is classified into three parts—translation, transaction, and economic—as highlighted in Table 12-1. Which of the three exposures needs greater attention of the management? Among the three, transaction exposure seems very important.

Briefly stated translation exposure, also referred to as accounting exposure, arises due to translation of assets and liabilities denominated in foreign currency. It does not have a cash flow implication but changes the complexion of financial statements as they are consolidated from time to time at the exchange rates prevailing at different times. Even though the economic utility of these assets and liabilities remains unaffected, the accounting standards warrant the translation of the value of foreign currency denominated assets and liabilities into local currency based on exchange rates.

Economic exposure is concerned with the changes in the competitive position of the firm due to changes in the exchange rates. Change in the exchange rates is a much wider phenomenon that alters the economic fundamentals and structure. Domestic firms do compete with foreign firms for raw materials, finished goods, technology, customers, etc. Changes in the competitive position of a domestic firm can be caused due to changes in the economic environment. A depreciating local currency would make imports costlier and make the local producer of similar goods more competitive.

While managers are required to manage all three exposures for effective control of risk, the management of transaction exposure is considered the most vital among the three for the following reasons.

Impact on Cash Flow Transaction exposure impacts the immediate cash flows of the firm affecting the liquidity. Continuing liquidity problems have potential to cause serious damage in the long run affecting valuations, solvency, etc. Translation exposure does not impact the cash flows, whereas economic exposure would affect industry as a whole. From the perspective of the firm, cash is the most crucial resource warranting immediate attention and intervention.

Style of Managing Exposures Management of foreign exchange transactions can be done either tactically or strategically. Since implications of transaction exposure are essentially short term, the tools and instruments available for managing transactions exposure are mostly tactical without losing the focus on the long term. Translation exposure is accounting only not changing the real economic potential of the firm, and economic exposure is wide spread for which an individual firm may have little control and requires strategic changes in position.

Interrelationship of Exposures Lastly and most importantly, management of translation exposure and economic exposure gives rise to transaction exposure. It is a moot point that should the exposures that otherwise do not impact the cash flows in the immediate future, be converted in the exposure-bearing risk of the cash flows in the immediate future.

Hedge or Not to Hedge: Selective Hedging

One of the crucial policy issues is concerned with whether the transaction exposure should be hedged or not. Though a naïve feeling would be to hedge always, the issue comes to fore because of the costs involved in hedging. Some believe that it is always advisable to hedge each and every transaction, whereas some may refrain altogether from hedging because either the exposure is too small or the chances of adverse movement in exchange rate are considered too remote. Such a philosophy of hedging some transactions while leaving others open is called selective hedging. Hedging renders stability to the cash flows which has a cost. Selective hedging enables cost reduction and is a conscious decision on part of the management to strike a balance between costs and benefits of hedging.

Selective hedging is dependent upon the likely exchange rate scenario in near future. In case of unidirectional movement of exchange rate and depending upon the confidence in the continuity of such directional movement, the following rules can be applied:

For receivables (Applicable for Exports):
Appreciating Foreign Currency/Depreciating Local Currency   Do Not Hedge
Depreciating Foreign Currency/Appreciating Local Currency   Hedge

For Payables (Applicable for Imports):

Appreciating Foreign Currency/Depreciating Local Currency	Hedge
Depreciating Foreign Currency/Appreciating Local Currency	Do Not Hedge

HEDGING STRATEGIES

Hedging against foreign exchange rate fluctuations can be done in two distinct ways—internally or externally—by using financial instruments and markets. Internal hedging methods attempt to control the amounts of transaction exposure by policy measures, whereas managing through financial markets implies taking suitable positions in the instruments meant for hedging. These instruments are derivative products. Such hedges normally have an explicit cost associated with them.

Internal methods have some advantages over the financial methods that include

1. *Containing exposure:* Prudence demands that the first attempt must be made to reduce or contain the exposure. Only after the efforts to reduce or eliminate the foreign exchange risk are exhausted, one must take recourse to financial markets to manage the exposure. This is based on the philosophy that prevention is better than cure.
2. *Reducing cost:* If the firm can contain the exposure by internal techniques, substantial cost saving can be made as hedging through financial products has explicit and/or implicit cost.
3. *Avoiding financial expertise:* Further, resorting to hedging with financial markets demands greater and deeper understanding of these markets, and the instruments meant for hedging. Such understanding may require special training and expertise.
4. *Avoiding monitoring cost:* The hedging with the financial markets also requires continuous monitoring of the exchange rate scenario and corrections in the strategies by subsequent actions, warranting full-time attention. Therefore, a firm may need a knowledgeable set of people to cover the transaction exposure through financial products.

INTERNAL HEDGING STRATEGIES

Internal hedging techniques are strategic policy initiatives that are easy to implement and comprehend. The attempt here is to contain foreign exchange exposures to the extent possible by adopting suitable policies. The following techniques of internal hedging are discussed briefly here:

1. Invoicing
2. Exposure netting
3. Leading and lagging
4. Risk sharing

Invoicing

The best way to avoid the foreign exchange risk is not to invoice in foreign currency at all. If invoicing for exports and imports are denominated in local currency, they are like domestic transactions with regard to currency exposures. However, adopting such a practice may not be feasible for several reasons. Business circumstances warrant that foreign exchange risk may be borne by the weaker of the two parties to the contract. In most cases, the suppliers/customers from developing nations are more desperate for business than the customers/suppliers from developed world. Naturally in such cases, the currency of invoicing is that of developed nation. Not only the relative size of the buyer and seller determines what would be the currency of invoicing, but it also matters how strong the nation is economically, politically, and financially in whose currency the transaction is denominated.

Firms from developing countries may prefer invoicing in foreign currency rather than their own domestic currencies because of greater acceptance of foreign currency a as medium of exchange. They seem to have more faith in international currencies, such as US dollar or euro, rather than their own. In certain countries, US dollar is as acceptable as the local currency. The reasons may be deeply rooted in economic, social, or historical factors. It may take long for the nation to shun such beliefs and build the same faith in its own currency. Currencies that have been subjected to high-inflation rates are regarded as weak and invoicing in these currencies is not done. It is perfectly normal to find that transaction is denominated in a currency that belongs to neither of the parties to the transaction but instead invoice in an internationally accepted currency. It is common to find invoicing in US dollar for a trade between a Chinese and an Indian party.

Another reason that the export transactions need to be invoiced necessarily in foreign currency or some internationally accepted currency is the legal environment imposed by the governments with the specific motive of building foreign currency reserves or to pay for the import bills for some essential commodities. Under such circumstances, invoicing in local currency for export transaction is ruled out. There apparently is a greater need to earn foreign currency because of import of essential commodity, like oil, or for servicing foreign currency loans, like from International Monetary Fund (IMF). In such cases, invoicing in foreign currency may be imposed legally. Governments in such nations may also offer some incentives to firms to earn precious foreign exchange.

In view of the foregoing, the option of invoicing in local currency is a strategy available only to large corporations belonging to developed nations. For firms in the developing nations, the strategy becomes difficult to implement, and foreign exchange risk would have to be borne and managed by alternative strategies other than invoicing.

Going beyond the operational constraints of invoicing in local currency, the strategy may not make much sense theoretically. It must be noted that the invoicing in local currency merely transfers the risk of foreign exchange to the counterparty who was hitherto not assuming the exchange rate risk. In case of Indian export to US importer the invoicing US dollar meant risk-bearing by Indian exporter. Now, if the buyer accepts the invoicing in seller's currency, that is, Indian rupee in this case, the exchange rate risk would be assumed by the buyer. Most probably in such a case, the price of the goods may have to be reduced so as to compensate the buyer for assuming exchange rate risk. Thus, the cost of hedging gets indirectly built-in into the price.

Exposure Netting

Exposure netting is identification and aggregation of exposures of similar and dissimilar nature. We use the concept of natural hedge here. What is considered good for exporters is bad for importers and vice versa. Appreciation of foreign currency is favourable for exporters as they realize more local currency for the same amount of foreign currency as time elapses. Accounts receivables, that is, the assets of the firm, rise in value when foreign currency appreciates. However, appreciation of foreign currency for importers is detrimental because costs rise as time elapses. Accounts payables, that is, the liabilities of the firm, rise in value with appreciation.

Accounts receivables and accounts payables behave in the opposite direction with the change in the currency rates. Being on the opposite side of the balance sheet, they offset the impact of each other. The export and imports (receivables and payables) provide a natural hedge against one another. When one loses on exports, exactly the same amount is gained on imports if exposures of export and imports are equal. Hence, receivables of US$10,000 and payables of US$8,000 both maturing at the same time, provide natural hedge to the extent of US$8,000. If US dollar appreciates, the value of receivables goes up and so does the value of payable. If US dollar depreciates, the receivables incur a loss but payable too reduces. The compensating effect of the receivable and payable would be to the extent of the lesser of the two. In the example, above US$8,000 is naturally hedged, and the foreign currency exposure is not US$18,000 (the sum of two) but only US$2,000 (the difference of two).

The concept of netting can be further extended to apply to the exposures in currencies that behave in similar fashion. It is observed that some currencies have tendency to move together and by approximately the same amounts. It is true for the currencies that are pegged. For example if Chinese yuan is pegged to US dollar, appreciation/depreciation of dollar with respect to rupee implies the same change in the value of yuan with respect to rupee. Similarly, Mexican peso though not pegged to US dollar can be assumed to appreciate or depreciate by similar amounts with respect to Indian rupee as does the US dollar. The implication of such relationship between currencies is that the exposures in these currencies can be combined for the purpose of hedging of the risks. If we assume exchange rate of yuan 8 per US dollar, then accounts receivable of yuan 16,000 is equal to an exposure of US$2,000. Further, if the same firm has accounts payable of US$2,000 with same maturity, then the exposures in yuan and US dollar can be netted.

Similarly, accounts payables in two different currencies that tend to move in opposite directions (negative correlation) can be netted. However, it is extremely unlikely to find negatively correlated currencies.

The success of netting the exposures of accounts payables and accounts receivables lies in matching the maturities of the exposures. In effect,

1. Accounts receivables and accounts payables in the same currency with same maturities can be netted, as their effects offset each other.
2. Accounts receivables with same maturities in two different currencies that are positively correlated can be aggregated.
3. Accounts payables with same maturities in two different currencies that are positively correlated currencies can be aggregated.
4. Accounts receivables and accounts payables with same maturities in two different currencies that are positively correlated can be netted, as their effects offset each other.

Another factor that governs the effectiveness of exposure netting strategy is the extent to which the operations of the multinational firm are centralized. Greater is the degree of centralization better would be the consolidation of assets and liabilities in different currencies with different maturities. With complete centralization of operations benefit of natural hedge of receivable against payable and vice versa can be derived completely.

Leading and Lagging

Leading and lagging is another policy initiative that can effectively bring down the explicit need to manage the transaction exposure through derivative instruments. Leading and lagging strategy can be said to be a corollary of selective hedging.

For receivables denominated in foreign currency, that is appreciating, the selective hedging principle recommended no hedging at all because the firm is expected to realize more as time elapses. By the same token, the more the firm delays its receivable denominated in appreciating foreign currency, more beneficial would it be. A deliberate strategy to defer or delay the receivable would lead to a greater realization in local currency. However, if the foreign currency is depreciating deferring the receivable would be detrimental and the effort must be to realize the receivable as early as one can. Therefore, the firm can be generous in granting a larger credit periods or extending the credit period for the receivables denominated in an appreciating foreign currency.

Similarly, if foreign currency is depreciating and the firm has payable in that currency, the later it pays, better would it be as the value of the foreign currency is diminishing with time. A conscious effort to pay as late as possible would save costs for the firm. In case the foreign currency is appreciating, the firm must pay as soon as it can. In such a case the costs mount with time. Though firms while buying tend to favour contracts that have longer credit periods but in case of an appreciating foreign currency such temptations would need to be avoided.

In a nutshell the leading and lagging of receivables and payables depending upon the likely exchange rate scenario can be an effective strategy to manage transactions exposure. It is summarized in Table 12-2 as follows.

Table 12-2
Leading and Lagging

	When foreign currency is appreciating
Lag the Receivable	Extend credit period and defer the collection without increasing default risk.
Lead the Payable	Do not accept longer credit period and pay as quickly as feasible.
	When foreign currency is depreciating
Lead the Receivable	Offer no credit period and collect as early as one can.
Lag the Payable	Accept longer credit period when offered and pay as late as feasible.

Implementation of leading and lagging strategy may be subject to several constraints, practical or legal. While advancing receivables, the firm should face no problems as it improves the cash flow and liquidity, but advancing payables may constrain the liquidity and, hence, the appropriateness of leading the payable. For want of funds, the firm may not wish to pay earlier especially if the cost of borrowing in local currency exceeds the savings to be made by paying earlier. Similarly, if the increase in cash flow on account of prolonging the collection of receivable is less, the cost of funding it may not be advisable to defer the receivable.

Policy of leading and lagging can be effective only when firms have adequate liquidity. Policy of leading and lagging cannot be taken in isolation and assumed to deliver favourable results. By extending credit in case of receivables denominated in appreciating foreign currency besides constraining liquidity also increases credit risk. The benefits have to be weighed against constraints of illiquidity, cost of funds, and assuming credit risk.

Further, the strategy is also subject to legal constraints, especially lagging of receivables as many nations may not permit undue extension of foreign currency receivables. For example, in India all foreign currency receivables must be realized in 180 days. Lagging payable may not be subject to legal constraints.

Therefore, leading and lagging strategy can only be implemented partially, when conditions otherwise permit such implementation.

Risk Sharing

The strategy of risk sharing is allocation of the burden of exchange rate risk partially on buyer and seller. It recognizes the fact that concentration of exchange rate risk on single party is unfair. Such strategy is normally adopted in cases of high-value contracts that extend over long periods of time involving several cash flows phased over time for a single contract. It recognizes that the burden of exchange rate risk needs to be shared by both the parties to the contract since forecasting exchange rate behaviour over-extended future is prone to error and deviation could be substantial. Under the strategy of invoicing the risk gets fully transferred from one party to another. The compensation for assuming exchange rate risk often gets built in the price. If the risk is shared by both the parties by linking the payments to the exchange rate, the situation should lead to more balanced and fair pricing of the contract.

Consider an illustration that how the risk of exchange rate gets built-in by adjusting the cash flow. Let us assume that an Indian exporter enters into a long-term contract for supply of garments over a period of two years for an aggregate value of US$24 million to be completed evenly in 24 months. Invoice would be raised every month. Since the contract is spread over a longer period of time, it is unreasonable to assume that exchange rate would not change substantially during the contract period. If the prices were to be fixed, the exporter would like to quote somewhat higher price to compensate for the risk of unexpected depreciation of US dollar. That would be detrimental to the buyer.

The possible and more realistic way out is to make invoice price a function of the spot exchange rate. One possible adjustment of price exchange rate can be as follows:

Exchange Rate at the End of the Month	Price Adjustment
₹46 or below	Invoiced at US$1.01 million
Between ₹46.01 and ₹46.99	Invoiced at US$1.00 million
₹47.00 and above	Invoiced at US$0.99 million

In the above payment structure linked to the exchange rate, we may conclude as follows:

(a) For the likely range of movement of the exchange rate (between ₹46 and ₹47.00), the seller bears the risk and normal contract value is paid.
(b) The price is adjusted upwards to the extent of 1% for the supply of the month when the exchange rate falls below ₹46.00. The extra price is expected to partly compensate the exporter for the unexpected fall in the value of rupee.
(c) Similarly, buyer pays less by 1% if there is an unexpected appreciation of Indian rupee. The benefit of rise in the value of rupee is partially passed by the seller to the buyer by accepting lesser number of US dollars.

The effective exchange rate realized by the exporter is depicted in Figure 12-1 for spot exchange rate varying from ₹44 to ₹49. Both buyer and seller stand to gain partially when exchange rate movement is beyond the expected range. None of the parties to the contract are at an extreme disadvantageous or advantageous position. The exporter does not suffer as much if exchange rate falls below ₹46. The buyer saves some cost by paying less if exchange rate moves above ₹47.

Such risk-sharing arrangements work very well for long-term contracts where there is an explicit recognition that forecast of exchange rate can deviate substantially from actual.

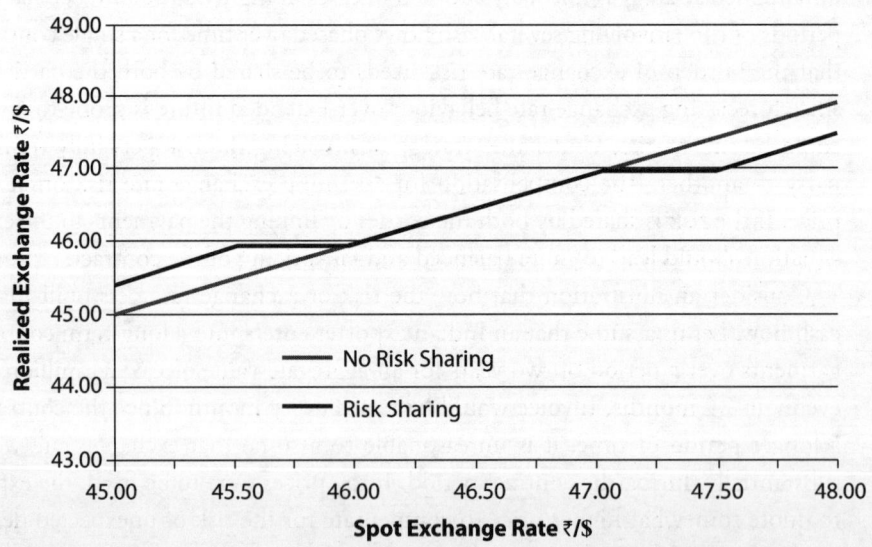

Figure 12-1
Exchange Rate Risk Sharing with Price Adjustment

For routine business, it may not be practical to implement such risk-sharing arrangements. Reserve Bank of India has issued comprehensive guidelines on risk management. Please see the Annexure given in the *Online Resource Center*.

HEDGING WITH FINANCIAL INSTRUMENTS

As long as transaction exposure can be managed by internal hedging techniques, the firm need not take any explicit action to cover the risk of foreign exchange rate fluctuations. Only after remedies of internal hedging get exhausted the firm wonders how the exposures can be hedged. For hedging explicitly, there exists wide array of financial instruments. These instruments are forwards, futures, options, and swaps as discussed in earlier chapters.

Given a unidirectional trend in the exchange rate movement, as has been the case with Indian rupee till 2008, the need for hedging had been rather low. Hedging makes more sense when there is equal likelihood of movement of exchange rate in either direction. The predictability of the direction of movement is crucial to the decision to hedge. For example, consider the case of an exporter in India invoicing in US dollar. If US dollar has been appreciating all the time in the past the exporter does not face the risk of receiving lesser than the spot rate. If the profitability planned is based on the spot rate, the exporter may not feel the need to hedge the receivable. On the contrary if the exchange rates were fluctuating either way, the risk of realizing lesser than anticipated becomes a distinct possibility and may prompt the exporter to hedge.

We illustrate hedging with various financial instruments through an example of receivables and compare their outcomes. This is done to facilitate a comparison of various instruments with regard to their functionalities, effectiveness, and suitability. Generalizations, if any, may be made with caution.

Assume a firm has receivables of US$10,000 due in three months' time. The hedging alternatives available to the firm are as follows:

1. Hedge with Forward Contract
2. Hedge with Money Markets
3. Hedge with Futures Contract
4. Hedge with Options Contract

Forward Hedge

The easiest way to hedge is through a forward contract. For receivables, the exporter needs to sell the receivables forward at the rates prevailing in the forward markets. Assume the spot rates quoted are ₹46.38 – 46.80. The 3-m forward rates offered by the bank are ₹47.23 – 47.55 indicating an annualized premium over spot of about 4.70%. The firm would be in a position to sell its receivables forward at forward bid rate. The only decision the firm is required to take is whether the offered forward rate is acceptable or not. If the firm believes that the future spot rate would be less than the forward bid rate of ₹47.23 it would go for the forward sell contract else not.

In case the firm decides to sell the receivables forward at ₹47.23 the realization is fixed in domestic currency too. The firm would realize ₹472,300 for US$10,000 irrespective of the spot rate prevailing after three months. The hedging outcome is depicted for possible range of spot rates between ₹45.00 and ₹48.00 in Figure 12-2.

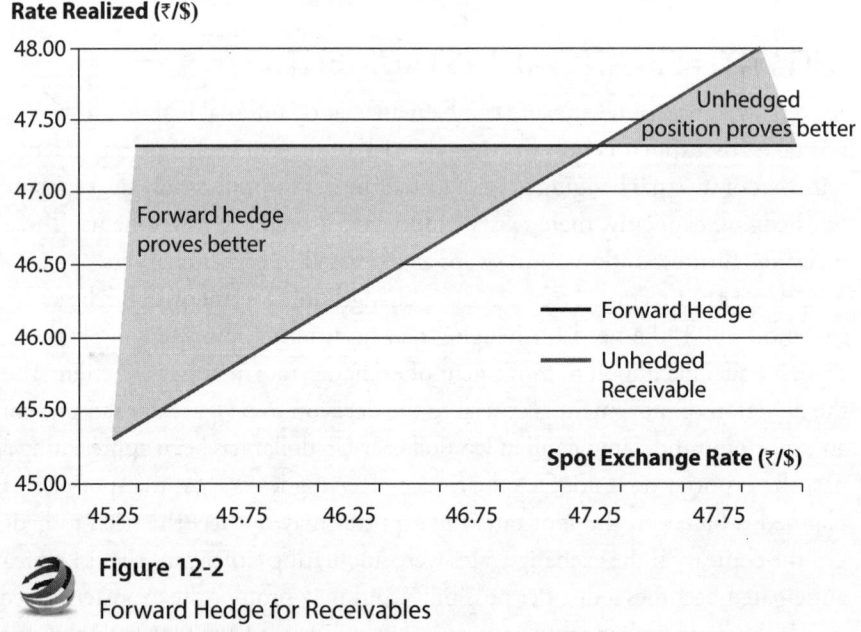

Figure 12-2
Forward Hedge for Receivables

Effectiveness of Forward Hedge Whether or not the forward hedge proved beneficial would only be determined at the expiry of the forward contract by comparing the forward rate with the spot rate at expiry. For the case of receivable, if the spot rate is less than the forward rate, the firm feels better off by taking the forward cover. In the example if the spot rate after three months were in excess of the forward rate of ₹47.23, the hedge would result in notional loss and is not effective. For payable the reverse would apply.

It must be mentioned that hedge was chosen to provide stability to the exchange rate and not to maximize (in case of receivable) or minimize (in case of payable) the local currency cash flows. In fact by taking the forward cover the potential for making profit was foregone in order to secure protection against the potential losses due to fluctuating foreign exchange. As such it would be wrong to blame forward hedging if the unhedged position yields a better cash flow in the end. It must be recognized *ab initio* that unhedged position may prove effective or ineffective than the hedged position. Forward hedge guarantees a fixed rate and does not maximize or minimize the cash flow.

Underbooking/Overbooking of Forward Contract In the example, the exposure in the spot and forward markets were identical, that is, US$10,000 each and the exporter was fully hedged.

In the circumstances that the forward rate offered by the market is not attractive enough, one has to take a speculative position in the foreign exchange market by either underbooking or overbooking the forward contract as compared to the position in the cash market. If forward contract is underbooked some of the receivables would be sold in the spot market.

Underbooking of the forward would be done when the exporters expect that the future spot rate would be in excess of the forward rate offered. This would enable the firm to sell part of the receivables at future spot rate but deliver only part against the forward contract. In such situations, one could rightly question the merit of going in for the forward hedge. Firms could still go in for the forward hedge so as not to remain completely exposed and keep the risks within the acceptable limits. For example, the firm believing that future spot rate would be in excess of ₹47.23, the forward rate it may decide to hedge only US$8,000 and may carry the risk of remaining US$2,000 for selling in the spot market presumably at an exchange rate of greater than ₹47.23. This would be the case of underhedging.

Alternatively, the firm could also overhedge by selling forward contract worth more than US$10,000. In such a case the firm believes that future spot rate would be less than the forward rate. In such situation, the firm would meet the excess delivery requirements under the forward contract by purchases from the spot market. If the firm believes that the future spot rate would be lower than the forward rate of ₹47.23, it may decide to sell US$12,000 at forward rate. At maturity, the commitment under forward contract would be met by US$10,000 from receivable and remaining US$2,000 by buying spot. In case the expectations of the firm come true, the realized rate would be in excess of the forward rate.

Underbooking or overbooking of forward contract amounts to taking speculative position on the differential exposure. The amount of overbooking or underbooking depends upon the hedging needs and risk appetite of the firm. In the example of underhedging, the firm covered US$8,000, whereas it was prepared to assume risk on remaining US$2,000 in the hope that future spot rate would yield better cash flow than the forward rate. However, the firm could not have assumed the risk worth US$10,000. Similar conclusion can be made for the situation of overhedging.

Exercise 12-2
Forward Hedge for Payable; Underhedging and Overhedging

An Indian consultancy firm availed the services of a British consultant for whom a payment of £30,000 is due after three months. The spot rate of British pound is ₹87.70, whereas 3-m forward is available at ₹88.90 suggesting about 5.5% annualized appreciation.

(a) What would be the exchange rate if the firm wants to remain fully hedged?
(b) What strategy should the firm adopt if it believes that (i) appreciation would not be as much as suggested by forward rate and (ii) appreciation would be more than as suggested by forward rate?
(c) What exchange rate would be payable by the firm if it underhedges by 50% and the spot exchange rate after three months turns out to be (i) ₹88.50 and (ii) ₹89.30?
(d) What exchange rate would be payable by the firm if it overhedges by 50% and the spot exchange rate after three months turns out to be (i) ₹88.50 and (ii) ₹89.30?

Solution
(a) To hedge the firm can buy a 3-m forward contract for £30,000 at ₹88.90, thus freezing an out flow in Indian rupees at ₹30,000 × 88.90 = ₹26,67,000. This amount shall be payable irrespective of spot rate prevailing after three months.

(b) In case the firm believes that appreciation would be less than 5.5% as reflected in forward rate, then the firm can underbook the forward contract.

In case the firm believes that appreciation would be more than 5.5% as reflected in forward rate, then the firm can overbook the forward contract.

The amount of underbooking or overbooking is dependent upon risk appetite of the firm and the confidence it has on its own forecast.

(c) **Underbooking by 50%:** If firm buys forward for £15,000 only and the exchange rate turns out to be ₹88.50, the cost of payable would be less. The firm would buy £15,000 at forward rate of ₹88.90 and remaining £15,000 at spot rate of ₹88.50 giving an effective exchange rate of ₹88.70/£.

If the spot rate at the end of three months turns out to be ₹89.30, the firm would end up paying more than the forward contract rate. The firm would buy £15,000 at forward rate of ₹88.90 as before and remaining £15,000 at spot rate of ₹89.30 giving an effective exchange rate of ₹89.10/£.

(d) **Overbooking by 50%:** If firm buys forward for £45,000 and the exchange rate turns out to be ₹88.50 the cost of payable would be more. The firm would buy £45,000 at forward rate of ₹88.90 and sell surplus of £15,000 at spot rate of ₹88.50 giving an effective exchange rate of (45,000 × 88.90 – 15,000 × 88.50)/30,000 = ₹89.10/£.

If the spot rate at the end of three months turns out to be ₹89.30, the firm would end up paying lesser rate than the forward contract rate. The firm would buy £45,000 at forward rate of ₹88.90 as before and sell surplus £15,000 at spot rate of ₹89.30 giving an effective exchange rate of (45,000 × 88.90 – 15,000 × 89.30)/30,000 = ₹88.70/£.

Hedging with Option Forward

We are aware that the obligations under forward contract are independent of the positions in the spot market. A firm expecting a receivable sells them forward to the bank hoping to settle obligations under forward contract from spot position maturing at the same time. In case the receivable is not realized at the time of maturity of the forward contract, the obligations made therein would have to be fulfilled. The only alternative for the firm would be to meet delivery obligations of the forward contract to buy from spot market. This may defeat the very purpose of the forward contract, with hedging of exchange rate risk getting annulled by default risk.

In business deals, one is never sure of the exact date on which the receivables would be realized unless under a letter of credit. In such cases, the realization date for receivables is known only on approximate basis, whereas the forward contract is an exact date contract.

To accommodate the uncertain business conditions option forward contracts are offered that allow for some flexibility for delivery date of foreign exchange. Instead of an exact date, a window is allowed for delivery of foreign exchange as shown in Figure 12-3.

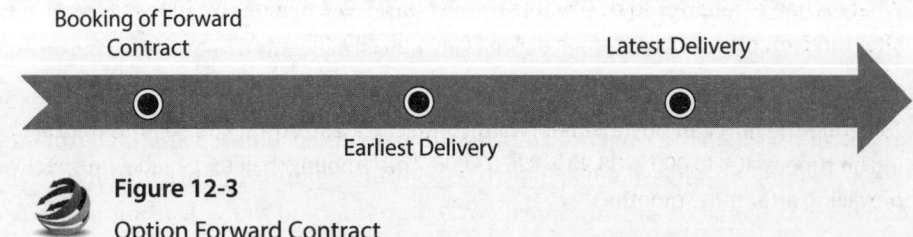

Figure 12-3
Option Forward Contract

For example, an exporter may expect to realize the receivable any time between 1 November and 30 November. An exact date forward contract is not suitable for the needs of the exporter. In such a case, the exporter can negotiate an option forward contract with flexibility to deliver the foreign exchange any time between 1 November and 30 November. Naturally, this option forward contract would be more expensive than the fixed date forward contract, in terms of the forward rate offered.

The delivery of foreign exchange under option forward contract can be made during the option window having the earliest and the latest dates. For permitting flexibility of delivery of foreign exchange, the banks quote rates on the basis of protection of bank's interest assuming worst case scenario. This would be dependent upon whether the foreign currency is at premium or discount. The bank would buy at the lowest possible rate and sell at the highest possible rate during the delivery option period. Hence, the rule for quoting the option forward rate would be

When foreign currency is at premium: Buy as early as possible and sell as late as possible
When foreign currency is at discount: Buy as late as possible and sell as early as possible

Such pricing policy makes option forward contract extremely expensive as reflected in the bid ask spread of the quotation. For illustration refer to Exercise 12-3.

 Exercise 12-3
Option Forward Rates

The following rates are prevailing in the foreign exchange markets for spot and forward transactions in respect of US dollars:

Spot	47.50	48.00
3-m Forward	49.00	49.75
4-m Forward	49.60	50.40

What rates would be quoted by a bank under an option forward contract with delivery window of one month starting three months from now?

Solution
The exchange rates of spot and forward rate indicate that US dollar is at premium. Therefore, in the delivery window the bank would like to buy dollar as early as possible and sell dollar as late as possible. Therefore, the option forward quote of the bank with delivery window of three–four months would be

Option Forward Rate (3 – 4 months)	49.00	50.40

MONEY MARKET HEDGE

Money market hedge is implemented by taking actions in the money markets of two currencies in question without resorting to forward markets, and yet freezes an exchange rate that is not subject to change. The firm adopts all those actions that the financial markets would take to arrive at the forward rate. It is a homemade forward contract.

One would recall the steps that are required in arriving at the forward rate. These actions would be replicated by the firm in its own capacity. The forward rate is arrived by (a) borrowing in one currency, (b) converting the borrowed currency into the other currency at the prevailing spot rate, and (c) investing the converted currency. These actions lead to the determination of forward rates. Here, the firm can take all these actions by itself and see what exchange rate is realized for receivables.

Money Market Hedge for Receivable Consider the following exchange rate and interest rate scenario:

Spot rate		₹/$	46.68	46.90
Interest rate	% p.a.	US dollar	4.00%	4.50%
		Indian rupee	10.00%	10.50%

The spot rates are bid and ask, whereas interest rates are for lending and borrowing.

To set up a money market hedge for US$10,000 receivable after 3 months, the firm must take the following three steps today:

(1) **Borrow foreign currency:** Borrow US dollar at 4.50% so that the maturity value of the borrowing after three months is US$10,000; the receivable amount. The amount borrowed is 10,000/(1 + 0.045/4) = US$9,888.75. By doing so the assets and liabilities stand matched for the dates of maturity of receivable and loan, and the liability of loan gets liquidated from the receivable.
(2) **Convert borrowing in local currency:** Convert in local currency (Indian rupees) in the spot market at the prevailing bid rate to realize ₹46.68 × 9,888.75 = ₹4,61,606.92.
(3) **Invest in domestic money market:** Invest Indian rupees for three months at 10% to have the maturity value of ₹4,61,606.92 × (1 + 0.10/4) = ₹4,73,147.10.

By doing so the firm would realize ₹4,73,147.10 while liquidating the dollar loan with dollar receivable on maturity. The loan would be paid back with interest. The realized money from the investment in the domestic money market can be regarded as the realized value of receivables. Hence, the effective realized rate for the receivable is

₹4,73,147/US$10,000 = ₹47.31/$

The process of money market hedge for receivable is shown in Figure 12-4.

Comparing Money Market Hedge and Forward Hedge The steps as shown in Figure 12-3 ensure that the money market hedge results in the fixed exchange rate for receivables, just as was the case with forward hedge. In the instant case, the exchange rate obtainable is slightly higher at ₹47.31 as compared to the forward rate of ₹47.23.

We have seen that by executing the steps of money market hedge, one can get the fixed rate. A natural question should then be why both forward hedge and money market hedge must not result into the same effective exchange rate. Under ideal circumstances, the results of forward hedge and money market hedge would be identical. The determination of forward rate

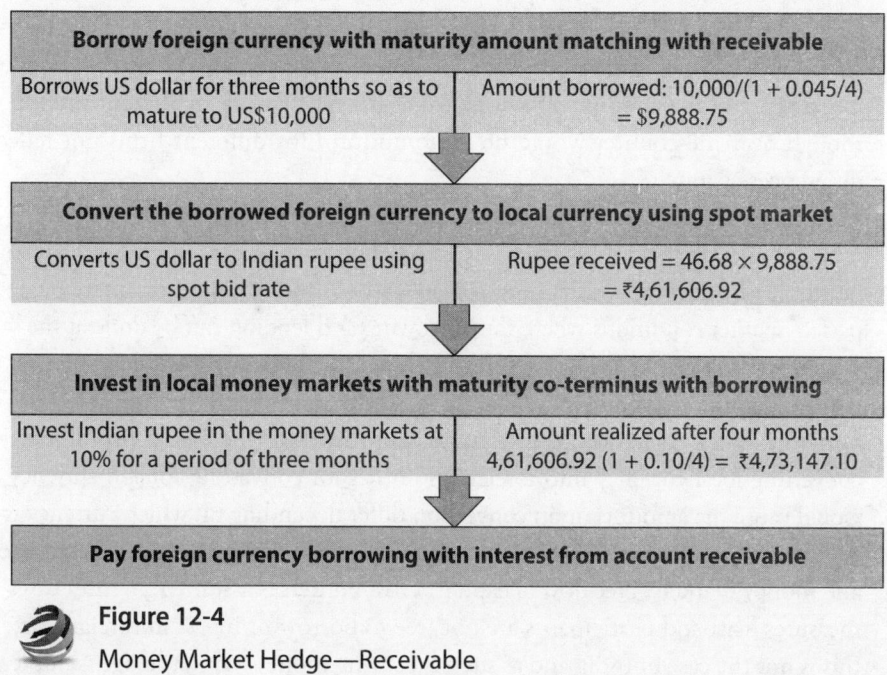

Figure 12-4
Money Market Hedge—Receivable

precisely follows the steps mentioned in the money market hedge. Interest rate parity forms the backbone of the forward rate determination. By taking the steps of the money market, one synthesizes the forward rate of own. The hedge with firm rate can be executed without resorting to forward market by accessing the money markets of the two countries/currencies.

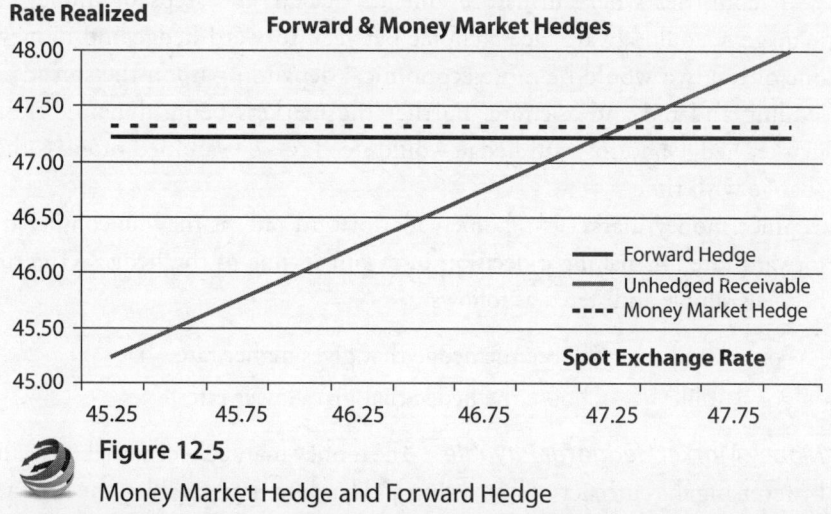

Figure 12-5
Money Market Hedge and Forward Hedge

The outcomes of money market hedge and forward hedge are depicted in Figure 12-5.

However, the real world is different than the perfect world which causes variation in exchange rate obtainable from forward markets and money markets. It is because the three

steps of borrowing one currency, converting to another and finally investing in the converted currency are done at different rates for different participants. Currency markets and money markets are over-the-counter and, hence, different firms face different rates. Forward markets though over-the-counter would be more uniform for different firms not reflecting corporate differences as much.

Another reason for the money market rate to differ from the forward rate is the presence of transaction cost. There are two types of transaction costs present in the execution of money market hedge: (a) borrowing and lending spread and (b) bid–ask spread. Interest rate parity assumes perfect market conditions where the borrowing and lending can be done at the same rate. In real situation, there would always be spread between the borrowing and lending rates no matter how large the amount of borrowing/lending is. The second type of transaction cost present is in the form of bid–ask spread in the foreign exchange market. There exist two different rates—one for converting local currency into foreign and other for converting foreign currency into local. This would cause the amounts upon conversion differ depending on which currency is converted.

Finally, the interest rate parity assumes complete integration of foreign exchange markets and money markets. Free flow of capital across borders is assumed. In most cases, capital control measures exist and participants are not free to borrow or invest in foreign currency. Currently, this is not the case in India and as such executing money market hedge is not feasible. Freedom to borrow and invest in currencies other than local at best is granted to select participants. There is absence of complete integration of money markets with the foreign exchange markets and different participants have varying abilities to participate in these markets at different rates. Therefore, forward rate and the synthesized rate with money market hedge would tend to differ from one another.

In countries where firms are able to execute the steps of money market hedge the managers would always face a choice between forward hedge and money market hedge as one of the two would be more economical depending upon the spreads in borrowing and lending and bid and ask rate. Further the markets being dynamic the choice of money market hedge and forward hedge would need to be examined often as the preferences may change with time.

Since money market is a homemade forward rate, it may be compared with the relevant forward rate for making a decision in favour of one of the hedges. The rule for selection of hedge is simple and stated as follows:

For receivable: Choose the hedge that gives higher rate
For payable: Choose the hedge that gives lower rate

Money Market Hedge for Payable   The money market hedge can be executed for payable too by reversing the currency of borrowing and lending. For payables, the firm needs a fixed sum of foreign currency in future. For money market hedge for payables, one would borrow in local currency, convert to foreign currency, and invest in such a manner that matures investment is equal to the amount payable. To facilitate comparison, the steps of money market hedge for receivables and payables are condensed in Table 12-3.

Table 12-3
Actions for Money Market Hedge

Money Market Hedge (For Receivables)	Money Market Hedge (For Payables)
1. **Borrow foreign currency** for a period and amount such that maturity amount of borrowing is equal to amount of receivable.	1. **Borrow local currency** such that after its conversion to foreign currency and investing for the period, the amount matches the value of payable.
2. **Convert to local currency** the borrowed foreign currency at spot bid rate.	2. **Convert to foreign currency** the borrowed local currency at the spot ask rate.
3. **Invest in local currency market** the amount so converted for maturity to coincide with the realization of receivables.	3. **Invest in foreign currency market** the amount so converted for maturity to coincide with the maturity of payable.

The amount of local currency to be borrowed for execution of money market hedge requires backward calculation. For the same data of the market as in case of receivable just discussed if the firm had to pay US$10,000, the amount of local currency to be borrowed would be arrived as follows:

Amount of payable required after three months	=	US$10,000.00
Amount of US dollar required today if invested at 4%; US$10,000/1.01	=	US$9,900.99
Amount of rupee required to be borrowed today at spot ask rate; 46.90 × 9900.99	=	₹4,64,356.43
Maturity amount of the rupee borrowed at 10.5%; ₹1.02625 × 4,64,356.43	=	₹4,76,545.79

The remaining steps of money market hedge for payable may be executed as depicted in Table 12-3.

Exercise 12-4
Comparing Money Market Hedge and Forward Market Hedge

With respect to British pound, the following scenario exists in the foreign exchange markets and money markets in India and Britain:

  Spot Rate (₹/£)   :   80.20 – 80.50
  6-m Forward Rate (₹/£) :   81.50 – 82.00
  Interest Rates
    Indian rupee   :   10.00 – 10.50%
    British pound   :   5.50 – 6.00%

(a) ITL Ltd expects to receive £10,000 in six months and faces a choice of covering the exposure either through money market or forward market. Find which hedge is more efficient.
(b) IPL Ltd has to pay a £10,000 in six months. It also has the option of covering the exposure either through money market or forward market. Find which hedge is more efficient.

Solution

(a) Hedge for Receivables of ITL Ltd

Forward Hedge:

ITL Ltd may book a 6-m forward sell contract for receivable and realize ₹81.50 (forward bid rate) per pound.

Money Market Hedge:

For the money market hedge, the firm shall take the following steps:

(1) Borrow pound at 6% (pound borrowing rate) for 6-m: pound borrowed = 10,000/1.03 = £9,708.74
(2) Convert spot; Get 9,708.74 × 80.20 = ₹7,78,640.78
(3) Invest rupees for 6 m; realize 7,78,640.78 × 1.05 = ₹8,17,572.81

The firm pays the loan raised from the receivable.

Effective rate of realization = ₹81.7572 (higher than forward)

Since realization under money market hedge is higher than forward hedge ITL Ltd must choose money market hedge.

(b) Hedge for Payables of IPL Ltd

Forward Hedge:

IPL Ltd may book a 6-m forward buy contract for receivable and undertake to pay ₹82.00 per £ (forward ask rate).

Buy pound forward at ₹82.00

Money Market Hedge:

For the money market hedge the firm shall take the following steps.

(1) Borrow rupees at 10.50% the borrowing rate for rupee.
(2) Convert spot to pound at spot ask rate.
(3) Invest pound at 5.50% (pound investing rate) for 6 m.

Investment required today = 10,000/1.0275 = £9,732.36
Equivalent rupees needed today = 80.50 × 9,732.36 = ₹7,83,454.99
Value of rupee borrowed today after six months = 10.525 × 7,83,454.99 = ₹8,22,486.37
Effective rate for payment = ₹82.2486 (higher than forward)

Since payment under money market hedge is higher than forward hedge IPL must choose forward hedge.

FUTURES HEDGE

Another alternative available to the firm to cover the foreign exchange risk is to operate in the currency futures market. Using the principle of hedging with futures, we need to take opposite position in futures market to that of spot market. By doing so, one hopes to neutralize the potential loss in the spot market with an equivalent profit in the futures market.

Futures Hedge for Receivables For accounts receivable, we initiate the hedge by taking the following actions now:

1. Since as receivable the firm is long in the spot market, it would go short in futures by selling futures now. It is known as short hedge.
2. The positions in futures and cash must be equal ideally or as close as possible in practice.

3. The maturities of the futures contract and the receivable must also be identical. The maturity of futures contract must be chosen as close as possible to the maturity of receivables.

The actions at the end of the hedging period would be as follows:

1. Square up the position in the futures by entering the opposite contract. In this case of receivables the short position in futures would be squared up by going long on futures.
2. Sell the receivable in the spot market.

The process of futures hedge is depicted in Figure 12-6.

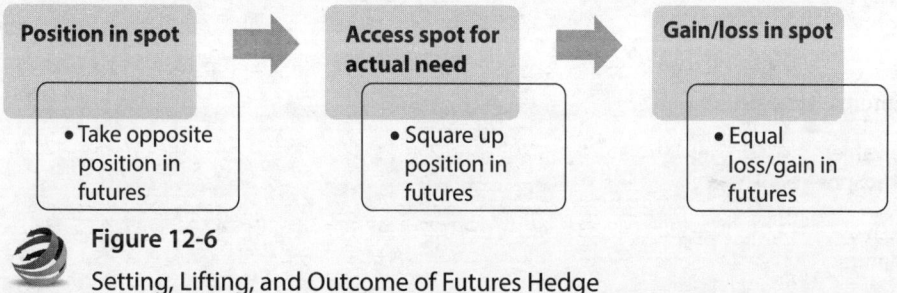

Figure 12-6
Setting, Lifting, and Outcome of Futures Hedge

Let us assume today is 20 July and receivable is due on 20 October. The futures contract closest to the maturity of the receivable is US dollar contract expiring on 27 October. The spot price is ₹46.68, whereas October futures contract is trading at ₹47.23 (assumed same as forward price for comparison purposes). Further, the contract size of each futures contract is US$1,000.

The exporter long on dollar spot would short futures contracts to hedge. The number of futures contract sold is US$10,000/US$1,000 = 10 trading at a price of ₹47.23/$. By doing so, the firm would realize a price close to the futures price now, that is, ₹47.23.

On 20 October, the receivables are realized and sold in the spot market. Short futures position would be squared up by buying it. On 20 October, the price of the October futures contract maturing on 27 October would be close to the spot rate prevailing then since cost of carry being proportional to the time remaining for maturity would be nominal. The spot exchange rate and the basis (difference of futures price and spot price) would determine the effectiveness of hedge. For various assumed spot exchange rates from ₹45.25 to ₹48.00 and the basis at the end the realized rate is shown in Table 12-4.

A look at the Table 12-5 would indicate that the realized rate would differ marginally from the target rate, that is, the initial futures price of ₹47.23 by the amount of basis at the end of the hedge. If the basis at the end of the hedge is zero (refer spot exchange rate of ₹46.25 in Table 12-4), the realized rate would be exactly equal to the rate at which initial futures position was taken.

Alternatively, the effective exchange rate may also be worked out from the initial contract price and the basis at the end. If initial futures price is F_0 and basis at the end is $F_1 - S_1$, then the effective exchange rate for receivable is

$$F_0 - (F_1 - S_1)$$

Table 12-4
Exchange Rate under Futures Hedge

											All figures in ₹
Spot Price	45.25	45.50	45.75	46.00	46.25	46.50	46.75	47.00	47.25	47.50	47.75	48.00
Basis (F – S) at End	0.10	–0.05	–0.10	–0.17	0.00	0.06	–0.12	–0.08	0.08	0.05	0.15	0.07
Futures Contract Bought	45.35	45.45	45.65	45.83	46.25	46.56	46.63	46.92	47.33	47.55	47.90	48.07
Profit/Loss on Futures	1.88	1.78	1.58	1.40	0.98	0.67	0.60	0.31	–0.10	–0.32	–0.67	–0.84
Receivables Sold at Spot	45.25	45.50	45.75	46.00	46.25	46.50	46.75	47.00	47.25	47.50	47.75	48.00
Effective Exchange Rate Realized	47.13	47.28	47.33	47.40	47.23	47.17	47.35	47.31	47.15	47.18	47.08	47.16

This is worked out in Table 12-5.

Table 12-5
Exchange Rate under Futures Hedge

											All figures in ₹
Futures Rate	47.23	47.23	47.23	47.23	47.23	47.23	47.23	47.23	47.23	47.23	47.23	47.23
Basis (F – S) at End	0.10	–0.05	–0.10	–0.17	0.00	0.06	–0.12	–0.08	0.08	0.05	0.15	0.07
Initial Rate Less Basis at End	47.13	47.28	47.33	47.40	47.23	47.17	47.35	47.31	47.15	47.18	47.08	47.16

Comparing Futures Hedge with Forward and Money Market Hedges Based on the spot rate and basis as assumed in Table 12-5 the exchange rate realized for receivables under futures hedge is compared with forward and money market hedges in Figure 12-7.

It may be re-emphasized that the futures hedge would seldom be perfect as compared to forward or money market hedges, where the realized rate was fixed and independent of the future spot rate. Futures price is indicative of future spot rate as well as the forward rate. Hence futures hedge would end at approximately at the forward price. The variation would be minimal depending upon the basis at the end of the hedging period. The variation would be

Measurement and Management of Transaction Exposure   389

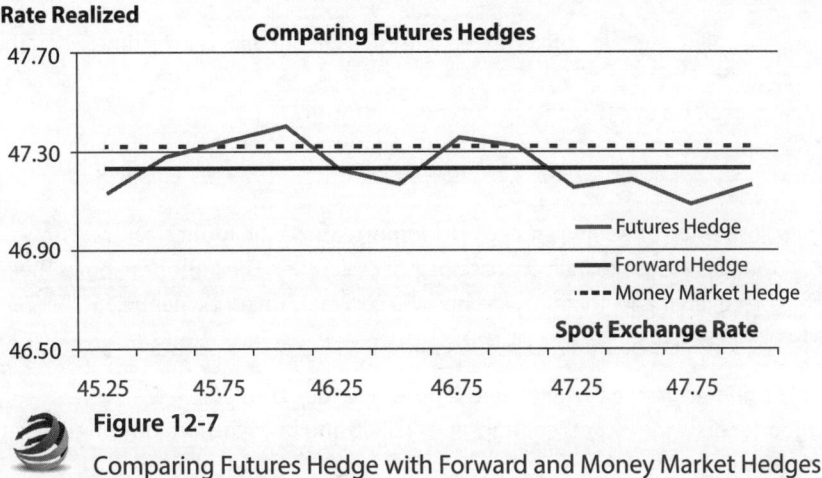

Figure 12-7
Comparing Futures Hedge with Forward and Money Market Hedges

equal to basis, and due to convergence of the futures and spot prices the basis at end should be very nominal. Therefore it is often said that under futures hedge the larger price risk is replaced by much smaller basis risk.

Futures Hedge for Payables   Futures hedge for payables would be implemented in the same manner as that of receivables with opposite actions. The actions in implementing the futures hedge would be as follows:

(1) As payable position is short in the spot, the firm should go long in futures by buying futures now. It is known as long hedge.
(2) The position in futures and cash must be equal ideally and as close as possible in practice.
(3) The maturity of the futures and the payables must also be identical. The maturity of futures contract must be chosen as close as possible to the maturity of payables.

The actions at the end of the hedging period would be

(1) Square up the position in the futures by entering the opposite contract. In this case of payables the long position in futures would be squared up by going short on futures.
(2) Buy the payable in the spot market.

> **Exercise 12-5**
> **Hedge for Importer—Long Hedge**
>
> An Indian importer buys a machine worth US$50,000 in June. Payment is due after six months in December. The spot exchange rate is ₹45.5625, whereas December futures is trading at ₹46.6500 indicating an appreciation of dollar by about 2.4% in six months.
>
> (a) If importer feels that dollar will appreciate much more, then how shall he hedge using currency futures? Assume futures contracts in rupee are available for US$1,000.

(b) Examine the following two different scenarios of exchange rates at the time when the payment becomes due in December.
   (i) US$ appreciates to ₹47.5600 and futures sells for ₹47.5700
   (ii) US$ depreciates to ₹44.5625 and futures sells for ₹44.5700

Solution

(a) *Hedging Strategy:* As hedging strategy the importer buys the futures contract now trading at ₹46.6500 and sells close to delivery date before December. The importer knows the exact amount of dollar to be covered and, therefore, he buys 50 contracts on an exchange.

   No. of contracts bought = Exposure amount/Value of one contract = 50,000/1,000 = 50

(b) *When US$ appreciates to ₹47.5600 and futures sells for ₹47.5700*

The importer exits the futures contract at ₹47.5700 and buys the foreign currency in the spot market at the prevailing spot rate.

Importer buys $50,000 at spot rate; Cost = 50,000 × 47.5600	= ₹23,78,000
Sells 50 future contracts booked earlier at ₹47.5700;	
Net gain on futures (47.5700 − 46.6500) × 50,000	= ₹46,000
Net rupee amount paid	= ₹23,32,000
Effective exchange rate (23,32,000/50,000)	= ₹46.6400

As against spot price of ₹47.5600 the importer ends up buying dollar at ₹46.6400.

When US$ depreciates to ₹44.5625 and futures sells for ₹44.5700

Importer buys $50,000 at spot rate; Cost = 50,000 × 44.5625	= ₹22,28,125
Sells 50 Future contracts at ₹44.5700;	
Net loss on futures (46.6500 − 44.5700) × 50,000	= ₹1,04,000
Net rupee amount paid	= ₹23,32,125
Effective exchange rate (23,32,125/50,000)	= ₹46.6425

As against spot price of ₹44.5625, the importer ends up buying dollar at ₹46.6425.

It may be observed that irrespective of appreciation or depreciation of US dollar, the effective cost of buying dollars remains close to the opening futures price, that is, ₹46.6500. The difference of actual cost and the futures price is on account of the differential of the spot price and the futures price when the hedge was lifted referred to as basis risk.

Cross Hedge Futures is an exchange-traded product and, hence, hedge is executed on the exchange. Exchanges offer futures contract on limited number of currencies that are most often traded and have sufficiently deep spot markets. At times the futures contract on currency of exposure is not available. In India, today we have futures contracts available in four currencies, namely US dollar, euro, British pound, and Japanese Yen. These contracts are introduced because most foreign trade is denominated in these four currencies and exchanges thought it fit to develop and offer futures contract in them. The exposures in other currencies such as Canadian dollar, Australian dollar, Mexican peso, or Chinese yuan cannot be hedged through futures because contracts on these currencies are not available in India. Firms having exposure in these currencies need to move to currency futures exchanges where such contracts are traded.

Another option available to the firms having exposure in such currencies where no futures contracts are available is to cover the exposure through a related currency on which futures are traded. Consider an Indian firm having an exposure in Canadian dollar. Ideally, it would like to cover its exposure through futures on Canadian dollar, which are not available. However, contracts in US dollar are available. Another fact known to the Indian firm is that there exists strong positive correlation between Canadian dollar and US dollar. Any depreciation or appreciation of Canadian dollar with Indian rupee should be same as that of US dollar; a strongly correlated currency with Canadian dollar. This hedge may not be a perfect hedge inasmuch as the percentage change in exchange rates of US dollar and Canadian dollar with respect to Indian rupee may not be equal. Such a hedge where exposures in the spot market and futures market are not on identical assets but are on related assets is called a cross hedge.

For estimating the effectiveness of cross hedge one needs to establish the relationship and find degree of correlation using past data. Greater the value of R^2 (explains the fraction of variation explainable) in the regression, better is the cross hedge. To make hedge more effective in case of lower degree of correlation the size of futures contract may be altered (overbook or underbook as the case may be) to offset the expected losses in the currency of exposure.

OPTIONS HEDGE

Another instrument of hedging is option. For our case of receivables, the firm needs protection against the falling exchange rate. If the spot exchange rate falls between now and at the time of maturity of receivables, the firm would be at a loss. To cover the exchange rate risk the firm needs to buy a put option that would provide the payoff when the exchange rate falls below the strike price of the put option.

The decision required in the options hedge would demand choosing the appropriate strike price of the option among the various strike prices available in the market, depending upon the protection level required. Assume that the firm chooses to protect its receivable below the exchange rate of ₹46.50. Therefore, it decides to buy a put option with exercise price of ₹46.50. Assume that such a put option is available at a premium of ₹0.20. By doing so, the firm assures itself of minimum realization price of ₹46.30 (strike price of ₹46.50 less premium of ₹0.20).

The payoff of the put at expiry with S as the spot exchange rate would be

	if	S > ₹46.50	0
		S < ₹46.50	46.50 − S

At expiry the firm would sell its receivables in the spot market and if the rate happens to be less than ₹46.50 the shortfall would be made good by payoff from the put option. For the spot price ranging from ₹45.25 to ₹48 the value of hedged receivables is worked out in Table 12-6.

Table 12-6
Options Hedge

												All figures in ₹
Spot Price	45.25	45.50	45.75	46.00	46.25	46.50	46.75	47.00	47.25	47.50	47.75	48.00
Put Option Strike	46.50	46.50	46.50	46.50	46.50	46.50	46.50	46.50	46.50	46.50	46.50	46.50
Premium	0.20	0.20	0.20	0.20	0.20	0.20	0.20	0.20	0.20	0.20	0.20	0.20
Payoff—Put Option	1.25	1.00	0.75	0.50	0.25	0.00	0.00	0.00	0.00	0.00	0.00	0.00
Rate Realized	46.30	46.30	46.30	46.30	46.30	46.30	46.55	46.80	47.05	47.30	47.55	47.80

Comparing Options Hedge Benefit of options hedge is that the firm retains the advantage of favourable movement of the exchange rate while simultaneously protecting itself from the risk of unfavourable movement. As can be seen from Table 12-6 the minimum realization would be ₹46.30. However, if the exchange rate goes up the firm retains the flexibility to gain. Such was not the case with forward, money market or futures hedges. In the other hedges the firm had foregone the potential profit to gain protection from unfavourable movement.

All the hedges discussed above for receivable are compared in Figure 12-8.

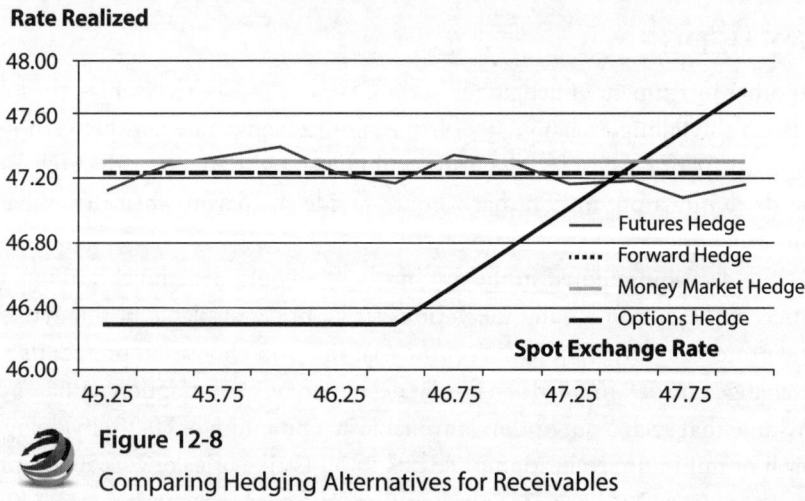

Figure 12-8
Comparing Hedging Alternatives for Receivables

As may be seen from Figure 12-8, the options hedge would prove beneficial as compared to forward hedge if the spot rate at the end of hedging period is in excess of ₹47.23. Similarly, options hedge would be beneficial as compared to money market hedge if the spot rate is in excess of ₹47.31. Similar conclusion cannot be made regarding futures hedge, as it is dependent upon the basis of futures at the end of the hedging period. However, if basis at the end is assumed zero then the futures hedge would be same as forward hedge.

Options Hedge for Payable The payables face the risk of rising exchange rate (appreciation of foreign currency). In order to cap the amount of payable, one would need to buy a call option with an appropriate strike price. The maximum exchange rate that would be payable by the firm would then be strike price of the call plus the call premium.

If we supposed that the firm had the payable rather than receivable and it did not want to pay more than around ₹46.50, then it could buy a call option with the strike price of ₹46. Assume that the call premium is ₹0.25. By doing so the total cost of payable would not exceed ₹46.75. This is shown in Figure 12-9.

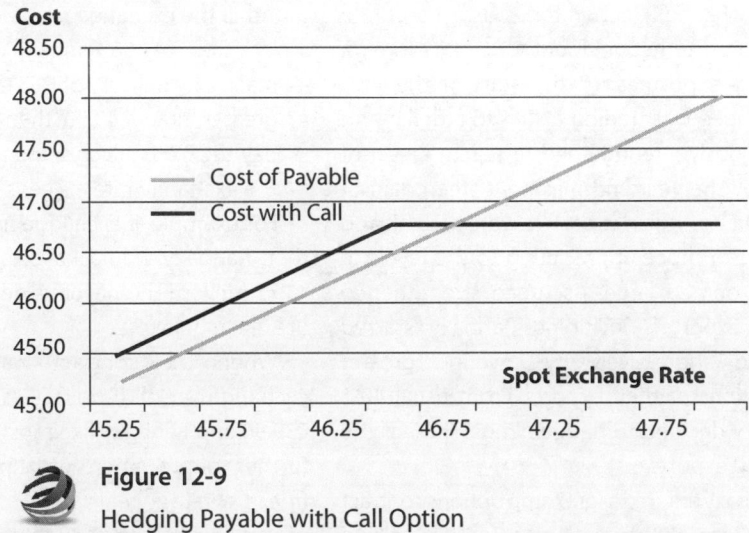

Figure 12-9
Hedging Payable with Call Option

Exercise 12-6
Hedging with Currency Option

Opto Electronics Ltd has imported a machinery worth £100,000 for which the payment is due in six-month time. The exchange rate prevailing is ₹85/£. In six months' time, British pound is likely to appreciate to an estimated level of ₹90/£. A call option and a put option with strike exchange rate of ₹87/£ are available at ₹1.50 and ₹3.00 respectively. What should Opto Electronics Ltd do to hedge its exposure of British pound? If it hedges, what would be the maximum exchange rate it would pay to liquidate the liability?

Solution
The firm is facing appreciating foreign currency. To protect against rise of British pound to as high a level as ₹90/£, the firm must buy the call option with strike of ₹87/£ at a price of ₹1.50. In case the exchange rate is more than 87, the firm would exercise the call option, else it lets the option expire worthless. For exchange rates of ₹85/£ and ₹90/£ the combined position of payable on due date would be as below:

Exchange Rate	Call Option	Call Cash Flow	Payable Cash Flow	Figures in ₹/£ Net Rate
85.00	Let call lapse	−1.50	−85.00	86.50
90.00	Exercise call	+1.50	−90.00	88.50

The firm can exercise its call option to buy the currency at strike of ₹87/£. The total cost of payable would then be limited to ₹88.50/£ including the premium for buying the call option.

CONCEPTS IN PRACTICE
Woes of Hedging

RANBAXY: HEDGING LOSSES!!!

One of the leading pharmaceutical companies of India Ranbaxy Laboratories as a corporate policy used to hedge about 40% of its foreign currency exposures. At the start of the year 2007, rupee was trading at ₹44 to a dollar and continuously strengthened to reach a level of 39.00 by the year end making a steep gain of around 11%. Indian exporters were hard hit and dangers of rupee appreciating to the levels of 35–37 loomed large. As rupee strengthened Indian exporters including Ranbaxy started hedging aggressively by covering greater proportions of their exports. From usual 40% Ranbaxy decided to hedge almost 80% of the targeted exports.

Ranbaxy entered a forex strip options contract in April/May 2008 for settlement for US$1 million at the end of each month for next eight years. The contract comprised 96 monthly strips with a leverage of 2.5 with each strip comprising the following options

| Long | 1 | Put with strike of ₹43.50 |
| Short | 2.5 | Calls with strike of ₹43.50 |

The contract meant that at the end of each month if the exchange rate is
- less than ₹43.50 Ranbaxy would get ₹43.50 million by delivery of US$1 million and
- greater than ₹43.50 then Ranbaxy would pay the ₹2.5 million × the amount by which the exchange rate exceeds ₹43.50.

For example, if exchange happens to be ₹45 then Ranbaxy would have to pay 2.5 × 1.5 = ₹3.75 million. The payoff is depicted in the figure given below.

When the contract was entered, the exchange rate of US dollar was hovering around ₹39.90 and Ranbaxy like most others expected further appreciation of rupee. Wanting to freeze a target realization of ₹43.50 a series of vanilla put option with strike of ₹43.50 as hedging strategy was too costly as put would be available for no less than ₹4. To recover part of the hedging cost Ranbaxy had to write options. Since call was out-of-money Ranbaxy chose to write 2.5 calls for every put bought to hedge receivables of US$1 million every month for next 8 years. Writing calls seemed

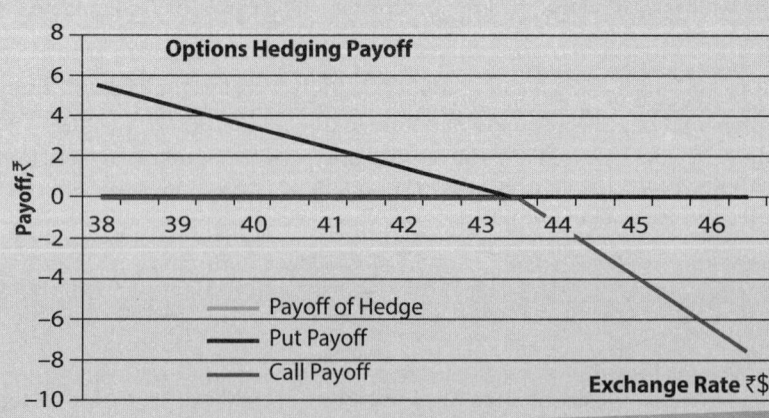

safe as it was rather deep out-of-money and, therefore, fetched very little premium. To offset cost number of calls were increased to 2.5 for each put.

Having committed potential liabilities by writing leveraged calls at strike of ₹43.50 Ranbaxy in its own estimate must have been very confident of further appreciation of rupee. Under no circumstances it thought that rupee would not only depreciate but also go below the level of ₹43.50 for considerable future. However, within months of the hedge the trend reversed substantially and by February 2009 rupee depreciated far beyond anyone's expectation to astonishing levels of 50 with Ranbaxy staring at marked-to-market (MTM) loss of around ₹600 crore.

What was considered a strategy to save hedging cost actually backfired miserably. In retrospect the prudence of hedging strategy was questioned in many ways. In the financial statement ending 31 December 2009 and December 2010, cumulative MTM losses on all derivatives used for hedging stood at ₹1606.218 crore and ₹999.632 crore as reported in the financial statement of Ranbaxy.

SUMMARY

MNCs have to deal with many currencies in day-to-day business. With flexible exchange rate systems prevailing in commonly used currencies, the exchange rates are changing too fast and too much causing uncertainties to the cash flows, accounting statements, and competitive positions of MNCs. The risks emanating from changing exchange rates, referred to as exposures, are of three kinds—transaction, translation, and economic.

Transaction exposure emanates from contracts denominated in foreign currency that are yet to be settled. Translation exposure concerns the changes in the value of assets and liabilities denominated in foreign currencies and are required to be translated in local currency from time to time at periodical intervals. Economic exposure relates to the change in the competitive position of the firm due to changes in exchange rates. Of the three, transaction exposure is considered most important for managing because of its implication on the immediate cash flows of the firm. The magnitude of transaction exposure is dependent upon (a) proportion of business in foreign currency, (b) time lag between cash flows and invoicing, and (c) volatility of exchange rate.

Management of transaction exposure can be done in two broad ways—by internal hedging policies or by using specifically designed financial instruments. Internal hedging techniques are invoicing, exposure netting, leading, and lagging are policy-oriented measures to contain risk that do not have an explicit cost. One way to eliminate the foreign currency risk is not to invoice in foreign currency. Changing currency of invoice merely transfer risk from one party to another. Further, it may be practically impossible for most firms to choose currency of invoice due to commercial, environmental, and legal constraints. Exposure netting uses the principle of natural hedge that receivable and payable provide. Since the effects of exchange rate changes are opposite on receivables and payable, they may be netted and only remaining exposure needs to be hedged, thereby bringing down hedging costs substantially. Leading and lagging is a strategy that attempts to manage transaction exposure by adjusting credit policy depending upon likely direction of currency movements. If foreign currency is appreciating, one may defer the collection and speed up payments to gain from appreciation. Reverse applies when foreign currency is depreciating. Under risk sharing strategy, the exchange rate risk is shared by two parties rather than borne by single party. It is normally achieved by adjusting the cash flows according to the exchange rate prevailing at the time of payment.

Market-oriented management of transaction exposure includes hedging through instruments such as forward contracts, futures, and options as also the money markets. A ready over-the-counter forward markets offering forward buy and sell of foreign currency exists in most countries enabling locking-in of exact exchange rate. Futures contracts are also available on select currencies on exchanges to allow hedging. The principle of hedging through futures is to take position in the futures market opposite to that of spot hoping to offset the losses from spot from gains in futures. Money market hedge can be implemented by borrowing in one currency, converting to another currency using spot market and investing. This allows individual firm to synthesize its own forward rate.

Options contract are available both over-the-counter and on exchanges on select currencies. Options hedge unique advantage over all other hedging strategies that it retains gains from favourable movement while simultaneously providing protection from unfavourable movement. Simplest of the hedging strategies are buying a put option for hedging accounts receivable and a call option for hedging accounts payable. However, many complex structures of options are also available to achieve desired risk return profile and containing cost of hedging.

QUESTIONS

12-1 Explain what different kinds of risks in foreign exchange are faced by multinational corporations.
12-2 Why do you think that management of transaction exposure is more important that management of translation of economic exposure?
12-3 What are the advantages of internal hedging techniques overhedging with financial instruments?
12-4 Briefly explain the following internal hedging techniques:
 (a) Invoicing and risk sharing
 (b) Exposure netting
 (c) Leading and lagging
12-5 Explain the mechanism of money market hedge for accounts payable.
12-6 Comment on the following statement: Under perfect markets forward hedge and money market hedge would yield the same outcome, and hence money market hedge is redundant.'
12-7 What are the advantages and disadvantages of futures hedge over forward hedge?
12-8 How would you execute an options hedge for (a) accounts receivable and (b) accounts payable?
12-9 Compare advantages and disadvantage of hedging with (a) forward, (b) futures, and (c) options.

PROBLEMS

12-1 **Forward Hedge**
An Indian exporter has supplied readymade garments to a retailer in Switzerland on six months credit invoiced at CHF1 million. The spot and 6-m forward rates in the Indian market CHF is quoted at ₹65.00 and ₹67.50, respectively. If the exporter believes that rupee would depreciate by no more than 7% p.a., should he hedge the receivable by booking 6-m forward contract?

12-2 **Money Market Hedge**
Refer to Problem 12-1 and assume that the exporter is free to borrow or lend in Indian rupee or Swiss franc. Borrowing rates and investing rates in Indian rupee and Swiss franc are 12% and 4%, respectively.

What steps should the exporter take to implement the money market hedge? Compare the outcome of money market hedge with forward hedge?

12-3 Option Forward

The following rates are prevailing in the foreign exchange markets for spot and forward transactions in respect of US dollars:

Spot	47.5	48.00
3-m Forward	46.0	46.75
4-m Forward	45.4	46.20

What rates would be quoted by a bank under an option forward contract with delivery window of one month starting three months from now?

12-4 Futures Hedge

Refer to Problem 12-1. The Indian exporter can also hedge through futures markets in India. Unfortunately no futures contract is available in Swiss franc. However, the value of Swiss franc is strongly correlated with US dollar as well as euro. Spot exchange rate of Indian rupee with respect to US dollar and euro are respectively ₹61.50 and ₹75.00. 6-m futures contract (contract size = 1,000 units of foreign currency) of US dollar and euro are available at ₹64.55 and ₹77.20, respectively.

(a) How should the exporter hedge his exposure in Swiss franc with futures on US dollar?
(b) How should the exporter hedge his exposure in Swiss franc with futures on euro?
(c) What risk would the exporter face with futures hedge with US dollar or euro?
(d) If value of Swiss franc is more closely related to euro than to US dollar, then should the exporter hedge with dollar or euro?
(e) After six months at the maturity of receivable as well as futures contract the spot rates of Swiss franc, US dollar, and euro are ₹67.55, ₹64.40, and ₹77.30, find out the effective exchange rate realized with futures hedge with US dollar and euro.
(f) Find out the effective exchange rate realized with futures hedge with US dollar and euro if at maturity of receivable as well as futures contract the spot rates of Swiss franc, US dollar, and euro are ₹63.55, ₹60.40, and ₹72.80, respectively.

12-5 Options Hedge

Ford, Japan owes $1 million payable in 3 months. Spot forward and options markets in Tokyo have following rates (all rates ¥/$):

Spot	120.00	3-m Forward	117.00

3-m options

Strike	Call Premium	Put Premium
124	1.40	5.70
122	2.00	3.80
120	3.00	2.50
118	4.00	1.80
116	5.10	0.70

Evaluate the following hedging strategies:
(a) Buy US dollar 3-m forward.
(b) Buy 3-m call with strike of 118.
(c) Buy 3-m call with strike of 120 and write a 3-m put with strike of 116.
(d) Buy 3-m call with strike of 122 and write a 3-m put with strike of 118.

13
Measurement and Management of Translation and Economic Exposure

LEARNING OBJECTIVES

This chapter aims at

- explaining translation, consolidation, and resultant exposures
- describing different methods of translation of financial statements such as current/non-current method, monetary/non-monetary method, temporal method, all current method
- quantifying the translation exposure
- highlighting management of translation exposure through balance sheet and derivatives
- explaining economic exposure and its implications
- describing methods of assessing economic exposure
- explaining the methods and desirability of management of economic exposure

CONTENTS

Introduction
Translation Exposure
Translation Exposure—Explained
Does Translation Exposure Matter
Determinants of Translation Exposure
Methods of Translation
    Current/Non-current Method
    Monetary/Non-monetary Method
    Temporal Method
    All Current Method
    Recognition of Translation Gain/Loss
Measuring Translation Exposure
Management of Translation Exposure

    Balance Sheet Hedge
    Derivatives Hedge
Economic Exposure
    Economic Exposure Explained
Measuring Economic Exposure
    Scenario Analysis
    Market Value of the Firm—A Proxy to Cash Flow
    Real vs Nominal Exchange Rates
    Pegging and Economic Exposure
Managing Economic Exposure
    Manage or Not to Manage
    Strategic Management of Economic Exposure

INTRODUCTION

In the previous chapter, we discussed transaction exposure. This chapter is devoted to the other two exposures related with changing foreign exchange rates—translation exposure and economic exposure. At the outset, it may be mentioned that while transaction exposure was important in terms of its implication on immediate cash flows, translation exposure and economic exposure also influence the value of the firm. Transaction exposure is present with all those firms having imports and exports irrespective of them being multinational firms. Translation exposure arises with firms that have subsidiaries or controlling interest abroad. Economic exposure is wide spread and affects all firms—some largely, specially the multinational corporations (MNCs).

TRANSLATION EXPOSURE

Translation exposure, also called accounting exposure, arises when multinational corporations incorporate the results of its subsidiary companies located abroad into its own performance. The MNCs usually have interest in several countries. They have subsidiaries or joint ventures abroad. They also have interest in firms abroad where they exercise significant control over the managerial decision-making of these firms by virtue of being a major supplier, crucial customer, or debt financiers and yet may not be a joint venture. These firms are separate legal entities incorporated in foreign lands, but directly/indirectly are controlled substantially or fully by the owner MNC.

These foreign legally separate entities draw their financial performance in the respective currencies of the nation where they are located or incorporated. For example, Tata Steel's subsidiary Corus in Europe (Rechristened Tata Steel Europe) would draw its financial performance in its *functional currency*, that is, euro. However, at the end of the year Tata Steel is required to present its performance and financial position to its shareholders, which must include the financial data of Corus too. Being an Indian company, it is mandatory for Tata Steel to present its performance in its *reporting currency*, that is, Indian rupees. Therefore, it is imperative to translate the financial data of Corus originally stated in euro to convert into Indian rupees. We are discussing the impact of such translation of financial statements on the value of the parent firm referred as translation exposure.

Likewise, if a parent firm has many subsidiaries, each of which uses its functional currency for its financial statements, the parent firm needs to convert subsidiaries' accounts to reporting currency. The process of integrating the financial accounts of different subsidiaries into parent's performance is called *consolidation*. While the parent's own performance is presented in *stand-alone accounts*, the combined performance with all the subsidiaries is called *consolidated financial statements*.

Need for Consolidation The performance of the parent on consolidated basis is mandatorily required because regulatory authority prescribes it in the interest of the owners of the parent firm, the shareholders. The shareholders of the parent firm are entitled not only to the financial data of the firm but also to all its subsidiaries, as owners or as majority stakeholders, despite the fact that the subsidiary by itself is a separate legal entity incorporated in a foreign land. The shareholders of the parent have extended arms to the subsidiaries located in foreign lands.

Besides being mandatory in the recognition of the rights of shareholders, the consolidation provides useful information to the managers of the parent firm with regard to interlinkages among its various subsidiaries. Since parent enjoys the control, a comprehensive view of all the activities is required for making decisions more effective and efficient and for devising suitable strategies for the group as whole rather than only for the parent firm. Though management discussion and analysis may be done even when the financial statements are drawn in functional currencies separately but consolidation to single denominator of reporting currency renders decision-making convenient, expeditious, and easily comprehensible.

Process of Consolidation Consolidation of financial statements appears to be a matter of arithmetic where functional currency is converted into reporting currency using an exchange rate. It seems a simple process of multiplication or division of financial figures with exchange rate. However, the simplicity ends here because of two reasons as mentioned here:

1. *Valuing same assets/liabilities on different dates*: When same assets and liabilities stated in the foreign (functional) currency of the subsidiaries are carried period after period and translated in domestic (reporting) currency, the foreign exchange rates are different at different points of time. This changes the value of these assets and liabilities even though the economic value has remained unchanged.
2. *Valuing different assets/liabilities on the same date but at different rates*: Different items of financial statements are converted in reporting currency on the same date but at exchange rate used for their translation are not identical. This causes the imbalance in the financial statements even though the balance sheet in functional currency is balanced.

TRANSLATION EXPOSURE—EXPLAINED

We demonstrate the first issue with an extremely simple example. An Indian firm remits euro 1 million to Germany to its subsidiary and invests the same in the acquisition of goods for trading. The exchange rate at the time of remittance was ₹60/euro. The balance sheet of the subsidiary stated in million euros and rupees would be

	Euro	Rupee		Euro	Rupee
Equity Capital	1.00	60.00	Stocks	1.00	60.00

The same would be reflected in the parent firm as reduction in bank balance by ₹60 million and an increase in investment in subsidiary by the same amount, both on the asset side. While consolidating the investment and equity of the subsidiary would cancel out each other, stocks in Germany worth ₹60 million would appear for reduction in bank balance.

Now, assume that a year elapsed with no further development. The balance sheet of the subsidiary remains what it was a year before. However, now euro depreciated to ₹55. The balance sheet of the parent incorporating the value of the subsidiary's stock would appear as follows:

	Euro	Rupee		Euro	Rupee
Equity Capital	1.00	60.00	Stocks	1.00	55.00
Loss on Translation		−5.00			

The stand-alone balance sheet of the parent that includes its financial performance shows no changes, but the consolidated financial statement would show the value of stocks at ₹55 million. The issue is what item in the balance sheet would be adjusted for the decline in the value of asset by ₹5 million? Natural answer would be adjustment in the net worth. Such change in the values of assets and liabilities affects financial performance, despite no changes in the economic performance, is called translation exposure.

DOES TRANSLATION EXPOSURE MATTER?

In the preceding section, we observed that the value of goods decreased on account of depreciation of euro and not due to any operational inefficiency. Is this indeed a risk? The opinion is divided on whether variations due to exchange rate changes on the foreign currency denominated assets and liabilities are threatening enough for the parent.

For some translation exposure is not relevant at all. According to them, the performance of the firm is reckoned by economic activity and not by illusory gain or loss due to changes in the exchange rates. It is illusory because the situation of depreciating euro may reverse in the next period bloating the performance. Over the long run, these changes must even out. Should the credit or discredit of the performance on account of transient exchange rate changes be attributable to management?

Profit or loss need not be repatriated or converted in the parent's currency on every reporting date. The assets and liabilities continue to rest with the subsidiary on continuing basis. The assets created by assuming liabilities in foreign country in its currency are required for continuing economic activity of the subsidiary. Objective of consolidation is to incorporate economic performance of subsidiary into that of parent and use of an exchange rate is a mere compulsion to present financial performance in a single currency.

Some others hold the contrary view and believe that translation exposure does matter. According to them, the financial earnings and position of assets and liabilities get affected. These have potential to impact accounting earning per share (EPS) and critical structural and liquidity ratios like debt equity and current ratios, which are considered drivers of the value of the firm. There have been instances where stock prices of multinational firm have reacted sharply due to volatility of exchange rates. When the performance of parent is dependent on the subsidiary's performance whose currency is weak, greater risk is attributed to parent's operations, thereby raising the discounting rate adversely affecting the valuation.

Those supporting the view of irrelevance counter argue that valuation of firms is driven by cash flow changes, and not on accounting profit. Exchange rate changes impact only the accounting profit having no immediate cash flow implications. However, current exchange rate scenario forms the basis of future projections and, hence, affects valuation.

DETERMINANTS OF TRANSLATION EXPOSURE

Without further dwelling on whether translation exposure is relevant, one is more concerned about its measurement and quantum. Factors affecting the parent's value would depend upon (a) the level of dependence on subsidiaries, (b) the strength of the functional currencies relative to reporting currency, (c) the economic situations of the nations where subsidiaries are located, and (d) the methods of translation used.

For example, Maruti Suzuki Limited, a subsidiary of Suzuki, Japan, in India contributes substantially to the revenue and profit of the parent and it is natural that the value of Suzuki in Japan would be greatly dependent on economic performance of Maruti in India as well as exchange rate of rupee and yen. The large ticket acquisitions of Corus by Tata Steel, JLR by Tata Motors and Zain by Bharti Telecom have started impacting the stock performance of parents in the Indian capital markets. It is believed that the value drivers for Tata Motors and Tata Steel are the performance of JLR and Corus and, hence, on rupee exchange rate with respect to British pound and euro. While economic performances of these subsidiaries are important for parents, it becomes critically dependent on the performances of the currencies involved when crises happen. Such has been the case during Asian currency crises in the past and more recently for the banks and the firms in Euroland. When currencies show signs of weakness due to any reason including recession, the earning in the parent's currency drop and stock value is re-rated. Weakness of Indian rupee must surely cause concern at Suzuki in Japan as with depreciating rupee they get lesser yens. Same would hold true for a US multinational having subsidiaries in Europe when euro continues to struggle.

The quantification of translation exposure is also dependent upon what method of translation is adopted. We discuss these methods next and demonstrate that a different method can lead to a different measurement of translation exposure.

METHODS OF TRANSLATION

The other issue relates to which exchange rate must be used in translating items from functional currency to reporting currency. To understand this, we must understand the various methods used for translation from one currency to another. There are four methods available for translation of financial statements:

1. Current/Non-current method
2. Monetary/Non-monetary method
3. All current method
4. Temporal method

Fortunately, accounts of subsidiaries need not be translated for every transaction. The requirement of translation arises at periodic intervals at each reporting date when consolidation of accounts is mandated. The question of using appropriate exchange rate arises then.

Current/Non-current Method

Under current/non-current method, different items of balance sheet are classified into two—current and non-current. Current assets and current liabilities are short-term in nature, that is, they mature within a year. All current items are translated at current rates, that is, closing rate as on the date of consolidation. Current assets and liabilities include accounts receivables, accounts payables, inventories, cash and bank balances, etc. All items of non-current nature whether assets or liabilities, such as fixed assets and long-term liabilities including equity capital, are translated at *historical rates*, that is, the exchange rate that prevailed at the time when the assets were acquired or liabilities created. It essentially means that the non-current items of long-term debt, fixed assets, and equity are not subject to change with time and with changes in the exchange rates. Once recorded at historical rates, the value of these items becomes fixed from one period to another. Current assets and current liabilities do change with time because exchange rate on various dates of consolidation would be different.

Items of profit and loss account are translated using average rates for the period under consideration, except those items related to non-current assets and liabilities where historical rate would be used. One such item is depreciation that relates to the fixed assets and is translated at historical rate; the rate applicable to the fixed assets.

The major issue with the use of this method is that exposure would be measured incorrectly since long-term liabilities of loans are subject to exchange rate risk, but they are translated at historical rate. If a loan is taken for US$1 million when the exchange rate was ₹35, the outstanding amount would continue to be reflected at exchange rate of ₹35/$, that is, ₹35 million even if the exchange rate moved to ₹25 or ₹45. It would not be a correct representation of liabilities.

Monetary/Non-monetary Method

The monetary/Non-monetary method classifies items of balance sheet into monetary or non-monetary rather on maturities, as was the case with current/non-current method. Monetary items are those that represent a claim, receivable or payable, for a fixed sum of foreign currency. They would include accounts receivables, accounts payables, both long-term and short-term loans, etc. The aspect to be considered is the monetary value and not maturity. Non-monetary items are physical assets and liabilities such as fixed assets and inventory.

For monetary items, current rate is used, whereas non-monetary items, including equity capital, are translated at historical rates.

With respect to current/non-current method, the difference arises in respect of (a) inventories of stocks, translated at current rate under current/non-current but at historical rate under monetary/non-monetary and (b) long-term debts, which are translated at closing rate under this method but at historical rate under current/non-current method. Since monetary assets and liabilities carry the risk of changes in the values with changing exchange rates, they must be translated at rates as recent as possible. Non-monetary assets and liabilities are assumed to maintain the same values because real rates do not change if assumptions of Purchasing Power Parity (PPP) hold.

Items of revenue and cost are translated at average rate during the period except those related to non-monetary assets and liabilities. The rates used here would be same as those used for relevant non-monetary assets or liabilities. Depreciation related to fixed assets is converted at the same rate as that of fixed asset. Similarly, the cost of goods sold pertaining to the inventory is also translated at the rate used for inventory.

Temporal Method

Temporal method is a variant of monetary/non-monetary method. The underlying principle in the temporal method is to use the same type of exchange rate for translation for items that are used for carrying an item in the balance sheet. Items are neither classified as current/non-current nor as monetary/non-monetary. If the market value is used in balance sheet, the translation would take place at current rate, and if assets and liabilities are carried at original cost, they would be translated at respective historical rates. This usually leads to a difference in the translation of inventories. Since they are carried to the balance sheet at market rates, the translation is done at current rate, unlike at historical rate under monetary/non-monetary method.

Profit and loss account would be translated at average rate for the period except those related to fixed assets for which the historical rate is used.

All Current Method

The simplest of all methods is the all current method where only closing rates are used for all items. However, equity is translated at historical rates. Items of profit and loss are translated at average rates during the period.

The major objection with this method is that it violates the principle of accounting for assets that are recorded at historical rate. While balance sheet items of parent as well as that of subsidiary are recorded at historical rates, in different currencies, there is little rationale for recording the same at current rate in consolidated accounts.

A summary of rates to be used for translation of various assets and liabilities under different methods is presented in Table 13-1.

Table 13-1
Comparison of Translation Methods

Item	Current/Non-current	Monetary/Non-monetary	Temporal	All Current
Cash	C	C	C	C
Debtors	C	C	C	C
Creditors	C	C	C	C
Inventory*	C	H	C	C
Fixed Assets	H	H	H	C
Term Liabilities	H	C	C	C
Equity	H	H	H	H

*Assumed at market rates, C = Current Rates, H = Historical Rates

Recognition of Translation Gain/Loss

While translating different items at different rates, the consolidated accounts would not be balanced, whereas stand-alone accounts are balanced in their respective currencies. This imbalance would either be a gain or loss. To re-balance accounts, the translation difference could be either (a) routed through profit and loss account or (b) adjusted in the equity account of the consolidated balance sheet.

If routed through profit and loss account, the consolidated profit and hence the earnings would get affected. Reported earnings would then be influenced by exchange rates. If the cumulative translation gains or losses are directly adjusted in the equity account by separately designated account as 'translation reserve account', the consolidated earnings would not be affected.

Foreign exchange rates fluctuate all the time like the prices of any other commodity or financial asset. Do we need to translate the financial statements all the time as the exchange rates change? Fortunately, not! Translation of balance sheet and profit and loss account is mandated only when the accounts of the parent owning the subsidiaries are published. The financial statements of the subsidiaries are required to be consolidated then. In most cases, this is required to be done on annual basis on the day of closing of books of accounts of the parent, when the parent prepares its financial statements.

Translation exposure relates to the assets and liabilities that are regarded as exposed to currency rates. Such items are translated at the closing rates.

The translation exposure is, thus, the difference between the exposed assets and exposed liabilities that are translated at current rate. Therefore, the definition of exposed assets and liabilities assumes significance. The amount of translation exposure would differ depending upon which assets and liabilities are regarded as exposed to currency rate changes.

We take an example to explain how translation is done, the difference after translation is adjusted, and how translation exposure is measured in different methods. Assume an Indian multinational has subsidiary in Europe preparing financial statement in euro. The following is the balance sheet of the subsidiary on a reporting date.

			Euro, Thousand
Shareholders' Fund	400	Fixed Assets	150
LT Loans	250	Current Assets	
ST Loan	210	Inventory	450
Current Liabilities	180	Receivables	400
		Bank & Cash Balance	40
	1,040		1,040

The Indian parent firm needs to convert the balance sheet in Indian rupee for consolidation purpose. This is done in Table 13-2 using three different methods, that is, current/non-current, monetary/non-monetary, and all current. Since different items of balance sheet are converted at different exchange rates, the translated balance sheet in home currency would not match. Even under *all current method* where all items are translated at uniform closing rate, there would be a mismatch because shareholder's fund would continue to be translated at historical rate.

Table 13-2
Translating Balance Sheet

	Euro, Thousands	Rupees, Thousands Current/Non-current		Rupees, Thousands Monetary/Non-monetary		Rupees, Thousands All Current	
Shareholders' Fund	400	H	24,000	H	24,000	H	24,000
LT Loans	250	H	17,500	C	18,750	C	18,750
ST Loan	210	C	15,750	C	15,750	C	15,750
Current Liabilities	180	C	13,500	C	13,500	C	13,500
Translation Gain/(Loss)			5,000		1,500		6,000
TOTAL	1,040		75,750		73,500		78,000
Fixed Assets	150	H	9,000	H	9,000	C	11,250
Inventory	450	C	33,750	H	31,500	C	33,750
Receivables	400	C	30,000	C	30,000	C	30,000
Bank and Cash Balance	40	C	3,000	C	3,000	C	3,000
TOTAL	1,040		75,750		73,500		78,000

Notes:
1. Historical rate for the shareholders' fund and fixed assets is ₹60/€.
2. The exchange rate prevailing at the time of availing LT loan was ₹70/€.
3. The inventory carried is for the period when exchange rate was ₹70/€.
4. Closing rate as on the date of reporting and translation is ₹75/€.
5. H and C denote translation at historical and closing rates, respectively.

The difference on translation needs to be adjusted in the shareholders' fund under a separate reserve account named 'translation reserve account' or like. An increase in translation reserve represents gain and a reduction would signify translation loss.

MEASURING TRANSLATION EXPOSURE

To what extent changes in the exchange rates from one period to another period would impact the financial statement is called translation exposure. To quantify the translation exposure, we use the concept of natural hedge. Assets and liabilities provide a natural hedge to one another for a unidirectional change of exchange rate. An appreciating foreign exchange would increase the values of assets and liabilities equally, nullifying each other. Therefore, translation exposure faced would be the difference of assets and liabilities that are translated at closing rate. For the data in Table 13-2, translation exposure under different methods is shown in Table 13-3.

Table 13-3
Translation Exposure under Different Translation Methods

Euro, Thousands

Item	Euro	Current/Non-current	Monetary/Non-monetary	All Current
LT Loans	250		250	250
ST Loan	210	210	210	210
Current Liabilities	180	180	180	180
TOTAL	1,040	390	640	640
Fixed Assets	150			150
Inventory	450	450		450
Receivables	400	400	400	400
Bank and Cash Balance	40	40	40	40
TOTAL	1,040	890	440	1,040
Translation Exposure		500 Asset	200 Liability	400 Asset

Note: Shaded cells indicate translation at historical rates.

Note how the translation exposure changes in value as well as in directional impact. The impact of appreciating currency would be opposite in two situations of where assets exceed liabilities and where liabilities exceed assets. Under current/non-current method, assets translated at current rate are higher than the liabilities at current rate by €500,000. If euro appreciates by 1%, then the translation gain would be €5,000. If monetary/non-monetary method is used, 1% appreciation of euro would result in translation loss of €2,000. We may generalize as follows:

When local currency depreciates	**Translation Gain/Loss**
and exposed assets > exposed liabilities	Gain
and exposed assets < exposed liabilities	Loss
When local currency appreciates	**Translation Gain/Loss**
and exposed assets > exposed liabilities	Loss
and exposed assets < exposed liabilities	Gain

MANAGEMENT OF TRANSLATION EXPOSURE

We may see that gain or loss on translation is rather trivial because it is merely an accounting exposure. Depending on the translation method used, the impact can be varying and opposite. Further, it does not impact the cash flows. The same logic of it being irrelevant is also forwarded for making the management of translation exposure a non-issue.

However, if some firms still feel the need for managing translation gains or losses, it is possible by (a) either managing the balance sheet of the subsidiary and/or (b) taking a position in derivative instrument to offset the impact of translation.

Balance Sheet Hedge

Managing the translation exposure by managing the balance sheet hinges around the concept of making equal the assets and liabilities exposed to current rates. If the quantum of assets and liabilities that are translated at current rate are equal, the translation exposure would be zero. In the example just discussed, and assuming that parent follows monetary/ non-monetary method, we have translation exposure of €200,000 on the liability side, that is, liabilities at current rate exceed the assets at current rate. If the parent decides to remit by way of equity as sum of €200,000 and use it for paying of any of the short term, long term, or current liabilities, then the liabilities exposed to the current rate would reduce by €200,000 without corresponding reduction in assets exposed. That would make translation exposure vanish, that is, for the next period variations in exchange rate, there would not be an impact on the value of the parent.

Thus, one way of managing the translation risk is to make cash move back and forth between the subsidiary and the parent to eliminate translation exposure. Further, assets and liabilities exposed to the current rate can be made equal in many ways. For example, it may require extending the credit period suitably, as a policy measure controlled by the parent, for increasing the account receivable by €200,000 again eliminating the translation exposure. This increases the credit risk. Would it be appropriate for a firm to replace translation exposure with credit exposure remains a question to be answered?

Regulatory impediments on capital flows would constrain the flow of cash back and forth. Policy measures that eliminate the translation risk but convert it into another kind of risk raise many questions, the most important being the financial prudence.

Derivatives Hedge

Another way to manage the translation exposure is to use the principle of hedging the potential losses with expected gains from another market that is independent and separate. Such a possibility exists with derivatives markets that would offer compensatory payoffs when uncontrollable factors turn adverse and provide a hedge. Continuing with monetary/ non-monetary method and translation exposure of €200,000 on liability side implies that the parent faces a translation loss if euro depreciated. From the perspective of Indian parent, the loss on account of depreciation of the foreign currency, euro, can be protected by selling a forward contract now or by buying a put option.

A more convenient way of looking at the derivatives hedge is to focus on expected profit in the coming period. Under normal course, the change in the value of the firm is driven by changes in the level of future profit. In case of a subsidiary, it also becomes dependent upon the exchange rate changes. If foreign currency in which financial statements of subsidiaries are made depreciates, the translated profit would be less in the parent's balance sheet.

Consider, for example, a British subsidiary of an Indian firm expecting a profit of £1 million in the next quarter. At current exchange rate of ₹90/£, the parent expects ₹90 million as profit. If British pound appreciates to say ₹95, there would be a gain but if it depreciates to say ₹85, the Indian parent faces translation loss for the same level of economic performance. To protect against the depreciating pound, Indian parent can sell £1 million 3-m forward. If the forward rate is ₹89, the parent locks a profit of ₹89 million irrespective of exchange rate prevailing three months later.

The management of translation exposure either through managing the balance sheet or through derivatives raises a fundamental question. Is it prudent to convert a notional loss into a financial transaction with immediate cash flow implication? If cash travels back and forth or a forward contract is booked to manage translation exposure, we give rise to transaction exposure. In managing translation exposure, we end up converting it into transaction exposure. Justification for doing so lacks merit because transaction exposure is the real loss, whereas translation exposure is notional.

Therefore, it is not unusual to find some MNCs leaving the translation exposure unattended except for disclosing the gain or loss in consolidated earnings due to exchange rate changes, especially when cash flows generated at subsidiaries are retained locally for meeting local needs. If earnings are in surplus, they are usually invested till the time opportunities for organic or inorganic growth are identified.

ECONOMIC EXPOSURE

Economic exposure is concerned with the impact of changes in exchange rates on the competitive position of the firm. It can be measured through the changes in the cash flows of the firm due to change in the exchange rate on an aggregate basis rather than for individual transactions. As the exchange rate changes, the economic environment in which the firm operates too changes. This causes changes in the relative competitive position of the firm as changes may be favourable for some firms but unfavourable for others. It is a broader issue than both transaction exposure and translation exposure.

In an increasingly integrated world, the operating domain of firms has been expanding from domestic to global. This makes the firm compete on global basis rather than on local basis. The resources used by the firms in terms of raw materials, manpower, etc. are being procured internationally. Similarly, customer base too has expanded. The financial performance of firms is becoming increasingly dependent on global conditions of which exchange rate behaviour is a significant part.

Even when a firm is a pure domestic one in terms of its input and output being denominated entirely in local currency, its competitive position gets affected by changes in exchange rate because goods and services of imported substitutes become either expensive or cheaper. Such a change would alter competitive position of a pure domestic firm because the cost and revenue model of a competing MNC firm dependent upon global inputs and outputs undergoes a change. The MNCs and firms whose inputs and/or outputs are largely denominated in foreign currency are more susceptible to the exchange rate movements as compared to the firms dealing purely in the domestic markets.

For example, most firms in India in the area of information technology and software development are export-oriented and cash flows and profits are critically dependent on the exchange rates of major currencies like US dollar, euro, etc. Similarly, firms in petroleum sector depend too much on imports of oil again denominated mostly in US dollars. The cash flows of such firms become heavily dependent on the exchange rates. The changes in cash flows are reflected in the value of the firm, that is, the stock price.

Let us examine the impact of depreciation of local currency on the values of a pure domestic firm. Consider the position of a local automobile manufacturer that produces and sells cars with all indigenous suppliers and customers only in India. A competitor is a trading firm that imports entirely and markets different automobiles. Due to depreciation of local currency, the cars supplied by importers would become expensive as compared to the ones supplied by domestic producer, thereby likely to affect its cash flows favourably. The competitive position of the firm has improved despite no direct reliance on the import or export and, hence, exchange rate. As a result, the value of the firm should increase benefitting shareholders.

With the appreciation of local currency, the domestic firm should face increased competition from foreign products as imports become cheaper. Local sales of the local firms are expected to decline. The value of the firm should see an adverse impact.

Situations of depreciating or appreciating local currency may not be as simple and straight forward as described above. The cost structure too plays an important role as the value of inputs too changes. If markets for imported inputs are also competitive, the local firm may see a decline in the cost of inputs with appreciation of local currency.

The net impact of appreciation of local currency would depend on the level of competitiveness in the markets for finished goods and raw materials. The exposure of the firm with respect to foreign currency rates is, thus, dependent upon several vastly different factors such as market structures, competitiveness of import substitutes, and elasticity of demand. Therefore, even in the absence of transaction exposure, the stakeholders of the firm—particularly the shareholders—are not insulated from the happenings in the foreign currency markets. Economic exposure is faced by all the firms, whether pure domestic or MNCs, on a continuous basis unlike transaction exposure or translation exposure, which occurs only when firms undertake transactions denominated in foreign exchange. However, MNCs may exhibit more sensitivity with exchange rates.

MEASURING ECONOMIC EXPOSURE

With increased complexity of cost structure, revenue model, environmental sensitivities of the firm, and interdependent macroeconomic variables, it would be hazardous to make simplistic predictions about the direction and quantum of impact of exchange rate changes on the competitive position of any firm. Further, foreign exchange markets behave exactly like stock markets where information keeps flowing on a continuous basis and prices keep adjusting for the new information. Though the changes may appear to be random, they are driven by complex structure of economies and cause–effect relationship may become difficult to establish, posing difficulties in the measurement of economic exposure. We defined economic exposure as the impact of the changes in the exchange rates on the competitive position of the firm. The primary determinants of the strength of the firm are its cash flows and its net income. If they undergo a change for any reason, the competitive position of the firm changes.

Scenario Analysis

One way of measuring economic exposure is to conduct a scenario analysis, examining the cash flows with different exchange rate scenarios. Cash flow projections may be made under different exchange rate scenarios. A proforma cash flow statement may be prepared with major heads of revenue and cost. This facilitates the analysis of exchange rate changes on each item of revenue and cost. An extremely simple exposition is shown in Table 13-3, which examines three possible exchange rate scenarios described as follows:

Scenario I   The present exchange rate is ₹50/$. The firm makes a sale of ₹2,100 and $20. The costs in rupee and dollar terms are ₹800 and $30, respectively. With overheads of ₹300, it has a profit of ₹400.

Scenario II   Let us examine the scenario of rupee appreciation by 10%. If rupee appreciates, the import substitute of finished goods becomes cheaper and, therefore, local sales decline to ₹1,800. On the same front, inputs from abroad become cheaper too and firm replaces domestic input of ₹100 with imported input of $2. The costs also reduce but not as much as the sales. The profit declines to ₹170 as shown in Panel II of Table 13-3.

Scenario III   Now assume that rupee depreciates 10% to ₹55/$. This makes import substitutes of inputs and outputs more expensive. Since import substitute of output is more expensive, the firm makes increased sales at ₹2,300. For the same reason, import content comes down. The net profit increases to ₹615. This is shown in Panel III of Table 13-4.

By analysing various possible situations, the sensitivity of the cash flows with changing exchange rates can be estimated. Scenario analysis can become easier if the firm has past data available with respect to changes in cash flows with given percentage change in exchange rates. Improvement in cash flow may be construed as improvement in competitive position. In the aforementioned analysis, the depreciation of Indian rupee seems favourable for the firm. Expected cash flow may be found by assigning the probability to each exchange rate scenario.

Scenario analysis is a good way of finding the dependence of the firm on exchange rate volatility. However, it has its own limitations. One major limitation is that only limited number of scenarios can be analysed, and none of which may actually occur. Another limitation is that it tests the domain knowledge of people. Without domain knowledge and without being conversant with the linkages of firm's operations with exchange rates, cost structure, import substitutability of input and output, etc. scenario analysis becomes difficult and unreliable. Scenario analysis establishing the changes in the cash flow position of the firm due to changes

Table 13-4
Measuring Economic Exposure

	Rupee Component	Dollar Component	Equivalent Rupee	Total (₹)
Panel I: Present Forecast at Exchange Rate of ₹50/$				
Sales	2,100	20	1,000	3,000
Variable Cost	800	30	1,500	2,300
Overheads	300	–	–	300
Cash Profit				400
Panel II: Rupee appreciates to ₹45/$ causing decline in domestic and export sales as well as cost of inputs				
Sales	1,800	18	810	2,610
Variable Cost	700	32	1,440	2,140
Overheads	300	–	–	300
Cash Profit				170
Panel III: Rupee depreciates to ₹55/$ causing decline in domestic and export sales as well as cost of inputs				
Sales	2,300	22	1,210	3,510
Variable Cost	1,000	29	1,595	2,595
Overheads	300	–	–	300
Cash Profit				615

in the exchange rates presupposes the understanding of the business intricacies of the markets for the finished product and raw material markets the firm deals with.

Market Value of the Firm—A Proxy for Cash Flow

Scenario analysis can be done only by those having knowledge and access to firm's internal policies. We may find the dependence of firm on exchange rate much in the same manner as we find beta of the firm, that is, by regression. Assuming that cash flows of the firm derive the value of the firm, we may use its stock price as proxy for cash flow. Further, stock price changes would truly and independently reflect the changes in competitive position of the firm in the eyes of all stakeholders. Stock price is an aggregate measure of competitive position of a firm in the domain in which it operates. However, we need to decipher the component of stock price changes that depends on foreign exchange rates to find economic exposure.

A regression of the past data of stock price with different exchange rates would help establish a relationship and dependence of the firm on the exchange rates. This historical analysis can be used to find the likely changes in stock price with the anticipated exchange rate in future.

We may plot returns measured by the changes in the stock price as dependent variable and percentage change in the exchange rate as independent variable for the past and do regression. The regression equation would have the following outcome:

$$R = a + b \times \Delta ER + c$$

where R = Returns on the stock, ΔER = Percentage change in exchange rate, b = Sensitivity of R with exchange rate changes, a = Y intercept, and c = Random error terms.

The advantage of using the stock price as a measure of economic exposure of the firm is that such analysis may be carried out without the in-depth understanding of (a) currency markets, (b) economic conditions, and (c) access to the information specific to the firm.

Measurement of economic exposure with the changes in the stock price also serves another useful purpose, which possibly is difficult to account for in the scenario or sensitivity analysis. An exposure is defined as changes in the competitive position due to unanticipated changes in the exchange rates. Since stock prices already discount anticipated events, including the expected changes in the exchange rates, the measurement based on changes in the stock price would only account for the new information that has not been discounted in the existing price.

Real vs Nominal Exchange Rates

What kinds of changes in the exchange rates matter and alter the competitive position of the firm is a key question. Economic exposure relates to changes in the competitive position. If the changes in exchange rates are such that they affect all the firms in a uniform manner, then there would be no change in relative competitive position. For example, depreciation of local currency would indicate higher inflation rate. While depreciation makes import substitute costlier, they also increase the cost in accordance with inflation rate, making no difference to market dynamics with respect to a domestic producer and an importer. Consider, for example, that inflation in India is 5% more than in Japan. A television set manufacturer in India competes with a firm that imports televisions from Japan. As per PPP, Indian rupee must depreciate by 5% with respect to Japanese yen. If so, imported television from Japan would cost 5% more. However, the cost of television sets in India would also rise by 5% because of increased inflation. This would mean no change in the competitive positions of domestic producer and importer.

Changes in the exchange rate as per PPP as highlighted above mean change in nominal rates but not in real rates. Changes in nominal exchange rate are immaterial for economic exposure unless they signify the change in the real exchange rates. If the changes in the nominal exchange rates are consistent with the changes in the inflation rates—as would happen if PPP holds—the competitive position of local firm with respect to foreign firm remains unchanged. What is lost by way of increase in the nominal exchange rates is compensated by increased inflation rate. Therefore change in real exchange rate only causes economic exposure.

For illustration purpose consider a small example. Assume there are two suppliers of shirts—one manufacturing locally and the other importing entirely from Britain. The cost of manufacture of shirt for a domestic producer is ₹1,200, whereas the imported shirt cost £20. With the current exchange rate at ₹60 per pound, the cost of imported shirt is exactly equal to ₹1,200 keeping the competitive positions of domestic producer and imported supplier at par with one another.

Now assume that the inflation rates in India and Britain are 20% and 10%, respectively. According to PPP, the new nominal exchange rate after one year should be ₹65.45 (60 × 1.2/1.1). This would imply that the real exchange rates have not changed. Under the circumstances where the real exchange rates remain unchanged, it can be demonstrated that the competitive positions of domestic producer and importer remain unaffected. While local manufacturer faces increased cost due to inflation in India, the imported supplier faces impact on two counts—one, inflation in Britain and, two, increased exchange rate. The combined impact of inflation and exchange rate changes for importer is exactly equal to increased inflation faced by the domestic producer, as may be seen by the analysis done in Table 13-5.

However, the relative competitive position would be affected if the change in nominal exchange rates is not consistent with PPP, causing depreciation or appreciation of the currency in real terms. As per PPP, the depreciation of rupee should be equal to the differential of inflation rates in two countries, that is, 10%. Assume that the actual depreciation of rupee is more than 10%, say the exchange rate is now ₹70 rather than ₹65.45. In such a case, the importer would face additional cost in the form of extra depreciation of rupee, making his products more expensive relative to the domestic producer.

Table 13-5
Change In Real Rates Only Have Economic Exposure

	Cost Today	Cost a Year Later	
		Real Rates Constant	Real Rates Change
Exchange Rate	₹60/£	₹65.45/£	₹70.00/£
Local Manufacturer	₹1,200	₹1,440 (increased by 20% due to inflation)	₹1,440 (increased by 20% due to inflation)
Importer Equivalent ₹	£20 ₹1,200 (@ ₹60/£)	£22 ₹1,440 (@ ₹65.45/£) Increased by 10% due to inflation and remaining 10% due to change in nominal exchange rate	£22 ₹1,540 (@ ₹70.00/£) Increased by 10% due to inflation and remaining due to change in nominal exchange rate
Impact	Competitive position is identical costs being same	Relative position remains same if changes in nominal exchange rates are consistent with PPP, i.e., real rates do not change.	Relative position of local manufacturer improves as rupee has depreciated more making product of importer relatively more expensive as compared to the domestic producer.

Pegging and Economic Exposure

We just concluded that if the exchange rate changes are in accordance with PPP, there should be no economic exposure. There is a common belief that if exchange rates are not allowed to change, the economic exposure would be non-existent. Under pegged exchange rate system, the local currency value is tied to an anchor currency, for example, Chinese yuan to US dollar. Since the value of currency is fixed in terms of another, the competitive position should remain unchanged. However, such logic is flawed because for economic exposure it is the change in the real rates that matter. The fact remains that when exchange rates are fixed, the risk associated with transactions denominated in foreign exchange is eliminated, that is, transaction exposure does not exist. However, economic exposure continues because fixing nominal exchange rates does not imply that real rates are also fixed.

By fixing the exchange rate by law, we are defying the law of one price, that is, not letting PPP prevail. Exchange rate can be regulated through exchange control laws but not inflation. The inflation rates of the two countries in all probability would differ. By fixing the exchange rate in nominal terms, there is no appreciation or depreciation of currency in nominal terms. The fact is that by fixing the exchange rate in nominal terms, the currency would appreciate or depreciate in real terms by the differential of inflation rates in real terms. Hence, it would give rise to economic exposure.

MANAGING ECONOMIC EXPOSURE

The management of economic exposure is complex because the sources of changes in the operating cash flows causing the firm's competitive position to change are too many. The responses of customers, competitors, suppliers, lenders, investors, etc. to a given change in the price level are difficult to predict since economic rationale does not prevail all the time. Behaviour of people to the changes in the economic, political, and social environments is too complex to be formulated into a mathematical model capable of analysing the impact of a change. Therefore, management of economic exposure becomes more of strategic nature concerned with stabilizing the future cash flows over a long period of time, unlike management of translation and transaction exposures that focus on the stable cash flows in the immediate future.

Manage or Not to Manage

There is a debate on the need to manage the economic exposure. Few argue that as long as transaction exposure is managed well, there is no explicit need to manage the economic exposure. Since individual transactions cause variations of cash flows collectively, they represent the economic exposure. The argument is valid only partially. Transaction exposure and translation exposure are subset of economic exposure. Economic exposure is much broader than any of transaction exposure and translation exposure. Sales and purchases in foreign currencies can be hedged through variety of financial instruments available. Similarly, balance sheet exposure of the assets and liabilities denominated in foreign currency too can be managed though they do not affect cash flows unless liquidated. However, changes in the cash flows due to consumer behaviour, competitor's reaction, etc. to exchange rate changes forming part of economic exposure are not hedged. Economic exposure is a superset that encompasses transaction and translation exposures, besides many other factors and, therefore, needs to be managed besides hedging transaction and translation exposures.

Strategic Management of Economic Exposure

Management of economic exposure is strategic in nature. It has to encompass all functions of an organization and cannot be confined to finance function alone. All other functions like marketing, production, purchase, etc. and the respective strategies are equally responsible and concerned about the risk posed by changing exchange rate causing changes in the competitive position.

From production function viewpoint, one possible strategic way of managing economic exposure is to spread the manufacturing locations of various plants. Most MNCs manage economic exposure by locating the manufacturing plants in many countries rather than export from a single location. Besides expanding the marketing base by increased geographical coverage such spreading of plant locations reduces volatility of the aggregate cash flows of the firm due to exchange rate changes since products are invoiced in local currencies rather than in foreign currency. The use of several currencies in the invoicing would offset negative effects of some with positive effects on remaining currencies.

From marketing viewpoint, economic exposure can be managed by diversification of product range. Product variants may be launched meant for different nations and nationalities. If markets are segmented on geographical basis, the responses of customers in different nations for a given change in exchange rate too would be nullifying. Diversification of products and markets, though primarily done to increase the sales and the profits, also renders stability to operating cash flows. Launching products into new geographical territories, pricing strategies in the new markets are some of the marketing-based interventions that are seldom thought as risk reduction strategies. The currency diversification is automatically achieved as a by-product of marketing strategies focussed on new product and new market development.

Purchase-based activities that lead to reduced economic exposure are vendor development, cultivating domestic vendors to reduce dependence upon foreign vendors, entering into fixed price long-term contracts for supplies. All these activities are aimed at certainty of cash outflows.

Though cash flows of most firms are primarily dependent upon the operating activities of sales and purchases, the role of finance is often overlooked in managing the economic exposure. Financing structure too can expose firms to wider fluctuations in operating cash flows than one expects. From financing viewpoint, the management of economic exposure is to follow a golden rule to borrow in the currency in which the cash flows of the firm are generated. This would match the currencies of inflow and out flow reducing the differential and hence the economic exposure.

Economic exposure can also be managed by currency derivatives. We know that derivatives give payoff that can compensate for the likely losses due to adverse exchange rate movements. Taking a suitable position in derivatives would reduce the variability of the combined cash flows. However, management of economic exposure by taking derivative position exposes the firm to real loss of cash. Again one faces the question of managing a macroeconomic threat with microeconomic and tactical tool of derivatives.

SUMMARY

Translation exposure results from the conversion of accounts denominated in one currency to another currency. Seemingly, it is a simple process of multiplication of accounting number by exchange rate. However, it is naive to assume that such a process can give rise to no risk. Changing exchange rates poses a threat to the performance of MNCs because the same economic performance would look different at two different points of time when exchange rates undergo a change.

The need for translation of accounts of subsidiary arises due to the legal requirement of presenting the consolidated accounts to the shareholders that warrant the use of a common currency. It raises a problem of mismatch of balance sheet due to usage of different exchange rates for different items on the balance sheet. The problem is solved by adjusting the shareholders' fund through specially created account as 'currency translation reserve'. Translation exposure is a function of (a) level of dependence on subsidiaries, (b) strength of the functional currencies relative to reporting currency, (c) economic situations of the nations where subsidiaries are located, and (d) methods of translation used.

There are four methods of translating the accounts from one currency to another—current/non-current, monetary/non-monetary, all current, and temporal. These methods classify various items of financial statements for the purpose of using historical, average, and closing rates. In India, monetary/non-monetary method is used which prescribes translation of non-monetary items at historical rate and remainder at closing rate.

Translation exposure is measured by the difference of assets and liabilities exposed to closing rate. Translation exposure can be managed through balance sheet hedge, that is, equating the assets and liabilities translated at closing rate to nullify the effect of exchange rate changes. Execution of balance sheet hedge may be impractical due to legal hurdles. Another way of managing the translation exposure is to take a derivative position in such a manner so as to offset the likely adverse impact of exchange rate movement. However, the merit of managing translation exposure is challenged because such attempts convert the notional exposure to real cash flow implications.

Economic exposure is concerned with the changes in the competitive position of a firm due to fluctuations of exchange rate movements. It affects all firms in varying degrees though the impact of economic exposure on MNCs is more as compared to a pure domestic firm. To assess economic exposure, changes in exchange rate in nominal terms are irrelevant. Economic exposure is assessed by changes in real exchange rates. Under pegged exchange rate system, the value of currency is fixed to an anchor currency in nominal terms. Since the inflation rates in the pegged currency and anchor currency are going to be different, the pegged exchange rates would surely imply change in real exchange rate. Pegging eliminates transaction exposure but gives rise to economic exposure.

The management of economic exposure is mostly strategic in nature, though tactical tools of derivatives too can be used. Economic exposure is much wider in scope and, therefore, managing it requires participation from all functional areas of an organization. Multiple plant locations, increasing product range, diversifying markets, etc. are strategies that help reduce economic exposure though these strategies are motivated by and formulated to achieve other objectives.

QUESTIONS

13-1 What do you understand by translation exposure?

13-2 Why do you think that management of translation exposure is more important than management of economic exposure?

13-3 Critically evaluate the statement 'Managing translation exposure is a waste of precious time of management'.

13-4 Briefly explain the following translation methods:
   (a) Current/non-current method
   (b) Monetary/non-monetary method
   (c) All current method

13-5 'Translation exposure would be same irrespective of the method used for translation.' Discuss.

13-6 How is economic exposure different from transaction exposure?

13-7 China has pegged its currency to US dollar and, therefore, Chinese companies do not face any economic exposure. Do you agree with the statement? Give reasons.

13-8 How would you measure economic exposure by scenario analysis, and what are the limitations of such an exercise?

13-9 Comment on the statement, 'Economic exposure can be managed only strategically'.

PROBLEMS

13-1 Translation Methods

Assume an American firm has a subsidiary in Germany having the following assets and liabilities denominated in euros:

Balance Sheet			Euros in Thousands
Fixed Assets	12.00	Net Worth	12.00
Stocks	5.00	Term Liabilities	5.00
Debtors	4.00	Trade Creditors	6.00
Cash	2.00		
	23.00		23.00

The current rate of exchange is 1 euro = US$1.20. The US parent is required to consolidate its subsidiary's accounts with it.

(i) Find out the exposure of the US parent if it follows (a) current/non-current method and (b) monetary/non-monetary method.

(ii) What translation gain/loss would result if US$ appreciates to 1.12 per euro?

13-2 Hedging Translation Exposure

A British subsidiary of a US parent is expecting a profit of £1 million in six months. Current exchange rate is £1 = $1.8 and 6-m forward rate is £1 = $1.78. British pound is expected to depreciate to £1 = $1.6. Explain what forward position the US parent can take and what would be the payoff from forward contract if the forecast comes true.

Political and Country Risk

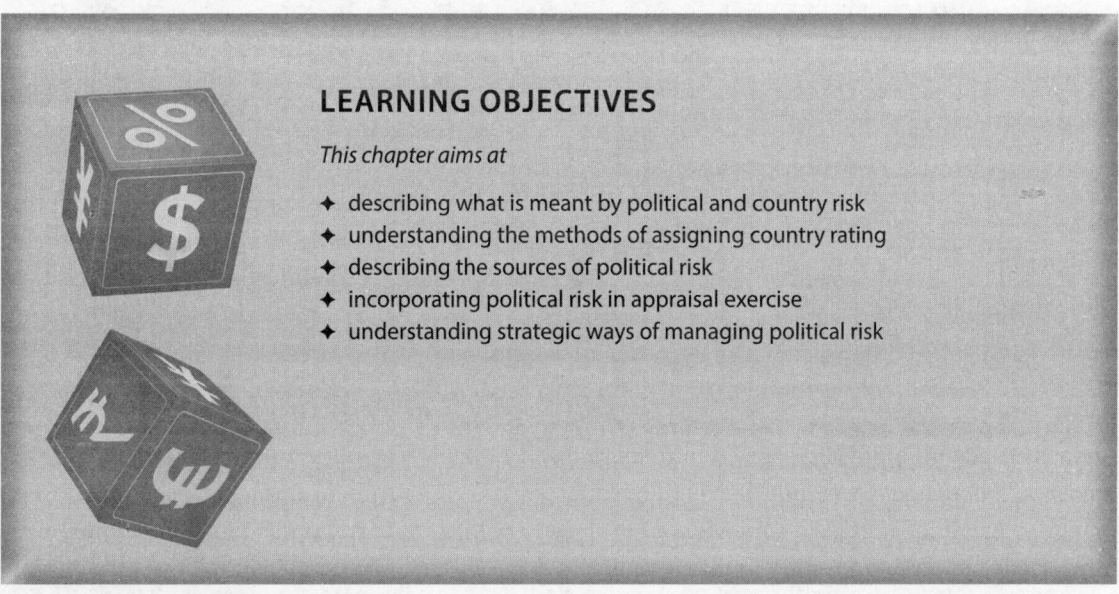

LEARNING OBJECTIVES

This chapter aims at

- describing what is meant by political and country risk
- understanding the methods of assigning country rating
- describing the sources of political risk
- incorporating political risk in appraisal exercise
- understanding strategic ways of managing political risk

CONTENTS

Introduction
Sources of Political Risk
Measuring Country/Political Risk
    Economic Risk
    Financial Risk
Sovereign Rating and Political Risk
Forms of Political Risk
    Expropriation
    Managing Expropriation
    Politics and Business

Political Risk and Capital Budgeting
Managing Political Risk
    Hire Locals
    Seek Local Listing
    Borrow Locally
    Repatriate Quickly

INTRODUCTION

Multinational corporations (MNCs) face a unique situation due to the political and economic scenarios in the country of operation, which is predominantly absent from the decision-making framework of a domestic corporation in that country. For domestic companies, the political and economic situations remain static, and it is not a matter of choice or variable to commence a project. However, MNCs are concerned with (a) whether or not to start business in a foreign land, (b) how to protect the existing assets for continued operations, (c) how to continue to derive the economic and financial benefits from host nation to home nation where the MNC is domiciled, and finally (d) the freedom to close down in case operations prove unviable. These issues are named as political and country risks that an MNC faces.

The sources of these risks are numerous and possibly extremely difficult to quantify. Most decisions are subjective in nature and made on the basis of qualitative judgement. The threats to the entry, existence, expansion, and repatriation of profits may emanate from vastly different factors that are seemingly unrelated. They include (a) current economic condition and future outlook such as development level, likely policies, and growth estimates of an economy, (b) fiscal and monetary policies and degree of openness, (c) political situation, (d) cultural differences and attitude towards foreigners, (e) governance standards and legal recourses available, (f) transparency of government actions, etc.

Political risk assessment is mainly concerned with the actions of government that can impact the cash flows of the project. These actions or policy initiatives by the government adversely affecting the entry, continuity of operations, or exit of MNCs from a nation may be voluntary or involuntary arising from delicate economic environment, extreme political instability, dangerous social unrest and riots, terrorism, etc. The MNCs need to consider these factors while making a choice of locating a project. Since projects are usually long-term in nature, the forecast of political, economic, and social factors that would unfold in distant future are extremely difficult to measure.

SOURCES OF POLITICAL RISK

Political risk or country risk lacks a formal or comprehensive definition. It connotes different meanings. In the definition of earlier periods, it usually referred to *transfer risk*, which meant possibility of government's restrictions on repayment obligations of foreign debts. Sovereign risk refers to the inability of the government to honour its external debt repayment obligations arising out of bad economic situation and imprudent economic and monetary policies. It normally excludes failure to repay domestic debt because no government is expected to default on its dues due to its unique ability to print money, and honour commitments.

Sources that give rise to political risk are too vast to enumerate and perhaps unique to every economy. Yet a demonstrative list of factors is presented below:

1. Political situations such as war, terrorism, dictatorship, civil war, and riots
2. Economic situations such as recession, inflation, loss of export competiveness, fiscal imprudence, and tardy growth rate

3. Monetary situations such as rising interest rates, public debt, external debt, credit squeeze, and rapid devaluation/depreciation of currency
4. Social conditions such as labour unrest, xenophobia, call for nationalist policies, and being self-reliant
5. Natural calamities such as flood, draught, tsunami, and earthquake

Any of these mentioned factors have potential to become a sufficient cause of deterioration of business conditions affecting resident and non-resident firms. While some of these factors are completely unpredictable, some factors relating to economic and monetary policies can forewarn the potential threat to business and help in assessing the risk, at least in the short and medium term. As we gauge the health of the business enterprise from its financial statements, a nation's health and conduciveness to business can be assessed, partly subjectively and partly objectively from the soundness of economic and financial policies pursued. The deterioration of economic, monetary, and trade policies of the nation often forces the government to exercise its power to make laws aimed at protection of economy. These laws such as increased taxation, unilateral acquisition of business, freezing of accounts, forcing procurement from local sources, etc. are often passed in larger public interest.

The risk of loss due to political reasons that arises in a particular country due to changes in the country's political structure or policies, such as tax laws, tariffs, expropriation of assets, or restriction in repatriation of profits is considered political risk. Political risk is distinct from other commercial risks. Examples of political risks include licence cancellation, exchange control regulations, sanctions, confiscation of assets, etc.

MEASURING COUNTRY/POLITICAL RISK

The measurement of political or country risk may be done from economic and political conditions. Deteriorating economic conditions and unstable political situations would indicate increased risk. There are a number of international agencies involved in the measurement of country risk such as Business Environment Risk Intelligence (BERI), Euromoney, Control Risks Information Services (CRIS), Standard & Poor's (S&P), and Moody's. Most agencies involved in political risk measurement have different economic, monetary, and political factors along which subjective assessments coupled with some measurable indicators are evaluated. These factors are assigned a weight, which are used to assign a numerical score or alphabetical symbol that provides an overall impression of political risk. The risk assessment has to be a relative measurement in the set of countries being considered. However, there is no unanimity amongst various rating agencies on the factors to be included and weights to be assigned in the measurement of country risk. Each one of them has its own method, rationale, and scoring system.

We present here a broad idea of the factors that go to decide the country rating. It revolves around the same or similar concepts as used in corporate finance to assess the risk associated with a firm. The risk of a firm is often segregated as (a) business risk and (b) financial risk. Business risk deals with variability of the reward to the shareholders due to changes in the business environment. The ability of the firm to withstand the competition, changing technologies, market conditions, etc. is quantified as business risk. The business risk becomes analogous to economic risk in the context of a country. It would measure the ability of an economy to respond to global environment changes.

The financial risk of a firm is dependent upon the use of debt to propel the growth and enhance the returns to shareholders. By seeking greater returns by deploying borrowed funds, the firm also makes these returns more volatile. Likewise, a developing nation too borrows to have desired economic growth, which otherwise cannot be met with domestically generated resources only.

Technically, business and financial risks are measured in terms of degree of operating leverage and degree of financial leverage, respectively, which are described in terms of ratios available in the financial statements of the firm. On similar lines, we may assess the country risk along two parameters: (1) the ability of the economy to cope with the economic and environmental changes in the world, which is referred to as *economic risk*, and akin to business risk in the context of firm, and (2) the ability of the economy to service external debt sought for the speedier and higher growth of the economy, which is referred to as *financial risk*. The measurement would be made in the form of similar ratios representing the structure, composition, and stability of the economy available in the form of national data.

Economic Risk

The economic factors that affect the country risk are concerned with the ability of the nation to attract, retain, and absorb the economic benefits of a multinational firm making an investment. It is a function of the level of gross domestic product (GDP), its growth rate as against the planned and historical, incentives for investment, level of savings, consumption levels, etc. The orientation of the government with regard to foreign investors can be measured from their fiscal, monetary, and trade policies, and may be answered from questions such as

- What has been the level of fiscal deficits in the past and are they sustainable in the long term?
- Does the fiscal management represent financial prudence?
- What has been the growth of money supply and resultant inflation, and are they too sustainable in the long term?
- What has been the trade policy, tariff levels, and the degree of protection provided to local industries?
- What have been the policies for portfolio and foreign direct investment (FDI), and are they progressively relaxing?

Besides the aforementioned subjective judgement of questions, the numerical measurement is possible in terms of any or more of the following indicative list:

1. Ratio of savings and domestic investment to GDP indicating inherent strength of propensity to save and invest in an economy. Higher rates of savings and investment usually connote better ability to cope with adverse situations, as the economy has self-sustained growth.
2. Ratio of fiscal deficit to GDP indicating financial prudence and government's impetus to economic development. A reasonable fiscal deficit may be considered as acceptable and

good, whereas large deficits are not desirable. The trend of fiscal deficit over immediate past is of critical relevance here in making the assessment.
3. Ratio of public debt to GDP again indicating financial prudence with regard to government's orientation towards borrowing and sustainability of economic development.
4. Imports and exports as per cent of GDP, indicating propensity to consume imported products and export competiveness of the nation. The elasticity of imports and exports too would be considered in the ability of the economy to sustain external threats.
5. Current account deficit as per cent of GDP, as per cent of earnings in foreign exchange, as per cent of foreign exchange reserves, etc. indicating an ability to bear external shocks.

Financial Risk

Similarly, there are some monetary or financial indicators that can throw some light on the political risk. It is concerned with the ability of the economy to generate foreign exchange adequate to meet the payment obligations to service foreign debt. Nations that borrow from international markets, and put them to non-productive use are more susceptible to default on the borrowings. Therefore, the end-use of the funds borrowed in foreign currency becomes important. If the generation of foreign currency cash flows exceeds the repayment obligations of the borrowing, the nation becomes safer with time. If so, the country becomes inherently strong with the passage of time. Some of the quantitative measures of financial risk are as follows:

1. Total external debts to exports, GDP, reserves
2. Imports as per cent of reserves or the number of months/years reserves would cover the import requirements
3. Total debt service to GDP
4. Interest obligations to exports
5. Growth rate of exports and imports

The financial risk is often segregated in terms of maturity of foreign debt, that is, over short term and over long term. Foreign investment in a country can broadly be classified in two ways: the portfolio investment in financial assets of the country, and FDI made for creation of tangible assets. Portfolio investments are fast and easy to divest as compared to FDI. The financial risk therefore must be considered from service obligations of short-term debt as well as of long-term debt. The ability to meet short-term and long-term service obligations may differ substantially. The nature of foreign debt therefore has the following four components:

1. Interest obligations falling due over short term usually defined as within next 12 months
2. Principal repayment falling due in next 12 months
3. Interest obligations over long term falling due after 12 months
4. Principal obligations due after 12 months

Another distinguishing feature of external debt is whether the debt is owned by government or guaranteed by it, or the debt is taken by private enterprises. While aggregate level of debt is important irrespective of backing by sovereign or not, the assessment of financial risk as a component of country risk is mainly concerned with debt by government or guaranteed by government.

SOVEREIGN RATING AND POLITICAL RISK

Sovereign credit rating is one way of understanding how risky it is to do a business in a foreign country. Prominent credit rating agencies such as S&P's, Moody's, Fitch, and DBRS publish ratings of various countries, undertake surveillance to constantly upgrade/downgrade, and issue warning signals that can help MNCs take decisions on investing abroad. Sovereign credit ratings give investors insight into the level of risk associated with investing in a particular country and also include political risks.

Developing countries seek credit rating because rating often decides the cost of finance for the firms located in the sovereign as financiers add premium in the financing cost in accordance with the risk associated. Another common reason for obtaining sovereign credit ratings, other than issuing bonds in external debt markets, is to attract FDI. To give investors confidence of investing in their country, many countries seek ratings from credit rating agencies such as S&P, Moody's, and Fitch to provide financial transparency and demonstrate their credit standing.

The threats to existence and growth of MNCs operating in foreign lands emanate from several factors. These factors range from political conditions, external threats, and economic and financial position of the nation. Sovereign ratings are one way of assessing political and country risk, which is an attempt to convert subjective factors into objective numbers. Different rating agencies adopt different methods though somewhat similar to assign credit ratings.

S&P classifies sovereign rating of nation along five scores: political, economic, external, fiscal, and monetary. These ratings apply to sovereign's ability and willingness to serve financial obligations assumed from commercial creditors, and does not apply to obligations to other governments or intergovernmental debt, debt by supranational agencies such as International Monetary Fund (IMF) or the World Bank, sovereign-guaranteed debt, or commitments by public sector enterprises, government-related entities or local and regional governments.

Each of the five scores ranges from 1 (strongest) to 6 (weakest).

Political Score Political score is based on past track record of the sovereign in managing the financial crises and delivering the economic growth, ability, and willingness to implement reforms, and stability of policies and institutions. Other factors include effective checks and balances, free flow of information, and timely and reliable public finance data and statistics.

Economic Score Economic score is primarily concerned with (a) income levels, (b) growth prospects, and (c) economic diversity and volatility. An income level of more than US$35,000 is assigned score of '1', whereas income level of less than US$1,000 is weakest at '6'. Adjustment is made for undervaluation or overvaluation of the currency. A sustained current account surplus indicates undervaluation and per capita GDP understates prosperity. Higher per capita GDP is better because it reflects the higher tax base available that lends credence to credit worthiness. The score is further modulated for the growth prospects; with growth rate higher than peers help improve the rating. Growth rate is seen over a longer period of time to eliminate situations of increased inflation or creation of asset bubbles, and to cover at least one economic cycle. Economic diversity is gauged from the dependence of growth on multiple sectors. If one single activity constitutes 20% or more of GDP, it is not supposed to be diversified enough. The ability to cope with extreme weather conditions and natural disasters is also considered.

External Score External score is concerned with ability to generate receipts from abroad (current account receipts), external indebtedness of the sovereign and liquidity, and the international investment position. The external debt is compared with current account receipts. The other dimension of external score is the status of sovereign's currency. If the currency of sovereign is used by others as *reserve currency*, it reflects vast and open capital markets with interest rates and foreign exchange rates determined by market forces. The currency is considered a reserve currency if it constitutes more than 3% of the world's allocated reserves. The currency is considered as *actively traded* if it constitutes more than 1% of the world's foreign exchange turnover.

Fiscal Score The fiscal performance of a nation is usually ascertained in terms of fiscal deficit as percentage of GDP. However, the ratings by S&P consider fiscal performance as changes in the government debt as percentage of GDP rather than fiscal deficit. It is believed that fiscal deficits are affected by political compulsions and considerations that skew the expenditure. Fiscal performance is adjusted for flexibility gauged qualitatively in terms of sovereign's (a) ability and willingness to raise the tax rates and tax base, and (b) ability and willingness to cut the expenditure.

The second dimension of the fiscal score is the debt burden focusing on debt levels and its cost. Debt level is measured as percentage of GDP and cost of debt is measure as percentage of revenue. A debt less than 30% of GDP and interest cost comprising less than 5% of government revenue is the best and assigned a rating of '1'. Increasing debt level and increasing interest cost reduces the rating, with more than 100% of GDP as debt and interest cost accounting for more than 15% of revenues is assigned the poorest rating of '6'. While assessing level of debt due consideration is also given to the liabilities that have potential to become government debt, such as systemic risk in financial sector.

Structure of debt also influences the fiscal score. The structure of debt is measured on the basis of currency and status of debt holder. Higher proportion of debt denominated (typically more than 40%) in foreign currency exposes the nation to global uncertainties and exchange rate changes. Similarly, if debt holders are non residents (typically more than 60%) or local banks (typically holding more than 20%) are considered constraining factors for better fiscal performance and are viewed negatively. The structure of debt is considered as government's ability to refinance.

Monetary Score Monetary score focuses on the exchange rate system the country has, and whether the monetary policies have credibility. It is governed by the nation's ability to control the money supply and domestic liquidity conditions. The credibility of monetary policy is measured by inflation trends. The effectiveness by which the monetary policy can be delivered is dependent upon the depth and diversification of the domestic financial system and capital markets.

The highest score of '1' is assigned where the monetary authority is able to lower interest rates effectively or even expand its balance sheet significantly, and therefore, ease tight liquidity conditions without stoking inflationary pressures. This would happen when the country has deep and diversified credit and capital markets. The lowest score of '6' is assigned where sovereigns use the currency of another, or have extensive foreign exchange controls affecting the current account, or have persistent high inflation. Under such conditions, a sovereign has very limited or no flexibility to affect domestic economic conditions, and cannot provide any meaningful buffer against domestic financial stress.

Exchange rate regimes determine the freedom of monetary policy. Floating exchange rate system provides absolute flexibility to adjust monetary policy, and therefore it is considered best, whereas pegged system of exchange rate determination constrains the monetary policy, and so is accorded lowest rating. Credibility of monetary policies is a subjective assessment, and assessed from whether the monetary authority is independent of political scenario. Effectiveness of monetary policy is measurable in terms of consistent low rates of inflation. For sovereigns with the highest level of monetary flexibility, the inflation is expected to remain well contained (defined as averaging between 0% and 3% per year).

The efficiency of capital markets determines the transmission of monetary policy in the economy. Capital markets respond to changes in interest rate (a potent tool of monetary policy). If markets are developed, changes in economy and business would be effective and true as desired by monetary policy. If markets are not as developed, the intended changes would not fructify. Efficiency of capital markets can be accessed from (a) government's ability to issue, at market-determined rates, long-term fixed-rate nominal local-currency bonds, (b) existence of an active money market and corporate bond market, and a developed banking system (c) share of bank intermediation in local currency. They provide an indication of the confidence in a market's long-term liquidity. Better scores are associated with a higher proportion of local-currency fixed-rated bonds with a long maturity. Better banking system and capital markets provide multiple sources of funding.

FORMS OF POLITICAL RISK

The influence of actions of government over operations of MNCs usually come in the form of (a) expropriation or nationalization, (b) increased taxation, (c) constraints on repatriation of profits, (d) imposing conditions of licensing, (e) allocation of resources, and (f) commitments for capacity, prices, exports, etc.

Standard & Poor's Rating Symbols and Meaning

Letter Grade	Meaning		Ratings as on 30 Sept 2013*
INVESTMENT GRADE			
AAA	Extremely strong capacity to meet financial commitments		Australia, Canada, Denmark, Finland, Germany, Hong Kong, Luxembourg, Norway, Netherlands, Sweden, Switzerland, Singapore, UK
AA	Very strong capacity to meet financial commitments	AA+ AA AA–	Austria, France, New Zealand, USA, Belgium, Kuwait China, Chile, Japan, Saudi Arabia, Taiwan
A	Strong capacity to meet financial commitments, but somewhat susceptible to adverse economic conditions and changes in circumstances	A+ A A–	Israel, Korea Malaysia Mexico, Poland, Thailand
BBB	Adequate capacity to meet financial commitments, but more subject to adverse economic conditions	BBB+ BBB	Ireland, Peru Brazil, Italy, Russia, South Africa
BBB–	Considered lowest investment grade by market participants		India, Spain
SPECULATIVE GRADE			
BB+	Considered highest speculative grade by market participants		Indonesia, Romania, Turkey
BB	Less vulnerable in the near-term, but faces major ongoing uncertainties to adverse business, financial, and economic conditions	BB BB–	Hungary, Portugal Bangladesh, Greece, Jamaica
B	More vulnerable to adverse business, financial and economic conditions, but currently has the capacity to meet financial commitments	B+ B B–	Kenya, Sri Lanka, Uganda Lebanon, Ukraine, Venezuela Belarus, Pakistan
CCC	Currently vulnerable and dependent on favourable business, financial and economic conditions to meet financial commitments	CCC+	Argentina, Cyprus, Egypt
CC	Currently highly vulnerable		
C	A bankruptcy petition has been filed or similar action taken, but payments of financial commitments are continued		
D	Payments default on financial commitments		
Ratings from 'AA' to 'CCC' may be modified by the addition of a plus (+) or minus (–) sign to show relative standing within the major rating categories.			

*As published by S&P on 30 Sept 2013, www.standardandpoors.com.

CONCEPTS IN PRACTICE
Sovereign Rating

POLITICS AND ECONOMICS OF CREDIT RATING: ITALY AND INDIA

Politics of Italy: In the wake of uncertain verdict given by Italian voters in the elections held in March 2013, the sovereign rating of Italy was downgraded. Political development thereafter threatening the survival of the coalition government raised serious doubts about its ability to implement structural reforms. Sensing trouble over approval of 2014 budget rating firm DBRS threatened a downgrade of sovereign rating. The DBRS rating on Italy determines how much margin the European Central Bank charges on borrowing against Italian government debt. The ECB uses the best rating out of those issued by Moody's Investors Service, S&P's Ratings Service, Fitch Ratings and DBRS, when determining collateral margin charges. DBRS rates Italy at 'A' that is highest among the four rating firms. A rating downgrade could mean a higher margin on the debt Italian banks avail from ECB or else reduce their borrowing, which could escalate financial tensions in the region.

The approval of budget is supposed to show how the government intends to implement key fiscal policies and structural reforms to help in bringing down Italy's long-term debt loan. Italy's public debt was forecasted at 132% of GDP by the end of 2013.

All four ratings companies had Italy's rating on a negative outlook. Moody's rated Italy at Baa2, two notches above junk bond territory. S&P cut its rating on Italy in July 2013 to bring it in line with Moody's. Fitch had Italy at BBB+, three notches above junk. Fitch also said that Italy faced a downgrade if prolonged political uncertainty derails the country's fiscal targets.

Economics of India: In May 2013, S&P had warned that it may downgrade India's existing sovereign rating at BBB–; the lowest investment grade, to junk grade if the government fails to pursue reforms, and check deterioration in fiscal and current account deficits. S&P said its future credit rating action would depend upon the response of policymakers to the latest economic developments. In mid-August 2013, when Indian rupee depreciated against US dollar to about ₹69 against usual ₹59 in short span of a month the global rating agency S&P said it will maintain negative outlook for the country as currency depreciation is adversely impacting investor confidence and capital outflows. A downgrade would mean pushing the country's sovereign rating to junk status, making overseas borrowings by corporate costlier stifling down the investment growth further. Also depreciating rupee was likely to inflate the fuel subsidy bill, weaken the credit quality of oil companies, and put pressure on the fiscal deficit. Besides fiscal deficit, the current account deficit at $88 billion (4.8% of 2012–13 GDP) too was at a record high level.

Expropriation

Expropriation is the most severe form where the assets of a firm are taken over by the government by paying much less compensation than the true value, or not paying at all, or paying market-based compensation, but the entity is forcibly acquired against the wishes of the existing owner. Nationalization of assets is perhaps a more respectable word for expropriation. It is a forceful confiscation of assets by the state outside the common law. In the past, confiscatory taxation, denial of access to infrastructure or necessary raw materials, imposition of unreasonable regulatory regimes, among others have been considered to be expropriatory actions. At the same time, governments must be free to act in the broader public interest through protection of the environment, new or modified tax regimes, the granting or withdrawal of government subsidies, reductions or increases in tariff levels, and imposition of zoning restrictions.

Expropriation may take many forms, direct as well as indirect (or 'creeping' expropriation). Nations can resort to a wide variety of techniques to achieve increased control of a foreign investment so as to deny the effective control to the foreign entity. The most common types of measures that have given rise to claims of indirect expropriation are: assuming management control, increased and differential taxation, regulation and forced restructuring of investment contracts, etc. Foreign owner is no longer able to participate in the enterprise's day-to-day management, and control or the situation where the actions permanently and irrevocably deprive the foreign company to make use of its investment.

Classic examples of outright expropriation include the nationalization of entities owing debts to foreigners or having outstanding contractual relations with them, the direct annulment of debts or claims, measures denying the foreign owner access to its funds and profits, and the appointment of administrators to manage the foreign property in the enforced absence of the owner.

Managing Expropriation Expropriation or nationalization is an event, and hence, can be managed by insurance. The risk of expropriation and nationalization may be transferred by investors to an insurance firm. There are governmental, quasi-governmental, multilateral, and private insurers that offer policies to cover political risks, including expropriation and nationalization. Governmental and quasi-governmental insurers offer protection to investors from their countries when investing in other jurisdictions. Some of these entities include

- Multilateral Investment Guarantee Agency (MIGA), which is sponsored by the World Bank, and offers coverage to businesses investing outside their home country
- Overseas Private Investment Corporation (OPIC)
- Export Credits Guarantee Department (ECGD) of UK
- Export Development Canada (EDC)

Insurance companies provide political risk covers. These may be purchased for covering only political risk on the sale to a particular country, for a portfolio of political risks or as part of a credit insurance policy.

The other alternative for dispute resolution is to seek arbitration. In order to recover losses caused by government actions, MNCs may directly approach International Center for the Settlement of Disputes (ICSID), which was created through the Convention on the Settlement of Investment Disputes between States and Nationals of Other States (the ICSID Convention) to facilitate the arbitration and conciliation. There can be clauses in Bilateral Investment Treaties, and Free Trade Agreements if such remedies are available therein.

CONCEPTS IN PRACTICE
Indirect Expropriation

METALCLAD IN MEXICO

Metalclad Corporation case in Mexico is a well-cited case of expropriation by Mexican government. Metalclad, a US corporation operating through its Mexican subsidiary received a permit by the Federal Government of Mexico to construct hazardous waste landfill in Guadalcazae. The place where the landfill was allocated had an unstable soil allowing for easy filtration and contamination of deep waters. The location was also an area of unique biological diversity. Five months after the company started construction, it received a notice that the company required an additional municipal permit. The company applied for the permit and it was turned down by the municipality of Guadalcazae. Additionally the Governor issued a decree declaring that the area of construction was a protected natural area. Metalclad issued proceedings before the International Centre for Settlement of Investments Disputes (ICSID) claiming 'Expropriation'. The Tribunal held that the actions of local government and the ecological decree were to be considered as an indirect expropriation. As a result, the investment made by Metalclad was held to be totally lost. The compensation ordered by the tribunal, payable by Mexico, was US$16.7 million.

Politics and Business

In the context of growth and expansion of multinational corporations, the political stability is a major decision-making parameter. As we know, the businesses are dependent upon how politicians perceive its role in the development of an economy and welfare of people. Accordingly, politicians divide themselves into different political parties with significant differences in the philosophies, objectives, and models of achieving these objectives. Political stability in a nation for expansion plans of MNCs are not as much concerned about the right or wrong of a policy, as it is with the continuation of such policies. Changes in the philosophies, objectives, and models of growth and developments over a period constitute political risk. A shift in political power often means shifts in policies and business environment. From the perspective of risk, the policy per se is not as important as the changes in the policy.

Amongst many political philosophies, capitalism and socialism are perhaps two well-known and researched political philosophies that are substantially different from each other regarding the ownership of resources, methods of their exploitation, and finally the distribution of benefits in an economy amongst various sections of the society. In the process, they govern the right to own the property, the manner of its utilization, and sharing of the benefits. It is not what political philosophy a country has that impacts the multinational firms, but it is the change that imparts risk to the operations. Continuity of political philosophy would make decision making easier and MNCs would adapt to the ongoing political thought. Any change in political philosophy would make operations of multinational riskier and warrant change in the decision-making framework.

CONCEPTS IN PRACTICE

Cost of Political Orientation in Business

YUKOS OIL COMPANY: PAYING HEAVY PRICE FOR POLITICAL ORIENTATION

Yukos Oil Company (Yukos) was a very prominent and successful Russian petroleum company headquartered in Moscow, and was controlled by Russian oligarch Mikhail Khodorkovsky and a number of other prominent Russian businessmen till 2003, when the company faced the threat from Russian government. Yukos was one of the world's largest non-state oil companies, producing about 20% of Russian oil—about 2% of world production.

In December 2003, the Russian tax authorities ordered re-audit of Yukos, just months after a previous audit had been completed and signed off. The re-audit—conducted at a lightning pace of just 15 days—claimed Yukos had underpaid its 2000 taxes due by RUB 79.6 billion, (€2.27 billion). Yukos was also ordered to pay fines of 40% of the tax arrears and penalty interest, leaving an additional tax burden of RUB 99.4 billion (€2.9 billion). In July 2004, Yukos was charged with tax evasion, for an amount of over US$27 billion. The Russian government accused the company of misusing tax havens inside Russia in the 1990s so as to reduce its tax burden. These tax havens were set up by most major oil producers in outlying areas of Russia, which had been granted special tax status to assist in their economic development. These havens were used to plan taxes, resulting in Yukos having an effective tax rate of 11% as against statutory rate of 30%. Yukos claimed its actions were legal at the time, and that the company used the same tax optimization schemes as other Russian oil companies, such as Lukoil, TNK-BP, and Sibneft. However, Yukos was the only one to be charged with tax evasion and penalized. A general crackdown on such tax evasion practices began with Putin's presidency, with numerous companies closing or purchasing their trading vehicles. It is

widely believed that Yukos severe treatment at the hands of the tax authorities was due to its attempt to purchase a large block of Duma deputies so as to block oil tax reform legislation.

To recover tax dues Yukos' assets were frozen by the government, as the company was not able to pay these tax demands. Most of Yukos's assets were sold at low prices to oil companies owned by the Russian government, *Rosneft*. The Parliamentary Assembly of the Council of Europe has condemned Russia's campaign against Yukos and its owners, as manufactured for political reasons and a violation of human rights.

This is considered one of the starkest examples of state expropriation of corporate assets. The former management of Yukos also contend that, in addition to the tax process being a sham, the manner of the tax enforcement was arbitrary and disproportionate. The most flagrant example of this was the fact that Yukos' assets were all frozen by the tax authorities, preventing any payment from being made, even though the initial liabilities could in fact have been met.

Khodorkovsky was convicted of fraud and sent to prison for 10 years, and was released only in December 2013. Khodorkovky's imprisonment and the subsequent dismantling of his business empire were believed to be caused by his funding of Vladimir Putin's opponents, and his public accusations about state corruption. Khodorkovsky's jailing was seen by many as sending a warning to Russia's big businessmen to keep out of politics. A former Putin aide, Igor Sechin, now runs Rosneft, the world's top listed oil firm by output thanks to Yukos legacy assets. There is widespread concern internationally that the trials and sentencing were politically motivated. On 20 December 2013 following his release, Khodorkovsky addressed the media and referred to himself as a 'political prisoner', and stated he would not re-enter business or politics. The Permanent Court of Arbitration in The Hague in July 2014 ruled that Russia is liable to pay $50 billion, i.e., almost half of $103 billion plus interest to former owners of Yukos.

Similarly, amongst many systems of governance, the two forms of authoritarian rule and democratic system are well debated. These governance systems, which have little in common, decide the rights of people, setting public policy objectives and rules, and processes and forms for governance, and grievance redressal. Again, it is not the form of governance that impedes operations of MNCs, but the change in such system would cause instability and imparts political risk.

POLITICAL RISK AND CAPITAL BUDGETING

Recognizing the presence of country or political risk the investment exercise by the MNCs must find ways of incorporating it in the project appraisal process. The initial appraisal requires only two vital inputs:

1. The cash flows for the life of the project
2. The discount rate to be used for arriving at the present values

The cash flows of the project can be projected with scenario analysis against different possible government actions that may affect cash flows to the parent. Such actions normally include increased levels of taxes, limits on repatriation of profits, etc. Under each such scenario, cash flows may be projected with likely probability of each event. The assessment of likely probability of the event is subjective. Using probability of each scenario the expected NPV can be worked out that serves as benchmark for decision-making. The drawback of such exercise is that it is also a tedious one. Also only limited number of scenarios can be examined, whereas in real life unanticipated situations are huge in number.

The other method to incorporate the country risk is to increase the discount rate by adding the risk premium, under Capital Asset Pricing Model (CAPM) model. One of the approaches to handle the uncertainty of the future cash flows is to increase the discount rate that effectively brings down its present value. The risk premium for each uncertain factor can be added in the cost of capital as hurdle rate to be crossed for acceptance of the project. Projects with high political risk would have higher discount rate, and therefore, to justify the riskier foreign investment one would require a correspondingly higher cash flow.

MANAGING POLITICAL RISK

Since risk is political, its management too can be political. Insurance is one explicit action that provides protection against political risk. However, there are many tactical and strategic decisions that help avoid the threat of nationalization of expropriation as also reduce loss in case an unlikely action is taken. Though complete protection from actions of the government cannot be assumed by any of the suggested strategies, using them would deter actions by governments. These strategies are also aimed at creating perception among people that MNCs objectives are congruent with national interest.

Hire Locals

One of the best ways of protecting their own interests by MNCs is to hire local labour as much as possible. For most developing nations, employment creation has always been a major political consideration for attracting foreign investment, and a very appealing argument for justifying the FDI policy to the population at large. Involvement of local labour acts as a deterrent to any action by government that directly or indirectly affects the viability of the operations of a multinational corporation.

Seek Local Listing

Extending the scope of the philosophy of involving the local stakeholders as much as possible the MNC must favourably consider joint venture mode rather than adopting wholly owned subsidiary structure for doing business abroad. The presence of local shareholders again serves as deterrent for any politically motivated action that can cause damage to the foreign shareholders, as their interest are aligned with those of local shareholders too. Presence of local shareholders also helps in changing perception that the firm is not foreign but local. While it is

easy for governments to act against a wholly owned foreign enterprise, the actions would stand diluted if multinational firm has local shareholders too.

Borrow Locally

Though most multinational firms are heavily skewed towards equity financing and are self sufficient in financial resources to fund the foreign operations, it is strategic to borrow from local banks and financial institutions as much as possible to manage political risk. The financial loss because of any government could translate into a potential loss for local lenders. Seeking loans from international or foreign banks does not provide protection from political risk. Even though borrowing may be against the corporate philosophy and distorting the target capital structure, the local borrowing is highly preferable in the initial stages of the foreign investment as tool of managing political risk because the local lender would also act as lobbyist for the multinational.

Local borrowing also helps in managing the exchange rate risk to the extent the debt service payments can be met from locally generated cash flows.

Repatriate Quickly

Most foreign operations are long-term in nature with periodic infusion of foreign funds. As a tool of managing the political risk, a short-term approach must be adopted. Any surplus interim cash flows must be repatriated as soon as possible even though subsequently these funds may be required for further infusion for the growth. If so, the funds can be remitted back when needed at a later date. Even though it may increase the cost of remittance, it would be worth incurring it. This short-term approach is consistent with saying 'a bird in the hand is better than two in the bush'.

SUMMARY

Multinational corporations operating in countries other than where they are domiciled face a unique set of risk called political risk or country risk. Being strangers in the economy they operate in, they may face discriminatory practices for not being politically aligned with the government because of the supreme powers of the government to pass legislations in larger public interest. Besides politics, there are dangers of country being downgraded because of several reasons such as following imprudent fiscal and monetary policies, hyperinflation, extraordinary debt burden—public or external, labour unrest, riots, etc. Such happenings, some of which are observable, are neither measurable nor can be forecasted, but can be sufficient reason to render foreign operations unviable.

The measurement of country risk is normally done by assigning a letter grade by several rating agencies after careful considerations to economic, fiscal, monetary, and political factors each of which are assigned a weight and measurable parameter. The exercise of measuring country risk is similar to that of assigning a credit rating to a firm. Economic growth, inflation, budget deficits, levels of external debt, debt service payments, savings and investment patterns, balance of payment situation, level of reserves, and stability of exchange rate form complex maze of parameters that go into determination of country risk.

Expropriation or nationalization of assets of a firm is the most serious form of political risk that results in total loss of assets and future generation of cash flows. There can be direct expropriation or indirect expropriation by regulation or taxation that makes MNCs incapacitated. Few agencies worldwide provide insurance against such expropriation.

Foreign investment projects by multinational firms usually incorporate the country risk in appraisal of projects by increasing the discount rate by adding a risk premium, thereby, raising the bar for acceptance of the projects. Unless increased returns are justified, the project is not undertaken.

There are other strategic ways of managing the political risk in a foreign land. These strategies are aimed at increasing local participation of the host nation. The stakeholders to the firm in the form of labour, shareholders, and lenders must belong to the host nation as far as possible to deter any damaging action, and to remove the feeling that objectives of the MNC are opposed to national welfare.

QUESTIONS

14-1 What are the similarities and dissimilarities in assessing a corporate rating and country rating?
14-2 What are the different factors considered in assessment of country risk?
14-3 What are the strategic ways of managing political risk?

Part V
International Financial Markets and Controls

15. International Debt Markets
16. International Equity Investment
17. Foreign Direct Investment
18. Managing Capital Flows

International Debt Markets

LEARNING OBJECTIVES

This chapters aims at

- understanding of international bond and debt markets
- realizing motivation of accessing and investing in international bonds
- understanding differences between foreign bonds and Eurobonds and their markets
- knowing about different types of bonds
- realizing how to decide coupon rate, nature of coupon, and currency of denomination of a foreign bond
- knowing about considerations of investing in Eurobonds
- comparing cost of different international bonds
- comprehending risks in international bonds
- familiarizing with environment of foreign bonds in India

CONTENTS

Introduction
International Debt Markets
International Bonds Market
Types of Bonds
Deciding Features of Foreign Bond
    Nature of Coupon and Coupon Rate
    Currency of Denomination
Eurobonds Market
    Issue Process
    Dual Currency Bonds
    Composite Currency Bonds
Features of Eurobonds
Considerations of Investing in International Bonds

Yield on the Bonds
Comparing Costs of Foreign Bonds
    All-in Costs for Bonds
Risks in International Bonds
    Exchange Rate Risk
    Interest Rate Risk
    Inflation Risk
    Political Risk
International Banking
    Syndicated Loans and Project Finance
    Offshore Banking
    Development Banks
Foreign Currency Loans in India

INTRODUCTION

Large multinational corporations (MNCs) with worldwide operations have huge appetite for funds. At the same time, they also have large internally generated financial resources. Any gaps in the funding of investments are met by borrowing. If confined to access only the domestic financial markets, these MNCs face two critical issues: (1) the domestic market may not be large enough to meet the huge requirements, and (2) the cost effectiveness of such borrowings is questionable. Sometimes these borrowings may become prohibitively expensive due to exposure limitations of lenders. Accessing global markets would not only meet the huge requirements of funds, but it would do so at competitively lower cost by expanding the investor base and menu of a variety of instruments.

Besides meeting financial needs, having investors from diverse nations is beneficial for MNCs from strategic point of view because it helps to improve their visibility across the globe, and results in greater acceptance of the products of the firm.

Financial markets for equity and debts have become increasingly open to offer ample funding alternatives for finance managers in governments, institutions, and MNCs. The varying needs of these MNCs have also led to development of new financial products and innovations in financing. The funding of World Bank and IBM in 1981 is a classic example that gave birth to a new product called swap.

Such developments and product innovations are leading to faster integration of world's financial markets too. With increasing mobility of capital across the world investors as well as borrowers in the capital markets have wider choices available. This has enabled the process of equalization of risk-adjusted returns across the world in different currencies. While on one hand capital is finding alternative usage for better utilization, on the other hand the increased level of contagion has increased the transfer of evils of one economy to spill over to the rest of the world. Several currency crises in recent decades such as Asian currency crisis, Mexico peso crisis, and more recently the troubles of Eurozone are cases where increased integration of financial markets and contagion have impacted the world as a whole, sometimes leading to systemic risk. It remains a moot point whether isolated financial markets would have prevented the global damage. However, both benefits and suffering of integrated markets to be shared on the global basis should make financial markets more robust and shockproof in times to come.

Increased integration of financial markets would promote convergence of fiscal and monetary policies across the world because any structural impediments in an economy would cause arbitrage opportunities, elimination of which finally must lead to increased convergence.

With reduced interference by the central banks, the pricing of financial products has become market driven and competitive enough to provide reduction in cost of capital, and hence, production of goods and services at lower cost. Technology too has played its part in making financial transactions faster, smoother and less prone to errors facilitating cross-border mobility of capital. Increased mobility of capital from local to global must go a long way in strengthening the financial markets because as investors become more aware, literate and investment friendly the resource base widens. Deregulation of financial markets must induce greater savings, increasing the market size. This too helps in bringing down the cost of capital.

An integrated financial system or financial deregulation around the world can do lot of other good for the investors and borrowers. Absence or reduced controls tend to promote competition not only among lenders, but also among those seeking funds. To attract competitive investments from global markets, the borrowers need to demonstrate highest standards of governance and ethics. Thus, those seeking attention of global investors would voluntarily improve governance standards rather than merely following the minimum standards set by regulatory authorities in a nation.

It is often said that globalization only helps large multinationals, and small- and medium-scale enterprises do not benefit. It would be wrong to presume so. The availability and cost of credit in domestic market should see a positive impact of globalization. The extent to which an MNC seeks to replace funding from international markets implies release of equivalent funds in the domestic financial markets. Additional availability of funds in the domestic markets would find alternate uses, and would in turn be made available to smaller and medium enterprises that are confined to local financial markets.

According to Bank of International Settlement (BIS), global debt markets have increased in size from US$70 trillion in mid-2007 to about US$100 trillion in mid-2013. Primarily, the growth has come due to significant expansion of government expenditure to fill the budget deficits in the local debt markets.

INTERNATIONAL DEBT MARKETS

As we know, capital has two forms—debt and equity. International debt can be mobilized through loans from commercial banks, and by issuing debt securities with the financial intermediation of international investment banks.

International financing decisions are largely motivated by (a) interest rate differentials in various currencies in case of fixed rate loans, (b) expected changes in the interest rate of the currency borrowed in case of floating rate loan, and (c) expected changes in the exchange rates over the life of the loan. Besides, various other subjective factors enter the decision making process. These include terms and conditions of the loan, grievance-redressing mechanism in vogue, prospects and strength of the currency in times to come, political situation, as also the need for natural hedge such as matching currencies of revenue and cost, as well as assets and liabilities.

International debt market mainly consists of (a) bank loans, and (b) international bonds. We focus on bonds first.

INTERNATIONAL BONDS MARKET

International bonds are normally referred to as bonds denominated in a currency other than the currency of the issuer or the country in which the issuer resides. These bonds are characterized by issuer, currency of denomination, nature and periodicity of coupon payments, maturity, etc. International bonds are either issued by foreign entities or in foreign currency or traded in foreign markets.

The issuers of international bonds are governments, organizations supported by government, MNCs, multilateral agencies such as World Bank, and Asian Development Bank. Although the USA has traditionally dominated the world's bond markets, bonds issued in the US dollar now account for about 36% of the international bond market.

Bond markets are open to both institutional and individual investors, but there is much more participation generally by institutional investors. A majority of bond market participants in Europe are institutional investors, such as pension funds, insurance companies, and banks. The largest market for foreign bonds is London.

The primary benefit of international bonds is that issuers including the governments of emerging and developing economies gain access to extremely liquid pool of funds, and therefore, most competitive pricing on global basis. In developing economies, the domestic markets are not as developed. From cost effectiveness point of view, external borrowing may make better sense for firms and governments of developing nations. Further, such issues would go a long way in integrating the world markets, and better alignment of domestic returns with global factors impacting the cost of capital in a favourable way. Increased number of issues of international or Eurobonds by developing economies may ultimately force governments to follow policies that promote international flow of capital. The barriers to movement of capital would tend to reduce as time progresses.

Government Bonds Government bonds, also referred to as sovereign bonds are the bonds issued by central governments to borrow money from non-residents to bridge the fiscal deficit, to retire existing debt, to shore-up reserves, etc. These bonds are of highest quality commanding lower yields because of the promise of the government issuing them. In view of the national pride associated, the governments would not default on the promise of payment of coupon or principal, though there have been some instances in the history where sovereign bonds have defaulted. Of course, the premium for default risk gets incorporated in the yields of the bond. Lower the yield lower is the risk of default. Also higher the issue price lower is the yield.

The bonds issued by governments are known by different names around the world such as treasuries in USA, gilts in UK, and Bunds in Germany. It is far easier for governments to issue securities in their own currency, and sell them to residents because of the unique advantage the governments have in their authority to print money. In the unlikely event of the inability of the government to pay, it can simply print money and meet the obligations. However, this would prove to be inflationary and investor may lose wealth in real terms despite earning nominal returns. To prevent the temptations of having seignorage gains and subjecting residents to high rates of inflation, governments, mostly in emerging and developing countries, tend to issue bonds in foreign currency, supply of which is not controlled by them.

From the viewpoint of investors, who mostly come from developed economies the yield offered on these bonds are very attractive because most developed nations are having zero or near zero rates of return on investment. With loss of national prestige attached in case of default, most investors consider foreign bonds issued by sovereign as safe, whereas they provide better returns, if they are to invest in domestic bonds.

CONCEPTS IN PRACTICE
International Bonds

ZAMBIA, RWANDA ISSUE BONDS TO INTERNATIONAL INVESTORS

In April 2013, Rwanda successfully issued its first international bond of a moderate size of US$400 million. After the 1994, genocide when about a million of minority tribe, Tutsis were killed by the majority tribe Hutu, Rwanda has been viewed as fragile economy in the sub-Saharan region. The successful issue of bonds at lower than expected yield of 7% was a sign indicating the change of global perception about the country, dearth of bonds, and investors' appetite for increased return with commensurate risk. The appetite for higher yielding debt is helping a swath of countries make their debuts on global bond markets. These countries include Honduras, Angola, Paraguay, Mongolia, Zambia, Albania, Montenegro, and Bolivia, who have issued inaugural bonds recently. From African continent, Rwanda joined other recent Eurobond issuers that include Gabon, Ghana, Namibia, Nigeria, and Senegal.

Investors piled into the deal, placing orders equivalent to almost half of Rwanda's estimated nominal gross domestic product (GDP) in 2012, as they sought exposure to one of Africa's most striking turnaround stories. The facts that economic growth has averaged about 8% since 2003, and inflation has been subdued, thereby, explaining the enthusiasm of the international investors. As a result, Rwanda has attracted more than US$3 billion of orders for its US$400 million 10-year bond sale, allowing bankers to tighten the yield to just 6.875%, comfortably below the 7% to 7.5% that was initially expected. In contrast to this, the yield on Portuguese bonds soared to 8% in July 2013.

Rwanda had capped the size of its bond sale prudently to US$400 million as against the typical benchmark of not less than US$500 million, and used the proceeds to repay several government loans, complete the construction of a convention centre in Kigali, and finance a hydropower project. They raised only as much as was needed.

Prior to Rwanda, in September 2012, Zambia who made its debut Eurobond at 5.625% with proposed programme of US$500 million actually ended by increasing it to US$750 million in view of large demand of as high as US$12 billion. S&P and Fitch assigned a rating of B+ to the bond, the same as the country's long-term foreign currency rating. Oversubscription at lower yields simultaneously with rising yield on Portuguese bonds is reflective of changing perception of international investors. Does it imply that Sub-Saharan Africa a safer bet than the Eurozone?

Semi-government Bonds The bonds may also be issued by organizations that are in some way backed by governments, such as municipal corporations, and public sector organizations. In terms of default, these bonds are considered riskier than the government bonds.

Corporate Bonds The corporate bond market sector is second largest after the sovereign government bond sector. Nearly 30% of outstanding bonds in the global market are corporate bonds, according to Merrill Lynch. Corporate bond markets continue to grow and develop although recent market volatility has slowed growth.

Unlike government bonds, corporate bonds are more prone to default. The assessment of credit quality of corporate bond issuers is particularly important. The only way to objectively and subjectively gauge the credit quality is by the credit rating assigned to the bond by reputed credit rating agencies such as Moody's and Standard & Poor's (S&P).

Table 15-1 gives the break-up of the international debt securities by residency, nature, and currency of issue. It is abundantly clear from the data in the table and the figures that (a) of the

Table 15-1
International Debt Securities (US$ billions)

	Dec. 13				
	Total Outstanding 22,793.7				
By Residence of Issuer			**By Instruments**		
Developed	17,781.5	78.01%	Money markets	870.9	
UK	3,490.9	15.32%	International bonds	21,922.8	
USA	2,061.5	9.04%			
Others	12,229.1	53.65%	**Total Bonds Outstanding**	21,922.8	
Offshore	1,826.2	8.01%	**By Type**		
Cayman Islands	1,249.3	5.48%	Floating rate	6,000.8	27.37%
Hong Kong SAR	159.5	0.70%	Fixed rate	15,546.1	70.91%
Others	417.4	1.83%	Equity related	375.9	1.71%
Developing	1,716.2	7.53%			
China	51.5	0.23%			
India	23.1	0.10%	**By Currency of Issue**		
South Africa	32.7	0.14%	US dollar	7,847.4	35.80%
Korea	175.5	0.77%	Euro	9,910.9	45.21%
Russia	127.9	0.56%	Pound sterling	2,079.3	9.48%
Brazil	156.6	0.69%	Yen	486.2	2.22%
Mexico	175.1	0.77%	Swiss franc	357.0	1.63%
Others	973.8	4.27%	Others	1,242.0	5.67%
International Organizations	1,469.9	6.45%			

Source: 'International Debt Statistics', *BIS Quarterly Review*, March 2014.

total of US$22.80 trillion, the developed nations constitute about 78% of the international debt outstanding, whereas developing nations merely have 7.5% share, (b) money market securities have only a miniscule share of total international debt outstanding, (c) there is an overwhelming preference to issue fixed rate instruments rather than riskier instruments with floating coupon or convertibles, and (d) US dollar and euro are the most preferred currencies of denomination of debt comprising more than 80% of total.

TYPES OF BONDS

Apart from issuer based distinction international bonds can be classified in many ways—along different types of issuer, different markets, different characteristics, etc. Bonds are characterized by coupon, maturity, frequency of coupon, and currency of issue. They can be classified as follows:

Conventional or straight bonds This is the most simple and popular bond with a fixed coupon (usually paid on a semi-annual basis), and at maturity the entire principal is repaid. The repayment of principal in a single tranche is called bullet repayment.

Floating rate bonds/floating rate notes (FRN) Floating rate notes/bonds have a coupon/interest rate linked to a variable benchmark rate such as London Interbank Offer Rate (LIBOR) and Euro Interbank Offer Rate (EURIBOR) plus some additional 'spread' reflecting the credit quality of the issuer. Interest rate is reset periodically based on a benchmark rate prevailing, and they provide market based returns to the subscribers. For issuers, the cost remains linked to the market conditions.

Zero-coupon bonds Zero coupon bonds have no coupon, and therefore, do not have any interim interest payments. They are issued at discount and re-deemed at par. The entire return consists of capital gains. These bonds usually have some tax advantage attached.

Index linked bonds To cover risk of inflation many governments issue inflation-indexed or index-linked bonds to preserve purchasing power of investors. The coupon is denominated in terms of 'inflation plus'. They offer real rates of return to investors. Such indexing is often done for bonds of longer maturities when forecast of inflation for extended period of time is difficult to make, and may deviate substantially during the tenure of the bond.

Convertible bonds A bond that provides the investor an option to exchange the bond for a preset number of shares of the issuer at a preset price and time is called a convertible bond. Such a feature is available only in respect of corporate bonds.

Equity linked bonds Corporate bonds also have flexibility to attach equity warrants as sweetener, where part or whole of bond is converted into equity after some time. It helps bring down the cost of fixed capital for the issuers, as the coupon in such bonds can be reduced as compared to an equivalent straight bond.

Figure 15-1 shows the composition of foreign bonds market in terms of nature of coupons, currency of issue, and type of issuer as on Dec 2013.

International Debt Markets

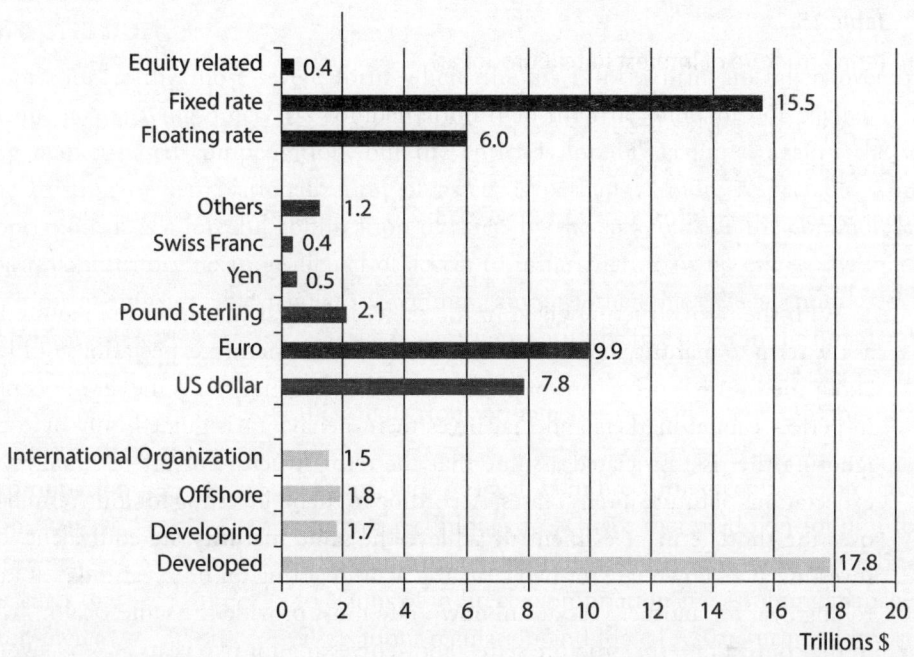

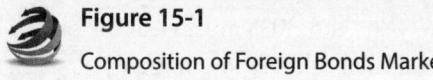

Figure 15-1
Composition of Foreign Bonds Market

FEATURES OF FOREIGN BOND

We know that features of bond include face value, redemption value, coupon rate, periodicity of coupon, and maturity. These features affect the issue price of the bond. The issue size and maturity of the bond are decided by the constraints of requirement of loan. In case of foreign bond, the issuer faces two other important decisions: (i) currency of issue, and (ii) choosing between fixed rates or floating rates. Both the decisions are interlinked because of varying interest rates, and term structure of interest rate in different currencies.

Nature of Coupon and Coupon Rate

Let us first examine the decision of fixed or floating coupon rate. It is dependent upon expectations of future interest rate. Is there a relationship between the fixed coupon and variable coupon or equivalence between the two options? It all depends upon how the issuer feels about the behaviour of future interest rate, and the fixed coupon that prevails today. To illustrate, we consider a numerical example. Assume that a firm wants to issue Eurodollar denominated debt for five years with annual coupon payment. We take the principal amount of borrowing of US$100 to be redeemed at par after five years and a choice of issuing fixed rate debt or floating rate debt. The yield curve reflecting the return expectations of investor with term to maturity is as shown in Table 15-2.

Table 15-2
Term Structure of Interest Rate (Eurodollar)

Years	1	2	3	4	5
Term Structure	3.00%	3.50%	4.00%	4.60%	5.30%
Discount Factor	0.9709	0.9335	0.889	0.8354	0.7724

With the term structure given in the table, it is clear that investors require higher returns as the term to maturity of investment goes up. Do the return expectations of investors foretell about the future expectations of interest rate? May or may not. One set of people who believe in perfect capital markets and that investment behaviour is guided only by expected returns ignoring the risk associated assume that the term structure of interest rate reveals investors' expectations of future interest rates. According to them, investing for long term now and rolling over the short term investment to achieve the same maturity are equivalent. It implies that investing at a known rate for two years today or investing for one year today at known rate and rolling over for another year at unknown rate must provide the same wealth. Mathematically, in the context of term structure stated above investing for two years at 3.5% would yield same wealth than if one invested for one year at 3% and then rollover for another year at rate not known say, $_1r_2$. Similarly, investing for five years at 5.30% must yield the same wealth as would be by investing at 4.60% for four years and then rollover for another year at an unknown rate say $_4r_5$. These are referred to as forward rates.

If so, we can arrive at one-year interest rate expected by investors given in the above term structure. For example, to solve for $_4r_5$ the equation used would be

$$(1.046)^4 \times (1 + {}_4r_5) = 1.053^5; \qquad {}_4r_5 = 8.15\%$$

We get all the forward interest rates as shown in Table 15-3.

Table 15-3
Forward Interest Rates (Eurodollar)

$_0r_1$	$_1r_2$	$_2r_3$	$_3r_4$	$_4r_5$
3.00%	4.00%	5.01%	6.42%	8.15%

The interest rates so arrived represent the expected one-year rate at the beginning of each year and would be the expected coupon payment at the end if one were to issue floating rate bond. These floating rate payments must be equivalent to a bond with some fixed rate coupon. This can be arrived by equating the present value of the payments of fixed coupon bond to the face value. We can determine the fixed rate using the formula

$$\text{Fixed Coupon Rate} = \frac{1 - \text{Last Discount Factor}}{\text{Sum of all Discount Factors}} = \frac{1 - 0.7724}{4.4012} = 0.0517 \equiv 5.17\%$$

The example solved above provides valuable insight to the determination of coupon rate, and nature of bond. These are summarized here:

1. If fixed rate bond is to be issued, the coupon must be 5.17%. This coupon rate satisfies the expectations of the investors. Though it may appear high when compared with the current one-year rate of 3% but more than expected coupon payment in the initial years would be offset by the less than expected coupon payments in later years.
2. With the given term structure as in Table 15-2 if the issuer can place the fixed rate bond at a coupon lower than 5.17% it must be done.
3. For the floating rate bond the issuer must forecast the interest rate for future. If the forecast rates are less than the figures shown in Table 15-3 floating rate bond must be issued. If the forecast rates are higher than the one depicted in Table 15-3 fixed rate bond at coupon no more than 5.17% would be more beneficial.
4. From the perspective of interest rate risk both fixed rate and floating rate bonds are equally susceptible. The issuer would end up paying more (a) in case fixed rate bond with coupon of 5.17% is issued and the interest rate fall subsequently, and (b) in case floating rate bond is issued and interest rate rise subsequently. In both cases the issuer has option to hedge later through interest rate swap.

Currency of Denomination

Another decision with the issuer of foreign bond is the currency of denomination of the bond. There is a tendency to issue bonds in a currency with lower rates of interest. In case of foreign bonds, the currency of issue and the utilization of mobilized funds are in different currencies implying that service payments would be generated in a currency different than the currency of issue of bond. For example, a Japanese issuer of dollar denominated bond would collect funds in US dollar, convert to yen for putting to use, and service dollar obligations from the cash flows generated in yen. Therefore, exchange rate of yen with US dollar at the time of service payments has cash flow implications.

Again, we examine the decision with an example of a Japanese issuer choosing to denominate bonds in Eurodollar rather than in yen. The bond issue in yen with fixed or floating coupon can be analysed on the same lines, as discussed in the preceding paragraphs depending upon the term structure of interest rates in yen, and forecast of future interest rates.

Like the term structure of interest rates impacts on decision of floating or fixed coupon the exchange rate projections affect the choice of currency in which to denominate the bond. If the exchange rate behaved exactly as per the term structure of interest rate in two currencies the choice of currency of denominating the bond becomes irrelevant, just in the same fashion as the choice of floating or fixed coupon becomes trivial, if the interest rate moved exactly as per the term structure available at the time of the issue.

For example, consider the same term structures of interest rate in Eurodollar (same as in Table 15-2) and Japanese yen as given in Table 15-4. Remember the term structure of

Table 15-4
Term Structure of Interest Rates (Eurodollar and Yen)

Years	1	2	3	4	5
Term Structure, Eurodollar	3.00%	3.50%	4.00%	4.60%	5.30%
Term Structure, Yen	0.50%	0.70%	0.73%	0.76%	0.80%
Discount Factor, Yen	0.9950	0.9861	0.9784	0.9702	0.9609

Eurodollar equated a fixed coupon of 5.17%. On similar lines, we can find that fixed coupon of 0.80% in Japanese yen equates the term structure of interest rate of Japanese yen. Japanese issuer is now faced with two choices—issue a yen denominated 0.80% fixed coupon bond or issue dollar denominated 5.17% fixed coupon bond.

The two bonds are analysed in Table 15-5. The cash outflows of 0.80% fixed coupon yen denominated bond with face value of ¥100 in the first panel shows that present value of outflows are same at ¥100. If Eurodollar bond with fixed coupon of 5.17% with face value of US$100 is issued, the bond obligations would be serviced in US dollar by converting receipts generated in Japanese yen at the exchange rates prevailing when the service payments are due. The cash outflows, therefore, are dependent upon the exchange rate forecast.

The current spot exchange rate is ¥100/$. Assuming interest rate parity (IRP) applies and the forward exchange rates as unbiased predictor of exchange rate, the forecast of exchange rates for tenure of the bond are projected using the term structure of interest rate in Eurodollar and yen are as below:

Year	0	1	2	3	4	5
Forecast Exchange Rate (¥/$)	100.00	97.57	94.66	90.86	86.10	80.38

For example, the expected spot exchange rate for the fifth year is ¥80.38/$ arrived as follows:

$$\text{Expected Exchange Rate (¥/\$)} = S_0 \left[\frac{1 + {}_0r_5(\text{yen})}{1 + {}_0r_5(\text{dollar})} \right]^5 = 100 \times \left[\frac{1.008}{1.053} \right]^5 = ¥\,80.38/\$$$

With IRP-based exchange rate forecast five-year, 5.17% fixed coupon dollar denominated bond is equivalent to 0.80% fixed coupon yen denominated bond as shown in Panel II of Table 15-5.

From the date in Table 15-5, it is evident that preference of currency of denomination of the bond is dependent upon the expected behaviour of the exchange rate. We make the following observations:

1. If exchange rate moved exactly as per the IRP, the issuer is indifferent to the currency in which to denominate the bond.
2. If the local currency (yen in this case) appreciated more than expected based on term structure, the issue of bond in foreign currency is preferable.

Table 15-5
Equivalence of Yen and Dollar Denominated Bonds

Years	0	1	2	3	4	5
Term Structure, Eurodollar		3.00%	3.50%	4.00%	4.60%	5.30%
Term Structure, Yen		0.50%	0.70%	0.73%	0.76%	0.80%
Panel I: 5-Year Yen Denominated 0.80% Fixed Coupon Bond with Face Value of ¥100						
Equivalent Fixed Coupon, Yen		0.08%				
Cash Outflow, Yen		0.80	0.80	0.80	0.80	100.80
Discount Factor		0.9950	0.9861	0.9784	0.9702	0.9609
Present Value, Yen	100.00	0.8000	0.7900	0.7800	0.7800	96.8600
Panel II: 5-Year Dollar Denominated 5.17% Fixed Coupon Bond with Face Value of $ 100						
Equivalent Fixed Coupon, Eurodollar		5.17%				
Expected Exchange Rate (¥/$)		97.57	94.66	90.86	86.10	80.38
Cash Outflow, Yen		504.44	489.39	469.75	445.14	8453.56
Present Value, Yen	10,000	501.92	482.59	459.6	431.87	8123.03

3. If the local currency (yen in this case) depreciated more than expected based on term structure, the issue of bond in local currency is preferable.

If the currency appreciation/depreciation happens at uniform rate then the effective cost of bond in the issuer's currency may be found using the following:

$$(1 + \text{coupon in local currency}) = (1 + \text{coupon in foreign currency})(1 \pm \text{\% Annual depreciation/appreciation of local currency})$$

Issuing bonds in foreign currency carry the foreign exchange risk. Just as interest rate risk in case of fixed/floating rate bonds can be managed with interest rate swaps, the currency risk in foreign bonds too can be hedged with financial swaps that enable in transformation of the liability from one currency to another.

EUROBONDS MARKET

In international bonds market a distinction is made between foreign bond and Eurobond. International bonds are those where the nationalities of issuer and subscribers are different. When the bond is denominated in the currency of the subscriber's (not that of issuer), it is called a foreign bond. For example, GE that is a US firm issues bonds in Germany denominated in euro would be a foreign bond. When the issuer denominates the bond in his own currency but issued to foreigners, it is called Eurobond. For example, GE issues bonds denominated in

US dollars to Germans. It would be termed as Eurodollar issue. Similarly, if a Japanese firm issues yen denominated bonds to a US investor in USA, it would be called Euroyen issue.

The primary centre for Eurobond is London that gained prominence in 1960. The first issue of Eurobond was made in 1963 by Autostrade, an Italian motorway network. The market got boost following recycling of petrodollars.

The name Eurobond is a misnomer, as it may lead to an impression that they relate to European bond markets, or bonds denominated in European currency, euro. Eurobonds are actually bonds that are denominated in a currency other than that of the country of issuer. These foreign and Eurobond have been given interesting names. For example, *Bulldog* bonds are sterling denominated bonds issued in the UK by a non-UK issuer. *Yankee* bonds are dollar denominated bonds issued in the USA by a non-US issuer. *Rembrandt* bonds are issued in the Netherlands by non-Dutch issuer; *Matador* bonds in Spain issued by non-Spanish, *Samurai* bonds in Japan, that is, yen denominated bonds in Japan by non-Japanese borrowers. Japanese borrowers issuing foreign currency bonds in Japan are called *Shogun* bonds. Just as Eurodollar is US dollar off shore, Eurobonds are the bonds issued by residents and non-residents of a country in a foreign currency. The currency in which the bonds are denominated is not that of the potential subscribers of a country whose resident are aimed at.

Traditionally US bonds have dominated the world's bond markets because of the ready availability of US dollar worldwide spread during the era of Bretton Woods. In the 1960s, when US government imposed interest equalization tax and other restrictions on foreign bonds issues, Eurobonds gained prominence. Eurobonds have become extremely popular instruments of fund raising, and today command about 80% share of the international bond.

Governments, international organizations, international banks, and corporations are major issuers in the Eurobond market. Supranational organizations (such as the World Bank or the European Bank for Reconstruction and Development) use such bond issues for financing the development of emerging markets or to support developing countries. Governments use foreign/Eurobonds for financing projects of national importance, or to meet the deficits. Corporations, including banks and multinational entities, issue Eurobonds for many purposes including financing for capital and other projects. International banks need resources in various countries or onward credit, and hence, need to mobilize funds in different currencies. This enables diversification too.

Eurobonds are usually issued in more than one country, and are traded across international financial centres such as London, Zurich, Paris, Frankfurt, and Amsterdam. These bonds are intended towards broader investor base in various countries rather than one single country. For example, a German firm can issue dollar denominated bonds to investors all over Europe, USA, and Asia.

One feature of Eurobonds that has implication on its value is that they conventionally give annual coupon, whereas most foreign bonds have practice of making semi-annual coupon payments. Therefore, a 5% foreign bond is more valuable than its equivalent 5% Eurobond.

The relationship of annual and semi-annual rates is as below:

$$(1 + \text{Annual Rate}) = (1 + \text{Semi-annual Rate}/2)^2$$

For example, a 5% semi-annual foreign bond is equivalent to 5.0625% annual rate Eurobond in terms of value. Similarly, a 5% Eurobond is equivalent to a 4.939% semi-annual foreign bond.

Issue Process The process of issue of Eurobonds involves appointment of lead manager to the issue, who form a syndicate of international banks, obtain credit rating, determine the offer price, conduct due-diligence, place the issue with individual investors from their base of clients, and underwrite the issue. The underwriting means subscription of the issue by syndicate members in case of non-subscription. Naturally this would take place at a discounted price to the actual value arrived by the syndicate.

The Eurobond market is largely a wholesale, institutional market with bonds held by large institutions. The bonds are available in the secondary markets too that again are over-the-counter. Some bonds are listed on London and Luxembourg stock exchanges.

Dual Currency Bonds Dual currency bonds are the bonds that promise payments in two currencies. The usual structure is to pay interest in one currency and the principal in another currency. These bonds make a great sense to an emerging MNC that is expanding with a project in a new territory and has to wait for cash generation. For example, an Indian multinational in aluminium may like to fund acquisition of a loss making plant in another nation, say in Canada. It can do so by issue of dual currency bond where interest payments, which are frequent and small, may be made in Indian rupee from the existing operations in India, whereas the principal, which is at maturity and large, is repaid in second currency, that is, Canadian dollar, when it falls due on the hope that by that time the loss making unit would be generating enough cash flows in Canadian dollars to provide repayment of the principal.

It is not far to reason that such dual currency bonds would carry coupon higher than a straight single currency bond. The exchange rate risk would certainly be present in such bonds warranting promise of greater return for bearing additional risk by the investors.

The dual currency bonds were first issued in 1963, but they became popular during the 1980s. Some Japanese corporations commencing their operations in USA issued dual currency bond where coupons were paid in yen because they could not generate dollar funds in USA in the initial years, and principal paid in US dollars when the US operations were expected to generate adequate cash flows in US dollars.

Composite Currency Bonds In contrast to dual currency bond are the composite currency bonds also referred to as *currency cocktail bonds*, the bonds that are issued perhaps in a hypothetical currency such as SDR, or basket of currencies, the erstwhile ECU. The advantage of issuing bonds denominated in a basket of currencies is the reduction in currency risk. Naturally, a basket of currencies would be less volatile than any of the currencies comprising it, as few currencies in the basket would appreciate whereas some would depreciate. Hence, the coupon in such cases can be lower than a comparable dual currency bond.

FEATURES OF EUROBONDS

As we know, bonds are the instruments of borrowing promising a fixed interest at periodic intervals and the principal at promised dates. All bonds do not follow this definition as we have bonds with variable coupon (floating rate bonds) or deep discount bonds that have no coupon at all. Yet these are classified as bonds because they are fixed income securities. A few typical features of Eurobond, though may not be present in all bonds, are as follows.

Unsecured   Eurobonds are unsecured, that is, in case of default the holders have no recourse to the assets of the issuer because they are issued by a non-resident. Therefore, success of Eurobond issue and its issue price are dependent on the rating. Higher the rating less risky is the bond. With higher rating, the price is higher and the yield is lower.

International rating agencies such as S&P, and Moody's assign rating by letter grades such as AAA and BB to indicate safety or risk associated with these bonds. Most Eurobonds are rated very high on the credit rating because these markets are available to either sovereign entities or highly respected, reputed and established multi-national corporations with excellent track record and brand equity. The factors considered in the rating exercise are numerous. In case of sovereign bonds the political climate, stability, fiscal and monetary policies, GDP growth rates, proportions of public and external debts to GDP, etc. are considered.

Issued in Bearer Form   Eurobonds are bearer bonds, that is, no record of holders is maintained for the purposes of payment of periodic coupon and principal. The one, who holds the bond is the owner. Holders have to present coupons to claim interest payments, and the physical certificate for redemption of principal to the issuer.

Tax Advantage   Eurobonds are issued in a currency other than the currency of the place of issue, thereby avoiding regulatory controls as well as tax jurisdiction. This makes the markets for issuers as well as for investors very conducive and attractive in terms of pricing. There is no withholding tax applicable for the interest paid to the investors.

Unregulated   Eurobonds, being issued to non residents, escape the rigorous scrutiny and disclosure requirements placed on local issuers by the regulatory bodies of the issuer's country. For example, a dollar denominated bond for US investor would have to comply with registration process, detailed scrutiny of indenture and disclosure requirements under the laws of USA. Indeed this is onerous, expensive and time consuming. Instead, the offering outside USA through Eurodollars can be made rather quickly with little procedural hassles.

OTC Secondary Markets   Eurobonds are traded actively in the secondary market. Listing on an exchange is rare. These bonds can be bought and sold by investors through the counters available with most prominent banks in major financial centres.

Normally Eurobonds are fixed rate coupon and mature in three to seven years. Coupon are payable annually as against convention of semi-annual in other bonds.

Due to ease of issue and its bearer nature providing tax advantage, Eurobonds have become extremely popular. The proportion of Eurobond is estimated at about 80% of international bond market.

The disadvantage of Eurobonds is that they are unsecured. Therefore, they are issued only by respected corporations and governments which are considered devoid of default.

INVESTING IN INTERNATIONAL BONDS

The primary advantage of considering investing in international bonds is comparative safety of the investment, in particular, the promise that interest and principal will be paid on time because they are issued by governments, reputed corporate, and multilateral agencies. These bonds provide a fixed dependable stream of income. There are a number of key variables to look at when investing in bonds. These include the bond's maturity, redemption features, credit quality, interest rate, price, yield, and in some cases tax or fiscal status.

Investors use bond swaps to realize a variety of benefits. A swap, the simultaneous sale of one security and the purchase of another, may be done to change maturities, change assets, change from fixed to floating rates (or vice versa), upgrade the credit quality of the portfolio, increase current income, realize tax benefits, or achieve a number of other objectives. These are frequently called switches, as well as being called swaps.

YIELD ON THE BONDS

Yield on the bonds refers to the returns the bond holders can earn. The total return on bond comprises (a) a reward for holding them by way of earning coupon, and (b) a capital gains arising when investors decide to divest them equal to the difference in purchase and sale/redemption value.

There are two commonly used measures of yield—current yield and yield to maturity (YTM)

Current Yield The current yield is the annual return on the amount paid for a bond, regardless of its maturity. If you buy a bond at par, the current yield equals its coupon. Thus, the current yield on a par-value bond paying 6% is 6%.

However, if the market price of the bond is more or less than par, the current yield will be different. For example, if you buy a €1,000 bond with a 6% stated interest rate after prevailing interest rates have risen above that level, you would pay less than par. Assume the price that you paid is €900. The current yield would be 6.67% (€1,000 × .06/€900).

Yield to Maturity A more meaningful figure is the yield to maturity because it tells you the total return you will receive if you hold a bond until maturity. It also enables comparison of bonds with different maturities and coupons. Yield to maturity includes all interest payments, and any capital gain that would be realized upon maturity, if purchased below par or any capital loss in case of purchase above par. Current yield does not represent the bond's real value.

Realized Yield When a bond is sold prior to its maturity, the returns consist of the coupon earned during the period of investing, and the gain or loss incurred by disinvesting.

COMPARING COSTS OF FOREIGN BONDS

Most issuers face the question of comparing the cost of financing with domestic and foreign bonds. Can this be compared right away on the basis of the coupon rates offered in domestic and foreign currencies? The answer is yes if the exchange rates are assumed constant over the tenure of the bond. A 10% rupee bond in domestic market as compared to 6% coupon bond denominated in Singapore dollars is expensive as long as it is presumed that exchange rate of

454 International Finance

Indian rupee with respect to Singapore dollar is pegged or remains constant over time. However, in real life, are 10% coupon on Indian rupee bond and 6% coupon on bond denominated in Singapore dollars comparable? The answer depends upon the behaviour of exchange rate during the tenure of the loan.

Let us consider a 5-year bond of ₹100 in India with 10% coupon payable annually (for simplicity only, in practice coupons are paid semi-annually) with a similar bond of S$4 at 6% coupon when exchange rate is ₹25/S$. We consider the following three scenarios.

Stable Exchange Rate One of the easiest ways of comparing the cost of bonds in different currencies is to directly compare the interest rate prevailing in those currencies. The coupon rate would be equal to the interest rates prevailing. A 10% coupon on Indian rupee denominated loan and 6% coupon on Singapore dollar denominated loan are equivalent, and meet the expectations of subscribers in two countries. The cost of loan in each currency would be equal to respective coupon rates provided. How much 6% Singapore dollar loan would cost in rupee terms is dependent on the equivalent rupee cash flows on the coupon payment dates and redemption dates payable in Singapore dollar and exchange rates prevailing then. Rupee cash flows remain unaffected with changes in exchange rates. If exchange rates remain constant, the cost of foreign currency bond in domestic currency would be same as the coupon rate in the foreign currency as shown in Table 15-6.

Table 15-6
Cost of Bonds and Exchange Rates (₹/S$)

Year	Rupee Cash Flow	Foreign Currency Cash Flow	Constant Exchange Rate		6% Appreciation of Foreign Currency		6% Depreciation of Foreign Currency	
			Exchange Rate	Rupee Cash Flow	Exchange Rate	Rupee Cash Flow	Exchange Rate	Rupee Cash Flow
0	100.00	4.00	25.00	100.00	25.00	100.00	25.00	100.00
1	−10.00	−0.24	25.00	−6.00	26.50	−6.36	23.58	−5.66
2	−10.00	−0.24	25.00	−6.00	28.09	−6.74	22.25	−5.34
3	−10.00	−0.24	25.00	−6.00	29.78	−7.15	20.99	−5.04
4	−10.00	−0.24	25.00	−6.00	31.56	−7.57	19.80	−4.75
5	−110.00	−4.24	25.00	−106.00	33.46	−141.85	18.68	−79.21
Cost	10%	6%		6%		12%		0%

Appreciating Foreign Currency (Depreciating Local Currency) When foreign currency starts appreciating, the coupon payments on a foreign bond would cost more in terms of local currency. Assuming that Singapore dollar appreciates at 6% p.a., the cash outflow every year would be 6% higher than the previous year. The foreign currency denominated bond would cost as much more as appreciation of foreign currency. Therefore, the cost of Singapore dollar bond would be 12% in terms of rupees (6% coupon in Singapore dollars and 6% due to its annual appreciation), a shown in Table 15-6.

Depreciating Foreign Currency (Appreciating Local Currency) When foreign currency starts depreciating, we need lesser number of domestic currency units to service the coupons and principal. If Singapore dollar now depreciates by 6% p.a., the effective cost of bond must reduce by the same extent. Observe last column of Table 15-6 depicting the cash flows in rupee terms with 6% annual depreciation of Singapore dollar. The internal rate of return (IRR) of rupee cash flows gives the cost of the bond at 0%. The coupon payments in Singapore dollar are completely offset by its depreciation.

Therefore, we may conclude as follows:

1. Vastly different interest rates (yields) in different currencies are not the true differentials of costs of funds in different currencies unless exchange rates remain constant.
2. It is not necessary that low yields in strong foreign currency would signify lower cost of funds, as compared to issues in local currency.
3. It is also not necessary that high cost of borrowings in weak currencies mean higher cost of funds, as compared to the cost in local currency.

The effective cost of borrowing in local currency should be equal to coupon rate in denominated currency ± likely annual appreciation/depreciation of denominated currency with respect to local currency.

All-in Cost for Bonds

Foreign bonds or Eurobonds have several features, which make comparison of different bonds for the investors as well as issuers difficult. We have already seen that interest rates, and therefore, coupon rates are vastly different in different currencies. The behaviour of exchange rates is another fact that makes cost comparison difficult. To compare cost one needs to forecast the future exchange rate. Other factors that need to be considered in cost comparison are periodicity of coupon, maturity, arranger's fee, underwriting commission, etc. The best way to compare the costs of different bonds is to find the cash flows of the bond and then find its internal rate of return. This is referred to as all-in cost.

As an example of cost comparison, lets us compare the costs of four bonds denominated in four different currencies, with features given as follows:

Bond Features	Bond 1	Bond 2	Bond 3	Bond 4
Currency	Eurodollar	Euro	Yen	Pound
Coupon, %	5.00%	6.00%	1.50%	5.50%
Periodicity of coupon	Annual	Semi-annual	Semi-annual	Semi-annual
Maturity, *years*	3	5	4	4
Issue expenses, % *of face value*	0.50%	0.53%	1.00%	0.75%

Depreciation of INR, % *per annum*	4.00%	2.50%	6.00%	4.50%
Current spot, ₹/Unit	60.00	82.00	0.50	100.00
Face value, *Foreign currency*	100.00	100.00	10,000.00	100.00

To compare the cost of each of the four bonds above, we project the cash flows in Indian rupee. These are projected in Table 15-7. The calculations are as follows:

1. The initial cash inflow is equal to face value × current spot exchange rate less issue expenses.
2. Periodical interest payments have been projected at coupon rate specified on the face value. The rupee cash flow is determined by multiplying the foreign currency coupon with the expected exchange rate at the time of payment using the estimated depreciation of Indian rupee against the foreign currency. For example, third year interest amount for pound denominated bond is

$$= \text{Face Value} \times \text{Current Spot} \times \text{Coupon} \times (1 + \text{Depreciation})^{years}$$
$$= 100 \times 100 \times 0.055/2 \times (1 + 0.045)^3 = ₹313.82$$

3. Cash flow at maturity consists of final coupon payment and redemption of face value. The rupee cash flow is projected at expected exchange rate using the given annual rate of depreciation.

Table 15-7
Comparing Costs of Foreign Currency Denominated Bonds   Cash Flow, ₹

Year	Eurodollar	Euro	Yen	Pound
0	5,970.00	8,156.95	4,950.00	9,925.00
0.5	–	−249.06	−38.61	−281.12
1.0	−312.00	−252.15	−39.75	−287.38
1.5	–	−255.28	−40.93	−293.77
2.0	−324.48	−258.45	−42.14	−300.31
2.5	–	−261.66	−43.38	−306.99
3.0	−7,086.64	−264.92	−44.66	−313.82
3.5	–	−268.21	−45.98	−320.8
4.0	–	−271.54	−6,359.73	−12,253.13
4.5	–	−274.91	–	–
5.0	–	−9,555.87	–	–
Cost, Semi-annual	4.59%	4.34%	3.86%	5.15%
Annual Cost, %	9.39%	8.87%	7.87%	10.55%

4. The IRR of cash flows can be found by using IRR function in EXCEL.
5. The IRR is arrived for the semi-annual period. It is converted to annual cost using the following:

$$\text{Annual Cost} = (1 + \text{Semi-annual Cost})^2 - 1$$

A look at Table 15-7 indicates that yen denominated loan is least expensive whereas pound denominated loan is most expensive. The all-in cost is approximately equal to foreign coupon rate plus rate of depreciation of Indian rupee with respect to the foreign currency. The excess cost represents the apportionment of issue expenses over the life of the bond.

RISKS IN INTERNATIONAL BONDS

Bonds have two kinds of risk associated with them—default risk and interest rate risk. Default risk is the risk of non-payment of delayed payment of coupon or principal. As stated earlier, bonds issued by governments of developed nations are regarded as free from default risk. However, the bonds issued by emerging economies have varying degree of risk reflected in the varying yields of the bonds issued by various governments. The other risks faced in bonds are exchange rate risk, inflation risk, and political risk.

Exchange Rate Risk

When the bonds are denominated in the currency other than the home currency of the investor, the value of bond could go down as well as up depending on what happens to the currency exchange rate/interest rate/inflation rates.

Assume a US investor purchased a £1,000 par value British bond with a 5% coupon. At the time of investment, the currency exchange rate was $1.50/£ and paid $1,500 for acquiring the bond.

Several years later, when bond matures the investor receives £1,000. If currency exchange rate has fallen to $1.40/£, therefore, one gets only $1,400 for a bond purchased for $1,500. The loss of $100 is entirely due to currency risk. It is also possible to profit from currency risk. Had the dollar fallen in comparison to the pound say to $1.80, the investor would have received $1,800 or $300 more than he paid.

Unfortunately, currency risk remains just a speculation. Currency exchange rates are moved by a number of macroeconomic factors including interest rates, unemployment data, and geopolitical events, none of which can be accurately predicted with any reasonable certainty. Investors and institutions can guard against currency fluctuations by engaging in certain hedging practices.

Interest Rate Risk

While investors are effectively guaranteed to receive interest and principal as promised, the underlying value of the bond itself may change depending on the direction of interest rates. There is inverse relationship of bond prices and the interest rates. If interest rates in general rise after a Government bond is issued, its value will fall because bonds paying higher rates

CONCEPTS IN PRACTICE
Exchange Rate Risk and International Bonds

INTERNATIONAL FINANCE CORPORATION ISSUES FIRST-EVER RUPEE INTERNATIONAL BONDS

After successfully issuing local currency bonds in Chinese renminbi, Russian rouble and Brazilian real, in November 2013 International Finance Corporation (IFC) received an overwhelming response from global investors to its first tranche of US$160 million Indian rupee denominated bond, when it received more than double the amount it lower yields than the comparable G-sec yields. The tranche was under the proposed $1billion 10-year program to raise funds in Indian rupee. The repayment was linked to the exchange rate of Indian rupee.

The three-year bond of IFC offered a yield of 7.75%, which was about 70 bps lower than the G-sec reference rate prevailing then. This was a remarkable response because investors must expect higher yields compensating them for bearing the exchange rate risk on these rupee denominated bonds. The high interest rate in Indian rupee was extremely attractive for global investors absorbing the additional exchange rate risk. IFC would convert bond proceeds from dollars into rupees on the domestic spot exchange market, and use the rupees to finance private sector investment in India.

Encouraged by whopping response, IFC may decide to issue second tranche early 2014, and may also increase the tenor of the bond consistent with their objective of providing long-term project financing at as cheap cost as possible. The proceeds of the issue would be utilized to finance private sector projects in India.

will come into the market. Similarly, if interest rates fall, the value of the older, higher coupon bond will rise in comparison with new issues. Interest rate risk in case of bonds is also known as market risk.

Inflation Risk

In a period of low inflation and moderate shifts in interest rates, investors often are content to hold their bonds to maturity, ignoring the changes in market value of their bonds. However, some investors strive to structure their bond holdings to minimize market risks and take advantage of market opportunities. Governments extremely conscious of inflation rate tend to issue inflation indexed bonds.

Political Risk

One of the major risks in a foreign bond is that it represents an unenforceable claim. An investor that owns the bonds of a company in his or her home country has specific legal recourse in the event of default. Foreign bonds, however, offer no such protection. An extremist political movement (e.g., Iran in the 1970s) could come to power and seize or deny all foreign assets and claims. A country may become engaged in a military conflict and may impose currency controls. In such a case, even if the coupon is paid it cannot be converted in the foreign currency, that is, the home currency of the subscribers of the bond. After World War II, for example, investors holding bonds in Great Britain were paid interest in pounds yet were unable to convert those pounds to dollars; the money could only be reinvested in pound-denominated investments or spent within the borders of Britain.

Government bonds are largely free from political risk, but not entirely from credit risk, as government bonds are always subject to downgrades in credit ratings. Some functions in the economy are not a central government's direct responsibility, but the government needs and wants to develop and strengthen the way those fields function. The most common fields on which government focuses such attention are mortgage loans to strengthen affordable housing, loans to students for educational purposes, loans to farms or small businesses, etc. To finance these efforts, a central government may create something called a government agency and finance this quasi-government agency by issuing bonds. Since they are indirectly or directly guaranteed by the government, these bonds are called quasi-government or sub-sovereign or agency bonds. Such agencies can be publicly or privately owned.

CONCEPTS IN PRACTICE

Political Risk and Yield on International Bonds

YIELDS ON EGYPT'S INTERNATIONAL BONDS FOLLOW POLITICAL UNREST

Since the time of political unrest against the rule of President Mohamed Morsi gathered momentum in Egypt, the yield on its international bonds is continuously falling. The bonds worth $1 billion are due for redemption in 2020. The yield had fallen steeply in line with continuously deteriorating political uncertainty to 11.07% on 27 June 2013 from a respectable 5.84% six months back in December 2012.

Within the first two weeks of July 2013, army intervened to remove the incumbent president, who was the first democratically elected President of Egypt, the yield started improving. The improvement was by roughly 200 basis points, indicating that the army could be far stable politically for Egypt than the democratically elected government. Even though the volumes were small it was an indication enough for cautious return to political stability and expectations about the interim government to rule effectively till the next general elections.

Besides rendering temporary political stability, the analysts seem to have more confidence in the interim government's ability to have fiscal reforms to contain soaring budget deficit, than Mohamed Morsi. This increased confidence seemed to emanate from the support the interim prime minister got from many

Islamists, and the pledge of $12 billion financial aid from Gulf governments such as Saudi Arabia, Kuwait, and UAE. The amount is considered good enough to surmount any balance of payment problems in the short term.

Another factor that seemed to work in improving the yield was the fact that much of the debt is believed to be owned by Egyptian banks, who intend to hold it for the long term, viewing it as a hedge against depreciation of the Egyptian pound. It is important for them because Eurozone debt crisis has already weakened their balance sheets. Selling these bonds and booking losses on them would be a further dent in their performance. Hence, they have been unwilling to sell. Also foreign debt is small relative to its economy at under $35 billion at the end of 2012 or about 15% of GDP.

A steep drop in yield is seen as a buying opportunity by many because if Egypt does stabilize the yield may fall by further 300–400 basis points, as has been witnessed in the history. Since 2012, yields on emerging market bonds have risen around the world, often by more than 100 bps, because of climbing US Treasury yields.

INTERNATIONAL BANKING

In today's increasingly integrated world the domain of banking has expanded from local/domestic markets to global market. The depositors and borrowers of the banks now are looking for avenues that offer better returns on deposits and lesser cost of borrowing.

The beginning of international banking possibly can be traced to creation of Eurodollars (Refer to the *Online Resource Centre* for details) when large amounts of US dollar was circulating amongst banks outside USA. These funds in US dollars were subjected to minimal regulation that led to market-driven pricing of the banking products. European banks saddled with sizable dollar deposits had to find way to lend them to have positive spread. Hence, US dollars were made available to borrowers outside Europe. Absence of regulations made deposits and lending attractive because banks could offer higher returns to depositors and charge lower interest from borrowers. Under the Bretton Woods era both the supply and demand for US dollar was very high resulting in market oriented pricing of deposits and borrowings.

The second impetus to international banking came when Organization of Petroleum Export Countries (OPEC) priced oil to earn extra-ordinary profits. The surplus of OPEC parked in international banks was used for financing the trade deficit of oil importing nations by way of sovereign debts. So called petrodollars comprised a significant source of internationally liquid money in the banks.

In today's world, the imbalances in the balance of trade in various countries create demand and supply of money in the form of currencies that are internationally acceptable. Countries such as Japan, China, India, and Taiwan have significant foreign exchange reserves that find its way back in the international banks. These nations are more focused on safety of money rather than earning handsome returns, making available a cheap source of money.

Global business firms constantly looking for natural hedges for their international operations create demand for foreign currency borrowings. Increased activity in large cross-border acquisitions has created the demand for foreign currency loans. Trade credit requirements of MNCs who form the customer base provide banks a ready market for demand of foreign money.

Syndicated Loans and Project Finance

Long-term financing by banks is provided in the form of syndicated loan, or medium-term Euronotes.

Syndicated loans are the loan provided by several banks to single borrower. Banks join together to finance large credit requirements of the MNCs and other highly reputed firms. Syndication is a form of risk sharing amongst banks by limiting exposure of each participating bank to single borrower. One bank assuming the responsibility of mobilizing the required sum is called the lead bank. The functions performed by the lead bank are to (a) make/assess the funding requirements, (b) conduct due-diligence, (c) arrange for the other banks to participate in the credit, (d) decide on the proportion of credit each bank can assume, (e) fix the interest rate structure, (f) negotiate a fee structure, etc.

The time required to arrange the syndicate varies according to the size of the loan, rating of the borrower, etc. The tenure of the loan is also a huge consideration. In international markets, the problem of asset liability mismatch is magnified as compared to domestic banking. Syndicated loans have longer maturities than the deposits. Most international source of money is in the form of demand deposits. Therefore, maturity mismatch of source and use of funds for the banks is a serious concern.

Further most syndicated loans are on variable rate with LIBOR as most commonly used benchmark. Since source of funds is a demand deposit with banks paying market rates, the pricing of loans too has to be dynamic and market based. Banks negotiate a spread over the varying LIBOR with the borrowers. Banks dealing in Eurodollar or other Eurocurrencies normally hedge for the spread through Eurodollar futures, for which active markets are available in USA, Europe, and Singapore.

Besides interest income, syndicated loan generate many other fee based sources of income. Lead manager charges a variety of fee named in several ways such as a syndication fee, legal fee, out-of-pocket expenses, front-end management fee, and annual fee, for various activities the banks perform. There are usually commitment charges that are levied on unutilized funds. Besides, there is underwriting fee that guarantees availability of the required funding. All these charges are normally shared amongst the syndicate members depending upon the functions each syndicate member performs. These fees raise the effective cost of loan for the borrower.

Terms and conditions of the syndicated loan include clauses regarding disbursement procedure, mode and place, method of repayments, jurisdiction, indemnity, etc. Because of differing locations of asset and flexibility of end-use of funds, the syndicated loans do not have security. At best, syndicate bank may have collateral in the form of a bank guarantee from another bank.

For large borrowers who can access bond markets find syndicated loans expensive and inconvenient, as compared to issue of foreign bonds. Therefore, syndicated loans are apt for rather smaller firms that are internationally known but are not large enough to launch a bond issue of their own.

Project finance is non-recourse credit secured only by cash flows of the project. It helps in isolating the other activities of the borrowing entity that implies delinking of risk and capital structure. The project is segregated as a legally separate entity created for an exclusive purpose of execution or implementation of a single project. The cash flows of the project are used for service of loans and equity. Providers of equity are called sponsors of the project. Since project finance is non-recourse, the credit risk is higher. The cost of credit is, therefore, greater because other assets of the sponsors are delinked from the project.

Offshore Banking

Related to international banking is a term offshore banking. Banks are subject to wide array of regulations such as statutory ratios, limit on lending, deposit insurance, and selective credit control. These regulations impact the profitability of the banks adversely. Offshore banking is a conscious attempt to locate banking operations to avoid various banking regulations of the host country. Both depositors and borrower in such offshore bank would be largely non-residents.

For example, in a prominent offshore centre such as Bahamas there are minimal banking regulation and tax rates, which has prompted lot of banks world over to establish branches there. Such offshore centres are mostly tax heavens. In the absence of financial regulation and taxes, while offshore banking helps free flow of capital across international borders at most efficient costs, they are also serving as hub of financial malpractices ranging from money laundering, tax evasion, financing of criminal activities, and unethical practices.

CONCEPTS IN PRACTICE
Small Country Bloated Banking—Cyprus

SHOULD TAXPAYERS BEAR THE LOSSES OF THE BANK FOR ITS RECKLESS BEHAVIOUR?

On Monday 25 March 2013, the troika—International Monetary Fund (IMF), European Union (EU) and European Central Bank (ECB)—granted €10 billion bailout package to Cyprus's flagging economy in exchange of closure of 'LAIKI', the second largest bank of Cyprus. Healthy assets of *LAIKI* were to be transferred to Bank of Cyprus; the largest bank of the nation, whereas the non-performing assets were to be disposed off. Cyprus agreed to inflict losses on its big depositors in the banks. All deposits above €100,000 not guaranteed by EU all across banks in Cyprus were frozen and a part of it (estimated around 30%) would be expropriated.

In the absence of the bailout package the banks in Cyprus would have collapsed and threatened the economy of Cyprus and a pull-out from Euro. Banks in Cyprus have substantial exposure in the financial crisis of Greece. The banking sector of Cyprus was extremely oversized at about 10 times of its GDP. Failure of banks would mean a lot to Cyprus, as a nation and the risk of being thrown out of the Eurozone.

The losses of the banks were of the order of €20 billion. Facing bankruptcy in 2011, Russia pumped a low interest loan of €2.5 billion hoping that remaining would come from EU.

Cyprus has been serving as tax haven for Russia. The ill-gotten money in Russia has found its home in Cyprus to avoid high taxation in Russia. The size of Russian money in Cyprus is huge (estimated at €20 billion). It is estimated that about 40% of the capital invested in Russia is routed through Cyprus. Cyprus offered high interest rates to its foreign depositors to attract capital besides being a low tax destination. EU has felt that depositors of the banks are lenders, and hence, must suffer the consequences of failure when it is granted the bailout package with a condition that high value depositors must bear the losses. The bailout package of €10 billion seems small, but it is significant in terms of the GDP of Cyprus estimated at €18 billion.

The bailout demanded raising of €5.8 billion by Cyprus. By all means a very high proportion of the GDP the contribution could come only by forcing losses on the wealthy depositors (€10,000 and above). The shortfall in the contribution can be made up by increasing taxes and privatization. Austerity, privatization and financial sector reforms are the other pre-requisites of the bailout package. Capital control measures would include suspension of credit card payments for purchases made overseas.

The bailout package of Cyprus making banks pay for their risky behaviour rather than taxpayers shelling out the losses can be applied in times to come for all banking system. The Cyprus bailout can serve as template for tackling banking crises in future. This may obviate the need of creating European Stability Mechanism to recapitalize banks in times of trouble.

Perhaps for the first time the depositors of a bank are being made to pay for the sins, greed, and recklessness of the bank managers. Earlier bondholders of the bank and not its depositors have been made to pay. No depositor lost money in the bailout of banks in Greece, Ireland, or other European nations. But in case of Cypriot banks, there are no bond holders. Not many are objecting to such a solution because it is widely believed that Cyprus banking system has served for long as money laundering arm for Russian oligarchs, and many believe the conditions of the package are just and fair. Also one must not forget that perhaps the solution in case of Cyprus could only be implemented with less serious disruption to the banking system because of its overall size as compared to Eurozone and ability to manage 'run on the bank'.

Source: Business Line and *The Economic Times,* 26 March 2013.

Development Banks

Another source of long-term funding available is development financial institutions. International developmental financial institutions provide finance in developing nations and specific projects of public interest financing of which may not find favour with domestic commercial banks due to stretched viability, or they may simply be too big for the resources banks have. Development finance is mainly focused on infrastructure sector such as building roads, irrigation facilities, power generation, ports, and communication infrastructure.

World Bank came into existence primarily for rehabilitating war devastated countries post World War II, and is today engaged actively in financing of projects in developing nations with the broader and holistic objectives of poverty alleviation, reducing income disparities of nations, overcoming balance of payment crises, and economic development.

International Finance Corporation provides finance to private sector projects by loan and equity contributions in developing countries augmenting their financial resources. The funding is normally available for larger projects, which in turn releases domestic capital to be used for many smaller projects.

There are several regional developmental banks, who concentrate on specific regions such as Africa and Asia. Asian Development Bank and African Development Bank provide credit and developmental financing in their respective regions on soft terms, which includes protracted repayment schedule, increased moratorium period and concessional interest rate.

FOREIGN CURRENCY LOANS IN INDIA

Prior to 1991 when India was a highly regulated economy the external borrowings were at minimal level primarily driven by national needs rather than commercial considerations. They could not be termed as external commercial borrowing because interaction with foreign markets was confined to few select purposes and participants. Government was focused on solving issues of national importance such as balance of payment problems and dangerously low foreign currency reserve eroding the confidence of international community. With first primary step towards integration and liberalization of Indian economy post 1991, the commercial consideration started gaining ground.

The features that govern the mobilization of external funds is dependent on (a) global factors such as global liquidity, emerging markets allocations, and capital mobility, (b) national factors such as sovereign rating, national growth, inflation, political stability, regulatory environment, availability of domestic credit, and stability of exchange rate, and (c) investment needs of corporate sector, project profitability, credibility of local borrowers, desire for corporate for cross border acquisitions and becoming global player, etc. Factors affecting the demand and supply of foreign credit directly decide the interest rate and risk premium, and determine the growth of external commercial borrowing.

Subsequent to crisis of 1991 and initial liberalization measures thereafter the environment for foreign credit in India is becoming increasingly relaxed with respect to (a) need for approvals and dismantling of red-tape, (b) ceiling on amount of credit, (c) cost of credit, (d) maturity of credit, (e) end-use of funds, etc. Since then several changes have been made in the regulatory environment of external commercial borrowings guided by Reserve Bank of India. The latest guidelines for external commercial borrowings (ECBs) in India as on 1 July 2013 are presented in the *Online Resource Centre*.

Till 1991, Indian issues in the Eurodollar bond market and other international bonds markets were limited to the few issuances by Public Sector companies such as ONGC, IDBI, and State Bank of India (SBI). IDBI raised funds in Deutsche mark whereas SBI preferred Japanese yen. All these were fixed rate non-convertible bonds. These offerings were backed by sovereign guarantee.

India's trade deficit caused by import of large quantities of crude oil, continuously increases its demand for dollars to meet its import requirements. A majority of India's foreign currency convertible bonds (FCCB) issuances have been dollar denominated, and traded on the Singapore and Luxembourg stock exchanges. Reliance Industries Ltd. (RIL) and SBI have been accessing international bonds market frequently, and have created several milestones. In 1996 and 1997, RIL made several forays in the international bonds market, and successfully placed Yankee bonds of US$100 million with 100 years maturity and US$210 million with 30 years maturity, and US$100 million with 50 years maturity.

Most issues were fixed rate fixed maturity bonds. Few floating rate notes were issued with variable coupon rate pegged to a LIBOR in US dollar. Since the time, Indians were allowed to raise equity abroad the preference shifted to issue of convertible bonds called FCCBs.

While these bonds integrated Indian debt markets with the world, the issuing firms carried exchange rate risk for coupon and principal. Some of the companies that had issued FCCBs and Eurodollar bonds prior to 2007, and faced repayment issues include Suzlon Energy Limited, Wockhardt Group, etc. Most of these FCCBs were issued in 2007 when exchange rate was ₹42, which plummeted to a low of ₹57.

CONCEPTS IN PRACTICE
External Commercial Borrowings, Capital Structure, and Value of the Firm

DEFAULT BY SUZLON

Suzlon Energy, one of the world's leading manufacturer of wind turbines and a darling of Indian investors, in order to expand by acquisitions abroad, launched FCCB issue of US$300 million in May 2007. The zero-coupon bonds were convertible at ₹1,800 per share (at about 60% premium to the average price of around ₹1,125) at maturity of debt after 5 years. The proceeds were to be used for acquisitions abroad in Hansen Transmission in Belgium and RE Power Systems in Germany.

Suzlon defaulted on repayment of $201 million due on 11 October 2012 when it failed to get an approval for rescheduling debt from the investors.

Suzlon got a lifeline by ₹9,500 crore loan restructuring programme. Domestic lenders suspended principal repayment and interest for two years, reduced interest rate by 3%, and advanced fresh working capital loan of ₹1,800 crore. In February 2013, when promoters sold 10.99 crore shares the stock had fallen to abysmal ₹16 to raise ₹240 crore to lenders as part of debt restructuring plan.

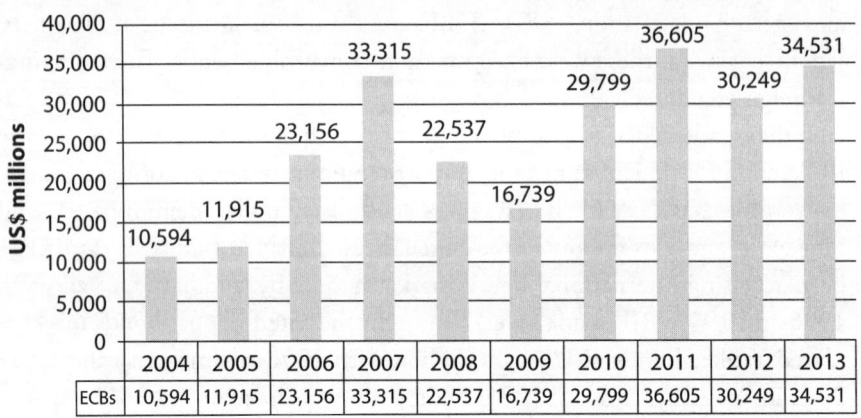

Figure 15-2
Growth of External Commercial Borrowing in India

Figure 15-2 depicts the pattern of ECBs working in India since 2004.

SBI also made several forays in the international bonds market. It issued India Development Bond (IDB) of US$1.6 billion in 1991, Resurgent India Bond (RIB) worth US$4.23 billion in 1998 both with maturities of 5 years. The currency of denomination was US dollar. It also mobilized another US$5.5 billion by way of certificate of deposit called India Millennium Deposit with maturity of 5 years. The exchange rate risk on these bonds was shared with RBI and Central Government. Also some of the issues contained clause of premature withdrawal, but to be made in Indian rupees only and not US dollar reducing exchange rate risk. The proceeds were used for lending (a) to other banks, (b) to Indian firms, and (c) to government by way of subscription to government securities.

In December 2004, SBI announced issue of $1 billion medium term note (MTN) programme with maturity of 5 years. It had many firsts to its credit. It was (a) largest in size by Indian firm, (b) at the lowest ever cost with c) rating of Baa2 higher than India's sovereign rating of Baa3. The bonds were listed on the Singapore Stock Exchange.

With substantial gap in the borrowing costs in domestic and foreign markets, and booming stock markets with high prospects of growth Indians firms were rushing for borrowings abroad. The preferred mode of raising the foreign debt was by way of convertibles. With stock markets in India offering substantial returns, the conversion price usually were fixed at a premium ranging between 25–150%. Indian firms were successful in placing debts with foreigners are very nominal or sometimes even with zero coupon. Since tax rules in India did not consider debt conversion into equity, as capital gains the convertible route rather than straight debt was very popular. During the period 2005–08 about 200 firms in India raised approximately US$16 billion through FCCBs.

From national economy viewpoint conversion option is better than repayment because at maturity conversion into equity implies no foreign exchange outflow. Redemption of ECB can be done by four modes: injecting fresh equity, raising domestic debt, buyback, and restructuring.

Raising equity is dependent upon the stock price prevailing at the time of redemption. Raising domestic debt is subject to comparative borrowing rate in Indian rupee. Restructuring requires approval of the original investor.

SUMMARY

With ever-increasing needs of funds from MNCs, free movement of capital, and convergence of international capital markets, firms are accessing international debt markets more and more. The recourse to international markets is motivated by reduction in cost of capital. At global level it helps in integration of capital markets and allows better availability of domestic credit to smaller firms.

Issuers of international bonds are governments, semi-government organization and multinational firms. Governments of developing nations mobilize funds from international markets to reduce cost of funds whereas subscribers get advantage of getting higher returns than domestic bonds offering near zero returns. Though there are wide varieties of bonds and currencies of denomination available, the overwhelming preference is for fixed rate bonds denominated in US dollar or euro.

Two critical decisions in issue of international bonds are determination of nature of coupon, and currency of denomination. If global markets are fully integrated then it does not make any difference if the bonds bear a fixed or variable coupon or the currency of denomination.

Eurobonds became popular in 1960s with London as most prominent centre. Besides, there are dual currency bonds where coupons and redemption amount are paid in different currencies, and composite bonds that are denominated in a basket of currencies rather than a single currency.

Eurobonds are unsecured, rated, and bearer instruments. They offer tax advantage, not constrained by regulation, and are traded in secondary markets.

Considerations to invest in bond include enhanced yield, and risk reduction through diversification.

For the issuer, the cost comparison of different bonds is governed by expectations of interest rates in various currencies, and expected exchange rate behaviour. International bond face interest rate risk and exchange rate risk, but these risks can be hedged with derivatives such as swaps.

Bank finance by way of syndicated loans and project finance are other modes of raising international finance. Offshore banking centres have developed to meet these financing needs. International developmental financial institutions also provide long-term finance at relatively concessional terms to select projects of national importance and of infrastructure development, which otherwise do not find favour of commercial banks.

The mobilization of funds from international markets for Indian firms is governed by guidelines from Reserve Bank of India. With increasing integration of Indian economy, these guidelines are becoming more and more relaxed in terms of eligibility, all-in cost, ceiling amounts, end-use of funds, etc.

QUESTIONS

15-1 Why do you think that governments in developing countries could prefer issuing foreign bonds than in their own currency?
15-2 What are the advantages of Eurobond over foreign bond?
15-3 What are the differences in fixed rate, floating rate, and convertible bonds?

15-4 What are the risks associated with issue of foreign bond? Describe them briefly.

15-5 How do term structure of interest rate in different currencies impact the decision to choose floating rate or fixed rate bond and currency of its denomination?

PROBLEMS

15-1 to 15-4 Choosing Currency of Bonds

An Indian firm needs to raise ₹10,000 million for its capital expenditure programme. The requirement is for five years. The firm is facing two choices, either issue pound denominated Eurobond in London market or access local markets in Indian rupee. Ironically, one-year yield in sterling pound and Indian rupee is identical at 6.60%. The firm is banking on subscription by non-resident Indians for Eurobond. In case of both the bonds, the maturity is five years with annual coupon. The firm is faced with the following term structure of interest rates in British pound and Indian rupee:

Time	1	2	3	4	5
Pound sterling	6.60%	6.10%	5.80%	5.50%	5.30%
Indian rupee	6.60%	6.75%	7.00%	7.40%	7.80%

Answer Problems 15-1 to 15-4:

15-1 For issuing bond denominated in Indian rupee, what fixed coupon rate could it offer?

15-2 For issuing bond denominated in pound sterling, what fixed coupon rate could it offer?

15-3 Given a choice between rupee denominated and pound denominate, which of the fixed rate bond would be easier to market? Why?

15-4 If the firm were to issue a floating rate bond and the term structure remained same as prevailing today, what would be the rupee cash flows toward coupon and principal for (a) rupee denominated bond and (b) pound denominated bond with current spot exchange rate at ₹ 100/£.

15-5 All-in Cost for Bonds

You have choice of issuing any of the four bonds features of which are described here:

Bond Features	Bond 1	Bond 2	Bond 3	Bond 4
Currency	Eurodollar	Euro	Yen	Pound
Coupon, %	6.00%	6.50%	3.50%	4.50%
Periodicity of coupon	Annual	Semi-annual	Semi-annual	Semi-annual
Maturity, years	3	5	4	4
Issue expenses, % of face value	0.50%	0.53%	1.00%	0.75%
Depreciation of INR, % per annum	4.00%	2.50%	6.00%	4.50%
Current spot, ₹/Unit	60.00	82.00	0.50	100.00
Face value, Foreign currency	100.00	100.00	10,000.00	100.00
Annual management fee, %	0.50%	0.10%	–	0.35%

Find all-in cost for each of the bond.

International Equity Investment

LEARNING OBJECTIVES

This chapter aims at

- understanding the features of international capital markets
- familiarizing with composition of secondary markets worldwide
- understanding how returns undergo change in international investment
- realizing how risk is compounded in international investment
- understanding the rationale for international investment
- understanding what Sharpe ratio is and trade-off between risk and return
- knowing about the trends of foreign institutional investors (FII) investment in India

CONTENTS

Introduction
Equity Markets
International Investment
    Returns and Exchange Rates
    Risk in International Investing

Rationale for International Diversification
International Portfolio—The Risk Return Trade-off
Foreign Portfolio Investment in India

INTRODUCTION

The growth of the multinational corporation (MNC) in the twentieth century has been demanding increased access to international capital markets. Large firms are making public issues to mobilize capital worldwide with national boundaries losing relevance. The trend of increasing access to international capital market is upwards only with firms having global outlook for their products, brands, technologies, personnel, etc. The norms of nationalities for workers, managers, etc. are getting relaxed with time. Like products, technologies, manpower, etc., the ownership of the firms is no more confined to geographical boundaries of nations. Multinational firms are becoming less and less concerned about the ownership status, and developing greater and greater competitiveness by way of mobilizing capital at least cost. The cost of funds is overshadowing other considerations.

As the demand for capital grows globally, the investors too are looking beyond national boundaries to earn better returns on their investment. The increased awareness and development of equity cult and reduction in capital controls by nations, help capital markets integrate faster than ever before. With increased activities in stock markets world over, the stock exchanges provide an excellent platform to those wanting to raise capital and those willing to invest globally. Technological developments for faster and real-time dissemination of information is another factor that has increased the efficiency and effectiveness of international equity investment by (a) making arbitrage opportunities visible, (b) reducing transaction costs, and (c) quick transfer of ownership.

Development of financial intermediation, innovations in financial products to suit needs of investors' niche, and better corporate governance standards too are contributing greatly, removing the home bias on part of investors and firms alike.

EQUITY MARKETS

Equity markets can be classified as (a) primary and (b) secondary. Primary markets are the offerings by the firm directly to their investors. When the firms place equity with the investor, it provides an exit and entry route to investors by getting the stock listed on a stock exchange, which provides a platform for transfer of ownership of the stock from those wanting to exit to those wanting to invest.

International primary capital markets would be the one when a firm makes an offering on global basis and seeks listing of its stock on international stock exchanges. According to a study by PricewaterhouseCoopers (PwC), cross-border initial public offerings (IPOs) from 2002 to 2011 claimed that 13% of all IPOs by value were cross-border offerings. The most prominent firms came from China perhaps because of their limitation of not being able to make offering in local market dominated by public sector firms and stipulation of track record of three year profitability.

In contrast, the success in international markets is guided by credibility of the firm and highest level of corporate governance and information disclosures. Besides strategic reasons to seek international listing such as creating brand awareness and aiming for larger market share, the financial reasons included (a) the desire of firms to access larger pool of investors to help bring down the cost of capital and hence improve financial standing, and (b) seeking natural hedge against currency risk in case of an international acquisition. Cross-borders IPOs are subject to much greater technical and financial scrutiny by more aware and knowledgeable analysts. Therefore, once accepted the international offering goes a long way in serving the long-term objective of growth of the firm.

According to the PwC study, the most preferred centres for listing are London and New York accounting for 41% and 23% of all IPOs, respectively. In value terms, London accounted for US$110 billion and New York had US$56 billion during the period 2002–11. Singapore and Hong Kong were the next preferred destinations that served as cross-border IPO listing hubs in Asia.

Domestic stock markets provide residents with the choice of investing in domestic companies. When these markets are opened for non-residents, the width and depth of the market widens. While the secondary markets provide increased investor base to the firms seeking capital, the open markets also make available a variety of investments to investors.

The market capitalization of stock markets around world was estimated at US$55 trillion in 2012 as shown in Table 16-1, which provides information about major stock markets of the world. The 23 stock exchanges account for about 90% of market capitalization worldwide. Though the gap between the developed world and the developing world remains substantial, it

Table 16-1
World's Stock Markets: A Snapshot

Country	Market Capitalization				% Share of World Market Capitalization	
	US$ million		% of GDP			
	2005	2012	2005	2012	2005	2012
Australia	804,074	1,286,438	116.1	84.6	1.86	2.42
Belgium	288,515	300,058	76.5	62.0	0.67	0.56
Brazil	474,647	1,229,850	53.8	54.6	1.10	2.31
Canada	1,480,891	2,016,117	130.6	110.7	3.43	3.79
China	780,763	3,697,376	34.6	44.2	1.81	6.95
Hong Kong SAR	693,486	1,108,127	381.9	420.9	1.60	2.08
France	1,758,721	1,823,339	82.3	69.8	4.07	3.43
Germany	1,221,250	1,486,315	44.1	43.7	2.83	2.80
India	553,074	1,263,335	66.3	68.6	1.28	2.38
Italy	798,167	480,453	44.7	23.9	1.85	0.90

(Contd)

Table 16-1 Contd

Country	Market Capitalization				% Share of World Market Capitalization	
	US$ million		% of GDP			
	2005	2012	2005	2012	2005	2012
Japan	4,736,513	3,680,982	103.6	61.8	10.96	6.92
Korea, Rep.	718,180	1,180,473	85.0	104.5	1.66	2.22
Mexico	239,128	525,057	28.2	44.6	0.55	0.99
Netherlands	592,906	651,004	92.9	84.3	1.37	1.22
Russia	548,579	874,659	71.8	43.4	1.27	1.65
Singapore	316,658	414,126	256.4	150.8	0.73	0.78
South Africa	565,408	612,308	228.9	159.3	1.31	1.15
Spain	960,024	995,095	84.9	73.7	2.22	1.87
Sweden	403,948	560,526	109.0	106.6	0.93	1.05
Switzerland	938,624	1,079,022	244.0	170.7	2.17	2.03
Turkey	161,537	308,775	33.4	39.1	0.37	0.58
United Kingdom	3,058,182	3,019,467	133.2	124.0	7.08	5.68
United States	16,970,865	18,668,333	135.1	119.0	39.28	35.11
World	43,209,736	53,163,894	96.2	76.8	90.41	88.90

Source: Compiled from http://data.worldbank.org/indicator/CM.MKT.TRNR

is shrinking with time. In 2005 three markets of the USA, UK, and Japan contributed to more than 50% of global market capitalization. Even in 2012 they contributed slightly less than 50% of global market capitalization.

However, the share of developed markets such as the USA, UK, and Japan has declined in 2012 as compared to 2005, whereas the share of developing markets such as China, India, and Brazil has increased during the same period signalling increased interest and awareness in equity. According to World Federation of Exchanges, the global market capitalization in 2013 has increased to more than US$64 trillion registering a growth of about 17% and touching the peak activity that prevailed in 2008 prior to Lehman Brothers collapse. Trading volume too has grown by about 12% in 2013.

Table 16-2 presents the activity levels of the major stock exchanges as measured by market liquidity as per cent of GDP, turnover as per cent of market capitalization and number of listed stocks. Trading surpasses GDP in case of developing countries such as Hong Kong and Korea matching those of developed markets of Switzerland, UK, and USA.

Table 16-2
World's Stock Exchanges

Country	Market Liquidity — Value of Shares Traded % of GDP		Turnover Ratio — Value of Shares Traded % of Market Capitalization		Number of Listed Companies	
	2005	2012	2005	2012	2005	2012
Australia	89.0	69.2	78.0	84.7	1,643	1,959
Belgium	33.3	21.3	44.8	39.0	222	154
Brazil	17.5	37.0	38.3	67.9	381	353
Canada	74.5	66.3	63.6	61.6	3,721	3,876
China	26.0	69.7	82.5	164.4	1,387	2,494
Hong Kong SAR	162.0	467.0	43.3	123.1	1,020	1,459
France	71.4	43.1	92.0	66.4	885	862
Germany	63.7	36.0	146.0	91.8	648	665
India	52.0	33.8	92.2	54.6	4,763	5,191
Italy	62.4	37.7	140.5	166.6	275	279
Japan	109.3	60.5	118.8	99.8	3,279	3,470
Korea	142.4	134.0	209.8	139.2	1,620	1,767
Mexico	6.2	10.0	25.7	25.3	151	131
Netherlands	130.9	57.1	147.7	70.8	237	105
Russian	20.9	36.3	39.0	87.6	296	276
Singapore	97.0	57.0	40.4	43.3	685	472
South Africa	81.2	81.1	39.3	54.9	388	348
Spain	137.7	79.8	163.9	106.3	3,300	3,167
Sweden	125.2	71.6	118.9	73.0	252	332
Switzerland	229.6	101.4	100.1	63.7	263	238
Turkey	41.7	44.2	154.9	136.5	302	405
United Kingdom	181.5	102.2	141.9	84.0	2,759	2,179
United States	171.2	136.3	129.2	124.6	5,143	4,102
World	105.5	72.4	116.5	99.8	50,936	47,520

Source: Compiled from http://data.worldbank.org/indicator/CM.MKT.TRNR

INTERNATIONAL INVESTMENT

International portfolio investment means investors taking positions in markets in another country—directly or indirectly. The exposure is not only in two markets but in two currencies too. Therefore, investing in foreign markets is regarded as portfolio of two assets, that is, position in equities abroad and position in foreign exchange, even though entire capital is invested in single market abroad. The investment is subject to returns obtained in the securities markets abroad in foreign currency as well as loss or gain made on exchange rate while converting those returns to home currency.

Since return consists of two components, the risk of investment abroad too has to be seen as portfolio risk comprising the variability of returns in investment, variability of exchange rate, and the correlation in foreign exchange returns and securities returns. We examine the return and risk of foreign investment in detail now.

Returns and Exchange Rates

The key difference in domestic investing and international investing is the currency exchange. An American investor investing in US equity shares is not concerned with the interest rates, inflation rates, or any other broad economic factors while comparing different investments in different stocks. However, when the same investor expands the investment canvas to world markets, the issues of differences in interest rates, inflation rates, political uncertainties, unemployment, growth rates, etc. come to the fore, which affects the expectations of returns and risks associated. Under conditions of free economy and international trade, these different factors of economy and political situations would get reflected in the changes in the exchange rates (assumed floating rates and no pegging).

International investing essentially involves conversion of currency twice—one at the time of investing and the other while divesting. An American investor deciding to invest in India would need to first convert its US dollar to Indian rupee, then invest in Indian securities, divest at the end of investment horizon say one year, and reconvert the Indian rupee proceeds back to US dollars. If rupee return in India is r_R and the spot rates at the beginning and at the end of investment horizon are S_0 and S_1, respectively (expressed as number of Indian rupees per US dollar), then dollar return $r_\$$ is given by Eq. 16-1.

$$1 + r_\$ = \frac{S_0}{S_1}[1 + r_R] \tag{16-1}$$

Therefore, returns in dollar terms for an American investor investing in India would get influenced by (a) returns in the Indian markets, and (b) foreign exchange markets in India with respect to US dollar, as shown in Figure 16-1. The returns earned in rupee terms would increase or decrease depending upon the appreciation/depreciation of rupee.

For example, in the beginning an investor brings in $1 when the spot rate is ₹50.00/$ and Indian securities market provides and expected return of 20%, the ending value of the investment is expected at 50.00 × 1.2 = ₹60.00. To know how much the investor earned in dollar terms, the

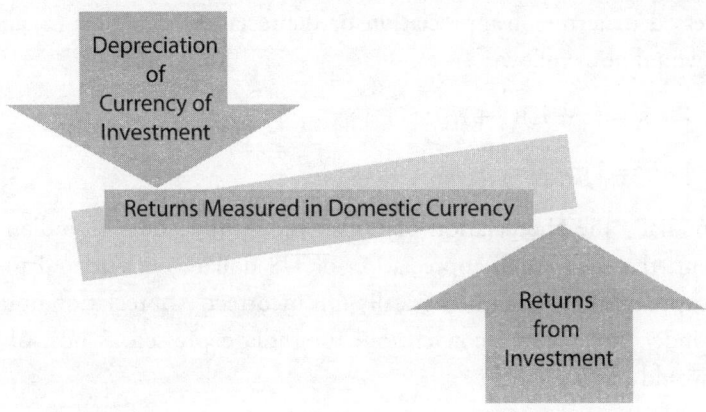

Figure 16-1
Offsetting of Investment Returns by Currency Depreciation

rupee proceeds need to be converted back to US dollar. If in the meantime rupee depreciated by 10% to ₹55, then equivalent US dollar would be 60/55 = $1.0909 and the dollar return would be 9.09% against the rupee return of 20%. The difference in the dollar and rupee return is attributable to rupee depreciation. Instead if rupee had appreciated by 10% to ₹45.00/$, the investor in the USA would get 60/45 = $1.33 boosting the dollar return to 33.33% against rupee returns of 20%. In this case, the increased dollar return is attributable to appreciation of Indian rupee. Only when the exchange rate remained unmoved, the dollar return and rupee return would be identical.

Exercise 16-1
Returns and Exchange Rates

A pension fund in the USA wants to invest in Indian equity expected to yield a 20% return. The current spot exchange rate is ₹50/$. Find out the dollar return after one year if (a) INR appreciates by 10%, (b) there is no change in the exchange rate, and (c) INR depreciates by 10%.

Solution
Assuming at the start of the investing period the American investor brings in US$1.00. He converts them at the spot exchange rate of ₹50.00/$ and invests in Indian equities. After a year he obtains a return of 20% and maturity value of investment becomes ₹60. His dollar returns under different circumstances of exchange rate are as follows:

	Rupee depreciates by 10%	Value of rupee is unchanged	Rupee appreciates by 10%
Spot Exchange Rate after One Year	₹55.00/$	₹50.00/$	₹45.00/$
Numbers of US Dollars Received after One Year	1.0909	1.2000	1.3333
% Return in Dollar Terms	9.09%	20.00%	33.33%

Expressed in terms of appreciation or depreciation of dollar ($a_\$$ and $d_\$$ respectively) the returns would be as follows:

$$1 + r_\$ = (1 + r_R)(1 + d_\$)$$
$$1 + r_\$ = (1 + r_R)(1 - a_\$) \qquad (16\text{-}2)$$

Colloquially the appreciation of dollar and depreciation of Indian rupee are considered equivalent, that is, a 10% appreciation of US dollar is considered to 10% depreciation of Indian rupee. However, mathematically it is incorrect. Appreciation or depreciation for Indian rupee (under direct quote convention; for India expressed as nos. of Indian rupee per US dollar) would be

$$\text{Appreciation }(+)/\text{Depreciation }(-)\text{ of Indian rupee} = -\frac{S_1 - S_0}{S_0} = \frac{S_0 - S_1}{S_0} \qquad (16\text{-}3)$$

Appreciation of Indian rupee implies depreciation of the other currency, that is, US dollar and vice versa. However, they are not equal due to base effect. The base in Eq. 16-3 is S_0, and it changes to S_1 while computing appreciation/depreciation of foreign currency (US dollar in this case). Exchange rate quotation to the format of number of units of foreign currency per unit of domestic currency would be obtained by inverting the direct quote, that is, $1/S$, and the appreciation or depreciation of US dollar would then be given by

$$\text{Appreciation }(+)/\text{Depreciation }(-)\text{ of US dollar} = \frac{S_1 - S_0}{S_1} = -\frac{S_0 - S_1}{S_1} \qquad (16\text{-}4)$$

To illustrate consider that rupee depreciates by 10% from the current level of ₹50/$ to ₹55/$. This depreciation of Indian rupee means appreciation of US dollar. But let us find how much the appreciation is. The appreciation of US dollar is from initial exchange rate of 1/50 is to 1/55. This is equal to 9.09% as can be obtained using Eq. 16.4.

$$\text{Appreciation }(+)\text{ of US dollar } = \frac{S_1 - S_0}{S_1} = \frac{55 - 50}{55} = 9.09\%$$

Appreciation of US dollar, $a_\$$, expressed in terms of depreciation of Indian rupee, d_R, is

$$a_\$ = d_R/(1 + d_R)$$

Therefore, a 10% depreciation of Indian rupee corresponds to 10/1.1 = 9.09% appreciation of US dollar.

Depreciation of US dollar, $d_\$$, expressed in terms of appreciation of Indian rupee, a_R

$$d_\$ = a_R/(1 - a_R)$$

A 20% appreciation of Indian rupee corresponds to 20/0.8 = 25% depreciation of US dollar.

Exercise 16-2
Foreign Investment Returns and Exchange Rate

A German investor needs to invest in British equities expected to provide a return of about 15%. What would be his expected return if British pound (a) appreciates by 10%, (b) remains unchanged, and (c) depreciates by 10%?

Solution

The returns to German investor in terms of euro would be given by

$$(1 + r_\euro) = (1 + r_£)(1 \pm d_\euro/a_\euro)$$

where $r_\euro$ is return in terms of euro
$r_£$ is return in terms of pound
$d_\euro$ and $a_\euro$ is depreciation/appreciation of euro with respect to pound

(a) A 10% appreciation of pound is equal $10/(1 - 0.1) = 11.11\%$ depreciation of euro.
Therefore $(1 + r_\euro) = (1 + 0.15)(1 + 0.1111) = 1.2777$ or $r_\euro = 27.77\%$.
(b) If exchange rate remains unchanged euro return would be same as pound return, that is, 15%.
(c) A 10% depreciation of pound is equal to $10/(1 + 0.1) = 9.09\%$ appreciation of euro.
Therefore $(1 + r_\euro) = (1 + 0.15)(1 - 0.0909) = 1.04545$ or $r_\euro = 4.55\%$.

For investing in foreign markets we need to make two estimates—the expected return on the securities in the foreign markets and expected appreciation/depreciation of foreign currency. One way of forecasting the expected returns and exchange rate returns is based on stock returns and exchange rates in the recent past using regression.

The sensitivity of dollar returns with respect to spot exchange rate changes for US dollar and rupee returns for one year period from 9 May 2012 to 7 May 2013 is given in the *Online Resource Centre*. The parameters of regression equation for rupee and dollar returns, rupee returns and exchange rate returns, and dollar returns to exchange rate returns are summarized as Eqs 16-5, 16-6, and 16-7, respectively, and in Table 16-3.

$$\text{Daily Dollar Returns} = 1.2997 \times \text{Daily rupee returns} - 0.0260 \quad (16\text{-}5)$$

$$\text{Daily Rupee Returns} = -0.7042 \times \text{Daily Exchange Rate Returns} + 0.0868 \quad (16\text{-}6)$$

$$\text{Daily Dollar Returns} = -1.7102 \times \text{Daily Exchange Rate Returns} + 0.0917 \quad (16\text{-}7)$$

Regression parameter, the coefficient of determination of dollar returns with rupee returns has strong bondage at 83% and correlation coefficient at 0.91.

It is noted that stock markets and currency markets have negative correlation. Depreciation of Indian rupee has a tendency to suppress the equity returns while appreciation of would tend to make stock prices rise, as revealed in Figure 16-2. Appreciation of Indian rupee is good for US investor even when Indian stocks yield no return. Any positive returns on the equity investment in India coupled with appreciation of Indian rupee would be very attractive for foreign investors, as may be seen from Figure 16-3.

Table 16-3
Returns, Risks, Covariance, and Correlations of Rupee, Exchange Rates, & Dollar Returns

	Rupee Returns	Exchange Rate	Dollar Returns
Average Daily Return, %	0.082495	0.006117	0.081214
Annualized Return %	20.29	1.50	19.98
Standard Deviation, %	0.821990	0.533131	1.169719
Annualized Standard Deviation, %	12.89	8.36	18.35
Annualized Variance, %	166.21	69.92	336.59
Regression Parameters			
	Slope	Y Intercept, %	Coefficient of Determination, R^2, %
Dollar Returns to Exchange Rate	−1.7102	0.0917	60.76
Rupee Returns to Exchange Rate	−0.7046	0.0868	20.88
Dollar Returns to Rupee Returns	1.2997	−0.0260	83.42
Covariance Matrix			
	Rupee Returns	Exchange Rate Returns	Dollar Returns
Rupee Returns	1.00	−49.06	215.15
Exchange Rate Returns		1.00	−119.09
Dollar Returns			1.00
Correlation Coefficient Matrix			
Rupee Returns	1.0000	−0.7763	0.9096
Exchange Rate Returns		1.0000	−0.4551
Dollar Returns			1.0000

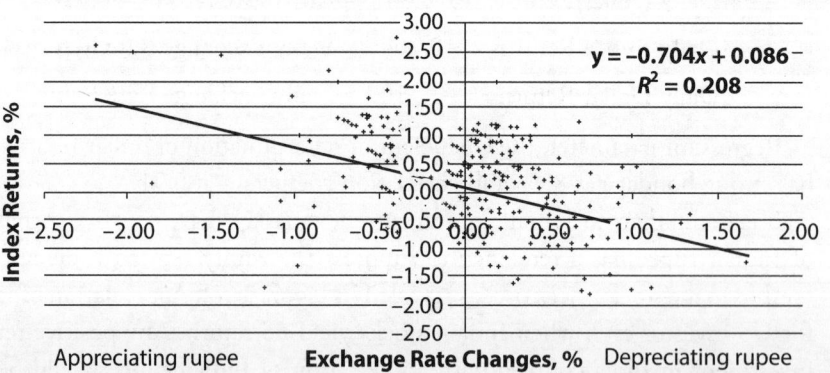

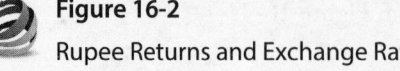

Figure 16-2
Rupee Returns and Exchange Rate

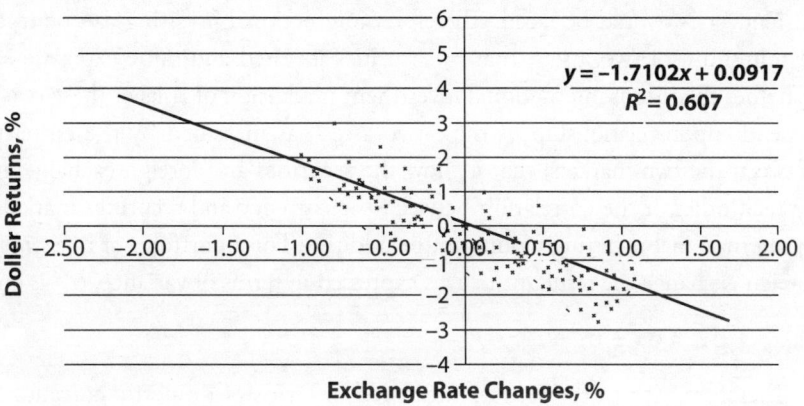

Figure 16-3
Dollar Returns and Exchange Rate

Dollar returns and rupee returns have very strong correlation and coefficient of determination. It perhaps indicates high degree of integration of Indian economy and markets with the world. The scatter diagram and regression equation is depicted in Figure 16-4.

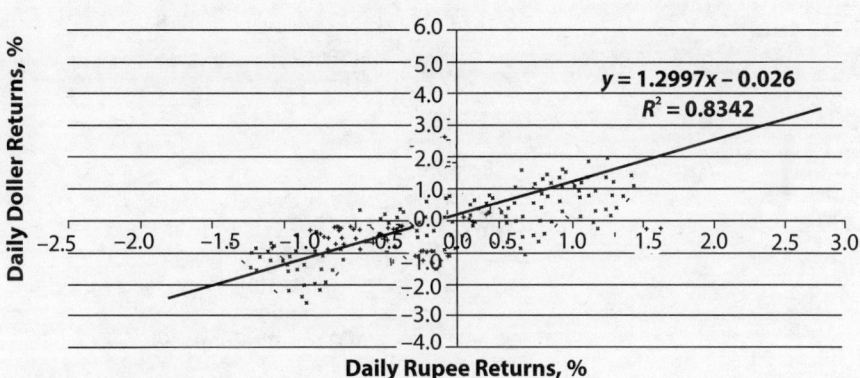

Figure 16-4
Dollar Returns and Rupee Returns

Risk in International Investing

The other side of the coin for any investment is risk. In case of international investing, the added dimension to the risk is the change in the exchange rates which is absent in domestic investment. Therefore, one may tend to conclude that international investing would be invariably more risky than domestic investing. It is not so necessarily. To find an exact answer we resort to portfolio theory.

If one were to invest in any securities, the risk faced would be measured by the standard deviation of such investment. Similarly, if one were to trade only in the foreign exchange market, the risk faced would be the volatility of foreign exchange rates. When one is investing in the international markets both the risks—volatility of securities invested in, σ_s, and volatility of exchange rates of currency, σ_c—would be faced. Therefore, international investing can be regarded as a portfolio of minimum of two assets, that is, securities invested and same exposure in foreign exchange. Whether the risk of international investment is addition of risks of these two assets or not would depends upon relationship of these two assets, as measured by the correlation coefficient, ρ_c, between the two markets, that is, how the securities and foreign exchange markets are affected by each other. If the correlation between the currency and securities markets is small, then risk in international investing would not be additive. For a portfolio of investment in securities and foreign exchange the resultant risk, as expressed in terms of variance, σ_p^2 is given by Eq. 16-8.

$$\sigma_p^2 = \sigma_s^2 + \sigma_c^2 + 2\rho_c\sigma_s\sigma_c \tag{16-8}$$

Therefore, risk in the returns measured in terms of domestic currency of the investor is a function of (a) volatility of returns in foreign currency, (b) volatility of exchange rate, and (c) correlation of returns with exchange rate. The complexity of risk in international investing is characterized in Figure 16-5.

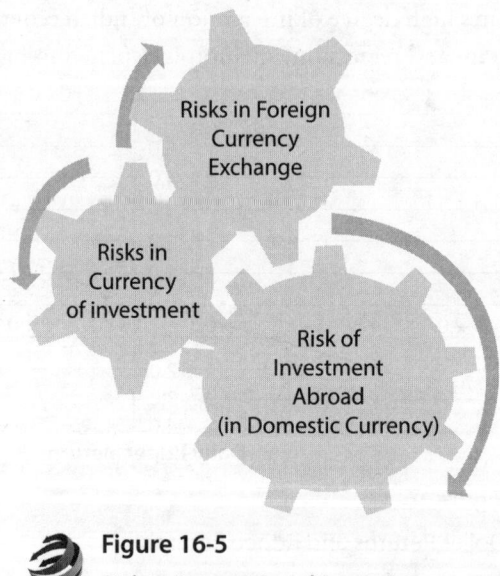

Figure 16-5
Risk in International Investing

In general unlike returns, the risk of a portfolio is not weighted average of assets comprising it. In case of perfect positive correlation between the securities and foreign exchange markets the risk would become additive. Where the relationship between the securities markets and foreign exchange markets is low the risk would not be as great as sum of the risk in securities and foreign exchange. Lower the correlation between the two, lower would be the risk.

Negative Correlation In fact there could be possibility of the two markets especially those of developing economies being negatively correlated. In developing economies currency depreciation is normally seen reducing returns in the foreign exchange markets. But such currency depreciation may be accompanied by increased competitiveness of the industry and stock returns may be positive. Under such situations volatility of returns in the domestic currency would be marginally more than the volatility of returns in foreign currency. If currency markets and security markets have sufficiently high negative correlation it is possible to obtain risk of returns denominated in domestic currency to be less than the risk faced in foreign currency. Mathematically we have

$$\sigma_p^2 = \sigma_s^2 + \sigma_c^2 + 2\rho_c\sigma_s\sigma_c \leq \sigma_s^2 \tag{16-9}$$

$$\rho_c \leq -\frac{\sigma_s}{2\sigma_c} \tag{16-10}$$

Exercise 16-3
Risk of Foreign Investment

A study of risk of investments in different markets and exchange rates reveals the following data:

	Volatility of Equity Returns	Volatility of Exchange Rate of US Dollar	Correlation Coefficient between Stock Market and Foreign Exchange Market
India	20%	15%	−0.2
England	10%	5%	+0.3
Germany	12%	7%	+0.4

(a) Find out the risk an American investor would face if he invests in equity markets of India, England, and Germany.
(b) At what level of correlation would the dollar returns of American investor face a smaller risk than that of the rupee returns faced by an Indian investor?
(c) What would be the risk of dollar returns if the coefficient of correlation in the Indian stock market returns and currency markets for US dollar is −0.4?

Solution
(a) Variance of returns for an American investor for investment in international markets is given by Eq. 16-8

$$\sigma_p^2 = \sigma_s^2 + \sigma_c^2 + 2\rho_c\sigma_s\sigma_c$$

Volatility of dollar returns for investment in India
  Variance of Dollar Returns = 400 + 225 − 2 × 0.2 × 20 × 15 = 505; Volatility = 22.47%
Volatility of dollar returns for investment in England
  Variance of Dollar Returns = 100 + 25 + 2 × 0.3 × 10 × 5 = 155; Volatility = 12.45%
Volatility of dollar returns for investment in Germany
  Variance of Dollar Returns = 144 + 49 + 2 × 0.4 × 12 × 7 = 260.2; Volatility = 16.13%

(b) For the correlation coefficient of less than − 15/2 × 20 = −0.375 the dollar returns from investment in India would face a risk lower than 20% that is faced by Indian investor.
(c) For correlation coefficient of −0.4 the risk of dollar returns would be

  Variance of Dollar Returns = 400 + 225 − 2 × 0.4 × 20 ×15 = 385; Volatility = 19.62%

Referring to the correlation matrix in Table 16-3, the covariance of equity returns and exchange rate returns is found to be −49.06% indicating a negative correlation between currency markets and stock markets with a value of correlation coefficient of −0.4551.

An American investor investing US dollar in Indian equity market would face risk of returns of 12.89% in rupee terms, and a risk of exchange rate of 8.36%. Can the risk of the two be aggregated? Since there is correlation of less than 1.00 between equity and exchange rate returns the risks of the two markets cannot be aggregated. The risk of dollar returns measured by its variance would be given by

$$\begin{aligned}\text{Risk of dollar returns} &= \text{Variance of Rupee Returns} + \text{Variance of Exchange Rate Returns} \\ &\quad + 2 \times \text{Covariance of Exchange Rate Returns and Rupee Returns} \\ &= 166.21 + 69.92 - 2 \times 49.06 = 138.01 \\ &\equiv \text{Standard Deviation of } 11.75\%.\end{aligned}$$

Hence an American investor is facing lesser risk than an Indian investor by investing his dollar in India due to negative correlation between dollar exchange rate and stock returns.

CONCEPTS IN PRACTICE
International Diversification

CASE FOR INVESTING IN AFRICA

Investors diversify their portfolios to boost returns and manage risk. However, the benefits of diversifying across geographic regions are reduced if markets are highly correlated. An analysis of the trends over the past two decades revealed, as expected from global market integration, that regional indices have become increasingly correlated with the S&P 500 index. Sub-Saharan Africa is also part of this trend, but is a notable laggard. For instance, in 2010 the correlation with the S&P500 was 0.86 for markets in Latin America, 0.79 for Asia, and just 0.31 for Sub-Saharan markets (excluding South Africa). Additionally, correlations among African markets are generally very low. While there remain barriers to exploiting this trend, Africa's integration lag may present opportunities for investors seeking regional diversification—and policymakers seeking to attract greater portfolio investment to the continent.

Source: Moss, Todd and Ross Thuotte, Abstract of Working Paper *Nowhere Left to Hide? Stock Market Correlation, Regional Diversification, and the Case for Investing in Africa*, http://www.cgdev.org/publication

RATIONALE FOR INTERNATIONAL DIVERSIFICATION

The rationale for international investment without resorting to quantitative analysis is the investors' clamour for international diversification because of the belief that foreign stocks may move in opposite direction with another or would react differently with one another for same cause. So when one market is depressed by 10%, the other markets may deliver good performance or may not be as depressed as 10%. Therefore, portfolio consisting of local and foreign stock must show steadier performance of return and hence less volatility. Correlation coefficient is the quantitative way of saying the belief that how different markets would behave differently at different times.

The relationship of different markets changes with time. About 50 years back possibly the markets were isolated for variety of reasons—economic and political. The study of correlation is often segregated between developed markets of the world like those of USA and Europe with those of developing markets such as Asia and Africa. The differentials in growth rates, inflation rate, interest rates, education levels, market efficiency, etc. contribute towards low degree of correlations. Most researchers have observed and argued that with increased openness of the world markets the correlation among them tends to rise with time. The trend is expected to continue as the world becomes more and more integrated.

Other factors besides converging economies include (a) presence of large MNCs who are now more globalized, (b) increasing role of firms in developing markets going abroad to do business rather than being dependent purely on home economy, and (c) increasing number of nations responding to factors that seemed local but had global impact such as collapse of Lehman Bros and Greece crisis. With time, the correlation among markets is set to increase rather than decline with increased interdependence of economies of the world.

With increased correlations among the markets would the international diversification be effective? It is a difficult question to answer. But the attractiveness of international diversification should reach a plateau and not diminish because correlation coefficients would peak out at much less than 1.00. The reason is clear. Howsoever large MNCs may become, they would continue to be more influenced by policies of home nations, more and more local firms would develop as part of industrialization and make home markets more dominated by local firm listings, business cycles would remain asynchronous irrespective of level of integration. Therefore, international diversification would not lose its relevance just because correlations are increasing. They would tend to flat out. Therefore, investors would continue to look abroad.

Figure 16-6 presents a sample correlation matrix of different markets of the world. One finds that because of geographical proximity, cultural affinity, converging living standards, high literacy levels, and free flow of labour and capital as also the same currency, the European markets show very high degree of correlation (France with Germany and Switzerland) but is less than 1.00. One would perhaps guess that should be the upper limit to correlation. Most developing nations in Asia such as India (maximum of 0.54 and 0.50 with Singapore and Hong Kong) and China (maximum of 0.51 with Hong Kong) have correlation no greater that 0.35 with markets in the developing nations.

Correlation Matrix: Daily % Chg Correlation Current Bull Market (Since 3/9/09)

Country	Australia	Brazil	China	Canada	France	Germany	Hong Kong	India	Japan	Malaysia	Mexico	Russia	Singapore	S. Africa	S. Korea	Spain	Sweden	Switz.	Taiwan	UK	US
Australia	1.00	0.21	0.34	0.27	0.33	0.31	0.66	0.31	0.60	0.45	0.23	0.40	0.60	0.39	0.64	0.27	0.30	0.34	0.61	0.35	0.22
Brazil	0.21	1.00	0.19	0.64	0.56	0.55	0.30	0.33	0.09	0.18	0.64	0.43	0.32	0.45	0.26	0.49	0.51	0.49	0.21	0.55	0.70
China	0.34	0.19	1.00	0.19	0.18	0.16	0.51	0.24	0.29	0.29	0.21	0.25	0.37	0.26	0.36	0.13	0.15	0.15	0.36	0.20	0.13
Canada	0.27	0.64	0.19	1.00	0.61	0.62	0.31	0.32	0.16	0.23	0.65	0.49	0.38	0.52	0.26	0.53	0.59	0.54	0.23	0.60	0.78
France	0.33	0.56	0.18	0.61	1.00	0.94	0.37	0.39	0.22	0.25	0.56	0.63	0.45	0.66	0.30	0.87	0.84	0.83	0.24	0.89	0.69
Germany	0.31	0.55	0.16	0.62	0.94	1.00	0.37	0.39	0.22	0.25	0.56	0.64	0.45	0.67	0.31	0.79	0.85	0.81	0.25	0.87	0.69
Hong Kong	0.66	0.30	0.51	0.31	0.37	0.37	1.00	0.50	0.53	0.52	0.30	0.48	0.74	0.43	0.64	0.31	0.35	0.36	0.63	0.40	0.23
India	0.31	0.33	0.24	0.32	0.39	0.39	0.50	1.00	0.25	0.32	0.35	0.44	0.54	0.43	0.35	0.33	0.37	0.37	0.35	0.41	0.29
Japan	0.60	0.09	0.29	0.16	0.22	0.22	053	0.25	1.00	0.42	0.15	0.30	0.50	0.27	0.55	0.18	0.20	0.27	0.51	0.23	0.13
Malaysia	0.45	0.18	0.29	0.23	0.25	0.25	0.52	0.32	0.42	1.00	0.23	0.35	0.53	0.29	0.47	0.20	0.23	0.25	0.49	0.26	0.15
Mexico	0.23	0.64	0.21	0.65	0.56	0.56	0.30	0.35	0.15	0.23	1.00	0.43	0.35	0.53	0.25	0.47	0.53	0.50	0.21	0.55	0.69
Russia	0.40	0.43	0.25	0.49	0.63	0.64	0.48	0.44	0.30	0.35	0.43	1.00	0.53	0.63	0.39	0.52	0.60	0.57	0.34	0.63	0.49
Singapore	0.60	0.32	0.37	0.38	0.45	0.45	0.74	0.54	0.50	0.53	0.35	0.53	1.00	0.49	0.57	0.37	0.43	0.44	0.60	0.47	0.32
South Africa	0.39	0.45	0.26	0.52	0.66	0.67	0.43	0.43	0.27	0.29	0.48	0.63	0.49	1.00	0.36	0.54	0.64	0.63	0.33	0.70	0.49
South Korea	0.64	0.26	0.36	0.26	0.30	0.31	0.64	0.35	0.55	0.47	0.25	0.39	0.57	0.36	1.00	0.24	0.33	0.32	0.68	0.33	0.23
Spain	0.27	0.49	0.13	0.53	0.87	0.79	0.31	0.33	0.18	0.20	0.47	0.52	0.37	0.54	0.24	1.00	0.72	0.69	0.19	0.76	0.60
Sweden	0.30	0.51	0.15	0.59	0.84	0.85	0.35	0.37	0.20	0.23	0.53	0.60	0.43	0.64	0.33	0.72	1.00	0.77	0.25	0.81	0.64
Switzerland	0.34	0.49	0.15	0.54	0.83	0.81	0.36	0.37	0.27	0.25	0.50	0.57	0.44	0.63	0.32	0.69	0.77	1.00	0.26	0.82	0.62
Taiwan	0.61	0.21	0.36	0.23	0.24	0.25	0.63	0.35	0.51	0.49	0.21	0.34	0.60	0.33	0.68	0.19	0.25	0.26	1.00	0.26	0.19
UK	0.35	0.55	0.20	0.60	0.89	0.87	0.40	0.41	0.23	0.26	0.55	0.63	0.47	0.70	0.33	0.76	0.81	0.82	0.26	1.00	0.66
US	0.22	0.70	0.13	0.78	0.69	0.69	0.23	0.29	0.13	0.15	0.69	0.49	0.32	0.49	0.23	0.60	0.64	0.62	0.19	0.66	1.00

Source: http://www.bespokeinvest.com/thinkbig/2014/3/14/global-equity-market-correlation-matrix.html, accessed on 9 April 2014.

Figure 16-6
Correlation of World's Markets

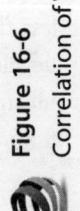

INTERNATIONAL PORTFOLIO—THE RISK RETURN TRADE-OFF

Constructing a global portfolio requires adjustment of returns commensurate with risk assumed. We know that risk profiles for investment in several economies would be substantially different due to heterogeneous economic, social, and political conditions. Assuming that these heterogeneities would be accurately reflected in exchange rate movements on the assumption of free flow of capital, the exchange rate risk would be one comprehensive and consolidated measure of risk of cross-border investing. The uncertainties of return measured in domestic currency would be function of (a) risk of returns of investment in securities abroad, (b) risk of exchange rate fluctuations, and (c) correlation of returns in foreign exchange markets and securities markets.

To understand the desirability of investment abroad, we need to balance the expected returns with the risks assumed. The trade-off between returns and risk is usually measured by the ratio of expected return and expected risk. Investment with higher return and lower risk are preferred. Investors, therefore, tend to choose investment that improves the ratio of expected return and risk. One such measure is Sharpe ratio defined as the ratio of excess returns to the standard deviation. If the new investment improves the Sharpe ratio of the portfolio, it is desirable else not.

To know whether investment abroad is desirable we examine the outcome of return and risk if out of the total investment in home country a marginal investment is made abroad. Assume that entire corpus is invested in home market with an expected return of r_h and risk of σ_h. A marginal sum, Δ, is invested in markets abroad. The market abroad has expected return of r_a and risk of σ_a measured in terms of home currency. Such a portfolio would have expected return, r_P, and risk, σ_P, as follows:

$$\text{Expected Portfolio Return } r_P = \frac{1}{1+\Delta} r_h + \frac{\Delta}{1+\Delta} r_a$$

$$\text{Variance of Portfolio } \sigma_P^2 = \left(\frac{1}{1+\Delta}\right)^2 \sigma_h^2 + \left(\frac{\Delta}{1+\Delta}\right)^2 \sigma_a^2 + 2\rho_s \left(\frac{\Delta}{1+\Delta}\right)\left(\frac{1}{1+\Delta}\right) \sigma_h \sigma_a$$

Note that expected return of the portfolio is weighted average of returns in the markets at home and abroad. The risk of the portfolio is not weighted average but instead is determined by the coefficient of correlation, ρ_s between the securities markets at home and abroad. Whether or not an investor must invest in the markets abroad would depend on risk and return trade-off. One measure of risk and return trade-off is the ratio of expected return and its risk, as measured by standard deviation. Investment abroad is desirable if risk return trade-off of the portfolio of investing abroad improves that of domestic investment, that is,

$$\frac{r_P}{\sigma_P} \geq \frac{r_h}{\sigma_h} \qquad \text{or} \qquad \left(\frac{r_P}{\sigma_P}\right)^2 \geq \left(\frac{r_h}{\sigma_h}\right)^2$$

Putting the values of portfolio return and risk, and ignoring the terms containing Δ^2, being negligibly small we get

$$\left(\frac{r_h^2 + 2\Delta r_h r_a}{\sigma_h^2 + 2\rho_s \Delta \sigma_h \sigma_a}\right) \geq \left(\frac{r_h}{\sigma_h}\right)^2$$

Simplifying further we get

$$\frac{r_a}{\sigma_a} \geq \rho_s \frac{r_h}{\sigma_h}$$

$$r_a \geq \rho_s \frac{r_h}{\sigma_h} \sigma_a \qquad (16\text{-}11)$$

In terms of Sharpe ratio, the trade-off between return and risk is measured through excess returns over risk free rate. Equation 16-11 can easily be modified by replacing the returns with excess returns over risk free rate without changing the conclusion. Therefore, in terms of excess returns, that is, the Sharpe ratio the Inequality 16-11 becomes

$$r_a - r_f \geq \rho_s \frac{r_h - r_f}{\sigma_h} \sigma_a$$

$$r_a \geq \rho_s \frac{r_h - r_f}{\sigma_h} \sigma_a + r_f \qquad (16\text{-}12)$$

From Eq. 16-12 we can conclude on the desirability of investment abroad when (a) home market returns are less, (b) home market risk are high, (c) risk in markets abroad is less, and most importantly (d) the degree of correlation of the securities markets of home and abroad is low.

The opportunities for investment abroad need to be analysed in a systematic manner in a step-by-step process as follows:

1. Find the expected return and its volatility (standard deviation) of the investment abroad as percent.
2. Find the expected return and its volatility of foreign currency markets abroad with respect to home currency.
3. Find the relationship (coefficient of correlation) of return of investment in securities market abroad and foreign exchange market abroad, ρ_c.
4. Find Sharpe ratio of investment at home using expected return and volatilities in the home market.
5. Convert the expected return and volatility of investment abroad to home currency using Eqs 16-2 and 16-8, respectively.
6. Find the coefficient of correlation between securities markets abroad and home, ρ_s.
7. Compute the minimum required return for investing abroad so as to improve the portfolio performance in terms of Sharpe ratio given by Eq. 16-12.

International Equity Investment

Refer to Exercises 16-4 and 16-5 for better understanding of analytical framework for investment abroad.

Exercise 16-4
Analysing Investment Abroad

An Indian financial institution is exploring to diversify its domestic portfolio to other Asian markets specifically Hong Kong and Singapore. The expected returns and the volatilities of the securities market, volatilities of foreign exchange market with respect to Indian rupee, and the correlation coefficients of securities market with the foreign exchange markets are as given in the following table:

	Expected Returns in Stock Markets	Volatility of Stock Market Returns	Volatility of Exchange Rate with Respect to INR	Correlation Coefficient between Stock Market and Foreign Exchange Market
Hong Kong	12%	8%	6%	+0.2
Singapore	11%	9%	4%	+0.1

The investor expects to earn 20% return with a volatility estimate of 10% in Indian securities market. The risk free rate of return in India is placed at 5%.

An analyst on whose forecast the financial institution relies, of foreign exchange markets predicts appreciation of Indian rupee by 3% against Hong Kong dollar, and depreciation of Indian rupee by 4% against Singapore dollar.

(a) What are the expected returns and volatilities for the Indian financial institution if it decides to invest in securities markets of Hong Kong and Singapore?
(b) What explanations can be offered for return and risk in Indian rupee being different than those inherently present in the respective markets?
(c) What observations can be made regarding desirability of expanding the portfolio to securities from Hong Kong and Singapore?

Solution

(a) Expected return from investment abroad in Indian rupee terms after adjustment of expected appreciation/depreciation of Indian rupee using Eq. 16-2:

From Investment in Hong Kong = $1.12 \times 0.97 - 1 = 0.0864 \equiv 8.64\%$
From Investment in Singapore = $1.11 \times 1.04 - 1 = 0.1544 \equiv 15.44\%$

Expected volatility of rupee returns from investing abroad is given by Eq. 16-8.

Variance of Investment in Hong Kong = $8^2 + 6^2 + 2 \times 0.2 \times 8 \times 6 = 119.2$
or standard deviation = 10.92%

Variance of Investment in Singapore = $9^2 + 4^2 + 2 \times 0.1 \times 9 \times 4 = 104.2$
or standard deviation = 10.20%

(b) Note that expected return from investment in Hong Kong is lower due to depreciation of Hong Kong dollar (appreciation of Indian rupee), and that from Singapore is higher due to appreciation of Singapore dollar (depreciation of Indian rupee).

488 International Finance

Similarly risk of investment in Hong Kong and Singapore become different from those inherent in the respective securities markets when translated in terms of Indian rupee, due to interplay of securities markets with currency markets.

(c) It may seem that since the returns are lower than the expected return in India while the risks of investment in markets abroad is comparable to that of India, investment abroad is not desirable. However this could be a misleading conclusion. Desirability of investment abroad must be analysed in terms of improvement in the portfolio performance when expanded abroad.

Exercise 16-5
Analysing Investment Abroad

Continuing with the data of Exercise 16-4, a further study of the securities markets suggests a correlation coefficient of Indian securities markets with Hong Kong and Singapore securities markets are at 0.40 and 0.60, respectively.

(a) What are the minimum expected returns that would improve the portfolio performance if it is expanded to include securities from Hong Kong and Singapore?
(b) What would be the decision with regard to investment in securities from Hong Kong and Singapore?
(c) What would be the Sharpe ratio if 10% of funds are moved from India to (i) Hong Kong market and (ii) Singapore market?
(d) What would be the Sharpe ratio if 50% of funds are moved from India to (i) Hong Kong market and (ii) Singapore market?
(e) What is the reason for difference in values of Sharpe ratio obtained in (c) and (d)?

Solution
Portfolio performance measured by Sharpe ratio lays requirement of minimum return. With expected return for an Indian investor in India at 20% with risk free rate of 5%, the minimum return desired from investment abroad that improves the risk return trade-off is given by Eq. 16-12.

(a) For investment in Hong Kong the minimum equivalent rupee return required is

$$r_a \geq \rho_s \frac{r_h - r_f}{\sigma_h} \sigma_a + r_f \geq 0.4 \frac{15}{10} \times 10.92 + 5 \geq 11.55\%$$

For investment in Singapore Hong Kong the minimum equivalent rupee return required is

$$r_a \geq \rho_s \frac{r_h - r_f}{\sigma_h} \sigma_a + r_f \geq 0.6 \frac{15}{10} \times 10.20 + 5 \geq 14.18\%$$

(b) The expected rupee return from investment in Singapore is 15.44% and hence it is desirable to expand the portfolio to include stocks from Singapore markets. However, the expected rupee return from investment in stock markets of Hong Kong is 8.64%, and hence it is not advisable to invest in Hong Kong.

(c) If investor in India moves 10% of the funds in the Hong Kong market, the expected return would be

$$0.9 + 20.00 + 0.1 \times 8.64 = 18.864\%$$

And the variance of such portfolio would be

$$\sigma_P^2 = \left(\frac{9}{10}\right)^2 10.0^2 + \left(\frac{1}{10}\right)^2 10.92^2 + 2\times 0.4 \times \left(\frac{9}{10}\right)\left(\frac{1}{10}\right)\times 10.0\times 10.92 = 90.0544$$

$$\sigma_P = 9.49\%$$

The Sharpe ratio is $\dfrac{18.864 - 5.00}{9.49} = 1.46$

If investor in India moves 10% of the funds in Singapore market, the expected return would be

$$0.9 + 20.00 + 0.1 \times 15.44 = 19.544\%$$

And the variance of such portfolio would be

$$\sigma_P^2 = \left(\frac{9}{10}\right)^2 10.0^2 + \left(\frac{1}{10}\right)^2 10.2^2 + 2\times 0.6 \times \left(\frac{9}{10}\right)\left(\frac{1}{10}\right)\times 10.0\times 10.2 = 93.058$$

$$\sigma_P = 9.65\%$$

The Sharpe ratio is $\dfrac{19.544 - 5.00}{9.65} = 1.507$

(d) If investor in India moves 50% of the funds in Hong Kong market, the expected return would be

$$0.5 + 20.00 + 0.5 \times 8.64 = 14.32\%$$

And the variance of such portfolio would be

$$\sigma_P^2 = \left(\frac{1}{2}\right)^2 10.0^2 + \left(\frac{1}{2}\right)^2 10.92^2 + 2\times 0.4 \times \left(\frac{1}{2}\right)\left(\frac{1}{2}\right)\times 10.0\times 10.92 = 76.64$$

$$\sigma_P = 8.75\%$$

The Sharpe ratio is $\dfrac{14.32 - 5.00}{8.75} = 1.065$

If investor in India moves 50% of the funds in Singapore market, the expected return would be

$$0.5 + 20.00 + 0.5 \times 15.44 = 17.72\%$$

And the variance of such portfolio would be

$$\sigma_P^2 = \left(\frac{1}{2}\right)^2 10.0^2 + \left(\frac{1}{2}\right)^2 10.2^2 + 2\times 0.6 \times \left(\frac{1}{2}\right)\left(\frac{1}{2}\right)\times 10.0\times 10.2 = 81.65$$

$$\sigma_P = 9.04\%$$

The Sharpe ratio is $\dfrac{17.72 - 5.00}{9.04} = 1.407$

(e) The Sharpe ratio for domestic investing is $(20 - 5)/10 = 1.50$. With some investment going to Singapore Sharpe ratio improves despite decreased returns of Singapore due to reduced risk. This does not happen in case investment is made in securities in Hong Kong. However, when substantial investment moves to Singapore Sharpe ratio declines because portfolio derives substantial returns from investment in Singapore with less than proportionate reduction in risk.

CONCEPTS IN PRACTICE
Risk Perspective

RISK PERSPECTIVE OF FOREIGN AND DOMESTIC INVESTORS

India is one of the major emerging markets where foreign investors choose to invest. One of the key sectors in India is information technology (IT). IT stocks in India form a major part of index and these stocks are among the most cherished ones because of the growth potential and impeccable corporate governance that is distinct from other sectors of the Indian economy. IT companies in India serve as global hub for IT needs of the world.

The foreign institutional investors (FIIs) as well as domestic institutional investors (DFIs) hold substantial holding of the major IT firms in India. During the period of one year (FY 12–13) the holding of the FIIs and DFIs changed in four major IT firms as follows:

Shareholding (%)	FII Holding				DFI Holding			
	June 2012	Sept 2012	Dec 2012	Mar 2013	June 2012	Sept 2012	Dec 2012	Mar 2013
Infosys	37.89	39.42	40.55	40.52	18.28	18.32	18.70	17.51
TCS	14.63	14.83	14.96	14.14	6.70	6.49	6.45	5.44
Wipro	6.59	6.54	7.02	7.30	3.47	3.49	3.06	3.32
HCL	19.97	20.31	21.80	24.32	9.51	9.33	8.40	6.56

Source: Data taken from *Hindu Business Line*, 20 April 2013.

The general trend of holding was that while DFIs decided to prune their holding in these firms, the FIIs increased their holdings. Both DFIs and FIIs are intelligent and learned investors who take positions based on potential of the firms they invest in. Clearly when DFIs were selling, FIIs were buying. The data reveals that while FIIs increased their stakes in HCL from 19.97% in June 2012 to 24.32% in March 2013, the DFI reduced their stake from 9.51% to 6.65% during the same period. The pattern is more or less similar in other IT firms too.

The motives of intelligent and learned investors for altering the holding can be many but one plausible explanation reflecting the contrasting behaviour of the two classes of investors may lie in their perspective of risks associated. While the risk perception of DFIs remains local the risk is seen on global basis by FIIs. When choppy conditions in the global markets such as recession in USA, crises in Eurozone, natural calamities in Japan, etc. were affecting the portfolios of global investors during this period, the domestic investors in India were focused on finding investment avenues in sectors other than IT as its growth had toned down being dependent upon global factors. Global investors perhaps perceived investment in Indian IT firms as safe bets in the context of the portfolios they held. DFIs were possibly looking for more attractive investment bets in India as they became apprehensive of the growth potential of IT firms due to challenging global economic conditions representing risk levels greater than their appetite.

FOREIGN PORTFOLIO INVESTMENT IN INDIA

The FIIs are those institutional investors which invest in the assets belonging to a different country other than that where these organizations are based. Foreign institutional investors play a very important role in any economy. These are the big companies such as investment banks, mutual funds, etc., who invest considerable amount of money in the Indian markets. With the buying of securities by these big players, markets trend to move upward and vice-versa. They exert strong influence on the total inflows coming into the economy. Market regulator SEBI has over 1,450 foreign institutional investors registered with it. The FIIs are considered as both a trigger and a catalyst for the market performance by encouraging investment from all classes of investors, which further leads to growth in financial market trends under a self-organized system.

FII investment in India plays a key role in the Indian stock markets. The market fortunes fluctuate directly with the FII activity—making gains upon the purchases by them and losing with the sales by them. With the exception of 2008–09 the Indian equity markets has been attracting positive net flows as depicted in Figure 16-7 and the aggregate inflow has topped US$140 billion in 2011–12 as can be seen in Figure 16-8.

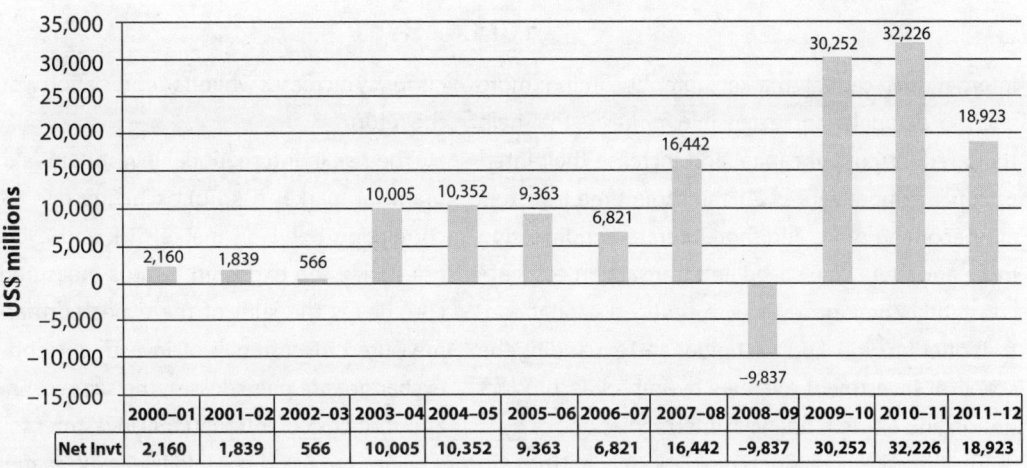

Figure 16-7
Net Portfolio Investment by FIIs

The environment for foreign investment in financial markets and securities is governed by Securities and Exchange Board of India (Foreign Institutional Investor) Regulations, 1995 (as amended from time to time), and Foreign Exchange Management Act, 1999 and regulations framed thereunder. The approvals and registration are granted by Securities and Exchange Board of India (SEBI) and in case of a bank or its subsidiary by Reserve Bank of India.

Subject to certain condition all kinds of investors such as pension funds, mutual funds, investment trusts, insurance companies, banks, or institutional portfolio managers are eligible as FIIs.

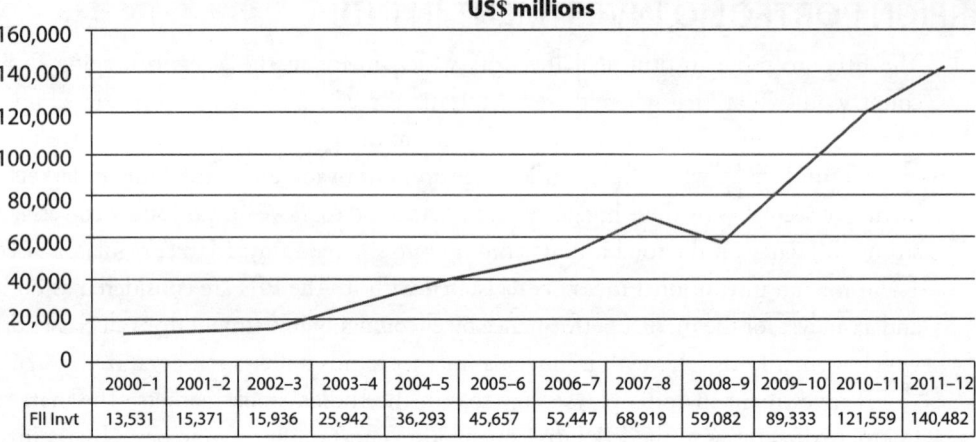

Figure 16-8
FII Portfolio Cumulative Investment

SUMMARY

International capital markets are becoming more and more popular and accessible for MNCs that help them reduce cost of capital and increase their International competiveness. At the same time investors are becoming more and more literate and investing more and more. The speed and transaction costs are constantly coming down with reduced capital controls offering global opportunities and expanding the scope of investment avenues by improved product design and efficient financial intermediation.

The firms are increasingly mobilizing capital through cross-border offerings in the primary markets and listings on international exchanges providing liquidity and depth to markets. The market capitalization of stock exchanges of the world is estimated at US$64 trillion in 2013 with about the same volume of trading. The capital markets of developing nations though far behind that of developed nations are fast closing the gap in share of market capitalization as well as in volume of trading. The returns on international investment get modified by the appreciation or depreciation of the currency of investment. If currency of investment appreciates the return in the home currency increases while its depreciation would reduce the return.

The risk in international investment is dependent upon (a) market risk, (b) exchange rate risk, and (c) correlation between market risk and exchange rate risk. While the expected returns measured in home currency is the sum of the expected market return measured in currency of investment and expected exchange rate gains/losses, the same cannot be said about the risk of international investment.

Since the risk is not additive in international investment, it forms the basis of international portfolio diversification. The rationale for international diversification is the low coefficient of correlations between stock markets of the world. Despite financial market integration, the capital markets of a country continue to be largely governed by the local factors rather than global factors.

The risk return trade-off is measured by Sharpe ratio and is dependent upon the correlation coefficient. International investment is desirable when (a) risk premium in currency of investment is more, (b) foreign investment has low risk (standard deviation), and (c) if there is low correlation in home and foreign markets.

QUESTIONS

16-1 In terms of risk a domestic portfolio of equity shares is always less risky than an international portfolio of stocks. Do you agree with the statement? Provide justification.

16-2 How would returns in the home currency change if (a) investing currency depreciates, and (b) investing currency appreciates?

PROBLEMS

16-1 **Home Currency Returns**

An investor from the USA is contemplating investing in one of the following four markets abroad. The expected return in local currency and expected change in the exchange rate with US dollar are as follows:

	India	Britain	Germany	China
Expected returns, %	12.0	8.0	9.0	10.0
Expected change in exchange rate, %	−2.0	+2.0	+1.2	−0.5

Note: ± means appreciation/depreciation of currency with respect to US dollar.

The investor has allocated the funds of US$10 million in the ratio of 4:3:2:1 in order of highest to lowest expected return. Find how much should be invested in each market.

16-2 **Volatility for Investment Abroad**

Refer to P 16-1. The markets in the four countries have the following:

	India	Britain	Germany	China
Volatility, %	15.0	6.0	5.0	10.0
Exchange rate volatility, %	10.0	2.0	8.0	0.5
Correlation between stock market and exchange rate	−0.5	0.2	0.3	0.05

Find out the volatility the US investor faces in each of the four markets.

16-3 **Risk Premium for Investment Abroad**

Continuing with the data given in P 16-1 and P 16-2 a further study of securities markets has revealed the following coefficients of correlation with US securities markets:

	India	Britain	Germany	China
Correlation with US markets	0.3	0.6	0.5	0.2

Find what minimum risk premium is required to invest in each of the markets if the US risk premium is 8% and the US market volatility is 12%.

Foreign Direct Investment

LEARNING OBJECTIVES

This chapter aims at

- explaining the theory of absolute and comparative advantage as basis for international trade
- describing the meaning of terms-of-trade and how benefits of foreign investment may be shared
- understanding why multinational corporations make foreign investment
- describing how foreign investment benefits the recipient nation
- describing why nations control foreign investment
- understanding the various modes of making an entry into a foreign nation
- understanding the trends of foreign direct investment capital flows worldwide and in India

CONTENTS

Introduction
Theory of International Trade
Theory of Comparative Advantage
    Sharing Benefits of International Trade
    Exchange Rate and Terms-of-trade
    Limitations of Theory of Comparative Advantage
Motives for Foreign Investment
    Imperfect Market
    Horizontal Expansion
    Vertical Expansion
    Risk Diversification

Benefits of Foreign Direct Investment
Barriers to International Trade and Foreign Direct Investment
    Tariff Barriers
    Non-tariff Barriers
    Protection and Need
Modes of Foreign Direct Investment
Foreign Direct Investment in India

Annexure A17-1: Trends for Foreign Direct Investment in India

INTRODUCTION

MNCs invest in several locations and countries as a strategic policy. These investments relate to moving not only to stable, developed countries but large inflows also sometimes take place in developing and poor countries not having stable political and economic environments. Expansion to these locations is perceived to be more risky because of the unknown environments, language barriers, cultural gaps, differences in legal systems, social customs, and practices. Yet MNCs have been growing at a fast rate.

At a macro level, nations impose several restrictions on foreign direct and portfolio investments, and trade due to several political and economic reasons, which are very appealing to public. These impediments to foreign investment have their roots in several interrelated and complex factors. The restrictions are imposed sometimes in the name of associated national honour and prestige like the need to be self-sufficient. Sometimes foreign investment is checked to protect domestic producers preserving technology and employment. Foreign import is often discouraged by imposing tariffs not only as a policy of protectionism, but also as raising resource base for the government to permit developmental expenditure and reallocation of wealth from the rich to the poor. Yet another reason justifying imposing controls for foreign investment and trade is the need to prevent the perceived misuse of national resources if handed over to foreign nationals.

THEORY OF INTERNATIONAL TRADE

Leaving apart the political, cultural, and financial reasons controlling the foreign trade, we examine here the economic theory that justifies promotion of international investment and trade in the perspective of increasing national and world welfare. The most ancient theory that highlighted the basic principles of international trade was propounded by the famous economist Adam Smith. Called the theory of absolute advantage, it emphasised that nations should export goods that they can produce more efficiently than others, and import goods that others can produce more efficiently than them.

For simplicity of exposition, let us assume that there are only two nations in the world, that is, India and the USA, and only two commodities, that is, grain and cloth. The cost as measured in terms of the number of labour units required to produce one unit of each in the two nations are as follows:

Labour Units or Cost/Unit	Grain	Cloth
USA	4	6
India	8	8

The USA can produce one unit of grain with four labour units while India takes eight labour units to do the same. Similarly, to produce one unit of cloth, the USA and India take six and eight labour units, respectively. Since the USA can produce both grain and cloth with lesser units of labour (lesser cost), it is said to have absolute advantage over India in both the products. Therefore, India should produce none and the USA must produce both. With no international trade, both the nations would produce both the products only for themselves and meet their own requirements, without engaging in trade with one another. According to the theory of absolute advantage, if one nation could produce one product more efficiently than the other, there would have been scope for international trade. Since India held no absolute advantage over the USA in either of the products, there was no scope for international trade.

Under such circumstances both the economies would be in balance meeting their own requirements from indigenously produced goods by deploying the labour workforce among the various products needed. Assume that labour force in India and the USA are deployed as shown in Table 17-1. It is further assumed that allocation of labour is such that economies are at full employment achieving the prosperity as they could by themselves. No need of products from other nations is felt. Under such circumstances, trade among nations would neither be felt nor take place.

Table 17-1
Cost of Production, Deployment, and Production in India & USA without Trade

	Labour Hours or Cost/Unit		Labour Units Deployed in		Total Production	
	Grain	Cloth	Grain	Cloth	Grain	Cloth
USA	4	6	800	1,800	200	300
India	8	8	2,800	800	350	100
Total Production/Requirement					550	400

We observe from Table 17-1 that requirement of grain in the USA is 200 units, which is met by deploying 800 labour units, of the total labour units of 2,600 available in the USA. The remaining 1,800 labour units are allocated for production of cloth meeting their full requirement of 300 units. Similarly, in India the total requirements of 350 units of grain and 100 units of cloth are met by deploying 2,800 units of labour in grain production and remaining 800 labour units in cloth production.

THEORY OF COMPARATIVE ADVANTAGE

The view propagated by Adam Smith was held as correct for long till a different view was given by another economist David Ricardo. He demonstrated that despite a nation holding absolute advantage in both the products there existed a scope of trade provided the cost are measured in relative terms, that is, price of one commodity in terms of another, rather than in absolute terms.

Using the same data we may measure the cost of grain and cloth in terms of one another in a nation. If the USA has to produce one extra unit of grain it has to give up $4/6 = 0.67$ units of cloth. If India has to do the same, it foregoes $8/8 = 1.00$ units of cloth. Therefore, in relative terms grain production is cheaper in the USA than in India. Similarly to produce one extra unit of cloth, the cost paid is sacrifice of $6/4 = 1.5$ units of grain in the USA, and $8/8 =$

1.00 units of grain in India. Therefore, relatively it is cheaper to produce cloth in India than in the USA.

In terms of relative prices, the USA holds comparative advantage in production of grain and India has the same in production of cloth. Accordingly, the following reallocation of resources should be done:

1. Since it is cheaper to produce grain in the USA than in India, the former must deploy all labour to grain production.
2. Since India can produce cloth cheaper than the USA in terms of relative prices, it must allocate all resources to cloth production.
3. After meeting all their requirements of the products produced in the respective nations, the surplus can be exported to the other nation.

If done so, all the workforce is deployed in production of grain in the USA, whereas India allocates all its labour force to cloth production. The outcome of such reallocation would be as shown in Table 17-2.

Table 17-2
Production, Requirement of Products with Deployment Based on Comparative Advantage

	Relative Prices		Labour Units Deployed in		Total Production	
	Grain	Cloth	Grain	Cloth	Grain	Cloth
USA	4/6 = 0.67	6/4 = 1.50	2,600	–	650	–
India	8/8 = 1.00	8/8 = 1.00	–	3600	–	450
Total Production					650	450
Total Requirement					550	400
Excess of Production over Requirement					100	50

It may be observed from the reallocation of resources based on comparative advantage that production of all the goods would be in excess of aggregate requirements. Despite USA holding absolute advantage in both the products, it would have comparative advantage in producing and exporting one product. Further even when India has no absolute advantage over the USA in either of the products, it too has comparative advantage in producing and exporting. Extra grain of 100 units is available and 50 units of extra cloth are available from the earlier position. Increased production of goods should enhance public welfare in both the economies. Without loss of conclusion this can easily be extended to all products and all nations. Therefore, international trade would be beneficial because of the following reasons:

1. The extra availability of the goods would lead to enhanced consumption by present users and/or introduce new users deprived of these goods earlier. Both these aspects would be good for the economies for growth of GDP and welfare of people in both the nations.

2. Producing larger quantity at one place rather than producing lesser quantities at two different places would make the learning curve advantages and economies of scale exploited, leading to further reduction of cost, making products cheaper and more affordable.
3. As one scales the learning curve the nations would develop specialization and product improvement due to innovations would take place. Therefore products of better quality with lesser price would be available.

Sharing Benefits of International Trade

The gains of extra production need to be shared between two countries through trading of commodities among themselves. In our case grain and cloth need to be exchanged for one another between India and the USA. This essentially implies determining the exchange ratio for cloth and grain, that is, how much grain for how much of cloth. This is referred to as **terms-of-trade**.

The benefits of trade, that is, sharing of surplus production would depend upon the ratio of exchange of goods in terms of one another. We examine two extreme scenarios if the terms-of-trade are settled at (a) US prices or (b) Indian prices. At relative prices of USA, 1.5 units of grain equal 1.0 unit of cloth. If the trade between India and the USA is done at the exchange rate of 1.5 units of grain for 1.0 unit of cloth, the USA imports its requirement of cloth of 300 units from India by exporting 450 units of grain. At relative prices of the USA, the trade causes no detriment to the USA. The exchange ratio of trade at 1.5 units of grain per unit of cloth USA gets the same quantity of cloth as it can replace by shifting grain production. Under such a case the entire benefit of surplus production goes to India with no loss to USA as may be seen from Table 17-3.

Table 17-3
Terms-of-trade at USA Prices: 1.5 units of Grain for 1.00 unit of Cloth

	Available	Export (−) /Import (+)	Required	Benefit
USA's Position				
Grain	650	−450	200	−
Cloth	−	+300	300	−
India's Position				
Grain	−	+450	350	100
Cloth	450	−300	100	50

However if the terms-of-trade are done at the relative prices of India, that is, 1.0 units of grain for 1.0 units of cloth, the situation reverses and the benefit of surplus production goes entirely to the USA. Here the terms-of-trade are same as what India can do of its own, and hence the benefit goes to the USA but at no detriment to India. The trade at exchange ratio determined by relative prices in India is demonstrated in Table 17-4.

Table 17-4
Terms-of-trade at Indian Prices: 1.0 unit of Grain for 1.00 unit of Cloth

	Available	Export (−)/Import (+)	Required	Benefit
USA's Position				
Grain	650	−350	200	100
Cloth	−	+350	300	50
India's Position				
Grain	−	+350	350	−
Cloth	450	−350	100	−

While it is established that international trade would enhance the world welfare, the issue of sharing of the surplus remains contentious. In extreme exchange ratios the benefit belonged to one nation but it did not imply loss to another. Terms-of-trade would decide the sharing of the benefits among the nations. In the context of current example it is likely that the each country values its own product more than what it actually deserves. By the same token the same country values the other's products less valuable than what it deserves. Terms- of-trade would indeed be a question of bargaining between the nations involved.

If the benefits of the international trade are to be shared equally the exchange ratio that needs to be made is 400 units of grain for 325 units of cloth, that is, 1.23 units of grain per unit of cloth. Refer to Table 17-5.

Table 17-5
Terms-of-trade for Sharing Benefits Equally

	Grain	Cloth	Grain	Cloth
	USA's Position		India's Position	
Consumption	250	300	350	100
Surplus Shared	50	25	50	25
Available	650	−	−	450
Export (−)/Import (+)	−400	325	400	−325

Exchange Rate and Terms-of-trade

We may simply replace the labour hours by the cost of production on monetary terms and examine changes in the exchange rate. Assume that after accounting for all factors of production paid in local currency the cost which reflects the same relative prices as was the case in terms of labour hours, are as follows:

Cost/Unit	Grain	Cloth
USA (US$/Unit)	1.00	1.50
India (₹/Unit)	100	100

Further assume that terms-of-trade is fixed at 1.25 units of grain for 1 unit of cloth. If the initial exchange rate were to be ₹50/$ both grain and cloth would be cheaper in USA creating huge demand for both grain and cloth in India. This is clearly unsustainable because the terms-of-trade of 1.25 grains per cloth provides two exchange rates. For goods to cost same in monetary terms India exporting cloth gets US$1.50 spending ₹100. For importing 1.25 units of grain India pays $1.25 saving ₹100. Therefore, India pays extra $0.25 at the prescribed terms-of-trade. India runs a huge trade deficit with equivalent trade surplus in USA. Also there is huge unemployment in India.

This clearly warrants that initial exchange rate must change, or terms-of-trade must change or a combination of changes in both. The market forces with no government intervention would create huge demand for US dollars in India raising its value. Similarly, labour and other factors of production with huge pressure on them would become more expensive in USA raising cost of production. This would continue till both the countries find comparative advantage and terms-of-trade.

Imposing Tariff Intervention by government by imposing tariffs would inhibit trade in quantity and comparative pricing of the products. This would cause the prices of the same commodity differ in two countries. While grain costing US$1.00 in USA costs ₹100 in India and exchange rate is ₹50/$ India may impose 100% import duty on grain so as to cost $2.00 in India to maintain purchasing power of Indian rupee.

Limitations of Theory of Comparative Advantage

One may find several holes in the theory of comparative advantage in this modern era. We examine some of them here.

Mobility of Factors of Production In this simple exposition, we assumed migration of labour from one industry to another at no cost. At the same time we assumed complete immobility of labour across borders. In modern age this indeed is not true. We often find people moving to different locations keeping their job profile same rather than changing job profile at the same location. We see software engineers in India moving all over the world keeping profession same rather than remaining in India and change profession. The sacrifice for the free international trade and development of specialization cannot come free of cost.

Product Differentiation Another feature of modern age may also defy the theory of comparative advantage is the product differentiation that causes consumption patterns to change despite the commodity or product serving the same basic need. What may apply for basic commodities may not hold good for highly differentiated products, such as automobiles, television sets, and mobile phones. Several brands with varied features have created vastly different and highly segmented markets with different perceived values, not measurable in monetary terms, of the same product.

Shifting Relative Advantage The theory of comparative advantage rests on the premise that international trade takes place through movement of goods across borders, creating specialization and deriving economies of scale. Over time the relative advantage may shift from one nation to another. For example, the advantage of producing cars in the USA first shifted from the USA to Europe, then to Japan, and how sourcing components from India and China. Similarly, advantage in textiles has moved from affluent USA and Europe to poorer nations of Asia.

Technology and Services The theory of comparative advantage is based on movement of goods. With increased share of GDP coming from services sector, which perhaps are not as mobile as goods, the advantage may shift from one nation to another. With technological advancements, the jobs can shift from one location to another, for example, software services, call centres, etc.

Tariffs and Barriers to Trade Imposition of tariff and other barriers to trade are not necessarily governed by preserving the comparative advantage. Instead they are guided by exactly the opposite inasmuch as developing skills, learning and reducing dependence on others. They create artificial difference in the relative prices. Imposition of tariff has been defended on the grounds of (a) providing protection to domestic industry, (b) creating employment, (c) developing human resources, (d) generating revenue for government for propelling growth through development expenditure, etc. All these reasons have similar economic consequences as propagated by the theory of comparative advantage. Which of the philosophy is more desirable is a moot point.

However in conclusion we may say that the merits of the comparative advantage to determine international trade remain intact despite several conflicting policies. All the deficiencies as mentioned above cannot replace the argument of the theory of comparative advantage in entirety because all policies would remain transitory in nature, and would ultimately have to be guided by comparative advantage.

MOTIVES FOR FOREIGN INVESTMENT

Besides the theory of comparative advantage explained earlier, the motives for FDIs can be many. Not necessarily opposing the comparative advantage principle these motives are easier to see and strategize. These factors include desire to grow, cut costs, increase market share, avail incentives, exploit technology, command supply chains, etc.

Imperfect Market

Motives for investment abroad mostly have their origins in the imperfect markets—for products, factors of production, and capital. The markets for factors of production such as labour, capital, and technology are imperfect across the world as they do not cost the same everywhere. In Asia, Africa, and Latin America while labour is cheap, capital is scarce. Minerals are abundant in Africa but they lack technology and infrastructure to exploit them. The literacy level in terms of English language is high in India but opportunities for commensurate employment are few and scarce.

Capital, education, and skills are high in the USA and Europe but they are too expensive. These distortions and differences in availability and pricing of factors of production create investment opportunities for MNCs. Different nations are endowed differently in terms of natural resources, human skills, and capital. The motivations to expand to markets abroad are mainly governed by exploitation of these opportunities created by imperfect markets for factors of production. On a broader scale, MNCs are only attempting to bridge the gap due to imperfect markets.

Imperfect markets for factors of production lead to strategies centred around cost reduction.

With growing competition the margins of multinationals are shrinking and hence the need for survival gains priority. Almost all multinationals from Japan, such as Sony and Panasonic in electronics, and Toyota and Honda in automobiles have set up operations in other Asian countries like Thailand to exploit cheap but skilled labour to compete on cost of production globally. Volkswagen of Germany started producing cars in China to exploit huge market which possibly was too expensive to be served by export.

Imperfect markets are not confined to factors of production alone. There could be imperfect markets for the finished products as well. What is considered unwanted in one part of the world may be useful to other parts of the world. Products become obsolete in developed economies, while the same product remains useful in the developing world. Examples include automobiles, mobile phones, computers, etc. which continuously become obsolete in the developed world but are continued to be used in the developing world.

Horizontal Expansion

Initially, MNCs resorted to horizontal expansion, that is, setting up facilities to meet needs of specific geographical areas. It was essentially a duplication of facility. It emphasized on serving different markets and the underlying motive is expansion of revenue and markets. The MNCs aim at creating new sources of demand for their products in new and unexplored market. When the markets become saturated at home, the firms have to find new avenues of demand abroad. Japanese auto makers Toyota and Honda set up facilities in the USA to cater to American markets. The trade-off was between allocation of fixed cost at new location and the saving of transportation cost. The strategy of horizontal expansion was also followed to overcome trade barriers. The transportation cost with tariffs increased the cost of export to a point where MNCs chose to set up facilities for production abroad rather than export.

Vertical Expansion

Of late MNCs have started using vertical expansion, that is, exploiting cost advantages in various locations deriving home the economies of scale and catering to all locations. The motive is driven by reduction in cost by specialization and allocation of fixed overheads over larger volume. The reduction in cost is supposed to overcome the shipping cost. A large number of MNCs are following this strategy where successive stages of production are carried out at different locations with output of one serving as input for another.

Sony of Japan presents a classic example of both horizontal and vertical expansion. They have several plant locations stretching from Brazil to China, South Korea to USA, and India to England producing different items all over and meeting demands for their products worldwide.

CONCEPTS IN PRACTICE
Trading Old as New

TOYOTA AND HYUNDAI: REFURBISHING FOR POOR NATIONS

World renowned car manufacturers such as Toyota and Hyundai have found a new strategy to create a new source of demand for their products in less developed countries, which are otherwise large but lack purchasing power. On the other hand, they have established markets in developed economies characterized by good purchasing power fancied with newer and newer features in the products. These car manufacturers are aggressively adopting strategies to exploit purchasing power differentials that have created imperfections in the finished goods markets.

These automakers buy used cars from rich and developed nations in exchange of new and superior models, refurbish these old/used cars, attach a warranty to them, and offer services as if they would do for the new ones, and sell them to users in developing world at substantially low prices. These models are extremely popular world over but new cars would not be affordable in less developed nations of Asia and Africa. By adopting such strategies these car manufacturers achieve dual purpose of satisfying customers with newer and improved versions in the rich developed world and maintain the brand loyalty in developed economies, while at the same time create their own brand in the emerging economies.

Risk Diversification

Besides making strategic decisions for investing in a foreign country for the purpose of cost reduction or revenue/market expansion, another natural outcome of such investment is reduction of risk. Because world markets are not integrated the coefficient of correlation between them is rather low. This is because the business cycles in two countries are likely to be asynchronous. This would render stability to revenue, profit and cash flows of the multinational corporation.

In case of investment in two countries, we may apply the portfolio theory. The combined return would be weighted average of the returns. However, the risk is not a weighted average

CONCEPTS IN PRACTICE
Diversifying through Foreign Direct Investment

BHARTI BIDS FOR ZAIN SUCCESSFULLY

Bharti Airtel's quest to become an international telecom player got a boost when it successfully bid $10.7 billion for acquiring Zain's African assets in an all cash deal. Only two months back in January 2010 Bharti had acquired 70% in Warid, the telecom operator in Bangladesh for $300 million—a meagre amount as compared to Zain's acquisition. Recognizing the fact that Africa has huge reserves of untapped resources and investment opportunities, Bharti ventured in the African markets despite the increased perceived risk with African continent. Earlier it had failed twice in the attempts to acquire a larger player in Africa namely MTN, the South Africa based telecom operator. The attempts failed due to legal and other administrative hassles.

The perception of risk in the markets can be estimated by the following remarks made by some merchant bankers immediately after the announcement:

Morgan Stanley: The acquisition would increase Bharti's net debt to earnings before interest, taxes, depreciation, and amortization (EBITDA) to 2.4x in FY 2011, assuming full debt funding, and lower EPS for next two years by 25% and 17%, respectively.

Credit Suisse: By improving operations and through adequate investments, Bharti could help Zain gain 1,300–400 basis points market share and improve EBITDA margins 400–500 basis points in the next three years. This could lead to EBITDA of $1.2 billion by 2012.

Bank of America Merrill Lynch: Monetizing their rich valuation of Zain-Africa will require a complex interplay of consumer behaviour, capex intensity, marketing skills, and regulatory support.

Goldman Sachs: The deal is 5–26% dilutive in the first year. Bharti's return on invested cash should decline for the next couple of years, implying its investment in Zain would impact its ability to generate an immediate return in near term.

According to Sunil Mittal, CMD of Bharti, the agreement is a landmark for global telecom industry. 'More importantly with this acquisition Bharti would be transformed in to a truly global company. We believe that strength of our brand coupled with our unique business model will allow us to unlock the potential of emerging markets. This is the continent to watch out for future,' said Mr Mittal.

The comparative of Bharti and Zain are as follows:

	BHARTI	ZAIN
Market Capitalization	$26.70 billion	$16.20 billion
Subscribers	125 million	70 million
Revenue		$6.96 billion in 2008
Countries	India	24 countries (15 countries in Africa)

What Bharti has obtained for $10.7 billion are (a) footprint in Africa in 15 nations, (b) 42 million customers out of total of 70 million Zain's customers in Africa's 15 countries, (c) revenue from African operations of $2.73 billion, and (d) EBITDA of $869 million and Net Profit of $112 million.

Some of the risks associated with the acquisition would not look as high if one considers the position in which Bharti is in. In its domestic market in India it was facing declining Average Revenue per User (ARPU) with Reliance Communications and Vodafone competing very hard. Further Bharti has been successful in operating a low-cost business model that is extremely suitable for African operations and rules out threats from telecom operators in West or USA. Bharti's tariffs are 10 times lower in India than in Africa. Also if Bharti upgrades to 3G network simultaneously in India and Africa it would offer significant advantage of increased purchasing power with telecom equipment suppliers, that is, Ericsson, Alcatel, etc. However, the challenge is to execute the low-cost model because of the user density. African market is significantly less than Indian markets in size and hence ability to replicate low-cost model is doubtful. Population density is 5–20% of Indian circles implying more investment in reaching the same customer base. Capex needed would be 3–5 times of Indian operations.

The threats in the environment included (a) slowing growth in African markets, (b) loss making Zain Africa despite 35% penetration, (c) significantly increasing investment from other operators in Africa (MTN and Globacom), and (d) high proportion of intangibles (40% of Zain's assets) resulting from many takeovers in the past which are difficult to put them in productive use.

Source: Compiled on the basis of news articles in *The Times of India*, *Hindustan Times*, and *Business Line*.

of the individual risk but instead depends upon the coefficient of correlation. Consider a multinational firm that has operations in two countries that have coefficient of correlation at 0.40 with the following returns and risk:

	Country 1	Country 2
Expected return, $\check{R}$	12%	18%
Expected risk, σ	10%	15%
Coefficient of correlation, ρ_{12}	0.40	

Assuming 40% is invested in Country 1 and remaining 60% in Country 2 the returns would be

Portfolio return, $\check{R}_p = w_1\check{R}_1 + w_2\check{R}_2$
$= 0.40 \times 12\% + 0.60 \times 18 = 15.60\%$

The portfolio risk, given by variance is

Portfolio risk, $\sigma_p^2 = w_1^2\sigma_1^2 + w_2^2\sigma_2^2 + w_1w_2\rho_{12}\sigma_1\sigma_2$
$= 0.40^2 \times 12^2 + 0.60^2 \times 15^2 + 0.60 \times 0.40 \times 0.40 \times 10 \times 15$
$= 118.44$

Portfolio risk, standard deviation, $\sigma_p = \sqrt{118.44} = 10.88\%$

It is interesting to note one would have expected the portfolio risk of the asset to be somewhere between 12% and 18%. However, the portfolio risk is 10.88%, that is, lesser than the lower of the standard deviations of returns in two countries. The portfolio risk would be weighted average only when the two markets are perfectly positively correlated (coefficient of correlation = 1).

Exercise 17-1
Rupee Return for Bharti

With Bharti's acquisition of Zain, the firm shall be operating in 15 African nations. The profits of all 15 currencies would be converted in US dollars before repatriation to India. In some of these countries, US dollar is acceptable as their local currency. The returns in US dollar are estimated at 13%. What would be the returns for Bharti in rupee terms if rupee is expected to depreciate against US dollar by 5%? The standard deviation of exchange rate is 12%. If the returns of African operations have correlation with exchange rate of 0.50, what is the risk of rupee returns for Bharti?

Solution

The rupee return of Bharti would be

$$R_e = \frac{S_1}{S_0}(1+R_i) - 1$$

$$= (1+g)(1+R_i) - 1 = 1.05 \times 1.13 - 1 = 0.1865 = 18.65\%$$

$$\sigma_e^2 = \sigma_i^2 + \sigma_g^2 + 2\rho_{ig}\sigma_i\sigma_g = 20^2 + 12^2 + 2 \times 0.50 \times 20 \times 12 = 664$$

$$\sigma_e = \sqrt{664} \equiv 25.77\%$$

Exercise 17-2
Diversification of Risk for Bharti

With Bharti's acquisition of Zain, the firm shall be operating in Africa besides domestic markets of India. Assume that risk of operation in African markets as measured by standard deviation is 20% while for Indian markets it is 10%. Business from Zain would constitute 30% of the total. The coefficient of correlation between Indian and African markets is low at 0.30. What do you think is the risk faced by Bharti after its acquisition of Zain?

Solution

The portfolio of Bharti now consists of two assets—the Indian operations with 70% proportion and African operations with 30% proportion. The aggregate risk of the portfolio would be

Portfolio risk, variance $\sigma_p^2 = 0.30^2 \times 20^2 + 0.70^2 \times 10^2 + 0.70 \times 0.30 \times 0.30 \times 10 \times 20 = 97.60$

Portfolio risk, standard deviation, $\sigma_p \equiv \sqrt{97.60} \equiv 9.88\%$

It is interesting to note that despite entering a more risky market, the aggregate risk faced by Bharti is less than that of its Indian operations.

BENEFITS OF FOREIGN DIRECT INVESTMENT

The FDI is a key element that represents economic integration of the world. Increased flow of capital across nations should reflect that imperfect markets of the factors of production as well as inequality of consumption and purchasing power across nations are being exploited by multinational corporations. Ultimately, it must lead to increased economic convergence and gaps between developed and developing worlds must come down over a period of time. Of course if barriers to trade and investment were to be absent, the free market forces governed by business considerations alone would enhance the welfare of the world in a faster and better way.

From Figures 17-1 and 17-2 we observe that FDI inflows and outflows, respectively for USA, European Union, and BRICS showed increasing trend from 2004 to 2007 but declined thereafter for the next two years possibly due to financial crisis of 2008. However, it has again started looking up.

The growth of inward FDI has been good for both EU 27 and BRICS nations; perhaps for different reasons. Major destinations of FDI in EU 27 are Germany, France, and Belgium which are having a rather liberal and smoother capital flows attracting investment, whereas for BRICS the motivation of FDI inflows are their larger markets and better growth rates though the regulatory regimes may not be as conducive as that of EU 27.

The benefits of FDI for recipient nation are manifold. With increased globalization the nation stands to gain many tangible and intangible advantages. Besides providing wider consumer choices in terms of improved products, FDI inwards

(a) provides employment to local residents and contributes greatly to human development,
(b) increases capital base and equivalently releases domestic capital to be put to alternate use,

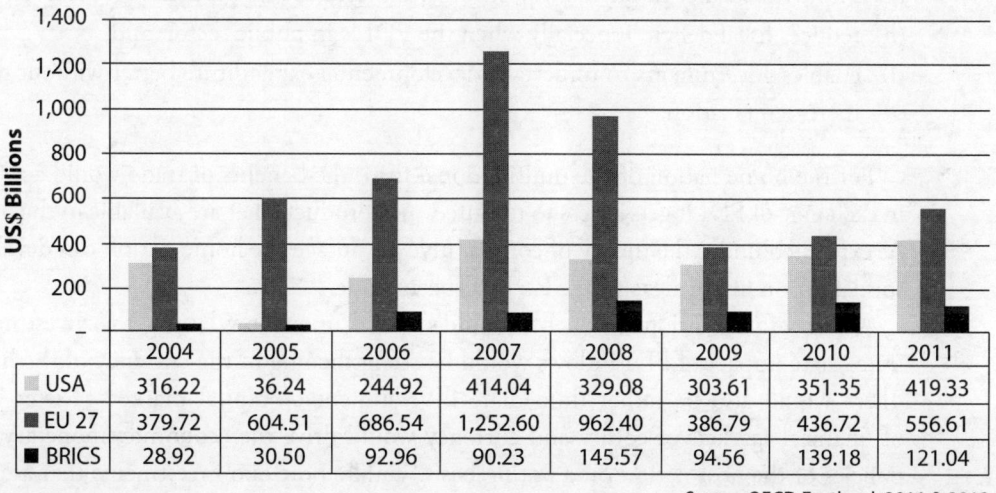

	2004	2005	2006	2007	2008	2009	2010	2011
USA	316.22	36.24	244.92	414.04	329.08	303.61	351.35	419.33
EU 27	379.72	604.51	686.54	1,252.60	962.40	386.79	436.72	556.61
BRICS	28.92	30.50	92.96	90.23	145.57	94.56	139.18	121.04

Source: OECD Factbook 2011 & 2012

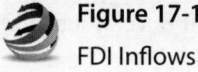

Figure 17-1
FDI Inflows

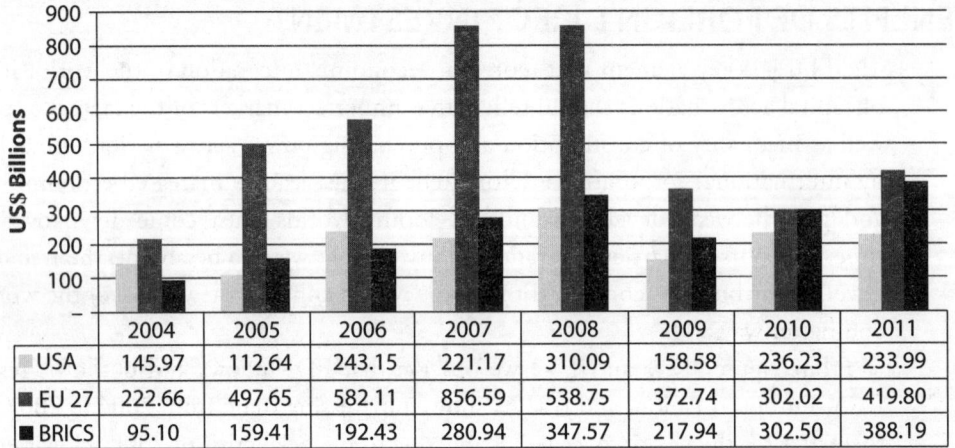

	2004	2005	2006	2007	2008	2009	2010	2011
USA	145.97	112.64	243.15	221.17	310.09	158.58	236.23	233.99
EU 27	222.66	497.65	582.11	856.59	538.75	372.74	302.02	419.80
BRICS	95.10	159.41	192.43	280.94	347.57	217.94	302.50	388.19

Source: OECD Factbook 2011 & 2012

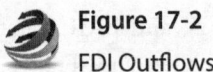

Figure 17-2
FDI Outflows

(c) makes domestic industry more competitive and efficient, both locally and globally, due to increased competition,

(d) brings improved and better technology increasing efficiency, producing better products at lower prices,

(e) results in use of hitherto unexploited resources due to lack of capital or technology or skills,

(f) enhances income and consumption levels propelling all round economic growth,

(g) improves balance of payment position and increases foreign exchange reserves,

(h) reduces fiscal deficit, especially when the FDI is in public sector, and

(i) enables governments to undertake developmental expenditure better without resorting to increased taxation.

For the home nation of the multinational firm, the benefits of trade would accrue because in exchange of FDI it gets access to resources and products that are available in the host nation. As explained under the theory of comparative advantage the home nation can develop further specialization in the areas where FDI has been made.

All the aforementioned benefits would depend upon how lasting the investment is. The immediate impact of FDI inflows would be strengthening of the currency of the host nation. There would also be rather immediate development of capital markets. Better integration of financial markets of equity and currency would drive the economic, monetary, and trade policies of the host nation on a lasting basis. Unlike portfolio investments that are essentially volatile in nature, FDIs provide a more stable, longer lasting, and more beneficial impact on the economy. Figure 17-3 depicts FDI inflows to some prominent developing nations.

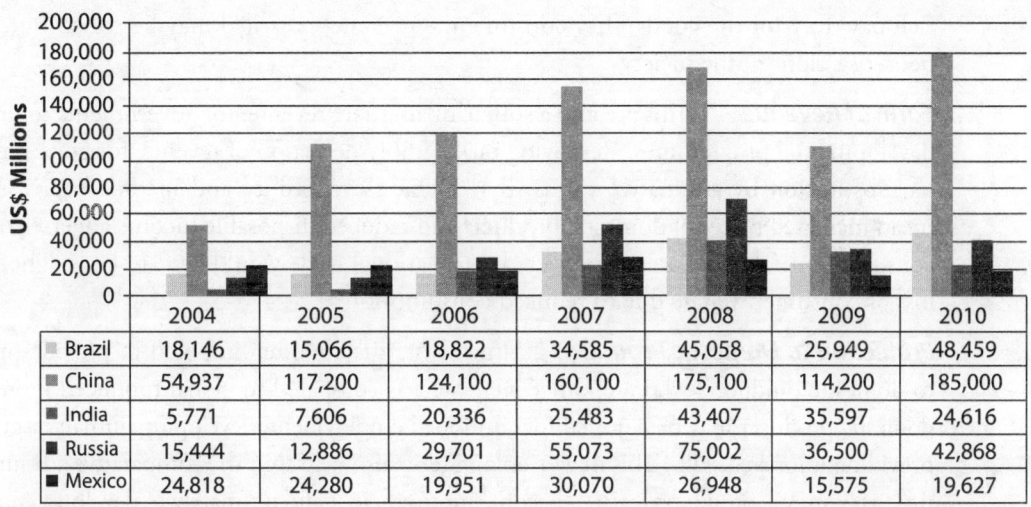

Figure 17-3
FDI Inward Select Countries

	2004	2005	2006	2007	2008	2009	2010
Brazil	18,146	15,066	18,822	34,585	45,058	25,949	48,459
China	54,937	117,200	124,100	160,100	175,100	114,200	185,000
India	5,771	7,606	20,336	25,483	43,407	35,597	24,616
Russia	15,444	12,886	29,701	55,073	75,002	36,500	42,868
Mexico	24,818	24,280	19,951	30,070	26,948	15,575	19,627

Source: OECD Factbook 2011

BARRIERS TO INTERNATIONAL TRADE AND FOREIGN DIRECT INVESTMENT

Governments in various nations impose several restrictions on free trade and foreign investment, both inward and outward. Such restrictions no doubt take away the benefits the society gets through free international trade. These barriers to trade create further imperfections in the markets of products, factors of production, and capital. National priorities and compulsions such as employment creation, skill development, and raising resources overshadow the supposed benefits of international trade that are sacrificed. These restrictions are also aimed at creating a level playing field for trading nations.

These barriers are often in the form of imposing quantitative and qualitative restrictions referred to as tariff and non-tariff barriers, differential tax rates, sectoral caps on foreign investment, outsourcing norms, minimum export commitment, employment to local personnel, restriction on capital flows, etc. It is hard to say that these restrictive policies on foreign trade and investment achieve the objectives as stated above.

Tariff Barriers

Tariff-based restrictions may be justified on the grounds that these are imposed not with the intentions of restricting foreign trade. As tariffs serve several other purposes too though adversely affecting foreign trade and investment, the benefits may outweigh the loss due to restrictive foreign trade. Some of the benefits justifying tariffs are as follows:

Socialistic Objective Imposition of tariffs on luxury goods may be defended to achieve equality of income and bridging the gap between rich and poor sections of the society. While

rich pay duty for the goods, they consume the revenue so earned may be redistributed in the poorer sections of the society.

Form of Revenue Tariffs are also a source of alternate revenue for governments to undertake developmental programmes. Removing tariffs imply depletion of revenue for government and its substitution by alternative forms, that is, raise excise duty and income tax. This would mean increased prices of domestic products and reduced disposable income adversely affecting consumption. The loss due to restricted international trade would have to be weighed against loss of consumer welfare due to reduced consumption.

Protection to Domestic Producers Similarly, tariffs are often imposed to provide protection to domestic producers who are rather inefficient as compared to global producer. Protection to domestic producer may be required for continued employment, developing human resource, and providing improved skills. This may over long term also help shift the comparative advantage over time as domestic producers learn to become more efficient and ultimately to develop a competitive advantage. Unless given the opportunity in the form of protection local producers cannot demonstrate their willingness to learn and outperform more efficient producers around the globe.

Non-tariff Barriers

Non-tariff barriers are in the form of regulations that impose restriction of foreign investment and attempt to direct the flow of FDI in specific sectors. This invariably adds to the red tape which becomes a deterrent for MNCs to expand. The process of controlling the flow of FDI is subjected to various regulatory approvals of the projects and placing limitations on foreign ownership and management by prescribing extent of equity holding.

Other constraints for FDI inwards in a nation are conditions such as (a) hiring of local people, (b) binding export commitment, (c) local sourcing of raw materials (d) limiting repatriation of earnings, and (e) a differential and discriminatory tax structure that are more in the nature of ascertaining that the foreign investment should not only be beneficial but also must be perceived to be so by serving the other social causes. These conditions also assure a nation that benefits of international trade, which are futuristic and uncertain do indeed serve the national cause by providing protection to local industry and creating employment.

Organisation for Economic Co-operation and Development (OECD) has developed an index of restrictiveness for the openness of the economy. The FDI Regulatory Restrictiveness Index (FDI Index) measures statutory restrictions on FDI in 57 countries and is used as a summary measure of openness of the economy.

Four types of measures are covered by the FDI Restrictiveness Index: (i) foreign equity restrictions, (ii) screening and prior approval requirements, (iii) rules for key personnel, and (iv) other restrictions on the operation of foreign enterprises. The highest score for any measure in any sector is 1 (the measure fully restricts foreign investment in the sector) and the lowest is 0 (there are no regulatory impediments to FDI in the sector). The score for each sector is obtained by adding the scores for all four types of measures, with the constraint that their sum is also capped at a value of 1. The Index covers 22 sectors. It excludes implementation and institutional quality. Table 17-6 briefly describes the scoring system of OECD for developing FDI Restrictiveness Index.

Table 17-6
Scoring of Restrictions of FDI Index 2010

Scoring Parameter	Score
(i) Foreign equity limits scores	
New Investments	
No foreign equity allowed	1.00
Foreign equity < 50% of total equity	0.50
Foreign equity > 50% but < 100% of total equity	0.25
Acquisitions	
No foreign equity allowed	0.50
Foreign equity < 50% of total equity	0.25
Foreign equity > 50% but < 100% of total equity	0.125
(ii) Screening and approval	
Approval required for new FDI/acquisitions of < USD100 mn or if corresponding to < 50% of total equity	0.20
Approval required for new FDI/acquisitions above USD100 mn or if corresponding to > 50% of total equity	0.10
Notification with discretionary element	0.025
(iii) Restrictions on key foreign personnel/directors	
Foreign key personnel not permitted	0.10
Economic needs test for employment of foreign key personnel	0.05
Time bound limit on employment of foreign key personnel	0.025
Nationality/residence requirements for board of directors Majority must be nationals	0.075
At least one must be national	0.02
(iv) Other restrictions	
Establishment of branches not allowed/local incorporation required	0.05
Reciprocity requirement	0.10
Restrictions on profit/capital repatriation	0.10
Access to local finance	0.05
Acquisition of land for business purposes	0.10
Land ownership not permitted but leases possible	0.05–0.01

For further details refer to www.oecd-ilibrary.com

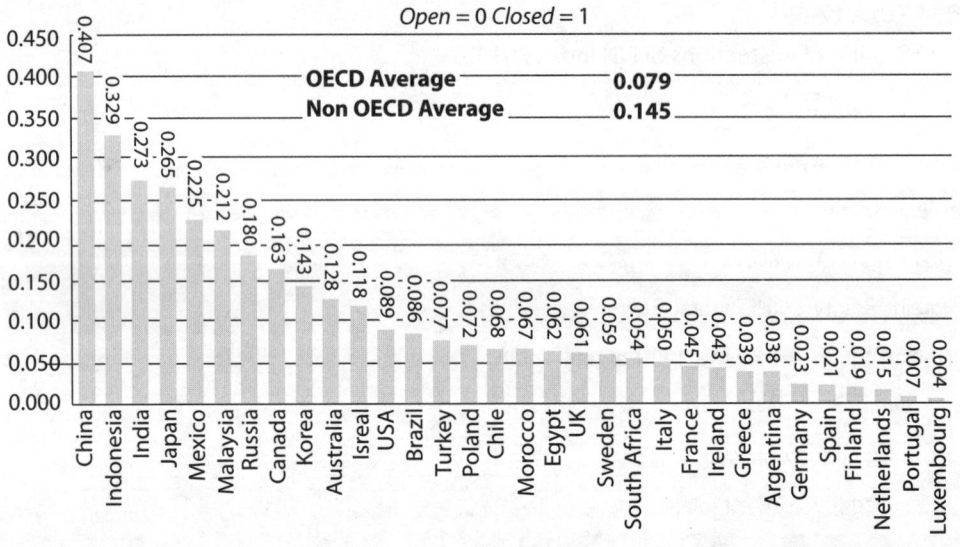

Figure 17-4
OECD's FDI RR Index 2012 Select Countries

Source of Data: www.oecd.org

CONCEPTS IN PRACTICE

Foreign Direct Investment Policies and Domestic Economy

VODAPHONE GETS FULL CONTROL OF INDIAN OPERATIONS

In December 2013 consequent upon changes in the FDI policy in India permitting 100% FDI in telecom sector, Vodafone Group plc sought permission to have total control over its Indian operations, Vodafone India Limited. Vodafone is the second largest player in telecom in India behind Airtel with Vodafone Group plc owning 64% stake. The parent firm negotiated a deal to buy out the remaining 36% shareholding in the hands of two local investors.

Ajay Piramal through his firm Piramal Enterprises had picked up the 10.97% stake in two tranches, in August 2011 and February 2012, paying a total of $955 million (₹5,864 crore at ₹1,290 per share). On 10 April 2014 he sold at ₹8,900 crore (₹1,960 per share) a more than 50% return over two years. The sale of stake in Vodafone bolstered balance sheet of Piramal Enterprises by ₹10,000 crore. Ajay Piramal said, 'In an environment where most companies are starved for cash, it will open up more opportunities. We will redeploy the cash in financial services, healthcare, and information management.'

Similarly, the second investor Analjit Singh, the owner and founder of Max India, sold 24.65% holding for much less at ₹1,241 crore with different terms and conditions. Singh plans to use the funds to raise his stake in Max India.

A mere change in FDI policy has augmented the domestic base of capital by approximately ₹10,000 available for other entrepreneurial activity or consolidation of domestic firms.

Figure 17-4 graphically displays the restrictiveness in descending order. It is worth investigating that China being highest in FDI restrictiveness index still attracts substantial and possibly the greatest FDI inflows. Perhaps the benefits of the FDI for the multinational corporation in terms of vast markets of China, growing economy accompanied with cheap labour to make them globally competitive are the reasons good enough to overcome the FDI restrictiveness.

World Trade Organization (WTO) is attempting to enhance international trade and help negotiate trade agreement with the objective of reducing trade barriers without creating side-effects of such opening up of the markets worldwide. Besides helping set trade negotiations, WTO is also involved in monitoring fair implementation of such trade agreements, resolving disputes as and when they arise, and creating a level playing field for trade among developing and developed nations.

Protection and Need

Some of the barriers to international trade and foreign investment are based on the perception of the nation and its government on what is required and what is not required for the nation. For example a nation may deny foreign investment by multinational firms, such as Coco-Cola, Pepsi, and McDonald's as these investments may be considered unwarranted while policy may provide for open and free foreign investment in the area of manufacturing like automobiles, computers or technology like Internet, communication, etc. where the nation may be deficient and a need is felt to invite foreign participants. In such cases, FDI may become sector specific.

OECD Commentary on FDI in 2010

FDI activity recovered in 2010 after two years of sharp declines following the global financial crises.

FDI outflows worldwide picked up in 2010 by around 13% from 2009, to USD1,282 billion, as compared to the sharp decline in investments in the two previous years (−40% and −12% in 2009 and 2008, respectively). OECD investors accounted for around 80% of global FDI outflows (USD1,004 billion) representing a 10% increase from 2009 (compared to the decline in 2009 by 44% to USD912 billion and in 2008 by −15% to USD1,633 billion). The top three investing countries were the United States (USD351 billion), Germany (USD107 billion), and France (USD84 billion). The United Kingdom, the second largest OECD investor in the pre–crisis period, was in 18th position in 2010. Investors from the European Union as a whole accounted for 34% of global outflows in 2010, at USD437 billion (34% in 2009 and 51% in 2008).

OECD countries hosted only 53% (USD650 billion) of global FDI inflows (as compared to 87% of inflows in 2000). The large majority of OECD inflows went to America and Europe.

The United States accounts for 36% (USD236 billion) of the OECD's FDI inflows in 2010.

The United Kingdom, Germany, and France in total accounted for 19% (USD45 billion, USD46 billion, and USD34 billion, respectively). OECD investors have continued diversifying the destination of their investments, with around 34% of their investments hosted outside the OECD area. The largest non-OECD recipients were China (USD185 billion), Brazil (USD48 billion), the Russian Federation (USD43 billion), and India (USD25 billion). Indonesia and South Africa received in total USD15 billion.

Source: OECD iLibrary.

MODES OF FOREIGN DIRECT INVESTMENT

Foreign investment can come in various forms. Starting from exports it may extend to licensing, joint venture, or acquisition of a firm. These forms of foreign investment have varying degrees of risks and investments. They also depend upon several other factors—both host nation specific factors and firm specific factors. Factors specific to host nation relate to policy and regulatory environment permitting or restricting FDI, cultural outlook, legal framework, commercial and taxation environment, developmental stage of the nation, safety and security available, etc. Firm specific factors relate to the position of the MNC intending to make investment, such as maturity of the multinational corporation, resources available with the firm, management philosophy for expansion and growth, willingness to share technology, and managerial expertise.

Typical Life Cycle of MNC Modes of entry can be best explained on the basis of the life cycle of a firm. It essentially means how firms become multinational over time. If we study the stages of growth of a multinational firm, we find that firms start small catering to limited geographical needs and gradually expand from city to province to nation. As the competition at home grows and margins erode a need to explore markets beyond is felt. As a matter of strategy and driven by need to expand markets and profits, the firm typically looks for newer and newer markets. The easiest, fastest, and least risky way of entering a fresh market is to start exporting to a neighbouring nation. Typically, a firm does the same. That is the beginning of a firm becoming multinational from a pure domestic corporation.

As the export markets expand in size the local competition and imitations begin to develop forcing the firm to set up production facility abroad. This helps in meeting greater demand, carry out product improvements adapting to local conditions, and better control over pricing decisions to meet local competition. Setting up of the production facility abroad throws two choices—by licensing to a local firm or have control over operations. If the size of the market is large enough one desires to have control over operations abroad.

Subject to local regulatory environment the control can be either partial through a joint venture with a local partner or full through a wholly owned subsidiary. Again an MNC is faced with minimum of two choices, that is, to have the green-field venture or go for inorganic growth through acquisition of a facility that perhaps has already been set up by a competing local firm.

The options for the modes of entry for a multinational firm to expand business in another country are presented in Figure 17-5 and are described briefly here.

Licensing

Licensing rather than setting up a facility of production abroad has several advantages. In terms of investment levels and political risk licensing is the safest mode. Besides it is quick for introducing a product and helps build the brand. To the MNC, it provides a fast feedback on the acceptability of the product abroad, and enables assessment of future potential. It is a safe strategy and is akin to test marketing of projects which firms usually take before committing a large scale investment. The disadvantage of the strategy is that cheap imitations may develop

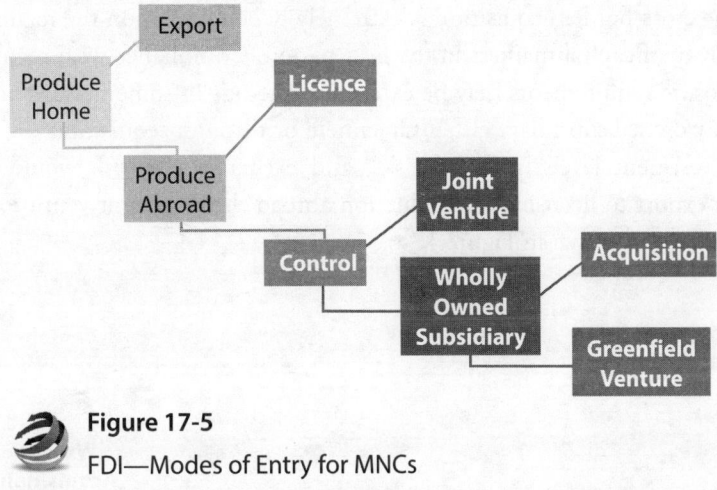

Figure 17-5
FDI—Modes of Entry for MNCs

and pose difficulties later. In many of the developing countries, it may be a serious handicap in the absence of laws protecting intellectual property and patents or enforcement of such laws even when they exist.

Joint Venture

Production abroad opens up the question of going with a joint venture or setting up fully controlled subsidiary. Joint venture besides reducing the equity investment offers advantages of capitalizing on the knowledge of local partner, who is better aware of cultural and business aspects of the host nation, providing necessary managerial and technical skills, and suitable adaptation of the product for local needs. It may also lead to better acceptability of the product if it is jointly produced by with a local partner. Involvement of local partner greatly reduces political risk for the MNCs if the threats of nationalization or confiscation of assets is a potential threat. Local participation in a joint venture would be a deterrent for government to take punitive action or acquire the assets in national interest. Further joint venture as against wholly owned subsidiary is likely to face lesser administrative hurdles and red tape, speeding up the investment. On the negative side, a joint venture may give rise to agency problems, dividend policies, control of finances, and payments of royalty or technical fee. The divergence of the views on these matters emanate from differing nationalities of the two partners attempting to control operations.

Wholly Owned Subsidiary

The control of production facility abroad can be done either by setting up a Greenfield venture or by acquiring asset of similar firm by buying controlling stakes. A Greenfield venture would be an exercise ab initio and involves gestation period. The inorganic growth could be expensive but provides a head start to the project. Acquisition in the host nation helps improve competitive position of the MNC as at least one local competitor is acquired. The feasibility of the cross-border acquisition is extremely dependent upon the regulatory environment, and maturity of capital markets in the host nation. Compliance with regulatory environment and disclosure requirements may be extremely onerous in some nations and serve as deterrent for wholly owned subsidiary either Greenfield or through acquisition.

Investment levels, political risks, and exchange rate risk would increase as one moves from export to licensing to production abroad through joint venture, through wholly owned subsidiary as shown in Figure 17-6.

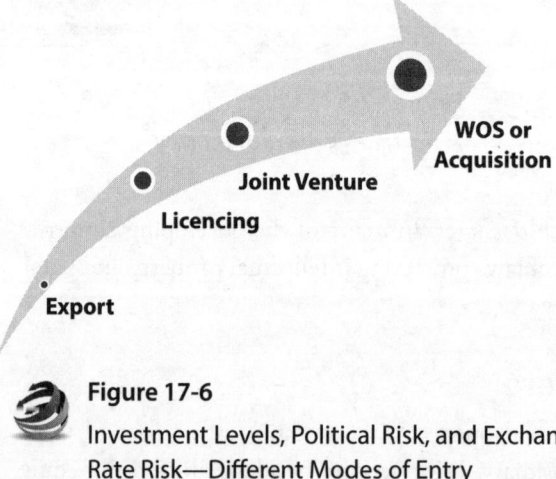

Figure 17-6
Investment Levels, Political Risk, and Exchange Rate Risk—Different Modes of Entry

FOREIGN DIRECT INVESTMENT IN INDIA

India has been amongst the more favourable destinations in the world for FDI. It has been attracting investment in all sectors. The trends of FDI are given in Annexure A17-1. The extant policy governing the FDI in India are discussed in the *Online Resource Centre*.

SUMMARY

International capital markets are becoming increasingly more popular and accessible for MNCs, which helps them reduce cost of capital and increase their international competiveness. At the same time investors are becoming more and more literate and investing more and more. The speed and transaction costs are constantly coming down with reduced capital controls offering global opportunities and expanding the scope of investment avenues by improved product design and efficient financial intermediation.

An essential way for the MNC to grow is to make investment in countries other than its own. These investments abroad are inherently risky due to unknown environments, language barriers, cultural gaps, differences in legal systems, social customs, and practices. At the same time MNCs also face considerable regulatory hurdles in making foreign investments.

The rationale for nations to permit international investment comes from theory of competitive advantage. The theory of comparative advantage proves that even though one nation is inefficient in all respects to another there exist a scope to have trade between them. The disadvantage of one nation over the other has to be measured not in absolute terms but in comparative terms, that is, in terms of the sacrifice made. While the theory of comparative advantage is well recognized and understood in terms of improved economic and social welfare, other considerations such as national honour, self-sufficiency, and national security continue to dominate policies regarding openness of the economy to foreigners. The terms-of-trade, that is, how much of one commodity for another of gets dominance over the broader objective of joint economic welfare.

Factors, such as shifting of immobility of factors of production, relative advantage over time, imposition of trade barriers and tariffs, and creation of employment diminish the argument of comparative advantage though its merits cannot be taken away altogether.

Motives for foreign investment are many. Exploitation of imperfect markets for factors of production, economies of scale through horizontal and vertical expansion, control over supply chain, increased market share, and diversification of risk by having globally steadier revenue and cash flow etc are among the reasons for MNCs to invest abroad.

The country receiving the FDI also stands to gain in many ways. Foreign investment creates employment, increases capital base, brings latest technology and products, improves balance of payment position, propels consumption driven growth, reduces government expenditure and fiscal deficit causing tax rates to decrease and disposable income to rise, and shores up the foreign currency reserves.

Barriers to international investment including direct investment include tariffs, regulations restricting foreign ownership through sectoral caps, and direction of flow of foreign capital, administrative approvals.

The initiation of foreign investment in most cases start with trading before opting for full-fledged manufacturing base in a foreign country. Such trading often provides learning experience and better understanding of the environment before a larger commitment can be made. The modes of entry in a foreign market include licensing, forming a joint venture, acquisition abroad or starting a Greenfield venture. Each of these modes of entry has different risk–return trade-off.

QUESTIONS

17-1 What is the theory of absolute advantage and why it does not form the basis of international trade?
17-2 How is the theory of comparative advantage different from the theory of absolute advantage? Describe with an example.
17-3 What do you understand by terms-of-trade?
17-4 Discuss briefly some of the motives for MNCs to invest abroad.
17-5 Describe briefly how a recipient country benefits from foreign direct investment.
17-6 What causes nations to regulate the inward foreign direct investment?

Annexure A17-1

TRENDS FOR FOREIGN DIRECT INVESTMENT IN INDIA

The trends of foreign direct investment (FDI) in India are presented in the following by way of tables and graphs depicting year-wise growth, sectoral distribution, and countries contributing towards FDI.

FDI in India	US$ Billions	
Financial Year	Equity Flows	Total FDI
2000–01	2.463	4.029
2001–02	4.065	6.130
2002–03	2.705	5.035
2003–04	2.188	4.322
2004–05	3.219	6.051
2005–06	5.540	8.961
2006–07	12.492	22.826
2007–08	24.575	34.843
2008–09	31.396	41.873
2009–10	25.834	37.745
2010–11	21.383	34.847
2011–12	35.121	46.556
2012–13	22.423	36.830
Cumulative since April 2000	193.404	290.078

Annexure A17-1

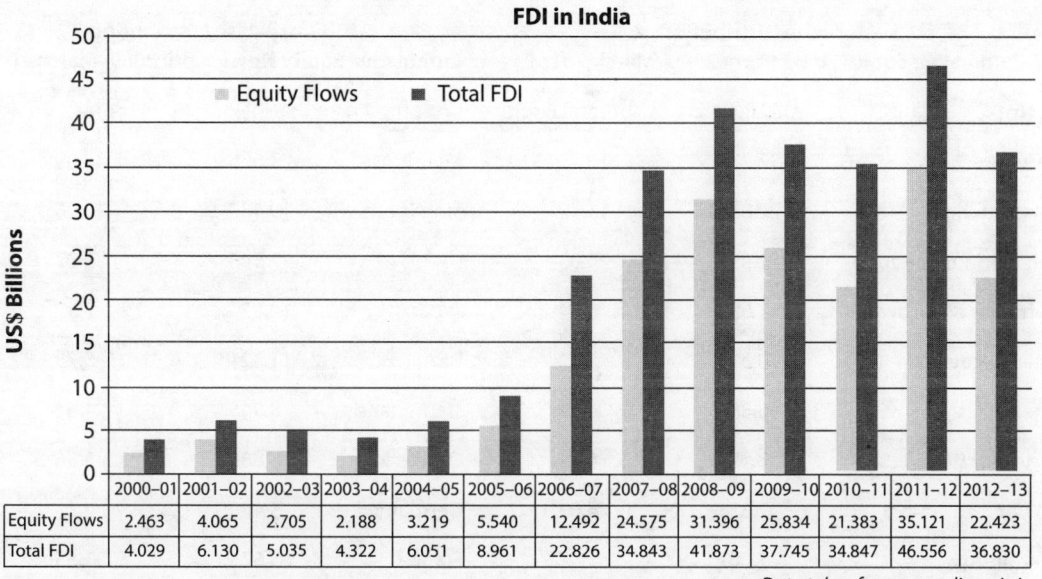

	2000–01	2001–02	2002–03	2003–04	2004–05	2005–06	2006–07	2007–08	2008–09	2009–10	2010–11	2011–12	2012–13
Equity Flows	2.463	4.065	2.705	2.188	3.219	5.540	12.492	24.575	31.396	25.834	21.383	35.121	22.423
Total FDI	4.029	6.130	5.035	4.322	6.051	8.961	22.826	34.843	41.873	37.745	34.847	46.556	36.830

Data taken from www.dipp.nic.in

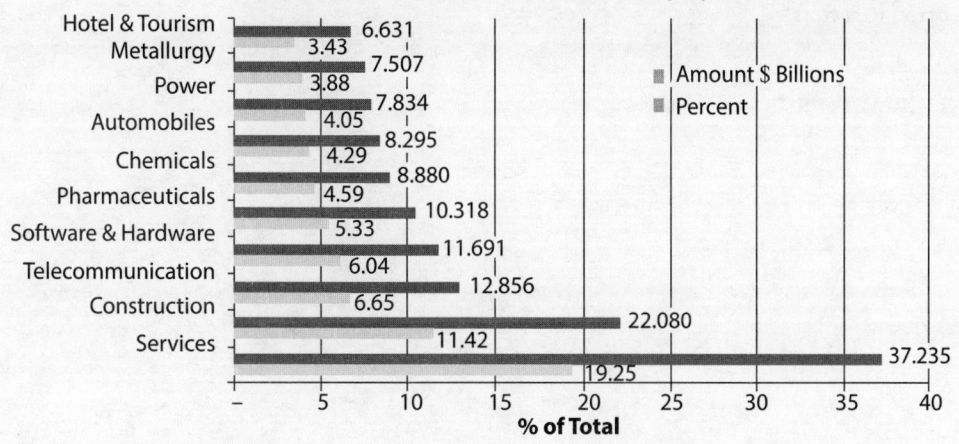

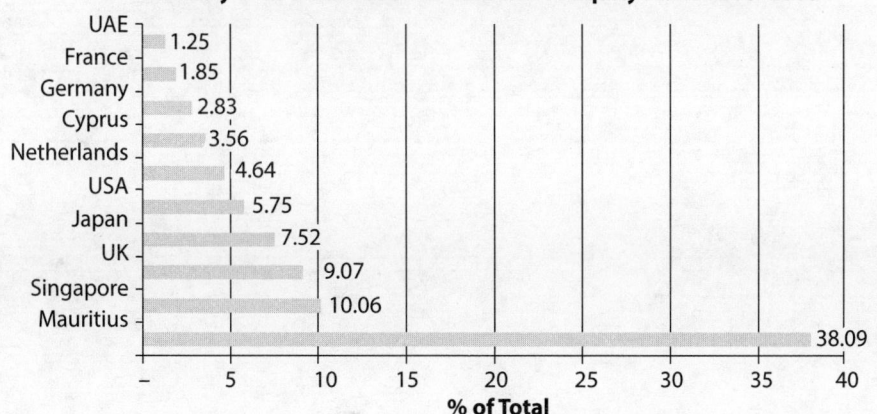

Sector-wise Distribution Cumulative Equity Flows (April 2000–March 2013)			Country-wise Distribution Cumulative Equity Flows (April 2000–March 2013)		
Sector	US$ Billions	% of Total Equity	Country	US$ Billions	% of Total Equity
Services	37.235	19.25	Mauritius	73.666	38.09
Construction	22.080	11.42	Singapore	19.460	10.06
Telecommunication	12.856	6.65	UK	17.548	9.07
Software & Hardware	11.691	6.04	Japan	14.550	7.52
Pharmaceuticals	10.318	5.33	USA	11.121	5.75
Chemicals	8.880	4.59	Netherlands	8.965	4.64
Automobiles	8.295	4.29	Cyprus	6.889	3.56
Power	7.834	4.05	Germany	5.480	2.83
Metallurgy	7.507	3.88	France	3.573	1.85
Hotel & Tourism	6.631	3.43	UAE	2.422	1.25
Total % of top 10 sectors		**68.94**			**84.63**

Managing Capital Flows

LEARNING OBJECTIVES

This chapter aims at

+ discussing the need for capital controls measures especially for emerging economies
+ describing the brief history of capital controls with a view to understand the objective achieved in different times
+ explaining the kind of capital flows that are desirable or undesirable
+ understanding what the implications of imposing capital controls are
+ discussing the theoretical underpinning of capital controls in terms of 'impossible trinity'
+ explaining the circumstances and the stage of economy at which capital controls are effective
+ highlighting the popular ways of managing capital flows and how and why different emerging economies have chosen such measures
+ explaining how India has responded to surging flows of foreign capital

CONTENTS

Introduction
Nature of Capital Flows
    Foreign Direct Investment
    Commercial Borrowings and Other Inflows
    Portfolio Investments
History of Capital Controls
Implications of Capital Flows for Domestic Economy
Capital Controls and Impossible Trinity
Features of Capital Control Measures
Ways of Capital Control
Effectiveness of Capital Control Measures
Capital Controls in India

INTRODUCTION

In the last two chapters, we discussed foreign portfolio investment, borrowing in foreign currency, and inward foreign direct investment (FDI). All the three modes cause an inflow of foreign capital in an economy but have substantially different implications in terms of macro policy responses related to fiscal and monetary policies, and exchange rate management. Any kind of inflow of foreign capital causes local currency to appreciate, increases money supply, leads to inflationary pressures or imposes sterilization costs, while the outflow would have reverse implications. This chapter is more focused on the issues related to inflows of foreign capital into developing or emerging economies rather than outflows from developed nations since issues faced by emerging markets have more serious implications than the developed markets, which are already strong enough to absorb negative implications, if any.

The inflows of capital are considered beneficial for an economy as it eases financial constraints for improving productive capacities leading to greater growth. It also facilitates faster and market-oriented financial integration, and economic development. Though long-term benefits of free and unfettered flow of capital across borders are undisputed, they are often perceived risky and sometimes considered extremely destabilizing to the economy by the developing nations, who do not have strong enough macroeconomic structures in place to effectively deal with inflows that are large.

The capital flows on capital account are different from the capital inflows of foreign exchange from exports. The difference is that in case of exports the foreign exchange has been already earned by the existing production capacities available, while in case of flows on capital account in the nature of FDI, borrowings or portfolio considerations the required capacity to service the repayment obligations is yet to be created and make the nation earn the foreign exchange in future. Whether or not a nation would be able to create such repaying capacities remains doubtful as one may face several impediments in implementation. Further the service commitments to these capital flows are not voluntary, whereas export inflows or import outflows are voluntary. Therefore, flows on account of capital account are futuristic in nature. The assessment about the ability of the nation to execute the utilization of foreign capital inflows in an effective and efficient manner forms the key to the policy of managing foreign capital flows.

The direction of flow of international capital follows no specific pattern but the focus of managing capital flow remains on the (a) massive inflows for developing and emerging economies, and/or (b) massive outflows for developed or advanced economies. The flow of capital from developed nations to developing nations is motivated by (i) above normal growth offered by developing nations, who often face scarcity of capital, and (ii) developed nations pursuing policies of monetary easing have surplus money not finding attractive uses at home.

NATURE OF CAPITAL FLOWS

We here distinguish between three kinds of inflows on capital account that have vastly different economic implications and require different policy responses on part of the recipient nation. From the balance of payment (BOP) categorization, the foreign capital inflows and outflows may be segregated into three different kinds as described here.

Foreign Direct Investment

The FDIs that are direct investments in equity are long-term movement of international capital resulting in enhancement of productive capacities of the recipient countries and equivalent release of domestic capital for alternative uses. The FDIs more often than not bring in new products and new technologies, improve human skills, and promote consumption-driven growth. The FDI inflows are considered good by developing nations in general and are mostly welcome. Yet developing nations put several restrictions and conditions before such investments are allowed. The conditions and restrictions may emanate from several considerations, such as political compulsions, national safety and honour, objective of achieving self-sufficiency, protection of local industry, and jobs. Therefore, controls on such capital flows are often imposed with respect to (a) limiting of ownership patterns to ensure that national interest are not compromised with over-enthusiastic corporate objectives of multinational corporations (MNCs), (b) end-use restrictions to achieve growth in sectors that are capital intensive and/or technology starved, (c) repatriation of profits to ensure continued supply of capital and sustained development, (d) preserving national, cultural and religious sentiments, etc.

Commercial Borrowings and Other Inflows

Other inflows include planned borrowings by nations by the government, public, and private sectors. It also includes equity inflows of foreign capital by way of depository issues or direct equity offerings. These inflows have impact of net investment position of the nation, level of external debt and consequent service obligations which often place an upper limit to such mobilization of funds. At the level of individual firms, such mobilization of external equity or debt puts them under greater pressure to generate enough to service the foreign repayment obligations than they do for domestic sources of funds. Thus, foreign inflows of capital promote greater efficiency. In addition, private firms get access to deeper and larger pool of financial resources and enable them to optimize cost of capital and capital structure.

Most of these funds are routed through the regulated financial institutions. For domestic financial institutions, the foreign inflows create pressure on them to be more efficient in channelizing and distribution of finances, develop superior and faster appraisal processes and systems, and effective monitoring. Despite the obvious advantages to the firms and financial institutions the foreign flow of capital cannot be left unchecked due to larger objective of containing external debt of a nation to a reasonable levels that can be serviced keeping in mind the limits of efficient utilization that a nation has.

The controls of capital flows of such nature are imposed with respect to containing debt levels of the firm, end-use of foreign funds, hedging conditions, repayment periods, and all-in costs. These controls involve additional administrative costs in approval and monitoring.

Portfolio Investments

The third category of cross-border flows of capital is for portfolio investment. These investments are primarily aimed at debt securities where practice of *carry trade* is prevalent but is not confined to debt markets alone. As such portfolio investments can affect any asset class. To the recipient nations, the portfolio investment make asset markets more efficient and pricing of the financial products consistent with world markets. To the investors, these investments help in diversifying risk and earn better risk-adjusted returns. With slightest of adversity, these capital flows are subject to sharp and massive reversal.

Such investments have potential threat of making exchange rates volatile, rapidly deteriorating foreign exchange reserves position when outflows take place, and creating asset price bubble when large capital inflows take place. Asset price bubble relates to the unrealistic high values of the assets than what the fundamentals can support.

HISTORY OF CAPITAL CONTROLS

Prior to World War I, there was little history of capital controls of any significant nature. Capital controls were used to finance the war time expenditure. The purpose of capital controls was to contain the outflows to other nations; thereby keeping wealth within the nations enhancing the tax base as also to hold interest rates lower. They again came to the fore in managing the depression during the 1930s to provide impetus to the economies and to have greater freedom on monetary and exchange rate policies. Under fixed exchange rate system that prevailed then the nations could devalue currency to encourage exports, discourage imports, and correct BOP deficit. Under the fixed exchange rate system if a country wanted to retain monetary independence, it could be possible only by exercising capital controls (as highlighted in the impossible trinity). However, they gradually vanished thereafter.

At the end of World War II, the financial stability of the world was felt necessary. With the introduction of Bretton Woods system, the official interventions in the currency markets got legitimacy and led to acceptance of the fact that stable exchange rates are good for international trade and world's welfare. The capital controls were aimed at containing the volatility in the exchange rates. During the Bretton Woods' era of fixed exchange rates, many countries limited asset transactions to cope with BOP difficulties. However, recognition of the costs and distortions created by these capital flow restrictions led to their gradual removal in developed countries.

Dismantling of the Bretton Woods system saw beginning of floating rate regimes and free market forces that applied to capital too. The capital controls were phased out in the 1960s and the 1970s resulting in substantial increase of cross-border flows. International capital flows fuelled a global expansion that enabled developing countries to repay the borrowings of the International Monetary Fund (IMF) and other official creditors, and to accumulate foreign exchange reserves.

In the recent past several currency crises notably Asian currency crisis of 1997 started a debate over desirability of capital controls. The global economic crisis that began with the collapse of mortgage-based lending in the United States in 2007 and spread around the world in 2008 was preceded by large imbalances in global capital flows. Global capital flows fluctuated between 2% and 6% of world gross domestic product (GDP) during 1980–95, but since then they have risen to 15% of GDP. In 2006, they totalled $7.2 trillion—more than a tripling since 1995. The most rapid increase has been experienced by advanced economies, but emerging markets and developing countries have also become more financially integrated.

The volume of capital flows as measured by percentage share of GDP has been on the rise. Though the flows are more within the developed world than in the developing economies in absolute terms, but as proportions of GDP the capital flows are far higher for developing and emerging markets. During the period 1980–1999, the average cross-border flows were around 5% of global GDP. They peaked to 20% in 2007 and thereafter dropped significantly due to global liquidity crisis.

Realizing the benefits of free capital flows to the world economy certain international organizations have placed a binding commitment on its member nations to pursue policies of open economy. There is a binding obligation on European Union (EU) members to have no capital controls. The Organization for Economic Cooperation and Development (OECD) too has called for high level of openness to cross-border flows of capital. Capital flow control measures can reduce discipline in financial markets, tighten financing constraints by restricting the availability of foreign capital, and limit diversification benefits.

However, there is recognition of the fact that complete openness cannot be advocated in view of the experiences of several currency crises and during recent global liquidity crisis when developed and highly open economies were subjected to greater risks.

IMPLICATIONS OF CAPITAL FLOWS FOR DOMESTIC ECONOMY

Capital inflows have both positive and negative implications for the domestic economy. Free flow of capital has substantial benefits through financial market integration but is risky too. If flows are smooth, then they are easily manageable and desirable. However, when inflows are massive and rapid they can cause outflows that are disruptive and pose policy challenges. Some of these implications, not necessarily the benefits, are as follows.

Reducing Cost of Capital   Foreign capital inflows augment the financial resource base for the recipient country by widening the investor base and currencies of borrowing. Motivated by interest rate differentials the inflows would help bring down such cost of borrowing in local currency because the substitute foreign currency borrowings must be available at cheaper rate. Even the portfolio investments motivated by differential of stock and debt market returns would bring down cost of equity by freeing the equivalent local capital. Overall, the cost of capital both for borrowing and equity in the recipient nation should come down making domestic industry more competitive on global basis.

Deepening of Financial Sector   With capital inflows the financial sector of the recipient nation must become more efficient and open, the outcome of which would be speedier availability of capital to domestic borrowers. Inflows if routed through financial sector would create pressure on financial intermediaries to make use of funds faster and thus promote efficiency. With cheaper and speedier availability of credit, the productive investment must increase in the recipient nation. The financial sector would develop sound appraisal and supervision mechanisms.

Allocation of Credit   With enhanced base of capital available, it becomes easier for the government to provide sectoral direction to credit. It can even out the sectoral differences in the availability of capital to different sectors within the economy and removing the regional imbalances. The prudential measures can be directed towards attracting capital inflows as well as restricting outflows. Since outflows would be guided by prospects of increased returns abroad, greater availability of domestic credit can be ensured by containing the outflows.

Real Appreciation and Export Competitiveness A major problem associated with the inflows is the appreciation of local currency caused by foreign currency inflows. If the currency is not overvalued, the export competitiveness of the nation would be adversely affected. Capital flows would tend to reduce inflows by way of exports. Hence, the choice would be to have inflows on capital account or on current account. For developing nations foreign currency receipts on current account are structurally more sound that than the receipts on capital account.

Preserving Reserves and Maintaining Balance of Payment By restricting the outflows a nation can have desired levels of foreign exchange reserves if its depletion is considered damaging to rating of the nation and is a cause of dwindling confidence of international community. If so, the benefit of reduced cost of capital would get eroded by decreased country rating. For foreigners increased levels of reserves infuse confidence in them with regard to shock absorption capacity of the recipient nation. To the residents reserves provide a sense of security and a comfort level to meet needs of imports.

Macroeconomic Instability Portfolio flows are extremely volatile in nature especially when the flows are leveraged, as happens in case of carry trade. A little decline in returns can trigger massive outflows with reserves eroding much faster than the speed they were built up. Managing these disruptive outflows is a challenge and can cause pressure on macroeconomic fiscal and monetary policies. The case of Mexico highlights the strains that the country had to go through when they tried to control the outflows of foreign capital by raising interest rate stifling growth and investment with adverse effect on employment.

Creation of Asset Bubble Massive inflows can lead to overvaluation of asset prices much beyond their true values. Referred to as asset bubble, they are likely to burst sooner or later. While increasing asset prices create an illusion of well-being seldom do nations realize the danger and harm they can cause to the economy, when these investments are withdrawn. There have been several instances in the history that have caused serious damages to the economy. Boom in the real estate prices may lead to false sense of well-being without increasing the real welfare. Many nations have suffered such asset bubble situation in the Eurozone since 2007 onwards.

Credit Growth, Overheating, and Inflation For countries with flexible exchange rates, the local currency appreciates with capital inflows, raising the relative prices of the goods of the recipient country. This makes exports less competitive and imports more attractive. For countries with fixed exchange rates, the increased demand for domestic assets leads the monetary authorities to buy foreign exchange (sell domestic currency), increasing the domestic money supply, which is inflationary unless sterilized. Ultimately, the prices of domestic goods and assets rise. In either case, the prices of domestic goods and assets rise relative to those in the rest of the world—a real appreciation—making domestic exported goods less competitive in the world markets and hurting exports and industries focussing on import substitution.

CONCEPTS IN PRACTICE
Destabilizing Capital Flows

CAPITAL CONTROLS GAIN CREDENCE

Capital controls are back in fashion. In June 2010 South Korea and Indonesia announced measures to regulate potentially destabilizing capital flows affecting their economy. In October 2009 Brazil had announced a 2% tax on investment in financial securities by foreigners. Taiwan also restricted foreign investors from buying time deposits. South Korea introduced three control mechanisms:

1. Restriction on trades in currency derivatives including trades in non-deliverable forwards, and cross currency swaps
2. Enhanced restrictions on end-use of loans in foreign currency
3. Tightening of existing regulation on foreign currency liquidity ratio

The objective of such capital controls is to (a) limit the likely sharp reversal of capital flow as large outflows (about $65 billion in five months preceding September 2010) were seen in South Korea, (b) to curb the rapidly rising short-term foreign debt (standing at $154 billion equivalent to 57% of foreign currency reserves).

Indonesia's capital control focused on retention of foreign currency. In contrast to outflow of foreign currency in South Korea, Indonesia faced large inflows. Same had been the case with Brazil. Indonesia witnessed sharp gain in stock markets of about 85% (from November 2009 to September 2010) due to large foreign portfolio investment. Its currency also gained 17% during the period. With a view to check the potential and sudden outflow Indonesia enforced a minimum lock-in period for short-term debt instruments that were extremely popular with foreign investors. It also decided to extend the maturity of instruments to retain foreign exchange for longer periods. Such measures are expected to prevent asset bubble, appreciation of local currency, and rising inflation.

Despite recognition of the fact that capital controls distort the economic theory of market based pricing and efficient allocation of resources, both developed and developing nations have been using capital controls to direct the flow in desired direction. Capital controls can protect an economy from volatile capital flows. India and China, the two large economies still exercise capital controls despite attractive growth rates.

Source: Compiled on the basis of an article by Kavaljit Singh, *Business Line*, 18 September 2010.

CAPITAL CONTROLS AND IMPOSSIBLE TRINITY

The argument for free capital flows are same as those forwarded for free international trade that attempt to justify removal of various kinds of trade barriers. By the same token, the rationale for imposing trade barriers can be extended to manage capital flows.

Capital controls are aimed at limiting the rights of the residents to enter into capital transactions with non-residents. While the objective of capital control is to eliminate the

ill-effects of such capital flows but at the same time the economy must make good use of the inflows. It is recognized that unless a nation achieves a certain threshold of financial and institutional development it cannot capitalize on the benefits of free flow of capital. In view of pros and cons attached with capital flows, there is a need to develop a comprehensive yet flexible and balanced approach to management of capital flows.

As well understood the impossible trinity says that all three—fixed exchange rate, independent monetary policy and free flow of international capital—cannot exist simultaneously. Coexistence of all three would be destabilizing the economy. Since it is not possible to have all three, developing nations have to pick any two of them. It is natural for emerging market economies to pursue fixed exchange rate system to have price stability and promote international trade, and also have monetary freedom to better guide the development of nation with planned and acceptable level of inflation. Therefore, they necessarily have to exercise capital controls. Even when a country is having managed float regime the capital inflows would have to be absorbed by intervention to maintain the exchange rate in the desired band. To contain inflation the intervention has to be sterilized.

Sterilization is the most popular policy response and has been virtually used by all countries facing capital surges during the 1990s. It also avoids the burden on the banking system of higher reserve requirements. Moreover, by limiting the role of banking system in intermediation of the flows, sterilization operations reduce bank's vulnerability to sudden reversal of flows.

CONCEPTS IN PRACTICE
Cost of Sterilization

COST OF STERILIZATION IN INDIA

To absorb additional liquidity arising out of interventions the sterilization in India is done in three ways:

1. Market Stabilization Scheme (MSS) under which dated securities of T-bills are sold exclusively for the purpose of stability and where government bears the cost
2. Open Market Operations (OMO) conducted by Reserve bank for the sole purpose of controlling equity implies cost for Reserve Bank
3. Increase in Cash Reserve Ratio (CRR) impounding a fraction of funds of banking system the cost of which is borne by commercial banks.

These costs measured as percentage of GDP are substantial with implication for conduct of future monetary policy. These costs are direct outcome of capital inflow surges. Larger the foreign inflows, larger would these cost be. The costs are measured as follows:

- Cost under MSS is the interest borne by government as securities under MSS are issued exclusively for the purpose of achieving stabilization of exchange rates.

- Cost of OMO is measured by the difference of yield earned and paid. Under OMO Reserve Bank offers the securities typically are sold at a higher yield than the yield earned by Reserve Bank of the foreign currency denominated securities acquired in the process of intervention. It is the differential of the yield earned and yield paid that impact the balance sheet of the Reserve Bank.
- Increase in CRR places a burden on banking system as the proportion of money does not earn interest raising the interest rate to borrowers. Since CRR is otherwise also used as monetary tool and not only for sterilization purposes, the entire cost cannot be attributed to sterilization cost.

The table below presents the cost of sterilization borne by government, Reserve Bank and commercial banks during the period 2004–05 to 2006–07 when capital flows into India were high and later periods when capital inflows were nominal.

Costs of sterilization mount as continuous sterilization bids up the rates at which successive issuances can be made. This erodes the profitability of the central bank and several central banks have suffered losses—Chile (1.0% of GDP per annum during 1993–98), Colombia (0.5–0.7% in the early 1990s), Mexico (0.2–0.4% during 1990–92) and Poland (1.0 to 1.15% of GDP during 1995–97.

Cost of Sterilization in India			% of GDP
Year	Reserve Bank	Government	Commercial Banks
2004–05	1.7	0.1	0.2
2005–06	0.4	0.1	0.3
2006–07	0.6	0.1	0.3
2007–08	0.2	0.2	0.5
2008–09	0.0	0.2	0.4

Source: Report on *Currency and Finance 2009–12*, Reserve Bank of India.

Both on fundamental consideration of impossible trinity and on practical consideration of exorbitant costs of fiscal and monetary measures that developing economies can ill afford, the best possible option for emerging economies is the take measures of capital control.

Removing imperfection in markets of products and for factors of production is a long drawn strategy. However, removing imperfections in the capital markets can be done rather easily and in a faster way by adopting prudential measures gaining precious time to make macroeconomic changes. The capital flows across borders are instantaneous as capital chases higher returns. Though in the long term the free flow of capital across borders moves capital

from surplus to deficit nations equalizing returns across globe, developing nations see these capital flows as more threatening, destabilizing, and damaging to their economies because of extremely volatile nature of such flows and problem of real appreciation. Further, the size of foreign capital flows if left unchecked may be large enough to outstrip the domestic money supply.

Here we are primarily concerned with capital flows not on account of FDI but largely the investment in financial assets like stocks, bonds, derivatives and non-productive asset like real estate normally referred as portfolio investments. Design of capital control measures are constrained by export competitiveness, financial stability, sterilization costs, risk of reversal of flow, etc.

Though in the long term capital flows should have beneficial impact by channelizing and optimizing the use of capital from surplus (developed) nations to deficit (developing) nations, but they carry great risk in the short term, especially for developing nations. For long two decades from the 1960s to the 1980s, Korea used foreign funds heavily to augment resources and propel growth in excess of 10%. While capital flows by way of FDI are considered long term in nature, the capital flows on account of portfolio considerations are considered volatile and therefore worthy of control.

FEATURES OF CAPITAL CONTROL MEASURES

It is often suggested by economists that before imposing capital controls the economy must exhaust macroeconomic policy measures. Capital control measures should not be regarded as substitute of macroeconomic policy changes but should be a time gaining tool to prepare the nations better for affecting policy changes. The objective should be to develop sufficiently deep macroeconomic and financial structure to absorb the benefits of foreign capital inflows. IMF suggests that capital flow control should be imposed only when (a) currency is not undervalued, (b) reserves are adequate or sterilization costs are too high, or (c) economy is not overheated (credit growth or asset price bubble). The economy must let the local currency appreciate when it is undervalued. It must shore up reserves and sterilize if inflation is a concern. Lastly, lower the policy rates and allow monetary easing if overheating is not a concern. Finally, consider fiscal tightening if growth objective can still be met. Only when such efforts are considered impractical or exhausted, capital flow controls are advisable. This is depicted in Figure 18-1.

However, there are limitations to this suggestion. There has been increasing share of portfolio investment as opposed to FDI in the international flow of capital. Such capital flows are more likely to cause asset price bubbles, appreciation of local currency to retard export led growth, credit booms with dilution in appraisal processes and perhaps leading to crony capitalism, distortions in the capital, and money markets, etc. The major issue that a developing nation faces is the real appreciation of local currency causing loss of export competitiveness. Policy measure that can reverse the loss of export competitiveness is sterilization. Massive inflows would shore up the reserves causing buying of foreign currency (increasing supply of local currency).

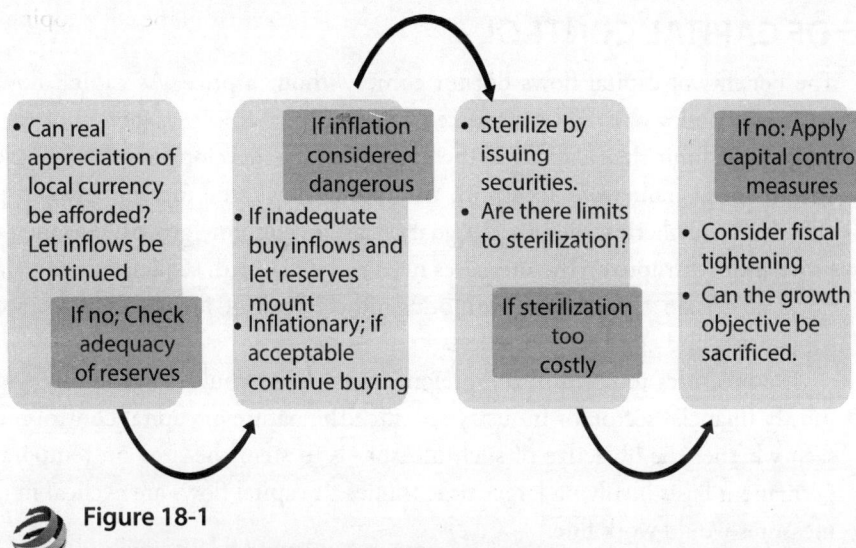

Figure 18-1
Desirability of Capital Control Measures

To offset the inflationary pressure created by massive inflows and official intervention the governments would have to sell bonds with rising yields. The interest rate differential that attracted the portfolio investment in the first place would remain as wide and may not stem the inflows. Therefore, sterilization intervention could lead to further increase in the foreign capital inflows.

The other remedy of preventing the real appreciation of local currency is fiscal contraction achieved by either raising taxes or reducing developmental expenditure. Raising taxes would cause serious pains to the society in developing nations by reducing the disposable income, reducing consumption, and making growth tardy. It is well established that developmental expenditure works as a catalyst for growth in a developing economy. Reducing developmental expenditure would take away the impetus so vitally needed for the economy. With macroeconomic policy measures expensive, painful, and politically undesirable, the governments in developing nations have to resort to newer ways of handling the problem of real appreciation of local currency.

Economist advocating free markets oppose the capital controls much in the same way as they oppose the imposition of tariff that inhibits or distorts international trade. The justification of imposing trade barriers comes in the name of protection to infant domestic industry which is underdeveloped and needs time to grow to compete in the world markets. Same argument can be extended to financial markets of the emerging economies which are in infancy and need protection by way of capital controls. Just as tariffs protect the economy, capital controls restrict the pace of flow of capital providing enough time to absorb and developing a sustainable model of growth and ability of the nation to deal with external shocks. However, there is one difference in trade barriers and capital controls. While trade barriers seem to extend indefinitely in time because of the argument of providing protection to the industry being infant who never becomes adult, the capital controls have been used only temporarily to postpone difficult monetary and fiscal responses.

WAYS OF CAPITAL CONTROL

The benefits of capital flows do not come without a price. As capital flows can complicate economic policy or even be a source of instability themselves, governments have used capital controls to limit their effects. If the countries have developed sufficient level of institutional and financial framework to absorb the capital flows, the measures would prove to be more effective in furthering the broader goal of faster economic growth else the capital flows could prove more disruptive. The measures need to be planned, sequenced, and aimed at restricting flows of certain types while promoting other types of flows. They require sound financial supervision and effective regulation.

The measures to control the foreign capital flows could be economy wide, sector specific mostly financial sector, or industry specific. The nature of capital control measure can also be seen whether the objective of such measure is to stem the flow on temporary basis or rather permanent basis involving larger time frames. If capital flows are cyclical in nature, temporary measures would work fine.

The economy wide measures would aim at reducing systemic risk. They regulate credit growth if the policy makers believe that economy is overheating. Such measures include (a) placing limits on domestic credit growth rate, (b) placing sectoral limits on lending, (c) having a conservative loan to value ratio, (d) increasing capital adequacy requirements, and (e) enforcing stricter rules for asset classification and provisioning.

Measures of capital control are directed most towards bonds and least towards FDI.

Capital flow measures are advised when there is no time available to make macro-policy adjustments. Because capital flows are much quicker and macro adjustment has its own inertia temporary measures may be warranted. Therefore, to avoid potential adverse effects of such capital flows developing countries impose rather unilateral and temporary controls over inflows and outflows of foreign capital through policy measures mostly achieved by any of the following ways:

(a) Placing end-use restrictions on capital inflows
(b) Taxing the inflows/outflows based on transactions
(c) Prohibiting outflows for certain time prescribing minimum holding period
(d) Prescribing enhanced reserves levels possibly varying with time

Besides, governments in developing economies impose several restrictions on the residents to regulate the outflows from the country. Capital flow controls must complement macroeconomic policies and are country and situation-specific. Another feature is that these measures are temporary and are removed when the circumstances become appropriate.

End-use Restrictions End-use restrictions generally prohibit investment in financial assets such as portfolio investments in equities and bonds, as also investment in real estate. The restriction on end-use of capital is intended to prevent creation of asset bubbles. These large and rapid inflows challenge the capacity of the developing nations to absorb the capital inflows that in the absence of finding usage in asset creation get diverted to cause overvaluation of existing assets beyond their fair value. Inflows of foreign capital mostly end up in purchase

CONCEPTS IN PRACTICE
Ways of Capital Controls

CAPITAL CONTROLS—DIFFERENT WAYS

Capital controls are desirable to avoid excessive debt and asset price bubbles. Many developing nations have imposed variety of capital controls both on inflows and outflows for different reasons and situations. Some of these are highlighted as follows:

Brazil In October 2009 Brazil imposed a 2% tax on financial transactions on foreign investment in equity and debt portfolios at the time of making the investment with the intention of containing the appreciation of local currency, real. It also imposed 6% tax on foreign purchase of bonds. In July 2011 the government imposed a 1% tax on currency futures transactions.

In June 2013 Brazil dismantled capital controls to prevent depreciation of real that fanned inflation, which touched the high end of the target rate at 6.50%. Brazil first increased the interest rate to curb inflation. It decided to tax foreign purchase of bonds almost immediately followed by removal of 1% tax in the currency futures market. The removal of taxes would increase foreign currency flows stemming the depreciation of its currency: real.

Brazil had used capital controls before during the period 1993–98 but entirely for different reasons and in different circumstances. During 1993–98 the foreign inflows were motivated by carry-trade phenomenon when investors borrowed in currencies with low interest rate and invest in real with high interest rate capitalizing on interest rate differential, with real pegged to US dollar. In 2009 the situation was different. Brazil was a fast growing economy with not as high interest rate as earlier period with floating exchange rate system and low domestic savings rate that warranted foreign capital infusion to fund the growth. The capital controls of Brazil were uncharacteristic of an open and growing economy.

Argentina In 2012 Argentina placed a 15% levy on credit and debit card purchases abroad in foreign currency to stem the outflow of dollars, placed restrictions on buying dollar for travel abroad, and practised dual rate forcing citizens to buy dollars at an exchange rate that was extremely unfavourable for purchase of dollars.

Malaysia Malaysia imposed capital controls in September 1998 during the contagion regional currency crisis in efforts to bring stability to the economy, rather than accepting IMF bailout conditions in the aftermath of Asian currency crisis, in contrast to other affected nations like Korea, Thailand, and Indonesia. These capital flow controls prohibited transfers from domestic account to foreign accounts and vice versa, limited credit facilities to offshore parties. The capital controls that included pegging the ringgit to RM3.80 to a US dollar, were lifted in July 2005. Before the onslaught of the crisis in July 1997, the ringgit was trading at a high of RM2.42 against a US dollar but fell after regional currencies, starting with the Thai Baht and Indonesian Rupiah were attacked by speculators.

of financial assets such as stocks and bonds or real estate distorting true values. The asset bubbles go unnoticed as they keep domestic and foreign investors happy and complacent but ultimately burst to cause extremely damaging consequences. Therefore, as a prudent measure the governments in developing nations place restrictions for the end-use of funds especially in stock markets and real estate.

Taxing Foreign Capital Flows Taxing the inflows and outflows are aimed at reducing the returns on capital and close the gap of interest rate differential; a major motivating factor. Developing nations, due to their lower base and large markets, have shown greater growth rates as compared to developed nations and therefore serve as attractive destinations for investment purely motivated by earning better returns. Carry trade has been used for long to exploit the differential in returns of developing and developed markets by borrowing in currencies with low interest rates and investing in currencies with high returns.

Taxing the inflows and outflows of foreign capital reduces the arbitrage opportunities and therefore the volatility of such flows. While in good times the capital inflows are fast but during bad times, the outflows are even faster. This makes the host nations more vulnerable to external shocks. It could be extremely damaging not only for host nations but also for investing nations. Taxing financial transactions of non-residents has also served the purpose of revenue generation for governments.

During 2010 Peru increased fee from 10 bps to exorbitant 400 bps on purchase of central government securities to check massive and rapid inflows. Similarly, in the same year Thailand too subjected the interest income and capital gains to a 15% withholding tax on government bonds. In 2011 Korea too adopted similar measures to counter inflows.

Brazil has been using tax as tool of managing inflows and stem real appreciation of local currency for long time.

Holding Period Requirements Placing time restriction on outflows by prescribing minimum holding period is primarily concerned with both (a) absorbing the inflows in the economy by giving itself more time, and (b) de-motivating investors to make very temporary investment for getting better returns. By ensuring a longer term commitment of the foreign investor the host nation prepares itself to absorb better as well as limit volatility in financial and currency markets. It has been observed that large capital inflows not only have a tendency to stop suddenly but also reverse too. During the 1990s, Chile placed restrictions on sale and repatriation of investment in foreign currency by prescribing a minimum waiting period to check the outflow of capital.

In 2010 there was a five-fold increase in the inflows in Indonesia crossings $26 billion mark with about 89% deployed in short-term bills of Bank of Indonesia which were sold under sterilization programme. While Indonesia continued with sterilized intervention, raising reserves substantially yet the Rupiah; the local currency appreciated by 29%. In 2011 Indonesia resorted to capital control measures by prescribing a 6-month holding period for non-residents for the purchases of the bonds. The capital control measure was aimed at (a) solving problem of asset liability mismatch as short-term deposits were being used for long-term financing and

(b) by extending the maturity of the investments the volatility in the exchange rate was spread over time with gradual appreciation rather than sharp changes.

The classic example of capital controls is China, which encourages FDI with incentives but restricts other forms of capital flows. While investing in China is easy, it is extremely difficult to take it out. Due to the potential damage the foreign capital inflows and outflows can cause, it is extremely doubtful whether a country irrespective of its level of development can ever afford to have complete liberalization of capital flows.

CONCEPTS IN PRACTICE
Taxing Foreign Capital Flows

THE CHILLY CHILEAN *ENCAJE*

For long period of more than a decade, Chile practised capital controls to avoid real appreciation problem and unwarranted build-up of short-term debt on Chilean economy by unique way of reducing the attractiveness of increased returns while simultaneously ensuring a long-term flows. During the late 1980s and early 1990s, international capital began to return to Chile because of its sound economic policies and low levels of debt as also due to slow growth and low interest rates in the developed world.

The Chilean authorities feared that these capital inflows would complicate monetary policy decisions—perhaps causing real appreciation of the exchange rate—and they also were wary of the danger of building up short-term debt. Chile had long restricted capital flows and these limits were updated in the early 1990s to deal with the surge in capital inflows. Direct investment was made subject to a 10-year holding requirement in 1982; this period was reduced to three years in 1991 and to one year in 1993. Portfolio flows were made subject to the *encaje*—a one-year, mandatory, non-interest paying deposit with the central bank—created in 1991 to regulate capital inflows. The *encaje* was initially 20% but was increased to 30% in 1992. The penalty for early withdrawal was 3%. This effectively ensured long-term capital flows to Chile while reducing the gap in returns between developed and developing world. The effect of the *encaje* was to tax foreign capital inflows, with short-term flows being taxed much more heavily than long-term flows.

Source: Federal Reserve Bank of St Louis Review, November/December 1999.

Unremunerated Reserve Requirements Another popular measure of controlling the foreign capital inflows is to subject them to higher than normal reserve requirement. These reserve not earning returns help in reducing the interest rate differential just in the same manner as does the tax on inflows.

Referred to as unremunerated reserve, the nation requires that part of the inflows be deposited with the central bank for varying duration. For remitter of foreign capital the part of funds are not available for earning returns, thus discouraging flows. The reserve requirements have time dimension attached to it and therefore in can help lengthen the maturity of the capital inflow reducing problems of maturity mismatching for the bank as well as contain volatility of exchange rate. It is an attempt to make temporary inflows more permanent. Thus, unremunerated reserve requirements (URR) can achieve both the objectives with what is achieved by taxing the inflows and prescribing the minimum holding period. As the proportion placed as reserve does not earn returns, such a measure is classified as price based capital control.

Subjecting inflows to taxes or to URR have similar outcomes on the capital flow. However, there are substantial administrative differences between the tax and URR. With respect to exchange rate management the URR is a better control measure because reserve amount is not required to be converted in local currency at all while the taxes that are payable in local currency the full amount is required to be converted into local currency. Second, URR is a deadweight loss not being used by anyone while taxes contribute to the local economy as they become part of the revenue in the fiscal budget. Third, the management of reserve offers more flexibility because monetary authorities are able to control the features of URR at periodical intervals in terms of proportion and length of time. For taxes to be withdrawn or amended the exercise would be more onerous administratively having budgetary implications. Table 18-1 describes various ways different nations have implemented URR.

Besides three categories of capital controls as discussed earlier, there are other ways too depending upon the objectives of putting such controls. One may lower interest rates, or resort to intervention in the foreign currency markets to build reserve or manage currency value at a desired level. Feasibility or desirability of such actions is dependent upon the inflation rate, foreign exchange reserve level, growth target rate, etc.

The signals for imposing capital flow control are usually provided by changes in the exchange rates and levels of foreign exchange reserves. Increase in foreign exchange reserve not accompanied by decreasing current account deficit usually signals accumulation of volatile capital making the nations more vulnerable for external shock. Building foreign exchange reserves is expensive.

The contagion effect of capital flows is severe. There are several examples that have caused extensive damage to the economies of the world due to unchecked capital flows that went unabsorbed by host nations. The financial crisis of 2008 clearly demonstrates that unchecked capital flows could be very destabilizing for the world. It perhaps makes a case for the need for capital controls, because capital flows unless accompanied by suitable structural reforms could create greater troubles. Due to contagion effect inordinately large capital flows give rise to banking or currency crises.

Capital controls often discriminate between residents and non-residents. Capital flow controls on residents are indicative of lack of faith of residents in the macroeconomic policies of the governments, or lack of confidence in their own currency. Capital flight by residents is often adopted to escape high rates of taxes, fear of confiscation or nationalization of private property. In 2008 Iceland prohibited conversion and transfer of domestic currency asset. Ukraine in 2008 also adopted similar controls on outflows to prevent banking and currency

Table 18-1
Unremunerated Reserve Requirements by Different Nations to Manage Capital Inflows

Country	Year of Surge	Period of Capital Control	Description of Unremunerated Reserve Requirement
Argentina	1991	August 1993	From 40% to 43% (On domestic and foreign currency demand deposits. In addition, a 3% reserve requirement was also introduced on domestic and foreign currency 30–89-day time deposits.
Brazil	1992	July 1994–December 1994	From 10–15% to 30% on savings deposits; 100% marginal reserve requirement on demand deposits, 20% (subsequently increased to 30%) on time deposits and 15% reserve requirement on loans for the purchases of goods also introduced
Chile	1990	January 1992–May 1992	Non-remunerated 20% reserve requirement on deposits and loans in foreign currency to be maintained for one year and a 30% marginal reserve requirement on inter-bank deposits introduced
Colombia	1991	Jan 1991–Sept 1991	Marginal reserve requirement of 100% imposed on all new deposits; subsequently, replaced by an increase in reserve requirements on most deposits
Czech Republic	1992	Aug 1994	From 9% to 12%
China		April 2004	Reserve requirement increased in two-steps: from 6% to 7% (effective 21 September 2003) and further to 7.5%. In addition to increase in reserve requirements, a differentiated reserve requirement system was also put in place whereby the reserve requirements applied to financial institutions were dependent upon a number of criteria, such as capital adequacy, asset quality, and non-performing loans.
Kenya	1992	Oct 1993–Mar 1994	From 12% to 20%
Malaysia	1989	May 1989–1994	From 3.5% to 5%, the base for reserve liabilities was extended to include (i) all outstanding ringgit received through swap transactions with non-residents (effective 16 September 1991) and (ii) foreign currency deposits and transactions, such as foreign currency borrowing from foreign banking institutions and inter-bank borrowing (effective 3 January 1994).
Mexico	1990	April 1992	Compulsory liquidity coefficient for dollar liabilities set at 15%
Sri Lanka	1991	Nov 1991–Feb 1994	From 13% to 15%
Thailand	1988	Aug 1995	From 0% to 7%

Source: Report on *Currency and Finance 2009–12*, Reserve Bank of India.

crises. Similarly, in 2001 Argentina too had placed limits on the withdrawal of deposits from banks by residents (referred as *corralito*) and loans in foreign currency. Whether capital controls differentiate on the basis of the transactions or on the basis of resident status, the investors have been able to overcome these measures by several innovative ways. Transactions can often be disguised to avoid capital controls. Similarly, the discrimination between residents and non-residents can be overcome by disguising identities of investors.

EFFECTIVENESS OF CAPITAL CONTROL MEASURES

The effectiveness of capital controls to avoid the problem of real appreciation of exchange rates has its own cost. It increases the cost of monitoring, which in turn gives rise to corrupt practices. On the other hand, capital controls can provide considerable freedom in following economic and monetary policies independent of capital flows. Nations have used such measures on a sustained basis though arguably it is believed that implicit costs of capital controls could be prohibitive if followed on sustained basis. Effectiveness of capital control measures is more when it is not a substitute for macro policy responses.

The efficacy of capital controls and other prudential measures is also dependent upon the ability of resident to circumvent the control measure. It is observed that over a period of time volumes of capital flow regain the levels that existed prior to implementing control. However, capital control can help in transforming the short-term flows into long-term, spread out volatility, and provide much needed time to adjust macroeconomic policies and build financial sector efficiencies. If inflows are not stemmed another policy response could be to relax controls over outflows.

Internationally, especially among developed nations capital controls are considered undesirable. World Trade Organization (WTO) allows capital controls only under the conditions of balance of payment crisis. Most Bilateral Investment Treaties and Free Trade Agreements provide legal protection to foreign investment and its repatriation. The OECD's *Code of Liberalization of Capital Movements* is a legally binding instrument focusing comprehensively and exclusively on international capital movements. Members of the EU are prohibited from imposing any restrictions on cross-border movements of capital among EU members and third countries. However, there are safeguards that allow for the temporary imposition of restrictions. However, once an EU member joins the currency union, these safeguards may only be imposed by the EU Council and are limited to non-members.

CAPITAL CONTROLS IN INDIA

India had been focused on the strategy of self-reliance and import substitution that inhibited capital inflows prior to the 1980s. There were numerous restrictions on capital flows—both inward and outward. Even the current account transactions were subjected to establishing the need (licensing), clearances from foreign exchange perspective (reserve adequacy), imposing import duties (fiscal constraint), etc. Foreign currency inflows were mainly on account of bilateral or multilateral funding sought by government.

With full convertibility on the current account since 1994 and enactment of Foreign Exchange Management Act, 1999 (FEMA), India cautiously treaded the path of removing controls on the capital account because of structural imbalances in the BOPs. However, the philosophy and the form of controls have evolved over time. Reserve Bank of India (RBI) had commissioned two reports on capital account convertibility in 1997 and 2006, which provided a roadmap for full convertibility of Indian rupee. In the aftermath of the Asian currency crisis, other crises in several Latin American countries highlighted the destabilizing effect of capital account openness. The removal of capital controls has to keep pace with strengthening of domestic financial sector.

During the 1990s, a number of measures were taken to widen, deepen, and integrate its various segments in financial markets. Over a period of time India is continuing its transformation from a closed economy to an open economy with cautious approach to capital account convertibility, exchange rate management, and trade liberalization. Capital account transactions are closely monitored to ensure an orderly process of liberalization and macroeconomic stability.

During 1993–95, India had strong capital inflows for portfolio investments. Sterilization was the policy responses to handle these inflows and keeping inflation under control. To absorb additional liquidity Cash Reserve Ratio (CRR) was increased and export refinance limits were reduced. During 1995–96, there was a deceleration in capital inflows. Period from 1996–2001 witnessed return of capital inflows with BOP surplus with heightened volatility in capital flows on account of Asian currency crisis and other political events This necessitated policy initiatives to manage the volatility in capital inflows which included increases in the bank rate, the repo rate, and the cash reserve ratio, sales of foreign currency in the market. Monetary measures were temporary, often reversed within a period of two to three months, consistent with the policy objective of ensuring orderly conditions.

The foreign exchange reserves increased phenomenally due to persistent inflows as also the surplus in the currency account from 2001–02 onwards. The reserves doubled to cross US$100 billion mark in March 2004. To manage inflows India resorted to increasing the outflows by prepayment of high cost official debt and rationalization of interest rates on non-resident Indian (NRI) deposits. With the changing profile of capital flows, the traditional approach of assessing reserve adequacy in terms of import cover has been broadened to include number of parameters which take into account the size, composition, and the risk profiles of various types of capital flows as well as the types of external shocks to which the economy is vulnerable.

A number of steps were taken to offset the expansionary impact of external flows on domestic money supply. These included the following:

- Increase in the minimum maturity of non-resident deposits to one year to attract stable flows as also to minimize the country's short-term external debt.
- LIBOR-linked interest rate ceilings on foreign currency denominated deposits.
- LIBOR-linked interest rate ceilings on non-resident rupee deposits.
- Substantial expansion of the automatic route of FDI abroad by Indian residents.
- Greater flexibility to corporates on pre-payment of their external commercial borrowings.
- Liberalization of surrender requirements for exporters enabling them to hold up to 100% of their proceeds in foreign currency accounts.

- Allowing banks to liberally invest abroad in high quality instruments.
- Pre-payment of debt owed to multilateral and bilateral agencies by the Government of India during 2002–03 and 2003–04.

The broad key policy response to inflows has been sterilized intervention as close to two-thirds of the inflows were absorbed by sterilized intervention. Realizing the limited stock of securities available for sale to sterilize, a market stabilization scheme was initiated in April 2004 for government to bear the cost, which hitherto was borne by RBI. The CRR was also considered as monetary policy response as substitute for sterilization. As a result of these timely and coordinated measures, India was successful in containing the contagion effect of the Asian crisis. In addition, safeguards developed over a period of time also helped in limiting the contagion. These included low current account deficit, comfortable foreign exchange reserves, low level of short-term debt, and absence of asset price bubble or credit boom.

These positive features were the result of prudent policies pursued over the years notably, cap on external commercial borrowings with restrictions on end-use, low exposure of banks to real estate and stock market, insulation from large intermediation of overseas capital by the banking sector, close monitoring of off-balance sheet items and tight legislative, regulatory, and prudential control over non-bank entities.

In effect the sterilized intervention as response to capital inflow has suited other needs of the country by enabling the accumulation of foreign currency reserves, and facilitating an expansionary fiscal policy by selling of government securities to fund the budget deficit and achieve satisfactory economic growth.

During 2010–11 rupee was relatively stable despite global financial crisis. India's capital controls are more inclined towards regulating inflows rather than outflows and converting short term into long term. This augments investment base beyond domestic savings. The following is the current status of capital controls in India:

1. FDI is welcome and there exist only sectoral limits.
2. For portfolio investments, rules and regulations are being simplified as the time progresses, like opening of government securities market for foreign portfolio investment.
3. External commercial borrowing (ECB) has fairly liberal automatic route with some restriction of all-in cost and end-use with hedging compulsion for those who do not have natural hedge by prescribing higher capital requirements.
4. Gradual opening of the issue of rupee denominated bonds indicating that India is heading for full capital account convertibility. In view of adequacy of reserve the control over outflows are getting relaxed with time by permitting resident individuals to invest in financial assets abroad.
5. Over the years, to enable the firms to manage their foreign exchange risk flexibly and efficiently, several relaxations have been introduced, such as carrying out derivative transactions on the basis of past performance rather than on the basis of individual underlying contracts, cancelling derivative contracts even as the underlying exposure exists, and hedging up to a limit without documentation.
6. Introduction of cash settled derivatives contracts on currencies available on exchanges.

SUMMARY

Free flow of capital across nations is considered beneficial for an economy in improving the capital allocation and even out the differences in the cost of capital across nations. However, this unchecked flow of capital is also considered risky when the inflows or outflows are massive and rapid. They have potential to disrupt the financial markets and impact macroeconomic policies. The capital flows are characterized by herd behaviour that puzzles policy makers to find ways of managing such spurts of inflows and outflows. While long-term inflows of foreign capital coming by way of FDI is welcome the flows on account of portfolio investment motivated by interest rate differentials is considered disruptive due to their volatile nature. Most developing nations or emerging economies who do not have very sound financial structure in place consider capital control as necessity.

Capital controls have gained prominence and have been considered appropriate because they allow much needed time required to strengthen the macroeconomic structures to absorb the benefits of cross-border flows. The implications of cross-border capital are both positive and negative. While they can help reduce cost of capital in developing nations, they can be disruptive too to cause asset price bubbles, inflationary pressure, or increased cost of sterilization. Inflows cause local currency appreciation adversely affecting the balance of payment and erosion of export competitiveness, which is vital for a developing nation. For nations pursuing pegged exchange rate system or a managed float and wanting monetary freedom must have sufficient capital control measures in place; as established by 'impossible trinity'.

Economist believe that the problem of capital flows must be addressed first by macroeconomic policy measures and only after exhausting them one must consider specific tool to contain the international capital flows. At best these measures must only be temporary to permit time for macroeconomic adjustment to take place. They should not be regarded as substitute of macroeconomic policy interventions.

The popular ways of controlling the flow of foreign capital are (a) placing end-use restrictions on capital inflows, (b) taxing the inflows/outflows based on transactions, (c) prohibiting outflows for certain time prescribing minimum holding period, and (d) prescribing enhanced reserves levels possibly varying with time. Different nations have used different ways of controlling the inflows and outflows of foreign capital.

Like most emerging economies India too has faced surges of capital inflows but its policy response to such flows has been through sterilized intervention which has enabled increase in reserves and maintaining the exchange rate, and providing fiscal stimulus vitally needed to achieve good growth.

QUESTIONS

18-1 Why do you think capital control measures are desirable for developing nations?
18-2 What are the benefits of free flow of capital for emerging market economies?
18-3 Why do you think surges of foreign flow of capital is risky for a nation?
18-4 Do capital control measures befit the 'impossible trinity'? Justify.
18-5 Can the capital control measures be a permanent feature of a nation? If so what consequences is it likely to face?
18-6 Briefly describe four capital control measures.
18-7 Differentiate between taxing of inflow of foreign capital and prescribing unremunerated reserve requirement as a tool of managing the foreign capital flow.

Part VI
Multinational Financial Management

19. Capital Asset Pricing Model—Local and Global
20. Cost of Capital and Capital Structure for Multinational Firms
21. International Capital Budgeting
22. Financing Foreign Trade
23. Taxation and Transfer Pricing in India
24. Accounting for International Operations

Capital Asset Pricing Model— Local and Global

LEARNING OBJECTIVES

This chapter aims at

- revisiting the concepts of CAPM
- highlighting the differences and complexities of CAPM to extend it in the global context
- differentiating between systematic and unsystematic risks in local and global contexts
- explaining how to find global beta
- discussing how to incorporate exchange rate risk in CAPM
- explaining segmented and integrated financial markets
- discussing how a county-specific CAPM can be arrived in segmented markets
- explaining dual listing and depository receipts as modes of integrating the financial markets

CONTENTS

Introduction
Domestic Capital Asset Pricing Model Revisited
   Return and Risk of a Portfolio
   The Efficient Frontier
   Capital Market Line
   Risk Premium on Market Portfolio
   Risk of an Asset in a Portfolio
   Pricing the Asset: The Expected Return
   Benchmark Values
   Portfolio Diversification—Domestic Markets
   Relevant Risk Measure, the Beta
Global/International Capital Asset Pricing Model
   The Efficient Frontier
   Portfolio Diversification—Global Markets
   Systematic and Unsystematic Risk for
     Global Portfolio
   Global vs Local Betas of Firms
Exchange Rate Risk
   Incorporating Exchange Rate Risk
Segmented and Integrated Markets
   Country-specific Capital Asset Pricing Model for
     Segmented Markets
Integrating Capital Markets
   Dual Listing
   American Depository Receipts and
     Global Depository Receipts
   Indian Depository Receipts
Diversifying Globally

INTRODUCTION

We all are familiar with the capital asset pricing model (CAPM), which is regarded as an extremely useful and robust model to find the risk adjusted expected returns for equity holders for any project. As long as the project is in the same environment as that of the firm, the applicability of CAPM is well established and accepted. The capital market theory deals with the aspect of how an individual asset would be priced in the efficient markets. CAPM is one such model that establishes the formal relationship between risk and return. Recall that the risk adjustment in CAPM is for business risk alone and does not include adjustment for financial risk emanating from the capital structure deploying debt in financing of the project.

The understanding of CAPM that helps investors identify assets to invest in is based on two-decision variables called return and risk. It also clarifies to the investors regarding which risks get rewarded and which do not. It also helps in knowing what returns to expect and what not to. CAPM helps managers of the firm establish the minimum cost of capital the project must earn to satisfy shareholders who are assumed to hold diversified portfolios, and are concerned with only the market risk of the project. CAPM allows managers to focus their attention on market risk and not on the project-specific risk if they are investing globally.

CAPM is also considered an appropriate model for finding the cost of equity for international projects. The reason for acceptance of CAPM as a valid model for determination of cost of equity and hence cost of capital is the recognition of the fact that return and risk are intricately linked. In other price-based models such as dividend discount model, the trade-off between risk and return is reflected in the price of the financial security. In case of a situation of single economy, the observed price can serve as a measure of cost of equity. However, in case of international investment this observed price would need to be translated in another currency. Since risk profiles in two economies are different, such derived price would not be a true reflection of cost of equity.

In this chapter, we shall be examining the basic underlying thought of CAPM first in the local context and subsequently extend it in the global context.

DOMESTIC CAPITAL ASSET PRICING MODEL REVISITED

CAPM states that returns must be commensurate with risk assumed. It consolidates risk in a single parameter called beta—a measure of systematic risk. It ignores unsystematic risk on the assumption that investors hold diversified portfolios. It replaces standard deviation as measure of total risk indicating that the variability of returns can be arrived with a simplified measure of risk, called beta that measures variability of returns of a stock in terms of variability of market as a whole.

Return and Risk of a Portfolio

In case of a single stock, the risk is measured by standard deviation of its returns. However, when combined with other stocks it becomes a portfolio. The return and risk of the portfolio exhibit different behaviours than individual stock. While the portfolio return is weighted average of the securities comprising it—as one would expect—the portfolio risk is not aggregated in the same manner. The risk of the portfolio returns, that is, standard deviation of the portfolio, in addition to the individual risks of the asset, is dependent upon how one stock behaves with respect to others. The portfolio risk in case of two-asset portfolio would be dependent upon

1. risk of individual assets measured by their standard deviations,
2. proportions of investment in each asset, and
3. covariance of the two assets.

Several combinations of two assets are possible to form portfolios by assigning different proportions of investments. Not all portfolios are equally desirable in terms of expected returns and risks. Investors either maximize return for a given risk or minimize risk for a given return.

As the size of the portfolio increases, the portfolio risk becomes increasingly a function of covariances amongst the assets comprising the portfolio, while the contribution of risk of individual assets, that is, their standard deviations diminish.

The Efficient Frontier

Of the several combinations of two assets possible, a few are more desirable than others. The portfolios that offer the greatest returns for the same risk or the least risk for the same return are called *efficient portfolios*, whereas others are inefficient and discarded by rational investors. The locus of such efficient portfolios is called *efficient frontier*. The efficient frontier of two risky assets, *A* and *B* is depicted in Figure 19-1 as *Arc ASMB*.

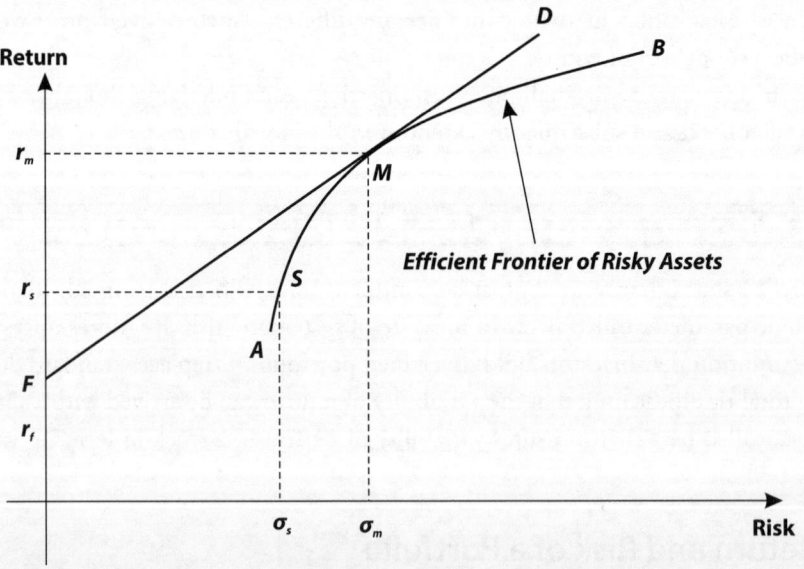

Figure 19-1
Efficient Frontier of Risky Assets and with Risk-free Asset

The assumptions of CAPM include that the only two parameters of the asset, that is, the expected return and the risk form the basis of investment. All investors attempt to maximize the utility of money that is assumed to grow with expected return but places a penalty on the risk associated with the investment. The amount of penalty depends upon the degree of risk aversion—a factor that is investor-specific. Thus, the efficient frontier would necessarily provide maximization of excess returns over the risk-free rate per unit of risk faced. The portfolios on efficient frontier would have either maximum return for a given risk or least risk for a given return.

If we expand the scope of investment beyond the risky securities to include the risk-free asset as one option it has significant influence on the shape of the efficient frontier. With the introduction of borrowing and lending at risk-free rate the efficient frontier changes dramatically. Here the lending can be thought as investment in T-bills.

Let us assume two stocks A and B with given expected returns and risks. Any investor can form numerous portfolios with the two stocks simply by changing the proportions of the money in each of them depending upon the risk and return combination that is feasible. A few of these portfolios would be efficient. With the risk-free asset, F, one may draw a capital allocation line through F and any asset on the efficient frontier of risky assets. If the amount allocated to risky asset, S is f then the portfolio return, r_p, and portfolio risk, σ_p, are represented by the following Eqs 19-1 and 19-2.

$$r_p = (1-f)r_f + fr_s \tag{19-1}$$

$$\sigma_p = f\sigma_s \tag{19-2}$$

where r_p and σ_p are the return and risk of the portfolio comprising risky asset, S, and risk-free asset. r_f is the risk-free rate, r_s and σ_s are the return and risk of risky security S, and variance of risk-free asset and its covariance with S is zero.

Capital Market Line

The existence of portfolio M and the risk-free asset has very significant and important implication in portfolio management. The straight line joining the risk-free asset and the portfolio M becomes the efficient frontier. The line joining F and M is the tangency line that has maximum slope. It implies that for a given increase in risk the increase in return would be largest if the portfolio is on this tangency line. As all investors are guided by same trade-off of risk and return they all necessarily must choose portfolios that lie on the *straight line FMD* in Figure 19-1.

Any combination of risk and return that lies on the *line FMD,* called capital market line, that is, the line passing through risk-free asset and the market portfolio, is achieved by merely adjusting the proportions of investment in the two assets, that is, the risk-free asset, F and the portfolio, M. Therefore, all investors must necessarily choose portfolio M and F rather than S and F.

The Market Portfolio, M From the foregoing it is evident that if all investors have homogeneous expectations, identical holding period, and only market assets to invest in, then all the investors would choose the same risky portfolio, M. The portfolio M remains common to all investors irrespective of their attitudes towards risk. The desired risk and return can be obtained by changing proportions of investment in F and M. What could be this common portfolio? This risky portfolio, M shall be nothing but the market portfolio (a portfolio consisting of all securities that are traded in proportion of their market capitalization). This portfolio shall be on efficient frontier and will also be on maximum slope line from F along which capital allocation to F and M can be done.

Risk Premium on Market Portfolio The next question that needs to be answered is that what extra returns over and above the risk-free rate must be provided by the market portfolio? The excess return over the risk-free rate is referred to as risk premium. The market risk premium must be proportional to the risk contained in the market portfolio. If σ_m is the standard deviation of market return then the risk premium must be proportional to the risk of market portfolio

$$\text{or Market Risk Premium} \propto \sigma_m^2$$

Risk of an Asset in a Portfolio We are aware that the portfolio risk is given by sum of all the covariance of all the securities comprising the portfolio. Each security in the portfolio contributes to its overall risk. The contribution of risk of an individual security to the portfolio risk is dominated by its covariance with other securities in the portfolio, and not as much by its own variance.

Pricing the Asset: The Expected Return

How would an asset be priced in an efficient market? We continue to assume that all investors are holding the risk-free security and the risky security namely the market portfolio, M. Suppose after some research we are able to identify some security, S, that seems to offer a better return than the risky security, M, already in the portfolio. It has an expected return of r_s and standard deviation of σ_s.

To capture increased return the investor would reallocate the existing portfolio by borrowing some money to invest in S. Let us compare the two strategies A and B which involve borrowing a fractional and equal amounts, Δ and act as follows:

Strategy A: Borrow Δ and invest in market portfolio M
Strategy B: Borrow Δ and invest in security S

Strategy A: Borrow Δ and Invest in Market Portfolio The investor opting for incremental borrowing invested in the market portfolio would face some extra returns and risk due to change in the portfolio.

$$\text{Increase in return for the investor would be} = \Delta(r_m - r_f)$$

The new risk of the portfolio too would change and would be equal to the proportional amount multiplied by risk of the risky asset. Therefore,

$$\text{New risk, the variance} = (1 + \Delta)^2 \sigma_m^2 \cong (1 + 2\Delta)\sigma_m^2 \text{ (Ignoring the } \Delta^2 \text{ term being small)}$$

The earlier risk the investor faced was σ_m and therefore the increase in risk is

Incremental risk $\cong 2\Delta\sigma_m^2$

The reward per unit of risk assumed by the investor due to increased outlay of investment, referred to as incremental risk premium, would be

Incremental risk premium $\cong \Delta(r_m - r_f)/2\Delta\sigma_m^2$

Strategy B: Borrow Δ and Invest in Security S If investor opts for investment in the newly found security, S, he would face some extra returns and risk due to change in the portfolio.

Increase in return for the investor would be $= \Delta(r_s - r_f)$

Likewise the risk of the portfolio too would change. The new risk would be

$$= \sigma_m^2 + \Delta^2\sigma_s^2 + 2\Delta\text{Cov}(s,m)$$

Again ignoring the Δ^2 term being too small the increase in risk is $\cong 2\Delta\text{Cov}(s,m)$

And the incremental risk premium

$$\cong \Delta(r_s - r_f)/2\Delta\text{Cov}(s,m)$$

If any of the strategies of the two is more rewarding, that is, it offers greater incremental risk premium than the other the investors would prefer that. If strategy B is more rewarding than the strategy A the investors would rush for buying security, S either by borrowing more and more or by divesting the market portfolio. This would drive up the price of security S bringing down its returns. This process would continue till such time the incremental risk premium of the two strategies becomes equal. In an efficient market, this would happen more quickly than one would imagine.

Therefore, for equilibrium in the prices the incremental risk premium under strategy A and strategy B must be identical. We equate the two to get Eq. 19-3 what is known as Capital Asset Pricing Model.

$$\frac{\Delta(r_s - r_f)}{2\Delta\,\text{Cov}(s,m)} = \frac{\Delta(r_m - r_f)}{2\Delta\sigma_m^2}$$

$$r_s = r_f + \frac{\text{Cov}(s,m)}{\Delta_m^2}(r_m - r_f)$$

$$= r_f + \beta(r_m - r_f) \tag{19-3}$$

because $\beta = \dfrac{\text{Cov}(s,m)}{\Delta_m^2}$ by definition

Benchmark Values

CAPM as given by Eq. 19-3 requires three critical inputs namely market return, risk-free rate of return, and the beta of the security which is being valued. Of these two inputs are common to the valuation of all securities. We need the value of market return and risk-free rate. The following are considered reasonable approximations and proxies for the values of the risk-free rate and market return:

1. T-bills (ST Govt. security) is assumed to have zero risk, β = 0, and risk premium of 0, and a return of r_f. This is regarded as reasonable estimate of the risk-free rate. The yields on the T-bills would therefore replace the risk-free rate.
2. The market portfolio is assumed to have β = 1 and risk premium of $(r_m - r_f)$ is taken as reward for taking the market risk. As a reasonable substitute to the market, an index serves as best proxy.

The risk of all the securities is measured in terms of their relationship with the chosen market index. If the relationship of the security with the market indicates greater sensitivity the β value would be greater than one. If it is less sensitive than market its beta would be less than one. For securities that exhibit same risk in returns and move in exact tandem with the market, the beta would be 1.00.

Expected risk premium of any security, $S(r_s - r_f)$ varies directly with its beta as given by Eq. 19-4.

$$r_s - r_f = \beta^*(r_m - r_f) \tag{19-4}$$

Portfolio Diversification—Domestic Markets

The virtues of portfolio diversification for risk reduction are well established. The risk of the portfolio reduces as we add new securities to it. Lesser the degree of correlation, better is the outcome. However, as we add securities to the portfolio the risk reduction takes place at a decreasing rate. Simply stated the risk reduction achieved by adding 5th stock to a portfolio of four is far higher than the risk reduction due to addition of 55th stock to a portfolio of 54 stocks. As the portfolio grows in terms of number of securities, the risk reduction by induction of new security into the portfolio becomes lesser and lesser.

Would adding new securities to a portfolio continue to reduce portfolio risk and make it zero? The answer is that it would not because different securities react differently to different situations.

Systematic and Unsystematic Risks We are aware that the risk of investment in equities consists of systematic and unsystematic risks. The systematic risk arises from the factors that impact the returns of all the stocks. The impact of factors, such as growth rate, fiscal policies, monetary policies, and tariff affects large number of stocks if not market as a whole. The unsystematic risk comprises factors unique to a particular firm, such as expansion plans, financing structure, management, and technical know-how. These factors are firm-specific that alter the return of the firm in question.

The portfolio theory suggests that by increasing the number of securities in the portfolio the unsystematic risk can be diversified away. Therefore, the risk of combining two stocks would be smaller than the risk of single stock. As we increase the number of stocks in the portfolio, the proportion of unsystematic risk reduces. After sufficiently large number of stocks in the portfolio the component of unsystematic risk would become almost negligible. This is called diversification effect.

The portfolio risk for sufficiently large number of stocks would then consist of the systematic risk alone. Empirical studies suggest that for effective diversification the number of stocks could be as low as 20–25, where the unsystematic risk becomes almost negligible. The selection of the stocks should be based on coefficient of correlations of the stock returns. Negative coefficient of correlation is desired but such negatively correlated securities are difficult to find. In such case, we choose stocks with low degrees of correlation with one another. The diversification effect in a portfolio as function of number of securities in it is depicted in Figure 19-2. It exhibits that some residual risk would remain no matter how large the portfolio becomes. This residual risk is called systematic risk and portfolio considerations would entirely be guided by it.

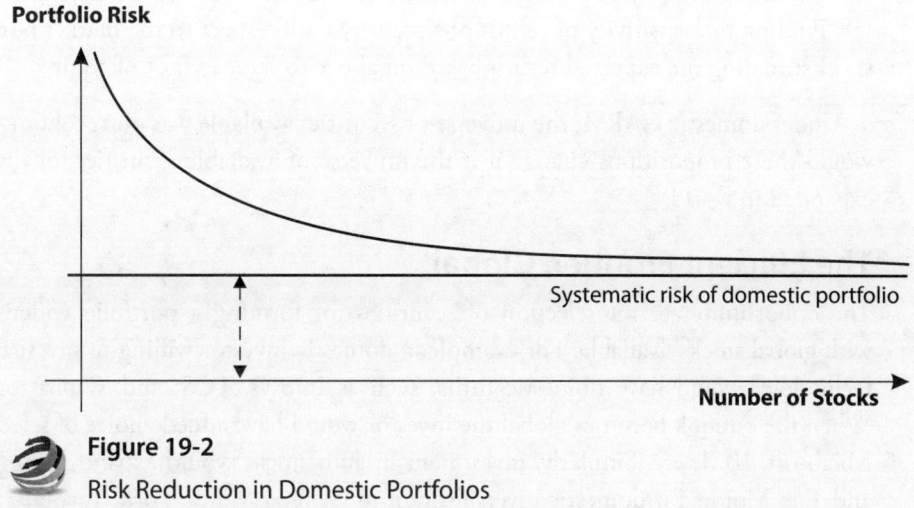

Figure 19-2
Risk Reduction in Domestic Portfolios

Systematic risk, the sole risk in the well-diversified portfolio is measured from its beta, β. β signifies the changes in the returns of the portfolio with respect to changes in the market. It is the sensitivity of the returns of the well-diversified portfolio devoid of unsystematic risk. Both for local and global portfolios, the sensitivity of returns would be given by the β of the portfolio. How is beta of global portfolio different from that of local portfolio is the question when we extend the CAPM model to the global situation.

Relevant Risk Measure, the Beta

CAPM bifurcates risk into two elements—the systematic risk and the unsystematic risk. CAPM does not concern itself with unsystematic risk assuming efficient markets and adequate diversification on part of all investors. The only concern addressed by CAPM is the systematic risk, which becomes relevant for determination of pricing of the financial asset. In efficient markets, the investors would get rewarded for only the systematic risk as the unsystematic risk can be diversified away. Therefore, for measurement of cost of equity the relevant risk that needs to be rewarded is measured by beta and not standard deviation.

GLOBAL/INTERNATIONAL CAPITAL ASSET PRICING MODEL

CAPM in domestic or single country context assumes that all investors hold a market portfolio that lies on the efficient frontier as well as on capital allocation line that provides the most efficient trade-off of highest increase in returns for a given increase in risk. The domestic CAPM essentially involved the following:

(a) Identification of efficient frontier
(b) Estimating the risk-free rate—returns on T-bills was a good proxy
(c) Finding the tangency portfolio with risk-free rate and market portfolio, and market portfolio as represented by index was considered suitable substitute
(d) Assuming the market portfolio as efficient eliminates the need for finding efficient frontier
(e) Finding the sensitivity of return of a security with respect to the market portfolio
(f) Estimating the expected return based on above to serve as cost of equity

Under domestic CAPM, the universe of securities available was one economy/nation. How would these propositions change if it the universe of available securities for diversification is expanded to world?

The Efficient Frontier, Global

The opportunity set for selection of securities for forming a portfolio widens considerably with global stocks available. For example, a domestic investor willing to invest in information technology would have domestic firms, such as Infosys, TCS, and Wipro to choose from. When the outlook becomes global the investor would have added choice of selecting firms like Microsoft, IBM, etc. Similarly, investment in auto stocks would expand from Maruti Udyog and Tata Motors for domestic diversification to General Motor, Ford, Toyota, Honda, etc. for international diversification. Due to the smaller correlation among international stocks, the diversification effect would be greater in case of the global portfolio. A portfolio consisting of stocks across the globe would result in greater reduction of risk for same level of return, or greater increase in returns for same level of risk, as compared to a pure domestic portfolio. Therefore, for global portfolio the efficient frontier should shift upwards as shown in Figure 19-3.

One implication of upwards shifting of efficient frontier and consequent delegation of domestic market portfolio (proxy by the local index) is the inability to use the local beta for estimation of cost of capital when firms diversify into another country. For example, Bharti Telecom would be right in using its beta for evaluating acquisition of another telecom circle in India but it would be improper to use the same beta when it acquires African operations of Zain.

The Market Portfolio The optimal portfolio would now lie on this global efficient frontier. The domestic optimal portfolio substituted as market portfolio of domestic securities only would lie below this new efficient frontier, and would no more be optimal. Instead global market portfolio would be optimal. The global market portfolio would have lesser risk and

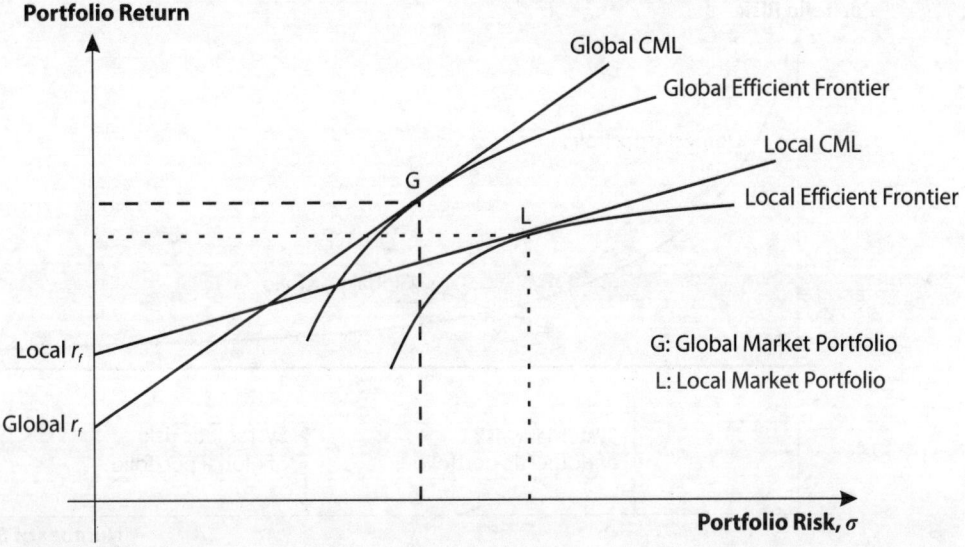

Figure 19-3
Markowitz Efficient Frontiers of Local and Global Portfolios

higher return than the local market portfolio. This may again be seen from Figure 19-3 comparing local and global optimal portfolio, *L* and *G*, respectively.

With upwards shift of the efficient frontier the capital market line would now be steeper than the domestic capital market line, even if the same risk-free rate is assumed to prevail internationally as that of domestic (which would not be the case). Since the global CML would be steeper the reward to risk ratio is higher for global diversification, which can easily be visualised from Figure 19-3. The global efficient frontier would have both, that is, lesser risk and higher return as compared to local efficient frontier.

CAPM as a model to measure risk adjusted cost of equity assumes that all investors not only hold the same market portfolio but also agree on the same expected returns and risk characteristics of the security being valued. The assumption of homogeneous expectations limits the applicability of CAPM more severely in the international context. All investors at global level must agree for the same expected return and corresponding risk for an investment; a situation hard to visualize.

Portfolio Diversification—Global Markets

Figure 19-4 depicts the difference in the diversification effects of the portfolio consisting of local stocks and the portfolio comprising global stocks. Since the number of factors that would affect the stocks on worldwide basis is smaller a well-diversified global portfolio would have smaller β as compared to the portfolio comprising only local stocks. The effect of diversification would be more pronounced and faster in portfolio of global stocks because of the following reasons:

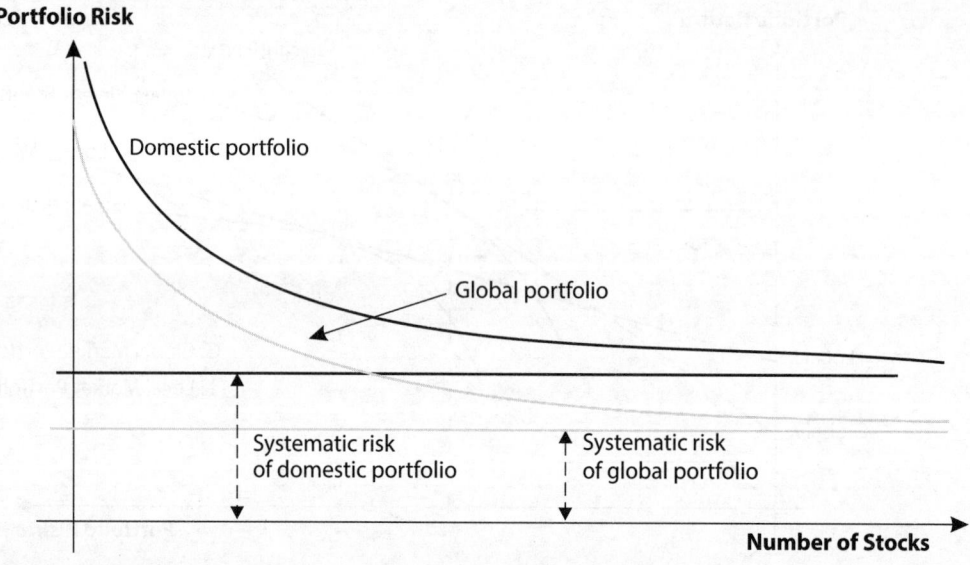

Figure 19-4
Risk Reduction in Global and Domestic Portfolios

(a) The portfolio of global stocks would have lower risk as the number of factors affecting global markets would be significantly lower. For example, government policies in the India would impact returns in the Indian markets. However, the impact of changes in the policies by government of India would have lesser impact on the returns if portfolio consisted of global stocks rather than Indian stocks. As such what is systematic in local environment may become unsystematic in global scenario and hence is diversifiable.

(b) Another factor that helps risk reduction in global portfolio is the improved probability to find stocks with low degrees of correlation on global basis. For example, returns of Microsoft in USA and Infosys in India would be rather less correlated than the returns of Infosys and Wipro in India. Hence, it is easier to construct a portfolio with desirable risk reduction features on global basis.

Hence, portfolio of global stocks would have lower β as compared to portfolio of local stocks.

Investing globally offers wider menu of stocks to choose from. With several multinational corporations (MNCs) establishing worldwide network with increased specialization in the product and services offered the diversification would demand a portfolio consisting of many industries and products. For example, a Japanese investor would not have software-based firm in his portfolio, as firm as large as Microsoft may not be available in their domestic markets. Similarly, US investors may face a lack of suitable investment opportunity in consumer electronics if confined to US stocks alone. For effective diversification, one would have to access the Japanese stock markets for investing in likes of Sony, Panasonic, etc. Similarly, for diversifying into aviation one has to include stocks of Boeing or Airbus. Hence, more effective diversification can be achieved by investing internationally as variety available increases. The trade-off between risk and return would be better with international investing.

Systematic and Unsystematic Risk for Global Portfolio

In case of a domestic portfolio, the systematic factors would comprise economy wide events, such as fiscal, monetary, and trade policies. These factors are common to all stocks impacting their returns. However, these policies around the world are not aligned with one another due to diverse national objectives. For a global portfolio the events that would impact most stocks in such a portfolio should only constitute the systematic risk. Thus, fiscal, monetary, and trade policies of different economies or nations not being aligned, become unsystematic factors for a global portfolio. Therefore, what is considered systematic for domestic portfolio could indeed become unsystematic for global portfolio. Factors that have the potential to influence returns of global portfolio would be too few. These would include global events, such as recession, currency crises, political instabilities, wars amongst nations, and earthquakes.

Due to lesser number of events that impact the global portfolio returns, the level of systematic risk for a global portfolio consisting of international stocks should be lower than that of a domestic portfolio comprising stocks from single economy.

Global vs Local Betas of Firms

Systematic risk of a stock is measured by its beta. Beta of a stock is defined as ratio of its covariance with the global market, and the variance of the global market, σ_m^2 as given by Eq. 19-5.

$$\text{Beta for stock, } s = \frac{\text{Covariance }(s, m)}{\text{Variance}} = \rho_{sm} \frac{\sigma_s \sigma_m}{\sigma_m^2} = \rho_{sm} \frac{\sigma_s}{\sigma_m} \qquad (19\text{-}5)$$

Benchmarking for betas for global and domestic portfolio too would become different. The relationship of returns of the security against the benchmark index would govern the value of beta. For domestic portfolio an index, such as NIFTY or SENSEX for India, serves as an ideal proxy for the market. In the context of global portfolio, we need to benchmark the portfolio returns against a global index. Several such indices from MSCI (promoted by erstwhile Morgan Stanley and Capital International) are available.

The measurement of sensitivity of returns of each security with respect to returns of global portfolio, proxy by a global index, would provide the global beta of the stock. The local beta of the same stock measured against a domestic benchmark would be different, and should be higher than when measured against its global equivalent on the presumption that returns of a firm must be more correlated with the economy it operates in. Even global firms such as IBM, Coca-Cola, and Pepsi which derive considerable revenues and profits from operations in several economies and in several currencies are likely to have higher beta locally in USA than globally because significant proportion of their operations are still driven by policies and

CONCEPTS IN PRACTICE
Global Market Portfolio

WORLD INDICES

MSCI indices are free float-adjusted market capitalization weighted indices that are designed to measure the equity market performance of various markets. They have several indices focusing on different domains and most prominent of them are all markets world index, developed market index, and emerging market index.

The MSCI ACWI consists of 45 country indices comprising 24 developed and 21 emerging market country indices. The developed market country indices included are*: Australia, Austria, Belgium, Canada, Denmark, Finland, France, Germany, Greece, Hong Kong, Ireland, Israel, Italy, Japan, Netherlands, New Zealand, Norway, Portugal, Singapore, Spain, Sweden, Switzerland, the United Kingdom, and the USA. The emerging market country indices included are Brazil, Chile, China, Colombia, Czech Republic, Egypt, Hungary, India, Indonesia, Korea, Malaysia, Mexico, Morocco, Peru, Philippines, Poland, Russia, South Africa, Taiwan, Thailand, and Turkey.

The MSCI World Index measures the equity market performance of developed markets. The MSCI World Index consists of the following 24 developed market country indices*: Australia, Austria, Belgium, Canada, Denmark, Finland, France, Germany, Greece, Hong Kong, Ireland, Israel, Italy, Japan, Netherlands, New Zealand, Norway, Portugal, Singapore, Spain, Sweden, Switzerland, the United Kingdom, and the United States.

Similarly, the MSCI Emerging Markets Index is designed to measure equity market performance of emerging markets. The MSCI Emerging Markets Index consists of the following 21 emerging market country indices*: Brazil, Chile, China, Colombia, Czech Republic, Egypt, Hungary, India, Indonesia, Korea, Malaysia, Mexico, Morocco, Peru, Philippines, Poland, Russia, South Africa, Taiwan, Thailand, and Turkey.

*As of 31 December, 2012

Source: www.msci.com, accessed on 23 April 2013.

markets of USA. In exceptional cases where the returns of the stock are more driven by global events rather than local events one may find global beta to be higher than local beta.

If stock of Hindustan Unilever has a beta of 1.10 when measured against NIFTY or SENSEX, then its beta should be lower when the same share is included in a global portfolio.

International diversification is recommended for its potential to lower the risk of portfolio returns because of the fact that stock markets of different nations exhibit low degrees of correlation that tend to even out the returns of one market with another rendering stability. These correlations are low because of many factors. Different nations are at different levels of

Table 19-1
Risks of Emerging Stock Markets and Their Correlation of Indian Stock Markets

Country	Index	Standard Deviation, %	Correlation Coefficient of Returns of Stock Indices with NIFTY
India	NIFTY	5.64	1.00
China	Shanghai Composite	19.87	0.02
Hong Kong	Hang Seng	3.38	0.22
Indonesia	Jakarta Composite	11.52	0.37
Malaysia	KLSE Composite	4.70	0.07
Japan	Nikkei 225	3.43	−0.04
Singapore	Straits Times	2.44	0.20
Korea	Seoul Composite	5.74	0.11
Taiwan	Taiwan Weighted	4.11	−0.03
Israel	TA 40	8.57	0.22
USA	DJIA	1.82	−0.06
USA	S&P 500	2.06	−0.01

Source: Siddique, Saif (2009), *Examining Association between Select CNX Nifty and Selected Asian and US Stock Markets*.

economic development, varying growth rates, phased out or asynchronous business cycles, different levels of market efficiencies, extent of capital controls, etc. Table 19-1 presents risks associated with returns of different stock markets and their relationship with Indian markets as measured through various stock indices during the period of June 2004 to May 2009.

EXCHANGE RATE RISK

While low degree of correlation would encourage portfolio diversification for risk reduction, investing globally adds one more dimension that goes to increase the risk, that is, the exchange rate risk. One major hurdle in transforming the expectation of returns to same level is the exchange rate movement.

Assume that all investor agree that return in the Indian market would be 20%. Would this return be same for all global investors? Due to uneven changes in the exchange rate it would not be so.

Let us consider an example. Assume two investors, one from USA and another from Europe, who have homogeneous expectation of 20% return in Indian markets invest one unit at prevailing exchange rates of ₹50/€ and ₹60/$, respectively. However, at the end of one year US dollar appreciates by 5% while appreciation of euro is 10%. If so the returns realized by them in their respective currencies are 9% and 14% by European and American, respectively, as is depicted in Table 19-2.

Table 19-2
Differential of Expected Return due to Exchange Rate Movements

Return and Exchange Rate Scenario	European Investor	American Investor
Initial Investment	€1.00	$1.00
Equivalent Rupee	₹60.00	₹50.00
Final Value of Investment	₹72.00	₹60.00
Exchange Rate after 1 Year	₹66.00	₹52.50
Equivalent Home Currency Amount	€1.09	$1.14
Return in Home Currency	9%	14%

Despite unanimity about the rupee returns by both investors, their returns in the respective home currencies would be different. Even if they have homogeneous expectation of rupee returns the homogeneity would not exist due to exchange rate risks. For all investors—Indian, European, and American in this case, the return at 20% would remain same if the exchange rate did not move at all. However, if they did then returns would be different depending upon the how the exchange rates behaved.

If returns are not measured in nominal but in real terms (net of inflation) the realized returns in respective currencies would depend on whether the exchange rates moved according to the relative purchasing power parity. If relative purchasing power parity holds then the real returns would be identical. It is indeed difficult to assume that relative purchasing power parity would hold.

Nominal vs Real Returns In terms of real returns, CAPM is stated as Eq. 19-6.

$$(r_s - r_f) = \beta(r_m - r_f) \tag{19-6}$$

From Fisher effect, we have the relationship of real and nominal returns stated as Eq. 19-7.

$$1 + r = \frac{1+R}{1+I} \tag{19-7}$$

Where r is real return, R is nominal return with I as inflation rate.

In case of small periods of time inflation rate does not change much. In addition, for small inflation rates the real and nominal rates are approximated as $r \approx R - I$.

In terms of nominal rates, the CAPM then becomes

$$(R_s - I - R_f + I) = \beta(R_m - I - R_f + I) \text{ or}$$
$$(R_s - R_f) = \beta(R_m - R_f) \tag{19-8}$$

Beta with Real and Nominal Returns Therefore, as long as time periods involved and inflation rates are small CAPM as given be Eq. 19-6 is same as the one given by Eq. 19-8, remains valid irrespective of whether returns are real or nominal. Regression analysis for determination of beta too could be performed with nominal excess returns data for market and security. It would be no different if the returns were real. Due to high volatility of equity returns, stability of inflation rates the betas based on real and nominal rates would not be different.

Relative Purchasing Power Parity (PPP) and Capital Controls For international investing the guiding principle is not the nominal return but real return. Let us examine how the returns for the foreign investor would differ. Suppose Indian stock markets have an expected return of 20% and there exist no capital flow controls. Assuming an inflation rate in India as 5% the real returns obtained by an Indian investor is 14.28% as given by Eq. 19-7.

$$1+r = \frac{1+R}{1+I} = \frac{1.20}{1.05} = 1.1428 \quad \text{or} \quad r = 14.28\%$$

For an American investor would the return be same as that of Indian investor? Assume current spot rate of ₹55/\$ and investment horizon of one year. With investment of \$1.00 his ending wealth in Indian rupee would be ₹55 × 1.2 = ₹66.00. If the spot rate after one year is ₹60/\$ the equivalent US dollar are 66/60 = \$1.10. With inflation rate of 2% in USA the real return would be 7.84%. Hence, the returns for foreign investors are dependent upon (a) the exchange rates and (b) inflation rates. Further these returns are also dependent upon the rates of taxes, treatment of tax on dividend, and capital gains. Here we have assumed same rates of taxation and same treatment of capital gains and dividend across all nations.

Proceeding in the similar manner the real rates of returns for French, British, and Japanese investors in their respective currencies with assumed exchange rates and inflation rates have been worked out in Table 19-3.

Varying real rates of return in the last column of Table 19-3 clearly establish that capital markets are not in equilibrium even when the markets are fully integrated, that is, there are absolutely no barriers to the flow of capital across borders. Hence, asset prices in various markets would continue to exhibit different returns in different markets even when the financial markets are fully integrated.

Table 19-3

Nominal and Real Returns from International Investing

Investor	Currency	Exchange Rate Now, (₹ per unit of invested currency)	Exchange Rate after One Year, (₹ per unit of invested currency)	Nominal Return, (% p.a. in invested currency)	Inflation Rate, (% p.a.)	Real Return, (% p.a. in invested currency)
US Investor	\$	55.00	60.00	10.00	2.00	7.84
French Investor	€	72.00	75.00	15.20	3.00	11.84
British Investor	£	84.00	86.00	17.21	4.00	12.70
Japanese Investor	¥	0.55	0.54	22.22	1.00	21.01
Indian Investor	₹	1.00	1.00	20.00	5.00	14.28

These returns would be equalized, that is, asset price equilibrium be achieved if in addition to free flow of capital signifying integrated markets, the exchange rates in the currency markets moved exactly per relative PPP. If relative PPP were to hold the exchange rate at the end of investment horizon of one year would be 55 × 1.05/1.02 = ₹56.6176/$ and dollar return for American investor would be 14.28%, that is, same as what the Indian investor earns. Readers may verify if the returns for French, British, and Japanese investors too would be identical at 14.28% if exchange rates moved exactly as per relative PPP.

With regard to application of CAPM for international investment the returns would comprise (a) absolute returns in the currency of investment, and (b) returns on exchange rate. CAPM would only establish asset price equilibrium in a single economy where the risk is condensed in single factor, beta. International markets would be in equilibrium when real rates of return are equalized. This would happen only when relative PPP holds and capital markets are integrated with no capital controls existing across borders.

Incorporating Exchange Rate Risk

Knowing well that PPP in any form is not likely to hold the international investment decision based on assumed equilibrium of asset prices as per CAPM would be erroneous. Does that mean that we abandon CAPM? Mechanical application of CAPM in international situations may not be advised. However, we may extend the underlying principle of CAPM that attempts to consolidate risk in a single factor called beta for pricing of assets. CAPM is a single factor model and it clubbed all the risk into a single parameter of excess market returns proportional to the sensitivity of returns with respect to market portfolio.

In extending the CAPM to global markets another dimension of risk, that is, exchange rate risk was added, which in no case be clubbed with the market risk. Since there are two facets of risks in international investing—returns in the markets invested in, and returns on the exchange rates—we may segregate risks on two factors and assign a premium to each. Just as the sensitivity of with market portfolio is termed beta we may define sensitivity of return with respect to exchange rates as gamma, γ. Extending the central idea of CAPM we may state the CAPM in international context as excess return on an asset consisting of (a) beta times excess return of global portfolio and (b) gamma times the excess returns on exchange rates. Thus, CAPM may be stated as

Excess Return on Asset = Beta × Excess Returns on Market Portfolio + Gamma × Excess Returns on Currency Markets

As the benchmarking of excess returns over market portfolio is done with risk-free rate in the economy the benchmarking for return in the currency market can be done with the forward premium/discount, fp prevailing in the currency markets. For a portfolio of investment in n currencies, we may state the CAPM as Eq. 19-9.

$$r_s - r_f = \beta(r_m - r_f) + \sum_{1}^{n} \gamma_i (s_i - fp_i) \qquad (19\text{-}9)$$

Each of the terms of the Eq. 19-9 is briefly described here:

- The excess returns on asset, $r_s - r_f$, are measured in home currency of investor, that is, US dollar for an American, euro for a German, Indian rupee for an Indian investor, etc.
- Risk-free rate, r_f, would be return on government securities of the home country of the investor.
- Market excess returns, $r_m - r_f$ is measured in the home currency on the world market portfolio. A suitable proxy for market portfolio could be any of the MSCI World indices.
- Currency returns for ith currency, s_i, is the percent change in the exchange rate for ith currency measured in terms of direct rates.
- Forward premium, fp_i, is the percent premium in ith currency in the currency markets if they are vibrant. In case of inefficient currency markets lacking depth the forward premium can be replaced by differential of risk-free rates of home currency and foreign currency.
- Sensitivity of returns with market portfolio, beta would be obtained by regression slope of market excess returns with security's excess returns using historical data.
- Sensitivity of returns with currency markets, gamma would be obtained by regression slope of excess returns of security with currency market excess returns using historical data.

Beta and the Risk-free Rate   We already discussed that beta of the global portfolio would be smaller than that of domestic portfolio in the preceding section and as depicted in Figure 19-4. The risk-free rate for the domestic portfolio would be set equal to returns on the government securities considered devoid of any risk. The securities issued by governments in different countries offer return consistent with economic conditions prevailing in the region. For example, returns on short term government securities in India could be 6% while those in USA could be 3%. How do we explain the difference in returns? The difference in returns could be attributed to difference in economic conditions of two countries, mainly gauged by inflation rates. If so the nominal returns may differ by differential of inflation rate (the purchasing power parity) but not the real returns.

If measured in terms of nominal returns the global risk-free rate could be more/less or equal to the local risk-free rate as it should be computed as weighted average of risk-free rate across the globe. That must bring down the risk-free rate for developing nations, that is, not all but half of the world. For developed nations the risk-free rate would be smaller than the weighted average risk-free rates across the globe.

Another added dimension is the perception of risk-free rate. While the assumption of returns on government securities as risk-free may be valid for local investors, it may not be perceived so by international investors. There are instances when foreign investors have burnt their fingers while lending to developing nations and governments on the premise that 'firms fail but nations do not' because of the unique position of all governments to print the local currency and honour commitments. That precisely was the premise when US banks lent to several Latin American nations in the 1980s. Hence, for international investors some part of the returns on government securities may be perceived as premium for default risk.

SEGMENTED AND INTEGRATED MARKETS

The validity of international/global CAPM would depend upon the state of capital markets across the globe. In two extreme situations they can be seen as *fully segmented* or *fully integrated*.

Segmented markets would be those where neither a domestic investor is allowed to diversify in another nations nor a foreign investor is allowed to participate in the domestic markets. If we assume segmented markets then the local CAPM works fine. If markets are segmented no MNC would be permitted to set up operations. The portfolio investment in the capital markets are simply out of question.

At the other extreme, we may have fully integrated markets where irrespective of nationalities and currency, all are allowed to have diversification through projects or through portfolio investments in different capital markets around the world. No capital controls exist in fully integrated capital markets. In such a situation, international CAPM would determine the cost of equity in for MNCs in their project diversification endeavours. This warrants use of risk-free rate, beta, and risk premium on global basis. All these parameters would not be difficult to determine.

Markets are integrated if asset prices in the world market offer identical returns irrespective of the domicile or currency of investment. Any kind of restriction in free flow of capital would distort the returns in various markets.

Recognizing that beta based on global portfolio is lower than the one based on domestic market portfolio the global cost of equity is lower. Using a global beta for determining the cost of equity therefore would lead to lower hurdle rate to be overcome for acceptance of the project. For example, an Indian telecom firm for an expansion project needs to know the desired rate of return by the potential investors predominantly Indian. This hurdle rate may be computed by CAPM by either using local or global beta. Using global beta would lead to lower hurdle rate.

Country-specific Capital Asset Pricing Model for Segmented Markets

If Indian markets are segmented then all securities would be priced as per local CAPM. Modifying Eq. 19-6 by substituting market returns specific to India the CAPM for India becomes

$$\text{India-specific CAPM: } (r_s - r_f) = \beta(r_{\text{Ind}} - r_f) \tag{19-10}$$

Where r_{Ind} is the market return on an index in Indian capital markets, and beta is covariance of the security returns with the chosen index, that is,

$$\beta = \frac{\text{Cov}(r_s, r_{\text{Ind}})}{\sigma^2_{\text{Ind}}} \tag{19-11}$$

Substituting value of beta in India-specific CAPM, we get price of security in terms of coefficient of risk aversion, A defined as excess returns of the market portfolio divided by variance of the market. Risk aversion indicates the price of risk for Indian investors and can be specific to each nation depending upon the several macroeconomic variables, stage of development, diversification opportunities, level of market efficiency, etc. Re-arranging the CAPM on an aggregate basis, we get Eq. 19-12.

$$\begin{aligned} r_s - r_f &= \frac{\text{Cov}(r_s, r_{\text{Ind}})}{\sigma_{\text{Ind}}^2}(r_{\text{Ind}} - r_f) \\ &= \text{Cov}(r_s, r_{\text{Ind}})\frac{(r_{\text{Ind}} - r_f)}{\sigma_{\text{Ind}}^2} \\ &= A_{\text{Ind}}\text{Cov}(r_s, r_{\text{Ind}}) \end{aligned} \quad (19\text{-}12)$$

Equation 19-12 attempts to price one asset in terms of its covariance with the market and risk aversion. If all traded assets in an economy are aggregated return, r_s is aggregated, and right hand side of Eq. 19-12 changes from security-specific return to market return expected by Indian investors. Similarly, the left hand side comprising the covariance of individual security when aggregated for all securities becomes market variance. Therefore, for a single economy of India Eq. 19-12 transforms to Eq. 19-13.

$$r_{\text{Ind}} = r_f + A_{\text{Ind}}\sigma_{\text{Ind}}^2 \quad (19\text{-}13)$$

Therefore, in segmented markets, the expectation of returns of Indian investors is a function of (i) variance of the Indian markets—the risk measure and (ii) risk aversion—the excess return desired per unit of variance. Since financial markets are segmented there would be small covariance with world markets.

If Markets are Integrated When capital can flow across borders freely without any regulatory controls or promotion, international investing would be guided purely by commercial considerations leading to pricing of financial assets in most efficient manner. Globally competing resources would tend to increase the efficiency of capital markets worldwide. Under equilibrium with capital markets fully integrated the decision with regard to domicile and destination of investment would lose its relevance. In terms of mobilization of capital, the hurdle rate to be overcome for capital budgeting decisions should become identical across the world. Assets would be priced so as to provide same returns in all markets. Domestic factors influencing the returns in the financial markets are overshadowed by global factors.

Even though capital markets may impose no restrictions, the currency markets would influence the expectations of returns and hence asset pricing. Therefore, one most crucial prerequisite of complete financial integration is validity of relative purchasing power parity. Its validity is not solely determined by integration of capital markets but is more dependent upon distortions in the economic, monetary, and trade policies as well as differences in social, cultural, logistics, political, and legal environments. Political differences, regulatory barriers, lack of liquidity, information asymmetry, etc. are some of the reasons that cause markets not to be integrated.

Whether or not capital markets across the world are integrated is a moot question. The most likely answer is that markets are neither fully integrated nor fully segmented. Besides reduction in barriers to flow of capital, there are many more reasons that are leading to increased convergence of capital markets. With increased flow of business across world, emergence of global companies, increased literacy levels, fast developing information channels, more instantaneous flow of information, and converging standards of living, etc. the returns in various financial markets of the world are moving in tandem. It is not uncommon to predict the behaviour of local markets next day on the basis of what happened in the markets abroad after the local markets closed and foreign markets were still open.

Starting the day with opening of Japanese markets in Tokyo the information flow is continuous throughout the day as it progresses to Australia, Hong Kong, Singapore, India, London, Zurich, Paris, etc. to New York and Chicago, which in turn would set the tone for the next day in Tokyo markets. Overflow of information and spilling of prices from one market to another is becoming increasingly seamless in stocks, commodities, currencies and other tradable assets.

Despite conscious efforts to decontrol the markets many handicaps still remain. These handicaps would have origins in information asymmetry, fear of treading the unknown markets, cultures, different environments socially, politically and legally home bias. Different nations of the world are still segmented in many ways, such as developed or emerging economies, capitalistic or socialistic, literate or illiterate, rich or poor, and ancient or modern. Different cultures, religions, values, and ethical systems would continue to exist and keep financial markets segmented enough. It must be borne in mind that segmented market does not mean inefficient local markets. Securities may be priced correctly in domestic markets yet may defy equilibrium in the context of global markets.

INTEGRATING CAPITAL MARKETS

There are many strategies that are being increasingly adopted by MNCs, though motivated by reduction of cost of capital and risk, and diversification, that are attempting world markets to become increasingly integrated. These strategies allow participation of foreign nationals in the capital markets of another nation—primary and secondary both. To the MNCs, these strategies increase global visibility and increased credibility that make them more competitive besides rendering financial advantages of reduced cost of capital and diversification of risk. Some of these strategies are discussed here.

Dual Listing

Dual listing means listing of the same company at two bourses maintaining the different identities of shareholders. In practical terms the company has the same set of cash flows that must drive its valuation in both the bourses. In fact this could be achieved by mergers of the two companies. The motivations for not merging the two and instead have dual listing are several. Cross-border merger where two firms in different jurisdictions require exchange of cash/shares of one firm for the shares of surviving firm could become impractical due to (a) differential tax treatment, (b) local regulations not permitting investments by residents in foreign firms, (c) valuation and its currency, (d) exchange rate risk in remittances of dividends, (e) ownership by foreigners, etc.

These operational hurdles can be successfully overcome by dual listing in two nations maintaining the same dividend and valuation driven by same set of cash flows. Several companies in the past and present have successfully had dual listing. Prominent examples include Unilever, an Anglo-Dutch firm listed in the UK and the Netherlands, ABB listed in

Sweden and Switzerland, BHP Billiton listed in Australia and the UK, SmithKline Beecham in the UK and USA, etc. Dual listing therefore allows direct participation of foreigners in the fortunes of a multinational firm.

In theory since same cash flows are the underlying assets the valuation in each nation must be identical. However, in practice these valuations have differed sometimes significantly. Liberal flow of capital across borders should ideally remove discrepancy in valuation through arbitrage by buying in the market that undervalues and sell in the market that overvalues. However, it has not been so. A classic example that distortions in valuation can persist for long comes from the example of LTCM; a large hedge fund managed by Noble Prize-winning experts in finance. In 1997 Royal Dutch NV listed in the Netherlands traded at a premium of about 8–10% over Shell Transport and Trading plc listed in the UK despite having same underlying cash flows. LTCM set up an arbitrage position by buying in the UK and selling in the Netherlands hoping for the price correction and booking of profits. However, in 1998, default by Russia on its debt forced LTCM to unwind its original position. The gap in price rather than shrinking had actually widened to around 22% resulting in losses running into hundreds of millions of dollars.

American Depository Receipts and Global Depository Receipts

Another tool that promotes integration of financial markets is issuance of depository receipts (DRs) that enables shareholding by foreigners. A DR is a negotiable financial security issued by a depository in lieu of shares that can be traded by foreign investors either in over-the-counter (OTC) mode or on an exchange abroad, if listed. Depository receipt represents a firm that is a domicile of other nation. The DRs are issued in foreign currency and are equivalent to the underlying shares issued in local currency that are traded in the national markets where the issuing firm is domiciled.

Normally, a firm mobilizes capital from local investors by issuing shares to the residents and have them listed on the local stock exchanges for trading facilitating entry and exit of individual investors. Depending upon the regulatory environment of the nation foreign investors may or may not be allowed to subscribe to such issues. Non-residents are normally not permitted to subscribe to the shares. Further even if permitted the foreigners may not be willing to participate for other reasons such non-familiarity with foreign capital markets.

The DR is one way of inviting participation by foreign investors in raising capital overcoming investors' inhibitions by denominating the equity in freely convertible currency and offering an entry and exit route abroad. The investor base can be expanded to include global investors by issuance of DRs. The mechanism of issuance of DRs is described here and depicted in Figure 19-5:

- An international bank, called depository purchases shares in the local stock exchanges.
- Against the shares purchased the bank issues a DR representing equivalent number of shares.
- These receipts are denominated in foreign currency and are issued to the investors in other countries.
- These receipts would then be traded by subscribers either OTC or over the exchanges abroad if listed.

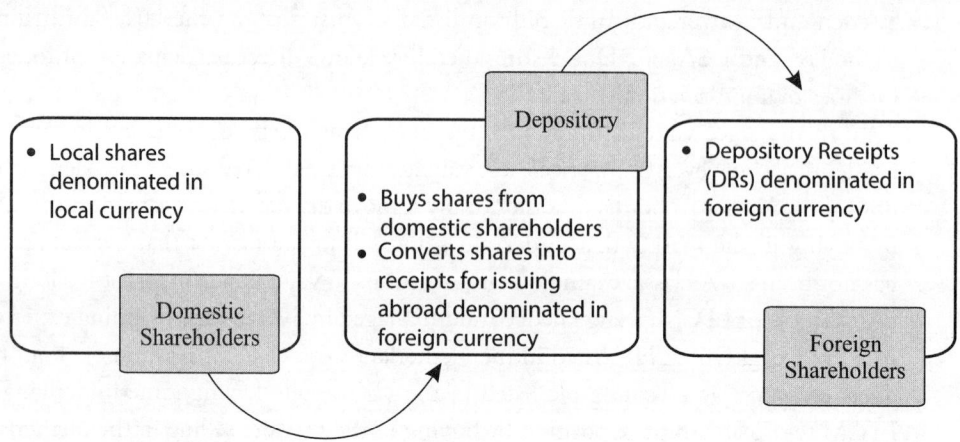

Figure 19-5
Process of Issue of Depository Receipts

The underlying shares remain with the custodian (depository), and the DRs issued are not on the records of the company. The benefit of dividend would be passed on by the depository to the individual holders. The dividend payable in local currency by the firm would be converted into foreign currency by the depository for making payment to foreign investors.

The DR holders do not enjoy voting rights as names of the holders do not appear in the records of the firm's shareholders. Voting rights vest with the depository bank which may exercise voting rights. The benefits of bonus, rights issue, etc. are exercised through the depository.

A firm that is listed on a local exchange decides to invite participation from global investors would follow this route as described in Figure 19-5. Firms that adopt depository route get the expanded investor base, increased visibility, and perhaps better valuations decreasing the cost of equity. Firms from emerging markets adopt this route. Investors benefit by diversification of their portfolios perhaps reducing portfolio risk, and obtain better returns by equity participation in firms from emerging markets. The DRs offer an opportunity for foreign investors to participate in the growth of firms listed abroad. Issuing firms get foreign participation without fulfilling the formalities normally required by foreign regulatory bodies. Hence, an American or European can reap the benefits of growth offered by Indian or Chinese firm that has ADRs or GDRs without being a resident.

It is a kind of dual listing of a security of a firm in two different exchanges. First ADR was issued by JP Morgan in 1927 for British retailer Selfridges. These are generally classified in two ways—Global Depository Receipts (GDRs) and American Depository Receipts (ADRs). ADRs are specifically meant for American investors while GDRs pertain to other investors.

Sponsored and Unsponsored Issues ADRs or GDRs may or may not be a fund raising exercise. A depository acquires shares in local market and issues equivalent receipts to the foreign investors. It merely replaces domestic shareholders with foreign shareholders. There is no fresh issue of securities by the firm. Such an exercise would be termed as *unsponsored* where the firm whose shares are converted to DRs has no role to play in the process. Where a firm issues fresh shares, or appoints a depository who in turn issues DRs and offers them for subscription by foreigners is called *sponsored*.

The DRs are required to meet the less stringent compliance standards of the exchanges where they are supposed to be traded, just in the same manner as the firms are required to meet the disclosures and informational requirements before listing at local exchanges. The disclosure and informational requirement are more stringent in developed markets such as those in USA or Europe than emerging markets, such as India, China, and Brazil. Most stringent requirements are supposed to be that of Securities Exchange Commission (SEC), USA applicable for US firms protecting American investors. Therefore, ADRs are classified in several ways varying with the level of compliance with the regulations of USA as described in Table 19-4.

Table 19-4
Classification of ADR Issues

Type of ADR	Features
Unsponsored	Issued by depository banks by purchasing equivalent shares in the local markets with no involvement of the firm; there can be more than one depository; issues receipts denominated in foreign currency to foreign investors; trading in receipts is restricted to OTC mode; subscribers may not get full benefits as that of local shareholders.
Sponsored Level I	Least stringent compliance and disclosure requirements; firms need not follow US GAAP but must file financial statements with US GAAP reconciliation; trading is allowed over-the-counter.
Sponsored Level II	Issuer must file for registration with SEC meeting disclosure requirement; used by firms desirous of listing only and not raising funds; ADRs can be listed at US exchanges such as NYSE, NASDAQ or AMEX.
Sponsored Level III	It is a fresh offering with compliance level same as that for a US firm mobilizing capital from US investors; it is followed by listing on any of the US exchanges.
Privately Placed Under SEC Rule 144	Offering is restricted to Qualified Institutional Buyers who are supposed to have better financial literacy. This can be done without going through the registration process of SEC.

From the perspective of market integration the DRs abroad and the local shares domestically must be valued identical because the fundamental drivers of value remain the same. The business and revenue models as well as economic environment of the firm remains same irrespective of whether the DRs are issued or not. It merely distinguishes the nationalities of shareholders.

Difference in values of DR and the underlying shares would give rise to arbitrage opportunities. Mispricing can be corrected by selling the overpriced shares/DRs and buying the underpriced DRs/shares. Arbitrage opportunities may be restricted by not permitting the fungibility, that is, conversion of DRs into local shares and vice versa. This is called two-way fungibility. Please see Figure 19-6. Where DRs held by foreigners abroad can be converted into local shares and sold in local markets but vice versa is not allowed, it is referred to as one-way

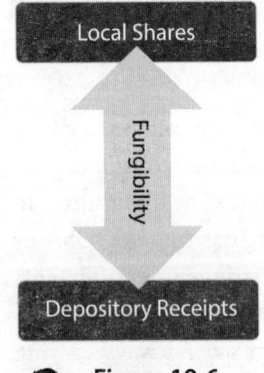

Figure 19-6 Fungibility of Depository Receipts

fungibility. Foreign investors holding DRs can always trade in the foreign markets among themselves but in case of need to trade in the original market, they must tender DRs for exchange of local shares. This may be permitted. However, re-conversion of the shares back into DRs may not be permitted. As such one-way fungibility may let the discrepancy in values to prevail in two markets.

If local shares are overpriced depository holders would like to convert DRs into local shares rather than sell them in their own markets. After conversion into local shares, they can be sold in local markets at higher prices. If GDRs/ADRs are overpriced investors would like to convert the local shares into DRs and sell in the markets abroad. Two-way fungibility would permit arbitrage and should improve liquidity in local as well as overseas markets. Two-way fungibility should enhance liquidity and renew interest in some of the GDR listings from India.

A large number of Indian firms, especially those in information technology sector, have accessed the US and global markets by issue of ADRs and GDRs. With the exception of few scrips GDR markets for Indian equity issues has been dormant. Since India is serving as a global hub of information technology the firms in the sector perceive advantages of issuing DRs more than mere mobilization of capital. Floating of ADRs and GDRs tends to increase the visibility of the issuing firm that creates synergies for business development, besides better valuation in domestic markets, and better access to capital markets by expanding investor base.

CONCEPTS IN PRACTICE

Integrating Capital Markets

ADRs BY INFOSYS TECHNOLOGIES LTD

In March 1999 a landmark was made for integration of Indian capital markets with the most vibrant, literate, and advanced markets of the world when India's leading technology firm, Infosys Technologies (INFY) made an offering of 1.8 million ADRs representing 0.9 million shares (1 ADR = ½ Share) at offer price of $27.88. This Level III sponsored ADR with Deutsche Bank acting as depository and ICICI Bank as custodian was offered at about 22% premium to the stock price in local markets. After exercising 15% Green Shoe option INFY mobilized $70.38 million by issuing 2.02 million ADRs at US$34 each.

The features of the ADR and Indian stock were same in terms of underlying cash flows, dividend, and other corporate benefits. Issue at

22% premium in the US markets over local price was perhaps an indication of (a) segregated markets where investors from India and USA could not participate in each other's markets, (b) perception differences in valuation of by two different set of shareholders. Subsequently in July 2003, May 2005, and November 2006 INFY came out with three more sponsored issues of ADRs from secondary market wherein it asked its local shareholders to surrender their shares for divestment and offer the same to the American investors. Unlike the first ADR issue of March 1999, these exercises were not aimed at raising fresh capital from abroad but instead give benefit to Indian investors to capitalize on the overvaluation of the ADRs. This led to the enrichment of Indian shareholders who obtained 26%–34% premium over local prices as shown in the following table.

American investors while subscribing to ADRs got an opportunity to participate in an emerging market firm growing at phenomenal rate of 25–30% as against firms in developed market offering modest growth rates. Potential for enhanced returns with diversification benefits perhaps explains the premium paid by the US investors.

Each of these sponsored secondary issues of ADRs meant transfer of liquidity from Indian markets to American markets. With increased liquidity of ADRs to American investors the price differential in the American markets and Indian markets has been falling. By August 2009 the premium had shrunk to about 1–5%. The prices continued to converge. As on 13 May 2013, the closing price of ADR was US$42.80. At an exchange rate of ₹55.00/$ this is equivalent to ₹2,354 per share. On 14 May 2013 the price of Infosys in the Indian market was indeed ₹2,354. Should this signify that global cost of equity and local cost of equity for Infosys have become identical?

	Nos of ADRs (millions)	Shares/ADR	Price of ADR (US$)	Amount Collected* (US$ million)	Premium over Local Share Price
July 2003	6	½ share originally but 1 share after issue of 1:1 bonus	49.00	294	26%
May 2005	16	1	67.00	1,072	34%
Nov 2006	30	1	53.50	1,605	34%

*This amount was collected by Indian shareholders and not by Infosys.

Indian Depository Receipts

Indian Depository Receipts (IDRs) are exactly opposite of ADR or GDR in context of India. While ADRs and GDRs by Indian firms enable participation by foreign equity investors in Indian companies, IDR allows participation by Indian investors in foreign companies. In an otherwise closed environment, IDRs allow some access to Indian investors to invest in select foreign equities if foreign companies desire to mobilize capital from Indian markets.

The IDR would be denominated in Indian rupee against the shares of the foreign company and would have to comply with the guidelines of regulator in India, that is, Securities Exchange Board of India (SEBI) which in 2009 issued guidelines for issuance of IDRs. These guidelines include stipulations regarding minimum net worth, minimum track record of distributable profits, cap on amount of offering based on net worth, etc. Besides the company making an issue of IDR shall also be the issuing company listed in its home country, not prohibited to issue securities by any regulatory body and has track record of compliance with securities market regulations in its home country.

CONCEPTS IN PRACTICE
Integrating Indian Markets with the World

OPENING INDIAN MARKET FOR FOREIGN FIRMS: INDIAN DEPOSITORY RECEIPTS

In the first ever case in the history of Indian capital markets, a multinational company—Standard Chartered Bank—sought approval from regulatory authority in India—Securities Exchange Board of India (SEBI) to raise $500 million by listing its Indian Depository Receipts (IDRs) on bourses. Foreign companies are now permitted under the automatic route to issue IDRs in India subject to complying with the IDR Rules and Disclosure and Investor Protection (DIP) Guidelines. Foreign financial services companies/banking companies having a presence in India (either through a branch office or a subsidiary) are also permitted to access the automatic route.

The current regulatory framework governing the issuance of IDRs include (a) pre-issue paid-up capital and free reserves of at least US$100 million and average turnover of US$500 million during the three financial years, (b) limit of 15% of the paid-up capital and free reserves of the issuer company, and the size of the IDR issue shall not be less than ₹500 million (c) earning of profits for at least five years and declaring of dividend of not less than 10% (d) pre-issue debt-equity ratio does not exceed 2:1 (e) listed in its home country (f) the IDRs denominated in Indian rupees must be immediately repatriated outside India by the issuer foreign company (g) the IDRs cannot be converted into underlying foreign shares before the expiry of one year from the date of their issue.

The UK-based company filed a Draft Red Herring Prospectus to obtain approval for subscription of 220 million IDRs to raise minimum of US$500 million. The principal rationale for IDR is *brand building and business development in India, its second largest market*, Standard Chartered said in a statement.

Mr Peter Sans, the CEO of global Standard Chartered said, 'Our intention to be the first company to list IDRs demonstrates how important India is to Standard Chartered. India is our largest and fastest growing markets and achieved over $1 billion in profit in 2009. This is the unique opportunity to raise our profile and allow investor in India to participate in our future.'

Standard Chartered plc already listed in London and Hong Kong became the first company to issue IDRs in May 2010. The price band for the offering was ₹100–115 (£1.47 or $2.10) per IDR while it finally issued at ₹104. 10 IDRs were equivalent to one share of the bank. The bank, which makes most of its profits in Asia, issued 240 million IDRs through the offer amassing ₹2,490 crore equivalent to US$530 million. According to the CEO Standard Chartered plc the issue was made not as much to raise capital but to communicate their long-term interest and commitment towards India.

The IDRs opened at the Bombay Stock Exchange (BSE) and National Stock Exchange (NSE) on 11 June 2010 and listed at ₹106; a premium of ₹2.00 (1.92% premium) over the issue price.

The IDRs shall not be automatically fungible into underlying equity shares of issuing company. The IDR holders could convert IDRs into underlying equity shares only with the prior approval of the Reserve Bank of India (RBI). Upon such exchange, individual persons resident in India are allowed to hold the underlying shares only for the purpose of sale within a period of 30 days from the date of conversion of the IDRs into underlying shares.

DIVERSIFYING GLOBALLY

Recognizing that internationally diversified portfolio would be less risky and could have a better risk reward ratio as compared to a domestic portfolio, it must be an endeavour of investor to expand internationally. Such international diversification places many limitations. Most investors face regulatory hurdles that prohibit unfettered investments abroad. These regulatory hurdles are more often imposed by governments of developing nations restricting free flow of capital. It is often done on grounds of conserving foreign exchange, maintaining stable exchange rates, steady security prices and avoiding creation of asset bubbles, etc.

Since money always chases higher returns people find ways and means of investing in foreign markets in most convenient manner. One innovative and convenient way of deriving the benefits of higher returns from emerging markets of India has been through Participatory Notes circumventing the laws.

Even if regulatory hurdles are absent most investors face operational bottlenecks for diversifying internationally. The background, understanding, and knowledge of retail investors for investment in a foreign land are limited. Most investors either do not have the time or lack skills to understand foreign markets. They often resort to investment through organized bodies, which complete regulatory requirements as well as fill the knowledge gaps.

Invest in Global Firms One simple way to achieve international diversification is to invest domestically only in firms that are truly global. Firms, such as Coca-Cola, IBM, Sony, and Nestle derive revenues and profits from their global operations and investing in them amounts to investing globally. Whether such a portfolio indeed has lower beta remains a mute question. Further even these corporation may be truly multinational in operations but seldom they have financial securities available across the globe. These firms tend to operate worldwide through holding companies rather than held publicly. Hence, a large part of the world does not have such diversification feasible.

CONCEPTS IN PRACTICE
Charms of Indian Capital Markets

OPENING INDIAN MARKET FOR FOREIGN FIRMS: PARTICIPATORY NOTES

As on	PNs	Assets Under FIIs	% of PNs
Dec–03	29.030	148.011	19.6%
Jun–04	29.702	138.090	21.5%
Dec–04	67.886	222.674	30.5%
Jun–05	67.187	261.334	25.7%
Dec–05	104.179	366.970	28.4%
Jun–06	120.595	397.835	30.3%
Dec–06	189.951	565.549	33.6%
Jun–07	367.330	659.570	55.7%
Dec–07	381.120	1027.141	37.1%
Jun–08	181.238	612.268	29.6%
Dec–08	71.320	417.476	17.1%
Jun–09	97.885	631.047	15.5%
Dec–09	168.632	848.333	19.9%
Jun–10	168.016	927.468	18.1%
Dec–10	200.927	1124.352	17.9%
Jun–11	153.291	1086.388	14.1%
Dec–11	138.711	917.930	15.1%
Jun–12	129.851	1090.492	11.9%
Dec–12	151.084	1335.189	11.3%

Crore, '000s
Source: Data from website of SEBI.

Participatory Notes (often called P-Notes or PNs and to be confused with Promissory Notes) are the financial instruments issued by Foreign Institutional Investors (FIIs) in India to overseas investors who are interested in investing in Indian securities markets but do not want to follow the required rules stipulated by regulatory bodies. Investment in Indian securities is allowed for FIIs that are registered with its regulatory body, the Securities Exchange Board of India (SEBI). These FIIs would take positions in Indian securities and issue PNs to their clients.

PNs are a convenient route of off-shore investment with underlying as Indian securities either in cash or derivatives. Hedge funds and High Net worth Individuals (HNIs) who are unregulated in their homeland and do not wish to disclose their identities can hide them through PNs which are negotiable and can be traded otherwise.

To mitigate the acute crisis of balance of payments in 1991, Government of India sought capital account flows by permitting participation in Indian securities markets by FIIs. The investment route was provided by Mauritius treaty which eliminated capital gains tax in India by residents of Mauritius trading in Indian securities. Since Mauritius had close to nothing corporate tax the investment in India would be free from tax if FIIs routed investment through Mauritius, which was as high as 40% in the past for on-shore transactions. Tax arbitrage was significant in the 1990s. With long-term capital gains at zero and short term capital gains at 10% now the tax arbitrage has reduced significantly.

The bonafide of PN holders and the source of funds have always been in doubt. Suspecting money laundering by Indian business by channelizing the ill-gotten money through PNs, RBI has been constantly demanding a ban of use of PNs. The stand of various regulatory bodies in India has been wavering. With about 25% of Indian securities held by FIIs who in turn have issued significant proportions of PNs, the uncertainties of regulation make Indian stock market extremely volatile.

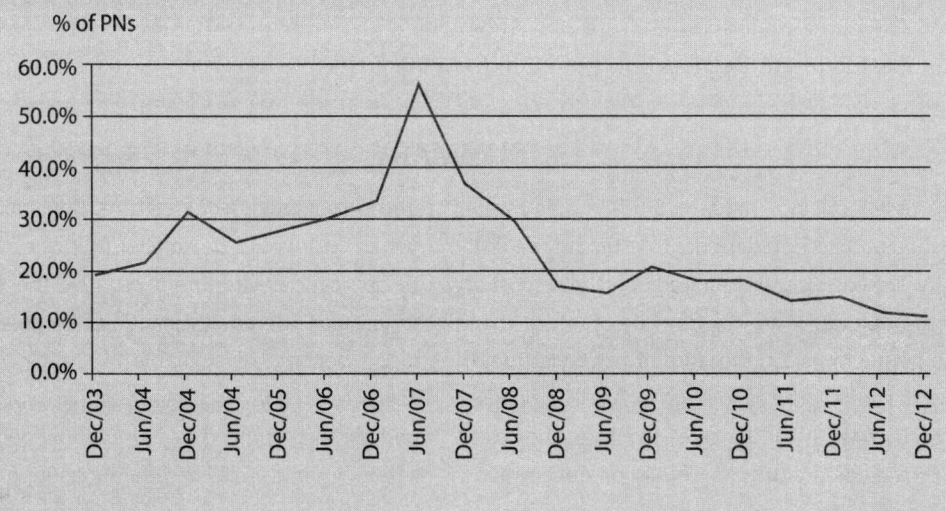

Invest in Country-specific Funds or ADRs/GDRs Other ways of diversifying internationally is to invest in (a) country-specific funds, and (b) subscribe/trade in the ADR/GDR issues of the multinational firms. Each of these alternatives leaves a doubt as to whether such strategies are available to all investors in the world, and whether or not it would constitute adequate diversification.

We have seen that in the real world markets are neither fully segmented nor fully integrated. With time the capital controls are being eliminated but they would always exist in some form/degree or the other. Depending upon the domestic economic conditions and ability to sustain adversity, governments in various nations place several types of capital controls for regulating the inflows or outflows of foreign currency. Each country has its own peculiarity in terms of economic conditions, political scenario, and social values. A fully integrated world seems a utopian concept because in such a world the concept of a nation and nationality would lose relevance.

Since in the real world we face neither fully segmented markets nor fully integrated markets, we can neither apply domestic CAPM nor international CAPM with confidence. With progression of time one may say that world is becoming more and more integrated but whether capital would ever be completely mobile remains a moot point. Measuring beta, finding market portfolio and determining risk-free rate of return become extremely subjective depending upon the perception of the evaluator. How do we find appropriate model for such situations? Despite the limitations as enumerated earlier, CAPM remains a robust model which academicians, researchers, and practitioner have been using alike. The underlying principles of CAPM remain sound and the idea is widely accepted. The difficulty of measurement of determinants is an issue but should not discourage the usage of CAPM. One simple way to extend the underlying concept of CAPM would be to add the risk premium for exchange rate risk too just as we added the premium for market risk.

SUMMARY

Capital asset pricing model (CAPM) is a well-established and accepted model to estimate the cost of equity. The basic inputs required to estimate cost of equity through CAPM are risk-free rate of return, market risk premium, and a measure of risk called beta. For a domestic firm, the estimation is based on proxies used for risk-free rate and market. For domestic firms, these proxies are returns on T-bills or government securities and a stock market index. Beta as measure of risk is benchmarked with index. However, for a global firm attempting to mobilize capital from shareholders of different nationalities or for the projects located in a foreign environment the use of local proxies and benchmarking beta against them is inappropriate. Therefore, the global version of CAPM is not same as its domestic counterpart.

Extending the CAPM to global markets raises several conceptual changes. The benchmarking changes and so does the beta of the firm. The concept of systematic and unsystematic risk also needs to be reviewed. Further one additional dimension that is absent in domestic version of CAPM is the exchange rate risk. CAPM consolidates all risk in a single variable called beta. The benchmark for estimating the beta of global basis would have to change from local index returns to global index returns. The value of beta thus arrived would be smaller than the one used in the domestic environment because the few factors that are considered systematic in domestic scenario indeed become diversifiable in the global context. The risk reduction in a global portfolio would be more rapid and pronounced because of low degree of correlation among stocks of different economies.

Another handicap in the application of CAPM is its assumption of consolidating all risk in a single factor. In domestic situation, the exchange rate risk does not exist. When estimating cost of equity on global basis where the return expectations and cash flow generations are in different currencies the exchange rate risk arises. This may necessitate adding another risk premium for exchange rate risk as we do for market risk in arriving at cost of equity.

The application of CAPM on global basis becomes difficult because world markets are neither fully segmented nor fully integrated. Fully segmented markets do not permit investments by foreigners, while in fully integrated market there is seamless movement of capital across the world. With increased liberalization and globalization firms are finding ways to increase participation by global investors. There are strategies like dual listing, issue of depository receipts, etc. available to invite attract foreign investors to derive benefits of increased returns and risk diversification by investing in financial assets. Under dual listing the MNC lists it stock in two different exchanges. In the issuance of DRs, the local shares are converted in another form and listed in a foreign market. Such strategies would lead to greater integration of financial markets. Investors willing to diversify the portfolios to global level also have options of buying stocks of MNCs, invest in country-specific funds to achieve indirect diversification.

QUESTIONS

19-1 Describe the inputs required for estimating cost of equity under CAPM model for local markets and what proxies would be used in applying CAPM.
19-2 Compare the diversification effect in local and global portfolios.
19-3 What changes in the local version of CAPM will have to be made if one wants to use it to determine the cost of equity on global basis?
19-4 How would you incorporate exchange rate risk in determination of price of a financial asset that is denominated in foreign currency?
19-5 How would you arrive a country-specific CAPM in segmented markets and what conclusion can be drawn for estimating the cost of equity in a foreign country with segmented markets?
19-6 Differentiate between dual listing and depository receipt as ways of attracting foreign investors.
19-7 What do you understand by segmented markets and integrated markets?
19-8 What are sponsored and unsponsored ADRs?

20

Cost of Capital and Capital Structure for Multinational Firms

LEARNING OBJECTIVES

This chapter aims at

- distinguishing features of cost of capital and capital structure of a multinational corporation (MNC)
- understanding how cost of capital and capital structure are interrelated
- discussing the limitations of capital asset pricing model (CAPM) in determining the cost of equity for an MNC and the ways to modify CAPM to incorporate the features of MNC
- understanding the meaning of pure-play approach and its application
- learning how to incorporate foreign exchange risk and country risk in cost of equity
- understanding how the capital structure of a subsidiary could be irrelevant for capital structure of an MNC at global level
- describing how to assess cost of debt for a foreign currency loan
- explaining the practical considerations in determining the capital structure of a subsidiary
- understanding how to value a concessional loan

CONTENTS

Introduction
Weighted Average Cost of Capital
Review of Weighted Average Cost of Capital and Capital Structure
    Cost of Debt
    Cost of Equity
Direct Investment in Multinational Corporations
Cost of Equity for a Foreign Project
    Capital Asset Pricing Model and Foreign Project
Beta of a Foreign Project
    Market Risk Premium for a Foreign Project
Pure-play Approach
    Cost of Capital for Foreign Project
Exchange Rate Risk and Sovereign Risk

Cost of Foreign Currency Debt
Capital Structure of Foreign Subsidiary
    Capital Structure of Multinational Corporation on Global Basis
    Irrelevance of Capital Structure of Subsidiary
Practical Considerations in Deciding Subsidiary's Capital Structure
    Managing Political Risk
    Desire for Control and Management Decision-making
    Currency Convertibility
    Eliminating Currency Risk
    Taxation
Low Cost Financing
    Valuation of Tax Holiday

INTRODUCTION

With increased globalization and liberalization of international trade, not only goods and services markets are becoming increasingly integrated but financial markets too are becoming more and more accessible and open. Opening up of capital markets widens the scope of mobilization of financial resources both in terms of cost of funds and a variety of instruments that are available. Diversity of needs of global investors has led to development of maze of financial instruments catering to the needs of a variety of investors. Global institutional investors are primarily focused on enhanced return with reduced risk besides other features.

An effective way of risk reduction is the well-established principle of diversification. While the investors on global basis are on the lookout for diversification opportunities that expands the portfolio from local to global, the MNCs on their part would like to include such investors in their endeavour to become more and more acceptable worldwide by having diverse customers, suppliers, investors, and other stakeholders. Besides strategic reasons of expanding the base of stakeholders, the diversification needs of the investors help reduce the cost of capital for the MNCs too.

Enhanced competition and desire to survive and succeed on part of MNCs has caused increased emphasis on reducing cost of production and marketing. The survival and growth of MNCs is extremely critical and is crucially dependent upon their ability to minimize cost of capital, both for funding the working capital and expansion projects.

Cost of capital for multinational firms is one of the most crucial subjects as it is a critical input required for strategic decision making of implementation of various cross border projects. The cost of capital is the hurdle rate that the returns of the project must cross to keep the shareholders of multinational firm interested in foreign projects. MNCs normally have access to larger sources of funds and instruments both in the form of equity and debt. This makes the choice more efficient but difficult too. With global access to funds the MNCs are likely to have advantage over pure domestic firms as the MNCs would be able to cut down on the cost of capital. Coupled with deep financial resource base such wide access to cheaper funds increases international competitiveness of the MNCs.

The cost of capital for multinational firms is the basis of acceptance or rejection of foreign investment. In most cases the environment of foreign nations is likely to be different than that faced for domestic projects. The risk characteristics for foreign investment, if higher would demand a higher discount rate and vice versa. For acceptance of the project a positive net present value (NPV) is desired. The determination of discount rate requires cost of capital as input.

WEIGHTED AVERAGE COST OF CAPITAL

The discount rate to be used for the cash flows must be chosen in a manner that reflects the aspirations of all categories of capital suppliers. The two broad kinds of suppliers of capital to a firm are (i) those who lend funds and expect a fixed return irrespective of success or failure of project, called debt holders, and (ii) those who are willing to settle for residual earnings after meeting all obligations, called equity holders.

Weighted Average Cost of Capital (WACC) is a single number that incorporates the combined expectations of debt and equity holders. This is used as a hurdle rate that must be overcome if the project is to be accepted. Crossing of this hurdle rate will ensure that return expectations of all capital suppliers are met through the benefits of the project. In order to develop such a consolidated and single number, we need to consider the cost of suppliers of all kinds of capital separately. Then depending upon the proportions of each kind of capital a weighted average may be found that could serve as a single number for evaluation of the project. Mathematically, this can be represented as WACC, as given in Eq. 20-1.

$$\text{WACC} = w_e \times r_e + w_d \times r_d(1 - T) \tag{20-1}$$

where

w_e = Proportions of equity $\quad r_e$ = Cost of equity
w_d = Proportion of Debt $\quad r_d$ = Cost of debt $\quad T$ = Marginal tax rate

Since we live in world of taxes and cost of debt is tax deductible, the effective cost of debt is $(1 - T) \times$ coupon rate. WACC is found on post-tax basis.

REVIEW OF WEIGHTED AVERAGE COST OF CAPITAL AND CAPITAL STRUCTURE

The framework for minimizing the cost of capital is hidden in the value of the firm. As we know, the central idea of finance is maximization of shareholders' wealth, and therefore the cost of capital that maximizes the value of the firm should be optimal. The value of the firm is the net present value of the projects arrived at by discounting the cash flows at a specific rate. The value of the firm increases as discount rate is lowered. For most cases the discount rate used is WACC assuming unchanged risk profile and capital structure. Lower the WACC, higher the NPV and hence the value of the firm. WACC is dependent upon capital structure, that is, the level of debt used in financing. Maximization of value of the firm would take place at a point of capital structure that minimizes WACC.

The emphasis on minimization of WACC rather than maximization of the value of the firm is due to the difficulties one faces with the measurement of impact on value of the firm of managerial decisions of changing the capital structure. It is difficult to estimate how the market values will change with the changing capital structure. However, it is far easier to see how the cost of capital would change with the changing mix of debt and equity in financing of an enterprise. Therefore, it is assumed that minimization of cost of capital would coincide with optimal capital structure.

In the world of taxes, the optimal capital structure is 100% debt as debt provides the tax shield that accrues to shareholders increasing their value. However, this ignores the cost of financial distress and agency cost of debt which mount as proportions of debt start increasing.

The traditional theory of capital structure suggests that as a firm replaces equity with debt, the weighted average cost of capital falls initially because of the tax shield of debt that accrues to the shareholders. This increases the value of the firm. The increase continues till certain level of debt is reached. When debt mounts beyond a certain level the equity holders start feeling threatened of the free cash flow available to them due to prior claim on it by the debt holders. With increased perceived risk by the shareholders with increased proportions of debt the cost of equity rises faster than the benefit of tax shield provided by debt. Hence, beyond a point the weighted average cost of capital starts rising, and firms must stop borrowing beyond this level. The traditional theory of capital structure relates debt ratio to WACC as depicted in Figure 20-1.

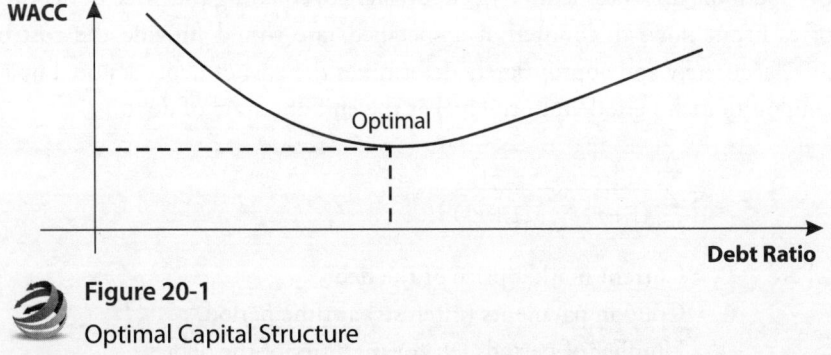

Figure 20-1
Optimal Capital Structure

Diverse Product Range A comparison of cost of capital of MNC and a pure domestic firm is in order. There are some favourable and some unfavourable factors influencing the cost of capital for MNCs. Since most MNCs are diversified in terms of their product lines, geographical segments and different economies, currencies, etc. as compared to a domestic firm the risk associated with MNCs are perceived to be lesser by capital suppliers. With decreased perception of risk, the equity and debt suppliers must demand a lower risk premium from MNC firms as compared to domestic firms. In contrast most domestic corporations are single-product single-market firms and are subject to greater risk in the eyes of international suppliers of capital. Investors in MNCs would possibly benchmark their returns against global market portfolio, and would expect global market risk premium that would be lower than the domestic market risk premium.

Access to Global Markets Further in most cases MNCs have greater access to the capital markets due to their global presence. The choice of markets and currency of denomination for raising capital by debt or equity is wider in case of MNCs. As against this a domestic firm normally has access to their domestic markets alone. Simply because of wider choices an MNC is in a better position to negotiate more favourable terms for raising capital. In addition, for pure domestic firms, access to international markets is also constrained by national polices on currency convertibility.

If capital controls deny access to funds denominated in foreign currency the domestic firm has no choice but to raise capital domestically irrespective of its cost. Where capital controls do not exist the access to foreign currency resources are constrained by the inability of domestic firms to generate cash flows to service capital in the same currency. Besides, the investors too would perceive more risk because they are exposed to political risk as service payments have to be remitted periodically that become subject to changes in the policies regarding capital control. Additional risk would demand additional risk premium. MNCs perhaps do not face such situation because of their ability to generate cash flows in several currencies.

Cost of Debt

Normally debt is issued with certain coupon and fixed maturity. The principal is payable either as bullet payment upon completion of the period of borrowing or is payable in installments over periodic intervals. Under all circumstances equating the price of debt to the present value of cash out flows discounted at a specified rate would provide the cost of debt. Equation 20-2 accurately and appropriately determines the cost of debt, denoted by r_d that pays a fixed coupon in each period and principal at the end of tenure of debt.

$$P_o = \sum_{t=1}^{N} \frac{C_t}{(1+r_d)^t} + \frac{R}{(1+r_d)^N} \qquad (20\text{-}2)$$

where P_0 = Current market price of the debt
C_t = Coupon payments (interests) at time period, t
N = Number of periods left for maturity of the debt
R = Redemption amount normally equal to face value of the debt
r_d = Cost of debt

Cost of Equity

There are two popular of ways of measuring cost of equity–dividend discount model and CAPM. Both are used for finding expected return by the equity investor. As per the dividend discount model, the cost of equity r_e is given by Eq. 20-3.

$$r_e = \frac{D_1}{P_0} + g \qquad (20\text{-}3)$$

where D_1 is expected dividend in next period, P_0 is the current market price, and g is the expected growth rate of dividend.

According to CAPM, the cost of equity is given as Eq. 20-4.

$$r_e = r_f + \beta \, (r_m - r_f) \qquad (20\text{-}4)$$

where r_f is risk free rate of return, r_m is the market rate of return, and β is measure of systematic risk.

However, CAPM is preferred way of finding cost of equity because it (a) is a market based model requiring no company specific inputs of expected dividend and its growth rate, and (b) provides for the risk based assessment of return expectations.

DIRECT INVESTMENT IN MULTINATIONAL CORPORATIONS

In the previous chapter we concluded that at their own level the individual investors can reduce risk by diversifying investments across many countries. The possible routes available are

(a) direct investments into the equity markets of several countries, (b) subscribing to country-specific or region specific mutual funds, (c) investing in ADRs/GDRs, etc.

Yet another way of achieving diversification individually by the shareholders would be investing directly in MNCs as against investing in domestic firms. Does direct investment in MNCs is of any significant advantage? Despite availability of other avenues of diversifying globally, direct investing in MNCs could make sense because of the following reasons:

1. Direct investment in MNCs would provide diversification benefits to those shareholders who cannot diversify on their own because of (a) inability to overcome home bias, (b) access to and lack of reliable information to make informed investment, (c) fear of unknown markets, etc.
2. Further the markets where barriers to international portfolio diversification exist, individual investors are handicapped and cannot reap benefits of international diversification. In such circumstances the MNC provides an opportunity to shareholders to diversify by subscribing to their capital rather relieving them the burden of allocating capital across different sectors, different nations, different currencies, etc. and yet face greater political and exchange rate risk. In case of direct investment in the equity of MNC, all these risks are managed by the multinational itself.
3. Direct investment in MNC may result in better risk adjusted return because with presence in several countries the size of the firm becomes larger and larger bringing down the cost of capital. Hence, the capacity of an MNC to reward the shareholders becomes better. Improved and stable cash flows reduce the risk too; an ideal combination for shareholders to have direct investment in MNCs and yet own a diversified portfolio without making much analysis and selection.

COST OF EQUITY FOR A FOREIGN PROJECT

The cost of equity for a project can be defined as the minimum rate of return that shareholders expect from the project/firm. Through CAPM we know that expected return from the investment is a function of risk. Higher the risk, greater is the expectations of return.

Usually, a multinational firm is a basket of projects. As long as the individual projects constituting the basket belong to the same risk class the return expectations of investors remain unchanged. So does the cost of capital for a specific project. As long as the proposed project belongs to the same risk class cost of capital of the firm can be taken as cost of capital for the project.

In case of multinationals, the spread of projects is in different countries. Even though the line of business may remain same, different locations spread worldwide makes the risk profile of the otherwise identical projects different simply because they operate in vastly different economic conditions, legal frameworks, political environments and cultural attitudes. For example, Coca Cola remains in the same business of cold drinks world over but the risk profiles of their operations in USA, Europe, Asia, and Africa could be substantially different from one another. Same applies to other MNCs, such as IBM, Vodafone, Toyota, and Sony.

Arguably the best method to arrive at cost of equity for a project is the capital asset pricing model that links the expected return with the risk associated. The basic underlying assumption

of the CAPM is that investors hold a diversified portfolio to minimize/eliminate unsystematic risk, and therefore the returns sought by investing in a project must only be compensated for its systematic risk. This systematic risk is dependent upon the variability of project's return relative to the market return. In case the MNC is diversified enough, the observed beta of the firm may serve also as a reasonable and fair estimate of the project risk.

The determinants of the cost of equity for project, that is, r_f, r_m, β_i, are easy to determine in case of a domestic project. Risk free rate is taken as returns on government securities, the market return is assumed to be the return on market index and beta of the project would be the same as beta of the firm if the project has similar risk as that of the firm.

For example, if Bharti Telecom were to expand its services within India either as fresh project or as acquisition, the cost of equity would be same as the present cost of equity of Bharti Telecom.

Exercise 20-1
Cost of Equity for Bharti

Consider Bharti is expanding to another telecom circle in India. If beta of Bharti is 1.2, the risk free rate of Indian market as reflected in the return on government securities is 6%, and market return as determined by the return on NIFTY is 14%, what is the appropriate cost of equity for adjudging the viability of the acquisition of new circle?

Solution
Since the proposed project bears the same risk as that of the firm, the determination of the cost of equity for the project may be done using the beta of Bharti itself. Applying CAPM we get the cost of equity as

$$r_i = r_f + \beta_i(r_m - r_f) = 6.00 + 1.20(14.00 - 6.00) = 15.60\%$$

Capital Asset Pricing Model and Foreign Project

Even though CAPM remains the most robust and accepted method of finding cost of equity for any project, there are great bottlenecks in its implementation in the context of international projects of an MNC. These issues are extremely fundamental in nature and are difficult to resolve with a conviction that could make usage of CAPM as universally acceptable tool for assessing cost of equity, and hence the discount rate for a foreign project of MNC.

Salient features and assumptions of the CAPM in international context have some significant implications.

Reward for Systematic and Unsystematic Risks CAPM is based on classification of risk into two—systematic and unsystematic. One implication is that of the two risks only systematic risk is relevant from the point of view of the investors. It also bases that systematic risk elements are contained and represented in a single parameter called beta. The investors would be rewarded only for systematic risk and not for assuming unsystematic risk. Even if an investor desires reward for the unsystematic risk, it would simply not be available in an efficient market. The reason for such a position is the fact that unsystematic risk can be diversified away by simply holding a diversified portfolio rather than a single asset. Therefore, the reward for taking risk should only compensate the investors that cannot be diversified away. The risk that matters in pricing of asset is the systematic risk. Thus, the cost of capital for a project must consider only its systematic risk and not the unsystematic risk.

Classification of Unsystematic and Systematic Factors For computing the cost of capital using CAPM, one needs to segregate the risk factors which are systematic and unsystematic (or diversifiable). In case the project happens to be in the same economy where the firm is domiciled, the bifurcation of risk factors is rather easy and has been resolved rather unanimously in CAPM in local or domestic context. What are considered systematic in the CAPM in domestic context include fiscal policies, monetary policies, trade policies, political factors, etc. that impacts returns of most stocks in an economy. Unsystematic factors are firm-specific.

In an international context, the risk must be viewed at global level. In the global context, the systematic factors would be the events that are capable of influencing global stocks. Such events would be acts of terrorism, tsunami, currency crises due to contagion, events leading to systemic risk, such as euro crisis. What could be termed as systematic at local level may actually be unsystematic at global level. Country-specific factors become unsystematic much in the same manner as firm-specific factors are unsystematic in the context of domestic portfolio. In the context of a global portfolio consisting of stocks from across the globe, the returns would not be as much affected by economic policies of one nation, say Japan as the returns from Japanese stocks may be compensated by returns from stocks belonging to other countries. Therefore, what is systematic for a Japanese holding portfolio of domestic stocks may actually be unsystematic for a global investor holding a portfolio of global stocks. For global investors, recession in Japan does not bother as much as it concerns a Japanese investor confined to domestic portfolio.

Majority and Minority Shareholders While undertaking a project in a foreign land an MNC needs to view the risk preferences and reward expectations in the context of shareholders domiciled in the same country. It is indeed rare or impossible to find an MNC which has investors from all across the globe evenly dispersed. Though it is common to find investors in MNCs with different and many nationalities but they do not have controlling stakes or are able to influence the decision making process. The control of the MNC essentially remains confined to residents of the country where the multinational company is domiciled. Therefore, we have multinational firms addressed as American, British, French, Dutch, German, or Japanese, etc. signifying that majority shareholding is controlled by residents of a single country even though residents of other countries could be shareholders too but they have only minority stake not capable of influencing management decisions.

Agency Problem—Nationalities of Shareholders Different nationalities of shareholders pose another issue in estimation of the cost of capital. Should the risk emanating from an overseas project of an MNC be viewed from the perspective of all its shareholders belonging to different nationalities or the shareholders of the nation where the MNC is domiciled? Indeed it is difficult and seems impossible to address concerns of all groups of shareholders especially when each group though in minority, has substantial stake but only one group can have controlling stake. An imminent question arises. In the interest of controlling stakeholders, should the interest of other group of investors be sacrificed? The so-called basic and fundamental principle of capital budgeting decision of maximizing shareholders' wealth faces a serious conflict here.

We all have recognized the agency problems between managers and shareholders, when we emphasize that not all actions of managers are in the interest of shareholders. Agency problem also exists between debt holders and shareholders, when debt holders impose covenants restricting the freedom of shareholders. Third kind of agency problem arises in case of MNCs having shareholders with different nationalities—with more than one group involved in managerial decision-making. The capital structure in terms of shareholding pattern poses the agency problem where amongst the shareholders too when there exist several groups.

Most MNCs have joint ventures with local partners with shareholding pattern at 51:49 between MNC and local partners. With controlling interest resting with MNC with 51% holding it is not necessary that all management decisions result in enhanced value to all shareholders. There are ample instances in joint venture where royalty payments from the subsidiary to the parent MNC have been increased. This undoubtedly results in increased cash flow for the parent shareholders but amounts to an equal loss of cash flow to the remaining and minority shareholders of the subsidiary.

Motives of Foreign Projects Most MNCs make an entry in a foreign land through joint ventures with local partners especially in less developed countries. The reasons for having a local partner rather than having independent operations with 100% ownership can be many. It may be done to overcome the local laws placing cap on foreign direct investment (FDI), to understand the local markets, to meet local competition, to earn extra-ordinary profits not available in matured and developed economies, to genuinely help develop a nation in terms of fulfilling the technology gap (though seldom), etc.

The considerations of an MNC are guided by enhancement of the risk adjusted value of the firm in the eyes of majority shareholders rather than risk-adjusted value of the global investors. CAPM propagates risk adjusted returns. The question 'Would the risk-adjusted returns of global investors and those holding controlling stakes be identical' is bound to be challenged. Such conflict of interest does not arise in case of pure domestic firms. There are ample incidents where increased royalty demanded by the parent multinational has resulted in decreased value of the subsidiary's firm in the local markets.

Application of CAPM for determination of cost of equity for a foreign project would require three inputs: (1) beta of the project, (2) market rate of return, and (3) risk free rate of return. CAPM requires benchmarking of project return with a market portfolio and its expected return. These issues pose serious challenges in application of CAPM for determination of cost of equity. We discuss them now.

BETA OF A FOREIGN PROJECT

Project beta for a foreign project of an MNC may be defined as

$$\text{Project Beta}, \beta_s = \frac{\text{Cov}(s,m)}{\sigma_m^2} = \rho_{sm}\frac{\sigma_s}{\sigma_m} \qquad (20\text{-}5)$$

where $\text{Cov}(s,m)$ = Covariance of return of project S with market portfolio
  ρ_{sm} = Coefficient of correlation between returns of Project S and market
  σ_s = Standard deviation of returns on Project S
  σ_m = Standard deviation of returns on market

Measurement of beta and hence cost of capital for a foreign project of an MNC poses many issues. There are three inputs required for assessing cost of equity—project beta, risk premium, and risk free rate of return. These three input raise three pertinent questions as follows:

1. For measuring beta of the project which one of the three benchmark portfolios should be used—foreign subsidiary's market index, parent's home market index, or global index?
2. The risk premium too has three choices—foreign market risk premium, parent's market premium, or global risk premium.
3. What risks must be incorporated in cost of capital, that is, what is systematic and unsystematic?

Many MNCs domiciled in a developed nation consider that the political and economic risks are very high especially when the proposed project is in a developing country. However, in a global context these risks would be unsystematic and hence diversifiable. Further due to asynchronous business cycles and many other divergences in economic, monetary, and financial structures, the coefficient of correlation of project's return with market return should be very low. Hence, even if political and economic risks are high leading to higher standard deviation, σ_s, the project beta should be low because of dominance of low correlation between economies. Ironically, high political and economic risk may not translate into high cost of equity due to low correlation. Discount rate may still be lower than that for a comparable project implemented in domestic market. It is indeed strange and difficult to comprehend that despite higher risk the effective discount rate may still be lower.

The unsystematic risk is considered relevant in case of foreign projects. The underlying concept of CAPM would suggest that diversification effect is greater if an MNC from developed nation sets up a project in a developing country rather than a developed country. Relatively speaking, the coefficients of correlation among developed economies are larger and hence diversification benefits would be smaller. Low correlation coefficient results in larger benefits of diversification. However, the component of unsystematic risk is higher for projects in developing economies. Therefore, contrary to general belief, the risk of a project in a developing country may be lower than that of a comparable venture at home despite larger unsystematic risk.

Benchmarking of project return against a portfolio—foreign, home, or global—does not seem to have an answer that is universally acceptable. The projects that are tied to the world economy rather than to local economy are likely to have similar risk profile irrespective of the location. For example, a steel plant located in India, Europe, China, etc. should exhibit similar systematic risk as steel output is more linked to global supply and demand conditions. The risks in such ventures would rather be high on a global basis. On the other hand, some projects are more tied to local economic conditions. For example, Japanese multinational Sony setting up a plant for producing and marketing LED TVs and other electronic products in India would face business risks that are linked to the Indian economy and its correlation with Japanese economy. If the coefficient of correlation between Indian and Japanese economies is expected to be low, it may not warrant a higher discount rate even though the project risk is greater in India.

From the foregoing it is surmised that a foreign project by an MNC has the following characteristics:

(a) The foreign project faces economic and political risks similar to those faced by similar firms in the same foreign economy. Fortunes of the project are intricately linked to the economic development and policies of the foreign country.
(b) The return expectations of investors domiciled in the parent country are relevant, and not of those domiciled in foreign country where the project is located. Therefore, cost of capital must be considered from the perspective of majority shareholders of MNC (ignoring the agency problem among different group of shareholders).

Due to (a) above the most preferred starting point for estimation of beta of foreign operations is the beta of proxy firm in foreign location. Since this beta is in relation to the market portfolio of the foreign country, it cannot be said to be applicable for the investors of MNC in the home country. What we need is the variability of the returns of the project benchmarked against home portfolio and not a foreign portfolio. The required beta is

Required beta, β

$$= \frac{\text{Covariance of Project's return with parent's market}}{\text{Variance of parent's market}} \quad (20\text{-}6)$$

$$= \text{Correlation of project with parent's market} \frac{\text{Standard deviation of project}}{\text{Standard deviation of parent's market}}$$

For illustrative purposes, consider Hyundai of Korea that wants to set up a plant for producing cars for Indian market through a new venture *Hyundai India, HI,* as 100% subsidiary. 100% ownership is assumed for simplicity to avoid the agency problem among different groups of shareholders. However, as long as a Korean investor has controlling and majority stake, the methodology would remain same.

Assuming that shareholders of Hyundai are essentially Korean their expectations of return are relevant. However, the risk faced by *HI* would emanate from Indian economy and not from Korean markets. Therefore, for estimating the cost of capital for Korean investors the covariance of returns of *HI* with reference to Korean benchmark market index, say KOSPI is relevant.

Since *HI* is a new venture the historical returns and its volatility are not available. This is the likely scenario in a majority of expansion projects of multinational firms. Hence, we need to use a proxy that exhibits the risk profile of the contemplated venture (pure-play approach discussed later). One such proxy could be Tata Motors Ltd (TML) or Maruti Udyog Limited (MUL) whose risk profile in Indian market is available based on past performances of their returns with the Indian benchmark, say NIFTY or SENSEX.

The observed betas of MUL or TML are relevant to the understanding of return expectations of Indian investors whose benchmark of risk measurement is Indian market, say SENSEX or NIFTY. Therefore, the available foreign proxy beta is the beta of a proxy firm in foreign market (Indian markets in this case for *HI*) given as follows:

Available foreign proxy beta, β

$$= \text{Correlation of project with foreign market} \frac{\text{Standard deviation of project}}{\text{Standard deviation of foreign market}} \quad (20\text{-}7)$$

$$= \rho_{sf} \frac{\sigma_s}{\sigma_{fm}}$$

For modulating the risk profile with return expectations of Korean investors, the benchmark needs to be changed from NIFTY/SENSEX to KOSPI, the market benchmark applicable for Korean investors. This can be done through correlation of Indian and Korean markets. The relationship of Indian and Korean markets is defined as ratio of their covariance and variance, defined as foreign market beta from the perspective of Korean investors.

Foreign Market Beta, β_f

$$= \frac{\text{Covariance of foreign market with parent's market}}{\text{Variance of parent's market}}$$

$$= \text{Correlation with parent's market} \frac{\text{Standard Deviation of foreign market}}{\text{Standard Deviation of parent's market}} \quad (20\text{-}8)$$

$$= \rho_{fp} \frac{\sigma_{fm}}{\sigma_{pm}}$$

If proxy beta and foreign market beta are available, then the required beta as described in Eq. 20-6 can be found as follows:

Required beta, β

$$= \frac{\text{Covariance of Project's return with parent's market}}{\text{Variance of parent's market}}$$

$$= \text{Correlation of project with parent's market} \frac{\text{Standard deviation of project}}{\text{Standard deviation of parent's market}}$$

$$= \rho_{sp} \frac{\sigma_s}{\sigma_{pm}}$$

Required beta is the product of *foreign proxy beta* and *foreign market beta* as may be seen.

$$\text{Required beta, } \beta = \rho_{sf} \frac{\sigma_s}{\sigma_{fm}} \times \rho_{fp} \frac{\sigma_{fm}}{\sigma_{pm}}$$

$$= \rho_{sp} \frac{\sigma_s}{\sigma_{pm}} \quad (20\text{-}9)$$

$$= \text{Foreign Proxy Beta} \times \text{Foreign Market Beta}$$

An Example Assume that MUL and TML have all equity (unlevered) betas of 1.3 and 1.2, respectively. Note that observed betas are levered betas that include the impact of debts taken by the firms. These observed betas would have to be unlevered to get unlevered betas. Observed betas of the firm can be converted to equivalent unlevered beta after knowing the values of debt, D and equity, E and the marginal tax rate, T of the firm whose beta is observed using Eq. 20-10. Refer section on pure-play approach discussed in the next section for detailed elaboration.

$$\text{Beta}_{(\text{All Equity})} = \text{Beta}_{(\text{Debt})} \frac{D(1-T)}{E + D(1-T)} + \text{Beta}_{(\text{observed})} \frac{E}{E + D(1-T)} \quad (20\text{-}10)$$

HI believes that risk profile of auto industry in India is represented by a composite of 60% of MUL and 40% of TML. Therefore, for foreign proxy beta of 1.26 is applicable for Hyundai's operations in India. The beta of 1.26 implies that Indian investor would desire compensation in accordance with risk of 1.26 for his exposure to auto sector.

Further, the coefficient of correlation of Indian and Korean markets is estimated at 0.6 with standard deviations of Indian and Korean markets at 16% and 12%, respectively the foreign beta as given by Eq. 20-8 is 0.80 (0.60 × 16/12).

Hence, applicable beta for Korean investors for its Indian operations as given by Eq. 20-9 is 1.008 (1.26 × 0.80).

Market Risk Premium for a Foreign Project

The cost of equity for the foreign project is also dependent on the risk premium, that is, the excess return over risk free rate for compensating the risk assumed by the investor. Thus, the cost of equity investor is the return expectation of the equity investor as given here:

$$r_e = \text{Risk-free Return} + \text{Beta} \times \text{Market Risk Premium} \quad (20\text{-}11)$$

The market risk premium, MRP, that is, the excess return for taking one unit of risk, demanded by the investors cannot be assumed to be same since the base itself for measurement of market or its definition is different in different countries. Further, since beta is estimated relative to the parent's market the risk premium too should correspond to investor's market. With respect to Hyundai's Indian venture, the risk premium should be the one that is demanded by its predominantly Korean investors. The risk premium demanded by the Indian investors is irrelevant simply because they are not the investors in the venture.

CONCEPTS IN PRACTICE
Cost of Equity and Capital Structure

BHARTI'S ACQUISITION OF ZAIN

In February 2010, Bharti Airtel (Bharti), the largest telecom operator in India finally succeeded in its third attempt to globalize its telecom operations beyond India in order to become a leading telecom operator in the world when it acquired Zain, another telecom form operating in 26 African countries. The all cash deal was placed at US$10.7 billion. Its earlier two attempts to acquire South Africa-based MTN had met with operational hurdles and could not fructify despite prolonged negotiations. Sunil Bharti Mittal immediately after acquisition summed up the motivation for this rather aggressive buy in following words '…the deal will leave India's stamp on very important continent and the company would become an MNC in one stroke'. The comparative of Bharti and Zain is as follows:

	Bharti	Zain
No. of Subscribers	125 million	70 million
No. of Countries	3	23
Market Capitalization	$26.7 billion	$16.2 billion

The takeover of Zain's assets worth $9 billion and its debt of $1.7 billion was funded by two Special Purpose Vehicles (SPVs) created in the Netherlands and Singapore. In December 2009 the debt equity ratio of Bharti was 0.40 of its EBITDA and would have shot up to 1.2 if Bharti availed the loan on its own books, and perhaps jeopardize its ability to bid and pay for 3G spectrum payments in India. The deal was funded as follows:

- $1.3 billion by Standard Chartered Bank
- $1.5 billion by State Bank of India
- Remaining by consortium of banks (BNP Paribas, Bank of America, Credit Agricole CIB, DBS, HSBC, Bank of Tokyo, Barclays, ANZ, Mitsui)

Most analysts thought that a price of US$255 per subscriber (only 62% of subscribers, that is, 41.89 million in Africa) paid was high and it would take a long time to recoup. Among the risk factors were the intangibility of most of the assets of Zain, losses incurred in the business, lower population density requiring larger capital investment for increased penetration casting doubt on the ability of Bharti to replicate low cost model of India, etc. Bharti justified the high price of acquisition in the potential to expand the low penetration and high average revenue per user.

Subsequent to the acquisition, Bharti—a predominantly equity financed firm—transformed to a leveraged firm with 40% debt equity ratio (10.7/26.7). The capital structure of Bharti underwent substantial changes from predominantly equity to debt resulting in fall in the stock price in India to a 16-m low of ₹272 expecting a fall in EPS for the next two years. The cost of equity had risen due to risk in business as well as financial risk emanating from increased debt.

The next question that arises is that should the Korean investor demand the same risk premium for all projects irrespective of their locations. The obvious answer is 'No'. The risk premium demanded by the Korean investor for an expansion project in Korea itself is given in the perspective of Korean market represented by its index, KOSPI. One way to account for the risk assumed in a foreign project is to adjust the market risk premium of parent in the ratio of risk of foreign market to the risk of home (parent's) market.

$$\text{Required MRP} = \text{MRP of Parent's Market} \ \frac{\sigma_{fm}}{\sigma_{pm}} \qquad (20\text{-}12)$$

If Hyundai's investors in Korea expect a market risk premium of 9% (with market return of 13% and risk free return of 4%) for present and future expansion projects in Korea, the risk premium demanded for Hyundai's venture in India would be

$$\text{Required MRP} = \text{MRP of Parent's Market} \ \frac{\sigma_{fm}}{\sigma_{pm}} = 9\% \frac{16\%}{12\%} = 12\%$$

Therefore, cost of equity for Hyundai's venture in India, r_e should be

$$r_e = \text{Risk-free Return} + \text{Beta} \times \text{Market Risk Premium}$$
$$= 4\% + 1.008 \times 12\% = 16.096\%$$

PURE-PLAY APPROACH

In the previous section we discussed the issues concerning the determination of cost of equity for a foreign project. The starting point of the exercise was the identification of a proxy firm in the foreign market which resembles in the business risk of the proposed venture. We proceeded on the assumption that such proxy is available and its beta is observable. Is this observed beta the correct base for estimating cost of equity for a foreign project?

The cost of equity incorporates (1) the financial risk, that is, the threat to returns on equity because of debt, and (2) business risk, that is, the variability or equity returns due to changing business environment. The observed beta not only reflects the business risk but is also affected by the financial risk. Beta is a function of capital structure too. More levered the firm is greater is its beta, because increased level of debt poses increased risk to the shareholders' return.

Most widely used method for projects of varying risk profiles is pure-play approach, that is, identifying a proxy as close as possible to the proposed new business activity. As stated earlier the risk adjusted cost of equity capital as per the CAPM based approach is determined by β of the proxy firm. Though this beta of the proxy firm correctly reflects the business risk but is superimposed by its capital structure, that is, the level of debt. We need to construct the beta we desire artificially by super-imposing it with the proposed capital structure of the project. Continuing with the example of Hyundai India we proceed under the pure-play approach as follows:

Step I: Identify a pure-play firm engaged in same/similar activity As a first step Hyundai Korea needs to identify a publicly traded firm purely engaged in automobile business in India. A reasonable similarity would also serve the purpose as long as it is safe to assume that the business risk of the new venture is identical to the pure-play firm. More the number of pure-play firms the better it is. It will provide more accurate estimate and remove the structural bias that exist if we use single firm. Let us assume that Tata Motors Limited (TML) is one such pure-play firm.

Step II: Find beta of the pure-play firm Next step is to know the beta of TML. Since TML is publicly traded firm its β is either publicly available or can be obtained directly by performing regression analysis on the price/return data of TML and market index say NIFTY.

Step III: Unlever the observed β β obtained in step II is applicable to the equity shareholders of TML. The observed β of TML not only reflects the business risk the TML but also considers the financial risk faced by its equity shareholders. We need to adjust the observed β for the capital structure of TML. The observed β needs to be converted into a β that depicts the risk of shareholders of TML as if its operations were financed wholly by equity. This is called unlevering of observed beta. This can be done by using the following Eq. 20-13.

$$\beta_u = \beta_d \frac{D}{D+E} + \beta_L \frac{E}{D+E} \qquad (20\text{-}13)$$

where β_u = Beta of the unlevered firm β_d = Beta of debt
β_L = Beta of equity for levered firm; the observed beta
D = Market Value of Debt E = Market Value of Equity

Equation 20-13 makes use of additive property of beta, which means that β of assets is simply the weighted average of the individual sources comprising the asset, that is, the beta of the asset created with some equity and some debt will be equal to weighted average of betas of the equity and debt. This weighted average is computed using market value proportions.

Equation 20-13 needs to be modified for the tax shield the firm enjoys with debt. Since interest is a tax deductible the value of debt, D needs to be replaced by $D \times (1-T)$; the post-tax value of debt. In most cases, the beta of debt can be assumed to be very low as value of debt does not change much with change in the equity market conditions. Assuming β_d equals to zero and adjusting for tax shield of the debt in Eq. 20-13 we get a relationship between levered and unlevered beta as Eq. 20-14 (which is identical to Eq. 20-10):

$$\beta_u = \beta_d \frac{D(1-T)}{D(1-T)+E} + \beta_L \frac{E}{D(1-T)+E} \qquad (20\text{-}14)$$

In case beta of debt is considered as zero Eq. 20-14 reduces to

$$\beta_u = \beta_L \frac{E}{D \times (1-T)+E} \qquad (20\text{-}15)$$

or $$\beta_u = \frac{\beta_L}{\{1+(1-T) \times D/E\}}$$

Assume that observed beta of TML is 1.5. Besides reflecting the business risk of the automobiles in India the observed beta of TML also represents its financial risk. Therefore, the observed beta is levered beta. And this has to be unlevered, that is, converted into β of equity as if TML was all equity financed.

If the debt equity ratio based on market values of TML is 1:3 and its marginal tax rate is 25% the beta of TML as if it were all equity financed will be 1.20 using Eq. 20-15.

$$\beta_u = \beta_L \frac{E}{D \times (1-T) + E}$$

or $\beta_u = \frac{\beta_L}{\{1 + (1-T) \times D/E\}} = \frac{1.50}{1 + 0.75 \times 1/3} = 1.20$

Step IV: Relevering Beta The beta arrived at in Step III represents the sensitivity of TML stock as if it were wholly financed by equity. Unlevering of beta implies segregation of the two components of the risk, that is, the business risk and the financial risk that are present in observed beta. Unlevered beta represents only the business risk.

This now needs to be relevered with the proposed financing pattern of the project. This can be done again using Eq. 20-15 incorporating the capital structure (debt equity ratio (D^*/E^*) and tax rate (T^*) of the proposed project.

$$\beta_L^* = \beta_u\{1 + (1 - T^*) \times D^*/E^*\} \tag{20-16}$$

If Hyundai proposes to finance its Indian operations with debt equity ratio of 2:5 and has a tax rate of 35% the beta of the project using Eq. 20-16 works out to 1.512.

$$\beta_L^* = \beta_u\{1 + (1 - T^*) \times D^*/E^*\} = 1.20(1 + 0.65 \times 2/5) = 1.512$$

This is the appropriate beta that must be used for computing the cost of equity of the Indian operations of Hyundai, Korea.

Note that in case we consider the risk profile of Indian operation of Hyundai as 60% of MUL and 40% of TML, then we also need to find unlevered beta of MUL and then find weighted average of unlevered betas of MUL and TML before relevering.

Cost of Capital for Foreign Project

With unlevering and relevering of beta, the correct beta for Hyundai India would be 1.512. From the perspective of Korean investors, the beta shall be 1.512 × Foreign Beta 0.80 = 1.2096. With market risk premium as modulated by risk of Indian venture, the revised cost of equity would be

r_e = Risk-free Return + Beta × Market Risk Premium
    = 4% + 1.2096 × 12% = 18.5152% ≈ 18.52%

Beta with Respect to Parent's Home Market Portfolio The aforesaid procedure described to find cost of equity based on beta measured against foreign portfolio and then adjusting the same for parent investors may be challenged by many. One may argue that if the project bears the risk of economy where it is located while the shareholders are domiciled in a different nation, the reward sought for the risk would be dependent upon beta of the project measured against the parent's home portfolio. Definitionally, this would simply be the ratio of covariance

Exercise 20-2
Cost of Equity and Capital Structure

Consider Bharti's acquisition of Zain with all of $10.7 billion through debt over its market capitalization of US$26.7 billion in India. Assume Bharti has no existing debt. A pure telecom operator in Africa is MTN listed at Johannesburg, South Africa, which is observed to have beta of 1.26 and has debt equity ratio of 1:3 with tax rate of 40%. The tax rate or Bharti is 30% in India.

The markets of India and Africa have a correlation coefficient of 0.7 and stock indices of South Africa and India have standard deviations of 25% and 16%, respectively. Risk free rate in India and Africa are 6% and the risk premiums desired are 10% and 8%, respectively. Find out the following:

1. If an African investor wanted to acquire Zain with 100% equity what would be the expected return on equity?
2. If an African investor wanted to acquire Zain with debt level as envisaged by Bharti what would be the expected return on equity?
3. What would be the cost of equity for equity investors of Bharti in India?

Solution

1. The pure-play for Bharti to consider business risk of Zain is MTN operating in African nations. Its observed beta of 1.26 is levered with debt equity ratio of 1:3. The unlevered (all equity beta of MTN reflecting only the business risk of telecom in Africa is found using Eq. 20-15

$$\beta_U = \frac{\beta_L}{\{1+(1-T) \times D/E\}} = \frac{1.26}{1+0.60 \times 1/3} = 1.05$$

An African investor funding entirely by equity faces only the business risk and his desired return on equity would be

$$r_i = r_f + \beta_i(r_m - r_f) = 6.00 + 1.05 \times 8 = 14.40\%$$

2. With debt equity ratio of Bharti as 0.40 (10.7/26.7) the relevered beta incorporating business risk of telecom in Africa and financial risk of debt using Eq. 20-16 is

$$\beta_L^* = \beta_U\{1 + (1 - T^*) \times D^*/E^*\} = 1.05(1 + 0.7 \times 0.4) = 1.344$$

$$r_i = r_f + \beta_i(r_m - r_f) = 6.00 + 1.344 \times 10 = 19.44\%$$

3. Incorporating the linkages of African market and Indian market the beta applicable to investors in India using Eq. 20-8 would be

Foreign Market Beta, β_f

$$= \text{Correlation with Indian market} \frac{\text{Standard Deviation of South African market}}{\text{Standard Deviation of Indian market}}$$

$$= \rho_{fp} \frac{\sigma_{fm}}{\sigma_{pm}} = 0.70 \frac{25}{16} = 1.09375$$

Required beta, β = Foreign Proxy Beta × Foreign Market Beta = 1.344 × 1.09375 = 1.47

With market risk premium of 8% and risk free rate of 6% in India the cost of equity for Bharti shareholders after Zain's acquisition is

$$r_i = r_f + \beta_i(r_m - r_f) = 6.00 + 1.47 (14.00 - 6.00) = 17.76\%$$

of returns of the project and variance of the market portfolio of the parent's nation. This means we measure beta relative to the parent's market portfolio.

The linkage of foreign project risk with its own market is stronger than with a distant market, that is, the parent's home market. In addition, statistically the linkage of the foreign market with the domestic market is more meaningful and makes better sense than the linkages of the foreign project with home market. Understanding of risk of the foreign project with home market is better understood by an indirect route through the foreign market. Therefore, to estimate the risk of Hyundai India with respect to Korean investor, it is considered more prudent to find relationship with Indian benchmark, NIFTY and then relationship of NIFTY with Korean benchmark KOSPI as compared to Hyundai India risk directly with Korean benchmark. This is shown in Figure 20-2.

Figure 20-2 also depicts a realistic position of world markets are neither fully integrated nor fully segmented. In such a situation the global markets would find integration at broader economy level through indices rather than at micro level of the project.

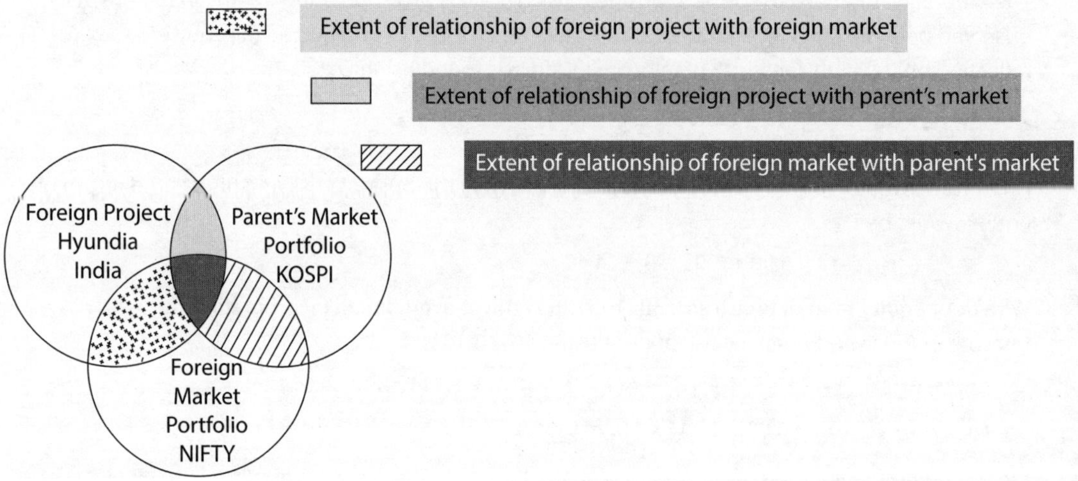

Figure 20-2
Linkages of Project Risk—Neither Integrated Nor Segmented

Beta with Respect to Global Portfolio Yet another choice available for the measurement of project beta is to use global portfolio, that is, measuring Hyundai India or its proxy's returns against returns of global index such as MSCI. This would imply that we assume global markets to be integrated and all investors hold global portfolio. At best this seems utopian. Even if all nations permit their residents to invest anywhere in the world, the investors would not go global due to home bias. ***Home bias*** relates to the inherent tendency of holding investment in securities issued at home even when they are free to invest globally.

Since global portfolio consists of stocks across the world some of the systematic risk at local level becomes unsystematic at global level. For example, Hyundai India returns affected by Indian economic conditions would be systematic when measured against NIFTY but would become unsystematic (hence diversifiable) when measured against MSCI. Against a global portfolio the foreign project would show a lower beta and hence would lead to lower required return on equity and hurdle rate. This is because risk of Hyundai India perceived by a global investor would be smaller than by an Indian or Korean investor.

With increased globalization world markets are integrating rapidly. The integration would at best occur at capital markets level in aggregate rather than at individual project's entity level. Only when all investors become global would benchmarking against a global index make sense. That is the reason one would prefer beta computation in the host nation and translate that to parent's nation using linkages at macroeconomic level.

EXCHANGE RATE RISK AND SOVEREIGN RISK

In the aforementioned analysis for the desired rate of return by investors, we have not considered (a) exchange rate risk and (b) sovereign risk.

Exchange rate risk arises when the returns are provided by the cash flows generated in a currency different than the currency in which returns are desired. The cash flows generated in foreign currency need to be converted in the currency of desired return. This would involve exchange rates at different times which again are volatile. In the context of our example the expected return on equity estimated for Korean investor for their Indian operations is placed at 18.52%. This return is required in Korean currency, won while the cash flows would be generated in Indian rupee by Hyundai India. The net present value would be calculated by discounting the cash flows at expected rate of return both expressed in parent's currency as follows:

$$\text{NPV} = \sum_{1}^{N} \frac{\text{FCF}_n \times \tilde{S}_n}{(1+\text{r}_e)^n} - \text{I}_0 \qquad (20\text{-}17)$$

where FCF_n = Cash flow in foreign currency for period n
 I_0 = Initial investment
 $\tilde{S}_n$ = Expected exchange rate at period n

Therefore, the desired rate of return becomes dependent upon (a) exchange rates volatility and (b) correlation of exchange rate with market. Sovereign risk arises due to handicaps faced in a foreign operation in making initial investment and subsequent remittances of cash flows. The desired return while including the premium for systematic risk does not provide for sovereign risk. One way of including the premium for sovereign risk is to add another spread. The spread may be calculated through the difference in inflation adjusted yields of bonds issued by two countries. In case both the host country and investing country have issued securities in same currency say US dollar the difference in yields can be attributed to sovereign risk.

Fundamentally adding another premium for sovereign risk based on differential of yields of the bonds issued by host and parent nations, in cost of equity lacks rationale. Since equity investment is inherently risky and there exists no promised return adding risk premium in desired rate of return would be fallacious. There cannot be any default in equity. Equity holders are owner of residual cash flow which may be negative, zero, or extremely positive. The compensation for default arising from inadequacy of cash flows is provided by the probability

of increased cash flows. Therefore, a better approach would be to modulate cash flows for sovereign risk rather than modifying the discount rate. However, this may be impractical.

COST OF FOREIGN CURRENCY DEBT

The second component of cost of capital is the cost of debt. When one takes a loan in domestic currency, the cost of loan is simply the interest rate, I, payable on loan. On a post-tax basis the cost of loan is $I(1-T)$ where T is the tax rate.

For a loan of one unit with an annual interest of I for a period on N years the cash flows of the loan would consist of an inflow of one unit, an annual outflow of interest every year for N years, and finally a repayment of one unit at the end of N years assuming a bullet repayment. The internal rate of return of these cash flows would give the cost of loan. From the perspective of lender, the solution of Eq. 20-18 would give the rate of return. For borrower the cash flows would be opposite and return would imply cost of debt.

$$-1+\sum_{1}^{N}\frac{I}{(1+r_d)^n}+\frac{1}{(1+r_d)^N}=0 \qquad (20\text{-}18)$$

The solution to Eq. 20-18 is simply $r_d = I$. The return earned by lender is I and the cost of debt for borrower too is I. It must be reminded that repayment in a bullet or phased the cost of debt remains unchanged. Hence, for a loan repayable in installments the cost continues to be $r_d = I$.

For WACC computation it is the post-tax cost of debt that is relevant. Because of the tax shield the interest has the post-tax cost of debt effectively reduces by the tax saved. The post-tax cost of debt can be computed by finding the Internal Rate of Return (IRR) of the modified Eq. 20-19.

$$-1+\sum_{1}^{N}\frac{I(1-T)}{(1+r_d)^n}+\frac{1}{(1+r_d)^N}=0 \qquad (20\text{-}19)$$

The post-tax cost of debt would simply be $I \times (1-T)$.

When a debt is raised in foreign currency, the cost of debt becomes dependent upon exchange rates too. Cash flows of debt are spread over time. Because exchange rates do not remain constant the cash flows in foreign currency even though constant become variable when converted in another currency. For example, consider a loan of US$100 for an Indian firm at interest of 5% for one year. In dollar terms, the cost of this loan would be 5% and if the tax rate is 40% the post-tax cost of loan would be 3% (5% × 0.6). In rupee terms, the cost becomes dependent upon the exchange rates. Assume that at the time of taking the loan if the exchange rate was ₹50/$, the firm received ₹5,000 as an inflow. After a year if the exchange rate is ₹52/$, the firm pays ₹5,460 (105 × 52). Therefore, in terms of Indian rupee the cost of the loan is 9.20%.

$$\frac{5,460}{5,000}-1=0.092\equiv 9.2\%$$

Considering the tax effect the post-tax interest payment would be $3 with 40% tax. The rupee outflow after one year would be ₹5,356 (103 × 52) giving post-tax cost at 7.12%. This is somewhat strange because post-tax cost of debt at $I \times (1 - T)$ must be 5.52% (9.2 × 0.6). The explanation is simple. The extra cost is due to rupee depreciation of Indian rupee with respect to US dollar. The total cost borne by the borrower may be seen as $d\%$ more in case of local currency depreciation. For annual depreciation of d the cost of foreign currency loan is:

$$\begin{aligned}\text{Cost of Foreign Currency Loan} &= \text{Interest Paid} + \text{Principal Repayment} - \text{Amount of Loan} \\ &= I \times (1 - T)(1 + d) + (1 + d) - 1 \\ &= I \times (1 - T)(1 + d) + d \end{aligned} \quad (20\text{-}20)$$

For the given data the depreciation of Indian rupee is $(52 - 50)/50 = 4\%$. Therefore, the cost of foreign currency loan using Eq. 20-20 is

$3(1.04) + 4 = 7.12\%$

The change in exchange rate must be computed in terms of direct quote convention, that is, $(S_1 - S_0)/S_0$. In case of appreciation, the exchange rate change would have negative sign, and the cost of loan in local currency would be less as compared to the cost of loan in foreign currency.

Pre-tax cost of loan would simply be $I(1 + d) + d$. In the instant case, it is $5 \times 1.04 + 4 = 9.2\%$

For a foreign currency loan of N years, the pre-tax and post-tax cost of loan would be given by solutions to Eqs 20-21 and 20-22, respectively.

$$\text{Pre-tax cost of loan, } r_d; \quad -1 + \sum_{1}^{N} \frac{I(1+d)^n}{(1+r_d)^n} + \frac{1(1+d)^N}{(1+r_d)^N} = 0 \quad (20\text{-}21)$$

$$\text{Post-tax cost of loan, } r_d; \quad -1 + \sum_{1}^{N} \frac{I(1-T)(1+d)^n}{(1+r_d)^n} + \frac{1(1+d)^N}{(1+r_d)^N} = 0 \quad (20\text{-}22)$$

The solution to these equations would be the internal rate of return and lead to the cost of loan same as Eq. 20-20. Table 20-1 exhibits the pre-tax and post-tax cash flows of a loan of €100 for an Indian firm with 7% interest and 35% tax rate both in euro and Indian rupee. The internal rate of return of these cash flows would give the cost of loan.

The cost of loan in euro is 7%. The post-tax cost is $7 \times (1 - 0.35) = 4.55\%$.

The cost of loan would be same as given by Eq. 20-21. In terms of Indian rupee depreciating by 5% annually pre-tax cost is $I \times (1 + d) + d = 7 \times 1.05 + 5 = 12.35\%$. And the post-tax cost is $I \times (1 - T)(1 + d) + d = 7 \times 0.65 \times 1.05 + 5 = 9.78\%$.

The cost of loan measured in Indian rupee is heavily dependent upon exchange rate changes. If Indian rupee were to appreciate by 5% rather than depreciate, the cost of loan would change drastically. The cash flows of the same loan with 5% appreciation on Indian rupee are shown in Table 20-2. Again IRR of these cash flows would indicate the cost of loan.

The cost of loan in euro would remain same as before at 7% on pre-tax basis and 4.55% on post-tax basis.

Table 20-1
Cost of Foreign Currency Loan—Depreciating Local Currency

Year	Principal (€)	Interest in Foreign Currency, (€)		Foreign Currency Cash Flow (€)		Local Currency Cash Flow (₹)	
		Pre Tax	Post Tax	Pre Tax	Post Tax	Pre Tax	Post Tax
0	−100.00			−100.00	−100.00	−7,500.00	−7,500.00
1		7.00	4.55	7.00	4.55	551.25	358.31
2		7.00	4.55	7.00	4.55	578.81	376.23
3		7.00	4.55	7.00	4.55	607.75	395.04
4		7.00	4.55	7.00	4.55	638.14	414.79
5	100.00	7.00	4.55	107.00	104.55	10,242.16	10,007.64
		Cost of Loan		7.00%	4.55%	12.35%	9.78%

The cost of loan in rupee terms would be given by Eq. 20-20 with $d = -0.05$. In terms of Indian rupee appreciating by 5% annually, pre-tax cost is $I \times (1 + d) + d = 7 \times 0.95 - 5 = 1.65\%$. In addition, the post-tax cost is $I \times (1 - T)(1 + d) + d = 7 \times 0.65 \times 0.95 - 5 = -0.68\%$.

Sovereign Risk In case of debt, a premium for the sovereign risk as determined from the differential of inflation adjusted yields on the government securities may be added. The rationale is that since debt promises a fixed rate of return with no extra reward for the excess generation of funds the protection against the sovereign risk is required. The differential in the

Table 20-2
Cost of Foreign Currency Loan—Appreciating Local Currency

Year	Principal (€)	Interest in Foreign Currency, (€)		Foreign Currency Cash Flow (€)		Local Currency Cash Flow (₹)	
		Pre Tax	Post Tax	Pre Tax	Post Tax	Pre Tax	Post Tax
0	−100.00			−100.00	−100.00	−7,500.00	−7,500.00
1		7.00	4.55	7.00	4.55	498.75	324.19
2		7.00	4.55	7.00	4.55	473.81	307.98
3		7.00	4.55	7.00	4.55	450.12	292.58
4		7.00	4.55	7.00	4.55	427.62	277.95
5	100.00	7.00	4.55	107.00	104.55	6,209.59	6,067.41
		Cost of Loan		7.00%	4.55%	1.65%	−0.68%

inflation adjusted yields is representative of likely compensation on account of investing in a country. It is different than investing in a project in that country.

CAPITAL STRUCTURE OF FOREIGN SUBSIDIARY

It is well recognized that capital structure and cost of capital are intricately linked. The capital structure of a project has its implications on the cost of equity and weighted average cost of capital. With increased level of debt, the equity holders of the project feel more threatened with respect to the residual cash flows available to them because of the prior claim of the debt holders. Accordingly, the risk perception of the equity holders increases with rising levels of debt. This gets imbibed in the value of beta. Therefore, value of levered beta is higher than the unlevered (all equity) beta.

All capital budgeting decisions including those of the foreign projects are taken with a view to maximize the shareholders' wealth. Capital structure decision too is guided by the same principle of maximization of shareholders' wealth. A debt ratio that maximizes the value of the firm is the optimal capital structure. Value of the firm is mostly gauged by the stock price assuming that the number of shares pre and post project remains same.

Since most foreign projects are often executed through a subsidiary a natural question of optimal capital structure for the subsidiary arises. The optimal capital structure is often decided in terms of well-established norms about debt ratios for a firm and industry based on multitude of subjective factors and experiences gathered in the past rather than a mathematically optimizing model. These norms about desirable debt ratios evolve over time as industry develops and finances are made available. Apparently, these norms based on experiences are devoid of mathematical modeling.

The subjective factors regarding permissible or acceptable levels of debt include project specific factors, such as its profile, tangibility of assets, availability of collateral and primary security, and management. They also include general factors concerning the economy, such as the business environment of a country, past experiences of failed and successful projects, comfort level of lenders, developmental needs of a nation, stage of economic development, availability of financial resources at national level, level of local competition, social needs of the product, and desirability of technology and products.

The desired capital structure is also governed by orientation of management towards debt. Management philosophy regarding debt, their desire for control, and interference-free decision making, rate of growth planned, etc. also play a great part in determination of the capital structure. Some MNCs also believe in building a debt capacity over a period of time so as to capitalize on any business opportunity as and when they arise in the environment. Hence, it not uncommon to see a drastic change in capital structure pre and post big-ticket acquisition, when the acquisition is through a leveraged buy-out (LBO).

The norms for debt ratios for an industry in an economy as well as capital structure of the firm evolve over a period of time. Therefore, existing capital structure of any firm becomes somewhat a non-factor in determination of cost of capital. As firm borrows the debt ratio increases. With time it repays debt and adds to the reserve. Under normal course of business with normal profits, the debt ratio of the firm declines from one period to another. With time the firm builds a debt capacity which may be used as and when required. Therefore, while determining the cost of capital the usual practice is to work on the target capital structure rather than on existing capital structure.

For an MNC having many subsidiaries a natural question as to their capital structure arises. These subsidiaries mostly operate as separate legal entities in their respective countries. The regulatory environment as well as norms for debt ratio prevailing in the country hosting the subsidiary become important.

Capital Structure of Multinational Corporation on Global Basis

The issue of capital structure of an MNC on global basis may be addressed in two ways—a top-down approach or a bottoms-up approach. With top-down approach we decide a target capital structure at apex level and then replicate it in every subsidiary. Under bottoms-up approach we let each subsidiary decide its own capital structure in accordance with project risk, political risk, the norms of the country hosting it, and then aggregate all subsidiaries to get to the overall capital structure of the MNC. In such a case, the issue of capital structure of the subsidiary is rather independent of the overall capital structure of the MNC at global level.

Top-down Approach In top-down approach, the philosophy of management at apex level of the MNC regarding debt ratios, the economic environment, and capital structure norms as prevailing in the parent's nation become key determinants of the capital structure of each subsidiary. Such an approach ignores local conditions altogether. It may be recognized that perceptions of debt ratios and risk in two different nations would most probably not be identical. From the viewpoint of diversification setting subsidiaries in dissimilar rather than similar economies makes better sense. In developing nations where capital markets are not as developed and efficient as in the developed world there is a greater tendency as well as acceptance to use higher levels of debt in financing growth. In developed economies where equity cult is better developed, funding of projects favours equity and lesser use of debt. In developed world, venture capital finance and private equity are well-established vehicles of growth.

Developing economies, such as India have promoted establishment of developmental financial institutions providing cheap source of debt capital with extended repayment periods to achieve desired levels of economic and industrial growth due to lack of private capital and rather under-developed capital markets. Besides cheaper and relaxed source of finance the system of subsidies and allocation of land at controlled rates tilted the capital structure towards higher proportions of debt. They have implications on project cost and hence the capital structure. It would not be strange to find cost of debt in developing economies to be lower than developed nations. Capitalization norms too favour debt in developing nations. In East Asian economies '*keirutsu financing*' eases availability of debt capital and hence acceptance of greater levels of debt. Lesser levels of maturity and efficiency of capital markets in developing countries make debt a better and more efficient option than equity.

Growth in a developing nation is propelled by debt while developed economies see growth equity-propelled.

Besides different capital structure norms in different countries, the replication of capital structure of parent at the level of subsidiary may not be possible due to regulatory reasons. Equity investments in a country are governed by policies regarding FDI, stock market regulations, currency controls, repatriation of profit, etc. Besides there can be operational constraints regarding minimum local participation in equity, markets, employment, procurement, etc. These factors not only impact the decision to have subsidiary but also its capital structure and shareholding pattern. The top-down approach to capital structure would be more focused on the corporate characteristics rather than country characteristics.

Bottoms-up Approach Under bottoms-up approach of capital structure determination the country-specific aspects come to the fore eclipsing the corporate philosophy regarding debt levels. Therefore, capital structure of the parent MNC becomes residual. Following capital structure norms of host nations tend to increase the acceptability of the subsidiary by local residents. Besides, such a policy of better compliance with existing legal framework of host nation facilitates speedier implementation of projects rather than consuming time in lobbying for regulatory and administrative changes as per the corporate policies. The benefits of early-bird are too well known to be repeated here. Following local norms for financing of the project would also provide cheap source of finance in case subsidiary is in a developing nation and parent comes from developed nation.

If greater levels of debt in host nations are permissible, it allows the MNC to conserve own resources alternatively to be used elsewhere or distributed as dividend. Greater use of local financing also reduces exchange rate risk because to the extent debt service payments are generated locally the MNC does not need to convert currencies. Since the amount of exchange rate risk is reduced, the corresponding risk premium should fall decreasing the cost of capital. Therefore, the value of the firm must increase. On the contrary, if increased debt at the level of subsidiary does not increase availability of funds elsewhere (perhaps due to capital outflow controls in the host nation) the value of the MNC may be adversely affected due to increased cost of equity.

Irrelevance of Capital Structure of Subsidiary

As stated earlier, optimal capital structure decision concerns maximization of shareholders' wealth, that is, maximization of stock price. For shareholders of an MNC the performance is viewed on consolidated basis and capital structure inclusive of subsidiaries becomes relevant.

With the help of an illustration we demonstrate that it is possible to have any capital structure of a subsidiary keeping the capital structure of the MNC constant. Assume an Indian Firm A desirous of having a subsidiary has following simplified balance sheet:

Balance Sheet of Firm A		Figures in ₹	
Equity	100	Assets	200
Debt	100		

It proposes to have a subsidiary with an asset base of ₹50. The equity contribution required for this subsidiary would be raised as loan by Firm A. Among numerous capital structures of subsidiary possible, we consider following three possible capital structure scenarios:

1. *All equity structure of subsidiary* Firm A borrows ₹49 to remit as equity and subsidiary raises remaining ₹1 as loan, with subsidiary having a debt ratio of 1/50.
2. *Leveraged structure of subsidiary* Firm A borrows ₹25 to remit as equity and subsidiary raises remaining ₹25 as loan, with subsidiary having debt ratio of 1/2.
3. *All debt structure of subsidiary* Firm A borrows ₹1 to remit as equity and subsidiary raises remaining ₹49 as loan, with subsidiary having debt ratio of 49/50.

The stand-alone balance sheets of parent Firm A, its subsidiary and consolidated balance sheet of Firm A under three possible capital structure scenarios of the subsidiary are presented in Table 20-3 with remarks.

From the remarks made it may be observed that with a given acceptable capital structure of the parent Firm A (with debt ratio of 3/5) at consolidated level any capital structure of the subsidiary firm can be achieved. Hence with the objective of maximization of shareholders' wealth for Firm A, the capital structure of subsidiary becomes irrelevant. Any capital structure of subsidiary should be acceptable to the shareholders of Firm A as long as its consolidated debt ratio does not change.

In the analysis presented in Table 20-3, we made two assumptions—(i) financing of subsidiary required use of debt and (ii) the cost of raising debt by subsidiary and parent were identical.

If debt is required to fund the subsidiary, it really did not matter on global basis who of the subsidiary or parent borrows. As long as the parent feels responsible for debt repayment, it is immaterial who borrows. Increased borrowing by subsidiary means lesser use of debt by parent and vice versa. If financing of subsidiary did not require additional debt there would be no debt at subsidiary level. The cash available at parent would fund the subsidiary. The aggregate amount of assets would remain same except that the location and form of assets change from parent to subsidiary, again keeping the capital structure unchanged.

Even though the capital structure remains unchanged, the cost of capital for the MNC may undergo a change if costs of borrowings by subsidiary and parent are not identical. The one who can borrow at cheaper rate must resort to borrowing to keep cost of capital lower. It should not be presumed that MNCs because of their size or reputation would be able to mobilize capital in home nation at a cheaper rate than what the subsidiary can in the host nation. Since cost of capital is a function of country characteristics too it is possible that subsidiary while using the advantages of the MNC may also be able to simultaneously exploit domestic conditions of the host nation to avail better financing deals.

The flexibility to mobilize capital in either home country or host nation requires an additional assumption of absence of capital flow controls between the host country and the parent's

Table 20-3
Balance Sheets with Different Capital Structures of Subsidiary

Figures in ₹	Parent	Subsidiary	Consolidated	Remarks
All Equity Financing of Subsidiary				
Liabilities				
Equity	100	49	100	
Debt	149	1	150	Firm A borrows required equity of ₹49 for the subsidiary while remaining ₹1 is borrowed by subsidiary. The consolidated borrowing is ₹150
Assets				
Parent's own	200		200	
Subsidiary		50	50	
Investment	49			
Debt Ratio	1.49/2.49	1/50	3/5	
Levered Financing of Subsidiary				
Liabilities				
Equity	100	25	100	
Debt	125	25	150	Firm A borrows required equity of ₹25 for the subsidiary while remaining ₹25 is borrowed by subsidiary. The consolidated borrowing is ₹150
Assets				
Parent's own	200		200	
Subsidiary		50	50	
Investment	25			
Debt Ratio	1.25/2.25	1/2	3/5	
All Debt Financing of Subsidiary				
Liabilities				
Equity	100	1	100	
Debt	101	49	150	Firm A borrows required equity of ₹1 for the subsidiary while remaining ₹49 is borrowed by subsidiary. The consolidated borrowing is ₹150
Assets				
Parent's own	200		200	
Subsidiary		50	50	
Investment	1			
Debt Ratio	1.01/2.01	49/50	3/5	

country. If there were capital controls on flow of funds across borders, then the capital structure decisions of parent, subsidiary, and consolidated become rather independent of one another.

PRACTICAL CONSIDERATIONS IN DECIDING SUBSIDIARY'S CAPITAL STRUCTURE

Given that the capital structure of the subsidiaries is rather irrelevant for determination of the value of the MNC and there seem many limitations in implementing top-down approach, the recommended approach to the capital structure of the subsidiary is guided by several factors. Some of these fundamental factors that must be considered are discussed here.

Managing Political Risk

One of the practical considerations that can impact the capital structure of an MNC is management of political risk. Each MNC operating in another country faces a political risk of expropriation to some extent being a foreign national. In case of failures on account of conditions of investment the government in foreign country due to its political compulsions may decide to expropriate assets of the subsidiary firm. To deter expropriation and contain loss of wealth of shareholders an MNC may decide to borrow as much as possible from local banks and financial institutions. When local financing gets involved expropriation means loss to local banks and financial institutions as well. This may be strong enough reason for governments not to take extreme step of expropriation. Large stakes by local banks may work as saviour. Therefore, the decision to borrow is guided by strategic reasons that may force the MNC to deviate from its target capital structure.

Besides avoiding loss due to expropriation, the financing by local banks may help the subsidiary perceived more as local entity rather than foreign. Greater stake by local banks would permit use of local influence on other matters too. There is considerable operational ease in garnering other resources, such as labour, raw material, and utilities and help better acceptance of finished products.

Desire for Control and Management Decision-making

The FDI regulation often places a cap on the level of foreign equity in a project. More often than not such rules are placed to permit control of firms by local residents as also to attract foreign investments. MNCs would have to cede control of the subsidiary if it is mostly or entirely financed by equity. An alternative emerges through use of debt. For example, consider a stipulation of maximum of 49% foreign ownership for a project of $100 by an MNC in a developing nation. With 100% equity financing the MNC would contribute $49 towards equity and yet not have management control. By having a leveraged capital structure of debt equity ratio of 1:1, the MNC may contribute US$50 as loan and US$24 through equity while remaining US$25 being contributed by local partner. Though in terms of majority control the local partner continues to have the control but practically participation of MNC may be increased by appointing additional director on board in the capacity and representative of lender.

Currency Convertibility

Several countries impose a variety of restriction on the convertibility of local currency into foreign currency. This may be motivated by political and/or economic factors. They either prohibit remittance of profit or place a cap on them or are put to additional taxes. Any of these restrictions limits the dividend receipts by MNC parent. Under such circumstances equity-oriented financing may leave larger surplus, which cannot be repatriated or makes repatriation too expensive. A high leveraged capital structure of subsidiary with interest cost would leave lesser for distribution of profit (in terms of absolute amount and not as percent of equity contribution) and may become more desirable. Again the MNC may have to deviate from the target capital structure.

Eliminating Currency Risk

The MNC often float in a subsidiary in a nation in pursuance of growth objective. This may require frequent to-and-fro movement of cash with excess being repatriated and infused back to subsidiary when needed. Such transactions would be subject to exchange rate fluctuations. Besides there would be transaction costs in the form of bid-ask spread. Alternatively, the MNC may decide to change the capital structure of the subsidiary from time to time by holding back the surplus for future growth needs, and when fall short may resort to borrowing. Only when absolutely sure that funds would not be needed for some time to come repatriation of surplus may be done. This essentially means matching the cash inflows and outflows in the currencies eliminating transaction costs and currency exchange rate risk.

Such practice would make capital structure of the subsidiary as well as parent flexible and would require balancing of (a) loss of value due to deviation from target and optimal capital structure against (b) the savings of transaction cost and increased value due to reduced currency exchange rate risk.

Tax Considerations

Repatriation of profits back to parent is normally subject to additional tax as well as withholding tax deducted at the time of remittance. In most cases the taxes deducted in host nation are provided as credit in the parent's home nation under Double Taxation Avoidance Agreements. As long as tax credits from subsidiary's host country combined with the tax on profit do not exceed the amount of tax payable the issue of remitting profit is acceptable. However, if the tax credits available result in a greater cash outflows than required by the marginal tax rate the remittance of profit is not financially prudent. The issue can be addressed by modifying capital structure in favour of debt. Financing subsidiary entirely by equity would place demand on repatriation of larger dividend to service higher base of equity mobilized at home. Financing through debt would result in greater cash outflows on account of interest, reduce initial funding through equity and hence have lesser pressure on remittance for servicing extra equity raised at home.

Tax considerations often become complex due to differential rates of taxes applicable in different nations depending upon the nature of income or expense. While interest income is tax deductible, dividend is not in most countries. For example, in India dividend are tax exempt in the hands of investors but dividend distribution tax is payable. Therefore, retaining earnings may be preferable option as compared to its distribution and then infusing further funds at a later point of time. If funds are surplus now but required later then dividend distribution tax is the cost that is completely avoidable. In addition, returns in the form of dividend or in the form of capital gains are taxed differently, with capital gains either exempt or taxed at lower rate. It may be reiterated that for comparison of different strategies the framework must always be post-tax returns from the perspective of owners/shareholders.

Tax considerations also often form the basis of investment in foreign countries as well as for raising capital or debt. Despite increased convergence of financial markets the taxes in different countries would continue to remain different, because the taxation policy is guided by several domestic conditions. Therefore, tax arbitrage would continue to be one of the primary motives of foreign investment and resource mobilization. Removing the tax differential among various nations perhaps is not a subject matter of international negotiations.

LOW COST FINANCING

Most developing nations in order to attract foreign investment offer a variety of incentives to multinationals to set-up projects. These incentives include grant of capital subsidy, sanction of soft loans, preferential allocation of land, tax holiday, preferential or exclusive access or rights to resources, guaranteeing minimum returns, etc. All these incentives have financial values and have implications on capital structure of the subsidiary. Should the subsidiary forego these benefits to defend the target capital structure?

The question of availing the incentives hinges on the difference of the values of the incentive at concessional rates and value of the same resource obtained at market rates. The NPV framework provides the worth of a concession in monetary terms.

Assume that an MNC has been offered a concessional loan of ₹500 at 8% instead of usual 15% with moratorium of 5 years. Thereafter the loan is repayable in five equal annual installments. The total tenure of the loan is 10 years. With tax rate of 40% the worth of loan can be computed by discounting the cash flow of the loan at 15% as shown in Table 20-4.

For the first year, the interest is ₹0.08 × 500 = 40. Post-tax interest is 0.6 × 40 = ₹24. For five years till the repayment begins, the amount remains same. From year 6 onwards, the interest payments would reduce. The last column of Table 20-4 gives the present value of cash flows of loan discounted at 15%. The present value of the cash outflows of the loan is ₹273.33. Subtracting it from ₹500 we get the benefit of loan at ₹226.67.

The benefit of the loan comprises two elements—the subsidized interest rate as against commercial rate and the tax shield on the interest. The interest saved is 7% (15% – 8%) on the principal outstanding. The value of the tax saved is ₹155.56. The tax saved is 0.40 × 8% (tax rate × subsidized interest rate). The worth of tax shield is ₹71.11. Both the savings discounted at commercial rate would add up to provide the aggregate value of the concessional loan at

Table 20-4
Value of Concessionary Loan

Year	Outstanding Beginning	Repayment	Interest	Post Tax Interest	Present Value of Cash Flow
1	500.00		40.00	24.00	20.87
2	500.00		40.00	24.00	18.15
3	500.00		40.00	24.00	15.78
4	500.00		40.00	24.00	13.72
5	500.00		40.00	24.00	11.93
6	500.00	100.00	40.00	24.00	53.61
7	400.00	100.00	32.00	19.20	44.81
8	300.00	100.00	24.00	14.40	37.40
9	200.00	100.00	16.00	9.60	31.16
10	100.00	100.00	8.00	4.80	25.90
	Present Value of Loan Cash Flows				273.33
	Worth of Concessionary Loan				226.67

₹226.67 as was estimated in Table 20.5. The working of interest and tax benefits is shown in Table 20-5.

Valuation of Tax Holiday

Most developing nations offer tax holiday for promoting industrial development and creation of employment to induce MNCs to set up operations. Normal mode of providing this benefit is to exempt profits for few initial years of operation. Is this incentive attractive enough for MNCs to make a policy decision in favour of expanding in a nation granting tax holiday?

The decision is dependent upon the tax regime prevailing in the home country of parent MNC. If the MNC is subject to tax in the home country on its global income the tax holiday apparently has no value because for the tax benefit in the host country would be offset by the additional tax paid in the home country. If the MNC is not taxed on global income the value of the tax saving can be computed by difference of profit after tax at full and concessional rates of taxes discounted at cost of equity. For example, if a Puerto Rico subsidiary of an US MNC is subject to 2% tax instead of normal 30% tax in Puerto Rico for the next 10 years, then the worth of tax benefit of US$100 as pre-tax profit is 98 – 70 = US$28. This must be discounted at cost of equity for the US investors.

Table 20-5
Value of Interest Subsidy and Tax Shield

Year	Outstanding Beginning	Repayment	Interest Paid	Interest Benefit			Tax Benefit	
				Interest at Market Rates	Interest Saved	Present Value	Tax Saved	Present Value
1	500.00		40.00	75.00	35.00	30.43	16.00	13.91
2	500.00		40.00	75.00	35.00	26.47	16.00	12.10
3	500.00		40.00	75.00	35.00	23.01	16.00	10.52
4	500.00		40.00	75.00	35.00	20.01	16.00	9.15
5	500.00		40.00	75.00	35.00	17.40	16.00	7.95
6	500.00	100.00	40.00	75.00	35.00	15.13	16.00	6.92
7	400.00	100.00	32.00	60.00	28.00	10.53	12.80	4.81
8	300.00	100.00	24.00	45.00	21.00	6.86	9.60	3.14
9	200.00	100.00	16.00	30.00	14.00	3.98	6.40	1.82
10	100.00	100.00	8.00	15.00	7.00	1.73	3.20	0.79
Present Value of Cash Flows						155.56		71.11
Worth of Concessionary Loan								226.67

SUMMARY

The cost of capital and optimum capital structure are intricately linked. Optimal capital structure is one that maximizes the shareholders' wealth. To obtain optimal capital structure once focuses on cost of capital and it is presumed that least cost of capital would maximize shareholders' wealth. Therefore, the debt ratio that minimizes the cost of capital is the optimal capital structure.

As compared to a domestic firm the decision for cost of capital for a multinational corporation is more complex because MNCs have access to wider and larger global markets, offering a variety of instruments for capital mobilization, in various currencies with investors in many countries with diverse expectations of risk and returns. The cost of equity for a foreign project is complex because the project faces risk in different economic and political environment while the investors are domiciled in another environment. There is a mismatch as risk and return expectations are not priced in the same environment.

CAPM is the model of choice to measure cost of equity that consolidates risk in a single parameter called beta. Use of CAPM as model of determination of cost of equity poses many problems. These include classification of systematic and unsystematic risk, conflicts between minority and majority shareholders due to different nationalities, etc. The project executed through a subsidiary in a different nation is subjected to risk from the environment not belonging to the parent investor. Measure of risk and risk premium pose benchmark problems. While the risk of the project can be readily assessed from the host environment using their benchmarks, the same cannot be reliably measured in the parent's environment due to segmented markets and extremely low degrees of correlation of project's risk.

Therefore, an alternative is found. We first measure the project's risk, that is, beta in the host environment. Then the linkage of project's risk with the parent's environment is found at macro level, that is, the correlations of host and home nations markets called foreign market beta. Using foreign market beta permits quantification of project's risk for the investors in the home market.

The project's beta calculated in the roundabout manner provides only for the business and financial risk. In foreign projects we also face (a) exchange rate risk and, and (b) political/country risk. The CAPM or beta does not account for such risk. But extending the same concept that a risk premium is desired for each class of risk we may add some premiums for (a) exchange rate risk based on exchange rate volatility, and (b) political risk based on country rating.

Cost of debt taken in foreign currency is dependent upon its appreciation/depreciation besides the coupon rate. If the currency in which the loan is denominated appreciates the cost of debt would be greater than the coupon rate by the amount of foreign currency appreciation.

The capital structure of a subsidiary throws two options:(1) follow the global target capital structure of the MNC and replicate it in all the subsidiaries, and (2) adopt capital structure as per the norms of the host nation of the subsidiary and let the global capital structure be decided by aggregate of all subsidiaries. Both the options have limitations in the environment imposed by the host nation. For a fixed capital structure of MNC at global level it can be established that capital structure at the level of subsidiary is irrelevant as long as the parent feels ultimately responsible for debt and its servicing.

Among the practical considerations impacting the capital structure decision are political risk, extent of control, orientation towards debt, availability of concessional finance, convertibility, currency risk, taxation, etc.

QUESTIONS

20-1 How do you think that cost of capital and capital structure decision are interrelated?
20-2 What factors differentiate the determination of cost of capital for a multinational corporation as compared to a domestic firm?
20-3 What limitations do you anticipate in the application of CAPM model for determining the cost of capital for a foreign project implemented by an MNC in a foreign country?
20-4 What limitations do you anticipate in determining the beta for a foreign project implemented by an MNC in a foreign country?
20-5 Describe pure-play approach of arriving at true measure of risk for a project in foreign country.
20-6 How do you account for country risk and exchange rate risk in a project located abroad and generating cash flows in foreign currency?

21

International Capital Budgeting

LEARNING OBJECTIVES

This chapter aims at

- understanding the basic framework used in capital budgeting exercises
- understanding three approaches to capital budgeting
- appreciating the requirements and limitations of WACC model and FTE model
- knowing about mechanics of APV method of appraisal
- learning the differences of cash flows for parent and subsidiary
- understanding the relevance of using the correct discount rates in different currencies and different situations
- learning why APV method is useful in international scenario
- knowing how to value debt tax shield, depreciation tax shield, and other project-specific cash flows

CONTENTS

Introduction
Capital Budgeting: A General Framework
Differences in Domestic and International Capital Budgeting
   Differences in Cash Flows
   Cash Flow—Subsidiary or Parent
   Currency of the Cash Flow
   Discount Rate
Illustration: Euronet—Equivalence of Net Present Value in Foreign and Home Currency
   Properties of Discount Rate
Review of Net Present Value Framework
Illustration: Equivalence of Weighted Average Cost of Capital and Flow to Equity Methods
   Flow to Equity Approach
   Weighted Average Cost of Capital Approach
   Limitations of Weighted Average Cost of Capital and Flow to Equity Models

Adjusted Present Value Method
   Debt and Discount Rate
Illustrative Case: DVS Limited—Adjusted Present Value Method
   Economic Indicators and Financial Markets
   Exchange Rate Projection
   Cash Flow Projection
   Tax Considerations
   Post-tax Incremental Cash Flow
   Discount Rate for Operating Cash Flows
   All Equity Net Present Value
   Depreciation
   Concessionary Loan
   Use of Blocked Funds
   Value of Debt Capacity
   Value of Royalty to Parent
   Value of Inputs Supplied

International Capital Budgeting

INTRODUCTION

With increased globalization, the firms are competing internationally. Their domains no more remain confined to the national boundaries. The order of the day is increasing size of operations, magnifying volumes of sales, diversifying customer base, expanding product range, increasing value addition to existing products, etc. Any or more of such strategies are increasingly deployed by firms in the international arena. Competition of finding a place in Fortune companies has increased over a period of time.

The accuracy and validity of capital budgeting decisions play a key role in the growth and achieving of global ambition of a firm. Those with greater and careful effort and extensive examination of growth opportunities are likely to succeed more than others who merely leave the capital budgeting exercise to chance.

While there is an increasing desire on part of corporations to expand beyond national horizons, there is increased risk emanating from necessity of fast decision-making. The compulsion of quick decision-making especially in takeover cases has made the managers of the firm to act in haste and hence they have become more prone to errors. In this perspective, the exercise of international capital budgeting needs to be done more diligently than what is required for domestic capital budgeting scenario. Under domestic capital budgeting exercise, a domestic corporation is dealing with an environment that it is completely familiar, and risk factors are consciously or unconsciously incorporated. To that extent the due diligence exercise is implicitly or explicitly completed. In contrast, the exercise of internationl capital budgeting involves dealing with new environment, different cultural background, unfamiliar business conditions, and commercial environment.

CAPITAL BUDGETING: A GENERAL FRAMEWORK

We all are familiar with golden rule of net present value (NPV) of capital budgeting represented as Eq. 21-1:

$$NPV = \sum_{1}^{N} \frac{CF_n}{(1+r)^n} - CF_0 \qquad (21\text{-}1)$$

where CF_n represents free cash flows for period n over the life of the project on N years and r is the discount rate.

The rule of acceptance and rejection of the proposal is clear—accept projects with positive NPV and reject those with negative NPV. NPV is the value that would be added to the shareholders' wealth. Table 21-1 demonstrates simple rule of NPV for acceptance of a project. The project has initial cash outlay of ₹100 with a life of five years with the cash flows given in Column 2 of Table 21-1. The discount rate used is 10% and the net present value is ₹18.44 as shown in the last row.

The projection of two inputs in the capital budgeting decision, that is, the free cash flows and discount rate presents difficulties. Besides limitations of forecasting of the cash flows a lot of attention and thought is required in selection of cash flows and discount

Table 21-1
Net Present Value

Year	Cash Flow (₹)	Discount Factor	Present Value (₹)
0	−100	1.0000	−100.00
1	25	0.9091	22.73
2	25	0.8264	20.66
3	35	0.7513	26.30
4	35	0.6830	23.91
5	40	0.6209	24.84
Net Present Value			**18.44**

rates. These limitations and interplay of cash flows and discount rate become increasingly complex if the capital budgeting exercise is concerned with multinational corporations involving situations of setting up a Greenfield venture in locations abroad or in a cross-border acquisition.

DIFFERENCES IN DOMESTIC AND INTERNATIONAL CAPITAL BUDGETING

Multinational corporations (MNCs) have operations in various countries. These operations overseas may range from mere export to an agent to a branch office to joint ventures to production/manufacturing set up. For establishing operations in locations other than the MNC's own nation the controlling office invariably has to make a decision with regard to desirability of the operations in a different country. At the first sight, this may appear to be a regular capital budgeting decision as if it were a local capital budgeting exercise with the change in the currency. In practice however, due to various complexities in the international arena this decision indeed is not that simple.

The capital budgeting decision in another country involves situations that are often absent in the domestic environment but have significant impact on the acceptance or rejection of the project. These factors have extreme influence on the international capital budgeting decisions, such as

- Political risk of operating in different country ranging from xenophobia to expropriation,
- Uncertainties with respect to culture, norms,
- Working conditions and laws relating to labour productivity and minimum wages,
- Different levels of protection based on nationalities of stakeholders,
- Availability of technical manpower and expertise,
- Greater hurdles and scrutiny by local governments in case the operations belong to MNCs rather than to the so-called tag of 'son of the soil' for domestic firms for similar projects,
- Different legal and administrative environment of labour markets, capital markets, economic environment,

- Business commitments to be made with respect to export, remittances that MNCs have to make, and
- Availability of various kinds of incentives, such as tax breaks, concessionary loans, and preferential allocation of resources of production.

All the aforementioned factors warrant special treatment in the capital budgeting framework and we shall be dealing with some of them in the case that that follows later in the chapter.

Differences in Cash Flows

Under conventional and domestic capital budgeting exercises, the projections of cash flows start from projection of earnings before interest and tax (EBIT). After providing for taxes, T, the non-cash expenses such as depreciation, D, are added back. Finally to arrive at free cash flows capital expenditure, $CAPEX$ and increase in working capital, ΔWC is provided for. Thus, free cash flows for any year are expressed as

$$\text{Free Cash Flow} = \text{EBIT} (1 - T) + \text{Depreciation} - \text{Capital Expenditure} - \text{Increase in Net Working Capital}$$
$$\text{FCF} = \text{EBIT} (1 - T) + D - \text{CAPEX} - \Delta WC \qquad (21\text{-}2)$$

It is worth mentioning here that in the projection of free cash flow the tax on interest is provided though interest is tax deductible. The impact of interest on earnings is not treated under the assumption of all equity financing.

Cash Flow—Subsidiary or Parent

While the process of arriving at the free cash flows for international capital budgeting remains the same as for domestic exercise, the question that whose cash flows—subsidiary or parent—should be used remains. This is often a debatable issue in case of international joint ventures where we have two owners—the parent MNC from home country and the local joint venture partner belonging to the host nation. The conflict of interest arising out of different nationalities of the two sets of shareholders cannot be ruled out. Under such an arrangement, it is often common to see that local day-to-day functioning is managed by people from host nation while major policy decisions are controlled by parent. We recognize the agency problem of employees not acting in the interest of shareholders, or conflict of interest of debt holders and shareholders. In international project, there is strong likelihood of having another kind to agency problem—national interests conflicting with shareholders' interest—as local managers or shareholders may not act in the interest of the parent who comes from a different nationality.

In case of international projects, while it is the subsidiary that generates the cash flow but its ownership lies with the parent. From the principles of capital budgeting we know for sure that only the cash flows of the owner matter. This raises an important question—do all the cash flows generated by subsidiary belong to parent? The answer to the question decides which cash flows to consider. While the process of forecasting cash flow emanates from the cash flows of the subsidiary as given by Eq. 21-2, there are often several differences in what is generated at subsidiary and what accrues to the parent. There are certain items that are included in the cost of subsidiary reducing the cash flows but actually are sources of cash inflows to the parent such as

1. Royalty payments, technical, or management fee are the cash outflows for the subsidiary but are actually cash inflows for the parent.

CONCEPTS IN PRACTICE
Subsidiary's Loss, Parent's Gain

ROYALTY PAYMENTS FOR UNILEVER

On 22 December 2012 the stock of Hindustan Lever Ltd, India's largest consumer product firm and a subsidiary of Unilever Plc, the Anglo-Dutch multinational, the world's second largest consumer goods firm fell by 2% on Indian stock markets on the apprehension that the royalty payments to the parent would be increased just on the lines of the decision of Indonesian subsidiary PT Unilever Indonesia who affected the increase in royalty from 3.5% to 5% of revenue.

On 22 January 2013 the apprehension came true when Indian subsidiary followed and announced a progressive increase in royalty from current 1.4% to 3.15% by March 2018. Amidst huge negative sentiments and reactions of the analysts the next day's loss in the stock price was another 4.4% and the stock hit a six-month low of ₹448. The gain in London was 2.7% in Unilever's stock; presumably compensating the loss of value of Unilever's holding in Indian markets by an equal increase in the London markets confirming the conservation of cash flow.

2. Inputs provided by parent in the form of supplies mandated under the joint venture agreements are cash outflows for the subsidiary but the profit earned by the parent on such supplies, that is, cash price less cash costs, accrue to the parent.

Such costs which are cash outflows for the subsidiary but are inflows to the parent must be added to the cash flows for the parent. For reasons of convenience, it is better to start from the profitability or the cash flow statement of the subsidiary and then modify it from the parent's viewpoint rather than attempt a direct cash flow forecast.

Currency of the Cash Flow

Using the same approach for international projects the starting point for the cash flow projection would be the after tax cash flows of the project/subsidiary in foreign location using Eq. 21-2. The cash flows of the project are denominated in local currency of the subsidiary and not the currency of the parent. Since the capital budgeting exercise is viewed from the perspective of shareholders of the parent the cash flows denominated in foreign currency need to be converted to home currency. Here we have two alternative approaches available to find the NPV:

1. Forecast cash flows in foreign currency (the currency of the subsidiary), discount them at rate consistent with foreign currency to find the present value and convert the NPV arrived in foreign currency into home currency using spot exchange rate, or
2. Forecast cash flow in foreign currency over the life of the project, forecast exchange rates for each period, and convert foreign currency cash flows of each period to the home currency cash flows, discount them at rate appropriate to home currency and find NPV.

In either case, we must have identical NPVs.

Discount Rate

In the two aforesaid approaches, the discount rates cannot be identical. The principle of capital budgeting demands the cash flows and discount rate used are consistent with each other. There are several differences in the cash flows projected in foreign currency and home currency in terms of riskiness of the cash flows due to different economic and political environments, risk premium, cost of capital, etc.

The outcome of the capital budgeting exercise must lead to identical NPVs irrespective of currency of denomination of the cash flows. Trying to work out discount rates in foreign currency is rather a difficult task and may lead to inaccurate and inconsistent NPV. Rather than independently finding the discount rate applicable in foreign currency it is a better approach to start with the discount rate in home currency for two reasons. First, cash flows have to be viewed from parent's perspective irrespective of where and in what currency they are generated, and second, the parent has a fair idea of the return expectations of investors in the home currency that forms the basis of discount rate. Therefore, it would be a better approach to convert the foreign currency cash flows in home currency using forecast exchange rates and then discount to find present values.

In case we proceed with the cash flows in foreign currency and avoid forecast of exchange rate, we need to have appropriate discount rate in foreign currency. The problem would be to find an appropriate discount rate in foreign currency equivalent to discount rate in home currency that leads to the same NPV. If cash flow in foreign currency for period t is CF_t, the projected spot exchange rate is S_t, the discount rates in foreign currency and home currency are r_a and r_h, respectively, then the discounted value of the cash flows would be

With discounting foreign currency cash flow at foreign discount rate:

$$\text{Present Value} = \frac{CF_t}{(1+r_a)^t} \times S_0; \quad \text{and}$$

With discounting home currency cash flow at home discount rate:

$$\text{Present Value} = \frac{CF_t \times S_t}{(1+r_h)^t}$$

For the present values under the two approaches to be identical, we must have

$$\frac{CF_t}{(1+r_a)^t} \times S_0 = \frac{CF_t \times S_t}{(1+r_h)^t} \qquad (21\text{-}3)$$

Simplifying Eq. 21-3, we get a relationship between the foreign and home currency discount rates as Eq. 21-4.

$$\frac{S_t}{S_0} = \frac{(1+r_h)^t}{(1+r_a)^t} \qquad (21\text{-}4)$$

Note that the condition dictated by Eq. 21-4 is similar to international Fisher effect discussed earlier or the uncovered interest rate parity. The difference is that the uncovered parity condition here is applied to the discount rate applicable for the parent's cash flows and subsidiary's cash flows; which among other things would incorporate riskiness of the cash flows and corresponding risk premiums. Since we shall be using APV approach (discussed later) cash flows would be discounted at a rate assuming all equity financing. Hence, these discount rates would include riskiness of the cash flow measured by beta and the risk premium. These would be project-specific. Uncovered interest rate parity could hold only at an aggregate level of an economy.

This simple description of alternative approaches to choice of currency of the cash flow is fraught with risk and can lead to divergent estimates. The divergence could be on account of our inability to find the consistent discount rates with respect to foreign currency and home currency. Since (a) it is difficult to find an equivalent discount rate in the foreign currency, and (b) MNCs have a fair idea about the return and risk expectations of the home investors, it would be a better idea to project the cash flows in foreign currency and convert them to home currency using currency forecast and discount at a rate appropriate to home currency. With the help of an example, we now demonstrate the equivalence of approaches using cash flows in foreign currency discounted at foreign discount rate and cash flows in home currency discounted at home currency discount rate.

ILLUSTRATION: EURONET—EQUIVALENCE OF NET PRESENT VALUE IN FOREIGN AND HOME CURRENCY

Assume that a US multinational firm, USNET, is planning to invest in Europe in a project called EURONET with investment of €100 million. Here US dollar is the home currency and euro is foreign currency. The incremental post-tax cash flows of the project denominated in euro over the life of 5 years are given in Table 21-2.

It is assumed that the base year $t = 0$ we have estimated a cash outflow of €100 million with the post tax incremental inflow at $t = 0$ prices to be €22 million. The post tax incremental cash flow is expected to grow at constant prices by 10% annually therefore first year cash inflow is €24.20 million. To have cash flows in nominal terms, we need to forecast the expected inflation rate in Europe because the project and parent operate in different economic environments.

Table 21-2
Cash Flows of EURONET

	Euro millions		
Year	Cash Flow in Real Terms	Forecast Inflation in Europe	Nominal Cash Flows
0	−100.00		−100.00
1	24.20	2.50%	24.81
2	26.62	2.40%	27.94
3	29.28	2.20%	31.41
4	32.21	1.90%	35.21
5	35.43	1.80%	39.43

Remember we do not do this exercise in domestic capital budgeting exercise because project operates in the same economy as that of parent. The forecast is provided in the column 3 of Table 21-2. After the forecast of inflation rate these cash flows are converted in nominal terms by multiplying the real cash flows with (1 + forecast inflation rate) as is done in the last column.

Converting Foreign Currency Cash Flows to Home Currency As a next step we need to convert the cash flows in euro to US dollar since the parent of the project EURONET belongs to USA. To do so we need to forecast the exchange rate. It can be done on the basis of interest rate parity where we find the forward rates for each period and then assume these forward rates to be unbiased predictor of future spot rates.

To find forward rates two inputs—current spot rate and the term structure of interest rates, that is, the yield curve in two currencies are required. These are assumed given and shown in Table 21-3. The current spot rate (i.e., $1/S_0$ being indirect rate for US parent) is given as

Table 21-3
Forecast Future Spot Exchange Rate (EURONET)

Year	Yield Curve		Forecast Spot Exchange Rate (€/$)	Forecast Spot Exchange Rate ($/€)
	USD	Euro		
0			0.7500	1.3333
1	3.00%	5.00%	0.7646	1.3079
2	3.50%	5.50%	0.7793	1.2832
3	3.80%	5.80%	0.7942	1.2591
4	4.30%	6.10%	0.8031	1.2452
5	4.80%	6.40%	0.8090	1.2361

€0.75/$. Using term structure of interest rates the forward rate (expressed as number of euro per dollar) for the period t can be found using the Eq. 21-5.

$$\text{For direct convention } F_t = S_0 \frac{(1+y_h^t)^t}{(1+y_a^t)^t}$$

$$\text{For indirect convention } F_t = S_0 \frac{(1+y_a^t)^t}{(1+y_h^t)^t} \qquad (21\text{-}5)$$

where y_a^t and y_h^t represent yields for time t abroad and at home in the respective currencies.

Using Eq. 21-5 the forecast exchange rates are shown in the last column of Table 21-3. For example, the forecast exchange rate for Year 3, S_3 would be equal to F_3 and is $1.2591/€ or €0.7942/$ as worked out as follows:

$$S_3 = F_3 = 1.3333 \frac{(1+0.038)^3}{(1+0.058)^3} = \$1.2591/€$$

Discount Rate in Home Currency It is a common practice to use a common discount rate for cash flows of all periods. Perhaps it is done for reasons of convenience. The changing expectations of investors with term of investment are ignored. Ideally the discount rate must be the one that corresponds to the timing of the cash flow. The NPV of EURONET in terms of home currency, that is, US dollar can be found by first converting the nominal cash flows in euro into US dollar and then by discounting them at discount rate that incorporates the expectations of US investors. If we assume that risk premium of 8% is desired over the yield curve, the discount rate applicable for US dollar for period t is

$$r_a^t = y_a^t + 8\%$$

Here the risk premium is held constant but the investors' expectations with term to maturity are incorporated in the discount rate using term structure of interest rate.

NPV of Project in Home Currency The NPV of the project EURONET in home currency works out to $7.29 million as shown in Table 21-4.

In a nutshell, the process of finding NPV in home currency involved (a) projecting cash flows in foreign currency, (b) converting them to home currency using the exchange rate forecast, (c) finding appropriate discount rate using the yield curve in home currency, and finally (d) finding the present values of the cash flows.

Equivalent Discount Rate and NPV in Foreign Currency For finding the value of the Project EURONET in foreign currency, that is, euro we need the discount rate that is applicable for euro. Equation 21-3 provides relationship of equivalent discount rates for foreign currency r_a and home currency, r_h as rearranged here by Eq. 21-6.

$$(1+r_a)^t = \frac{S_0}{S_t}(1+r_h)^t \qquad (21\text{-}6)$$

Table 21-4
NPV of Project EURONET

Year	Nominal Cash Flow (€ million)	Spot Exchange Rate ($/€)	Nominal Cash Flow ($ million)	Discount Rate (%)	Present Value ($ million)
0	−100.00	1.3333	−133.33		−133.33
1	24.81	1.3079	32.44	11.00%	29.23
2	27.94	1.2832	35.85	11.50%	28.84
3	31.41	1.2591	39.55	11.80%	28.30
4	35.21	1.2452	43.84	12.30%	27.56
5	39.43	1.2361	48.73	12.80%	26.69
Net Present Value (US$ Millions)					**7.29**

With forecast exchange rates known we can arrive at appropriate discount rate for euro cash flows. Alternatively, we may also use term structure of interest rate since we projected the exchange rates using it. Equation 21-5 used for projecting the exchange rate is restated here

$$S_t = F_t = S_0 \frac{(1+y_h^t)^t}{(1+y_a^t)^t}$$

Substituting the value of forecast exchange rate in Eq. 21-6 we get

$$(1+r_a)^t = \frac{(1+y_a^t)^t}{(1+y_h^t)^t}(1+r_h)^t \text{ or}$$

$$(1+r_a) = \frac{(1+y_a^t)}{(1+y_h^t)}(1+r_h)$$

(21-7)

With Eq. 21-7 and given discount rate in the home currency we can find the equivalent discount rate in euro that can be used to find the NPV of the cash flow in euro. For example, the discount rate that is equivalent to US dollar discount rate of 11.8% in euro is 13.95% as follows:

$$(1+r_a) = \frac{(1+y_a^t)}{(1+y_h^t)}(1+r_h) = \frac{1.058}{1.038}1.118 = 1.1395 \text{ or } r_a = 13.95\%$$

Likewise we find discount rate for each period and use it for finding the NPV. Cash flows in euro, the relevance and equivalent euro discount rate, and the present value for the project EURONET are shown in Table 21-5. The NPV comes to €5.46 million. This is equal to US$7.29 million when converted at currency spot rate of $1.3333/€.

Table 21-5
NPV of Project EURONET

Year	Nominal Cash Flows (€ million)	Discount Rate		Present Value (€ million)
		Home Currency ($)	Foreign Currency (€)	
0	−100.00			−100.00
1	24.81	11.00%	13.16%	21.92
2	27.94	11.50%	13.65%	21.63
3	31.41	11.80%	13.95%	21.23
4	35.21	12.30%	14.24%	20.67
5	39.43	12.80%	14.52%	20.01
Net Present Value (€ million)				5.46
Net Present Value ($ million) (NPV euro converted at current exchange rate of 1.3333)				7.29

Properties of Discount Rate

With the aforementioned situations the exponents of finance would soon and easily appreciate that selection of appropriate discount rate is the key to find the NPV. The discount rate is a function of several factors and would be different for (a) different risk profiles, (b) different capital structure, (c) changing preferences and expectation of equity and debt suppliers, and (d) constraints of tax and remittances affecting dividend decision.

The three decisions of finance—capital budgeting, capital structure, and dividend—are so closely interlinked that they cannot be seen in isolation with each other. Under conventional domestic capital budgeting decisions, the discount rate, capital structure, and dividend decisions are known, constant, and given. In most cases, firms take decisions to expand business are in the same line of business in broadly the same economic and political environments. Therefore, the risk profile, capital structure and dividend policies of the firm do not undergo a substantial change. If at all they do change then they are too gradual to have remarkable impact on the capital budgeting decision itself.

Unfortunately, in international capital budgeting cases the conditions with respect to cash flows and their riskiness, capital structure and payment of dividend to non-residents comes to the fore that need to be tackled appropriately while choosing the discount rate.

Perhaps the only similarity between domestic and international capital budgeting exercise is the objective of such exercise. Irrespective of the location of the project and currency of evaluation, the objective of the capital budgeting exercise remains that of maximization of shareholders' wealth. There are many frameworks and guiding principles available for evaluation of the projects, but the NPV approach has been the most acceptable framework for its superiority over other methods. The NPV method clearly has the following three advantages over other methods that come in handy in evaluation of international projects.

1. NPV method has the ability to quantify the increase/decrease in the shareholders' wealth. The NPV measures the absolute increase in the shareholders' wealth and in case of listed firms must reflect in increased stock price.
2. The aggregate NPV of the project is the sum of NPVs of its all parts. It is known as additive property. This enables us to examine the desirability of individual components of the project by quantifying net contribution each element makes to the value of the project.
3. The NPV method allows us to use different discount rates for different cash flows. We need to have different discount rates that are appropriate to value such cash flows. A well-established principle of adjusting the riskiness of the cash flows by adjusting the discount rate is considered better than certainty equivalent approach. Since in international capital budgeting proposals the streams of cash flows have different sources and have different risk profiles we need to be flexible in choosing the discount rates.

REVIEW OF NET PRESENT VALUE FRAMEWORK

Standard capital budgeting exercise warrants calculation of NPV. If positive the project is accepted and if not we reject the project. NPV accrues to equity holders and reflects the accretion to the value of value of equity. International capital budgeting exercise follows the same theoretical framework as is applicable for domestic capital budgeting proposals. The steps involved include (a) projection of initial capital outlay, (b) projection of cash flows for the estimated life of the project, (c) estimation of salvage value or terminal value, (d) choosing an appropriate discount rate of arrive at the present value of cash inflows, and (e) arriving at net present value by subtracting the initial outlay. If NPV is positive, then accept the proposal else reject it.

There are at least three different ways to arrive at NPV. All the methods must lead to identical figure of NPV if we use the numbers correctly. These methods are called Flow to Equity (FTE) approach, Weighted Average Cost of Capital (WACC) approach, and Adjusted Present Value (APV) approach. Before we discuss the APV approach, which is considered most appropriate for evaluating international capital budgeting projects, we review the other two methods, that is, WACC method and FTE method.

(a) Under FTE approach the cash flows accruing to equity holders are discounted at cost of equity to get the present value of inflows. To arrive at NPV we subtract the initial outlay contributed by equity holders.
(b) Under WACC approach cash flows accruing to equity as well as debt holders are discounted at weighted average cost of capital to get the present value of the cash inflows of the project. To arrive at NPV we subtract the total cost of project.

Table 21-6 gives the comparison of the two methods with respect to cash flows and discount rate. Irrespective of the method used we must reach not only identical conclusion but identical figures of NPV.

Table 21-6
Cash Flows and Discount Rates

Method	Cash Flows	Discount Rate
WACC Method	Cash flow to all investors PBIT (1 – Tax Rate) + Depreciation + Non-cash Expense – Capital Expenditure – Increase in Working Capital	WACC
Flow to Equity (FTE) or Equity Residual Method	Cash flow to equity investors PAT + Depreciation + Non-cash Expense – Capital Expenditure – Repayment of debt – Increase in Working Capital	Cost of Equity

ILLUSTRATION: EQUIVALENCE OF WEIGHTED AVERAGE COST OF CAPITAL AND FLOW TO EQUITY METHODS

To demonstrate the equivalence of the two methods we take a simplified example. Assume a project costs ₹450 million that generates earnings before depreciation, interest, and taxes (EBDIT) of ₹120 million. The depreciation is ₹20 million. With tax rate of 40% and all equity financing the income statement that forms the basis of projecting cash flows is given in Table 21-7.

For simplicity of computation but without losing the sanctity of argument we assume that the income statement is perennial without any growth. The assumption made only simplifies the calculation. Under all equity financing, the entire project cost of ₹450 million is funded through equity.

Table 21-7
Income Statement under All Equity Financing

Cash Flow	₹ Millions
Earnings before Depreciation, Interest, and Taxes (EBDIT)	120
Depreciation, d	20
Earnings before Interest and Taxes, (EBIT)	100
Interest, I	–
Earnings before Taxes, (EBT)	100
Taxes, T @ 40%	40
Profit after Taxes, PAT	60

Cash flow to equity holder can be found in many ways. One universal way is the find the cash flow that eliminates the effect of debt financing is to eliminate taxes on all earnings before interest and add back non-cash expenses such as depreciation. Post-tax incremental cash flows to shareholders is

$$\text{Cash Flow to Equity Holders} = \text{EBIT}(1-T) + \text{Depreciation} \qquad (21\text{-}8)$$

Sometimes due to depreciation differences it is easier to work with cash flow estimates before depreciation. In such a case, we add tax shield on depreciation after providing for taxes on all earning prior to depreciation as given by Eq. 21-9. This would be the same as shown in Eq. 21-8.

$$\begin{aligned}\text{EBIT}(1-T) + \text{Depreciation} &= (\text{EBDIT} - \text{Depreciation})(1-T) + \text{Depreciation}\\ &= \text{EBDIT}(1-T) - \text{Depreciation}(1-T) + \text{Depreciation}\\ &= \text{EBDIT}(1-T) + T\,\text{Depreciation}\end{aligned}$$

$$\text{Cash Flow to Equity Holders} = \text{EBDIT}(1-T) + T \times d \qquad (21\text{-}9)$$

However, when we do not wish to exclude the financing impact and look at the cash flow to the shareholder it is simply profit after tax (PAT) plus depreciation being a non-cash expense. Therefore,

$$\text{Cash Flow to Equity Holders} = \text{PAT} + \text{Depreciation} = 60 + 20 = ₹80 \text{ million}$$

We get the same figure using Eqs 21-8 and 21-9.

$$\begin{aligned}\text{Cash Flow to Equity Holders} &= \text{EBDIT} \times (1-T) + T \times d\\ &= 120 \times (1 - 0.4) + 0.4 \times 20 = 72 + 8 = ₹80 \text{ million}\end{aligned}$$

$$\begin{aligned}\text{Cash Flow to Equity Holders} &= \text{EBIT}(1-T) + \text{Depreciation}\\ &= 100 \times (1 - 0.4) + 20 = ₹80 \text{ million}\end{aligned}$$

The present value of a constant flow for ever can be found by

$$\text{Present value of cash flow to equity holders} = \frac{\text{Cash flow to equity holders}}{\text{Cost of equity}} \qquad (21\text{-}10)$$

Assuming under all equity financing the equity suppliers warrant a return, r_o of 16% the present value of cash inflows given is Eq. 21-10 is ₹500 million.

$$\text{PV of cash inflows} = \frac{80}{0.16} = ₹500 \text{ million}$$

The value of the firm is ₹500 million. We refer this as value of unlevered firm, V_U.

The Net Present Value is 500 − 450 = ₹50 million.

This indicates that the upon the acceptance of the project the value of equity would rise from ₹450 million to ₹500 million.

Flow to Equity Approach

With all equity financing the debt did not have any role in deciding the value of the firm. When a firm decides to finance the part of the project with debt replacing some of equity it changes the evaluation process in the following two ways:

1. *Increased cost of equity:* With fixed and prior claims of debt holders over the cash flows of the firm the cash flows to equity holders become more and more uncertain. This additional risk is reflected in the desire of equity suppliers to seek greater returns increasing the cost of equity demanding a premium over the return under all equity financing. The relationship of fresh cost of equity in a levered firm is a function of (i) differential of cost of all equity return and cost of debt, (ii) levels of debt reflected in the debt equity ratio, and (iii) tax rate. The relationship is given by Eq. 21-11.

$$r_e = r_o + (r_o - r_d)(1-T)\frac{D}{E} \qquad (21\text{-}11)$$

where r_e = cost of equity in a levered firm, D and E are market values of debt and equity respectively, T is the marginal tax rate, and r_d is the cost of debt.

2. *Increased value of the firm:* The other impact of debt is over the value of the firm. As per Miller and Modigliani proposition under taxes, the value of levered firm, V_L would increase by the amount of tax shield the debt provides. The levered firm saves the tax over the interest paid on the debt. With perennial debt, the value of levered firm is increased by the amount of tax saved ($T \times D$) on debt. Therefore, the value of levered firm increases by that amount over and above the value of unlevered firm. It is given by Eq. 21-12.

$$V_L = V_U + T \times D \qquad (21\text{-}12)$$

Under FTE approach, the cash flows to the equity holders must be discounted at cost of equity. To find the value of the firm with debt we now assume that the project is funded by 50% debt available at 8%, providing a debt equity ratio, D/E as 1 based on market values. Using Eq. 21-12, we can find the value of such levered firm as ₹625 million.

$$V_L = V_U + TD = 500.0 + 0.4 \times V_L/2 \text{ gives } V_L = ₹625 \text{ million}$$

Therefore, the value of debt is 625/2 = ₹312.5 million. And the value of equity too would be ₹312.5 million. With cost of debt at 8% the cost of equity given by Eq. 21-11 is 20.8%.

$$r_e = r_o + (r_o - r_d)(1-T)\frac{D}{E} = 16.0 + (16.0 - 8.0) \times (1 - 0.4) \times 1 = 16.0 + 2.8 = 20.8\%$$

The revised income statement for the levered firm would be as given in Table 21-8.
The value of equity as per the cash flow accruing to the equity holders is

$$\text{Present value of cash flow to equity holders} = \frac{\text{Cash flow to equity holders}}{\text{Cost of equity}}$$

$$= \frac{45 + 20}{0.208} = ₹312.50 \text{ million}$$

Table 21-8
Income Statement under All Equity Financing

Cash Flow	₹ Millions
Earnings before Depreciation, Interest, and Taxes (EBDIT)	120
Depreciation, d	20
Earnings before Interest and Taxes, (EBIT)	100
Interest, I	25
Earnings before Taxes, (EBT)	75
Taxes, T @ 40%	30
Profit after Taxes, PAT	45

Initial investment through equity is cost of the project less debt financing, that is, 450.0 − 312.5 = ₹137.5 million. Therefore, NPV is 312.5 − 137.5 = ₹175.0 million. As the benefit of tax shield would accrue to equity holders, the value to them can also be arrived by adding the value of tax shield, that is, TD (0.4 × 312.5) of ₹125 million to the NPV found under equity NPV that is, ₹50 million.

Weighted Average Cost of Capital Approach

The NPV of ₹175 million arrived through FTE approach can also be computed using WACC approach. Here the cash flows to both types of capital suppliers, that is, debt and equity are discounted at WACC. The WACC given by Eq. 21-13 with debt equity ratio of 1:1 is 12.8%

$$\text{WACC}, r = r_e \times \frac{E}{E+D} + r_d \times (1-T) \times \frac{D}{E+D} \qquad (21\text{-}13)$$

WACC, r = 20.8 × 0.5 + 8 × 0.6 × 0.5 = 10.4 + 2.4 = 12.8%

And, the cash flow to equity and debt suppliers are

= Cash Flow to Equity Supplier + Cash Flow to Debt Suppliers
= 65 + 25 × 0.6 = ₹80 million

The present value of the total cash flows discounted at WACC is

Present Value of Cash Flows = 80/0.128 = ₹625 million

Therefore, NPV is 625 − 450 = ₹175 million

Limitations of Weighted Average Cost of Capital and Flow to Equity Approaches

WACC or FTE approach is widely used in domestic project appraisal primarily for the following reasons:

1. The market values of debt and equity (in case the debt and equity of the firm are listed on the exchanges) are readily available.
2. Cost of equity incorporating the business risk and financial risk (the risk due to debt impacting the capital structure) and cost of debt are directly observable. This eliminates the need for estimating the correct cost of equity; an extremely difficult task alike for practitioners and academicians to perform.
3. Most domestic capital budgeting exercises relate to expansions in the same line of business that keeps the risk profile of the firm almost the same, and hence existing cost of capital serves as appropriate discount rate for valuing the cash flows of the project.
4. Most firms expand gradually and as such these expansion projects are small relative to the overall size of the firm. Hence, even though the projects that are financed not in the same proportion of debt and equity, the target capital structure of the firm essentially remains same over long term.
5. The implication on appropriate discount rate for use in valuation is that the (a) capital structure can be assumed to be constant and (b) risk profile of new investment remains almost same as before. Therefore, the cost of capital need not be adjusted either for financial risk of the firm or the business risk of the fresh investment.

In contrast to the capital budgeting exercise for domestic projects, the international capital budgeting exercise could be significantly different due to likely changes in the risk profile of the firm. Even though the expansion activity remains in the same line of business the fact that project is outside the economic environment where the parent firm operates renders uncertainty of the cash flows of the new project in unfamiliar conditions. The acquisitions of ZAIN by Bharti, CORUS by Tata Steel, JLR by Tata Motors, etc. were all in the same line of business as that of parent firm, yet the risk profile faced by each of the firm becomes distinctly different because the new operations were in vastly different political, economic, social, and cultural environments. Therefore, even for same and/or similar businesses international capital budgeting proposals are likely to have different business risks, which is normally not the case if the exercise is taken in the domestic context.

What about financial risk? More often than not international expansions by MNCs are motivated by several incentives offered in the host countries. These incentives normally relate to preferential allocation of resources, such as land, grant of concessionary loans, providing tax holidays, guaranteed off-takes, and assured minimum returns. Besides having effect on business risk, these incentives have considerable bearing on the capital structure of the project that may not be in conformity of stated target capital structure of the MNC. This alters the financial risk of the project having implications on the cost of equity as well as on WACC. Both cost of equity and WACC need to be moderated for the changed capital structure.

Further the operations of MNCs in locations other than their own are also subjected to various kinds of commitments in the form of exports, remittances of cash surplus, compulsions of investing further, prohibiting entry in certain domains to protect domestic firms, etc.

Exercise 21-1
WACC and FTE Methods

ABC Limited is evaluating a project costing ₹800 lakh which is expected to give an Earnings Before Interest and Tax (EBIT) of ₹200 lakh per annum forever. Assume no depreciation or any other non-cash expense. The firm faces a tax rate of 40%.

(a) Using Weighted Average Cost of Capital (WACC) of 12%, find the NPV of the project.
(b) Assuming that the project is funded through perpetual debt of ₹400 lakh (50% of original cost) at 10%, re-compute the NPV of the project using Flow to Equity method.

Solution
(a) **Using WACC Approach:**

	₹ lakh
Earnings Before Interest and Tax	200
Taxes @ 40%	80
Profit After Tax (Cash flow available to all suppliers of capital)	120

Using the WACC of 12% as discount rate for the cash flows available to all capital suppliers, we find the NPV of the project as ₹200 lakh.

Net Present Value = Present Values of Inflows − Initial Cost
= 120/0.12 − 800 = 1,000 − 800 = ₹200 lakh

(b) **Using Flow to Equity Approach:**

Assuming that 50% of the initial cost of ₹800 lakh is funded through a perennial debt at 10%, the market value of the equity will enhance by the NPV of ₹200 lakh. The total value of the firm will increase by ₹200 lakh.

Value of the firm 'V' = Value of Debt 'D' + Value of Equity 'E'
= 400 + 400 + addition of NPV = 400 + 400 + 200 = ₹1,000 lakh

We now find the cost of equity r_e for a levered firm with cost of debt r_d and tax rate of T as follows (Remember that WACC uses market values of debt and equity):

$$WACC = r_e \times \frac{E}{V} + r_d(1-T) \times \frac{D}{V}$$

$12 = r_e \times 0.6 + 10 \times 0.6 \times 0.4$

$$r_e = \frac{12 - 2.4}{0.6} = 16\%$$

The cash flow available to equity shareholders is

	₹ lakh
Profit before Interest and Tax	200
Interest on Debt (10% of 400)	40
Profit before Tax	160
Taxes @ 40%	64
Profit after Tax (Cash flow to equity shareholders)	96

Net Present Value = Cash flow to equity shareholders/Cost of equity − Equity capital
96/0.16 − 400 = 600 − 400 = 200 lakh (Same as obtained with WACC approach)

ADJUSTED PRESENT VALUE METHOD

The conditions of business risk and financial risk are not likely to remain same in case of international capital budgeting exercise, and the conventional frameworks of NPV using WACC approach or FTE approach may prove difficult to implement. The APV approach attempts to address the issues of changes in business risk and financial risk complementing conventional NPV approach and is imminently suitable for evaluation of international capital budgeting proposals.

Recognizing the fact that WACC as discount rate can be used only when the business risk and financial risk remain same, APV approach begins with the assumption that the project is undertaken with all-equity financing. It first finds the value of the project assuming all-equity financing and determining the NPV by subtracting the initial equity outlay. With all-equity financing only business risk is supposed to be present and financial risk emanating from capital structure is absent. Therefore, adjustments for financial risk in the cost of equity and hence the WACC are not required.

In the second and subsequent stages, we value each of the financing alternatives separately and adjust the NPV accordingly. With financing of the project valued separately, the MNC can determine whether a financing incentive is worth availing or not.

The value of debt financing can be found using Miller Modigliani proposition that value of levered firm is greater than the value of unlevered firm by the amount of tax shield offered by debt. It may be worth recalling that value of levered firm is not increased by cheaper debt replacing expensive equity but because of the tax shield offered due to tax deductibility of the interest payable on debt.

WACC and FTE approaches work well in circumstances where firm continues to strive for (a) fixed target capital structure (b) without any significant change in the risk profile no matter how a particular project is financed. It is not uncommon to find a particular project financed entirely by equity or debt, yet the firm would be well within the acceptable norms to discount the cash flows of the project at WACC. As long as a firm over long-term period attempts to maintain a specific capital structure by rebalancing the financing structure periodically, the use of WACC as discount rate is appropriate. By rebalancing the debt ratio is meant that if the project does well the firm creates borrowing capacity for future use and if it fails the firm repays debt. Under such a scenario, the amount of debt and hence the value of the tax shield varies according to the value of the firm determined by its cash flow. As debt and its tax shield become as risky as its cash flow, the correct discount rate would be WACC. In case of APV approach, the appropriate discount rate would be r_0.

In international capital budgeting exercise, the assumption of constant target capital structure as well as unchanged risk profile of the firm are more likely to be violated rather than maintained, due to availability of various financing incentives and unfamiliar political and economic environments.

We have seen above that though the basic framework of evaluation of projects remains that of NPV but substantial modifications were required to make the NPV framework adaptable to international capital budgeting situations. The critical inputs for the NPV framework are

(a) projection of cash flows, and (b) selection of suitable discount rate. In terms of input requirements, there are many aspects that need specific attention when evaluating international projects.

Differences in Cash Flows While considering the parent's cash flow, many environmental constraints arise. These are related to restrictions on remittances, payment of dividends, considerations of transfer pricing laws, etc.

Differences in Capital Structure Besides differences in the cash flows of the subsidiary and parent, the financing pattern too may be dictated by environment. Domestic capital budgeting proposals carry the similar financing pattern as that of the firm. Subsidiary and parent being separate legal entities operating in different legal and economic environment the capital structure of the parent may not be replicated in the subsidiary's capital structure. These may be due to legal compulsions or availability of finance that are project-tied. Therefore, the universal principle of capital budgeting of segregating the operational and financing cash flows may not be implemented in international capital budgeting exercise.

Differences in Risks The inflation rates in the host nations would be different from the inflation in parent's nation. High inflation rates render more uncertainties and hence make project in such locations inherently more risky. Further due to different inflation rates the term structure of interest rates in host nation and home nation are likely to be different. This aspect is highlighted in the case of EURONET discussed earlier in the chapter.

Political Risk Foreign investors invariably face political risk which includes the extreme form of expropriation or nationalization of assets. Milder forms of political risk emanate from red-tape, licensing, restrictions on remittances and dividend payment, onerous export obligations, greater scrutiny of management and stricter standards and adherence to corporate governance, etc.

Transfer Pricing Another area of concern that is growing of late is the issue of transfer pricing in case the MNC either supplies inputs or consumes output of the subsidiary. Disputes regarding avoidance of taxes are growing because the laws regarding transfer pricing are still evolving and leave a lot of ambiguity in interpretation of rules and methods that become controversial.

Concessional Financing To attract foreign investment for industrial and economic development many developing nations offer various kinds of incentives, such as allocation of land at subsidized rates, tax holidays, concessionary loans in terms of interest rate and extended repayment periods, and capital subsidies. These incentives are often attractive enough and cause deviations from target capital structure. Besides each of these benefits is to be evaluated as to what value do such benefits add to the project.

Debt and Discount Rate

Here amount of debt is fixed and has a fixed repayment schedule. Therefore, the amount of tax shield is certain. The only pre-requisite is that the firm is profitable enough to pay required taxes and avail the tax shield available on interest paid on debt. In such a case the appropriate discount rate is post tax cost of debt. If the availability of tax shield due to inadequacy of cash flow is questionable then either a higher discount rate could be used or a lower tax rate is taken. Under both cases, the value of tax shield would decline.

ILLUSTRATIVE CASE: DVS LIMITED—ADJUSTED PRESENT VALUE METHOD

To consider the application of APV method, we take an illustrative case and highlight various steps used in the method and provide valuation of each element of the project.

An Indian firm DVS Limited (DVS) is a leading manufacturer of two-wheeler automobiles in India. Besides having a fairly dominant position in the local markets of India DVS is also very active in export markets. In view of high population density and congested roads, DVS believes that Bangladesh would constitute a major market for two-wheelers in times to come. Presently they are exporting motorcycles to Bangladesh. In the current year, they expect to export 5,000 vehicles there. This market is growing at about 5% per annum due to import regulations prevailing in Bangladesh. Dealers are constantly asking for faster deliveries. According to them current level of exports to Bangladesh indicates an acceptance of the product.

With strong similarities in the consumer preferences in India and Bangladesh, DVS believes that they are very well placed to capture a better market share by expanding their presence. The current regulation in Bangladesh for importing vehicles is constraining the market growth to a modest level of 5%. With proximity to India and opportunities available they need to widen the scope and graduate from mere exporter to a producer by establishing a manufacturing facility in Bangladesh. Besides overcoming the import regulations, this would help in expanding market and improving profit margins.

Project Details and Features

A strategic team of DVS has drawn up a detailed plan to set up a project to produce motorcycles in Bangladesh. The select data is given as follows:

At Today's Value	In Bangladeshi Taka (BDT)
Capital cost of the project	1,000,000,000
At Year 1 Value	**In Bangladeshi Taka (BDT)**
Expected price per vehicle	40,000
Cost of production per vehicle	32,000
Cash flow per vehicle	8,000

During the first year of its operation DVS targets to produce 20,000 vehicles. The market for motorcycles in Bangladesh is growing at handsome rate of 12% per annum and with accepted product already in the market DVS too would grow at the same rate. Ramping up of the capacity and production therefore would not pose much constraint.

The current exchange rate is BDT 1.40 per Indian rupee (INR). The inflation rates in India and Bangladesh are 8% and 11%, respectively. Though there exist currency controls in Bangladesh the future exchange rate are expected to follow inflation rates. Accordingly the prices, cost of production, and cash flows can be increased in accordance with the inflation rates in Bangladesh.

The marginal rate of taxation in Bangladesh is same as that of India. The marginal tax rate is 35% in both the countries. Double Taxation Avoidance Treaty between the two nations permits credit for tax paid in one country to another. The rates of depreciation permit Straight Line Method (SLM). The planned horizon for the project is eight years and salvage value is negligible. Based on SLM, depreciation of BDT 12,50,00,000 can be claimed.

DVS intends to fund the project in Bangladesh by internal accruals except for availing the concessional loan that Bangladesh government is offering. The headquarters of DVS in India believes that of the total project cost of BDT 1,000 million 25% is readily available by way of debt but does not want to avail such loans. It perhaps would utilize such borrowing capacity in Bangladesh for expansion of the same project or some other project in future.

At present DVS has funds of BDT 70 million locked up in Bangladesh on account of motorcycles supplied which it intends not to remit and instead use it towards meeting capital expenditure of the proposed project. It is required to pay only 20% tax on these funds if retained in Bangladesh. If repatriated then the sum would be subject to usual tax rate of 35%.

The concessional loan of BDT 100 million is available at concessional rate of 8% against normal commercial rate of 14% that would be applicable to DVS if it were to mobilize such loan from the market. The loan is repayable in eight annual equal installments.

Other important features of the project include royalty payment of 1% of sales. The project in Bangladesh would require the engine of the motorcycle; the vital component to be supplied by DVS in India. The current price of the engine is ₹5,000. It provides 10% cash profit to DVS. These profits generated from exports are subject to reduced rate of tax of 10% against usual 35%.

We are required to find the desirability of implementation of the project in Bangladesh.

Exchange Rate Projection

We need exchange rate for converting cash flows from BDT to INR and vice versa. With the current spot rate of BDT 1.40 per INR as the base the expected exchange rates for the life of the project for the next eight years are projected according to purchasing power parity, that is, exchange rate in the nth year is

$$S_n = S_0 \left[\frac{1+I_b}{1+I_a} \right]^n \tag{21-14}$$

Where I_b = Inflation rate of home country, that is, India and taken as 8%,
I_a = Inflation rate of abroad, that is, Bangladesh and taken as 11%.

For example, the projected exchange rate for 5th year would be

$$S_n = S_0 \left[\frac{1+I_h}{1+I_a}\right]^n = 0.7143 \left(\frac{1.08}{1.11}\right)^5 = 0.7143 \times 0.8720 = ₹0.6228/BDT$$

Based on purchasing power parity the exchange rates till Year 8 are as given in Table 21-9.

Table 21-9
DVS Project—Projection of Exchange Rates

Year	0	1	2	3	4	5	6	7	8
INR per BDT	0.7143	0.6950	0.6762	0.6579	0.6401	0.6228	0.6060	0.5896	0.5737
BDT per INR	1.4000	1.4389	1.4788	1.5199	1.5622	1.6056	1.6501	1.6960	1.7431

Cash Flow Projection

The cash flows of the project would be the cash generation in BDT by production there. The cash flow per vehicle is BDT 8,000 in Year 1. This is increased by the inflation rate every year to keep the real value of cash flow constant. The BDT cash flow for each year is converted to INR using the exchange rate of that year. For example the cash flow in fifth year would be the product of production and the cash flow per unit as moderated by production growth estimates and inflation rates, respectively BDT 382.20 million.

Cash Inflow for Year 5 = Production in Year 5 × Cash flow per vehicle × (1 + Inflation rate)^5
= 20,000 × (1 + 0.12)^4 × 8,000 × (1 + 0.11)^5 = BDT 424.24 million

However, DVS would have to forego the cash flow through exports from India. The net cash flow from the project should be reduced by the loss of cash flow from the viewpoint of parent. The loss of cash flow is in INR and not BDT. Pre-tax cash flow generated per vehicle exported is BDT 5,000 at Year 0 price level. For Year 1 the quantity increases by 5% while increases the cash flow increases by 11%, that is, the inflation rate of Bangladesh. For example the loss of cash flow in Year 5 is

Cash Inflow Lost in Year 5 = 5,000 × (1 + 0.05)^5 × 5,000 × (1 + 0.11)^5 = BDT 53.77 million

Tax Considerations

For evaluation of desirability of the project post-tax cash flows are required. In an international capital budgeting exercise, the cash flows generated in host country are subject to host nations' tax rate while the cash flow in parent' country is subjected to their tax jurisdiction. Further consideration need to be given whether or not tax paid in one country laws is allowed the credit for the same in another country. More often than not the cross-border investments are guided by tax arbitrage available. Savings in taxes make certain negative NPV project a positive NPV one.

The NPV of the project depends on post tax cash flows. The project is required to pay taxes of the host nation on the assumption that the MNC would incorporate a separate legal entity in the host nation. If dual taxation avoidance treaty between the host and home nation exists then the cash flows must be subjected to the tax rate prevailing in the home nation. It is presumed here that if tax credits are not available an MNC would not be consider investing in foreign nation because by paying taxes in two nation the NPV of the project is more likely to remain negative.

If the tax rates in home nation is more than the tax rate in the host nation with tax credit available then the NPV on post tax basis must be computed after providing of taxes of the home nation.

To keep the exposition simple, in the instant case the tax rates in Bangladesh and India are assumed equal with credit for tax paid in one country available to offset the tax liability in the other country. If so the cash flows and NPVs arrived in BDT and INR would not differ on account of tax considerations.

Post-tax Incremental Cash Flow

Post-tax incremental cash flows in BDT are shown in Table 21-10. The calculation for cash flow generated and cash flow lost for the 5th year are shown above.

Table 21-10
Incremental Post Tax Cash Flow—DVS Project

(Figures in million BDT unless specified)

Year	1	2	3	4	5	6	7	8
Forecast Exchange Rate (INR/BDT)	0.6950	0.6762	0.6579	0.6401	0.6228	0.6060	0.5896	0.5737
Vehicles produced (Nos.)	20,000	22,400	25,088	28,099	31,471	35,248	39,478	44,215
Cash flows	177.60	220.79	274.49	341.25	424.24	527.43	655.70	815.16
Export lost (Nos.)	5,250	5,513	5,789	6,078	6,382	6,701	7,036	7,388
Cash flows lost	29.14	33.96	39.59	46.13	53.77	62.67	73.04	85.13
Incremental cash flows	148.46	186.83	234.90	295.12	370.47	464.76	582.66	730.03
Tax	51.96	65.39	82.22	103.29	129.66	162.67	203.93	255.51
Post tax cash flows	96.50	121.44	152.68	191.83	240.81	302.09	378.73	474.52

The incremental post tax for 5th year is worked out as follows:

	BDT millions
Cash flow generated	424.24
Cash flow lost	53.77
Incremental cash flow at EBDIT level	370.47
Tax @ 35%	129.66
Post tax incremental cash flow; EBDIT (1 – T)	240.81

Discount Rate for Operating Cash Flows

Under APV method we compute the NPV of the project from the perspective of the parent firm. The DVS being in Indian firm the cash flows in INR are important. The discount rate used is the opportunity cost of capital for Indian firm. With project assumed to be funded entirely by equity the cost is assumed with a risk premium of 5% over inflation rate. Hence, all equity cost of capital is 13%. We discount incremental post tax cash flows in INR to arrive at NPV. Alternatively, the BDT cash flows too can be used to arrive at the present value using discount rate for all equity financing applicable for Bangladesh for similar projects. From the perspective of parent the equivalent all equity discount rate in BDT can be arrived as

All Equity Capitalization Rate, in BDT

$$= \text{All Equity Capitalization Rate in INR} \times \frac{1+\text{Inflation Rate, Bangladesh}}{1+\text{Inflation Rate, India}} \quad (21\text{-}15)$$

$$= 13.00 \times \frac{1.11}{1.08} = 16.139\%$$

The discount rate of 16.139% in BDT is equivalent to 13% in INR under the assumption that financial markets are fully integrated. In case all equity discount rate in BDT is different than 16.139% the cash flows in two currencies would not yield the same NPV representing structural differences in the financial markets that are segmented.

All Equity Net Present Value

With cash flows and discount rates for all equity financing available we can find the NPV of the project. Table 21-11 presents the discounted value of cash inflows in BDT and INR. The cash inflows are discounted at 16.139% and 13.00%, respectively for the cash flows in BDT and INR.

The present value of cash inflows in BDT is −889.34 million providing NPV of the project at −BDT 110.66 million. Converted at current spot exchange rate of INR 0.7143/BDT the NPV translates to −INR 79.04 million. The same NPV can be arrived by discounting the rupee cash flows at discount rate of 13%. The value of cash inflows in INR is 635.26 million while capital expenditure is INR 714.30 million (1000 × 0.7143). The project has negative NPV of INR 79.04 million.

Depreciation Tax Shield

The NPV of the project computed in Table 21-11 is based on discounting the operating cash flows, which are considered as EBDIT (1 − T), where EBDIT is profit before depreciation, interest and tax. We have found the NPV at EBDIT level prior to depreciation for two reasons. First depreciation being fixed cannot be assumed to grow with inflation. The charge of depreciation remains same for all years. Second, depreciation as source of cash is certain and is not subjected to any uncertainty like the operating cash flows. Therefore, the same discount

Table 21-11
Discounted Cash Flows and NPV—DVS Project

(Figures in million unless specified)

Year	1	2	3	4	5	6	7	8
Forecast Exchange Rate (INR/BDT)	0.6950	0.6762	0.6579	0.6401	0.6228	0.6060	0.5896	0.5737
NPV in Bangladeshi Taka, BDT								
Cash flow	96.50	121.44	152.68	191.83	240.81	302.09	378.73	474.52
Discount rate				16.139%				
Discounted value of cash flows	83.09	90.03	97.46	105.44	113.97	123.10	132.89	143.36

Present values of inflows 889.34
Capital outflows −1,000.00
Net Present Value (BDT) −110.66
Current Spot Rate (INR/BDT) 0.7143
Net Present Value (INR) −79.04

				NPV in Indian Rupee, INR				
Cash flows	67.07	82.12	100.45	122.80	149.99	183.07	223.31	272.23
Discount rate				13.00%				
Discounted value of cash flows	59.35	64.31	69.62	75.32	81.41	87.93	94.92	102.40

Present values of inflows 635.26
Capital outflows = 1000 × 0.7143 714.30
Net Present Value (INR) −79.04

rate used for operating cash flows cannot be applied to depreciation. The APV method allows use of different discount rates for different types of cash flows.

We consider borrowing rate as appropriate for discounting the depreciation tax shield. It is found in Table 21-12 in BDT and INR. While borrowing rate for India is taken at 10% as known the equivalent rate for BDT cash flow has been arrived at 13.056% just in the same manner as used for finding the capitalization rate through Eq. 21-15.

$$\text{Cost of Debt, in BDT} = \text{Cost of Debt in INR} \times \frac{1 + \text{Inflation Rate, Bangladesh}}{1 + \text{Inflation Rate, India}}$$

$$= 11.00 \times \frac{1.11}{1.08} = 13.056\%$$

Table 21-12
Valuing Depreciation Tax Shield—DVS Project

(Figures in million BDT)								
Year	1	2	3	4	5	6	7	8
Depreciation	125.00	125.00	125.00	125.00	125.00	125.00	125.00	125.00
Depreciation foregone	–	–	–	–	–	–	–	–
Tax saved	43.75	43.75	43.75	43.75	43.75	43.75	43.75	43.75
PV of tax saved	38.70	34.23	30.28	26.78	23.69	20.95	18.53	16.39
PV of Depreciation Tax Shield, BDT				209.55				
PV of Depreciation Tax Shield, INR				149.68				

The depreciation available is BDT 125 million for eight years over capital investment of BDT 1,000 million on SLM basis. With tax rate of 35% the tax saved each year is BDT 43.75 million. There is no loss of depreciation as the project is a new one. Therefore, depreciation is incremental. The tax saved on incremental depreciation is discounted at 13.056% equivalent to cost of debt in India of 10%. The value of tax shield is INR 149.68 million arrived from BDT 209.55 million using spot exchange rate.

Concessionary Loan

The Government of Bangladesh in order to attract foreign investment and to create employment avenues is ready to offer a loan of BDT 100 million at concessional rate of 8% as against market rate of 14%. The loan is repayable in eight equal annual installments.

The appropriate rate of discount for loan is the market rate of interest and the value of the loan is given by discounted cash flow of the loan with market rate of debt as discount rate.

If the loan is at market rate itself the value of the loan is given by the tax shield on the interest. If the loan is available on subsidized rate then the value of the loan has two components—the tax shield on the loan and the interest subsidy. This may be shown very conveniently with a one period loan. Assume a firm borrows amount D at subsidized rate of r_s against the market rate of r_d for one period. The cash flow of the loan would be (a) cash inflow of D in period 0, (b) cash outflow of $(1 + r_s) D$ in period 1, and (c) cash inflow of tax saved on interest of $T \times r_s \times D$. Therefore, value of loan is

$$\text{Value of subsidized loan} = D - \frac{(1+r_s)D}{1+r_d} + \frac{Tr_s D}{1+r_d} = \frac{(r_d - r_s)D}{1+r_d} + \frac{Tr_s D}{1+r_d} \quad (21\text{-}16)$$

Value of Subsidized Loan = Present Value of Interest Difference + Present Value of Tax Shield

From Eq. 21-16, it is easy to see that if loan is at normal rate of interest, that is, $r_s = r_d$ the value of the loan would only be the tax shield on interest.

Concessional debt financing by Bangladesh government adds value to the project because of (a) the interest is tax deductible and provides a tax shield and (b) DVS pays lesser interest than the market rate. The DVS pays interest of 8% on BDT 100 million in the first year and saves tax of 35% on it. Therefore, the value of tax saved in the first year is BDT $100 \times 0.08 \times 0.35 =$ BDT 2.80 million. Similarly, it pays reduced interest of $100 \times (0.14 - 0.08) =$ BDT 6.00 million. Both the tax shield and interest rebate need to be discounted to arrive at its present value. The worth of loan is found by discounting the cash flows of the loan at commercial rate of interest and subtracting it from loan amount. This is shown in Table 21-13.

Table 21-13
Valuing Concessional Loan—DVS Project

(Figures in million BDT)

Year	1	2	3	4	5	6	7	8
Loan Amount	100.00	87.50	75.00	62.50	50.00	37.50	25.00	12.50
Repayment	12.50	12.50	12.50	12.50	12.50	12.50	12.50	12.50
Interest	8.00	7.00	6.00	5.00	4.00	3.00	2.00	1.00
Tax saved on interest	2.80	2.45	2.10	1.75	1.40	1.05	0.70	0.35
Loan cash flow	17.70	17.05	16.40	15.75	15.10	14.45	13.80	13.15
Discounted value	15.53	13.12	11.07	9.33	7.84	6.58	5.51	4.61
Value of the Loan, BDT					100 − 73.59 = 26.41			
Value of the Loan, INR					18.86			

The break-up of the loan value in terms of interest subsidy and tax shield on interest is shown in Table 21-14.

Table 21-14
Value of Interest Subsidy and Tax Shield—DVS Project

(Figures in million BDT)

Year	1	2	3	4	5	6	7	8
Loan Amount	100.00	87.50	75.00	62.50	50.00	37.50	25.00	12.50
Repayment	12.50	12.50	12.50	12.50	12.50	12.50	12.50	12.50
Interest	8.00	7.00	6.00	5.00	4.00	3.00	2.00	1.00
Tax saved on interest	2.80	2.45	2.10	1.75	1.40	1.05	0.70	0.35
PV of tax shield	2.46	1.89	1.42	1.04	0.73	0.48	0.28	0.12
Value of tax shield, BDT					8.41			
Interest saved	6.00	5.25	4.50	3.75	3.00	2.25	1.50	0.75
PV of interest saved	5.26	4.04	3.04	2.22	1.56	1.03	0.60	0.26
Value of interest saved, BDT					18.00			
Value of the Loan, BDT					8.41 + 18.00 = 26.41			
Value of the Loan, INR					18.86			

The NPV of loan arrived is BDT 26.41 million (100.00 – 73.59) equivalent to INR 18.86 million at spot exchange rate of INR 0.7143/BDT. If availed the NPV of the project would be increased by INR 18.86 million comprising tax shield of INR 6.00 million and interest rebate of INR 12.86 million.

Use of Blocked Funds

The DVS has unremitted funds of BDT 70 million available in Bangladesh out of the exports made in the past. On this 20% tax is already paid. If repatriated the amount is subject to full tax of 35% in Bangladesh. However, if not repatriated and instead deployed in financing of the proposed project no further tax would be payable. Hence, the value of the retained funds is differential of tax payable and tax paid. Again if used in financing of the project the value would stand enhanced by this amount.

		BDT in Millions
Amount available		70.00
Tax paid	20.00%	
Gross amount available	70.00/(1 – 0.20)	87.50
Tax payable	15% of gross amount	13.13

Therefore, if used in financing of the project the value would rise by BDT 13.13 million equivalent to INR 9.38 million at spot exchange rate of BDT 1.40/INR.

Value of Debt Capacity

Acceptance of project leads to greater borrowing power since asset base as well as equity base increase. Assuming a debt ratio of 25% (debt equity ratio of 1:3) for DVS the project in Bangladesh would add debt capacity of BDT 250 million (0.25 × 1,000). The same capital structure can be followed to fund this project as long as the risk profile of the parent firms largely remains same. The value of concessionary loan has already been captured at BDT 26.41 million (INR 18.86 million) by which the present value of the project would increase.

Assuming that concessionary loan of BDT 100 million is availed, the remaining debt capacity available is BDT 150 million. This loan is available at market rate of 14%. With tax rate of 35% annual interest tax shield is BDT 7.35 million (150 × 0.14 × 0.35) for life of the project of 8 years. In subsequent years, it is assumed that debt capacity would increase by the amount of repayment of concessional loans. Therefore, with annual repayment of BDT 12.5 million the debt capacity is increased. The tax shield on the interest is discounted at market rate of debt in BDT. The value of debt capacity comes to BDT 42.13 million which translates to INR 30.09. Calculation of benefit of debt capacity created is shown in Table 21-15.

Table 21-15
Valuing Debt Capacity—DVS Project

(Figures in million BDT)

Year	1	2	3	4	5	6	7	8
Debt capacity	150.00	162.50	175.00	187.50	200.00	212.50	225.00	237.50
Interest	21.00	22.75	24.50	26.25	28.00	29.75	31.50	33.25
Tax saved	7.35	7.96	8.58	9.19	9.80	10.41	11.03	11.64
Present value	6.45	6.13	5.79	5.44	5.09	4.74	4.41	4.08

PV of Debt Capacity, BDT	42.13
PV of Debt Capacity, INR	30.09

Value of Royalty to Parent

In the proposed scheme of the venture, there are two provisions that make the cash flow of the project differ from the cash flow of the parent—the payment of royalty on sales to the parent, and supply of engines for the motorcycles from India. While these are cash outflows from the project but they are cash inflows for the parent. The value of these cash flows must be added for project evaluation from the perspective of parent.

Table 21-16
Value of Royalty—DVS Project

Year	1	2	3	4	5	6	7	8
Vehicles produced (Nos.)	20,000	22,400	25,088	28,099	31,471	35,248	39,478	44,215
Price, BDT	40,000	44,400	49,284	54,705	60,723	67,402	74,817	83,046
Million BDT								
Revenue	800.00	994.56	1,236.44	1,537.16	1,911.01	2,375.80	2,953.61	3,671.90
Royalty	8.00	9.95	12.36	15.37	19.11	23.76	29.54	36.72
Withholding tax	1.60	1.99	2.47	3.07	3.82	4.75	5.91	7.34
Post tax cash flows	6.40	7.96	9.89	12.30	15.29	19.01	23.63	29.38
Million INR								
Equivalent INR	4.45	5.38	6.51	7.87	9.52	11.52	13.93	16.86
Present value	3.94	4.21	4.51	4.83	5.17	5.53	5.92	6.34

Value of Royalty INR Millions	40.45
Value of Royalty BDT Millions	56.63

Under the arrangement between the parent and its project, the parent would charge royalty at 1% of the sales. This is subject to a 20% withholding tax in Bangladesh. Further the royalty being related to exports it is tax exempt in India but the credit for withholding tax is not available for offsetting against other income earned domestically. The value of royalty is found in Table 21-16. In present value terms, it is INR 40.45 million. Equivalent BDT amount is 1.40 × 40.45 = BDT 56.63 million.

Value of Inputs Supplied

Similarly, DVS would supply engine of the motorcycle to the project. Each engine is priced at BDT 7,000 equivalent to INR 5,000 at Year 0 prices. This would grow with production at 12% each year and the price too is inflation adjusted at 8% in India. After taking cash cost into account the gross profit margin is placed at 10% of the price. Being export profit it is subject to reduced tax rate of 10% in India. While engine exported by DVS remains a cost for the project in Bangladesh it provides additional post tax cash flows to the parent. Being operational cash flow this is discounted at 13% as applicable. The present value of the component supplied from India is INR 88.39 million or BDT 123.75 million as arrived in Table 21-17.

After valuing all elements of the project we find the NPV of the DVS project in Bangladesh as ₹275.83 million. The value of each element is tabulated as follows:

Adjusted present value in millions	INR	BDT
Free cash flow	−79.04	−110.66
Depreciation tax shield	149.68	209.55
Loan		
Interest tax shield	12.86	18.00
Interest rebate	6.01	8.41
Blocked funds	9.38	13.13
Debt capacity	30.09	42.13
Royalty	40.45	56.63
Local supplies	88.39	123.75
TOTAL NPV	**257.82**	**360.94**

After going through the illustration one can easily appreciate the utility of APV method in appraisal of international projects. It helps avoid the complex issues related to dependence of discount rate based on capital structure and business risk by permitting the use of different discount rates more apt to the different nature of cash flows. Remember that we used different rates of discount for depreciation tax shield, debt capacity, etc. Conventional DCF methods using WACC or cost of equity attempt to treat each cash flow with same level of business and financial

Table 21-17
Valuing Supplies from Parent—DVS Project

(Figures in million INR)

Year	1	2	3	4	5	6	7	8
Nos. of vehicles	20,000	22,400	25,088	28,099	31,471	35,248	39,478	44,215
Export revenue	108.00	130.64	158.02	191.14	231.21	279.67	338.29	409.19
Export profit	10.80	13.06	15.80	19.11	23.12	27.97	33.83	40.92
Tax	1.08	1.31	1.58	1.91	2.31	2.80	3.38	4.09
Cash flow	9.72	11.76	14.22	17.20	20.81	25.17	30.45	36.83
Present value	8.60	9.21	9.86	10.55	11.29	12.09	12.94	13.85
PV Cashflow of Engines Supplied, BDT				123.75				
PV Cashflow of Engines Supplied, INR				88.39				

risk by using a single discount rate. Besides flexibility of choosing the appropriate discount rate APV method also provides valuable managerial input when it tells how important each element is to the overall desirability or otherwise of the project, by attaching a value to each element.

SUMMARY

Most multinationals have operations in several countries and they keep exploring options to expand in several nations implementing growth strategies. Therefore, identification, selection, and evaluation of cross-border project are key activities of most multinational corporations. Evaluation of projects in a country different than the home country is characterized by several constraints that prohibit the use of conventional capital budgeting methods. The general framework used for evaluation of domestic capital budgeting can hardly be used in international situations.

The complexity in capital budgeting exercise for international project arise on account of (a) vastly different political, economic, and social environment affecting the risk profile of the project, (b) currency of cash flows (c) vastly different expectations of investor in terms of desired returns, etc. These parameters make projections of cash flow and selection of discount rate—the two vital inputs required to implement the NPV framework—extremely complex and difficult. The conventional methods of using WACC or cost of equity as universal discount rate for arriving at NPV become inappropriate or difficult to implement.

An alternative method known as Adjusted Present Value (APV) method is used. This method enables use of different discount rates for different kinds of cash flows and finds value of each component of the project, rather than its aggregate value. It uses the property of additivity of NPV which says the sum of the components equals whole. In international projects there are several incentives and constraints present that need to be evaluated separately to make a conscious decision.

The basic framework of APV framework starts by computing the value of the project as if it were to be financed entirely by equity, thus eliminating the financial risk from the assessment. After arriving at all equity NPV other components that affect either the cash flows or capital structure are evaluated separately and the NPVs arrives so is added to the initial value. Since cash flows of the international projects are most often denominated in a currency different than the currency of the parent, all cash flows need to be converted to home currency. This is essential because the project is evaluated from the parent's viewpoint. In addition, discount rate applicable in one currency cannot be used for another currency because of differences in inflation rate, interest rates, and risk characteristics of two nations. Under APV method, it is easier to incorporate such flexibility.

Due to the segregated approach APV method allows separate valuation of depreciation tax shield, interest tax shield, loans at subsidized rates, cross cash flows of subsidiary and parent, different tax rates and treatments, etc. which are perhaps absent in domestic capital budgeting exercise but form essential part of international projects. Each of these segregated components needs to be valued separately to analyse the contribution an element makes to the overall NPV.

QUESTIONS

21-1 Why do you think WACC approach is not suitable for evaluating international project?
21-2 Compare WACC approach and FTE approach in terms of requirements of cash flows and discount rate.
21-3 What are the features that discount rate must satisfy before it can be used to find the present value of the given cash flow?
21-4 In terms of risk profile how are international projects different from domestic projects?
21-5 What is meant by net present value under all equity financing?
21-6 Describe APV method in brief.
21-7 What are the advantages of APV method over WACC or FTE method of project appraisal?

Financing Foreign Trade

LEARNING OBJECTIVES

This chapter aims at

- discussing various modes of payments in international trade
- explaining letter of credit, its purpose, and operation
- discussing documents and their purposes under letters of credit
- explaining different types of and different parties involved in letter of credit
- discussing how financing is facilitated under letter of credit
- explaining packing credit on pre-shipment and post-shipment
- discussing bill financing under bill discounting, factoring, and forfaiting
- explaining countertrade, its variants, and its advantages for nations

CONTENTS

Introduction
Supply and Terms of Payment
Letter of Credit Explained
Documents under Letter of Credit
    Invoice
    Packing List
    Inspection Certificate
    Bill of Lading
Bills of Exchange (Drafts)
    Insurance
    Certificate of Origin
Types of Letter of Credit
Advantages of Letter of Credit

Financing under Letter of Credit
Financing International Trade
Packing Credit—Pre-shipment and Post-shipment
Bill Discounting
    Banker's Acceptance
Factoring
    Invoice Financing
Forfaiting
Countertrade
    Countertrade without Money
    Countertrade with Money/Credit
    Objectives of Countertrade

INTRODUCTION

All business transactions involve at least one buyer and one seller. In international business scenario, the buyer and the seller are not likely to be in the same location/country. They are located far apart, possibly belonging to different nationalities characterized by different cultures, varying trade practices, conventions, and standards. They also are likely to have different languages. They are not only separated geographically but are also separated by business ethics and cultures as prevailing in different regions.

Normally, business moves on trust, that is, the seller is expected to sell the goods/services at reasonable price, meeting the quality standards as promised and set by the buyer, and the buyer is expected to pay according to the terms and conditions settled. It takes a long time for the buyer and seller to develop mutual confidence. It is purely a function of for how long the buyer and seller are having the business together. Longer the business relationship, greater is the mutual trust.

International trade has many peculiarities even though the business model essentially remains same as the one that applies to domestic transactions. In international trade, buyers and sellers are not only separated by large distances, there are also wide gaps in areas of business practices, conventions, legal frameworks, languages and cultures, etc. Unlike in domestic business the buyers and sellers in international business situations do not meet as often as may be required to build a reasonable trust between the two. Due to physical distances and different legal jurisdictions of buyers and sellers impeding the grievance redressing process, international business requires adequate care on part of buyers and sellers to safeguard their mutual interests. Apprehensions about fulfilment of each other's commitment always linger in the minds of both the seller and the buyer.

SUPPLY AND TERMS OF PAYMENTS

Most trade transactions have mismatch of supply and payment in terms of time. Possibly retail sale is the only circumstance where payment and delivery of goods are made simultaneously. In international transactions, this gap between supply and payment widens due to logistics involved. Either payment precedes supply or supply precedes payment.

Basic sale purchase contract is displayed in Figure 22-1. Seller despatches goods and prepares documents which confer the title of the goods to buyer. The buyer in turn agrees to make payments as agreed upon. Note that physical delivery/possession of goods/services and its payment are independent of each other. The ownership of goods in question should not be

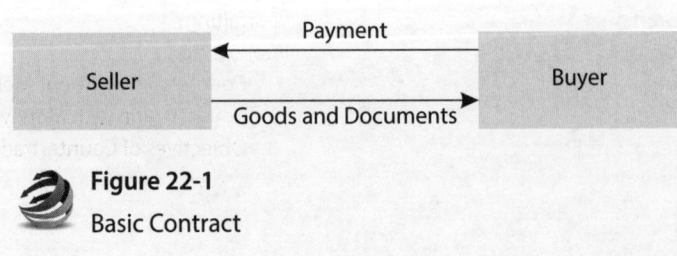

Figure 22-1
Basic Contract

confused either with physical possession of goods or having made the payment for the same. The transfer of ownership of goods from the seller to the buyer is determined by what is stated in the contract between the two. The title of the goods is transferred only when the relevant documents are handed over.

In international transaction, the transit period involved in despatch of goods from seller and its ultimate receipt by the buyer is fairly large. In addition, goods and documents conferring the title do not travel simultaneously. Usually, banks perform the task of making documents reach from the seller (exporter) to the buyer (importer) and collecting payment for remittance to the seller (exporter).

In relation to payment and documents the following may be noted.

Advance Payment Advance payment terms refer to the situation where the supplier needs payment before making despatch of goods. In day-to-day life, we find subscription to magazines follows these terms of payment. In commercial situations, advance payment terms indicate suppliers' market where demand is met only when full/partial payment is received. Such is the case for custom-built products.

Documents against Acceptance These payment terms mean that documents that signify title of the goods such as invoice are handed over to the buyer only after he accepts to make the payment within the time agreed to between him and the seller.

Documents against Payment These payment terms mean that documents that signify title of the goods such as invoice are handed over to the buyer only after he makes the payment.

It may be easily realized that advance payment terms or documents against acceptance (DA) terms do not bridge the trust deficit between the buyer and the seller. Advance payment favour the supplier whereas DA terms favour the buyer. The documents against payment (DP) terms seem to put the buyer and the seller at parity as goods are passed only when the payment is received (protecting the seller), or payment is made only when goods are in sight (protecting the buyer). The payment from buyer to seller can flow directly or through financial intermediaries, who perform the task of collection of money.

Besides dealing with documents and collecting payment, international financial community comprising banks and financial institutions can also work to resolve the trade dilemma faced by buyers and sellers. Mutual trust deficit between buyers and sellers is partially compensated by the financial community by lending its support to the transactions. Financial community being very closely knit and having gained the respect and confidence with each other can admirably fulfil the gap of credibility.

LETTER OF CREDIT EXPLAINED

Any trade transaction domestic or international requires (a) assurance of supply from seller to buyer and (b) assurance of payment from buyer to seller. Till both the parties are reasonably satisfied with each other's credibility, the trade transaction does not fructify. Yet they both need each other. The transaction can be facilitated by an intermediary who enjoys the trust of both. Banks are able to fulfil this role admirably as most businesses operate through banks. Both buyers and sellers need banks for various other needs. Banking moves on trust that has been built over a long period of time. The mutual trust among bankers can also help bridge the mistrust between buyers and sellers and resolve the trade dilemma by actively participating and becoming a party to the commercial transaction.

One instrument that creates trust and confidence between the buyer and the seller, and is purely a financial document is a letter of credit (popularly called LC). A comprehensive definition of letter of credit is extremely difficult to find because of the huge variety and the number of parties that get involved in the transaction supported by a letter of credit. As a brief description a *letter of credit can be defined as a guarantee by an intermediary, typically a bank on behalf of buyer (importer) to honour claims made by seller (exporter) according to the terms and conditions mutually agreed between the buyer and seller.* How a letter of credit operates and facilitates the trade transaction is depicted in Figure 22-2, showing various steps involved from initiation to conclusion of letter of credit.

The terms and conditions with regard to price, quantity, quality, delivery dates, and payment dates are finalized between the importer and the exporter. This underlying contract forms the basis of opening a letter of credit. The importer approaches his bank for opening of the credit line to the exporters stating terms and conditions that have already been agreed upon. The bank opening the letter of credit advises the exporter the amount and time limits of the credit along with the documentary requirements.

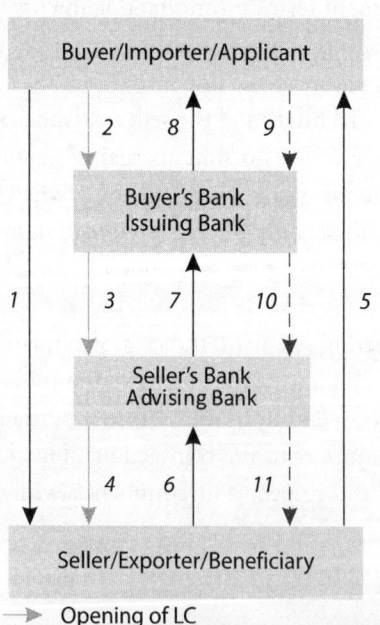

Figure 22-2
Letter of Credit

1. Finalization of terms of the contract between buyer and seller.
2. Opening of letter of credit by importer favoring exporter.
3. Issuing bank advises opening of LC to exporter's bank
4. Exporter's bank advises the exporter the availability of credit with terms and conditions.
5. Exporter dispatches goods and obtains documents from shipping company.
6. Exporter hands over documents relating to the title of the goods and payments.
7. Exporter's bank presents documents to issuing bank.
8. Issuing bank presents documents for payment or acceptance to the importer. Issuing bank releases documents of the title of the goods to importer.
9. Importer makes payment.
10. Issuing bank pays to exporter's bank
11. Exporter receives payment

After obtaining the required documents that indicate execution of order the exporter presents these for negotiation. Banks perform the validity check on the documents and if found in order makes payment to the exporter either immediately or on expiry of credit period.

The need for fulfilling the gap of trust between the buyer and the seller is greater in case of an international transaction as compared to a domestic transaction. We shall therefore explain the features and operations of a letter on credit in the context of international trade transactions involving both importer and exporter. However, these features would apply equally well for a domestic transaction conducted through a letter of credit.

The salient features of the letter of credit are that it (a) guarantees payment, (b) on behalf of the importer (applicant), (c) to the exporter (beneficiary), (d) up to a specified sum (credit), (e) up to certain time (validity), (f) upon submission of documents specified in the credit. Letters of credit used in international transactions are governed by the International Chamber of Commerce Uniform Customs and Practice for Documentary Credits. The general provisions and definitions of the International Chamber of Commerce are binding on all parties. A letter of credit thus protects interest of importer by not releasing the payment till the goods are dispatched, as well as that of the exporter by assuring the payment on behalf of the importer on completion of the terms of the credit.

Terms of credit are mutually decided by the exporter and the importer. Before a letter of credit is formalized as a document the contracting parties, that is, exporter and importer, agree to the terms of the contract with regards to physical goods involved. They decide the price, quantity, quality, delivery schedule, and payment terms. The most complex issue in international transaction is the time of payment. While the exporter wants guaranteed payment, the importer needs to assure supply before payment is released to the exporter. The importer, referred to as *applicant*, approaches the bank to open a letter of credit favouring the exporter, called *beneficiary* for a required sum. The purpose is achieved by the importer's bank communicating to the exporter that the sum mentioned has been earmarked for release upon producing evidence of dispatch of the goods in question. The importer makes clear the terms of supplies and payments as agreed by him with the exporter. Since the bank deals only in the documents of the title of the goods and not in physical goods, the letter of credit is called documentary letter of credit.

A sample letter of credit is displayed in Figure 22-3.

DOCUMENTS UNDER LETTER OF CREDIT

The letter of credit is secondary to the commercial contract entered between an importer and an exporter. The terms and conditions of the letter of credit are primarily driven by what has already been agreed to between the importer and the exporter. Normally, these terms and conditions involving quantity, quality, price, dispatch of goods, payment, etc. are translated in terms of documents that establish the basis of issuing letters of credit.

Typically, the documentary requirements of the LC may be classified in following ways:

- **Commercial:** Invoice, Packing List, Inspection Certificate
- **Transport:** Bill of Lading

INTERNATIONAL BANKING GROUP ORIGINAL

Megabank Corporation

P.O. BOX 1000. ATLANTA, GEORGIA 30302-1000
CABLE ADDRESS: MegaB
TELEX NO. 1234567
SWIFT NO. MBBABC 72

OUR ADVICE NUMBER: EA00000091
ADVICE DATE: 08MAR97
ISSUE BANK REF: 3312/HB/22341
EXPIRY DATE: 23JUN97

****AMOUNT****
USD****25,000.00

BENEFICIARY:
THE WALTON SUPPLY CO.
2356 SOUTH N.W. STREET
ATLANTA, GEORGIA 30345

APPLICANT:
HHB HONG KONG
34 INDUSTRIAL DRIVE
CENTRAL, HONG KONG

WE HAVE BEEN REQUESTED TO ADVISE TO YOU THE FOLLOWING LETTER OF CREDIT AS ISSUED BY:
THIRD HONG KONG BANK
1 CENTRAL TOWER
HONG KONG

PLEASE BE GUIDED BY ITS TERMS AND CONDITIONS AND BY THE FOLLOWING:
CREDIT IS AVAILABLE BY NEGOTIATION OF YOUR DRAFT(S) IN DUPLICATED AT SIGHT FOR 100 PERCENT OF INVOICE VALUE DRAWN ON US ACCOMPANIED BY THE FOLLOWING DOCUMENTS:

1. SIGNED COMMERCIAL INVOICE IN 1 ORIGINAL AND 3 COPIES.
2. FULL SET 3/3 OCEAN BILLS OF LADING CONSIGNED TO THE ORDER OF THIRD HONG KONG BANK, HONG KONG NOTIFY APPLICANT AND MARKED FREIGHT COLLECT.
3. PACKING LIST IN 2 COPIES.

EVIDENCING SHIPMENT OF: 5000 PINE LOGS—WHOLE—8 TO 12 FEET
FOB SAVANNAH, GEORGIA

SHIPMENT FROM: SAVANNAH, GEORGIA   TO: HONG KONG
LATEST SHIPPING DATE: 02 JUN 97

PARTIAL SHIPMENTS NOT ALLOWED   TRANSHIPMENT NOT ALLOWED

ALL BANKING CHARGES OUTSIDE HONG KONG ARE FOR BENEFICIARYS ACCOUNT.
DOCUMENT MUST BE PRESENTED WITHIN 21 DAYS FROM B/L DATE.

AT THE REQUEST OF OUR CORRESPONDENT, WE CONFIRM THIS CREDIT AND ALSO ENGAGE WITH YOU THAT ALL DRAFTS DRAWN UNDER AND IN COMPLIANCE WITH THE TERMS OF THIS CREDIT WILL BE DULY HONORED BY US.

PLEASE EXAMINE THIS INSTRUMENT CAREFULLY. IF YOU ARE UNABLE TO COMPLY WITH THE TERMS OR CONDITIONS, PLEASE COMMUNICATE WITH YOUR BUYER TO ARRANGE FOR AN AMENDMENT.

Figure 22-3
Sample Letter of Credit

Source: www.mushroomtrade.com, accessed on 23 July 2013.

- **Financial:** Bill of Exchange, also called Drafts
- **Insurance:** Insurance Cover Note for the transit
- **Regulatory:** Certificate of Origin

Invoice

For the supply of goods, the exporter raises a commercial invoice indicating specification and description of goods, quantity, price and value, etc. Commercial invoice is an evidence of sale of goods and indicates transfer of the title of goods from exporter to importer.

Packing List

Packing list details how goods are packed. Packed goods are dispatched to the importer on the specified mode of transport. A packing list contains the description of goods being exported, the number of containers, and goods contained in each of them. This must be in accordance with the description of goods mentioned in the accompanying invoice.

Inspection Certificate

Certain letters of credit are opened by importers with the condition that goods prior to dispatch would be inspected by the representatives of the importer to ascertain whether the quality of goods being sent matches with the quality required. Since letters of credit deal only with documents and not goods, the banking system is not responsible if the goods are later found to be defective or of inferior quality. In case the letter of credit specifies the inspection certificate issued by some representatives/agency, then it must form the part of documents.

Bill of Lading

The second category of documents relates to evidence of shipment of goods. A bill of lading (BL) or an air way bill (AWB) is issued by shipping/airline. This serves as proof of dispatch of goods. The bill of lading issued by the shipping company is considered as adequate evidence of shipment in international commercial transactions. The shipping company however, does not certify the content of the shipment. It is merely an evidence of receipt of a certain number of boxes or cartons for delivery to the consignee. The consignee is the person who is expected to receive the goods and may be different than the importer/buyer.

The BL is obtained by the exporter who submits it to his bank. The BL reaches the buyer through the importer's bank. The shipping agency is required to deliver the consignment to the consignee (importer) upon receipt of freight charges if not prepaid.

Besides evidencing the shipment of goods, a BL serves other purposes too. Its most important feature is its negotiability. BL is a negotiable instrument implying that with mere endorsement and delivery of BL the property mentioned therein stands transferred. Therefore, the one who possesses an endorsed bill of lading becomes the owner of the goods. This feature helps in financing of the international trade when the goods are in transit. The lender when entitled to have the endorsed bill of lading becomes secured with the consigned goods held as primary security against the funds lent. Therefore, negotiable form of bill of lading is most popular in international trade and financing.

There are many terms associated with bill of lading. These are described here to facilitate understanding of how international trade is financed.

Straight vs Order Bill of Lading A straight bill of lading essentially means that it is not negotiable. The consignee of the goods cannot endorse it for transfer of title of goods mentioned on it. Since a **straight bill of lading** is devoid of title, the goods can be delivered to the consignee even without it. In contrast an **order bill of lading** is negotiable and bears the title of the goods. The ease of transfer of the title of the goods makes the order bill of lading an instrument apt for financing.

In a *straight bill of lading* the goods can be claimed only by the consignee. Such a bill of lading would be used by an exporter who wishes to retain title of the goods till the time the payment is made or assured. A straight bill of lading can also be used in the situations where no financing is sought, for example, payment received in advance by exporter.

An order bill of lading is used when financing of the trade transaction is sought by any of the parties. Mostly exporters need financing for the goods supplied and therefore they would make an order bill of lading with themselves as consignee. By becoming the consignee the order bill of lading can be endorsed and handed over to the financing bank/intermediary with goods mentioned in the bill of lading as security for funds.

Clean vs Foul Bill of Lading Goods are delivered to the shipping company by the exporter in suitable boxes/packaging. The shipping company makes an assessment of the prima-facie condition of the goods. A cursory, visual look at the containers the shipping company makes a judgment about the condition of the goods. If considered good the shipping company issues a clean bill of lading. If prima-facie the goods appear in good condition the bill of lading is stamped *CLEAN* by the shipping company. Note that the stamp of 'clean' is in no way a certificate of the quality or quantity of the contents or its worthiness. If the condition of the packaging raises a doubt that goods inside may have been damaged, then such a bill is referred to as foul bill of lading. Naturally a foul bill of lading becomes non-negotiable as the financing party is not clear about the extent of damage that could have occurred.

On-board and Received-for-shipment Bill of Lading When an exporter delivers the goods to a shipping company at the port, it is not necessary that the vessel for the destination port is available or ready. Therefore, the consignment might have to wait at the port till the vessel arrives. In such a case, the shipping company issues a bill of lading called *received-for-shipment* meaning that goods have been received at the port are actually not loaded in the vessel. In contrast, we have *on-board bill of lading* which signify that goods have been loaded on the vessel. The name of the merchant vessel appears on the bill of lading. A received-for-shipment bill of lading is not an appropriate form for financing due to uncertainty involved regarding when the shipment would be made.

From the foregoing it is clear that for financing of international trade bill of lading must be **ORDER, CLEAN,** and **ON-BOARD**. Any other form of bill of lading is not acceptable due to any of (a) inability to take delivery of goods, (b) doubtful condition of goods, and (c) uncertainty of shipment and its timings.

BILLS OF EXCHANGE (DRAFTS)

When a documentary credit is opened, it is a promise by the opening bank to honour the claim of payment made by the exporter for supply of goods and on satisfactory completion of documents as specified in the letter of credit. This claim of money is made in the form of a document called bill of exchange. A bill of exchange is a claim of the payment that accompanies the documents drawn under letter of credit. While the importer gets the documents to the title of the goods with which it gets the goods released from the carrier, the exporter gets the payment at the terms already set in the bill of exchange. On due date the amount in question flows from the importer to the exporter passing through banks.

From the financing viewpoint, a bill of exchange (alternatively referred to as *draft*) is the most important document. The exporter for receiving payment would draw a bill of exchange, which is an instrument in writing signed by the drawer (exporter) containing an unconditional promise to pay a definite sum payable on demand to his order or bearer. The order is usually made to the bank that has opened or confirmed the LC.

The other prominent feature of bill of exchange is its negotiability. As in the case of bill of exchange negotiability means that the property mentioned in the instrument is transferable by endorsement and delivery. In simple terms, it means that the one who possesses the bill of exchange duly discharged by the drawee, then on the due date, that is, the maturity of bill of exchange the holder can claim the amount mentioned on it. For negotiability to be practical it is implied that the order to pay must be unconditional.

Sight and Usance Bill of Exchange Bill of exchange may be classified by (a) maturity, and (b) security. Maturity implies the due date of payment. When the exporter wants the payment immediately, he would draw a draft that orders payment upon sight. A sight draft requires payment of the required sum mentioned on seeing it. The bill of exchange would then be phrased *on sight*. When a credit period is involved the payment is due on expiry of credit period. In such a case the draft would be made payable after expiry of credit period after sight. Such a bill of exchange is called a *usance bill of exchange*. A usance bill of exchange needs to be accepted by the drawee before it can be used for financing. If the drawee is a bank who accepts the bill for payment on due date, it is called *banker's acceptance*.

In case the draft is drawn on the basis of the underlying trade transaction as evidenced by the invoice or bill of lading, it is called a *documentary bill of exchange*. If the draft is drawn without the evidence of trade transaction, it is called *clean* bill of exchange.

The drawer (exporter) is usually the person entitled to receive payment from the drawee (the importer or his bank), who is obligated to pay on due date the mentioned sum. With negotiability the holder on due date is entitled to receive payment. This feature allows

financing. If exporter wants a payment prior to the due date he can hand-over the accepted bill of exchange to a financier who can pay the exporter now after deducting the desired returns. This is referred to as discounting.

A sample of documentary usance bill of exchange is shown in Figure 22-4 that depicts a payment of US$25,000 with interest at 10% due from Continental Bank after 90 days of date (27 February 2011) to the drawer (exporter) or to his order (upon due identification by drawer). The draft for negotiability must be accepted by the drawee (Continental Bank).

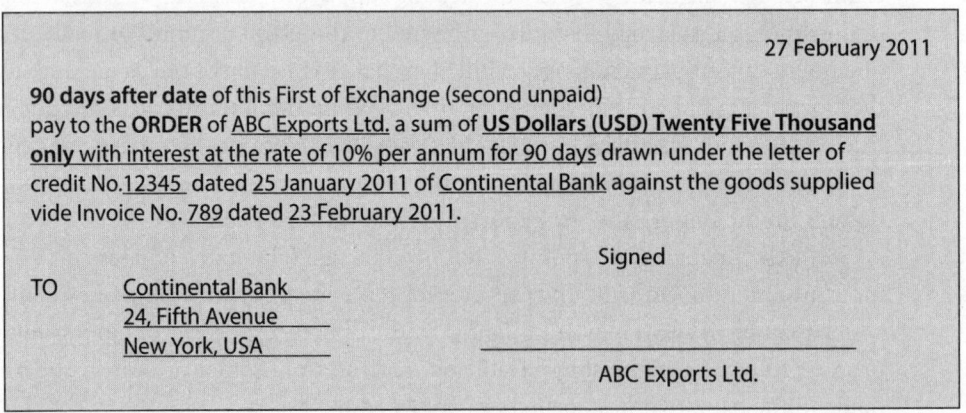

Figure 22-4
Sample Documentary Usance Bill of Exchange

Insurance

Goods to be supplied under letter of credit need to be insured. It facilitates financing because any financier holding the underlying goods as security against funds lent would like to be compensated in case any damage occurs to the goods. Even when financing under letter of credit is not desired the opening bank would insist for insurance because letter of credit substitutes the importer with opening bank for the payment.

Certificate of Origin

Certificate of origin is another document that is usually insisted upon in the letter of credit. It is issued by the consular of the importing nation located in exporting nation. Many nations offer varying rates of customs duty depending upon where from the goods are being imported. It serves regulatory purpose of determination of customs duty, and facilitates clearance of goods by the importer. In addition, such certificates also have statistical value in determining the imports and exports made by a nation.

The aforementioned documents are most common in letters of credit. Besides, importers and exporters may agree for more number of documents to form the part of letter of credit. These may relate to design and drawing in case of technical goods, sea worthiness of the vessel used in shipment, etc.

TYPES OF LETTER OF CREDIT

The usage of letter of credit has become very common and hence a huge variety of letters of credit is used to meet the specific business needs. Some of the types of letters of credit are briefly mentioned here.

Irrevocable and Revocable Letter of Credit An irrevocable letter of credit is the credit that cannot be modified or cancelled without the consent of all the parties to the credit. It is particularly in the interest of the beneficiary, that is, the exporter. A revocable credit can be modified or cancelled by issuing bank without the consent of all the parties. Most letters of credit are irrevocable. Revocable letters of credit do not serve the purpose of financing because it may be cancelled at any time leaving the financier with no security/recourse.

Confirmed Letter of Credit Sometimes the exporter is not sure of the credibility of the bank opening the letter of credit. The opening bank may not be that well known in the exporter's country. Further, the exporter has no knowledge of the relationship of the opening bank and the importer. The exporter also has no legal jurisdiction in the importing nation against the importer or his bank. If the same bank is also the paying bank, the bill of exchange would have to be drawn on them for acceptance. In such a case, the exporter may want another bank on whom it trusts to become a party of the trade transaction, and specify that another bank must add its confirmation to the payment. If another bank confirms the payment, the letter of credit is called confirmed letter of credit. Confirmed letter of credit is safer as it involves two banks for the payment. The confirming bank would add confirmation to the letter of credit for a fee and therefore confirmed letter of credit become more expensive. A revocable letter of credit cannot be confirmed.

Revolving Letter of Credit Normally, a letter of credit is issued for a specified sum for which the bills are paid. A revolving letter of credit automatically replenishes to a level after a bill has been submitted. It is used for repeated purchases spread over a period of time and obviates the need for opening separate and several letters of credit for every transaction.

Transferable Letter of Credit A letter of credit usually allows payment to the beneficiary, that is, the exporter. If the original beneficiary of the credit needs to transfer fully or partly, the amount of the LC to another party it can be done. Letters of credit having such a provision are called transferable LCs. It is useful when first beneficiary is not in a position to supply the entire order and instead sub-contracts part of the order to another supplier. In such a case the documents under the LC could be of second beneficiary.

Back-to-back Letter of Credit A letter of credit that is issued on the strength of another letter of credit is called a back-to-back letter of credit. The terms and conditions, for example, amount, time, etc. of the back-to-back letter of credit cannot exceed those of the first credit. Such LCs are useful when the original beneficiary procures the goods from different suppliers, and makes payment to them. These sub-contracted parties may insist on letters of credit being opened in their favour. The exporter then makes one consignment for supplies to the importer. Documents under the LCs are drawn by the original beneficiary.

Red Clause Letter of Credit When the credit is required at the pre-shipment stage, the importer may extend an unsecured advance to the exporter. This amount (usually specified in red ink) is deducted from the face amount of credit when exporter presents final bills for payment. This LC is used primarily to finance the exporter to facilitate the execution of order.

Stand-by Letter of Credit A stand-by letter of credit is a guarantee issued by the bank on behalf of the creditor/importer to pay in case the importer fails to pay the bills of the exporter. The primary liability to pay remains with the importer. A stand-by letter of credit may not be tied to a specific trade transaction, and can serve as guarantee for payment to the exporter, and may reflect financial standing of the buyer/importer. This is also known as bank guarantee or non-performing letter of credit. It is a secondary payment mechanism.

Banks in Letter of Credit

Due to various reasons, such as the distances involved, time zone differences, absence of branch network, and lack of credibility, there are usually several banks involved in a letter of credit who perform different functions in issuance, advice, negotiation, and payment of credit. These banks depending upon the role performed by them are classified as follows.

Opening/Issuing Bank The bank that issues the credit on the request of the applicant (importer) favouring a beneficiary (exporter) for the required sum and valid for some time is called opening bank.

Advising Bank The issuing bank not having its own office in the location of the beneficiary cannot communicate directly with the beneficiary being unknown to him. Instead it may communicate through a correspondent bank, who advises the beneficiary of the availability of credit. Advising bank renders credibility to the letter of credit. The advising bank and the beneficiary may have a business relationship already existing.

Confirming Bank A confirming bank is the one who in addition to the issuing bank undertakes to pay the sum mentioned in the credit in the event of non-payment. However, the terms and conditions of the credit would have to be met. A confirmed letter of credit is desired by the exporter in cases where the opening bank is not very well known. The confirmation normally comes from more established and credible banks. Confirming bank charges a fee for guaranteeing credit. From financing viewpoint a confirmed letter of credit is better than the unconfirmed letter of credit.

Paying Bank The issuing bank may not pay the bills of the exporter and instead may make another bank pay the bills. Such a situation may arise due to non-availability of credit for the importer by the issuing bank. The bank who pays is called the paying bank.

Negotiating Bank A negotiating bank is the bank that examines the documents submitted by the exporter whether or not they have been submitted in accordance with the terms and conditions stipulated in the letter of credit. Paying bank makes the payment only after negotiating bank confirms the validity of documents negotiated. This involves the bank checking the documents for compliance with the terms and conditions of the LC, handling and resolution of discrepancies and obtaining reimbursement. These bills may be treated as Export LC Bills Purchased where the banks will advance the bill amount negotiated to the beneficiary, or a Collection Bill where the payment is made to the beneficiary upon receipt of funds from the Issuing/Reimbursement Bank. Negotiation is done with recourse to the beneficiary unless the bank confirms the LC or accepts the usance bill of exchange as a drawee.

ADVANTAGES OF LETTER OF CREDIT

Letters of credit are a great facilitator of international trade that assures the payment to the exporters on completion of tasks specified in the LC. Since a bank replaces the importer, the creditworthiness of the importer becomes secondary to the trade transaction. The time and the effort required for conducting the due-diligence is reduced considerably if a letter of credit is opened. Though it costs money to open the letter of credit it may ultimately be extremely cost effective because inherent risks assumed by both buyer and seller stand reduced considerably. This risk reduction has bearing on the price. Once an irrevocable LC has been opened the exporter is sure that the order cannot be cancelled or amended and on completion of conditions specified in the LC he would get the payment.

Like the exporter is assured of payment, the importer too benefits through letters of credit. An importer is assured that supplies would be made in time, and if the exporter does not meet documentary requirements under the LC which are laid down to protect the buyer's interests the payment would not be released. The importer may also benefit from better pricing as the risks of insolvency or default are practically absent in a transaction backed by letter of credit.

The major disadvantage of letter of credit is that it adds to the cost in the form of charges and fees levied by various banks for performing their respective roles. However, these should be considered against the advantages of increased volume and reduced risk.

On the broader front of economy, letters of credit promote international trade because of the reduced political risks. In circumstances where political uncertainty is large, nations resort to capital controls. In such cases, the commitment made by the bank is treated differently than those made by ordinary residents who may be prohibited to make payments in foreign currency. Regulatory or political embargos normally spare the commitments made by banks and financial institutions because failure to do so causes much larger and irreparable damage to national pride and reputation.

FINANCING UNDER LETTER OF CREDIT

A transaction backed by letter of credit becomes much more credible than without it. Enhanced credibility of the trade transactions opens up avenues for financing. Financing is accomplished due to substitution of customer credit by bank. Segregation of documents of ownership and financing enables different modes of financing for exporters and importers. On receipt of a large order the exporter faces working capital constraints. When the order is backed by letter of credit, the exporter can seek finance from his bank. With assured payment by another bank under letter of credit, the advance made becomes self-liquidating when the payment is ultimately realized through banking channels. The advance against LC augments financial resources of the exporters and can help in speedier execution of supplies.

Post-shipment credit is done on the basis of acceptance of bill of exchange when a credit period is involved. The face value of the bill of exchange represents a claim of the holder on the importer or his bank. The value of bill of exchange discounted at the required rate of return can be made available at any point of time. This is referred to as bill discounting. The discounting rate is a function of risk. In case of banker's acceptance the risk is nominal and to that extent financing becomes cheaper.

It must be clear that letter of credit as such is not a financing mechanism but is a mode of payment. In other modes of payment, that is, DA or DP, the banks do not get involved in the payment guarantee though they may serve as couriers of documents and transfer of payment from the importer to the exporter.

Under letters of credit the risks attached are much less as compared to other modes of payment, that is, DP or DA. Under payment mode of DP, the collecting bank hands over the shipping documents including the document of title (bill of lading) only when the importer has paid the bill. The drawee is usually expected to pay within three working days of presentation. The attached instructions to the shipping documents would show 'Release Documents against Payment'. Under DP terms the exporter keeps control of the goods (through the banks) until the importer pays. If the importer refuses to pay, the exporter can either take legal recourse, which may be expensive and difficult to control from another country, or find another buyer or arrange a sale by an auction. Under both cases the price obtained may be lower but probably still better than shipping the goods back.

Under Documents against Acceptance, the exporter allows credit to the importer called usance. The importer is required to accept the bill to make a signed promise to pay the bill at a set date in the future. When he has signed the bill in acceptance, he can take the documents and clear his goods. The exporter loses control of goods. The exporter runs more risks than with DP terms. Under DA additional risks are that later importer might refuse to pay on the due date on the grounds that the goods are not what he ordered. Further between the time of delivery and scheduled payment date the importer might go bankrupt.

The features of negotiability and irrevocability of letters of credit makes financing possible. It is not necessary that LCs be established to meet financing needs. The mode of payment of DA or DP is a direct contract between the buyer and the seller, whereas a letter of credit is a composite instrument involving at least three parties, that is, buyer, seller, and bank.

Documents not in conformity with the terms of letter of credit become ineligible for financing. Since financial institutions and banks involved in the process of issuance and financing of LC are non-technical, the correctness of documents is the only way of ascertaining the genuineness of the underlying commercial transactions. Discrepancy in documents is quite common. These include supposedly minor and typographical errors, such as misspelling of description of goods, non-matching of invoice amount with bill of exchange or insurance, and bill of lading dated later than the date of dispatch allowed. For these reasons of discrepancies, the documents may be referred to the applicant. Such discrepancies are discovered at the negotiation stage. Exporters are advised to strictly follow the instruction and documents mentioned in the letter of credit if obtaining finance is one of the objectives.

FINANCING INTERNATIONAL TRADE

We discussed financing of international trade under letter of credit. It must be emphasized that letter of credit is only a mode of payment making extensive use of banking channels. The negotiability, irrevocability and separation of title documents from financing are the features that can be used for making letter of credit a financing vehicle.

PACKING CREDIT—PRE-SHIPMENT AND POST-SHIPMENT

Packing credit is a facility to exporters to meet their working capital needs for execution of export orders. These needs relate to procurement of raw materials and meeting manufacturing expenses for meeting export orders.

It can be denominated in Indian rupee or in foreign currency. To promote exports and make Indian export competitive, the rate of interest is in line with international markets. If the loan is in foreign currency, the rate of interest is linked to London Interbank Offer Rate (LIBOR). According to the extant guidelines, the final cost of exporter must not exceed 0.75% over 6-month LIBOR. The exporter can choose to avail credit in convertible currencies, such as US dollar, pound sterling, euro, and yen. However, the risk associated with the currency exchange rate fluctuations is borne by exporter.

Banks are able to lend funds in foreign currency at LIBOR linked rate due to availability of deposits in foreign currency in the form of balances in Exchange Earners' Foreign Currency (EEFC) account, accounts of non-resident Indian (NRI) and residents in foreign currency, etc. To augment foreign currency resource banks may negotiate a line of credit for themselves from foreign overseas banks.

For short-term needs, the packing credit is divided in two parts—pre-shipment stage and post-shipment stage. Pre-shipment packing credit is an advance made to an exporter for purchase, processing, manufacturing, or packing of goods prior to shipment. Packing credit needs are assessed on the basis of value of letter of credit opened or confirmed and irrevocable orders for the export. Post-shipment credit is meant for financing of export receivables, that is, after the goods have been despatched on credit.

For availing packing credit, the banks advancing the loan need to conduct an appraisal exercise with regard to eligibility, quantum of finance based on LCs or value of confirmed orders in hand, past track record, capacity to execute order, financial strength of the exporter, etc. To monitor the proper end-use of funds, the payments are normally released to the suppliers of the exporters.

Pre-shipment packing credit is given for specific duration depending upon the manufacturing process and time involved. Generally, the duration of the credit is limited to a maximum of 180 days with a provision to extend it by another 90 days in case of unforeseen delays in execution of orders. The availability of credit is progressive, that is, funds are released as per the progress made in the execution of orders. Therefore, costs of monitoring the loan increases.

Once the order is executed, the pre-shipment advance is liquidated by converting it into a post-shipment credit. Post-shipment credit is liquidated upon receipt of payment from the importer, and any incentives that are made available by Government of India.

BILL DISCOUNTING

We have seen under letter of credit bills of exchange are drawn on importer/his bankers by the exporter. These bills are presented by exporter to his bankers for acceptance and collection. Bills involving credit period would be paid only on expiry of such credit period.

Bill discounting refers to the lending by banks to the drawee (exporter) against the bills. Under this type of lending, the exporter's bank takes the bill drawn on the importer and pays the exporter immediately the face value of the bill after deducting some amount as discount/commission. The bank then presents the bill to the importer on the due date and collects the total amount. If the bill is delayed, the exporter pays the bank a pre-determined interest depending upon the terms of transaction.

Financing post-sale operations against bill of exchange is always considered beneficial for the bank because of the following reasons:

(a) Bills represent the receivables stage of the cash cycle and hence nearest to cash.
(b) Bills are shorter in term from other working capital modes of financing and therefore carry lesser risk because risk is supposed to compound with time.
(c) Bills are self-liquidating in nature as they are presented by the bank for payment on due dates to the importer adjusting the advance made to the exporter.
(d) Bills provide credit enhancement through acceptance by the importer, a third party, besides the discounting bank and exporter.
(e) Bills offer liquidity to the bank because of the availability of re-discounting with central bank.

The benefits to the exporter are as follows:

(a) Increasing competitive advantage due to their enhanced financial ability to offer more attractive forms of payment and credit period.
(b) Improving upon liquidity and other structural ratios that are extremely important in creating value for the firm.
(c) Replacing credit-based sales with cash sales.
(d) Enhancing borrowing capacity due to off-balance sheet financing in bill discounting when without recourse.
(e) Limiting the risk related to unreliability of debtors.

Commercial bill has distinctive characteristics of easy transferability and negotiability, contributing to rapid growth in international trade. Therefore, bill discounting became the principal means of settlement in international trade.

Bill discounting has been in vogue for a long time. In India, bankers and other business houses have been historically using some kind of bill-like instruments written called 'Hundies' to pay and receive the value of goods exchanged in the course of trade. However, with the development of organized financial markets over the years, and the spread of commercial and organized banking, Hundies gradually started losing their status as the principal instrument of credit and were replaced by Bill.

Banker's Acceptance

Banker's acceptance is a usance draft or bill of exchange drawn on and accepted by a bank as its commitment to pay a third party. It lends credibility and adds to the comfort level of discounting bank if the bill under question is accepted by a bank, usually importer's bank. Banker's acceptances add to the ease of negotiability and transferability as compared to the bill of exchange accepted by an importing firm. Refinancing or re-discounting of banker's acceptance by central bank is also easier.

On banker's acceptance a bank becomes the primary obligator of the draft or bill of exchange drawn on and accepted by it. In effect, banker's acceptance involves substituting the bank's creditworthiness for that of a borrower. The accepted bill bears an irrevocable, unconditional guarantee of a bank to pay the bill on maturity. It helps in the process of creating a negotiable instrument that is also attractive to investors as short-term paper. Banker's acceptance compares favourably as a funding avenue in terms of cost vis-à-vis short-term LIBOR-based loans.

Banker's acceptance, being a tradable money market instrument, its liquidity and pricing in the secondary market would largely hinge upon the rating of the bank that grants the acceptance.

FACTORING

Bill discounting and banker's acceptances are apt for payment methods and financing of tangible goods. These modes of payments and financing require financial discipline and are suitable for specific trade transactions involving goods. The tangible goods serve as security providing comfort level to financiers.

With rapid pace of development the proportion of trade is shifting towards intangible services from tangible goods. In the absence of tangible security bill financing or banker's acceptances lose appeal as safe lending mechanism. Even though financiers hardly ever exercise their right to take possession of goods, the psychological comfort of being owner of goods makes financing secured and attractive. In case the bill represents services the psychological comfort is missing. In such case, the financing is based on the strength of the drawer (exporter) rather than importer drawee or banker.

Besides bill discounting requires a lot of financial discipline and coordination effort among the various parties involved. To avoid the compulsions of discipline as well as the operational hassles entailed in bills financing, it is but necessary that a cost effective flexible alternative system to bill finance is evolved and introduced with appropriate legal framework to aid the creditor recover his dues with least hassles. With open account sales becoming the preferred mode, there are practices obtaining in some developed countries where banks extend working capital finance on an ongoing basis against invoices raised by their clients' on their buyers. One such financing arrangement is factoring.

Factoring can be defined as the conversion of credit sales into cash. An exporter supplies goods to the importer and raises invoice. While the goods are received by the importer, the factor (usually a bank) buys the accounts receivable of the exporter and then pays up to 80–85% of the invoice amount immediately on agreement. At the end of the credit period, the importer pays to the factor and not the exporter. The remaining amount is paid to the exporter when the importer pays the invoice value to the factor. Factor deducts his commission and expenses. The flow in factoring is shown in Figure 22-5.

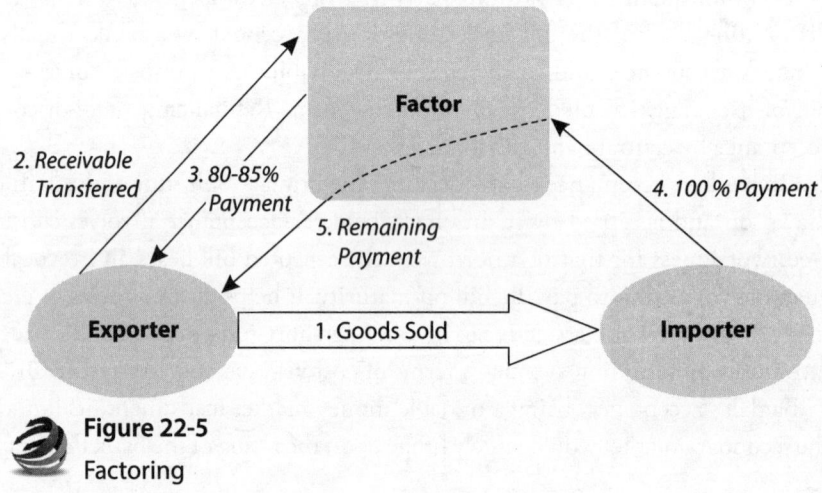

Figure 22-5
Factoring

Besides financing, a factor performs many other roles. The factor becomes a party to the transaction at the initial stages when the importer and the exporter are negotiating the terms of supply. Factor conducts credit investigation in the country of importer through his network, usually consisting of banks, and establishes the credit worthiness and solvency of the buyer importer. This information is shared with the exporter client. The credit check can be with regard to a specific order or on aggregate basis prescribing the maximum credit limit that can be given to the importer. Exporters cannot afford a representative in all the countries where they intend to export. Even if they do such representatives who are generally technical may not be well equipped to understand the intricacies of credit assessment and financial solvency.

Besides undertaking the credit investigation a factor can also perform sales administrative tasks related to invoice preparation, monitoring and follow-up for collection, cash flow projections, as also the legal action in case of default. This can save cost for exporting firms by delegating the sales administration work. Legal cost which could be prohibitive in an unknown country can be saved. The delegation of sale administrative work is akin to sub-contracting of payroll accounting.

Another important service that a factor can provide is managing the political risk for the client exporter. In the agreement with factor the exporter can negotiate that in the event of political move of prohibiting foreign currency cash flows, the factor pays the exporter irrespective of whether the payment has been made by the importer. Factoring effectively protects cash flows of the exporter. Thus factoring can save cost of insurance against late payment or non-payment by importer.

Factoring can be classified as *with recourse* or *without recourse*. Factoring with recourse means that in the event of non-payment by the importer the factor would have recourse to the exporter for the amount advanced. Here the risk of delayed payment may be borne by the factor but the credit risk is assumed by the exporter. In factoring without recourse the credit risk or default risk is borne by the factor. The factor has no recourse to the exporter for non-payment of the shortfall in payment. The exporter would be entitled to full amount of invoice less fees of factor.

Another classification is *disclosed* or *undisclosed* factoring. Under disclosed factoring, the importer knows that the invoice is being paid for by the factor. Therefore, the importer makes payment to the factor and not to the exporter supplier. Upon receiving the invoiced sum, the factor pays the balance to the exporter, as indicated in Figure 22-5. Under undisclosed factoring, the importer is not aware that exporter is availing finance from the factor. On due date the importer pays to the exporter, who in turn settles his accounts with the factor. It is natural that factoring without recourse must be disclosed. Recourse factoring can be disclosed or undisclosed.

Factoring therefore has benefits of effective and efficient management of receivables, providing a sort of insurance cover against political and default risks, enabling better planning and assured deterministic cash flows to the exporter. Like bill discounting factoring too can be off-balance sheet improving upon the critical ratios supposedly determinants of value of the firm. With these benefits the factoring usually is expensive because it not only involves funding cost but also absorbs administrative overheads, collection cost, credit investigation effort, and finally the insurance cover.

The main difference between factoring and loan is that funding is based on customer's (importer's) ability to pay rather than client's (exporter's) financial strength. Bank loan for working capital is assessed on borrower's capacity to pay, and the collateral being offered. Weak exporters can cash in on strength of importers for funding working capital through factoring. Factoring is off-balance sheet unlike loan. Since factoring is off-balance sheet, it helps not so strong exporting firms, which is typical of firms in developing countries.

Invoice Financing

A variant of factoring is *invoice financing*, which is also becoming popular in mature markets.

Invoice financing, as a loan product, offers the financial benefits of factoring, while allowing the exporting firm full control over the receivable management.

This will be ideally suited to the services sector, where due to the inherent nature of its operations not involving movement of tangible goods, drawing of bills of exchange is not generally in vogue.

Under invoice financing, there is also scope for flexibility as to the quantum of potential funding, as it is based on the level of debtors. Like factoring credit line under invoice financing to the exporter is based on the financial strength of the importer and not as much on the borrowing exporter's own financial strength. Invoice financing is provided on 'undisclosed' basis, which implies that the importers would not be aware of the arrangement, as long as there is no default.

The bank has a right to disapprove debtors/any invoice raised and make them ineligible for financing under this scheme for reasons of adverse credit report or their payment record.

In many industries, it is observed that sales do not occur on a uniform basis and fluctuate from month to month. Hence, the present system of receivable financing through cash credit is found to be inappropriate, leading to intermittent over-financing or under-financing.

Invoice financing would be more appropriate to cater to new enterprises with irregular sales. New enterprises do not have much borrowing power due to lack of track record or other financial strength. They can leverage the credibility of their importer customer under invoice financing.

FORFAITING

Forfaiting is a word derived from the French phrase *forfait et sans guaranties* meaning that legal right of recourse has been forfaited.

Operation of forfaiting is similar to factoring where forfaiter bears all commercial and political risk. The basic difference between the forfaiting and factoring is that forfaiting manages long-term receivables (over 90 days up to 5 years) while factoring manages short-term receivables (up to 90–180 days) and is more related to receivables against commodity sales.

Forfaiting is used for deferred payment sales of capital goods. It came into vogue in the 1960s when west European capital goods suppliers wanted to supply capital goods to their customers in developing countries, especially east European countries involving credit period ranging between three and five years. Centrally planned economies of east Europe faced resource crunch to finance economic development. The suppliers (exporters) faced substantial commercial risks due to rather weak standings of the customers as well as political risk due uncertainties of governments. Due to larger credit period involved it was difficult to forecast customers' ability to pay as well as political developments.

In those days, forfaiting was seen as a highly specialized technique whose main purpose was fixed rate medium term financing of cross border sales of capital equipment without recourse to the exporter, eliminating all commercial and political risk. These risks would be carried by the forfaiter.

Forfaiting works as follows (not necessarily in the same order):

1. The exporter and importer agree for supply of goods where payment is made in periodic intervals usually semi-annual or annual.
2. The obligations normally have freely negotiable debt instruments, such as LCs, Bills of Exchange, and Promissory Notes.

3. The notes are endorsed by exporter as 'without recourse' and handed over to the forfaiter.
4. The forfaiter discounts the promissory notes of importer at an agreed fixed rate, and makes funds available to the exporter. These notes are contingent upon the exporter performing his obligations. The discount rate is a function of risk which is assessed by the forfaiter. Since discount rate has implications on the cash flow of the exporter the price of goods is quoted only after the risk assessment is done and rate of discount ascertained.
5. These notes are avalized (European term for irrevocably and unconditionally guaranteeing the payment) by a bank for the political risk. Once avalized, the political risk gets segregated from the commercial transaction.
6. At maturity the notes are presented for payment to the importer.

By discounting the trade receivables without recourse to the exporter the forfaiter obtains a freely negotiable debt instrument that can either be retained within the forfaiter's own portfolio or sold on to an investing institution in the secondary forfaiting market.

The forfaiting typically involves the cost elements of (a) commitment fee, payable by the exporter to the forfaiter 'for latter's' commitment to execute a specific forfaiting transaction at a firm discount rate within a specified time, and (b) discount fee, interest payable by the exporter for the entire period of credit involved and deducted by the forfaiter from the amount paid to the exporter against the avalized promissory notes or bills of exchange.

Benefits to exporters are (a) 100% financing, (b) without recourse, (c) not exhausting the exporter's existing credit line, (d) improved cash flows, (e) reduction of interest rate risk, currency risk, credit risk, and political risk, and (f) increased trade opportunity.

COUNTERTRADE

Countertrade is exchange of goods and services with or without the use of money. Countertrade is perhaps the oldest form of trading between two parties/nations. When there was no currency, the trade was done by exchanging one good for another. Silk, spices, cloth, wheat, rice, etc. being goods of universal use were being exchanged between needing parties. Today we have currency yet countertrade takes place. The commodities too have changed ranging from oil, automobiles, aircraft, defense equipments, and food grains. Monetary values may be used for accounting purposes.

Countertrade without Money

Countertrade can be broadly classified in following ways: (1) without money, where no financing may be involved, and (2) with money, where financing may be involved. In each category, there are a number of ways that the transactions can be structured.

Barter It is the exchange of one form of goods and services for another form of goods and services without any use of money like the trade relationship between India and erstwhile USSR exchanging MIGS for onions. Trade is balanced when the value of export becomes equal to the value of imports. Though money is not involved it can be used as numeraire to account for value.

A single contract covers both flows and no cash is involved. In practice, however, the supply of the principal export is often released only when the sale of the bartered goods has generated sufficient cash.

Barter is often the main means of trading in subsistence economies and in cross border trade in undeveloped regions of the world. More developed markets use it in international trade where they have commodities to offer which are accessible to world markets. Barter may also be introduced into existing contracts to recover debts, that is, when the original payment terms have failed.

Clearing Arrangement In barter, there was simultaneous and single deal. When barter is arranged with time lag in imports and equivalent exports, a clearing account needs to be established. If the arrangement has specific time period under which the trade balance must become zero, then at the end of the period the final settlement must be done by shipment of the goods equivalent to remainder amount from deficit party to surplus party, and make trade balance zero.

Switch Trading Sometimes, it is not possible for two parties in barter to make trade balance zero. This results in imbalances in bilateral trading agreement and causes accumulation of credit surpluses in one country and debit deficits in other country. For example, consider that oil and wheat are exchanged between India and Kuwait. If India has imported more oil than the wheat exported, then Kuwait would have surplus. For any reason, such as no more need of Indian wheat in Kuwait, the surplus may be sold, perhaps at discount by Kuwait, to a third party/nation. The third party/nation would then lift wheat from India to be sold in the world markets. Such transactions are known as 'switch' or 'swap' deals because they typically involve switching the destination of goods on the high seas.

This situation arises when the goods are traded for services. For example, China may build infrastructure for import of minerals from an African nation and that leaves trade balance in favour of China.

Countertrade with Money/Credit

Like countertrade without money, the countertrade with money/credits too has three forms namely buyback, counter-purchase, and offset.

Buyback Buyback is similar to tolling structure where fuel supplies are made and power output bought. In buyback the compensation for input is in the form of buyback of output. For example, a firm may build a plant, supplies technology, imparts training, etc. to a developing nation and in exchange takes a part of the output of the plant. The most cited example of buyback perhaps is the when the payment for construction of gas pipeline by Western European countries for transporting natural gas from Soviet Union was made in the form of buyback of the gas delivered by Soviet Union to Western European countries. Similarly, an exporter of equipment for a chemical plant may be repaid with part of the resulting output from the factory. This practice is most common with exports of process plant, mining equipment, and similar orders. Buyback arrangements tend to be much longer term and for larger amounts than counter-purchase or barter deals.

Counter-purchase Under counter-purchase, goods and services are supplied on explicit condition that payment in return would be made in the form of some other goods and services, as distinct from buyback where payment is made from the output being produced from the goods and services rendered. The contract of supply of goods or services is obtained on a pre-condition of reciprocal basis. Naturally, it would involve credit period for reciprocal arrangement to be fulfilled. A recent example of this is the ongoing trade between Congo and China where infrastructure is being traded for a supply of metals. In a counter-purchase agreement, a foreign supplier undertakes to purchase goods and services from the purchasing country as a condition of securing the order. They can be in the form of two separate but binding agreements with penalties specified in case of non-performance.

Counter-purchase is generally resorted for two reasons—first, to stimulate exports and second, to alleviate the balance of payment deficit resulting from imported goods.

Offset Commonly used in defence or aircraft procurement, offset strategy of countertrade is an agreement by one nation to buy a product from a company in another subject to the purchase of some or all of the components and raw materials from the buyer of the finished product, or the assembly of such product in the buyer nation. Offset has traditionally been used by governments around the world when they have made major purchases of military goods but is becoming increasingly common in other sectors. Under *direct offset* the supplier agrees to incorporate materials, components or sub-assemblies which are procured from the importing country. In some large contracts, successful bidders may be required to establish local production. Under *indirect offset* the purchaser requires suppliers to enter into long-term industrial co-operation and investment in an unrelated sector.

The overall objective of offset either direct or indirect in the defence sector is generally to promote import substitution and to minimize the balance of payment deficit by developing an indigenous industrial defence capability. The objective of stimulating civil investments is to increase, diversify, and support the industrial base.

Whilst there are various forms of countertrade, deals seldom fit these categories precisely. It is not unusual for a large export deal to involve several countertrade arrangements, for example, some long-term buyback plus counter-purchase or barter to finance initial down payments.

Objectives of Countertrade

There can be several reasons for a nation to choose countertrade over cash imports and exports. Some of them are as follows.

Lack of Reserves International trade is settled in hard currencies; the currencies accepted worldwide and freely available. The amount of hard currencies available with the central bank of nation is called reserve. High level of reserves provides comfort level to exporting firm/

country. Reserves can be created by exporting. Developing nations face the problem of lack of exportable commodities and therefore reserves. For example, African nations may be rich in natural resources but do not have means of technology of extracting them to make into an exportable commodity. Only countertrade can help overcome the problems.

Protect Local Industries By engaging in countertrade, nations ensure that as they give business to a foreign nation that also creates business and job opportunities for their own people by promoting the traded commodity.

Adverse Balance of Trade Maintaining a positive balance of trade is very important for every nation. A negative balance of trade results when export is less than import. The excess imports need to be settled. Adverse balance of trade is regarded as a factor retarding economic growth. Countertrade is a great way for nations to ensure that the import and exports in the nation are balanced as every commodity that is being bought is equaled with some commodity being sold.

Competitive Advantage When it comes to trading, there is also competition between various nations. By providing the opportunity of countertrade to another country a nation can gain a competitive edge over other nations selling or trading the same product.

Besides the aforesaid reasons, there could be several other political, economic, and structural issues that necessitate countertrade. Each nation is faced with typical problems of its own. It may (a) have surplus capacity which is not being exported otherwise, (b) have no credit available due to doubtful capacity to service the debt, (c) not be equipped with well-developed private sector, (d) have currency controls which cannot be relaxed for other economic reasons, etc.

Countertrade can provide benefits of (a) allowing entry into difficult markets, (b) overcoming currency controls and exchange rate problems and yet have import and export of goods, (c) improving on debt service capability by not borrowing, (d) create markets for otherwise non-salable product in cash, etc.

One of the disadvantages of countertrade is that it is a rather costly way of doing trade. If trade is done on cash/credit basis the pricing would be competitive and fair. In case of countertrade, the compulsion of one nation may have an adverse impact on the price of the import or export product for the nation which is compelled by circumstance to engage in countertrade. Negotiations under countertrade are often stretched in time. It also creates problems of valuation because a numeraire is required to make the trade balance.

SUMMARY

Trade between buyers and sellers is inherently risky because of a lingering doubt in the minds of each about the likely default the counterparty can commit. In international trade this gap of credibility widens substantially due to different environments, varying commercial practices, large distances, different legal jurisdictions, and absence of recourse, etc. This is compounded by the fact that in international trade it seems practically impossible to synchronize delivery of goods with payment.

Many modes of payment such as advance, DA, and DP are available to exporters. But the most commonly used method is by way of letter of credit. It overcomes the credibility gap by substituting the payment by importers by guarantee of a bank. The letter of credit segregates ownership of goods with payment by making them separately negotiable. While title of goods is attached with invoice and bill of lading (during transit) the credit payment is segregated by another instrument called bill of exchange.

Complex business situations have made the letter of credit complex in terms of documents and number of banks involved and hence the types of letters of credit. An irrevocable LC is one whose terms of credit can be changed only if both exporter and importer agree to a change. It cannot be changed unilaterally. A confirmed letter of credit is one where payment is guaranteed by another bank. A confirmed and irrevocable is ideal instrument for least cost of financing.

Amongst the documents under letter of credit, perhaps the bill of lading and bill of exchange are two most important documents. Bill of lading is a document letter of credit which confers the ownership of the goods to its holder during the transit of goods. Bill of exchange is the document that relates to the payment of supplies made. This too is a negotiable instrument. With segregation of delivery and payment of goods financing is made possible. From financing viewpoint a bill of lading that is order, clean and on-board is ideal. If a bill of exchange is accepted by a bank becomes least risky and hence most apt for financing.

Credit facilities for meeting working capital needs for execution of export orders is normally granted by way of pre-shipment or post-shipment credit. These are done at internationally competitive rates and may be based on letters of credit or confirmed orders in hand. A refinance is available from central bank to augment financial resources of the bank.

For financing of export receivable factoring and forfaiting are the other two modes of financing. Factoring is management of entire sales ledger providing credit investigation and collection services. Most payment against a bill raised on the importer is made available to the exporter upfront. The remaining amount after deduction of factoring fee are paid when the bill is actually realized. Under factoring without recourse the risk of non-payment is borne by factor. The mechanism of forfaiting is similar to factoring except that it pertains to longer credit period to cover sale of capital goods and bills are avalized by bank to assume political risk.

Countertrade is the exchange of goods and services without involving cash. There are many forms of countertrade. It is the most suitable form of international trade for nations having inadequate reserves, having balance of payment (BOP) deficit or lack technology to make products exportable, etc.

QUESTIONS

22-1 What do you understand by trade dilemma? Can an intermediary help resolve it?
22-2 Differentiate between payment modes of documents against payment and documents against acceptance.
22-3 What is the purpose of (a) invoice, (b) packing list, (c) certificate of origin?
22-4 Differentiate between the following terms:
 (a) Clean bill of lading and foul bill of lading
 (b) Straight bill of lading and order bill of lading
 (c) On-board bill of lading and received-for-shipment bill of lading
22-5 Differentiate between the following terms:
 (a) Sight and usance bill of exchange
 (b) Confirmed and unconfirmed letters of credit
 (c) Applicant and beneficiary
 (d) Transferable and back-to-back letters of credit

22-6 Briefly describe how a documentary credit is opened.

22-7 'Letter of credit makes financing of receivables easy.' Comment.

22-8 'Factoring goes beyond mere financing of receivables.' Comment.

22-9 What is bankers' acceptance and how is it useful in financing of receivables?

22-10 Describe forfaiting and draw its difference with factoring.

22-11 'A factor wrongfully considers ability of importer to pay rather than financial strength of the exporter.' Do you agree with the statement? Give reasons.

22-12 Differentiate between the following terms:
  (a) Factoring with recourse and without recourse
  (b) Disclosed and undisclosed factoring

22-13 What do you understand by countertrade? Mention few circumstances where countertrade can prove beneficial for a nation.

22-14 Differentiate between the following terms:
  (a) Barter and switch trading
  (b) Buyback and counter-purchase

Taxation and Transfer Pricing in India

LEARNING OBJECTIVES

This chapter aims at

- discussing the Indian income tax environment and its few salient features, with types of taxes, rates of corporate tax, and tax incentives
- explaining transfer pricing regulations in India
- explaining arm's length price and the methods of determining it
- explaining tax havens and how multinational corporations use them for their advantage
- discussing General Anti Avoidance Rules, their rationale and implications on international business
- understanding Double Taxation Avoidance Agreements, their features, and how they promote international business
- understanding Advance Rulings and how they help in removing uncertainties about tax rates, laws, and obligations

CONTENTS

Introduction
Income Tax
Types of Taxes
Taxable Income
Residential Status
Tax Rates
    Minimum Alternate Tax
    Capital Gains
    Transactions in Securities
    Dividend Distribution Tax
    Withholding Tax
Tax Incentives
Transfer Pricing
Introduction
Transfer Pricing Regulation in India
Associated Enterprises
Nature of Transactions Covered
Arm's Length Price
Methods of Determining Arm's Length Price
    Comparable Uncontrolled Price Method
    Resale Price Method
    Cost Plus Method
    Profit Split Method
    Transactional Net Margin Method
    Any Other Method
Relaxations in Transfer Pricing and Arm's Length Price
Tax Havens
General anti Avoidance Rules
Double Taxation Avoidance Agreements
Advance Rulings

INTRODUCTION

With increased globalization multinational corporations (MNCs) are spreading out activities in various nations around the world taking advantage of competencies available in different parts of the world to gain competitive edge and strengthen their positions. Exploiting inherent advantages available in different nations helps improve product quality and reduce price. Each region or nation is characterized and endowed with different amounts of natural resources, capital, labour proficiencies, and skill sets. In an integrated world these resources and skill sets can be put to better use by MNCs for overall welfare of consumers around the world.

The usual model adopted by MNCs is to perform various manufacturing operations in different locations adding value to the product making use of the inherent advantages of different nations. For example, a Japanese corporation may own ore mines in India to exploit the best quality raw material, ship ore for conversion into steel to take advantage of superior steel-making technologies, and again ship them to all parts of the world to convert ingots into sheets, bars, etc., closer to the market. All or part of the activities from raw material to finished goods may be performed at different locations around the world but may be controlled by single entity. We have seen that most manufactured goods are now produced in China taking advantage of the huge labour force available possibly at fraction of the wages prevailing in the developed world. From the same token, most information technology development work is concentrated in India to take advantage of the relatively less expensive engineers and technologists available.

The integration of various activities along the value chain has advantage for the world community as a whole because benefits of each nation or society do not remain confined to local residents of the area.

Ironically different parts of the world are also subject to different tax laws and jurisdictions. While taking advantage of the inherent competencies across the globe MNCs can also effectively take advantage of the different tax rates, laws, and jurisdictions for its universal objective of enhancing shareholders' wealth. While there can be no objection to the stated goal of the MNCs, the question whether the enrichment is at the expense of another stakeholder, that is, the government, needs to be answered.

The shareholders' claim on the cash flows of the firm is residual. Before shareholders can lay a claim on the profit, the taxes on it need to be paid. Since multinationals operate in different legal and tax jurisdictions across the world, understanding of environment of tax in various nations is an important decision for an MNC for maximization of shareholders' wealth. MNCs therefore are entitled to make decisions to locate operations where tax liabilities are less. Tax arbitrage often becomes the basis of decision-making.

In this chapter, we examine a few important issues related to taxes that arise in case of international transactions with a bird's eye view of tax environment in India.

INCOME TAX

TYPES OF TAXES

There is multitude of taxes at each level or phase of production, marketing, and distribution. Taxes are levied in India at the national and state levels and can be categorized into three—direct, indirect, and transactional.

Direct Taxes Direct taxes include corporate income tax, capital gains tax applicable for profits in transaction in capital assets, dividend distribution tax applicable when firms distribute the dividend, wealth tax, etc.

Indirect Taxes Indirect taxes are value added tax (VAT), excise duty, import duties, service tax, sales tax, and R&D tax.

Taxes on Transactions Transaction in securities, commodities are subject to taxes which arise due to transaction of financial assets.

We here concentrate only on direct taxes.

TAXABLE INCOME

Income tax in India is based on residential status of the taxpayer. All firms including MNCs if incorporated in India are considered resident Indians. A resident Indian is taxed for the worldwide income including capital gains while a non-resident is taxed on the income arising in or received in India, or deemed to arise or accrue in India. Income that is deemed to accrue or arise in India includes

- Income arising from a 'business connection', property, asset, or source of income in India;
- Capital gains from the transfer of capital assets situated in India; and
- Interest, royalties, and technical service fees paid by an Indian resident, non-resident, or the Indian government.

In general, a company's taxable income is determined by aggregating the income from all of the heads, that is, business connections, capital gains, interest, royalty, etc. The computation of business income is normally based on the profits shown in the financial statements, after adjusting for exempt income, non-deductible expenditure, special deductions, and unabsorbed losses and depreciation.

Payments made to a non-resident for the provision of services are taxable in India even if the services are rendered outside the country. Where the fees are payable in respect of services used in a business or profession carried on by such a person outside India or for the purpose of making or earning income from a source outside India, they are not taxable in India.

Losses arising from business may be set off against income from any source in that year. A business loss may be carried forward and set off against future business profits for the next eight assessment years. Losses arising from the transfer of short-term capital assets are set off against capital gains (whether long-term or short-term) arising during the same year and may be carried forward for set off against capital gains for the next eight years.

Long-term capital losses may be set off only against long-term capital gains during the year, and can be carried forward for eight years for set off against long-term capital gains.

Unabsorbed depreciation can be carried forward indefinitely.

Advance Tax Taxes on income of an assessment year are usually paid in installments by way of advance tax on quarterly basis. A company must make a prepayment of its income tax liabilities by 15 June (15% of the total tax payable), 15 September (45%), 15 December (75%), and 15 March (100%). Any overpaid amount is refunded after submission of the final tax return.

RESIDENTIAL STATUS

Taxable entities are divided into three categories depending upon their residential status. These categories are Resident, Resident but not ordinary resident, and Non-resident. The categorization is based on the amount of time spent in India during a period usually a financial year from 1 April to 31 March.

An individual is a 'resident' if (a) he has been in India during the previous year for 182 days or more or (b) the individual has been in India during the previous year for less than 182 days but has been in India for an aggregate of 365 days or more in the four years preceding the previous year and his stay in India during the previous year is 60 days or more. The tax status is determined on the basis of residential status and not citizenship. Thus, an Indian citizen can be non-resident or a foreign citizen can be resident Indian for tax purposes.

Individuals, who are not resident in accordance with the above are treated as non-residents under the Income Tax Act.

A company is considered resident in India if it is incorporated in India or if control and management of its affairs take place wholly in India. The residential status is also decided on the basis of 'permanent establishment' resulting in tax liabilities for foreign enterprises. Permanent establishment is deemed if any of following conditions prevails:

- Offices negotiating and concluding contracts for and on behalf of its head office
- Activities of office is closely involved with revenue generation activities
- Activities of the office are similar to that of the overseas head office
- Appraisal of the employees of the Indian office based on sales target achieved in India

Revenue authorities in India are closely monitoring activities of Indian offices of foreign companies in India. Long-term presence in India on account of multiple contracts of the employees of foreign companies and negotiation of contract in India are being deemed as 'permanent establishment' and resulting in tax liabilities on the portion of income of head office in India.

TAX RATES

The tax rates for resident and non-residents are somewhat different in India. In addition to normal income tax rates there is (a) surcharge applicable if income exceeds certain thresholds and (b) a cess on the amount of tax. The tax rates are as follows:

	Tax	Surcharge	Cess	Effective Tax Rate
Resident Firms				
Income ≤ ₹10 million	30%	Nil	3%	30.900%
Income > ₹10 million		5%		32.445%
Non-resident Firms				
Income ≤ ₹10 million	40%	Nil	3%	41.200%
Income > ₹10 million		5%		43.260%

The taxable income of non-resident companies engaged in certain businesses (i.e., prospecting for, extraction or production of mineral oils, civil construction, testing and commissioning of plant, and machinery in connection with turnkey power projects) is deemed to be 10% of the specified amounts. Similarly, for non-residents in the business of operating ships and aircraft, profits and gains from the operations are deemed to be 7.5% and 5%, respectively, of the specified amounts.

Minimum Alternate Tax

Income statements of the firms are prepared under Indian Companies Act and as per the Accounting Standards prescribed in India. Taxable income is arrived under Indian Income Tax Act, which can be different from the stated income on books. The differences in stated income and taxable income arise due to several factors, such as tax incentives available, different rates of depreciation prescribed in Companies Act and Income Tax Act, and accounting inconsistencies in stating income and expenditure on accrual or cash basis, etc.

A minimum alternate tax (MAT) is imposed on resident and non-resident corporations on profits stated on books. As from 1 April 2011, where the income tax payable on the total income by a company is less than 18.5% of its book profits, the book profits are deemed to be the total income of the company on which tax is payable at a rate of 18.5%, further increased by the applicable surcharge and cess. Thus, inclusive of surcharge and cess the effective MAT rate for a domestic company (which most often be the case of an Indian subsidiary of an MNC) is 19.06% where the total income is less than or equal to ₹10 million, and 20.01% where the total income exceeds ₹10 million. For non-resident companies, the effective MAT rate is 19.06% where the total income is less than or equal to ₹10 million, and 19.44% where the total income exceeds ₹10 million.

Tax paid under the MAT provisions may be carried forward to be set off against income tax payable in the next 10 years, subject to certain conditions. The scope of MAT has been broadened by making developers of special economic zones (SEZs) and units in SEZs liable to pay MAT.

The MAT also applies at the same rate of 18.5% on limited liability partnerships.

Capital Gains

Capital gains arise on disposal of capital assets. These are further categorized as short-term and long-term depending upon the period the capital asset is held prior to its disposal.

If the capital asset is disposed after holding it for more than three years the capital gains arising therein are categorized as long-term capital gains; and if the asset is held for less than three years the gains on such disposal is classified as short-term. For long-term capital gains the tax rates are less as compared to short-term as shown as follows:

Short-term capital gains	At normal rates
Long-term capital gains with indexation	At 20% plus applicable surcharge and cess

Gains from the sale of long-term capital assets are exempt from capital gains tax if they are reinvested in certain securities (subject to an annual investment cap of ₹5 million) within six months and locked in for three years.

Transactions in Securities

For foreign institutional investors (FIIs) registered with Securities and Exchange Board of India (SEBI), the following taxes are applicable for the portfolio investment:

Income	Company Defined Under Section 2(17)		Non-company
	Income ≥ ₹10 million	Income ≤ ₹10 million	
Dividends	Exempt under Section 10(34) if *Dividend Distribution Tax is paid by the company declaring the dividend.*		
Income from Units	Exempt under section 10(35)		
Income (other than above) in respect of securities	21.012%	20.60%	20.60%
Capital Gains where Securities Transaction Tax (STT) is chargeable			
Short-term	15.759%	15.45%	15.45%
Long-term	Exempt under section 10(38) of the Income Tax Act, 1961		
Capital Gains where Securities Transaction Tax (STT) is not chargeable			
Short-term	31.518%	30.90%	30.90%
Long-term (without indexation)	10.506%	10.30%	10.30%
Income from transfer of such securities if chargeable under the head business income			
Business Income If there is permanent establishment	42.024%	41.20%	30.90%
Business Income (where no permanent establishment	NIL	NIL	NIL

Under Section 90(2) of the Income Tax Act, 1961, where Double Taxation Avoidance Agreement (DTAA) has been entered then the taxpayer can choose tax rates that are more beneficial to the taxpayer. For removing any confusion regarding treatment of tax on transactions, any non-resident can approach 'Advance Rulings Authority' to determine the tax implications in India for the transaction proposed to be entered.

Dividend Distribution Tax

A domestic company is required to pay dividend distribution tax of 16.2225% (15% plus a surcharge of 5% and 3% cess) on any amounts declared, distributed, or paid as dividends. Dividends are exempt from tax in the hands of recipients if dividend distribution tax is paid.

Withholding Tax

Payments made by a firm are subject to tax deduction at source. The following rates of withholding taxes are applicable.

Dividend There is no withholding tax on dividends. However, the company paying the dividends is not subject to dividend distribution tax then 10% withholding tax is applied with no surcharge or cess. In case of non-resident, the rate is 20% unless reduced by tax treaty.

Interest Interest paid to a non-resident is generally subject to a 20% withholding tax, plus the applicable surcharge and cess (2% surcharge if payment exceeds ₹10 million and 3% cess, for a withholding rate of 20.6% or 21.012%). In case of non-resident, the rate is 20% unless reduced by tax treaty.

Royalties The withholding tax on royalties and fees for technical services paid to a non-resident is 10% unless reduced by treaty. Additionally, a surcharge (2% if the payment exceeds ₹10 million) and cess (3%) are imposed, increasing the withholding tax to 10.3% or 10.506%.

TAX INCENTIVES

Government of India provides several incentives in taxes for having balanced industrial growth, that is, promoting underdeveloped sectors, and balanced regional development and promoting exports. India offers a number of benefits, including tax and non-tax incentives for establishing new industrial undertakings; incentives for specific industries, such as power, ports, highways, electronics, and software; incentives for units in less-developed regions; and incentives for units producing exports or in export processing zones and SEZs.

These incentives keep varying from time to time, place to place, and industry to industry. Some of these benefits are as follows:

- 200% deduction allowed for in-house scientific research
- Deduction of business profits from export of services for units located in SEZs 100% for first 5 years and 50% for next five years and another five years subject to certain conditions
- 100% deduction of business profits for 10 years for units located in North East India
- Accelerated depreciation for certain categories, such as energy saving, environmental protection, and pollution control equipment
- Investment allowance of 15% for manufacturing firms if investment exceeds ₹1,000 million

A lot of changes in the Income Tax structures are proposed under a new Direct Taxes Code Bill, 2010 (DTC) that is expected to replace Income Tax Act, 1961 and aimed at facilitating voluntary compliance and simplifications.

TRANSFER PRICING

INTRODUCTION

In a large organization where its various divisions have supplier–customer relationship, the tool of transfer pricing is used to monitor the divisional performances of profitability. The price at which the output of a division is transferred to another division is called the transfer price. For example, a packaging unit may have polyester film making division producing films and a printing division that uses films as raw material for printing before it is sold to the end-users. The total profits of the firm would be the sum total of the profits of both the divisions. However, the question which division is more profitable can only be answered when a price of films to be supplied to printing division is fixed. In situations where output of one division serves as input to another division in the manufacturing/production process, it is imperative on part of the organization to measure the value addition made by each division, which can be done only when transfer price from one division to other division is fixed. This is often done by the same management.

In the context of an MNC these divisions are likely to be located in different countries subject to different legal jurisdictions. These divisions often take the form of separate legal entities by way of joint ventures, wholly owned subsidiaries, etc. For example, an Indian automobile producer belonging to an MNC may import engines from the parent organization. Here the parent is not only controlling the Indian subsidiary but also acts as supplier. Though separate entities from each other, these firms may be controlled by the same parent that sets policy guidelines. The price at which the engine would be supplied to the Indian subsidiary would impact the profit of parent. There would be opposite impact on the profitability of the subsidiary. However, on a consolidated basis the profit would remain unchanged irrespective of the transfer price used.

If the parent increases the price of engine, the profits of the parent would go up and to that effect the profit of subsidiary would come down. If the price of the engine is decreased the opposite would happen with aggregate profit (pre-tax) of the two remaining same. In case the parent and subsidiary have different tax rates, the post-tax profit can be increased by adopting suitable transfer pricing policy at the expense of revenue authorities.

As an illustration, consider a parent in Eurozone supplying engines at a price of €1,500 (called transfer price) to its subsidiary in another country in Eurozone as key part of the automobile being manufactured there. With input costs of €1,000 the profit of parent is €500. With taxes at 40% the post-tax profit is €300. The subsidiary sells the finished automobile for €10,000 with input of €8,500 including the cost of engine at €1,500. With 20% tax rate the contribution of €1,500 by subsidiary adds to the post-tax profit of the parent by €1,200. The aggregate post-tax profit of the parent is therefore €1,500. This is depicted in Figure 23-1.

Irrespective of the transfer price used the consolidated pre-tax contribution would remain unchanged as revenue of parent is cost to the subsidiary nullifying the impact. However, since parent and subsidiary are subject to different tax rates the post-tax profit is subject to change by using suitable transfer pricing policy. To save tax the parent may decide to shift profit to low-tax nation by decreasing the transfer price of engine. To the extent of price decrease the contribution of parent would fall resulting in higher saving in tax. By the same extent, the contribution of the subsidiary would rise resulting in increase outgo of tax. However, increased tax incidence in the low-tax region would be lesser that the savings of tax made in high-tax region increasing the post-tax profit.

Assume that new transfer price fixed is €1,200. The aggregate impact of transfer price revised from €1,500 to €1,200 is shown in the table in Figure 23-1. The enrichment of shareholder by €60 is at the expenses of revenue authorities of parent's nation losing €120. The remaining €60 is gained by revenue authorities of subsidiary's nation.

While revenue authorities of the subsidiary's nation and shareholders of the parent have no reason to complain about the new transfer price of €1,200, the loss of the revenue authorities of the parent's nation can challenge the transfer price. It may disallow the claims of the parent firm and re-calculate the profit using the fair price the loss of the revenue authorities would be compensated. Under these circumstances, the parent would end up making lesser profit because the revenue authorities would not recognize the increased cost as determined by the revenue authorities of the parent's nation. If so the powers of revenue authorities would serve as deterrent to the parent to arbitrarily fix the transfer price.

The issue of shifting profit from high-tax regions to low-tax regions by changing the transfer price along the value chain to increase the wealth of shareholders at the expense of revenue collection of the nation has wider economic implications for the economy by way of fiscal and monetary policies of the nations. It has impact on the developmental expenditure, subsidies, social security funding, etc. of developing and developed nations alike who may be practising high tax rates.

The arbitrariness on (a) part of parent firms to fix the transfer price and (b) disallowance of the same by revenue authorities needs to be eliminated for gaining unjust advantage by shareholders at the expense revenue authorities and vice versa. Since issues related to transfer price are global in nature there is a need to have uniform practices and guidelines. With the consistency of approaches in mind Organization of Economic Cooperation and Development (OECD) has been doing substantial work in drafting guidelines of transfer pricing that may have global acceptance.

The issues in transfer price are as follows:

1. Whether any party in the international transaction was in a position to dominate the process of price determination, that is, are they associated enterprises?
2. If yes, whether the price at which the transaction took place was actually influenced?

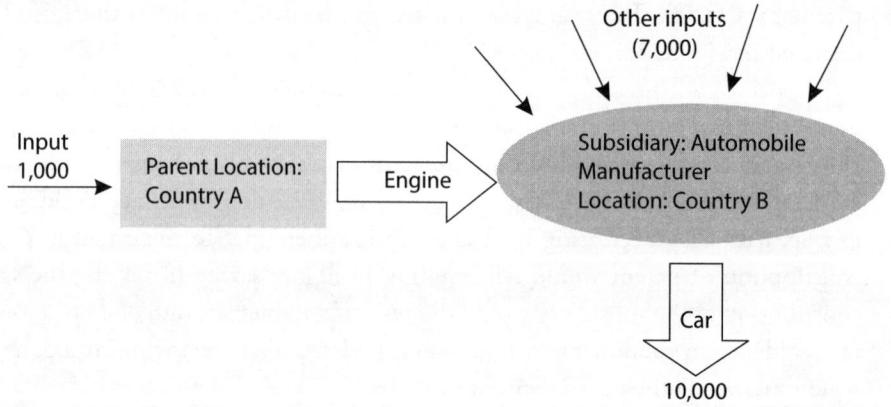

	Parent	Subsidiary	Total
Tax rate	40%	20%	
Selling price	1,500	10,000	10,000
Input price	1,000	8,500	8,000
Contribution	500	1,500	2,000
Tax	200	300	500
Post-tax contribution	300	1,200	1,500
Transfer price reduced to €1,200			
Selling price	1,200	10,000	10,000
Input price	1,000	8,200	8,000
Contribution	200	1,800	2,000
Tax	80	360	440
Post-tax contribution	120	1,440	1,560

Loss Suffered by Revenue Authorities in Parent's Nation	120
Gain to revenue authorities in subsidiary's nation	60
Net gain to shareholders	60

Figure 23-1
Impact of Transfer Price Policy on Aggregate Profit

3. If yes, what should have been the fair price (referred to as Arm's Length Price or ALP) that could be substituted to re-compute the profit and tax thereon?

A common framework to answer these questions that has gained universal acceptance is the transfer pricing guidelines of OECD.

TRANSFER PRICING REGULATION IN INDIA

Transfer pricing issues remained unaddressed in India till 2001 when for the first time a regulation relating to transfer pricing issues were incorporated by way of insertion of Section 92 in the Income Tax Act. Prior to 2001 the issue of transfer pricing was addressed only indirectly and in an arbitrary manner by authorizing the assessing officer to disallow certain expenditure, withdrawal of tax benefits, etc. if the taxpayer is suspected of misusing the transfer pricing. Disallowance of expenses and tax holiday benefits were discretionary and penal in nature and were devoid of rationale providing a lot of discomfort to taxpayers.

The problem was specifically addressed in a systematic manner for the first time in Finance Act, 2001, when Section 92 was inserted exclusively dealing with the transfer pricing. Besides defining the scope of transactions covered and the methods of computation of fair price, the act also provided usage of a specific method to justify the transfer price and dealt with the documentary requirements to support the claim. These guidelines are broadly based on OECD guidelines on transfer pricing.

The provisions of transfer pricing regulations can be divided in three areas:

1. The definition of *associated enterprises*
2. The scope of products and services to be covered
3. Computation of *Arm's Length Price (ALP)*

Associated Enterprises

Transfer price used as a tool of escaping higher tax rate for unjust enrichment has meaning only when it is established that the two parties to the transaction are related/associated. Associated enterprises are those common entities that can exercise influence on pricing decisions in two enterprises. The influence on the pricing decisions need not be derived from mere majority shareholding or management control but it must be recognized that firms can exercise considerable influence by other roles too, such as lender, a major supplier, or a key customer. We all know that wholly owned subsidiaries or majority shareholding (≥51%) by MNCs in a venture abroad are associated firms.

Expanding the scope of associated enterprises Section 92A of the Indian Income Tax Act defines meaning of associated enterprises as an enterprise which participates, directly or indirectly, or through one or more intermediaries, in the (a) management, or (b) control, or (c) capital of the other enterprise. It also covers situations in which the same person (directly/indirectly) participates in the management, control, or capital of both the enterprises. In addition to this definition, certain other specific parameters have been laid down, based on which two enterprises would be deemed as associated enterprises. These parameters include

1. Direct/indirect holding of 26% or more voting power in an enterprise by the other enterprise or in both the enterprises by the same person;
2. Advancement of a loan, by an enterprise, that constitutes 51% or more of the total book value of the assets of the borrowing enterprise;
3. Guarantee by an enterprise for 10% or more of total borrowings of the other enterprise;

4. Appointment by an enterprise of more than 50% of the board of directors or one or more executive directors of the other enterprise or the appointment of specified directorships of both enterprises by the same person;
5. Complete dependence of an enterprise (in carrying on its business) on the intellectual property licensed to it by the other enterprise;
6. Substantial purchase of raw material/sale of manufactured goods by an enterprise from/to the other enterprise at prices and conditions influenced by the latter;
7. Where one enterprise is controlled by an individual, the other enterprise is also controlled by such individual or his relative or jointly by such individual and relative of such individual; and
8. The existence of any prescribed relationship of mutual interest.

Besides the aforesaid parameters, there are certain deeming provisions where a third party is deemed as associated enterprise. This rule aims to counter any move by taxpayers to avoid the transfer pricing regulations by interposing as third parties between group entities. For example, if A and B are associated enterprises in USA and India, respectively, and if A enters into an agreement with C in USA on behalf of B, then any transaction between B and C based on such agreement would be deemed as transaction between the associated enterprises.

Nature of Transactions Covered

Indian transfer pricing rules do not include domestic transactions between two associated enterprises within India, because one way or the other they would be taxed in India irrespective of shifting of profits in two associated firms. The rules mainly apply to cross-border or international transactions.

Section 92B of the Act defines the term 'international transaction' to mean a transaction between two (or more) associated enterprises involving the

1. sale, purchase, or lease of tangible or intangible property;
2. provision of services; cost-sharing arrangements;
3. lending/borrowing of money; or
4. any other transaction having a bearing on the profits, income, losses, or assets of such enterprises.

The associated enterprises could be either two non-residents or a resident and a non-resident; furthermore, a *permanent establishment* of a foreign enterprise also qualifies as an associated enterprise. Permanent establishment includes fixed place of business through which business of the enterprises, partially or wholly, is carried out. Accordingly, transactions between a foreign enterprise and its Indian permanent establishment are within the ambit of the code.

ARM'S LENGTH PRICE

Challenging the transfer price used is not enough. If the transfer price is inappropriate it has to be replaced by the fair price, that is, the price ought to have been charged. This is called arm's length price. The basic issue in transfer pricing is the determination of ALP so as to make the controlled and uncontrolled transactions indifferent to tax. Section 92F defines the ALP as the price applied between two persons other than associated enterprises in an uncontrolled condition.

One limitation faced in arriving at the ALP is the comparability of the controlled and uncontrolled transactions. In real life, no two products are absolutely identical. They differ in many ways even tough performing the same basic function. The differences in quality of two products cause huge price variations. For example, different soaps can be priced in the variation range of 100% to 1,000% on account of brand value, fragrances, packaging, etc. that makes the process of comparison difficult. In industrial products, these variations could be magnified and functional comparison with price may not hold good.

Pricing is also a function of the risks associated. When goods are supplied by a parent firm to another related firm (a subsidiary in another nation) the aspects of after-sales service, providing warranty, etc. are normally incorporated in the contract and accordingly price changes. Whether the parent or subsidiary bears the risk would seriously impact the price charged in the transactions/supplies between the two related parties. In such circumstances, normally the parent is required to train the manpower, the cost of which may not be explicitly stated but manifested in the price.

The quantity of the product supplied too has impact on prices. The contract between parent and subsidiary may not be at the same price at which the product may be available in the open market. Normally, substantial volume of business is exchanged between two associated enterprises. In fact volume is often the cause of one enterprise to control the other enterprise. Most MNCs establish production facilities in different nations by way of subsidiaries only when volume of the product sold becomes large enough. Due to the substantial off-take constituting major proportions of business between two related parties, the pricing may be significantly different from what it would have been in an uncontrolled transaction.

The difference in prices in controlled and uncontrolled situations is often based on risks shared and resources deployed, that forms the basis of favourable treatment in pricing policies. Research, technology, materials, after-sales support, etc. are some of the functions and components in the price that become extremely difficult to segregate to attaching monetary values that are included in the price.

METHODS OF DETERMINING ARM'S LENGTH PRICE

According to Section 92C, the arm's length price in relation to an international transaction shall be determined by any of the following methods:

(a) Comparable uncontrolled price (CUP) method
(b) Resale price method
(c) Cost plus method
(d) Profit split method
(e) Transactional net margin method
(f) Such other method as may be prescribed by the Board

Transfer price regulations become applicable when a business or commercial transaction is entered between two parties that are related with each other and there is a reasonable chance that the prices are influenced or controlled by either party, which does not reflect the true or fair value of the transaction being undertaken. The motive of controlling the price could be managing profits between two associated enterprises that are subject to two separate tax rates and jurisdictions. Shifting profits in among associated enterprises can enrich the shareholders by at the expense of revenue authorities.

Comparable Uncontrolled Price (CUP) Method

As the name suggests, the price of the transactions between two associated enterprises (deemed to be a controlled price) is compared with that of the same/similar transaction in an uncontrolled environment. By uncontrolled environment is meant a price that would have been charged between two parties as if they were not related in any manner to the extent of determination of value of the transaction.

Comparable Uncontrolled Price method of determining the ALP is to find what would be the price if the transaction was not controlled. Suppose firm A supplies a product X to an associated enterprise B; then there are three possible ways as shown in Figure 23-2 that a comparable uncontrolled price may be obtained:

1. At what price firm A supplied the product X to an unrelated firm C, or
2. At what price firm B could buy product X from an unrelated firm D, or
3. At what price unrelated firm D would supply product X to firm C.

For comparability, adjustments to the uncontrolled price are allowed for material differences in the controlled transaction.

Comparability Analysis The concept of establishing comparability of controlled and uncontrolled transactions is central to the application of the ALP. An analysis under the arm's length principle involves study of

1. characteristics of the property or services
2. functional analysis, that is, *FAR (Functions, Assets, and Risks)* analysis

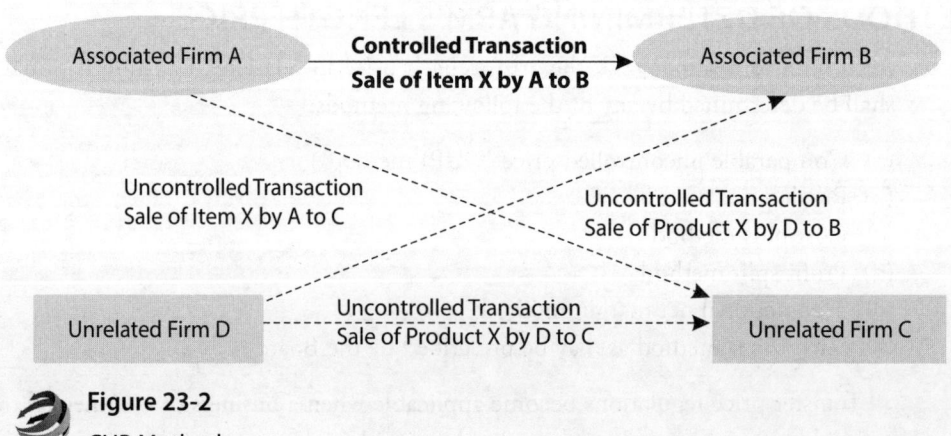

Figure 23-2
CUP Method

In dealings between two independent enterprises, the compensation usually reflects the functions that each enterprise performs, taking into account the assets used and risks assumed. The price is dependent upon all the three factors. Functional analysis also named FAR analysis, is the key element in a transfer pricing exercise. It is the starting point and lays down the foundation of determination of the ALP analysis.

Functions that may need to be accounted for in determining the comparability can include technical aspects of product design, engineering, marketing and distribution aspects, and logistics. Risks analysis includes financial risks including method of funding, funding of losses, foreign exchange risk, product risk including design and development of product, after-sales service, intellectual property risk, risks associated with obsolescence, market risks including fluctuations in prices and demand, business cycle risks, credit and collection risks, etc. It is important to price the risk and identify who bears it.

It is often difficult to find an uncontrolled transaction that has identical features of the transaction, the price of which is being questioned. Market prices for the transfer of the same or similar property may vary across different markets owing to cost differentials prevalent in the respective markets due to locations, government regulations regarding price controls, interest rate controls, exchange controls, subsidies, antidumping duties, etc. Study of contractual terms often reveals the reasons for differences in the price or the profit margins.

Ideally, application of the arm's length principle must be done on a transaction-by-transaction basis but since it becomes cumbersome to do so, the practical recourse is to 'aggregate' such transactions.

The ALP in the method is equal to the price paid in comparable uncontrolled environment.

The CUP method is considered most direct and reliable method of finding ALP. The key to applicability of CUP lies in comparability. Where it is possible to find a suitable comparable there cannot be a more suitable method than CUP. From Figure 23-2, one can make out that it is the most useful method when the associated firm A sells the same product to an unrelated party, or associated firm buys the same product from an unrelated party. In addition, when the product is fairly standardized and available in the market with minor variations where the transaction is done by two unrelated parties (i.e., firm C selling to firm D in Figure 23-2) the price becomes ALP under CUP method.

The comparability under CUP must include (a) quality of product, (b) contractual terms, (c) date of transaction, (d) level of market, that is, wholesale/retail, (e) location, etc. The need for price to be determined by free market forces is utmost in CUP method. One of the situations where CUP may not be applicable is the controlled market conditions where regulated prices prevail.

Resale Price Method

Assume that firm A sells a product to its associated firm B who in turn sells to an unrelated firm C at price P as depicted in Figure 23-3 . Under resale price method, the ALP for firms A and B would be determined on the basis of reselling price less reseller margin. The starting point for ALP would be end-product price that perhaps is transparently established with known reseller margins. For example, assume that a shoe manufacturer has its own distribution firm

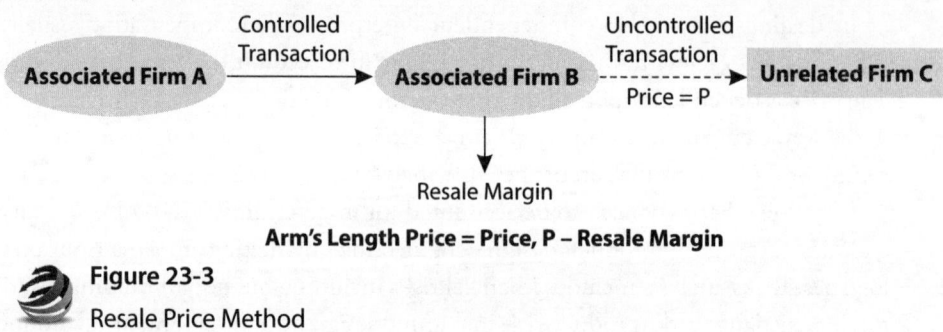

Figure 23-3
Resale Price Method

through which it sells its products. If the distributor margin established in the footwear trade is taken as 25% inclusive of selling and distribution costs and the profit for distributor, the ALP would be

Uncontrolled Price − Reseller's margin = 100 − 25 = 75% for final price

Reseller margin is taken as selling price less cost of goods sold. Therefore, situations where reseller margins can be readily established using cost of goods sold are apt. The method is applicable to situations where the (a) firm performs no or very little value addition to the product (b) it is easy to establish uncontrolled price of the final product, and (c) reseller's margin is reliably available either as market practices or from the financial statements. Reseller margin should be found not by using the transfer price between associated firms A and B but by the price at which firm B would obtain the product in an uncontrolled transaction. Reseller margins are also subject to functions performed by the firm (such as advertising cost in the example) and the risk assumed (such as replacement of product). Exclusive reselling arrangements and general agents have different reselling margins. Resale price method of obtaining ALP is more based on functional comparability and not product comparability.

Cost Plus Method

Under cost plus method, the ALP would be given by adding gross profit margin to direct and indirect costs, that is,

Arm's Length Price = Direct Cost + Indirect Costs + Gross Profit Margin

Direct and indirect costs can be taken from the supplier of goods and services involved in a controlled transaction while the gross profit margin can be established through comparable uncontrolled transactions. This is the mark-up for the cost that is incurred by the supplier. The costs would be actual and not estimated. The costs would include direct cost, such as labour and material and indirect costs would include items, such as depreciation and repairs. Operating costs, such as marketing and general overheads are excluded. The gross profit margin, that is, the mark-up on the cost should include compensation for the functions performed and the risks undertaken. These could best be ascertained on the basis of comparable uncontrolled transaction.

It is similar to resale price method where gross profit margins are established through uncontrolled transaction. In cost plus method, it is a mark-up on cost while under resale price method it is deduction from the end price.

Cost plus method is applied (a) where cost data is transparently available (b) when transactions involve contract manufacturing, or (c) when semi-finished goods are sold between associated firms.

Cost plus method is applicable only for items sold and not for items bought.

Profit Split Method

Under profit split method, the combined value of the total profit of the two related enterprises controlling the transaction is split on the basis of functions performed, assets used, and risks assumed by each party. External comparison as to how two unrelated parties would have shared the profit in similar circumstances would form the basis of splitting the profit between related enterprises. The method directly addresses the basic reason of transfer pricing regulation by implying that profit allocation by associated enterprises is done for tax planning purposes, and does not reflect the true values.

The method is extremely dependent upon availability of reliable comparable data between unrelated parties to form the basis of allocation of profit among related firms. In complex technical, intangible, and innovation-based industries, it is extremely difficult to obtain such data.

The method can be applied in joint venture circumstances for integrated operations or where one sided methods are not appropriate. It would be useful in circumstances where profits arise from intangible activities.

Though fundamentally strong, the method has serious limitations. It requires access to information on total profit of related enterprises. These associated enterprises in the international scenarios are likely to be independent legal entities falling under different tax jurisdictions. This would give rise to several disputes. For example, assume two related firms—one located in USA and another located in India with aggregate profit of US$100. Indian tax authorities determine that ratio of profit is US$60 in USA (against US$70 shown in books) and remaining US$40 (against US$30 shown in books) in India. While Indian revenue department may be justified in increasing the profit, the US revenue authorities may not be willing to correspondingly adjust the profit downwards for the US firm because their tax revenue would stand reduced.

Generally, splitting of profit is done on the basis of some broad allocation keys. These allocation keys can be assets/capital deployed or costs incurred. The allocation keys can also be some parameter which is considered value determinant and profit drivers. Examples would include headcount in a call centre setting, floor area in retail operations, production capacities in manufacturing set ups, etc. One of the most commonly used allocation key is capital employed.

Transactional Net Margin (TNM) Method

This method of determining the ALP is similar to cost plus method or resale price method, under which gross profit margin was either added to the cost or subtracted from the price. In TNM method the net profit margin is applied to an appropriate base, such as cost, assets, and revenue, therefore it is less direct method as compared to cost plus or resale price method. The method is applied as follows:

(a) Find the net margin realized in controlled transaction between associated firms.
(b) Compare the net margin in the controlled transaction with that of uncontrolled transaction between two unrelated firms.
(c) Make adjustment for the differences (a) and (b).
(d) Find the arm's length price.

Profit level indicators could be (i) PBT to sales, (ii) EBIT to sales, (iii) EBIT to assets, (iv) EBIT or PBT to net worth, (v) operating profit to revenue, etc.

The major advantage of TNM method is that it is least controversial as the issue of comparability is less complex in TNM method. This is because profit level indicators are generally available in public domain for comparable uncontrolled transactions. The comparison of controlled and uncontrolled transactions at the net profit level would be easier as different characteristics of the firm, product features, cost composition, allocation of fixed costs on different products, etc. need not be analysed and compared. Net margins are less affected by functional differences than the gross profit margins. Comparability for functions performed, assets used, and risks assumed would be less strenuous.

The TNM method is less applicable for the firms that are engaged in several products or functions because it can be used on an aggregate basis where profit level indicators are generally available and perhaps does not distinguish among different segments.

Assume that firms A and B are associated enterprises and firm A supplies a component to firm B at ₹120. The operating cost before interest and after depreciation is ₹100. Suppose another firm not controlled by either firm A or B in the same product line earns a net profit margin defined as margin over cost before interest but after depreciation (a profit level indicator) is 40%. If so the ALP should be ₹140 (Cost of ₹100 and net profit margin of 40%) as against transfer price used by firm A of ₹120. Therefore, the income of firm A would rise by ₹20.

Any Other Method

The Income Tax Act in India besides providing for five methods that are recognized by OECD also allows any other method for determination of ALP as long as the principle of its determination follows the principle of an uncontrolled transaction conducted between non-associated enterprises. This flexibility would permit use of other valuation techniques such as discounted cash flows.

The most appropriate method for a situation would be governed by several factors, such as nature of transactions, availability of reliable cost data, and extent of comparability of transactions. It may be observed that due to several possible methods and their applicability in determining ALP there is plenty of scope for differences to arise between the taxpayer and revenue authorities. These differences of opinion with regard to application and suitability of method having revenue implication may result into prolonged and perhaps avoidable litigations. In addition, transfer pricing rules if implemented arbitrarily have potential to contaminate the investment climate and serve as deterrent to foreign investment. With these implications in mind there are several provisions incorporated in the rules where arbitrariness is reduced, and litigation avoided.

RELAXATIONS IN TRANSFER PRICING AND ARM'S LENGTH PRICE

From the previous discussions on transfer price and ALP, it is evident that there is considerable scope for ambiguous interpretations and applicability of methods. This creates ample scope for controversies while the very objective of such rule was exactly opposite. In order to reduce controversies and resulting litigation, there are certain provisions that intend to put the controversies at rest. Some of these are mentioned here.

1. **No Adjustment**   No adjustment to the ALP computed by the taxpayer would be made if the price computed by the tax department is within ±5%.
2. **Advance Pricing Agreements**   Provisions for Advance Pricing Agreements (APAs) have been made in Finance Act, 2012, where an agreement between the tax authority and any taxpayer regarding method of determining the ALP or specifying the manner in which the ALP is to be determined would be reached in advance and remain binding on both parties for a set of transactions for a fixed period, if there is no change in the law. APAs are likely to (a) provide certainty on the treatment of its international transactions, (b) eliminate tax leakages arising on account of double taxation, (c) proactively avoid transfer pricing controversies, and (d) eliminate/reduce risk of economic double taxation.

    The maximum period for which advance pricing agreements can be entered is five years. There is no threshold minimum either for duration or monetary value for APAs. These APAs can be unilateral (agreement between taxpayer and tax authority in India), bilateral, (agreement between tax authorities in two countries where associated enterprises are located) or multilateral (agreement involving several tax authorities and associated enterprises).
3. **Safe Harbour Rules**   Since September 2013 India provided for 'Safe Harbour Rules' to reduce transfer pricing audits, and prolonged disputes. Safe Harbour Rules mean that if certain standards are met the transfer pricing as determined by the taxpayer would remain valid and unchallenged. These rules would increase transparency and help improve investment climate. These rules would present revenue authorities as investor and business friendly. Taxpayers can opt for safe harbour rules for justifying that international transactions between associated enterprises are done at ALP. For certain transactions, these rules are as given in the following table.

Safe harbour rules applicable to international transactions are at the option of the taxpayer. They are applicable for five years beginning from financial year (FY) 2012–13.

Taxpayer has flexibility in electing the years to be governed by safe harbour. They can opt to apply safe harbour rules and if opted, they are not entitled to make any comparability adjustments nor allowance of range benefit made.

Nature of Transaction	Transaction Value	Safe Harbour Ceilings
IT and ITeS Services with Insignificant Risk	Value up to ₹500 crore Value > ₹500 crore	OPM ≥ 20% OPM ≥ 22%
KPO with Insignificant Risk	No limit	OPM ≥ 25%
Loans to Wholly Owned Subsidiary	Value up to ₹50 crore Value > ₹50 crore	Interest ≥ SBI Base rate (30 Jun) + 150 bps Interest ≥ SBI Base rate (30 Jun) + 300bps
Corporate Guarantee to Wholly Owned Subsidiary	Value up to ₹100 crore Value > ₹100 crore	Commission > 2% p.a. Commission > 1.75% p.a.

Contract R & D with Insignificant Risk
    Software Development
    Generic Pharma Drugs
	No limit	OPM ≥ 30%
		OPM ≥ 29%

Manufacture and Export of
    Core Auto Components
    Non-core Auto Components
	No limit	OPM ≥ 12%
		OPM ≥ 8.5%

Note: OPM: Operating Profit Margin

TAX HAVENS

Most people including corporates want to save tax, and they are constantly on the lookout for ingenious means of doing so. Tax arbitrage is a big consideration for MNCs as they make choice of locating the operations in tax efficient locations and transferring profits there to the extent possible. The debate of using tax havens to one's advantage is on ethical grounds rather than on legal validity of such practices.

Tax havens are the countries or regions that have zero or low tax rates. Switzerland, Singapore, Hong Kong, Mauritius, and Netherlands are few locations that are prominent, besides a large number of other territories, such as Luxembourg, Cayman Islands, Cyprus, British Virgin Islands, and Bermuda. These locations are characterized by their liberal regulations and secrecy laws that provide protection to funds and confidentiality to the identities of depositors. Delaware is one tax haven located in USA where the number of firms registered is more than the number of residents living there because Delaware levies no tax on subsidiaries of holding companies. Similarly, Ireland too has very different laws for taxes.

Most of the tax havens were small countries with little natural resources and any other kind of competitive advantage that would enable them compete. They had to devise means of attracting foreign capital and talent. The objective seems defeated today because of the ingenious ways in which MNCs and wealthy individuals have used these tax havens to gain maximum advantage themselves by simply using these countries as conduit. Today, these locations are seen as not merely as tax havens only but also as *safe harbours* to protect illegal and black money, and unethical activities of money laundering, drug money and terrorist funding.

The fact that India attracts maximum foreign capital of about $4.5 billion from a rather small economy like Mauritius raises a doubt that the money actually is doing a round trip where black money leaving shores of India is routed back via Mauritius.

The practices adopted by multinationals exploiting the gaps and loopholes in the law are becoming increasing cause of concern for revenue authorities world over. Firms are structuring the deals in a manner that are tax efficient and yet they remain within the ambit of the local laws.

CONCEPTS IN PRACTICE
Tax Havens and Tax Avoidance

DOUBLE IRISH DUTCH SANDWICH

Tax havens present a route that is cherished by multinational firms because that allows them to reduce tax liabilities on the profits earned and yet remain within the legal bounds. Global corporations, such as Microsoft, Apple, and Google have used these laws to their maximum advantage. US-based multinational corporations (MNCs) have to pay taxes at 35% on the profits earned and retained in USA. However, if the profits are retained outside USA they are not taxable. Therefore, most US multinationals for their sales outside USA would like to keep profits abroad in tax havens to escape US taxes.

Ireland has been one of the most preferred nations of MNCs of USA to operate from there. Ireland as a nation has the following advantages:

1. It has a low tax rate of 12.5%.
2. There is no withholding tax on royalty if the transaction is with European Union countries.
3. The tax in Ireland is based on control or management of the firm and not residential status. An Irish subsidiary of an MNC though located in Ireland is not taxed because its control or management is outside Ireland.
4. There are no transfer pricing rules to determine if the price used is fair market price, and hence costs, such as goods bought, services rendered, management fee, and royalty can be transferred to tax havens to effectively reduce the tax rate of 12.5% to close to zero.

Profits in Ireland are taxed at a low rate of 12.5%. This becomes even more attractive in the absence of transfer pricing rules in Ireland. This provides flexibility to MNCs from USA to transfer intellectual property right at whatever price they wish to and in accordance with the amount of profit they want to shift out from USA to abroad.

Even the 12.5% tax in Ireland can be reduced further by having a second Irish firm that buys intellectual property rights from the first Irish firm and sells to non-US customers. The payment of royalty to the first Irish firm is not made directly because it would attract Irish withholding tax. Instead it routes this payment through a Dutch firm to make use of two provisions that exists: (1) No Irish withholding taxes are deductible if the transaction involves a European

Exhibit: Double Irish Dutch Sandwich

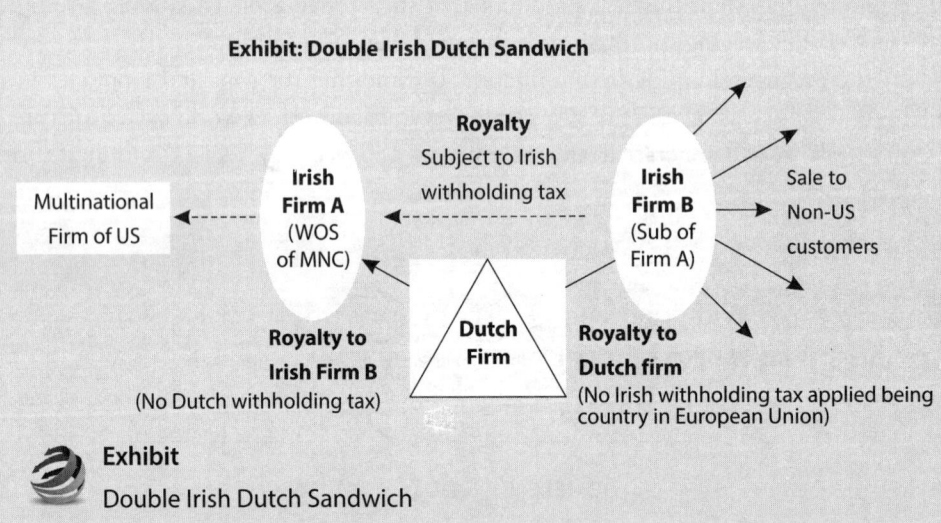

Exhibit
Double Irish Dutch Sandwich

Union country and (2) Withholding tax rate is nil in Netherlands for payments of royalty. Thus, both inflows and outflows from a Dutch firm are tax-free. This is depicted in the exhibit. It is easy to guess that both the Irish firms as well as Dutch firm are only 'shell companies'.

According to Permanent Subcommittee on Investigations, US Senate in a study in 2012 have revealed that 17 largest US corporations hold about US$300 billion in cash outside USA virtually paying no or very nominal taxes, most of which is managed through tax treaties, lack of transfer pricing rules, loopholes in taxation systems, negotiated special tax rates in developing countries. Some of the highlights are as follows:

1. Apple has US$74 billion in foreign countries of the total of US$110 billion and effective tax rate of 13.8%. Apple has a subsidiary in Ireland that pays no tax in any country.
2. Microsoft has negotiated a deal with Puerto Rico to pay just 2% tax on its profits, and invoices sale to US customers from there.
3. Amazon sells goods worth £4 billion in the UK but pays only £2.4 million (0.06%) tax because these profits are earned by an arm of Amazon located in tax haven of Luxembourg.

GENERAL ANTI AVOIDANCE RULES

Revenue generation for government has always been important for pursuing desired fiscal objectives, such as implementing developmental plans, even out the income differentials, reduce regional disparities, and fund social security programmes. At the same time, other objectives of nations, such as capital formation, job creation, and industrialization are in private hands. With both public and private enterprises important for achieving social objectives and also promote private enterprises to achieve a balanced development, the government endeavours nation building by providing tax breaks and incentives.

Private firms use these fiscal incentives for planning taxes and the government hopes that the purpose for which they are granted would be achieved. When these fiscal incentives are availed tactfully without meeting their underlying objectives, the validity and purpose of such fiscal incentive are challenged. While withdrawing these incentives is definitely not the solution because it would discourage private capital formation, the government can establish whether use of these incentives was purely done with the intention of tax avoidance.

We need to differentiate between tax evasion and tax avoidance. Tax evasion is a term usually used to mean illegal arrangements where tax liability is hidden or ignored, that is, the taxpayer pays less than he is legally obligated to pay by hiding income or information from tax authority. Thus, here the tax liability is reduced by 'illegal and fraudulent' means. Tax avoidance refers to the legal means so as to avoid or reduce tax liability, which would be otherwise incurred, by taking advantage of some provision or lack of provision in the law. Thus, in this case taxpayer tries to reduce his tax liability but here the arrangement will be legal, but may not be as per intent of the law. Thus, in this case, the taxpayer does not hide the key facts but is still able to avoid or reduce tax liability on account of some loopholes or otherwise.

It is indeed difficult to draw a fine line of demarcation between tax avoidance and tax evasion. Tax avoidance is an area of concern across the world. The rules are framed in different countries to minimize such avoidance of tax. However, clever business enterprises are innovative enough to avail tax benefits to reduce tax liabilities. To counter such rules or loopholes being used specific measures are taken to prevent such misuse. The rules that are made with the intentions of plugging the loopholes in the law are referred as Specific Anti Avoidance Rules (SAAR). When the rules are generalized these are called General Anti Avoidance Rules (GAAR). Such rules are aimed at denying the tax benefits where revenue authorities feel that transactions involved are a sham only and are structured to avail the tax benefits lacking commercial substance. Aimed at preventing the tax abuse, the provisions of GAAR itself are capable of greater abuse by administration.

The implications of GAAR in international business are serious because they are presumed to be a tool of harassment in the hands of revenue authorities. Since these rules are general and broad in scope, they impart substantial discretion to revenue authorities, and as such are considered arbitrary by MNCs. When transactions of the MNCs are challenged and rejected to deny tax benefits attached with these transactions, the long drawn legislative process begins which has adverse impact on the MNCs in particular and on investment climate in the nation in general. While few developed nations have implemented GAAR some others such as USA and UK have refrained from doing so because of the potential harm these rules may cause to the investment climate to which foreign inflow of capital is an important constituent.

In March 2012 India announced implementation of GAAR to prevent tax avoidance but hastily had to defer its implementation at least by two years in view of the severe criticism of such a need. The apprehensions are that it would be misused by tax authorities in India which as it is not considered investment friendly. It was felt that arbitrary nature of GAAR would have greater nuisance value rather than protection of government's revenue. Further to ensure that

provisions of GAAR are not misused by tax authorities to harass small businesses a threshold of tax benefits of ₹3 crore is placed. In addition, transactions prior to August 2010 would be out of its purview to ensure that old cases are not dug out simply to accumulate more taxes.

Striking a balance between wide coverage and uncertainty, it is imperative that the government issues detailed guidelines on inherent principles and on the type of transactions/arrangements they may consider as 'avoidable transaction'. A mechanism similar to an advance ruling may be considered to avoid uncertainty, protracted litigation, and disputes.

In view of the ongoing debate over its desirability at present, the status of GAAR is hazy and business entities are not sure when and in what form GAAR would be implemented in India.

DOUBLE TAXATION AVOIDANCE AGREEMENTS

As the name implies, Double Taxation Avoidance Agreement (DTAA) is aimed at elimination of taxation of the same income twice.

These treaties benefit institutions and individuals who earn in countries other than their own where they are domiciled. Taxes are chargeable on the basis of residential status and the place where the income originated, nature of income etc. Due to varying laws in different countries, the same income may become chargeable twice in two different nations. For example, an American earning income in India would have to pay tax to Indian authorities because it was earned in India (based on source of income), and may also have to pay tax on the same income because it was earned by American (based on residential status). This dual taxation is a deterrent to international trade.

A relief may be granted by nations aimed at mitigation of taxes. This may be unilateral or bilateral. Unilateral relief, as the name suggests are the measures taken by one country alone. Mostly such measures are taken to increase the attractiveness of the nation as an international investment destination. Unilateral reliefs may take many forms. The country providing unilateral relief incorporates laws that (a) exempt foreign income from taxes, (b) provide credit for the taxes paid in foreign country to be adjusted against the tax liability, (c) treat taxes paid abroad as tax deductible expense, and (d) incentivize investment by providing investment allowance.

Bilateral reliefs focus on treaties that avoid double taxation. Such treaties between nations prescribe general rule for determining income, tax rates applicable for different types of income, rates of withholding taxes, etc. For example, to promote international trade between India and USA, the two nations may enter into an agreement on bilateral basis to avoid dual taxation. These agreements are usually drawn with the principles laid down under Vienna Convention on the Law of Treaties. While the intention is to avoid double taxation at the same time it has to be ensured that these agreements do not become a tool of tax evasion.

Broadly, under DTAA, the country where the income is generated has the right to tax it according to its laws. The country of residence gives credits for this tax and taxes the income at a lower rate.

In the European Union, member states have concluded a multilateral agreement on information exchange. This means that they will each report (to their counterparts in each other jurisdiction) a list of those savers who have claimed exemption from local taxation on grounds of not being a resident of the state where the income arises. These savers should have declared that foreign income in their own country of residence. If there is any difference it suggests tax evasion.

India has comprehensive Double Taxation Avoidance Agreements (DTAAs) with 84 countries as of 2013. The major countries with which it has signed the DTAA are the US, the United Kingdom, the UAE, Canada, Australia, Saudi Arabia, Singapore and New Zealand. The rules vary from country to country depending upon the taxation policies of the two nations involved. If the DTAA exists one can avail benefits. The benefits of DTAA are lower withholding tax (tax deducted at source or TDS), exemption from tax, and credits for taxes paid on the doubly-taxed income that can be enchased at a later date.

There are three ways to treat taxes paid in another nation. One can claim credit for taxes paid abroad against the total taxes payable. The other is to claim tax paid abroad to adjust against the income. Yet another way is to claim exemption of the income earned abroad. A sample of three methods of avoiding double taxes is shown here in a tabular form.

Double Tax Avoidance—Methods			
	Tax Credit	Tax Deduction	Tax Exemption
Indian Income	100	100	100
Foreign Income	100	100	100
Tax paid in India @ 20%	20	20	20
Taxable Income in Country of Residence	200	180	100
Tax on Global Income in the Country MNC is Domiciled, 30%	60	54	30
Tax Credit	20	–	–
To be Paid	40	54	30
Total Tax Paid	60	74	50

In exemption method, the income earned in other countries is exempted from tax of the country where taxpayer is domiciled. Therefore income is taxed only in one country and not both. This is usually followed in respect of profits attributable to foreign permanent establishments and income from immovable property.

Under tax relief method income is taxed in both countries as per laws of the two nations and DTAA. However, tax credit is allowed in another country under the assumption that liability to pay tax arises on global income in the country where the taxpayer resides. However, to the extent the tax is paid in another country the credit is allowed against the tax liability where the taxpayer is resident.

Indian law on taxes provides that the provisions of DTAA would override the provisions of domestic tax laws. One has the option of choosing the provisions of either DTAA or Indian

Income Tax Act, whichever is beneficial to the taxpayer. Benefits of DTAA are available upon completion of some formalities such as establishing the tax residency status.

Most DTAAs provide that incomes from interest, royalty or fee for technical services are taxed on net basis. Tax deduction at source (as different from tax payable) is normally at a lower rate. To eliminate the procedural delays in claiming refunds, the lower of the TDS rate or rate mentioned in DTAA is applied.

Tax Sparing is another feature of DTAAs in India. There are certain tax incentives available in India which are passed on to the foreigners operating in India. The tax credit normally is confined to the amount of tax actually paid. In tax sparing the tax credit is allowed against the tax foregone in India due to incentives.

The model for taxation can either be residency-based usually referred as OECD model followed by developed nations, or source-based referred as UN model followed by developing nations. Under the Income Tax Act, 1961 of India, there are two provisions, Section 90 and Section 91, which provide specific relief to taxpayers to save them from double taxation. Section 90 is for taxpayers who have paid the tax to a country with which India has signed DTAA, while Section 91 provides relief to taxpayers who have paid tax to a country with which India has not

CONCEPTS IN PRACTICE
Double Taxation Avoidance Treaty

MAURITIUS DTAA

India signed Double Taxation Avoidance Agreement with Mauritius which worked as superfast vehicle for portfolio investment in Indian capital markets. Under Article 13 of the Agreement capital gains from transactions in Indian shares at bourses were to be taxed only under Mauritian laws. But under the Mauritian laws capital gains are exempt. Hence capital gains made out of trading in Indian shares are neither taxed in India nor in Mauritius.

This made Mauritius an excellent platform for routing investment in Indian capital markets. All that was needed to be done was to form a firm under Mauritius law and route foreign capital for portfolio investment in India. With Indian exchequer at loss with this treaty posed many questions to deny the tax advantages under the treaty. It was in the form of demonstration of commercial substance and proof of beneficial ownership. To remove such ambiguities the government of India in 2000 issued Circular 789 vide which Tax Residency Certificate (TRC) issued by Mauritius would serve as conclusive evidence for claiming benefit under the DTAA.

Introduction of Section 90 Sub-section 5 proposed to be effective retrospectively from 1 April 2012 attempts to nullify the assurance of TRC as sufficient evidence for claiming DTAA benefits. It makes TRC as necessary but not sufficient condition for claiming benefits of DTAA.

signed a DTAA. Thus, India gives relief to both kinds of taxpayers. A large number of foreign institutional investors who trade on the Indian stock markets operate from Mauritius. According to the tax treaty between India and Mauritius, capital gains arising from the sale of shares are taxable in the country of residence of the shareholder and not in the country of residence of the company whose shares have been sold. Therefore, a company resident in Mauritius selling shares of an Indian company will not pay tax in India. Since there is no capital gains tax in Mauritius, the gain will escape tax altogether. The Indian and Cypriot tax treaty is the only other such Indian treaty to provide for the same beneficial treatment of capital gains.

The rules vary from treaty to treaty. For example, the tax treaty with Mauritius has zero tax for capital gains on equities, but that with the US taxes capital gains. For example, if India taxes long-term capital gains at 20%, the country of residence where such gains are taxed at 30% will levy only 10% tax on such income. In many cases, if an individual establishes his residency in a country with which India has signed DTAA, then income generated in India will be taxed at the rate mentioned in the treaty. For example, if a person is resident of the US in an assessment year, TDS on interest earned on fixed deposits in India will be 15% instead of the domestic rate of 30%.

ADVANCE RULINGS

The provisions of the Income Tax Act in India and existence of DTAA with many countries are subject to multiple interpretations, which results in doubts about the taxability of transactions that MNCs may undertake. In order to provide the facility of ascertaining the income tax liability and to plan taxes well in advance, and to avoid long drawn and expensive litigation, a scheme of Advance Rulings has been introduced under the Income Tax Act, 1961.

An Authority for Advance Rulings (AAR) has been constituted consisting of a Judge, and two other members where MNCs can obtain binding rulings towards the tax liabilities arising out of any transaction or proposed transactions. The advantages of advance rulings are that it

- helps the applicant in planning his income tax affairs well in advance;
- brings certainty in determining the tax liability;
- helps avoiding long drawn and expensive litigation; and
- is inexpensive, expeditious, and binding.

The advance ruling can be sought on any question of law or fact specified in the application in relation to a transaction which has been undertaken, or is proposed to be undertaken, by the non-resident applicant. However, an advance ruling cannot be sought where the question

- is already pending in the case of the non-resident applicant before any income tax authority, the Appellate Tribunal or any court;
- involves determination of fair market value of any property; or relates to a transaction which is designed prima facie for avoidance of income tax.

The advance ruling is required to be pronounced by the Authority within six months of the receipt of a valid application.

CONCEPTS IN PRACTICE
Advance Ruling and DTAA

BOOZ & COMPANY WITHOUT THE BOOZE

Booz & Company (India) Pvt. Ltd was required to pay fee for the technical services to its associates in 10 countries (Australia, USA, UK, Netherlands, France, Cayman Islands, Japan, China, Italy, and Germany) with whom (with the exception of Cayman Islands) India had Double Taxation Avoidance Agreements. Booz India sought advance ruling on whether the technical fee payable by them to their associates for the work to be done by them in India would be chargeable to tax as 'business income'. They sought that since none of the associate has permanent establishment in India the income derived by them in India should not be subject to tax as 'business income' and instead by treated as 'Fee for Technical Services' and charged with 10% tax under Section 115A.

The stand taken by Booz Group was contended by revenues authorities that ground of 'no permanent establishment' in India is misplaced. The various terms and conditions governing the relationship between the Booz Group companies and its Indian affiliate Booz India, the global character and profile of the Booz Group, the interdependence amongst the various companies of the Booz Group, the nature of the services rendered and exchanged between the companies of the Booz Group, and the location of Booz India's office in India combine give rise to a case for Booz India being a permanent establishment in India on several grounds. The revenue authorities stated as follows:

1. The Booz Group is a global network of group companies and in order to optimize the benefits of Booz Group's global business network and expertise, affiliates of Booz Group provide/avail services from each other.
2. It was observed that the entire Booz Group is being catered by a basket of approximately 2,200 technically/professionally qualified personnel which is utilized for executing any project won by the group/its affiliates.
3. Booz India would execute the client's project using its own employees and to the extent required, and procure services of technical/professional/personnel from its group companies around the world. These professionals would work together as one team to execute the projects.
4. The group companies also have the power to recall its technical/professional/personnel and replace them with others.
5. The team would work under the supervision of Booz India with respect to the concerned project with overall control resting with the group as a whole and the personnel would abide by the employment agreement entered into with the group.
6. Any financial and/or other responsibility in respect of any claim made by the third party on Booz India for an actual or alleged infringement of any industrial or other rights of third parties made available by the group to Booz India will be borne by the group.
7. The group will also impart on-the-job training to the employees of India.

In view of the position highlighted by the revenue authorities it was held by Advance

Ruling Authority that permanent establishment does exist and hence the incomes received by them from the Indian company are taxable as business profit under the Tax Agreement of India and the respective countries except Booz & Co. (ME) Ltd, Cayman Islands with which there is no tax treaty by India.

On 14 February 2014 an advance ruling was given that the technical fee/royalty is subject to tax under 'business income' because Booz (India) is deemed as *permanent establishment* of Booze group in India. The payments by Booz India to other group companies were also subjected to withholding of tax under Section 195 of the Act.

SUMMARY

Taxes and related issues play a vital role in growth and decision-making for multinationals because various operations and subsidiaries operate in different countries and have separate legal and tax jurisdictions. Because shareholders' enrichment comes only after paying taxes the laws relating to them often come in conflict with shareholders' interest. The considerations of taxes in various countries therefore become strategic in nature with long-term implications. The chapter is devoted to understanding of tax environment in India.

In India there are three kinds of taxes—direct tax, indirect tax, and transactional tax. Of these the corporate tax which is part of direct tax is most important. The corporate tax in India is applied on income from business, capital gains and other income, such as royalty and interest. The tax rates are (a) based on residential status of taxpayer, (b) payable in advance, (c) subject to minimum tax, (d) different for business income, capital gains, and dividend distribution, and (e) subject to withholding taxes. For promoting investment from private sector, there are several incentives and tax breaks available in order to have balanced regional development and employment generation.

Another related issue that affects MNCs the most is the transfer price—the price used in transfer of goods and services from one subsidiary to another, which are located in different tax jurisdictions. The transfer price used by MNCs is always suspected for manipulation of profit by shifting major part of it to low-tax jurisdiction to the detriment of revenue for nation with high tax rate. The transfer pricing regulation in India provides for (a) ways of establishing relationship amongst the firms, (b) the transactions that would be under scrutiny, and (c) methods of determining the fair price, that is, Arm's Length Price (ALP) for determining the taxable profit. These are essentially same as prescribed by OECD.

There are five different methods of determination of ALP are (i) CUP, (ii) resale price, (iii) cost plus, (iv) profit split, and (v) transactional net margin. The MNCs have the discretion of choosing any method but are required to have sufficient documentation to prove their claim for the transfer price used and appropriateness of method used for ALP. Despite regulations the business complexities are large enough to cause controversies. In order to have convenience and avoid unnecessary litigation there are facilitating provisions of (a) ignoring less than 5% difference between ALP and transfer price, (b) obtaining advance price agreements, and (c) safe harbour rules.

Tax havens are territories or regions with low or zero taxes, which are used by several MNCs as conduit to route funds and investments in several countries, which though perfectly legal but are challenged on moral and ethical grounds. Unfortunately, these tax havens are also used for parking, and routing illicit money and money laundering.

Reflecting concerns of governments to raise revenue and realizing that MNCs do use sham transactions to avoid paying taxes, most nations have provided for General Anti Avoidance Rules. Commonly called GAAR, these rules are aimed at discovering practices that help avoid taxes by availing reliefs available in law without providing benefits for which these reliefs were given. GAAR is aimed at empowering revenue authorities to disallow the tax benefits claimed if they believe that transactions were structured so and defeated the objectives of such benefits.

While GAAR is aimed at discouraging sham practices to Double Taxation Avoidance Agreements (DTAAs) are aimed at encouraging international trade and investment by ensuring that same income is not taxed twice. In order to ensure that taxes paid on income in one nation gets due recognition in tax liability in another nations, DTAAs are signed where two nations agree to recognize and provide credit to the taxes paid in each of the nations. The DTAAs for most nations signed by India provide for lower rates of taxes than normal.

Since tax laws by themselves are complex and applicability of DTAAs may add to the confusion there is a provision in the law to obtain a ruling in advance to remove any misinterpretation regarding the treatment of a business transaction for tax purposes. As the advance ruling is binding on tax authorities as well as the MNCs, it helps in providing clarity of tax implications before the transaction is undertaken and structured.

QUESTIONS

23-1 Why do you think that taxes are an important considerations for MNCs to plan their growth?
23-2 What is transfer pricing? With the help of an example show how transfer pricing can be used by MNCs to maximize shareholders' wealth.
23-3 What do you understand by Arm's Length Price? Describe any two methods of finding ALP, their merits, and demerits with applicability to the circumstances they are best suited to find ALP.
23-4 Transfer pricing is applicable only when two enterprises involved are under common management. Describe the various ways in which such common interests can be established.
23-5 What are (a) Advance rulings, and (b) Safe harbour rules?
23-6 What are tax havens? Describe their advantages and disadvantages.
23-7 What are General Anti Avoidance Rules? How do these rules affect the foreign investment in a country?
23-8 What are the benefits of (a) Double Taxation Avoidance Agreements, and (b) Advance Rulings?

Accounting for International Operations

LEARNING OBJECTIVES

This chapter aims at

- explaining how to account for transactions denominated in foreign currency and treat exchange rate differences
- discussing accounting for foreign currency loan
- describing principles used in translating accounts from one currency to another, and treat the differences arising due to exchange rate variations
- incorporating exposure of foreign operations
- explaining hedge accounting and its differences with conventional accounting
- highlighting the difference between cash flow hedge and fair value hedge
- explaining the equity method of accounting for investment in associates
- explaining proportionate consolidation for representing interest in joint ventures
- describing procedure for consolidation of account of various subsidiaries

CONTENTS

Introduction
Accounting for Transactions in Foreign Currency
    Accounting with Forward Contract
    Transactions in Non-monetary Items
Accounting for Foreign Currency Loan
Translation of Foreign Operations
Accounting for Net Investment in Foreign Operations
Hedge Accounting for Foreign Currency Exposure
    Cash Flow Hedge
    Fair Value Hedge
Accounting for Investment in Associates
    Equity Method
Accounting for Interests in Joint Ventures
    Proportionate Consolidation
Consolidation of Accounts of Subsidiaries

INTRODUCTION

As we know, multinational corporations (MNCs) operate through several subsidiaries in different nations due to a variety of reasons. These subsidiaries are normally separately incorporated bodies in the host nations, where they are required to follow the laws of the host nations just as its other residents do. MNCs exercise control through shareholding or by other business means, and do not seek immunity status of a foreigner to escape the legal or other environments of the host nation.

One of the environments that challenges MNCs the most is the adherence to the accounting standards and practices of the countries where their subsidiaries are located. Since economic, political, and legal environments are different in each nation, the accounting practices too are different in each nation. These practices relate to (a) methods of recording business transactions, (b) ways of presentation of financial statements, (c) disclosure requirements, (d) audit procedures, rules, and practices, (e) penal provisions of non-adherence to accounting standards, etc.

The factors that cause the divergences in accounting standards of various nations are different levels of financial literacy, investor awareness and investor protection laws, transparency standards, efficiency of capital markets, etc. There are substantial differences in the accounting practices in different nations especially between developing and developed. Each nation has a set of accounting rules prescribed by way of accounting standards collectively referred to as Generally Accepted Accounting Principles (GAAP), which all business organizations registered have to follow. The GAAP for different nations are somewhat different in terms of treatment of income, expenses, assets and liabilities, and disclosure requirements.

Accounting standards and practices in India are laid down by the Institute of Chartered Accountants of India. Accounting professionals from various nations are attempting to make accounting standards and practices harmonious all over the world. However, this perhaps is extremely difficult to achieve and therefore understanding of differences in various accounting standards is essential for reconciliation of financial performances when presented in different economic environments using different currencies and different accounting practices.

Due to divergence of accounting standards MNCs face an uphill task of achieving convergence in financial statements for reasons of achieving harmonization of practices leading to similar interpretation of business activities by their shareholders. Another reason for MNCs to have financial performance to be reflected truly is the diversity of nationalities of shareholders. MNCs mobilize capital worldwide and therefore would like that their financial performance be interpreted uniformly and without ambiguity by those providing capital. Any misgivings or misinterpretations are likely to have an adverse impact on their reputations and damage capital mobilization effort. Therefore, levels of transparency, consistency, and truthfulness are absolutely essential given the fact that international investors have high levels of financial literacy.

It is impossible to provide a comprehensive exposure to accounting variations of different nations, but a brief attempt is made here to explain some key differences in key areas that affect MNCs. It is presumed here that readers are familiar with general principles of accounting. These are as follows.

1. *Accounting Transactions in Foreign Currency* Since most multinationals do business globally and transactions in various currencies need to be recorded in single currency, they are required to follow practice to convert foreign currency into local currency.
2. *Accounting for Associates, Subsidiaries, and Joint Ventures* Since global businesses are implemented by making subsidiaries, associates, or forming joint ventures, the understanding of differences between accounting practices for associates, subsidiaries, and joint ventures is desired.
3. *Consolidation* Since MNCs are required to present their accounts in single reporting currency while their subsidiaries use different currency, the accounting standards governing methods of translation and procedures for consolidation of financial performance is essential.
4. *Hedging Accounting* MNCs invariably face foreign exchange risk besides other risks. The accounting for hedging has become substantially different from accounting for other business transactions. An exposure to difference of hedge accounting and accounting for routine transactions is also necessary.

ACCOUNTING FOR TRANSACTIONS IN FOREIGN CURRENCY

We discussed transaction exposure previously in a separate chapter. Transaction exposure arose when the contracts were denominated in the foreign currency and were not settled. As and when these transactions of foreign currency are settled, the gain or loss is recorded and reflected in the financial performance of the firm. The resultant gain or loss on account of variations in the exchange rates on the date of recording the transaction and date of its maturity are shown separately from the actual transaction.

The accounting treatments for transactions denominated in foreign currency are contained in Accounting Standard (AS) 11, The Effect of Changes in Foreign Exchange Rates, or Ind AS 21 with the same title. There are the following three issues in transactions that are denominated in foreign currency:

1. At what exchange rate to recognize the initial transaction,
2. How to treat the exchange rate gain or loss when the transaction is settled, and
3. At what exchange rate to translate the transaction and its gain or loss if it is outstanding on any interim reporting date.

Initial Recognition Consider the following illustrative example on how the transactions denominated in foreign currency are recorded in the financial statements. Assume on 12 January an Indian importer receives invoices of goods worth US$1,000 for payment to be made after one month. The spot exchange rate is ₹50/$. On 12 January initial transaction would be recorded in the books of importer in Indian rupees, at the exchange rate prevailing on the date of transaction, called spot rate as follows:

        Dr Purchases   (50 × 1,000)   50,000
            Cr Vendor   (50 × 1,000)   50,000

The initial recognition for a monetary item (account payable here) is done on spot rate prevailing. Sometimes average rate over a period may be used for the convenience of all transactions in the period.

Exchange Rate Differences on Settlement When the payment is actually made after a month, the exchange rate could be anything and most likely be different than ₹50/$, the exchange rate of the day of the transaction. Different exchange rates on date of transaction and date of settlement would give rise to variation in the expected and actual cash flows. This variation, resulting in gain or loss, is solely on account of exchange rate changes.

There are two possible treatments for recognizing the difference in exchange rates of date of transaction and date of payment—(a) recognize changes as part of initial transaction, or (b) recognize the changes as gain or loss separately and independent of initial transaction.

In the first case, the value of purchase would be undergoing a change by the amount of change in the exchange rates. On the date of payment if exchange rates were ₹49 purchases would get reduced and in case it is ₹51 purchase would increase. However, such treatment is not permitted.

Under the second case of recognizing the gain and loss separately, the initial transaction remains unaffected. For two cases of exchange rates of ₹49 and ₹51 on the date of payment (settlement) as distinct from the initial rate, (referred as historical rate), the following would be recorded:

When exchange rate is ₹49/$

Dr Vendor 50 × 1,000	50,000	
Cr Bank 49 × 1000		49,000
Cr Foreign exchange fluctuation account (49 – 50) × 1,000		1,000

When exchange rate is ₹51/$

Dr Vendor 50 × 1,000	50,000	
Dr Foreign exchange fluctuation account (51 – 50) × 1,000	1,000	
Cr Bank 51 × 1000		51,000

In the first case there is a gain (credit), while in the second case there is a loss (debit) on account of variation in the exchange rates on dates of transaction and maturity. Note that Purchase Account and Vendor Account are not affected by the variations in exchange rates. The initial transaction remains unchanged. The cash flow implications of settlement due to exchange rate changes are reflected in the profit and loss account of the firm.

In accordance with the Indian as well as international standards Accounting Standard AS 11 and IAS 21 it is the practice to recognize the exchange gain or loss in the profit and loss account separately and leave the initial underlying transaction unaffected by such changes.

Effects of Exchange Rates on Reporting Date In the aforesaid example, the initial transaction and its settlement took place in the same accounting period. However, under continuing operations there would always be some outstanding transactions that have been recorded at historical rate and not yet settled as on the reporting date of financial statement.

Multinational firms are required to report financial performance periodically, quarterly more often than not, depending upon the laws in the host nation.

Assume that the transaction of purchase on 12 January remains unpaid till 31 March which is the closing date for presenting the financial performance in India. Here again there are two alternatives available—(a) do nothing on the reporting date and let the impact be recognized only on the settlement date, and (b) the spot rate on the reporting date be given cognizance and gains or the losses be recognized for the period. Under alternative (a) where no entries would be recorded on 31 March is not permitted.

However, here again the practice is to recognize gain or loss on the reporting date. Assume the spot exchange rate on 31 March is ₹50.50. In such a case there is a loss of ₹500 {US$1,000 × (50.50 − 50.00)}. This would be debited to Foreign Exchange Fluctuation Account with an equal credit to Vendor Account. Whenever the transaction is finally settled the gain or loss would be reckoned from the new base of ₹50.50 (the exchange rate on the previous reporting date). Assuming that the payment is made on 10 April when the exchange rate was ₹51.50 following entries would result:

On 31 March (when exchange rate is ₹50.50/$ and payment is outstanding)
    Dr   Foreign Exchange Fluctuation Account   500
        Cr   Vendor Account   500
(The loss on account of depreciation of rupee for the period is recorded on notional basis and vendor is marked to the exchange rate of 31 March)

On 10 April (when exchange rate is ₹51.50 and transaction is settled)
    Dr Vendor Account   50,500
    Dr Foreign Exchange Fluctuation Account   1,000
        Cr Bank   51,500
(Loss on account of further depreciation of rupee for the period is recognized)

By accounting in the manner just described the loss attributable in different accounting periods is segregated. The aggregate loss of ₹1.50 is now split in two accounting periods, that is, pre and post 31 March. If we do not give recognition to the exchange rate that prevails on reporting date of 31 March the aggregate loss of ₹1.50/$ would be accounted for in the single period of post 31 March.

Accounting with Forward Contract

We considered the recording of foreign currency denominated transactions without hedging through a forward contract. However, if a firm hedges through a forward contract, there would be changes in the way of the transaction is recorded. Once a forward contract is booked to hedge against the foreign exchange fluctuations, the uncertainty about the exchange rate on settlement date and therefore the resultant gain/loss on the transaction is resolved. The spot rate on the date of settlement becomes irrelevant to the transaction due to firm rate available under the forward contract.

The initial transaction is recorded as before, that is, at the spot rate on the date of transaction. On the maturity of the transaction which coincides with the maturity of the forward contract, the foreign exchange gain or loss is recognized on the basis of the forward rate rather than the spot rate prevailing then. The accounting entries for an export transaction worth US$1,000 when the spot rate was ₹50, booking of forward sell contract at ₹51.00 are shown in Table 24-1 as follows.

Table 24-1
Accounting with a Forward Contract—Transaction and Settlement in the Same Period

	Dr	Cr	Explanation
On the date of export (spot rate = ₹50.00/$)			
Dr Customer Account Cr Sales	50,000	50,000	Recording export of goods at the spot rate of ₹50.00
Dr Forward Contract Bank B Cr Forward Contract Payable of $1,000	51,000	51,000	Recognizing sale of dollars under forward contract with Bank B at forward rate of ₹ 51.00.
On the date of realization of export (spot rate = ₹52/$)			

Dr Bank A
   Cr Customer Account
   Cr FEF Account
	52,000	50,000
		2,000
			Recording realization in Bank A indicating increase in bank balance

Dr Bank A
Dr Forward Contract Payable
Dr FEF Account
   Cr Bank A
   Cr Forward Contract Bank B
	51,000
	51,000
	1,000
		52,000
		51,000
			Buying US$1,000 from Bank A at ₹52.00, liquidate liability under forward contract with Bank B, and depositing rupee amount in Bank A.

Note: FEF Account stands for Foreign Exchange Fluctuation Account.

It may be noted that gain/loss on account of changes in the exchange rate is independent of spot rate prevailing at the time of maturity, that is, ₹52.00/$.

Transaction with Forward Contract and Intervening Reporting Date Accounting illustrated in Table 24-1 would apply if initiation and settlement of transaction were in the same accounting period. Under the circumstances of date of settlement falling in the subsequent accounting period for a transaction on which forward cover has been taken the gains or losses would have to be treated in following manner:

1. Under the provisions of Accounting Standard AS 11 the exchange gain or loss would have to be apportioned on the basis of time elapsed in each accounting period, and

2. Under the provisions of Accounting Standard AS 30 the gains and losses on the exposure and the hedging instrument (forward) should be clubbed.

Continuing with the same initial transaction we assume the following:

The initial transaction occurs on 1 January with spot rate of ₹50.00/$.
The credit period is four months and customer would pay of 30 April.
The export is covered by booking a forward sell contract of US$1,000 maturing 30 April.

Based on the above the accounting entries on the dates of transaction, reporting, and settlement are shown in Table 24-2.

Table 24-2
Accounting with Forward Contract—Transaction and Settlement in Different Periods

	Dr	Cr	Explanation
On the date of exporting, 1 January; Spot Rate = ₹50.00/$			
Dr Customer Account 　Cr Sales	50,000	50,000	Recording export of goods at the spot rate of ₹50.00.
Dr Forward Contract Bank B 　Cr Forward Contract 　　Payable of $1,000	51,000	51,000	Recognizing sale of dollars under forward contract with Bank B at forward rate of ₹51.00.
On the date of closing of period, 31 March; Spot Rate = ₹52.50/$			
Dr Customer Account 　Cr FEF Account	750	750	Recording proportional gain/loss of forward premium/discount for the time elapsed in the accounting period.
Dr Forward Contract Bank B 　Cr Forward Contract 　　Payable of $1,000	750	750	In addition, bringing the forward transaction to the proportionate premium allocable to the period being closed.
On the date of realization, 30 April; Spot Rate = ₹52/$			
Dr Bank A 　Cr Customer Account 　Cr FEF Account	52,000	50,750 1,250	Recording realization in Bank A indicating increase in bank balance, and realization of export receivable.
Dr Bank A Dr Forward Contract Payable Dr FEF Account 　Cr Bank A 　Cr Forward Contract Bank B	51,000 51,750 1,000	52,000 51,750	Buying US$1,000 from Bank A at ₹52.00, liquidate liability under forward contract with Bank B, and depositing rupee amount in Bank A.

Note: FEF Account stands for Foreign Exchange Fluctuation Account.

It may be noted that on the date of reporting, that is, 31 March the aggregate foreign exchange gain of ₹1,000 {(51.00 – 50.00) × 1,000} is split in two periods according to the time elapsed in each accounting period. Of the total gain of ₹1,000 the transaction has remained outstanding for three months (1 January to 31 March) in this reporting period. Therefore, the gain of ₹1,000 be split in the same proportion, and ₹750 is the foreign exchange gain deemed to have accrued in the previous accounting period. The remaining gain of ₹250 would be recognized in the subsequent period. It may be noted that the actual spot exchange rate on 31 March becomes irrelevant once the forward cover has been taken. If the forward cover was not there, then the gain/loss would have been recognized on the basis of spot exchange rate prevailing on the date of reporting.

The accounting treatment just described is allowed when the forward contract is booked for covering exchange rate risk for an existing asset/liability and does not apply if the forward is booked for covering a firm commitment or a forecast cash flow, which can be accounted for under *hedge accounting* described later in the chapter.

Transactions in Non-monetary Items

Non-monetary items such as inventory and fixed assets are measured in terms of historical cost in a foreign currency which shall be translated using the exchange rate at the date of the transaction or on the date of determination of fair value, if done.

For reporting date the carrying amount of the non-monetary item is first determined on the basis of Accounting Standard applicable to such item. Different standards are applicable for determining the carrying amounts for fixed assets and inventory. The carrying amount in foreign currency is determined first and then translated in local currency.

For inventory the applicable standard prescribes carrying value as lower of cost and net realizable value. While cost would be determined on the basis of historical exchange rate the net realizable value would be obtained using current rate. As an example consider a value of US$10,000 in a foreign location that needs to be translated. The historical exchange rate is ₹50/$ and therefore the value of inventory is ₹5,00,000. However, on the date of valuation the net realizable value of inventory is US$10,100 but the exchange rate is ₹45/$ which translates to a value of ₹4,54,500. Should the inventory be carried at ₹4,54,500 being lower of cost and net realizable value? Such presentation would be incorrect. The correct position is that cost or net realizable value would be compared in the denominated currency and converted to local currency later. If cost is lower historical rate would be used, and if net realizable value is lower current rate would be used. Therefore, the correct value of inventory after conversion is ₹5,00,000. Instead if the net realizable value was US$9,090 and exchange rate were ₹60, the inventory would be valued at ₹5,45,400 (9,090 × 60).

ACCOUNTING FOR FOREIGN CURRENCY LOAN

Due to attractive interest rates in the international markets in different foreign currencies most firms like to borrow abroad. This is especially true for reputed firms in developing countries where interest rates are rather high in domestic markets but due to its good standing the firm can get loans at very competitive and attractive rates in the international markets in foreign currency.

Loans are monetary items because the number of units of money payable is determinable. They can be either short term (repayable in one year) or long term (repayable in more than one year).

Accounting standard provides an option to recognize unrealized exchange differences arising on translation of certain long-term monetary assets and long-term monetary liabilities, such as foreign currency loan from foreign currency to functional currency.

Initial Recognition Initial recognition of a transaction denominated in foreign currency must be recorded at the spot rate prevailing on the date of the transaction.

Reporting in Subsequent Periods At each reporting period the transaction in foreign currency that are outstanding on the date of reporting must be adjusted as follows:

Monetary item	At closing rate
Non-monetary items measured at historical rate	At historical rate
Non-monetary items measured at fair value	At rate that prevailed when fair value was determined

Assume that an Indian firm has borrowed on 1 April 20X1 for five years US$1,000 at an interest rate of 8% p.a. repayable in 10 semi-annual instalments. The spot rate prevailing at the time was ₹50/$ at which the loan is credited in bank account. The initial recognition of loan on 1 April 20X1 would be as follows:

Dr	Bank ($1,000 @ ₹50/$)	50,000	
	Cr Loan Account		50,000

Treatment of Exchange Variations on Reporting Date Assume on 30 September 20X1; a reporting date, the exchange rate is ₹55/$ and the firm pays $100 towards principal and $40 (8% on $1,000) towards interest. The average exchange rate during this period was ₹52/$. The carrying amount of loan on 30 September 20X1 is US$900 × ₹55/$ = ₹49,500.

Repayment

Dr	Loan Account ($100 @ ₹50/$)	5,000	
Dr	FE Fluctuation Account [100 × (55 – 50)]	500	
	Cr Bank ($100 × 55)		5,500

Interest payment

Dr	Interest ($40 @ ₹52/$)	2,080	
Dr	FE Fluctuation Account [40 × (55 – 52)]	120	
	Cr Bank		2,200

The loan liability would be valued at closing rate as follows:

Dr FE Fluctuation Account [900 × (55 – 50)]	4,500	
Cr Loan Account		4,500

Suppose in the next semi-annual period ended 31 March 20X2 the exchange rate was ₹48/$ while the average during the period was ₹51/$. The firm made repayment with interest as scheduled.

Repayment

Dr	Loan Account ($100 @ ₹55/$)	5,500	
	Cr Bank ($100 × 48)		4,800
	Cr FE Fluctuation Account [100 × (55 – 48)]		700

Interest payment

Dr	Interest ($36 @ ₹51/$)	1,836	
	Cr Bank ($36 × 48)		1,728
	Cr FE Fluctuation Account [36 × (51 – 48)]		108

The loan liability would be valued at closing rate as follows:

Dr Loan Account [800 × (55 – 48)]	5,600	
Cr FE Fluctuation Account		5,600

The aggregate gain or loss on foreign exchange would be as follows:

In Indian rupee	Semi-annual period Ended 30 Sept 20X1	Semi-annual period Ended 31 March 20X2
On repayment	–500	700
On interest	–120	108
On fair valuation	–4,500	5,600
Total FE Gain/Loss	**–5,120**	**6,420**
Carrying value of loan liability		
At the beginning	50,000	49,500
Repayment	5,000	5,500
+/– FE loss/gain	4,500	5,600
Ending value	49,500	38,400
Ending value	$900 × 55 = 49,500	$800 × 48 = 38,400

The accounting for a foreign currency loan as highlighted above recognized the gain or loss on the exchange rate in the profit and loss account. However, there is an exception in case of monetary items of long-term nature (maturity more than 12 months from date of initial recognition) where the unrealized exchange rate differences can be accumulated in a separate account as distinct from any other account of foreign exchange difference) directly under equity, and then transferred to the Profit and Loss Account over the period of maturity.

In the previous example, the foreign exchange difference was on fair valuation dates, that is, ₹4,500 and ₹5,600 were charged to FEF account in the profit and loss. As the loan matures in five years, it could be classified as long-term liability. If so, the amounts need not be routed through the profit and loss but instead could be taken to equity in a separate account designated as 'FE Translation Reserve' or like. Then the journal entries would be

On 30 September 20X1
  Dr FE Translation Reserve [900 × (55 − 50)] 4,500
   Cr Loan Account   4,500

On 31 March 20X2
  Dr Loan Account [800 × (55 − 48)]   5,600
   Cr FE Translation Reserve   5,600

At the end of period on 31 March 20X2 the FE Translation Reserve would have credit balance of ₹1,100. This could be spread over five years (the maturity of loan) by transferring 1,100/5 = ₹220 to the profit and loss leaving ₹880 in the reserve as follows:

On 31 March 20X2
  Dr FE Translation Reserve [1,100/5] 220
   Cr FE Fluctuation Account   220

CONCEPTS IN PRACTICE: WOES OF FOREIGN CURRENCY LOANS

Local Currency Depreciation

HIGH COST OF FOREIGN CURRENCY LOANS

With fast depreciating Indian rupee in the latter half of 2012 the Indian firms having resorted to borrowing in foreign currencies at attractively low interest rates were facing exorbitant cost of loan. Though the interest rates were very low the profitability of the Indian borrowing firms stood exposed due to exchange rate losses on account of rising values of the foreign currencies in which interest and repayment liabilities were to be paid. What was contemplated as beneficial due to lower interest rates actually turned out to be more expensive due to depreciation of local currency.

Corporate India has been demanding that accounting relief (deferring the foreign currency losses in profit and loss account) granted to them in respect of long-term foreign currency loans be extended to short-term foreign currency loans too. The law currently requires companies to mark-to-market every quarter the exchange fluctuations on their short-term foreign currency loans. Responding to Assocham's request for accounting relief on short-term foreign currency loans, the Corporate Affairs Ministry has conveyed in December 2012 that accounting relief provided in the Accounting Standard 11 are available only to long-term borrowings. Instead they were advised to hedge their foreign exchange risks by entering into hedging transactions which are at present available particularly in the context of short-term foreign currency monetary items. According to them the firms must follow prudent risk management policies/practices to mitigate the foreign exchange risks by obtaining hedges under the conditions where the volatility in the exchange rates is probable.

The Corporate Affairs Ministry had in December 2011 had issued two notifications to provide relief for firms that had sizeable long-term foreign currency loan exposure in their balance sheets. This was a huge respite for large corporate houses, such as Reliance Group and the Tatas as well as public sector majors, including Indian Oil Corporation (IOC) and Gas Authority of India Limited (GAIL). The relief meant that these firms would not be required to expense the foreign exchange losses on their long-term debt in the profit and loss account every quarter/year.

The denial of same treatment for short-term loans would mean that firms would have to continue taking their forex losses to the profit and loss account every quarter/year.

TRANSLATION OF FOREIGN OPERATIONS

In an earlier chapter, we discussed translation exposure and various methods of translating the financial statements denominated in foreign currency using different exchange rates. The treatment of differences arising from fluctuating exchange rates and the process of incorporating the financial results of a foreign operation are linked.

The accounting standard distinguishes foreign operations as *integral* or *non-integral*. A foreign operation is integral when it conducts business as if it were an extension of the MNC. For example, a foreign operation might be selling goods imported and remitting the proceeds to the parent. In such cases, a change in the exchange rate between the reporting currency and the currency in the country of foreign operation has an almost immediate effect on the MNC's cash flow from operations. Therefore, the change in the exchange rate affects the individual monetary items held by the foreign operation rather than the net investment in that operation.

In contrast, a non-integral foreign operation accumulates cash and other monetary items, incurs expenses, generates income, and perhaps arranges borrowings, all substantially in its local currency. It may also enter into transactions in foreign currencies. When there is a change in the exchange rate, there is little or no direct effect on the present and future cash flows from operations of either the non-integral foreign operation or the parent MNC. The change in the exchange rate affects the net investment in the non-integral foreign operation rather than the individual monetary and non-monetary items held by such foreign operation.

Translation of the financial statements of a non-integral foreign operation for incorporation in its financial statements uses the following procedures:

1. the assets and liabilities, both monetary and non-monetary, of the non-integral foreign operation should be translated at the closing rate;
2. income and expense items of the non-integral foreign operation should be translated at exchange rates at the dates of the transactions, that is, historical rate; and
3. all resulting exchange differences should be accumulated in a foreign currency translation reserve until the disposal of the net investment.

The translation of the financial statements of a non-integral foreign operation results in the recognition of exchange differences arising from

(a) translating income and expense items at the exchange rates at the dates of transactions and assets and liabilities at the closing rate;
(b) translating the opening net investment in the non-integral foreign operation at an exchange rate different from the one used previously; and
(c) other changes to equity in the non-integral foreign operation.

These exchange differences are not recognized as income or expenses for the period because the changes in the exchange rates have little or no direct effect on the present and future cash flows from operations of either the non-integral foreign operation or the MNC. When a non-integral foreign operation that is not wholly owned is consolidated, accumulated exchange differences arising from translation and attributable to minority interests are allocated to, and reported as part of the minority interest in the consolidated balance sheet.

Financial position of foreign operations can be included in the parent's financial statement by using consolidation, proportionate consolidation or the equity method depending upon the nature of foreign operation.

The incorporation of the results and financial position of a *foreign operation* follows normal consolidation procedures, such as the elimination of intra-group balances and intra-group transactions of a subsidiary. However, an intra-group monetary asset/liability, whether short-term or long-term, cannot be eliminated against the corresponding intra-group liability/asset without showing the results of currency fluctuations in the consolidated financial statements. This is because the monetary item represents a commitment to convert one currency into another and exposes the MNC to a gain or loss due to exchange rate fluctuations. Accordingly, in the consolidated financial statements such exchange rate difference is recognized in profit or loss.

However, if the exchange rate difference arises from *monetary item that forms part of net investment in a foreign operation*, it is recognized as

1. Profit or loss in the separate financial statements of the parent,
2. Profit and loss in the individual financial statements of the foreign operation, and
3. *Other Comprehensive Income* (OCI) as a separate component of equity in the consolidated financial statements till disposal of foreign investment when it is reclassified from equity to profit or loss.

Any goodwill arising on the acquisition of a foreign operation and any fair value adjustments to the carrying amounts of assets and liabilities arising on the acquisition of that foreign operation shall be treated as assets and liabilities of the foreign operation. Thus, goodwill of the foreign operation shall be translated at the closing rate.

Any contingent liability disclosed in the financial statements of a non-integral foreign operation is translated at the closing rate for its disclosure in the financial statements.

ACCOUNTING FOR NET INVESTMENT IN FOREIGN OPERATIONS

A net investment in a foreign subsidiary is a monetary item that is receivable or payable from/to foreign subsidiary for which settlement is neither planned nor expected in near future. Trade receivable and trade payable are excluded from net investment in foreign operations. The existence of formal arrangement is immaterial for determination of net investment in foreign operations.

Translation of net investment in foreign operations from foreign currency to local currency follows monetary/non-monetary method wherein (a) assets and liabilities are translated at closing rate, and (b) income and expenses are translated at exchange rate prevailing on the date of transactions, that is, the actual exchange rate. The foreign exchange gains or losses are recognized in the profit and loss accounts of the stand-alone statements of both the subsidiary and the parent, and in *OCI* in the consolidated financial statement and accumulated under a separate component of equity and then reclassified from equity to profit and loss account on disposal of net investment.

There are three possibilities in net investment with respect to exchange rate differences—(a) net investment is denominated in parent's currency, (b) net investment is denominated in subsidiary's currency, and (c) net investment is denominated in currency other than that of parent or subsidiary. We examine three scenarios of net investment by an Indian firm.

When Net Investment is Denominated in Parent's Currency

Assume that an Indian firm, A has net investment in its foreign subsidiary, B in Europe denominated in Indian rupee for ₹10,000. The functional currencies of A and B are Indian rupee and euro respectively. Indian firm's presentation currency too is Indian rupee. The exchange rate at the time of recognizing net investment was ₹80/€.

Initial recognition The amount would be initially recorded as (a) investment in books of parent Indian firm A at ₹10,000 and (b) unsecured loan in books of foreign subsidiary B at €125 (10,000/80).

Subsequent reporting—Carrying amount and exchange rate differences Assume that after a year when accounts are reported euro appreciated to ₹85/€. The net investment would be valued at closing exchange rate and any fluctuation would be recorded as follows:

- Since loan is denominated in Indian rupee the stand-alone financial statement of A would continue to show investment at ₹10,000. The question of exchange rate gain or loss does not arise.

- The investment in stand-alone financial statement of European firm B prepared in euro should now be carried at 10,000/85 = €117.65, with the foreign exchange gain of €7.35 reflected in its profit and loss account.
- In the consolidated financial statement of parent A the exchange rate gain of ₹624.75 (€7.35 × 85) would be reflected in *OCI* in a separate account under equity. This would continue till such time the net investment lasts.

When Net Investment is Denominated in Subsidiary's Currency

We consider the same situation except that now the net investment is now denominated in functional and reporting currency of B as €1,000. The exchange rate was ₹80/€.

Initial recognition   The amount would be initially recorded as (a) investment in books of A at ₹80,000 (€1,000 × 80) and (b) unsecured loan in books of B at €1,000.

Subsequent reporting—Carrying amount and exchange rate differences   After a year when accounts are reported euro appreciated to ₹85/€. The net investment would be valued at new exchange rate and exchange rate fluctuation would be recorded as follows:

- Since loan is denominated in euro the stand-alone financial statement of subsidiary B would continue to show a liability €1,000. The question of exchange rate gain or loss does not arise as reporting currency for B is euro.
- The investment in stand-alone financial statement of Indian parent firm A should now be carried at ₹85,000 (€1,000 × 85), with the foreign exchange gain of ₹5,000 reflected in its profit and loss account.
- In the consolidated financial statement of Indian parent A the exchange rate gain of ₹5,000 would be reflected in *OCI* in a separate account under equity. This would continue till such time the net investment lasts.

When Net Investment is Denominated in Currency Other Than That of Parent or Subsidiary

We consider the same situation except that the net investment is now denominated in US dollar, functional, and reporting currency of neither A nor B as $1,000. The exchange rate was ₹60/€ and $1.35/€.

Initial recognition   The amount would be initially recorded as a) investment in books of A at ₹60,000 ($1,000 × 60), and b) unsecured loan in books of B at €740.74 (1,000/1.35).

Subsequent reporting—Carrying amount and exchange rate differences   After a year when accounts are reported, euro appreciated to $1.40/€ and rupee depreciated to ₹62/$. The net investment would be valued at new exchange rates and exchange rate fluctuations would be recorded as follows:

- Since loan is denominated in US dollar the stand-alone financial statement of European subsidiary B would show unsecured loan at €714.29 (1,000/1.40) registering a gain of €26.45 in its profit and loss account.

- The investment in stand-alone financial statement of Indian parent firm A should now be carried at ₹62,000 ($1,000 × 62), with the foreign exchange gain of ₹2,000 reflected in its profit and loss account.
- In the consolidated financial statement of Indian parent A the exchange rate gain of ₹2,000 of its own, and equivalent rupee of € 26.45 of ₹2,295.86 (26.45 × 62 × 1.40) aggregating to ₹4,295.86 would be reflected in *OCI* in a separate account under equity. This would continue till such time the net investment lasts.

Disposal of Net Investment Under all cases of loans denominated in different currencies, the accumulated amount in OCI under separate head in the equity would be transferred to consolidated profit and loss account when the net investment is disposed. If there was a gain in the OCI the consolidated profit and loss account would be credited with the equivalent debit to OCI account bringing the balance in OCI account to nil. Similarly, if there were a loss in OCI it would be transferred to profit and loss account at the disposal of the net investment in foreign operations.

Treatment of Intra-group Assets and Liabilities and Exchange Rate While consolidating the financial statements of subsidiary and/or joint venture (other than net investment in foreign operations), the exchange rate differences that arise in intra-group monetary assets and liabilities are accounted for in the profit and loss account, and then eliminated.

HEDGE ACCOUNTING FOR FOREIGN CURRENCY EXPOSURE

For Indian firms the framework for accounting for hedging the exposures in foreign currency is contained in two accounting standards AS 11 and AS 30. Principles of hedging and its accounting are contained in the IAS 39. We first discuss hedge accounting in the Indian environment.

Accounting Standard AS 11—The Effect of Changes in Foreign Exchange Rates Accounting Standard AS-11 prescribes amortization of the forward premium of discount over the forward period to be shown as profit or loss and offsets the exchange rate difference in the value of the underlying asset or liability appearing in the balance sheet. As an example, consider Indian exporter having exported goods invoiced as US$1,000 with spot exchange rate of ₹50/$ for a three-month credit. The exporter books a 3-m forward contract to sell US$1,000 at ₹53/$. While the receivable would be recorded at ₹50,000 the exchange rate gain of ₹3 would be routed through the profit and loss account.

Hedge Accounting AS 30 Framework for hedge accounting is provided in Accounting Standard AS 30—Financial Instruments, Recognition, and Measurement. As of now, the adoption of AS 30 is voluntary. Hedging is normally done through taking positions in derivative instruments for an underlying exposure that otherwise renders uncertainty to cash flows. Conventional accounting would demand presentation of gains/losses on the exposure and the derivatives separately. Hedge accounting permits a presentation of gains or losses of the combined position of exposure and the derivatives used for hedging.

Hedge accounting distinguishes between a *cash flow hedge* and a *fair value hedge*. A fair value hedge is intended to protect fair value of an asset or a liability already created or a firm commitment made, while cash flow hedge is aimed at protecting a forecast cash flow. An example of asset or liability already created would include goods sold or bought on credit and denominated in foreign currency where a firm is exposed to risk for foreign currency denominated asset (account receivable) or a liability (account payable). An order received from a buyer and accepted would be an example of firm commitment. When this order is denominated in foreign currency it gives rise to exchange rate risk on a firm commitment. A foreign currency transaction likely to be incurred in future such as sale or purchase in foreign currency would be a forecast cash flow that faces risk of exchange rate. When a hedge protects the changes in fair value it is referred to as fair value hedge, and a hedge aimed at protecting the forecast cash flow is termed as cash flow hedge.

Under a hedge, the derivative instrument that protects the firm from the risk of changing fair value or changing cash flow is designated as *hedged instrument* and the underlying exposure is called *hedged item*. Hedged item can be an asset, liability, a firm commitment, highly probable forecast transaction or net investment in foreign operations which exposes the firm to the risk of changing fair value or cash flow in future.

Fair value hedge can be said to be protecting the balance sheet while cash flow hedge is aimed at smoothing the income statement. Under both the hedges the firm takes a position in a derivative designated as *hedging instrument* intended to offset the adverse impact on the values of assets/liabilities or cash flows in future. It is up to the firm to classify a hedge either as fair value hedge or a cash flow hedge except that hedge for forecast cash flow cannot be termed as fair value hedge. Accounting treatment and procedural requirements would be different under fair value hedge and cash flow hedge. Since procedural requirement is more onerous under fair value hedge most firms are likely to classify hedge as cash flow hedge.

Marking-to-market Foreign exchange exposures that are not represented on the balance sheet such as exposures arising due to forecasted sale or purchase transactions, if hedged with a forward contract or any other derivative product, are required to be marked-to-market at the end of each reporting period. This gives rise to difference in values due to exchange rate changes. On each reporting date, both the hedged item and hedged instrument are marked-to-market. In case of loss, it is routed through the profit and loss account, but if MTM results in profit it would not be recognized on the principle of prudence to provide for anticipated (unrealized) loss but recognize profit only when realized.

Cash Flow Hedge

Under cash flow hedge, the firm can defer the gains or losses on the derivative position till the underlying transaction affects the profit and loss account. For example, a firm intending to import materials worth US$1,000 in 12 months books a 12-m forward contract to buy US$1,000. The recognition of profit or loss on the forward contract would be deferred till the contemplated purchase takes place. Till then profit/loss would be recognized through equity. Such treatment permits (a) simultaneous recognition of profit or loss on the physical and derivative, and (b) booking of income or expense under appropriate account rather than foreign exchange gain or loss. The effect of changes in the foreign exchange in this case would be recognized in the purchase head and not as a separate item in the profit and loss account.

Fair Value Hedge

Under fair value hedge, the changes in value of hedged item and hedged instrument can be combined and the resulting gain or loss is routed through profit and loss account.

To avail the benefit available under AS 30 for hedge accounting one has to comply with the conditions laid out therein. There has to be (a) identification of hedged item, (b) hedging instruments, and (c) test of effectiveness of hedge documented before the hedge is undertaken. This requires preparation for hedging programme and it approval at the highest management level. This may prove to be problematic in view of vast choices of derivatives available and frequent and drastic changes in their values.

The hedge has to satisfy the criterion for its effectiveness. As long as hedge results remain within the limits of effectiveness (normally set between 80% and 125% of value) the treatment as stated above may be accorded. The portion beyond test of effectiveness would have to be routed in the profit and loss account.

Hedging for Net Investment in Foreign Operations The portion of gain or loss on the hedging instruments is recognized directly into equity through OCI. The amount would be transferred to profit and loss account on disposal of investment.

ACCOUNTING FOR INVESTMENT IN ASSOCIATES

Accounting Standard AS 13 applies to accounting treatment of investment in associates for separate financial statements.

It provides for use of equity method for treatment of investment only for consolidation purposes. The equity method is not applicable for firms that do not have subsidiaries or joint ventures. Therefore, they do not prepare consolidated statement.

An associate is defined as an entity where a firm called investor exercises *significant influence*. If an investor holds more than 20% of the voting power, it is presumed to have significant interest in the firm unless it can be clearly demonstrated otherwise. With less than 20% voting power significant influence is not presumed unless demonstrated otherwise. The existence of significant influence can be evidenced in one or more of the following ways:

- Representation on the Board
- Participation in policy making
- Material transactions between the investor and investee
- Interchange of managerial personnel, etc.

Holding of warrants, options that have potential future voting rights, etc. are considered as exercised when deciding whether the significant influence exists.

If significant influence does not exist (i.e., holding less that 20% equity of a firm) the investment would be recorded with cost method. Cost method allows for following:

1. Initial recognition at cost,
2. Dividend from investment is recorded as dividend income,
3. For subsequent reporting investment is valued on each date of reporting and differences in value are adjusted in the carrying amount of the investment, and
4. Unrealized gains or losses due to adjustment in fair market value are routed (a) through income statement if the investment is classified as 'held for trading' and (b) through equity if classified as 'available for sale'.

Indian accounting standard permits use of cost method for passive investment with some modification to the cost method just described. If the investment is classified as 'available for sale' then only loss is recognized in the income statement, while unrealized profit goes unrecorded.

Adjustments to the carrying amount may also be necessary for changes in the investor's proportionate interest in the associate arising from the changes in the *Other Comprehensive Income* of the associate. Such changes include those arising from the revaluation of property, plant, and equipment and from foreign exchange translation differences. The investor's share of those changes is recognized in other comprehensive income of the investor.

Equity Method

If the investor has significant influence then equity method of accounting is applied (except in cases of venture capitalists or mutual funds) for including the performance of associate in the consolidated financial statements. Once the investor ceases to have significant influence, the application of equity method would discontinue. When significant influence ceases to exist, the remainder investment would be revalued on that date and profit or loss on the divested portion would be recorded in the income statement.

Under equity method of accounting, the following accounting treatments are made:

1. *Initial investment* is recorded at cost, identifying any goodwill/capital reserve arising at the time of acquisition. If cost is in excess of fair value there would be goodwill. Goodwill appearing as part of investment would not be amortized. If cost is less than the proportionate share of fair value then the difference would appear as capital reserve directly in equity. However, international accounting standard would treat it as income in the profit and loss account.
2. The *carrying amount* of the investment is adjusted thereafter for the post acquisition changes in the investor's share of net assets of the investee. The consolidated statement of profit and loss reflects the investor's share of the results.
3. Distributions received from an investee reduce the carrying amount of the investment.

4. Adjustments to the carrying amount may also be necessary for alterations in the investor's proportionate interest in the investee arising from changes in the investee's equity that have not been included in the statement of profit and loss. Such changes include those arising from the
   - revaluation of fixed assets and investments,
   - foreign exchange translation differences, and
   - adjustment of differences arising on amalgamations.

To illustrate the application of equity method of accounting, we consider an example. Assume that firm A (Investor) invests in firm B (Investee) acquiring 30% interest at a cost of $500 on 1 April 20X1. The fair value of the firm B is placed at $1,000. The initial recognition of the investment would be made at fair value of net assets. Assume that extra $200 paid comprised $100 towards extra value of the plant, while remaining extra $100 was not identifiable with any asset. Any excess of price over fair value is recognized as goodwill while if fair value exceeds the price the difference would go as capital reserve. The accounting treatment is shown in Table 24-3.

Table 24-3
Equity Method of Accounting for Investment

Recognizing Initial Investment in an Associate	$	Journal Entry		
Initial cost of investment	500	Dr Investment in Firm B	500	
30% share of fair value	300	Cr Cash		500
Excess paid by the investor	200			
Excess value identified with the plant and equipment*	100			
Goodwill**	100			

* Extra depreciation would be provided over the excess amount with remaining useful life of 5 years.
** The amount of goodwill will not be amortized.

Treatment of Value Paid in Excess of Fair Value in the Initial Recognition Since the investor paid more than the fair value, the excess of payment over fair value would be goodwill. However, of the excess amount of $200 it was identified that plant and equipment with remaining life of 5 years was undervalued by $100. The investor firm A would have to provide for extra depreciation on the increased value identified with plant and equipment over its remaining life. Therefore, annual additional charge of $20 on extra value of plant and equipment would be debited to investment income and credited to investment for next five years.

The remaining amount would be shown as goodwill. The goodwill remains merged with investment and is not amortized. However, if the cost of investment were to be less than the fair value the gain would be separately classified as capital reserve in the equity account under Indian accounting standard or recognized as income under international accounting standard.

Treatment of Income and Dividend of Investee Firm For the year ended 31 March 20X2 firm B declared an income of $200 and an extraordinary income of $50. It also disbursed dividend of $40 pertaining to the previous year. For the year ended 31 March 20X2 it had declared and paid an interim dividend of $60 and provided for final dividend of $50. The dividend received would be deducted from investment, and the proportionate share of income should be added to the carrying amount of investment.

Therefore, 30% share of income and extraordinary income of firm B for the year ended 31 March 20X2, that is, $60 and $15 would be added to the original investment. Likewise final dividend received of previous year of $12 and interim dividend of $18 for the current year would be deducted from the income. The final dividend for the current year would be adjusted when paid. The accounting treatment of income and dividend for the investor firm is shown in Table 24-4.

Table 24-4
Equity Method of Accounting for Investment

Computation of Carrying Amount of Investment		$	Journal Entries		
Initial Investment in Firm B (on 1 April 20X1)		500			
Add:	Share of income of B for the year ended 31 March 20X2	60	Dr Investment Firm B Cr Investment Income	60	60
	Share of extraordinary income of B the year ended 31 March 20X2	15	Dr Investment Firm B Cr Investment Income	15	15
Less:	Final dividend received for the previous Year 20X0–01	12	Dr Cash Cr Investment Firm B	12	12
	Interim dividend received for the current Year 20X1–02	18	Dr Cash Cr Investment Firm B	18	18
Less:	Extra depreciation for the excess paid over fair value for the year 20X1–X2	20	Dr Investment Income Cr Investment Firm B	20	20
Less:	Share of unrealized profit in the closing stock of Firm B as on 1 April 20X2	3	Dr Investment Income Cr Investment Firm B	3	3
Carrying amount as on 1 April 20X2		522			

Treatment of Transactions between Investor and Investee Profits and losses resulting from 'upstream' and 'downstream' transactions between the firm and an associate are recognized in the financial statements only to the extent of unrelated interests in the associate. 'Upstream' transactions are, for example, sales of assets from an associate to the firm. 'Downstream' transactions are, for example, sales of assets from the firm to an associate. The firm's share in the associate's profits and losses resulting from these transactions is eliminated.

As an example consider that during the year firm A supplied goods worth $100 to firm B that included profit margin of 20%. These goods were sold by firm B partially and the goods worth $50 were included in the closing stock of firm B on 31 March 20X2.

The investor firm has to recognize the profit or loss on such closing stock to the extent of unrelated investors' interest in the investee firm. Alternatively put, the profit on the closing stock has not been realized. The unrealized profit needs to be adjusted in the investment by debiting the 'income from investment' and crediting to 'investment'. The unrealized profit in the closing stock is $10 (20% of $50) and investor's share is $3 (30% of unrealized profit).

The carrying amount of the investment in firm B as on 31 March 20X2 would be $522 as shown in Table 24-4 after incorporating the income, dividend, extra provision of depreciation on increased value of fixed asset and upstream transactions.

ACCOUNTING FOR INTERESTS IN JOINT VENTURES

Joint ventures are very common in international businesses. Joint venture means a contractual arrangement whereby two or more parties, called venturers, carry out an economic activity with share of income, expenses, assets, and liabilities agreed upon. Each party agrees to perform certain functions complementing the other exercising joint control over strategic matters and decision-making.

The contracts for joint control and be categorized into three—*jointly controlled operations, jointly controlled assets*, and *jointly controlled entities*.

Jointly controlled operations are characterized by use of assets and other resources of the venturers without forming a separate entity, for a joint objective. Each venturer uses own assets, incurs own expenditures, and creates own obligations. Most joint ventures are either based on revenue sharing or profit sharing.

The accounting for *jointly controlled operations* is fairly straightforward where each venturer recognizes (a) the assets it controls (b) liabilities it creates (c) expenses it incurs, and (d) the income it earns. No separate accounting records are mandatory because each venturer keeps all its records for the satisfaction of the other co-venturers.

Jointly controlled assets involve control of some specific assets for the purpose of achieving joint objectives. The most commonly cited example of jointly controlled asset is the sharing of gas pipeline by several refineries or oil-producing firms for transporting output. Again this form may not require setting up of a separate entity. Records of expenses may be kept to the extent they are required for sharing.

The accounting for interest in *jointly controlled assets,* a venture recognizes, (a) its share of the jointly controlled assets, classified according to the nature of the assets; (b) any liabilities which it has incurred; (c) its share of any liabilities incurred jointly with the other venturers in relation to the joint venture; (d) any income from the sale or use of its share of the output of the joint venture, together with its share of any expenses incurred by the joint venture; and (e) any expenses which it has incurred in respect of its interest in the joint venture.

Jointly controlled entity is a joint venture that sets up a separate legal entity where joint control is exercised, which maintains separate books of accounts and that need to be incorporated in the financial statements of the venture on proportionate basis.

Proportionate Consolidation

Accounting for jointly controlled entity can be done under International Accounting Standard IAS 31 either on *proportionate consolidation* basis or on *equity method* (as explained earlier under 'Investment in Associates'). Accounting under proportionate consolidation implies line by line addition of the proportionate share of all items of income statement and balance sheet of the joint venture to those of the venturer. Accounting for joint venture based on equity method though allowed is discouraged because proportionate consolidation better reflects the substance and economic reality of the joint venture. An example of proportionate consolidation is presented in Table 24-5 where the venturer X Ltd holds 40% share in JV Ltd.

As is evident from Table 24-5 the financial statements of A Ltd are consolidated on proportionate basis by adding 40% of assets and liabilities of JV Ltd to the respective line items.

Table 24-5
Proportionate Consolidation

	X Ltd	JV Ltd 40% Share of X	X + JV Proportionate Consolidation
Income Statement			
Revenue	1,500	390	1,656
Cost of Goods Sold	1,200	260	1,304
Overheads	120	65	146
Financing Cost	30	15	36
Profit before Tax	150	50	170
Tax	45	15	51
Profit after Tax	105	35	119
Balance Sheet			
Fixed Assets	300	180	372
Investment	20		
Inventory	200	50	220
Account Receivable	300	50	320
Cash	100	20	108
Total Assets	920	300	1,020
Equity	500	50	500
Long-term Debt	220	80	252
Account Payable	200	170	268
Total Liabilities	920	300	1,020

Treatment of Inter-venture Transactions Under proportionate consolidation, we add the proportionate share of the joint venture in the financial statements of the firm. However, profit and loss of the firm that belongs to the firm itself is required to be adjusted in the carrying amounts of the assets and liabilities as follows:

(a) When a firm contributes or sells assets to its joint venture, the firm must recognize only that portion of the gain or loss which is attributable to the interests of the other venture partners eliminating its own. However, the firm should recognize the full amount of any loss when the contribution or sale provides evidence of a reduction in the net realizable value of current assets or an impairment loss.

(b) When a firm purchases assets from its joint venture, the firm should not recognize its share of the profits of the joint venture from the transaction until it resells the assets to an independent party. However, the firm should recognize its share of the losses resulting from these transactions in the same way as profits except that losses should be recognized immediately when they represent a reduction in the net realizable value.

The aforesaid rules apply only to the preparation and presentation of consolidated financial statements and not in the preparation and presentation of separate financial statements of the firm.

In the separate financial statements of the firm, the full amount of gain or loss on the transactions taking place between the firm and the jointly controlled entity is recognized. However, while preparing the consolidated financial statements, the firm's share of the unrealized gain or loss is eliminated. Unrealized losses are not eliminated, if and to the extent they represent a reduction in the net realizable value of current assets or an impairment loss. The firm, in effect, recognizes, in consolidated financial statements, only that portion of gain or loss which is attributable to the interests of other venture partners.

Assume that X Ltd supplied equipment worth ₹80 that is included in the fixed assets of the joint venture. The equipment was supplied at a profit of 25%. While consolidating on the proportionate basis 40% of the fixed assets, that is, ₹32 is included in the financial assets of X Ltd. However, it includes profit earned by X Ltd. While it can take the profit of the other partners in the venture in its books X Ltd would have to exclude its own profit in the proportionate consolidation of the joint venture. The value of asset needs to be modified as below:

	Figures in ₹
Value of equipment supplied by X Ltd included in the fixed assets of JV Ltd	80
Profit of X Ltd in the equipment supplied @ 25%	20
Share of X Ltd in the fixed assets of JV Ltd @ 40%	32
Profit of X Ltd in its share of the equipment supplied @ 25%	8
Value of equipment to be shown in proportionate consolidation	24

In addition, assume that of the total inventory of ₹50 of the joint venture comprised ₹20 supplied by X Ltd, which included 30% profit for it. Based on the similar lines as for fixed assets, the profit share of X Ltd would have to be eliminated from the carrying amount of inventory that X Ltd is required to show in its proportionate consolidated financial statement. This amount works out to ₹0.96 as shown below:

	Figures in ₹
Value of inventory supplied by X Ltd	20.00
Profit included in inventory @ 30%	6.00
Share of X Ltd in the inventory @ 40%	8.00
Total profit included in the inventory share of X Ltd	2.40
Share of profit in the inventory belonging to X Ltd @ 40%	0.96
Value of inventory to be included in proportionate consolidation	7.04

CONSOLIDATION OF ACCOUNTS OF SUBSIDIARIES

The MNCs have several subsidiaries through which they operate in different nations. Consolidated financial statements (CFS) are presented by a parent firm to provide financial information about the economic activities of its group. Users of the financial statements of a parent are usually concerned with, and need to be informed about, the financial position and results of operations of not only the enterprise itself but also of the group as a whole. The CFS precisely fill this gap. CFS present financial information as a single economic entity to show the economic resources controlled, the obligations and results the group achieves with its resources. Most MNCs operating have several subsidiaries in several countries, and shareholders need to know the performance of the MNC as a whole rather than separately for each subsidiary.

A subsidiary does not mean that it is 100% owned. Control exists when an MNC owns more than 50% of the voting power of an enterprise. Control can also exist by means other than shareholding.

The performance of the subsidiaries could be shown by way of a single line disclosure by applying equity method of accounting for investment reporting the value of the investment. However, this would be inadequate disclosure lacking in providing the comprehensive view of the share of assets, liabilities of the associates (subsidiary that the parent firm has. When control of the subsidiary is assumed then complete disclosure of all assets and liabilities is desired. Therefore, it is considered mandatory to consolidate the financial positions of all subsidiaries, rather than showing share of income and value of investment as associates.

Accounting standard AS 21 prescribes the following consolidation procedure:

1. Financial statements should be consolidated by combining on a *line by line* basis by adding together like items of assets, liabilities, income, and expenses of the subsidiaries with the parent's accounts.
2. The cost of investment in subsidiary and the parent's portion of equity, at the date of investment should be eliminated.
3. Any excess of the cost of investment in a subsidiary over the parent's portion of equity should be described as goodwill and recognized as an asset in the consolidated financial statements.

4. When the cost to the parent of investment in a subsidiary is less than the parent's portion of equity of the subsidiary, then the difference should be treated as a capital reserve in the consolidated financial statements.

In case the subsidiary is 100% owned all the assets, liabilities, income, and expenses are part and parcel of the parent MNC. However when the subsidiary is not 100% owned the claim of parent MNC over net assets of the subsidiary is only to the extent of shareholding, while the remaining belongs to the other shareholders who are in minority. For example, an MNC may hold 80% capital of a subsidiary. Under accounting standard, the MNC is required to consolidate financial statement on line to line basis, while ideally it must do proportionate consolidation to the extent of their holding. An alternate way to consolidate is to do 100% consolidation and then recognize claim of remaining 20% separately, called minority interest. A 100% consolidation with minority interest recognized is preferred over proportionate consolidation because with majority holding the control is exercised by the parent MNC, while remaining shareholders have the objective of mere investment.

Table 24-6
Consolidating Accounts on Date of Acquisition   ₹ lakh

	MNC, A Ltd	Target, T Ltd		Intragroup Balances	Consolidation
		Book Value	Market Value		
Cash	250	15	15		265
Account Receivable	275	25	25	5	295
Stocks	375	30	30		405
Land	200	15	15		215
Building	500	50	60		560
Equipment	600	30	40		640
Investment	160				
Goodwill					48
TOTAL	2,360	165	185		2,428
Current Liabilities	250	20	20	5	265
Long-term Debt	450	25	25		475
Capital	1,150	70			1,150
Reserves	510	50			510
Minority Interest					28
TOTAL	2,360	165	45		2,428

As per the accounting standards minority interest is that part of the net results of operations and of the net assets of a subsidiary attributable to interests which are not owned, directly or indirectly (through subsidiaries), by the parent MNC.

1. Minority interests in the net income of subsidiaries for the reporting period should be identified and adjusted income attributable to the owners of the parent.
2. Minority interests in the net assets of consolidated subsidiaries should be identified and presented in the consolidated balance sheet separately from liabilities and the equity of the parent's shareholders.

To highlight the principles of consolidation, let us consider an example. Assume an MNC A Ltd acquires a target firm T Ltd by paying ₹150 lakh in cash and incurring fee of ₹10 lakh for 80% share. The financial positions of A Ltd and T Ltd are shown in Table 24-6. The net worth of T Ltd is ₹120 lakh (₹70 lakh of capital and ₹50 lakh of reserves) in the books.

The value paid by A Ltd to acquire 80% of T Ltd is compared with market value. The excess amount over market/fair value must be recognized as goodwill (if paid less than the market value then difference as capital reserve) in the consolidated accounts. The market value of net assets of T Ltd is ₹140 lakh (185 – 45). A Ltd has paid ₹160 lakh to acquire 80% share which is worth ₹112 lakh. Hence, the amount of goodwill is ₹48 lacs (160 – 0.8 × 140), which shall be shown in consolidated accounts.

	T Ltd	Value of A's share
Book Value of Net Assets	120	96
Market Value of Net Assets	140	112
Price paid for 80% share		160
Excess of price over book value		64
Excess of price over market value, **Goodwill**		48
Minority Interest, 20% of market value of net assets		28

Since under line by line consolidation the entire assets and liabilities of T Ltd are added to those of A Ltd against its 80% holding the consolidated account must reflect minority interest of 20% that is not owned by A Ltd. The minority interest is 20% of the market value of net asset, that is, ₹28 lakh which is reflected as separate line item.

Further in the process of consolidation all intergroup assets and liabilities have to be eliminated. This implies that investment in the books of A Ltd on asset side and the net worth of T Ltd on liability side must be eliminated against each other to have true view if A Ltd and T Ltd were to be treated as single entity. Similarly, if there are any such reciprocal assets and liabilities they too must be eliminated in consolidation. In Table 24-6 it is assumed that ₹5 lakh are receivable by A Ltd from T Ltd, which respectively are included in account receivable of A Ltd and accounts payable (under current liabilities) of T Ltd. They stand nullified in the consolidated financial statement.

Consolidation Post Acquisition Post acquisition the acquirer MNC firm would continue to record its investment in its books as investment in associates. The consolidation would take place on same lines as before in all subsequent periods, where investment as modified by the profit and loss in the associate would have to be set off against equity of the subsidiary. Besides offsetting of investment against equity following too must be adjusted:

1. Re-computing the fresh value of investment, and minority interest
2. Elimination of intra-group transactions such as sales and purchases transactions between MNC and its subsidiary, of account receivable and payable from one another
3. Elimination of profit from intra-group transactions
4. Amortization of excess of cost over book value

As a simple example assume that T Ltd earns an income of ₹50 lakh and pays a dividend of ₹20 lakh in the year following the acquisition. Assuming that A Ltd follows equity method the new value of investment in T Ltd would be ₹184 lakh as follows:

Opening value of investment		₹160 lakh
Add: Proportionate share of profit	(80% of ₹50 lakh)	₹40 lakh
Less: Proportionate dividend received	(80% of ₹20 lakh)	₹16 lakh
Closing value of investment		**₹184 lakh**

This value of investment would be offset against new value of equity of T Ltd to ₹170 lakh (140 + 50 − 20). The value of goodwill would remain unchanged. Similarly, the minority interest too would increase by 20% of increase in net worth of T Ltd by ₹6 lakh (0.2 × 30) to ₹34 lakh from earlier ₹28 lakh. The consolidated position on account of these transactions would be as follows:

	A Ltd	T Ltd	Consolidated	Remarks
Increase in cash	16	30	46	Dividend received by A Ltd, and rise in cash of T Ltd
Increase in Investment	24	–	–	As explained earlier
Total	40	30		
Increase in net worth	40	30	40	80% share of profit of T Ltd
Increase in minority interest	–	–	6	As explained earlier

In addition to the aforesaid transactions related to the income of T Ltd as shown in the previous table, there would be more transactions in the books of A Ltd due to extra depreciation on building and equipment that are on enhanced value in the books of A Ltd, which are not shown here.

Minority interests in the net assets consist of

(i) the amount of equity attributable to minorities at the date on which investment in a subsidiary is made; and
(ii) the minorities' share of movements in equity since the date the parent–subsidiary relationship came in existence.

Where the carrying amount of the investment in the subsidiary is different from its cost, the carrying amount is considered for the purpose of aforesaid computations. Minority interests should be presented in the consolidated balance sheet separately from liabilities and the equity of the parent's shareholders. Minority interests in the income of the group should also be separately presented.

A subsidiary is excluded from consolidation when (a) control is intended to be temporary because the subsidiary is acquired and held exclusively with a view to its subsequent disposal in the near future, which is usually a period less than 12 months; or (b) it operates under severe long-term restrictions which significantly impair its ability to transfer funds to the parent.

In such cases, investments in subsidiaries should be accounted for in accordance with equity method as prescribed under Accounting Standard (AS) 13, *Accounting for Investments*. The reasons for not consolidating the financials of a subsidiary should be disclosed in the consolidated financial statements.

SUMMARY

The MNCs conduct their business in several countries where they are required to draw financial statements in the currencies of the respective host nations and need to be translated in the functional or presentation currency of the MNC. Besides all these subsidiaries also have transactions which are denominated in foreign currency. The accounting issues in (a) recording foreign currency transactions, (b) incorporating financial performances of the subsidiaries by translating accounts from one currency to another, and (c) treatment of resulting exchange rate gain or loss and hedging thereof are complex, cumbersome, and controversial because of different accounting practices prevailing in different countries.

Transactions denominated in foreign currency are recorded in local currency by using spot exchanges rate of the day, referred as historical rate. Since such transactions are settled in foreign currency at a later date the amount in local currency is likely to be different than what is recorded. Such differences are recognized separately through foreign exchange fluctuation account. If the settlement in not done in the same accounting period then the outstanding transaction is marked to the exchange rate that prevails on the intervening reporting date. Similarly, if the transaction is covered by a forward contract the premium/discount on it is also recorded in foreign exchange fluctuation account in the respective periods prorated according to the time in each period. The treatment of exchange gain/loss is different if the transaction involves a non-monetary item, such as inventories, or a monetary item of long-term maturity such as foreign currency loans.

Foreign operations of MNCs are classified as integral or non-integral. Integral operations are those where the foreign arm of the MNC operates as an extension and treatment of exchange gain/loss is same as explained earlier. Non-integral foreign operations conduct and control business as a separate entity or otherwise with some control/decision-making, then accounting is performed with equity method if a subsidiary, with proportionate consolidation if a joint venture, and full consolidation if a subsidiary.

Translation of financial statements of a foreign entity is done using monetary/non-monetary method where monetary items are translated at closing rate and non-monetary items are translated at historical rates. The translation again or loss is recorded either in the profit or loss account or in Other Comprehensive Income (OCI) as part of equity in the consolidated accounts.

Upon disposal of net foreign operations the balance in the OCI is transferred to profit and loss account.

Under hedge accounting if the transactions in foreign currency are hedged with derivatives instrument, the exchange gain or loss on the underlying transaction and the derivative can be netted and charged to profit and loss account. Hedge accounting distinguishes between fair value hedge, cash flow hedge, and net foreign operations.

When an MNC acquires between 20% and 50% equity of a firm it is said to have *significant influence* over the firm. In such a case, the investment is treated as investment in associate. Value paid in excess of fair value is recorded as goodwill. The value of investment in the books of the MNC is recorded by using equity method of accounting where carrying amount of investment is increased by proportionate share of income and decreased by dividend received. If there are transactions between the MNC and the firm, then profit of the MNC is required to be adjusted.

When an MNC operates an asset, operation, or an entity through a joint venture with other participants, the accounting treatments are different. For jointly controlled assets and operations, the accounting is fairly straightforward but in case of jointly controlled entity the performance of such entity is incorporated using proportionate consolidation method. Any upstream of downstream transactions between the MNC and the jointly controlled entity are adjusted for profit of other joint venture partners.

When an MNC has more than 50% equity in a firm it is classified as subsidiary. The performance of the subsidiary is incorporated on full consolidation basis and not by the proportionate share. The value of investment determined by equity method is offset against the capital of the subsidiary. Similarly, all intra-group balances of assets and liabilities are offset against each other. The claim of other shareholders is shown separately as minority interest in the consolidated financial statements.

QUESTIONS

24-1 How are the transactions of a firm denominated in foreign currency recorded in local currency (a) initially, (b) on intervening reporting date but transaction not settled, and (c) upon settlement? Illustrate with an example.

24-2 Repeat 24-1 with the forward contract in foreign currency booked.

24-3 The accounting for a foreign currency loan is allowed to be treated differently from regular revenue transactions. Explain the difference of the accounting for a foreign currency loan.

24-4 What do you understand by net investment in foreign operations? How are the exchange rate differences accounted for in the books of a firm having net investment abroad and denominated in foreign currency?

24-5 Differentiate between fair value hedge and cash flow hedge.

24-6 Explain equity method of accounting for an investment in an associate.

24-7 What do you understand by proportionate consolidation?

24-8 Explain the meaning of goodwill and minority interest when an MNC consolidates account of a subsidiary which is not wholly owned.

Selected ISO Currency Codes

Country	Currency	Code ISO 4217
Austria, Belgium, Cyprus, Estonia, Finland, France, Germany, Greece, Ireland, Italy, Latvia, Luxembourg, Malta, the Netherlands, Portugal, Slovakia, Slovenia, and Spain	Euro	EUR
Afghanistan	Afghani	AFN
Argentina	Peso	ARS
Australia	Dollar	AUD
Bangladesh	Taka	BDT
Bhutan	Ngultrun	BTN
Brazil	Real	BRL
Brunei	Dollar	BND
Cambodia	Riel	KHR
Canada	Dollar	CAD
China	Renminbi/Yuan	CNY
Croatia	Kuna	HRK
Czech Republic	Koruna	CZK
Denmark	Krone	DKK
Egypt	Pound	EGP
Hong Kong	Dollar	HKD
Hungary	Forint	HUF
India	Rupee	INR
Indonesia	Rupiah	IDR
Iran	Rial	IRR
Iraq	Dinnar	IQD
Israel	Shekel	ILS
Japan	Yen	JPY
Kenya	Shilling	KES
Kuwait	Som	KGS
Laos	Kip	LAK
Lebanon	Pound	LBP
Malaysia	Ringgit	MYR
Maurituius	Rupee	MUR
Mexico	Peso	MXN
Nepal	Rupee	NPR
New Zealand	Dollar	NZD
Nigeria	Naira	NGN
Norway	Krone	NOK
Pakistan	Rupee	PKR
Philippines	Peso	PHP
Poland	Zloty	PLN
Qatar	Riyal	QAR
Russia	Ruble	RUB
Saudi Arabia	Riyal	SAR
Singapore	Dollar	SGD
South Africa	Rand	ZAR
South Korea	Won	KRW
Sri Lanka	Rupee	LKR
Sweden	Krona	SEK
Switzerland	Franc	CHF
Taiwan	Dollar	TWD
Tanzania	Shilling	TZS
Thailand	Baht	THB
Turkey	Lira	TRL
UAE	Dirham	AED
United Kingdom	Pound	GBP
United States	Dollar	USD
Venezuela	Bolivar Fuerte	VEF
Vietnam	Dong	VND
Zimbabwe	Dollar	ZWD

Index

% Spread
Absolute purchasing power
  parity 158
Absorption approach 34
Accounting exposure: *See*
  Translation exposure 399
Add-on yield 347
Adjustable peg 54
Adjusted present value
  method 628
ADR 567
  Classification of 567
  Sponsored 566
  Unsponsored 566
Advance pricing
  agreements 687
Advance rulings (AAR) 695
Agency problem 8, 583
All current method 402
American depository
  receipts 565
American option 284
Amortizing swap 317
Anchor currency 86
Arm's length price (ALP) 678, 680
  Methods of determining 681
Asian currency crisis 91
Asian options 306
Ask rate 117, 340
Asset swap 317
Assignment 288
Associated enterprises 679
Asynchronous business
  cycles 11
Authority for Advance
  Rulings 695
Avalized 663
Average strike option 307

Backwardation 267
Balance of payment 15, 16, 17, 24, 31
  Correction of 31
  Definition of 16
  Imbalances in 24
  Structure of 17
Banker's acceptance 659
Barrier options 305
Barter 21, 663
Basis 262
Basis points 119
Basis risk 263, 264
  Sources of 264
Basis swap 317
Beta 551, 555, 558, 561
  and Risk-free rate 561
  Global vs local 555
  Real and nominal returns 558
  Relever 592
  Unlever 591
Bid–ask spread 118
Bid rate 117, 340
Big Mac study 161
Bill buying rate 136
Bill discounting 658
Bill of exchange
  Discounting 652
  Documentary and clean 651
  Sight and usance 651
Bill of lading 649
  Clean vs foul 650
  On-board and received-for-shipment 650
  Straight vs order 650
Bill rate 135
Bill selling rate 135
Bills of exchange (drafts) 651
Bimetallic standard 46

Bonds 444, 455
  All-in cost 455
  Types of 444
Borrower's FRA 342
BP curve
  Shape of 205
  Slope of 206
Bps 119
BP schedule 205
Bretton Woods System 53
  Features of 53
Broken date contracts/
  odd date contracts 128
Bulldog bonds 450
Burgernomics 162
Buyback 664

Call option 274, 276
  on interest rate 349
Cap
  Relationship with floor 356
  Relationship with swap 356
Capital account 18, 19
Capital account balance 25
Capital asset pricing
  model 549, 562
  Country-specific for segmented
    markets 562
  Foreign project 582
Capital control 530, 531, 532
  Desirability of 531
  Features of 530
  Ways of 532
Capital control measures 538
  Effectiveness of 538
Capital controls 527
  and Impossible trinity 527
Capital flows 522
  Nature of 522

Capital flows and
   Domestic economy 525
Capital gains 673
Capital market line (CML) 547, 553
   Global 553
   Local 553
Capital structure 578, 600, 604
   Multinational corporation 600
   Political risk 604
   Weighted average cost of capital 578
Capital structure and 604
   Currency convertibility 605
   Currency risk 605
   Desire for control 604
   Political risk 604
Capital structure decision in MNC 5
Caplet 352
   Payoff of 353
Caps 352
Carry trade 40, 176
Cash flow hedge 715
Cash rate 125
Cash settlement 255, 257
Centralized vs decentralized control 9
Certificate of origin 652
Classical gold standard 46
Clean float 76
Clearing arrangement 664
Cocktail swap 317
Coefficient of risk aversion 562
Collar 356
Comparable uncontrolled price (CUP) method 681, 682
Comparative advantage 331
Concessionary loan 607
Consumers' lag 36
Contango 267
Controlling capital flows 38
Conventional peg 83

Convergence 267
Convertible bonds 444
Cooperative interventions 103
Corralito 538
Cost method 717
Cost of debt 580
Cost of equity 580, 581
   for a foreign project 581
Cost plus method 681
Counterparty risk 253
Counter-purchase 665
Countertrade 21, 663
   Objectives of 665
   with money/credit 664
   without money 663
Covered interest arbitrage 176
Crawling bands 84
Crawling pegs 83, 97
Credit default swap 317
Credit quality spread 321, 330
Cross hedge 265, 390
Cross rates 119
Currency basket 63
Currency board 86
Currency devaluation/depreciation 31
Currency futures 251
   Arbitrage 267
   Hedging with 259
   Pricing 265
   Speculation 269
Currency swap 317
   Fixed-to-fixed 323
   Fixed-to-floating 324
   Floating-to-floating 324
   Reducing cost of funds with 321
Current account 18
Current account balance 24
Current account multipliers 30
Current/non-current method 402
Current yield 453

Delor's plan 66
Demonetization of gold 58
Depreciation
   Impact on BP schedule 208
   Impact on IS schedule 208
   Impact on LM schedule 208
Development banks 463
Direct rate 118
Direct taxes 671
Dirty float: *See* Managed float 98
Discount rate 4, 615, 620
   Properties of 620
Divergence indicator 63
Dividend decision in MNC 5
Dividend distribution tax 675
Documents against acceptance 645
Documents against payment 645
Dollar bloc 53
Dollarization 84
Double Taxation Avoidance Agreement (DTAA) 692
Down and in 305
Down and out 305
Draft: *See* Bills of exchange 651
Dual listing 564
Dual-rate system 145
Dutch disease 82

Economic convergence 66
Economic exposure 367
   Management of 415
   Measurement of 410
Economic risk 422
Efficient frontier 546, 552
   Global 552
Elasticity approach 33
Equity linked bonds 444
Equity method 717
Equity swap 317
Errors and omissions 20
Eurobonds 449, 451
   Features of 451
   Market 449

Euro dollar 153
  Instruments of 154
Eurodollar futures 346
  Hedging with 347
  Value of 346
Euromarkets 188
European currency unit 61
European monetary cooperation fund 61
European monetary system 60, 62
European option 284
Exchange rate and terms-of-trade 499
Exchange rate mechanism (ERM) 61
Exchange rate pass-through 168
Exchange rate risk 6
Exposure netting 371, 372
External balance 195
External commercial borrowings (ECBs) 464

Factoring 659
Factoring, types
  Disclosed or undisclosed 661
  with recourse or without recourse 661
Fair value hedge 715, 716
FDI and 502
  Horizontal expansion 502
  Risk diversification 503
  Vertical expansion 502
FDI restrictiveness index 510
Fiat money 51
Financial risk 422, 423
Fiscal expansion
  Effect of 204
Fiscal policy 195
Fisher effect 170
Fixed exchange rate
  Fiscal expansion 212
  Monetary expansion 211

Flexible exchange rate
  Fiscal expansion 216
  Monetary expansion 214
Floating arrangement 84
Floating exchange rate system 78
  Advantages of 78
Floating rate bonds/floating rate notes (FRN) 444
Floor 355
  Relationship with cap 356
  Relationship with swap 356
Floorlet 355
Flow to equity approach 624
  Capitalation of 625
Foreign bond 445, 453
  Costs of 453
  Features of 445
Foreign currency loan
  Accounting for 706
Foreign direct investment 507, 509, 514, 523
  Barriers to 509
  Benefits of 507
  Modes of 514
Foreign operations
  Translation of 710
Foreign project 592
  Beta 585
  Cost of capital 592
Foreign project 585
Forfaiting 662
Forward and futures hedge 261
Forward contract 125, 126
  and Futures 254
  Cancellation of 241
  Hedging payable 238
  Hedging receivable 238
  Limitations of 252
  Obligations under 240
  Payoffs of receivable and payable 233
  Speculation with 243
  Underbooking/overbooking of 378

Forward discount 183
Forward–forward swap 128, 133
Forward hedge 377
  Cost of 242
  Effectiveness of 378
  Market hedge and 382
Forward market hedge
  Money market hedge and 385
Forward positions
  Payoffs of 234
Forward premium 183
Forward premium/discount 126
Forward rate 125, 446
Forward rate agreement 340
  Features of 340
  Pricing 344
Forward swap 317
FRA: See Forward rate agreement 340
Free float 76, 102
Free floating 84
Fungibility 568
Futures
  Terminology of 255
Futures contract 254
  and Forward 254
Futures hedge 386
  for payables 389
  for receivables 386
  Forward hedges 388
  Money market hedges 388
Future style options 286

General Anti Avoidance Rules 690
Global depository receipts 565
Gold bloc 53
Gold bullion standard 48
Gold exchange standard 48
Gold pool 57
Gold specie standard 45, 48
Government bonds 441

Havala 145
Hedge accounting 714

Hedged instrument 715
Hedged item 715
Hedge for importer—long hedge 389
Hedging instrument 715
Hedging payable with call option 298
Hedging payable with forward contract 238
Hedging receivable with forward contract 236
Hedging receivable with put option 295
Hershatt risk 125
Home bias 594
Horizontal bands 83
Hundies 659

Imperfect market 10, 501
Implied volatility 286
Importing inflation 79
Impossible trinity
   Capital controls 527
Independently floating 102
Index linked bonds 444
Indian depository receipts 569
Indirect rate 118
Indirect taxes 671
Interbank rates 119
Interest rate option 349
   Call 350
   Payoff 352
   Put 351
Interest rate parity 176, 184, 248
   and NDF 248
   Transaction costs 184
Interest rate swaps 317
   Applications of 326
   Features of 324
Internal balance 195
Internal hedging strategies 371
International banking 460

International bonds 440, 453, 457
   Investing in 453
   Market 440
   Risks in 457
International diversification 483
   Rationale for 483
International Fisher effect 171
   Home bias 175
   Pegged exchange rate 175
   Risk premium 174
International Swaps and Derivatives Association (ISDA) 314
Intervention mechanism 62
Investors' FRA 342, 343
Investment decision 4
Investment decision in MNC 4
Investment in associates
   Accounting for 716
Invisibles 18
Invoice financing 661
IS-LM-BP approach
   Limitations of 217
IS-LM-BP schedule
   Effect of exchange rate changes 208
   Fiscal expansion and contraction 200
   Monetary expansion and contraction 202
IS schedule 199

J-curve 35
Jamaica Agreement 58
Jointly controlled assets 720
Jointly controlled entity 720
Jointly controlled operations 720
Joint venture 515, 720
   Accounting for 720

Keynesian multiplier 28
Knock-in options 305
Knock-out options 305

Law of one price 157
Lead bank 461
Leading and lagging 371, 374
Letter of credit 645
   Advantages of 655
   Applicant 647
   Beneficiary 647
   Bill of lading 649
   Document under 647
   Financing under 655
   Types of 653
Letter of credit, role of banks
   Confirming bank 654
   Negotiating bank 654
   Opening/issuing bank 654
   Paying bank 654
Letter of credit, types of 653
   Back-to-back 653
   Confirmed and unconfirmed 653
   Irrevocable and revocable 653
   Red clause 654
   Revolving 653
   Stand-by 654
   Transferable 653
Licensing 514
Life cycle of MNC 514
LM schedule 201
Long hedge 261
Louvre Accord 104

Maastricht Treaty 66
Managed float 98, 99
   Benefits of 99
Managed gold standard 52
Marginal propensity to consume 27
Marginal propensity to import 28
Marginal propensity to save 27
Margins in options 289
Margin system 257

Index

Market maker 116
Market portfolio 547, 548
   Risk premium on 548
Marking-to-market 258
Matador bonds 450
Merchandise 18
Merchant rates 119, 135
Mexican peso crisis 90
Minimum alternate tax 673
Minority interest 724
Monetary expansion
   Effect of 204
Monetary models 217
Monetary/non-monetary
   method 402
Monetary policy 195
Money market hedge 381
   for payable 384
   for receivable 382
Moneyness of options:
   in-the-money, at-the-money,
   out-of-the-money 283
Motives for foreign
   investment 501
Mundell–Fleming Model: *See*
   IS-LM-BP approach 199

Natural hedge 366
Net investment in foreign
   operations
   Accounting for 712
Nominal and real exchange
   rates 165
Nominal effective exchange
   rate 137
Nominal exchange rate 413
Nominal return 170
Non-deliverable forward 248
   Hedging with 245
   Interest rate parity 248
Non-deliverable forward
   contract 244
Non-monetary items
   Accounting for 706

Non-sterilized intervention 101
Non-tariff barriers 510

Objective of multinational
   corporation 7
Offset 665
Offshore banking 462
Open interest 258, 288
Open market operation 101
Optimum currency area 70
Option forward 133, 380
   Hedging with 380
Option forward rates 381
Options
   Commitments under 282
   Payoffs 276
Options and forwards/
   futures 289
Options hedge 391
   for payable 393
Outright forward 130

Parallel loans 313
Parity grid 62
Participating forward 304
Participatory notes 572
Par value 53
Path-dependent options: *See*
   Barrier options and Asian
   options 305
Pegged exchange rate
   system 88
Perfect and imperfect
   hedge 263
Permanent establishment 672
Peso problem 83
Pips 119
Plaza Accord 104
Points-in-points 119
Political risk 6, 420
   Capital budgeting 432
   Forms of 426
   Management of 433
   Sources of 420

Portfolio diversification 550, 553
   Global 553
   Local 553
Portfolio investments 523
Post-shipment packing
   credit 657
Premium style options 286
Pre-shipment packing credit 657
Price effect 33
Price specie flow 48
Producers' lag 36
Profit split method 681
Project finance 461, 462
Proportionate consolidation 721
Protectionism 37
Purchasing power parity and
   Exchange rate 161
   Exchange rate pass-
     through 168
   Non-tradable goods 160
   Time lag in changes 161
   Trade barriers 160
Pure-play approach 590
Put option 274, 278
   On interest rate 351

Quanto swap 317
Quasi-govt bonds 459

Ratio range forward 303
Real effective exchange rate 137
Real exchange rate 413
Realized yield 453
Real returns 170
Relative purchasing power
   parity 163, 559
   and Capital controls 559
Relevering 592
Rembrandt bonds 450
Resale price method 681
Reserve account 19
Residential status 672
Returns 558
   Nominal vs real 558

Safe harbour rules 687
Samurai bonds 450
Scenario analysis 411
Selective hedging 370
Semi-government bond 442
Sharpe ratio 485
Shogun bonds 450
Short hedge 261
Significant influence 716
Silver standard 46
Smithsonian Agreement 60, 61
Snake in the tunnel 60
Sovereign rating 424
Sovereign risk 420
Sterilization 101
Sterilization cost 528
Sterilized intervention: *See* Sterilization 101
Sterling bloc 53
Sticky price model 220
Swan diagram 196
Swap
  Basis swap 335
  Counterparty risk 333
  Definition 313
  Effective date 325
  Fixed-to-floating 335
  Floating-to-fixed 335
  Hedging strategies 330
  Need for intermediary 332
  Rationale for 331
  Reducing cost of funds 330
  Reset date 325
  Types of 316
  Warehousing 333
Swap quotes 131
Swap transaction 128
  Rationale for 129
SWIFT 116

Switch trading 664
Syndicated loans 461
Systematic risk 550, 582
Systemic risk 255, 439

Target zone arrangements 103
Tariff barriers 509
Taxable income 671
Taxes on transactions 671
Tax evasion and tax avoidance 691
Tax havens 688
Tax sparing 694
Temporal method 402
Terms-of-trade 498
Term structure of interest rate 344
Theory of absolute advantage 495
Theory of comparative advantage 496, 500
  Limitations of 500
Tick size 257, 284
Tom rate 125
Trade account balance 25
Transactional net margin method 681
Transaction exposure 363, 367
  Factors affecting 364
  Management of 368
  Measurement of 365
Transit period 136
Translation exposure 367
  Determinants of 401
  Management of 407
  Measurement of 406
Translation gain/loss 404
Triangular arbitrage 176
Triffin's dilemma 58
TT buying rate 135

TT selling rate 135
Types of taxes 671

Uncovered interest arbitrage 176
Uncovered interest rate parity (UIP) 207
Unremunerated reserve requirements 535
Unsystematic risk 550, 582
Up and in 305
Up and out 305
Usance period 136

Value date 125
VaR (value at risk) 367
Vehicle currency 119
Volume 288
Volume effect 33

Weighted average cost of capital 577
Weighted average cost of capital approach 625
  Limitations of 625
When to hedge 240
Wholly owned subsidiary 515
Withholding tax 675
World indices 556
World Trade Organization 513

Yankee bonds 450
Yield curve: *See* Term structure of interest rate 344
Yield to maturity 453

Zero cost collar: *See* Range forward 301
Zero-coupon bonds 444

About the Author

Rajiv Srivastava is currently Professor, Finance, at the Indian Institute of Foreign Trade, New Delhi. An engineer and dual MBA by qualification, he possesses a vast experience of 35 years in corporate finance having worked in senior and top positions with various corporates such as Uflex Ltd, CMC Ltd, and Rajasthan Breweries Ltd.

In the earlier part of his career, Prof. Srivastava worked with the State Bank of India for a span of 14 years where he was involved with credit appraisal, consultancy, and training of industrialists and bankers. He also served as ICCR Chair Professor of Finance at Jinan University, Guangzhou, China for a semester in 2012. He is the co-author of *Financial Management, Second Edition* and author of *Derivatives and Risk Management, Second Edition*.

Related Titles

FINANCIAL MANAGEMENT, 2/E
[9780198072072]

Rajiv Srivastava, *Professor, IIFT, Delhi*; Anil Misra, *Associate Professor, MDI, Gurgaon*

The second edition of *Financial Management* is a comprehensive textbook designed specially to meet the requirements of management students specializing in finance. It deals with the core concepts of finance with an emphasis on specialized sub-areas, such as working capital, capital markets, investment decisions, international finance, derivatives, mergers and acquisitions, and risk management.

Key Features
- Focuses on managerial applications through case studies, exhibits, and illustrations of well-known Indian companies
- Contains review questions, practical assignments, numerical problems, and practice problems with each chapter

ACCOUNTING FOR MANAGEMENT
[9780198093312]

S. Ramanathan, *Visiting Professor, Institute of Chartered Accountants of India, Institute of Cost Accountants of India, and Institute of Management Studies (Kanpur University)*

Accounting for Management is a comprehensive textbook designed for postgraduate students of business management. It follows a practice-oriented approach to explain the core concepts of accounting, with the help of numerous illustrations and solved examples.

Key Features
- Covers important contemporary accounting concepts of product life cycle costing, target pricing, activity-based costing, among others
- Includes appendices that provide useful analysis of IFRS, Indian GAAP, and US GAAP guidelines

STRATEGIC FINANCIAL MANAGEMENT
[9780198095187]

Palanisamy Saravanan, *Associate Professor, IIM Shillong*; Jayaprakash Sugavanam, *Co-Founder and Vice President, NanoBI Data and Analytics Pvt. Ltd, Bengaluru*; Bharathy Jayaprakash, *Practising Chartered Accountant, Bengaluru*

Strategic Financial Management is a comprehensive textbook designed to meet the requirements of postgraduate management students specializing in finance. It aims to familiarize readers with the theoretical and practical aspects of managing finance in an organization to maximize its value through examples and exhibits.

Key Features
- Includes in-depth coverage of corporate valuation, capital budgeting, and financial engineering
- Discusses global factors that impact finances in organizations, such as inflation, currency rate changes, liquidity crunch, and increasing focus on enterprise risk management and approaches to handle them
- Explains factors leading to corporate restructuring and its forms in detail
- Provides solved and unsolved numerical problems to give an idea about application of techniques such as working capital, economic order quantity, and operating cash flows

DERIVATIVES AND RISK MANAGEMENT, 2E
[9780198089155]

Rajiv Srivastava, *Professor, IIFT, Delhi*

Derivatives and Risk Management, 2e is a comprehensive textbook designed to cater to the syllabi requirements of students specializing in finance. Advanced topics such as credit risk, securitization, and credit derivatives are covered in detail along with discussion on other corporate finance-related topics such as corporate securities seen as derivatives and real options. In addition to covering regular subject material, the text covers weather and energy derivatives and accounting for derivatives. A few cases that throw light on the dangerous side of derivatives are also discussed.

Key Features
- Explores new issues in derivatives such as volatility and value at risk, credit risk, and also relatively complex products such as option on bonds, options on swaps—swaptions, etc.
- Provides examples and boxed exhibits for illustrating the key applications of derivatives and risk management
- Includes case studies on derivatives used by various organizations that led to disasters

Other Related Titles

9780198077039	Shah: *Financial Accounting for Management, 2/e*	9780198066903	Khatua: *Project Management & Appraisal*
9780195683608	Sekhar & Rajagopalan: *Management Accounting*	9780198064510	Aurora, Shetty & Kale: *Mergers & Acquisitions*
9780195695250	Shah: *Management Accounting*		